1 MONTH OF
FREE
READING

at
www.ForgottenBooks.com

By purchasing this book you are eligible for one month membership to ForgottenBooks.com, giving you unlimited access to our entire collection of over 1,000,000 titles via our web site and mobile apps.

To claim your free month visit:
www.forgottenbooks.com/free506320

ISBN 978-0-365-21384-0
PIBN 10506320

THE

SOUTHERN STATES.

MARCH, 1893.

SOUTHERN STATES AND COTTON MANUFACTURE.

By J. S. Jeans,

Secretary of the British Iron and Steel Institute.

It has probably been a source of surprise to not a few who have considered the question that the cotton industry of the American Continent, instead of having established its principal *habitat* in the localities where the cotton has grown, should have taken up its chief location in the New England States. And it must have surprised a good many more that Great Britain, which has no raw cotton at command, and has to import every ounce of its raw material from foreign countries and chiefly from the Southern States, should have taken the lead in this industry for so many years. On the face of the matter, it would naturally be supposed that cotton could be most cheaply and conveniently manufactured on the spot where it was grown, just as iron and steel are most conveniently produced where the raw coal and iron ores are at hand. The main reason, of course, for the supremacy of Great Britain in the cotton manufacture has been the fact that it has been the home of the most important applications of machinery to that industry, and consequently the centre in which the mechanical appliances required for its development have been most readily accessible. But now that other countries, and notably the United States, have almost come abreast of England in reference to the manufacture of mechanical appliances, the aspect of affairs is undergoing a change. Lancashire is falling back, while the United States is coming forward, and among the recent advances of the United States no feature is more conspicuous than the remarkable growth of this industry in the New South.

According to the most recent returns at command, the supply of raw cotton furnished by the world has grown from an average of 1,110,700,000 pounds in the five years ending 1850, to 5,047,200,000 pounds in the year 1891. Of the former quantity the United States supplied 964,200,000 pounds, or eighty-seven per cent. while of the latter quantity that country provided 4,068,000,000 pounds, or eighty per cent. The remainder of the raw material supplied in both periods is shown below:

	Average 1846—1850. Pounds.	Year 1891. Pounds.
Brazil................ ..	23,800,000	45,700,000
West Indies...........	6,300,000	17,900,000
East Indias...........	87,600,000	566,500,000
Egypt, Smyrna, &c.....	29,700,000	582,600,000

In spite, therefore, of the fact that other countries have been supplying raw cotton in increasing quantities, there appears to be no country so well suited for furnishing the requirements of the world as the Southern States of America. But while America furnishes eighty per cent. of the raw cotton consumption of the world, that country retained for its own consumption in 1891, 1,215,-600,000 pounds, or a little more than one-third of the total quantity there produced. The remainder was used by England and by the Continent of Europe·in almost equal proportions. Why should not the United States alter this condition of things and become the cotton emporium for neutral nations, as England has hitherto been? If we look closely at the facts we shall see that this event is probably nearer than is generally supposed, and that it is to the South that the rest of the world is likely to look in the future, as the centre of the American cotton manufacture.

The recent statistics of American cotton manufacture issued from the census office, show that great strides have been made by the Southern States between 1880 and 1890. The amount of capital invested in that industry in the Southern group has advanced from $21,976,713 to $61,124,096; the number of hands employed has advanced from 20,827 to 41,481, and the value of the manufactured products has been raised from $21,038,712 to $46,971,503. This compares very favorably with the progress made by any other group of States within the same interval. Of the total advance made by the United States in reference to the value of· the cotton manufactures produced in this interval, the South contributed more than thirty-three per cent.

This, however, is not surprising.

What is perhaps a good deal more remarkable is· the fact that the South has not done even better. The States of Georgia and North and South Carolina are specially well adapted for the carrying on of the cotton manufacture. They have the raw material on the spot, and they have, moreover, the command of exceptionally cheap labor. The census returns show that in 1891 the average wages paid to each cotton operative in the Southern States was $210, as compared with an average of $335 in the New England, and an average of $332 in the Middle States. Obviously, therefore, if it depended alone on the nominal cost of labor, the South should hold the field.

Returns made to the commissioner of labor in the United States showed that the cost of spinning one pound of cotton yarn (No. 18 and under) in the Manchester district was 0.02786 cents, and in Alsace 0.04093 cents, so that the cost on the continent was about forty-seven per cent. more than in England. When we come to higher numbers in the English scale (say No. 80) the cost was 0.28647 cents in Alsace and 0.19132 cents in England, showing a difference of forty-nine per cent. against the continent. The items of expenditure in each case were as under (for No. 80):

	England. Cents.	Alsace. Cents.
Labor.....................	.08697	.10231
Fuel	.01023	.03069
Interest and Depreciation.. .	.05627	.09209
Other Expenses.......... .	.03785	.06138
Total	.19132	.:8647

These figures make it tolerably plain that success in the cotton industry does not depend on the mere nominal cost of labor, inasmuch as the English operative is paid at least thirty per cent. more than his congener in Alsace, as measured in terms of a day's pay. On the other hand fuel is much dearer in Alsace, and other expenses take up a larger proportion of the cost of the finished product. The same remark applied until quite recently, if it does not still apply to some extent to a comparison between New York and Georgia, as shown in the following statement, collated from the same source, giving the cost of producing one yard of sheeting (36 inches wide, 44x42):

	Amount of cost in		Per cent of unit cost in	
	New York.	Georgia.	New York	Georgia.
Labor	.00914	.00909	21.71	17.65
Materials	.02644	.03770	62.80	73.17
Administration.	.00088	.00046	2.09	0.89
Other expenses.	.00565	.00427	13.41	8.29
Total.........	.04211	.05152	100	100

If this showing be true, it behooves the Southern cotton spinners to see whether it cannot be altered in favor of Georgia. The greatest difference against the South appears to lie in the cost of materials. This can hardly apply to cotton, but it may, of course, apply to fuel and other stores. If so, it may not be easily altered to the extent that could be desired. But the difference in the cost of labor is not so much in favor of Georgia as it should be, having regard to the average wages paid as above stated.

It would be very interesting, if it were possible, to make an exact comparison of the efficiency of the Southern cotton mills and cotton operatives with those of the North and other countries. That however is an extremely difficult task, on account of the differences that are found in the character of the goods manufactured. Some mills spin fine and others spin coarse numbers. Some have more looms and others have more spindles. These and other matters have to be taken into account in considering the following statements, showing the number of employes in the cotton mills of the United States and the number of pounds of cotton used per employe:

Group of States.	No of employes.		Pounds of cotton used.	
	1880.	1890.	1880.	1890.
			1=1000.	
New England....	127,185	148,718	541,373	714,691
Middle	28,367	32,344	109,389	128,184
Western.........	2,366	3,355	15,120	24,232
Southern.... . .	16,741	37,168	84,528	250,637

Group of States.	Pounds of cotton per employe		
	1880.	1890.	increase per cent.
New England	4257	4805	13
Middle	3856	3994	03
Western..........	6390	7223	13
Southern	5090	6748	32

Assuming that the description of cotton produced in each group remained fairly constant as between the two dates, it is manifest that the Southern group has made considerably more progress in this interval than any of the others. In the New England and Western groups the percentage of advance as between the two dates has been much the same, but there is a remarkable difference in the quantity of raw cotton worked up per employe, the Western mills being about fifty per cent. ahead of the New England factories, but this, of course, may be, and most likely is, due to the causes already referred to, inasmuch as it is highly improbable that the oldest centre of the trade should, under similar conditions, be so far behind the least industrial group of the whole. The technical conditions of manufacture are assuredly more advanced in New England than they are in any of the States in the West, although it is more than likely that the Western mills, which are chiefly of very recent origin, will be constructed with the newest forms of labor-saving machinery. It is to the advances made by the mills of the South in this latter regard that the remarkable increase of efficiency in 1890 over 1880, as measured by the quantity of cotton spun per operative, is principally due.

So far as access to the principal markets of the world is concerned, the South has obvious advatages over any other important centre of the manufacture in either Europe or America. The great cotton markets of the United Kingdom are India, China, Japan, and other countries in the East. Most of these countries are now being equipped with mills and machinery which are expected, before long, to place some of them—India especially—in a position to meet their own requirements. But this is not likely to happen for a good many years to come, and in the meantime, India takes something like forty per cent. of the total cotton manufactures of Great Britain. The Southern States are a good deal nearer to China and Japan than England, and if the Nicaraguan canal be completed, as seems most probable, the geographical position of the South in reference to these markets will be improved.

The mill owners of Lancashire appear to be much more apprehensive of the march of India than of any other competitor. The Indian cotton industry has made truly remarkable progress during the last twenty years. In that interval, the number of spindles employed in Indian cotton mills has advanced from 400,000 to about 3,125,000, and the number of people employed in cotton mills has increased from less than 20,000 to upwards of 105,000. The mills now in operation number 137, and consume annually some 375,000,-000 pounds of cotton. The progress achieved has mainly been made during the last five or six years. As a test of this fact it may be stated that the total exports of twist and yarn from India, during the five years ending 1889, amounted to not less than £18,250,000,

as compared with only £7,750,000 for the five years ending 1884. Manufactured goods have been largely increased, alike as regards production and exports during the same period, the total advance as between 1884 and 1889 having been over £2,750,000. The progress of the cotton mills of Bombay has been attributed to the command of cheap labor, but while this is no doubt an element in their favor, it should not be overlooked that the Bombay mills have been built with English capital and are managed by Englishmen who know their business.

The total value of the cotton manufactures of Great Britain has been roughly computed at £82,500,000, of which some three-fourths are exported. Of the latter proportion, again something like one-half goes to silver-using countries, where the cotton goods are not sold for money but bartered for silver, which must afterwards be sold for gold in order to become money to the vendor. The recent course of events, and especially the great depreciation in the value of silver, has compelled cotton manufacturers to face a declining value in that for which nearly one-half of their products are exchanged.

London, England.

AGRICULTURAL RESOURCES OF GEORGIA.

By R. T. Nesbitt,

Commissioner of Agriculture of Georgia.

Georgia is essentially an agricultural State, but in the abundance of her resources she may also be called a variety State, and quoting from the Encyclopdia Britannica, "Texas possibly excepted, no Southern State has a greater future than Georgia." Since this assertion was made our material progress has more than verified its correctness, and in the march of progress, Georgia has more than kept pace with her sister States. It is not our purpose, however, to make this article one of comparisons, nor is it within its scope to consider generally the resources of the State, but rather to confine it to the agricultural interest, its progress and possibilities.

Aside from the soil and climate, the quantity and quality of labor has the greatest influence in shaping the agricultural policy of a country and in governing the selection of crops. This being the case Georgia, in common with other Southern States, has by the conditions of her labor system, been driven into the cultivation of large field crops, and more especially the great staple crop, cotton. When the slave became a freedman no radical change could be immediately effected by reason of large land ownership and because of his previous training. The excellent plowman or hoe hand became an agricultural butcher when placed in the vineyard or orchard, and the rice-field darkey was found utterly inadequate to the duties of a truck farm. The land owner himself was a novice when it came to horticulture for profit or to illustrating the principles of "ten acres enough."

Therefore in viewing the agricultural development of the State as contrasted with the development of manufacturers,

railroads, etc., these facts should be considered. It should also be borne in mind that artificial agricultural progress is rare and of slow growth. With the farmer changes are not the work of a day, old methods being discarded with every recurring season and new ones adopted. In the agricultural world there are no booms, but a natural, steady growth. Experiment must precede development, and not merely experiment, but demonstration. Once the demonstration is made and adopted progress becomes sure and rapid. Viewed in this light, Georgia agriculture has not lagged, and we are now beginning to feel the impetus which improved methods, the result of some bitter experiments, are throwing into every artery of trade. Intense and diversified farming is becoming more and more popular as experience proves its wisdom. This much by way of premise in order to call attention to the circumstances surrounding Southern agriculture, and under which its advancement has taken place.

To consider Georgia immediately from an agricultural standpoint let us first inquire into the quality and character of the soil. To ascertain this the scientific investigator turns to the geology of the State and finds formations represented which embrace:

1. The *Metamorphic* of Middle and Northern Georgia.

2. The *Paleozoic* of Northwest Georgia.

3. The *Cretaceous*, lying South and East of Columbus on the Western boundary of the State.

4. The *Tertiary* and *Quarternary* of Southern Georgia.

The variety of soil that must accom-

A CORN FIELD IN GEORGIA.

pany the disintegration of these formations is shown to the popular mind in the red and brown loams, gray-gravelly lands, sandy lands and flatwoods of extreme Northwest Georgia; the red-clay lands and gray-sandy lands of Middle and Northeast Georgia; the red-clay lands (marl beds); the sandy lands of Middle and Southern Georgia and the Savannahs and palmetto flats of the coast.

Climate is the controlling condition in the growth of natural and cultivated vegetation, and it can be better understood and more intelligently dealt with in connection with the soil than apart from it. It is doubtful if there is any State in the Union which presents a greater variety of climate than Georgia. In the extreme Southern portion of the State we have a sub-tropical climate; in the North a decade scarcely passes without a snowfall of from twelve to eighteen inches, while in Middle Georgia we have all the variations which these two extremes imply. For every three hundred feet of elevation there is a fall of one degree in temperature; this cause would make a change in Georgia of about sixteen degrees. The annual mean for the State is 65.1 degrees, the summer mean 79.7 degrees, the winter mean about 50.1 degrees. The mean temperature of Atlanta corresponds with that of Washington (D. C.), Louisville and St. Louis. The extremes are seldom as great as in the Northern cities, sunstrokes being far less frequent. The range of choice in climate is wide, from the exhilarating atmosphere of the mountains to the somewhat enervating summer climate of the South, which is modified, however, by the sea-breezes. It is readily seen that with a soil and climate so varied, it is difficult to present concisely the agricultural conditions of the State.

In order that a better view of the present production and future capabilities of the soil may be obtained, we will adopt the methods of the Department of Agriculture and divide the State into sections with reference to soil and climate.

The varieties of soil in Northwest Georgia are greater than in any other portion, and perhaps the richest uplands in the State are the brown and red loams of this section. These loams differ greatly in appearance, but in adaptation to vegetation and productiveness are much the same. Sands of this character, which have been in cultivation for years, produce from thirty to forty bushels of corn to the acre, and when properly rotated, that is where leguminous crops precede it, a yield of from ten to twenty bushels of wheat per acre is not hard to obtain. It is only in the last twenty-five years that cotton, as a crop, has been planted in this portion of the State, and north of Floyd county it is seldom attempted, even now. In that county and farther south the usual yield is about 600 pounds of cottonseed per acre. Further divisions of these lands might be made for those who desire to study more minutely their character, but this is beyond the limits of the present article. It would be well to say, however, that the drainage of these lands is almost perfect, and that they are susceptible of very high culture. The forest growth is red, white and Spanish oak, hickory, dogwood, chestnut and pine; the agricultural products are corn, oats, wheat, clover, grasses and cotton. The gray gravelly lands of the ridges have never been highly regarded, but they have been found to be profitable for cotton, easy to cultivate and give a fine return upon the value at which they are held. On these the production of cotton with fertilizers is about 1,200 pounds per acre. All of these lands are exceptionally fine for fruit culture, the ridges being exempt from the frosts, which destroy the fruits on the low lands. The lands of the flatwoods of this section are not held in very high esteem, but where the streams leave the mountains and flow through the valleys very rich bottom lands are found, varying in width from one-eighth of a mile to two miles. Here the grasses are at home, and corn produces from forty to seventy-five bushels per acre. In these bottoms cotton does not succeed well, except on alluvial lands with a large proportion of sand.

The lands in Northeast Georgia are

MOORE HAY FARM, NEAR AUGUSTA, GA.

very similar to those of Middle Georgia, though their adaptability to vegetation is different on account of the difference in temperature. The red lands of this section are especially fine for small grain and grasses, and are usually devoted to these crops. The gray, sandy and gravelly lands are of much larger extent, and, while cotton on these lands is usually late in maturing, it produces more, and the plant seems better able to withstand the drouth. In the extreme northern portion of this section little cotton is planted. Of the usual field crops the yield under fair conditions is: corn, twenty bushels; wheat, fifteen; oats, twenty-five; barley, twenty-five; hay, two to three tons; sorghum syrup, seventy-five gallons. The fruits adapted to this section are pears, apples, peaches, grapes, cherries, strawberries, gooseberries, raspberries.

The settlement of Middle Georgia followed immediately upon the coast settlements, and here therefore the lands are more worn. Under a system of clean culture, without renovation, pursued year after year, the lands of this section were greatly depleted, but new methods are being adopted and waste places are being built up. The chief products of this section are cotton, corn, oats, wheat and all the grains and grasses. Tobacco is also grown. The land yields readily to fertilization, and under proper methods the renovation is rapid and thorough. In this section the peach is grown to perfection, and yields a handsome profit. The trees rapidly reach a bearing state, and new orchards can easily be brought in when old ones become unprofitable. The development of the fruit industry of this section has been remarkable, and in season there is hardly a market throughout the country without peaches from Middle Georgia. The watermelon, strawberries, grapes, all other fruits, do well here, and pleasant and profitable employment with a healthful home are offered to the agriculturist and horticulturist.

We will not attempt to present the different characteristics of the several distinct localities of Southern Georgia, but only call attention to very marked features. It is here we have the long leaf pine and wire grass region, with its immense resources of lumber and turpentine. In this division there are about eighteen whole counties with portions of others. Agriculturally these lands have not heretofore been much considered, and farm labor, owing to the fact that the lumber and turpentine interests offered so much higher wages, has been hard to obtain. Within the last few years more attention has been paid to agriculture, and the results under systematic and intelligent culture have been remarkable. To those unfamiliar with the wire grass, which gives its name to this section, it appears perfectly worthless; but when the old stubble is burned off and the new grass shoots up, all kinds of stock thrive and do well on it. I doubt whether a place is to be found where sheep can be more profitably kept, and there are flocks roaming through this region that are numbered by thousands. Those in a position to know have calculated the cost of keeping them as low as fourteen cents a head.

Around Savannah in Southeast Georgia is the great trucking district of the State, having immense advantages over Florida and many other trucking districts, and destined at no distant day to become the centre of the South Atlantic trucking industry. Around Thomasville and Albany we have the home of the famous Le Conte pear, thousands of which are shipped to different markets.

It is evident from what has already been said that aside from the great money crop, there are other crops which can be easily raised on Georgia soil, and there are many farmers looking to melons, fruits and vegetables for their profits. It may also be mentioned that there is in the southwestern portion of the State an area now profitably devoted to tobacco culture. No accurate information as to the value of these crops is at our command, but their aggregate value is several millions of dollars.

The values of the standard crops as published in the United States census reports for 1890 are:

Cotton, 1,191,919 bales, valued at $50,000,000.

Corn, 37,829,000 bushels, valued at $26,102,071.

Wheat, 2,323,000 bushels, valued at $2,555,380.

The usual combined value of these principal crops is about $79,000,000.

Georgia is the third State in the production of cotton; second in the production of rice; first in the production of watermelons. It has the largest area of any State adapted to long staple cotton, on which large profits are realized; the present production is about 18,000 bales, and it is increasing each year, and the possibilities in the development of this resource are immense. I have before me a letter from one of the largest melon growers in Georgia. He says: "The melon acreage in Southern and Middle Georgia last year was about 28,540 acres, cultivated by 987 farmers; and this crop netted the farmers as near as I can estimate about $489,000, while it paid to the railroads in gross revenue about $1,000,000." On Georgia soil the melon has attained its highest perfection and, in season, it finds its way into the markets of nearly every city in the Union. The following gives some idea of the peach industry and its value: "The Fort Valley region in Georgia was up to a few years ago given up to cotton farming. If the cotton farmers there had been told that they could do better raising peaches, and that their worn-out lands would soon become famous and worth perhaps a thousand dollars an acre for the cultivation of that familiar but neglected fruit, they would probably have smiled at the suggestion. Many of them, however, smile now every day because somebody did make the suggestion and they tried what virtue there was in it. Mr. Garlington states, with full knowledge of the facts, that an acre of peaches will yield $300 net in a good year, and shows that at that rate one crop in seven years pays better than a cotton crop every year, with cotton at ten cents a pound, and the chances are good for a peach crop one year in every three years."

From the foregoing, which is necessarily but a cursory view of the agricultural possibilities of Georgia, it will be seen that our State offers an inviting field to the careful, painstaking farmer. With a climate unsurpassed, a soil that responds readily to intelligent treatment, and many other elements for building up happy homes, she opens her doors and asks the help of enlightened immigration in making her agriculturally second to no State in the Union.

GEOLOGICAL RESOURCES OF GEORGIA.

By J. W. Spencer,

State Geologist of Georgia.

A short account of the geological features and resources of Georgia will give the best idea of the State—as the physical features, minerals and agriculture, are all dependent on the geology. As shown in the small accompanying map, Georgia is characterized by four distinct belts, representing (*a*) the Archaean and other crystalline rocks, occupying a large portion of the State; (*b*) the Paleozoic group occurring only in ten counties; (*c*) the Mesozoic

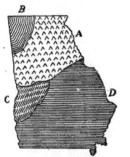

GEOLOGY OF GEORGIA.

group; (*d*) the Genozoic or Tertiary group covering about half the State.

A large portion of the country, underlaid by the Archaean formations, consists of the so-called Piedmont plains, or a gently rolling country with an altitude of from 700 to 1200 or, 1300 feet above the sea; but in the more northwestern portion of this belt the crystalline rocks rise into bold mountains intercepted by valleys. The Paleozoic country consists of a number of broad valleys from 800 to 1000 feet above the sea, traversed by many ridges a few hundred feet high,

and some narrow mountains rising from 1500 to 2000 feet above the sea. The Mesozoic country occupies a rather small triangular area, 500 or 600 feet above the sea, and consists of plains intersected with many deep valleys. A considerable portion of the Tertiary country has an altitude of from 400 to 600 feet and consists of plains with, however, some higher ridges; but the country gradually descends to near sea level.

These physical features give rise to characteristic industries and life. The Mesozoic and Tertiary country is traversed by rivers which are navigable throughout that belt, until the streams are ascended to the "fall line" at the margin of the Archaean formations. Above this line, the rivers and streams are characterized by rapids and shoals, which furnish one of the resources of the State in the numerous water powers which are frequently located in convenient relation to shipping facilities. These powers at the present time are utilized to only a very small proportion of their capacity, although extensively harnessed up at Columbus, Augusta and some other points. Near Atlanta alone the unused water powers of the Chattahoochee are greater than all those at Lowell, Mass. With modern distribution of power by means of electricity, there is no reason why this river should not be utilized throughout nearly its length. The same holds true with regard to the numerous other streams throughout the Archaean belt. The rivers which traverse the Paleozoic country have fewer powers than those of Middle Georgia, and are often navigable; although at present interrupted by shoals, still, along the margin of the Pale-

STONE MOUNTAIN, NEAR ATLANTA, GA.

ozoic belt, there are water powers.

As to the character of water for domestic purposes, the springs and many other streams throughout the Archaean and Paleozoic country supply excellent water. Of course, throughout the Archaean country no true artesian wells can be obtained. Throughout the Paleozoic country, while deep wells are often a necessity, yet artesian water is not demanded at present, although obtainable in some places. In South Georgia, artesian water is often desirable, and can be obtained in many portions of the country and at available depths, according to the presence or absence of water-bearing strata.

Closely connected with the physical conditions are the roads. The lands of Georgia are more favorable for making good roads than those of the States of the Mississippi valley, except, perhaps, a portion of the extreme northwestern part of the State, where abundant road-making material is obtainable. This arises from the fact that our clays contain a large percentage of sand, are more easily drained, and do not generally produce excessively deep mud. In South Georgia the clays are more or less of a sandy character, although in places somewhat more muddy than in Middle Georgia.

The soils of Georgia are equally dependent on the distribution of the geological formations; those over the Archaean belt are simply the result of the decay of crystalline rocks, and vary accordingly. The soils of the Paleozoic region are characterized by narrow belts varying with the geological formation and form some of the best lands in the State. In Southwest Georgia the surface lands are mostly loams of different degrees of consistency and sandy soils; these, however, vary greatly according to the nature of the underlying rocks which, in places, are calcareous, or, again, of a more clayey or sandy nature.

Nothing is more important than the distribution of building materials. Throughout the belt of crystalline rocks, which is divisible into several sections, there are enormous quantities of granite of various kinds. Marble of various colors occurs in abundance. Good slates are found in quantities.

In the Paleozoic country, limestones, of almost any character, are conveniently located. Sandstones, from beautiful gray to brown, may be easily obtained.

Throughout the broad plains of South Georgia, the question of construction materials is important, but at various localities, there are exposures of light Tertiary limestones, sufficient to afford an abundance of lime and building material. Sandstone of various textures occurs in some localities; and also flinty rocks suitable for road-making.

The clays of the State are extremely variable; thus we have fire clay in all the great groups or formations described, and some of these are naturally white and form kaolin; others again are tinted. Some of the most extensive deposits of these clays occur along the northern belts of the Tertiary strata in the southern part of the State. The clays suitable for brick purposes are valuable, and capable of producing bricks, equal in beauty to the Philadelphia pressed brick, and others, through all the grades to bricks of poor quality. Some of the clays or mixtures of clays are capable of making vitrified brick, and roof tiling as well as underground tiles. White sands are abundant, especially on the northern border of the Tertiary rock.

The crystalline formations produce mica, in workable sheets, feldspar, which is now used in fine grades of porcelain manufacture, and of course, an abundance of quartz. Corundum is found in many localities, the most valuable being adjacent to North Carolina. Garnets, which are also used for grinding purposes are found. Asbestos occurs in several localities; soapstone and talc are mined to a considerable extent. Graphite, in scales, occurs in rocks in such a proportion as to be workable. Gold is widespread throughout several belts and is found both in the gravels and sands derived from the disintegration of older rocks, and in veins traversing schistose rocks. The gold appears to be derived from pyrites, but in the deposits above the drainage levels, the gold is free milling, but below the drainage levels often passes into pyrites. More than $10,-000,000 of gold has already been obtained in the State.

Pyrite, or sulphide of iron, occurs in extensive beds sufficient to supply the whole country. This mineral has hitherto been imperfectly utilized, owing to the former low price of sulphur, and the preference of the acid manufacturers, many of whom are now changing their furnaces. From the quantity of pyrites of good quality, there seems no reason why the State should not supply its own and neighboring demands, and the demand is steadily increasing with the rapidly growing use of fertilizers. Much of the pyrites has a small percentage of copper associated with it to such an extent as to increase its value.

Among the iron ores, magnetite occurs in various beds, as also does hematite or specular ore, but the most abundant ore of iron in this belt at present conveniently located for shipment is limonite, or brown ore. Akin to the iron ores, is chromic iron, which is used for extraction of chrome. Ochres are also found throughout this belt.

Manganese ores have been found in several localities of the metamorphic rocks, but from one locality alone extensive shipments have been made even to the extent of 9000 tons in one year.

Nickel ore occurs in Northeast Georgia.

Barite or heavy spar is found. Argentiferous gelena occurs in the State. Molybdenite, beryl, and many others of the rarer minerals are also found.

The Paleozoic formations are represented by enormous thickness of deposits of the Cambrian and of the Lower Silurian systems and limited thickness of the Upper Silurian, a very small development of the Devonian, and considerable thickness of the Carboniferous systems. Of these systems, the most important, from the mineral standpoint, is the Knox or lower division of the Lower Silurian, the Upper Silurian and the Coal Measures.

In the Knox formations, there are enormous deposits of limonite or brown ore, which are extensively worked, and can be mined and put on board cars at a very low cost, from fifty cents to one dollar a ton. In the country where the iron occurs, manganese ores are found in many localities. Brown ores also occur in a portion of the Lower Silurian, equivalent to the Trenton series, and in the Sub-Carboniferous series. The Knox formation is also important as a source of extensive beds of bauxite. This mineral is now extensively sought for, as the source from which aluminum and alum compounds are most economically obtained. This mineral is known to extend into Alabama, but elsewhere in America at present it is only found in Arkansas. Our deposits of bauxite frequently contain from 55 to 62 per cent. of alumina, and some individual pockets have been known to reach even 70 per cent. Somewhat akin to bauxite is halloysite, which can be used as a substitute for bauxite, or as a fine porcelain clay, but this last mineral occurs in the Sub-Carboniferous series. The Knox formation also contains some valuable dolmitic limestones.

The Upper Silurian system, represented by the Red Mountain series, is valuable on account of containing red fossil ore. This ore above the drainage level is not calcareous, but below the drainage level is apt to be calcareous and even self-fluxing. It is the same ore which is most extensively used in the South for iron manufacture, but in furnace practice the iron producers prefer to mix brown ores with the fossil ore.

The Devonian system is represented by only a few feet of black shale, which is often mistaken for coal. The coal system of Georgia is confined to the northwestern corner of the State, where about nine different seams are known, several of which are workable. Some of these coals are equal in quality to any bituminous coals on the continent.

Our iron ores are largely shipped to Alabama and to Tennessee, but there are four large furnaces in the State.

Turning to South Georgia, besides the resources already named, there are valuable deposits of marl, used for agriculture, some green sand, and also beds of phosphates.

The above description of resources is an index to what the State contains and the relationship existing between the material welfare and the geological structure of the State.

IMMIGRANTS' OPPORTUNITIES IN GEORGIA.

By C. J. Haden.

Does Georgia want immigrants, and if so what attractions has the State to offer them ?

In my judgment Georgia has all to gain and nothing to lose by immigration. Between the State and the prospective settler there exist reciprocal inducements which ought to unite the two in life-long wedlock. Unfortunately at this juncture the match maker finds both parties hardly acquainted. They are shy and apparently indifferent; they have much to learn of each other. The hope of those who urge and agitate the union rests in the fact that Georgia is ready to move in the direction of substantial progress whenever led to see the way. The present plan of campaign is to awaken the land owners to a sense of their opportunity.

Considering that Georgia was one of the original thirteen colonies and classed among the older States, it is positively startling to know how sparse is her population. In Southeast Georgia the population in 1880 was only twelve persons to the square mile and in Southwest Georgia only twenty-one. Even in the most thickly settled portion of the State (Middle Georgia) it was forty-three persons to the square mile, and the average throughout the State was twenty-six persons to the square mile. The increase from 1880 to 1890 was 20 per cent., which would make at this writing the population to the square mile throughout the State averaging slightly over thirty persons.

It is well to say that the southeastern and southwestern parts of the State have the smallest proportions of waste lands, and those sections are the best capable of supporting a large population. England and Wales, which together comprise the same area as Georgia, with equally as much waste land, with a soil differing but slightly in fertility and a climate not so good for the production of vegatation are the home of 30,000,000 people, an average of 555 persons to the square mile. It will take 28,000,000 additional people to make a population in our State as dense as that of our mother country. Georgia could receive and assimilate every immigrant that lands on our shores at the present rate of influx for the next sixty-four years before our State's population will equal that of England and Wales. And while these figures are cited purely for the purpose of contrast, it shows that the absurd fear of over-population is worse than a phantom.

It is wasted energy for us to eulogize our resources in banquet speeches and newspaper discussions unless we bring more people. Wealth is produced by labor alone. We have no reason to complain in Georgia for lack of foreign capital. Europe and the North have within the past twenty years invested in railroad properties in this State nearly a billion dollars, and increased our railway mileage from 1800 miles to nearly 5000 miles. From the same sources have come vast sums of money which have been loaned or invested in town and city property and manufacturing industries. The spirit of growth has made every hamlet ambitious to be a town and every town eager to be a city. The truth is now apparent that our industrial system is becoming too top-heavy. More than two-thirds of our railway mileage is operated by receivers. The melancholy truth is that we have more railroads than we properly support. We have too much town and too little farm ; more transportation facilities than freight.

What is the remedy? This is the problem which confronts us. It is to restore a disturbed equilibrium that the advocates of immigration are in the field.

In 1880 Georgia had 7,690,292 acres of cleared land, which yielded $70,000,-000, according to the best accessible data. Of this cleared land it is safe to say that not more than one-half is in active cultivation, and it is fair to say that not more than one-half of this half is "half cultivated." Thus it will be seen that only about 20 per cent. of Georgia is out of the woods and only about 10 per cent. of it is actively employed. Turn upon these lands 100,000 industrious English, Scotch and German farmers and calculate the result. The average Georgia acre will produce $30 with only reasonable attention. Every immigrant farm laborer will till at the lowest estimate ten acres. Thus with only a fragment of the immigrants who enter Castle Garden in one year Georgia can extract from her now idle soil $30,000,000. ·

Contemplate $30,000,000 of new money turned into the arteries of our State's commerce! Then we could have activity that would abide with us; real business and not bubbles. In all these calculations I have leaned to the smaller side. It is not my purpose to attempt to excite or even to give what in my judgement are the full facts. What I here outline as our possible future is a mere picayune compared to the rapidly augmented fortunes which came to each of the States of Iowa, Nebraska and Minnesota under the benign influence of European immigration.

And the immigrant may ask what we have to offer more than the great Northwest, whither his friends and relatives have already gone. This question involves a voluminous answer. I shall not undertake any more than its outline now. First, a better climate. On this point argument is superfluous, in view of a series of disastrous blizzards which have scourged the extreme Northwest within recent years. Again we have an ocean front, which gives us

a market "as wide as the waters be." It costs the corn-grower in Dakota as much to transport corn to the Atlantic seaboard as it does the farmer in Georgia to grow it. I concede the fact that the soil of the Northwest is much more productive of corn and wheat than ours, but here the advantage ends. What they gain in fertility they lose in freight. When corn is seventeen cents in Minnesota it is fifty cents in Georgia; whenever the farmer in the former State gathers seventy-five bushels to the acre the farmer in the latter harvests twenty-five. Manipulate the facts as you will, they are in favor of Georgia.

And turning to fruits and vegetables, which yield more to the acre than staple crops both in gross value and net profits, the odds are enormously in favor of the Southeast. One acre of Le Conte pears in South-central Georgia produces more clear money than the average Minnesota farm. The South Georgia pear tree works for nothing and boards itself. An acre of land in Wilcox, Dooly or Irwin counties in Georgia will grow, with fair treatment, 300 pounds of sea island cotton, worth on a low market twenty cents per pound, or $60. The acre which makes this record in Georgia can be bought as it comes from the hands of the saw mill operator almost entirely cleared for from $2 to $5 per acre, or if in cultivation for from $5 to $10, and the taxes are eighty-five cents on $100. One $5-acre in Georgia yields a larger net return if planted in sugar cane than five $50-acres in Minnesota planted in wheat, and the percentage of taxation is much less than in any of the Northwestern States. Bear in mind, I emphasize the fact, that it is upon the net profit and not the gross results that we found our argument. It is quite common for 500 gallons of syrup to be grown upon one acre in South Georgia, which at the lowest market price is worth $150 at the nearest railroad station, and the cost of production differs very little from ordinary corn.

Before my mental vision I see bristling an army of interrogation points. Men will wonder how a country that will do all this has remained dormant, and will attack these statements with a hundred doubting questions. The simplest defence which I can put forth by way of anticipation is, let them come and see for themselves. Truths are being constantly unfolded that had been hidden since creation. The gold of California, the diamonds of South Africa, the mahogany of Honduras, the phosphates of Florida, all had the breath of life breathed into them by discovery. Some day the lands of the Southeast will catch the public eye, and suddenly rise in popular esteem and market value. A little tide of immigration would speed this movement and bring to an early consummation the development which we have long desired.

The question of immigration is not wholly new in the South. It came to us from Europe, planted colonies along our coasts and penetrated the interior during the last half of the eighteenth century. The best blood in our country took root here during that period. This current continued to flow until the slave ships of Liverpool and Boston began to dump African captives upon our country. It was a melancholy day for the South when our immigration changed color. Eventually it caused us to lose the political prestige which we so long enjoyed. The best, the quickest and the easiest way to bleach the tint of our body politic and regain our lost dominion is by repeated hyperdermic injections of good settlers from the fatherlands of Europe and from the North.

Reduced to a business footing the plan of settling immigrants is simple. There are a great many individuals and corporations who own large tracts of land which they are willing to parcel up into farms of small and moderate size and sell on easy installment payments at a low price. In many cases they will furnish material to build the houses and fences on the same easy terms, and even build the houses for settlers and include it in the land sale. The settler can begin with a very small amount of cash. There are a number of successful colonies in the Southeast already. A Swiss colony has been growing grapes at Mt. Airy, Ga., for several years with great success. A number of immigrants from Ohio, mainly German, have made the Fort Valley district in this State noted for its fruit and market garden products. Mr. Robt. Viewig, of Godwinsville, Dodge county, is a splendid specimen of an industrious German settler, and his work has been a prodigy of thrift and enterprise. The colony of Germans who settled Cullman county, Ala., have made it one of the thriftiest counties in that State.

If the people in Georgia can once become thoroughly aroused over this subject victory is ours. If they will co-operate to make themselves known in Europe and then to prepare for immigrant colonies when they arrive, the immigrants will do the rest, and I believe that these things are to be in the early future. I have an abiding faith in both the soil and the people of Georgia.

Atlanta, Ga.

FRUIT CULTURE IN GEORGIA.

By Henry R. Goetchius.

The close of the struggle between the States left the South in an impoverished condition, and the story of its quick resuscitation reads like a tale from the Arabian Nights. Its manifold natural advantages make the secret of its development. A less favored section would not have stood the shock of revolution. The figures illustrative of the South's progress, as shown by the comparative statistics of 1880 and 1890, tell a story that reads like a romance of development, and make an unassailable plea for every power of trade and money.

It is not within the province of this article to enter into detail as to the causes which have produced these results. They are numerous; the phosphate beds, the lumber and naval stores, the sugar plantations, the Florida fruits, the Alabama minerals, the Texas wool and cattle, and the great staple which, though dethroned, is still a factor of wealth within the borders of every Southern State; these all combine to make the story. The growth has been steady and rapid and in the face, too, of the most adverse surroundings. The section has been engaged in working the gravest social and political problems, while building up her waste places and restoring her broken fortunes, and with it all she has shared with others the measures of her bounty. The political changes wrought by the war have made the South a payer of tribute to other sections of the Union.

This tribute she pays in many ways; foremost are the taxes of the general government, so few of which find their way back. To these add the interest upon her railroads and other securities held by Northern capitalists; the unceasing stream of life and fire insurance premiums, and the millions which the money centres North and West annually appropriate from cotton and grain futures. It is gratifying to the Southern man, however, to reflect that his great section prospers in the face of these things and that already a change of conditions is taking place which in the near future will restore the equilibrium of the flow of capital. The wealth-producing agencies are to be found on every hand, and cotton is no longer sole monarch. The conditions of the cultivation of this crop are such that, while it produces annually an enormous sum of ready cash, it is only permitted the producer to handle the proceeds for a very short while. There are other sources of wealth which are giving to the South its substantial prosperity; chief among these is the culture of fruit, an industry which is assuming such proportions as to attract great consideration and which, from its results, especially in the State of Georgia, is attracting the most widespread attention.

It is not my purpose to write of the subject generally, or to go into details as to the cultivation of all the fruits capable of being produced in Georgia. The soil and climate are favorable for the growth of any product which can be produced in the temperate zone, the coffee plant excepted. All of the sub-tropical fruits can be and are grown in abundance for domestic uses, but the special products for commercial purposes are melons, peaches and grapes. Melons are produced in great abundance in Southwest Georgia, and thousands are annually shipped by rail and steamer. In 1891 more than 5000 car loads of melons were shipped from Southwest Georgia and Southeast Alabama to northern and western markets, and in 1892 the estimated shipment was 7000 car loads. It is to the culture of peaches and grapes in Georgia to which I desire to call special attention.

If the reader will look at his map of Georgia he will note the city of Atlanta at a point about 100 miles northwest from the centre of the State. The city is located at an elevation above tidewater of about 1000 feet on the hills which form the Southern limits of the Blue Ridge ranges of mountains. To the north and northeast is a rolling hilly country, increasing in elevation till you cross the Georgia line into the "Land of the Sky," the beautiful Ashville country so familiar to the tourist. Below Atlanta lies a plateau of land extending about 140 miles to the southeast and 100 miles to the southwest, the base of which section would be a line drawn from the city of Columbus on the west to the town of Fort Valley on the east. The country embraced in this triangle is the home of the grape and the peach and has within its limits the finest fruit lands in the world.

As yet practical developments have been made only in limited areas, of which Griffin in Spalding county and Fort Valley in Houston county are the centres. One of these places is within forty miles of Atlanta and the other is a little more than 100 miles distant. They are both within fifty hours of the great northern and western cities, and fruit

LE CONTE PEARS, GROWN IN GEORGIA.

shipped from their depots, shot through in refrigerating cars along the great Southern trunk lines, is within reach of a population of 30,000,000 of people within full time to be enjoyed in all its freshness and lusciousness. This fact has caught the attention not only of the fruit-grower but of the capitalist, and the lands about Griffin and Fort Valley today present an unbroken scene of peach and grape plantations. At the one place they extend north and south along the Central Railroad of Georgia, and southwest along the Georgia Midland & Gulf Railroad, and at the other they reach north, east, south and west along the Southwestern and the Atlanta & Florida Railroads.

At Fort Valley the acreage is devoted almost exclusively to peaches, and covers a space of some eight square miles.

There are about 1,000,000 trees planted and about half a million dollars invested in the orchards. The profits on the peach crop of Houston county, in which the town is located, for the year 1892 amounted to $350,000. Here some of the largest orchards are cultivated by joint stock companies and the capital invested is mostly from the Western States, notably Ohio. The largest orchard, however, is owned by a native of the county. Ten years ago he did not have a dollar. As an experiment he planted 20,000 peach trees which, within three years, began to bear. His net profits from his crop in 1889 were estimated at $50,000, and in the year following they were proportionately large. The orchards vary in the number of trees, from 5000 to 200,000, but there are many small farms, all of which go to swell the acreage.

The yield from the trees, on an average crop, is from one to one and one-half crates of three pecks each. In a full crop the yield is from two to four crates. The estimated cost of a crate from tree to market is about one dollar. This includes the cost of the crate, gathering and packing and carting the fruit, and transporting it by rail. The crates will sell for a price varying with the quality and condition of the fruit, ranging from two to seven dollars each. With 190 trees to the acre, and an estimated yield of two crates to the tree, the fruit-grower may count on 380 crates, and at the very low estimate of two dollars each in the sale, and with one dollar off for expenses, he would have a profit of $380 from one acre. With a low average crop, and that too only every third year (if such an unusual event should happen as two successive failures), this would be a profit of about $125 per annum for each acre in cultivation. But it is by no means an unfair estimate to expect even in the most unfavorable year a profit of $100 per acre.

The above figures are very conservative. Sometimes the profits on the fruit are so large as to be almost incredible. Last season the owner of an orchard had a half-acre of ninety-seven trees, and sold the fruit thereon for five hundred dollars as it stood upon the trees. The purchaser gathered 580 crates from these trees, for which he was offered by a Philadelphia firm two dollars per crate delivered on the cars. Deducting the cost of gathering, packing and carting and also the original purchase price of the fruit, this man had a clear profit of four hundred and fifty-seven dollars in this half acre, or very nearly at the rate of one thousand dollars per acre. We cannot go further in detail in writing of the Fort Valley peach farms. The industry at that point has grown to such proportions that it has begun to attract outside capital and is so extensive as to well repay one for a visit

to the locality. The land in that entire section is peculiarly adapted to fruit. It is of a red clay formation, with a loam sub-soil, (chocolate top soil), and even the worn-out cotton lands can be made to produce fine fruits by proper fertilization.

Leaving Fort Valley and passing northward on one of the lines of railway mentioned, we arrive in a few hours at Griffin in Spalding county. Here the tourist will find a veritable garden spot. On an elevated ridge some thousand feet above the ocean level, he looks around upon a beautiful country well watered by sparkling streams, which upon the one side flow westward towards the Gulf and on the other eastward towards the Atlantic. The climate is perfect, and the soil seems intended by nature for the growth of fruit. It is the red metamorphic clay overlaid with the detritus of granite and gneissic rock, and will produce the finest flavored fruits of all kinds grown upon this continent. One of the strongest evidences of the truth of this statement is that there are now to be found among the fruit growers of this section people from Florida, California, Montana, Michigan, Illinois, Ohio, Canada, Maine and Massachusetts.

About ten years ago the pioneer of this interesting colony happened there in quest of a climate favorable for weak lungs. This he found, for the thermometer never gets below zero, and even when it reaches (which it rarely does) twenty-five degrees above, "the oldest inhabitant" begins to look up his memorandum of what year in the misty past this unusual event transpired. In the decade that marked the coming of this pioneer, peach plantations and vineyards have grown to perfection. Last year, within a radius of seven miles of Griffin, more than a hundred car loads of fruit went North in June and July to gladden the eye and tickle the palate of people who at that time were permitted only to enjoy the fragrance which escaped from the blossoms of their own trees. These shipments consisted of both peaches and grapes, for the conditions are as favorable for the growth of peaches in this vicinity as at Fort Valley. There are now about one thousand acres in peach trees in the neighborhood of Griffin, and the cultivation of this fruit is successfully made a specialty by many. That section has also an advantage in that it is the home of the grape. A carefully compiled directory of the grape growers of the United States, published in 1891, gives for the State of Georgia one hundred and two grape growers and an average of six hundred and fifteen acres, of which four hundred and fifty three acres were in Spalding county alone. Since that year fully three hundred

SKETCH MAP OF FRUIT GROWING SECTION OF GEORGIA.

acres have been added, and the traveler on either of the railroads leaving Griffin, as he looks from the car window, will have his eye delighted with acres of flourishing vineyards.

In viewing the beautiful fruit farms about Griffin last summer, I was led to talk with a successful fruit grower who lives at Vineyard in Spalding county, and I gathered from him some very interesting information. The name of the farmer is Rudolph Oetter.

He is a native of Germany and spent the early years of his life in his native province of Bavaria. His father gave

some attention to fruit growing, and it was there that the son first gained practical information in horticulture. Rudolph Oetter came to America when he was about seventeen years old and first lived in Boston, Mass. After accumulating enough money by work to travel on a prospecting tour he went through the West and the South in search of a suitable place for the establishment of a fruit farm, and he says that of all the places that have come under his observation in the United States, the country in the neighborhood of Griffin, Middle Georgia, and the section contiguous thereto, is the most suitable for fruit growing. In 1883 he settled upon a tract of land near Griffin, in Spalding county, at a place called Vineyard, and in the fall of 1884 and spring of 1885 cleared six acres of ground and planted the same in grapes. These vines bore a full crop in 1889, and from the six acres he sold $1260 worth of grapes and 1800 gallons of wine. The grapes were sold at five cents per pound on the railroad track at the vineyard, and the wine was sold at a net profit of seventy-five cents per gallon, making a total profit of $2610 on the six acres, or $435 per acre.

In 1890 the crop from the six acres was not as good as in the year previous and price was lower, the net average profit being $150 per acre in grapes and wine.

In 1891 the six acres had increased by previous planting to nine acres, and from the nine acres there were shipped 30,000 pounds of grapes at a net price of three cents per pound, making $900, and 750 gallons of wine at a net profit of $1 per gallon, making $1650 total on net sales of grapes and wines, or an average of $163 per acre.

Mr. Oetter says that what is known as the Norton grape in full bearing condition with a favorable crop year, will make as a net income $400 per acre.

The following is an estimate of the cost of development of a vineyard and the probable yield. The figures in estimating the cost are liberal, and in stating the yield have been placed at a minimum. Taking grapes first: The first year's estimate, assuming that Norton vines, which are the best, will be planted, will be as follows, taking twenty-five acres as a basis, which would be a sufficient quantity to start on:

25 acres of land valued at $10 per acre.	$ 250
Clearing of 25 acres perfectly clean, $10 each....	250
Plants for 25 acres, at a cost of $50 per thousand, (500 plants to the acre)	625
Planting and staking......	75
Replacing stakes with posts second year........	350
Lumber for trellis.......	20
Wire................	375
Cultivating for three years.....................	375
House and barn.................................	500
Implements....................................	100
One mule........	150
Wagon...... ,.................................	40
Three years' living of a man and his family at $250 per year.................................	750
Total..	$3860

This farm should yield in the third year in Norton grapes three pounds of grapes on each vine, making a total of 37,500 pounds of grapes, which at four cents per pound, would be $1500. The fourth and fifth years would increase until it reached six pounds to the vine. If it were desired to add the necessary arrangements for making wine the following items of expense would be needed:

For building of vats.............................	$ 400
Presses.........,...............................	50
Casks and fermenting tubs......................	1000
Extras...............	50
Total............	$1500

Cost of vineyard................................	$3860
Cost of wine-making plant......................	1500
Total...	$5360

Assuming that the vineyard is in Norton grapes, in the fourth year the yield would be ten pounds to the vine or 125,000 pounds of grapes, from which could be made 10,000 gallons of wine, worth in bulk in Boston $1 per gallon, in the year following (which is as soon as the wine can be marketed), showing an income of $10,000 in five years from the investment of $5360. After the vineyard has attained its growth such items of expense as construction of the plant for the manufacture of wine and the building of the house and barn and the purchase and clearing of the land need not be estimated in the annual cost. If Delaware grapes should be planted instead of Norton grapes the yield could safely be estimated at three pounds to the vine for 20,000 vines and this would be 60,000 pounds. (The Delaware average more than 500 vines to the acre, as they are planted more thickly than the Norton). This 60,000 pounds of grapes at four cents per pound would yield $2400 on the investment of $3860. In the fourth year and subsequent years the yield would be six pounds or 120,000 pounds of grapes, which at four cents per pound would be $4800. , Assuming that the annual fixed charges on the plant would be $1800, the annual income therefore would be $3000 on an investment of $3860, and proportionately larger if there were an investment in a wine plant.

The above figures are from a practical fruit grower, and this man also says that the area of country contiguous to Griffin, and which we have described as lying on the high plateau below and within a hundred miles of Atlanta, is as much adapted to the growth of fruit as the country in which he lives. We have given actual results at Fort Valley and Griffin. There are thousands of acres of just such land within a short distance of either of these points and contiguous to rail, and it can be obtained for prices ranging from ten to twenty-five dollars per acre. When we remember that of the ten years passed it required four to bring the fruit into bearing condition and that therefore only six years can be allowed in the reckoning, the progress that fruit culture has attained in Georgia is wonderful. It is yet in its infancy, but its possibilities are immense. Early seasons, climate and soil are all favorable. Quick and satisfactory transportation is assured, and the teeming population of the North and West is ready to take and consume the crop. Of the five hundred car loads of peaches and grapes shipped out of Georgia last year nearly all went either to New York or Philadelphia, while Boston, Baltimore, Cincinnati, Chicago, St. Paul, Minneapolis and other large places got none. It is estimated that the twelve larger cities of the Union could handle sixty car loads a day, not to mention what minor places could consume. For early fruit shipped in good condition, the market is unlimited, and the assured consumption lies in the fact that this southern fruit can be placed in the markets while the northern fruit trees are only in blossom.

If I have succeeded in holding the attention of the reader I will, in conclusion, invite his consideration of three propositions:

First. That there is a very desirable section of Georgia suited in soil, climate and in every other natural advantage for the successful cultivation of fruit on either a small or a large scale.

Second. That the figures given by men now engaged in its cultivation show beyond question that there is a very large profit in it.

Third. That the industry has progressed sufficiently to prove that it is safe, and its possibilities are at present beyond estimation.

The facts and the figures will convince the doubtful that there is a great future for Georgia in this one special feature of her many advantages.

COTTON IN GEORGIA.

By H. H. Hickman.

In 1891 we had in Georgia 479,863 spindles. In 1892 50,000 were added to this number, giving us a total of 529,-863 spindles at the beginning of this year, with about 12,000 looms, or about one-fifth of the entire spinning and weaving capacity of the Southern States. When we take into consideration the large territory embraced by Georgia; the beautiful climate, for the most part very healthy and in every way favorable to the manufacture of cotton; an inexhaustible water power, running through the cotton fields whose product is more than a million bales per annum, and an abundant supply of the best of labor, it seems that Georgia's progress has not been what it should be. The State will regain its position at the front of the Southern cotton industry, however, after a while. We had a poor cotton crop last season and consequently we have had very little surplus money for investment. It is gratifying, however, to know that all the mills worthy of the name in the State are doing fairly well and are paying reasonable dividends. Of course, old worn-out mills without means and with poor management must go to the wall. Running such mills is like running an old worn-out plantation with lame mules thirty years old, "daddy gopher" plows and reaping hooks and scythes to gather the grain.

Two years ago I was criticised by the able president of the Bibb Manufacturing Co., who predicted loss and destruction to the Southern cotton mills on account of bad management and overproduction; but from that time to the present we have had a good demand for all the goods we could make. As far as the mills I represent are concerned, I could have sold twice the output at fair profits. Two years ago, when I predicted that we would spin our entire cotton crop in the South in half a century, I was perhaps somewhat enthusiastic. If I had included the entire United States and made my limit of time three-quarters of a century, it would have been nearer the mark, but I do not hesitate to say that the time will come when this country will be the greatest manufacturing centre in the world.

The accomplished editor of *Dixie* has promised to surpass my most sanguine expectations, proposing a clean sweep. To revolutionize cotton-spinning in the South, he proposes to make a perfect combination of all the Southern mills, sweeping out all New England by making all the fine goods in the South. This must be discouraging to our Yankee brothers. *Dixie* states that we have been going from bad to worse, until the majority of our mills have ceased to declare profits and are absolutely fronting loss and failure.

The *Manufacturers' Record* replied to *Dixie*, giving a long list of dividends paid by Southern mills, and showing that all was not lost, showing, too, that the cotton manufacturing industry of the South is steadily improving in its methods and machinery and advancing surely towards the higher standards of excellence maintained in the older manufacturing sections of the North. But *Dixie* is not willing to have our Eastern mills make all the fine goods and pocket all the big profits. This pugnacious advocate of the South would demolish all the New England mills, knock all the intelligence, ingenuity and energy out of our Yankee brother, erect fine-goods cotton mills down South and pocket all the large profits. This would indeed be a great victory, but when all these battles shall have been fought and won, then we may look for the millenium. . There is a natural field which the New England cotton manufacturing industry must continue to occupy for some years to come,

Columbus are the chief centres of the industry, the two cities containing a dozen mills, with about 240,000 spindles and nearly 8000 looms, considerable more than one-half of the industry of Georgia. The other mills are scattered among the smaller cities and towns.

A word now about the culture of cotton in Georgia. The production of cotton may be familiar to many who read this, but for the benefit of those who have never seen a cotton field I will outline the growth of a crop. To produce and market a cotton crop requires about the full twelve months. All contracts for labor expire at Christmas, and when the holidays are over the first

ENTERPRISE COTTON FACTORY, AUGUSTA, GA.

and there is a natural channel in which the development of the Southern cotton industry must progress. In the North the tendency is steadily away from those grades of goods that can be made to the best advantage in the South, while in the South the industry is gradually advancing to the finer products made in New England and thereby encroaching upon the industry of the North. The ultimate outcome of these tendencies is obvious to all, except those who persistently refuse to see it; the Southern industry will expand while the Northern industry must contract into narrower limits.

Georgia is peculiarly adapted to the requirements of cotton manufacturing, particularly in the Piedmont section — the northwest counties of the State. In this region the climate more nearly approaches that of New England than elsewhere, and the river and mountain streams supply ample water power for all needs of the industry. Augusta and

half of January is occupied to a great extent in making the necessary changes and settling new tenants. This once accomplished, part of the hands are put to cleaning the ditches and fields, repairing the premises and breaking down the old cotton stalks, preparing the way for the plows. Plowing begins as soon as

JOHN P. KING COTTON MILL, AUGUSTA, GA.

the land is ready, and by spring all the land that is to be cultivated should be nicely turned over and a proper proportion of small grain should be sown. Corn is planted and all attention is then turned to cotton.

Broad and deep furrows are opened where each row is to be, and the fertilizer is spread along the bottom of each row. A plow then covers the fertilizer with the soil and forms smooth beds ready for the seed. In the Gulf States the

AUGUSTA COTTON FACTORY AUGUSTA, GA.

seed from a former crop, with refuse from the stables, forms the chief fertilizer used, but in the Atlantic States it is necessary to supplement these largely with various manufactured compounds. As soon as the season for killing frosts has passed, planting begins, varying from the last of March to the last of April, according to latitude. The beds are opened with a shallow furrow, the seed is carefully sown in a continuous row, either by hand or machine, and then lightly covered. If the season be propitious, the plants come up quickly, appearing in narrow green bands down each row. When they attain a height of two or three inches a furrow is run on the side of each row with a narrow plow, and the laborers start in with hoes "chopping out" the larger portion of the young cotton, but leaving at regular intervals clumps of two or three stalks. These are thinned down to one stalk in each interval, on a second and more careful working. Some earth is thrown to them by a suitable plow to form a soft bed in which the roots may extend, and the crop is fairly started. The distances

between the rows and between the plants in each row are such that the plants when full grown may about touch each other, covering the entire field. The crop once started needs frequent workings, keeping the ground free from grass and slightly stirred so that the roots may penetrate it freely. Deep plowing is very injurious, as it cuts the roots.

If the season be favorable the growth is rapid. By the first of May the plants almost cover the ground and blooms begin to appear. All cultivation must now cease, as plows would damage the plant, and for a month nothing is done in the cotton fields. Six weeks from the appearance of the blooms the bolls mature and open, and picking begins early in August in more Southern latitudes, and by the middle of the month bales of new cotton begin to come into market in appreciable quantity. From that time until Christmas the work of gathering and preparing the cotton for market is continuous and urgent. After September 1 the fields are white with open bolls, while blooms continue to appear and new fruit forms until frost

SIBLEY COTTON MILLS, AUGUSTA, GA.

kills the plant. It is this continued bearing from July 1 to November that always ensures a moderate crop at least, unless an exceptional disaster destroys all calculations. The extended use of fertilizers and more skillful cultivation has greatly increased the yield. Ten years ago the total crop of the South was about 6,000,000 bales, while last season it was over 9,000,000 bales, although then all the conditions were exceptionally favorable. In the same time the crop of Georgia has increased from 800,000 bales to 1,200,000 bales.

Augusta, Ga.

THE SCHOOLS OF GEORGIA.

By S. D. Bradwell,

Commissioner of Schools of Georgia.

The progress that Georgia is making in educational matters entitles her to take rank with any of the Southern States.

In higher education, the State University and numerous colleges afford ample opportunities. State aid is extended, under the restrictions imposed by the organic law, only to the State University, the colleges being left entirely to private enterprise and the commendable zeal of the different religious denominations. The influence of the University has been greatly extended in the last decade by the creation of branch colleges, which are dependent upon the University in all matters of general government. Among these branch institutions are numbered the School of Technology, the Girls' Normal and Industrial College, the branch of the University for colored students, the agricultural colleges, and the law and medical departments of the University. Money for higher education can be appropriated only to the University through these channels.

The strides made by the State in the diffusion of education—primary education—among the masses have been wonderful. But little more than twenty years has elapsed since the birth of the public school system At first the small sum of $170,000 was appropriated for its support, and a few thousand were the recipients of its benefits Now the fund amounts to a million and a quarter, and seventy-five per cent. of the children of the State will express the figures which stand for those who attend the schools. By means of this fund every child in the State, white and colored, can obtain five months' schooling free of cost. By the "children of the State" we mean those who are within the ages prescribed by statutory enactment—six to eighteen years. This fund is made up from different sources, some of which are variable in amount each year. They are as follows: Tax on whisky, shows, fertilizers, oils, the hire of convicts, lease of oyster beds, besides a direct property tax. This last item for 1893 is fixed at $600,000. Another source of revenue to the school fund is the poll-tax, fixed by the constitution at one dollar. Last year this amounted to $208,000.

It should be stated that the fund alluded to is the State fund. This is largely increased by local taxation in the cities and towns,, which in addition to the State fund, is sufficient to maintain the schools in these favored localities for nine or ten months each year. There is scarcely a town of 2000 inhabitants in the State which has not availed itself of this privilege to levy an additional tax for the support of the schools. As a result, the public schools of many of the cities in Georgia will compare favorably with any common schools in any part of the country. In return, the State confers special privileges upon these cities and towns in allowing them to manage, under the general provisions of the law, their own schools. There are at present about forty-five of these local systems, and the number is increasing each year. They constitute a part of the common school system of the State, but they are independent in all matters of local control and government.

While the schools in the country districts, where the people are comparatively sparsely settled, are limited to five months, yet in many localities the patrons supplement the State fund, and the teachers are employed for a longer period. The State encourages the patrons to do this in order to make the schools permanent. Even in the five months' schools the parent is invited to add to the salary the State pays in order that the best teachers may be employed. In this way a partnership is formed between the State and the parent, and the school and the teacher are not entirely dependent upon the State.

Among the agricultural population the experiment of establishing "farm villages" is being tested. From this much good is expected to be derived, especially in making the schools permanent and in securing better schoolhouses.

The common-school system of Georgia is admirably designed in its general provisions. Each county is a school district, over which is placed a county board of education, consisting of five members selected by the grand jury and commissioned by the Governor. This board selects from the citizens its executive officer, who is called the county school commissioner. He is the superintendent of all the schools of the county, and to him are entrusted also the school finances, and the performance of certain ministerial as well as clerical duties. In all local matters, under general rules and regulations prescribed by the central authority, the county board has full control. It also sits as a court for the trial of all matters of local controversy. The right of appeal to the higher school courts is provided for.

The central authority is vested in the State Board of Education, of which board, composed of five members also, the Governor of the State is the president, and the State School Commissioner the executive officer. To this latter officer is entrusted the general management of all common or public schools of the State. He apportions the school fund to the different counties, construes the law, issues instructions to the subordinate school officers and examines the teachers. He has certain judicial powers, and from his decisions and rulings an appeal may be taken to the State Board of Education, and the decision of that body shall be final.

It will readily be seen that there is a nice adjustment in the system of the relative powers of the local and central authorities in accordance with the spirit of all our laws. There are certain rights reserved to the counties, in the exercise of which the State has no power to interfere; and in all matters of general nature the authority of the State is supreme. Where the scales are evenly balanced between the local and general government there is but little friction in the execution of the laws which control the system.

There are, as parts of this great system, about 10,000 teachers and 600,000 children. These figures are only approximate, as it has been five years since a census of the school population has been taken. It is proper to add, however, that arrangements are now completed for taking a census. When this work is finished—and it will be by the first of June—from statistics thus carefully collected, the assertion that Georgia has made wonderful progress in the diffusion of education among the masses, white and colored, will be clearly demonstrated.

No difference or discrimination is made between the races, the same facilities as to length of public school term, efficiency of teachers and other requisites, being guaranteed to colored just as to white; and yet the schools for the races must be separate, and under no circumstances can white and colored attend the same school. This is as emphatic as the law prohibiting intermarriage between the two races. The color line, to the entire satisfaction of both races, is drawn here; but the white and negro teachers undergo the same examinations and are under the same rules and regulations. The white and colored children study the same text-books and enjoy the same advantages always in separate schools.

Atlanta, Ga.

GEORGIA'S TRADE AND TRANSPORTATION.

By Col. I. W. Avery.

The railroad system of Georgia has grown from 643 miles in 1850 to 2937 miles in 1893. The stages of growth have been as follows:

Years.	Miles.
1850	643
1860	1420
1870	1845
1880	2459
1890	4600
1893	4937

In the three years 1889, 1890 and 1891 Georgia surpassed in increase of railroad mileage every other State in the Union, save Washington, in the far Northwest. In 1889, 338 miles of new railroad were built in Georgia; in 1890, 356 miles, and in 1891, 294 miles, an aggregate of 988 miles. In the same three years Washington built 1035 miles, or only 46 miles more than Georgia. Pennsylvania came next with 824 miles.

The relation of Georgia's railroad system to other portions of her autonomy is as follows: area, 59,475 square miles; total population, 1,837,353; population per square miles, 30.89; area, per mile of railroad, 12.4 square miles; population per mile of railroad, 374; assessed valuation, $415,328,945; valuation per capita, $226.

Two places in Georgia have ten railroads centering in them—Atlanta and Macon; two have seven roads each—Savannah and Rome; three have six each—Augusta, Columbus and Albany; five have five each—Americus, Cordele, Fort Valley, Griffin, and Waycross; while numbers have four among them—Dalton, Gainesville, Union Point, Millen, Tennille, Jessup, Riverside, Thomasville, Newnan and Valdosta.

Georgia has the finest system of ocean and railway transportation in the United States, and the equal of any in the world. Her two Atlantic seaports are Savannah and Brunswick. Savannah has twenty-one feet of water, and $3,300,000 appropriated by Congress to give twenty-six feet of water, this harbor being regarded as a national necessity, and the nation's commerce requiring that it should be perfected. Brunswick has a fine natural harbor and is connected with two powerful systems of railway, the Plant system, running into Florida and the Southwest and maintaining a line of steamers to Cuba; and the great East Tennessee Virginia & Georgia Railroad, with its nearly three thousand miles of track and its connections North, West, and Southwest; Brunswick being the South Atlantic terminus of the system, and Norfolk, Va., the Middle Atlantic terminus.

Savannah is the Southern terminus of four great radiating steamship lines to Boston, New York, Philadelphia, and Baltimore, the four greatest American ocean ports, under the Ocean Steamship Co. This magnificent steamship service, with its eleven fine steamships, makes Georgia a great entrepot for national and international commerce. These ships do a vast business, and have great and completely equipped wharves with every trade convenience.

In considering Georgia's geographical position, her commercial advantage becomes strikingly manifest. Her seaport cities are nearer by railroad than New York to San Francisco, Cal.; Portland, Oregon, Omaha, Neb.; Salt Lake City, Utah; Memphis, Nashville, and Chattanooga Tenn. Birmingham and Montgomery, Ala. Little Rock, Ark.; and Waco, Tex. Thus the South through Savannah and Brunswick, is in closer touch than New York with the grain and flour and meat marts of the West, making Southern direct trade with foreign countries sure, necessary and profitable, and rendering it inevitable that Georgia, the South and the West and Europe shall and will use this trade advantage, and secure short Southern railway transportation in competition with the longer Northern routes.

Savannah and Brunswick are so much nearer than New York to the grain and meat marts of the West, and richest cotton fields of the South, by existing and possible lines of railway, that the grain, meat and cotton, if they have a chance; will seek this best, shortest, cheapest and quickest route to Europe, their largest market. Georgia has now superior conditions to secure direct trade and to furnish a quick and paying trade over every other point in the full factors of commerce, products, negotiable exchange, terminal facilities and railways, Europe having a plethora of merchant marine.

Closer to most of the commercial centers of the West than northern Atlantic ports, connected to those centers by complete and direct railway systems thoroughly equipped, that are never blocked in winter by snow and ice, and running through territory rich in every farm and mineral wealth, it is inevitable that foreign commerce will seek this favored route of transportation through Georgia to the South and West, instead of by the longer, more circuitous way of the North, with its frozen perils and obstacles of the bleak northern winter.

The nearer stretch of Georgia's seaports is already getting substantial recognition, and a good tide of shipment is pouring from the West through Savannah to New York by the Ocean Steamship Company, which carries steadily and regularly wool and other goods from Colorado, Nebraska, Illinois, Arkansas, Missouri, and other Western States; and this growing tide of Western stuff is but the precursor of a great current of Western trade to the old world through the sunny South, and by these more convenient Georgia gateways of Savannah and Brunswick. The fact of this beginning of Western passage of stuff to New York through Georgia is enormously significant and presages large home commercial competition, and a vast future Southern trade, with Georgia to the front as the conduit and immediate beneficiary of the new tide of fructifying commerce. And tariff reform, with its policy established, will open the doors and let in a rich and increasing tide of affluent foreign commerce through Georgia's ports to the broad Pacific, making Southern direct trade a tremendous reality.

Savannah's railway connections with every part of the country are thorough and many. Besides her four imperial ocean steam lines, firmly established, largely profitable, and steadily growing, carrying great currents of freight and passengers to the North, she has the best-established railway trunk lines North, Northwest, West, Southwest and South. She has also an excellent and profitable fruit steamship line to South America. The beauty of Georgia's system of railways is that to all points there are rival lines of railroads, ensuring the wholesome benefits of competition.

Tracing out the Georgia railroad systems it will be seen that they are an almost perfect network for freight and passenger traffic. The lines cross and recross, giving short reach to all points, and establishing the most convenient trade communications and easy commercial relations. From each leading city new straight tracks to important points are projected and building. Many great centre systems have their termini in Georgia, the State thus being their headquarters, and the controlling focus of railway operations and trade progress.

Besides her unsurpassed and unequalled through transportation for commerce and travel, Georgia has the finest local support for railroads in the United States. The leading cotton-raising State in the South, the largest naval stores producer in the world, the chief fruit, melon, peach, vegetable State of the Union, growing all the time and supplying the whole country, and with direct trade about to supply Europe; a vast lumber State with a splendid variety of timbers; one of the chief fertilizer States of the South, doing an immense and increasing business, and shipping all over the world; building up foreign trade in cotton yarns; the possessor of mighty quarries of marble, slate and granite, now being successfully worked; a region of vast grain and hay areas and stock country. Georgia in her own varied and matchless scope of productions can support her railways, and presents irresistible inducements to settlers, home-seekers and investment hunters.

A brilliant and momentous fact· in Georgia's record in connection with transportation, and as signal a distinction as the invention of the cotton gin, is that in 1819, a Georgia merchant, Mr. William Scarbrough, of Savannah, Ga., built and sent across the Atlantic ocean the first steamship that ever crossed the seas, thus inaugurating ocean steamship navigation, which has revolutionized the commerce of the whole world. This was a great triumph for human practical progress. This steamship was named the "City of Savannah." The full account of this crucial event and the life of Mr. Scarbrough can be found in the second volume of the National Cyclopedia of American Biography. It was a fitting thing that Georgia, that is lead-ing the South in her transportation annals, should have thus led in ocean service for trade.

Some of Georgia's rivers are usefully navigable, and are being used for trade, the Savannah, the Coosa and Ocmulgee rivers all being used for commerce.

But the crowning achievement of Georgia's transportation advantages will be the establishment of a short trans-Atlantic, trans-American and trans-Pacific mail route from England, through Savannah, Ga., and San Diego, Cal., to Australia, New Zealand, Japan and China, shorter by 800 miles of rail and 2,500 miles of ocean passage than any other route. This will be a magnificent contribution to the convenience of the world's commercial correspondence.

Again, the completion of the great Nicarauga Canal will bring Georgia to the front, and add infinitely to her commerce.

Georgia today is the Southern leader of local and national transportation, and has every basis for a continuance of her carrying supremacy.

Atlanta.

THE LUMBER INDUSTRY OF GEORGIA.

By Walter Pope.

Yellow pine forests constitute one of the most valuable resources of the State of Georgia, probably the most valuable, and certainly no element in the natural wealth of the State has made Georgia so widely known. Georgia "pitch pine" is known and esteemed in lands where few people know whether Georgia is a State, a city, or a family name. The saw mill industry of Georgia is of enormous extent, representing millions of dollars of capital invested in land and plants and yielding a product greater in value than comes from any other single industry in the State. So seemingly exhaustless are the forest resources of Georgia that lumbermen have slaughtered timber in a wasteful manner, and to those who are familiar with the industry it is apparent that the great inroads upon the Georgia forests must soon enhance the price of the lumber until it will equal if not exceed the value of the white pine of the North and Northwest, as it has been thoroughly tested, principally by the car manufacturers of the North and Northeast, and has been found to take the place of white pine in the finishing of their cars. It has also been found to be more durable, which of course is quite an item.

I have based my estimate of the coming value of Southern pine upon the fact that the demand is greater than the supply, and further upon the superior strength and durability of this lumber.

The manufacture of lumber is a very interesting sight. Watching a train load of logs, six to twelve cars long, come rolling in, drawn by a full-grown locomotive, and seeing from one hundred and fifty to two hundred men working away apparently at perfect ease, one would suppose it an easy job to work at

a saw mill. But like all other manufacturers they have their hardships, such as getting out at day-break and putting in steady time until dark. And then, as the men say, "The work ain't hard but so regular." A great many of the larger mills work convicts, but of course it is necessary for them to have their skilled men and a large number of free laborers, who attend to the logging of the mill, which is also a very interesting study. It takes about twelve teams, each composed of a big cart with broad-tired wheels, four mules and a driver, to go into the forest and bring logs to the railroad and place them convenient for the train and for the crew to load. The train is loaded by means of a long loop chain thrown around the log, one end being securely fastened, and a team of mules hitched to the other end rolls the logs on the cars. By this method a small crew and one team can load six or eight cars of logs in a very few minutes.

On account of there being very little undergrowth and the trees not very thick, averaging about eighteen trees to the acre, it is very easy for the logging teams to get about in the forest without having to stop and cut their way through, and in this way the mill men can select the larger trees, say from eight inches and over in diameter, and leave the younger ones standing to grow up with the new crop. And where they have a sufficient amount of timber to keep them cutting for fifteen or twenty years, they can go back over this and start anew. But cases of this kind are very rare.

It takes from fifteen to twenty years for a forest to grow up, and since the farmers of the South have learned the value of the land they are following very closely behind saw-mill men, clearing up the young forest for cord wood and rails and cultivating the ground. And at the rate the lumbermen have been utilizing the timber, trying to supply the demand of the manufacturer and consumer, and being so closely followed by the farmer, allowing now and then for the new towns that are so rapidly growing through Southern Georgia, it will not be many years before our forest

In this lumber section the farmers are comparatively few, though prosperous. This I cannot account for unless it is only of late years that they have learned the value of these timber lands, and have found it much to their interest to go to the extra expense of clearing them up and cultivating them while this cost is very small. It certainly cannot be on account of the healthfulness of the country, for it is a very common thing

A GEORGIA PINE FOREST.

will be remembered as a thing of the past.

There are about four hundred mills in this section of the country. About sixty-five of these are large first-class merchant mills. The gross output of the South is about four hundred million feet a year. Of this whole amount about two-thirds goes by the ocean, estimated about one-half foreign and and one-half coastwise. The remaining one-third is equally divided between the home trade and the North and West.

to see old settlers with gray-haired children.

The timber lands of South Georgia contain more or less sand, which makes them quite productive of fruit and cotton. It grows more level toward the coast and is very easily cultivated. There is but very little, if any, undergrowths on these lands, and when the saw-mill men finish an acre, taking from it such trees as can be worked to advantage, there is very little work left for the farmer in preparing it for cultivation.

The marketable value of these lands for farming purposes, after timber has been taken off, has a tendency to cause a great many of the manufacturers to hurry through their forests and work their timber into such material as is easiest cut, regardless of value, and for that reason the older and better saw-mill men have had an up-hill fight to

LONG-LEAF PINE, NEAR AUGUSTA, GA.

keep up the market price, but of course the days of these little mills, better known as "Pepper-boxes," are limited, and then the steady, careful manufac-turers will be able to obtain a price for their material that the superior quality of it should command.

In addition to the timber itself the pine forests of Georgia yield a valuable product in turpentine and rosin, the preparation of which forms an extensive industry. Turpentine orcharding, as it is called, is an interesting process, al-though crude and wasteful in its methods. These two valuable products are ob-tained by scarring the tree trunks and distilling the gum which exudes. The first step in commencing operations in a new turpentine orchard is to clear the ground of leaves and underbrush in or-der to facilitate operations. This is usually accomplished by burning over the ground, care being taken to protect the trees and to keep the fire well under control. Then the trees are systemati-cally gashed or boxed, as it is termed, by axes made for the purpose. The law fixes the time for doing this work between the middle of November and the middle of March. As soon as the boxing is done the crude, thick gum be-gins to ooze from the wounds and is collected for distillation. The wounds made in boxing heal quickly, so that it is necessary to chip the trees frequently to continue the flow of gum. The gum is gathered in buckets and emptied into barrels and these are collected by teams and taken to the still. The still is a crude affair and the process of distilla-tion is very simple. The gum is emptied from the barrels into a covered copper kettle with a furnace beneath it. A neck leading from the kettle terminates in a worm surrounded by cool water for the purpose of condensing the vapors from the boiling gum, water also being added to the gum in the still to facilitate distil-lation. The steam and turpentine pass off together and separate in condensing, the spirits of turpentine rising to the top. This is dipped off and barreled for market. The gum left in the kettle after distillation is rosin, which is skimmed, strained and put into barrels. A great amount of this rosin is used in the making of varnish and soap. The manufacturers of Pear's soap consume more than double the amount of any other soap manufacturer, which is of itself good proof of its superior quality.

The best market for our yellow pine has been South America, chiefly the ports of Rio Janeiro and Buenos Ayres, but on account of the financial trouble which occurred about the time of the dethronement of Dom Pedro, producing

LOGGING SCENE IN A GEORGIA PINE FOREST.

A GEORGIA PINE SAW MILL.

a depression of that market from which it has never rallied, the manufacturers have been forced to seek other markets. Having direct shipments to the North and Northeast, they have been able to lay lumber down at the car works at such a small cost that they have established quite a business among them.

It has been used for a number of years by the car works for sills for their freight cars, and has lately taken the place of white pine for their sidings and roofing, and I dare say that when they have given it a thorough test and found its superior lasting qualities they cannot be persuaded to use any other wood in the construction of their cars.

There is nothing prettier than our Southern curly pine for finishing sleeping cars. It is true that the scarcity of this curly pine makes it very expensive, and for that reason it is not so well known through the North and Northeast as some more inferior and less beautiful wood. But when once used the cost will not be considered, as we have often found to be the case in some of our Southern cities where it has been used in finishing residences and office buildings. The growth of this curly pine is something that our oldest lumbermen have not been able to account for, as it is the rarest thing that you find more than one or two boards in a tree, and these boards often come from two to five inches from the bark. What has most puzzled the manufacturer is the fact that the board coming from either side of this curly board will likely be of perfectly straight grain, and while the timber will cut from four to eight thousand feet of lumber to the acre, it will not average two hundred and fifty feet of this curly pine.

There is very little round timber, that is timber that has not been turpentined, in this part of the country. The saw-mill men and the forestry experts of the government, after making a careful study and repeated tests of the tapped timber, find that it is superior in many particulars to that which has not been tapped.

As a slight explanation we will first take the car sills, which are mainly manufactured by the Southern mills.

These, one will readily see, are not in any way affected by turpentining the tree, as they are generally cut from the heart and their strength and durability remain the same, as the turpentine only comes from the sap of the tree. Next, we have our car siding and boards, which are greatly benefited by the tree first being turpentined before it is cut, for in drying these boards the heat causes the greater portion of the rosin to ooze out of the pores of the lumber and thereby not only deface the lumber but make it much harder to work to a smooth and glossy finish. The remainder of the rosin which is left in the pores of the lumber becomes crystalized, which makes it more or less brittle and less apt to absorb paint and varnish used in finishing, also causing it to split and break with less weight, while a board cut from the turpentined tree is more flexible and less liable to break and split when finished and will absorb the paint, thus making it last much longer where it is exposed to the weather. So the consumer will readily see that it is not only with a view of saving the value of the turpentine and rosin, but to enhance the value of the material that the trees are turpentined.

Occasionally saw mill men get an order for virgin timber, and were they so disposed they could very safely fill it from their tapped trees and give perfect satisfaction, as this country boasts of very few experts who are able to tell the difference between a sill sawed from turpentined timber and one sawed from a virgin tree. But of course saw mill men, being famous for their honesty and straightforward way of doing business, always first explain to the buyer the impossibility of detecting the difference between the lumber, and they never lose an order on account of not being able to fill it from a virgin forest. The only instance where the virgin pine has been found preferable is in the use of large pieces that naturally contain a certain amount of sap, and these pieces are generally used in places where they are not exposed to bad weather, and in that case the difference in the lasting qualities is such a small item that it would not justify the consumer in paying the extra cost of having them gotten out of round timber. On this subject, as on many others, opinions vary, but that is largely due to the fact that buyers have never made a thorough test of the material.

RANDOM IMPRESSIONS OF GEORGIA.

By Frederic Jewett Cooke.

William Edgar Nye's good-natured slander on Georgia railroad trains being slower than her famous razor-back hogs will hardly stand practical test, particularly after one has taken a trip on the "Nancy Hanks" express train running between the cities of Savannah and Atlanta. This train runs the distance of 294 miles in six hours and forty minutes, including eighty minutes consumed in stops and water-taking, making an average speed of sixty miles an hour, and in some cases running as fast as eighty miles an hour. It is claimed by the railroad officials as the second fastest train in America, the "Empire State" express, from New York to Buffalo, being the speediest. However this may be, the speed attained by the flying "Nancy Hanks" is great enough to refute Mr. Nye's remark, and places Georgia in the front rank in railroad traveling. It is a good sign, this awakening of Southern railroads to the demand for rapid travel, as it puts the South in touch with the greater railway systems of the North and West, and demonstrates that Southern railways are abreast of the times.

In a flying trip through so great a State as Georgia, the character of the cities forms an interesting study. In Atlanta, for instance, one sees all the rush and whirl incident to a Northern city. Taking the centre of the city and drawing a half-mile circle around this point, during business hours the streets are as crowded as those of Chicago. Atlanta people are fond of show, love fine equipages, point with pride to the city's magnificent business structures and superb private residences, dress stylishly and work heart and soul for anything and everything tending to improve Atlanta. Every man, woman and child talks for Atlanta at home or abroad, and is a walking advertisement of the capital city. Added to these, the citizens are broad-minded, charitable and public-spirited, and these characteristics, coupled with the most intense energy and absolute unanimity where the city's interests are concerned, have made Atlanta what it is today.

Macon, the central city of Georgia, differs from Atlanta in marked lines. It is not a whit less progressive in ideas, and was for years a most formidable rival to Atlanta both in population and trade. In spite of this rivalry the relations existing between these two cities have always been of the most cordial character both socially and commercially. Macon occupies a commercial situation which no other Georgia city can invade, and its great wholesale establishments do an annual business which is the envy of the other Georgia cities. These houses have grand buildings and warehouses, the pride of every Maconite, and the territory for a hundred miles about Macon is most asssiduously cultivated. Macon's banking-houses are models of strength and prudence, and the business men are imbued with progress, spirit and a determination to keep Macon abreast of sister cities in influence. For beautiful suburbs Macon, in company with Augusta, easily leads the State, and to fall in love with natural scenery one has only to go to College Hill and see the beautiful homes and the exquisite landscapes in every direction. Macon's people are thoroughly Southern in characteristics, delightful entertainers, hospitable to a fault, and ready to throw open their homes to the stranger, whether on business or pleasure bent. The buildings are modern and the streets broad, well kept and delightfully shaded, and the citizens are proud of the city and fully alive to its future possibilities.

Augusta, that charming garden city on the eastern edge of Georgia, is half Georgian and half South Carolinian in complexion. Nestling on the elbow of the upper Savannah river, the city's church-spires point heavenward by the dozen, the great cotton factories clatter from daylight to dark, the broad, shaded streets weary the eye in their length of houses, while the flight of the electric cars shows enterprise and gives Augusta the sobriquet of the Electric City. The half-sleepy Augusta of years ago is now no more, for in the soft atmosphere for which the city is celebrated the people have put on new life and are pushing the city in every possible manner. Outside of New Orleans, Augusta is the only Southern city celebrating a carnival for nearly a week every winter, and Broad street, paved with asphalt for over a mile, offers a spectacle rarely seen save in some great parade on Pennsylvania avenue, Washington. On carnival occasions Augusta is filled with gay maskers, and Broad street is ablaze with fire as the floats move down the line. The carnival, started as an experiment a few years ago, is now an annual event and an interesting spectacle. Augusta's people combine the rare trait of entertaining and attending to business at the same time. Club life is popular and the Commercial Club building is a beautiful structure. Augusta women are famed the country over for their soft, rare Southern type of beauty, and the promenade on Broad street on a pleasant evening reminds one of the south of France, so far as beautiful women are concerned. Augusta, with its location, soft climate, progressive spirit, and great industrial record (according to the last United States census leading all Southern cities), is going to keep on improving. It is an old city, the Augusta *Chronicle* being 108 years old, and the city is now in the hands of those who know how to develop it, commercially and socially.

Savannah, the great port of Georgia, throbs with shipping activity along the docks and wharves extending in front of the city on the Savannah river. The great steamships lie lazily against the wooden wharves, the negro roustabouts chant weirdly as they pass to and fro loading and unloading the cargoes, the odor of the salt sea creeps up through the haze from the Tybee light, twenty miles across the rice marshes, and behind all this shipping activity Savannah stands, the city of public squares and monuments, peerless as the Atlantic cotton port, and distanced only by New Orleans and Galveston as a cotton-shipping centre. Proud of her aristocracy, proud of her wealth, proud of her people, proud of her position, she has every cause to feel so. One is impressed with the dignity with which the city even carries on its business; that calm, deliberate dignity which denotes high breeding and easy manners. Savannah's citizens conduct business as they would conduct a great entertainment, with exquisite grace and ease, and with none of the rush and whirl characterizing the northern Georgia cities. Great wealth exists in Savannah; the people are cosmopolitan, the city is in closer touch with New York than are other Georgia cities, and is moving forward in its own way, quietly but unerringly. Backed by the great line of Atlantic coasting steamers and Georgia's greatest railroad, Savannah stretches out her hands and gathers from every section of the State for her export and coast trade, and, differing as she does from other Georgia cities in methods and ideas, stands a successful yet curious centre of enormous business development and quaint social life.

Columbus, in the extreme west of the State, lies along the Chattahoochee waterway (to the Gulf of Mexico), and her people have seized this stream in the firm grasp of the huge dam to drive her cotton mills. In her people, Columbus resembles Macon, for they are lavish yet unostentatious entertainers. One is impressed with more of the ante-bellum architecture in the houses than is found in the other Georgia cities, her homes having escaped the severe ravages of the war from which other cities suffered, and modern architecture is the exception. This is, perhaps, the greatest charm of Columbus. The people are earnest in their endeavor to keep in touch with the State's progress; they occupy a commercial territory of great area along the Chattahoochee river, and they push trade as widely as possible with three such aggressive cities as Atlanta and Macon on the one side and Montgomery, Ala., on the other. Nearly every railroad running into the city was built by Columbus capital, though some are now absorbed in the greater systems of the State. Socially, no city in Georgia boasts of grander lineage or prouder inheritance, though lacking the slightest element of arrogance or display. Everybody, rich or poor, seems to possess a jolly, good-natured, happy-go-lucky temperament, and after spending a few days there I found myself dropping into the habit of "taking it easy" and appreciating that haste was not always necessary to make a living. In the language of a Columbus citizen, who must have adapted from the Hoosier poet Riley: "When God made Columbus He took a day off and just sat around and felt good."

These are Georgia's five large cities, and, while every place has its own characteristics, one may form some idea of the State's people and their peculiarities and hobbies from this sketch of my impressions.

SOUTHERN PROSPECTS FOR ENGLISH CAPITAL.

It is not every country which possesses an abundant endowment of natural resources that affords a safe and remunerative investment from a commercial point of view. The great controlling factor is the relative position in which these endowments are placed. Distance, even in this age of railways, is capable of discounting the value of mineral and other natural products. The element of competition is such a potential one nowadays that the cost of production must be reduced to the minimum, and transport charges must likewise be sunk to an almost irreducible rate compatible with an adequate return to supply a dividend. Small profits, if extensive trading, is a *sine qua non* of industrial undertakings in this era of our history. Monopolists are as rare now as the antediluvian icthyosaurus. One nation may retain the sole manufacture of a special description of produce for a large number of years, but the last decade of the nineteenth century will assuredly be the one in which that exclusive benefit is snatched from its grasp. All movements in commercial and industrial labor tend to this end. Thus the country which can produce materials and labor for the supplying of the best and cheapest commodity will be the one to occupy the foremost place in international progress, and, therefore, this is the country where the greatest accumulation of capital will be observed. Again, capital is so keenly sensitive that unless either antecedent results or a well-authenticated report on the character of the natural resources and the possibilities and facilities for their due development can be given, to prove its value as a commercial enterprise, it will be found wanting in such regions.

The Southern States of the American Union can satisfy both demands upon their capabilities. The natural wealth is of the most abundant kind; the climate is favorable to the successful cultivation of all commodities absolutely necessary to the world's requirements; transport is almost if not quite the lowest in either hemisphere; labor can be obtained cheaply and of good quality. These are items which will secure new markets against most competitors, whilst retaining the supply of home demand. We are not desirous of painting a picture, the original of which cannot be found of exactly the same tone and tint in the facts themselves. A great deal has been said in behalf of the great capabilities of the South by writers and speakers of authority. If too much has been uttered, it only remains to remark that the South is capable of accomplishing a great deal more than has already been done. If we can cast a horoscope of the future of the South and its industrial undertakings, to say that it would be in inverse ratio to the period of time that has passed to develop these States to what they are, we should not be far away, on the side of exaggeration at any rate. The past is a faint shadow of the future, and with the Nicaraguan Canal in prospect the latter becomes brighter still. Up to the present the States have undoubtedly been somewhat hampered in the transportation problem, for either it meant transmitting goods via railroads or adopting the circuitous sea route via Cape Horn to reach Asiatic countries and Australasia. With a path through Central America the obstacles will greatly disappear.

With such a plentitude of natural endowments as the States, and especially the Southern States, possess, it is pretty well a surety, all things being equal, that capital will thrive and investments be remunerative. The more the land is cultivated and utilized the greater will be the value of the surrounding areas. How has the South grown in this respect? Between 1860 and 1870 the assessed value of property in the Southern States suffered a decline, on account of the ravages of the war which crippled all enterprise and endeavor, of some $2,000,000,000. A year or two ago the assessed value stood at over $3,800,000,000. This means an enormous development of the various occupations of Southern workers. Another sign of the inherent power of the Southern States is the fact that on most railway lines throughout the States the mileage has been doubled within the last ten years.

As regards the various resources of the South there can be little doubt to all impartial observers that the facilities of the Northern States are not so great for the production of cheap iron manufactures. That there is the power to gain the pre-eminence is proved fairly well by the competition that has arisen and is likely to arise between the manufacturers in New England and the South. But, as a writer upon the Southern district of the Union as regards the possibilities existent in reference to iron manufacture there, has remarked in a contribution appearing in the volume which records the visit of the British Iron and Steel Institute to America: "To fully appreciate the position and future of the South we have to imagine a coalfield yielding ten times as much coal as the whole of the United Kingdom, unmeasured deposits of iron ores, and that both coal and ore are being won for say 4s. per ton; we must grasp the facts that pig iron can be produced at 40s. per ton; that the cost of long distance railway carriage is one farthing per ton per mile, and that the bulk of the produce of pig iron is already delivered to the Northern district. Having these things in our mind, we can arrive at no other conclusion than that in the future the Southern district will develop an export trade which will hurt the United Kingdom more severely than any other competition has done."

As regards coal, the assumption that coal in the Southern States can be raised for 4s. per ton is entirely borne out by the figures given in the census, and it is also true that the cost of coal is much lower in the American States than in England, and this is a fact that will tell considerably in favor of American advancement. Iron ore prices run on parallel lines for cheapness. American ores of the best quality are much cheaper than in England. Hematite iron ore in the States varies from 3s. 2d. to about 7s. 1d., in some mines running as high as 9s. per ton. In Great Britain, hematite ore raised from Cumberland mines averages 11s. 4½d. per ton and Lancashire ores average 8s. 10½d. per ton, the lowest price being 8s. 6d. These prices are, of course, inclusive of all charges, which are greater, especially as regard royalties, in the United Kingdom than in the States. Capitalists investing in iron mines are, therefore, much freer in America than in England in more ways than one, the prospective future of the industries in the respective countries not being of the least important among them, whilst transport charges, as has already been mentioned, are more greatly in favor of the manufacturers in America.

The staple product and manufacture of the South, however, is cotton. In most States this necessity is cultivated generally to a large extent. South Carolina will yield some 800,000 bales annually; North Carolina about half that quantity; in Georgia is situated the celebrated and growing port of the cotton trade—Savannah, and which has exported as many as 1,000,000 bales in a year; Mississippi supplies something like 900,000 bales annually; Louisiana some 560,000 bales. These are the records of what has already been accomplished, but they exhibit to no great extent the possibilities of the South in this way. Since the year 1870 this industry has made phenomenal growth throughout the States, which has been but the awakening of the latent energies. English capital has already gone to the States in considerable quantities and has been remuneratively employed, and from an economical point of view, as well as from a national point of view, this is beneficial to British trade. In the majority of the States the climate is favorable and the soil well adapted for the planting and growth of cotton. The cotton-seed industry, which yields the oil so considerably used as a substitute for olive oil, etc.; the raising of corn, wheat, oats, tobacco, rice, sugar, are carried on in the various Southern States, Georgia especially, by reason of the various latitudes of the State, and therefore the diverse temperatures possessing facilities for the growing of a great variety of fruits, the very life of the tin-plate trade of Great Britain.

The industries which we have dwelt upon briefly are in such a condition and stage of development that capital and labor would have exceptional facilities to lay a foundation for future exertions. Perhaps too much stress cannot be laid upon the canal that is to unite the two oceans, when one regards the impetus given to the eastern trade of Great Britain by the construction of the Suez Canal. Undoubtedly it will, at least, be a bonanza to the manufacturers of the States, especially the Southern States, if they are sufficiently prepared to take full advantage of its benefits. Concurrently with this English capitalists in the States will receive like and enduring blessings, provided they are in a position to receive them.

TOBACCO CULTURE IN THE SOUTH.

By H. S. Fleming.

From the earliest days of the settlement of the South, tobacco has been one of the main agricultural crops. It was long the chief source of wealth in Virginia and Maryland, and for nearly 200 years was the principal currency of the colonies. Upon it all other values were based, and, because of the greater profit in growing it, the other agricultural interests were neglected. Prior to the Revolutionary war exports of tobacco had rapidly increased with each year, but during that period its culture in other countries attained considerable proportions, and when peace was restored the foreign market presented a new element of competition and American tobacco exports have not since that time increased in nearly so great a ratio as before. Its cultivation, however, has extended over all of ·the Southern States, some growing small and others large quantities, and since 1870 Virginia, which up to that time had been the greatest producer, has ranked second, Kentucky taking the lead.

After the introduction of the gin, cotton quickly assumed the position of the. leading agricultural staple of the South and tobacco-raising did not increase much in the principal cotton-growing States. Until 1860, however, it held a high position in the agricultural products of the South, the crop in 1850 being 167,870,122 pounds (83.5 per cent. of the total grown in the United States), and in 1860 this had increased to 350,189,-808 pounds. During the civil war nearly all agricultural pursuits were at a standstill, and, at its close, because of the impoverishment of the country and the disorganization of labor, as well as the relatively greater value of cotton, tobacco-growing decreased in all States,

particularly in those furthest South, and in 1870 the total product was but 194,-202,856 pounds (73.9 per cent. of the country's crop). During the following decade it increased again to 338,249,206 pounds, but the increase in States other than Kentucky, Maryland, North Carolina, Tennessee and Virginia was small, cotton being the leading product. The production in 1880 and 1890 was as follows:

TOBACCO CROP OF THE SOUTHERN STATES.

	1880. Pounds.	1890. Pounds.
Alabama	452,426	162,430
Arkansas	970,220	954,640
Florida	21,182	470,443
Georgia	228,590	263,752
Kentucky	171,120,784	221,880,303
Louisiana	55,954	46,845
Mississippi	414,663	61,511
Maryland	26,082,147	12,356,838
North Carolina	26,986,213	36,375,258
South Carolina	45,678	222,898
Tennessee	29,365,052	36,368,395
Texas	221,293	175,706
Virginia	79,988,868	48,522,655
West Virginia	2,296,146	2,602,021
Total	338,249,206	360,463,695
Total of United States	472,661,157	488,255,896
Per cent. from the South	71.5	73.8

During the past year, owing to increased interest in diversified crops, largely induced by the depression in cotton for the two previous years, tobacco growing has received a larger share of attention than usual, and in almost every Southern State there have been formed local associations, whose aim is to urge the farmers to cultivate the plant, and also to provide the necessary warehouses in which to store the crop.

A cursory review of the history of tobacco-growing presents many points of interest. Probably the first mention of it was made by Columbus on his first voyage in 1492, when he found the natives using it, and later, on his second voyage in 1494, Friar Pane, who accompanied him, spoke of its use for both chewing and as snuff. Columbus told further that these natives chewed and smoked an herb having a pungent yet aromatic smell and bitter taste, called *cogiaba* or *cohiba*. In 1503 the Spaniards found the natives of Paraguay using it, and in 1519 or 1520 it is mentioned at Tobasco. In 1559 some leaves were sent from San Domingo to Europe by Hernandez de Toledo, and a little later Jean Nicot, envoy from the Court of France to Portugal, sent to Queen Catherine de Medicis some seed. Through this circumstance it was named *Herba Regina* and, in honor of the minister, *Nicotina*. Still later, in 1565 Sir John Hawkins carried some leaf from Florida to England, and in 1584 a member of Sir Richard Grenville's expedition, which, under the auspices of Sir Walter Raleigh, discovered Virginia in 1585, told of the herb, saying that the natives called it *"uppowac,"* but that in the West Indies the Spaniards called it *"tobacco."* He goes on to say that the "leaves thereof being dried and brought to powder, they (the natives) used to take the fume or smoke thereof, by sucking it through pipes made of clay, into their stomache and head."

In 1610 the first secretary of the Virginia colony wrote: "Here is a great store of tobacco which the salvages call *apooke*, howbeit, it is not of the best kind; it is but poor and weak, and of a byting taste. * * * The salvages here dry the leaves of the *apooke* over the fier, and sometimes in the sun, and crumble it to powder—stalks, leaves and all—taking the same in pipes of earth, which they very ingeniously can make." In 1585, when Sir Richard Grenville returned to England, he carried with him both pipes and tobacco, as did also Sir Ralph Lane, who was sent out by Sir Walter Raleigh as the first governor of the colony, and returned to England in 1586.

The first efforts at cultivating the plant appear to have been made in 1612, by John Rolfe, husband of Pocohontas. So successful was he that tobacco cultivation became a mania with the colonists, and within a short time little else was grown or thought of. In 1617 Captain Samuel Argall, the new governor, says that all the public works and buildings in James Town had fallen to decay; "the Market-Place, Streets and other Spare Places planted with Tobacco and the Colony dispersed all about, as every man could find the properest place and best Conveniency for planting." Shortly after, in 1619, a lot of 20,000 pounds was shipped to England. In this same year James I placed a disproportionally heavy duty on the Virginia product, and, in 1620, when 40,000 pounds were sent to the mother country, owing to this heavy duty and the carelessness shown in selecting, the greater part did not bring over eight pence per pound, and the remainder not above two shillings.

About this time, because of much complaint among the colonists, most of whom were young unmarried men, and the return of a number to England, a shipment of "ninety respectable young women" was made to supply them with wives and induce a permanent residence; each man who selected a wife paying 120 pounds of tobacco for her transportation.

The production of tobacco steadily increased and that of other crops diminished. Efforts were made by the Virginia Company to restrict production, but they were only partially successful, as the crop had become a most profitable one by means of improved tillage and an increase in price. In 1622 the crop was about 60,000 pounds, most of which was sent to Holland, none going to England because of the excessive import duty. By 1632 the crop had increased so that there was considerable suffering because of overproduction. Later, in 1639, laws were passed providing for inspection of all tobacco offered for sale, and such as was rejected was burned. From this time until 1730 Virginia tobacco growers were alternately harassed by severe laws, heavy duties, and even with these, of overproduction, though owing to the rigid inspection the leaf took higher rank and brought better prices than in the earlier years. In 1732 a tobacco manufactory was started on the Rappahannock river, and about 1769 one was erected in Mecklenburg county, the first south of the James river. In 1845 the exports from Virginia amounted to 42,841 hogsheads of about 1000 pounds each. This increased until 1853 when 59,544 hogsheads were sent abroad, and after that time the exports declined somewhat until the revolution. After the war exports were light for some years, not reaching their former figure until nearly 1800. Since that period Virginia tobacco culture has passed through many periods of depression. In 1850 the crop amounted to 56,803,227 pounds, in 1860 to 123,968,312 pounds, but in 1870, after the long struggle during the civil war and consequent disorganization of labor and impoverishment of the people, it was only 37,086,364 pounds. In 1880 there was a considerable gain, the production being 79,988,868 pounds, but in the ten years between that period and 1890 it had again fallen to 48,522,655 pounds. This has been owing to two causes: First, competition of the ordinary grades with those of the North and West, and second, the greater profit found in mixed crops and truck farming. At present the tendency in Virginia is to give up the commoner varieties of leaf and produce special grades. There are now five distinct qualities produced in the State. To the trade these are known as "Dark Shipping," "Red and Colored Shipping," "Sun and Air-cured Fillers," "Bright Yellow," and "Flue-cured Fillers." Each of these is subdivided into a number of grades and each has its particular uses.

Maryland, like Virginia, has always grown large crops of tobacco, and in its early history the trade passed through the same troubles. The plant was first grown in the settlement on Kent Island, now in Queen Anne county, in 1631, and from that time its cultivation in the eastern and southern portion of the State extended rapidly. The leaf has not the same qualities as that grown in Virginia, and in its early days did not hold so high a position in the market. The amount produced has fluctuated widely, and of late years has been steadily declining. In 1850 the crop amounted to 21,407,-

497 pounds, in 1860 to 38,410,965 pounds, in 1870 to 15,785,339 pounds, in 1880 to 26,082,147 pounds, and in 1890 had dropped to 12,356,838 pounds.

Tobacco cultivation in North Carolina dates from a little later than in Virginia. By 1669 it had grown to considerable importance, and England passed laws prohibiting the sale of the leaf in Virginia except in payment of debts. This did not prevent it from coming in, however, and for many years Virginia growers suffered from their own overproduction, with the added load of a large share of the North Carolina product. The development of fine tobacco culture in the latter State dates from a much later period. In 1852 two brothers owning a farm in Caswell county grew some yellow leaf tobacco on high, sandy land. After two or three crops it was noticed that the leaf had a peculiar flavor, and this was attributed to the method of curing. Further trials demonstrated that it was primarily the soil, and only in smaller part the curing process. From this the cultivation of yellow tobacco extended over Caswell county and into Pittsylvania county, Virginia. The stimulus given to tobacco culture by this may be appreciated from the fact that in 1850 the total product of the State was but 11,984,786 pounds, whereas in 1860 it had grown to 32,853,250 pounds.

During the war tobacco culture was practically abandoned, and after that period the growers suffered the same hardships and troubles experienced in Virginia and other Southern States. By 1870 the crop only amounted to 11,150,-087 pounds, but since then, notwithstanding the competition with Northern and Western tobacco, it has steadily increased, amounting to 26,986,213 pounds in 1880, and in 1890 to 36,375,-258 pounds.

Tobacco was first cultivated for market in Florida in 1829 in Gadsden county. A Virginia tobacco planter who had settled there found that the soil was peculiarly adapted to the plant, giving it a fine, silky texture and yielding a large return per acre. His efforts in raising it were followed by others, and the production for the State was 75,274 pounds. From this time until 1850 the culture extended into Calhoun, Jefferson, Leon and Marion counties, and in the latter year 998,614 pounds were grown in the State—776,170 pounds in Gadsden, 109,000 in Marion and the remainder from the other counties. In the decade from 1850 to 1860 tobacco-growing first increased, and in the latter years declined, owing to increasing efforts to raise Sea Island cotton and sugar-cane, so that in the last-named year the total production of the State had dropped to 828,815 pounds. Following this came the practical abandonment of agricultural pursuits during the war, and from its close to 1870 tobacco culture received but a small share of attention, the amount grown in the latter year being but 157,405 pounds. From 1870 to 1880 many causes acted against it—the difficulty of obtaining reliable labor for a crop which demands such care and attention, the relatively higher price of other products and the increasing difficulty of raising a fine leaf on lands which had long been under cultivation. How greatly these factors impeded the work can be realized from the fact that in 1880 the total yield of the State was but 21,182 pounds. From this time, however, new lands were opened and tobacco-planting received a further stimulus, and with the introduction of a number of new varieties which are held in high favor by cigar manufacturers has been steadily gaining ground, the production in 1890 being 470,443 pounds. With the erection of cigar and tobacco factories, which are seeking Florida both because the climate is so well suited for tobacco manufacturing and on account of the high-grade leaf grown there, it is probable that within the next few years the State will be producing more tobacco than ever before in its history, and with the very material advantage of working all its leaf into shape for the market.

In Louisiana tobacco was one of the principal staple productions 170 years ago. As early as 1718 the "Western Company," then settling and building up New Orleans and the contiguous territory, introduced its cultivation, and later, in 1752, the royal government of France offered to receive into the king's warehouse all tobacco raised in the province at the rate of about $7.00 per hundredweight. The same plan was followed by the Spanish authorities in 1776, and during 1793 and 1794, owing in large measure to the ravages of insects on the indigo plants, which formed one of the staple products, tobacco growing received additional attention. In 1802 there were 2000 hogsheads of tobacco exported from New Orleans, and its culture had become general along the river up as far as Natchez. There was not, however, enough care given in curing the product, and competition with better-appearing leaf grown along the Ohio river caused a decline in the industry. About 1824 the Acadians introduced a new process of curing which gave their tobacco a peculiar flavor and brought it into immediate favor, which it has never lost, and its name—perique—is known throughout the markets of Europe and America. This tobacco was grown almost exclusively in the parish of St. James, some fifty miles above New Orleans, and represents almost the entire production of the State. In 1850 this amounted to 26,878 pounds, in 1860 to 39,940 pounds, in 1870 to 15,541 pounds, in 1880 to 55,954 pounds and in 1890 to 46,845 pounds. From this it will be seen that there has been but little effort to develop the tobacco industry in this State. Sugar, cotton and rice form the staple articles of production, and though it is known that excellent tobacco can be grown in many parishes, there has been an indisposition to make the experiment of raising it.

In Arkansas tobacco-growing began prior to 1840, and in that year the product of the State amounted to 148,439 pounds. In 1850 this had increased to 218,936 pounds and in 1860 to 989,890 pounds. In 1870 it decreased to 594,886 pounds, but in 1880 had almost regained its position, producing 970,220 pounds. In 1890 the production was slightly less, amounting to 954,640 pounds. The greater part of this was grown in Randolph, Izard, Newton, Boone, Madison, Carroll, Benton and Washington counties, which in soil and climate are excellently adapted for the cultivation of this plant. Arkansas tobacco is well known in the market, and some varieties for plug use hold a high position. Growers in a few of the counties take particular pains in curing and assorting the crop, and it is in such places that the industry has yielded exceedingly remunerative returns.

Kentucky easily takes the first position of all tobacco-producing States in this country. From its early settlement, tobacco, introduced probably by Virginia settlers, became one of the staple crops. As early as 1785 General Wilkinson, of Lexington, entered into a contract with the Spanish government to deliver several boatloads at New Orleans, and in so doing opened a market for this product which eventually drove Mississippi and Louisiana producers out of the business, except in such special varieties as they produced. From 1810 to 1820 its cultivation extended over the central and southern portion of the State, but facilities for reaching a market were so poor that the increase of production was not very rapid. Nearly the entire crop was transported to the Ohio or Cumberland rivers by wagon and thence by flatboat to New Orleans. During 1827 and the years following, a number of local dealers established themselves in different counties, and in 1840 more extended marketing facilities were secured and with them a number of factories for making the tobacco into shape for sale. This gave a great impetus to the business and tobacco culture rapidly increased during the years following, the total production of the State in 1850 amounting to 55,501,196 pounds. This has steadily increased since that time, in 1860 being 108,126,840 pounds; in 1870, 105,305,869 pounds; in 1880, 171,120,784 pounds, and in 1890, 221,880,303 pounds.

Kentucky is divided by the trade into eight districts, each producing, through peculiar qualities of the soil and methods of curing, tobacco of different varieties. These are known as the "Paducah," the "Ohio River," "Lower Green River," "Green River," "Upper Green River," "Clarksville," Cumberland River," and "White Burley" districts. Each embraces several counties, but has no fixed limits, expanding or contracting as one or another variety of leaf is grown.

In Tennessee, like Kentucky, tobacco culture commenced with the settlement of the State. The early pioneers in the northeastern portion of the State raised sufficient for their own needs. Those who settled along the Cumberland river, having access to the New Orleans market by means of this waterway, commenced planting on a somewhat larger scale, and about 1810 tobacco began to form one of the staple products of the State. In Montgomery, Smith and Sumner counties this crop was grown to a very large extent, and each year several thousand hogsheads were sent to New Orleans. When, in 1819, the Indian titles in Western Tennessee were bought up and this land opened to settlers, the cultivation of tobacco increased rapidly and extended through nearly all of the counties which were within reach of the river. From 1830 to 1840 the greatest increase took place, and in the latter year nearly 26,000,000 pounds were produced. About 1834 factories were erected at Clarksville, and several establishments for making strips followed. Later, about 1842, an effort was made to establish a market here for the sale of tobacco in casks, but it met with strong opposition both from the farmers and agents of New Orleans houses, and it was not until 1845 that the warehouse was opened. From 1846 to nearly 1850 the prices received for tobacco were low, and its cultivation declined somewhat, the production in the latter year being but 20,148,932 pounds. After this, with an increase in tobacco factories, warehouses and better prices, it increased until in 1860 it was 43,448,097 pounds. Following the civil war the production was again reduced, amounting in 1870 to but 21,465,452 pounds, in 1880 to 29,365,052 pounds and in 1890 to 36,368,395 pounds. The State is divided practically into three districts, West Tennessee, Clarksville and the Upper Cumberland river. Of these the Clarksville district is the best known and most widely celebrated for the excellent leaf grown in it.

This briefly reviews the growth of to-bacco culture in the principal producing States. Like all other industries it has met periods of depression. These have resulted from overproduction and other causes met with in any business, and, as is usually the case, those who produced the ordinary grades, bringing the least money, suffered the most. Tobacco-growing presents one great difficulty which, unless overcome, will inevitably lead to failure. The plant requires intelligent and constant attention during growth, harvesting and curing, and if this is not given the product will not even be up to the average of that particular district. In this fact lies the conditions of success, as only the leaf that is above the average will make the crop a profitable one.

HOW THE SOUTH STANDS A CRISIS.

By Edward H. Sanborn.

That there has been a marked change in business conditions in the South during the past four or five months, and that the outlook now is probably more favorable than at any previous time, are facts that are well known to the reading public—thanks to the amount of space that has lately been devoted to the subject by the newspapers. The improved conditions in the South have been eagerly heralded by the Southern papers and the newspapers of the North, the West and the East have responded quickly. So marked has been the change in the South, by reason of contrast with the preceding two years of depression and financial stringency, that it has attracted the attention of the nation. When first the improvement manifested itself it was viewed by many as a sort of commercial spasm, a sudden effort to regain lost ground and to prevent further recedence, but the events of the past two months— the steady increase in activity and the constantly improving financial conditions —have inspired confidence and have convinced the world that the South is approaching a state of greater stability than it has ever enjoyed before.

A new country, with small population, with uneven development, with crude methods in manufacture, finance and commerce, with insufficient capital and with industries yielding products but one stage above the raw materials, is subject to violent reverses as phenomenal as its remarkable strides of progress. Such fluctuations in business are inevitable, but they are modified by the conditions that characterize the region in which they occur. If productive industry, based upon local resources, be the foundation upon which a community

rests, reverses can be temporary only, and a restoration of normal conditions is sure to restore activity and prosperity. If, however, dependence be upon external and uncertain resources, growth is rarely staple or healthy. This reasoning is strikingly substantiated by a comparison of Southern growth with the magic rise and sudden collapse of numerous Western towns. There have been booms in the South which have suffered collapse and have not yet been revived, but in nearly every instance even the wrecked or uncompleted scheme contains all the elements essential to success. There exist as a basis natural resources in the shape of coal, iron ore, timber or other raw materials which are unaffected by times or seasons. The success or failure of the enterprise is merely a question of management and means. Failures of development projects in the South have not been caused by lack of resources, but they are traceable to either incompetent management or insufficient funds. But when we turn to the West, to Kansas, Nebraska, and Iowa, we find, in addition to the thriving cities that have been created by the railroads, scores of towns that have been abandoned as lacking the essentials for successful existence. When the Western fever was raging most violently, a wave of development swept out across the plains and towns sprang up in a day, created and sustained for a brief time by the speculative mania, but the subsidence of the first excitement left nothing for the towns to exist upon, and they simply collapsed. There are scores of such wrecks in the West, with streets of deserted and decaying houses standing as monuments of the folly of those who tried to build cities where not even a single house was needed. Of course, this condition of affairs must not be accepted as a type of Western growth any more than the unsuccessful enterprises in the South are to be regarded as specimens of progress in that section. The failures in the West and South represent the result of misdirected energy in these two sections, with this difference: the collapse of the Western boom town was complete and final, while the failure of the Southern town-building schemes meant merely the temporary suspension of enterprises for which there is reason and which sooner or later will be completed.

An appreciation of these conditions is necessary to a full understanding of the depression which has lately visited the South and the return of activity and prosperity, now so marked. It should ever be borne in mind that depression did not come to the South because of any unfavorable conditions characteristic of that section. On the contrary the South has suffered chiefly from extraneous causes which have aggravated the defects usually found in a newly developed country. The pressure was from without rather than from within. Had the rest of the world maintained its equilibrium the South would not have been disturbed. This is capable of easy demonstration. When the Baring failure startled the world and precipitated a panic whose effects have not yet been removed, the South was in the period of its greatest activity in matters of development and progress. The recognition of the opportunities for profitable investment then existing in the South had drawn thither a great amount of capital from all parts of this country and from abroad, and, in addition to the generally prevailing activity in established enterprises, many projects for industrial development upon a scale of great magnitude were in the formative stage when the panic descended. The ensuing financial stringency and the timidity of investors crippled many enterprises then in operation and necessitated the suspension of projects in contemplation or process of development.

Then followed a year of depression and stagnation, in many respects the most trying and most critical period through which the South has ever passed. Under the circumstances it was not to be expected that much progress would be made by Southern industries, but the records show that the South has not stood still even during the period of greatest depression. The scarcity of ready money, the inability of investors in Southern enterprises to use their holdings as collateral, and the rigid restriction of credit by the banks and money-lenders, rendered exceedingly difficult the maintenance of newly-established industries and almost prohibited extensions of business. When the depression seemed to be in its worst stage the burden of the South was still further increased by the production of the greatest cotton crop ever raised—the 9,077,000 bales of the season 1891-92. This enormous crop, greater by 400,000 bales than the largest previous yield, caused a decline in price to the lowest point reached in half a century, so that but few planters reached the end of the season without finding themselves in debt, in spite of the fact that they had sold more cotton than ever before. Only those who are familiar with Southern conditions and understand the position of cotton as the great staple cash crop can realize the effect of the decline in cotton to the losing point. To the planter who put every acre in cotton and depended upon the proceeds for money with which to buy food and clothing it meant standing face to face with want. It meant a loss on the work of a year and starting the next year in debt. The effect of this unprecedented cotton crop was hardly less severe than the influence of the financial panic, so close to which it came.

The factors that have wrought the present improvement in Southern conditions can be clearly defined. They are:

1. A smaller crop of cotton, produced at less cost than ever before and sold at an advanced price.

2. The introduction of more economical and systematic methods of conducting business.

3. The change in the national administration.

4. Increased confidence in the South, due to the proof of its stability during the critical period.

The reduction in the production of cotton involves several conditions of advantage that do not appear at first sight. In round figures the cotton crop of the season 1891-92 amounted to 9,000,000 bales, which sold at an average of 7½ cents per pound, making a total of $337,500,000, to which is to be added the value of about 1,000,000 tons of seed sold to the oil mills at an average of about $9 per ton, or a total of $9,000,000, which brings the aggregate value of the crop up to about $346,500,000. The crop of the present season will not be far from 6,000,000 bales and the average price will be about 9¼ cents per pound, which will make the cotton alone worth about $277,500,-000. The scarcity of hogs and the consequent high price of lard has created an enormous demand for cotton-seed oil, so that the crushing this season will probably reach 1,500,000 tons, for which planters have received from $7 to $25· per ton, $18 representing a fair average. Adding $27,000,000 for seed to the value of the cotton itself makes the present crop worth about $305,000,-000 to the planters, or about $40,000,000 less than last year. But this does not represent a loss to the planters, for it cost them less per pound to raise the present crop than the preceding one, and while the aggregate value shows a decrease of $40,000,000, the smaller proceeds include a good margin of profit, whereas the larger value in 1891-92 represented about the actual cost of production, and in many cases a loss. In some sections of the Mississippi valley the crop was largely reduced or wholly ruined by overflow and the absence of compensating circumstances has inflicted great hardship upon the planters. Taking the South as a whole, however, the planters have made more money out of less cotton this season. An incidental advantage of the reduced cotton crop is found in the increased production of foodstuffs. During the past season, instead of devoting all their acreage and all their energy to cotton, and buying

their food and supplies on credit under most usurious terms, the planters undertook to raise their own food and relied upon a smaller amount of cotton to yield sufficient cash to discharge their obligations. This was the characteristic feature of Southern agriculture in 1892, and in that year many of the cotton-growing sections raised enough corn, hay and hogs to supply home consumption, and in several instances there was a surplus of these products for sale.

Evidence of these favorable conditions is not wanting. A Mississippi cotton factor says in a recent letter: "The planters have made large crops of corn, potatoes and other home produce and plenty of forage. A great many in this section have hay and corn to sell in large lots." Another merchant in the same State writes: "There have been raised throughout the valley during the present year abundant corn and forage crops, and, best of all, the crops of 1892 of all kinds have been made on an exceedingly limited amount of supplies." A Georgia cotton factor writes: "Farmers are in better condition, due to having raised provisions—principally corn—to a larger extent than for many years." An Alabama fertilizer manufacturer presents this view: "We have made calculations for several of our farming friends, and find that the increased supply of corn, peas, potatoes and hay raised this year more than offsets the loss on the cotton crop this year over last."

The lull in the active development of Southern resources, which came during the past two years, gave opportunity for the reorganization of business methods and the adoption of more economical means of conducting industrial operations, the effect of which has been exceedingly beneficial to the South. There has been a revision of credit, evidenced by the accumulation of money in Southern banks and the greater caution of bankers in making loans. While this has caused more or less hardship, and has had a tendency to restrict legitimate operations, it has also prevented speculation and has exerted a beneficial influence upon a people whose tendency has been to depend rather too much upon the credit system. Consumers and merchants have limited their purchases to their actual necessities or less, and the enforced economy has been accepted with good grace. In industrial affairs the past two years have been a period of great improvement in methods, and in every branch of productive industry distinct progress has been made towards the more efficient and more economical practices that prevail in the older manufacturing sections with which the South comes directly in competition. Particularly is this noticeable in the iron industry, which, by reason of improved methods and greater economy, has been enabled to follow a falling market with profit. Despite the low price of pig iron several of the largest Southern producers made more money during the late period of depression than in any preceding time of general prosperity. Southern lumber manufacturers have had to face severe competition, but economical methods and improved machinery have enabled them to hold their own and continually move forward. Southern cotton mills benefited in a very large degree by the depression in cotton, which gave them cheaper raw material than they had ever enjoyed before. Their indisputable advantage in the manufacture of the coarser grades of cotton fabrics is being gradually extended to the higher grades of product by the introduction of better and more efficient machinery. This progressive step has been especially prominent during the past year, when the construction of new mills has been unusually active. The more recently built mills in the South are equipped with the best classes of machinery and are capable of producing better grades of yarn and cloth than have ever before been made in the South. Throughout every branch of industry this effort to reach a higher standard has been conspicuous during the dull times, and now that the industrial revival has come the gain is unmistakable.

The change in the national administration gave the South a decided impetus. The benefits which the South was expected to derive from this change may or may not have been largely imaginary; the effect has been unmistakable. During the latter part of the past administration the South undoubtedly suffered severely from the threatened enactment of laws designed to perpetuate by measures of force the rule of the party then in power. The framers of these laws aimed to eradicate an evil that did not exist, save in their own imagination, and the means proposed were such as threatened the security of every investment in the South. In the anticipation of such inimical legislation there was l.ttle encouragement for the investment of additional capital in the South, and much money then invested in Southern industries undoubtedly would have been withdrawn had it been possible. The change in administration, however, removed all danger of such legislation and the return to power of the party most in sympathy with the South restored general confidence in that section, and gave encouragement to all interested in its development. The danger thus averted was far more of a disturbing element than most observers are willing to recognize, but its reality has been impressed upon the writer by personal observation and by the testimony of those who felt the depressing influence of the pending Force Bill.

Had there been a general and complete collapse of Southern industrial enterprises during the late critical period, it would have been no surprise to the onlookers; but the manner in which the South has stood the strain has opened many eyes to a realization of the solidity of that section. Bradstreet's figures of commercial failures furnish some interesting evidence on this point. During 1891, the year of greatest financial stress throughout the country, the failures in the South numbered 2412, or 19.4 per cent. of the total of the United States, with liabilities amounting to $35,578,000, 18.4 per cent. of the total. In 1892 the aggregate liabilities declined uniformly about 50 per cent. in the Eastern, Middle and Southern States, and in that year the South had 18.6 per cent. of the failures and 16.6 per cent. of the total liabilities. It is interesting to note that 731 out of 2412 failures in the South in 1891 were due to lack of capital and 431 were attributed to disaster, under which are embraced failure of crops, commercial crisis and other external causes, show-ing that the troubles were due to causes that were not peculiar to that section of the country.   In the West lack of capital caused 1368 out of 2602 failures; in the Middle States 1345 out of 3002; in the Eastern States 462 out of 1789; in the Northwest 478 out of 1262, and in the Pacific States 431 out of 1182. While this is a cause likely to predomi-nate in a newly developed country, the South makes a better showing on this point than any section except the old and settled Eastern States.   During the most trying period in many years the business interests of the South have demonstrated their stability in such a manner as to secure a larger share of public confidence than they have ever before enjoyed.

Now that the removal of depressing influences has restored normal conditions in the South, there is a notable increase from week to week in industrial and commercial activity.   The march of progress has been resumed and new enterprises are rapidly assuming definite form.   Beyond the steadily diminishing influence of the late depression there seems to be no element of disadvantage that can retard the growth of the South in every direction—commercial, financial and industrial.

THE SOUTHERN OUTLOOK.

Population Needed by the South.

The greatest need of the South is for more population in order to give to that section a larger consuming capacity and thereby greater productive possibilities than now exist. Except at a few conspicuous points, where great cities are growing, the population of the South is not increasing in proportion to the advantages and possibilities of that section. There is opportunity for the accommodation of the entire present population of the United States south of the Ohio river and east of the Mississippi without crowding or without overtaxing the resources of the territory indicated. The Southern States contain the largest undeveloped area in the United States, and this region presents unlimited possibilities for the production of everything that is made by nature or man. There is a range of soil and climate that presents the conditions essential for the growth of everything that is required for food or clothing, and in and upon the ground there is every raw material upon which manufacturing industries depend. There is no other section of our country in which are grouped together natural resources of such extent and diversity of character.

The East and the West have their own peculiar advantages and their characteristic resources, but nowhere outside of the Southern States has nature placed so many and so diverse resources in close juxtaposition. The East, small in area and with limited natural resources, supports the densest population upon this continent—supports its people by trade and industry, the basis of which is the resources of remote States and countries. The West, with limitless areas of productive agricultural country, yields food for millions, but this is the limit of its possibilities. The South, however, combines with its industrial resources agricultural possibilities that guarantee support to a population as great as any portion of the world now knows. The South has made pro-

digious strides in every line of development during the past ten years or more, but the growth of agriculture and industry has not had an appreciable effect upon the resources of the country. The progress thus far made represents merely the utilization of opportunities immediately accessible and requiring little effort. Only the timber nearest to the river and railroad has been cut; only the upper and thicker coal seams have been opened; only the exposed ore banks have been touched; only the most readily productive soil has been tilled; only the overflow of nature's abundance has been grasped, while the greatest resources of all are practically still untouched. The application of the more efficient and more economical methods that are required where conditions are less favorable will bring results in the development of Southern industry that we cannot now comprehend.

This leads us back to our starting point—the need of the South for more people—men who will apply themselves industriously and intelligently to the utilization of the natural resources everywhere so abundant. Money is needed less than brains and muscle. The industrious mechanic or the thrifty farmer is of more value to the South now than is the millionaire, who sits afar off and shifts his capital from place to place as opportunities present themselves or vanish. The South needs men who will make themselves integral parts of the community, and consider the land as their home and abiding place. More than all else, perhaps, is the small farmer needed, the man who will devote his little means and large energy to inducing the soil to yield for him all of its wealth, not alone cotton or corn, but a full round of food and raiment. For such men as this the South presents rare opportunities, and guarantees health, happiness and prosperity. The next need of the South is for the skilled artisan, the trained worker who can make his own skill profitable to himself and the community, and at the same time render productive

1.8

the great supply of unskilled, untrained labor which is found on every hand, and which can be had at nominal cost. There is urgent need of men such as these to impart to the industries of the South the system and methods which compel success in the older, more advanced sections of the country.

The Investor's Opportunity.

"The time to buy is after a panic" is an old saying that we occasionally hear, the credit for which is generally given to Jay Gould. Whether Gould was the author of this or not matters not. It is true in many cases, and so it is immaterial whether Mr. Gould first uttered it or whether it came from some less noted financial genius. It is emphatically true as relates to the South at present. For two years or more we have been passing through a financial depression which has strained the ability of many to carry properties that are intrinsically worth many times what they can be bought for to day. There are mineral and timber lands, town properties, water powers, newly-established industries, all of the best character, whose values are just as certain to advance as the growth of the United States is to continue. The laws of trade based on supply and demand, on the enormous expansion of all the business interests and the increase in the population of our country, make certain a steady increase in the value of well-selected Southern properties.

The more the South has been studied and the more closely the effect of the panic upon its industrial interests has been watched, the more deeply impressed with the wonderful resources and the great future of this part of our common country have been the moneyed people of other sections. Here is a country of boundless natural wealth, a country which will inevitably develop very rapidly, where great fortunes are going to be made, not only by active operations, but also simply by the "unearned increment" of land, about which we hear so much these days. The wise man who has money to invest will invest it now, before the reaction from the two years of depression takes place.

Property of all kinds in the South, improved and unimproved, city and country, can be bought at a very much lower price now than it will command a few years hence. The scarcity of money and the difficulty in meeting deferred obligations during the last

year or two make the holders of many very valuable properties willing to sell at a very much lower price than they would have accepted a few yeare ago, and very much below the real value of the property. There are well-located industrial enterprises, started without sufficient capital, which can be bought for one-half or even less of the original cost. Timber and coal properties which in a few years will rank in selling value with similar properties in the North and West can in many cases now be purchased at prices ranging all the way from a couple of dollars to ten dollars an acre, the latter figure being sufficient to secure some of the finest undeveloped coal tracts in the entire country; while the former will cover the cost of a good many valuable timber tracts. Opportunities for the establishment of new industries on the most valuable conditions are without number. If you want to build a cotton mill—a business which must necessarily move South, where the profits are uniformly, under good management, very large—you can secure from dozens of well-located places exemption from taxation for ten years, a free site, and in some cases a bonus of land which, with the natural growth of the town, will in a moderate length of time be worth almost as much as the mill cost. Iron-making must constantly increase, even if prices have been low for two years, and the South certainly has greater advantages for this industry than any other section. If you want to build a furnace, a rolling mill or any ironworking enterprise you can secure concessions which will go a long ways towards returning the entire investment whenever general business revives. In woodworking interests, and, in fact, in every line of productive industry, inducements of the most liberal character in the way of tax exemption, land bonus, etc., can be had.

The South wants the aid of outside capital to establish new banks; to open mines; to build factòries, and for every kind of legitimate enterprise. The conditions surrounding such investments never were more favorable than they are at present.

How the World's Fair Will Help the South.

This Columbian year is a season of great opportunities from which the South must reap advantages in many ways, and the exceedingly favorable turn which Southern affairs have taken during the past three or four months adds greatly to the value and importance of the opportunities. The World's Fair, of course, is the event of the year upon which the attention of the world is fixed, and propitious conditions will bring to Chicago in midsummer and early fall such a congregation of sightseers as never before has been assembled in any city. Naturally Chicago and its tributary territory will enjoy the concentrated effects of this mighty gathering of people, and there can be no doubt that the direct benefits will more than equal the millions of dollars that have been and will be expended in the creation and maintenance of this greatest of all expositions. But it is not reasonable to expect that such a volume of energy will expend all its force at Chicago, or that its effects will be confined to the West and Northwest. Undoubtedly its influence will be felt to the farthermost limits of the country. Already, even while the opening of the exposition is still several months distant, its quickening influence is felt in many lines of business. Nearly every branch of industry is receiving more or less of an impetus from the approach of this great event.

The South will be benefited by the World's Fair in many ways. The eight or nine Southern States that will have buildings of their own upon the exposition grounds will create an impression in the minds of visitors which the unrepresented States will have cause to regret. It is a great misfortune that every Southern State has not made provision for its own building and collection exhibit, and particularly is it regrettable that States of such great resources as Alabama, Tennessee and North Carolina will have no suitable representation. The failure of these States to avail themselves of this great opportunity makes it more incumbent upon them to reach out for the indirect benefits of the exposition. The World's Fair not only will bring to this country thousands of sightseers from other lands, but also it will set in motion a large proportion of our home population. Very many of those who visit Chicago, whether they come from other parts of this country or from abroad, will not end their travels at the chief objective point, but will continue their journeyings into the Northwest, throughout the East and West and into the South. As the section of the country embracing the greatest undeveloped resources, as a region of rare picturesque beauty and historical interest, and as the scene of the most remarkable industrial development this country has ever known, the South will receive a large share of attention from those

who will extend their travels from the World's Fair for pleasure, information or business.

The incidental opportunity is of great importance to the South, and it is to be hoped that its value will be fully appreciated by the people of the South, particularly in those States which will have no direct representation at Chicago. We hope that many parties will be made up in Chicago for the purpose of visiting the South at the close of the exposition, when very much of what is most interesting in that section can be seen under favorable conditions. This is a matter to be kept well in mind by intending visitors to Chicago and also by the people of the South.

Where Brains and Money Pay.

There is no section of this country in which judicious investments will pay larger returns than in the South. In a rapidly developing country there are always good opportunities for the man who has ready money to use, and in the South, where cash is less abundant than in the North, there are possibilities for the investor that are not found elsewhere. The best opportunities are open to practical men who can supplement their money with energy and brains, men who can conduct their own business and deal intelligently with changing conditions as they present themselves. A cotton manufacturer who will invest $100,000 in a mill in the Carolinas or Georgia and assume personal direction of its operations, can obtain a larger return for his investment and services than he could get in the North. An experienced iron manufacturer who will build a blast furnace or a rolling mill at any one of a hundred advantageous locations in the South and manage it himself, will find a larger balance of profit on his books than in Pennsylvania. A capable fruit grower who will cultivate a tract of Georgia land will get better returns in actual cash than in California. A mill man who will build himself a saw mill in any of the recognized timber regions will find a ready market for his output at prices that will leave him a larger margin of profit than he could find elsewhere. This argument is capable of indefinite extension and application to every branch of business. The chief requisites are intelligence, discretion and personal attention to the direction of one's own affairs. The application of such principles is a guarantee of success in any branch of business a man may choose to enter in the South.

Notes on Southern Progress.

THE annex building for the collective exhibit of Virginia's products at the World's Fair is now well under way, and will afford abundant room for the interesting exhibits to be presented. The space on the lower floor will be 1600 square feet; on the upper floor 1200 square feet, and a wall space of 2500 square feet. Besides this there has been alloted to Virginia 1600 square feet floor space in the agricultural building, 1440 square feet in the mines building and 418 square feet in the horticultural building.

A PLAN is being considered in Houston, Texas, of holding a cotton carnival during the coming fall. The idea is to organize an association with a capital stock of $30,000 to take the matter in hand, using the large auditorium building, soon to be erected, for exhibits. Premiums will be offered for county displays, and, as it would continue for two weeks, low rates would be secured from the railroads.

ARRANGEMENTS are about completed in Memphis, Tenn., for the erection of a large auditorium having a seating capacity of 6000 people. The capital stock of the company organized to build it will be $20,000, and work will be commenced as soon as $15,000 has been subscribed.

THE extensive deposit of asphalt near St. Jo, in Montague county, Texas, is being operated by a local company having a capital stock of $200,000. The product is being shipped all over the country, and has been pronounced equal to any in use. Its development promises to become a large industry, as it is the only mine now being worked in the Southwest.

THE Thomasville Exchange & Banking Co., of Thomasville, Ga., is rapidly developing the suburban town of La Cubana City. The property comprises over 800 acres adjoining Thomasville, and the company is offering great advantages to manufacturing enterprises. The A. del Pino Co., manufacturer of cigars, etc., is to locate at once a factory in La Cubana City. Its building will be of brick, three stories high, 40x150 feet, and will employ 150 Cuban cigarmakers. Work has been begun cn an electric street railroad to connect La Cubana City and the Savannah, Florida & Western depot. The officers of the Thomasville Exchange & Banking Co. are as follows: D. I. MacIntyre, president and general manager; T. C. Mitchell, vice-president, and D. I. MacIntyre, T. C. Mitchell, A. T. MacIntyre and W. H. Mitchell, directors. The company is a strong one personally and financially.

THE tract of land known as Bolivar Point, containing 2978 acres of land on the peninsula opposite Galveston, Texas, was recently sold for $600,000. The purchaser was John R. Lewis, who represents Kansas City and Minneapolis capitalists. It is understood that the new owners expect to build a town on the tract, and will become interested in the proposed railroad from Galveston to Beaumont.

THE sales of loose leaf tobacco on the Danville (Va.) market for February amounted to 6,077,766 pounds, being the largest sales ever made in a single month. The sales for the first five months of the fiscal year were 16,200,000 pounds, an increase of 1,488,000 pounds over the same period last year.

CITIZENS of Nolan, Mitchell, Fisher, Coke, Scurry, Howard, Borden, Martin, Glasscock, Midland, Ector, Ward and Pecos counties, in Texas, propose organizing a bureau of information for the purpose of inducing immigration to these counties. The land in this section is extremely rich, fertile and cheap, and every inducement will be offered to secure desirable settlers.

A SYNDICATE represented by Col. Harry Thompson, of Winchester, Ky., and Col. H.

T. Groom, of Lexington, Ky., has recently purchased the Reeves lands, aggregating some 40,000 acres, in Jackson county, Fla. The price paid was $2.50 per acre. It is the intention of the purchaser to convert part of the land into tobacco farms as fast as possible, and if necessary will import Swedish and German laborers. The soil has been carefully examined by expert tobacco-growers and pronounced suitable to the growth of the finest cigar leaf, equal in every respect to that grown in Cuba. Samples of the tobacco grown on the land were examined and found to be exceptionally fine, although grown by new beginners and cured by a crude processs. Fruit-growing will also be entered into.

FOR some time past there has been an effort on foot in New Orleans to erect a large and finely-equipped hotel. The project is gradually assuming definite shape, and has proven an attractive investment for capital, as already there has been a number of bids for blocks of stocks by investors in New York and Chicago. The hotel as planned would cost about $1,000,-000, and be one of the finest in the South.

AN extension of the sewage system of Memphis, Tenn., so as to drain the suburbs is under consideration, and Geo. E. Waring, Jr., the sanitary engineer who constructed the present excellent sewage system there, has examined the plans and submitted a report to the city council, in which is embodied suggestions for carrying out the work. A committee has been appointed to confer with the property owners relative to the financial side of the question, and when this is satisfactorily adjusted a bill will be presented to the legislature of the State asking it to authorize a levy of a special tax of one cent on each $100 for sewer purposes in Memphis.

E. A. LINDSEY, a tobacco grower and cigar manufacturer near Jacksonville, Fla., has shipped to the United States Department of Agriculture a box of his best leaf tobacco for a place in the government exhibit at the World's Fair. The tobacco was grown on his farm, and the samples weighed three and a quarter pounds, there being eight varieties, as follows: Vuella Abajo (Havana), Comstock Spanish (Havana), Sumatra, Connecticut seed, Missouri, Sweet Oronoco, Hester and Hyco. These samples were all of the crop of 1892, and have been cured with the greatest possible care. During the last year he had four acres

in tobacco, the average yield being over 1000 pounds per acre.

THE Washington *News* in an editorial on Southern prosperity says: "All evidences point to the conclusion that the South is entering upon an era of unexampled and deserved prosperity, and its achievements promise to commensurate with its splendid opportunities and resources. The revival is not in the nature of a "boom," and the progress is not spasmodic or transient, but healthy, substantial and natural. With advantages peculiarly its own, and with citizens who appreciate them and have the judgment and energy to profit by them, the immediate future of the South is more than promising. The *Evening News* believes that the record of its advancement will be more surprising with each succeeding week. The South has a magnificent destiny, and all sections of the country will rejoice in the accumulating evidences of its triumphal progress."

DURING 1892 there were packed in the United States 3,223,165 cases of tomatoes, against 3,322,365 cases in 1891. Of the output in 1892 the South packed 1,055,498 cases, against 885,110 cases in 1891. The corn pack of the country in 1892 was 3,417,190 cases, against 2,837,153 cases in 1891. Of the 1892 pack the South furnished a little over 500,000 cases. The canning and packing industry offers a wide field in which the South can engage in profitable business. While the export trade in canned goods is growing, it has never been pushed as it ought, and there is a market for much more goods than are consumed in this country. No section of the United States offers such advantages as the South for the growing and packing of fruits and vegetables. The necessary apparatus for a small canning factory can be purchased at moderate cost and the business yields a good return upon a small expenditure of capital. The rapidly increasing number of canneries in the South indicates the extent to which the opportunities are being recognized and appreciated.

THE phosphate miners of South Carolina and Florida are taking steps to have a suitable collective exhibit of the industry prepared for the World's Fair. The miners in both States are contributing liberally to a fund that is being raised for the purpose and the project is meeting with hearty support from the many people interested in this important industry.

A GOOD illustration of the rapid appreciation in values of real estate in New Orleans is shown in a sale of 616 acres recently consummated. In 1890 this tract was purchased for $33,000, and now it has just been sold for $160,000. No more convincing evidence of the rapid growth of the city could be found than is contained in this incident.

THE approach of spring is stirring real estate matters actively in Baltimore, and, if indications mean anything, this spring and summer will show some surprising developments in and about the city. Baltimore is singularly destitute of suburban places of residence, although possessing suburbs of infinite beauty and charm which offer every condition requisite to growth and progress on a large scale. It is only within the past year that the delightful surroundings of the city have been recognized in a practical manner, and whatever of energy and appreciation have been manifested is due chiefly to external influences, to capitalists in other cities who have been quicker than Baltimoreans to grasp the situation and improve its opportunities. This year will probably witness developments that will surprise the people of Baltimore and set them a pace to work up to.

THE manufacture of paper from cottonseed hulls is a new industry that is just being established in New Orleans by the Cottonseed Hull Fibre Co., a recently organized company with $250,000 of capital stock. The mode of operation is to digest the hulls for about six hours with soda ash, thereby producing a pulp which is washed, bleached and then put through the same process used in paper mills. The entire process requires about thirty-six hours.

A CORRESPONDENT in Arkansas writes as follows: "We are inclined to take a sanquine view of the situation, inasmuch as we are just passing out of a three years' hard experience—the hardest the South has known since reconstruction days. These have been years of anxiety, and we have come out of them with an experience born of suffering, with a broad knowledge of cause and effect. Among the many lessons we have learned, the most valuable, we think, are:

1. The evils of our credit sistem.
2. The excessive growth of cotton to the exclusion of other crops.
3. That the plantation system is wrong and

a hindrance to the healthy growth of the country.

To expatiate briefly on these three lessons: We believe the merchants have determined to adopt nearer a cash system of business, and thus force our farmers to produce many of the necessaries of life which they have formerly bought on credit at excessive prices. This will necessarily cause them to grow less cotton, which will in turn cause the plantation owner either to dispose of some of his land on easy terms to his renters or let it lie idle, an occurrence we do not anticipate.

The effects of these changes in our credit system are already apparent, most noticeable in the decreased sale of "side meat" and flour and the corresponding increase in the home production of these articles.

If the merchants continue this idea of education the South will within the next ten years experience an era of prosperity equal to that of *ante-bellum* days, without any of the attending social dangers.

THE Cumberland Inland Co., composed of stockholders in Macon, Atlanta and other places, is getting ready for the approaching season. During last season the gross receipts of the hotel were $24,859 and expenses $18,130, leaving a net profit of $6729. A considerable amount was expended in making improvements on Cumberland island and in advertising, neither of which will be so great this season, and consequently it is expected that the hotel will prove a paying investment. The entire property, hotel, furniture, etc., is estimated as worth about $130,000.

PROF. WILBUR R. SMITH, of Lexington, Ky., has recently been appointed one of the commissioners from that State to the World's Fair. The other commissioners are: W. H. Dulaney, banker, of Louisville; Hon. John D. Clardy, of Hopkinsville; Hon. John W. Yerkes, of Danville; Hon. A. James, of Penrod, and Judge J. D. Black, Barboursville. The appropriation for the Kentucky exhibit is $100,000.

THE space assigned to the Baltimore public schools at the World's Fair is sufficient to make a fine display, being in size 38x20 feet. The exhibit is almost finished, the work of getting it into shape being now in progress. The exhibit will include the school work of pupils from the beginners' grade in the primary school to the graduating class in the city college, covering a period of thirteen years. It will be divided into several branches, such as literary, drawing, modeling, photographs of schools, etc.

NEW ORLEANS real estate agents have just closed a deal with Northern capitalists which is of more than ordinary interest, involving the purchase of a tract of land fronting on St. Charles avenue, and is directly opposite Audobon Park. The purchasers are a party of St. Louis and Chicago capitalists who were attracted to New Orleans some time ago, but hesitated in purchasing on account of the lack of transportation facilities. The introduction of the electric motor at once decided them to seek investment, and after a personal inspection they concluded to purchase the tract as above stated, and as one of the most suitable for their purposes. Negotiations were opened with Judge J. M. Bonner, the owner, and the contract was finally closed, the price paid being $160,000. This tract has a frontage on St. Charles avenue of 616 feet, with a depth of 8000 feet. It is to be laid off with a broad avenue running the entire length 130 feet wide, with a fifty-foot park in the centre. The roadway will either be paved with asphaltum or gravel, with concrete curbing and gutters. The parks will be beautified by trees, flowers and fountains, and other improvements introduced which will make it the most attractive as well as exclusive residence portion in New Orleans. The property will be restricted for residence purposes only. The company intends to call it Beauregard Park.

THE climate of Charleston, S. C., seems to be conducive to long life. The death records of that city for 1892 show that twenty-eight white people who died during last year had reached ages upwards of eighty years, while forty-eight colored people were over eighty years old at the time of their death, ten of them being upwards of ninety years.

THE South is at once old and new, whether we regard it from a political, social or industrial point of view. Its conservative temper remains, but it is adjusting the distinctive elements of its old life to new lines of progress. Whatever may have been its mistakes and its misfortunes, it has held fast to certain great principles of government until their validity has been everywhere recognized. Its white population is the most homogeneous of any in the Union, and is the most largely descended from a revolutionary stock. And our people are as little tinctured with alien ideas as with alien blood. They are thoroughly American. For this reason they prefer to share their lands to American immigrants. But they have come to understand the importance of fostering communities of small freeholders—the social, political and industrial value of a middle class. This consummation bids fair to be, pre-eminently, the new feature in Southern life. Circumstances have been for years gradually bringing it about, and the tide of immigration will both welcome and confirm it. This old quarter of the Union is new also in the fact that it is still so sparsely peopled. Slavery not only prevented immigration, but limited the expansion of native enterprise. In a great part of the South industrial advance could only keep step with the increase of its slave population. Hence vast regions of fertile and heavily timbered soil have remained to this day untouched almost at our very doors. But it is obvious that this state of things cannot much longer continue. A pleasant climate, abundant and cheap lands, are attractions which cannot be ignored. Adventure has pushed its way to the farthest West and is turning back. There is no such abundance of cheap and available land, there is no such combination of the conditions of comfort and prosperity anywhere else in the Union, or for that matter in the world as may be found here in these Southern States.—*New Orleans New Delta.*

PEN SKETCHES OF GEORGIA CITIES.

ATLANTA.

The Gate City of the Southern Empire State.

Atlanta is the capital of the State of Georgia, in which the increase in value of property during the last decade, by official report, was $210,000,000. The city has an elevation of 1085 feet above sea level, greater than any other city of equal population in the Union save Denver.

Atlanta is the practical centre, geographically, of a section of the ten States of Virginia, West Virginia, North Carolina, South Carolina, Georgia, Florida, Alabama, Mississippi, Tennessee and Kentucky, which contain 450,515 square miles and over 15,000,000 people. Around it, within seventy-five miles, is a greater mineral variety and a larger abundance of many minerals than the same environment of any city in the South, if not in the world.

Atlanta's health, under scientific observation and test of temperature and rainfall proven by its wonderful low death rate, shows it one of the most salubrious climates on the globe. Its trade area is mainly agricultural, with soil fit for all grains, grasses, cotton, fruits, truck and dairying. It is rich in varied and proximate minerals and timbers, while its manufactures embrace a territory from the Potomac to the Rio Grande. Its transportation facilities, with its eleven railroads, are unequalled.

With these and many more rare advantages, Atlanta's real estate has made rapid and steady enhancement in value. Every new railroad and industry has brought people, creating greater demand for homes and business sites. The growth of the city in population, business and manufactures is the sure test of the steady increase in the value of real estate. The official and reliable record on these points proves that property has moved continuously up in prices.

The census reveals the following figures of Atlanta:

	Population.
1880.............................	37,409
1853.............................	44,517
1885..............	56,837
1892, by directory........	112,000

	Real estate values for taxes.
1880....	$12.000,000
1883....	18,896,620
1885....	21,712,930
1890....	30,729,894
1891....	34,502,618

Real estate increase 1891 over 1890......... $3,772,721
Personalty increase 1891 over 1890........... 2,298,747

Total realty and personalty increase one
year, 1891 over 1890..................... $5,071,451

This is a greater increase than ever known before in a single year of Atlanta's life.

The remarkable fact in Atlanta's real estate growth is that it has not only been rapid but certain and continuous, and hence there has never been any "boom" or spasmodic appreciation in the prices or valuation of her real estate. Property brings uniformly more money every year, and buyers have never lost on legitimate transactions. Let me verify this by actual sales and bona fide offers of particular pieces of real estate, as might be done by every piece.

In 1879 the "Seltzer Block," on Peachtree street, four acres, was bought for $2500; in 1889 it sold for over $40,000, and in 1890-91 parts brought prices that showed it worth $100,000. Just beyond it ten acres cost in 1881 $4500, and since then the buyer has sold part of the ten acres for over $100,000, and the part sold would bring now proximately $200,000, as indicated by actual sales, and the remainder of the ten acres unsold is worth now in the open market $75,000.

Sixty acres on Peachtree road, three and a half miles from the centre of the city, cost $3000 in 1881, and in 1890 sold for $60,000, and the owners are getting a handsome advance on that. Across the road twenty-one acres in 1884 brought $9000, in 1889 $20,500, and now, in 1892, $65 a front foot for about 400 feet. $26,000 has been declined for about five acres. These prices are common for north side property.

Our lists of east side lots on the boulevard show lots that were selling at $10 to $20 a front foot from five to eight years ago are now bringing from $70 to $100 a foot. So on the south side, lots held in 1885-86 at $150 a front foot are in 1890-91 selling at $500 to $600 a foot. In the west, southwest and northwest, both city and suburbs, lots held at $300 to $500 an acre then are selling now at from $1200 to $2000 an acre.

In West End I think of a tract of twenty acres that was listed in 1884 at $2500, and in 1889 a bona fide offer of $20,000 was declined. In 1892, a quarter of a mile beyond, property sold at auction at $2000 an acre, showing the twenty acres worth $40,000 to-day.

Central business property shows almost as great increase in value. A triangular lot fronting the Methodist church, corner of Peachtree and Pryor streets, sold at auction in 1882 for $2500; was offered in 1888 with a $1500 house on it for $8000, and since then offers of $10,000, $12,000, $16,000 and $20,000 have been successively refused for it. In 1890 a lot corner of Wheat and Pryor streets sold for $6000, and six months later for $20,000. Three years ago a ninety-foot lot on Whitehall street, between Mitchell and Trinity avenue, was offered at $300 a front foot, and recently $1000 a front foot has been refused.

In May, 1892, an eleven-acre tract on the Central Railroad (Bonnybrae), near West End, which cost the owner $11,000 in 1889, was sold at auction by lots for $19,800, and many lots have since been resold at from 20 to 25 per cent. advance, and more than half a dozen homes are being built on the tract.

These instances are enough to demonstrate the advance in price and value in all parts of the city, and this general enhancement has been the result of actual improvements, as in the case of Bonnybrae. The demand for all classes of real property has been sustained by increased population and business, and not by "booms" or over-speculation, and as the increase of real estate value is greater each year than the previous year, and the city income thus grows yearly, the permanent improvements increase annually and this is another cause of enhancing real estate values.

Atlanta's real estate has never retrograded in value, and there are more evidences of its future increase in value to-day than at any time of its history. It has the universal confidence of all Atlanta people, as well as of the citizens of the State of which it is the capital.

All this shows Atlanta to be a safe place for investment in real estate by the capitalists of the whole country.

There is an important history connected with Atlanta's soubriquet of the "Gate City of the South" that carries great significance, and embodies in the name the distinction of the city as the chief railway centre of the whole South.

As far back as the year 1857, only ten years after the place was incorporated as Atlanta, having been dubbed "Terminus" in 1837 and chartered as "Marthasville" in 1844, a great gathering of practical business men was held in Charleston, S. C., and after a thorough review of the whole Southern section, impartially and unanimously settled upon Atlanta as the leading railroad point of the South, and christened the vigorous young giant of a municipal infant as the "Gate City," which name it has enjoyed ever since undisputed.

This distinguished title was won and has been held by her threefold qualities of centrality, accessibility and unequalled network of railways, existing and prospective, of which the city is the centre. No other city has just such a location.

Atlanta to Atlantic cotton belt ports, air line, 260 miles.

Atlanta to Gulf of Mexico ports, air line, 270 miles.

Atlanta to the Mississippi river, air line, 340 miles.

Atlanta to northern line of cotton belt, air line, 200 miles.

Atlanta is thus by nature and without a rival the interior commercial market of this great and favored section.

Resting on a plane 1085 feet above the sea-level, with its perfect climate, delightfully breezeful even in the hottest months, absolutely free from malarial taint, and with its unqualified healthfulness, Atlanta, by an inevitable destiny, must become what she is swiftly striding to be, the coming manufacturing city of the South.

Her railway facilities already surpass those of any other Southern point. Eleven great railroad lines centre here:

1. The Central Railroad system, to the sea.

2. The Richmond & Danville system, north.

3. The Atlanta & West Point, to the Gulf.

4. The Atlanta & Florida Railroad, to Florida.

5. The Georgia Pacific Railroad, to Birmingham.

6. The Western & Atlanta, now Louisville & Nashville, west.

7. The East Tennessee, Virginia & Georgia Railroad, west and to the sea.

8. The Marietta & North Georgia Railroad, northwest.

9. The Georgia, Carolina & Northern Railroad, north,

10. The Atlanta, Covington &. Macon Railroad, to the sea.

11. The Georgia Railroad, north and to Charleston and Port-Royal.

Other lines' are contemplated, and work is actually going on· to complete branches that will be prolific feeders for the city.

It will thus be seen that Atlanta affords a sure spot for location or investment.

Atlanta is the centre of thousands of miles of railway. track, linked in symmetrieal connection with great ocean steamship schemes, ramifying the South, riveting the South Atlantic ocean to the West, Northwest, North and the Gulf. Ponderous steamers bind it to New York, Boston, Philadelphia, Baltimore, and now soon to Liverpool and Bremen, through Brunswick.

The Southern Railway and Steamship Association has its headquarters in Atlanta, and controls freight for all the railroads south of the Ohio and east of the Mississippi rivers and ocean steamship lines between the Southern ports and Eastern cities. The commissioners of the Southern Passenger Association are also in Atlanta, and control Southern passenger traffic. Atlanta's possibilities from her railway environment cannot be estimated. She must become the greatest interior mart of the South.

I. W. Avery.

SAVANNAH.

The Great Seaport City of the South Atlantic States.

Beautiful and prosperous Savannah is one of the most historic as well as loveliest cities on the American continent. It was the germ of one of the original colonies, the greatest of the Southern section of the United States, that has ripened into the Commonwealth which has won and held undisputed from every other Southern Commonwealth the proud name of the Empire State of the South.

Nature fashioned the ground of this place for the site of a great river and ocean metropolis, whose advantages have no rival South or North. The spot captured the eye of the farseeing Oglethorpe, the founder of Savannah and Georgia, and he seized promptly the providential location for his future great city.

A healthy bluff rises clear above the highest flow of the river and goes back gently with salubrious pine forests on pure sand to the rear, affording restful basis for attractive homes and delightful living, and its lowest environments are drainable by the flowing river into phenomenal truck farms and blooming gardens.

The city, while growing steadily to its present exquisite loveliness and commercial power, has shone with unfading historic renown. Its annals are lustrous with great events and characters,· and every spot of city and surrounding country is rich in chronicles of enterprise and valor.

Savannah is the first naval stores mart in the world.

Savannah has been for years the second cotton port of the United States.

Savannah is the chief South Atlantic seaport of the American continent.

Savannah is the third port in the United States in the value of its exports.

Savannah has the smallest white record of mortality in the United States (seventeen to 1000), proving its health; ample pure artesian well water, and average summer heat of 80^b to $90°$ and winter cold of $30°$ to $40°$.

Savannah is the creator, head and pivot of the largest connected system of ocean steamships and railroads in the Western Hemisphere. linking Savannah by separate sea steam lines to Baltimore, Philadelphia, New York and Boston, every ocean mart of the North, and by the best iron tracks to the West and Gulf, the route giving a railroad freight line from great Western and Southwestern marts shorter and cheaper than to New York by from eighty-seven to 691 miles.

Savannah is the terminus of the great Plant system of railway and steamships that taps with iron spider web the orange sanitarium of Florida and makes the West Indies tributary by close ship lines to this country.

Savannah is the centre of one of the three rice sections of the South and one of the important rice marts, and the culture of tobacco is growing.

Savannah is the best truck region of the South, and furnishes spring vegetables to the North by its steam lines.

Savannah is one of the prolific oyster and fish markets in the Union.

Savannah is the distributing point, through its ships North and abroad, and through its railways to the interior, of the famous yellow pine and other lumber which Georgia has beyond any other State in the Union or the world.

Savannah has as fine an art academy as the United States can show, and is the art centre of the South, as well as a literary centre, having the Catholic library and the Historical Society library, the oldest and most valuable in the State.

Savannah was the first Southern city to light with electricity.

Savannah is especially well equipped with hospitals and other charitable institutions.

Savannah has the largest volunteer military in the South and a coterie of fine military clubs.

Savannah has around it as fine salt water suburbs, historic and beautiful, as can be found on the continent—Tybee, Thunderbolt, Bonaventure, Isle of Hope, Beaulieu and others—all reached by railroads of the city's complete electric car system, which also threads and circles the place with an economical service.

Savannah, in a word, attracts the world for homes, business and investments.

Savannah has one of the best schemes of trade transportation, not only in the United States, but in the world. Its connected and complete system of Atlantic navigation north, with railway trunks west to the Pacific, is unequalled.

That genius of transportation, Wm. M. Wadley, foresaw the great commercial importance of Savannah and conceived and created the great "Central Railroad and ocean steamship system," that is the heart of the carrying network which is working out Savannah's commercial destiny.

Look at the map and mark the four regular ocean steam lines of passenger and freight service radiating from Savannah to Boston, New York, Philadelphia and Baltimore, the four chief American Atlantic ports and greatest Northern commercial ocean marts.

Then note the magnificent and well-equipped schemes of connected iron railway tracks running without a break from Savannah to the Gulf, the West and the North, reaching every interior city, and the great Pacific ocean ports distributing her water cargoes.

You have in the symmetrical combination of these great water and rail plants, through this elevated, healthful and favored Savannah, the natural leader of the South Atlantic seaports of this continent, an instrumentality of commercial growth and power whose results cannot be measured.

The Central Railroad's vital lines leading to Augusta, Atlanta, Columbus, Chattanooga, Montgomery, Birmingham and Albany are supplemented by other important railways from Savannah. We have the Savannah & Charleston Railroad, the Atlantic Coast Line to the North, the Savannah & Columbia, the "South Bound," the middle line to the North and short line to the Carolina mountains ; the Savannah, Americus & Montgomery, the direct line to the Gulf and the Southwest ; the East Tennessee, Virginia & Georgia to Macon and Rome, and the Savannah, Florida & Western, the short line to the orange land and the West Indies, all modern lines in successful operation.

There are building the Macon, Dublin & Savannah by Dublin, the Middle Georgia & Atlantic by Eatonton from Atlanta to Savannah, and the Savannah & Jacksonville by Darien, all short and through new and rich territory to feed Savannah's commerce and afford competition with existing lines, ensuring low fares and freights.

Within a year under the operation of the lease of the South Bound Railroad to the Florida Central system, the Florida Central and the Jacksonville, Tampa & Key West will have direct connection through Savannah with the North and West, centering all of the Florida railway systems in Savannah, shortening the distance between Jacksonville and Savannah nearly sixty miles, and giving tourists to Florida the nearest route both from Cincinnati and New York.

All of the Savannah railway lines have close, direct and great railway connections—Chattanooga, Nashville & Louisville, the Kansas, Memphis & Birmingham, the Richmond & Danville, the Texas Pacific and others—trunk lines from the Atlantic to the Pacific oceans, shorter and of easier grades than the great Northern trunk lines, and free from snow and ice.

The Central Railroad system has about 2000 miles of track in Georgia, Alabama and South Carolina, with thirteen magnificent steamships to Atlantic ports.

The Savannah, Florida & Western, the "Plant system," has over 900 miles of track in Georgia, Florida and Alabama, with almost 1000 miles of steam water lines.

Timber, cotton, coal, iron, naval stores, rice, phosphates, grain, truck and fruit of our own load these lines, which connect the Atlantic, Gulf and Pacific coasts and the

West Indies and South America, using the vast Union, Missouri and Southern Pacific Railroads.

I. W. Avery.

MACON.

The Central City of the State of Georgia.

Macon is the handsome and thriving "Central City" of the State of Georgia, the pivotal centre of the "Empire State of the South," located on the Ocmulgee river, navigable to Brunswick on the ocean, and the converging point of twelve lines of railroads that feed its commerce and contribute to its trade and prosperity.

Macon began its prosperity in 1806 as Fort

UNITED STATES COURTHOUSE, MACON, GA.

Hawkins, an Indian trading-post, that was an important place in the war of 1812, when the navigation of the Ocmulgee was started. In 1822 Bibb county was organized and Macon authorized to be made the county site, and the city was incorporated in 1824. The first railroad survey in the State was for a line from Macon to Milledgeville in 1825. Macon's first bank was the Bank of Darien in 1825; the first steamboat navigation was in 1828; the first railroad in 1837 from Macon to Forsyth, and the Central Railroad was completed in 1843.

Macon is 380 feet above the sea level. It is on a site of hills, crowned with smooth plateaus dotted with beautiful homes, environed by fruit and grain fields, threaded by the serpentine Ocmulgee, winding through rich corn and cotton bottoms. This lovely site is on the ground into which 300 miles of southerly plains blend into granite hills.

The rainfall has averaged 48.75 inches for ten years. The temperature has averaged: Spring, 63.33; summer, 79; autumn, 64.93; winter, 46.88. The comparative annual temperature has been: Macon, 63.33; Jacksonville, 69.10; Atlanta, 60.90; Cincinnati, 55.30; New York, 51.20; Boston, 48.20. The average death rate for six years was 9.41. Macon has never had an epidemic. The percentage of impurities per gallon in the city water as compared with other cities was: Macon, 1.12; Philadelphia, 3.50; Boston, 3.96; Atlanta, 4.05; New York, 4.78; Chicago, 6.68; Rochester, 13.25; London, England, 15.41. Purity of water is a vital element of health. Macon's water comes from springs in her hills, pure, cold and sparkling, and never affected by drought or surface water.

The growth and extent of Macon's manufacturing industries is shown by the following comparative statement:

	1880.	1890.
Number establisments.	54	161
Capital	$651,800	$3,608,977
Hands employed	1,115	3,142
Wages paid	$301,022	$1,085,716
Materials used	$936,196	$2,534,144
Value of products	$1,724,125	$4,974,914

The percentage of increase in Macon's manufacturing interests compares with other Southern cities as follows:

Percentage of increase in number of establishments—Macon, 215; Atlanta, 64; Nashville, 27; Savannah, 52; Augusta, 525.

Percentage of increase in capital—Macon, 454; Atlanta, 215; Nashville, 99; Savannah, 169; Augusta, 241.

Percentage of increase in employes—Macon, 172; Atlanta, 92; Nashville, 43; Savannah, 43; Augusta, 247.

Percentage of increase in wages paid—Macon, 260; Atlanta, 235; Nashville, 134; Savannah, 88; Augusta, 320.

Percentage of increase in cost of materials used—Macon, 170; Atlanta, 58; Nashville, 40; Savannah, 5; Augusta, 121.

Percentage of increase in value of products—Macon, 188; Atlanta, 117; Nashville, 51; Savannah, 31; Augusta, 174.

Macon led in the percentage of increase in capital, materials and products, but was second to Augusta in number of industries, employes and wages. Macon put more money into manufacturing and bought more material, with but little less products than came from Augusta's more numerous establishments with more hands and more wages. Macon left behind all but Augusta, and led that city in increase of capital and materials used and nearly equalled that city in products.

Macon's largest industrial interest is textiles; four establishments, representing $1,-

employes, $95,390 in wages, $40,436 of materials and $231,600 of products.

The liquor industry, with three establishments, represents $313,750 of capital, employing 48 hands, paying $27,531 in wages, using $85,198 of materials and turning out a product valued at $186,600.

Five furniture factories show $128,015 of capital, 122 hands, $42,687 of wages, $44,175 of material and $118,610 of products.

Five carriage and wagon shops have $65,050

WESLEYAN FEMALE COLLEGE, MACON, GA.

430,390 of capital, employing 1038 hands to whom wages amounting to $219,135 were paid, consuming $722,356 worth of materials and producing goods valued at $1,115,366.

Five planing mills, with only $152,500 of capital, employed 202 hands, paid $95,030 in wages, used materials costing $446,400 and turned out a product of $669,780.

Nine brick and tile works, with $253,150 of capital, employed 448 hands, paid $142,199 in wages, consumed materials to the value of $75,722, and yielded $594,500 of products.

Foundries and machine shops, five in number, come next, with $344,200 of capital, 173

of capital, employ 73 hands, with $32,243 of wages, $37,657 of materials and $100,585 of products.

In the contest between Macon and Atlanta for the Technological Institute it was shown that Macon could be reached by the greatest number of people in less time and at less expense than Atlanta, and that a line equidistant from both at any point had fifty-seven counties, 1142 miles of railroad, and 647,475 population nearer Atlanta, as compared with eighty counties, 1798 miles of railroad and 894,200 population nearer to Macon, giving Macon the advantage of twenty-three more counties, 655 more railroad miles and 246,725 more population than Atlanta, and $45,000,000 more of wealth accessible.

Macon is central ; has at her door unlimited material of all kinds, twenty-five kinds of valuable woods on the Ocmulgee, clay and kaolin for brick, pipe, terra-cotta and crockery inexhaustible, twelve railroads leading in all directions, close relations with country around, growing fast and dependent' on her fine climate and success in all her industrial enterprises.

Macon has among her industries, cotton mills, knitting mills, foundries, machine works, guano and phosphate works, a brewery, ice works, furniture factories, barrel factories, wheel works, flour and corn mills, cotton com-presses, candy and cracker factory, publishing

A TYPICAL SOUTHERN HOME, MACON, GA.

and printing house and large railroad shops, aggregating $7,000,000 annually in business.

Macon's railroad situation is well worthy of study. The city is the centre of twelve rail-road lines tapping important regions of trade.

1. The Central to Savannah, southeast.

2. The Macon & Atlantic to Savannah, southeast.

3. The Macon & Dublin to go to Savannah, southeast.

4. The East Tennessee, Virginia & Georgia to Brunswick, southeast.

5. The Georgia Southern & Florida to Pa-latka, South Florida.

6. The Southwestern to Eufaula, Ala., south-west.

7. The Macon & Columbus to Columbus, west.

8. The Macon & Birmingham to· Birming-ham, northwest.

9. The Central to Chattanooga, northwest.

10. The East Tennessee, Virginia & Georgia to Chattanooga and Knoxville, northwest.

11. The Covington & Macon to Gainesville and Athens, north.

12. The Georgia to Augusta, northeast.

Of Georgia's railroads 75 per cent. centre in Macon. Macon has given to the railroads of Georgia $3,300,000 in money, besides large grants of land and valuable privileges. An examination of the country her railroads tap shows that she draws from fruit, grain, cotton, stock, gold, granite, marble, iron, coal, lum-ber, turpentine, rice, and other sections. Her traffic is simply magnificent in its variety and value.

Macon is in the middle of the richest cotton section of Georgia. The city is the largest inland cotton market in the State, and is sur-rounded by the best cotton counties of the State or the South. Houston county, tributary to the city, is the first cotton and peach county of Georgia. Macon's receipts run to 175,000 bales, the warehouse storage is over 80,000 bales, and the three immense ware-houses and compresses are expected this year to handle nearly a quarter of a million bales. The Alliance warehouse has received in one day 500 bales. Macon is also one of the best markets in the State, giving better prices than any city save Savannah and Brunswick, the seaports. ·

Macon has in the. city and suburbs about 45,000 people. The census of 1890 shows a larger percentage of increase of population than any other city of Georgia. The percent-age of increase in 1890 was 79 per cent.; Atlanta, 75; Columbus, 71; Augusta, 63; Savannah, 40.

Macon has an immense and growing whole-sale trade in proportion to her people, proba-bly the largest of any in the South, that is, in proportion. The city has nearly 100 whole-sale houses, embracing· dry goods, groceries, hardware, shoes, hats, liquors, bags, paper, crackers, candy, tobacco, cigars, and all else in wholesale traffic. The wholesale trade amounts to nearly $50,000,000. One dry goods house does over $2,000,000 of business, and has a great building of six floors, each 60 by 150 feet. Macon's superior railroad envi-ronment and connections explain the city's remarkable wholesale advantages and power. Macon has 500 retail houses, doing a successful trade of especial enterprise. These live merchants have built up a large business in orders from the wealthy sections tributary to the city. One house occupies a building of five floors 50 by 200 feet. Three retail houses employ 120 men and women.

Macon's tax valuation in 1889 was $11,300,-423; in 1891, $14,623,999, and the bonded debt only $568,800. The city tax was $1.25, and her whole tax only $2.35. The postoffice

MERCER UNIVERSITY, MACON, GA.

receipts in the year ending March 31, 1890, were $45,390, and in 1892, $53,590; a conclusive index of the growth of trade and population.

Macon has eight banks, strong institutions, with $1,660,000 of capital. The strongest financial institution is the Exchange Bank, located in its own magnificent building.

Macon is especially affluent in educational facilities of the highest order and greatest variety. This city has the honor of founding the first female college in the United States, the Wesleyan Female College, chartered in 1836, costing $125,000, that has sent out 2,039

graduates and thousands of other students. Its building is 255 by 85 feet, five stories high. Mercer, the great Baptist university, Pio Nono, now St. Stanislaus Catholic College, Mt. de Sales Convent, the State Academy for the Blind, the Alexander Free School, and a magnificent system of forty-five public schools, with 100 teachers and 5419 pupils, form an unsurpassed scheme of instruction and educational equipment.

But Macon's crowning celebrity and value is that the city is the centre of a region of land that has 90 per cent. of the fruit orchards and vineyards of Georgia, which are attracting the attention of thousands of people in the North and West, and which bid fair to be the giant industry of the State. In this circle will be found the large orchards at Marshallville, Fort Valley, Elberta, Forsyth, Barnesville, Tifton, Montrose, and Danville, where is probably the greatest peach orchard in the world—a thousand acres.

The fruit lands make to perfection all the fruits. Ffteen dollars an acre will buy dirt that will bring from $100 to $500. Peaches bear the third year. A 1000-acre peach farm will in five years cost $40,000, and a single full crop will net the owner $300,000 and last for ten to fifteen years. This Macon section has no competition from May 25 to August 10, and direct trade now consummating will make Europe a market for this fruit. A million dollars comes from the fruit of this region, and in three years it will go to three millions. It looks as if this industry must overshadow everything. With what benefit to Macon may be understood.

Macon's government, charitable institutions, churches, suburbs, public buildings, electric car service, etc., are all excellent. She has as handsome fair grounds as the world can show, a fine academy of music, stately residences, and a picturesque site.

As great a critic as Henry Ward Beecher declared Macon 'one of the most beautiful cities of the South."

I. W. Avery.

OCMULGEE PARK.

A Suburb of Macon Where Nature Has Been Lavish.

Macon, typically a city of beautiful suburbs, possesses none more beautiful, so far as lavishness of nature is concerned, than the Ocmulgee Park properties. These properties, comprising over 600 acres of rolling land, hills, dales, flowing streams and gushing springs, lie within ten minutes' ride of the heart of the city, and are now being developed. When finished, Macon will have an ideal suburb, so near the business centre of the city that electric cars will reach one's home in a quarter hour, and so beautiful that home-seekers will flock to this delightful spot. For natural landscape beauty Ocmulgee Park posesses unrivalled advantages, and with the work now in progress fully completed this suburb will grow and thrive in accord with the healthy pulse of Macon's growth.

Perhaps no other property around the city has a greater future before it than Ocmulgee Park. The land, comprising over 600 acres, lies on the northern edge of Macon, and is now a part of the city. It stretches a distance of 8000 feet in length, and is flanked by the Ocmulgee river. The East Tennessee, Virginia & Georgia Railroad runs through the

CITY HALL, MACON, GA.

property parallel with the river, affording magnificent opportunities for the locating of manufacturing plants. From the railroads the lands are hilly and at present are laid out in lots for suburban homes. The company has already finished six miles of broad, well-graded streets, running through the park in graceful curves, and iron for the electric street car line has been ordered. This line will be in operation by April 1st, and other work completed which will enable the company to begin active work in disposing of lots.

Ocmulgee Park is modeled after the famous Llewelyn Park, near Orange, N. J., and the principal streets will be made with the idea of retaining all the natural beauties of the land, and will run in serpentine curvings through

the properties. Fifty acres have been donated by the company for parks, and these are now in the hands of landscape engineers to be beautified and improved. The electric railroad will follow the principal streets and explore the park in such a manner that every resident and home builder will have easy access to the cars, whether his home be large or small in pretension, for Ocmulgee Park is a suburb of the wealthy as well as the middle classes, the lots ranging from several acres each down to the average building site of 50x100 feet.

With the high hills and rolling landscape of these properties, Ocmulgee Park is a beautiful spot, and with the progressive men who constitute the board of directors of the company it will become a most desirable suburb of the city of Macon. Its great advantages are: First, proximity to the business centre of Macon; second, great natural beauty; third, thorough and careful development and permanent improvements, and fourth, the adaptability for grand residences or modest homes without conflict. A feature of the suburb is a clause in the charter of the company prohibiting the sale of liquor in the park, though in the city limits and under city protection.

Macon, with her steady growth and forward march among Georgia's cities, is blessed with many beautiful suburbs. She will need them all in the next few years. But, among all, Ocmulgee Park will be found along with the most ambitious, and as the city grows in population, influence and wealth, this park will possess some of the handsomest residences and homes in the city, and those who invest early will have no cause to regret the step either from a speculative standpoint or from that of owning a permanent home in a beautiful section of Macon.

IN MACON'S SUBURBS.

The Gunn Tract, Rich in Clay and Timber.

Macon abounds in opportunities for profit in lands. The suburbs, though being developed rapidly, still possess unusual advantages for investors and syndicates of capital. It may seem strange that a city of over 40,000 people, including the suburbs, should have valuable timber lands of hard wood almost at its very doors at a cost which is comparatively a mere song. Yet such is the case. For instance, the Gunn property is only one mile from Macon and 1000 acres of it are offered for sale by Messrs. Dunwody & McLennan, real estate agents at Macon, the price being only $100 per acre for the entire tract. This property possesses great advantages for fine brick making, 700 acres of the valley land abounding in the best brick clay south of Philadelphia and so testified to by an expert from the Philadelphia Clay Works who prospected for clay from Philadelphia to Tampa, Fla. Already five brick yards are located on this property, yet all are failing to supply the demand in the territory from Macon to the Atlantic and through Florida, where there is practically no competition. This clay being from five to seven feet deep, produces an output of $30,000 worth of brick and about $100,000 worth of tile drain and terra-cotta goods per acre.

In addition to the brick-manufacturing facilities of this tract there is a very large area of hard-wood land, including such varieties as oak, hickory, beech, elm, maple and gum, adapted to furniture and cabinet wood-working. One or two small factories in Macon are now using these woods, and there are millions of feet of them along the Ocmulgee river, now navigable. The valley land of this property is rich and the upland well adapted for factories. Two trunk lines—the East Tennessee, Virginia & Georgia, and the Georgia Southern & Florida railroads—traverse the property. With such suburbs, Macon only awaits the touch of new capital and factories to lead her sister cities, for she has twelve operated railroads, pure water, an equable climate and this rich back support.

BEAUTIFUL BELLEVUE.

A Village of Homes on the Hills That Overlook Macon.

Macon has grown, is growing, will grow, in spite of the croakers, who never built a city, nor extended one's limits, and pessimistic prophets who never did aught save to discredit the efforts of progressive men with foresight to see coming needs and faith enough to go forward and meet them.

Macon needs more space in which to exercise her lusty growth. The circumscribed limits of the city proper are as much too small for present needs as would be the first pants of boyhood when made to cover the robust limbs of manhood.

Every growing city in the country has had the same experience, and with it has come the same result in each case, rapid transit and the springing up of suburban annexes.

The reason for this bubbling over, as it were,

of home-builders from the crowded city is not hard to trace out. Land in the city proper becomes too valuable except for strictly business purposes, and then, too, it is a trait of all men to hope at one time for a home in the country. It is impossible, however, to do business in the city and follow fully the bent toward a home in the country. Here it is that the suburban home offers a happy blending of the best features of city and country life.

While Macon has been growing the growth of her suburbs has fully kept pace with that of the city, and as a result close-in suburban property is today on a parity with what city property was ten years ago, and new suburbs are a necessity. With the need always comes a remedy, however, and the formation of the American Investment and Loan Company, and the building of an electric line to its property marked a new era for Macon, the opening of a new and charming suburb to home-builders and investors.

The building of the car line was in the nature of an experiment, and there were not lacking croaking wiseacres who, with dubious headshakes, foretold that it would never pay. These same doubters further said that the gentlemen who bought Bellevue and proposed to open up and offer it for sale had shown more faith than judgment. Verily these sceptics have had their day, and the bright and cheerful homes that have sprung up on the property have answered their doubts and emphasized the judgment of the projectors and promoters of Bellevue.

It is but a short twenty minutes' ride from the Exchange Bank building to Bellevue, and it is one that will afford more than usual pleasure. Take a car one of these bright, sunny afternoons and you will see on the way to Bellevue at least a full share of distinguishing landmarks and representative institutions of the city. On one hand the tall spires of the Wesleyan Female College point heavenward. On the other side a little later the buildings of Mercer University overtop the trees that surround it, and then the massive outlines of St. Stanislaus College stand out in bold relief against the blue dome of heaven.

Then Huguenin Heights is passed and the steep ascent of the plateau, on whose summit nestles Bellevue, is begun. A little later the grounds of the Log Cabin Club are reached, and they present a pleasant half-way house by the wayside. The grounds are laid off with gravel walks that wind in among flower beds, while overhead majestic oaks whose foliage never yields to the touch of the frost king, whisper of breezes that are charged with ozone fresh from nature's crucible. The club-house is modeled after an old style southern homestead, with broad halls and wide verandas that can woo a cooling breeze even on summer's warmest days. After nightfall, when myriads of incandescent lights play hide and seek amid the foliage of the trees and cast weird shadows over the sleeping flowers, the scene is one of rare beauty.

A mile beyond Log Cabin Club the summit of the plateau is reached and nearly a hundred homes tell the story of Bellevue's growth of a year. Twelve months ago Bellevue was an open plantation, with alternate strips of forest and field. Now wide and well-graded streets and avenues, fringed with rapidly-growing elms and maples, have taken the places of the unkempt hillsides, and alongside these thoroughfares the roof trees of Bellevue's new inhabitants have been built.

It would be hard to picture a residence suburb that combines more substantial advantages than Bellevue. The natural drainage is perfect, and below the surface at a depth ranging from thirty to fifty feet there are subterranean streams of water as pure as gushes from the slopes of the famed Piedmont section. Its height, something like 200 feet above the level of the city, raises it above the dangers that come from the noxious vapors that rise from a densely crowded community, and the miasma that is exhaled from the lowlands that skirt rivers in a southern latitude.

Leaving out of view the practical advantages of Bellevue, the landscape that is spread out from its summit is as charming as can be found anywhere outside a mountainous section proper. Hills and valleys are spread like a map, the smoke from suburban homes rises here and there, and in the distance the spires and domes of the city are seen far below.

Bellevue has unquestionably one of the greatest futures of any suburban developments in the South.

The work of twelve months has wrought wonderful changes in this property. A year ago it was cut off from the city, and while adjoining the corporate limits, it was yet isolated in consequence of not being penetrated by a single street or roadway. Today an electric railway goes through the entire length of this beautiful crescent-shaped property, and three sixty-foot boulevards, Bellevue, Mercer and Melrose run parallel through this embryo residence point. These are crossed by beautiful avenues running from east to west. Rows of shade trees line broad boulevards of Bellevue.

Fifty thousand dollars worth of lots have been sold at private sale, and without the least effort.

Bellevue Boulevard, in addition to being coursed the entire length by an electric line, possesses the additional advantage of having been declared a public roadway by the Board of County Commissioners. This is a magnificent drive running from Macon through the property and has a full electric front of three and a-half miles. In fact there is not a lot in Bellevue that is more remote than one block from the electric line, which gives the entire investment the advantage of easy access.

The location of Bellevue is grand. It possesses a magnificent elevation, being 200 feet above the level of Macon and on a line with the spires of Mercer and Wesleyan.

All of the surroundings are attractive and conditions desirable and healthful. Two beautiful small parks grace intermediate points on the property, and one large park makes an attractive terminus. Then the Central Railroad is all that separates Bellevue from the aristocratic suburb of Vineville, and this has been obviated by spanning the Central with a bridge, thus joining two of the most beautiful suburbs in the South.

It will be seen from this that Bellevue is to be equally distinctive for its social and healthful environment.

The most attractive club-house in Georgia is the Log Cabin, at Bellevue. It is built on the old-fashioned plan, and the whole conception is novel and pleasing. Two broad hallways cross the length and breadth of the building, forming an elegant dancing place; a comfortable room is cut off in each corner of the structure, making four in all, and these are used for ladies' reception room, dining room, billiards, etc. Straight chairs with rawhide bottoms are used in the house, and rustic willow chairs grace the broad colonnade that encircles the building. In the second story a balcony, set aside for chaperons and spectators, overlooks the capacious dancing halls, a colonnade and dormer windows give the second story a pleasing exterior, while the interior of the building is finished with Georgia pine. The cost of the building alone was

$5000. The ground was donated by the company. The club house stands in the centre of a four-acre lot, surrounded by water oaks and beautiful evergreen shrubs, and a lovely lawn stretches on the western approach, all going to make the Log Cabin Club House and grounds peculiarly attractive.

The club has a membership of 150, and every few nights Bellevue is the scene of some brilliant social event.

Bellevue values are obliged to increase when one considers Macon's central location and great railroad and educational facilities. She has eleven railroads; two of the most famous seats of learning in the country; a list of industries that show an annual output of $7,000,000; a wholesale trade of $50,000,000; tax values representing $15,000,000, and a tax rate of $1.45; has a population, including her suburbs, of 40,000; spends $70,000 annually on her public schools; and shows the low death-rate of 9.41 among the white population. One of the best evidences of the soundness of Macon's growth is presented in the fact that her post-office receipts are $53,590.60, having nearly doubled in seven years, while the last census gives her a greater percentage of growth than any Georgia city.

Macon is growing, and will continue to grow. From 1880 to 1890 the ratio of increase of population was 79 per cent., while Atlanta, the famed Gate City of the South, only showed 75 per cent. The growth of Macon's suburbs was in greater ratio than that of the city proper, and the next ten years will show a still more wonderful increase.

The home-builders and investors of the city must look to a new suburb, and Bellevue being the first one to offer cheap, reasonable and well-drained lots, with rapid transit to and from the city, must receive first attention, and the property is worthy of it. All of the conditions that can make a desirable home are found there, and nothing unpleasant pertains or can pertain to its surroundings.

Home-builder, renter, dwellers in narrow homes, where only a modicum of sunlight can come, go and see Bellevue, and you will say, as did the Ethiopian queen, after she had viewed the matchless glories of Solomon's temple and kingdom that the half has not been told.

✝ ✝ ✝ ✝ ✝ ✝ ✝ ✝

AUGUSTA.

The Chief Manufacturing City of the South and a Great Commercial Centre.

The old and elegant city of Augusta, a commercial metropolis, the chief manufacturing city of the South, both a railroad focus and a head of Savannah river navigation, the largest interior cotton market of the whole Southeast of the United States and the convergence of three railway lines leading to important South Atlantic direct trade seaports, is one of the historic and most · ambitious cities of the South; and a type of its best citizenship and most progressive civilization.

CONFEDERATE SOLDIERS' MONUMENT, AUGUSTA, GA.

Augusta's advantages may be set forth thus:

1. A manufacturing center and the South's industrial leader.

2. An agricultural centre of the best farm section of Georgia.

3. A magnificent cotton market.

4. The heart of a great railway web.

5. River connections with the sea, and the direct terminus for three direct trade lines; besides less direct for two others.

6. The South's healthiest city in low mortality.

7. Suburbs with climatic antidote to malaria and lung and throat ills.

Augusta is a beautiful place, nestling in a picturesque environment. It has broad streets that carry an idea of luxury, and that are lined with handsome residences, suggestive of wealth and culture.

Broad street, fitly named, the main business thoroughfare, has been paved for a mile with

GREEN STREET, AUGUSTA, GA.

aristocratic asphalt, the ideal pavement, in felicitous keeping with the spirit of the city, and there is no handsomer street in the United States, and it is doubtful if it can be surpassed in the world. It is 120 feet wide from sidewalk to sidewalk, surpassing the famous Pennsylvania avenue in Washington, D. C., the national capital, and when it is blazing at night with electric illumination, and brilliant with one of its glittering carnivals, it 'is a spectacle of municipal splendor.

The suburbs are in keeping with the city proper. Summerville, known as the Sand Hills, and including Monte Sano ; North Augusta, over the river, looking down from its rising and picturesque eminence of observation upon the lovely panorama of the river-bordered city; and the fine grounds of the Carolina Land Co. constitute a trio of suburban surroundings, most attractive.

The Sand Hills have grand groves of stately old trees, lordly old dwellings set in spacious

and ornate grounds, and the modern and well kept Bon Air hotel filled in the winter with happy millionaires. North Augusta is under Mr. W. M. Jackson's management, and sweeps up from the river, which is crossed by its splendid iron bridge, and is full of promise with its wide hard boulevards and imperial building sites.

In 1733 the Georgia Colony was founded and Augusta was laid out in 1735, becoming the most important trading point of the colony.

Augusta was the seat of government from 1776 until 1795, save when in the hands of the English in the Revolution. In 1788 she held the convention that ratified the United States Constitution, and George Washington visited it in 1791.

Augusta was incorporated in 1789. In 1825 there were fifteen steamboats plying on the river between Augusta and Savannah, and she shipped 100,000 bags of cotton. Her first rail-

COTTON EXCHANGE, AUGUSTA, GA.

road—the Charleston & Augusta—was completed in 1836 ; the Georgia to Atlanta in 1845 ; the Central to Savannah in 1854; the Columbia in 1860, and the Macon and Port Royal each in 1873.

The city of Augusta is in a region that is

not exceeded in its native elements of wealth and progress nor outstripped in its development. Twenty-six Georgia and nine South Carolina counties, the very cream of two great States, are tributary to Augusta, with their million of thrifty and progressive people, $200,000,000 of property, $75,000,000 of fertile land, blooming with fine farms, divided by a great river, threaded by modern railroads, alive with prosperous towns and cities, worth $45,000,000, growing half a million bales of cotton—the South's exclusive and imperial staple.

The Savannah river, which runs by her

been the terminal point of the first Southern railroad—the South Carolina—from Charleston, and the starting place of the second—the Georgia—from Augusta to Atlanta.

Critically studying Augusta's railroad situation, she is seen to possess an extraordinary endowment of railway facilities: Three lines connect her with the best and strongest South Atlantic seaports, Port Royal, the finest harbor in the South, and Savannah and Charleston, the two oldest and wealthiest ocean marts of the South,

Port Royal is linked to Augusta by the Port Royal Augusta Railroad, and it is simply in-

CANAL LOCKS AND DAM ACROSS SAVANNAH RIVER, AUGUSTA, GA

door, and connects her with the ocean, extends 450 miles from its start to the sea, and is an affluent tributary to her trade and greatness. The river is navigable by large ships eighteen miles from Savannah to the ocean, 230 miles from Savannah to Augusta by steamboats, and 150 miles above Augusta by small steamboats, 398 miles all told of commercial waterway.

On this river lie twelve Georgia and six South Carolina counties, with $100,000,000 of wealth, making $30,000,000 worth of farm crops, raising 350,000 bales of cotton and a million bushels of grain. Augusta has a rare region to feed her trade.

Augusta enjoys the distinction of having

evitable that with this imperial harbor Port Royal must become one of the great commercial seaports of the United States, and as Augusta is her exclusive interior connection with the great West and its granaries, established Southern direct trade, now a certainty, must give Augusta a phenomenal growth.

But in addition to Port Royal, solely hers, Augusta has direct railroads, to Savannah by the great Central Railroad of Georgia, and to Charleston by the South Carolina Railroad, both running successful lines of ocean steamers to Northern ports, and Savannah already enjoying direct trade with Europe and South America. Thus is Augusta the immediate beneficiary of three splendid ocean ports—two with established ocean commerce on a large scale, and the other the coming ocean port of the South Atlantic.

Turning northward, we find the road to Columbia, northeast, connecting with two great through lines north, the Richmond & Danville by Charlotte, and the Atlantic Coast Line by Wilmington. Then comes the Savannah Valley Railroad to Walhalla, Greenville, and Spartanburg on into Western North Carolina. The Georgia Railroad, one of the best managed in the whole country, runs directly west to Atlanta and southwest to Macon, tapping northwardly the Air line, and connecting Augusta with the greatest railway systems and richest farm sections of the South. The nar-

BROAD STREET, AUGUSTA, GA.

row guage road from Augusta to Sandersville is the seventh of her railway lines.

In addition to these seven important railway feeders, linking Augusta to the full points of the compass, other lines are contemplated. The new and valuable South Bound from Savannah to Columbia is the short line into Florida, and is to have a branch to Augusta. The Augusta and Knoxville is to give a new western connection, and the Augusta and West Florida another southern outlet through Thomasville to Florida. The projected Augusta and Chattanooga railroad will give a straight shoot to the West, saving the round-about run through Atlanta.

Augusta's electric railway in the city and out to its beautiful suburbs, with its investment of a third of a million dollars, and its twenty-

five miles of track and public-spirited management, under Col. D. B. Dyer, is a powerful factor in Augusta's prosperity and progress. It is one of the best-handled city railway systems in the South. A line is projected to North Augusta into Carolina.

Work on the Murray Hill Electric Line began a few days ago, and will be pushed rapidly. The rails, wires, poles and cars have all been ordered. This suburb will soon be dotted with lovely homes and ornamented with a handsome park. The Murray Hill company is composed of Washington, Philadelphia and Augusta capitalists.

It is a convincing proof of the possession of surpassing advantages for manufacturing and of their successful use, as well as of her certain and great industrial future, that Augusta has beaten every city of the South in manufacturing growth in the decade from 1880 to 1890, according to the census. The following figures show the proportion of Augusta's growth in manufacturing in the ten years: Percentage of increase in number of establishments — Augusta, 595; Atlanta, 64; Nashville, 27; Savannah, 52; Chattanooga, 388.

Percentage of increase in capital invested—Augusta, 241; Atlanta, 215; Nashville, 99; Savannah 169; Chattanooga, 388.

Percentage of increase in number of hands employed—Augusta, 247; Atlanta, 92: Nashville, 43; Savannah, 43; Chattanooga, 140.

Percentage of increase in wages paid—Augusta, 320; Atlanta, 235; Nashville, 134; Savannah, 88; Chattanooga, 325.

Percentage of increase in materials used—Augusta, 121; Atlanta, 58; Nashville, 40; Savannah, 5; Chattanooga, 128.

Percentage of increase in value of product—Augusta, 174; Atlanta, 117; Nashville, 51; Savannah, 31; Chattanooga, 31.

Augusta has twelve cotton mills, with 4,500 hands, spinning 80,000 bales of cotton annually into products worth $6,000,000. There are four lumber companies, producing annually

A COUNTRY DRIVE NEAR AUGUSTA, GA.

$1,000,000 of manufactured product, and fertilizer works whose product is worth $1,000,000 per annum. The business in fertilizers runs close up to $2,000,000. There are two large ice factories, and another is in course of erection. Beyond these there are large iron foundries, car shops, flour and grist mills and many smaller industries.

Augusta sells 275,000 bales of cotton and consumes in her own mills 80,000 bales, raising prices by her home competition for the staple, and thus always furnishing a steady rival buyer in her own home demand. English buyers come to the Augusta market, increasing her importance.

COMMERCIAL CLUB, AUGUSTA, GA.

Augusta has eight banks, with a capital and surplus of $1,750,000, a deposit account of $3,000,000, and a total of loans and discounts of $4,500,000. The Georgia Railroad Bank is the continuation of the old powerful Georgia Railroad & Banking Co., and has all the solidity and strength of the parent institution. The banking house of Fleming, Thomas & Co. is one of the younger financial institutions of the city that has gained a strong hold, and exemplifies the best financial talent of the place.

In addition to the vast water power on the Savannah river above Augusta, estimated at 400,000 horse power, nearly equalling that of New England, her famous canal of seven miles length, eleven feet deep, 150 feet wide at surface and 106 feet at bottom, begun in 1845, completed in 1847 and enlarged in 1871, costing $1,500,000, furnishes the city with ample and convenient water power, besides water way for large flatboats from the upcountry. On the canal 7400 horse power are in use. And through the canal comes the water into the large reservoir that gives the city 8,000,000 gallons of water a day, and can supply half a million people. The water power of the canal is rented at the low rate of $5.50 per horse power—a great advantage over steam.

Augusta has as fine a system of public schools as the South affords. Over 7000 children are enrolled, the school fund is $70,000 and 125 teachers are engaged. The Houghton Institute, the venerable old Richmond Academy and the Tubman High School all add to Augusta's educational advantages. Paine Institute and Haines Industrial School afford higher education for the colored. Other schools are St. Mary's and Sacred Heart Academy, the business colleges of Prof. Belot, Prof. Osborne and the St. Patrick's Commercial Institute, and also the Medical Branch of the University of Georgia. These educational institutions afford complete instruction in every department of culture.

The health of Augusta is shown by the official fact that the annual death-rate among the white people is only 13.17 per 1000, and this death-rate has been steadily decreasing under good sanitation and with the fine water. The climatic advantages of Augusta's suburbs have become historic and proverbial as anti-pulmonary and anti-malarial. The pure pine atmosphere as a healing is noted. The Sand Hills and North Augusta will be as famous and popular as Florida and less enervating.

Augusta owns $2,050,000 of property and owes only $1,748,000 at 4½ to 7 per cent., showing $301,200 over her debts. And the income from her canal and its water-power very nearly pays the interest on the public debt, practically leaving her without the burden of a dollar's debt, which could be cancelled at any time. As industries increase the income from the water-power will grow.

Of Augusta's homes, owned by her citizens and not rented, only 2.6 per cent. are encumbered with mortgages, against from 3.2 to 8.7 per cent. in the other cities of the State.

Augusta's real estate grew from 1882 to 1892 69 per cent., while her public debt decreased

52 per cent. in proportion to increase of population.

Manufacturing establishments increased in ten years 595 per cent., while wages increased 320 per cent., a great benefit to merchants.

Augusta has a soil that makes a hard surface on clay or sand, and the boulevard of the North Augusta plant is a hard drive from the use of two or three inches of this dirt. There is a fortune in this dirt for road purposes.

The wholesale commerce of Augusta runs to $72,000,000, including a very large grocery, dry goods and shoe trade. The firm of Mulherin, Rice & Co. is a representative house of this great and increasing business.

The real estate of Augusta, never having been raised to speculative prices by boom methods, presents an attractive field for solid investment by capital.

One of the great industries of the city of special value and attraction is the lumber manufacture, which has perhaps the strongest plant in the State—the Jesse Thompson Co., covering seven acres, owning great mills and miles of railroad and doing $300,000 of business over an area from New York to Texas. This concern deals in the yellow pine lumber that is one of the staples of Georgia, and its head is one of the leading industrial spirits of the South.

The daily newspapers of Augusta occupy a unique position, the oldest being over a century in age, dating from 1775, and the youngest, the *Evening Herald*, being scarcely two years old. The *Chronicle*, which is the centenarian, mirrors Augusta in a conservative manner, more in line with the old regime, while the *Herald* is progressive and aggressive, championing the younger element of the city. It is to the *Herald* that the term unique might properly be applied, for it was conceived and first published as a co-operative daily newspaper, the editors, managers, printers and pressmen sharing the expenses and the profits. From the beginning the *Herald* was a fighting element in local matters, agitating reforms and internal improvements, which neither of the other dailies cared to espouse, and almost instantly it struck a popular chord. From this beginning the *Herald* became almost as communistic (in a broad sense of the term) with the people, as it already was with itself, and shared with the people all the reforms it agitated. The first year found it a success, and at the present time the *Herald* stands firm in its principles and

faithful to the trust of its constituency—a rare example of a daily newspaper conducted on the lines of co-operative profits.

I. W. Avery.

COLUMBUS.

The City of the Chattahoochee, With Its Water Power and Factories.

"Chattahoochee tells the story,
    Chattahoochee sings the water;
Chants the sad *memento mori*
    Of the chieftain's dusky daughter;
Tells her love, its tragic ending,
    And her loyalty undying,
The brave story ever blending
    With the river's surge and sighing."

The city of Columbus, Georgia, and the Chattahoochee river are two factors in the western portion of the State which are not only interesting from an historical point of view, but also as showing how the South has taken advantage of natural water power and seized the opportunity to manufacture the product of her cotton fields tributary to Columbus for miles around. Here is a river, God's gift to Georgia for mills and factories, with half an hundred miles of water power, and here is a city which has utilized it. The great dam, roaring athwart the greatest cotton mill in the South—a mill of 60,000 spindles and the employer of 2,000 operatives— starts the wheels of cotton mills, aggregating over 80,000 spindles, and a total capital of over three millions of dollars, and is a monument to the prosperity of Columbus. And from this single instance of the importance of the Chattahoochee river, regardless of the traffic by steamboat and the vast unused water power above the city, it is not difficult to see in what position the City of Columbus stands as compared with other Georgia cities so far as natural location is concerned, and how she has utilized it.

From time immemorial it has been the custom, in describing the characteristics of cities or States, to use the superlative, and to picture in extravagant phrases every hill-top, back-street, public building or creek within her environs. To the reader who expects such a description of Columbus, he is warned in time, for this sketch will deal in cold, hard facts. Sometimes the naked truth outshines the subtlest flattery, and Columbus is willing to stand on the facts. She has never made as much noise in voicing her advantages as have her sister cities, yet the city is fifth in population in the State, lowest in the tax rate, first in cotton manufacturing, and equal to all in social and educational development. For these and other good reasons, it is therefore quite unnecessary to sing her praises in high sounding adjectives, when a truthful portrayal is stronger in itself.

The strongest points touching Columbus are the fruit of a collection made by the Board of Trade, and they give a good bird's eye view of the city:

Population—(1890 census) 18,650.*

Manufactures—Cotton mills, iron works, cotton compresses, flour mills, fertilizers, brick yards, wagon factories, oil mills, ice and refrigerating factories, bagging, paper boxes, clothing, barrel factory, planing mill, etc.

Transportation—Eight railroads, and the navigation of the Chattahoochee river by steamboat.

Trade—Wholesale groceries, boots and shoes, dry goods, hardware, lumber, flour, clothing, guano, wagons, furniture, crockery, etc.

Cotton receipts—From 75,000 to 120,000 bales, more than 20,000 being consumed annually by the local mills.

Schools—White and colored public schools, with an average attendance of whites, 937; colored, 1125; total 2098. Private schools and colleges of a very high character.

Churches—Sixteen churches for whites of various denominations, and various suburban churches, besides the churches for the colored people.

Tax rate—One per cent.

Water power—Equal to 1,000,000 horsepower at the lowest stage of the Chattahoochee river.

Real estate holdings of manufactures exempt from taxation, $1,053,000; of other manufactures, $1,632,300. The former includes the cotton factories, and the latter the iron, fertilizer, ice, bagging and smaller industries,

The increase in taxable values is from $3,357,835 in 1880 to $9,446,930 in 1891, showing a steady and rapid growth in the value of city real estate, aided by the erection of new buildings in all parts of the city.

It may be interesting to compare the tax rate of Columbus with other surrounding cities. It is as follows:

	Tax Rate. Per Ct.	Bonded Debt.
Columbus.............	1	$480,800
Augusta.....................	1½	1,787,800
Macon......................	1¼	585,800
Savannah....................	2¾	3,654,500
Atlanta.....................	1½	2,220,000
Montgomery....	1⅜	492,500

The sale of merchandise and manufactures exceed $23,000,000 annually, including over $5,000,000 of groceries, $3,000,000 of dry goods, $4,000,000 of cotton cloths, etc., $4,000,000 of cotton and $1,000,000 of iron products.

The banking capital exceeds $500,000, with over $3,060,000 in deposits.

The relations between capital and labor are of the most cordial kind, a strike never having taken place, though thousands of operatives are employed in the various mills. Many of the laboring classes own their own homes, and wages are paid in spot cash weekly or fortnightly.

The climate of Columbus is not oppressive during the summer and is delightfully soft and pleasant during the winter. The city water is brought from hills outside the city by a good system of water works, and the drainage is excellent. Chills and epidemics have never afflicted the city. The death rate, according to the Secretary of the Bureau of Vital Statistics, is 15.3 per thousand per annum.

Columbus is a city of homes, and possesses many beautiful residences, as well as innumerable less pretentious homes for the middle and laboring classes. The city is famous for her splendid social qualifications, no undue distinction existing, nor any social ostracism on account of religion or politics. With such characteristics on the part of her people, and such advantages as she possesses from her water power and commercial location, there

*Columbus stands in a peculiar position regarding her population, the Chattahoochee river being the dividing line between the States of Georgia and Alabama. Across the river, in Alabama are the two suburbs of Columbus—Girard and Phenix City, with a population in 1890 of 7636 people, almost entirely composed of Columbus wage-earners and merchants, but which population is not included in the census of Columbus. Adding this to the census population, with all its acknowledged inaccuracies, there is a total population of 26,286, even according to the Porter figures. As a matter of fact, however, the directory canvass displays an actual city population of nearer 26,000 than the census figures of 18,500, and with the legitimate suburbs of Girard and Phenix City, across the river, Columbus is really entitled to a total of 32,000 to 35,000 people. In justice to the geographical location of the city, it is proper to append this. For all commercial purposes the two Alabama towns mentioned are a part of the city of Columbus.

can be no reason why the city should not continue in her career of prosperity and keep abreast of the other Georgia cities.

ROME.

The Picturesque River-Circled and Seven-Hilled City of Cherokee Georgia.

In the northern part of Georgia, in the land of the Cherokee Indians, sixty-five miles northwest of Atlanta, seventy-five miles south of Chattanooga and 126 miles east of Birmingham, on a group of hills, and at the confluence of the Etowah and Oostanaula rivers, whose union forms the Coosa river, the city resting upon a tongue of land jutting into the junction, and a sentinel upon three rich valleys, Rome reposes in scenic beauty, the undisputed Queen City of this affluent Cherokee valley. The Coosa flows southwest through Alabama to the Gulf.

Rome has colonized DeSoto, across the Oostanaula; East Rome, over the Etowah; West Rome, and South Rome, fronting southerly the Coosa—four typical suburban children. Seven strong, handsome iron bridges, costing $200,000, and two with draw bridges, connect her with all of her trans-river suburbs.

Rome is a strikingly attractive place in her physical features. Her mixture of sweet, rich valleys and beautiful hills, crowned with lovely homes, and threading by and through her rushing rivers, ornately bridged, make a spectacle of real city charmfulness.

For her growth no city in the South has a finer transportation endowment. Seven railroads and three navigable rivers do her trade and warrant her future prosperity—ten strong arteries of commerce and expansion.

The East Tennessee focuses in Rome and sends out four trunk tentacles of traffic, north to Knoxville, northwest to Chattanooga and Memphis, southwest to Vicksburg, and south to Brunswick. Its 2200 miles of iron track revolve around this favored city with myriads of daily trains as trade feeders.

The Rome Railroad runs as part of the Western & Atlantic of the Nashville & Chattanooga system.

The Chattanooga, Rome & Columbus goes 180 miles to Griffin, and is part of the great Central System of Georgia, and when done to Columbus, with new links to Albany and Tallabassee, joining to the Plant plant, it will be a through way from Chicago to Havana sixty hours shorter than now.

The Rome & Decatur, sixty-five miles of the

135 now done from Rome to Attala, will make Savannah or Brunswick Southern direct trade seaports fifty-seven miles nearer to Decatur than by Chattanooga and forty-nine miles nearer than by Birmingham, and the shortest route from these South Atlantic ocean ports to Memphis, St. Louis, Kansas City and the grain, flour and meat centres of the Northwest.

The Rome & Northeastern to Gainesville is projected and will penetrate the rich mineral region of North Georgia.

The White Star Line of steamers, five in number, plies on the Coosa 225 miles to Gadsden, with an outlet through the Alabama river to the Gulf of Mexico, 800 miles waterway, 500 miles nearer the sea than Chattanooga by the Tennessee river. The Oostanaula is navigable 105 miles.

With this imperial railway and water equipment Rome has a sure future.

Rome's rivers are bordered with fertile and exhaustless bottoms, whose crops of cotton, grain, hay and all farm stuff make a vast volume of traffic, never failing. There is no finer fruit region anywhere. Surrounded herself by iron and marble in her hills, and with her railways penetrating the finest coal, iron and cotton sections of the South, reaching the stock and grain belt of three States, with their fine farm and timber resources, and a wide mineral area, the trade tributary to Rome is large and growing.

The commerce of Rome far outruns her population. Her banking capital runs to $800,000. Her wholesale grocery trade is $3,500,000; dry goods trade, $1,250,000; drug trade, $300,000. The cotton business has leaped to 100,000 bales in a year, worth $4,000,000. The whole annual trade is estimated at $15,000,000. The city markets 150,000 bushels of oats, 175,000 bushels of corn, 5000 tons of hay, and uses and ships 10,000,000 feet of lumber. Bradstreet and Dun, the great and careful commercial authorities, quote Rome as "the safest and steadiest city in the South."

Rome is inevitably to become a powerful city of manufactures. She has the only scale works, turbine water wheel works and cotton tie works in the South, and these useful adjuncts of industry typify and show her fibre of enterprise, and that she does not pattern after other folks. Rome has a huge tannery, brick plant making 100,000 brick a day; a stove foundry, plow works, cottonseed oil mill, cotton factory, cotton compress, steam cotton gin, excelsior works, rubber packing works, gas and electric light works, two ice factories, rolling mill, foundry and machine shops, two furniture factories, two big planing mills, bauxite and aluminum works, charcoal iron furnace, large acid phosphate works, two guano factories and two stave and buckler factories. Her manufactured products run to $2,500,000. Her industrial enterprise is remarkable. The turbine water wheels made in Rome have sold in Oregon and crossed the continent 4000 miles to San Francisco. The Towers & Sullivan Plow Co. make the entire plow, from wood-work to iron-work, from North Georgia forests and mines, fashioned by Rome mechanics.

Professor Spencer, the State geologist of Georgia, has just officially announced that Floyd county has large deposits of the clay

ARMSTRONG HOTEL, ROME, GA.

that will make vitrified brick for paving streets—a rare and valuable thing. This is the coming pavement for cheapness, smoothness and durability; as smooth as asphalt and far less expensive, and as lasting as belgian block and infinitely less rough and noisy. It is the ideal residence pavement. In this clay Rome has a mine of wealth. The demand for the perfect vitrified brick will be without measure.

The variety of Floyd county's resources and accomplishments has been exemplified in her capturing for years in succession the first premium at our State fairs and greatest expositions for the best and most complete county display against some formidable competition. These marvelous displays have embraced a diversity of production and merit that no other country could equal. But the most extraordi-

nary single matter of this great display was a bale of cotton, raised on Floyd county soil, of her cottonseed, by her farmers, manured with her fertilizer, plowed by plows whose wood and iron came from her land and made by her labor in her factory, ginned by gins made in her own gin factory, baled in her own compress, in cotton bagging made in her own factory, and bound by cotton ties of her own iron manufactured in her own mill. This is an example of Southern thrift, independence and enterprise, worthy of all honor and universal imitation, and a practical object lesson of Floyd's versatility and pluck.

Rome can be proud of her school facilities. Her public school system is complete. She has three large buildings, valued at $25,000, Shorter Female College is a magnificent institution, in a superb structure, poetically located on a picturesque eminence that commands the whole country. The college has 225 pupils, and is under the charge of that distinguished educator, Dr. A. J. Battle, for seventeen years the successful president of Mercer University, with Prof. I. W. Duggan as business manager. The Rome Female College, the Rome Business University, the Rome Military Institute and the East Rome High School are all valuable institutions.

Rome has peerless water works. The clear, crystal fluid comes from a spring four miles off in the hills, with a capacity of 5,000,000 gallons daily, flowing through Silver creek. The water tower is seventy feet high, and there are six miles of main piping. The ore came from mines in sight, the wood from near forests, the brick and piping out of home clay, all made by home labor in home concerns.

Red and brown iron ore and manganese exist all around Rome in inexhaustible quantities, and several furnaces are operated around and in Rome. Quarries of exquisite marble come to the very borders of the city. An Egyptian marble (black) is being quarried. There is also mottled and white marble. There is no other deposit of this black marble known in this country. Rome has an abundance of fine water power on her rivers, adequate to any demand.

Rome has one of the finest hotels in the

THE HOLMES SANITARIUM, ROME, GA.

South, the Armstrong, 170 by ninety feet, costing including land $175,000. Rome has two excellent daily papers, the morning *Tribune* and the evening *Hustler.* Rome has a fine fire department of three companies, and the losses in three years averaged $3,000 a year only.

Rome has perfect health, or as near perfect as can exist. The summers are cool, slight covering being needed at night. The winters are mild, the river never being frozen over. The death rate is eight and one-half per thousand, something phenomenal, In seven years, the highest average temperature was eighty-two degrees. July, and the lowest, thirty-four, January. The yearly average ran

agencies of water and fuel to the most complete transportation and markets, and with them all every charm of climate and food and convenience of living. Timber, iron, coal, marble, cotton, &c., are all here native to the land. The miner can mine and the mechanic make, and all can have the best educational advantages as free as the air.

Rome lastly enjoys a charming variety of exquisite scenery. An enchanting prospect for miles upon miles in every direction stretches out before the delighted view, blending in harmonious and æsthetic combination, mountain and meadow, vale and forest, river and field, forming a lovely picture. The landscapes constantly reveal varying tints,

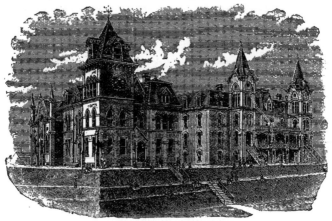

SHORTER COLLEGE, ROME, GA.

between fifty-seven and a-half and sixty-two and a-half.

Rome presents as fine a field for general profitable investments and healthy, delightful homes as any portion of the United States. Whether business is desired in farming, gardening, fruit raising, mining, quarrying, manufacturing, transportation or trade, this favored place offers unsurpassed attractions.

Floyd county is what might be termed an "all-around" county, affording advantages for every labor. The farmer or gardener can get the best farm, garden and fruit lands in the United States, covering an unusual and varied range from cotton to grain and hay. The commercial man has the best facilities for trade. The manufacturer has every factor of industries from raw material, and the primal

changing skies and dawns, sunsets of gold and twilights of silver, and are never-ending sources of pleasure to the vision.

I. W. Avery.

NEWNAN.

A Thriving Town Surrounded by Agriculture and Industry.

Among the counties in Western Georgia, between Atlanta and the Alabama line, and which may be termed the garden district of the State, is the county of Coweta, with the City of Newnan as the county seat. This section of Georgia is a very rich one. It is in this part of the State that great plantation fortunes were amassed in earlier years, and the old homes, still existing, show evidences of grandeur rarely seen in other portions. The changes, too, of later years show that while agriculture is still a great factor in Coweta county, and still is a powerful auxiliary to the City of Newnan, her citizens have also developed valuable manufacturing advantages, and that Newnan holds a high position in the State as a factory centre.

The railroads have had much to do in bringing about this result, for Newnan is located at the crossing point of two of the great trunk lines of the South, the Atlanta & West Point Railway (a part of the Richmond & Danville route from Washington to New Orleans), and the Central Railroad of Georgia (from the West to Savannah. With two such powerful railway systems running through the town, Newnan has become a manufacturing centre such as few towns in the South can claim to be, and, to the city's credit, these enterprises are owned by local capital.

With an altitude of 955 feet and situated on the watershed between the Chattahoochee and the Flint rivers, Newnan possesses splendid natural drainage and a rare freedom from epidemics, and within a radius of three-fourths of a mile, a population of nearly 4000 people, about 500 of which are operatives or connected in some capacity with the city's manufacturing interests.

The tax rate of Newnan is the lowest of any city in Georgia, regardless of size, being only four mills ($4 per thousand), and the county tax only two mills ($2 per thousand). This is less than one-fourth of the tax rate in any other city and county in the State. The taxable property of Newnan is $1,900,000, and the tax books show that the city's wealth increased over 170 per cent. in ten years in the same territory. The debt of Newnan is only $16,000, less than 1 per cent. of taxable values.

Newnan is one of the best-governed cities in the South and has much to show for its expenditures, its public school property, and chalybeate springs, and park, alone being worth more than double its indebtedness.

Newnan has handsomer churches than any city five times its size in the State, a magnificent public school and a fine public library.

Newnan has in manufactures two planing mills, one iron foundry, an engine and boiler works, a flouring mill, two grist mills, two cotton mills, an oil mill, furniture factory, carriage factory, tannery and harness factory, cotton compress, acid chamber and guano factory, two distilleries, shoe factory and an electric light plant, two hotels and a commodious opera house.

The country surrounding Newnan raises fruit in every variety, and grape culture is very profitable. Land can be purchased for this industry from $10 an acre to $40.

Newnan wants a woman's college, and there is now an unrivalled opening for such a school in the South. All the necessary buildings, laboratory and apparatus are standing, such a college having been conducted at Newnan for forty years until the death of the former proprietor closed it.

Newnan wants to double her manufactures in the next two years. The low tax rate and other advantages already mentioned are invaluable auxiliaries to this end. An ice factory, canning factory, agricultural works or more shoe and cotton factories would be good paying enterprises. Every manufacturing plant in the city is paying handsome dividends.

Newnan wants good immigrants—homeseekers—and every reasonable inducement will be given to such, and to capital locating in the county seat of Coweta county.

Outrunning the Blizzard.

The Central fast train left Atlanta the other day when the snow lay twelve inches thick. Numerous sleighs had been improvised in that city and gay parties dashed over the frozen crust of white. One or two trim "clippers" appeared upon the streets with as much style as if upon the speedway in Central Park. Trains were snowbound, wires and schedules were in a tangle, and men shook their heads at the station when asked if the Nancy Hanks would get through to Savannah that night. It was just 1.30 P. M. when the big engine rolled over Whitehall street and puffed under the Hunter street bridge. The snow, which had been falling steadily two days, lightened up and behind cold banks of cloud the sun streamed over the white surpliced earth. Myriads of colors flashed from the white crystals, as seas and boulders of snow billowed away to the right and left. The trees were coated with ice, and the famous orchards between Atlanta and Griffin were cracking under their wintry weight. Through all the ceaseless glacial scene the Nancy Hanks plunged like a reindeer. Stone culverts spanned frozen streams and the pretty flower gardens at the stations were long sheets of ice. Men talked of the big grain crop and fruit yield we should certainly have this year, while the Nancy Hanks kept her nose to the wind and made her sixty miles an hour without trouble. The pilot sped, like a snowchute, along the track, and the hoarse signal echoed over the white waste like a blast from the Thetis on an Arctic journey. The thermometer was below twenty degrees, but the boxes were steaming. The ice-cased telegraph wires had sagged in many places to the ground, and here and there a pole had snapped short off. But the fast flyer shot over the snow like a cannon ball in ricochet, and when the big Mogul rolled into Savannah on time, a thin fringe of snow lay around the edges of the streets and the land of the blizzard had been cleared.—*Savannah Press.*

NATURAL GAS IN INDIANA.

Readers of the article in this magazine for February on the wonderful growth of towns in the Indiana gas district, will be interested in the following summary of industries at Alexandria, which is in the centre of the area of greatest flow in the gas field, and has become now the most conspicuous of all the towns in the gas district.

	No. of hands employed.
*De Pauw Plate Glass Works	450
†Lippincott Lamp Chimney Works	375
Alexandria Window Glass Works	175
Neily Oar Works	22
Adams Lumber Co	25
Branum Lumber Co. and mill	20
Hoover & Irish Lumber Co	22
Hall Planing Mill	17
Gips & Mullen Carriage Works	6
Terre Haute Brewing Co.	5
Indiana Brick Co	62
Alexandria Brick Co	35
West Alexandria Brick & Tile Co	35
Ward Brick Mfg. Co.	15
Booth & Free Quarry	18
Nicosin Quarry	52
Mt. Vernon Quarry	18
Fairmont Milling Co	14
Young Flour Mill Co	15
Contractor on United Window Glass Works.	100
Contractor on De Pauw Plate Glass Works— addition	262
Contractor on De Pauw Window Glass, Jar and Bottle Works	190
T. Brooks, well contractor	10
Fifteen building contractors	179
Five street contractors	85
Three gas and pipe contractors	14
	2227

*Works being quadrupled in size.
†Works about to be doubled in size.

There are now in course of erection and under contract to be built immediately the following plants:

	No. of hands to be employed.	
De Pauw Window Glass Works	900	men.
De Pauw Bottle and Jar Works	200	"
De Pauw Plate Glass Works—enlargement of present plant	1000	"
New Albany Rail Mill	1000	"
Wetherold Rolling Mill	200	"
Findlay Chain Works	300	"
Addition to Lippincott's Glass Works	250	"
United Glass Works	2000	"
Minor industries	150	"
Total	6000	"
Employed by works now in operation,	2227	"
Grand total.	8227	"

Even these figures, however, do not tell the full story, because most of these concerns will employ more hands than they are given credit for. These are the minimum figures. The New Albany Rail Mill for instance, contracts to employ 2000 to 2500 men in twelve months, but it is only reported in this list to employ 1000, which is to be the minimum number with which it will start in August. In addition to the long list of enterprises, contracts are pending for many concerns, some of which will soon be closed, which will greatly increase the number of hands.

The total wages of the mechanics and laborers to be employed by the enterprises mentioned in the list will foot up about $150,000 a week, or $7,500,000 a year. What a pay roll of this size means in town-building can be realized when it is remembered that it is three times as much as the aggregate annual wages in Terre Haute, Ind., a place of 30,000 people, employing, as reported by census, 5200 laborers, with a pay roll of $2,100,000 a year, and would nearly equal the pay roll at Holyoke, Mass., which has a population of 74,000 and pays $8,000,000 a year to 22,800 laborers, the average rate of wages being very low because so large a proportion of the hands are women and children working in cotton mills. Even Indianapolis, with 105,000 population, pays out only $7,000,000 a year in wages, or not as much as Alexandria will be paying just as soon as these enterprises can be built; and in 1880, when Louisville had 125,000 population, its total annual wages to factory hands were $5,800,000. These comparisons will show what Alexandria's future will be with 8000 to 10,000 mechanics at work, receiving $7,000,000 to $8,000,000 a year.

Readers of the daily papers probably remember an interview with Postmaster-General Wanamaker, which was published a few months ago, just after his return from a trip through the natural gas regions of Indiana, and they will recall his enthusiasm regarding the marvelous advance that was already under way in this, the greatest natural gas region ·in the world, and his predictions as to the continued progress and prosperity of this section. In November last the Washington correspondent of the Indianapolis *Journal*, referring to the return of Postmaster-General Wanamaker and Secretary Foster from a trip to Indiana, quoted them as saying that if there should be any change in the tariff laws to the disadvantage of the manufacturing interests of ·the country, the result would simply be a still greater concentration of manufacturers in the gas regions, and in that way even a reduced tariff would prove of advantage to this section. Their statement was : "The manufacturers in the Indiana gas belt can operate and make money, and their employes can thrive to a degree when those of other sections suffer disaster from adverse legislation from competitive free trade, for the difference between coal or wood fuel and the nominal expense of leasing a gas well is so great as to protect the manufacturers in the gas belt against any reasonable competition from our own countrymen. In fact a reasonable reduction in the tariff, or a reduction which would be almost disastrous to other sections, might prove of advantage to many persons in the natural gas belt, as it would compel many manufacturers in other sections of the country to move in and seek free fuel in order to compete at all with European products, and no manufacturer outside the gas belt could make any money at times when those in the gas belt would be reasonably successful."

The truth of this is being realized by manufacturers in various parts of the country, and the disposition to get into the gas region and to locate in Alexandria, which is the very centre of the gas field and consequently has the greatest supply on which to draw, is becoming every day more pronounced. The simple statement of the DePauws, whose great glass and iron works are being removed from New Albany to Alexandria, that their saving

in fuel would be over $400,000 a year, is all the argument that is needed to cause manufacturers to investigate the advantages of this section. The whole country is waking up to the magnitude of the developments that are going on here, and many of the leading capitalists in America are beginning to make heavy investments. Mr. Russell B. Harrison, son of the late President, has been in many of the towns in the gas region during the last few weeks negotiating for a very comprehensive electrical railway system to connect all the towns in this district. It is claimed that Mr. Wanamaker, Secretary Foster and others are interested in this scheme. From Indianapolis come reports of an organization of Chicago, New York and Boston capitalists to form a gigantic combination, and the Indianapolis *News* says : "If the plans do not miscarry, a great natural gas combination will be formed in Indiana. The amount of money it will handle is said to be a Monte Cristo-like dream." This will simply give emphasis to the value of all the gas operations in this whole territory, and will help to attract attention to what is being done in the way of utilizing natural gas.

Fortunately there has been no real estate boom yet, and values have wisely been kept down to a point where every mechanic can buy a lot and own a home, but this condition of low prices cannot be maintained much longer. The vast concentration here of industrial concerns, the great building activity and the interest aroused throughout the country are sure to have their natural effect in bringing about a much higher range of prices in the near future.

The indications are that there will be a readjustment of values in the spring, and a continued advance in prices. It will be very difficult to build stores and dwellings fast enough during the next twelve months to accommodate the rapidly growing population. The Alexandria Company, Alexandria, Ind., is giving site and free fuel to desirable factories.

FOUTZ'S MEDICINES

A LOUISIANA SUGAR PLANTATION.

THE

SOUTHERN STATES.

MAY, 1893.

THE "QUARTERS" ON A LOUISIANA SUGAR PLANTATION.

IN THE LOUISIANA SUGAR BELT.

By Reginald Dykers.

Just a great waving expanse that melts away and becomes strangely vague and unreal as the eye tries to reach its limit; just a pure unsullied carpet of the tenderest green, streaked here and there by an unsteady line that marks a ditch—such is a sugar plantation in Louisiana.

Set somewhere in it, surrounded by trees from which the moss hangs in long, fantastic, almost weird pennants, is the dwelling of the planter, built in the queerly-fashioned style of the old regime; the style of broad balconies and broad halls and broad windows, and sheltering broader hearts within.

Some of these old residences are crumbling away; their moldy foundations can scarcely stand the burden of age and neglect that has been laid upon them. Others, again, have been tended with a careful hand. Strong arms have supported their ancient walls and propped their veering chimneys. Paint, fresh and bright of hue, has smoothed away the wrinkles on their poor old faces and brought them back to youth again. Here and there one meets with a dwelling that has been erected by some planter of today, possessing every modern convenience, but lacking the quiet stateliness of its venerable neighbors.

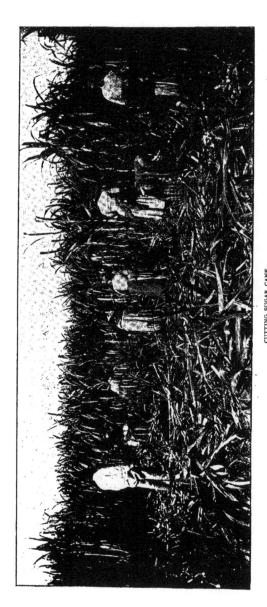

CUTTING SUGAR CANE.

Obtruding itself upon the scene, not far removed from the residence, blackened somewhat by the sombre belching of its great grimy smokestacks, is the sugar house, where the process of sugar making is carried on; where the hard, woody fibre of the cane is robbed of its sweet contents and then cast into a seething furnace to help make the steam that will rob still other cane of its riches. During only about three months out of the year is the machinery in motion. All the rest of the time spiders weave their webs about it and try to bind the giant wheels together so that they may never move again. Poor little brave ambitious spiders!

A sugar planter in Louisiana may be one of two types. He may be a descendant of the old creole race, full of old-fashioned notions and prejudices, resenting innovation on his time-honored methods, seeing year by year his substance sapped away by more enterprising competitors, yet looking down upon them all with a haughty scorn that one has to see to understand, or he may be a thorough

American full of energy and vim, always trying to find somebody who knows more about his business than he does himself so that he can learn something from him. The second type is fast pushing the first out of existence, and where he doesn't quite eliminate him he manages to bring him over to his own way of thinking, and instil into him some of the broad ideas that fill his own brain.

Louisiana is, and is likely to remain for some time to come, the principal sugar-producing State of the Union, though several of her neighbors are steadily climbing up in the scale. A Northern company, at the head of which is Mr. Hamilton Disston, of Philadelphia, has been busily engaged in reclaiming the swamp lands in the Florida Peninsular, and on a portion of these reclaimed lands they are now operating the St. Cloud sugar plantation. These filled-up swamps are said to be admirably adapted for the growth of sugar cane, and as they are situated below the frost line there is every reason to believe that an almost ideal location for the sugar planter has been found. Time is necessary, however, to determine whether they will continue to bear out their brilliant promises. Dr. H. W. Wiley, chemist of the United States Department of Agriculture, in a letter published in the *Florida Farmer*, says: "It will require a longer experience than has yet been had to determine whether or not such lands will continuously grow a high grade of cane." The doctor evidently inclines to the belief, however, that they will.

In Texas there are about 500,000 acres suitable for cane-growing, and the industry is making rapid strides, especially in Fort Bend county. Louisiana alone, though, is capable of producing sufficient sugar to supply the entire population of the United States.

There are over 4,000,000 acres of land in the State suitable for the production of sugar cane. Of this only about 175,000 acres are at present devoted to its cultivation. That there should be so much available land for this purpose now lying idle or planted in cotton, of which there has recently been such an overproduction, is at first sight a source of considerable wonder, yet on careful investigation the main cause of it can be easily perceived. Since time immemorial, ever since Etienne de Bore first made his queer-looking sugar on the old Bore plantation in 1792, it has been regarded as absolutely necessary for those who cultivated cane to invest in ponderous and expensive machinery for crushing out the juice and converting it into

SUGAR MILL, BELAIR PLANTATION.

MILL FOR GRINDING SUGAR CANE.

sugar. There were the massive mill, the iron kettles, or, perhaps, a costly vacuum pan, the clarifiers, the syrup tanks, the filter presses and a great number of other appliances, to say nothing of the powerful engine and battery of boilers necessary to put all the great plant into motion. Until very recently to be a sugar planter has been synonymous with being a man of considerable affluence. To plant cotton, corn or potatoes it was only necessary to have land, a mule and a plow, but with sugar cane it was different. A trip through the sugar belt, showing each plantation in posession of its own factory, will make this plainly manifest.

Of late, however, a complete change in the order of things is fast coming about. At this present moment there are hundreds of small farmers in Louisiana and Texas who raise cane and sell it by the ton to some central factory. They are paid for it at the rate of about four dollars per ton, and twenty tons to an acre is considered an average yield. These farmers possess no machinery whatever, and merely cultivate their land and sell their crops of cane just as the beet-growers of the West sell their product to the beet-working establishments. Under this system a great deal of land that formerly lay idle simply because there were no more men left with the necessary combination of in-

clination and capital to erect a sugar-house is now being cultivated in cane.

The advent of central factories, although it took place long ago in Cuba, is of comparatively recent date in Louisiana, and there are at this time only about half a dozen in operation; but it is quite certain that this system will eventually supersede all others. Its advantages are so manifest, and it offers to inhabitants of other States such strong inducements to immigrate hither that it is much to be regretted by Louisianians that the movement was not started sooner. In every instance the factories are equipped with machinery of the most improved pattern, constructed regardless of everything but a thorough extraction of the juice and its conversion into sugar. Every operation is subjected to a rigid chemical test in the laboratory, where every unnecessary loss, however small, is noted, and steps are taken to prevent it. This perfect equipment and supervision will accomplish much towards augmenting the total output of sugar, a great deal of which is lost every year in the somewhat antiquated sugar houses that have been operating since ante-bellum days.

Sugar cane is planted either in the spring or in the fall. The canes are laid lengthways, sometimes two or three abreast, in long trenches or furrows. The new canes sprout forth from the

FILTER PRESSES.

eyes or joints and are very slow in their growth when they first make their appearance, requiring strict care and attention until they are, as one might say, fairly on their feet.

Seed cane that is to be planted in the spring has to be carefully guarded from the action of frost during the winter months. In Louisiana and Texas, where several severe frosts usually occur during winter, it is preserved in "windrows." Windrowing consists in cutting the cane off near the ground and throwing it into the furrows between the rows, allowing the leaves to remain upon it. The canes are laid so that the foliage of one set overlaps the cut ends of the next set, and assists greatly in protecting the stalks from the ravages of the cold. When a windrow is properly arranged there is nothing visible but a long ribbon of leafy tops. Over this two furrows of dirt are thrown from opposite sides, and the sensitive canes are thus effectually protected until spring arrives and they are exhumed for planting purposes.

If, instead of cutting the whole crop in the autumn, that portion intended for seed cane were allowed to remain in the field until the time to plant it, the juice in the stalks would freeze and the stalks themselves would split and be utterly useless. Windrowing is sometimes resorted to when frosts occur during the grinding season, while a quantity of cane, mature and ready to be ground, is still standing in the field, as it is claimed by many planters that unless it is cut immediately after the frost touches it, it will make a poor yield of sugar. In fact it is only recently that any one has become skeptical on this point, and in years gone by the approach of freezing weather was the signal for all hands to invade the fields where cane was still standing and windrow all that remained of the crop, in order that whatever deterioration the cold might cause should be arrested. It is, however, an expensive system of insurance. Windrowing under these conditions is not performed with the same care that is bestowed upon the cane intended for planting in the spring. The whole operation is necessarily very hurried, and no dirt is thrown over the fallen stalks. They are simply thrown in the row, protected by their own leaves, and the mill driven to its utmost capacity in order to get it all crushed as quickly as possible.

Cane that is planted in the fall does not, of course, make its appearance above ground before spring, but if properly fertilized it will send out strong, hardy roots during the winter. After the crop makes its appearance it receives very careful attention in the way of plowing and fertilizing, the last plowing being generally done some time in June. From then until the time for beginning the harvest in the autumn, say in October or early November, is the planter's holiday, and if he is a prosperous planter and has no other pursuits to engross his attention, he generally goes to some resort in a cooler latitude and recuperates.

With the harvest his hardest work begins. His sugar-house and fields become a busy hive where laborers, black and white, and every other hue known to the census-taker, swarm promiscuously. Every stalk has to be cut by hand, as there has never been any machine devised for the successful

with slats fixed across it bears the cane into the factory in a continuous stream and drops it into a set of huge iron rollers, sometimes as many as six, or even nine being grouped together, where it is squeezed with tremendous force. Sometimes a bright genius will permit a rock or a coupling pin to go along with the cane, and the result is a general smash-up, unless the mill is equipped with a hydraulic device for regulating the pressure and allowing it to respond gracefully to the imperative demands of hard and unyielding substances. The practice of shredding, cutting or macerating cane before it is fed to the mill is

A SUGAR SHED ON THE LEVEE.

cutting of sugar-cane. In fact, it grows so thick and matted and is blown by the wind into such an inpenetrable jungle that no machine can get through it. So into the fields goes a motley army. With one blow—a great rending cut, like the swing of a Berserker's axe —the cane is cut at the top at the last red joint, and with deft, swift strokes the leaves are stripped from it with a hook-like arrangement on the back of the knife. Then, with another terrible cut, it is lopped off at the ground and thrown into piles across the rows, and then loaded on huge wagons which transport it to the sugar-house. A carrier, composed of an endless chain,

becoming very popular, some ten per cent. better extraction being obtained thereby.

The juice from the mill is generally subjected to a process of purification and bleaching by means of sulphur fumes. It is passed through a receptacle filled with a number of shelves and partitions so arranged as to retard the flow as much as possible, and the fumes are generated in a small furnace underneath. This sulphuring process renders the juice extremely acid, and it has to be mixed with lime to neutralize its acidity and remove further impurities before it is cooked. This is done in square tanks called clarifiers. From the

clarifiers the juice goes into the evaporators which consist, in a first-class house,
of what is called a double effect. This
is composed of two large vessels, like
covered pans or kettles, in which a partial vacuum is maintained. In the first
effect the vacuum is such that the boiling point of the juice is 180 degrees,

The juice is cooked in all these successively, the scums being carefully removed and its density increasing as it
goes along. In the last, the "*Batterie,*"
it remains until the boiling point is about
250 degrees Fahrenheit. It is then
deemed to have cooked sufficiently and
is emptied into coolers. The cooling,

THE LAST LOAD BEFORE DINNER.

and in the second it is 130 degrees. The
juice is boiled in these two effects until it
shows a density of thirty degrees
Beaume, which is ascertained by means
of a hydrometer. It is then carried into
the vacuum pan proper, where the process of cooking is continued and the
granulation takes place. From the vacuum pan the cooked mass goes into a
mixer and from there into the centrifu-
gals, which are perforated iron bowls
that revolve with great rapidity. By
means of this apparatus the drying can
be so quickly accomplished that the
sugar can be seen to change in color
while one is watching it. After being
dried out the sugar is ready to be packed
in bags or barrels and shipped to market. In small establishments the "open
kettle" method is generally followed, and
instead of the expensive machinery
above described there are four large
kettles called the "*Grand,*" the "*Flam-
beau,*" the "*Sirop*" and the "*Batterie.*"

coagulated mass is called "*cuite*" or
"*masse-cuite,*" and the little ragged darkies, of which every sugar plantation
has a full quota, think it is immensely
superior to the nectar of the gods. To
eliminate the molasses from this "*cuite*"
is the operation next in order, and a simple and effective method of achieving
this is to put the "*cuite*" into vessels
having outlets in the bottom, suspended
over a water-tight trough. In the course
of a week or so almost all the molasses
will have dropped through into the
trough, leaving a residue of tolerably
dry and merchantable raw sugar.
Every large plantation has a large
output of molasses, which, in the last
few years, has brought such a low price
as hardly to pay the cost of barrels and
freight. In fact, a great number of
planters have poured it into the ditches
or fed it to the stock, as it makes a very
healthful and nutritious food for cattle
when mixed with ensilage. The pro-

duction of this almost valueless by-product amounted in 1891-92 to 16,-429,868 gallons, and during the same season the 575 houses operating in the State of Louisiana turned out 360,499,: 307 pounds of sugar, those using modern apparatus obtaining an average extraction equal to 2343 pounds of sugar per acre, while those using machinery of a primitive type averaged 1494 pounds per acre. There are about fifty establishments in Louisiana using horse-power only for the operation of their mills.

The sugar industry has been dragged into considerable prominence during the past few years. What importance it has failed to achieve through its own efforts has been thrust upon it by political machinations. It is to be hoped that the outcome of it all will be to put it on a broad, firm basis, so that after awhile it can supply the people of the United States with an article for which they are now paying to foreign countries several millions of dollars annually. When this is done and when the central factory system becomes thoroughly established, and small proprietors abandon their crude apparatus, a new era of prosperity will dawn over the sugar belt.

A SACRIFICE TO THE RIVER GOD.

THE CLIMATE OF NORTH CAROLINA.

By H. B. Battle,

Director of the North Carolina Experiment Station.

Man can live anywhere, but nations only can attain their best development in countries posessing a variable climate. This variation must not embrace too great extremes. Man can live in localities with the lowest temperature just as he can exist in regions having the highest. After being sufficiently acclimated to these extremes of temperature he can live with more or less comfort, according to his surroundings and his peculiar nature. The high, frozen latitudes of Greenland or Siberia support a hardy people, who have been inured to the desolate wastes of those countries. The blazing sun of the equator likewise gives life to races that have apparently flourished. These climates develop races, not nations. In neither have nations ever been developed that have made themselves felt in the world's history, and it is doubtful if they ever will be. The temperate zones offer to man regions that yield him the best development, and nations powerful and long-lived are the result. Besides pleasing to man, the variable climates of these regions are essential to progress, in furnishing seasons necessary to the growth of plants and all vegetation. One continuous summer, fall, spring or winter would be destructive to the best development of these growths. The eternal summer of some latitudes would be productive of continuous growth were it not for some necessary consequences. The lack of atmospheric currents and the inevitable result of the

absence of moisture, which would be brought by these currents from localities where there are bodies of water and where evaporation is going on, would be very detrimental to the growth of many plants. Plants, as well as man, need climatic changes with periods of cold and warmth, moisture and dryness. Plant growth, which is absolutely essential to the existence of man as well as all animal life, requires these changes. Cold at the same time decomposes the rocks to form necessary soil and unlocks food materials needed by plants.

Warmth and moisture are needed to assist germination, and in future growth by the absorption of plant food in the movement of soil moisture with its life-giving constituents, until full development is reached, and the fruit is the result. Alternate periods of dryness are essential to growths, as without it warmth cannot be secured to the degree required by many plants. Thus vegetable growth is maintained and the life-giving and comfort-giving crops of corn, wheat, cotton, rice, oats, tobacco, etc., are returned to man for the care he bestows upon them.

Man for his best development likewise needs these variations of seasons. He is too much a creature of change not to receive invigoration and needed rest from the effects produced by non-recurrence of any long-continued single or double seasons. The result of an autumn and winter season is needed to overcome the effects of the heat of summer upon his constitution. In the same way summer follows the winter and gives restful change from the too great severity of the previous cold. The

Note.—In the preparation of this article I have not hesitated to draw on "The Climatology of North Carolina," published by the North Carolina State Weather Service of the North Carolina Agricultural Experiment Station, for many facts and recorded data.   II. B. B.

intermediate seasons, fall and spring, furnish an admirable arrangement for the tempering of the change between two severe seasons as they pass one into the other, thus preserving health and life to animals and plants. The ravages of certain diseases, both of man and of vegetation, resulting from one season, or

The location is most admirable, for its contact with the ocean on the east and the southeast, and the occurrence of the double range of high mountains in its western portion are the prime causes of our unexcelled climate. In its borders is located the highest land east of the Rocky Mountains. Mount Mitchell is

MOUNT MITCHELL, ELEVATION 6711 FEET.

else due to natural surroundings, are stopped or mitigated by the other. It is thus that all life flourishes. In the temperate zone, therefore, where the seasons recur in beautiful sequence, nature provides the best means for development. Man lives easily and flourishes, and nations are the natural result.

Nowhere do these natural climatic conditions occur in better combination than in North Carolina, with its area of 52,286 square miles (of which 3600 square miles is water surface), located between the parallels of 33° 49′ and 36° 33′ North latitude, and the meridians of 75° 27′ and 84° 42′ west from Greenwich. Its extreme length from east to west is 503 miles and the greatest width is 187 miles.

6711 feet above the level of the sea and 423 feet higher than far-famed Mt. Washington. In fact, there are in North Carolina forty-three mountain peaks higher than 6000 feet, and eighty-two which are over 5000 and almost 6000 feet in height. From this altitude there is a gradual descent to the sea level, rendering possible within a comparatively short distance all the climatic conditions usually attending a descent of nearly 7000 feet to the sea level. Roughly speaking, this is the equivalent of nearly eight degrees of latitude, which would extend almost to the Northern limit of Vermont. The general direction of the streams and rivers is easterly, and the continual erosion of the mountains and elevations during past ages by their action, has caused the eastern shore line to project far out into the Atlantic Ocean. This effect is increased by the high annual rainfall which courses back through these streams to mother ocean, and also because the rainfall from more than one-half the State reaches the sea coast in North Carolina through streams that rise, flow and empty entirely within her borders. The numerous sounds, bays and estuaries thus formed by this fortunate combination, give to the east more of insular or peninsular climate than would naturally be found with a plain shore line, which is more noticeable south of us. This result is to some extent intensified by the nearness of the Gulf Stream, with its volume of water fifty miles in width, and an average annual temperature about fourteen degrees warmer than the water through which it flows. Its effect would be more felt but for the intervening body of water, fifty miles in width, between it and the coast, and also for the natural direction of the wind from the southwest to the northeast, which tends to carry away from the coast the warm moist air arising from the surface of its heated waters.

In these natural conditions of high mountains, gradual descent to the sea, numerous water surfaces and peculiar contact with the ocean, and drainage areas, North Carolina is not excelled by any State in America. They give her an incomparable climate and many results which follow from favorable climatic conditions when combined with soil and favorable location. The water

areas give moisture on exposure to the evaporating influences of the sun, which yields both a higher temperature in the winter and a lower temperature in summer, and also is almost the sole cause of the large and valuable rainfall which blesses this region. The ascent from the sea coast to the mountains gives the usual decrease of temperature of one degree for 300 feet of elevation and the additional result of causing a condensation of the

SUB-TROPICAL FLORA, EASTERN NORTH CAROLINA.

moisture already formed. It is to be expected that this moisture would condense, with favorable conditions, soon after forming, and would only be transferred ·to localities farther west by the action of favorable winds. Such is approximately the case, for the annual rainfall is greatest in the eastern coast regions, and decreases somewhat when the central district· is reached, and still further diminishes as the mountain region is touched. The mountains easily tend to condense the moisture by the lower temperature of ·the mountain sides, and the winds after passing them are dry. It is for this reason that here the west winds are generally dry and the east winds moist. The average prevailing direction of the wind over the whole State is mainly southwest, though during the last four months of the year they are from the opposite direction, the northeast. The winds accordingly blow parallel to the mountain system and not across, as is the case with the coast range of California.

Another very important benefit of the high mountain range on· our western border is to prevent the frequent inroads of those ·extreme cold waves which have their origin in central British America, and roll on irresistibly over the levels of the Mississippi basin eastward until the Appalachian chain is reached and its high peaks offer effectual barriers to their further progress in that direction. They are thus deflected to the right hand and oftentimes reach other Southern States before being felt here. If of much magnitude, a cold wave may roll over this natural barrier, and, like the crest of a large water wave, break over it and roll eastward, or else by the more circuitous routes reach the main portions of the State by proceeding around these mountain chains by the north or the south. Such, however, is the efficiency of the United States Weather Bureau and of the State Weather Service, that by ascertaining the velocity of their progress, these waves can be foretold with almost exact certainty and information disseminated throughout the State to the advantage of our people. Frosts also are foretold in the same way, and fruit, trucking

and tobacco interests thus protected.

The natural location is also of benefit in warding off cyclones, and this is so notably the case that rarely do tornadoes occur with serious consequences. The average visitation of a true tornado of funnel-shaped clouds is less than once in six years. It has now been sixteen years since a tornado has visited Raleigh in Wake county that can be said to have been destructive. Even in this case only a few trees were uprooted, and with no attendant accident to life. In 1884 the southern tier of counties in the central portion of the State was visited by a tornado of some violence .and destruction, and some loss of life followed its path. With the exception of here and there an isolated storm of small dimensions, the State is•remarkably free from the disastrous effects of tornadoes, so common in many of the Middle and Western States.

For convenience of comparison the State is divided into three districts, the eastern, the central and the western, each occupying approximately one-third of the State. Of the ninety-six counties, there are thirty-six in the eastern district, embracing nearly the whole of the geologically Cenozoic or Recent formation. It includes the coastal plain rising from the sea level to an average elevation of 250 feet at the western limit. In this region are found all the navigable waters of the State, including sounds, bays, inlets and rivers. The central district of twenty-six counties belongs mainly to the Laurentian and Huronian formations, with belts of Triassic formation, and includes the rolling portions between the coastal plain region and the foot-hills of the mountains. In the western limit of the district the elevation varies from 800 feet to 1000 feet. The western district with the remaining thirty-four counties includes the foot-hills and the mountains, and belongs practically to the same geological formation, excluding the Triassic, as the central district. It is, however, composed more largely of such dense compact rocks of these early eras as still retain in a measure the distinctive form produced in the immense mountain upheaval of eras gone by. The elevation of parts of the

ROUND KNOB, NEAR THE SUMMIT OF THE BLUE RIDGE.

district varies from 800 to 1000 feet on the east to nearly 7000 feet in the centre, at the summit of the Blue Ridge, gradually decreasing through the surrounding table-land, averaging 4000 feet, to the west, where the Smoky Range is reached on the extreme western limits, and with elevations almost as high. The mountains are nearly all densely wooded to the very peaks, and in scenery they rival that of Switzerland. Round Knob, on the Western North Carolina Railroad, near the top of the Blue Ridge, is a picturesque example. Numerous cross chains are found connecting the main chains through valleys 1500 to 2000 feet elevation and upward.

The climatic conditions of these districts will be considered separately and the State as a whole. In the compilation of these figures, records from 128 stations, in seventy counties, were used. Of this number forty are in the eastern, thirty-six in the central and forty-seven are in western districts. The period of observation extends from the year 1820 down to the present, with varying periods for each station. It is interesting to know that the first observations of which we now have record were made by Dr. Joseph Caldwell, president of the University in 1820, and with the exception of a period of years previous to 1844 and during three years of the late war, we have an almost unbroken record down to the present. The periods of observation are therefore sufficiently long at the various stations to give reliable data in arriving at normal weather conditions in various sections of the State. Some records, which might give a preponderance to certain districts, have not been included in the calculation of the normals.

The mean (or average) annual temperature of the whole State is 59.0 degrees, which is the normal (average for long periods) for twenty years. Comparing with the normal annual temperature for the whole Northern hemisphere, which is 59.5 degrees, it is readily seen that the claim that North Carolina embodies the average temperature of the whole hemisphere is verified. The annual mean temperatures of the districts are as follows: For the eastern,

60.7 degrees; for the central, 59.5 degrees, and for the western, 55.9 degrees. The figures below give also the seasonal mean temperatures for the State and its different portions.

	Spring	Sum'er.	Aut'mn	Winter
Eastern district. ...	58.2	77.0	62.5	44.9
Central district.....	59.1	70.8	59.4	42.7
Western district....	55.5	72.5	55.7	40.0
For the State........	57.5	76.0	59.5	42.6

The mean annual temperature of a few important stations are given below:

Asheville........... 54.5		Lenoir.............. 55.6
Charlotte........... 59.9		Morganton......... 57.6
Chapel Hill........ 59.5		Newbern........... 61.5
Cape Lookout...... 62.8		Raleigh............. 60.1
Franklin........... 54.2		Southport.. .... 64.5
Fayetteville 61.0		Statesville 56.3
Greensboro........ 59.4		Tarboro........... 59.6
Goldsboro 61.5		Weldon............ 59.0
Highlands......... 50.5		Wilmington 63.1
Hot Springs....... 57.8		Webster............ 53.4
Kitty Hawk....... 59.7		

For comparison the annual mean temperature of a few large cities in other States are given, as well as for some foreign cities of note:

Augusta, Ga....... 64		Palermo 64.2
Boston, Mass.... 48		Venice............. 56.3
Charleston, S. C.... 66		Edinburgh......... 46.8
Chicago, Ill....... 48		Paris...,........ 50.5
Jacksonville, Fla... 69		Berlin............ 48.2
Little Rock, Ark.... 62		Lisbon............. 60.1
Los Angeles, Cal... 61		Naples............. 60.6
Mobile, Ala........ 67		London............ 50.5
New Orleans, La... 69		St. Petersburg...... 36.7
New York, N. Y.... 51		Mexico............ 62.1
Omaha, Neb....... 49		
Philadelphia, Pa.... 53		
Portland, Ore...... 52		
St. Louis, Mo...... 55		
San Francisco, Cal.. 56		
Savannah, Ga....... 67		
Washington, D. C.. 55		

In reference to the extremes of heat and cold, the different portions of the State are extremely fortunate. Only in a few localities does the thermometer ever record below zero and then only during the more intense cold waves. With the exception of the last winter, no weather colder than two degrees below zero has been recorded in the last six years. In the central and eastern districts it is comparatively a rare thing to find it colder than ten or twelve degrees above zero.

As to the extreme heat of the summer, the State is likewise most fortunate. Rarely is 100 degrees reached and then only for a very short period. These temperatures are found, as would be expected, in the central district, though occasionally high temperatures are noticed in the eastern district.

The wonderful thermal or frostless belt must not be passed over. In certain mountain localities, especially noticeable in Burke, Polk and McDowell counties and elsewhere, in the valleys and along the sides of the mountains at a height of 1200 to 2000 feet, where the contour of the mountains admits of the phenomena, occurs the celebrated paradox of a frostless belt. Even above and below this belt may be seen the effect of blighting frosts in sharp contrast with the untouched foliage and flowers in the more favored localities. A writer (Dr. C. Mills), in the New York *Evening Post*, graphically describes the phenomena noticed at Tyron Mountain, in Polk county: "All through January the mountain tops above this valley were white with snow, but in the valley the jessamine bloomed and roses budded. What is more striking, the line of demarcation is distinctly visible to the naked eye. In apple blossom time the difference is so marked as almost to startle one. Here, for instance, is an orchard on our side of the line, a mass of fragrant blossoms. Yonder is another just over the line in which the buds are peeping timidly out between the half-formed leaves. A little later, while the wild flowers without are still asleep, the azaleas and rhododendrons make the valley a garden of delight. The season is known to be nearly a month earlier in the spring and later in the autumn than in the valley below."

The cause of the phenomena is probably the stratification at night of the atmosphere of the regions below and above the belt. By reason of the movement of air ascending and descending, caused by effect of the previous day's sun and of the containing mountain sides, the humidity of the air is controlled by the rise of the heated air from below and the descent of the cooler air from above, and the formation of frost is thus delayed until the rising of the next day's sun, which entirely prevents it. The curvature of the mountain sides also shelters these spots from the cold and wintry wind, and heat is so stored up by the sides during the day as to increase at night the movement of the air surrounding the favored belt.

The average annual precipitation (including rain, hail, sleet and snow) for the whole State is 53.29 inches. In the different portions it is as follows: The eastern district, 55.23 inches; the central, 49.85 inches, and the western, 53.32 inches. The seasonal averages are as follows:

	Spring.	Sum'er.	Aut'mn	Winter
Eastern district.....	12.85	17.04	13.10	12.24
Central district.....	12.18	13.99	11.35	12.28
Western district....	13.19	14.95	10.61	14.07
For the State........	12.94	15.87	11.71	12.77

It is a very noteworthy and providential fact that the months of October and November are the dryest, when staple crops are in more need of dryness than moisture to mature thoroughly; and when the reverse is required, and more moisture is needed, we find the heaviest precipitation in the summer months of July and August.

The average annual snowfall is about five inches or less, and the falls are far from being nearly equally distributed. The Piedmont region east of the Blue Ridge has the greatest snowfall, and rarely is the snow seen in portions of the eastern district. It remains but a short time upon the ground, and hardships from snowfalls are rare. During the past winter, when the snowfall was exceptionally heavy in the central district, the curious spectacle was noticed of a heavy fall of six inches on December 27, 1892, when barely a vestige remained on January 3, 1893, just one week later.

The average date of the first killing frost is October 10, but this varies in different localities, as might be supposed, owing to temperature and humidity. Light frosts often occur, however, before this time. The latest killing frosts occur in April, but may, in exceptional cases, be delayed till May.

The main causes, due to location in respect to ocean and mountains, which affect the climatic conditions of North Carolina, together with a brief study of those conditions, have already been included. It now remains to mention in what way these conditions affect the life, character and general well-being of those

VICTORIA REGIA, GROWING IN OPEN AIR, SALEM, N. C.

who are so fortunate as to reside within her borders. Enumeration will be made under three headings, all mutually dependent upon each other, and upon the causes of their existence.

1. In relation to plant and animal life.
2. In relation to water-power.
3. In relation to healthfulness.

1. *Plant and Animal Life.*—The existence of such a varied flora in the State is evidence of the possibilities for very great extension in the growth of staple crops of assistance to man, as well as the utilization of such natural growths as can be turned to man's advantage. In reference to the fauna, under which broad term is included all animal life, whether existing on land or in water, the same will apply; for their natural occurrence in such great numbers indicates that the climate and the temperature of the waters are especially suitable to their development. This fact can also be utilized in the further growth of domesticated animals or marine life.

The different altitudes from the sea coast to the mountain top, with resulting climatic conditions, render possible the greatest profusion of plant growth, from the lowly herb of value for medicinal purposes, to the lordly timber tree of the forests. All have uses, and are, in many instances, the bases of large and profitable enterprises. On the mountain tops, the balsam, white pines, and the rhododendrons, natives only of high latitudes, are found in abundance; and stretching in beautiful gradation to the sea, where the live oak and the palmetto flourish, are a profusion of varieties of plants and timber trees from semi-alpine to semi-tropic in character. At Salem can be seen growing in the open air the mammoth water lily, Victoria Regia, that native of the Amazon, which heretofore has not been grown outside of conservatories. Mr. Gerald McCarthy, botanist of the North Carolina Experiment Station, on the basis of Dr. Curtis' list, estimates that the plants of the State embrace between 5000 and 6000 specimens, nearly all of which are native to the State. There are 600 species of woody plants, including the forest trees,

of which number the long-leaf pine, the short-leaf pine, oaks, cedar, cypress, gum, hickory, walnut, chestnut, maple, locust, ash, cherry and poplar, are of great commercial importance, and of each several varieties are found. Of medicinal herbs, barks and berries 2100 species are utilized.

The growth of staple crops likewise is possible in varieties, ranging from buckwheat of the mountain top to rice of the tidewater. Corn, oats, upland rice, the grasses, tobacco, peas, wheat and sorghum, find a foothold in almost every portion of the State, while cotton is confined to the eastern and central districts. Fruits can be grown in almost every section. Grapes, of which the Scuppernong, Lincoln and Catawba are natives, flourish. In the middle belt of the central district, owing to the climatic and soil conditions found there, they are ready for shipment ten or fifteeen days in advance of localities further South. In the eastern district, owing to mild winters and early spring, the cultivation and shipment of trucking crops has assumed enormous proportions, and the canning industry is springing up in their path. The soils of the State, in conjunction with the natural advantages of climate, respond well to judicial management.

The natural stock ranges of the mountains are found to be very beneficial for domestic animals, and show possibilities for extension in cultivated areas. Similar conditions are met with in other localities, and the experienced hand only is needed to develop them. Marine life in the rivers, sounds, estuaries and bays of the east is very abundant. The warm waters of that region, combined with the peculiar formation of land-locked water areas render the fishing interests of great importance. Shad, mullet, herring, blue fish, sturgeon, bass and mackerel are the principle kind that abound. A single haul in the steam fisheries of Albemarle sound has been known to bring in 380,-000 herrings. In addition to fish, the oyster interest is becoming immense; and the wild fowls, terrapin, etc., of the region find votaries among the epicures.

2. *Water-Power.*— Elevation and rainfall are the sources of the tremendous

water power of the State. The descent from the high mountain elevations and plateaus to the sea coast, in such a comparatively short distance, combined with the result of 53.29 inches of precipitation annually, must make itself felt in the development of great water-powers. The total length of the principal rivers is 3300 miles and the total fall is approximately 33,000 feet. The water power developed by these rivers, world, as they have for generations been known to our people. In the east, on the coast at Southport, Carolina Beach, Wrightsville, Beaufort, Morehead City, Nag's Head and Avoca, are watering places which are much frequented in the summer seasons. In the central district, among others, are Kittrells, Southern Pines and Raleigh, recognized as winter resorts. In the mountain section of the west are Asheville, Morganton, Hender-

ORTON RICE FARM, LOWER CAPE FEAR RIVER.

as estimated by Dr. Kerr, former State geologist, is 3,370,000 horse-power. This power is capable of turning 130,000,000 spindles. This power is more and more being utilized in manufactories, and in the future will be developed more largely.

3. *Healthfulness.*—In no other direction is the beneficial effect of the State's superb climate better felt than in the healthfulness it offers to all who make their residence here. In all localities of the State can be found resorts that are fast becoming known to the outside sonville, Mount Airy, Blowing Rock, Linville, Roan, Mount Waynesville, Cleveland Springs, Catawba Springs, Connelly Springs, Glen Alpine, Hot Springs and others—all resorts of established and growing reputation, particularly frequented in the summer season, though many are visited continuously throughout the year. At many of these, where natural advantages of scenery and climate are combined, are found mineral springs of great therapeutic value. The dryness of many mountain locali-

ties, notably at Asheville, which during 1889 recorded only 66 per cent. of humidity, is especially beneficial to many classes of diseases; other points in the central district, Southern Pines, for example, possess similar advantages. The varied character of these resorts but gives an indication of the general healthfulness of all sections. Only the lower portions of the eastern district and the flats of river bottoms and swamps can be said to be unhealthy, and these only during the warm period of the summer months. By a judicious use of cistern water for drinking, and care as to nonexposure to the night dew, these localities are rendered far more healthy, and inhabitants enured to them exhibit typical specimens of health and vigor. Contagious diseases are seldom met with, and epidemics are practically unknown. The natural healthfulness is still further increased by the occurrence of large bodies of pine trees. The effect of their growth is well established in the production of ozone, that oxidizing agent which is so useful in nullifying many germs of disease, which might, under favorable surroundings, obtain a foothold.

In summing up a description of the State's climate, Dr. Kerr has well said: "Middle and eastern North Carolina correspond to middle and southern France, and western North Carolina to northern France and Belgium. All the climates of Italy from Palermo to Milan and Venice are represented."

In a word and in conclusion, North Carolina possesses the cream of America's climate. This fact, and the many results attendant upon it, will surely make themselves known the world over, and eventually will transform the State into a veritable garden spot.

EDUCATION IN NORTH CAROLINA.

By Geo. T. Winston,

President of the University of North Carolina.

During the last twenty years in North Carolina greater progress has been made in education than in other directions. The public school system has been developed and strengthened, until now a child can enter one of the best city schools at the age of six, and go steadily forward with his education in public schools until he graduates from the University. The private schools have multiplied and grown until scarcely a prosperous county in the State lacks a good academy, while here and there may be found classical academies of high grade, drawing large patronage from other States. The colleges and seminaries have increased their endowments and patronage to the point that enables them to do creditable work in higher education. The State has established and endowed a college for the training of young men in agriculture and the mechanic arts, and also a school for the normal and industrial training of young women.

The public school system is wisely planned and arranged. Two things are lacking—increased revenues for the support of the country public schools during longer terms, and increased facilities for the special training of teachers. These wants will be supplied as the State grows in industrial prosperity. The general sentiment is favorable to universal education. Although criticism is heard occasionally, directed against the establishment of high-grade public schools in new localities, or the expansion of the work of those already established, or against the policy or management of individual State institutions for higher education, the time has passed in North Carolina when any one dares to manifest openly an active spirit of opposition to public education. The people have taken hold of the idea of public education, and they are beginning to comprehend its true significance. Its beneficent results are already manifest. The public school is now established beyond possibility of destruction. Its growth and maturity are merely questions of time.

Nor is there less enthusiasm for higher State education. The obligations of the State to maintain and support the University are not only incorporated in the constitution, but are becoming universally recognized among the people. The institution is rapidly gaining a strong hold upon the affections of the people, and is doing a work for the people and for popular education that entitles it to receive their confidence and support. The various religious denominations also have manifested practical zeal and large generosity in endowing and enlarging their colleges. The work of establishing and endowing denominational high schools in different sections of the State has also begun. Altogether the educational status of North Carolina is very encouraging.

The development of the system of private schools has kept pace with that of public schools. The idea of public education has by no means supplanted that of private education. This is one of the most hopeful signs in the educational future of the State. There is a kind of training which public schools cannot furnish. There is a class of people that public schools cannot reach. There is imperative need of both systems, and each system is stimulated and improved by the other. For some generations the State has suffered greatly from lack of an efficient public school system. Other States that began with well-equipped public schools have suffered almost equally in other ways from lack of efficient private schools.

There is a great change in public sentiment regarding universal education. Even the incubus of the negro is seriously considered no longer. When in the capital of North Carolina the old governor's mansion was torn down, and in its stead was erected the Centennial graded school for whites, and by its side was erected a medical college for negroes, a new era began in education.

Many of the most energetic and talented young men in the State during this generation have devoted themselves to education, and by voice and pen, as well as by pedagogic skill, have aroused among the people widespread and growing interest in education. The University sends out annually from fifteen to twenty active, enthusiastic and competent young teachers. The colleges are equally as helpful in this great work. The schools are equally fortunate in the character of the young women whose services are given to education. Many a schoolroom in North Carolina is presided over with the refined grace, the tender courtesy, the lady-like gentleness, that belongs to refined homes. The social and industrial upheaval has thrown into the school-room, and frequently into the log-cabin school-house, the still blossoming and fragrant flower of an honorable and gentle family, now uprooted and prostrate.

Changes are taking place in our industrial system which demand better schools, more schools, and universal education; in other words, these changes demand skilled labor and educated labor. Agriculture is no longer profitable in North Carolina except with the most intelligent application of the most intelligent labor. The farms are growing smaller year by year, or are being deserted, while the towns are rapidly swelling in numbers. Manufactures are springing up. There is greater intellectual activity as a neces-

sary result. It is manifested most clearly where its power is massed and where instruments exist for its employment. Special taxes are voted in all these centres of industrial and intellectual growth for educational facilities; and high-grade schools are secured for both races, with terms averaging nearly ten months a year. From these schools the best scholars may go direct to the colleges or to the State University. The school at Goldsboro sent to the University a scholar who not only stood the best entrance examination for that year, but also kept at the head of his class afterwards. He will graduate this year from the United States Military Academy at West Point, number one in his class.

These schools, popularly known as graded schools, exist in nearly all the largest and most active towns. The chief are at Raleigh, Asheville, Wilmington, Goldsboro, Fayetteville, Tarboro, Greensboro, Wilson, Durham, Charlotte, Salisbury, Concord, Statesville, Reidsville, Murphy, Shelby and Winston. At other places the establishment of such schools has been delayed or rendered unnecessary by the existence of well-equipped and competent private schools and academies, already doing the work of education. This is notably the case at Oxford, where the Horner School and the Oxford Female Seminary have for years done excellent work both for the community and for the State.

While the city schools are open nearly ten months, yet the average school term for the State is about thirteen weeks. The country districts have not as yet levied special taxes, but as soon as a beginning is made in this direction, there will doubtless be a general movement which will result in such increase in taxation as will enable all the schools to run at least four months. These districts are large in territory and sparse in population, making progress both slow and expensive. The number of districts is 7555, of which 5168 are for whites and 2387 for colored. During the last year, 1892, the schools taught were 6979 in number, being 4603 for whites and 2376 for colored. It will be observed that 576 districts had no schools during the year, of which only eleven were colored. The total valuation of school property in the State is not quite $1,000,000. Improvements are steadily making all over the State in the character of the houses, the furniture and the apparatus. This is strikingly so in the cities and large towns. Very handsomely built and equipped graded school houses have recently been erected in Durham and Asheville. Other places are being stimulated. Progress has already been made beyond the expectations or hopes of any educators in North Carolina twenty-five years ago. Another generation will see the entire system larger, stronger, better. "*Crescit eundo.*"

The great trouble is lack of funds. Good salaries are paid in the city graded schools, but in the country schools meagre wages too often attract gaunt and meagre talent. For 1892 the average salary for white males was $26.20 per month; females, $22.72; negro males, $23.23; females, $20.14. These wages will attract the best negro talent at present, but only inferior white talent, as a rule, will accept such small compensation. This is strikingly true of males.

The school age in North Carolina is from six to twenty-one years. This age includes thousands who have already passed through school and are in active business. Excepting those at college, very few boys or girls continue at school beyond the age of eighteen. Many parents do not send children to school at the early age of six. The total enrollment, therefore, is not a fair criterion of the educational situation, being only fifty-six per cent. of the school population in 1892. The superintendent of public instruction, Hon. S. M. Finger, estimates that about sixty-one per cent. of the school population was actually enrolled in 1892, in both public and private schools. It is safe to say that if we allow for those who had already been enrolled and had passed through school, as well as for those whose parents would not send them to school at the early age of six or seven years, we would find only about ten or twelve per cent. unenrolled of those who should have been enrolled. The actual enrollment for 1892 was: Whites, 215,919; negroes,

119,441; total, 335,358. The average attendance was thirty-four per cent. for whites and thirty-one per cent. for negroes.

In the private schools about 38,400 pupils were enrolled, of whom about 4000 were negroes. Over ten per cent. of the pupils at school in 1892 were in private schools. The number of private schools has steadily increased during this generation, and there has been marked improvement not only in the buildings and equipment, but also in the quality of the instruction. Some of them may safely challenge comparison with the best academies in other States. The Horner School, at Oxford, and the Bingham School, at Asheville, have educated three generations of scholars. The Raleigh Academy, the Oak Ridge Institute, the Davis School (Winston), the Tarboro Academy, the Cape Fear Academy (Wilmington), the Elizabeth City Academy, the Ravenscroft School (Asheville), the Rutherford Military Institute, the Gaston Institute (Gastonia), the Turlington Institute (Smithfield), the Laurinburg Academy, the Thompson School (Siler City), and others are doing good work not only in the school-room, but also in stimulating the public to appreciation of education.

The University is the head of the public school system of the State, as well as of the private school system. It is near 100 years old. It has twenty-three teachers, ten large buildings, 316 students, six scientific laboratories, a select library of 30,000 books, many societies for special scientific and literary culture, four general courses of study, six brief courses, professional courses in law, medicine and engineering, advanced courses and graduate courses. It has graduate students at Harvard, Cornell and elsewhere, who rank among the best scholars there. The University offers seventy scholarships to needy young men of talent, and loans of money to the very deserving. It is rapidly regaining its former position among the leading universities of America.

Among the colleges there is marked activity and growth. Wake Forest has steadily increased its endowment and its patronage, and has generously and intelligently enlarged its facilities for instruction, both of teachers and of apparatus, so that it may reasonably hope to become in a few years the leading Baptist college in the South. Its missionary educational work has been active and successful. Through its president. and professors and agents it has stirred up a wonderful zeal for education in North Carolina, and has been a potent factor in the educational and intellectual upheaval that has been so marked in this generation.

Davidson College maintains its long-established reputation for scholarly work and for conservative culture and parental discipline. Its facilities for education are constantly growing, and its student roll is now larger than ever before.

Trinity College, after many years of most useful work amid struggles with poverty, has moved into a new and elegant home at Durham, provided for it by the munificent generosity of Mr. Washington Duke and Mr. Julian S. Carr. Here it has caught the push and enthusiasm of that active town, and, under the wise and tireless management of its faithful and versatile president, it bids fair to rival the already famous college of the Methodist Church, and to stand abreast of any in uplifting and cultivating the Methodist people of the South.

Elon College has sprung up as if by magic, with large equipment, faithful and zealous teachers, extensive patronage, wise and active management. It belongs to the Christian denomination, and it is not only a monument to their zeal and liberality, but a practical and blessed institution of culture and refinement.

Guilford College, notwithstanding its quiet and modest unpretentiousness, is one of the most meritorious colleges in the State, whether we consider the quality of the work done, or the character of the students and faculty. Its graduates are often inspired with ambition to receive higher special training, and they may be found every year either at the University of North Carolina or at one of the great Northern universities. Guilford College belongs to the Society of Friends.

The Agricultural and Mechanical College, at Raleigh, affords a good general higher education in English, mathematics and the sciences, besides technical education in mechanics and such arts and sciences as relate to agriculture. The college is well endowed by the State, and it furnishes board at cost. Tuition is free to 120 students.

North Carolina College, at Mount Pleasant; Judson College, at Hendersonville; Catawba College, at Newton; Lenoir College, at Hickory; Concordia College, at Conover, and others, are exerting wholesome and stimulating influences upon education and upon the public.

There are many good female schools, seminaries and colleges in the State. The oldest and most widely known are Salem Academy (Moravian), and the St. Mary's School (Episcopalian), at Raleigh. The Salem Academy has probably exerted a wider and larger influence upon education than any female school in the South. It is now superior in equipment, in patronage, and in general excellence to what it has ever been before. St. Mary's School (Episcopalian), and Peace Institute (Presbyterian), both in Raleigh, represent a very high grade of intellectual culture and refinement. They draw patronage from all the Southern States. The Oxford Female Seminary (Baptist), and the Chowan Baptist Female Institute, at Murfreesboro, are both well known for the efficiency of their work and their most wholesome influences for culture and refinement. The Greensboro Female College (Methodist), under its recent new management, has surpassed its former reputation in all respects. It has added to its material equipment, its faculty, its scope of instruction, its area of patronage. It promises to be one of the leading Methodist seminaries in the South. Besides these are, Davenport College, at Lenoir; Claremont College, at Hickory; the Wesleyan Female College, at Murfreesboro; the Kinsey Female Seminary, at La Grange; the Littleton Female College, the Skyland Institute, at Blowing Rock; the Wilson Collegiate Institute, and others, which are steadily improving both the quality and quantity of their work.

The State Normal and Industrial School for women, at Greensboro, is a well-equipped and a remarkably well-organized institution recently established by the State for the special training of young women. Free tuition is given to all who intend to teach, and there are 120 free scholarships distributed among the counties. Board, books, etc., are supplied at cost. This school has met a wide-felt and earnest demand, as is shown by the fact that it was taxed by applicants beyond its utmost capacity even on the day of its opening. Its influence not only upon female education, but upon the general system of the State, will be marked and most wholesome.

The education of the negroes is well provided for in North Carolina. There is a large sentiment against negro education, under the idea, first, that it is an expense to the whites; second, that it is not good for the negroes. These ideas, however, are not formulated in active opposition. Meanwhile the education of the negro goes on, and the question seems likely to settle itself. During the year 1892 the negroes paid for one-half their education in public schools in North Carolina. Their property is assessed at about $8,000,000. The facilities for the higher education of the negro in North Carolina are comparatively better than those for the higher education of the whites. He has a thoroughly organized medical college in Raleigh and a law school in connection with Shaw University. Probably 1500 negroes are now receiving higher education in the State, such as will enable them to do the work for their race in the so-called higher professions. Their best-known institutions for higher education are: Shaw University, Leonard Medical College, Estey Seminary and St. Augustine Normal School, at Raleigh; Livingstone College, at Salisbury; Scotia Seminary, at Concord; Christian College, at Franklinton; Bennett Seminary, at Greensboro; Biddle University, at Charlotte, and Gregory Institute, at Wilmington. Besides these there are eight negro normal schools sustained by the State, affording not only general education, but also special normal training for teachers. It is doubtful whether the negro has better educational facilities anywhere on the globe than in North Carolina.

On the whole the educational outlook is most encouraging. The General Assembly, recently adjourned, made liberal appropriations to all the State institutions for higher education and increased the tax rate for public school purposes. Laws were passed making possible the establishment of several new graded schools. Before long we may hope for a constitutional amendment allowing taxes to be levied for the support of the public schools four months in the year. Progress in education promises to be as great during the next twenty years as during the last twenty; and the State, especially in her institutions for higher education, may hope to become an educating centre for the South.

NORTH CAROLINA'S RESOURCES.

By Hon. Elias Carr,

Governor of North Carolina.

During the first century of North Carolina's existence as a State her people were mainly engaged in agricultural pursuits, and it has been only during the past few decades that such other important elements of national prosperity and greatness as manufactures and commerce have begun to receive a considerable share of attention. This state of things has in large measure characterized the early development in all countries, but has been more especially true of this and neighboring States because the character of the labor and conditions of climate and soil have been more favorable to agricultural development. But our people are now recognizing the fact that their future prosperity depends upon the building up of diversified industries, and they are turning more attention to manufacturing, mining and commerce. A brief statement of existing conditions will serve to show that this tendency has a basis of fact and that its future is secure.

A diversity of agricultural products may be mentioned as the first important element in the present and future prosperity of the State. A country which depends for food so largely upon one product, such as potato or rice, may suffer from famine when this crop fails, and another which depends for its money supply upon some staple like cotton may be impoverished by the fall in price or partial failure of the crop. But in a region where exists the possibility of agricultural diversity, the failure in one crop is accompanied by the success of another. And it is claimed for North Carolina that her farmers cultivate successfully a greater variety of crops than are grown in any other American State.

This variety of products is due to an existing great diversity in soil and climate. The eastern margin of the State, but little above sea level, is pushed out into the ocean and comes in contact with the warm breezes; and along the southeastern border, where the influence of the gulf stream is most marked, sugar cane, the palmetto, the live oak and other semi-tropical plants attain a vigorous growth. Further inland, along the lines of the Atlantic Coast Line Railroad and the Atlantic & North Carolina Railroad, under the modifying influences of the sea, has grown up an extensive and profitable trucking business, supplying vegetables for early northern markets. In passing from the east with its lowlands near the coast, westward to the mountains, which lie 300 to 400 miles distant and rise to a height of over 6000 feet above the ocean, we find the same variations in temperature, soil and products as if this area extended from Eastern Carolina northward across Pennsylvania and New York, the forest trees and other vegetation of the mountain counties resembling that of these latter States. Intermediate between the coast region and the mountains lie the Piedmont counties, which, with their mild climate and fertile loam soil, are becoming the most important region of the State both in agriculture and manufactures.

Cotton is grown in nearly all the counties of the State; and in those best adapted to its cultivation—the eastern and midland regions—it continues to be planted so extensively as in large measure to exclude other crops. During past few years the price has been so low (eight and nine cents per pound) that even in case of the most careful farmers the margin of profit was reduced to a minimum; but the effect of this reduction has been in a measure counterbalanced by the increasing profits arising from the manufacture of oil and meal from the cotton seed. And yet it must be admitted that the "agricultural depression" in the cotton belt is quite marked and general. One important cause of this depression is clearly recognized—overproduction of cotton and underproduction of such farm supplies as constitute food for man and beast. Those farmers who are adopting a different policy of raising these necessary supplies as far as possible at home, and then cultivate cotton as a money crop, are finding less cause for complaint of "hard times," and are pointing to one of the ways by which thrift and prosperity may again be made to characterize farming in the Southern States.

To those who enter upon the subject with this latter plan as a guide cotton farming offers many inducements, for in addition to the profits arising from the sale of the lint and cottonseed oil, meal and hulls (or the use of the two latter for feeding stock and as a fertilizer), the farms of the cotton belt will also produce various other crops, corn, wheat, oats, clover, grasses, tobacco, potatoes, peanuts, etc. So that in Edgecombe, Wake, Mecklenburg and Forsythe counties, where the yield of cotton is often from one to one and a half bales per acre, there are some of the best stock farms to be found in the State, and in these regions yields per acre of twenty to thirty bushels of wheat, forty to seventy-five bushels of oats, fifty to seventy-five bushels of corn, 200 to 400 bushels of Irish and sweet potatoes, two to three tons of hay, or forty to sixty bushels of peanuts, are not uncommon.

In the lowlands of the eastern region, where the soils are too wet for this diversity of crops, corn, grasses and rice are the profitable substitutes, the latter crop being largely grown in the southeastern section. In the mountain counties, corn, wheat, oats, rye, the grasses, buckwheat,

Irish potatoes and tobacco all grow luxuriantly and compete for ascendency as profitable crops. In these counties stock raising is also an extensive and profitable branch of farming. The culture of tobacco, long common in the western and upper central counties, has of late extended rapidly into the eastern counties. This has long been the most skilled and the most profitable class of farming practiced in the State—the most painstaking farmers, under favorable conditions, often selling his crop of bright yellow tobacco at prices which yield from $2.00 to $4.00 per acre. A careful estimate shows the annual tobacco product of the State to approximate 75,-000,000 pounds with a valuation of about $10,000,000.

As an important element in this growing diversity of agricultural products, I may mention also that the areas devoted to trucking, vineyards and orchards have increased greatly during the past few years. Ten years ago trucking on a commercial scale in North Carolina was almost unknown; but the industry has developed so rapidly in the eastern counties, along the several lines of railway, that during the past year the area devoted to this industry amounted to many thousand acres and the financial returns reached several millions of dollars. During the same period the areas planted out in grapes and other fruits on a commercial scale have been considerably extended. In the eastern sandy soils the Scuppernong grape flourishes, and vineyards, like the Tokay in Cumberland and Medoc in Nash, have won a favorable and wide reputation for their wines. In the midland and western counties, other grapes like the Concord, Ives, Catawba, etc., flourish, and many vineyards have already reached large proportions and are shipping both wine and grapes to the markets of the country. Peach orchards on a commercial scale are being established in the central counties and in the "thermal belts" of the mountain region; and on the mountain slopes of the western counties apple orchards are growing in number and area, and the fruit has already become widely and favorably known.

But it is in manufacturing enterprises that North Carolina has shown the greatest development during the past few years. The numerous streams which, as they pass across the State descend from the mountains and hills to the lowlands, furnish water powers here and there, which in the aggregate are estimated to be equal to 3,500,000 horse-power. The abundant supply of wood furnishes a cheap fuel to supplement the coal; labor is cheap and satisfactory, and the climate mild enough to allow uninterrupted work. Under these favorable conditions manufacturing establishments have been springing up rapidly during the past few years, and are certain to increase in number, magnitude and variety in the near future.

There are in the State at the present time 160 cotton mills, located in thirty-eight different counties, operating about 10,000 looms and more than 500,000 spindles. The profits arising from many of these mills range from 10 to 25 per cent. on the capital invested. There are thirteen woolen mills, operating about 100 looms and over 1000 spindles. There are of tobacco factories, located at Winston, Durham, Reidsville, Henderson and elsewhere, 110 plug factories, nine smoking tobacco factories, and three cigarette factories, the aggregate business of which amounts to several million dollars per annum. There are fifty-seven carriage and buggy factories, located in thirty counties, thirty-two wagon factories, twenty-five furniture factories, six hub, spoke and handle factories, twenty-four sash, door and blind factories, three paper mills, eight knitting mills, forty-two canning establishments, including vegetables, fruits and oysters; fourteen cotton-seed oil mills, sixteen fertilizer factories, and a considerable number of miscellaneous establishments. Probably the greatest progress has been made in the growth of cotton factories, cotton-seed oil mills and tobacco factories, and these have continued to yield the largest profits.

The development of the cotton-seed oil industry illustrates the continued supremacy of the cotton plant in both the agriculture and manufactures of the Southern States. A few years ago the cotton seed had only a nominal value, and were used mainly to scatter over fields as a manure. At the present time they are hulled and pressed in the mills. The hulls make a valuable article of food for cattle, either being fed direct, or cooked, or mixed with other ingredients in silos. The meal (ground remains of the kernels after the oil has been pressed out) constitutes the richest food we have for cattle, and is extensively used in this way, and it is also largely used as a fertilizer, alone or mixed with other materials. The oil is used for a variety of purposes—replacing lard in one field, olive oil in another, and recent developments seem to show that one of its products will replace the "mineralized rubber" of commerce.

During the past few years there have also sprung up in many different counties lumber mills and wood-working establishments of various kinds, for the purpose of utilizing the great quantities of pine and hardwood timber which abound in the forests of the State. And it is a matter of no little importance to the State that everything possible be done to encourage these industries, looking to the manufacture of our timbers into finished products in factories established in our own State.

In portions of the extreme Eastern countries, where the conditions are less favorable for agriculture and manufactures, the fishery interests supplement these industries and contribute materially to the wealth of the region. Prominent among these fisheries may be mentioned the shad and herring fisheries at Avoca and Edenton, in the Albemarle Sound, which are among the largest fishing establishments in the country; the Beaufort and Morehead fisheries, where a variety of fish in large quantities are caught; and the Cape Fear fisheries, about the Lower Cape Fear and New rivers, which yield large quantities of mullets. There are also many intervening points where fisheries of lesser importance exist. Many of the shad and other fish are shipped to large markets packed in ice; others are salted for later shipments.

The oyster interest in North Carolina has come into prominence during the past few years. Careful surveys of the sounds in the eastern region demonstrated the fact that there exist in these waters already large natural beds of oysters, and other large areas well adapted to oyster culture. It is hoped that in the future the development of this industry may result in great benefits to the people of that region and to the State at large.

In the central and western counties the mineral resources—iron, gold, granite, sandstone, coal, corundum, mica, &c., are aiding materially to increase the wealth of the region.

In conclusion it may be said that the outlook for the increasing material prosperity of the people of the State is decidedly encouraging. Our people are making an earnest effort in this direction, and are offering a cordial welcome to intelligent settlers who may come among them with capital to invest or with skilled labor to be employed.

GRANITE QUARRY AT MOUNT AIRY—FORTY ACRES OF BARE ROCK SURFACE.

ECONOMIC GEOLOGY OF NORTH CAROLINA.

By J. A. Holmes,

State Geologist of North Carolina.

A line drawn from Weldon to Raleigh, and from Raleign to Hamlet, divides the State into two general geologic divisions — the eastern, or coastal plain region, the formations of which are comparatively recent in age and are composed mainly of sands and clays which have never been hardened into "rock," with occasional deposits of marl and limestone; and the western, the formations of which are made up of the older, hard and crystalline rocks, mostly granites, gneisses and slates, with two narrow and irregular strips of red sandstone.

Along the western border of this eastern region the surface of the country is undulating in character and has an elevation varying from 200 to 300 feet above the sea. Eastward, approaching the ocean, the elevation decreases to but a few feet above the sea, and the surface becomes nearly level, in many places marshy, and extensively intersected by the sounds and estuaries of the rivers. The western region, undulating along its eastern border, becomes more hilly westward through the middle and Piedmont counties until the hills become small mountains, and these in turn give place to the Blue Ridge and adjacent mountain chains.

The economic geology of the eastern region is comparatively limited. It contains large areas of the finest farming lands of the State and valuable forests of short-leaf and long-leaf pine. The principal economic mineral products are marls and limestone, phosphate, iron ores and building stone, the latter two of which will be mentioned further on.

Marls, commonly known as shell marl or blue marl, are found in numerous beds or patches near the surface, widely distributed through the majority of the eastern counties. They contain from twenty to ninety per cent. of carbonate of lime, and at one time were extensively used for agricultural purposes. But their use has been largely abandoned in favor of the stronger lime which is now manufactured so cheaply by burning the oyster shells from the coast region. Limestone of varying character, suitable for burning into lime and for other purposes, occurs along the Cape Fear river and its tributaries, and at intervening points as far north as the Neuse.

Phosphates much like the South Carolina rock have been found in several of the southeastern counties, Sampson, Dublin, Pender, New Hanover, etc., but the only place where they are now being worked is at Castle Haynes, New Hanover county, and at Rocky Point, Pender county, where the phosphate occurs in nodules varying from the size of a bean to several inches in diameter, thickly imbedded in limestone rock.

It is in the middle and western counties that the more important mineral products occur, and it is to these regions that the following notes relate. When the capitol building at Raleigh was planned, fifty years ago, and again when the postoffice building was ordered, nearly twenty years ago, it was proposed to bring granite from New England for building material, because it was not known that stone suitable for the purpose could be obtained at home; but a careful search in each case resulted in the use of home material, and as a result of this and later enterprises, North Carolina granite and brownstone are today being quarried at more than two dozen places and shipped as far north as New York and as far west as Chicago.

Granite and granitic gneiss suitable for building and monumental stone and paving purposes are widely distributed and abundant in many of the midland counties and in Henderson county west of the Blue Ridge. The most important of the granite quarries now being worked are those of the Greystone Granite Co. and P. Linehan & Sons, at Greystone, Vance county; those of the Hambley Granite Co., the Stone Mountain Granite Co., the Kirk Mountain Co., and the Pink Granite Co., of Salisbury; the Mt. Airy Granite Co., at Mt. Airy; the quarry of Durham & Elliott, at Mooresville, and of W. D. Troy, near Henderson.

The sandstone, brown, red and gray, now considered workable, is all located in one belt which starts in Granville county and extends in a southwesterly course across the State through parts of Durham, Wake, Chatham, Moore, Montgomery, Stanley and Anson counties, and the principal quarries are near Durham, Sanford, Egypt and Wadesboro. At each of these places quarries of considerable extent have been opened up, and at many intervening points stone of excellent quality and color abound.

Marble in workable quantities is to be found in McDowell county ten miles north of Marion, in Swain county in the gorge of the Nantahala river, and in Cherokee county along nearly the whole length of Valley river and southwest of Murphy on the Notteley river and beyond to the Georgia boundary line. Until recently lack of transportation facilities has prevented the development of these deposits, but now the Western North Carolina railroad runs through the deposits on both the Nantahala and Valley river regions, and the Marietta & North Georgia railroad passes through the region southwest of Murphy, and several quarries are being opened up, the most prominent being those of Rickard & Hewitt, and of the Nantahala Marble & Talc Co., on the Nantahala; of C. N. Hickerson, on Valley river, and of the Notla Consolidated Marble, Iron & Talc Co., at Kinsey and Culbertson, on the Marietta & North Georgia Railroad.

Slate suitable for roofing purposes has been found at several places in the State, and two quarries have been opened up recently, one in Montgomery and another in Stanley county.

The conglomerates of the triassic sandstone formations have been successfully and extensively used for millstones. The quarry in Moore county has produced a majority of these. The porphyritic granites and gneisses of several of the middle and western counties are largely used for this purpose, one of the most notable of these quarries being that of J. T. Wyatt, near Salisbury. The sandstones of some of the counties are fairly well adapted for use as grindstones.

Among the siliceous slates so abundant in the region described by Kerr as Huronian, there are frequent beds of novaculite or whetstone. One of the best localities is a few miles west of Chapel Hill, from which these stones have been carried in all directions. Other quarries are found in Person county, near Roxboro, in Anson county not far from Wadesboro, in Montgomery and adjoining counties on the great slate belt, and in fact many sections of the State have their own quarries which either do or might supply the local demand at least in part and as to articles of the commoner grade.

Kaolin is found in many of the midland and western counties of the State in deposits varying in quantity and quality, and suitable for various uses, for china and other wares, paper-making and for fire-brick. The largest deposits of pure white kaolin are found in the western counties as a product of decomposition of the feldspar in large veins. A number of these veins have been worked during the past few years. The largest is that worked

LAFAYETTE FORMATION IN EASTERN NORTH CAROLINA.

by the Carolina Clay Co., near Webster.

Beds of fire-clay and potter's clay also abound in the more recent geological formations of the eastern and middle counties. The two largest deposits of fire-clay at present known are one near Spout Springs, in Harnett county, on the Cape Fear & Yadkin Valley Railroad, and another on the Northwestern North Carolina Railroad, about four miles southwest of Greensboro. Fire-brick from both these beds have stood satisfactorily the severest furnace tests.

Foliated and fibrous talc occurs in many places, but the large workable beds of this mineral appear to be limited to Macon and Cherokee counties. Here on the Nantahala river, in Macon county, and on Valley and Nottely rivers, in Cherokee, massive fibrous and foliated white talc occurs in irregular lenticular masses in the beds of marble, and is being mined and ground at several points for use in the arts and manufactures.

Soapstone, an impure variety of talc, in the form of a greenish and grayish massive or slaty rock, is widely distributed in the State, and is mainly used locally for chimney and furnace hearths and linings.

Agalmatolite is found abundantly in Chatham and Moore counties. It is popularly called soapstone and has the soapy feel of that mineral, but contains only 3.02 per cent. of magnesia. This substance has been an article of trade to New York on a large scale and for many years. It is used in the manufacture of paper, wall-paper especially, soaps, cosmetics, pencils, etc., and for various adulterations.

Small deposits of baryte are to be found in many places in the State, but only a few deposits are worthy of mention here. A vein of very white compact granular baryte, of from seven to eight feet in width, has been found at Crowder's mountain. Another vein, eight feet in width in places, of the white granular variety, has been worked to some extent at Chandler's, nine miles below Marshall, in Madison county, and other veins occur in this region.

Corundum has been found in considerable quantities in several counties, notably Macon, Clay, Jackson, Haywood, Madison and Iredell, and in small quantities it has been found in many other places. During the past several years mining for corundum has been an important industry in Macon county, at Corundum Hill and on Buck creek. During last year extensive mining operations have been in progress at several places in Macon and Jackson, and on a smaller scale in Iredell and a few other counties.

Since 1869 mica mining has been an important industry in several counties of the mountain region, especially in Mitchell, Yancey and Macon, and to a smaller extent in Jackson, Buncombe and Haywood counties. The aggregate yield of cut mica to date has been more than 500,000 pounds, valued at not less than $1,000,000. A new branch of the industry is now springing up in the grinding of the waste mica (nearly nine-tenths of the whole) into a fine powder, which is used in lubricants and for other purposes. The mica occurs as large crystals, associated with quartz and feldspar, in veins of considerable extent, situated in the gneisses and crystalline schists.

The occurrence of coal in North Carolina is confined to the limited triassic areas. It is now being mined at Egypt, on the Cape Fear & Yadkin Valley Railroad and the Egypt Railroad, and mines are being opened up at several other points in the Deep river coal basin of Chatham county. A company has also been organized for opening up a mine in the Dan river basin, near Germanton.

Pyrite is one of the common minerals of North Carolina. In the gold mines the associated pyrite is generally auriferous. Large veins of compact pyrite are now being worked in Gaston county, and promising deposits are reported as occurring in several other counties, especially in Jackson county, near Balsam station, on the Murphy Railroad.

The discovery several years ago of emerald and hiddenite in Alexander county, where mining operations on a considerable scale have been carried on, may be fairly said to have inaugurated a new industry in Western North Carolina

—the search for gems. This industry has now grown to considerable proportions. The larger amount of mining has been done in the explorations for hiddenite, emerald, beryl and rarely and considerable value have been obtained. This gem has not been found elsewhere than at this locality. A beryl of emerald green color has been found in the North Carolina mica veins in

WATER POWER ON TAR RIVER AT ROCKY MOUNT.

tinted garnets, but a limited amount also has been done in searching for ruby corundum, sapphire, oriental emerald and topaz, kyanite, rock crystal, and other rare minerals. Only a few notes can be given here relative to the more important gems.

Fourteen or fifteen small diamonds have been found in the State, eight of which were discovered in the gold mining gravel beds in Burke, Rutherford and McDowell counties centering about the Brindletown region. Of the others, one has been found in Lincoln, two in Mecklenburg, two in Franklin and one in Richmond county.

Hiddenite is an emerald-green gem, a variety of spodumene, found at Stony Point, Alexander county, where it occurs in the soil and in cavities in gneissoid rock, along with emerald (beryl), monazite, rutile, allanite, quartz crystal, etc. A considerable amount of mining for these gems has been carried on during the past few years, and both hiddenites and emeralds of rare beauty

Mitchell and Yancey counties, and at Stony Point, Alexander county, as gem material of great beauty. Bluish-green, transparent beryl has also been found in small crystals and masses in many of the mica veins of Mitchell, Yancey, Alexander and other counties. This is more abundant than the emerald. Many fine beryl crystals of different colors, and ranging in size from very small specimens to those more than two feet long and seven inches in diameter, have been collected at these mica mines and some from other formations.

The ruby corundum has been found in Clay and Macon counties in considerable quantities, and to some extent in Jackson, Iredell, Mitchell and Gaston counties. Perhaps the most noted locality has been Corundum Hill, in Macon county, where many fine gems have been found.

The sapphire corundum has been found in many of the localities named for the ruby but is more rare, nevertheless a considerable number of pretty gems have been discovered. The same is true in regard to the oriential gems—emerald and topaz.

Rock crystal is abundant and widely distributed. Many rare and interesting forms have been found, and some remarkably large crystals, nearly 300 pounds in weight, have been found in Ashe county. Many and beautiful specimens of rutilated quartz, and smoky quartz (cairngorm), have also been found at a number of localities.

A number of specimens of opalescent quartz have been found in Cabarrus and other counties during the past few years, some of the specimens being of considerable beauty and value.

Specimens of common agate have been found in Cabarrus and Mecklenburg counties, and among them a few handsome gems. Some fine specimens of moss agate have been found in Orange county.

Garnet is widely distributed throughout the middle and western counties of the State. The most beautiful and perfect large crystals of the brownish-red color are found in Burke, Caldwell and Catawba counties. Some of these when cut show a peculiar play of colors. Large crystals and crystalline masses of reddish-brown garnet are found in Macon and Mitchell counties, and from this latter county most of the gem material is obtained. At a locality eight miles southeast of Morganton several tons of garnets were collected and used in the manufacture of sand paper. The rarest colored garnets for gem purposes are found in Macon county.

Small zircon crystals abound in the gold sands of Burke, McDowell, Rutherford, Caldwell, Mecklenburg and other counties in yellowish-brown and brownish-white, sometimes amethystine, pink and blue colors. Large greyish-brown crystals of zircon are found so abundant on the south side of the Blue Ridge, near Green river, Henderson county, that a few years ago over thirty tons were mined at this locality, where the crystals are found bedded in a decayed feldspatnic gneiss.

In addition to the above, it is worthy of mention that specimens of malachite, rutile, tourmaline, spinel, chrysolite, lazulite, carnelian and jasper, all of considerable beauty, have been found in different localities in this State and promise supplies of new gem material.

In the mussels in some of the creeks and ponds of the State are occasionally found pearls of fair quality.

Iron ores are widely distributed in the State, occurring in the most recent as well as in the oldest geological formations, and in several of the eastern as well as many of the middle and western counties. The ores of the eastern counties are mostly of the variety known as "bog ore," existing in isolated patches of limited area and thickness, but they have nevertheless proved useful in the manufacture of iron during both the Revolutionary and Civil wars. In many of the middle and western counties iron ores occur in considerable abundance and variety, including magnetites, hematites, limonites and spathic ore.

The most noted of these iron ore deposits is that at Cranberry, Mitchell county. In the development of this deposit, and in the building of a railroad connecting it with Johnson City, more than a million dollars have been expended during the past few years, and a very large quantity of magnetic ore suitable for the manufacture of Bessemer steel has been opened up. The length of the surface ore exposed is 1500 feet, and its width varies from 200 to 800 feet. In Ashe county there are three important belts of ore which will doubtless be opened up in the near future. Other large deposits of magnetic ores of high grade occur in other parts of Mitchell and more than a dozen other counties, the development of which only awaits better facilities for transportation. Ores also occur in Madison, Buncombe, Haywood, Mitchell, Macon and Swain counties. In Cherokee county, associated with the marble deposits, are numerous and extensive beds of limonite ores which give promise of large developments of good quality.

East of the Blue Ridge, in addition to the isolated ore beds, there are a number of ore belts of importance, such as the Gaston, Lincoln and Catawba belts, now being largely developed by the North Carolina Bessemer Company at Bessemer City, Gaston county, and the Stokes county belt with its most important deposits near Danbury. The extensive beds of brown hematite at Ore Hill, Chatham county, have recently been opened up to a considerable extent by the North Carolina Steel & Iron Company, which has erected a modern blast furnace at Greensboro. These and many other workable deposits of iron ores are described in detail in a report on this subject now being printed for distribution by the State Geological Survey.

While no extensive beds of manganese ore have as yet been opened up, several promising deposits are being explored and developed in Gaston, Lincoln, Madison, Mitchell, Jackson, Caldwell and other counties.

Chrome iron ore in considerable quantity occurs at intervals in the chrysolite beds of Mitchell, Yancey and Jackson counties, and other deposits have been found in Guilford and Wake counties.

Copper is not widely distributed nor very abundant in North Carolina, but there are several deposits in the State deserving attention. The most important and the most interesting of these is that at Ore Knob in Ashe county. This deposit was worked for a number of years, and the excavations reached a length along the vein of 2000 feet, and a depth of 400 feet, the vein varying in thickness from six to twenty feet. The fact that the ore from this mine had to be hauled by wagon a distance of forty miles, and the sharp competition with the more favorably situated Lake Superior mines, combined to make the working of this mine unprofitable, and it was discontinued in 1882. In Granville and Person counties a series of copper mines are located along the veins which extend from near the Virginia line southwest for a distance of ten to twenty miles near the line between Person and Granville counties. The more prominent among these are the Royster, Tuck, Blue Wing, Mastodon, Pool, Buckeye, Gillis and Copper World. The ore at the Ore Knob mine is mainly a yellow sulphuret or chalcopyrite; the ore at the Granville and Person county mines is a black sulphuret of copper and vitrius copper ore. Several of these latter mines are now being worked, the ore being partly treated at the mines and thus reduced to a concentrate containing from twenty to fifty per cent. of copper, which in turn is shipped to the Oxford Copper Works for complete reduction.

There are deposits of copper ore in Jackson, Haywood, Ashe and Allegheny counties, and in a considerable number of the gold deposits of the Midland counties copper ore occurs in considerable abundance, but the present prices and the cost of reducing these ores do not allow of their being worked profitably.

Silver ore is found in quantities worthy of mention in only one county, at the Silver Hill and Silver Valley mines in Davidson county, where it is also associated with lead and zinc. These deposits are now being operated and the ores reduced at Thomasville.

For nearly a century gold mining in North Carolina has attracted considerable attention, and for the first half of the present century it received as large a share of attention in this as in any other of the States of the Union. Interest was first attracted to the gold deposits of the South Atlantic States by the discovery of the Reed mine, in Cabarrus county, of gold nuggets in 1799, and a few years later (1803) a nugget was discovered in this mine weighing twenty-eight pounds avoirdupois, and for forty years thereafter a large number of nuggets were produced here. Indeed it may be safely said that both as to the size and as to the number of nuggets produced this mine has not been equalled on this side of the continent. The discovery of gold in California nearly fifty years ago took away much of the interest which had centered in the North Carolina gold mines, but nevertheless from that date down to this the gold deposits of the State have received more attention than all other kinds of mining put together. West of a line drawn from Weldon to Hamlet there is not a county in the State in which gold has not been found.

Perhaps the largest amount of attention has been given to the Midland counties, where in Mecklenburg county alone more than 100 mines have been operated.

Gold occurring in the State is generally found in one of the following conditions: (1) In surface gravel deposits along channels of the streams or in the ravines and depressions along slopes of the hills; or (2) distributed through the mass of the rock; or (3) in quartz veins which penetrate the rocks. One of the best illustrations of this first mode of occurrence is illustrated at the Portis mine in the northeast corner of Franklin county. Here no definite veins are to be seen but the surface soil, which in places is a finely divided sandy loam and in other places

is a pebbly gravel; all contains particles of gold and is taken up to a depth of from a few inches to several feet and washed for gold. From this mine alone in this way there has been gathered upwards of a million of dollars worth of gold. At various other points through the Midland counties, as in Montgomery and Stanley and others; in the Piedmont region as in Burke, McDowell, Rutherford and others, and in the mountain counties as in Cherokee, Jackson, Swain, Henderson and others, a large number of such gold bearing gravel deposits are known to exist and many of them have been worked or are being worked at the present time.

Of gold occurring distributed through the mass of the rock, a good illustration may be found at the Russell mine in

HYDRAULIC GOLD MINING IN MONTGOMERY COUNTY, NORTH CAROLINA.

Montgomery county. Here there is no indication of a vein, but the particles of gold are distributed through the talcose and chloritic schists and slates of the section. In other words, the rock itself is gold bearing, and certain seams of the rock, which are richer in gold than the rest, are worked in the mining operations, and the gold to the extent of from $3 to $10 per ton of rock, is thus secured. Many other mines of this character have been or are being operated in the Midland and Piedmont counties of the State. One of the most noted deposits of this central region is that in the Gold Hill District, which lies near the junction of Rowan, Cabarrus and Stanley counties. Veins at this point have been worked to a depth of nearly 800 feet, and for a linear distance of more than 1500 feet, and more than a million dollars' worth of gold has been removed from the mine.

The vein deposits are numerous through the Midland counties of the State, and have been worked to a large extent. The greatest difficulty which stands in the way of working them profitably at the present time is the fact that at a point below water-level these low grade sulphuret ores cannot easily be mined and reduced at a cost low enough to make the operation a profitable one, but by adopting economic methods a number of them are being worked successfully.

From the beginning of the present century down to date it is estimated that more than eleven millions of dollars' worth of gold have been taken from North Carolina mines. With improved mining and metallurgical machinery it is to be hoped that the gold mining in the future in this State will yield equally large results.

THE FORESTS OF NORTH CAROLINA.

By W. W. Ashe,

North Carolina Geological Survey.

For the past hundred years the forests of North Carolina have played an important part as resources of the State. Each new railroad opened a densely forested territory along its line for the lumberman. But so fast have these lands been made accessible that as yet the vast majority of them are still in their native state of sylvan grandeur.

The forests, so far as their distribution is concerned, extend from the very seacoast to the highest mountain, and embrace in abundance a series of the most valuable American trees. Naturally the forests fall in three divisions, more or less clearly marked. The first is the long-leafed pine belt, conforming roughly to the flat, sandy, tertiary formation and lying in the eastern third of the State. The second division extends from the western boundary of that to the foot of the mountains, and is covered by forests of mixed oaks, hickories and yellow pine. Beyond this in the mountains lies the great reserve of valuable hardwoods, walnut, cherry, the valuable oaks, ash, yellow poplar, locust.

In the long-leaf pine belt, the western limit of which extends from the bend the State makes to the southeast near Anson county, northeast to Northampton county, are found four very valuable trees—the long-leaf pine, cypress, white cedar or juniper, and short-leaf or rosemary pine. The long-leaf pine is, however, the most valuable of the region. Its timber is of two different grades—pitch, or very heavy and resinous, and clear, or yellow pine —and is sold from the State as lumber under many different names—Carolina, Southern, yellow long-leaf, Georgia, heart, clear pine. This grade is the great lumber pine. Pitch pine is largely used for naval architecture, and is confined to the counties more adjacent to the ocean, while the clear comes from those farther inland. The counties of Moore, Harnett and Johnston, and parts of Stanley, Montgomery and Chatham have large areas of virgin forest. The fact that boxed turpentine trees have been found to make lumber equally durable to the unboxed, and more capable of standing a transverse strain, has lately brought to market large tracts of abandoned orchards.

The short-leaf pine is found over the whole of the long-leaf pine belt, on wet clayey soil, being very abundant, and the chief lumber tree lying above the Tar river, where it attains a larger size than any of the yellow pines of eastern America, reaching a diameter of five and a-half feet, with a limbless bole eighty to 100 feet long. The chief unworked area of this tree is the neck lying between Tar and Chowan rivers, covering about eight counties. In the northeastern and central part of the State also occur large areas of sap pine, which, when kiln-dried, makes a beautiful lumber for interior work.

The cypress is another tree of great value, found in the deep swamps scattered through the eastern section. It is a large tree with a fine-grained, soft, durable wood. A company sawing in Columbus county put many logs on their carriage which will measure five feet through at the taper. Sixteen maritime counties have two-thirds of the cypress land, which approximates one-half of their area. It is used for shingles and all kinds of exposed wood work, cantilevers, brackets, frets, trimmings and about eaves, balconies, etc. Besides, it is much used for inside work.

White cedar or juniper is scattered in the swamps along with the cypress. The largest cedar swamps are the Green, in Brunswick and Columbus counties, Hyde swamp, Dismal swamp and Holly Shelter swamp. This wood makes the best shingles, pails, tubs and water-tanks.

Another tree of less importance, occurring in this district, is the sweet gum, which often has a diameter of five feet and clear trunk of sixty to seventy feet, and is used for furniture. There are several oaks, which are used extensively for staves—water, willow, laurel, Spanish, swamp white oak and over-cup oak.

Palmetto, used for piles in salt water, as it withstands the attack of the coral worm, occurs in the southeastern part. Red cedar, used for making shingles and posts, occurs over the whole State, but reaches its largest size, a diameter of three to four feet, in the neighborhood of the sea coast.

In the middle district the oaks largely predominate, being mixed in most places with yellow or short-leaf pine. This pine is a tree with fine grain wood and large heart, the same as that which is being shipped from Arkansas as long-leaf pine or yellow pine lumber.

The oaks of this region include a number of red and black oaks, very valuable for woodwork and furniture. White oak and post oak, which make excellent wagon timber and furniture, are very common and reach large size. Black walnut is common along with the oaks, but attains its greatest size in the mountains. There are found in this region four hickories growing abundantly on all kinds of soil and furnishing valuable wagon material. At present there are only eight manufactories of spokes and handles in the State and thirty-two wagon factories.

It is in the mountain counties, where the Appalachian system is most developed, that the valuable hardwoods attain their greatest development, not only reaching their largest size in this State, but in eastern America. There is still much walnut and cherry, especially in the extreme southwestern counties of the State. There are walnut trees still standing which have a diameter of five to six feet and a trunk of fifty to sixty feet. Cherries, with a diameter of four to five feet, are not uncommon. The tulip, or poplar, reaches a diameter of eleven feet and a height of one hundred and fifty feet; the chestnut a diameter of seven feet, and other desiduous trees attain proportionately large sizes on the cool, moist slopes of the mountains and in mountain coves and valleys. For veneering material, curly ash and black walnut are frequent, while the deep coves of most of the high mountains have large quantities of figured yellow birch and maple, both used extensively for veneering and inside finish.

Scattered in belts immediately adjacent to the Blue Ridge are bodies of excellent white pine. The lumber from this pine is the same grade as "No. 2" in the Albany market. The completion of the Charleston, Cincinnati & Chicago Railroad through Mitchell county will in the immediate future throw open 15,000 acres of white pine land lying in the eastern part of that county. So far McDowell county has been the centre of the white pine trade in the State.

Yellow poplar reaches its greatest development in the mountains. Trees containing 4000 feet are frequently cut. There is a church on Hominy creek, Buncombe county, all the woodwork of which came from one poplar tree, which contained over 8000 feet of lumber.

No Southern State has a larger amount of soft wood, suitable for paper manufacture, than this State. In the mountains there is an abundance of linn, the chief material used farther north for making paper, also buckeye and ash.

In the middle and eastern sections there are large areas of three kinds o ash suitable for this use and easily accessible. At present there are three large paper mills in the State, one only using ash entirely and the others a variety o woods. None are making use of linn or buckeye.

Locust is common in the western part of the State, and, besides the local use, it is being turned into insulator pins for telegraph wires. There are three pin factories located in the southwestern counties.

THE TOBACCO INDUSTRY OF NORTH CAROLINA.

By H. E. Harman,

Editor of the *Southern Tobacco Journal.*

 A LEGEND says that in the long ago, before State lines were drawn, an Indian warrior came a-wooing from the land of Pocahontas to what is now the county of Caswell in North Carolina. The father of the maiden whose hand he sought looked with ill-favor upon the young warrior's suit, and for a time the youthful brave despaired of winning the much-coveted prize. He made various presents to the irate father—presents of wampum and hides and arrows—but all to no effect. At last, recites the legend, he brought a hand of tobacco and a pipe. The unpacified chief at first looked upon it with disfavor, but at last was induced to test the weed which the young brave declared to be a solace for every Indian misfortune. The fumes of the comforting smoke soon pacified the irate father, who not only gave away his much worshiped daughter to the young warrior, but ordered that the plant from the land of Pocahontas be grown upon his own domain.

With the legend we have little to do, for it is enough to know that tobacco has brought to the people of North Carolina a degree of comfort in the shape of a paying crop and a remunerative manufacturing industry which no other branch of agriculture has yielded.

At the close of the war, tobacco growing in this State had made but little progress. At that time it was confined to a few counties bordering on the Virginia line, with Caswell as the centre. By degrees the industry spread. The new method of curing by flues, which so greatly increased the value of leaf, made it distinctly a money crop, and planters began to experiment in various sections. Granville county at once became famous for its yellow leaf, and reports went abroad of planters who made from $500 to $600 per acre. Then the new county of Durham became famous for its leaf. The great Piedmont section, with Winston as a centre, next caught up the idea and grew the weed successfully. Next the trans-mountain section around Asheville engaged in the business, and later the eastern counties, centering around Rocky Mount and Wilson, took the tobacco fever, until to-day the weed is grown from Murphy in the west to Greenville in the east, a distance of over 500 miles.

It is difficult to estimate the value of the tobacco crop to the planters of North Carolina. It is no doubt true that few crops have ever yielded a better return to the intelligent farmer. It is an ordinary thing for the planter to make from $150 to $200 per acre, while many instances are on record in which the yield per acre has reached from $400 to $600. Before the bright grades, known as cutters, were controlled by a trust, prices were much higher than they are to-day, but even yet, on the other grades, intelligent tobacco growers find the crop a most profitable one.

The average production of tobacco in the State is now estimated at 70,000,000 pounds per year, and under ordinary circumstances the price will average ten cents per pound. This brings to the growers of the State the round sum of $7,000,000 per year and shows the value of the crop to our planters. No crop is so susceptible to fine cultivation and care as tobacco. Many planters have made snug fortunes growing it, while

YOUNG TOBACCO IN THE FIELD.

others have grown poorer every year. While the average price for the entire product of the State is about ten cents per pound, some planters make their crops bring them twenty cents, while others fall below five cents. This shows that it is the intelligent and careful planter who makes money out of this crop, while the sluggard is generally a loser.

The increase in tobacco growing in grows the finest grade of leaf that is produced anywhere in this country. The bright tobacco of North Carolina has a higher commercial value than the leaf grown in any other State, and our total product sells for more money than that of any other State except Kentucky, which State produces such an enormous quantity of heavy leaf.

But it is not in the mere production of leaf that the tobacco industry has

STREET SCENE IN FRONT OF TOBACCO WAREHOUSE.

this State has been very rapid within the last dozen years. Taking the total increase in tobacco growing in the past thirty years in this country, it amounts to only 21,000,000 pounds, of which North Carolina contributed fully one-fifth. Many States have fallen off in their production from year to year, while North Carolina has gone steadily forward. The main reason for this steady increase in production is accounted for in the fact that this State been of greatest benefit to the State, but in the manufacture of leaf into the commercial article. While the growing of tobacco has made prosperous farm homes all over North Carolina, tobacco manufacture has built prosperous towns and cities. There are in the State to-day nearly 200 factories engaged in the manufacture of tobacco, all of which give profitable employment to a large number of operatives. Winston, Durham, Reidsville, Greensboro, High

Point, Mt. Airy, Kernersville, Salisbury, Statesville, Asheville and a number of other places have felt the quickening influence of the tobacco factory, and have prospered under its spell. The growth of some of these places has been wonderful—due entirely to the tobacco manufacturing business. Take Durham as an example. At the close of the war it was a way station on the railroad. The great smoking tobacco

to operatives thousands of dollars every week, and making the town one of the most prosperous and enterprising in the South. The manufacturers of this one place alone have paid into the national treasury for tobacco stamps within the past six years over $4,000,000.

The reputation of North Carolina plug and smoking tobacco and cigarettes stands very high in all the markets of the world. The plug is produced with

TOBACCO IN BULK IN FACTORY.

business started up, and afterward the cigarette industry. Operatives for these factories flocked to Durham, and to-day it is one of the hustling cities of the New South, with prosperous homes and a population of 10,000 people. Winston, in 1870, was a mere village with no factories of any importance. The plug tobacco manufacturing business began to take root and grew with amazing rapidity. To-day over thirty plug tobacco factories are at work, paying out

a smaller percentage of licorice and other adulterants than that made from Western leaf, and hence is purer. The leaf will not absorb sweetening and the plug comes nearer being natural leaf than that produced elsewhere. For smoking tobacco the factories of the State have an opportunity of selecting the best stock, which grows to perfection here. Not only this, but factories outside of the State send here for much of their stock. As for cigarette tobacco,

North Carolina produces 90 per cent. of this desirable type.

North Carolina's soil is especially adapted to the growing of the bright types of tobacco, a quality of soil which no other State possesses to such an extent as this. These bright tobaccos are found growing upon the mountain sides of Haywood and Buncombe counties with as much of a native feeling as upon the soil of Granville or Durham counties, where the golden leaf tobacco first won its reputation. To North Carolina many of the largest factories of the country look for their supplies of leaf. The great cigarette factories of Richmond, New York and Rochester buy practically all of their stock in this State. The large factories of the Northwest, which make a specialty of fine and long-cut tobaccos, get their choicest stock here; while the immense establishments in the West, which put up the bulk of navy goods, come here to buy wrappers for a large part of their product. And not only this, but the English trade has of late years learned that it gets its finest leaf from the Carolina fields, although, as yet, North Carolina gets little credit in foreign quotations for the fine tobacco produced in the State.

The tobacco trade of the State has a strong organization which looks after matters of general interest. It is known as the North Carolina State Tobacco Association, and was organized six years ago. It meets every summer, generally at Morehead City, and has done very much to bring before the world the high quality of North Carolina tobacco. There are over twenty separate tobacco boards of trade in the State, and these are usually represented by a number of delegates to the general meeting. Taking the State as a whole, it has no equal in the organization of its tobacco interests. No other State in the Union maintains a separate tobacco organization similar to the one here.

As noted in the outset of this paper, tobacco has done more toward building up the industrial interests of the State than any other product. It is the only industry in North Carolina which has produced millionaires and made so many poor young men independent in a few years. Tobacco manufacturing has been and still is quite profitable, owing largely to the fine quality of leaf produced. It is time that the geographies discard the old tar and pitch picture as a symbol of the State's industries and adopt instead a leaf of her gold producing tobacco.

THE UNIVERSITY OF NORTH CAROLINA.

This institution is in many respects one of the most interesting in the Union. It is one of the few whose history dates from the Revolution; one of the few which has turned out a president of the United States and a vice-president; one of the few which had over 450 students prior to 1861, and it was the only Southern State college which kept its doors open during the Civil War. The members of the faculty were at their posts when Kilpatrick's calvary rode into Chapel Hill, in April, 1865, its commanding officer, Brigadier-General S. D. Atkins, being himself soon a captive to the winsome daughter of President Swain, whom he carried off as a bride to his home in Illinois.

Its foundation-stone is in the State Constitution of 1776. Its charter was granted within a month of the adoption of the Federal Constitution. Its fathers were those strong men who secured that adoption. Its doors were opened for students in 1795, and soon 100 young men were gathered within its walls.

Up to 1861 the University had a distinguished career. Its first president, Rev. Joseph Caldwell, D.D., of New Jersey, was not only a strong executive officer, but a man of learning and progressive ideas. He built at Chapel Hill, prior to 1832, the first astronomical observatory connected with institutions of learning in the Union. He was one of the earliest advocates of public schools in North Carolina. He was a warm and successful promoter of the railroad system. He impressed himself strongly on his students, who were among the chief leaders in public and private life throughout the Southern States.

President David L. Swain, who had been a governor and a judge, succeeded him in 1836. Under his administration the number of matriculates reached 461, thus placing the institution, in point of numbers, near the top of United States universities. Yale gave him the degree of LL.D. in recognition of his eminent ability and success. He was a man of great executive power and *bonhommie*. He knew how to do the right thing at the right time. In 1865 he visited General Sherman in his military headquarters in order to obtain protection for the capitol and the University buildings. Sherman was so charmed with Swain

MEMORIAL HALL, UNIVERSITY OF NORTH CAROLINA.

that he made him the gift of a valuable horse to enable him to return home.

We can only mention a few of the professors of this University. Denison Olmstead, afterwards of Yale, and Elisha

170

Mitchell, a graduate of the same institution, were two of the most eminent. Mitchell fell a martyr to science while exploring the highest peak east of the Rockies, afterwards named in his honor.

SMITH HALL, LIBRARY, UNIVERSITY OF NORTH CAROLINA.

He conducted the first State geological survey in the Union, that of North Carolina. E. A. Andrews left the University and became in New England an eminent teacher of schools and writer of classical text-books. Wm. M. Green and James H. Otey became bishops of Mississippi and Tennessee, respectively. Charles F. Deems is now the eloquent pastor of the Church of the Strangers, in New York city, and author of many highly esteemed religious works. He has recently established at the institution of his early labors a most beneficent fund, to which the late Mr. W. H. Vanderbilt made a handsome contribution. This fund (about $16,000) is peculiar in this, that the principal is loaned in small sums on good security to needy and deserving students.

The insolvency of banks and individuals by reason of the Civil War destroyed the endowment of this University. It was reorganized in 1868 under the Reconstruction Acts of Congress, the old faculty being replaced by new, but the experiment was most unsuccessful, and its doors were closed in 1870. In 1875 they were reopened under a new government. Hon. Kemp P. Battle, once treasurer of North Carolina, was placed at its head. His eminent virtues, talents, learning, public experience, business talents and knowledge of

men raised the University to life. State aid and considerable endowments were procured, an excellent faculty of twelve professors and five instructors was secured, representing the culture of Harvard, Yale, Cornell, Universities of North Carolina and Virginia, of Gottingen, Bonn, Berlin and Paris, the most approved methods of instruction introduced, and the institution started on a noble career of expanding usefulness.

In 1891 President Battle resigned in order to accept the recently endowed chair of history, and George T. Winston, a member of the faculty, who had become eminent for his literary, educating and executive powers, was chosen unanimously to succeed him. Three hundred and twenty students are now in attendance, being a notable increase over the preceding year. The chair of political and social science has been created especially for President Winston.

While the instruction of the University of North Carolina is of a high order, the moral and religious influences are of the best, and the conduct of the students is wonderfully good. Intoxicating liquors are prohibited by law from being sold within four miles of the corporate limits of Chapel Hill, nor are students allowed to use them in any way, at their fraternity banquets or otherwise. All gymnastic exercises and games are encouraged, and visitors are surprised at the universal sobriety, good conduct and cheerfulness prevailing. Not only is hazing prohibited by law, but the students themselves have unanimously resolved to have none of it at Chapel Hill.

The influence of the University on North Carolina and the South generally can be seen from the fact that it counts among its alumni a president (Polk), a vice-president (King), an attorney-general (Mason), a solicitor-general (Phillips), fourteen United States Senators

(Benton, of Missouri; King, of Alabama; Eaton and Nicholson, of Tennessee; and of North Carolina, Branch, Mangum, Brown, Haywood, Graham, Bragg, Clingman, Ransom and Vance), six United States Cabinet officers (Branch, Graham, Dobbin, Thompson, of Mississippi; Brown, of Tennessee, and Mason, of Virginia), seven foreign ministers, twenty governors of States, sixteen State supreme court judges, besides numberless representatives in Congress, superior court judges, eminent divines, presidents and professors of colleges, successful merchants, farmers, manufacturers, and, in fact, the leaders of the people in all pursuits. At this time the two Senators from North Carolina (Ransom and Vance), five members of the house (Branch, Grady, Henderson, Alexander and Crawford), the governor of the State (Carr), the speaker of the house (Doughton), the president of the University (Winston), three out of the five supreme court judges (Avery, Shepherd and Clarke), the director of the State Agricultural Experiment Station (Battle), the president of the State Female Normal College (McIver), the president of the State Agricultural Society (Battle), the president of the longest railroad (Elliott), the president of the Farmers' Alliance (Butler), the owners of the largest factories in the State (Fries, Holt, Morehead), are all alumni of the University.

One of the most unique and beautiful college buildings in the Union is the memorial hall of the University, erected to the memory of its distinguished alumni. It was designed by Samuel Sloan, of Philadelphia, and is a grand auditorium, 130 feet long and 120 feet broad, without a column or pillar to mar the effect. On its walls are marble tablets, commemorating the great men and the benefactors of the University.

The University of North Carolina is doing a very large charitable work. At least one-half its students are either partially or totally self-sustaining. Economy is the fashion. Students have been known to obtain a year's education on the expenditure of only $100. Humble farmers are pushing their sons up to a higher plane. The University roll is full of obscure names, now taking their place among the names of the old rulers of the State and of society. These boys know how to submit to sacrifices, and many of them are at the head of their classes, are presidents of the literary societies, leaders of the football and other athletic teams, and of the Young Men's Christian Association. Pathetic stories could be told illustrative of the pluck of some of these sturdy fellows. An artist, whose work is bringing him into distinction, trudged on foot most of the way to Chapel Hill, sleeping under

SOUTH BUILDING UNIVERSITY OF NORTH CAROLINA.

trees, and paying five cents each for supper and breakfast in the shape of crackers and cheese, with only $3.50 in his pocket and one change, not of linen, but of homespun cotton. An honored teacher, superintendent of public instruction of Rutherford county, with one of his arms withered from infancy, all his fortune being $100, made by hard work, had the courage to go to the University and trust to his high purpose and to Providence. These, and scores of others like them, attained their object. God, through His large-hearted servants on earth, helps those who help themselves.

The University of North Carolina is situated at Chapel Hill. The name is most appropriate. This eminence, on which was located an old ante-Revolutionary chapel of the Church of England,

descriptions of North Carolina and of its University in the American supplement to the Encyclopedia Britannica, visited Chapel Hill, and was so struck with its advantages that he has bought valuable lots in the village. He has recently built a hotel designed for the comfort of those who must leave their homes for health in the summer, as well as of those seeking for a winter resort.

The University is rapidly expanding and growing. It aims to be the great Southern University. Its technical and professional schools are attracting students

OLD EAST BUILDING, UNIVERSITY OF NORTH CAROLINA.

land, is 250 feet above the basin to the east, which was once the bottom of an arm of the ocean, stretching from Staten island to Georgia. It is 500 feet above the sea. The rock which forms the eminence is of the Laurentian system. The spring and well waters are so pure that they can be used in the chemical laboratory for most purposes without filtration. The healthiness of the place is not surpassed by any in the Union. A New York lawyer, W. G. Peckham, in search of good climatic conditions for his winter's rest, attracted by the

from distant States. Its academic schools maintain students that are recognized everywhere as meritorious and elevated. It is in contact with and in sympathy with the life of the great people. It educates scholars and thinkers and scientists, but its chief purpose is to educate men of character, who will be useful to humanity. This spirit pervades the institution, and gives to its students an enthusiasm and a power that makes them succeed in life, whatever be their sphere.

NEW WEST BUILDING, UNIVERSITY OF NORTH CAROLINA.

SOCIAL AND INDUSTRIAL CONDITIONS IN ARKANSAS.

By Hon. W. M. Fishback,

Governor of Arkansas.

Under the genial and health-giving climate of our State, and in the face of almost every species of political obstacle, there has grown up in Arkansas a religious and social condition not inferior to that of any State in the Union.

We have in Arkansas some 3500 churches, or one to every 322 inhabitants, over one-half of which have been erected within the past ten years. Ten years ago the Methodist Episcopal Church, South, had about 525 churches, valued at nearly 300,000, and ninety-six parsonages valued at $45,000. Now they have 1033 churches and 195 parsonages, valued in the aggregate at about $1,000,-000; and during the same decade they have erected educational buildings valued at about $200,000. The colored Methodists have 173 churches and 27,956 members. Their church property is valued at $233,425. The Baptist denomination is conceded to be the largest in the State, having 1772 churches and 99,490 members. The colored Baptists have 558 churches and 37,405 members, but I have no other statistics concerning them. We have in all twenty-nine denominations.

Our educational advancement within the past ten years has been at an almost unparalleled pace. The school enrollment of our youth has increased at a rate of percentage from two to fifty times as great as that of any State admitted into the Union at the time of or prior to the time of our own admission. We have 3000 school-houses, or one to every 375 inhabitants, 1547 of which have been erected within the past ten years. We have one college or seminary for every 22,000 inhabitants,

over two-thirds of which have been erected within the past decade. A State University and three normal schools afford free education of a higher order. Two-fifths of our State tax and one-half of our county taxes support our public schools. We have in the negro districts about 900 separate schools for the colored people. Several of their school-houses cost from $10,000 to $20,000 each. They also have several colleges and the State supports one normal school for colored teachers.

About two years ago Hon. F. P. Laws opened, at his own expense, in the village of Bebee, a free daily Bible school, which has constantly grown in interest until it now has a membership of 235 and an average daily attendance of thirty-five. I know of no other such institution in the world. The good it is accomplishing should awaken general interest and general inquiry throughout Christendom. While within the past thirteen years the South has expended $216,000,000 in the free education of the youths of our section, in Arkansas alone we have expended during the same period $10,200,000, with an average of 350,000 children.

It were enough, perhaps, to say of our system of laws that two years ago the Congress, controlled by a political party not in sympathy with the majority of our people, selected from the statutes of Arkansas the entire body of laws by which one of the territories of the Union is governed. I am very much in doubt if there is a community in the world of equal population where the laws are more generally enforced and obeyed than in this State. The carrying of concealed weapons in Arkansas is a crime, and the officers of the law are themselves liable to prosecution if they fail to prosecute offenders against this statute.

Our temperance laws are said by competent judges to be in advance of those of any other State because, being the result of evolution, growing by degrees and taking hold of one community at a time, as public sentiment in that community is educated up to an appreciation of their importance, the laws upon this subject are easily and completely enforced. In every county the people vote at each biennial election for or against license, and even when the counties vote for license a majority of the male and female adults in any neighborhood may vote it away from within three miles of any church or school-house by petition to the county authorities. Under this process of evolution, and with the aid of female votes or petitions, we have gradually driven license out of some thirty-five of the seventy-five counties, and away from more than 2000 churches and school-houses.

Animated by such religious surroundings, enlightened by such educational facilities, and protected by such a system of laws, our people enjoy exceptional safety, both of life and property.

The colored race is found in numbers only in about a third of the State. The race problem is here no longer a problem. Matters have adjusted themselves in accordance with common sense. The Australian ballot has eliminated all danger from ignorance and the free public school system is fast educating the negro in the duties of citizenship. The Christian doctrine of the universal brotherhood of man has thrown around him the mantle of protection in all his rights, both as a man and as a citizen. He stands before our law the equal of all other men. Yet he has at last accepted the doctrine that the white man ought and will rule this country.

Our climate is proverbially genial and healthy in the greater part of the State. Our death rate is much smaller than in most of the Northern States, while our birth rate is nearly double that of most of our sister States of the North. The climate of Arkansas is so favorable to both animal and vegetable life that the census of 1880 (I have had no access to that of 1890 yet) shows the money value per acre of her farm products to be greater than that of any other State in the Union except Louisiana. In one portion of the State apples attain a perfection that has not yet been found anywhere else in the United States. They have excelled wherever displayed in competition.

A commissioner sent out by the Patent Office in 1859 reported to the Government that Arkansas is so well adapted to the culture of the grape that the rocky hill-sides of the State, if planted to the vine, would prove more valuable than our best cotton lands. He said also that wine made from one species of our native grapes had been taken to Europe and pronounced equal to the best foreign wines.

There will be on exhibition from Arkansas at Chicago soon a chunk of crystallized carbonate of zinc ore, having only about 10 per cent. of waste matter, weighing seven tons. It was, together with another similar chunk weighing 64,000 pounds or thirty-two tons, broken from a boulder upon the hillside, which has been cleared off until there has been exposed a surface block of 13,000,000 pounds, or 65,000 tons.

We have, according to recent geological survey, a distribution of 216 square miles of zinc ore, and overlying it and all around it we have 2199 square miles of marble, the same as Tennessee marbles.

We have 2347 square miles of coal. Ten years ago we mined only about 5000 tons of coal; in 1889 only 279,000 tons from twenty-seven mines. We have now in operation seventy-eight mines and the output is variously estimated from 750,000 to 1,250,000 tons annually.

We have thirteen square miles of granite; 305 square miles of novaculite or whetstone rock—famous all over the world; 126 square miles of manganese, not including ores of lower grade; 7300 square miles of limestone, available for lime and building stone; 1296 square miles of pottery clays; 2140 square miles of clays suitable for vitrified brick, and 612 square miles of clay for pressed brick of the highest grade. We have also alum shales, the outcrop of which is 375 miles in length. We have 200 acres of chalk, available for the manufacture of highest grade of Portland cement. We have 640 acres of beauxite or aluminum ore. And but the other day we discovered large deposits of red and yellow ochre. We have also inexhaustible beds of gypsum and marl. We have the largest hardwood trees yet discovered in the world.

LIZ; A CHARACTER SKETCH.

By Alice MacGowan.

Liz's paternal home was across the river from town, on Stringer's Ridge; but when I had the pleasure of making her acquaintance she was "staying with" Rachel on the street just below our house.

This "staying with" is a characteristic institution among the southern darkies; the hut is never so small or the inmates so numerous but there is room for one more.

You need not trouble yourself to threaten your worthless cook or handmaiden with discharge. It has no terrors for her, though she have not a relative in the world nor a cent in her pocket. She will simply go and "stay with" Sairy, or Mandy, or Unk' Jube, till another place hunts her up, or till the party upon whom she has billeted herself shows signs of restiveness.

Liz, however, was not thus destitute of home and belongings. Though her mother was dead, she had a father Uncle Josh Bivens, an ordinary sort of person in whom there was no observable trace of the talents with which we afterward found his offspring so plentifully endowed. But Uncle Josh had taken the liberty of providing Liz with a stepmother, which provision, though probably made with the best intentions, failed to meet with her approval.

It was found after a short and rapid trial that they could not agree, so Liz as she afterward informed us, "took her foot in her hand an' came over to Rachel's." She further said that she had "seed Rachel afore"—this in reply to an inquiry as to whether she was a relative of the latter.

The summer was unmercifully hot, the work dragged, and we told Rachel that we wanted a girl of twelve or fourteen to wash dishes and run errands. The day after we spoke to her about it Uncle Josh Bivens came in town, and later appeared at the house bringing Liz.

The first view of her, while not exactly engaging, was not discouraging. She was of stout squat figure, and looked bright.

She was what the negroes call a "regular Guinea"—small, active, black, with an ebon, dusky blackness that suggested the action of time, wind and weather on her features. She had a pert, apish countenance, with lips that were not thick, but were thrust out to an astonishing degree, forming a sort of shelf on the lower part of her face. In short, she was a typical African on the Guinea model, and would have seemed most at home in a tribe, with a waist-fringe for costume, a basket of mealies on her head, and a group of bee-hive-shaped huts for background; and had you met her while out walking some fine morning in Africa, you would have taken her for no less than a member in good standing of the Hooey-ooey tribe.

Her appearance was not deceitful—it was the only thing about her, we subsequently found, which was not. She was a queer, furtive, woodsy creature, about as comfortable in her clothes, though they were few and not at all confining, as some wild thing, a squirrel or a coon, snared and dressed up.

But she was clean; she had a certain bluff willingness and capability about her; my need was great, and so I took her. I thought sometimes afterwards it would have been better if the Hooey-ooeys had had her—they might have. understood her better.

Before Uncle Josh left her with me he "drawed her up in line" and lectured her exhaustively upon the duties, privileges and obligations of her new position, and I had a comfortable feeling when he closed his lengthened exhortation, that his council, instructions, warnings and threats certainly covered every imaginable exigency in her future career and left nothing of responsibility on my shoulders. I did not know then so well as I did later how much she resembled a Texas pony, having all the hardy, tireless endurance and ready ability to take care of herself of those little animals, and more than a little of their startling unreliability.

I found after she had been with me a short time, that most of the darkies in my neighborhood called her "Crazy Ca'lline." The adjective was a tribute to her peculiar talent and the extravagances into which it led her, the difference of name being a thing not uncommon among the darkies, who frequently have three or four names by which they are called, indifferently.

We soon found that, while we had hired her for more prosaic duties, Liz was an improvisatrice of unlimited range and ability—in fact, a dusky female Haggard, whose limber imagination scorned the realistic and sprang boldly into the empyrean of the impossible. Her inventions were of two kinds. The first seemed, like the impulse of the bird to sing or the plant to bloom, merely the spontaneous outgushing of a redundant power. The second was brought into use when she had reason to expect reproof; and like the flutterings of the mother partridge on pretendedly broken wing to allure you from her concealed nestlings, was intended, by a startling display of fancy, to divert your attention from some offending fact.

"Lizzie," I asked her, "how was it that you couldn't get along with your stepmother? Rachel tells me she is a good woman."

A mumble at the latter part of this remark, and then, "Mebby she is, mebby she is a good 'ooman; but her 'n me caynt live en one house. Daddy brung her oveh dah to boss me, 'n' 'bout de fus wu'd she gun me I levelled her wid

de skillet. 'Deed I did," in answer to my incredulous look. "I flattened heh. I lef' den; Ise 'fraid daddy'd git me, 'n' I run out 'n' clum up en de 'simmon tree. Stayed up dere two days—yaas."

"Why, Lizzie, you never went without eating two days, I know."

"No, I didn'; Daddy come out 'n' thowed up some braid t' me."

A few days after this conversation I saw Liz's stepmother, Aunt Clarissy. She came to peddle some buttermilk and vegetables. I found her a small yellow woman, dressed in second hand finery, with a smooth, insinuating voice and manner, and a fondness for big words, which she misused with unfailing accuracy—a sort of old-gold Mrs. Malaprop.

As soon as I saw her and heard her placid, oily tones my faith (if I had had any) in Liz's version of their differences was entirely destroyed; for, despite her small size and soft voice, she didn't look like a person who would lend herself readily to the flattening process described.

She told me she believed Liz was a "well exposed girl," (with which opinion I could see no reason to differ) but it took a "right smart hoopin'" to keep her down.

"She's right indiffe'nt now to what she was when I took hol' o' her," she added. "I made heh right smaht o' clo'es too; but she's allus a projickin' an' a raarin' 'roun' tell she t'ahs ev'rything of heh back; that's what's p'oduced heh down so."

My impression of the relative positions of the two was confirmed when Liz presently came in.

"How you come on, Liz?" said Aunt Clarissy, quite civilly; then suddenly and fiercely—"Don' you blow yo'se'f out an' commence a-lyin' to me," as Liz took the usual long breath and settled back on her heels to reply. And the girl, instead of resenting such language, answered meekly and briefly and drifted out of the room as unostentatiously as possible.

"I tell you, Mis'," said Aunt Clarissy, looking after her, "if all the good advice I'se gun that gal wuz writ out 'twould fill a bah'l, 'twould so! An' I do think she's doin' some betteh; look like the evil spe'it sort entehin' out o' heh."

II.

Liz had lived some time before she came to me with a family across the river near her home. We had every reason to suppose them quiet, respectable members of society, but some of her recitals in regard to them sounded like chronicles of domestic life among the noble redmen.

The grandmother of the family, who had taken on much flesh along with the dignity of advancing years, seemed, according to her account, to have been an intimate and gamesome playmate.

"Time de chimbly cotch afi," said Liz, "I's setting' top de gate pos', 'n ole Mis' come a-rackin' thoo a-hollerin' fi' ; 'n' I sez, 'Ol'. fatty ! ol' fatty ! Run, ol' fatty !' "

"You would'nt dare to say any such thing," said I.

"Well, I thunk it, anyway," she answered, making the only abatement I ever knew her to make in any of her narratives.

In this same family were two daughters, upon whose beaux, accomplishments and achievements, she frequently held forth. The elder and smaller of the two, Miss Norma, seemed to be her favorite.

"Miss Narmer know a heap," she used to say, "'n' she c'n jes' play de pe-anner fit to bus' hit. She got a song w'at she sings dat's made up 'bout heh, 'Yer me Narmer,' hit say. 'Yer me Narmer.' 'N' she's little; but she c'n hoop."

"Whip who, Lizzie ?" I asked.

"W'y, heh sisteh. Dey fouts all de time."

Here I demurred. "You musn't say such things as that, Lizzie; you know it's not true."

" 'Deed hit is true," she asseverated, "'n' Miss Narmer ain' got no call· t' keer fer me a teellin' hit, for she c'n hoop. Dey fouts 'n' pulls ha'r. Dey fouts at de table, 'n' breck de dishes ; 'n' dey fouts 'n' de baid ; and dey fouts all over house; 'n' Miss Narmer hoop all de time—she mos' got all Miss Ellen ha'r pull out—fouts 'bout dey beaux, too."

It was of no use to remonstrate with her about telling tales of this character. Indeed, it only made matters worse, for she would repeat what she had said over and over and over, like nothing so much as a chattering monkey, and I soon learned to disregard her talk entirely, though I did sometimes wonder what remarkable characteristics she would endow us with, when she went away and we passed into the Gotterdam-merung in which all her past associates met and wrestled daily.

We bought all our groceries from a man named O'Brien. He was known in Liz's vocabulary as "ol' Brine," and she addressed him as Mr. Brine.

One morning "de Cunnel," as she called the head of the house, was asked to make a number of small household purchases at O'Brien's on his way down to his office, and Liz was sent with a basket to trot along after him and bring them home. She got back some time near noon, and in response to my indignant, "Where have you been all this time," she drew a good breath, and, standing first on one foot and then on the other, and looking sideways at me to catch the first signs of mollification on my face, she began one of her amazing improvisations.

" 'Deed I wan' t' git back. I knowed you need them things ; but ol' Brine, he sayed, soon's Cunnel come in, 'W'y, Cunnel ! Ise proud ter see yeh. I hain' seed yeh sence Polk's time !' 'N' him and Cunnel dey talk, en dey talk. 'N' den he say, 'Cunnel we ain' had a good sing toge'r fer a long w'le.' 'N' he git out books—singin' books—'n' him 'n' Cunnel dey sing, en dey sing. 'N' a heap o' folks come in t' trade, 'n' ol' Brine tole 'em, 'Go 'way, go 'way! Me 'n' Cunnel's havin' a reg'lar ol' fashion sing toge'r.' 'N' heap o' chillen come in 'n' wanted chawin' gum, 'n' sich; 'n' he jis say, 'Go 'way ! quit yo' talkin'—cain' y' see me 'n' Cunnel's a-singin' ? I don't want my store all n'ised up.' 'N' dey ain' quit tell 'bout a minnit ergo ; 'n' I got my things 'n' cut for home."

Now, when I tell you that "de Cunnel" was a middle-aged gentleman, with a very dignified manner, and only so much acquainted with the busy grocer as one may be with a man from whom one makes daily purchases, you will understand why I was laughing long before Liz had put the finishing touches to her report.

When she saw these signs of returning good humor she pulled up her Pegasus in full flight, showed a row of ivory, and quietly turned to. build the fire, concluding, as usual, that I might "ast de Cunnel" if it wasn't all just so.

This I did not fail to do; and for a long time his duets with "ol' Brine" were a standing family joke.

When the circus came to town Liz was "neither to hand nor to bind." If, in the language of the song, we had "set a thousand guards upon her," I think she would have "leveled" them all, and held a straight path over them to that goal of all her hopes.

She could not be spared in the afternoon, and I seriously doubted the wisdom of letting her go at night; however, as all Rachel's folks would be going, too, I thought she might be trusted with them.

Ten o'clock came, that night, and no Liz. Eleven, and she had not returned. At half-past eleven I went down to Rachel's, to find them all in bed and asleep; and at two Liz herself came in, weary but triumphant. I was exasperated beyond measure. "Liz," I said, "where have you been?"

"To de succus," she responded, briskly; "but I come home 'fore 'twuz oveh. I got so ti'ed 'n' sleepy I couldn' stan' hit no mo', nohow."

This brazen effrontery staggered me. "What shall I do with you" said I, speaking as solemnly as anyone could when looking at Liz. "You know the circus was out hours ago—at 10 o'clock, or a little after."

"'Deed hit wuzn't; 'n' hit ain't thoo yit. Dey quit a-kickin' up dey heels a right smaht wile ergo, but dey jis taken down de tents wen I come erway, an' dey's lots o' hit out on de flat now."

It was plain that she felt she had sacrificed much of the show to which she was legally entitled, by coming home before she had seen the last straggler outside the corporate limits. I was too weary and exasperated to press the matter, but merely said with sleepy severity

that I should send her home to-morrow, and went to bed.

In the morning, after her work was done, Liz came in with her shoes on and her belongings in a bundle.

"What's that for?" I inquired.

"I thought you's goin' t' sen' me home—y'sayed y'wuz."

My threat of the night before came back to me, and the thought of the circumstances under which it was made brought a covert smile.

Liz, as quick to read a face as an intelligent dog, sat down on the floor and began taking off her shoes, all the while watching me furtively to see if I relapsed into severity or raised any objections to her remaining.

I thought necessary to attempt some sort of reproof, so I said: "And what will you do if I send you home, Lizzie? Will you behave yourself there?"

"I dunno," she answered, gloomily. "I 'specs I'll lay out dat ol' 'ooman 'bout de fust wu'd she guvs me—I thinks I's behave mighty nice here."

The conclusion of this remark caused me to laugh outright; so Liz considered the matter settled; and, gathering up her shoes and bundle, she carried them into her own room, nor was the question of her departure again raised till, with the introduction of several new members into my household, I needed more efficient help in her place, and let her go, thinking in spite of all her faults, that I "could have better spared a better man."

I saw Liz the other day, and she had a bit of a black baby on her arm.

"Why, Lizzie, whose child is that?" I asked.

"Mine," she answered promptly. "Hits paw ain' no 'count. He's done lef' me. Say he ain' gwine live wid no sich fly-up-de-crick—ma'y or no ma'y. But I gwine to fotch hit up right"—and indeed the little thing did look clean and well cared for, as it lay blinking on its mother's shoulder.

The idea of Liz "fotchin' up" anything right seemed irresistibly funny; though I've no doubt the monkey mothers that we watch through the bars fondling their wrinkled babies think

they are bringing them up irreproach-
ably.

I asked her how she was training it
just now.

"O, I hoops hit," she said, an assertion which was flatly disproved by her
look of fond pride at its small, aged-
looking visage. "I hoops it good; 'y
mus' 'y know. Dat w'at ail me—I
didn't git 'nough w'en I's little.—From
the New Orleans *Times-Democrat.*

THE SOUTHERN OUTLOOK.

The Governors' Immigration Proclamation.

The full text of the immigration proclamation which was issued by the convention of Southern Governors in Richmond, April 14, is as follows:

The States represented at this convention comprise substantially the Southern half of the American republic. The territorial area of these States is 875,720 square miles. The population as shown by the census of 1890 is 22,279,670.

Its eastern and southern exterior limits are bounded by the Atlantic ocean and Gulf of Mexico. The interior is traversed by many of the most important rivers on the continent and by some of the greatest in the world. The surface is diversified by mountain chains and beautiful valleys, by long stretches of fertile bottom lands and broad expanses of picturesque and productive prairies. The climate is temperate, changing more or less with the seasons, and is pleasant, invigorating and healthful. The resources of this vast area are distributed with wonderful and surprising equality, and its adaptation to natural and to industrial productions is almost limitless.

Minerals.—All, or nearly all, these States have inexhaustible deposits of coal, mostly bituminous, which can be mined less expensively, perhaps, than elsewhere in the world. In every section of the area embraced by these States are enormous and immeasurable supplies of iron, lead, zinc and other metals useful in the industrial arts. Multiplied thousands are already engaged in mining and reducing these metals. The value of these mines and mineral deposits have already long since passed the period of experimentation, and yet they are in the very infancy of their development.

Forestry.—Scattered throughout these States are also great areas of forest lands, on which are growing in super-abundance as fine timber as can be found in the world—cypress, oak, walnut, ash, maple, pine and the like—fit in the highest degree for ship-building, house-building, and for all the uses of manufacturing.

Agriculture.—The soil and climate unite to give these States unsurpassed adaptation and capacity for the productions of agriculture. Tobacco, cotton, sugar, Indian corn, wheat, rye, barley, oats—all the cereals—are grown here in profuse abundance. Nowhere in the world does the earth yield a more prompt, certain and abundant return to the vitalizing touch of the husbandman than in these Commonwealths.

Horticulture.—As much may be said likewise, of horticulture. Nowhere can richer or sweeter fruits—such as oranges, bananas, apples, peaches, plums, grapes, berries—be grown in greater profusion. Already are to be found here very many of the most extensive and profitable orchards, vineyards and gardens on the globe.

Such in brief are the climatic and topographical conditions, and such the natural and productive advantages of these great States of the South and Southwest. Hitherto immigration and capital have flowed towards the Western and Northwestern States. This was due, no doubt, largely to the fact that those were new States, where immigrants could find free homes by right of settlement on the public lands of the United States, and due partly, it may be, to the fact that most of the States represented in this convention were the theatre of war during the struggle between the States, and were interrupted in their progress by the somewhat turbulent conditions immediately following the cessation of hostilities, incident to the so-called period of reconstruction. But happily all these disadvantages are now at an end. The desirable public lands of the Northwest are practically absorbed; they have been taken up. Long since the old disturbing forces that prevailed in the South and menaced its well-being have disappeared. It has begun a new era of progress and prosperity. The tide of immigration has been directed Southward, and is pouring in upon us in a steady and an augmenting stream. Peace is smiling every-where, and is striving to win her victories no less renowned than those of war. At this auspicious period in Southern history the Gov-ernors of the States here represented have met to give the world assurance of their profound gratification that this new and brighter day has dawned upon their States, and, if possible, to accelerate the movement which is now so soon to develop the wonderful resources and wealth of the Southern States. They are anxious to have immigrants to settle among them; they are anxious to have capital make investments and develop enterprises. To the worthy immigrant they extend the hand of welcome, with the assurance that he will find an educated, warm-hearted, hospitable, pro-gressive people, among whom he can live in amity and peace, without regard to his religion, his politics or his nativity. Churches and school-houses are everywhere, and although these facilities for worship and education are already established upon a most liberal scale, they are constantly and rapidly increasing. The social, moral and religious life of the people of these States is upon a high plane.

To the capitalist these States offer special inducements for investments. The laws are favorable to the investor, and public order and private right are firmly upheld and maintained. Nowhere in the world are there such golden opportunities for investment in mining and manufacturing enterprises. Fuel, water, wood, metal, cane, cotton, tobacco, hemp, flax—all here together—one waiting to serve the other, almost without the cost of transportation. The South is bounding forward now. It is the field in which the immediate future will unfold the most marvellous development of the century. Here new homes are to grow, like spring flowers coming up out of the " winter of our discon-tent," and are to multiply with increasing rapidity as the years go by. Here capital is to find its most tempting and profitable field for investment. The Governors of the States named, in behalf of their several constituen-cies, extend a cordial and pressing invitation to home-seekers—farmer, mechanic, miner, workman—to come and cast their for unes with the South; as they do also a similar invi-tation to capitalists, whether in the United States or elsewhere, to examine our resources and to aid us in their development, to the end that they may participate in our prosperity.

A Plan for Stimulating Southern Immi-gration.

The general interpretation of the word im-migration does not convey the real significance of the present immigration agitation in the South. The present efforts are not designed to stimulate a southward movement of cheap foreign labor, but to secure a much larger in-flux of home-seekers. The South does not need more or ch aper laborers of the unskilled classes, for this element in our industrial economy already exists in abundance and at a cost that meets all present requirements. Furthermore, the introduction into the South of the cheap foreign-born labor which now exists in such large volume in the North would create another troublesome problem in the difficulty of effecting an affiliation of the col-ored race and the foreign-born laborer. From nearly every point of view extensive immigra-tion of mere day laborers is not desirable for the South.

The present need of the South is for small capitalists, industrious, frugal and intelligent men, possessed of moderate means and pre-pared to become citizens, owners of their homes and integral parts of our industrial, social and political economy. Such men add to the wealth and prosperity of any section, and constitute the most desirable factors in the development of any country.

Admitting this, the question resolves itself into one of ways and means by which such im-migrants can be brought into the South in greater numbers than heretofore. Leaving out of consideration what may be accom-plished among the present population of the North and West, and disregarding also the temporary opportunities that are presented in connection with the World's Fair this sum-mer, the most practical plan appears to be one involving work in those foreign centres from which the South must expect to draw its de-sirable immigrants. Efforts directed towards diverting immigrants southward after their ar-rival in this country are simply a waste of time, energy and money which can be made immensely productive when used in other directions. Most of the desirable immigrants come to this country with through tickets to destinations chosen before starting, and it is impracticable to change their plans. The only aimless immigrants are those whose means are sufficient only to pay their steamship passage. They are chiefly unskilled laborers of the lowest order, and they settle in the Eastern States, where they find employment in the mines, upon public works and about large manufacturing establishments, where cheapness of labor is the only consideration and skill is not a requirement.

To carry out the plan that seems to promise the largest and most satisfactory results it is necessary to have the co-operation of three factors, which are these : First, the joint efforts of all the Southern States that care to participate in the work ; second, the steamship companies, and third, the railroads in this country. In rough outline the plan is as follows : A number of immigration and information bureaus can be established at advantageous centres in Europe, each in charge of a competent agent, well supplied with the proper literature, railroad and steamship rates and the necessary information about Southern conditions and opportunities. An organization of this sort would make possible the selection of the most desirable classes of immigrants and make sure their settlement in the South by determining their destination before starting.

To make more clear the advantages of this plan it is necessary to consider more fully some of the essential practical details. First and most important of all is the preparation of the literature for such work. Intending immigrants want specific information, not vague generalities. It is necessary to specify localities and give prices of land and furnish very definite details. A few years ago the commissioners of agriculture of New Hampshire compiled and published, at small expense, a catalogue of farms in that State that had been abandoned by their owners on account of unproductiveness. In one year one-quarter of these farms were sold and reoccupied, many of the purchasers being foreigners of small means. If by such simple practical methods so great results can be accomplished among the bleak hills of New Hampshire, where every acre yields stone enough to fence it, how much greater accomplishments are possible under the favorable conditions that exist everywhere in the South ?

The selection of working centres abroad is another important detail, and one upon which the success of the whole plan largely depends. A brief study of the immigrants who are now coming to this country, or who have come here in years past, will give a preliminary idea on this point. Among the home-seekers who come to this country and locate in the West and Northwest the German and Scandinavian elements predominate, while the poorer laboring classes, who start at the landing point in search of work, or who settle in the great seaboard cities, are composed chiefly of Irish, Poles, Hungarians and Italians. These facts point to Germany and Sweden as the most productive fields in which to work, Germany probably offering the largest opportunities. England, Scotland and Switzerland are also good territory.

Agents maintained jointly by the Southern States offer the most economical and the most efficient means for conducting such work. The expense to each State for fourteen foreign agents, representing fourteen States, would probably be no greater than the cost of maintaining a single representative. With a division of the expenses of such an organization among a number of States and several transportation companies the cost to any one party in the arrangement would be slight, so small that it could readily be borne by private subscription in the event of any inability to provide for it out of public funds.

The co-operation of transportation companies in such a plan is essential, in order to add the inducement of low through fares by steamer and rail. In the successful operation of such a plan the transportation companies would be the first to reap direct benefits in actual cash.

Whether this plan as outlined requires modification in its details can be determined best by a thorough investigation and careful study of conditions at home and abroad. This plan, however, embodies principles that must be applied in order to accomplish the largest and most satisfactory results with the smallest expenditure of labor, time and money.

Bonuses for Manufacturers.

The failure of many industrial enterprises in the South has been due chiefly to the methods pursued by promoters in securing the location of manufacturing establishments. The greatest error in these methods is the granting of bonuses in various forms as inducements to manufacturers. No other practice has been so productive of legal complications, misrepresentation and dishonest dealings of various kinds. Bonuses have no place in common sense business dealings, and an offer or a demand for a bonus as a factor in determining the location of any industrial enterprise ought to excite suspicion of ulterior motives. The practice of offering bonuses, which has grown out of the competition between ambitious Southern towns and cities, has attracted to the South an unfortunately large number of business cripples—concerns either too weak or too deficient in honesty to get along without outside and unreasonable aid.

This question presents two definite propositions at the outset—first, a manufacturing establishment that cannot be located except through the instrumentality of a bonus is not a desirable addition to any community; second, a locality that would not be chosen by a manufacturing concern apart from the inducement of a bonus is not an advantageous location for a manufacturer. Bonuses are requested for two reasons—either because the concern is financially unable to meet existing business conditions, or because the seekers for bonus are prompted by dishonest motives. A concern that cannot conduct its business successfully without a cash gift, for which no equivalent is given, is of no benefit to an ambitious progressive community. A concern that demands a bonus practically as a bribe certainly is not an acquisition for which any self-respecting town would seek.

On the other hand, bonuses are given for one of two reasons—either to make up de-

ficiences in natural advantages or to secure a basis for a speculative movement. Every offer of a cash bonus is open to these suspicions, and properly so. We hardly need to say that the offer of a bonus under either of these conditions ought at once to determine a refusal on the part of the concern to which the offer is presented. A locality that does not offer every needed advantage for the conduct of a certain line of business receives no additional resource by the offer of a bonus. An industrial establishment which is permitted to become the basis of speculative operations invites well-deserved disaster.

By bonus we mean an offer of money for which no equivalent is given. Legitimate and honest business does not recognize the exchange of something for nothing. This kind of exchange exists only in gambling and thievery. If there be degrees of merit or demerit in bonuses, perhaps the least objectionable is the donation of land for factory sites, but we question the wisdom of even this form of persuasion. The whole matter can be boiled down to this· An advantageous location needs no offer of bonus to attract manufacturers, and a concern that is really desirable will not ask for and will not be influenced by an offer of money, land or similar inducements. A bonus has no place in legitimate business dealings.

NOTES ON SOUTHERN PROGRESS.

A CHARTER has been filed at Austin, Texas, for the Texas City Improvement Co., having for its purpose the construction and operation of a deep-water channel connecting the Gulf of Mexico along and across Galveston bay with the proposed Texas City, on the west shore of Galveston bay. The company has its capital stock placed at $2,000,000, and the incorporators are A. B. Walvin and others, of Duluth, Minn.; F. B. and F. L. Davidson, of Galveston, and E. B. Frederick, of Michigan.

. THE citizens of Houston, Texas, propose to hold a cotton carnival and exposition next November, and sufficient subscriptions have been secured to ensure the success of the enterprise. A permanent brick and iron building to cost about $30,000, and capable of seating 6000 persons, is contemplated in the plans. The building will be arranged suitably for accommodating large gatherings, such as conventions, concerts and public receptions.

A REAL estate movement of considerable magnitude has recently assumed shape in the Florida Land & Improvement Co., of Tampa, Fla. R. W. Easley, of Tampa, in company with several capitalists, has organized the company, and articles of incorporation have been filed with the secretary of state. The company is capitalized at $100,000, and its purposes are the purchase and sale of real estate, the negotiation of bonds and mortgages, and similar transactions. The president is R. W. Easley and the vice-president is W. W. Trier.

JNO. G. JAMES, president of the Panhandle Loan & Trust Co., of Austin, Texas, writes as follows in a recent letter to the *Manufacturers' Record:* "I am well convinced that the very best line of investments in Texas is small-capital national banks at good county-seat towns. They usually have no competition, get high rates for money, make small loans well secured, know all about their patrons' affairs and conditions. They have as directors good,

solid, safe business men, the best in the country, and are removed from 'booms' and speculative influences. Such banks all over Texas do well, and net 10 to 18 per cent., and are far safer and more profitable than the big-capital banks in our large Texas cities, most of which, I am sorry to say, in past three years have lost more money than they have made. I am sticking to the country bank, and any one at a fine county seat of a rich agricultural county should in a three years' run, if well handled, be able then to net 18 per cent. right along. If providence permits I expect to go on and put in five or six more such banks over in eastern Texas, where they are greatly needed and should be profitable, in counties in which there are now no banks at all."

GOV. HENRY L. MITCHELL, of Florida, in his message to the Legislature, says there has been a great influx of foreign capital into the State, and general prosperity reigns. Phosphate is being developed and mined, and promises in a short time to be a source of great wealth, being practically inexhaustible. The State is so favored by nature that a general failure of crops is impossible. The fruit crop has not been injured by cold weather, while the increased yield has met with ready sale at remunerative prices. The orange crop has on the whole brought good returns; while the pineapple crop has exceeded the most sanguine expectations, both as to size of crop and favorable prices; the value of the crop two years ago was only $147,000, and in one year it increased to over $600,000. The orange crop exceeds in value any other crop in the State. The planting of fruit orchards suitable to the middle and western parts of the State have progressed rapidly, and many of them are yielding the growers profitable returns on the investment.

IT is reported that a large amount of land near Macon, Ga., is being sold to English and Western people for settlement by colonists.

Quite recently 4000 acres have been sold on the line of the Georgia Southern & Florida Railroad to parties from Ohio who intend to raise fruit. A tract of land at Wellston, in Houston county, consisting of 17,000 acres, was sold recently for $20,000. Peach trees will be planted on the entire place. The 4000 acres mentioned above sold for from $7.00 to $12.00 per acre, and will be converted into orchards. Previous to this several large places have been sold in this region at sums ranging from $8000 to $16,000. This section of the State is the true home of the peach, and the lands along the line of the Georgia Southern Railroad are well adapted to the successful growth of fruit. It is estimated that next season 1,000,000 peach trees will be planted along the line of the Georgia Southern.

A CHAMBER OF COMMERCE AND INDUSTRY has recently been organized in Raleigh, N. C., for the promotion of public interests.

KNOXVILLE, TENN., is to have another college added to the institutions of learning for which that city is noted. The Holbrook Normal College is to be established in the suburbs of that city through the enterprise of the Knoxville & Fountain City Land Co. The contract has been awarded for the necessary buildings, which will represent an investment of $50,000.

THE citizens of Natchez, Miss., have organized an association to encourage the development of the manufacturing interests of the city. The officers have been chosen from among the representative business men of the city as follows: President, L. G. Aldrich; vice-presidents, Henry Frank, J. W. Lambert, A. H. Foster and George Brandon; secretary, James Farrell; treasurer, A. G. Campbell.

THE South is certainly faring well in the distribution of patronage under the present national administration. Representative Catchings of Mississippi recently pointed out the share of official appointments that the South had received up to April 15. So far only fifteen of the forty diplomatic missions under the State Department have been filled, and of these fifteen, nine have been given to residents of Southern States. Alabama has received the Spanish mission. Louisiana the French ambassador, Tennessee the mission to Chili. Texas that to Turkey Missouri the Swiss mission, Delaware the

most important of all, the embassy to Great Britain, Kentucky furnished the minister to Peru, Georgia the one to Gautemala, and Honduras and a North Carolinian has received the appointment to the mission which includes Greece, Roumania and Servia. These are not the only good berths in the foreign service which have gone to the south. Four consuls general, positions which are but little inferior in rank to those of ministers, have been chosen from below Mason and Dixon's line. They are those to Vienna and Mexico, both of which went to Missouri. Several other good foreign places have been given the south. In the domestic service of the government the south has been almost equally fortunate. Mississippi has furnished one assistant secretary of the interior and the recorder of the general land office. Maryland has the superintendent of immigration and one of the positions on the district court of appeals. Virginia supplied the solicitor of the State department. South Carolina a commissioner of railroads and the second auditor of the treasury. Tennessee a solicitor of the treasury. Georgia an assistant attorney general. Florida the deputy fifth auditor, and Texas got another of the court of appeals judgeships. Besides these, the three important cabinet positions held by Southern men must not be forgotten—the secretaryships of the treasury, navy and interior.

A KINDLY spirit of philanthropy speaks in this reflective paragraph from the *Iberville* (La.) South: "If they only knew. We refer to the people who live in the North country, who are now just emerging from the severest winter that has come to them in the course of three decades. If they only knew of the genial climate here in this gulf region, they might add to their lease of life years on years, and happiness would be augmented many folds. But, alas, they do not know, and how we pity them shivering with the cold penetrating to the bones, benumbing the muscles and chilling the blood. Now if they only knew the warm hearts and genial ways of our Southern people, as we know them from personal experience and observation, much of the dread of a change of habitation from the North to the South would be removed from their minds. They would come and enjoy the pleasure of new-made friends, good and true. We are now willing captives to the charms of this our southland and to the warm, generous and noble

FORT WORTH, TEXAS, holds a peculiarly advantageous position for the packing business in that it is the centre to which the cattle of Western Texas must be shipped to reach Northern and Eastern markets. Recently a number of Boston capitalists perfected arrangements to erect and operate a large packing establishment there, and this has been followed by Chicago people, who have decided to build an extensive packery and stock-yard. These two projects will represent over $3,000,-000, and their example will undoubtedly draw others to the place.

AT Newman Springs, Texas, the San Carlos Coal Mining Co. is developing a coal mine at a depth of 800 feet beneath the surface of the ground. The tract of land owned by the company comprises some 60,000 acres, all of which is underlaid at this depth by about five feet of coal. This is in two seams, the upper one three feet thick and the lower one two and one-half feet, the two being separated by a small seam of slate. The coal produces an excellent coke of a peculiar black color and dense structure, well suited for smelting furnaces. As this article is selling now for over $30 per ton in that region there is a good margin of profit in producing it, and with this there is a ready market for the product.

IN the recent election held in Colbert county, Ala., on the question of issuing bonds for road improvements, those favoring the issue won their point after an exciting contest, and now, as soon as the bonds can be prepared and sold, the much needed improvement on the roads will be commenced. The county could not have found any means which would lead to a more rapid appreciation in value of property or would be more likely to cause the settlement of a desirable class of farmers.

THE rapid extension of the market for Southern fruit and vegetables is shown in the comparison between the shipments of these products from Charleston, S. C., in 1890 and 1892. In the former year the total value of berries, potatoes, vegetables and melons shipped amounted to $1,680,000, and in 1892 to $2,-675,000, showing an increase of almost $1,-000,000 in two years, or about 60 per cent.

IN Florida the canning industry is being developed in a manner which is most encouraging. A cannery is to be started in Jacksonville; another at Key West; one at Chuluota; one is in operation at Tampa; another near Fernandina; still another at Cocoanut Grove, and several more in view at other points. Two canneries operating in the State have been making a specialty of canning pineapples, and the demand for this class of goods has increased to such an extent that each expects to enlarge during this season.

MT. AIRY, A THRIVING NORTH CAROLINA TOWN.

The town of Mt. Airy is situated in Surry county, North Carolina, in the centre of a great valley embracing about 1000 square miles, with an average altitude of 1400 feet above the level of the sea. Around this valley the Blue Ridge forms an almost complete circle, while to the southwest is the Pilot mountain, one of the loftiest spurs of the Blue Ridge. Mt. Airy occupies a position in the centre of this valley. It is just five miles south of the Virginia line and nine miles from the base of the Blue Ridge on a plateau which is separated from Pilot mountain by the Ararat river. The situation and elevation make the drainage unsurpassed, while the climate and scenery are as attractive as can be found in the Blue Ridge.

The northern half of the valley in which Mt. Airy is located forms the basin of the Ararat river, from the circuit of which basin many smaller rivers and creeks flow both eastward and westward. The resources of this basin, the territory immediately contiguous to the town of Mt. Airy, are varied and inexhaustible. Not the least of the advantages is the abundant water power above noted, and this is being utilized to a large extent by the many mills springing up throughout this section.

The climate is unsurpassed. The rigors of the Northern winters, and indeed of the winters in the plains below, are debarred by the lofty barriers of the mountain chains surrounding the valley, and, consequently, while snow and ice may cover the middle and eastern section of North Carolina, this mountain basin is singularly free from the cold. And while Mt. Airy is protected from the extreme cold it is also free from the severer heat of the summer season incident to most Southern towns, thus enjoying the rare advantage of being both a summer and winter resort.

The town is reached by the Cape Fear & Yadkin Valley Railroad from Greensboro. N. C., and, with a direct line from Wilmington, N. C., and Charleston, S. C., and close connection with the Richmond & Danville system and the Norfolk & Western Railroad, it is easily accessible from every point.

The growth in population has been rapid and substantial. In 1880 the town contained 490 people, in 1885, 800, in 1890, 2000, and now the official city census shows a population of 3000. This rapid increase has been largely due to the growth of manufacturing enterprises, the manufacture of tobacco being the chief industry of the town. A large number of warehouses, a dozen plug factories, two cigar factories and three leaf factories have attracted to the town a large percentage of its increase in population. Besides these, are cotton factories, woolen mills, saw mills, flouring mills, sash and blind factories, a spoke and handle factory, a foundry and machine shop and the largest granite quarry in the South. Mt. Airy has one newspaper, three schools and three churches.

The town is in the centre of a great tobacco growing section, the tobacco being not so light in quality, but of a finer grade than that grown further in the interior of the State. It is particularly suitable for manufacturing into plugs.

The most extensive granite mines in the State are found in this section. Indeed, there are hundreds of acres of various qualities. The largest granite quarry in the South is situated two miles distant, and from this staple the town has received the name of the "Granite City."

Mt. Airy is justly noted for its ample hotel facilities, there being three excellent hostelries, two of which especially cater to tourists in search of health and pleasure. Chief among these and on a bluff known as "Renfro Heights," in the centre of many acres of nicely laid out grounds and a grove of majestic oaks and other trees, all of beautiful foliage and natural growth, is the new and charming "Renfro Inn." From its spacious piazzas and each of its rooms a commanding view of the surrounding mountains forms a

RENFRO INN, MT. AIRY, N. C.

most delightful picture. To the south is seen the far-famed Pilot Mountain, to the north the Pinnacle of Dan, to the west, Fisher's Peak, 3700 feet high, to the east, Moore's Knob; in fact, giving Mt. Airy not only the advantage of attitude, but altitude with great breadth of plateau, surrounded by high mountains from six to twenty miles distant, which shut off all the warm breezes of the lowlands and allow one to enjoy the cool, dry and invigorating atmosphere of this favored spot, free from malaria, fogs and mosquitoes, with all the comforts of a well-kept and well-appointed hotel. The rooms are single or *en suite*, as required, are light, airy, pleasant and well furnished and connected with the office by electric bells. Plans have been perfected, not only to give an abundant supply of pure water, but to make faultless the sanitary arrangements.

The roads about Mt. Airy are exceptionally good, and numerous beautiful drives are found through this undulating country and by its mountain streams. Many points of interest could be visited in this pleasant manner. The White Sulphur Springs are three and a-half miles distant, the water of which is said to be fully equal, if not superior, to the White Sulphur Springs of Virginia. Flat Rock, a short distance away, is of special interest, and a drive of ten miles takes you to Devil's Den, a wonderful and capacious cave, with walls of solid rock, entering the side of the mountain for several hundred yards, and leading to the verge of a bottomless pit. Every facility for riding and driving can be enjoyed, as there is a well-equipped livery stable connected with the hotel. Tennis courts and croquet grounds, well laid off and kept in perfect condition, and other amusements, are offered. Excellent quail shooting abounds during the fall and winter months.

Renfro Inn will be open the entire year, under the personal management of Mr. W. A. Bryan, of the Montonese House, Branford, Conn., formerly of the Orton, Wilmington, N. C., the Bon Air, Augusta, Ga., and other leading resort hotels. The table and service are of the best, and careful attention is given in rendering to he patrons of the house every attention which contributes to their comfort and happiness, in order to establish for this new hotel a reputation which will be the best possible foundation for its future popularity and success. Rates are reasonable, and special to families. Connections can be made with Cape Fear & Yadkin Valley Railroad at Greensboro, N. C., from all points North and South; also from other points at Walnut Cove, N. C; The postoffice address of the manager is W. A. Bryan, Renfro Inn, Mt. Airy, N. C.

Sparger Bros. hold the supremacy in the manufacture of tobacco in Mt. Airy. In their new brick building, one of the best equipped in the State of North Carolina, they have a capacity of 2,500,000 pounds per annum, and their trade extends over the entire South.

Mt. Airy is soon to be the county seat. Although it does not as yet enjoy that distinction, it has its full quota of enterprising lawyers. Among these is W. F. Carter, who makes a specialty of the collection of claims and examination of titles. He is also a large real estate broker, the rapid growth of Mt. Airy making the real estate business very profitable.

GEO. W. SPARGER.

Geo. W. Sparger is another of Mt. Airy's enterprising lawyers. Mr. Sparger is an extensive dealer in real estate and negotiates the purchase and sale of lands.

S. P. Graves is one of the younger of the legal fraternity, and is considered to be one of the best attorneys in the town. He also deals in real estate.

The rapid growth of Mt. Airy and the solid character of this growth have led to a great increase in the prices of real estate. Plats of land that eight years ago sold for $100 are now worth $3000. Still there has never been a real estate "boom;" fictitious prices have never been made; there has never been any over-stimulation, and, consequently, there has never been a period of stagnation in the history of the town. Still real estate prices are not high. The citizens of the town realize that enormous charges will successfully debar immigration.

Therefore, to persons seeking investments Mt. Airy holds out inducements of a very inviting nature. The climatic advantages, the hotel facilities, the manufacturing enterprises and the innumerable resources of this favored town bid fair to bring to a realization the determination of its people that it shall have a population of 10,000 in the year 1900, or sooner.

THE SCHOOLS OF NORTH CAROLINA.

The Bingham School, Asheville.

"Among Southern Schools for Boys," says the United States Bureau of Education in its circular of information No. 2, 1888, "Bingham's stands pre-eminent." Founded in 1793, a century ago, by the grandfather of the present superintendent, it is the oldest school of any kind in the South, and the only one which has been transmitted from father to son during a century of successful experience in training boys to be men in the best sense. Its area of patronage for the last fifteen years, besides thirty-two localities in North America, including Mexico, has extended to South America, Europe and Asia, an area attained by no other Southern school, and probably by no American school.

Up to 1890, when a second fire in nine years drove it from its wooden buildings in middle North Carolina, it lacked an ideal situation and ideal comfort, safety, convenience, ventilation and sanitation in its buildings. For the purpose of a searching inspection the writer visited the school in January, and no one who makes such an investigation can doubt that in the new Bingham school at Asheville the ideal situation has been secured, and the ideal comfort, safety, convenience, ventilation and sanitation have been attained.

Asheville, the location of the new Bingham school, has been aptly termed the sanitary centre of the South, attracting, as it has done, a hundred thousand visitors in a single year by its beauty of situation and salubrity of climate, and retaining many of its wealthy visitors as permanent residents. The site of the school is on a bluff 250 feet above and across the French Broad river, sufficiently near to the city for convenience, and yet so isolated as to enjoy the advantages of the country. The drainage is perfect, and the supply of the purest mountain spring water is ample.

The buildings, with accommodations for 128 pupils, two in a room, are all of brick. They are in eight sections, separated by fire-proof parapet walls, and are placed on both sides of a street seventy-five feet wide. They are but one story high and but one story deep, so that each pupil gets air and light from two directions. Noises are above or below nobody. Dampness is prevented by a course of slate and cement under every floor, and the sun shines into every room at some time every day. The rooms, basements and attics are ventilated in the most efficient way. Each room is heated by an open grate, and has two single spring beds. Water is supplied in front of each range, both for drinking and for fire protection. But the most distinctive feature in the building is that a class-room, large, airy and thoroughly lighted and ventilated, with quarters for a teacher behind it, is placed in the centre of each of the eight ranges, so that the teacher is ubiquitous, and combinations for disorder in study hours are impossible. The sanitary arrangements are complete in every respect, and may well serve as a model for schools, colleges and hotels throughout the country. The gymnasium is also a model of its kind. It has a pitch of seventeen feet, and the largest main floor space in proportion to numbers in the United States. It has an elevated running track two hundred and twenty feet long, and ample space for two bowling alleys; it is thoroughly lighted, ventilated and heated, thoroughly furnished with the most approved apparatus and seems perfect for its purposes of physical culture. The kitchen is furnished with the best and most approved apparatus. The mess-hall is well heated, well lighted, well ventilated, and the tables are exceptionally clean and inviting, and are abundantly supplied with well-cooked food. The boarding department is in charge of an intelligent and efficient manager, whose sole business is to give it the attention it requires, and it has been put on the same high plane as the co-ordinate department of discipline, sanitation and instruction.

12

The leading physicians of Asheville, one a United States Navy surgeon, temporarily retired, affirm the writer's judgment as follows:

"ASHEVILLE, N. C., December 1, 1891.

"We have carefully examined the new school building on Bingham Heights, just without the city limits of Asheville, and take pleasure in bearing testimony as follows:

"1. The location in natural advantages leaves nothing to be desired.

"2. The buildings exceptionally fill the requirements.

"3. The sanitation is as perfect as scientific modern plumbing can make it.

"4. The water supply is abundant, the water of the purest, carefully collected from mountain springs and without a chance of contamination

"5. The all the year round climate of Asheville is world-renowned, and with the school's exceptionally excellent equipment and sanitation, gives Bingham's special advantages not enjoyed by another school in America.

"S. WESTRAY BATTLE, M. D., U. S. N.
"JOHN HEY WILLIAMS, A. M., M. D.
"JAMES A. BURROUGHS, M. D.
"WM. D. HILLIARD, M. D."

Lieut. John Little, 14th Infantry United States Army, the present professor of military science and tactics, writes over his signature as follows, under date of June 1, 1892: "The Bingham School begins its second year at Asheville, N. C., and the hundredth year of its existence with excellently equipped barracks, mess hall and gymnasium ; and the climate of Asheville is all that could be desired. This school possesses more attractive features and offers better opportunities for the mental and physical development of boys than any similar institution known to me."

Col. W. H. Lawton, Inspector General United States Army, in his annual report to the Secretary of War, for 1892, (p.p. 272, 273,) affirms this judgment as follows : "Bingham School is one of the oldest of the kind in the State. Its reputation is that of one of the best military schools in the South. In changing its location from Orange county, where it was recently destroyed by fire, to Asheville, Major Bingham has selected a beautiful and picturesque spot, where he has erected the college buildings : and while the establishment was not complete, in the work so far done the

ST. MARY'S SCHOOL, RALEIGH, N. C.

application of the superintendent's great experience and knowledge of the necessities and conveniences of such an institution were apparent on every hand. Every conceivable detail seems to have been anticipated, and all the

States as well. Its situation is one of the most delightful and pleasing and advantageous enjoyed by any college. Raleigh, the capital of the State, is easily accessible from all points, and the temperate climate, staid character of

ST. MARY'S SCHOOL, RALEIGH, N. C.

arrangements are unique and practical. The discipline of this school is to be commended. The service of the mess hall is excellent, and the gymnasium is a model in all particulars. The inspection was most satisfactory in all particulars."

Such opinions from such competent and disinterested judges are entirely conclusive, and the location, equipment and status of the new Bingham's have only to be fully known to make its present accommodations entirely inadequate for those who will soon fill its halls to overflowing.

St. Mary's School, Raleigh.

This school for young ladies, under the auspices of the Protestant Episcopal Church, is one of the oldest and best-established seminaries in the South, drawing its patronage from every Southern State and from many Northern

the population and literary atmosphere pervading the people make it peculiarly suitable as a home for a girls' school.

The situation of the school itself is all that can be desired for beauty and convenience. The buildings, six in number, are located in a grove of twenty acres, well shaded with native oaks, and one mile from the State capitol. These buildings are all of brick and stone, commodious and ample in accommodations in every respect, and the venerable gothic architecture renders them singularly attractive. The chapel, a beautiful building in the gothic style, will seat 200 students, and is furnished with a large pipe organ. It is devoted exclusively to religious purposes, the services of the church being held there on both Sundays and week-days. Particular care has been taken to render the dormitories comfortable. They are spacious, well ventilated, and each lady, with her room-mate, has a room to herself. The cuisine receives special attention, and is in every way satisfactory.

No young ladies' seminary in the South is better equipped than St. Mary's. As there is nothing gaudy or extravagant about the appearance of the buildings, so the aim and influence of the system of training is to make, not superficial students with a mere smattering of a few branches of literature and science, but scholarly, refined and thoroughly cultured women. The corps of teachers has always been noted for efficiency, while Rev. Bennett Smedes, the president, is an educator of the highest standing. All branches usually taught in such an institution are represented, and the departments of music and art are specially noted for their excellence and thoroughness. At the close of each academic year St. Mary's confers diplomas upon such members of the senior class as have satisfactorily completed the requisite examinations. This honor may be forfeited by unsatisfactory deportment.

Only a short time ago St. Mary's celebrated its semi-centennial. The *alumnæ* reassembled from all parts of the United States, and among these were many women whose names are familiar to the reading public. No greater attestation of the success of this school as a place for training girls into true womanhood could be produced than the catalogue of those graduates who assembled to honor their *alma mater*.

Salem Female Academy.

In the quaint old town of Salem, N. C., now a part of the city of Winston-Salem, which was settled over one hundred years ago by a band of Moravians journeying southward, there are many old and historic buildings, relics of another age. The stately Moravian church, the primal hotel in which George Washington passed a night when making his triumphal tour over the country, the Sister's house and many other buildings were all erected in the last century.

With her many elms adding to the effect of these quaint old buildings, Salem presents a scene of quiet and repose, well calculated to excite the interest of the scholar and to attract the student in search of a quiet retreat. To be sure the inevitable hand of progress has attracted business and enterprise to Salem to a degree not dreamed of by the early settlers. Side by side with the old buildings have grown up modern houses and the town now teems with manufactures.

In the old days, in an immense park, was erected the first building of the Salem Female Academy. In time, other buildings have been added, making the plant as complete as any in the South. While the institution is under the the patronage of the Moravian church, it is non-denominational in character, drawing students from every denomination and from every Southern State. It has long been celebrated for its excellent equipment and the thorough system of instruction, and of late years has added to its reputation by developing a musical department unexcelled in any female college in the United States.

The Salem Academy is unusually well equipped in all its departments. An industrial school has been added recently. The buildings contain accommodations for about 450 students. Dr. Clewell, the president, has presided over the destinies of the institution for the last eight years.

Davis School, Winston.

This preparatory military school for boys was removed from La Grange, N. C., to Winston about three years ago. The buildings, which are ample for the accommodation of 350 boys, are located in a large grove of forty acres and are reached from the depot by a car line. To the branches usually taught in a boys' preparatory school, Col. Davis, the superintendent has added military tactics, chemistry, elemental medicine and music. The Davis band is one of the best in the State of North Carolina.

Granville Institute, Oxford.

Last year Granville Institute was secured by the Misses Hilliard—one a former student, the other a graduate of the Woman's College of Baltimore. The situation of the school is excellent ; and the interior of the building having been thoroughly renovated and newly furnished throughout, offers attractive accommodations for students and instructors. The climate of Oxford is fine and the health of the school excellent.

The principals are well prepared for their work, both by their college training and by several years of experience as successful teachers. Their assistants are carefully chosen, and a high standard is maintained in every department, the curriculum corresponding with that of the best schools in the country.

Two courses of study are offered : a college preparatory, which gives thorough preparation

HORNER MILITARY SCHOOL, OXFORD, N. C.

for college entrance examinations, and an academic course, requiring one more year of science, history and English, with elective work in mathematics, Latin or modern languages. There are also provided thorough courses in music and art, under experienced and cultivated instructors.

Granville Institute is essentially a home school, the number of pupils being limited to twenty-four. This enables the principals to give personal attention to the mental, moral and physical well being of each pupil. A high, social and moral tone is maintained, and no girl will be maintained in the school whose presence would be morally injurious.

The Horner School, Oxford.

No argument is needed at this day to demonstrate the money value of an education. All are agreed that the cheapest and best investment that any parent can make for his son is in a thorough education. But the oft-repeated inquiry arises, where shall I educate my boy?

First, then, let us suggest to anxious parents that they are not likely to miss wide of the mark if they choose an institution with the prestige of success. Measured by an arduous s andard, the writer has seen with pride the position that the graduates of the Horner School, at Oxford, maintain.

Of such it may not be amiss to make mention of one living alumnus who stood well up with Aaron Burr at Princeton; of yet another whose mark was number one at Annapolis; of a third, who, as president of the University of North Carolina, as the head of the educational system of the State; another, the president of the most extensive and wealthiest railroad system in the South; of one whose name is the synonym of successful cotton spinning, himself the very first of a great industrial family; of two circuit judges; of two Congressmen; of a long list of college professors; of a brilliant array of young lawyers, and of one of these whose professional income exceeds that of any firm in the State. Should we leave the student roll and inspect the roll of patrons it will be found that among the number are the strong men of North Carolina and the South, embracing Senator Ransom, Judges Henderson, Ruffin, Pearson, MacRae, Burwell, Ashe, Bynum, Fuller, Faircloth and others.

The valedictorian at the university this year is and for several years past has been a Horner boy. And it is as true as it is common

that Horner's best men are the best men anywhere and everywhere. Her sons are eagerly sought by all the colleges.

This school was founded in 1857 by the late James H. Horner, M. A., L.L. D., and is now under the direct control and management of his two sons, J. C. Horner and Rev. J. M. Horner. They are both young men, under forty years, and the latter a graduate of Johns Hopkins University, and each has inherited a love of and tact for teaching. Col. Thos. J. Drewry, a distinguished graduate of the Virginia Military Institute, has control of the cadets, and such assistants are employed as the exigencies of the school require. But it is not of these things alone that one desires information. What of the climate, and of the health, and of the appointments of the school?

Oxford is situate fifty miles north of Raleigh and 120 miles south of Richmond. It is proverbially a school town—three flourishing boarding schools for young ladies are there, and in Oxford is the State Orphan Asylum, with its three hundred little children. They have no chills and fevers, no epidemics, and as little malaria as the most favored. The Piedmont section is rolling and broken, and is fair to the eye.

The school buildings are new and commodious, hot and cold baths are convenient, a steam laundry is attached, and the building is lighted with electricity. The table has the immediate care of the mother and sisters of the principals, who preside over and at the same. Twelve fine Jersey cows supply butter and milk for the cadets, and the dairy plays an important part in the domestic economy. Vegetables and fruits from a rich garden of four acres come fresh to the table, and clover and lucerne, and grass from nearly fifty acres are used for the stock. The buildings overlook a lawn of eleven acres, from which are cut the ball grounds, and under the spreading elms and oaks are arranged the tennis courts. Attached to the school property are three hundred acres of hill and dale that belong to the school, and here the cadets are free to enjoy themselves.

An infirmary separate from the buildings has been arranged in case of sickness, and in such cases the tenderest care is exercised.

To maintain the high standard of the school for scholarship, for accuracy and thoroughness has rather been the aim of its founder and his sons, than to unduly swell its catalogue. The

DINING HALL, HORNER SCHOOL, OXFORD, N. C.

number of students is now one hundred, ranging from Texas to Chicago. It is not a cheap school, in the vulgar sense of the word, for surely a cheap school will make a cheap man.

It seeks the best patronage from without and within the State, and feels confident that those parents who wish to make men out of their sons will be pleased in every respect. But such as have not this desire the principals do not care to trouble.

This map shows the geographical location of Alexandria, Indiana, the most conspicuou of the new towns in the gas district. The map is a photographic reproduction of th map published by the Geological Department of the State. Alexandria is in the centr of the area of greatest flow. Manufacturers from all parts of the country are locatin there to avail themselves of the saving in fuel. Free gas and factory sites are given t desirable factories. The town has grown in a year from a population of 1000 to 500(Real estate values are rising rapidly.

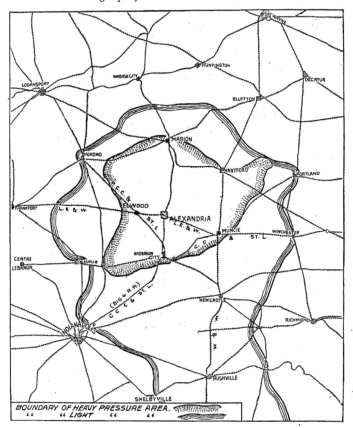

MAP OF THE INDIANA GAS DISTRICT.

THE FACTORIES

Now in Operation and Building Will Employ From 8,000 to 9,000 Operatives.

ALEXANDRIA

Will have during the next two years such a growth as no town in America has h

ATLANTIC——
——COAST LINE.

RICHMOND AND NORFOLK.
TO
CHARLESTON AND COLUMBIA.

Passing Through

VIRGINIA AND NORTH AND SOUTH CAROLINA.

**Special Attention Given to
MANUFACTURING INDUSTRIES.**

**The Finest Early Vegetable and Strawberry Section of the South
Adjacent to this Line.**

QUICK SCHEDULES OPERATED for Movement
to Northern Markets.

For information apply to

T. M. EMERSON,	**H. M. EMERSON,**
Traffic Manager,	Assistant General Freight Agent,
WILMINGTON, N. C.	WILMINGTON, N. C.

TURTLE POND FALLS, DEERFOOT PARK RESERVATION, TALBOT COUNTY, GEORGIA.

THE STATE OF GEORGIA.

By Hon. W. J. Northen,

Governor of Georgia.

The purpose of this article is to call the attention of investors and home-seekers to the advantages offered in Georgia and at the South.

Home-seekers considering the possibilities in change of location and capitalists seeking opportunities for investment naturally inquire first as to the character and intelligence of the people, second, as to the climate and consequent healthfulness, and finally, the benefits or profits to come, financially, under reasonable or ordinary efforts.

All these conditions will be found in Georgia to the satisfaction of the most exacting. The people of the State are cultured and refined, law abiding and progressive. The facilities for education have more than doubled in the last decade, while the very rapid advance in material prosperity marks the high character and progressive spirit of our people. No State with the same population shows a better record in the criminal courts or less lawlessness among the people.

The representative people of this State are not only cultured and intelligent, but they are hospitable and liberal minded. A representative Georgian wherever found is proverbial for his warmheartedness.

This much I have said first, because the people of this State deserve it to be said; second, those who come among us need to know it; and third, because some people have seen fit, for causes I will not now discuss, to say falsely to the contrary. No people upon this continent surpass the people of this State in whatever goes to make up a liberal-minded, cultured, law-abiding citizenship.

The climate of Georgia is healthful and invigorating; free from unusual excesses of heat or cold.

Upon my farm in Middle Georgia I oftentimes have fair grazing for stock during the entire winter. It is seldom the case that our hardy grasses in that section of the State fail longer than three months of the year to furnish grazing. In climate Georgia is a fairly representative State of the "Sunny South."

NOTE.—This interesting and forceful portrayal of the resources of the State of Georgia has been written for THE SOUTHERN STATES by Governor Northen, through the kind courtesy of the *Southern Cultivator*, of Atlanta, Ga., with which Governor Northen is under exclusive contract to write. The interest of the *Cultivator* in the welfare of Georgia, and the public spirit of Governor Northen, permit the present exception to this contract.—ED.

These primary points being settled largely in favor of the State, I desire mainly to call attention to investments and citizenship in Georgia. While it is true that the State is growing rapidly in wealth and population, it is also true that we have much room and many attractions for capital, and large and valuable territory for new settlers.

As an indication of the possibilities in Georgia, it may be well to say that the close of the war between the States found us owning but $120,000,000 in tax values, and that now—twenty-seven years later—we return $475,000,000, making an annual increase of more than $13,000,000 during the interval.

Besides these remarkable additions to our tax values in real and personal property, the manufacturing interests of the State have had a most gratifying growth. In 1881 the State had invested in cotton manufacturing $2,482,000. In 1886 this amount had steadily increased, and we had an investment of $5,709,000. This year we have invested in this State $10,839,000, more than 500 per centum increase in eleven years.

In 1881 the mining interests of this State were returned for taxes at $101,-000. A gentleman from Wisconsin has just invested $100,000 in mining for gold in the northeastern part of the State. A capitalist thoroughly familiar with gold mining in the West has just assured me that he knows no State with better prospects for gold mining.

Northwest Georgia abounds in iron ore and slate, while North Georgia proper has inexhaustible quarries of marble and granite. Many handsome residences in Chicago and other cities give evidence of the value and beauty of Georgia marble, while along the streets of many Western cities we find the solid granite pavements furnished by the enterprise and material of this State.

No State in the Union surpasses Georgia in timber and woods. The Georgia pine stands unrivalled for its uses, whether in furnishing naval stores or building material, while our hard woods are abundant and valuable and susceptible of beautiful finish and high polish. Along all these lines Georgia is rich in resources, and the convenience and cheapness of railway and water transportation, as well as the market demands, make profits easy and sure.

Whatever may be the conditions of the future, Georgia is to-day mainly an agricultural State. While there are great and undeveloped possibilities in manufactures, mining and lumber and naval stores, I am candid in the opinion that the agricultural possibilities of this State have never yet been approached.

Under the earlier system there was great wealth in cotton and other lines were not investigated. Under our present system of labor no general changes have been attempted and there are no general results to be reported. Being assured by my own experience that diversified agriculture could be made highly remunerative in the State, I was gratified to find similar results with others, some of which I will present to the readers of the SOUTHERN STATES as an evidence of the productiveness of our soil and the value of the crops.

With 800 pounds of gossypium spread upon an acre of land previously well prepared, Col. Geo. W. Scott sowed on September 20th half a bushel of clover seed and one bushel of orchard grass seed and cut the following May 9824 pounds of well-cured hay. This patch was immediately dressed with 400 pounds of gossypium and cut on July 5th, and made 3929 pounds of well-cured hay. This acre was mowed four successive years, being top dressed after each cutting with 400 pounds of gossypium, and averaged six tons per acre each year.

Col. George Scott says Georgia is the best clover country he knows. The first crop matures so early it is not damaged by the spring drouth. We are always certain of a fair second crop, and in wet seasons we can count on three good cuttings. In the proceedings of the State Agricultural Society of New York, I find a record of Mr. Allen B. Benham's premium farm, for which he received $50. I find reported a clear profit of $994 from ninety acres on this farm, or $11 an acre. I find also a record of Mr. Robert Harvey's dairy farm, for which he received a premium of $50, run by one team of horses and seventeen cows at a profit of $817.53, or an average of $48 to the cow. Major Warren's grass farm in Georgia, containing ninety-two acres, averaged $60 per acre. Mr. B. W. Hunt, of Eatonton, has a dairy farm of eighteen cows that made net proceeds in 1887, $1329.25, and in 1888, $1474, or about $75 per cow, against New York's $48.

With the enormous yield of grass and hay reported, and the known adaptation of our soils to grain, there is nothing to hinder enormous yields from stock-raising in Georgia at these prices. We need never buy a horse or mule from beyond our borders. Major W. A. Wilkins, of Burke, says he can raise a thorough-bred colt at $25 expense each year, and receive for him in Kentucky markets from $1500 to $2500. He says further, he can raise a mule colt for $15 to $20 and sell him when ready for market for $120 to $150.

Stock-raising is rapidly becoming one of the valuable resources of our farms. The next ten years will make astonishing developments on this line. Recent experiments in cattle feeding have brought astonishing results in the use of cotton-seed. Years ago we did not consider cotton-seed worth the handling for any purpose whatever. First we found they were good for manure. Next we discovered they contained a valuable commercial product in their oil. This has been wonderfully remunerative and has enriched largely those who have handled the seed. Without destroying either of these valuable elements we now find we can get from the cotton-seed fine products in beef and mutton and still preserve all the oil and most every particle of fertilization. Sir J. B. Lawes is authority for saying that one ton of cotton-seed meal fed to a steer will produce $30 worth of manure.

Col. W. M. Towers, of the cotton-seed oil mills at Rome, Ga., has had very satisfactory results in feeding beeves on cotton-seed meal and cotton-seed hulls, putting upon a steer of 1600 pounds about 100 pounds of flesh per month, using no food at all but cotton-seed meal and cotton-seed hulls properly mixed.

An average steer is expected to consume five pounds of cotton-seed meal and twenty pounds of hulls per day.

If space allowed I could give the remarkable results in fruit farming in the State, and the large amount of capital already invested from the outside in this business. Strangers passing through our State cannot believe these results possible from the exhausted and worn appearance of the land.

Upon many farms in Georgia the continuous clean culture necessary for the growth of cotton has exhausted the humus from the soil, and but little or no vegetable matter has been returned to it, but the most remarkable feature in our agriculture is the wonderful recuperative power of the soil under judicious treatment. We have only to abandon the culture of cotton, change our crops, or, even with continued cotton crops, furnish intelligent and abundant fertilization to obtain satisfactory yields and profitable results.

Without delaying to illustrate the recuperation under such cultivation as would furnish vegetable matter to the soil, it may be sufficient to give a notable success made by Mr. Furman upon his farm in Middle Georgia, while he continued the cultivation of cotton. Taking sixty-five acres of worn Middle Georgia land, fairly representing all sections of the State, under usual methods, Mr. Furman the first year produced eight bales of cotton, or one bale to eight acres. The second year, under intelligent improvement, he gathered twelve bales, an increase of 50 per cent. over the first year's production. The third year, under still more progress, he gathered twenty-four bales, an increase of 100 per cent. over the immediately preceding year. The fourth year he gathered forty-eight bales, an increase again of 100 per cent. upon the preceding year. The fifth year, the one immediately before Mr. Furman's death, he gathered eighty-eight bales, or just 1000 per cent. increase over the work of the first year.

Mr. Furman's land is simply representative of the other worn lands of the State and his experiment can be repeated over the State under similar conditions.

Farm lands in Georgia can be bought at very low figures, from five to twenty-five dollars per acre, except in close proximity to large cities, where they are higher.

The methods of farming are rapidly changing. Cotton is being abandoned as belonging more properly to the States west of us, and our farmers are giving more attention to fruit, grain, grasses and stock. One farm in peaches has netted in one year $50,000; one acre in Middle Georgia has produced 17,000 pounds of red clover, and no State in the Union is better adapted to grazing and stock-raising.

We will be glad to welcome to Georgia many times the amount of capital we have and multitudes of good people who come to identify themselves with our interests, while they seek for themselves satisfactory and profitable investments.

CHARLESTON.

By Robert Adger Bowen.

Charleston, thy brow is crowned with holier wreaths
    Than laureled ones that tell of victory,
    Though these be wanting not. There are to thee
The garlands woven from the love that breathes
From human hearts, where deeper down than seethes
    Tumultuous care and worldly vanity,
    There pulsates to the music of thy sea
The memory that suffering bequeaths.

Such sacred wreaths are fadeless, and endure
    Throughout Time's changes, mellowing more and more,
        Stained with the heart-throbs of humanity;
And as thy Southern skies above thee, pure
    And golden, and the ocean on thy shore,
        Shall this love crown thee to eternity.

Cordially Yours.

Jno. F. Goucher.

SOUTH CLOISTER OF FIRST METHODIST EPISCOPAL CHURCH, BALTIMORE.

THE WOMAN'S COLLEGE OF BALTIMORE.

By Frank Roscoe Butler,

Professor of English Literature in the Woman's College.

To the ideal of academic life and character in an institution. devoted to the education of men there seems of necessity to belong a certain flavor of antiquity. The new-born university may astonish us by the boldness of its innovations and the brilliancy of its achievements, but the light that shines from it is likely to be a somewhat garish one. It needs that softening which can come only of a certain venerableness in scholastic traditions connected with local memories of past generations of men.

But the fitness of things lays no such requirement of age and mossy memories upon institutions devoted to the education of women. Whereas the pursuit of wisdom turns men gray, women seem to assimilate knowledge only to be made by it eternally youthful. With woman reminiscences of the long past, so far as they are of intellectual things, are reminiscences of a narrow outlook, of mental dependence and servitude. Even now it is only the Anglo-Saxon race that has learned to ask respecting her:

"If she be small, slight-natured, miserable,
How shall men grow?"

As compared with the universities and colleges for men, women's colleges belong to an order of things still novel; they are the product and the promise of a new day. Hence while in the former we demand an element of the venerable,

197

and look for that charm which ivy and wall-flower give to the "studious cloister," in the latter we are more than content to find the freshness of the rose in gardens open to the sun; in the one case we expect a flavor as of rich wines long stored; in the other we have that bloom which is upon the grape clusters before the finger of man has brushed them.

In the social and intellectual life of our day, Vassar, Smith, Wellesley and Bryn Mawr are names to conjure with. Not only do they touch the imagination with semi-poetic effect, but they fill the mind with a multitude of expectations of the most practical nature,—expectations of better things in the homes of the land, in its schools, in social life, in church work, in every kind of philanthropy to which women give direction or assistance,—in fine, wherever a woman can exert a more effectual influence by virtue of increased knowledge and intelligence. Nor least among what they promise is the direct effect upon the individual lives of that large class of women who do not marry and who support themselves. To many of these life becomes, in consequence of a college education, a far better thing, not simply because they are enabled to obtain higher wages, but because the knowledge of books and the possession of cultivated tastes open up to them avenues of further self-culture, of enjoyment, and of helpfulness toward others, which of themselves give to life zest and a sense of personal independence, even when a large part of each day is filled with routine duties not altogether congenial.

Though younger than the four colleges mentioned, the Woman's College of Baltimore is born to the inheritance of an opportunity no less rich than theirs, and it has already, in the five years of its existence, taken an honorable position by their side. In its name it is, perhaps, not altogether fortunate. This seems to be too long and, since it inevitably suggests a type rather than an individual, lacks distinctive character. It wants the ease of utterance and the condensed suggestiveness which are needful in order that a mere name shall come to affect the imagination and the sentiment deeply. But who can tell

but that the recognition of this fact may one day lead some one to endow the college generously enough to bring about a change in its name? Meanwhile, the local designation attached carries with it much that is every way fitting.

If, however, anything is lacking in the name when a rallying note is needed for college mirth, the want seems in no way to hinder a spirit of devotion to the college idea in itself. An enthusiastic spirit always finds its surroundings rich in symbolism, and it does not long want names for its conceptions. Already there have grown up around the idea of "The College," present to the minds of the students, a hundred associations serving to define it. It is natural that these should be, first of all, associations of place, and it is a happy circumstance that the college buildings themselves possess such attractiveness for the eye as leads one almost inevitably to idealize the life that goes on within them.

The college is fortunate in that, though its buildings stand within the city, with blocks of brick houses rising around them on every side, they possess the advantage of wide lawns and of openness to light and air such as is usually to be found only in the country. The site was chosen, the buildings were planned and the spot was selected which each should occupy, while this entire district of Baltimore was little more than an open field. Since then the city has stretched a mighty arm northward and encircled the college in its embraces. It having early become necessary, however, to make provision for several more buildings than were at first planned, the trustees have purchased, within the last two or three years, all the available ground in the neighborhood. Upon lots thus acquired two large halls of residence have been erected, and a third is now being built. Thus the line of separation between the college as a whole and its surroundings is not easily drawn. Yet the central group of college buildings is quite distinct both in situation and in general appearance from all that surrounds them. They stretch along St. Paul street, up a gentle slope, from Twenty-second to Twenty-fourth street. The extent of the lawns in front and the proportions of each building by itself, together with the disposition of the different members of the group, unite to produce an admirable architectural effect. They are throughout in the Romanesque style, of the Lombard variety, with adaptations from that order to which Vitruvius gave the name of Tuscan. They are built of dark, undressed granite, and are surmounted by conspicuous roofs of Roman-red tiles.

Architecturally a member of the group is the First Methodist Episcopal church, standing farthest south, the tower of which is the most conspicuous object in the northern part of the city. This tower is almost an exact reproduction of a *campanile* to be seen just outside the ancient city of Ravenna. The church itself owes some of the most distinctive features of its architecture to suggestions taken from the celebrated San Vitale in

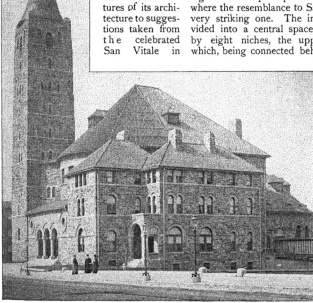

Ravenna, the church which, built in 526 A. D. upon the general plan of St. Sophia in Constantinople, became the model for Charlemagne's cathedral at Aix-la-Chapelle. Other North Italian churches, too, have furnished points of suggestion that have been worked into the design. The corbels, for instance, upon which rests the flat dome which, under the influence of the Byzantine style, is so distinctive a feature of Lombard architecture, are an exact reproduction of corbels found in the church of San Anastasia in Verona. The beautiful windows in the frieze which serve, after the model of San Vitale, to light the interior from above, are copied from mosaics in San Nazario e Celso, the mausoleum of Galla Placidia, the daughter of Theodosius the Great. The pulpit, too, is a reproduction in wood of an alabaster pulpit erected in 530 in San Apollinare Nuovo, the church of Theodoric the Great in Ravenna. The chapel, attached in the form of a half-ellipse at the rear of the church, is itself a gem. Here perhaps more than elsewhere the resemblance to San Vitale is a very striking one. The interior is divided into a central space surrounded by eight niches, the upper parts of which, being connected behind massive arches, constitute a continuous gallery semi-elliptical in form. This chapel is used by the college for devotional purposes as well as for public lectures and concerts. It is connected with Goucher Hall, the main college building,

GOUCHER HALL, WOMAN'S COLLEGE OF BALTIMORE.

by a short bridge on the north side.

The external beauty of this main building is well matched within by the dignity of the general plan and the light and cheerful character of the separate rooms. The Lombard style requires massiveness and simplicity of structure, and it is a distinct triumph in architectural design when, these qualities being made to stand out impressively, there is added to them, with the perfect congruity to be found here, an effect of grace and cheerfulness. By the depth and solidity of its foundations and the massy thickness of its walls, Goucher Hall seems built to last as long as colleges may be needed on this earth of ours, be that time ever so long, and yet the impression made upon one who wanders through its corridors and class-rooms is altogether a cheerful one. It seems as if even that depression of spirits which is perhaps an all but universal experience with those who are entering collegiate halls for the first time, as candidates for entrance examinations, might be expected to yield somewhat to the influence of so genial a light as comes in through these windows.

Here it is, in these class-rooms with their soft yet clear light, that all collegiate interests really center, that

collegiate life gives token of its reason for being. The throngs of students who already fill these rooms testify strikingly to the eagerness with which American young women respond to the intellectual opportunities which the age is throwing open to them. If mere numbers, however, are not a proof of this, proof of it may be found in the avidity with which these students seek to appropriate to themselves the culture that is offered them.

Yet five years ago, when the college was opened, there was doubt in many minds as to whether any real need of a woman's college of the highest grade existed in Baltimore. For twenty-five years the project had been mooted of founding here a young ladies' seminary of the common type, and when at last the hope of doing this seemed near realization, there were many among the friends of the proposed institution who felt that that would fully meet any existing requirement. It was more than a happy accident, more than a mere ambition to do something extraordinary, that led one or two of the most influential friends of the enterprise to insist that the new institution should be a college in the true sense, of a grade equal to that of any in the country. Five years' experience has amply justified their views as to the actual needs of the community in which the college is placed. Its success, so far as this is indicated by an ability to attract students to itself, has long been assured.

The college was founded by the Baltimore Conference of the Methodist Episcopal Church. The prime aim was, as a matter of course, to provide for the needs of the community which it represented. Hence, its success might have been measured simply by the readiness with which the young women within the borders of the Baltimore Conference responded to the opportunities thus brought to them. Yet at the present time only fifty-four per cent. of the students come from Maryland, while from the other Southern States come nine per cent., and from the North and West come no less than thirty-seven per cent. of the total number.

The significance of these facts is marked in several important respects. They serve to show that the Woman's College may hope to compete successfully with other colleges of the same

character in the North, that is, that it may expect to draw its patronage from all parts of the country. This practical independence of a purely local patronage frees it from the necessity of making the standard of its requirements for admission conform to local conditions. There having been hitherto in the State of Maryland little interest in the collegiate education of women, there have existed few, if any, distinctively college preparatory schools for girls. Hence a college depending for patronage upon this community alone would be compelled to receive students who are far from adequately prepared for college work. It is only by rigid adherence to its standards that the college can give the greatest possible impulse to the development of good preparatory schools throughout the State. Thus it is that the college, by that maintenance of its standards which comes of its having a patronage other than local, is able to be of use to its own community in the most effective way,—to say nothing of the benefit it provides its students in the

A LECTURE-ROOM IN GOUCHER HALL.

way of association with others coming from all parts of the country, in itself a great gain.

Another noteworthy fact is that, although the college is the offspring of a denominational body, fifty per cent. of its students come from families not affiliated with that body, being distributed among thirteen different denominations. Next in number to the Methodists are the Protestant Episcopalians, and next to them the Presbyterians. That so many of the students are from other than Methodist families would seem to be due to the fact that the college has from the outset pursued the liberal policy of placing the least possible emphasis upon its denominational relations, the aim of the church in founding the institution having been simply to secure to the young women of the community in which it exists certain intellectual advantages under conditions in no way subversive of their moral and religious welfare.

The time is not yet very remote when in speaking of an American college there was little need of any particular mention of its curriculum. The character of this could be taken for granted, since, whatever minor differences of detail might be found, the curriculum in all colleges was of the same general type. To-day the case is different. The type which was all but universal twenty-five years ago is hardly to be found, except here and there in some rural college which exists apart from those influences which affect the rest of the world. Not only have the modern languages and literatures and the natural sciences come to take their place beside the ancient languages, mathematics and the philosophical studies, but all of these older studies are now carried on in a way formerly not dreamed of among us. Furthermore, in many colleges the arrangement of the different studies in their relation to each other has undergone a change.

One of the most important innovations in the college curriculum is the introduction of the so-called "group system," first developed in the Johns Hopkins University. With that multiplication of the subjects of study suitable for treatment in college which inevitably followed upon the general development of scientific methods in all departments of thought, the college curriculum suffered imminent danger of over-crowding. The growth of the elective system, however, by which each student is permitted to select the studies which he wants to pursue, tended to afford some relief in this direction. But this system has at the same time made it possible for students to cover so wide a range of subjects as interferes with their obtaining more than a smattering of knowledge of any of them. The "group system" aims to correct this fault. It prescribes, as do other systems, certain studies for all students alike, and then, instead of permitting a miscellaneous choice of elective studies, it requires the selection of one out of several "groups" of subjects. In each group the studies are distinctly related, and,—in the belief that it is better for one to know much concerning a few subjects than to know very little about many subjects,—their number is so far limited as to bring about a concentration of effort on definite lines of work. There are in the curriculum of the Woman's College of Baltimore fourteen groups of studies, each group taking its name and distinctive character from the presence of two related studies, each of which is carried on continuously for a period of not less than two years. Thus the student who elects, for example, the German-French group, besides taking the other studies prescribed for all alike, carries on the study of German and French daily for a period of two years beyond the point at which other students drop them. The result is that the student who has chosen this particular group feels at the end of her course that, besides the knowledge gained and the discipline received from studying those other subjects that go to make up a college curriculum, she has such a knowledge of these two subjects as gives her a confidence in herself and her powers not possible to one who merely has a smattering of many things without having gone very deeply into any of them.

This system of group studies was devised by the Johns Hopkins Univer-

BENNETT HALL, WOMAN'S COLLEGE OF BALTIMORE.

sity for its under-graduate work, in order to make sure of having students who, on beginning that post-graduate work which is the chief feature of the university, would be properly prepared for advanced study in the two subjects to which it might be their purpose to devote themselves as specialists. Specialization for its own sake, within the limits of the college curriculum, is unquestionably a mistaken principle and subversive of that very "liberality" of culture which college education aims mainly to achieve. A system of liberal culture, however, which, without ceasing to be broad, provides an opportunity for just so much specialization upon one or two subjects as tends to develop that feeling of confidence in one's knowledge already spoken of, is thus rendered

more perfect rather than less so in its adaptation to its intended ends. The curriculum of the Woman's College is intended to provide so much of specialization as will answer this purpose and at the same time to conserve a real liberality of culture.

All studies after the freshman year are arranged, as far as possible, in courses of five hours per week, extending through the year, the older plan of putting in certain studies for courses of one, two or three hours per week, through perhaps a third or half of the year, having been abandoned.

Whether a curriculum constructed upon this plan is likely to seem so attractive to students who are looking forward to their college course as is the curriculum of the earlier type, might appear at first glance open to question. Ardent young minds are oftentimes eager for a little knowledge, if no more can be had, of many things, and is it not monotonous to pursue the same studies five days in the week throughout the year? Is there not, therefore, in such a curriculum a decided lack of variety? If the methods of college work were those of the high schools and academies, or even if the present college methods were the same as those of an earlier time, such a curriculum would beyond a doubt be open to this charge. So far as mere variety goes, however, that is obtained under present conditions in a way which an·outsider would not think of, and to a degree which he would find it difficult to understand. It was formerly an accepted opinion among us that almost any man of real intelligence who had been through college was properly eligible to a college professorship. Having studied the text-books, could he not teach them again? But at the present day college instruction is coming more and more to be placed in the hands of men who, after graduating from college,

have devoted three or four years in the higher universities of our own country or of Europe to advanced work of a kind such as cannot be done anywhere else, in that particular field in which they wish to make themselves specialists. Men so trained have at their command, or within easy reach, the whole field of knowledge, practically speaking, in their chosen departments. Thus their instruction ought to have a richness, an interest and a value which one less thoroughly prepared, whatever his general intelligence or his mere tact as an instructor, could never hope to impart to his teaching. Under the trained specialist, the study of French, for instance, from having been, perhaps, little more than the mechanical learning of idioms and irregular verbs and the mouthing of set phrases of supposed usefulness in conversation, becomes the introduction to a new world, in which the thought, the feeling, the whole life and history of a great people reveal themselves at every turn. Where words and phrases and even the vocables of a language become thus instinct with life, the mastering of

ONE OF THE COLLEGE HOMES.

A STUDENT'S ROOM.

them can be no longer in any sense mechanical, but must proceed with the inevitableness, and at the same time ·the sense of freedom, which belongs to all clear thinking. If the higher powers of vision which are produced by mechanical device have ability to reveal to us in a drop of water a whole world of varied life, with how much more truth may each of the great departments of human knowledge of which the college curriculum is made up be said to reveal a world of most varied elements, when its riches are displayed by one who has achieved anything like a real mastery of it. Under such instruction things new and undreamed of are brought to light every day, until the student comes to develop a true sense of the fact that a lifetime is not sufficient for exhausting the gold in any one of these mines of knowledge ; and to feel this vividly is itself something of an education.

But whatever pride the Woman's College may take in the character of its curriculum, the visitor will probably feel that its particular boast is in the system of physical training which it has introduced. This may be seen to have accomplished already the most excellent results. Bennett Hall, as the gymnasium is called, stands north of Goucher Hall, across Twenty-third street. Here every student has to spend certain hours in systematic training throughout the period of her residence. These exercises, coming in between hours of class work, afford an agreeable relief from the strain of other duties. The effect is easily seen in the changed aspect with which students often return from Bennett Hall to their class rooms.

The department of Physical Training is under the charge of an experienced physician, who has made a specialty of this work and who holds a regular professorship in the college. The Swedish system of training is used, and the instructors having oversight of all exercises are from the Royal Central Institute in Stockholm. The visitor who is fortunate enough to get sight of the classes is fascinated by the beauty and precision of movement which even a few months of training is able to bring about. Yet this beauty is not that of movements which are intended simply to be graceful in themselves, but the higher beauty of a perfect adaptation to worthiest ends. The first object aimed at is the development of the organs of respiration and the circulatory system. The second aim is a normal development of muscular strength and suppleness. As one watches the marching, running, jumping and vaulting, and the hundred other exercises—many of them seemingly indescribable—all of which are so full of life and yet without violence, he can hardly escape a sympathetic glow through the veins and tension of the muscles, which at least serves to give a suggestion of the good that must come to those who have this training.

Interesting as the class work here is, however, one gets but little idea from watching it what the real results obtained in this department are. At the beginning and middle of every year each student undergoes a complete physical examination. To any in whom this examination—which is to the last degree scientific—reveals physical weakness or deformity, special work is assigned with the Zander Swedish movement machines, which have for their purpose the correcting of such defects. All other students are assigned to the regular classes for general training. Some of the results of this work as shown by a comparison of the measurements of two successive years are interesting. For instance, the average lung capacity in 1891 was 94.95 cubic inches; in 1892 it was 116.13 cubic inches. The measurements of 1892 showed that thirty-six per cent. of the students had increased twenty-five per cent. or more in lung capacity. Twenty-four per cent. had increased forty per cent. or more. Four per cent. of the students had doubled their lung capacity. The average grip of the left hand in 1891 was 61.85 pounds: in 1892, 72.18 pounds.

That girls should enter into the work of the gymnasium as eagerly as boys do, is hardly to be expected. It would be in contradiction to all the traditions and habits of the lives of most of them to do so. Yet on the whole they show no little zest for it. In the spring, when the exercises that have been carried on since September begin to grow some-

A CORNER OF THE DINING ROOM IN ONE OF THE COLLEGE HOMES.

what wearisome, an entire change is made in their character. The swimming pool in the basement of Bennett Hall is then put to use, and nearly all the new girls learn to swim at once. Tennis, too, and archery are brought into requisition, the open ground lying north of Bennett Hall being used for this purpose.

A new piece of ground two squares west has been obtained to put to these uses henceforth, however, since upon this ground at the north of the gymnasium other buildings are to be erected, the plans of some of which, at least, are already made. Here are to stand a music and art building, a biological laboratory, and at the extreme north, opposite to the First Church tower at the south, an astronomical observatory, completing the central group of buildings as now planned. Yet practically a member of this group is the new building of the Girls' Latin School of Baltimore, the preparatory school of the college. This building stands diagonally across St. Paul and Twenty-fourth streets, opposite the spot to be occupied by the astronomical observatory, and is in the same general style as the other buildings already erected. In the hope that eventually a preparatory department may be dispensed with, it has been planned with reference to its possible use in the future for the

NORTH ENTRANCE OF GOUCHER HALL.

purposes of the scientific department.

That part of college life which goes on within dormitories would seem to admit of little in its general character that is unique. But even the common routine of a gigantic domestic establishment may take on the greatest differences of character, according to the material conditions to which it is subject and the spirit that pervades it. The two dormitories of the college, standing each a square away from Goucher Hall, one east and the other west, on Twenty-third street, leave nothing to be desired in the material conditions suitable for an agreeable home life. As respects sanitation and all other appointments upon which health and daily cheer depend, one cannot but feel that the residents of these homes have greatly the advantage over the dwellers in that famed summer palace presented by old King Gama to the Princess Ida in which to maintain her apart from the world. And the bright interiors, with the abundant life which they set off, present to the visitor spectacles no less fascinating than those which charmed the Prince and his comrades who intruded within those forbidden precincts.

As respects that spirit which pervades dormitory life, and upon which the very name of dormitory seems almost to throw a chill and a doubt, it is to be remembered that a woman's college has the advantage over the young ladies' finishing school and similar institutions. If it is a college in the true sense, only the serious and aspiring can succeed in entering it. If its standards are kept up properly, only the industrious can maintain themselves in it. The advantage of young women over young men in point of maturity at the same age, makes it an altogether different problem to deal with the former from what it is to deal with the latter. A community of this kind can be left for the most part to form its own rules and provide for their execution. The spirit that pervades the college work, the atmosphere and the feeling engendered in the recitation and lecture rooms, if this is a healthful one, must inevitably give the tone in the dormitory life also. If to inculcate love of truth in all its forms, to awaken earnestness and depth of purpose is the aim sought after and achieved in all class work, the student is sure to carry these qualities out of the classroom with her. If dignity and courtesy rule there, they will not fail to show themselves everywhere else. If the conduct of the work is such as to promote easy relations between teacher and student, and to avoid all danger of excessive demands upon the nervous energies, then the relaxation which shows itself in the home life need never be accompanied with anything which goes beyond the limits of good taste. The

college which hedges in its dormitory life by means of a multitude of minute restrictions would seem in doing so to betray a lack of confidence in the beneficent effects of that very system of education, the purpose to promote which is the sole justification of its existence.

It remains to say a word concerning the president of the college, the Rev. John F. Goucher, D.D., whose residence, one of the finest in the rich city of Baltimore, stands facing the college grounds, on the east side of St. Paul street. The pride would be an excusable one which he might easily take in looking out from his library window upon the sweep of buildings of which it commands a view, for more than to any other person the very existence of the college may be regarded as due to him. It was he more than anyone else, perhaps, who as a member of the Baltimore Conference, championed the cause of a college as opposed to the project of an academy for young ladies. It was his gift of Goucher Hall with the ground it stands on that made the college a possibility, and it is his planning and persistent energy, more than of any other person, which have given to the college the character it now sustains. What plans his busy mind may still be engaged with in the interest of further developments for the college, no one knows but himself, but he may be trusted to have plans not yet unfolded, the realization of which will transcend in importance anything as yet achieved.

SOUTHERN PROGRESS AND PROSPECTS;
A BRITISH VIEW.

By J. Stephen Jeans.

As one who has devoted a good deal of attention to the development of the resources of the United States, I am much pleased to have the opportunity of complying with the request communicated to me by the editor of the SOUTHERN STATES Magazine, that I should contribute an article on the position and prospects of the South from a British point of view, and more especially in reference to the most important of the material resources on which the prosperity of the New South is likely to depend next after cotton, if not even before that commodity, namely, the production of coal and iron ore and the industrial fabric that may be raised on those foundations. The mineral wealth of the South has been the envy and admiration of other States and of other countries for years past. Its progress has been rapid, phenomenal and continuous. A few years ago a comparatively weak and helpless infant, the South has today become an industrial octopus, stretching forward its Briareus-like arms in a hundred different directions, and seizing chances and opportunities with a firmness of grasp that it is difficult to elude.

The first thing that strikes a philosophical inquirer into the resources and circumstances of the Southern States is their wonderfully varied conditions of soil and climate. Within the area of 835,000 square miles embraced by the fourteen Southern States the climate is mostly all that could be desired for a great part of the year, and is entirely favorable to continuous and sustained labor, while the soil is not only prolific but produces in especial luxuriance crops that are not grown elsewhere to the same profit. The Southern States, however, cover nearly ten times the area of Great Britain, so that it is natural to look for variety of climate as well as of products. The soil is, of course, especially favorable to the growth of cotton and tobacco, but there is no good reason why other products should not be cultivated largely, and this will no doubt come with increase of population and of enterprise.

During the decade ended with 1890 the South made unquestionably greater progress in all the essential details of material well-being than in any other period in the history of the country. The population as a whole advanced from 16,369,000 to 19,600,000, being a much larger advance than any that is on previous record. The population of the Southern States is now about thirty-one per cent. of the total population of the country, whereas in 1870 it was about thirty-two per cent. of the total, which means that other parts of the country have made greater progress in population than the South with all its great record behind it. But in comparing the South with the North or the West, it should never be forgotten that it has had to pass through a period of trouble that has not been experienced by any other part of the Union, and that between 1870 and 1880 it had to make a slow and painful, and perhaps, on the whole, a not very complete recovery from the devastating effects of the Civil War. Its capital was gone ; its enterprise was sapped ; its credit was almost nil ; the main source of its wealth was at one stroke entirely obliterated; its labor was disorganized, and its economic condition had not a single redeeming feature. These serious ravages could not be repaired in a day.

Capital naturally fought shy of such a stricken community. What had they to attract it? The cotton-fields were still left, but the cotton-workers were in a state of complete anarchy and demoralization. No one knew what was to happen next. The centre of operations during the war was devastated; the property that the old Southern planter had in his slaves was utterly wiped out; there were next to no manufactures in existence, and the agricultural industry could not do much more than live from hand to mouth until the new order had succeeded to the old, a naturally tedious, and, under the circumstances of the South, a peculiarly delicate and difficult process. No locust-infested community ever experienced a more utter blight.

In 1880 the South was not much more than beginning to recover from these trials and disturbances. The process of building up the interests that had been so grievously hurt was slow, and many new problems were presented for solution that were more or less peculiar to the States in this region. But as the railway system extended, and as the labor question became better understood under the changed conditions necessitated by the war, capital was more and more attracted to mineral and agricultural resources that had previously been ignored and neglected. "Go South, young man!" came to be almost as favorite a shibboleth as Horace Greeley's well-known approval of the West. Population did not quite make such progress as in the other parts of the country, for the South has not hitherto been greatly attractive to immigrants, and the fecundity of the Southern whites is no greater than that of other parts of the United States, but still the promise of the Southern States under reconstruction was good enough to attract many settlers from other parts of the country, and more enterprise and vigor began to be thrown into the work of development. The results of this movement, which is but little understood

in England, may be traced in a few tables which are collated from the reports of the eleventh census.

The South Central group of States, which embraces eight of the principal States in the South, and includes Alabama, Tennessee, Kentucky, Arkansas and Louisiana, has made remarkable progress in wealth during the decade ended with 1890—more remarkable, indeed, than that achieved by any other group within the same period except the Western. What is known as the South Atlantic group, on the other hand, has not made anything like the same amount of progress—less so, on the whole, than any other group. The advances made in wealth, as measured by the increase of assessed valuation, and in population, during the decade are shown in the following table:

Group.	Assessed Valuation.			Population.
	Per capita.		Increase Per cent	Increase. Per cent
	1880.	1890.		
North Atlantic	$521	$610	40	19
South Atlantic	219	241	28	16
North Central	315	316	38	29
South Central.	153	215	73	23
Western	480	666	138	71
Total United States.	337	394	46	25

It appears, then, that the two groups which include the Southern States as a whole—the South Atlantic and the South Central—are considerably less wealthy than any of the other groups, the South Central having less than one-third of the average wealth per capita of the Western States, and not much over one-third of the average per capita wealth of the North Atlantic group. But in considering this relative position, two circumstances should be borne in mind—the fact that the Southern States started some twenty years ago from a much lower level of impecuniosity than any of the other groups, having been practically ruined by the war, and the next that the population of the Southern States is largely composed of the negro element, which is thriftless and poverty-stricken and apparently largely incapable of acquiring wealth. If the colored population is eliminated, the average assessed valuation for the whites would come out as about $320 per capita for the South Central, and $410 for the South Atlantic groups, a showing that compares much more favorably with that brought out for the other groups in the above table. Nor should it be forgotten that in former computations of the wealth of the Southern States, the colored population, instead of being reckoned as owners of wealth themselves, were dealt with as the possession of the white population. If this method of computation were still to be applied, the circumstances of the South would be very much altered in appearance. At the census of 1890 there were 3,262,000 colored people in the South Atlantic and 3,479,000 in the South Central group, making a total of 6,741,000. The value of a negro was estimated by different standards, according to his age, his capacity and his skill, but if it is put at $500, then the estimated wealth of these two groups of States at the present time, as measured in the terms adopted before the war, would be $3,370,000,000 more than the figures recorded for 1890, or fully eighty per cent. more than the amount actually returned. In short, the effect of the war was to reduce the South from the position of being the richest part of the country to that of being absolutely the poorest, and for nearly twenty years the South failed to make much progress.

What strikes one, however, as being a little remarkable in the records of assessed valuation for 1890, is the fact that some of the Southern States that have the richest mineral resources, and, therefore, presumably the greatest capacity for advancement, have in reality made the slowest progress. Between 1880 and 1890 the States of Kentucky, Tennessee and Alabama went ahead to an extent that excels the average of the whole country, as measured by the increase of assessed valuation, but the States of Virginia and West Virginia average less than one-half the general increase, and continue among the absolutely poorest States in the Union. The absolutely poorest States of all, in the order of their poverty, are Mississippi,

Alabama, South Carolina and North Carolina, and these, as might be expected, are among the States that have the largest relative colored population. Alabama, in 1880, was in the depths of poverty, having only a per capita assessment of $97, or less than one-fourth the average assessment of the United States in 1890. In the interval it has increased its assessment by over sixty per cent., and having regard to the extent of its mineral resources and its capabilities for development in other directions, there is every reason to suppose that its future progress will be solid and substantial.

In point of actual wealth the Southern States are still far behind the more easterly States, although they are improving in this respect every day. The census returns of the assessed valuation of the principal Southern States in 1880 and 1890, per head of the population, and the increase of assessed valuation between the two periods show the following:

	Assessed valuation per capita.		Increase per cent.
	1880.	1890.	
Alabama............	$ 97	$130	60
Arkansas............	107	152	99
Florida.............	114	196	148
Georgia	155	205	57
Kentucky...........	212	275	46
Louisiana...........	170	209	46
Maryland...........	531	462	decrease.
Mississippi....	97	122	42
North Carolina......	111	131	36
South Carolina......	134	114	decrease.
Tennessee...	137	196	64
Texas..............	201	311	117
Virginia.............	203	218	17
West Virginia.......	225	222	21

These figures compare with some of the principal Eastern States:

	Assessed valuation per capita.		Increase per cent.
	1880.	1890.	
New York...........	$521	$629	42
Massachusetts.......	888	962	35
Pennsylvania........	393	493	54
New Jersey.........	506	476	decrease.
Connecticut	525	480	decrease.

Another indisputable evidence of progress and prosperity is the amelioration of the general condition of the working classes, and the best evidence of this form of growth is the advance of the general rate of wages paid in industry. The census returns enable an estimate to be made of the average annual wages paid in the principal cities of the United States for each of the years 1880 and 1890. Dealing with the same thirteen Southern cities, from data so ascertained, it appears that there has been a great gain all along the line. The low wages paid in the South was formerly made a cause of reproach to that region. It must be admitted that the reproach is being very successfully wiped out, and it need not excite any surprise should the inducements held out to labor to gravitate in the direction of the South rise to as high a level as those found in the East or West. In every case the average of the wages paid per employe in the Southern cities shows a notable, and in some cases a phenomenal, advance betweeen 1880 and 1890, although there are still considerable extremes, as typified by an average of only $321 per head in Augusta and an average of $516 in Memphis. The details are appended at length in the table that follows:

City.	Hands employed.		Average wages paid per employe.	
	1880.	1890.	1880.	1890.
Norfolk	752	2791	$421	$462
Richmond............	14,047	18,151	213	384
Wheeling	5512	5439	397	448
Baltimore...........	56,338	83,091	268	425
Charleston	2146	5283	297	415
Mobile	704	2331	370	367
Memphis............	2268	5569	372	516
Nashville...........	4791	7434	273	446
New Orleans	9504	22,563	391	433
Louisville..........	17,448	24,807	334	444
Atlanta.............	3680	7680	241	429
Savannah...........	1130	1643	395	516
Augusta....	1680	5861	266	321

The census returns enable a comparison to be made of the above figures with those that similarly illustrate the progress of the central eastern cities in the same years. The average rate of increase has been higher in some of the Eastern States, but on the whole the cities of the South have no reason to be ashamed of their record.

Unfortunately the census returns of railway progress do not allow of a comparison of the Southern States as such

for different periods, in consequence of the fact that the country is grouped in an arbitrary manner into a number of divisions, which do not strictly correspond to the geographical demarcation. Thus, we find that Maryland and part of West Virginia are grouped with part of New York and New Jersey, Louisiana with Texas and part of New Mexico, Arkansas with Colorado, Kansas and Indian Territory, and so on. Only two complete groups deal with the Southern States exclusively—the first (group IV in the census classification) embracing Virginia, West Virginia and North and South Carolina; and the second (group V) including Kentucky, Tennessee, Mississippi, Alabama, Georgia and Florida. Adding the returns for these two groups of States together, we have a statement showing the progress of the railway interest in ten of the Southern States as between the years 1880 and 1889, the main facts of which are submitted in the following table:

	1880.	1889.
No. of passengers carried....	6,394,000	30,060,000
Passenger earnings..........	$12,818,000	$28,958,000
Tons of freight carried......	17,759,000	61,781,000
Freight earnings.............	$33,067,000	$70,007,000
Total income.................	$46,956,000	$103,061,000
Total expenditure............	$43,617,000	$69,526,000

This record makes it clear that the number of passengers carried on the Southern lines has in the interval increased nearly fivefold, that the passenger earnings have more than doubled, that the freight tonnage has increased more than threefold, while the freight earnings have more than doubled, and that while the total income from all sources has considerably more than doubled, the expenditure has only increased by about sixty per cent. This can hardly be regarded as otherwise than a very satisfactory record, especially when we bear in mind that the very large increase of income has been concurrent with a large reduction of both passenger fares and freight rates, and that while the expenditure in 1880 was almost abreast of the income from all sources, the income in 1889 was more than thirty per cent. in excess of the expenditure. Putting the matter in another way, it appears that while the expenditure in 1880 was ninety-three per cent. of the earnings, the working expenses in 1889 were only sixty-seven per cent. of the total earnings. No group of American States, and probably no other country or locality in the world can show a better result within so short a period.

We have remarked that the increase of gross income has been coincident with a substantial reduction of rates and fares. This is shown in the following figures :

PASSENGER RECEIPTS PER MILE.

	1880. Cents.	1889. Cents.
In Group IV............	3.024	2.207
In Group V......................	3.364	2.375

FREIGHT RECEIPTS PER MILE.

	1880. Cents.	1889. Cents.
In Group IV.....................	1.459	0.766
In Group V......................	1.923	1.087

Here we find that freight receipts have fallen to about one-half of what they were in 1880, and that passenger receipts have also been largely reduced. The same movement has been apparent throughout the United States as a whole, but nowhere in a more marked degree than in the Virginias and Carolinas, which had in 1889 the lowest ton-mile rates of any group of States in the country excepting only one. This is a very important matter as bearing on the future prospects of the region in question, for it is needless to remark that however abundant its natural resources may be, it cannot make progress in reference to the outside world unless it has the command of ample and economical means of transportation, and here we find that it has almost the cheapest transportation on the American Continent, which is merely another way of observing that it has practically the cheapest transportation in the world. In the future competition of the United States with the mother country this fact must be an element of much importance.

The present cost of production of pig iron at some of the Southern furnaces, as estimated by selling price and by the cost of the raw materials, is almost, if not quite, as cheap as the cost of production in the principal districts of Great Britain. That, unfortunately, has hitherto availed the Southern States but little, owing to the great distance of the furnaces from important markets. But the distance is apparently being shortened every day by the reduction of traffic rates, while in the mother country the rates are kept up to the old level, and are now probably on an average three times as high as they are in the group of Southern States just mentioned. The same low range of freights must equally operate in favor of the Southern States in their competition with other iron-making centres on the American Continent.

The remarkable movement that has been adverted to opens up the further inquiry : Can the Southern States afford to continue these low rates of freight, and is there any solid cause for believing that they are likely to be permanent? The census returns clearly show that the reduction of rates and fares on the Southern lines have not reduced their gross earnings, and that they have been coincident with a large amount of economy of working. The following figures support these propositions :

EARNINGS PER MILE OF LINE.

	1880.	1889.
From freight.................	$2075	$2573
From passengers.............	857	1079
From all sources.............	2932	3653

TRAFFIC CARRIED PER ENGINE.

	1880.	1889.
Tons of freight..........	21,299	32,753
Ton miles, per freight engine	1,885,000	3,694,000
Passengers carried..........	16,850	31,646
Passenger miles, per engine..	671,949	1,162,700

One of the most obvious advantages possessed by the Southern States is the command of practically unlimited supplies of good and cheap coal. In West Virginia, according to the reports of the eleventh census, the average price per ton of the 6,232,000 tons of coal produced in 1889 was only

82 cents at the pit's mouth. This was the cheapest price returned for any of the States on the North American Continent, excepting Pennsylvania, where the average was given at 77 cents, or five cents less. In the other Southern States the average price appears to be much under the average of the country as a whole. In Virginia the price for 1889 was returned at 93 cents; in Kentucky at 99 cents, and in Alabama it was $1.11, as compared with $1.44 for the country generally.

The coal of the Southern States appears to be mined under peculiarly favorable geographical and topographical conditions. The coal is not deep in the earth; in many cases it has only to be quarried near the surface. It occurs in thick beds, and as a rule it is not a very hard coal. Hence the average annual output of coal per employe is very high, much higher than in the majority of the American States or the European coal fields. Thus, for example, we find that in West Virginia the average annual output of coal per employe is 626 tons, which is more than double the annual average output of coal per employe in the British coal fields in the same year. The best result obtained in the coal fields of Continental Europe is about 280 tons per employe, but in most of them it falls much under this average. Alabama is considerably behind West Virginia in reference to the productivity of labor, the average annual output per employe having been no more than 512 tons in 1889, but this result is nearly ninety per cent. better than the average for the United Kingdom. Indeed, the only coal field that appears to produce coal more cheaply on a large scale than the coal fields of the South is that of Pennsylvania, where the ascertained average output for 1889 was 670 tons per employe; but the Pennsylvania field is of comparatively limited extent, having an area of only 9470 square miles, or little more than one-half the area of West Virginia, less than the area of Kentucky, and not much more than the proved coal area of Arkansas. The area of the Southern coal fields as a whole is more than six times that of the area of the Pennsylvania field, and as the latter is getting well on towards exhaustion over a large part of its area, it is fair to assume that its Southern rivals will come more and more to the front. It is not, of course, to be supposed that they will enjoy undisputed supremacy. They will have to reckon in the time to come with Illinois, which has the enormous area of 37,000 square miles of coal field, or more than twice the area of the British field, and with Missouri, which has an area of about 27,000 square miles, as well as with Kansas, Indian Territory, Iowa and Ohio, which have all large areas of coal-bearing strata, but they will nevertheless have their own distinct field, which will be likely to furnish them with a very considerable shipping business in the time to come, as well as their immediate local consumption, which is rapidly increasing.

Let it excite no great surprise if, in the not far distant future, Southern coal should be shipped to ports that are now supplied by England—nay, why should Southern coal not be shipped to England herself? The price of English coal at the pit's mouth for the last two or three years has been about double the average price of the coal of West Virginia, and it is not likely that English coal will get cheaper than it has been. Indeed, there is an increasing tendency to increase the cost of production in England from several causes—from the restrictions and conditions imposed by the State, from the increasing depth of working, from the shorter hours of labor, and from other influences—whereas, in virgin fields, like those of Virginia and Alabama, the contrary result may reasonably be expected, as the collieries become more opened out and production is attempted on a larger scale, with more perfect appliances and with a better labor organization.

There are probably but few inducements for good mining labor to go into the South up to the present time. The North and the Central States generally offer a higher rate of wages, and by that means secure the best class of workmen. This is an undeniable disadvantage to the South. Usually labor is cheap in proportion to its efficiency and not in proportion to its nominal cost. The Southern coal fields have natural advantages for the cheap production of coal that are certainly not surpassed in Pennsylvania or in any other coal field, and by and by those advantages are likely to become more apparent than now, when better systems of mining and more experienced labor are employed. As it is, however, the Southern States pay good wages for this class of work, as the following official figures show:

	Average daily wages.		
	Miners.	Lab'rs.	Boys.
Alabama......................	$2 15	$1.33	$0.66
Arkansas......................	2.20	2.00	0.71
Georgia......................	1 46	0.98	....
Kentucky......................	1.75	1.56	0.70
Maryland......................	2.45	1.86	1.06
Tennessee	1.98	1.26	0.72
Virginia......................	1.53	1.59	1 14
West Virginia...............	1.86	1.47	0.66

These figures appear to contain several rather anomalous features. Why, for example, should miners be paid sixty-two cents a day more in Alabama than in Virginia, and sixty-eight cents more than in Western Virginia? Again, why should laborers be paid about one-half the rate paid to miners in Alabama, and six cents a day more than miners in Virginia? Why, also, should laborers be paid ninety-eight cents a day in Georgia, and $1.56 in Kentucky? And why, in two adjoining States, with much in common, should the wages paid to boys under sixteen vary so much as forty-eight cents, which is the difference between Virginia and Western Virginia. It is clear that these variations are mainly due to temporary fluctuations in the supply of the necessary labor, and that

with adequate labor at command they would largely disappear, with the probable result of cheaper fuel than at present.

"It is a question of very considerable interest to us," wrote Cobden in 1835, "whether America will continue her career as a manufacturing country after the protective duties, which have professedly created her present cotton and other interests, shall have, in pursuance of the recent tariff law, been partially repealed." If we paraphrase these words to the extent of substituting "impending" for "recent" tariff law, we shall find that they are as applicable to the circumstances of the present day as they were to the time at which Cobden wrote. If anything, indeed, they are even more applicable to our present circumstances, because the issues involved to-day are much more important than they were at that time, and the interest is necessarily greatly intensified, not only by that fact but also by the singularly varied and eventful history of tariff legislation in the interval.

In a future article I hope to be able to enlarge upon the resources and prospects of the South as a manufacturing centre, with special reference to iron and textiles. Meantime, I may add that if the tariff of the United States were repealed to-morrow there does not appear to me to be any region in the United States that would miss it so little as the South. The principal industries of the country can be carried on in the Southern States quite as well without a tariff as with one, and where this is the state of affairs a tariff only gives artificial assistance to localities that would not be otherwise able to compete against those that are sufficiently strong to fight for their own hand.

LAUREL FORK FALLS, RHEA COUNTY, TENN.

THROUGH THE SOUTH WITH A CAMERA.

By H. S. Fleming.

I.—ALONG WALDEN'S RIDGE.

History tells us that when that hardy pioneer, Daniel Boone, started from his North Carolina home toward the almost unknown lands of Kentucky, his course lay up through the northeastern corner of Tennessee and across the Cumberland mountains, somewhere near the junction of the three States, Kentucky, Virginia and Tennessee, but so great is the honor of being located on one of his "trails" that nearly every town along the Cumberland mountains from Kentucky to Alabama has claims, if local tradition may be believed, to having been at one time a resting place for the great hunter. The one thing that gives just a shadowy substance of truth to some of these legends is, that Boone made a number of trips through this section and it is not known to a certainty that he each time followed his first trail. Even if we cannot have literal proof that he passed through all the places that lay claim to him, it is a pleasant fiction and the mountain country is so wild and unsettled that it does not need a vivid imagination to picture a figure clad in buckskin, carrying a long flint-lock rifle, silently stealing through the shadows of the great forest, with eye and ear on the alert for skulking Indians.

One little town in Tennessee, some fifty miles above Chattanooga, lying at the foot of Walden's Ridge, a great spur of the Cumberland mountains, claims to be right in the path that Boone followed through a gulch in the Ridge and across to the beautiful valley of the Sequatchee on the western side. In its early days this place was called Smith's Cross-roads, but when a railroad was built through it and an English company purchased lands and erected two furnaces, this name was considered by the inhabitants as not befitting its dignity, so it was re-christened after a prosperous city in the Buckeye State. The new name does not seem to have had much effect in bringing the town into prominence, however, and while, like all small Southern towns, it has grown by the addition of some small industries and has added to its population, it still lies nestled down in the valley, blinking sleepily at the sun, more than half satisfied with the present and dreaming, perhaps, of some future time when untold glories will come to it.

There is but one feature of the town which attracts attention and that, to use an Irishism, is not the town but the surroundings. To the west, just beyond a line of low foothills is Walden's Ridge, extending to the north and south as far as the eye can see. On the east there is a line of hills of considerable pretensions and beyond, though hidden by them, lies the Tennessee river. Both to the north and south there stretches out a beautiful and fertile valley all under cultivation. Passing through the town and winding its way between the hills to the river flows a beautiful stream of water which has its origin in a mountain brook on top of the ridge, and which, in opening its way to the valley, has carved into the heart of the mountain a deep and rugged gulch into which it leaps, plunging down past the fallen rocks that bar its passage and finally emerging placidly into the valley, rippling over stones and beneath the trees as peacefully as though it had not half an hour before lashed itself into foam over the rocks in its channel.

It was this stream, or rather the fall that it makes in leaping from the mountain top to its bed, that took me to the town. When I stepped off the train at the discouraging hour of half-past five in the morning the sun was barely perceptible, peering over the hills and

shining through the mist like a big red ball. A colored boy was at the station ready to carry my camera case up to the hotel and as soon as the train had drawn out we followed it half a mile up the track, across a trestle and bridge to the ramshackle inn. After about half the distance had been accomplished the porter's strength began to flag, and he finally ventured the remark: "Cap'n, yo' sho' mus' have ole pig iron in dis yere sa'chel." The fact was that the case was heavy. I had carried it many times—when I had to—and was painfully familiar with the faculty it seemed to have of growing more and more heavy with each step, until finally it felt like a ton weight. It was not over pleasant to look forward to carrying this load

some eight miles up the creek, climbing over and around rocks and through dense underbrush, but the photographic enthusiast readily forgets the difficulties to be encountered in the anticipation of successfully accomplishing his end.

When the hotel was reached, my baggage was deposited in the office and I proceeded to the back porch where a bucket of water, dipper, bar of soap and tin basin were at my disposal. After completing my ablutions, breakfast was announced and I seated myself at the table.

"Tea-er-corf'e?"

I turned to the girl who had put the interrogation and announced my preference for the latter beverage.

"N'eggs?"

I answered in the affirmative.

"Fried-er-biled; hard-er-soft?"

I satisfied her on this score, and she

A BIT OF COUNTRY ROAD IN TENNESSEE.

disappeared behind a partition in the lower end of the dining-room, where I heard her announce my wishes to the cook, with the added information that I was some drummer. Breakfast came in due time, and with it visions of indigestion. Nothing but the knowledge that I would have abundant opportunity for physical exercise would ever have induced me to eat. Nature was in too rampant a mood, however, for any qualms. The early hour of rising, with the taste I had of fresh mountain air, gave me an appetite that did not disappear at fried pork chops, greasy steak or leathery eggs. I ate heartily and never have had occasion to regret it.

After my meal a start was made for the mountain with horse and buggy and a companion who had volunteered to acccompany me, taking the same road Boone is said to have followed over a hundred years ago. Most of the old forest monarchs which shaded it then are gone. Between the lumberman and settler almost all of the large timber has been cleared out both in the valley and on the foothills, but on the latter there is a sturdy growth of young trees, which in time will grow to be fit representatives of their forefathers. The march of improvements and man's progress were visible all along the road from the hotel to the mountain. First the enormous slag heaps from the furnaces; then rows of neat and comfortable homes for the employes of the company, and further on, where we left our vehicle, just at the entrance to the gulch, a double row of grimy coke ovens poured out their brown and black smoke, through which shot an occasional red tongue of flame, casting a pall over the beautiful scene around them, and, withall, from their very silence giving to the place a certain air of mystery which added to its charm.

Near here the creek emerges from the gulch, forming a beautiful placid pool with a surrounding of rocks and forest which make it an almost ideal place, one where the imaginative might expect to see a naiad peering out from behind some brown rock, watching with alarm and curiosity the intrusion into her bower. A little further along in the gulch, at the terminus of a railroad built from the furnaces, were the coal mines, where, above the level of the creek, but several hundred feet below the top of the mountain, men were busily at work digging out coal for the coke ovens below.

As we advanced further up the gulch all traces of man's presence disappeared. On either side the ground rose abruptly to the foot of a high cliff, on the top of which could be seen the foliage and trees

growing on the mountain top. In some places, where the creek made a sharp turn, the gulch became wider, forming a little cove, in which was a perfect jungle of rocks, trees and underbrush, surrounded, as it appeared, by a solid wall of rocks, towering far above it. Just past one of these little coves a small stream, or branch, as it is generally termed in the country, found its way into the creek. This stream also originated on top of the mountain, and its ceaseless action on the rocks had worn out a cove, which extended back into the mountain for nearly half a mile, and of quite as great a depth as the main gulch in which we were. Its course was at an angle of some sixty degrees with our path, thus forming on top of the mountain an acute angle, the apex of which, a massive triangular-shaped rock probably 200 feet in height, had become detached from the main cliff and stood leaning forward like some grim giant, threatening destruction and desolation to the beautiful scene far beneath it. The mountain people, who are more matter-of-fact than poetical, have given this peak the euphonious name of Buzzard's Point, and, while this title cannot be considered as descriptive of the beauty or grandeur of the place, it seems that it may be appropriate otherwise, if one might judge from the number of these ugly, winged scavengers we saw around it.

Beyond this point the gulch became narrower, and the bed of the creek even more rough and rugged. Rocks of all sizes, from pebbles to boulders as big as a house, barred our passage, and here and there we came to a great barrier of driftwood, where whole trees, logs and small limbs and brush were piled together in indescribable confusion across the creek, and oftentimes high up on the precipitous bank of either side. Through these barriers the water gurgled and sang as though making merry at the destruction it had accomplished, and sometimes a twig standing partly out of the stream would be bent by the current and then spring back into place, giving a rythmatic swish which sounded oddly like a zither accompaniment to some weird song.

Not far above one of these barriers a

ON RICHLAND CREEK, RHEA COUNTY, TENN.

"wildcat" was found some years ago by the revenue officers. By way of explanation, it should be stated that "wildcat" is the mountain term for a private establishment making "mountain dew" without first asking Uncle Sam's permission. When the revenue officers came suddenly on this still, the mountaineers, seeing escape cut off, commenced firing, killing two and wounding several others of the attacking party, and kept up their defense until all of them were dangerously wounded. Of the six men captured, four died, and the other two, after serving a term in prison, returned to their homes and are now said to be hunting for the men who found them. These stills are now rarely found in the mountains in this section. In fact, the consequence of finding one is usually so unpleasant that people endeavor to avoid it. To come upon a still without warning means, in the majority of cases, sudden death to either the discoverer or the operator, depending on which shoots the quicker; and even if the unwary person should be allowed to depart, he will first receive some pretty rough handling, and may make up his mind that so long as he remains anywhere in that or any adjoining county his every movement is being watched as closely as a cat watches a mouse, and should he be seen communicating with revenue officers, or if the still be raided, he may expect a sudden demise. The chances of coming across these stills, however, are so remote that one may go anywhere in the mountains with perfect safety as to person and belongings, and always with the assurance that no matter how shabby or poor a cabin may look there is always a hospitable welcome awaiting the stranger and food and lodging for both him and his horse.

We were now approaching our destination, and after a hard climb in the bed of the creek for nearly half a mile up the side of the mountain we reached the foot of the falls. Here we rested, both to enjoy the beauty of the place and to refresh the inner man with food, with which we provided ourselves before leaving the hotel. Unfortunately there was not nearly so great a volume of water coming over the fall as we had expected to find, but there was enough to make an exquisite picture and amply repay us for the hard climb to reach it. From its bed on top of the mountain the water first fell some fifteen feet to a ledge, and from this took an eighty-foot leap below, dividing into spray and striking the rocks as a heavy rain, then collecting and dashing down beneath and around them on its way down the mountain. One large boulder almost under the fall, upon which the water struck when coming over in greater volume, was polished to as smooth and glossy a surface as might be made by the most skillful stone worker, and was as slick and slippery as any greased pole at the Donnybrook Fair. This latter fact we unintentionally demonstrated by trial, and it was the merest good luck that kept the camera case out of the pool in which we landed.

On either side of the falls the bluff stood up perpendicularly, and it was a matter of some doubt as to whether we were going to be able to get on top of the mountain and take a short cut back to town or would have to retrace our steps down the creek. Diligent search finally revealed a place where a part of the cliff had fallen, leaving a ledge at a considerable height above us, but within a foot or so of the blackened trunk of a partially burned tree. After assuring ourselves of its reliability, we "shinned" up the tree bear fashion, carrying the camera, and with not a little trepidation stepped from our extemporized ladder to the crumbling ledge of rock, climbing thence to solid ground. The creek was then called into service to remove the grime and dirt which we had collected, and a start was made for the hotel, striking through the woods across the top of the mountain for a path which led down to town.

The Cumberland mountains in Tennessee are a part of the great chain extending from Pennsylvania down through western Maryland, West Virginia, Kentucky and Tennessee into Alabama, where they terminate in a series of hills, in which the great mineral wealth of the latter State has been found. In Eastern Tennessee the range extends from the Kentucky line, near where the three States of Virginia, Kentucky and

A TENNESSEE MOUNTAIN CABIN.

Tennessee meet, in a south–south by west direction into Alabama, crossing the line just west of Chattanooga. The word mountain, as applied to this range is misleading as indicating, in its usually accepted meaning, a chain or series of rough and rugged crests, of little or no width. The Cumberland mountains, on the contrary, possess very considerable width on top, occasionally nearly thirty miles, and have an almost level surface heavily wooded with fine timber and an exceedingly fertile and productive soil. From the nature of the mountains, the range has been distinguished as the Cumberland Plateau region, and this name is far more appropriate as designating the character of the region.

The easternmost mountain of the range, commencing not far from the little town of Harriman and continuing to Chattanooga, is named Walden's Ridge, though why it should be called a ridge it is difficult to see, as it is nearly fifteen miles in width on the top. The entire mountain is formed of a series of parallel strata of rocks lying almost horizontal, the nearest to the top being a fine grained sandstone from fifty to three hundred feet in thickness, with a number of beds of softer rock running through it. Upon these the water has acted both in cutting out the the deep gulches and in carving the cliffs on the face of the mountain, undermining the harder rock above, until its weight finally causes it to break off from the main body and fall below, where the action of frost and vegetation completes the work of disintegration. On top of the mountain the soil appeared to be of a sandy nature, such as might be expected from the country rock, and its abundant fertility was shown in the rank vegetation everywhere.

Our walk led us · to an abandoned

wagon trail which we followed until it suddenly emerged from the forest and followed along the eastern brow of the mountain. The sudden change from the solitude and almost twilight darkness of the woods to the sunlit brightness of the view before us was wholly unexpected and almost startling in its effect. · There, stretched out before us, lay the valley of the Tennessee with its rolling hills and green vales, while beyond, at the edge of the horizon line and nearly sixty miles distant, stood out the Unaka mountains of North Carolina, their rough and broken peaks showing clearly against the sky even at this distance, while their sombre sides were veiled in a dark blue mist. Through the valley, winding like some great silver snake lay the Tennessee river, now disappearing behind the hills and again showing itself beyond them. At the base of the mountain just beneath us stood a log farm house where the cows and sheep were gathering for their evening meal. On beyond, Just across the

low foothill, lay the little town which, while we watched, was covered by the crawling shadow of the mountain and cast into sleepy silence. Off to the right rose the white smoke from the furnaces, floating lazily in the air above the gathering mist which was settling in white filmy streaks in the valleys.

As we stood there, the sun dropped lower behind us in the west, throwing the entire valley in shadow and blotting out the lines of hills and hollows; but its last rays rested on the distant mountains of North Carolina and touched the few light clouds floating above the valley, transforming them for the moment and giving to the scene a fairy-like glamour which made it seem as unreal as a dream.

It was now high time to make our way into the valley, so we struck out down the road and after a walk of a little less than an hour were at the hotel heartily enjoying the plain supper which had been kept waiting for us.

THE NIGHT THE PETERS BOYS COME DOWN THE ROAD.

A TALE OF THE KENTUCKY MOUNTAINS.

By James Tandy Ellis.

Tom Peters wuz a han'sum man,—
　No use disputin' that;
He warn't too lean an' lanky, nor
　He warn't too big an' fat,
But jest a happy medium, an'
　He stood six feet an' one,
An' when it come to bein' game
　He warn't afeard o' none.

An' when he walk'd he throwed his head
　Away up in the air;
The sunlight fairly glisten'd on
　His curly coal-black hair.
I've hearn a many feller say:
　"I'd give my weight in gold
To have Tom Peters' iron nerve,
　Along with his fine mold."

He had a brother—name wuz Chad—
　This Chad an' Tom wuz twins;
An' people said they look'd alike
　As much as two old pins;
But Tom he wuz the biggest, still
　They acted 'bout the same,
An' thar warn't any dif'rence when
　It come to bein' game.

Thar'd been a feud for sev'ral years
　A-goin' on between
The fam'ly of the Peters an'
　A fam'ly name o' Skeene:
Thar'd been a little killin', but
　It sorter simmer'd down
Till Tom commenced a goin' to see
　A girl name' Currie Brown.

Joe Skeene wuz goin' to see her too,
　But Tom he set the pace
So hot for Joe that purty soon
　Tom led him in the race;
An' then it warn't so very long
　'Fore things begun to warm,
'N' the neighbors put on quiet looks,
　An' waited for the storm.

An' purty soon Joe Skeene broke loose,
　An' said in town one day:
"Them Peters boys will need some salve
　If they git in our way;
For me an' brother Nat have been
　A layin' for the chance
To meet 'em face to face for once,
　An' lay 'em in a trance."

Of course the Peters boys they hearn
　About the bold remark,
But you kin bet it didn't keep
　Them in doors after dark;
For Tom he kep' a-goin' to see
　His sweet-heart Currie Brown,
But somehow you could always find
　His brother Chad around.

Let's see—'twuz on a summer night,
　About the last of June;
An' on the mountain riz that night
　A full an' glowin' moon.
The night was ca'm as one could wish,
　An' jest a little breeze
Wuz whisp'ring an' a makin' love
　To the old mountain trees.

The Skeene boys they had been in town
　A drinkin' purty free;
Old Nick wuz in the whiskey, whar
　He always likes to be.
They rode a-past the Peters house
　A usein' language bad,
A cussin' an' a throwin' out
　Their dares to Tom and Chad.

They rode past once or twice, an' then
　The door swung open wide,
An' Tom an' Chad come down the yard
　A marchin' side an' side.
Thar warn't no fumes of whiskey come
　Upon their steady breath;
Their grit wuz good without it when
　They stood in face of death.

The Skeene boys wuz a ridin' back,
  But when they chanced to see
The Peters boys, they made a halt
  Close by the old thorn trees,
An' Tom an' Chad come marchin' on.
  Old Death stood thar they knowed,
But nothin' could have turn'd them back
  As they come down the road.

And then—you've hearn it many time
  The pistols crack an' ring,
An' seen the fire a belchin' out
  An' hearn the bullets sing—
It didn't last so very long,
  The smoke soon cleared away,
The moon-beams lighten'd up the scene,
  An' thar three of them lay.

Joe Skeene an' Nat wuz still in death,
  An' by the old thorn tree
Tom Peters wuz a breathin' hard,
  An' Chad on bended knee
Wuz raisin' up his brother's head,
  An' wipin' off the blood
Which come a gushin' from his breast,
  An' spreadin' like a flood.

Jus' then a girlish form appeared
  An' stoopin' quickly down,
Between her sobs she whisper'd soft:
  "It's me Tom, Currie Brown."
He tried to raise his han'some head,
  His lips they tried to speak
Her name,—but that voice once so strong
  Had got too low and weak.

But from his noble eyes thar come
  A look she understood;
She kiss'd his lips, an' with her hand
  She staunch'd his streaming blood.
The wind sigh'd thro' the yaller pines
  An' seem'd to moan o'er head;
When Currie kiss'd those lips again,
  She kiss'd lips of the dead.

An' thar she knelt with broken heart,
  The moonbeams kiss'd her cheek;
The stars looked down in sympathy
  An' Chad he tried to speak.
Her cries rung out upon the night,
  Her tears in torrents flowed;
The Peters boys would ne'er again
  Come marchin' down the road.

JAMES RIVER ABOVE LYNCHBURG, VA.

PICTURESQUE VIRGINIA—FORTY YEARS AFTER PORTE CRAYON.

By Thomas P. Grasty.

'Who loves to live at home, yet looke abroad,
And know both passen and unpassen road,
The wonders of a faire and goodlie land,
Of antrest†, rivers, rocks and mountains grande,
Read this   *   *   *   *   *   *

The foregoing lines from Thomas McCarnasse (whoever he may be) form the prologue to the first of a series of illustrated articles in *Harper's Magazine* which made the writer's nom de plume, Porte Crayon, famous, and what was better, induced thousands to know the wonders, "the antres, rivers, rocks and mountains grande" of what is probably the most picturesque region in all the South. In that series of mingled descriptive, narrative and humorous contributions which appeared at intervals during several volumes of *Harper's*, beginning with the December number, 1854, Porte Crayon tells of a journey which he and his three cousins made through the mountains of Virginia, and the letter-press is enlivened and vivified by sketches from nature, whose accuracy has seldom been surpassed.

I have always called them the Porte Crayon "stories," probably because they were the first magazine articles that I ever found interesting enough to read;

†Caverns.

and there will ever linger in my memory the pleasant impression they made upon my boyish mind, which was intensified by the eagerness with which half the population of the village in Virginia's valley, beyond which my memory runneth not, looked for their appearance in *Harper's*—or, as I should have said, what then seemed half the population, but which as a matter of fact was only a small coterie composed of "friends or the family" who came regularly to borrow my father's magazines and return afterwards to discuss their contents. At all events, a great many people in that part of the Old Dominion were enthusiastic over Porte Crayon's productions and highly flattered by the attention which was being paid by the great New York magazine to scenes so near home.

These "stories," which is as good a name as any for such contributions of anecdote, character sketch, graphic description, table-talk, chat on the road, and all kinds of odds and ends likely to captivate the reader, would make good matter for a magazine like the SOUTHERN STATES if reproduced in their entirety, but as this cannot be done, I shall borrow from them according to my whim to add interest to what I started out to write concerning the beauties of the mountain region of Old Virginia.

As a sample of the light, breezy way Porte Crayon pursued as a writer I will first borrow the origin of the name of the colored Jehu who held the reins (not the ribbons, as they say nowadays) from start to finish in this mid-mountain journey.

In that day and time there were only two modes of travel in this region—one by private carriage, the other by stage-coach. The former was far the more "swell," as it is termed in this year of grace, 1893, or as they said then, the more aristocratic of the two. And as Porte Crayon (whose real name was Strother) set up to be a gentleman of quality, as well as an artist and man of letters, he and his three cousins went in their own conveyance. After telling about how a bag full of bullets were moulded for the slaughter of "varmints" and festive pheasants in the mountains, and how the old Crayon family carriage was revarnished and the roan and the sorrel sleeked up to the uttermost point of good looks, it was discovered that a suitable driver had yet to be selected. "Old Tom, Young Tom, Peter and a dozen others had successively been catechised and rejected. One morning a huge negro made his appearance in the hall, accompanied by all the negro household, and all in a broad grin.

'Sarvant, marster,' said the giant, saluting, hat in hand, with the grace of a hippo-potamus, 'I'se a driver, sir!' 'Indeed!' said Porte, with some surprise. 'What's your name?' 'Kc! Hi!' snickered the applicant for office, and looked toward Old Tom. 'He's name Little Mice,' said Tom. And there was a general laugh."

The story of their driver's name is thus told: "Why, d'ye see, Marse Porte," said Tom, "when dis nigga was a boy, his ole miss tuck him in de house to sarve in de dinin' room. Well, every day she look arter her pies and cakes and dey done gone. 'Dis is unaccount-able,' say old miss; 'Come here, boy, what goes wid dese pies?' He says: 'I spec, missus, little mice eats 'em.' 'Very well,' says she, 'maybe dey does.' So one mornin' arly, she come in, onex-pected like, and dar she see dis boy, pie in his mouf. 'So,' says she, 'I cotch dem little mice at last.' An' from dat day to dis, sir, dey call him nothin' but Little Mice, and dat been so long dey done forgot his oder name, if he ever had any."

And so, in the revarnished carriage, drawn by the roan and the sorrel, with the gigantic "Little Mice" for a driver, they started out—Porte Crayon and his three cousins, on the morning of the 8th of October, 1853, when Porte declared "a new era is about to commence in the history of women. The carriage was scarce driven up to the door when all three are ready cap-a-pie to jump into it! I thought the last wonder was achieved when they got all their baggage into one trunk and two carpet bags!"

Think of that, ye fashionable women of 1893—one trunk and two carpet bags holding the garments of three young ladies who doubtless had as many clothes, as clothes were counted in that day, as you will have when you start to the World's Fair!

The first object of interest visited by Porte Crayon's party was Weyer's Cave, on the Shen-andoah Valley division of the Norfolk & Western Railway.

PORTE CRAYON ON THE ROAD.

The illustrations in the first story of the series are made up almost entirely of interior cavern views. Then on to Staunton, whose public institutions received a grand free advertisement in *Harper's* for February, 1855. Journeying westward this unique party spent a night at Augusta Springs, now simply the

CANAL BASIN, LYNCHBURG, VA., BY PORTE CRAYON.

summer home of a rich Northern gentleman, and, strange to say, all mention of Elliott's Knob, next to Salt Pond Mountain the highest in Virginia, is omitted. This was no doubt due to the fact that they passed so close to it that they did not see it. It may, however, be seen from the left-hand windows, going west, on the Chesapeake & Ohio trains between the stations called Buffalo Gap and Ferrol, a half hour's ride west of Staunton.

Leaving Porte Crayon for a while, (who went thence to the Bath Alum, the Hot and the Warm Springs, of all three of which resorts sketches were made by Porte) it is worth while to consider the contrast between the hardships of the trip as made by even the wealthiest in those days—nearly forty years ago—and the luxury in which we *fin de siecle* people, of even moderate means, may see Virginia's curiosities and enjoy the grandeur of her mountain scenery. Then the "stopping places" were few and far between, and the accommodations often on the all-the-men-in-one-room and all–the–women–in–the–other order.

Today, at Weyer's Cave is a delightful hostelry, kept by Wright, the most famous host in Virginia. At Goshen, on the way to the great resorts, is an inn which in architecture, size and appointments would be a credit to Baltimore. At Clifton Forge, a few miles west, is another of almost equal elegance, while at Covington, where the Warm Springs branch of the Chesapeake & Ohio leaves the main line, is the Intermont, an inn fit to house the Duke of Veragua or any other duke who may choose to come that way. At the Hot Springs a bath house and swimming pool have just been completed at a cost of one hundred and sixty thousand dollars, which is probably more than the combined cost of all the improvements shown in Porte Crayon's sketches of the three adjacent watering places. This idea is made clear by comparing Porte Crayon's pictures of the Greenbrier White Sulphur reproduced from *Harper's* for August, 1855, with the illustrations from photographs of the Grand Hotel and a row of cottages taken last summer.

On the way to the famous resorts of Bath county, Porte Crayon crossed the beautiful Cowpasture, one of the two streams whose confluence forms James river—but he fails to mention it. In war times this noble stream was more talked

about and written about than the Mississippi itself, but since the war so little has
been said of it that few of this generation have had it in mind since their
geographies and school histories were
laid aside. But when the real history of
the war between the States shall come to
be written, its name will be found in so
many of that history's pages that future
generations will take a livelier interest
than do we in a stream whose banks for
miles and miles were the scenes of
heroism—American heroism. True, the
James, then called by the Indians the
Powhatan, was made historic by the first
settlement in 1607 at Jamestown on its
banks, and a little later by the affair of
Captain John Smith and the alleged
princess Pocahontas; but people have
got to looking on all that as a kind of
fairy tale.

The James is formed in the county of
Botetourt by the confluence of the Cowpasture and Jackson's rivers, both of
which rise in the county of Highland,
the northwesternmost county of Old Virginia, and run parallel southward, being
divided by the Warm Springs Mountain
almost all the way from their sources to
their confluence. And, by the way, one
of the most delightful drives in Virginia
is from Millboro Station to Warm
Springs Valley, the fine, firm road
threading its way over this mountain,

the summit of which affords one of the
four or five most magnificent views in
mountainous Virginia. Apropos of views
the most delightful and far-reaching in
the State, of those easily accessible, is
that from the Sharp Top, one of the
Peaks of Otter. Another, which some
consider even more magnificent, is the
view from Bald Knob or Salt Pond
Mountain. What was in Porte Crayon's
time called the Salt Pond is now known
as Mountain Lake, being a body of water
a quarter of a mile wide and about a
mile long and hundreds of feet deep,
4000 feet above the level of the sea.
This is in the county of Giles, and may
be reached by the Norfolk & Western
railroad.

But let us get back to James river,
which with its tributaries is flanked by
more picturesque scenery certainly than
any river in America, and I have heard
members of the globe-trotting fraternity
say that no river on the face of the earth
drained a region so rich in natural beauty
and grandeur.

In Porte Crayon's time there was a
canal from Richmond all the way to
Lynchburg, and a score or two of miles
above that meeting point of the "Tucka-
hoes," as the inhabitants of Piedmont
Virginia were called, and the "Cohees,"
the sobriquet of the dwellers in the Great
Valley and the mountain region.

NIGHT ON THE JAMES RIVER.

"There are no boats on the river now," observed our hero to his cousins, with a sigh. "This cursed canal has monopolized all that trade. I perceive, too, by that infernal fizzing and squealing that they have a railroad into the bargain. Ah, me! Twenty-five years ago these enemies of the picturesque had no existence. The river was then crowded with boats, and its shores alive with sable boatmen. Such groups! Such attitudes! Such costumes! Such character! They would have been worthy subjects for the crayon of a Darley or a Gavarni."

Porte then went on to tell about a trip he had taken on a flatboat, of which a certain Uncle Adam was commander, and a certain sable Caleb, first mate. "A delightful change it was," said he, "from the dusty monotonous highway, to find ourselves gliding down the current of this lovely river, stretched at ease upon a tobacco hogshead, inhaling the freshness of the summer breezes and rejoicing in the ever-changing beauty of the landscape. Then, what appetites we had! The boatman's fare of middling and corn bread was for a time a prime luxury. When in our idleness we grew capricious, we gave money to First Mate Caleb, who had an extraordinary talent for catering. Caleb would pocket our cash and steal for us whatever he could lay hands upon—an old gander, a brace of fighting cocks, a hatful of eggs or a bag of sweet potatoes. Occasionally we varied our fare by shooting a wild duck or hooking a string of fish, but fish, flesh or fowl all had a relish that appertains only to the omnivorous age of sixteen. But, after all, night was the glorious time, when the boats were drawn along shore in some still cove beneath the spreading umbrage of a group of sycamores. Then the fun commenced. The sly whiskey jug was passed about, banjoes and fiddles were drawn from their hiding-places, the dusky improvisatore took his seat on the bow of a boat and poured forth his wild recitative, while the leathern lungs of fifty choristers made the dim shores echo with the refrain."

If the memory of the good old flatboat days and nights made Porte Crayon lament the advent of the canal-boat,

what would have been his anguish had he lived to see the canal filled up and the tow-path turned into a railway track! The story of the rise and fall of the James River and Kanawha Canal is almost pathetic; for, after costing millions of money, an outlay which today constitutes a big fraction of Virginia's State debt, it was finally utterly abandoned and given away to a railroad company. Its tow-path is today the road-bed of the James river division of the Chesapeake & Ohio Railroad. The masonry in the locks and dams of this canal was so superbly substantial that, though left to the floods for the last twenty-odd years, most of it, except where broken up by blasting, stands to this day solidly intact; and as one rides on the cars and looks out upon dam after dam and lock after lock, abandoned to the elements, the first feeling, after a sigh for so much wasted labor and money, is one of admiration for what seems a veritable struggle for life by these adamantine structures.

The James flows for a longer distance through Botetourt than any other county, and its chief tributary, Craig's Creek, meets it within that county's limits. And right here I beg leave to regret that Porte Crayon was not something of a historian, for at the time he passed through Botetourt he might have obtained from men then living, but now gathered to their fathers, facts of which no record has been kept, but which, had he written them out, would have kept his memory green centuries after his entertaining stories shall have been forgotten. Named after Lord Botetourt, after having first been called Fincastle county, the whole State of Kentucky was carved out of it, and I am told that the title to the land on which the city of Louisville now stands cannot be traced without coming to Fincastle, the county seat of Botetourt. In this county, iron for Revolutionary cannon and iron for Confederate cannon was produced, and its legendary history, its folk-lore, is too rich to die for lack of a historian. However, though eleven years of my life were spent at old Fincastle, I know of but one living man who is sufficiently conversant with the history of this county to do it anything like justice, and if he would write out half of what he so delights his listeners by narrating, a most valuable contribution to Virginia's and Kentucky's history would be the result. I refer to Wm. A. Glasgow, of Lexington, Va.

If Porte Crayon could make the trip up the James today, he would be astonished at the industrial progress which may be witnessed from its banks—for instance, the growth of Lynchburg from six thousand souls to six times six thousand, due to its development from merely a tobacco mart into a considerable wholesale point and an important manufacturing centre. The difference between the Lynchburg of 1853 and the Lynchburg of 1893 is faintly suggested by contrasting the wood-cut made from a sketch by Porte Crayon with engravings from photographs taken recently for this article. Then, going up the river, huge coke furnaces have replaced the little charcoal stacks of 1853, there being of these above Lynchburg no fewer than eleven now in operation.

Of course all the world knows of the Natural Bridge, nevertheless, its grandeur entitles it to far more consideration at the hands of patriotic and nature-loving Americans than it is now receiving. I can pay it no higher tribute than to quote the words of a lady of high culture and one largely endowed with the artistic instinct, who had seen a great many of the so-called sights of the world. When I asked her what she thought of the Natural Bridge, her reply was: "It is the only great natural curiosity that

LYNCHBURG, VA., FROM A RECENT PHOTOGRAPH.

has not disappointed me." The sketch of it by Porte Crayon, reproduced in this article from *Harper's* of August, 1855, is almost as true to nature as any of the hundreds of photographs of it which have since been made. The only defect in the sketch is that it contains no human figure by comparison with which the immensity of this wonderful example of nature's greatness may be realized. Speaking of his efforts to portray the most striking features of this great natural wonder on paper, Porte Crayon declares that the task is impossible. He acknowleges that he has seen several sketches that rendered the general outline and even minute details with great accuracy, yet he avers he never saw one that conveyed even in a remote degree any idea of the majestic grandeur of the original.

Speaking of the Natural Bridge, I have of late years been struck with the preponderance of Western people over those from the East who visit it. Whether this is due to the activity of the agents who have charge of the western end of the passenger department of the railway that passes by the bridge, within twenty minutes' ride by 'bus, or whether it is due to the fact that the dwellers on monotonous, dead-level prairies have a keener relish than Easterners for such scenery as the mountains of Virginia contain, is a question I cannot answer.

Just below the Natural Bridge, at Balcony Falls, is a splendid combination view of green valley, rugged mountains and silvery streams. Here North river, on whose banks some twenty miles above stands Lexington, joins the James, and here the Blue Ridge was cut asunder by the resistless eagerness of the mountain waters to find the sea.

A striking view of an almost perpendicular cliff, rising nearly a thousand

RIVER BANK ROAD, NEAR LYNCHBURG, VA.

feet from the river's edge, is had at Eagle mountain, up stream toward Clifton Forge, which latter is a flourishing manufacturing town, where the main line of the Chesapeake & Ohio from Washington and Newport News joins the river branch, which, as has been stated, follows the tow-path of the old canal; and, after all, this river-bank freight road really does what the canal was intended to do—it links the coal fields of the Kanawha country and the grain fields of the Northwest with tide-water at Richmond and at Newport News.

Porte Crayon's party arrived at the Greenbrier White Sulphur late in October after the season had closed, and found the place all snowed under. As he puts it: "Field and forest were clothed in thin feathery white panoply, while rock, tree and lonely shrub, hanging with icycles, glittered like fancy glasswork, and icy cataracts hung from the hillsides, rigid and motionless as the sparry concretions of a cavern. But when the tardy sun began to illuminate the picture with his glancing rays, Crayon turned and thus addressed the inmates of the carriage: 'Look, girls! look and enjoy it while you may. It is but an evanescent scene, but one might live for a hundred years and never look on such a sight again. Welcome the day of storm and travail; welcome the night of cold and darkness, that like beneficent twin genii have wrought this scene of more than earthly splendor.'"

However splendid may have been the scene presented by the ideally picturesque environments of this king of Appalachian resorts, nevertheless I must confess that it is one in my estimation not to be compared with any summer-day scene to be witnessed here when the sun shines bright and the grass grows green and the foliage of the charmingly close mountains is at its richest. There are some people who claim that the Chicago Exposition will diminish the attendance this summer at the Virginia resorts, and perhaps this position may be correct so far as the stay-all-summer crowd is concerned; but of the thousands who will pass the White Sulphur on their way to the great fair, enough ought to stop over, if only for a

day or two, to keep every one of the five hundred rooms in the grand hotel, and all of the one hundred cosy cottages full all the time. There is no such place on the face of the broad green earth for rest as this. The air is so pure, the scenery so soothing, the water so sparkling.

From the White Sulphur, Porte Crayon's party journeyed backward. The next resort visited was the Rockbridge Alum Springs. Here are a few incidents of the journey: The first day was eventful on account of the abundance ot pheasants found feeding on wild grapes on the road-side, upon which Porte waged such bloody warfare that by night the carriage was loaded with game. The roads were "simply frightful," but Crayon took advantage of the situation to lecture in this wise: "That good roads were not to be desired by people in search of the picturesque; that there was no chance for adventures on a smooth, well-beaten highway; that robbers and bandits had become obsolete. Consequently he regarded a romantic, dangerous road, such as strikes the imagination with ——." Here he was interrupted by Little Mice, the big black driver:

"Bless de Lord, marster, what kind er men is dem?"

"At a little distance off," as Porte himself tells it, "six men were to be seen issuing from the wood and advancing toward the carriage in Indian file. Their hunting shirts and trousers were of mountain jeans, colored with hickory bark, but torn, stained and begrimed with dirt till the original dye was almost invisible. Some wore deerskin leggings and carried packs, while everyone was accoutred with a wicked-looking knife, a powder-horn, a bullet-pouch, and carried at a slope or trail a long rifle. As this formidable company approached with that swinging stride peculiar to the mountaineer, Mice turned of an ashy hue and spasmodically drew up his horses."

"S'pose dese is robbers, what we gwine do?"

"The forest was dark and lonely, and the suddenness of the apparition had taken Crayon quite off his guard. He began to entertain Mice's suggestion himself, and went so far as to push back the guard of his rifle-lock and loosen his knife in its sheath, and was fumbling in the sack for his revolver. By this time the men were beside the carriage, but instead of any hostile demonstration they saluted the travelers civilly and passed on."

"Done gone by and never totch us!" quoth the coachman, drawing a long breath, "and dere's deer tails and hind legs sticking out o' dere bundles."

But it is not my purpose to attempt to follow Porte Crayon too doggedly, and I will fill the rest of my space with incidents and anecdotes from his account of the journey.

One day Mice tied the reins to his leg, and drawing up his carpet-bag, with some hesitation pulled out a bundle about the shape and size of a man's head. "What!" exclaimed Porte, "have you turned naturalist, too? What are you going to do with that hornet's nest?"

THE NATURAL BRIDGE, BY PORTE CRAYON, 1855.

"Dis ain't no hornet's ness, Marse Porte; dem's bank notes, an please sir, I wants you to count 'em for me."

On examination of the bundle it proved to be a wad of one-dollar notes, a circulating medium then in tolerable repute in southwestern Virginia, furnished for the most part by Washington City bankers. When he saw of what material Mice's ball was composed, Crayon's countenance fell and vague suspicions of bank robbery crossed his mind.

"Where in the name of fortune did this come from? Did you find it or have you robbed a country store? Confess instantly."

"No, Marse Porte," replied Mice, with honest fervor, "I never stealed money in all my life—I didn't. Fact is, marster, I larnt dat way to thumb a Jack what you showed dem wagoners, so I skun dem nigger waiters at Lynchburg and Charlottesville outen dat money honestly, Marse Porte, honestly—dat money and dese two watches."

Here Mice produced a brace of copper watches that might have done duty at a New York mock-auction.

"Honor and honesty," Porte reflected, "like everything else, seem to be purely conventional."

"Dat's a fac, Marse Porte. Dem's my sentiments."

Before quoting any further from Porte Crayon, I desire to confess to misquoting his way of spelling the negro's abbreviation of master. It seems that he (or perhaps the editor of *Harper's*) had fallen into the Northern man's way of writing it "massa." Now, I beg to protest, and will leave it to the entire press of the South to decide if I am not right—that no genuine old-fashioned negro ever used this word "massa." They all said Marse Tom, Marse Dick, Marse Harry, and not Massa Tom, Dick or Harry. Porte Crayon being himself a Virginian ought to have avoided this error.

Who of us with a large early acquaintance has failed in later years to have an experience something like this:

As they put up one evening at a village tavern, a red-nosed, unshaven fellow approached Crayon and giving him a familiar poke in the ribs addressed him by name.

"I say, old hoss, how goes it? Don't remember me I reckon. Old schoolmate; look again."

Crayon shaded his eyes. "The face,"

GREENBRIER WHITE SULPHUR SPRINGS, AS SEEN BY PORTE CRAYON.

said he, "I don't recognize, but the voice reminds me of one Bill Montague."

"The same, old fellow, the same."

William Montague had commenced life some twenty years before with a small patrimony and a tolerable educa-

GREENBRIER WHITE SULPHUR SPRINGS IN 1893.

tion, both of which he drank up. With his means and respectability he also lost his good name, literally. From the sonorous William Montague (accent on the *gue*) it got to be Will Montage, then Bill Tage (pronounce g hard)— and by the time he arrived at the condition of complete vagabondism nothing was left of his title but Bill Taggs.

"Mr. Montague, I'm glad to see you."

"Mr. Montague? It wasn't Mr. Montague when we used to sit on the same bench at school. I have never forgotten our early friendship, old boy; how we used to catch flies together and drown kittens. Ah! those were rare times!" and William sighed as if the reminiscence was too much for him.

"Ah, Porte! we will never see such days again. To think of the windows we've broken, the bird-nests we've robbed, the hens' eggs we've sucked. And then the splendid lies we used to tell the school-master. You could beat us all at that, Porte; we all knocked under to you. Many a whopper I've

COTTAGES AT GREENBRIER WHITE SULPHUR SPRINGS.

borrowed from you to get myself out of a scrape."

"My friend," said Crayon with dignity, "since I left school I have been about in the world a great deal, and consequently have but a faint recollection of the matters to which you allude."

"At any rate you'll condescend to take a drink with an old acquaintance."

"Who's to pay?" said Boniface, looking significantly at Mr. Crayon, who slipped a quarter eagle into his friend's hand with delicate adroitness.

"I'd like to know," said Bill, addressing the landlord with an air of offended dignity, "why do you put that question to me when I ask a gentleman to drink? Set down your best." Here Mr. Montague flipped his coin on the table with the air of a millionaire. And when Bill asked for the change the landlord decided to credit it on Bill's bill, who rewarded Crayon's generosity by pretending that Crayon had owed him a small balance, "since, as you will recollect the night of the big spree, when you and I stole the miller's geese and got beastly drunk, etc." "No," said Crayon, blandly, "I recollect nothing of the sort—get out."

Porte Crayon's series of articles closes with an account of Berkeley Springs, and in the last pages he contrasts the style of entertainment in vogue there at the close of the last century with that which prevailed in his .day, and thus does he soliloquize: "But the old times have passed away. The old theatre has disappeared, the old bath-houses fallen to decay. The brave, the gifted, the gay, the beautiful of the old days have gone to one common resting-place." And then he says of Berkeley what we may say of some of the other resorts he sketched: "There are new times now, new hotels, new bath-houses, new fashions, new manners, new people at Berkeley. The new buildings are undoubted improvements on the old ones, and the fresh beauties that congregate here every summer pleasanter to think about than their great-grandmothers. For the rest we may quote Solomon and hold our peace: 'Say not thou, what is the cause that the former days are better than these? For thou dost not inquire wisely concerning this.'"

OLD VIRGINIA LABOR SAVING DEVICE.

THE NEED OF BEANS IN THE SOUTH.

By Edward Atkinson.

I have lately been once more through some portions of the Southland, and have observed the wreck of "busted booms" and the need of beans. Governor Wise once said of his native State that in the old times "the niggers skinned the land and the white men skinned the niggers." No offence can be taken from my making this quotation from a native orator. It has been made very manifest to me that Southern land needs beans, cow peas or other renovating plants, rather than booms, for its development. One of my friends has brought some of the land that Governor Wise described from five barrels of corn to fifteen per acre. He is a Yankee and he knows beans.

Peas are a variety of the same leguminous tribe; buckwheat is another. All are renovators of worn-out soil when rightly chosen. Who knows what kind of bean or pea is the best renovator, and why?

The coming man in the South is the pea-vine farmer. As "truth lies in the bottom of a well," so prosperity lies in the bottom of a pit or silo. The writer lately had occasion to remark to the Secretary of Agriculture that the main fault in this department for many years had been that "it didn't know beans." Time and money had been wasted in the attempt to substitute sorghum for sugar-cane and to divert needed labor from necessary work to the unprofitable occupation of reeling silk when the Chinese were ready to do that kind of work for us at a great deal less cost. I added that I hoped an assistant secretary might be found who should stand in the same relation to the South that the present Secretary himself held to the

West, so that he might lead Southern farmers to a true knowledge of beans, cow peas and peanuts. Maybe I am the ignorant person myself.

In order to justify what I am about to say I may first venture to remark that until about 1880 the South was as ignorant about cotton as we all appear to be at present about beans.

When I wrote a pamphlet on "Cheap Cotton by Free Labor" in 1861, in which I gave an analysis of cottonseed, I happened to remark that the free farmer of the future might get from an acre of good land:

500 pounds clean cotton, at ten cents............	$50 00
1200 pounds seed, yielding 600 pounds of kernel, giving twenty gallons of crude oil, at fifty cents................................	10 00
450 pounds of oil cake, at one and one-quarter cents.....	5 62
Total......................................	$65 62

Rather an extravagant prediction, when some of my friends were then putting woolen machinery into a cotton mill so as to have something to work with when the production of cotton should cease for lack of slave labor; but my proportions were about right even if cotton has become cheaper than I then dreamed it could.

It was, perhaps, a little presumptuous to predict the whole future of the cottonseed-oil industry, the conversion of the hulls into paper and the utilization of the root for dyeing and tanning not yet reached, when almost all the seed was wasted or used in a wasteful way for manure. What was the basis of the prophecy? Simply I knew the fact that the fibre of cotton consisted almost wholly of carbon derived from the atmosphere; that the oil was also carbonaceous, but that the seed produced with every bale of cotton would contain fifty pounds of phosphate of lime and potash, besides the nitrogen contained in the whole substance of the cotton plant.

When, about twenty years later, I made the statement at Atlanta that if we had a variety of the cotton plant in the North producing no lint but only seed it would long have been one of our most valuable plants, I was not myself aware that there was anything startling in this mere fact. Yet the whole cottonseed-oil industry has been developed since that date in 1880. The facts were then and had long been known to but a few men. Since then the facts have become commercially known to the whole country.

The facts about peas, beans and pea-nuts are now known in part to many, but is there any general or effective knowledge about the matter? Bean oil, I have reason to believe, is the principal oil of China. Bean meal is a great article of commerce in China, and has been used to fertilize sugar-cane in Formosa for centuries. Mountain rice, which grows on the Himalayas 8000 feet above the sea, is well known in India, and is cultivated without irrigation. The mountain rice of Japan comes up through the snow, and needs no irrigation. I have procured the seed and placed it in the Department of Agriculture. Every rice-fed nation must have beans, else the people would be starved for the nitrogen or albumenoids, in which rice is deficient. Is it not true that we as yet know little or nothing about beans and rice, either in the Department of Agriculture or among farmers in general—always excepting Yankee baked beans?

Among the food plants of India there is one which every farmer of the South, who knows even a little about the nutrient elements of food crops, will covet when it is described. In India it yields oil for men, and the cake is fed to cattle, while the refuse of the plant, being rich in nitrogen, is returned to the soil. It is one of the leguminous plants of the pea or bean variety and is called in Hindoo the *Mung-phullie* or *Bué-mung*. The pod is one and a-half inches long, each containing two or three seeds,

seventy-five of which weigh one ounce.

In these seeds there are the following elements:

	In 100 parts.	In one pound.
Water	7.5	1 oz. 87 gr.
Albumenoid	24.5	3 oz. 403 gr.
Starch	11.7	1 oz. 382 gr.
Oil	50	8 oz.
Fibre	4.5	315 gr.
Ash	1.8	126 gr.
	100	

Where maize has a food value at a certain standard of 88½, *Bué-mung* has a food value of 151. It is so rich that it must be extended with fodder when fed to stock. The plant is very prolific. Its botanical name is *Arachis Hypogœa*.

Another extremely valuable bean, very largely used in India and China as food for men and fodder for animals, is known as the *Bhut* or *Batwhan*. It has a food value of 105 against 88½ for maize.

The analysis, with the husk on or in the pod, for cattle feed is:

	In 100 parts.
Water	9.1
Albumenoid	40.4
Starch and sugar	25.1
Fat	15.8
Fibre	5.2
Ash	4.4
	100

After the oil is expressed the cake contains 40.7 per cent. of flesh formers and 7 per cent. of oil. If cut when the pods are first formed it makes a most nutritious hay. It is not attacked by any insect or parasite, and is fertilized with potash.

Another shrub pea universally grown in India, often in the same fields with cotton, is rich in albumen and starch but very free from oil. It is known as *Thur* or *Dul*.

Others are very hardy, growing far up on the hills. Some are climbers; others, which are bushy and very dense, are planted around the cotton fields for their protection.

Some of them grow on the poorest and sandiest soil. The qualities and values are all well known and defined in India, China and Japan. Those which contain the greatest amount of albumenoids are, of course, the best for renovating soil, as the nitrogen in them is now known to be drawn from the atmosphere by the microbes that live in the appendages which are found between the stalk and the root.

All these facts are well known in Asia. What do we know in America about beans? Who can tell the Southern farmer what bean or pea to plant for oil? What kind for fodder to mix with corn stalks in the silo so as to make a complete food? What kind to grow for starch? Perhaps all this is now a part of the common knowledge in the South as well as in India.

I may myself be the man who don't know beans, but the only bean oil I ever happened to hear of is castor oil, and I think there is no general knowledge about bean meal. Who knows beans? Let him reply.

Perhaps your readers will be somewhat surprised to know that *Mung Phullie or Bué-mung*, when translated into English, means peanuts. *Bhut* or *Batwhan* is the *Soy* or soya bean, lately introduced in the South. I suppose it was known before, but I imported several bushels, which were distributed, from the Atlanta Exhibition in 1881. *Thur* or *Dul* is the chick pea, corresponding closely to cow peas.

How much common knowledge is there in the choice of these varieties for renovating soil, for oil, for fodder or for ensilage?

Does the Agricultural Department yet know beans?

How about rice, the grain of largest consumption in the world, as a source of starch, of which there are over 200 varieties?

What does the Southern farmer know about upland rice that will sprout through the snow and needs no irrigation? What does the South yet know about the manufacture of starch and glucose from the sweet potato?

Soil, plant, beast and man must alike be nourished in due proportion with the nitrogenous element in food or in fertilizer. The pea and bean vine derive this element from the atmosphere without cost, but in very different proportions. The pea-vine farmer who knows which kind to choose will make the best soil and the biggest crops.

The experiment stations of the Agricultural Department may well be put upon the study of beans and rice, if the South now knows as little about beans as it did a dozen years or so since about cotton. It don't know much about cotton yet, else it would not bale it so barbarously or abuse the bale so wastefully.

A CABBAGE FIELD NEAR NORFOLK, VA., MAY 10, 1893.

TRUCK FARMING IN TIDEWATER VIRGINIA.

By Wm. F. Wise.

There is perhaps no industry of equal magnitude and importance that is so little known as the truck farms of tidewater Virginia. From more than a thousand farms within a radius of twenty miles from Norfolk $5,000,000 worth of early fruits, berries and vegetables are shipped every spring to the great cities of the North and West. How many New Yorkers knew, when they bought their early May peas, that 20,000 pairs of hands were picking early vegetables on the shores of Hampton Roads? How many Bostonians who enjoy early strawberries are aware that the berry crop of the Virginia truck farms is worth a million dollars this year? Few people East, West, North or South know that the eastern counties of Virginia embrace one of the most flourishing and most prosperous agricultural regions in the world. Here are enterprise and energy such as many people would believe do not exist in the South. Northern and Western people, never accustomed to slave labor and trained in ante-bellum days to believe that the Southern people were lavish only in the luxury of toil and labor performed by slaves, have never realized that the rebel soldier accepted the situation as he found it at the close of the war, and applied his hands and brain to the recovery of what the war had swept away. If a fair consideration of the facts herein set forth, and a visit to the great Virginia vegetable garden should not convince the unbeliever in Southern enterprise, then our efforts thus far would be in vain.

So little of the trucking industry existed around Norfolk before the war that its beginning may be located at the close of the war. Then there was no transportation from this region save by water, and four boats running to Baltimore and four to New York, all of them small, constituted about all the shipping accommodations. The people who engaged in truck farming had to learn the business from the start—how to grow vegetables and how, where and to whom to ship their produce when it was ready. The marketing of this truck was not the least of the difficulties, as no merchant desirous of maintaining a commercial or social standing was anxious to engage in a trade that branded him as a huckster, or some less respectable epithet. The capitalist looked upon our industry as temporary and hazardous, and was not inclined to keep the shipping facilities up with the continuous increase in the business. It was only when the truckers combined and demanded larger and better ships to New York that one was grudgingly given, but such was the success of this vessel that others rapidly followed, and then came fine steamers running to Boston, Providence, Philadelphia, Washington and Baltimore.

The first figures we have show that in 1879, fourteen years after the industry began, the value of the crops raised on these eastern Virginia truck farms amounted to $1,751,645. Eight years later Col. Thomas Whitehead, commissioner of agriculture of Virginia, put this on record: "The trucking business for the year 1887 for Norfolk county, and the value of fruits shipped, aggregated $2,287,042, exceeding the value of the entire iron industry of the State for that year." The Norfolk Chamber

PICKING STRAWBERRIES AT WEST NORFOLK, VA.

of Commerce gives the value of the truck raised in 1890 as $4,541,077. These are the latest figures obtainable, but the industry is still steadily increasing.

Truck farming in Virginia is a well organized and systematic industry. The farms are divided into sections of eighty to 100 acres, each being placed in charge of a competent manager, who receives a share of the profits as his compensation. This share ranges from little more than the wages of a farm hand to a quarter of the net proceeds, and finally reaches one-half the profits, when the manager becomes to all intents and purposes an equal partner in the enterprise, continuing upon this basis until he buys a farm and starts business on his own account. Quite a number of young men today have beautiful farms that were earned in this manner, and are worth from $25,000 to $50,000.

The entire crop to be raised is laid off on a diagram representing the section, and with each planting the crops travel around the farm in regular rotation. Radical changes in this plan are never made with success. The farmer is expected to furnish houses and wood for all labor; to pay in cash the regular hands once a week, and the pickers each day. This ends his obligations. The wages of the common laborer are from seventy-five cents to $1 per day; as a rule a white man who is not worth $1.25 per day is not desirable. With proper attention to his duties a good man should receive $40 per month the second year, in addition to house and fuel, and $50 the third year, after which he shares the profits. A section should net from $2000 to $4000 per season, according to the soil, location and management.

Tidewater Virginia owes its pre-eminence as a trucking region to peculiar climatic conditions, an exceedingly favorable combination of mild equable temperature and abundant rainfall. I am not a scientist but merely a practical man, and therefore I shall not undertake to advance any theories of my own about climate and rainfall. I shall merely quote from the statements of scientific men who have devoted thought and study to the subject. The statements of those who have noted conditions in this section for nearly a century show that there has never been a destruction of crops for the want of rain in the region between Lake Drummond and Old Point Comfort, embracing a width of twenty and odd miles. In a treatise on the hygienic and climatic conditions of

Norfolk, prepared for the Norfolk Chamber of Commerce, Dr. S. R. Jackson wrote: "The influence of the water is well understood here, for vegetation is much earlier on those farms which are directly located on the edge of streams, and for trucking purposes such farms are always most in demand. It may be asked 'Why has the water so much effect on the climate and vegetation?' It is owing not so much to our proximity to the Gulf stream as it is to the eddies from that great 'ocean river,' which are caused by the impediment to the northward flow of its western edge, which is produced by the great rush of water from the Chesapeake bay and from all of its tributaries through the narrow gateway between the Virginia capes. This immense outflowing body of water must have sufficient momentum to force the stream far out to sea, and thus by heading off the current of the western (which in this latitude is the warmer) edge of the Gulf stream, it causes a reflection of this warm water to our coast and into all the bays and estuaries with which it is indented. The Gulf stream is nearer to the American coast between Capes Hatteras and Henry than anywhere else, and this proximity, together with the eddies above alluded to, affords a satisfactory explanation of our climate."

Lieut. Henry H. Barroll, in charge of the branch hydrographic office in Norfolk, writes as follows about the temperature and rainfall of this section: "The climate is such an equable one that the three neighboring seaside resorts—Old Point Comfort, Virginia Beach and Ocean View—may well declare themselves to be either winter or summer resorts. The thermometer in summer ranges between 70° and 90° Fahr., and in winter rarely falls below 20°. The mean annual rainfall is about fifty-two inches, fairly distributed throughout the year, about thirty-five inches being precipitated during that period extending from the first of March to the first of October, the time when the crops are growing. Possibly it is due to this tempering of the climate by the Gulf Stream, and also to the certainty of an abundance of rain when most needed, that Norfolk has become a great trucking centre on the Atlantic coast. Be the cause what it may, those persons who have visited all parts of the globe concur in asserting that here is found a market which is equal, if not superior, to any other market in the world. The market for vegetables, game, poultry and fish is always excellent."

The growth of truck farming in this section of Virginia has caused the development of an extensive transportation service for carrying the produce quickly to distant markets by water or by rail. Formerly the truck and fruits were

PART OF A 200 ACRE STRAWBERRY PATCH NEAR NORFOLK, VA.

carted to the shores of the creeks and carried thence by sailboat to Norfolk, there to be shipped by slow vessels to Northern markets. In those days it usually took one day to gather the truck, another day to get it to Norfolk and two days more to reach New York. The country around Norfolk is now threaded

A TRUCKER'S HOME.

by the best of smooth shell roads, the streams are bridged and steam and electric railroads facilitate the shipment of farm products. Swift steamers and fast express service on the railroads put this great kitchen garden into quick communication with the innumerable family it feeds.

Last season the experiment of running solid trains of truck on fast trains from Norfolk to Cincinnati and Chicago was tried for the first time.

The average time to reach the principal markets is as follows:

Boston, twenty-four hours by rail and forty by water.

New York, twelve hours by rail and twenty-one by water.

Philadelphia, ten hours by rail and eighteen by water.

Baltimore, eight hours by rail and twelve by water.

Washington, seven hours by rail and twelve by water.

Richmond, two and one-half hours by rail and ten by water.

Cincinnati, twenty-three hours by rail.

Chicago, thirty-four hours by rail.

St. Louis, thirty-four hours by rail.

The average tourist coming to Norfolk sees but little of the truck-growing region, as the lines of railroads radiating from that city do not pass through the most extensive trucking section. East and south of Norfolk the amount of truck grown, while very considerable, does not compare with that grown to the west and across the Elizabeth river. This fact has caused many who have visited Norfolk and seen only the eastern region to disbelieve the statements made as to the amount of truck raised in the entire district, but a drive through the principal region west of the city would show more growing truck within a given time than any other single locality in the country.

The writer has been engaged in this trucking business ever since he doffed his grey uniform, and has watched its growth both from personal and patriotic interests. Since the commencement of work a regular book account has been kept, and this shows that during the last ten years the business has been fully as profitable as during any previous decade. While the product has not sold for as much money per package, a continuous curtailing of expense in many matters, taught by experience, has kept up the general average of profit. Instances of the remarkable success that has been achieved in truck farming as a business venture might be cited in numbers. In 1860 an immigrant German blacksmith and his wife settled near Norfolk, the purpose of the husband being to pursue his trade, but the four years of war drove him to farming for his support. Without detailing the steps that led up to success, it is enough to say that he is now reported to be worth nearly half a million dollars, all made by truck farming.

"Sunny Side" is a good specimen truck farm. A fair estimate of the proceeds previous to 1861 would give the owner not over $1000 for his services and rent of farm. The farm contains 100 acres, of which ten acres are occupied by the house and yard and by shore that is not available. Carefully kept book accounts for the seven years ended 1887 show that the farm netted an average of $4200 per year during that period. A section of 160 acres in Central Illinois, we will say, will sell readily at $100 per acre, although the owner must work all the year like a common laborer in order to get a thousand dollars for his work and rent of the land, and yet we are considered as demented because we think $200 per acre a fair price for Virginia truck land that will net $4000 to $5000 profit from the same area as the Western quarter section, and that with less hard labor.

"Poplar Hill" farm was one of the best managed thirty-five years ago, and carefully kept accounts, in which everything is itemized, show total expenses of $2057 for the year 1857, with estimated receipts of $2500, leaving a net profit, including rent for the farm, of $443. A careful estimate for the present would make the total expense $7000, with total receipts of $11,000 to $12,000, leaving net for profit and rent $4000 or $5000. In the first estimate, the object was to increase the value of the farm, educate the children, take care of the old slaves and raise the young, so as to add to the number of acres, mules and slaves, thus growing rich without making anything, and when the war swept away the slaves, becoming poor without losing anything. The latter estimate gives the fruit of education, when necessity compelled its practical application.

The truck farmers form a very important factor in the business interests of Norfolk and vicinity, as they figure prominently in many enterprises more or less directly connected with their business of vegetable farming. One of the truckers is president of a bank, several are bank directors. A fertilizer manufacturing company, a crate and box factory, a brick and tile works, several stores, a railroad, a warehouse and compress, a large land company and numerous other local enterprises are managed and largely owned by the truck farmers. The steam ferry between Norfolk and West Norfolk was created and is now managed by them. The truckers were the largest Southern purchasers of Peruvian guano while the agency was maintained in this country, buying a thousand tons at a single purchase, and when the agency in this country was discontinued they were the only direct Southern importers. The economy of soil and fertilizer has been carefully studied by the truck farmers, and they have probably reached a higher point in the application of science to practical agriculture than has been attained elsewhere in this country, if not in the entire world. Largely through their instrumentality the fertilizing value of the waste products of the great slaughter-houses of the West has been demonstrated. The finest mercantile buildings in Norfolk and Portsmouth belong to the truckers,

A TRUCKER'S HOME.

who are in fact a great power in money, brains and enterprise in this seaport. In every case, however, the farm itself is the principal business and all other interests are subservient thereto.

From the beginning of the trucking season in the spring there is a continuous

he a railroad official, banker or professional man. The son, while being
educated, is required to keep in touch
with the business, and a place is waiting
the moment his school days close.
There is no such thing as sons of truck
farmers seeking something to do.
Instead of farmers' sons seeking the
city, the merchants and professional

inflow of cash until fall, when the cotton,
peanut and oyster crops become productive and call for money. The large
population required to gather the truck
takes a brief rest before entering the
peanut fields and the oyster business,
thus enabling the banks to utilize the
money to the full extent. Constant
employment is given to a large population by the regular rotation of various
industries, and there is no season of the
year when profitable occupation cannot
be had for labor.

All the larger truckers have telephone
connections with their sections or farms,
and also with the telegraph office, thus
placing them in direct communication
with every part of their business. The
business itself is strictly a cash one,
and with check book, day book and
ledger in his pocket, the truck farmer
has "his office in his hat," as it were.
He is always at the head of his business
and in close touch with it.

The home-life of the truck farmer is
not without its distinctive features. His
family is as separate and distinct from
the business as would be the case were

men of the city love to engage in
trucking. It is owing to this fact that
while the population of Norfolk is only
34,986, in less than four miles of the
City Hall the population is estimated at
70,000. When the rush of the shipping
season is over, the trucker joins his
family at some mountain resort for rest
and recreation. As his own home is far
superior in many respects to seaside
watering places, the tourist will look in
vain for the Virginia truck farmer at any
watering place not in the mountains.

A few words about "Hatteras Point,"
the residence of the writer, may serve
to convey a better idea of a truck
farmer's life. Located on the western
branch of the Elizabeth river, adjoining
West Norfolk, with over a mile of water
front, its owner modestly regards it as
the finest truck farm in Virginia, and the
best in its equipment. The entire farm
is thoroughly tile drained, and every
building is in thorough repair, from the
mansion to the dog house. The mansion
contains all the latest improvements, hot
and cold water, hot-air furnace, conservatory, winter and summer dining-rooms

and kitchens, while the library reminds one of a minature telephone exchange, with its wire connection with all the various enterprises of its owner.

Railroad communication makes it possible to load truck in the fields and ship it direct to all the markets of the country. ·Likewise · supplies can be obtained in carload lots and unloaded from the cars at the farm. The importance of this will be appreciated when it is known that a season's supplies include 600 barrels of seed potatoes, twelve barrels of beans for seed, two barrels of cucumber seed, forty pounds of cabbage seed, 1000 berry crates, 10,000 boxes, 25,000 barrels, and over $12,000 worth of fertilizers. These give an idea of what

is handled on a truck farm. While writing these lines the telegraph office calls and states: "New York, April 24, W. F. Wise—Your grass asparagus sold to average five dollars per dozen.—J. J. Fredericks." This is the report of today's sales of asparagus shipped on the 22d—fifty-eight dozen, and this the first week on this crop.

These are but fragments of information about Virginia's great trucking industry. The reader must visit this great truck section and be his own judge, when he probably will learn that he is as much of a novice in truck growing as his informer is in writing articles for a monthly magazine.

JEFFERSON DAVIS AND HIS CAUSE.

By James R. Randall.

No man in the world's history has been more discussed relatively than Jefferson Davis, and as long as the bloody Confederate drama shall engage the attention of historians, his name and fame will inspire controversy tinctured with the praise or blame of friend or foe. Out of the immense mass of testimony now available and on record, a just digest will be made hereafter, and a proper verdict rendered of the cause he incarnated. I believe that future ages will hold him and his mission in greater reverence than the present time, because he was the champion of local self-government or home rule, as opposed to absolutism or centralization of power, and because the day will come when the conservative elements of the South must be appealed to for the salvation of constitutional government at the North. This appears visionary, but one of the most eminent of New England Republicans informed me that such was his opinion, based upon some of the unlooked-for results of the war and social antagonisms arising therefrom. There will be, as there have already been, startling mutations, gravitating from the public utterance of Andrew Johnson, who, when president, vehemently declared that the radical Republican ideas that he himself once veered toward, would, if carried to a logical conclusion, consecrate the ideal of the Southern Confederacy, and Wendell Phillips, of whom Foraker is the blatant imitator, at the other extreme, died proclaiming that the South had morally, if not actually, triumphed.

We have also lived to see James Redpath, the fiercest of abolitionists, recanting many of his preconceived sentiments, and even assisting in the compilation of a defensive biography of the great man who has just been permanently entombed at Hollywood. We have also lived to see, within a very recent period, no less a person than ex-Senator John J. Ingalls, of Kansas and Massachusetts, a former worshiper of that courageous lunatic John Brown, powerfully and insidiously advocating, in a far-pervading syndicate letter, the deportation of the negroes, who, in his conception, have proved, and continue to prove, a nuisance and a menace to the republic. In this connection, I am persuaded that the South takes no such view in the mass, and though abhorring black suffrage, comprehends the value of Ethiopian labor. I have, in other communications, declared that, in my humble judgment, the negro problem would be solved providentially, by natural laws. When, in the ripeness of time, the redundant white population of the East and West moves irresistibly southward to find a home and grave toward the tropic, the negro will retire before it to Mexico, Central and South America. Before he died, Hon. Alexander H. Stephens averred that, if the South were wise and discreet, there would come an epoch when the Southern Confederacy's constitution would, in the main, be preferred to that of the United States, and it is a pregnant fact that an overwhelming majority of the people, at the last presidential election, adopted almost identically the fiscal policy of the seceding commonwealths.

He is an audacious man, perhaps, who would make such positive statements, but more temerarious is he who should proclaim them impossible of fulfilment. Not to mention the amazing mutations of the remoter past, in proof of this contingency, let us look for a moment at what has happened in our own era. There dwells at Turin, in Italy, a venerable personage; who has, in a striking degree, a parallel case with that of Jefferson Davis. Let us see what Kossuth has survived to witness. He, in self-imposed exile, and physical defeat, has beheld Austria humbled in two wars; the Emperor compelled to restore to Hungary all she strove for in revolt, and all that was supposed to have been lost by subjugation. He has seen Hungarians, as prime ministers, controlling Austrian diplomacy. He has seen a monument of honor erected over the graves of his executed generals. He has seen Francis Joseph grow gray in agony, not simply because of martial adversity, but because of the tragic and appalling death of his only child and heir, and the consequential wretchedness of his imperial wife. He has seen Russia, whose intervention produced the catastrophe of his country, humbled in war, and the Norse giant of a Czar, who helped hound him down, die of a broken heart. He has seen another Czar dismembered by dynamite, and the reigning monarch the prey of Socialistic demonism. He has seen the butcher-general, Haynau, who slew on the gibbet or by musketry the heroes of his apparently lost cause of local self-government, dragged contumeliously by brawny English brewers through the slime of London gutters, and then commit suicide when disgraced by the nation he had so ferociously served. These things and many more has Louis Kossuth lived to witness, and yet less than fifty years ago no one ever dreamed of their happening. The chastening of a long-extended life has no doubt brought to him forgiveness of injury, as well as the revenges of time, but he still refuses amnesty on the terms of the conqueror, and, whether wise or not, prefers to die in exile, although honored and revered among his countrymen. I have mentioned these extraordinary facts simply to enforce the idea that though principles are eternal, nothing is so changeable as the mind of man.

There is no intention herewith to rouse ancient hopes or to encourage resentment, any more than to unsettle the fraternity of sections or impair the designs of a union of the States, or the perpetuity of the Union. The South in line with Jefferson Davis is content with the present status, has no desire to transform it, and, in case of emergency, would prove her sincerity. She recognizes the freedom of the negro and can stand his suffrage if the North can do so. She shrewdly comprehends that, if the North had known what was to follow, the negro would never have had the ballot at all, and she recollects that the first disfranchisement of the brother in black was engineered by a Republican congress and president to save the civilization of the District of Columbia. She admits that secession, however right in law, was inopportune and disastrous, when pushed to combat against overwhelming odds. She knows that her military honor is safe, and she will be forever proud of her heroic dead, however high or modest in rank or achievement. She knows that she committed no treason, and also that when treason itself prospers men call it patriotism. She knows that, under the new Union, she has development, materially, intellectually and politically, beyond what was practicable in the past. She knows that her future is boundless in promise. She has no quarrel with the North in any improper way, but, on the contrary, proposes, socially, diplomatically, martially and mentally, in all the avenues of copartnership, to seek the common glory and progress of the Republic and the majesty of the Union on sea and land. She would not take one fibre of the wreath from the brows of Lincoln or Grant, and remembers that her discomfiture came largely from the potency or prowess of a Kentuckian, a Tennessean and Virginian—Lincoln, Farragut and Thomas. Outside of all occasional gush and sentiment she is devoted to this Union. It suits her very well, and if she once forcibly attempted to dissolve it and was baffled in the enterprise, she perceives the providential thwarting, and only insists that, however unwise the effort may have been, the undertaking was not

treachery. And because of this inex-
pugnable insistence she pays her
last tribute to the dust of Jefferson
Davis.

Mr. Davis, strange to say, was born
in Kentucky, not far from the natal
place of Abraham Lincoln. It was a
curious coincidence, too, that when
Lincoln volunteered for the Black Hawk
war, Davis, then a lieutenant in the
regular army, swore him into service.
How little did either of them imagine
what marvellous relations they would
hold toward one another within three
decades! It is astonishing how fateful
men cross each other's orbits. Lamoriciere and Cialdini were schoolfellows.
The one a Frenchman and the other an
Italian. But, even in that early period,
Lamoriciere dreaded Cialdini. No one
could master him at sword play but the
Italian. Long afterward, when both
had become famous in their respective
nationalities as warriors, Lamoriciere
gave up his sword to victorious Cialdini.
Lincoln became the arbiter, in human
speech, of the destinies of Jefferson
Davis. When they met for the first
time nothing could have been more
preposterous in the fancy. Who could
have supposed for an instant that they
would "go sounding down the ages"
antagonistically as the civic champions
of their time?

The career of Jefferson Davis, up to the
war period of 1860, was exceptionally
brilliant. He won distinction in scholarly
youth. He did not fear to meet upon
the hustings, in early manhood, the
most renowned orators of the day, and
he kept the field in that contention.
He was not surpassed in skill and
daring by any officer or soldier in the
Mexican war. He was not outclassed
by any senator of the United States—
and there were giants in that senate
—nor by any secretary of war,
although, in partisan vindictiveness, his
name has been obliterated from the arch
of the grand bridge, near Washington,
which was constructed during his
official term. This was impotent rage,
for the removal of the statue of Brutus
made Brutus more memorable, and
Marino Faliero is all the more immortal because his picture as Doge of

Venice was turned insultingly to the
wall.

Because of his transcendent qualities
in all public duties, and in spite of the
fact that he protested against the extreme
secession wing of his people, and that
he was, up to 1861, so exalted a patriot
that no less an individual than Benjamin
F. Butler strove by multitudinous votes
in convention to nominate him over
Douglas for the presidency, he was
almost instinctively chosen to be chief
executive of the Confederate States.
He did as Mr. Stephens had done—
opposed secession with all of his powers
until his State withdrew from the Union,
and then, recognizing that paramount
allegiance, cast in his lot with her,
to sink or swim, survive or perish. I
refer the curious in such matters to
Bledsoe's little volume "Is Davis a
Traitor?," to Stephens's exhaustive
"War Between the States" and the
more pronounced fact that, when Charles
O'Conor proposed to try the issue of
treason in 1867 before Chief Justice
Chase and a Federal court, the victorious government who held him in
bondage cautiously retired from that
arbitrament, and though Mr. Davis
grieved at the failure of his captors to
meet the charge judicially no man ever
had a more strenuous or tremendous
verdict in his favor.

As to his conduct of the war, in a
civic station, men of prominence will
differ to the end. He had enormous
difficulties to surmount, and it may be
said that it is pure conjecture about any
one else being able to have done as well
as he did. There is no question of his
lofty intelligence and intrepidity. There
is occasional doubt of his judgment of
men and policies. According to Mr.
Stephens, the initial blunder, which did
not adhere to Mr. Davis, was secession
itself. Mr. Stephens compared it to the
abandonment of an almost impregnable
fortress, without spiking a gun, blowing
up the magazine or dismantling the ram-
parts, but quiet permission of hostile
occupation, and then attempting to retake
by storm what was voluntarily surrendered. General Wise was for fighting,
under the old flag, inside the Union.
General Dick Taylor declared that the

South lost because she did not, when she had the power, establish free trade. On the contrary, I once heard Senator Dawes, of Massachusetts, avow that if the South had, under a tariff for protection, developed her mineral, manufacturing and naval resources, the North would have invaded her in vain. When the blockade was virtually a success, the South, an agricultural country, with the sentiment of the world against her on account of negro slavery, was doomed to perish internally as well as externally. There was a limit to her resources of men and credit, while the North had boundless resources of both. And yet, several times, how near the South came to success, in spite of all odds and obstacles! Mr. Stephens insisted that had the South in time established financial credit abroad by her cotton, and resisted the temptation to invade Maryland and Pennsylvania, the result might have been changed. He also, I recollect, believed that had Toombs been president and Stonewall Jackson commander-in-chief the end, one way or another, would have come more speedily and with less desolation. Jackson is said to have bewailed the policy of scattering the precious forces of the South at the seaboard, and proposed, on the other hand, the formation of two mighty armies, East and West, for an onset when the North was half prepared and least able to endure the impact. It appears certain that had Sidney Johnston escaped wounding at Shiloh, General Grant and his army would have been captured. Bragg, in righteous indignation, broke his sword when Beauregard, instead of pressing the advantage, gave orders for retreat. He was sick at the time, and not himself. The impure water at Corinth, the point of retirement after a useless combat with Buell's fresh army, killed more men probably than fell by the enemy's bullets at Shiloh. By what is called the irony of fate, Beauregard was deprived of a prodigious victory at Bermuda Hundreds, through the temporary bewilderment of General Whiting. If that remarkable, but most unfortunate man, had stimulated his brain with a mild potation, General Butler and his whole

army would have been prisoners, as they were indeed effectually "bottled up." It is an unsolved problem about the first Manassas victory, and the propriety of an advance on Washington; but it brought about a regrettable feud between Mr. Davis and General Beauregard. I have often thought that had amity prevailed, and Beauregard been secretary of war, that master of strategy would have prevented many a blunder and saved many a battle. Mr. Davis might have improved opportunities if he had had a less dominant personality, and if he had not cherished the idea of his surpassing military talents. But he would have had many a bad quarter of an hour had he been a more plastic individual, confronted with several proud and dogmatic characters, and it is one of the grandest traits in the character of Robert E. Lee, although General Earl Wolseley does not think so, that he was sublime in proper subordination and obedience to one he considered his superior officer. Lee was great enough to take the failure of Gettysburg—so close to triumph—upon his own broad shoulders, although it is surmised by military critics North and South that a general now living lost the day by his want of enterprise in not occupying the strategic points as well as the town. General Pemberton is considered one of Mr. Davis' blunders, but Pemberton has been unduly reprobated. He was a skilful, brave and generous man. Why General Johnston never came to his relief at Vicksburg after he got into that snare, is something of a mystery. The substitution of Hood for Johnston in front of Atlanta appears to have been another cardinal error, but there was enormous pressure for a fighting man, and so Fabius was sacrificed. It is, in some quarters, believed to have been an error to make a long fight, when the North had everything to gain by delay and the South everything to lose. But what a record of glory that lengthened struggle consummated!

Frederick the Great, who had much of the skeptic in his composition, said that "great battles were fought beyond the stars." The Ruler of the Universe is also the Lord of Glory. The South was to be widowed and vanquished by the edict of the Almighty. Greatly may she have sinned. Tremendous were her punishment and expiation. The North was not sinless. She has not escaped unscathed. The South may be morally victorious if she be worthy of her best estate, and in the future the North may need her aid in many ways for the preservation of all that was ostensibly fought for in that section.

Many persons thought, perhaps some still think, that Mr. Davis should have remained at Richmond at the final catastrophe, and, amid the ruins of the Confederate capital, met his fate. It is idle to discuss this dramatic episode, and it is certain that, when Mr. Davis retired from the burning city, it was to carry out an intention to continue the contest beyond the Mississippi. Possibly, he recalled Napoleon's effort to persuade his old marshals to join him in further strife behind the Loire, but met with no favorable response. Mr. Davis received no countenance in his plan, and it was not practicable. When General Lee was similarly urged, he gave invincible reasons for pursuing an opposite course.

The pursuit and capture of Jefferson Davis were monumental blunders on the part of the Federal authorities, and but for the infamous assassination of Mr. Lincoln by Booth, who is said to have been made temporarily a madman by poisonous liquor, there might have been no arrest at all, and none of the deplorable incidents of incarceration. In the frenzy of the hour it is a wonder perhaps that a greater blunder still was not perpetrated. While Mr. Davis fiercely resented the imposition of manacles, and for a moment forgot perchance the perfection of Christian teaching, and did not imitate St. Vincent de Paul, who voluntarily assumed the place and chains of a galley slave, his dungeon experience proved the most fortunate event of his existence, and he could not then see what long years of repose and honor were ahead of him. He might, as a fugitive, have shared the comparative obscurity of Kossuth, and he might have encountered, as Belisarius did, the neglect and ingratitude of his countrymen. But just as a violent death made

martyrs of Lincoln and Garfield, imprisonment, with its humiliations and sufferings, made Davis heroic and immortal. He was the South in chains, the South in captivity, the South in agony. The eyes of the world were on him, and the sympathies of the universe were his. Even at the North he was lifted to an attitude of sublimity, and it will be to the undying honor of Horace Greeley and Gerritt Smith, redoubtable foemen and rabid abolitionists, that they not only insisted upon his release, but had the courage to offer to go upon his bond. Poor Greeley! The South, in her unworldly generosity and gratitude, and temporary want of political craft, nominated him for the presidency and broke his heart unwittingly, but her tears for him are sincere, and may he rest in peace.

Not the less pathetic was the detention of Mr. Davis after the shackles had been stricken from his limbs. The more lovable features of his nature emerged, and he became the Christian philosopher, calmly and patiently awaiting inevitable events. At that time, he was often visited by a young priest of Norfolk who had espoused his cause, as far as he could, and who, with dauntless, self-sacrificing zeal for the good of man and the glory of God, possessed a prodigious fund of learning and was, even then, a formidable logician and theologian. Though a staunch Episcopalian, Mr. Davis was a warm friend of Catholics, and remembered the loving message that Pope Pius IX, himself a sufferer for his faith, had sent to Fortress Monroe. Many an intellectual battle did Mr. Davis and Father O'Keefe wage with one another, and differing as they did radically, most tender was their friendship and respect for one another. It was in virtue of that friendship that the widow of Mr. Davis specially requested Father O'Keefe to be her guest at Richmond when the mortal remains of the old Confederate chief were to be grandly sepulchred. And very solemn was the scene when Rev. Dr. Minnegerode administered to him the communion of the Episcopal church. These soothing visitations refreshed his mind and calmed his spirit, so that he might say, as General William Preston quoted of General Lee:

"In my young days I freely shed my blood,
For what I deemed was my dear country's good.
In my old age, I only crave to be
Soldier of Him who shed His blood for me."

Emerging from his prison, with the vindication we have already mentioned, Mr. Davis sought, in several commercial ways, and by renting of his plantation, to support his family, but the task was not a gracious or successful one, even for him. He met with much encouragement, but it did not suit him, after what he had been and what he had endured. So it was a grateful relief when his friend, Mrs. Dorsey, in her will bequeathed him the beautiful estate at Beauvoir, on the Gulf of Mexico, in the State of Mississippi. There he lived to a very advanced age in quiet dignity and intellectual industry, comforted by his devoted wife and daughter. Many newspaper attacks were made upon him, especially when he, for comradeship, emerged now and then from his retirement. He rarely noticed such things, and only when the assailing party was a person of note or influence. His supremacy as a controversialist remained to the end, and his answers to Judge Black and Earl Wolseley were triumphant specimens of his forensic ability. Judge Black had never before met such an antagonist, and he never ventured to renew the contention. Mr. Davis, with logic and fact handled like a master, apparently struck him dumb. Here, too, he prepared his history of the events of the war. And then the end came at New Orleans. He passed away gently, serenely, trustfully. The whole South mourned him, and many kind and appreciative words were spoken and printed of him East and West. He had craved no pardon, asked no amnesty, made no excuse, and was, therefore, constructively not a citizen of the Republic, but he had urged his people to be loyal to the Union as it was, without apologizing for or being ashamed of what the men of the Confederacy had done and what the women of the Confederacy had endured. He no doubt had in mind the strident words of Owen Meredith:

"Be it so, though Right Trampled be counted as Wrong,
And that be called Right, which is Evil Victorious,
Here, where Virtue is feeble and Villainy strong,
'Tis the Cause, *not the fate of the Cause*, that is glorious."

It was most fitting that, after resting in the tomb for nearly four years at New Orleans where he died, his relics should be borne in reverential procession from the banks of the Mississippi to the shores of the James for permanent interment. His grave is hard-by the citadel he illustrated and defended, with such signal potency, for four historic years, and he sleeps with many thousands of the soldiers who once followed the banners of the Confederacy, and there let him rest in "the bivouac of the dead." Not far away the bronze imagery of Washington, Lee and Jackson keep watch and ward, and far below the roar and hum of industry speak of a revived people who, in the growth of opulence and power, hold intact what is most worthy of preservation in the past—the valor of their sires, the renown of their statesmen, the glory of their mothers, and the deathless love of local self-government in a Republic of freemen and a Union of States.

THE SOUTHERN OUTLOOK.

Alexander H. Stephens.

With appropriate ceremonies and before a vast concourse, on May 24th, at the little village of Crawfordville, which had for many years before been his home, the long-deferred memorial statue of Alexander H. Stephens was formally unveiled. The oration of the day, an elaborate production, was delivered by Hon. Thomas M. Norwood, of Savannah, who had a remarkable experience as senator and representative in Congress, and whose speeches and essays, from time to time, were masterpieces of their kind. The statue represents Mr. Stephens in his earlier manhood, and in the attitude of delivering his famous reply to Mr. Campbell, of Ohio, on the then relative merits of their respective commonwealths. The inscriptions on the monument are just such as he himself would have approved, and are largely drawn from his own declaration of his principles, motives and sentiments.

On one side is a passage from his Augusta speech:

"I am afraid of nothing on earth, or about the earth, or under the earth, except to do wrong. The path of duty I shall endeavor to travel, fearing no evil and dreading no consequences."

Another is:

"Here sleep the remains of one who dared to tell people they were wrong when he believed so, and who never intentionally deceived a friend or betrayed an enemy."

On another side is the following, written by Richard Malcolm Johnson, of Baltimore:

"Throughout life a sufferer in body, mind and spirit, he was a signal example of wisdom, courage, fortitude, patience, forbearance and unwearing charity. In decrepitude of age called to be Governor of the State, he died while in the performance of the work of his office, and it seemed fit that, having survived parents, brethren, sisters and most of the dear companions of his youth, he should lay his dying head upon the bosom of his people."

On the side of the monument toward Liberty Hall, Mr. Stephens' home, is written:

"The great commoner. The defender of civil and religious liberty. He coveted and took from the republic nothing save glory."

On the other side, fronting the gate and beneath the bowed face of Stephens, are the following lines inscribed:

"Born February 11, 1812; member of Georgia House of Representatives 1836 to 1840; member Georgia State Senate 1842; member United States House of Representatives 1843 to 1859; retired from Congress 1859; Vice-President of the Confederate States 1861 to 1865; United States Senator elect from Georgia 1866; member United States House of Representatives 1873 to 1882; Governor of Georgia 1882; died in Atlanta Sunday morning, March 4, 1882; author of the 'Constitutional View of the War Between the States' and of the 'Compendium of the History of the United States from Their Earliest Settlement Time to 1872.'"

In some respects Mr. Stephens was the most phenomenal man that Georgia or the South ever produced. From birth he was a sufferer in body and mind, and yet his capacity for labor within the orbit of his genius has never been excelled. It was as if he had taken a vow never to have an idle moment, and to perform with all of his might every task or duty set before him. He was so poor in youth that his education was partially an act of charity, but he paid back every dollar thus expended. He endured much humiliation in his college days, but he subdued the pride of others by surpassing them in oratory and scholarship. A vein of melancholy, largely the product of chronic disease, ran through his whole career like the wailing minor chord of music, but he learned, except in confidential correspondence or intercourse, to suppress it, and was as renowned for his anecdotical wit as for his profound statesmanship. Of political events he was a seer, but the death he anticipated from year to year eluded him until he had more than attained the limit of the Psalmist. Toward the end he used pleasantly and almost waggishly to say: "I will not die in watermelon time," alluding to the fact that the juice of this fruit had a wholesome effect upon the malady he most keenly dreaded. He did indeed pass away between the seasons. His memory was so retentive that he habitually recognized people whom he had not met for many years, and recalled circumstances they had nearly forgotten. He adumbrated the weather bureau and predicted storms when no visible sign portended them. Up to his seventieth year he could tell what kind of weather there had been on any day in Georgia during twenty years. This astonishing faculty was one of the secrets of his success, plus the training of a marvellous intellect, and it never failed him but once when he started an unfortunate controversy with Ben. Hill, who afterward became his close friend, and in lusty manhood preceded him to the grave.

From his struggling law practice in his younger days, to the very last week of his life, his powerful, subtle, luminous and comprehensive mind had harmonious and masterful deliverance. Now and then, in intervals of excruciating torture, the brain would seem to flutter, but it was restored gigantically when the crisis was passed. Always feeble, and almost corpse-like, he had to encounter physical injuries that would have made any other man lifeless and impotent for public life. But his spirit rose superior to all ills, and was over all triumphant while he survived. Even when he was apparently at the last gasp, his friends and neighbors came to him as to an oracle. His residence at Liberty Hall, in Crawfordville, was sought by the most distinguished men in the country, and to his room at the National Hotel in Washington—the room once occupied by Henry Clay, and where he died—party chiefs came for counsel and diversion. No man so formidable as an opponent on the stump, in the halls of legislation, and in written contention, ever had so many loving and admiring friends, and no man was ever more approachable to the lowest as well as the highest.

He was as particular in answering the letters of humble negroes, as presidents and cabinet officers. He kept himself poor by benefactions to others. He gave to worthy and unworthy alike, and not a few Georgians who have attained prominence owe the education to accomplish success to his bounty.

He found time to write a number of notable books, which will remain political classics. His "Constitutional View of the War Between the States" will be a text manual for future generations, and it embalms the cause of the South in an unrivalled shape.

He labored hard to save his people from civil war as a consequence of secession, and he foresaw that the defeat of Douglas for nomination by a united Democracy was the iliad of all his section's woes. But true to his convictions of State sovereignty, he went with his misguided people and prepared to share their fate. His counsels were not received at Richmond, as they had been overruled in his own State, and bitterly did the South have cause to regret it. His imprisonment was a dreadful ordeal, but it was only one of several terrible trials that he strangely outlived, and from which he sought deliverance in toil.

His people, or rather a part of them, even after the war, were often in violent antagonism to his policy or doctrines, but they feared and respected his prophetic vision, and they had memorable experience of his superior but unavailing wisdom. The masses, however, trusted him, even against their own prejudices and impressions, and so he never lost his place in their affections, and died in harness— the governor of the State.

His nature was complex, and good and evil waged contest for his soul. His strong individuality, iron will, exalted talents and resolute ambition impelled him to vanity, to conquest, to the pride of life; but he learned to be tolerant of the weakness of others, to practice charity, and, as he expressed it, "reverse revenge." There was always, too, an ever present reminder of the supremacy of God and his own inherent nothingness. The good deeds that he carried to the other existence were so numerous and potential that the foibles and faults of an exceedingly trying environment may readily be forgotten and forgiven. He loved his fellow men, his State, his country and his God, and he has gone to his account as one who "only feared to do wrong," and who "waged contention with his time's decay." He will be an imperishable memory. He will live in the tradition of his countrymen and in its history. He will inspire the young to vanquish the obstructions of fortune, and encourage the old to maintain the principles that never die. Very grand and beautiful and true are the many tributes paid to him by eminent persons, but none was more touching than the plaint, at the open grave, of his last negro body-servant : "Marse Aleck was kinder to dogs than most folks to humans !"

The Agricultural Products of the South.

There appears to be an impression among those who have seen but little of the South, particularly during the past two years, that the Southern planter or farmer is so absolutely dependent u on cotton that if that single crop fails, ruin and desolation to the entire farming community will follow. While it is true that a certain number of cotton planters still hold to the time-honored plan of planting nothing but cotton, so as to accumulate debts in a respectable manner, the time when this could be called a universal condition in the South has happily passed, and a new and broader farming industry has taken its place. To say a new industry implies that the South has always heretofore placed its dependence on the cotton crop. This may be misleading. Prior to the war there was a greater diversity in the crops of that section than even now, and it would be more proper to say that at this time the country is recovering the balance which was then observed between its various crops, and with this is feeling the advantages which have come through newer methods, improved machinery, better railroad facilities, and the development of its vast mineral resources.

In 1892 the cotton crop of the South was valued at about $315,000,000. The corn crop was valued at $248,000,000, wheat over $40,-000,000 and oats about $25,000,000. These three products then were of equal value with the cotton crop. Adding to them the value of tobacco raised, over $22,000,000 ; of rice, about $10,000,000 ; Florida oranges, about $3,500,000, and of garden truck, fruit and vegetables shipped North, between $40,000,000 and $50,000,000, the total value of the products named amounts to about $400,000,000.

It was only in the years immediately following the war that cotton was raised almost to the exclusion of other products. This was because the people were almost penniless and cotton was the one crop upon which advances could be secured. The condition of things has been steadily improving, and within the past two years the lesson taught by planting too much cotton has been so impressed upon everyone engaged in it that there has been a general effort to raise more

foodstuffs, and particularly to provide the food needed on each plantation or farm.

The Southern farmer today is not solely dependent upon his cotton crop for a living. In western Tennessee. Arkansas, Mississippi, Louisiana and Texas, while some few are following the old plan of purchasing food and planting cotton, the vast majority are raising diversified crops, and each succeeding year will see this plan carried out in a greater degree. In Georgia and th · Carolinas cotton-raising will soon hold second place, as to value, among the agricultural products of the States, not necessarily because less will be raised, but because of the increase in the production of cereals, fruits and vegetables. Through the western part of the cotton belt such a condition will not be likely to exist, but cotton will never again be raised in place of food products, as has been done in the past.

Why Immigrants Shun the South.

The editor of the *American Artisan* picked up a phrase-book for newly-arrived Swedish immigrants some days ago and ran across the following Scandinavian-American dialogue :

Q. "After 1 land in New York shall I there stay?"

A. "No. You should take a train and go West to Minnesota or Dakota, where you can get a big farm with little money."

Q. "Why shall I not go to Texas ?"

A. "Texas is not a good place for the Swedes for to go. The people are not good like in Minnesota, but bad and fierce. The people live in second stories and pull up the ladders at night, or else the cowboys would rob them. No Swede must go to Texas."

This is no joke, but a verbatim quotation, bad grammar and all, from a guide-book, with Swedish and English in parallel columns, and distributed broadcast over Sweden by the agents of a steamship company. Concerning its utter falsehood there can be no doubt at all. We give it merely as a straw to show that the trend of immigration is toward the Northwest.

We invite the attention of the Southern governors and all others who are interested in the Southern immigration movement to the above extract from an editorial in the *American Artisan* of May 20. This will give a hint as to the obstacles that must be confronted in stimulating Southern immigration, and it will serve to show how unfairly, how unjustly, yes, how dishonestly, the South is being treated by those who handle Western and Northwestern immigration. By systematic misrepresentation a widespread impression has been created to the effect that the South is no place for an honest, inoffensive and industrious immigrant. It is to counteract this slander and to spread the truth about the South that calls for vigorous work of a most practical character on the part of all who are interested in peopling the vast unoccupied areas of the South with desirable foreigners.

This text, furnished by the *Artisan*, gives another illustration of what we have endeavored to impress upon the minds of the people of the South, namely, that effective work in the immigration movement can be put forth only across the ocean, among the people who are the most desirable immigrants.

Impressions created in the minds of immigrants before they leave their homes are of the utmost importance, and a falsehood lodged there cannot easily be removed by any amount of argument when the immigrant has reached our shores. Upon such lines the mighty movement into the Northwest was started and still is maintained, and if the South desires to reap the benefits of such an influx of settlers it must be accomplished by methods that have already demonstrated their success, namely, missionary work abroad.

NOTES ON SOUTHERN PROGRESS.

LAND in the suburbs of Wheeling, W. Va., is in demand for residence sites. The West Virginia Building and Loan Association has recently secured an option on 100 lots on Wheeling Hill, where already over 100 lots have been sold to individuals. The land is to be improved with cottages, which will be owned by members of the association.

THE coffee industry of Mexico is being rapidly developed by the arrival of representatives of English, French and German syndicates, who have purchased extensive coffee lands in the States of Vera Cruz and Oxaca. These syndicates will invite immigration and engage extensively in the production of the best grades of coffee. The demand for land for the cultivation of coffee is increasing rapidly, over 1,000,000 acres having been sold during the past six months. Many Americans are among the purchasers.

IT seems very much like "sending coals to Newcastle" to manufacture cotton goods in this country and send them to England, and particularly when they go right into the heart of the cotton manufacturing district—Manchester. Yet that is what is now being done with goods made in a certain cotton factory in the South. Besides doing this, the same factory and others are making and shipping goods on the orders of concerns located at Fall River and other Northern cotton manufacturing points. The fact that the South is leading in the manufacture of certain classes of cotton goods, and is steadily forcing its way into the market with the higher grades, is universally admitted by spinners, and it is only a question of time when the finest grades will be made there and compete with the best material made in the world. Already the Southern product has more than a standing in the trade—it has a well-assured position, which the market has been forced to yield to

it, and one which it will always hold and advance.

THE board of health of New Orleans, after giving careful consideration to the proposed sewerage system to be adopted by the city, has passed a favorable report upon it, approving the plans and recommending that the work be carried on with all possible dispatch.

THE Georgia Exposition Co. has agreed to pay the Georgia State Fair Association $3500 to hold its fair in Augusta during the progress of the exposition, which opens October 17 and closes November 17. It is expected that the exhibits of Augusta's cotton factories, foundries, machine shops, factories, flour mills, marble works, brick and tile works and other manufacturing concerns will be more extensive than ever before, while the agricultural, horticultural and floricultural features of the exposition will be of a high order.

THE following allotments from the appropriation to improve the Mississippi river have been made by the Secretary of War: Levees $40,000, in addition to the $1,500,000 already placed at the disposal of the Mississippi river commission; for surveys, gages and observations $100,000; for first and second districts—Plum Point reach $240,000, Plant Point reach $179,000, dredging experiment $40,000, Hopefield bend $100,000, surveys, gages and observations $8000; third district—stone $100,000, plant $113,000, Lake Bolivar $15,000, surveys, etc., $12,000; fourth district—surveys, gages and observations $12,000; total $2,665,000.

AMONG the various laws passed by the Texas legislature at its recent session was one relating to roads, the chief feature of which is authorization of the issuance of county bonds for road purposes. The law is made to apply only to the counties of Cameron, Harris, Fayette, Dallas, Brazos, Coryell, Bexar, Rockwall and Ellis, giving to the county commissioners the general rights of eminent domain, including draining and ditching necessary for the building of public roads. It authorizes them by a resolution to fix an election at which a majority of the property holders of the county shall decide either for or against the issuance of county bonds for road-building purposes. Only property holders are allowed to vote. If a majority of these decide in favor of the road bonds, it shall be the duty of the commissioners to. issue bonds bearing not exceeding 5 per~cent. annual interest and redeemable in not less than ten or more than forty years. These shall not be sold for less than their par value, and shall not amouut to more than a levy of fifteen cents upon the $100 of such property valuation as will yield sufficient revenue to pay interest as it accrues and a sinking fund sufficient to pay the principal at maturity. The commissioners are prohibited from using the funds derived from the sale of the bonds or the tax levied for any other than their prescribed uses. It is provided that the State board of education shall purchase these bonds under the same conditions that it now invests the school fund in other county bonds. All roads and bridges built under this act are required to be constructed under the supervision of a competent civil engineer, the commissioners being directed to employ the county surveyor or some other competent person for the purpose. This act became a law without the executive signature.

FRUIT-GROWING is becoming a source of much profit in Georgia. Houston county is the base of operations of several fruit companies in which Ohio people are extensively interested. That section of the country seems to be extremely well adapted for raising fruit. The climate and nature of the soil are all that can be desired. To give an idea of the profits, J. B. James, superintendent of several large fruit companies, states that the profit on a carload of peaches often runs as high as $900, although freight rates to the North and West are from $250 to $300 per car. Shipments usually begin about June 1 and continue until August 1. Most of the varieties are marketed before the Maryland and Jersey fruit is ripened. The markets include Cincinnati, Chicago, New York, Baltimore, Philadelphia and Boston. Among the staple varieties of peaches for shipment are he Alexander, Shumaker, Waterloo, Early Rose and Craw-

ford. In the last three years six companies have started, owning nearly 5000 acres, which have been planted with peach trees. pear trees, nursery stock and melon vines. Around Fort Valley, Ga., fruit-growing has increased the value of land from $20 to $50 per acre. The companies are growing 3,000,000 plum cuttings for orchards and 250,000 peach seedlings. Fruit culture has resulted in the establishment of a crate factory at Fort Valley which employs 100 hands, while it is stated, a canning factory with a capacity of 20,000 cans per day will be running in a few weeks. Many of those interested are Ohio people, who were induced to locate in central Georgia through the efforts of Henry W. Grady and a number of Georgia farmers and newspaper men. Near Grand Junction, Tenn., is a country which is favorable for small fruit culture. A number of farmers have given up cotton planting and find a much larger profit in raising berries, melons, etc. Some growers realize $250 per acre.

A. L. JONES, an expert in the hop-growing business, has been traveling through North Carolina to ascertain if the section is favorable to raising hops. He went through Henderson, Kittrell, Raleigh, Southern Pines and other towns in that locality, and is reported as being highly pleased with the climate and condition of the soil. He believes that the ho 1 industry will be added to North Carolina's pursuits, and that some of the New York State growers will eventually locate there. In central New York thousands of acres are given up to hop yards.

THE immigration agent of the Norfolk & Western Railroad has purchased a small farm at Cozney Springs, near Roanoke, Va., and proposes establishing on it some German or Swiss truck farmers who are expected to arrive before long. If the effort is successful other farms will be purchased at desirable localities along the line of the railroad.

A NEW enterprise lately projected at Natchez, Miss., to be known as the Natchez Manufacturing & Aid Association, has just been incorporated. The object and purposes of this organization are the establishment of manufacturing enterprises in the city of Natchez and vicinity, and to afford aid thereto under the rules and by-laws of their charter. The capital stock of this corporation is placed at $1,000,000, divided into 10,000 shares of the par value of $100 each. The incorporators, who will also constitute a board of directors, are as follows: L. G. Aldrich, Henry Frank, Frank Gerard Brandon, Allison H. Foster, James W. Lambert, A. G. Campbell, James Farrell, P. W. Mulvihill, S. J. Perrault, E. A. Enochs, Henry C. Griffin, Abe Moses, J. H. Davis, C. L. Tillman and William Davis.

THE site for the New Orleans bridge has been selected, and the plans, which have been approved by the War Department at Washington, provide for a bridge located above Twelve-Mile Point, opposite Boisblanc on the east bank and Willswood plantation on the west bank. The branch road is laid out in the plans from the river through Willswood and Willow Grove plantation to the Texas & Pacific and Southern Pacific on the west and to the Illinois Central at Shrewsberry on the east bank. The greatest depth of water shown at the crossing is 100 feet, and the line strikes both banks at right angles. The width of the river at that point is 2290 feet. The plans show three spans, the centre being 1037 feet in width on the low-water line and 1070 feet between the middle of the piers, and the side spans are 610 feet each. The height of the bridge above extreme high water will be eighty-five feet and above low water 103.7 feet.

THAT New Orleans has entered an era of rapid growth and extension is indicated by the striking increase in the number of buildings erected during the last year. In the twelve months ended April 30 permits were issued for the erection or improvement of 1984 buildings, as compared with 1498 during the corresponding period of the preceding year, while the expenditures covered by the permits show an increase from $1,874,129 to $3,119,919. During the month of April alone the expenditures on new buildings in New Orleans amounted to $598,705. A marked improvement in the character of the new buildings is also noted.

THE business men of Louisville, Ky., are trying to accomplish two objects which will be of great benefit to the city, and in one case will have an important effect throughout most of the Western States, besides assisting to develop Southern commerce by water. The first object is to have the State capital removed to Louisville, and at the last meeting of the Louisville Commercial Club a resolution was passed favoring the issuing of $1,000,000 bonds by the city to be paid the State in consideration of the removal. By securing the capital the city would gain a large amount of trade, to say nothing of the many other benefits which would accrue to it. The other project is no less than a scheme to attract more trade from Central and South America by the way of Southern seaports and railway lines to the West. The recent establishment of a steamship line between Pensacola and Mexico is a part of this scheme, which in brief is to select a point like Pensacola and establish regular ocean routes to Porto Rico, Guadaloupe, Martinique, St. Lucia, St. Thomas, Barbadoes, Trinidad, Demarara, Para, Pernambuco, Bahia, Rio de Janeiro, Santos, Buenos Ayres and Montevido. It is a plain business plan of business men to open up new territories for trade, new lines of commerce, and especially to get their goods cheaper by a reduction in freight rates. A guarantee fund of $100,000 will be appropriated to pay any possible losses. It is believed, however, that the line just started will be a profitable one. In that case the guarantee fund will be used in extending the service. There is no desire to make a profit other than the cheapening of freight rates. Some figuring has been done on the estimated saving by the change of route from the present one via New York, and it is stated the one proposed will effect a saving of 30 per cent. Aside from this, there will be an average saving of four or five days in receipt of the commodities from South America.

THE Commercial and Industrial Association of North Carolina, which includes a membership from twenty-four of the principal towns of the State, is making special efforts to develop the resources of North Carolina through organized effort. Among the topics which the association is now discussing are the State at the Columbian Exposition, improvement of public roads, crops, municipal ownership of gas, water and light plants and encouragement of immigration. The State Press Association is working with the Commercial Association, and promises to assist it in every possible way.

A GLIMPSE OF FLORIDA IN CHICAGO.

THE

SOUTHERN STATES.

JULY, 1893.

SOME SOUTHERN EXHIBITS AT CHICAGO.

By Thomas P. Grasty.

In view of the immensity and diversity of Southern resources, plaintively calling for development, it was generally expected when the World's Fair was first broached that Southern exhibits would constitute one of its most interesting and conspicuous features. Far from this expectation being realized, the showing here made by the South is a source of congratulation only to the enemies of Southern progress. To those who love and are proud of the South, the situation, take it all in all, is one for sorrow and chagrin. This is all the more surprising when the great impetus given to Southern progress by the Atlanta Exposition in 1881 is remembered, and likewise the many benefits, fewer proportionately it must be conceded, flowing from the Cotton Centennial at New Orleans in 1884–'85.

Fortunately, however, this regrettable condition is not wholly irremediable, nor without omen of ultimate good. In fact, there is ground for hope that, just as the missing of a great opportunity has often been the means of arousing the individual to new activity, so it may now stir up the people of the South to unprecedented steps for their own and their country's welfare. Many a man has remained unenterprising all his life through exemption from competition, or

through a failure to see with his own eyes how others make the edges cut. The people of the South, naturally equal to any on earth in the elements that underlie thrift and progress, have but to come to this World's Fair in order to find out how they are sleeping away their sunshine while the West is making hay.

But there will be other days besides today. The great tide of immigration must be made to flow where it now belongs. There was a time when its natural drift was westward. That was when good land was cheaper there than anywhere else. Today land is cheaper in the South than in the West. Today it is easier to earn a dollar in the South than in the West. Nowhere else is energy or "gumption" capable of purchasing more of those things which civilized man desires or requires. For all that, however, the day is some distance off when this tide of immigration will of its own motion rush upon the South. The barriers of ignorance and prejudice and misconception on the part of the public must be got out of the way, and nobody will ever do this but the people now in the South themselves.

Therefore let us hope that as many Southern people as possible may come up here and get ideas of how to do the

KENTUCKY TOBACCO AND HEMP.

work that it is necessary for them to do before their section of this glorious Union will, at least for many years, begin to enjoy the measure of prosperity which nature designs it to enjoy. Let us urge them to come here and see how the new State of Washington has built a colossal cabin, every log in which is more than eloquent in praise of Washington's timber wealth — a cabin big enough to hold all the buildings of the Southern States put together, and filled with things calculated to make the home seeker long to plant his vine and fig tree in that alluring corner of the republic. Let us pray that our Southern friends may come here and see what a building California has, and compare the splendid fruit exhibit it contains with those of their own beloved States. The Southern man or woman, or I was about to say, ten-year-old child, who may come here and compare the exhibits made by the South with those made by the West and fail to go home longing for another chance to let the world know

what a rich and fruitful and heaven-favored land is ours, will be one of the kind the poet doubted the existence of when he queried:

"Breathes there a man with love so dead
Who never to himself hath said
This is my own, my native land!"

It would be unjust to the South to speak of the scantiness of its representation here without explaining the why and wherefore of it. Some Southerners have been heard by way of apology to say that it was due to poverty. No more erroneous or more unfortunate explanation could well be advanced. Poverty is one thing, temporary financial stringency another. Poverty proves one of two things, lack of resources or lack of industry. As a matter of fact there is lack of neither in the South.

One of the troubles was that the South, about the time appropriations ought to have been made for State exhibits, was seized with a retrenchment and reform spasm, which it did not get over in time. Candidates had to pledge themselves to oppose every sort of appropriation in order to get elected to legislatures. Nevertheless, the writer has always held that there would have been little difficulty in getting liberal appropriations even from "granger" legislatures had there been at hand men who knew how to collect and prepare State exhibits—men who could show just how the money would be spent. But, unfortunately, men at the South capable of presenting such practical plans and of carrying them out are scarce and generally have other work to do.

Another trouble in the way of adequate provision for Southern exhibits was, as has already been intimated, want of confidence, through inexperience, in the efficacy of advertising. The people generally did not realize that the settlement of the West had been accomplished only through the expenditure of millions of dollars for glorifying Western advantages. The truth is that the cost of all these magnificent Western exhibits is a mere bagatelle compared with the aggregate that has been invested in printer's ink for the same general purpose. Indeed, these exhibits go to show how well investments of that kind have paid. Let the people of the South make a note of this.

But the main trouble was the low price of cotton at the time the appropriations were under consideration. At that time the South was suffering the throes of monetary stringency, such as the country in general is groaning under today. But the South is now in better financial condition than any section of the Union. At the conference of bankers just held in Chicago, the reports made by Southern delegates were calculated to make those from the West open their eyes. One of the effects of the hard times resulting from the sudden fall in the price of cotton was the raising of more food products—the general diversification of crops. Thus necessity proved the mother of prosperity.

Governor Fishback, of Arkansas, who brought about the convention of Southern governors at Richmond a few months ago to devise ways and means to increase immigration, is of the opinion that much may yet be done to redeem the meagre showing made by the South at the World's Fair. He thinks that the widest publicity ought to be given to this paucity of Southern exhibits, so that public-spirited citizens may raise funds to supplement the deficiency. The bulk of the money for the Arkansas building and exhibit was raised by private subscription through the efforts of the women of that now rapidly developing State, and the usefulness of the exhibit is being enhanced by advertising done by private enterprise.

Speaking of the duty of our people in the present emergency, Governor Fishback in a conversation with the writer said: "A picture in the Kansas building, in whatever spirit it was conceived and from whatever invidious motive it is exhibited, furnishes at once an evidence of the false impressions prevailing in regard to the South, and an illustration of the duty of the South in making known the truth. This picture creates the impression that the South is adapted to nothing but cotton, and is intended to convey the idea that there is an entire absence of comforts in a home which relies upon cotton alone for its support. This latter proposition is as true of wheat as of cotton. No home can have many comforts which relies upon any single crop, and what is true of the individual home is also true of a community made up of an aggregation of homes."

"But," Governor Fishback went on to say, "the falsehood in the impression conveyed is that the South is not adapted to the cereals and grasses. The fact is the South is capable of more profits from grazing, to say nothing of the cereals and other agricultural products, than the colder and less hospitable North. Wherever a diversity of crops has been intelligently tried in the South the experiment has proven a financial success. In my judgment the ideal home is possible only in the South. Few will believe this because of the habit, which past conditions have superinduced, of confining agriculture to cotton. Let those of the South who raise wheat and oats and corn and the grasses have them brought up here and properly displayed so that all the world may see and believe."

Apropos of diversity of agricultural products, one of the most significant Southern exhibits here is a cow. A revelation to thousands and thousands every day is the story which this cow tells—a story short and true. Alabama is the State sending the cow which stands today as world winner in the production of milk and butter. Her name is Signal's Lily Flagg and she was born and bred and now resides at Huntsville. Her record from May 31, 1891, to June 1, 1892, was 13,092 pounds of milk and 1047 pounds of butter. The next best milk and butter cow in the world is Bison's Belle, of Columbia, Tennessee, and the fourth place is also held by a Tennessee cow. Stockraising in the South is on the increase, and there are parts of Mississippi, for instance, equal for grazing purposes almost to the famous bluegrass region of Kentucky.

Meagre as is the sum total of Southern exhibits in comparison with those of Northern States, there are a few which are well prepared and which will do a great deal of good. There are some States which have buildings and no exhibits of either raw material or products, and some with exhibits but no buildings. Where there was not money enough for both, the latter plan will prove to be the wiser. Kentucky, which appropriated more money than any Southern State, has both a building and exhibits of raw material. So, too, has Virginia. But it is surprising that Virginia's furnaces and iron works are utterly unrepresented. If Krupp, of Germany, could spend half a million showing his guns, surely the Tredegar works of Richmond, which made the Confederacy's guns, and now makes other iron products, could have afforded for the glory of Virginia if nothing else to make a display. The same may be said of the Richmond Locomotive Works.

One of the best represented of Southern States is West Virginia, whose legislature appropriated $60,000, which has been expended skillfully and judiciously. The display from this State in the Forestry building is especially commendable.

LILLY FLAGG, OF HUNTSVILLE, ALA., THE PRIZE BUTTER COW OF THE WORLD.

NORTH CAROLINA'S AGRICULTURAL EXHIBIT.

North Carolina's exhibit is the one which will probably take the prize offered for the best collective exhibit made by any State or nation. This exhibit is so meritorious that I shall have more to say of it directly.

South Carolina, immensely rich in resources,. and proportionately less developed than any Southern State, is entirely unrepresented, except by a little phosphate rock. Though too late to make up an exhibit, the South Carolinians ought to get up organizations all over the State and have prepared handsomely illustrated printed matter describing the natural wealth of their State.

Georgia, "the Empire State of the South," is without an exhibit.

Alabama, which makes more pig iron than any Southern State, and which supplies the Pennsylvania railroad with car-wheel iron, has no State display whatever.

Florida is represented only by what private corporations have done, notably the Okeechobee Land Company.

Mississippi, in whose soil flourishes everything that can be grown in the United States, has no exhibit except one made by a lumber company.

Texas, whose Bessemer ores are better than those of the Lake Superior region, and whose agricultural advantages are unsurpassed on the face of the earth, has a building but no exhibit.

Tennessee, which ought to have had one of the grandest displays on the grounds, is entirely unrepresented.

The Missouri exhibit is excellent.

The State of Virginia has a building filled with relics which are not likely to bring a single dollar or a single homeseeker within her limits. There are ores from Virginia in the Mining Building, but many of them bear no labels to show what they are or whence they come. There is reason to hope, however, that great improvements will soon be effected. Then will be time enough to describe Virginia more in detail.

Louisiana has a very creditable representation, including a handsome building and displays in the Agricultural, the

Mining and the Forestry Buildings.

The various exhibits of North Carolina, as has been said, show so much good management as to deserve a special description. Only $25,000 was appropriated and that did not become available till March 14, last. A State board of managers was created, composed of the board of agriculture and the national commissioners of North Carolina. Of this board Col. W. F. Green is president; Miss Florence Kidder, vice-president; P. M. Wilson, executive commissioner, and T. K. Bruner, secretary and commissioner of exhibits.

There was not money enough for a State building and for adequate exhibits in the four great departments in which North Carolina stood ready to compete with the world, namely, the Agricultural, Fisheries, Mining and Forestry. Accordingly every energy was bent upon preparing displays in these departments which collectively would stand a chance to win the prize, and which separately, each in its way, would indicate existing conditions and future possibilities.

In the forestry exhibit made by North Carolina, the plan adopted was to show planks four feet long and four inches thick; the upper half highly polished, the lower simply dressed. Above each plank is a photograph, 22x30 inches, of the identical tree from which the plank was sawed, and above this another photograph of the same size showing a section of the forest in which the tree grew. Over one hundred of these planks are in the display, each labeled with its proper scientific and popular name. To each is attached a map showing the portions of the State in which that particular kind of timber occurs. There are also in the exhibit full photographic illustrations of the turpentine industry in all its phases. There is besides a wonderful collection of medicinal herbs made by Wallace Brothers, of Statesville. Palmetto trees from Smith's Island shade the four corners of the space containing this forestry display from "the old North State." The timber was collected by Mr. Giffort Pinchot, forester of Mr. Vanderbilt's great estate in North Carolina. The maps were drawn by Mr. W. W. Ashe, of the North Carolina Geological Survey, who wrote an article for the May number of the SOUTHERN STATES Magazine on the Forestry of North Carolina. This exhibit is under the special care of Mr. George F. Greene. North Carolina has the advantage of a double exhibit, as there is a very beautiful and unique display of timbers and photographs sent by Mr. Vanderbilt from his Biltmore estate.

North Carolina's mineral exhibit occupies a large and conspicuous space at the corner of the two main aisles in the Mining Building. It attracts constant attention alike from technical and plain every day people on account of the great range and variety of its contents and the perfect system shown in classification and arrangement. The exhibit embraces both economic and precious ores, stones and metals. There are iron ores, copper ores, building stones, marbles, gold ore, gold nuggets and

NORTH CAROLINA'S AGRICULTURAL EXHIBIT.

NORTH CAROLINA'S FISHERIES EXHIBIT.

180 varieties of gems, including diamonds, hiddenite, sapphires, rubies, beryls, rose garnets, topaz, amethysts, emeralds and quartz crystals. These were collected under the special direction of Mr. 'T. K. Bruner, commissioner of exhibits. One of the most striking features of this mineral department of the North Carolina exhibit is a display of mica, one crystal among the many weighing over 300 pounds. The collection of the ores was superintended in part by Professor J. A. Holmes, State Geologist. Mr. H. B. C. Nitze, of the State Survey, made a technical collection of iron ores, and come here and put the exhibits in place, labeled carefully and correctly. Mr. R. Earnes, manager of the Gold Hill mines in Rowan County, made the larger part of the collection of gold, silver and copper ores. The sandstones, the cut and polished specimens of granite and marble are well worth investigation on the part of builders. A column of ashler work five feet in diameter, from the Mount Airy quarries, is another attractive feature of the display. It would be difficult to call for a mineral not to be found in this exhibit.

The Southern State exhibit, which causes the greatest surprise to sight-seers at the World's Fair, is that from North Carolina in the Fisheries Building. All the food fishes of the State are shown, not mere casts but mounted specimens. There are aquatic birds and game water fowl; a pen of living diamond-back terrapins; models of all the different kinds of nets and appliances for catching fish, among them one of the enormous seines, a mile and a half long by thirty feet deep, used on the North Carolina coast. The accompanying illustration shows a fisherman's hut made of salt-marsh bullrushes. Mr. H. H. Brimley, of Raleigh, is in charge of this fine display.

The agricultural department of North Carolina's exhibit embraces probably the largest variety of products shown by any State or nation. The portion of it devoted to tobacco contains the finest and costliest kinds grown in the United States. It is made up largely of what is known as "Virginia Bright", of which as much as 80 per cent. of the total product of the two States of Virginia and North Carolina is grown in the latter. It got to be called "Virginia Bright" because most of it was marketed in Virginia cities. There is cotton in every stage of growth, with cereals, grasses and truck-garden products in infinite variety. There are even live tea plants. Soils from various portions of the State are so arranged as to show the strata from the surface to a depth of several feet. There is a complete assortment of North Carolina's phosphate rock. This agricultural exhibit was collected under the supervision of Dr. H. B. Battle, director of the State Experiment Station, and is in charge of Mr. Joseph Gill of Raleigh.

The horticultural exhibit of North Carolina now contains only fruits in glass jars and thirty varieties of natives' wines, the principal vineyards represented being Hoyt's of Buncombe County, "The Tokay" at Fayetteville and "The Medoc" of Halifax. The wines include champagnes, clarets, imperials and scuppernongs. Fresh fruits of every kind will be shipped from the State and shown in this exhibit as they mature. Later on one of the features, which will be a novelty to most visitors, will be scuppernong grapes, discovered and made famous by Sir Walter Raleigh. Professor Saunders, of the United States Pomological Depart-

ment, recently said that North Carolina was the best apple orchard in the Union.

I have thus given special prominence to the display made by North Carolina, because it shows how much may be done with very little money; because it is in every respect significant and representative; because it embodies a correct idea. It says so much and says it so well that Mr. Wilson, the Executive Commissioner, and the experts in the several divisions who helped him prepare it and install it, deserve the meed of praise not only from the people of North Carolina but of the whole South. Good judgment and economy were exercised even in designing the cases, tables and racks, which are all of oak, and which, instead of being destroyed after the Exposition, will be taken back and used in a permanent museum at the State capital.

Although this article was intended to be suggestive rather than descriptive, it will be found that the only Southern State which has not been mentioned is Maryland; but, as Rudyard Kipling says, "that is another story"—and in some respects a good one.

PRIZE STORY I.
This story was awarded the First Prize
of Fifty Dollars, offered by the SOUTHERN
STATES Magazine for stories of Southern
life.

MATT: THE MOONSHINER'S DAUGHTER.

By Kathleen Gray Nelson.

The road was rough, the sun was hot, and it was with a feeling of intense satisfaction that Gaston Williams saw before him a rude house perched on the rocky hillside, so completely screened by the surrounding trees that he had not seen it until a sudden bend in the road brought him in full view. He stopped his horse in front of the tall rail fence and uttered a loud "hello!" For a moment all was silent save for the echo of his own voice that still lingered in the hills around, then a girl in a faded calico dress, a gingham sun bonnet shading her face, appeared in the doorway. She looked at the stranger suspiciously—visitors were rare in that section of the country—and nodded a careless "howdy."

"I have lost my way," he said politely, "and I have stopped to ask if you could give me lodging for the night."

"I don' know as we have any room," she answered cautiously, after a moment's hesitation, "the men folks went to town today an' ain' got back yit, an' you'd have to see them 'bout it anyhow."

"Is there any place near here where they would take me?" he questioned.

"Oh, yes," she said quickly, "thare's Ebenezer Milligan's, that's lesser 'n six miles from here. I reckon you could git thare afore dark, an' I mos' knows he'd take you."

He did not seem to notice her apparent eagerness to get rid of him, for, not at all daunted, he commenced again in an even more affable tone than he had hereto employed:

"I have had a long ride today and my horse is about played out. I don't think he can go much further. You see," he added confidentially, "I'm selling fruit trees through this part of the country and I'd like to show you my catalogue, as I have some very fine varieties."

The girl looked relieved at the mention of his business and said more cordially: "Mebbe Pap 'ud like to see 'em. Can't you light and come in awhile?" With that he dismounted, tied his horse to the fence, and taking his saddle bags on his arm he entered the yard. He was soon seated on the porch busily explaining the merits of various highly colored plates, showing trees bearing fruit of such enormous size and beauty as was never seen outside the Garden of Eden. So quickly did the time fly that the sun was almost gone when the girl said abruptly:

"I reckon we kin keep you fur the night as it's gettin' late now. Jes' take your hoss to the barn, right down thare across the road, and put 'im up," pointing to a roof that could be seen in a clump of trees. "You'll find feed a plenty in the crib."

When he returned to the house half an hour afterwards he found the girl in earnest conversation with two men, one a sturdy mountaineer of some fifty years, the other a tall, sullen-looking youth, who expostulated:

"Look a heer, Matt, you must be mighty keerful," and she looked apprehensively at the older man, and said:

"I think his squar,' Pap."

That night Gaston Williams fell asleep with a triumphant smile on his lips as he muttered to himself: "Thanks to a slick tongue, old boy, you are at last in the cabin of Lou Higgins, moonshiner." The next morning he breakfasted alone with Matt, and as

soon as he was seated she announced:
"Ike says as how sumthin's the matter with your hoss' foot this mornin'," an' he ain' able to travel."

"Indeed," he replied, as if rather pleased with the news. "Then I'm afraid I'll have to ask you to let me stay here today, as I see no way of continuing my journey."

"'Taint no trouble," she answered pleasantly, "fur we don' often have anybody passin' up heer, an' its kinder nice to see a new face 'casionally."

Something in her voice and a note of loneliness, of feeling perhaps, caused him to look at her with sudden interest. She was not pretty; he had decided that the night before, and with a man's disregard for details, he had not noticed anything further about her appeareance. But now, as he scrutinized her more closely, he decided there was something attractive about her face, with its heavy black hair coiled low on her neck and her eyes brown and appealing, a certain firmness about the lines of her mouth, with its full sensitive lips, a face that would have been full of passion and feeling had not its expression been one of constant repression.

She did not seem communicative, and finding that his efforts at conversation did not meet with any encouragement, he also relapsed into silence, which lasted until they had completed the morning meal. After he had gone out and examined his horse he sat for a long time on the front porch watching a daring red bird that flitted in and out among the trees, turning to look at him with a coquettish turn of the head, and then flying far away until it faded a crimson spark in the distance. Finally he thought of Matt, and the thought of her brought with it a little thrill of sympathy, so perceptible that he soon found himself seated on the kitchen doorstep watching her as she moved quickly about in her preparations for dinner.

"Don't you get lonely here?" he ventured, after he had watched her in silence for some time as she dexterously peeled potatoes, apparently unconscious of his scrutiny.

"Can't say as I do," she replied.

"Guess I'm use to it. Ma's been gone nigh onto five year now, an' I've live heer lookin' atter Pap an' Ike with no women folks 'bout 'tell I kinder like bein' by myself."

"It seems to me a terribly monotonous life for you," he persisted. "Just one woman living up here in the mountains apart from all her sex."

"Oh I'm a Georgy cracker by perfession," she said, with a slight touch of bitterness in her voice, "an' I ain' never knowed anything outside o' that. Don' know how I'd feel ef I'd been born in town whare folks don' see none uv God's makin's 'round 'em, nothin' but what they've done themselves, jes' houses an' sech like 'tell you mos' forgit God knows how to do anything."

"You don't like the city, then," he questioned, with some amusement.

"No," she replied, shaking her head emphatically. "I went down to Atlanty once, ain' never been thare sence, an' don' want to go no more. Folks wuz all so busy they did'nt seem to have no time to keer fur nobody, an' I never wuz so glad as when I got back heer whare thare wuz plenty of sky over me; an' the hills an' trees had'nt never looked so nice as they did atter I got 'way from that cramped up city whare thare did'nt seem hardly breath 'nough fur all them folks. But mebbe you like it?" she said, looking at him inquiringly.

"Oh yes," he answered carelessly. "I've always lived there."

"I s'pose you kin git use to anything," she said philosophically, "but it ud go mighty hard with me to have to live thare the rest uv my days. Why I loves ever'thing up heer jes' like it belonged to me; them thare hills that allus looks like they wuz wrapped up in a piece uv blue sky, the trees with the leaves a dancin' like they wuz so happy they couldn't keep still, an' it mos' looks like the birds knows me an' tries to call to me sometimes." She came to the door while she was speaking, and stood looking out upon the surrounding country with a contented smile.

"Whenever I gits to feelin' rebellious like, ur ongrateful," she continued, "all I has to do is jes' git out o' doors an' look 'round a bit; then my heart gits light agin."

"You are a loyal daughter of the mountains," he said, smilingly, "and your thoughts are the voice of nature in your heart." She turned away quickly at this remark, with a pleased blush, and he got up and sauntered toward the spring feeling that it would have been best had his pretty speech remained unsaid. From that time forth his man-. ner toward her was characterized by a patronizing chivalry that puzzled while it attracted her.

That afternoon he smiled quizzically as he found himself carrying the milk buckets for Matt, as they trudged along side by side, but her eyes were fixed on the golden sunset beyond. Presently she said softly: "I reckon the wrong side uv the clouds is jes' as pretty as this un, 'cause that's the one the angels looks at."

"I suppose so," he answered vaguely, and she went on confidentially:

"It don' look like folks thinks 'nough uv the lovely cover the Lord put over the earth; mebbe its the floor of Heaven an' we jes' see the glory a shinin' through." She gave him a quick, appealing glance as she continued: "I ain' never got religion, but they do say as how ever'thing's pow'rful pretty in heaven. We's all Baptists by nature up heer, but one Sunday I heerd a 'Piscopalian preacher wuz goin' to exhort down at Hick's Cross Road—that's 'bout five mile from here—an' somethin' tol' me to go to heer him, as we'd never had any o' his persuasion in these parts. Folks didn't like 'im. He didn't holler the gospel out loud like Brother Duncan, but mebbe he couldn't help that, fur he looked like his lungs wuz weak, an' didn't talk nothin' 'bout the fiery pit an' sech like, as we wuz 'custom to, so his preachin' warn't ginrally edifyin'; but somehow I felt like he wuz a talkin' to me, an' it done me more good 'n any sarmon I ever heerd."

"Yes," her listener said, with a sympathetic smile, as she hesitated, and thus encouraged she went on:

"He wuz a tellin' that day 'bout the joys o' Heaven—them clouds made me think uv it—an' he talked mos' like he

seed it right afore 'im. I guess he wuz shore uv gittin' thare. That night after I got home I set a long time, a thinkin' 'bout what he'd said, an' wonderin' ef I ever got thare, ef I wouldn't feel mighty lonesome 'mong all them fine folks. He said t'wuz a beautiful city, an' you know I ain' use to city ways, an' I was that pestered 'bout it all, that when Pap and Ike come home roarin' drunk I didn't say nothin' to 'em, an' ef it hadn't been fur what he said bein' in my heart, I'd a tarnationally went fur 'em."

They had reached the lot gate some time before, but Matt had leaned against it, pushing back her sunbonnet in her eagerness to tell someone the thoughts that were in her mind. She now pulled it back on her head until her face was lost in its spacious depths and said humbly: "Mebbe you can't understan' my feelin's, fur I've never had nobody to talk to sence I growed up. Pap an' Ike 'd never heer, and you looks so kind and knows so much I felt like it 'ud do me good to talk a bit; 'taint often I do." She did not wait for him to reply but opened the gate and went in quickly without looking at him.

As Gaston Williams lay awake that night thinking over the events of the day he decided to leave on the morrow if possible, and he also muttered to himself that for the sake of the girl he would never return. Then he closed his eyes and tried to sleep, but his dreams were haunted by a woman with appealing eyes, who held out her hands entreatingly to him, and from whom he could not escape, no matter where he turned. Then she led him along a narrow, dangerous path until they came to a high cliff where the waters foamed beneath, and in his anger he pushed her down, down, into the angry waves beneath, and she looked at him and smiled, and smiling sank. As daylight at last dispelled these unpleasant visions, he cursed himself for a superstitious fool and felt an unwarrantable sense of irritation towards his unwelcome dream visitor. Matt, all unconscious of her offense, told him while she fixed breakfast that "Pap says yore hoss is wusser" with a satisfied smile lurking around the corners of her mouth, a smile that changed to a sensitive quiver when he betrayed his impatience at the information. The work he had entered into with such zeal a week ago was now distasteful to him, and he had but one thought—to get away from this place as soon as possible. The monotony wearied him, he shuddered at the thought of another day spent in this dreary solitude, and he vented his ill humor on the girl, whom he felt was in some way responsible for his detention. When she quietly withdrew and left him alone with his breakfast and his wrath, he became more incensed than ever and vowed to get away from there if he had to walk. After he had tried in vain to read, the knowledge of his own injustice made him ashamed, and he found himself again seated on the kitchen doorstep watching Matt as she sat by the door knitting industriously on a coarse yarn sock.

"Is'nt there something I can help you do?" he inquired meekly, but she declined his aid, and apparently did not notice his penitence. He had in his hand a pocket edition of Tennyson that he had found on his desk the morning he left, and noticing her surreptitious glances at it he determined to try an experiment, so he said carelessly:

"I have been looking over a book of poetry, would you like me to read something to you?"

"I don't keer if you do," she replied, rather embarrassed by the novelty of the situation. He turned the leaves over idly for a moment, wondering what would best appeal to her understanding, and then he decided to try the sweet story of Elaine. She listened intently, finally letting her knitting drop unnoticed in her lap as she became more interested, but when he had finished she only said simply: "It wuz the best thing she could a done—jes' die," and she got up hastily and busied herself with the pans on the table. He closed the book with a feeling of disappointment and then he laughed at himself for expecting appreciation from this ignorant girl.

He did not see her again until dinner, and then she seemed preoccupied and only replied to his remarks in monosyllables. Later, however, she brought her knitting and sat down on the front porch, where he was moodily gazing at the distant hills and planning some means of returning to civilization.

"You're gittin' kinder tired bein' up heer, 'way from evr'body, ain't you?" she inquired.

"Yes," he replied, "I must find some means of getting away from here to-morrow."

"You might come back fur yore hoss some time," she suggested with a gleam of hope in her eyes. He made no reply to this remark except a negative shake of the head, and she went on with a bitterness in her tone that made him feel uncomfortable:

"Ef you ever come back agin I reckon I'll be married to Jim Watts, ·him what lives down thare," with a jerk of. her head down the road; "leastwise I will ef Pap an' Ike has their way. They's both sot on it. I ain' said what I'd do yit,"—he was conscious that she was watching him furtively—"fur I knowed Pap 'ud be that all-fired mad ef I went agin 'im that he'd be shore to git on a drunk. It seems a pity," she said, as if talking to herself, "that folks like us has got hearts an' feelin's an' sech like, fur it don' look like we had any partic'lar use fur 'em. We's wusser off than them cows down yander in the lot, 'cause they is content. It mos' makes me wish I'd been born a cow, but ef I had I reckon I'd still have this pure cussedness in my marrer, an' would allus been kickin' the milk bucket over, that bein' 'bout the only way I could a 'spressed my feelings."

"I should never judge you to be contrary," he said, lamely enough, not knowing exactly what to say to this strange speech, but she did not seem to hear him.

"I've allus heerd some folks is born kickin' agin Providence," she continued, "an mebbe I'm one o' that kind. I guess the Lord never intended me to be one o' the flowers of the earth—jes' one o' the nettles, an' He made me accordin'. We all believes up heer that we's what the Lord wants us to be," she said, raising her eyes suddenly to look at Gaston as if just aware of his presence. "Its kinder comfortin', fur we'd hate to think He wuz as dissatisfied with what He'd made as we is. I've allus had a notion that them what turns out failures on earth He'll patch up a bit when they git to heaven, leastwise I hope so, fur He would'nt want no critters up thare He wuz ashamed of, an' some uv us is mighty onery. I've had so much corked up in my heart I has to let it out sometimes," she said apologetically, and he felt relieved when she got up as if she did not want him to answer and started toward the gate. He watched her thin figure as it disappeared down a little mountain path, and he said softly, "poor girl," and sighed.

Matt had been gone probably an hour when she came hurriedly around the corner of the house, panting for breath, her face as white as the rose she had pinned on her bosom, and trembling in every limb she dropped down on the steps.

"They're onto you down at the still," she gasped, "Pap an' Ike an' Bill Watts. I went down thare jes' now, an' afore they seed me I heerd 'em talkin' 'bout you an' I laid low. Don' know how they found out yore business, but they's pow'ful riled, and Bill Watts wuz a snortin' wusser 'n any uv 'em." She stopped for breath, and placed one hand over her heart as if to hush its wild beating. Seeing that he made no attempt at denial, she continued hurriedly, intense disappointment in face and voice: "I see they wuz right. I couldn't hardly believe it at fust, but then thare's some folks we don' hate, I don' keer what they is." He was standing looking at her, his teeth firmly closed, a defiant expression on his face.

"It is true I am a revenue officer," he said quietly. She shuddered, and he was conscious of a certain regretful twinge at the knowledge of how he had fallen in this girl's estimation. With an effort she regained her self-control and said:

"You'd jes' as well set down an' take it easy. Some uv 'em is watchin' the house, but ef you'll stay quiet-like I'll git you 'way from here yit, see ef I don't, spite uv Bill Watts' smartness."

"You had better leave me to my fate, I do not deserve your kindness," he commenced, but she interrupted him.

"It come to me all uv a suddint what I'd do, an' 'taint no use to talk 'bout it. I reckon you thought you wuz a doin' right, 'taint fur me to say. They feels you ain' played exactly squar' with 'em, an' they're pretty hard on you. Spies don' hav' much uv a showin' up heer, specially when we've nussed 'em unbeknownst. What's ourn's ourn, an' nobody couldn't convince us 'twarent."

"Why do you try to help me," he commenced bitterly, stung by the reproach in her voice, but she again interrupted him.

"It's too late to be a talkin' 'bout that now. What I want to tell you is that they'll be heer a little atter dark, an' ef you go over thare to the barn you kin hear 'em afore they gits to the house—they'll be a ridin'. As soon as you heer 'em stop you jes' start off as fast as you kin down that road thare, it'll take you to the road that goes to Hiram Wilson's, an' then you'll know where you're at. It's a little outen the way, but you can't go to'ther road 'caus the creek's up an' the bridge has washed away. You oughter git to Johnson's station tomorrow night. Nobody from heer 'll follow you, I'll fix that," she said with a grim smile. Gaston seized her hand impulsively.

"Let me do something for you to show my gratitude," he pleaded, "take you away from here, send you to school. I have no sister, be one to me, and let me try to repay you for what you have done for me." Her face lighted up as he commenced speaking, but she shook her head sadly.

"The Lord put me whare He wanted me, an' I ain' fitten fur no other place." "Hol' on tell I git back," she added quickly, as she ran into the house. In a moment she was by his side again. "Here's my pistol in case you git into close quarters som'ers else. I 'lows that nobody from here will git onto your trail, but if they wuz to, promise me you won't use it on Pap. I don't feel like I oughter go back on him fur you."

"I promise," he said solemnly. "You have acted nobly by me, and may God punish me accordingly if I betray your confidence."

"You'd better be goin' now," she said nervously, as she started down the steps by his side. "Don' forgit to do jes' like I tol' you, an' git out o' the barn when they comes to the house. You might leave yore book uv fruit trees, as it 'll be , onhandy to carry," she added, with a wan smile. When they reached the gate she stopped and held out her hand.

"Good bye, I shall never forget you," he said, as he stooped and raised it reverently to his lips, at which a burning blush stained her face and neck.

"Believe one thing," he added earnestly, "whatever may have been my motive in coming here, I decided last night for your sake to keep your father's secret."

"I do believe you," she answered softly. "Good bye." He started hurriedly across the dusty road, and the girl stood watching him until he went into the barn. Then she wiped her eyes on the skirt of her sun bonnet, and walked slowly back to the house. She went first into his room, and when she saw on the table the little book from which he had read to her that morning, her lips twitched nervously.

"She did'nt do nothin' fur him," she muttered, "an' yit folks writ 'bout *her*. I allus thought God made me fur somethin' special, an' I'm glad I ain' afeerd when the time comes, but I wish he could a knowed it." She walked over to the little window and stood for a long time motionless, her eyes fixed on the far away clouds. "He'll never know," she moaned, "he'll never know."

It was quite dark when three men rode up in front of the house and dismounted in silence. The girl, crouching in the farthest corner of the porch, held her breath to still the rapid beating of her heart as she heard them enter the door. Then she ran swiftly, noiselessly down the walk, untied the horse nearest to the gate, mounted it, and was off. There was the sound of heavy footsteps, and oaths filled the air as two men jumped on the remaining horses and started in swift pursuit. On they went in the terrible darkness, over mile after mile of the rough mountain road, the horses' feet striking fire from the stones in their mad flight. At last they were gaining almost imperceptibly upon that flying figure ahead, a bullet whistled past her, and then another so close that its hot breath burned her cheek. The horses were straining every nerve, and no one noticed the sullen roar that fell upon the quiet darkness, coming nearer and nearer every moment. Suddenly there was a splashing noise, and the sound of one horse's steps had died away.

"The creek," one cried excitedly, "the bridge has washed away."

"He'll never git out o' thare alive," the other answered with slow satisfaction, and the pursuers turned their horses around and slowly started back.

The next night Gaston Williams boarded the train at Johnson's Station, and heaved a deep sigh of relief as he felt himself being rapidly whirled far away from the scenes of the past three days—far away from the moonshiner's lonely cabin.

And Matt was right—he never knew.

GREAT FALLS OF THE POTOMAC.

THROUGH THE SOUTH WITH A CAMERA.

By H. S. Fleming.

II.—IN THE PICTURESQUE POTOMAC VALLEY.

The valley through which the Potomac river flows from the Alleghany mountains to Washington possesses a peculiar charm both from its having been the scene of many stirring incidents during early pioneer days as well as throughout our Civil War, and from its beautiful scenery. In years gone past the valley was the home and favorite hunting ground of the Indians. Then as the hardy settlers pushed the natives further Westward and occupied their lands there came the dreadful deeds of savage warfare only too celebrated in the annals of our country. Along this river George Washington traveled when on his way to survey the lands of Lord Fairfax, in Virginia. Afterward he passed along the same route as an aid to General Braddock in the latter's ill-fated campaign against Fort Duquesne. Still later he was sent to the head of the valley in charge of the forces maintained by Maryland and Virginia to protect their frontier against the Indians and French, and after the Revolutionary War he made a trip through it on horseback to examine into the feasibility of opening the river so as to make navigation more easy. Gradually the valley was settled and lined with thrifty farms and became the seat of many industries. Then came the eventful four years of our Civil War, which carried destruction to this peaceful scene and made famous the names of Harper's Ferry, South Mountain and Antietam, and, after this, renewed activity in agricultural work and in developing the many other natural resources which nature has given so bountifully to this section.

One of the most important factors in the early development of the valley of the Potomac and country tributary to it was the Chesapeake and Ohio canal, running from Georgetown, D. C., to Cumberland, Md., a distance of some 187 miles, following the banks of the river for the entire distance and serving even in these days of railroads and rapid transit as a means of carrying a large portion of the coal and products of the upper valley to tidewater. It was the pleasure and privilege of the writer, by the courtesy of the canal company's officials, to travel by boat recently from one end of the canal to the other, and it is the purpose of this article to record by word and picture some of the beauties of nature and features of historic interest which abound throughout the valley of the Potomac.

Our start was made from Georgetown in a steam launch at noon on Monday, our party including the paymaster of the company, one of the supervisors, an engineer and the writer.

Settling ourselves in narrow quarters and dispos-ing of our traps to ad-vantage, the paymaster took the wheel and signalled one bell to the engineer to start at half speed, and at this rate we passed along the canal making as little wash as possible so as to avoid breaking loose the canal boats tied along the bank.

Along here the canal presented a busy scene, with many boats lining its sides, unloading coal, lumber, stone and other material brought down from above. At its lower end boats pass by lock down into the Potomac river and unload directly into vessels, coal being shipped in this way from Cumberland to New York and New England seaport towns. Gradually we left the city behind us and steamed along at full speed, a high stone embankment on one side, on top of which was the road over the aqueduct constructed by the government from the falls of the Potomac to Washington, furnishing the

A LOCK-TENDER'S HOME.

water used in the capital. On the other side was the towpath, and below it the Potomac river.

About three miles from Georgetown we passed a steam shovel busy at work dredging the bottom of the canal, and beyond this an old incline lock, at one time used to lower boats down to the river. The structure was something of a curiosity in its way. A long incline led from the river up to the canal, and on this stood a great iron tank large enough to hold a canal boat. At the head of the incline there was a lock, and against this the tank was held, filled with water and the boat pulled in. The gates were then shut and the tank and boat lowered down to the river where the boat was drawn out into tide-water and proceeded on to Washington.

No finer day could have been selected for the trip. The sun was bright and hot, but a gentle breeze was blowing and this increased by the motion of the boat made a seat on the shady side almost a dream of comfort. Ahead of us the canal wound along between the trees growing on its banks and to the left and below us flowed the Potomac river, its waters muddy from recent rains. Looking back over the course along which we had come the upper half of the Washington Monument could be seen in the far distance rising above the trees and reflecting the sun from its white sides and glistening top more like an imaginative creation from mist than a hard and substantial reality.

As we moved forward the country on either side became more and more wild and heavily wooded. On the Virginia shore the trees grew down almost to the water's edge, and here and there in the river a riffle showed where a ledge of rock lay. At several places the canal widened considerably to conform to the level surface of the country, and at one point in particular, known as the "log wall," the effect was charming, the width of the canal here and the abrupt sides giving the appearance of a lake, the effect being increased by several little rocky islands covered with trees and shrubs. Beyond, the canal narrows again to its usual proportions but still retains its picturesque appearance.

About five o'clock we reached the lower lock opposite the Great Falls of the Potomac, and here the supervisor and I landed, and after sending a young boy to call the ferryman, proceeded down the towpath a short distance and then through the woods to the river. Our purpose was to cross over to the Virginia side in order to get the best view of the falls, and as the ferryman kept both himself and his boat on that side we were compelled to sit down and wait until his attention had been secured by our messenger. Soon we heard the boy calling, and although nearly half a mile distant his voice reverberated down the river between the cliffs, sounding as clearly as though but a hundred yards away. After the call had been repeated several times we heard the ferryman's answer, and before long he appeared coming down a ravine on the other side of the river toward his boat. Reaching it he leisurely pushed off. When he reached us we stepped aboard and pushed out into the stream.

Reaching the Virginia shore we landed and made our way along a path, once an old wagon road, through the woods toward the falls. After a walk of possibly a mile we came to the remains of an old stone building, with two heavy walls still standing and a good-sized tree growing in the centre. In former days this was a jail erected by the Potomac

Company, probably about 1790. A little further on were the remains of several houses erected by the Great Falls Manufacturing Company at about the same date, and beyond these was the old office of the company, a commodious and substantial building, now used as a farm house. Turning in at a gate near the office we struck across a field to the line of the old Potomac canal, and following it for a short distance came in sight of the falls.

A sharp turn in the cliff enabled us to stand directly in front of the falls, and from this position the scene was grand and impressive. Beyond the falls the broad river, smooth and placid as a mirror, reflected the trees which grew on its banks. On both sides was the forest, and in the middle this enormous volume of water dashed around and over the great rocks which stand in the fall, lashing itself into foam in a mad endeavor to reach the narrow channel between the cliffs at the foot of the falls. Almost in the middle were two particularly large rocks, and between these the waters rushed, pouring down into a perfect cauldron of foam and mist and then dashing away down to the bottom, where the stream rushed along in great waves, lashing the base of the cliffs and forming eddies around every projecting rock and finally passing down the narrow gorge between the cliffs.

At the water's edge on the left sat a fisherman plunging his dip-net into an eddy, where both carp and shad are usually found in abundance. On the Maryland side the stream has cut a passage around the cliff, and sweeps through here in a series of small but very beautiful cascades, joining the main waters of the river just opposite where we stood.

Leaving the falls we retraced our steps to the road and, securing the services of a little girl from the farmhouse to guide us, we made our way through the woods in the direction of the locks built here by the old Potomac Company. After a short walk along a path densely overhung with foliage we reached the line of the old canal, now almost filled with earth and grown over with grass and trees, and in a few moments stood before

MONOCACY LOCK.

one of the old locks. The brown sand-stone of which it is built has stood the wear and tear of time remarkably well, and though the gates are gone and the joints between the stones green with grass and weeds, it looks as though it would be possible to put the lock in running order with very little trouble. Another of the ancient locks near by was much deeper and in an even better state of preservation.

In early days the control of the falls was a matter of great strategic import-ance, since from Cumberland down to Washington this was the only serious bar to navigation. So early as 1749 the idea of establishing trade between the headwaters of the Potomac and those of the Ohio was carried into effect

by a land and trading association known as the Ohio Company, which purchased a large tract of land from the Indians and constructed a warehouse at Fort Cumberland, now the city of that name. The goods came from Great Britain to Bellhaven, now Alexandria, Va., and were carried eighteen miles overland to the head of the Great Falls, then placed on barges and transported 170 miles to Cumberland. From there, by means of Indian paths across the moun-tains, an extensive trade was engaged in on the waters of the Monongahela, Youghiogeny and Ohio rivers.

In 1755, when General Braddock landed his army at Bellhaven, he marched to the head of the falls and then ascended the Potomac to Fort

Cumberland, from which place, accompanied by Washington, in the capacity of aid, he commenced his march to Fort Duquesne, opening ahead of him across the Alleghany mountains a wagon road which is still in existence and bears his name. The necessity for having a means of transporting material or men readily to and from the frontier of Maryland and Virginia was so apparent that eighteen years after Braddock's defeat, in 1773, Benjamin Franklin and Governor Pownall, with Thomas Walpole, Samuel Wharton and other English gentlemen, advertised in London for proposals for the improvement of navigation on the Potomac and endeavored to influence the British government to establish a new province

west of the Alleghany range on the waters of the Great Kanawha and Monongahela rivers. Following this, however, came our Revolution, during which such matters could not receive attention at home or abroad. At its close General Washington, who had always taken an active interest in plans looking toward the improvement of the river, and who was thoroughly familiar with the subject, wrote a letter regarding it to Thomas Jefferson on March 29, 1784, saying: "More than ten years ago I was struck with the importance of it, (the improvement of the river), and despairing of any aid from the public I became a principal mover in a bill to empower a number of subscribers to undertake at their own expense the

MONOCACY AQUEDUCT.

A CANAL-BANK STORE.

extension of navigation from tidewater to Mills Creek, about 150 miles." About this time General Washington took a trip along the river in the interest of Maryland and Virginia, and upon his return to Mount Vernon gave, as the result of his observations, the opinion that it was perfectly practicable to construct means of facilitating navigation along the Potomac from the east to the western waters of the Ohio.

Acting on this, these two States appointed a joint commission which met in Annapolis, Md., December 22, 1784, at which General Washington presided. The foundation of the Potomac Company was laid at this meeting, and both States subscribed liberally to the project. The joint act of incorporation stated its object to be "the extension of the navigation of the Potomac river from tidewater to the highest point practicable on North Branch," and authorized the president and directors to "construct canals and erect such locks and perform such other work as they may judge necessary for opening, improving and extending the navigation of the river above tidewater." General Washington was elected president of this company and held the position until he became President of the United States, thus being enabled to carry forward what he had often called a favorite plan of his.

The most serious obstacle to be overcome was at Great Falls, so work was commenced here upon a canal one mile long, six feet deep and twenty-five feet wide, descending seventy-five feet by means of five locks, each 100 feet long and twelve wide. Below Great Falls a canal two and one-half miles long was constructed on the Maryland side to overcome the fall of thirty-seven feet at Little Falls. On August 1st, 1799, the locks were opened with appropriate ceremonies, and from this time until August 1st, 1822, the records show that 13,924 boats transported 1,135,761 barrels flour, 38,382 barrels whiskey, 426 hogsheads of tobacco, 5,476 tons iron, and other articles of produce and sundries to the value of $395,649.04.

The rather limited knowledge of civil engineering at that time, but more particularly the small amount of money at command, ultimately caused the failure of the project. After forty years and an expenditure of over $700,000 and all the tolls received, with the exception of a single dividend of four per cent., the ascending navigation was almost as laborious and expensive as before, while descending navigation remained as it had been prior to any improvement, entirely suspended during the greater part of each year for want of sufficient depth of water.

But to return to our trip—we retraced our steps, again crossed the river and soon were aboard the launch. After supper at a hotel which accommodates visitors to the falls, we started forward again, our little engine chug-chugging along merrily. Hardly a breath of air was stirring, except that created by the motion of our boat, and as we advanced through the still water, so perfect was its reflection of trees and sky that but for the noise of the engine and rush of water it would have been easy to imagine ourselves sailing in midair. As the sun dropped lower its rays touched the light clouds floating in the sky, turning them into a golden mist. Gradually it sank out of sight behind the hills and now its light coming over their tops was a golden yellow, shading off through orange to crimson, then through purple to a sky of purest blue, the clouds standing out clearly in bright crimson where the light touched them and a deep, almost sombre, purple in the shadow. These colors reflected in the river and canal, with the setting of dark green trees on the bank, made the scene one of almost entrancing beauty, each twist and turn bringing before us a new picture. Soon the yellow light faded into orange, then crimson, and gradually, as the sun sank lower, the bright colors faded out and a sober blue spread over all. In the canal a thin layer of mist was floating on the surface of the water, and every breath of air disturbed it, raising a little column which

ON THE TOWPATH.

went trailing over the dark waters like the indistinct outline of spirit forms.

We· bowled along at a good rate, and as darkness settled down passed several canal boats making their way toward Washington. The canal regulations require each boat to have a head-light and by this means we could always tell when they were coming, but we came within an ace of running down one going in the same direction as ourselves, as its black shape was not discernable until it loomed up almost in front of us. It was so dark now that nothing could be seen on the water ahead except a little spot of sky between the reflection of the trees on either side, but we could gage our distance from the towpath by means of the most

brilliant and beautiful display of insect pyrotechnics I have ever witnessed. The trees were literally alive with fireflies which produced a continuous succession of brilliant sparkles as rapid as the scintillations of a diamond, seeming like a great piece of black velvet studded with resplendent jewels. Our enjoyment of this novel illumination was suddenly disturbed by a cry from the supervisor, who was steering. The wheel was instantly thrown hard over, and before the bell rope could be reached to signal the engine we struck the tow-line of a canal boat and came to a stop. The whole performance was so quick that we hardly knew anything had happened until it was all over, but had it not been for the promptness of our wheelman in throwing the boat around we would have been active participants in a collision and wreck in midcanal. The canal boat had been tied up for the night without any headlight showing, and the bow-line had allowed its head to swing out into midstream. It was now nearly eleven o'clock and we were anxious to reach a good point to tie up for the night. A short distance above Horsepen Culvert we found a place suited to our purpose and within a very few moments we were snugly settled for the night.

An early start the next morning took us through a rolling country all under cultivation, the fertile farms extending down to the river both on the Maryland and Virginia shores. About nine o'clock we reached Lock 27, better known as Monocacy Lock, and entering this we were soon raised to the level of the reach beyond, along which we continued to the Monocacy river, where a stone aqueduct 438 feet in length carries the canal across the river just below and in sight of an iron bridge on which the Baltimore & Ohio Railroad crosses.

The region around here was the scene of more than one contest during the civil war. North of us lay the historic grounds upon which the battle of South

Mountain was fought, and at the name of Monocacy the memory of the war veteran turns to this and the memorable fights at Fox's and Turner's Gaps, at Boonsboro, at Crampton's Gap, and General Jubal Early's advance on Washington. Before the investment of Harper's Ferry by the Confederate forces, General Lee ordered Major-General Walker to proceed to the Monocacy river and destroy the aqueduct; but, as General Walker said, "So admirably was the aqueduct constructed and cemented, it was found to be virtually a solid mass of granite. Dynamite had not been invented then, so we were foiled in our purpose." While time has done much toward accomplishing the end General Walker strove to reach, the aqueduct is still a solid and substantial piece of masonry capable of serving its purpose for many years to come. Beyond the aqueduct we passed along a stretch of canal without a turn in it for over a mile in length, producing an effect of perspective much like some of the long canals in Holland. Some distance further on we reached Point of Rocks, a bold bluff of the Blue Ridge mountains where General Walker crossed the Potomac after his failure to destroy Monocacy aqueduct.

All along here the country was rough and rugged, the mountains coming up to the river on both sides and terminating as abruptly as though cut off with a knife, sometimes with a great cliff towering above the water and again with a gentle slope surmounted by a massive bluff of rocks. The Baltimore & Ohio Railroad follows along the north bank of the canal nearly from the Monocacy to Harper's Ferry, and the sight of one of its fast trains dashing around curves and through tunnels, trailing behind it a column of dust, was in strong contrast to the slow canal boat just beneath it, gliding softly over the water, with the patient mules ahead tugging at the tow-line and the "crew," with the exception of the steersman, fast asleep under an awning on the deck. As our supervisor said, from one point of view, there was between the two just the difference between a dream and a nightmare.

In approaching Harper's Ferry on a railroad train the rapid rate of speed and the trees along the track prevent the traveler from fully realizing the beautiful country which surrounds it, but from our position we had full opportunity of seeing what a thoroughly picturesque and beautiful region it is. Lying in the lock almost beneath the railroad bridge we could see the rocky bed of the Potomac river extending far away back of us, shadowed by the mountains through which it has cut its way. Across the river lay the town, and high above it the hills from which the Confederate batteries poured down a storm of shot and shell into the works of the Union forces.

Soon we reached Antietam village, or rather what little remains of it, and passed through the aqueduct over Antietam creek. For several miles along here the canal passes through the Antietam battle field, bringing to mind the names of Lee, Stonewall Jackson, Hill, Hood and Starke, and of McClellan and Burnside. At Sharpsburg, a little distance above, some of the heaviest fighting was done, and between Antietam and this place was the ford where Lee cut the bank of the canal and with his army crossed the Potomac into Virginia. A large cement quarry and mill are now in operation at this place. Continuing on our way we reached the lock opposite Shepardstown, Va., passing under the Shenandoah Valley Railroad bridge, a fine structure which crossed the river high above our heads. Shepardstown is deserving of a place in history as being the home of James Rumsey, the first man to construct and operate in this country a vessel propelled by steam.

Rumsey was a native of Maryland, but moved to Shepardstown during the early years of his life and was employed by the Potomac Company while Washington was its president. While here he constructed a model of a steamboat which, upon trial in the fall of 1784, operated with a fair degree of success. In October of that year he obtained from the Virginia Assembly an act granting him the exclusive use of his invention in navigating the waters of that State for a period of ten years; and in January, 1785, secured from the General Assembly of Maryland a similar patent. During this year he worked on his boat and gave several trials, at one of which General Washington was present, and so convinced was the latter of the practicability of the invention that upon his return to Mount Vernon in March, 1785, he wrote to Hugh Williamson: "If a model of a thing in miniature is a just representation of a greater object in practice, there is no doubt of the utility of the invention. A view of his model, with the explanation, removed the principal doubt I ever had of the practicability of propelling against a stream by the aid of mechanical power; but as he wanted to avail himself of my introduction of it to the public attention, I chose previously to see the actual performance of the model in a descending stream before I passed my certificate thereto, and having done so all my doubts are satisfied."

During 1786 Rumsey gave further public trials of his boat and enlisted the interest of many people, but as usual with the inventor of anything that happens to be a radical departure from existing methods, all manner of fun was made of him and his work. His boat was named by the people the "flying boat," and the inventor "crazy Rumsey." The completed boat which he had in operation on the Potomac at this point was fifty feet in length, and propelled by a pump worked by a steam engine drawing water in at the bow and forcing it out at the stern under the rudder, a principle that has been similarly applied in recent years. The boiler was a miniature affair, holding only five gallons of water and requiring about six bushels of coal for twelve hours' operation. With all this crude apparatus the boat, when loaded with three tons in addition to the weight of the engine and boiler, or about three and one-half tons in all, was forced against the current at from four to five miles an hour.

Not far beyond Shepardstown we reached a stretch where on one side of the canal there is a high and steep cliff,

WHERE LEE CROSSED THE POTOMAC.

OLD FORT FREDERICK, BUILT ON THE MARYLAND

the place being known by the suggestive name of "Shades of Death." The occasion for this gruesome title was found a number of years ago when some of the boatmen struck for higher wages. In order to persuade others to join them they indulged in the merry sport of rolling great rocks down the cliff upon passing boats, sometimes totally destroying them and naturally interfering with navigation. Popular opinion, however, was against the rock rollers and they were soon compelled to forego their amusement, though the name then given to the place has clung to it ever since.

At a little before six o'clock we reached Lock 40, where it was our intention to spend the night. It was one of those quiet, still evenings when nature appeared to be resting after the fatigue of the day. Hardly a breath of air was stirring and the sun, partly obscured by light clouds, was slowly sinking toward the horizon. There was something in the situation that appealed to the instincts of a fisherman, so inducing the paymaster to accompany me, and borrowing from the lock-tender two rods, some bait, his boat and himself, we went down the bank to the river and were poled up stream to an inviting looking riffle. Baiting our hooks with minnows, we cast them afloat, but though it seemed that fish were jumping all around us we caught nothing but rocks, and after about half an hour our patience failed us and we went back to the launch. I was not yet

satisfied that there were no fish to be caught, especially as both the lock-tender and supervisor were well stocked with yarns of the big fish found here, so we arranged for another trial in the morning.

At an early hour the lock-tender called me and together we started out to fish. After whipping the stream along the bank without results, we stepped in the boat and moved down stream to a little triangular stone dam and pushed along to the fish-trap set at its apex. Upon this we mounted and proceeded to cast in the eddies around it.

While waiting patiently for a bite, a canal boat came along, and the skipper, in order to attract the attention of the man at the locks, commenced to blow his horn. It was at once made evident that he had artistic aspirations, as instead of merely giving a business-like "toot," he commenced playing a distorted version of Lottie Collins' now celebrated song, and after that branched off on "My Sweetheart is the Man in the Moon," and then a variety of other tunes, ending with an attempt at "Rock of Ages." He had hardly passed through the lock when we were hailed by our companions on shore and requested to come to breakfast; but just as I was laying my rod down there was that little tug and jerk which the angler always recognizes with a throb at the heart. I did not have time to play with my capture, so he was duly hauled out and proved to be a good sized speckled black bass probably ten inches long. Just a moment later Kerfoot had

FRONTIER DURING THE FRENCH AND INDIAN WAR.

as good luck, but as the breakfast call had been repeated from shore we made our way back and shortly afterward, bidding Kerfoot adieu and carrying away a most pleasant memory of his kindness, and the two fish, we continued our voyage.

A little before nine o'clock we reached dam No. 4 and passed through the lock into the wide sheet of water above it. Through here our little launch fairly raced and I was almost sorry when we again entered the locks to pass again into the narrow canal. Reaching the town of Williamsport, we replenished our stock of coal and ice and continued on our way. A little after noon we stopped at the side of a field, across which we walked and up a little eminence to the ruins of old Fort Frederick.

In May, 1756, when war was declared between England and France the former made every effort to strengthen the frontiers of Maryland and Virginia. At this time Governor Sharpe purchased one hundred and fifty acres of land some miles from the present town of Hancock and began to erect a substantial stone fort which he named Fort Frederick. The bastions and curtains were heavily built and faced with stone, and on each bastion he placed a six-pound cannon. The barracks were made large enough to accommodate a force of two hundred men under ordinary circumstances, but in case of need four hundred could be quartered in them. By the middle of August of the same year the fort was so far completed that

a garrison of two hundred men under a Captain Dagworthy was placed in it, and from that time until after the close of the revolutionary war the fort was always occupied by troops. No engagements of any importance took place near it, but the effect upon hostile Indians was sufficient to insure a greater degree of safety to settlers near by and between that place and Fort Cumberland. So well were the walls built that today they are standing almost intact, though the barracks and houses inside have given place to a peach orchard.

After a brief rest we pushed forward, and as evening began to fall we approached the little town of Hancock, and on arriving there strolled up to the hotel, where we had sent our fish, and soon sat at the table enjoying the result of my early morning's angling.

In the morning we roused early and after breakfast at the hotel started off again. We were now approaching the outlying spurs of the Alleghany mountains, and as the canal wound along the bank of the river each turn presented a new view, keeping one in constant anticipation of what was coming. At a number of places where the canal widened out into a good sized body of water, people living in Washington, Hagerstown and other places have erected neat little club houses, some of them quite pretentious. A little after noon we reached a lock when the supervisor and myself stepped out upon the towpath and walked forward to a tunnel by which the canal passes through the mountain. The country was rough, rugged and wild, a fit place for game, which, I was told, is quite plentiful. As the canal approached the face of the mountain it passed through a deep rock cut which cast the water into heavy shadow, beyond which the black mouth of the tunnel yawned. As our launch had not yet come up with us, we started through the tunnel upon the narrow wooden towpath. The sensations of this walk through thirty-five hundred feet of inky darkness will not soon be forgotten, nor do I long for their repetition. There was no light, and for sound there were only the dropping of water from the roof of the tunnel and the reverberations of our footsteps as we tramped along the muddy wooden way. As we approached the end there unfolded before us a view of rolling hills, broad fields and waving grain, framed by the half circle of the tunnel's mouth; a charming picture, made all the more beautiful by its contrast with the dense darkness

within. Emerging from the tunnel we awaited the arrival of the launch, which soon came steaming and puffing through the darkness like the spirit of some evil thing we had aroused. From here we moved forward through the beautiful country, stopping occasionally to pay off employes and pass a lock, and toward evening we reached Yorkers Bend where we tied up.

A bit of canal history, now, and the tale is told. The Chesapeake and Ohio canal is the direct outcome of General Washington's early efforts to open navigation between the Ohio and Potomac rivers. In 1820, when the affairs of the Potomac Company were in such bad shape, memorials were sent to Congress from Pennsylvania, Maryland and Virginia, requesting the government to give pecuniary aid to the project, and shortly after the States of Virginia and Maryland appointed a commission to examine into its affairs. The report to Congress by the committee having the matter in hand both sanctioned the

CRESAP'S CUT, NEAR CUMBERLAND, MD.

object of the memorials and recommended the suggestion of Maryland and Virginia that the canal be extended to the Ohio. From this time until 1825 the matter of a through canal was agitated by both of these States and the National Government, and finally, in the latter year, the Chesapeake and Ohio Canal Company was duly organized with charters from Virginia, Maryland, Pennsylvania and the United States, and on May 16, 1825, at Semmes' Tavern, in Georgetown, D. C., the Potomac Company executed a deed conveying its rights and privileges to this new company.

The charter stated its purpose to be the establishment of a connected navigation between Eastern and Western waters by constructing a navigable canal between tidewater on the Potomac river in the District of Columbia to some convenient point on the Ohio or its tributaries. The connection of the Ohio with Lake Erie, which had been a part of General Washington's original project, was not abandoned, a committee being appointed to confer with the legislature of Ohio relative to its accomplishment. Examinations of the route from the Ohio to Washington were instituted by the President of the United States and afterward by two celebrated civil engineers. On May 24, 1828, Congress appropriated one million dollars toward carrying out the project and both Virginia and Maryland, with Washington, and other cities and towns contributed liberally. On July 3, 1828, President John Quincy Adams, accompanied by members of his cabinet, foreign ministers and a great gathering of notables, dug the first spadeful of earth from the channel of the new canal. Work was pushed forward from this time, and though many difficulties were encountered, among them an injunction served by the Baltimore & Ohio Railroad, which effectually tied up all work for three years, by 1843 it was com-

pleted to Dam No. 6, 134 miles. Having no money with which to complete the work, a temporary arrangement was made with the Baltimore & Ohio Railroad by which the latter hauled coal from Cumberland to this point at a rate of two cents per ton per mile and loaded it on the canal boats for transportation to Washington. Further appropriations were secured, and on October 10, 1850, the canal was opened to Cumberland and five boats of coal loaded for the Eastern market passed through the locks. The occasion was celebrated by parades, the firing of cannon, and a banquet at which each speaker predicted a glorious future

A QUARTER DECK VIEW.

for the enterprise. Coal had been discovered in Alleghany county in 1804, but until about 1823 was not considered of much value; but now, with both railroad and canal to transport the product, coal mining became a most important industry, furnishing the greater part of the canal freight.

From 1850 until 1889 the canal enjoyed a period of prosperity, broken only by the years of the Civil War. In June, 1889, however, the great floods on the Potomac river, greater than any ever known before, completely destroyed some of the most important and expensive parts of the canal, leaving it almost a complete wreck. Strong efforts were made by a powerful railway corporation to secure the charter and use the canal for a railroad connection to Washington, but the price offered was so ridiculously small, when compared with the money which had already been expended—$11,000,000—and the immense value of the franchise, that the courts placed the property in the hands of the first bond-holders, and they set about repairing the damage done. In September, 1891, the canal was again opened for navigation, and its condition now reflects the greatest credit upon the engineering skill displayed and on the courage shown by those financially interested. Since it was reopened the tonnage carried has increased rapidly, and with the addition of more boats, which are now building, will before long be as great as before the disaster.

Leaving Yorkers Bend early in the morning we proceded through the ever-changing scenery, passing Old Town, a dilapidated village, which at one time had the reputation of being the most iniquitous place along the canal, and on to Old Town cut, a beautiful little stretch near a mill owned by the descendants of Thomas Cresap, the famous Indian fighter.

Beyond Lock No. 71 the scene is that beautiful one familiar to all who have traveled on the Baltimore & Ohio railroad, which passes along on the opposite side of the river, the great Alleghany mountains looming up all around, seeming to advance or recede at each turn of the canal, always presenting some new feature of beauty. Soon after passing under a bridge where the railroad crosses from the West Virginia to the Maryland side we came in sight of the steeples of Cumberland, and before long reached the wharf where our journey ended. A few hours later I stepped on a train and in five hours was whirled back to the starting point of our four day's ourney.

A TUNNEL VISTA.

PRIZE STORY II.
This story was awarded the Second
Prize of Twenty-Five Dollars offered by
the SOUTHERN STATES Magazine for
stories of Southern life.

THE STORY OF SAMANTHY WILLIAMS.

By Byrdie Herndon Hansbrough.

I.

Zeb Collins looked from his store door along the sandy street, with its shambling wooden houses; he bared his brow to the breeze that came sighing from the two placid lakes, that lay on either side of the village, winking in the sunshine.

As he gazed along the tiresome street his eye rested on a vision of beauty. Samanthy Williams, in her checked cotton dress and palmetto hat, was coming toward him, a silhouette of youth and grace surrounded by a glare of golden Florida sunshine, a suggestion of strength in her very movements.

Was it strength of will or endurance? Her voluptuous beauty, in shades of brown, from the light tan of her cheek to the black brown shadows of her hair, she inherited from her Spanish mother, whom old cracker Williams married in Key West and brought back to his Florida home to die when Samanthy was born; but her stolid indifference and independence, her slow plodding mind, her patient unmurmuring nature came from her cracker father. Never was a greater contrast combined in one person than the passion inspiring glow of Samanthy's beauty and the commonplace desires of her heart.

As she passed on Zeb Collins thought with pride that when the new house on the hill was finished he would ask Samanthy Williams to be its mistress.

She soon left the village behind and turned into the hammock road, swinging her palmetto hat in one hand and her basket of purchases in the other. High above her head the oaks and magnolias that lined the sides of the path met, and jessamine vines, yellow with blossoms, twined over them and hung in long festoons from their green boughs; tall ferns grew in the damp dark moss, and across the road a tiny stream trickled on, reflecting the sunlight's shredded gold and the flittering shadows of the trees.

As she passed through the varying lights that played upon her dark hair and tanned cheek with the crimson tinge of health beneath the brown, she looked like some tropical growth herself.

She paused, for coming to meet her was Professor Frankford, who owned the grove her father cared for, which included many acres of fertile hammock bordering the shores of shimmering lake Harris. Professor Frankford was a man of wealth and culture. He seldom troubled himself about his Southern property, but this winter he had applied himself to the task of writing a scientific treatise, and wanting seclusion he thought of his Florida estate and came down to occupy the cottage, which had been built years before but never occupied. He made arrangements with his overseer, old cracker Williams, to furnish his meals, and then settled his mind to rest and write, when lo! with his first breakfast appeared Samanthy Williams, a vision of the gods, a glorious Florida cracker.

The Professor was a nervous, sensitive man; the unexpected always worried him; he wanted all the events of life worked out on the plan of "ought to be." He was flurried; he put his glasses up, he put them down, he took them off. At dinner Samanthy reappeared; during the afternoon as he wandered around the grove he found her in a packing house wrapping oranges. When she came to bring his supper he spoke to

293

her, and shuddered at her want of culture when she replied.

Samanthy, with true cracker breeding, was indifferent to him; she spread his homely meals, took up her basket and departed. This very want of appreciation spurred him on to more intense desire to gain her friendship, until he found himself mastered by a passion which has more influence over the actions of men than any other emotion—the love of a beautiful face.

He could have gazed upon her face for hours, for hours have watched her graceful untaught movements, but he always shuddered when she spoke. He remained in another room until she had time to spread his meals and depart, but Samanthy always waited to ask in monotonous tones:

"Kin I do inything else fur you?"

He could have cried out: "Yes, for God's sake keep your mouth shut!"

The winter passed, the spring came, and still he lingered. His books and papers were neglected; he hated himself because ever between him and the pages of his manuscript would come a face filled with the sunshine of love, the shadow of despair. He told himself she was coarse and ill-bred, but immediately to his mind appeared the exquisite lines of her dainty chin, the sweetness of her tender mouth.

Pity him!

His life had always been cold, scientific; he had never known what it was to have a warm being, a beautiful woman, so constantly in his sight. One day he clasped her hand in his slim white fingers and told her he "loved her better than life." For one moment Samanthy eyed him with quiet amazement, then she threw back her head and laughed; a rare sound, for these people are grave and do not often laugh; then with one movement of her strong young hands she freed herself and departed.

Much to his astonishment this burst of feeling had no effect on Samanthy. He feared she would be shy, perhaps—O miserable thought!—she might even refuse to bring his meals again. Far into the night he paced his gallery and wondered how he could ever tempt back his beautiful wild bird.

But next morning Samanthy appeared at the usual hour with no confusion on her rounded cheek and a straightforward look in her honest young eyes, as she returned his eager greeting, and if there was any resentment in her heart the Professor failed to catch it in her blunt, "How is yer, Perfessor?"

So he said to himself: "I am a fool; I will say nothing more until I have made up my mind that the play is worth the price, until I can say this is the woman I will call wife, this is the one I will present to my proud mother and aristocratic friends as the crowning joy and blessing of my life," and a little shiver ran over him at the thought of Samanthy in the elegant home of the literary man of wealth. "Evidently she has never thought of me except as an added burden to the drudgery of her young life."

And then, strange inconsistency of man's nature, it made him feel indignant to think of Samanthy standing over the stove preparing his meals. But he was wrong in one premise, Samanthy had thought of the interview often and wondered in her slow way why it was Professor Frankford had made her "feel so small, if he even looks at me, and somehow I ain't got strength to git out and go till he gives me leave."

But as the weeks passed on and he said nothing more to her, she began to feel easier with him, though her manner never changed. So this evening when she saw him coming toward her she paused with her hands full of sprays of yellow jessamine and long ferns, and put her basket on the ground, for she knew by instinct he had something to say. His face was very pale as he came toward her through the hammock; he had made up his mind to sacrifice one principle of his life for another; he must possess this strange creature at the expense of ambition, fame and self-esteem.

He held out his arms to her and his eyes beneath his glasses flashed with intensity of feeling; he caught and held her eyes with his own, like a serpent charming a helpless bird.

"Samanthy, I love you, God help me. I want to make you my wife; a clergyman, a friend of mine is traveling through the South and will spend this night with me. Will you come?"

What power had he over this untaught girl; was it mesmerism, was it telepathy, the uncontrolled force of a strong mind over a weaker?

As if reading her answer in his eyes she replied faintly:

"I will come."

He clasped her eagerly in his arms, and told her it was necessary to keep their marriage secret and she must swear before God and the hosts of heaven never to reveal it until he gave her permission, and without a question, with utter dependence on his superior mind she swore, "as she hoped for salvation."

And that night when they stood in his little study and the pale young clergyman asked if he would take this woman to be his wedded wife, he thought to keep that vow; he had cast the die, he would give up everything for the possession of this woman, he would be true to her, he would educate her, she must learn for his sake, and Oh! she was so beautiful, with that queer startled look in her deep dark eyes and her strong young hand lying so quietly in his without a flutter.

After the ceremony Samanthy walked home alone, for the Professor did not wish to cause talk by being seen with her, until he had more fully matured his plans, so he swung himself into a hammock after seeing to his friend's needs and was soon lost in—shall we say it?—despondency and regret. For no sooner had he defied all obstacles and taken the fatal step, than these same obstacles rose up blacker and more forbidding than ever, but then Samanthy was not there with her glorious face and no mind picture could ever be anything but pale and lifeless compared with her glowing living self, so he thought all regret would vanish with to-morrow.

"For I shall see her again."

And in the study the pale priest leaned his head on his hand and coughed the dry husky cough which is the death knell for so many, and which told him he was not long for this life.

Shading his eyes from the glare of the lamp he gazed upon the place where Samanthy had stood by the window, half in the light, half in the shadow, and he thought of Helen of Troy, of Cleopatra, of Desdemona, of Amy Robsart, of Mary Queen of Scots, of all the women in history or poetry whose beauty had wrecked their lives, and he thought vaguely, "were they half so fair as this ignorant daughter of the Southland? If so, I wonder not that men went wild with admiration, for the women of today may pride themselves on educational and mental equality; they can force men to bow to these qualities, but the only feminine power is beauty. Education cannot erase this characteristic, for the nearer they live to nature and science the more their love for the beautiful increases." He heaved a little sigh as he banished the image of the fair cracker from his mind and thought of his few short years which consumption doomed him to spend alone.

Six weeks a wife, Samanthy was standing by the table preparing her father's meal, when he came in and told her she need not carry the Professor's dinner; he was gone.

"Gone!"

One word welled up from the heart too ignorant to express its woe:

"Where?"

"Wal, I can't say fur sure; told me to transact all my biz with his liyar; he was gone fur a furrin country."

With the true heroism of those uneducated people Samanthy said nothing; but while her father ate his dinner she went out and sat on the steps, where the cool wind from the lake, laden with the delicious acid odor of the orange grove, could blow in her face, and she looked with vacant eyes at the dancing waters, while ever through her startled mind these words came glancing:

"Gone without one word, and me bound by er oath."

All through the hot months of summer and the sad days of fall and the first cool weeks of winter her heart cried out in its agony:

"Surely he will come today."

Never once did she think of breaking her oath; with the superstition of her class she regarded the breaking of an oath as her doom for eternity. How often had she heard old cracker Williams say :

"A man can git furgiveness fur most inything but usin' the name of the Lord fur a lie, and that calls fur brimstone."

An oath with them is the most sacred thing in their lives, and never, until she had lost her hope in heaven, could she have broken that oath.

One night, when the fair face of Lake Harris was lashed by the wind, when black clouds swept across the sky and the waves rushed in agony and alarm to the shore and dashed themselves back foaming with anger and fear, when the orange boughs, laden with their golden fruit, creaked under their burden, Samanthy fell ill. When consciousness returned a tiny mortal wrapped in some of her old clothes lay by her side, and an old crone sat by the fire smoking a vile pipe.

Samanthy lay quite still until she had thought it all out; then a weary sigh escaped her lips and went echoing among the rafters; the old woman by the fire came to her side.

"Wall, yer ain't g'wing ter die. I told yer dad you'd git well; the likes ov yer never die, and yer wuz young ter be so bad—only seventeen this gone month. Wal your'n ain't the first pretty face has tuk its owner ter the devil."

The first day Samanthy left her bed and crept to the steps she saw her father ; he had never approached her during her illness. She heard him cross the hall and go into her room. He took up the sleeping baby, brought it to her and without a word pointed to the gate. Samanthy arose, she looked at the sleeping child, then into her father's face, and taking off her shawl she wrapped it around the baby and without a murmur passed from under her father's roof and out of his gate forever.

In his rough slow way old Williams had always been a kind father to Samanthy. He had reared her from a baby with the care of a mother. He had always regretted her great beauty, but had rejoiced in her strong young frame. He was a dull old man, but honest and with certain principles so

deeply founded in his nature that they had become part of himself. According to these principles there was nothing left for him to do but disown a daughter who had disgraced his good name, and even though it had been her death warrant Samanthy must have gone.

II.

Five years had passed.

Down by the lake, so near the waves could almost splash its steps, was a little two-roomed log cabin, with a small garden in the rear. Here lived Samanthy and her little daughter Hope, for by some strange impulse she had named her baby Hope. When Samanthy, now shunned alike by neighbors and strangers, was driven from home by her stern but upright old father, she had wandered to this then deserted cabin, too weak to work, nothing to live on, avoided by everyone. With a great contraction of pain at her heart, she had taken her child in her arms and walked into Zeb Collins' store. "Zeb," she said, "I am too weak ter work and I 'aint got nothing ter live on, so I have cum ter ask yer fur credit."

"Git what you need Samanthy," was all Zeb said, but Oh ! the pity, the pain, the misery that shone in his eyes for this fallen woman, once his ideal for all that was pure and good. Samanthy saw the look and understood it better than any language.

Soon after she received a letter :

"Smanthy, fur the sake uv what you once wuz ter me and fur the pity I feel fur you and the little waif, let me buy the cabin and strip ov land you live on fur you.   ZEB COLLINS "

Her answer was brief but full of untaught dignity :

"I kin take nothing from the hand ov iny man, Zeb, much less you."

Old Williams moved off the Frankford grove, for, though Samanthy's lips had been sealed, it was generally thought that the Professor was her betrayer. Soon after the grove changed hands, and her father died without seeing again the beautiful despairing face of his daughter.

At first no one would give Samanthy work, and she depended on the sale of the products of her small garden, but after awhile, as time soft-

ened the story of 'her disgrace, and
new people came in and the village
began to grow, the strangely beautiful
cracker woman was in demand for all
sorts of work; so she paid Zeb back,
and paid rent for her small garden, supported her girl and herself, lived alone,
seeking no one. Without one link of
love or friendship she struggled on.

Every night she would stand in her
cabin door and watch the white crested
waves on the lake and the long stretch
of dark, sad pines, with their drapery
of gray moss floating in the breeze, and
listening to the lonely call of the whip-
porwill, she would say to her sad,
expectant heart:
"He never cum today, but he'll cum
tomorrer."

Only one duty her life presented to
her, and that was to wait; but she did
this with a steadfast hope and patience.
All the love of her lonely life she
lavished on little Hope, who grew up
like some wild, shy animal, with all the
lovely outlines of her mother's beauty
and the sensitive intensity of her father's
nature, with a wild love for the beautiful
and a quick, fanciful mind. She loved
her mother with a passionate love which
sometimes frightened Samanthy by its
force. Today she was five years old,
and Samanthy had left her and walked
to the village to purchase her a birthday
gift. At the door she called:
"Here, Hope, is something fur you."

And she danced a gayly dressed doll
in her hands, but little Hope was lying
on the floor in the sun; her face was
crimson; her eyes were dull. Only a
few hours Samanthy had left her, and
now at one glance she saw the child was
ill. She took her up, the little gold
brown head hung over her arm weakly,
the curls all tossed and tumbled. She
took her in her arms and walked back
to the village. The doctor gave her
some medicine, but told Samanthy to
prepare for the worst.

Up and down, up and down, all night
by the lake shore, where the dull splash
of the waves sounded like clods falling
on a coffin, walked Samanthy with Hope
in her arms. Occasionally the little girl
would rouse herself to pet her pretty
mother's face and say:

"Oh, so hot, so hot!"

All next day, through dreary sunshiny
hours, Samanthy walked with her in the
house, for if she paused one moment the
little form would stir and the hot lips
murmur:
"So tired, so tired!"

The few remedies she knew of she
had given the child, but it seemed to
her she had already heard the summons
of fate for the life of her baby.

When the sun set, she went out by
the lake shore again, and in the pale
moonlight, with the softly glittering
waters on one side and the stern old
pines standing like sentinels on the
other, she walked up and down. Were
her muscles made of iron, was her
heart of stone, were her nerves of
strongest leather, that she could stand
this tension?

Up and down, up and down; the little form lay still now, and as Samanthy
came out of the shadow into the full
moonlight she looked into the dead face
of her baby. One moment she gazed,
then without a moan she went in and
prepared the little one for burial. Then
she laid her on the bed and crossed her
hands, locked the door and sped through
the woods. She looked like a spirit as
she passed in and out among the
shadows of the pines, till she reached
the road through the hammock that led
to the village.

Zeb Collins was sitting on his gallery,
smoking his pipe in the moonlight, when
he saw the shadow of a familiar form,
as if borne on wings of the wind, come
fleetly to his steps. She paused, the
pale moonlight fell across a white drawn
face, and hair which a few hours ago was
so dark and brilliant the sun loved to
linger there, now bleached to a snowy
whiteness.

"Samanthy, fur God's sake"—but he
asked no more, he only gasped—"the
child?"

"She is dead."

And Samanthy's voice was hollow and
thin.

"I want yer to bring a coffin, Zeb,
and help me ter bury her ternight. I
could'nt ask no one else," and like a
breath she was gone.

As Zeb Collins drove over the familiar

road, with the little coffin in the wagon, brave heart and strong man that he was, he bowed his head and wept.

At seven o'clock little Hope's soul had taken its flight, and as the first glow of dawn flushed the dusky pines and the placid lake, Zeb and Samanthy lowered the little coffin into a grave, out in the fragrant piney woods. Zeb filled the grave, while Samanthy knelt by with haggered face and wild eyes, while her form trembled with its pent up grief like some strong young pine bent by the blasts of the storm. The waters of the lake moaned in sympathy, and the pines tossed their branches above her head, and sighed and whispered together. Some water birds, aroused by the light of dawn, uttered their shrill scream as they rose and circled in the air. At last it was finished, and with a wild gesture of despair, she stretched her arms to heaven :

"O God, I have had er load of sorrow and disgrace on me fur a long time and I aint never grumbled; and now you have tuk the last thing that made me able to bear my misery ; give, oh give me strength fur the end, ter bide till he cums ; fur cum he will." Then with a wail she burried her face in her hands and wept. Zeb let her weep till exhausted, then he stretched his hand to her across the grave :

"Samanthy, I can't leave you here by yer self. Fur all yer shame I love yer ; come and be my wife."

Oh, depths of human love ! Could it be that this ignorant man had a great pure love in his heart which would have been impossible to his educated brother ?

She only raised her hands as if to shield herself from a blow, and cried :

"Don't, Zeb, I kin stand inything but kindness ; all yer scoffins I kin stand, but not yer pity, and what yer speak on kin never be."

III.

Thirty years Samanthy sat by her cabin door in the sunshine, looking out across the lake and listening to the monotonous croak of the frogs in the tall saw grass down by the marshy part of the lake, the drone of the early summer insects around her, and the sough of the wind in the pines, keeping guard over a little green mound out there.

She is an old woman now, with silver hair and soft brown eyes with a look of unrest and expectation in their depths.

Along the lake path came a man, an old man, but still carrying that distinguished air belonging only to a man of the world. He came up and stood before Samanthy. She looked at him, and a great light leaped to her eyes.

"You've cum ! you've cum ! I knowed you'd cum ; I've knowed it all the time."

"Yes, Samanthy, I have come. Thirty years have I wandered everywhere and tried to forget you, but my sin was ever before me. If it will comfort you, know that you have ruined my ambition and my success ; now, after thirty years, I am compelled to come back and claim you for my wife. If the few remaining years of my life can make amends, take them."

The cracker woman rose, tall and erect.

"You hev cum back, yes, you hev cum at last. I always knowed you'd cum, so I bore my burden. Thirty years of misery and shame hev you put upon me by binding me with er oath I couldn't break and then deserting me, and now you hev cum back you can make the only amends you could ever make—go with me to Zeb Collins and tell him what yer made me swear never to tell, that I am yer lawful wife and then—give me er divorce."

So for thirty years he had loved her and dreamed of her loving him alone and neglected. Her face had ruined his life which might have been so brilliant. At last he had given up the battle, a second time he had yielded to his love for the beautiful and had come back to her, and she—only asked a divorce so that she might *marry a cracker.*

THE GROWTH OF POETRY IN THE SOUTH.

By Harriet Peirce Sanborn.

In reviewing what may be called the rise and progress of our national literature, one is reminded of what James Russell Lowell has quaintly said of the growth of the nation itself. It grew

"Strong thru shifts, an' wants, an' pains,
 Nussed by stern men with empires in their
 brains."

A nation with a history to make has comparatively little of the leisure necessary for the development of the highest order of literature. That in spite of a home to make for itself, a government to establish, a civil strife to adjust, our nation has yet produced a literature worthy of the name is more a subject of congratulation and surprise than that the literature itself is not more extensive. In the South, for various reasons, the conditions were less favorable for the development of literature than in the North. The people were more widely scattered than in the North, and for years each family lived more unto itself than for the general good, and while cultivating each in its way the highest order of intellectual development, there was not offered to the rising poet and author the encouragement found in an appreciative home audience. Two of those best deserving the name of Southern poets were forced to turn Nortn, not only to find an audience but a market value for their poems. Poetry, unless it was the poetry of the ancient classics or models of the English classic lyrics, did not find much favor when uncombined with an ability in the poets to attend to more practical affairs with equal skill. Mr. Thomas Nelson Page, in his recent sketch of Southern authorship before the war, amusingly instances a case in point. One of Philip Pendleton Cooke's

neighbors said to him after he became known as the author of "Florence Vane:" "I wouldn't waste time on a damned thing like poetry; you might make yourself, with all your sense and judgment, a useful man in settling neighborhood disputes and difficulties." It seems that this was a typical example of the feeling towards the writers of literature pure and simple.

The more limited forms of literature have ever received appreciation and found their highest development in the South. Oratory, both judicial and political, has always flourished, and the speeches of the great Southern orators, before the war and since, rank with the best of that highly intellectual form of literature, so that whatever limit there may have been to poetical literature, it was not either from poverty of imagination or inability of expression. It was not that there was no genius, but there were generally no publishers and no appreciative public at home.

Again, it seemed to be the old feeling that no good could come out of this Nazareth. A poem written by a Southerner was trashy and that written by a Northerner was Yankee, both enough to condemn the effort as unworthy of consideration. Even at the present day such a feeling is not wholly lacking, as was amusingly commented on by the Norwegian novelist, Boysen, when he visited New Orleans a few years since. He became charmed with the atmosphere of poetry and romance which invested the ancient city and its surroundings. A resident appealed to Mr. Boysen, already intoxicated with the possibilities of the place from a literary point of view, and complained that there was no literature possible in the present day like that conjured by the magic wand of Walter Scott. He was indignantly rebuked by the novelist, who said: "Why, man, you don't half appreciate the wonderful possibilities that surround you. You are living in a perfect world of romance, and some day some one will reveal it to you." The novelist added, to his audience, "My prophecy has been fulfilled in the charming tales by George W. Cable."

In spite of adverse conditions, not altogether peculiar to the South, a goodly number of true poets adorn her native literature, and by virtue of the truth and beauty of their songs belong to the world literature as well. Some of the poets are perhaps best known by a single song, as in the case of Cooke, already mentioned, who wrote "Florence Vane," declared by Poe to be "the sweetest lyric ever written in America:"

    I loved thee long and dearly,
        Florence Vane ;
    My life's bright dream and early
        Hath come again ;
    I renew in my fond vision   .
        My heart's dear pain,
    My hopes and thy derision,
        Florence Vane.

            *   *   *   *   *

    Thou wast lovelier than the roses
        In their prime ;
    Thy voice excelled the closes
        Of sweetest rhyme ;
    Thy heart was as a river
        Without a main,
    Would I had loved the never,
        Florence Vane.

            *   *   *   *   *

    The lilies of the valley
        By young graves weep,
    The daisies love to dally
        Where maidens sleep.
    May their bloom, in beauty vying,
        Never wane
    Where thine earthly part is lying,
        Florence Vane.

Paul Hamilton Hayne, a soldier and poet, wrote many delicate nature poems. Hayne is regarded with great love by his people, and he is among the first of the Southern lyric poets. His favorite home was among the pines, and the following lines from a poem entitled "Forest Quiet," breathe the very spirit of "nature's stillness that can be felt:"

    So deep this sylvan silence, strange and sweet,
    Its dryad-guardian, virginial peace, can hear
    The pulses of her own bosom beat.

    No breeze nor wraith of any breeze that blows,
    Stirs the charmed calm; not even yon gossamer
            chain,
    Dew-born and swung 'twixt violet and wild rose,
    Thrills to the airy elements subtlest breath.

    What shadows of sound survive the waves' far
            sigh,
    Drowsed cricket's chirp, or mocking bird's
            croon in sleep,
    But touch this sacred soft tranquility
    To yet diviner quiet.

A poet whom the war brought out or developed was Henry Timrod, of South Carolina, who is entitled to a place among the leading poets of the South. His poetic imagination was strong, and his long poems as well as his verses for occasions gave promise of still finer work in maturer years. "Cotton Boll" is his most ambitious work, and its style allies him with a later poet, Sidney Lanier, whose poetical career was also cut off prematurely. "Katie" is the prettiest of Timrod's shorter poems. "Charleston" and "The Unknown Dead" are two of his poems that were written during the war. His "Ode for Decoration Day," from which a few lines are quoted, shows the grace and sweetness of sentiment which are characteristics of the Southern poets:

    Sleep sweetly in your humble graves,
        Sleep, martyrs of a fallen cause,
    Though yet no marble column craves
        The pilgrim here to pause.

    In seeds of laurel in the earth
        The blossom of our fame is blown,
    And somewhere waiting for its bi th
        The shaft is in the stone.

            *   *   *   *   *

    Stoop, angels, hither from the skies;
        There is no holier spot of ground
    Than where defeated valor lies
        By mourning beauty crowned.

Two Southern poets have endeared themselves to the nation as well as to the South by the contribution of a single song destined to endure because of patriotic sentiment—James R. Randall the author of "Maryland, My Maryland," and Francis Scott Key, author of "The Star Spangled Banner." A fact that gives pathetic interest to the poetry of the South is that, for the most part, it is the promise of what was to be. The sweetest and truest poets have died either before reaching maturity or when in the earliest fullness of their powers. .

A striking contrast in the life and personality of the men who represent the high water mark of Southern literature is presented by Edgar Allen Poe and Sidney Lanier. Both were poets endowed with power to express themselves in more than one of the forms of art. The life of Poe was prematurely cut off by habits of self indulgence; that of Lanier by fatal disease against which he struggled manfully, and in spite of which his musical songs were written and his notable lectures delivered. Poe was one of the first of our American writers to attract the attention of the literary world abroad. A high degree of poetic imagination was the characteristic of both these writers, and an exuberance which, in the case of Lanier, hardly knew whether to express itself in music or poetry. "Ligeia" and the "Fall of the House of Usher" are the most artistic and most imaginative of Poe's prose writings. "The Raven" and "Ullalume" show his richest poetic imagination. Poe himself regarded "Ligeia" as his finest tale. "Anabel Lee," "The Bells" and "The Haunted Palace" are three short poems that show Poe's gift of musical expression so that in many lines the words convey the very sound itself. These lines from "Anabel Lee:"

For the moon never beams without bringing
          me dreams
    Of the beautiful Anabel Lee,
And the stars never rise but I feel the bright eyes
    Of the beautiful Anabel Lee.

and these from "The Bells:"

    How they tinkle, tinkle, tinkle,
        In the icy air of night!
    While the stars that oversprinkle
    All the heavens seem o twinkle
        With a crystalline delight,—
    Keeping time, time, time,
    In a sort of Runic rhyme,
To the tintinnabulation that so musically wells
    From the bells, bells, bells, bells,
        Bells, bells, hells.
From the jingling and the tinkling of the bells.

illustrate Poe's peculiar gift of musical

expression which characterizes all his poetry.

In every literature there is a certain class of poets who seem to be essentially the poets' poets, such as Edmund Spenser and John Keats in English literature. The "Fairie Queen," "St. Agnes' Eve" and "Endymion" have been sources of rich suggestion and enjoyment to the poetical mind, and in these poets the modern poets have found inspiration and the quickening of their own imaginations. To a degree Poe and Lanier possess the high order of poetic endowment best appreciated by poets themselves, so that they are more poets' poets than popular poets. Poe had a weirdness of imagination to which he gave form in poems appealing more easily to the general taste, and his poems and tales will probably ever be read more extensively than those of Lanier, who wrote almost nothing of a popular character, save one or two nature and dialect poems. If these were better known he would be more loved by the general as well as the literary public.

From the restless and fervid spirit of Poe, whose poems and tales are as brilliant as the plumage of some tropical bird, it is a relief to turn to the tenderly fervid spirit of Sidney Lanier, whose life and words were in harmony, and whose beautiful thoughts were but the expression of the man himself. The earliest passion of Lanier was for music. As a child he learned to play, almost without instruction, on every kind of instrument he could find; he especially devoted himself to the flute in deference to his father who feared for him the powerful fascination of the violin, for it was the violin voice above all others that commanded his soul. He has related that during his college days the violin would so absorb him in rapture that presently he would sink from his solitary music worship into a deep trance, thence to awake alone on the floor of his room. This love of his soul for music is told by his wife in a memorial to his poems, and is mentioned because it shows the foundation for the conflict which was ever his, whether to express himself in music or verse. His subsequent effort in the science of English verse was an attempt to reconcile the impossible and to essay in verse what only the gamut can render possible. Lanier had a thorough belief in his own call to the mission of poet. Had this conviction been less steadfast he surely would have fainted beneath the burden it laid upon him. At a moment when an assured means of support for himself and his young family would have been most welcome, he set aside a most practical offer from his father because he felt the work he entered upon would conflict with the development of the higher work to which he was called. Sustained by the loving confidence of his wife, he gave up the opportunity for worldly prosperity, and with his flute and pen for a sword and staff he supported his little family in spite of failing health. His small book of poems and his incomplete but most suggestive course of lectures on the English novel amply justify his belief in his own calling. His poems do not form a large collection and the short nature and love poems are the most musical. Often the longer poems, such as "Corn" and "The Marshes of Glynn" are made somewhat obscure by an over-luxuriance of imagination and poetic expression. His "Song of the Chattahoochee" has been called as significant as Tennyson's "Brook" and voices the flow of the stream itself. Here are the first two verses:

> Out of the hills of Habersham,
> Down through the valleys of Hall,
> I hurry amain to reach the plain,
> Run the rapid and leap the fall,
> Split at the rock and together again,
> Accept my bed or narrow or wide,
> And flee from folly on every side
> With a lover's pain to attain the plain
>   Far from the hills of Habersham,
>   Far from the valleys of Hall.
>
> All down the hills of Habersham,
> All through the valleys of Hall,
> The rushes cried *Abide, abide,*
> The willful waterweeds held me thrall,
> The laving laurel turned my tide,
> The ferns and the fondling grass said *Stay,*
> The dewberry dipped for to work delay,
> And the little reeds sighed *Abide, abide,*
>   *Here in the hills of Habersham,*
>   *Here in the valleys of Hall.*

Another short poem, "Tampa Robins," is like a bird of bright plumage singing out from the orange groves of Florida. A mystical little poem, full of religious sentiment and the sympathy of nature, is the "Ballad of Trees and the Master:"

> Into the woods my Master went,
> Clean forspent, forspent.
> Into the woods my Master came,
> Forspent with love and shame.
> But the olives were not blind to Him;
> The little gray leaves were kind to Him ;
> The thorn trees had a mind to Him
> When into the woods He came.

A poem which is a beautiful picture of the love we know he bore his wife is called "My Springs." Of it he most naively admits that this one was written for the world, but he had another yet sweeter written for himself:

> In the heart of the Hills of Life, I know
> Two springs that with unbroken flow
> Forever pour their lucent streams
> Into my soul's far Lake of Dreams.
>
> Not larger than two eyes, they lie
> Beneath the many changing sky
> And mirror all of life and time,
> Serene and dainty pantomine.

The "Revenge of Hamish," "The Stirrup Cup" and "The Mocking Bird" are three other short poems in purely poetic style, unhampered by any theories of poetic expression. Lanier was a great admirer of Keats, and in the poetical wealth of his nature and the pathetic shortness of his literary career he well may be called our American Keats.

It is not alone upon his ability as a poet that the significance of Lanier's literary career is to be established. The collection of his lectures, delivered in great physical weakness very nearly at the close of his life, is full of the spirit of modern literary thought. If the course could have been completed the value would be more widely appreciated, but as they stand, twelve lectures upon the development of the modern novel, they are rich in suggestion, and again and again their influence is to be seen in the writings of the literary men of today. The lectures were written when all minds were full of the modern novel as developed by George Eliot, and in their unfinished condition seem, perhaps, to estimate unduly her significance in that most modern form of literary art. Had he lived to give us his thoughts upon the other great forms of modern literature, his otherwise extravagant view of George Eliot would have taken its relative place in the general scheme. As it is, his general view holds with the most modern of our writers as given in lecture and essay, and his voice was one of the first to be raised in the appreciation of the novel as one of the most potent modern educating influences.

The whole book is full of valuable suggestions as to the relation of art and life, and the temptation is to place too much significance upon his words because of his charming power to set his thoughts forth in a new and persuasive manner. Here is one significant passage from his poetical prose, which might take place beside some of Browning's poems as a lesson of warning against art for art's sake: "Can one not say with authority to the young artist, whether working in stone, in color, in tones, or in character-forms of the novel—so far from dreading that your moral purposes will interfere with your beautiful creation, go forward in the clear conviction that unless you are suffused, soul and body one might say, with that moral purpose which finds its largest expression in love, that is, the love of all things in their proper relation, unless you are suffused with this love, do not dare to meddle with beauty; unless you are suffused with beauty do not dare to meddle with love; unless you are suffused with truth do not dare to meddle with goodness; in a word, unless you are suffused with truth, wisdom, goodness and love, abandon the hope that the ages will accept you as an artist."

But literature in the South did not die with Lanier. The new-born South-

ern imagination exists in fresh and hopeful promise. Southern women, as well as men, are raising their voices in the revival of literature. Mrs. Preston, a student of Browning, Mrs. Townsend, a writer of tales of Louisiana life, the late Katherine McDowell, with her "Suwanee River Tales," Miss Murfree, with her stories of the Tennessee mountains, are a few whose works are best entitled to consideration. In dialect literature Joel Chandler Harris, Lanier and Thomas Nelson Page have amused as well as cultivated with their tales of local coloring. Of the modern novelists no more delicate imagination or more appreciative interpretation of the romantic atmosphere of the South can be found than in the works of George W. Cable. He has added a new element to our literature in his tales of the old traditions of the French in Louisiana.

We have no longer a question of a literature of the North or South, but of a national literature worthy or not of a place in the world-literature.

American literature has won a position in the literature of humanity. No foreigner now sneers at an American book. The future of our national literature is as assured as that of the nation itself. The younger writers of the day have begun to realize the possibilities of their own land to contribute material for the literary imagination. As the national life becomes more settled, the leisure necessary for the cultivation of letters and art will be more assured, and with unbounded fields for the imagination and an appreciative literary public the poets of the future will certainly have every opportunity to develop their highest powers.

STRING ME THE STRANDS.

By Charles J. Bayne.

String me the strands of her soft hazel hair,
    Tuned to the key of her laughter;
Give me some fairy-like, Ariel air
    For the light breezes to waft her.

Rhyme is too rude for such graces as her's,
    Rythm too strained for her freedom—
She the exquisite whose light treading stirs
    Flowers in life's herbless Edom.

Spread like the after-glow chromes of the skies,
    Give me her childish cheek's blushes,
Mixed with the tints of her autumn brown eyes,
    With her arched brows for my brushes.

She is too artless for art to portray;
    Gems with their own dust are burnished;
Umber and ochre her charms to display
    From her own charms must be furnished.

Then I shall ask not the sketchman his skill,
    Fret not with lords of the lyre;
One nectared kiss which her child lips distill
    Genius enough will inspire.

HAM JEFFERS.

By Thos. C. Harris.

"Talkin' about yer mean men," said old Uncle Bob, addressing a little knot of boon companions sitting on empty boxes and barrels around the door of a country store, "talkin' about yer mean men, I always allowed that Ham Jeffers was the dog-gondest mean man in the State of No'th Ca'lina."

"What did he do? Well, fust and last I don't know what he hain't done, but the last time I run agin him I got the best of him, though I thought fer a while I better hadn't a done it.

"Yer know that drectly atter the war everything was lively, and we tradin' men was a makin' money hand over fist. All the upper counties went to puttin' up plug tobaccer as fast as they could split. All through Granville, Person, Caswell and along thar was lots of factories a puttin' up plug tobaccer, which was mostly peddled out by waggins goin' down the country.

"Thar hadn't been no sale for leaf tobaccer all endurin' of the war, and thar was lots of it in the country. Same way about cotton. If yer ever noticed it, the folks in the cotton counties uses more tobaccer than whar it is raised and most of the wimmen dip snuff, puffectly scandilous, from mornin' till night. You may be a gwine erlong a piney woods road and pass a cabin when all the wimmen and half-grown gals will come to the do' to see who is passin', and the last one of them will have er tooth-bresh in their mouths.

"Well, we waggoners used to git a load of plug and peddle erlong till we got down to Albermarl Soun' or Little Washinton or summers down there, and take on a load of herrin' and shad to trade back home on. Yer see, the folks back from the water courses was mighty fond of fish, and it warn't no trouble to git shut of a load of fish on the way home, and so make busines a gwine and er comin'.

"How did we work the revenoo? Well that was a reg'lar picnic and as easy as rollin' off a log. I don't want no easier job than that was. Yer see, in them times there want no stamps to stick on the box, but when a factory wanted to ship a lot of plug they would notify the officer, and he would come and put his brand on the boxes with er hot iron and collect the tax, which was thirty-three cents er pound.

"Whar I was we used to send for the revenoo man and he gineraly got thar erbout 'leven er-clock. By time he got his iron good and hot and a few boxes branded all right the Madam would have dinner ready, and all hands would quit work fer an hour.

"The grub would shore ter be mighty nice, with plenty to drink and seegars and soforth atter dinner. All the time the boss and the officer would be er eatin' and er smokin' their seegars, the foreman up at the factry would be a slappin' the brandin' iron on to the boxes in the back room. And when yer reccolleck that every time he stuck it onto a box it saved thirty-three dollars yer may know he didn't let no grass grow under his feet.

"Atter dinner the boss and the revenoo man would come down and finish brandin' what boxes was out in the front room and settle up. Oh no, nothin' was said erbout his leavin' the brandin' iron and fire pot so handy, but them fellers was allers accommodatin' ter folks as treated them white. Traders as knowed the business allers made themselves solid with Cousin Isaac, as we used ter call him, or they'd git so pestered with them darned inspectors they couldn't make no money.

"Well, I started ter tell erbout Ham Jeffers and haint got to him yit. The last time I run ercross Ham was when I got to Jones county courthouse. Ham, he comes ter me and says his load and mine was all the terbaccer in the place and proposed to put the price up to a certain figger. I agreed and traded erlong slowlike till atter one er-clock, when I found out that Ham had been a sellin' under the price and had almost sold off his load. Well, I was mad at his underhand business but I never said nothin', and by sundown we both had sold out.

"We drove erbout a mile from town that evenin' and camped at er old saw mill place on er branch. Atter supper, Ham he comes over to my fire and puts at me fer a game of chuck-er-luck at five cents er game. Ham was always a mighty hand at gamblin' and didn't no more mind cheatin' than I'd mind takin' a drink uv corn licker right now, so I told him I didn't keer to play.

"Yer rickoleck that little, puny, taller-faced half-brother Joe I had? Well, Joe was 'long 'o me that trip and was erbout fifteen years old. Joe 'lowed he'd try him a few games, so I climed in the waggin and went ter sleep. I hadn't been ersleep long befor' Ham and Joe got into a fuss and Ham struck the boy so hard that the lick waked me up. Joe said Ham cheated and struck him. It riled me so I got down outen the waggin and asked Ham if he warn't 'shamed to hit a little boy like Joe, and he said he be durned if he was 'shamed of anything. As soon as he said that I snatched up a half a fence rail and fetched him a lick side his head and laid him out colder'n a wedge.

"Joe 'lowed I'd killed him shore 'nuff, and I waited for him to come to, but he didn't. Ham lay as limber as a dish rag and seemed to be as dead as a herrin'

and I begun ter git kinder skeered.

"I 'lowed we'd better be a gittin' away at once, so Joe and I hitched up and lit out fer home. We druv all nite and all next day, only stoppin' ter feed, until we got home. We never told a word about Ham, but I looked fer a constable with a warrant to arrest me any day.

"Bimeby I 'lowed I'd take a short trip and go to Smithfield court with another load, specially as I had'nt heard nothin of Ham. When I got thar about the fust man I see was old Jim Smith and with him was a lot of other fellers I used to run with. Jim took me erside and said he had bad news to tell me. He said that lick I gin Ham had put his chunk out fer good and I better be a makin' tracks.

"I tell yer, boys, I felt purty ashy, so I made Jim promise to take my load and team and sell it and send the money to the old woman, while I jumped on my lead horse and lit out. Well, I hadn't more'n crossed the bridge when I heard somebody a comin' as fast as he could split and a wavin' his hand for me to stop. That was the sheriff, I thought, so I laid the hickory on to old Jinny and just made her git up and hump herself.

"I tell yer, boys, fer about five mile I did some of the peartest ridin' I ever seen outside a circus and kept at it 'till Jinny stumbled and throwed me over her head, plum inter a big mud hole.

"By time I got the mud outen my eyes so as I could see, up rode Jim fairly bustin' his sides a laffin at me. 'You blamed old fool,' ses he, 'I was jest a trying to ketch up with you and tell you it was all a joke we boys put up on you. Ham is all right, only the lick you gin him has cured him of gamblin'; in other ways he is as mean as ever.'

"'Taint no use a talkin', boys, I shorely felt good when I heard that, and the boys at Smithfield made me set 'em up a right smart before they ever let me hear the last of it."

CHEAP LABOR IN THE SOUTH.

By John L. Black.

The slave labor of the South did not compete directly with the white labor of the North prior to 1860, because the negro produced exclusively cotton, sugar, rice and tobacco. That portion of the slave population used in domestic service was not a producing, but a consuming class, and barred from work at the South the laboring white man who aspired to as servile a position as that of domestic servant. The sentimental crusade of so-called philanthropy, directed against African slavery, led to its downfall; indeed, as a Southern man and an ex-slaveholder, the writer admits that the peculiar institution was in many respects objectionable, and its abolition is not to be regretted by any man of reflection, especially when, after the lapse of thirty years, it is now plainly demonstrated that the labor of the freed negro costs less than the former labor of the slave. The negro is now engaged in rearing himself, he pays his own doctor's bills and his funeral expenses, as it were, carries his own insurance and now even pays the parson to minister to his spiritual comfort, charges which humane masters formerly took upon themselves to pay. And thus insuring himself, the price of the free negro's labor is not over one-half of what it cost as a slave, considering money to be worth seven per cent. Therefore the South is now the great field for cheap labor.

Heretofore, since 1866, the great mass of this free negro labor has been concentrated on the production of cotton, sugar, rice and tobacco, and from the natural increase of this race too much cotton—and perhaps too much of the other products named—is being made,

the natural result being low prices. As a remedy, much of this labor is drawing itself from the cotton fields and is finding employment in other lines, in manufacturing, mining, building railroads and other so-called public works. With cotton at or under ten cents per pound the labor of an able-bodied black man can always be had in the South for fifty, sixty, or at the highest seventy cents per day. As a patient laborer the negro has no equal; he has no trades union or eight-hour law notions, but consents to work, and does work cheerfully, ten to eleven hours daily. His movements are not as quick as those of the white man, but his patient endurance is much greater, and as he toils he whiles away care with song.

In the colored race exists the great source of the South's future wealth. The sentimental abolitionist of the olden time, who wept and mourned in sackcloth and ashes while reading of the imaginary horrors of this black man-and-brother's state as he toiled in so-called chains and slavery, little imagined that abolition successful and the poor down-trodden negro emancipated, he would—not as a slave but as a free man and alongside of his old master —become the fertile means of enriching again the South. This sentimental class in the North has ever been clamorous for the elevation of labor, and they now have the fruits of it at home where the laborer has been elevated until he will not labor, but by trades unions and labor organizations aspires to rule and govern and control the capital he does not own. Hence the elevated, educated and enlightened labor of many portions of the North is not labor, but a clamoring horde of bosses who must needs control their employers.

When the Irishman was no longer available, the immigration of Chinese, Italians, Hungarians and such like was encouraged in order to supply the labor market in the North, and furnish the hewers of wood and drawers of water. But for the accession of these latter classes, many sections of the rich North would be in a collapsed condition even now. But at the South no foreign immigration finds its way; there the freed negro is present in sufficient numbers to supply all demands on the labor market, and he is likely to keep on in the even tenor of his way for a century yet to come. The Italian and the Chinaman in the North work cheaper than any other race, and why? Because they live on peculiar and cheap food, such as pleases them, but at the South the negro gets such food as best pleases him far cheaper than an Italian or a Chinaman can feed himself in the North. Hence the negro in the South can and will labor for less than either of the two competing classes referred to. The mildness of the climate and small cost of fuel make his housing and his clothing cheaper than the fuel and housing of any other laboring man in the Union. The cost of such clothing as he generally wears is so small that practically it amounts to nothing. At sixty cents per day for his labor, one day's work per week will feed him, and the wages of another day will, on an average, clothe and feed him. His wife, as a general rule, takes care of herself. Now this man is a free man and as a citizen of this great country he has a right to labor or not as he pleases, and he both can and will work more cheaply than even that so much talked of pauper labor of the Old Country.

Whatever free negro labor at the South produces can be produced no longer by the educated white labor of the North, unless the current rate of Northern wages be greatly reduced, as the negro can certainly underproduce his Northern laboring brother by forty to fifty per cent. In last October the writer saw one hundred and three able-bodied negro laborers, singing merrily at their work, making bricks and handling them for the erection of a cotton factory at Gaffney City in South Carolina. They were paid weekly in cash, sixty cents per day of eleven hours. In the same yard were thirty bricklayers and as many rough carpenters working on the mill building. Only four of these mechanics received over $1.00 per day and none over $1.25, the others ranging from seventy-five to ninety cents per day. The bricks were going into the walls of this factory at a cost of less than $6 per thousand, including cement foundations. In the yard were one and one-half million feet of Georgia pine, which was delivered there at a cost of $7.50 per thousand feet. This factory, with an outfit of looms and the best modern machinery, has been completed at a cost of about $18.50 per spindle. Where else in the United States can this be done except in the South? If any reader doubts the facts and figures I have stated, Mr. A. N. Wood, a banker at Gaffney City, and president of this mill, will verify them.

The poor white people live, thrive and keep fat at these wages, and are far happier than those engaged in the same calling in the North. They must live and have employment, for, although their welfare was never a matter of so much solicitude to the over zealous abolitionists and pious philanthropists, yet they are citizens of this great country and must have work. Some recent writers have spoken freely of this class as "Georgia crackers." Call them "crackers" if you will; they still are American citizens; they are patient and generally industrious and enjoy life to a greater degree than do the majority of the similar class in the North, toiling at the same kind of spindles and looms.

Poverty alone will make a man labor. If all were educated and rich, who would plow and dig, spin and weave, toil in mine and workshop? No one. But there is a natural law that should regulate wages, and it is higher than the law of any land—it is one of the laws of God. The laboring man should receive as the fruits of his labor enough to clothe him warmly, house him healthfully and another third equal to either . of these to supply his fanciful wants. If he receives less than the first two-thirds he will starve or die; if he does not have a little margin for fanciful expenditure he will become dissatisfied. Even at the low rate of wages in the South, the laborer has a larger margin left after being housed and clothed than has the laborer in the North. On the other hand, if so much is paid for wages as not to leave a good margin of profit on the employer's side, the laborer will soon find himself without an employer. The educated and elevated labor in the North in many cases now has left a slim profit to the capitalist employer.

The same labor the South now has will soon generate millions of wealth, amounts equal to the value of all the slaves emancipated in 1863*. The South is now the end of the union that holds the long lever in the labor supply, and the South will soon hold the plethoric bank account. Cheap pig iron, cheap cotton, cheaply manufactured cotton goods, sugar, rice, tobacco and many other products will help raise its fallen fortunes. No Congress can legislate to protect the Northern laboring man from the active competition of his black rival at the South. Thousands of these same white laborers faced death on many bloody battle fields to make these same negroes free, to bring them to the front as a . competitor in the labor market. Let such say who is to blame. This is the situation and the picture is not overdrawn. The South is now marching onward and most of this progress is due to an abundant supply of cheap, patient and contented labor.

The rapidly increasing population of the South supplies too much labor for the production of its staple crops. While other farm products can be added, such as increased grain and forage crops, still, even with a sufficient production of cereals and meats to supply all domestic wants, there will be too much cotton, rice, sugar and tobacco to insure remunerative prices. · The excess of labor, especially the whites, can be applied to cotton spinning to the

*$4,000,000,000 I say was the value of the slaves freed.

best advantage to laborer and employer. This is notably true in the Carolinas and in Georgia, which will be the great cotton spinning section of the South. These States will soon manufacture more cotton than they produce, even though the production be increased, as it will be. Evidence of the prospective increase in this line is found in the constant building of new mills, the published reports of profits in this business, and the quotations of the selling price of cotton-mill stocks in the Charleston, Atlanta and Augusta papers. Some of these stocks pay 20 to 35 per cent. per annum, and sell for $140 to $175 per share, $100 par. The white labor gathered into mills and other manufacturing enterprises, will but make more room for the free negro in the cotton fields. When it comes to iron ore mining and smelting, the free negro is in his proper element. Even now they are used in this work as far North as Sparrow's Point, Md., and in the iron works around Philadelphia, Pa. A recent press dispatch from Pittsburg, Pa., gives the following significant information:

About 250 negroes from the South arrived at Brinton station today. Colored laborers will have the first chance by the Carnegie Company at all its works in preference to foreigners who apply for work. James Galey, general manager of the plant, expects nearly 1000 others in a month This will mean that as soon as possible all the slaves will be dismissed. There are about 3000 foreigners altogether.

After Mr. Carnegie gets all he wants of Southern surplus labor there still will be more than enough left in the South to insure an abundance of cheap labor there. As the cost of clothing, housing and feeding the negro in the North will be in excess of the amount necessary in the South for his wages, clothing, food and housing, his labor still will be fifty per cent. cheaper in the South than in the North.

Said a New England shoe manufacturer to the writer: "I make no shoes that I can wholesale for less than $2.50 per pair, because my educated and organized labor costs me from $2 to $3.50 per day. I cannot apply such labor on coarse or common work.

"Who," I asked "will make shoes for the poor man?"

"It must be done," he replied, "where labor is cheaper." Now, while the free negro is a poor cotton mill hand, he is certainly a descendant of St. Crispin. He is the very best of shoe hands and soon must be utilized to make shoes for poor people. And this will be nothing new to Southern men of ante-bellum days, for the negro, then a slave, made some of the best hand-stitched work ever worn. He can and will do it again. In the tobacco factories of Richmond, Lynchburg and Danville, Va., and in the tobacco factories of North Carolina, the negro looms up in all his glory ; he is at home and makes himself useful.

Nor will this useful man, brother and citizen, be useful in these factories alone. He is the mudsill that grades railroads, the brakeman and train hand on the road, and the time may be speedily coming when the banded locomotive engineers and switchmen in the South shall become so exacting in their demands that they will have to stand aside, and the negro may not only fill every yard as switchman, but further still, he may play fireman as he has done on Southern roads for forty years past. He may even take the cab and run the engine. The great party of progressive ideas, which has held the reins of the national government for the last thirty years, has crammed every postal car on Southern lines full of negro mail clerks. All of this, done as a party measure, only proves that if the negro's faculties are sufficient to qualify him for a railway mail service position, he is certainly able to handle the throttle of a locomotive pulling a train. By all Northern theories he is the equal of the white man ; to carry out the purposes of a great party of moral ideas, he was made not only a free man but a citizen, and as such he has a right, equal with the rest of mankind, to employment and to enjoy the fruits of his labor. As some of the iron and steel men are turning to this race in order to escape the pressure of so-called organized labor, it may be well for railroad corporations to employ negro labor, which can be had cheaper than any other and will be about as efficient as any. And when again we have a mercantile marine, the negro can brave the briny deep as a sailor, for here he has often been tried and never found wanting, as shown in the British navy and merchant marine.

The great rich North has the money today ; the poor South has an abundant supply of the best labor on earth. A new era is dawning, and the next half century may make the South relatively the richest section of the Union.

CLIMATE AND CROPS OF TEXAS.

By Dr. I. M. Cline.

[From a report on "The Climate of Texas," by Gen. A. W. Greeley.]

As regards some of the undeveloped industries of the State and the advantages of the climate as a health resort, I will present the following as a brief result of some of my observations and study of these subjects during the several years I have been stationed in Texas:

The sugar-cane industry is one of the most promising fields for development in the State. In southern Texas alone, including the lower Rio Grande valley, there are over 1,000,000 acres on which sugar-cane can be successfully grown every year, and along the streams it is successfully grown for the manufacture of syrup north of the thirty-second parallel. An average of 14,000 acres have been cultivated in this product during the past three years; of this an average of 250 acres has been in the lower Rio Grande valley. The average yield for the State has been about four barrels per acre, while that for the southern portion of the State averaged about six barrels, and that grown in the lower Rio Grande valley about eight barrels.

The total value of the sugar-cane crop grown in 1889 amounted to over $1,500,000, and the average value of the product per acre was nearly $100. If the estimate as to the area on which sugar-cane can be successfully grown is placed at 1,000,000 acres and the product valued at $100 an acre, and it is taken into consideration that this would give a crop worth annually $100,000,000, an idea of the possibilities in this direction may be obtained. That the climate is suited to the production of sugar-cane has been established beyond question. This industry was successfully carried on along the Brazos river before the Civil War, but on the freedom of the slaves the plantations and plants were abandoned for want of capital to carry on the industry, and it is only within the last few years that it has been revived.

Wheat-raising is an industry which is comparatively in its infancy. There are at present less than 500,000 acres cultivated in wheat in the State, which yielded in 1889 something over 5,000,000 bushels (about thirteen bushels per acre), which is four bushels per acre greater than the average yield for the United States. North of the thirtieth parallel and west of the ninety-eighth meridian there is a large territory which promises to become one of the most important wheat-growing sections in the country. In this territory there are over 8,000,000 acres of arable land on which it has, within the last few years, been practically demonstrated that the soil and climate are particularly adapted to this product. Extensive and successful experiments in wheat-culture have been made in this section during the past five years on the strength of some climatological statistics, covering a period of ten years, published at Abilene in 1887, and these are being followed by a rapid development of this industry.

The average yield where experiments have been made in this territory is eighteen bushels per acre, which is twice that for the country generally, and the quality of the grain has been pronouncd by experts equal to any grown in the United States. In addition to the above territory it is estimated that there are over 3,000,000 acres in the section known as the Panhandle which will prove to be good wheat growing lands. Successful experiments have been made in this direction to a small extent, and the only question to be solved is whether the rainfall is sufficient, and it is generally believed that in some parts at least the climate will prove as favorable, as the soil is adapted to wheat culture.

In the northwest portion of the State and the Panhandle there are over 9,000,-000 acres, which give a prolific growth of sorghum cane, even in the dryest seasons. If the experiments in manufacturing sugar from this crop should prove successful this could and unquestionably would become a profitable industry in this State, as it offers a longer season in which to work up the crop than Kansas, while the climate of this section and that of that State are somewhat similar in other respects, and particularly as regards rainfall.

Gardening promises to become an important industry in the southern portion of the State. During the last year the area in gardens amounted to over 30,000 acres, and the total value of garden products amounted to over $4,000,000. Large gardens are operated in the vicinity of Galveston and Houston and vegetables are shipped to the Northern markets. The mild winters and early spring make this a paying industry.

The western portion of the State is adapted to grape and fruit culture, where in El Paso county alone it is estimated that there are 100,000 acres along the Rio Grande river which are susceptible to irrigation. Ysleta is the home of the domestic grape, and there is a large territory in the western portion of the State, where, it is believed, the cultivation of the grape, both for the manufacture of wine and raisins, will prove successful.

Experiments in the manufacture of wine have been made in Taylor county by a native grape grower of France, and he pronounces this section more favorable to that industry than his native country. Different varieties of the wild grape grow in abundance and are very productive in many parts of the State, and about 30,000 gallons of wine are manufactured from these annually. The total number of vines of the cultivated grape in the State is less than 900,000, of which one-tenth are in El Paso county. Grape culture, it is believed, will in the course of time become an important industry in northwest, central and west Texas.

It is believed than the cultivation of rice can be made a profitable industry over a large territory along the Gulf coast, but no attempt has been made in this direction. There is a vast number of acres along the coast in different localities where the ground may be overflowed almost at will, and there is very little question but that the climate and soil are suited to rice culture.

The production and manufacture of castor oil was entered upon in northwest Texas a few years ago. This plant has been found to thrive in all parts of the State where its cultivation has been attempted. It is perennial in the southern portion, and attains considerable size. It has been found to thrive as an annual in the northern portion as far west as the 100th meridian, and it is believed that it can be successfully cultivated much farther west than this. So far as I have been able to ascertain, the efforts to develop this industry have been successful. While it is hardly probable that the cultivation of this plant will ever become a leading feature in the industries of the eastern and southern portions of the State, it is most certain to become one of the important resources of the western portion on account of its capacity for withstanding drouth.

The ramie plant is being successfully experimented with in Galveston county, where the results as to product of fibre are very encouraging, and, as there is a large territory along the coast suited to the cultivation of this plant, it is expected to become a feature of decided economic and commercial importance.

Perhaps there is no industry which promises a more extensive development in nearly all parts of the State than the fruit crop, and this is being recognized and its cultivation pushed generally.

The pear is a sure crop of unusually large size and fine flavor near the Gulf coast, and it thrives in many other sections.

The northern and northwestern portions of the State appear to be particularly suited to the cultivation of the peach, some varieties of which often attain a size ranging from ten to fourteen inches in circumference, and the flavor is unexcelled.

In addition to the peach and pear, which promises to take the lead in the fruit culture, apples, plums and apricots, and several varieties of berries—blackberry, dewberry, strawberry, raspberry and gooseberry—and nuts, most prominent among which are the pecan, walnut and almond, are found to give a prolific growth and an abundant yield in different parts of the State. Canning establishments are being erected in sections where the fruit crop is being cultivated extensively, and the outlook is very favorable for the rapid development of this industry.

The value of the fruit crop put on the market at present amounts to about $2,000,000 annually.

In tropical fruits the orange is being successfully cultivated in some localities along the coast, and the lemon, lime, banana, date and fig are cultivated to some extent for individual use in gardens along the entire coast, and they give a prolific yield of a fine quality of fruit. The vanilla vine is indigenous to the southern part of the State. There is a large territory along the coast which promises resources in this line of decided commercial importance when developed, and the climate and soil of this section appear more favorable to the opening up of this industry than that of some sections of the country where it is being carried on successfully.

The olive has been found to thrive where cultivated in gardens as far north as the thirty-second parallel, and it is believed that the cultivation of this fruit will become a leading feature in the industries, particularly of the southwestern portion of the State, where the climate appears similar in many respects to that of those regions where the olive is successfully and extensively cultivated.

The Japanese persimmon is being successfully cultivated in many parts of the State and gives a very fine quality of fruit.

The beet of the mangel-wurzel variety gives a very prolific growth in many parts of the State. There is a territory embracing over 20,000,000 acres which extends perhaps as far west as the 102d meridian in some localities on which this product can be successfully cultivated. The beet has been produced extensively over parts of this territory for food for cattle, but its cultivation for the manufacture of sugar has never been attempted; yet this section offers an important field for the development of this industry. The fact that the beet can be planted at different seasons and made to grow almost throughout the year (on account of the open winters) is a feature worthy of consideration and one which should attract attention to this matter.

Among other crops, of which the value of the products amounts annually to from $100,000 to $4,500,000, and in favor of which the climate and soil are suited in different parts of the State, are barley, rye, millet, sweet potatoes, Irish potatoes, oats and broom corn, all of which appear susceptible of extensive development.

The cochineal or nopal cactus is indigenous to a great deal of that part of the State west of the ninety-ninth meridian, south of the thirty-second parallel. The cochineal insect is found on the plant in large quantities, but the development of this industry as one of the commercial resources of the State has never been attempted. The demand for cochineal is greater than the supply, and consequently there is an opening here for the development of an industry of great commercial importance.

No particular reference is made to cotton and corn as they are known to be the staple products of the State. The present yield of cotton is over 2,000,000 bales, and that of corn about 70,000,000 bushels annually. The area on which these two crops have in some instances been successfully grown extends as far west as the 100th meridian, but there are other crops which have already been mentioned (to which the climate and soil are better suited) that give much surer and more valuable crops than either of these west of the ninety-eighth meridian. Yet, as mixed farming is by far the most advantageous, these crops might be depended on to some extent in connection with other and surer crops over this territory.

Texas offers many prominent features of climate to the health seeker. The elevation varies from sea level to over 5000 feet above, and a great deal of the State is swept by the prevailing Gulf breezes, which temper both the summer and winter seasons to a very marked degree. The northers of the northwestern portion of the State have commonly been represented in darker colors than are actually found on experience. While there are to some extent unpleasant features, yet their short duration (twenty-four to forty-eight hours) and their rare occurrence make them far less disagreeable than is generally supposed. The climate generally is salubrious, and the disagreeable and dangerous periodical fevers are only found in small portions of the State, and then to no great extent.

The mortality of the State averages about fourteen deaths for each 1000 inhabitants annually. In this pneumonia is first, with one in fifteen deaths, which is followed closely by typhoid fever, with nearly the same ratio. The first-named disease is, as is well known, brought on by exposure; the last-named one is brought about by local unsanitary conditions, as is proven by the fact that in cities in the State where strict sanitary regulations are enforced it is the cause of less than one in each 100 deaths. Consumption comes third, with one death in each seventeen, which is about half as great as the average from this disease throughout the world. There are a few diseases which give an average slightly greater than one in every fifty deaths, while the majority of the remaining causes give an average of less than one in every 100 deaths.

The climate of that section of the State west of the ninety-eighth meridian and north of the thirtieth parallel is particularly adapted to the alleviation of pulmonary troubles. The elevation varies from 1500 to 5000 feet above sea level. The rare and dry atmosphere, an extraordinary amount of sunshine, with neither extreme of heat or cold, go to furnish a climate where outdoor exercise and recreation (which is so necessary in the treatment of pulmonary troubles) can be engaged in without inconvenience throughout the entire year. The condition of the soil in this section is favorable in a marked degree to the treatment of these diseases.

The topography of the country is undulating, with a regular and decided increase in elevation to the northwestward. This gives a natural system of drainage which is unsurpassed, thus rendering the soil free from stagnant and fermented water, which has been found to be one of the most prominent causes of pulmonary troubles. No cases of pulmonary consumption have been known to have had their origin in that territory.

A large per cent. of those who go there in search of relief are restored to health, and in others the progress of the disease is checked, while in the case of those in whom the disease is so far advanced that climate cannot cure or permanently check its advance, temporary relief is generally obtained. This has been the result in a number of cases which have come under my observation. A complete absence of malarial diseases and periodical fevers is also a striking feature of this climate.

The Gulf coast and the southwestern portion of the State offer unsurpassed advantages as a winter health resort.

The orange, banana, date and other tropical fruits thrive in this section, and with the exception of an occasional season with moderately low temperature, flowers bloom out doors in every month of the year. Excessive changes in temperature are rare, and the northers of northwest Texas never amount to more than a cool wave along the coast. The temperature ranges generally from 35 to 60, with pleasant, prevailing fresh to brisk southerly winds from the Gulf, which give an equable climate, where outdoor exercises and sports can be engaged in throughout the winter without the least inconvenience. The above, with other unexcelled natural facilities, such as boating, fishing and hunting, furnish advantages for recreation which cannot be appreciated until experienced, and they are of that character most desired by the pleasure and health-seeker.

The statement of Robert Russell in his "Climate of America" that the temperature has been known to fall in southern Texas with a norther from 81 to 18 in forty-one hours has not been verified here during the twenty years the record has been kept, and such changes have never been known to have occurred except in northern Texas a distance of 400 miles from the coast. January is generally the coldest month in the year and gives the lowest temperature.

The record at Galveston for this month for twenty years shows that the minimum temperature has been below thirty in eleven years and below twenty in one year only. From fifteen years' record it is found that the temperature during December, January and February falls ten degrees or more in twenty-four hours on an average of eight days in 188, rises ten degrees or more on six days in 100; and while the changes are probably slightly greater than the above for the entire coast region, yet they cannot exceed this to any great extent.

A fair idea as to the health of this section may be taken from Galveston as a base. The average annual death rate at Galveston is about fifteen per 1000 inhabitants. Pulmonary consumption leads with one in every fourteen deaths, which is one-third less than the average mortality from this dread scourge for the world. Pneumonia comes second, with an average of one in every twenty-eight deaths. Following these are a few diseases which give a death rate of one in fifty, and the remainder give one or less in 100 deaths.

No epidemic diseases have visited this section since 1870, except a few cases of smallpox, from which only seven deaths have occurred during the past seventeen years. Periodical fevers are not observed to any extent worthy of notice in this section, and, in fact, are almost entirely absent. Epidemic diseases are kept away by strict and systematic quarantine, which is carried on at the season without any material injury to commerce. It is a fact deserving mention that the more destructive epidemic diseases have never been known to have had their first origin here, and when transplanted to this section have not been propagated to anything like the same extent they have under other semi-tropical climates.

THE SOUTHERN OUTLOOK.

Prize Stories of Southern Life.

In the May issue of this magazine announcement was made of an offer of two prizes—fifty and twenty-five dollars—for the two best stories or sketches dealing with Southern life and conditions. The result of this offer appears in the two prize stories published in the present issue. These two stories, selected by a careful consideration of nearly one hundred manuscripts, are both striking in their force and originality. Both of them deal with the poorer classes of the South. In the story which was awarded the first prize—"Matt: the Moonshiner's Daughter," by Mrs. Kathleen Gray Nelson, of Atlanta, Ga., there is presented a tragical, yet touching, chapter of Georgia mountain life, the life of outlawed illicit distillers. The traits of genuine character in Matt, the vague yearnings of an untaught nature for something higher and nobler than could be found among her brutally ignorant kin and companions, present new phases of an element in nature that is often chosen as a basis for fiction. Mrs. Byrdie Herndon Hansbrough, of Leesburg, Fla., in her "Story of Samanthy Williams," finds in the humblest and crudest surroundings a character of strength equalled only by its extreme simplicity. It is the story of a character that was strong enough to adhere unflinchingly to a vow through thirty years of dishonor, sorrow and toil, and a faith that wavered not through thirty years of waiting and unrelieved expectancy.

While both of these stories are faithful in their treatment of Southern character, they cannot be considered as representavive of the the South any more than the life of a Michigan logging camp can be accepted as representing the social conditions of the West. Both of these stories deal with classes that have real existence in the South, and the writers find in these classes characters that are far above

their surroundings in purity, nobility and strength. These stories are striking in their portrayal of character, but it must be remembered that is not of such types as these that the South is composed. It is not by way of criticism that this warning is offered, but rather to prevent the acceptance of these stories and their characters for representative Southern people and conditions.

There is cause for much gratification in the more than average merit of a large number of the stories submitted for consideration. Several of them rank so close to the two that were selected for the prizes that the final decision was not reached without a careful weighing of the various points of merit. Among those that fell short of the prize standard were many well worthy of publication, and our readers will have opportunity to render their own decision regarding them upon their publication in these pages.

Jefferson Davis and "The Rebellion."

Editor The Southern States :

I note in your June issue an article upon "Jefferson Davis and His Cause" from the pen of our gifted townsman, James R. Randall. Several passages in it bring to my mind vividly a letter from Mr. Davis now in my possession, which illustrates forcibly his position with reference to the Lost Cause.

During the forty-fifth and forty-sixth Congresses, I was in an office in the House of Representatives and private secretary to the late Hon. Otto R. Singleton, of Mississippi. It was during that period and while a bill to pension the veterans of the Mexican War was under consideration that Colonel Singleton received the letter in question, and, at my request, gave it to me. The "more formal" one referred to has long since been published, but the one, a copy of which I append, has never yet appeared in print. Its postscript epitomizes the logic of his position on the secession question and confirms the conclusions reached by Mr. Randall:

BEAUVOIR, February 17, 1878.

My Dear Friend:

In the published proceedings of the 14th instant, I observe that a member of the House (Mr. Powers, of Maine) is reported to have used the following language : "He is also opposed to opening the door for the pensioning of all, including Jeff. Davis, who had been in the Mexican war, but had afterwards participated in the Rebellion." As this portends opposition to any measure granting pensions to the soldiers in the war with Mexico, which should include me, I wish, in the event of the fate of the bill depending upon my exclusion from its benefits that you or one of your colleagues, if you should be absent, would request the friends of the measure silently to allow the malignants to impose upon it the condition of my exclusion from the benefit of its provisions. For this purpose I will write a more formal letter appended to this to be used in the contingency described above. If Mrs. Singleton or either of your children are with you, please present to them my kindest remembrance and believe me to be Yours faithfully,

JEFFERSON DAVIS.

HON. O. R. SINGLETON.

P. S.— It was said the "Mexican Veterans are mostly in the prime of life yet;" add thirty years to mature manhood and you have the average age ; but many, myself included, are on the verge of the limit allotted to man. As to *"the Rebellion,"* I left the House of Representatives at the call of Mississippi and joined the regiment which had elected me when it was en route to Mexico ; at the expiration of their term of service I returned on crutches with them. At a later period I left the Senate at the call of Mississippi. In the one cause as in the other, I served my sovereign and perilled my life in obedience to her mandate. If sovereigns can rebel, then I may have "participated in" a "rebellion." J. D.

I think the letter well worthy of publication and take pleasure in sending it to you for that purpose. Respectfully,

C. J. WIENER.

Baltimore.

Stimulating Southern Industrial Growth

One of the most striking features of the Southern business situation at this time, when financial disturbances are everywhere uppermost in mind, is the activity of the numerous organizations that have for their purpose promotion of public interests. During the past six months boards of trade, commercial clubs and business mens' associations have been multiplying throughout the South at an unusual rate. Every large city and nearly every important town now has an organization of busines men whose prime object is the stimulating of industrial development. These associations are of varying character, and there is a wide diversity in the methods that they follow, but one and all are working for the advancement of the public welfare. The most gratifying feature of their work is the entire absence of the "boom" spirit. We are not aware of the existence of a single organization among them all that presents any indications of a speculative character, nor are any of them seeking to fulfill their objects by any other than legitimate business methods. There is a distinctive element of earnestness and practical business about their work that is exceedingly commendable. And the energy with which their work is being prosecuted is particularly significant under the trying conditions that now prevail.

The city of Atlanta, Ga., whose people are characterized by much of the dash and spirit of the West, is the latest of the Southern cities to inaugurate a vigorous and well-organized campaign for the promotion of industrial interests. The plan that is being considered in Atlanta differs radically from the methods applied elsewhere in similar work, its essential feature being a guarantee of principal and interest on stocks and bonds issued by manufacturing companies and representing no · more than one-half the actual cash invested in the property. In addition to this service the association will undertake to facilitate the transaction of business by every means within its power, securing advantageous freight rates, favorable corporation laws, and · also undertaking to raise the capital required for the establishment of new enterprises. The plan is broad and comprehensive, and, if carefully worked out, it should be productive of great good for Atlanta. The business men of that city are thoroughly awake to the opportunity that awaits them, and beyond doubt the movement now under way will greatly stimulate the growth of the city and its industries.

The city of Memphis, Tenn., enjoys the presence of the Young Men's Business League, an energetic organization that has just finished the first year of a useful existence. By making known to the world the opportunities presented in Memphis, and by persistently following every prospect of attracting new industrial enterprises, the association has succeeded in locating in Memphis four new factories, paying $300,000 yearly in wages and adding 2500 to the population of the city.

Helena, Ark., has a business men's league that is displaying much energy and earnestness in pushing the city forward. From this organization comes another new idea in development methods, being the application of the plan of building and loan associations to the erection of manufacturing establishments. It is a sort of instalment plan by which a small amount of money could .be made to accomplish much. We have yet to see the results of a practical application of the plan, but it evidently posseses advantages worthy of trial.

The citizens of Natchez, Miss., have recently organized the Natchez‾Manufacturing and Aid Association to promote the industrial interests of that city, and the work ·has been undertaken in an energetic spirit. This association has adopted the instalment plan of paying up its stock, and its capital will be used to assist manufacturing enterprises that desire to locate there.

At Jacksonville, Fla., the Industrial Development Co., a semi-public organization, is engaged in the work of industrial development, and has already made its influence strongly felt in this direction. An association of citizens is now in process of organization at Florence, Ala ; a commercial club has just been organized in Camden, Ark.; a board of trade has been formed in Waxahachie, Texas, and the business men of Raleigh, N. C., have organized a chamber of commerce and industry. These are a few of the recent steps in the direction of stimulating industrial growth in the South, and they indicate the widespread and earnest effort that is being put forth along this line.

Failures During Six Months.

A study of the statistics of business failures during the half year, as presented by *Bradstreet's*, reveals some interesting points about business conditions during the past six months. The number of failures, the estimated assets and the total liabilities have been greater than during any similar period in the last fifteen years, which means the greatest in the history of the United States. The failures since January 1 number 6239, or 133 more than in 1885, the greatest previous record. Compared with the first half of last year the past six months show an increase of 888 in the number of failures. While the total liabilities since January 1 are $170,860,222, as compared with $56,535,521 during the same period of last year, the estimated assets increased in the same time from $28,935,106 to $105,371,813. It is strikingly shown by these figures that the chief cause of failures

has been lack of ready money rather than insufficient assets, for the assets are figured at sixty-one per cent. of the liabilities during the past six months, as compared with fifty-one per cent. in the same time last year. It is worthy of note that the percentage of assets to liabilities in the failures of the past six months has been the highest on record as an average for the entire country.

Looking at *Bradstreet's* figures in detail we find that the largest increase in the number of failures appears in the West, where 1633 are recorded for the half year, as compared with 1037 in the corresponding months of last year. The liabilities increased in the same time from $12,415,040 to $40,765,888, and the assets from $6,847,226 to $30,564,991. The Northwest shows the · largest proportionate increase in liabilities from $6,355,793 to $29,154,069. About two-thirds of this increase, or $14,300,000, is contributed by Iowa, where havoc has been wrought by booms and speculation. One failure alone accounts for $6,000,000 of this indebtedness, another for nearly $2,000,000, one for $2,500,000, and another for $1,000,000, almost all of them in Sioux City.

The South and New England, popularly regarded as the poorest and the richest sections of the country, stand side by side in the record of failures, a remarkable demonstration of the strength and stability of the South. In New England the number of failures increased from 872 to 919, or 5.7 per cent.; the estimated assets increased from $3,313,814 · to $6,689.403, or just about 100 per cent., and the total liabilities increased from $8,944,637 to $17,346,440, or ninety-four per cent. In the South, the increase in number of failures was from 1043 to 1060, or 1.6 per cent.; assets increased from $5,849,462 to $11,428,867, or about ninety-five per cent., while liabilities increased from $9,263,201 to $18,297,454, or ninety-six per cent. The average liabilities of the failed firms in the South this year was $17,261, and in New England the average was $18,875. The average assets in the South amounted to $10,781, and in New England the average was only $7,279. The most striking feature of this comparison between New England and the South is the relation between assets and liabilities in the two sections. In the South the estimated assets amounted to 62.5 per cent. of the liabilities, or 1.5 per cent. higher than the average for the entire country. In New England the ratio was only thirty-eight per cent., or twenty-three per cent. below the average for the country as a whole.

Viewing these statistics from any standpoint, the showing for the South is strikingly favorable, demonstrating clearly the truth of what has been repeatedly asserted in these columns, namely, that the South is standing the strain of tight money and lost confidence better than any other section of the country, a fact that becomes more remarkable when viewed in the light of the adverse business conditions that have long hindered the development and progress of the South.

Missionary Work by Immigrants.

A well-informed correspondent, writing to us about the practical phases of the present Southern immigration agitation, has this to say about the manner in which the South is advertised by those who go there from the North and take up their abode :

I know the North thoroughly, having been raised on a farm and hired in different villages in four different States. I know the prices of land and crops, and also know that there are many thousands who are ready to move to a warmer climate, where there are cheaper lands and a greater variety of products. Here is another thing that I know—that it is necessary to convert only one man in a community to be effectual. I have a splendid illustration of this. A man went from my county to Louisiana and there planted and raised a crop of rice. The land was cheap and the crop big, and what was the result? Why, over a hundred people have gone there from Park County, Ill., alone within eighteen months, and many more are ready to go as soon as they can sell their property, and all because one man took the lead. There is now a whole town of these Northern people in Louisiana as the outcome of the efforts of one satisfied and successful settler from the North.

It was chiefly by such personal advertising that the West and Northwest were peopled with desirable immigrants from the East and from foreign countries. The pioneer settlers who met with success at the start were not slow in communicating with their friends in their old homes, and the missionary work thus done has ever been the most effective advertising that the West and Northwest have received. If those who are stimulating the immigration sentiment in the South would direct their energies into clearly-defined channels and locate here and there a sample immigrant, as it were, the seed thus sown would yield a hundred-fold in new settlers of the kind that the South needs. Personal influence counts for more by many hundred times than the indiscriminate, indefinite and generally aimless talk and argument that have thus far characterized the immigration agitation in the South.

Southern Profit from Western Disaster.

The question that is most frequently suggested by the financial disasters in the West is this : "What will be the effect upon the South of the Western panic?" The answer can be expressed in a single word—beneficial. In every respect the South is reaping, and will continue to reap, a great advantage from the wide-spread financial disturbances in the West. The immediate advantage is that resulting from the comparison of the South under the terrible strain with the collapse of Western enterprises and institutions, which have been falling like card houses during the past week. Bank after bank in the West has closed its doors under the terrific pressure of panic, and many financial institutions of high standing and years of great prosperity have gone down with the newer and weaker concerns. Out of the wreck many will doubtless arise and regain a measure of their business, but the experiences of the past few weeks have been a staggering blow to Western prosperity, particularly the far West.

The immediate gain to the South is by contrast ; the next benefit will arise from the diversion to the South of a great amount of capital withdrawn from the West by timid or cautious investors. The experience of the past few weeks will be sufficient to convince thousands of investors that their money is no longer safe in the West. Without passing upon the justice of such impressions, it is enough to indicate this sentiment as a fact that cannot be disputed. The manner in which the South has withstood the pressure of panic will attract to that section a large amount of the capital withdrawn from the West during these troublesome times. Popular distrust is an influence that is more difficult to counteract than any element that enters into the world of finance, and it will take years for the West to regain what has been lost in the past few weeks, even if there be no more events of a similar character to disturb still further the equilibrium of that section.

Still further advantage is likely to fall to the South from the agitaton of the repeal of the Sherman silver bill. The East has been foremost in the demand for the repeal of this law, and an intense enmity towards the people of the East has been engendered in the silver producing States of the far West. As a suggested means of retaliation, the Western people threaten to divert their trade as far as may be possible from the Eastern seaboard cities to the Southern ports. Regardless of the considerations by which the Western people are actuated in this retaliation, there is a steadily growing movement of Western trade towards the Gulf ports, and the stimulus of any such a sentiment as that expressed by the angry silver people will have a beneficial effect upon the trade of the South. Much of the Western trade must inevitably find its way through the natural inlet and outlet of the Gulf ports, and a determination on the part of the West to cease business with the East would be of immediate profit to the South. Without criticising the motive, this is the result of the wrath of the West.

The position of the South in all this tempest of trade is that of an interested spectator who views the storm from a point of safety and is sure to profit from whatever may be left when the cyclone passes.

Notes on Southern Progress.

THE city of Knoxville, Tenn., is keeping pace with the progress of improvements in the South. Some of the structures now under construction or to be erected in the city are an opera house to cost over $125,000, a normal school and dormitories to cost $55,000, a university school to cost $12,000, two churches which will cost $41,000, a $50,000 business block and four others aggregating $50,000, a $20,000 residence and six others ranging from $5,000 to $10,000 each. Nearly $500,000 will be spent in building operations in the city within the next year.

A DETAILED statistical account of the fisheries of the South Atlantic States is contained in the eighth report just issued from the department at Washington, D. C. This shows that in 1890 the number of persons engaged in the fisheries in this section was 16,001 ; the amount of capital invested was $1,688,286, and the first value of the products $1,573,704. The shad is by far the most important single object of capture, after which come oysters, alewives and mullet. The value of these four items is $1,086,285, a sum twice as large as that accruing from the sale of all the other products combined.

THE present wheat crop of Texas is estimated at 6,000,000 bushels. The acreage is larger than ever before. The upland yield is said to be much lighter than that in the valleys. An expert statement is that 700,000 acres are planted with the grain. President Brown, of the Galveston Wharf Co., says the Galveston elevators can handle all of this crop.

THE city of Lake Charles, La., is becoming an extensive site for shops and factories. Some of the plants now in operation are rice mills and a sugar refinery, while the Kansas City, Watkins & Gulf Railroad Co. contemplates erecting car shops, a foundry and a paint shop at this point. The Johns rice mill, located at Lake Charles, is said to be the largest in the country. When complete it will use 4000 sacks of rough rice every twenty-four hours. It is estimated that J. B. Watkins, the railway financier, has invested fully $1,000,000 in Lake Charles enterprises.

ACCORDING to President Fairbanks, of the Florida Fruit Exchange, the coming orange crop of the State will be 5,000,000 boxes, of which 4,000,000 boxes will be marketed. During the season just closed the product was 3,900,000 boxes, which sold at an increase of nearly 20 per cent. over the previous year.

THE citizens of Augusta, Ga., are already preparing for the proposed exposition to be held in that city in connection with the Georgia State Fair. What is known as the Augusta Exposition Co. has been formed, and at its last meeting selected the following named gentlemen as a committee on exhibits. H. W. Landram, Otis G. Lynch, S. P. Weisiger, L. A. Berckmans and A. A. Thomas. The following officers were unanimously elected: Manager and soliciting agent, John W. Clark; secretary, Martin V. Calvin; manager of advertising privileges and attractions, Sanford H. Cohen. The event bids fair to be a memorable one in the State's history, and all the individual concerns and trade bodies of Augusta have combined to make it a success. It is attracting much attention and receiving a liberal advertisement from the press throughout the country.

THE Camden Commercial Club, Camden, Ark., has effected a permanent organization with the following officers: President, J. W. Brown; vice-president, W. W. Watts; secretary, A. Felsenthal; treasurer, J. W. Holleman. All the merchants have joined this organization and it will be its special care to promote the business interests of the city.

BY the expenditure of over $500,000, the city of Atlanta, Ga., has been furnished with a complete water supply system, including a reservoir with a capacity of 156,000,000 gallons, two pumping stations and a filtering plant. The water is taken from the Chattahoochee river.

THE Louisiana Building at the World's Fair will be dedicated on August 10th with appropriate ceremonies. Governor Foster and his staff will attend in a body. Representatives of the legislature, national commissioners and State officials will also be present. The director-general, Mrs. Potter Palmer, members of the general commission and other distinguished people will take part in the ceremonies, and prominent Louisiana orators will deliver addresses.

THE Louisiana Land & Development Co., Limited, of Abbeville, La., has been incorporated for the purpose of encouraging immigration to Louisiana and securing industries of every kind and to aid in developing the resources of the State. The incorporators are M. B. Hillyard, W. D. White, W. O. Pipes, D. L. McPherson, Joel Moody and L. A. Minx, the two last named being respectively president and Secretary. The capital stock is placed at $100,000.

FROM data gathered by the *Manufacturers' Record* it is ascertained that 1355 new industrial enterprises were organized or established in the South during the first half of this year. There has been less than the usual activity in development projects because of the disturbed financial conditions, which have made money scarce. Had it not been for this, the first six months of this year would have been a period of great activity and progress in the South. The enterprises embraced in this record cover a wide range of industry, as may be seen from the appended list:

Iron furnaces................................	1
Machine shops and foundries..........	45
Stove foundries...........................	1
Miscellaneous iron and steel works...	18
Woodworking establishments..........	359
Furniture factories......................	18
Carriage and wagon factories..........	7
Agricultural implement factories	8
Mining and quarrying companies......	113
Flour mills..........................	38
Textile mills.............	75
Cotton compresses	9
Cottonseed oil mills...................	53
Brick works..............................	39
Canning factories......................	67
Ice factories	40
Electric light and power plants.......	51
Gas works..............	7
Water works.......	36
Miscellaneous, not in above...........	370
Total................................1355	

The lesson of these figures is that the South never stands still but ever goes forward, whether times be good or bad.

AN interesting phase of the present active progress of New Orleans is the interest manifested in that city by Western capitalists. Mr. Robinson, of the New Orleans real estate firm of Robinson & Underwood, spoke of this feature in a recent interview with a correspondent of the *Manufacturers' Record :*

"During a recent visit to Chicago I had the pleasure of meeting a large number of capitalists who are enthusiastic about the South, and particularly with New Orleans. They have carefully studied the situation of affairs in all the prominent cities, and their deduction is that New Orleans presents the greatest attraction for investment of capital and safer returns than any other city, which clearly indicates that the good work of the *Manufacturers' Record* for this place is asserting itself through the capitalistic world. The progressive yet conservative method that has actuated the establishment of values here, coupled with all the natural advantages that we possess, has had a most happy effect upon the investors of the West. It is safe to state that this coming winter a large and influential class of heavy operators will fetch their money bags here for distribution in our numerous fields for operation.

"One of the favorite schemes now under consideration among the Chicago people is the hotel project. They realize and fully appreciate the necessity for a first-class hotel here, and feel, and justly so, that it will prove a paying enterprise ; so that is within the near possibility. It was particularly gratifying to me, while enjoying the characteristic hospitalities of the Louisiana building at the World's Fair, to see the large crowds of Western lumbermen all eagerly inquiring about Louisiana lands, and all anxious to get information on that subject, as in every instance the knowledge sought was for the purpose of coming down here and locating, as land is cheap and more productive than in any other State, while our climate is mild and healthy."

As an indication of how it pays for a community to help along manufacturing industries, the city of Eufaula, Ala., may be mentioned. Not long ago the people voted to pay $50,000 towards building an addition to the mills. The business has increased so largely and is at present so prosperous, in spite of the general condition of trade, that a 5 per cent. semi-annual dividend has just been declared. An industrial investment that pays 10 per cent. yearly is something for any city to be proud of, and the citizens of Eufaula are to be congratulated for the display of business judgment they made in assisting to develop the mills.

IT is understood that the directors of the Tennesse Coal, Iron & Railroad Co. have definitely determined to construct a large steel plant near Birmingham, Ala, This decision has been arrived at after a series of experiments both with the Talbott process and others. At the Fort Payne steel plant it is said that an excellent quality of steel has been made from pig iron made by Little Bell furnace, at Bessemer, Ala. The details of the process used are not given, but it is understood to be but a slight modification of the usual open-hearth basic method.

A NEW line of steamers has been organized to ply between Europe and New Orleans. Through the effort of Messrs. G. de Key er & Co., of Antwerp ; Messrs. de Clerck and Van Hemberick, commissioners of the same city, and Capt. Leon Mannoni, of New Orleans, the first direct line of communication between New Orleans and Antwerp has been established. Captain Mannoni has decided upon Antwerp as perhaps the most important city of the northern portion of the European continent from its commanding commercial position. The ships of this new line will take consignments of merchandise directly from and to California, Mexico and the principal cities of the United States, the company having made special arrangements with the Southern Pacific Railroad and others of the principal railroad lines in the United States. The first steamer of this new line, the Brookside, carrying 2650 tons, left Antwerp on the 21st of June, and the regular time for the departure of steamers from Antwerp to New Orleans has been fixed for the 15th of each month. Captain Mannoni will act as agent in New Orleans.

A COMPANY of Wisconsin capitalists is engaged in building up a town on the west side of Galveston bay, about eight miles from Galveston, Texas. A contract has been left for the excavation of a channel 250 feet wide to deep water. Substantial stone docks will be built, and railroad lines will be constructed connecting with the Gulf, Colorado & Santa

Fe and the International & Great Northern Railroad systems at Virginia Point, and also to Houston for the purpose of tapping the roads centring there. It is stated that the president of a well-known trunk railroad has agreed to make the new town the southern terminus of the railroad system he represents.

SECRETARY DIRMEYER, of the Lumbermen's Exchange of New Orleans, gives an interesting statement of the progress in the building industry of that city. From August 1, 1891, to July 1, 1892, there were constructed 443 frame buildings and ninety-two brick buildings at a total cost of $1,831,867. During the same period from 1892 to 1893 1957 frame buildings and eighty-eight brick buildings were constructed at a total cost of $2,940,472. This shows the remarkable increase of over $1,000,000.

WEST END, a thriving and beautiful suburb of Atlanta, Ga., but for many years a regularly chartered city, is about to be annexed to Atlanta. Its rapid growth has made it practically a part of this city, and it will probably become so now in name as it long has been in fact. The annexation will give Atlanta quite an addition in territory and wealth.

MR. W. R. LAWSON, of the London *Financial Times*, who recently made an extensive tour of the South, said, before returning to England: "I am going back to England with quite a cheerful feeling in regard to Southern roads. In fact, I think the South looks as though it would be the most prosperous part of the country this year. Iron industries are bad, but almost everything else looks well. The truck farming has increased enormously since I visited the South last. It is becoming a great source of revenue for both the people and the railroads."

TEXAS lands continue to be a strong attraction to colonizers. The Rock Investment Co., which recently purchased 3800 acres of pasture land on the line of the Southern Pacific road, will make extensive improvements on the property. It is proposed to locate a colony of Swedish-Americans there. The Phillips Investment Co., of Kansas City, which has secured 6000 acres fronting on Lovaca bay, will divide the property into small farms and town lots. The water front makes the property unusually desirable, and a wharf is to be built to facilitate shipments of farm and other products. A bank is to be included among other enterprises in the development of this locality.

ENGLISH capitalists are interesting themselves in the scheme to build a dam on the Rio Grande near El Paso, Texas, for storing the waste water of the river. A. F. Spawn, of London, and several others have been examining the site of the proposed dam. It is roughly estimated that the cost of the dam will be about $4,000,000, including a 40-foot canal thirty-five miles long, to irrigate the Rio Grande valley, containing over 1,000,000 acres of rich land.

A GENTLEMAN who has recently travelled extensively in Georgia, is quoted by the Savannah *Morning News* as follows. "For the first time in twenty-five years the farmers are actually independent. They have all they need at home, and are not in debt to the merchants. At every small town in south Georgia the merchants report that they have sold less meat, corn and hay this year than in any year since the war, and what they have sold is chiefly to turpentine and millmen. In many counties the farmers have bought no meat at all. Instead, they are selling meat and corn to the merchants, a most unusual state of affairs. Corn and meat are to be had in large quantities in the wire grass, and the merchants, instead of selling these articles to the farmers, are buying from them and shipping to Savannah. There is plenty of corn to be had at fifty cents a bushel. One merchant who sold seventy-three boxes of meat last year said he had only sold one this year, and other merchants were found with meat in stock which they could not dispose of. At Cairo, down in southwest Georgia, the farmers seemed to be particularly well situated, having plenty at home and buying nothing. In Worth county it was asserted that the farmers had not bought a pound of meat this year, and that they had 5000 bushels of corn to sell. The consequence of this happy state of affairs is that the farmers are not worrying their minds about the financial situation, as the people in the cities are doing. One farmer sized up the situation pretty well when he said: 'I have fat horses and mules, fat cows, fat hogs and plenty of corn in the barn. I owe nobody, and I don't care a continental if every bank in creation bursts.'"

ON PEACHTREE STREET.

ATLANTA: THE GATE CITY OF THE SOUTH.

By James R. Randall.

For a period in many of the Eastern States, as well as in the West, nearly every prominent Georgian who traveled in those directions was presumed to be a resident of Atlanta. Other municipalities of the State had some more or less mythical existence in the popular memory, but Atlanta had real, practical and universal identity. This peculiar status was largely engendered by active spirits who constituted the energizing forces of the city and stamped their characteristics upon the intelligence of the time. A marked idiosyncrasy of the repre-

sentative Atlanta man, like the ancient Roman, "when Rome survived," was and is to claim the superiority of his residence in a phenomenal way, and to reflect in his own person the dominance of his habitation. This naturally excited the envy or displeasure of rival or would-be rival communities, and a very entertaining volume could be compiled of these unfavorable or carping criticisms, some of which were acute or humorous in an unusual degree.

It is said that Roscoe Conkling preserved, in a scrap book, all of the animadversions published about him, along with the formidable and multitudinous caricatures of the illustrated weeklies. His power and dignity were in no wise injured by these expressions or pictures, but, if anything, exalted, just as the good man is said to fear not the mighty legions of evil contending for his soul because of the mightier array of principalities of good who rally to his defense and rescue. Atlanta could well afford to gather and make public all of the hostile literature with which she has been bombarded, if only to demonstrate, by facts and history accomplished, how her antagonists have been discomfited and placed in the category of false prophets.

Atlanta is far from sanctity, perhaps, and not without faults, it may be, but she has shining virtues also, and her achievement demonstrates that the elements of nobility and worth are in the ascendant, and that her prosperity is the inevitable result of great opportunities grandly utilized. The people believed in the eminence of their city and compelled others to believe in it, and however much they may have differed among themselves upon every other topic, they were and are unified upon the prosperity of Atlanta. They not only claimed supremacy, but worked to prove it by prodigious coherence and exploit. Sentiment, which Disraeli said rules the world, animated these people, and had oracular music in the writing and speaking of a Grady; but behind sentiment marched the army of capital, brains, industry and thrift.

The men who united for such a purpose were chiefly and initially drawn from Georgia, Alabama and Virginia, but East Tennessee has proven a potent factor, and the North and Europe cannot be omitted from the muster-roll of nationalities. It is a popular legend that East Tennesseeans and North Georgians can more than match the Hebrew in money-making ability and that the combination of such potentialities has

THE STATE CAPITOL.

considerably helped Atlanta to supremacy. Luckily for Atlanta, nature had provided these elemental conditions with a munificent and exceptional domain. When the city was, as Metternich once declared of Italy, "a mere geographical expression," the clairvoyant vision of the illustrious John C. Calhoun discerned the grandeur of the future. He beheld the superb situation of an inevitable railway centre at this place, and he placed his finger upon the map where the focal point of traffic would magnetically approach and complete its material sorcery. Later on, Mr. Stephens, who had much to do with the suggestive building of the Western & Atlantic Railway, averred that Atlanta had every condition for a majestic municipality but one, that was the lack of water supply, which would at all hazards and expense be obtained. Only the other day this one defect was supplied by pouring into the city the abundant and salubriously filtered flow of the Chattahoochee river, some miles distant.

With such natural advantages, and with residents capable of exploiting them, Atlanta has, in a comparatively brief period, grown to be incontestably the first of Georgia cities, and seems destined to become the first city of the South in numbers, importance, wealth and influence. Once started on the road to superiority there was an inexorable and unimpeded gravitation of outside auxiliaries. Railway facilities and cheap fuel attracted capital and developed industries. Opulence expanded every avenue of profit and pleasure, and fashioned social as well as commercial attractions. The removal of the capital from Milledgeville fixed the political centre and drew to this favored enterprising arena many of the notable professional intellects of other localities, old and young, who might otherwise have remained inglorious if not mute.

None of these men had vaster ability for successful expansion of the city than the newspaper fraternity, and it may be capitally doubted if Atlanta could in so short a time have performed such wonders as are now everywhere in her limits or beyond them visible, had her press been of a different quality. In season and out of season, in peace and war, and reconstruction worse than war, and in staggering financial depression or the alluring temptations of prosperity, in storm and sunshine, the editors of Atlanta have never for an instant wavered in the performance of their higher mission, and their fame is deservedly national, as their reward has been correspondingly significant. Not a few of the eminent personages of the commonwealth owe their distinction in a large sense to the newspaper's loyalty and talent. The splendid list of remarkable men credited to Atlanta would seem to imply that the editors can well be proud of their favorites, whose laurels have been increased by the marvellous use of printer's ink.

More, perhaps, than any other Southern city, especially cities of comparatively recent origin, Atlanta is essentially modern in the sense that a Northern man would use the term. The people are practical and business-like. The papers are, with few exceptions East and West, equal to his home organs if not better. The hotel accommodation is mammoth and elegant in equipment. The rapid transit is nearly perfect. The ability to reach expeditiously every part of the world by railway is consummate. The club arrangements are genial and hospitable. Churches and church annexes are without stint, and, as a rule, most conservative. The public buildings and mercantile establishments are handsome and, in many cases imposing. The streets are well paved and gradually perfected. Schools are under first-rate management. Philanthropic institutions are numerous and growing rapidly. The suburban development is immense, quite abreast of the age, and of an alluring character, because of the foot-hills of the mountain region and magnificent arboreal growth.

The Northern man will find also that the fervid attributes of the South are not by any means devoured by the pursuit of the sordid dollar, but rather intensified. In many a lordly mansion along Peachtree street, where prosperous men of affairs have congregated, a genuine Southern welcome to all accredited visi-

HEADQUARTERS ATLANTA FIRE DEPARTMENT.

tors is still regnant, and the hearts and minds of the possessors of these palaces have not become cold or cynical or suspicious, as is only too frequently the case when swelled by plutocratic pride. And on this beautiful Peachtree street the Southerner's fondness for plentiful air and light for his residence holds fairy prominence. Not only are the majority of dwellings there artistic and expensive, but they are surrounded by ample grounds and lawns, lavish ·with foliage and flowers delightful to the senses and typical of the gentler and spiritual nature of the owner, who leaves the shop behind him when his abode is reached. The architecture of the Atlantian is like his character, eclectic, combining the excellencies and beauties from every source, ignoring monotony, and aspiring to new results all the time, and producing original styles and infinite variety. Every house-builder seeks to outdo his predecessor in home loveliness and comforts, and discards all patterns, blending all schools boldly. Every residence is different, and the result is a picturesque and exquisite aggregate of . differing architectural effects. Some of the owners of these lovely mansions have had thrilling experiences in war and peace ; and some of them, admirably cultured or naturally eloquent, delight to unfold to appreciative guests the marvels of their experience or understanding.

While no sensation is long-existent in Atlanta, because of successive sensations, the visit of President and Mrs. Cleveland to the fair of 1887 survived longer than anything else as a bauble of conversation, and· an account of it by the most brilliant talker in the State, who couches in a Peachtree elysium, is even yet a dazzling reminiscence. Eutaw Place, in Baltimore, might be regarded as superior to Peachtree street because of its width, its glorious parks and some of its superb residences, but it yields to the Atlanta thoroughfare in charms of disconnected dwellings and their wealth of landscape adornment. And it may be added that while property on Baltimore's most splendid street is rather startling in the modesty of selling prices, the figures obtained per front foot on Peachtree street are amazing for their altitude. If every American of a certain class hopes to go to Paris before he dies, every Atlanta man of a certain ambition contemplates moving to Peachtree street before shuffling off the mortal coil. There is a tendency at the South in all of the newspapers towards exalting local celebrity, and to live or die on Peachtree street is a record that fashion or its congener cannot easily resist. There are grand mansions and attractive homes on other streets, but Peachtree has a stamp that nothing obliterates, and the consciousness of it marks individuals like Napoléon's electric indication of the man "who had fought in the army of Italy."

Atlanta has to pay the penalty of her widespreading reputation. If anything uncanny—the common incidents of conspicuous and complex communities— happen there, it is more widely known, more vehemently heralded and more raspingly animadverted upon, than in any other Southern city. She invariably receives the most caustic moral lectures from some of her own vociferous guardians and from less boisterous and progressive localities. And yet no place can so readily and alertly offset and baffle one explosion with another, and, behind it all, she is robustly conscious that her sturdy, profound and solid virtues are not to be eroded by surface convulsions, which, after all, are productive finally of a healthier atmosphere, encouraging to the righteous and admonitory of the strayed or weak, who are halted or turned back from transgression. But nothing long endures for Atlanta astonishment, and, as one gentleman said, "If the big Equitable Building were to sink into the ground by some abnormal cataclysm, it would be forgotten in a fortnight because of some other portentous event." I well remember the building of the first Kimball House and its subsequent destruction by fire. A wag scrutinizing the ruins observed that "Atlanta looked as if she had lost her front teeth," and there was much chatter about the catastrophe ; but almost before the debris had ceased smoking a newer and grander caravansary was projected and pushed to rapid conclusion.

RESERVOIR, ATLANTA WATER SUPPLY.

THE GRADY HOSPITAL.

One of the great men of the State and one of the richest, who subscribed $2500 to the stock, was so well content to lose his money in a patriotic way that he made it a condition precedent for his cash to be expended in the foundation so as to typify his deep burial of it beyond the hope of dividend or recovery.

The approaches to Atlanta by railway are (as is not generally the case with other cities) exceedingly attractive. This is chiefly because its splendid suburbs have been persistently developed by a very alert and aspiring population, aided and abetted by rapid transit of a superior kind. This is specially true of the route from Augusta by the Georgia Railway, where for miles rustic palaces or cottages embowered in woodland delight the vision of the tourist. From Decatur to the corporate limits of the Gate City these charming scenes are of processional continuity, and it is something of a surprise when the sylvan paradise melts into the hurly-burly of an industrial panorama.

The fact is that Atlanta's environment of suburbs is something unusual, and it may be said, without exaggeration, almost phenomenal in number, variety and loveliness. There are fully twenty-five of them. As novel and attractive a one as there is among them is a manufactured lake, called East Lake, on the Georgia Railroad four and a-half miles from the city, covering forty-one acres, a crystal sheet of water furnished by cool springs, rippling merrily to every breeze, sparkling in the sunshine, bordered by a fine broad drive, and with commodious bathing-houses and row boats, that form an irresistible summer delight in the warm days. A new electric line carries the people to the charming resort. It may be observed in passing that the old town of Decatur, which has a reflected glory from Atlanta, narrowly missed being a metropolis just as Williamsport in Western Maryland had the consideration of no less a person than George Washington as the capital of the United States. It is also related in this connection that the statesmen

THE EQUITABLE BUILDING.

who flourished at Milledgeville in the middle of the century deliberately prevented the main line of the Central Railway from approaching that isolated place, and forever barred it from becoming, as was quite probable, the Southern terminus of the Western & Atlantic Line instead of Atlanta.

Only the other day, Atlanta, after much ⋅ coquetting, absorbed the West End, a beautiful suburb, and the next census will show the result in increased population. Sooner or later, what are now suburbs will be parts of the city, and at no very remote period it may be that Decatur will apply for corporate admission.

The most conspicuous object visible as one nears Atlanta is the new capitol, which is almost a reproduction in minature of the splendid edifice at Washington. This beautiful structure, admirably adapted for its purpose, is built of oolitic limestone from Indiana, with interior adornment of Georgia marble. As Georgia has an immense deposit of superior marble quite convenient by rail to Atlanta, many persons in the State were indignant because that native stone was not selected for the whole

construction. Economy, however, prevailed; the appropriation was limited to $1,000,000, and, to the credit of all concerned be it said, the capitol was completed within that bound of finance. The irrepressible American tobacco chewer has profaned the interior somewhat, and it was discovered not long ago that the odious American relic hunter had defaced the ornamentation. As a rule, the unadulterated Southern man or woman is neither a relic hunter nor an autograph fiend, so it would appear improbable that such vandalism could be traced to inhabitants of this section, unless they have recently acquired the detestable and reprehensible propensity of those persons who would have carried away piecemeal the tomb and home of Washington at Mount Vernon, had not bolts and bars and iron fenders prevented such spoliation.

The Union railway station at Atlanta is very conveniently situated right in the heart of the city's busiest mart and within easy reach of hotels. The commercial and travelling convenience of this cannot be measured. It has made the city the oasis of the drummer and the tourist. The trains of every railroad come here to the depot and interchange loads of people, who step from one line

THE CHAMBER OF COMMERCE.

to another without loss of time or cost of transfer. There is no confusion or worry in hunting distant depots for departure, and as the trains leave very much together it is possible to meet friends coming or going on different lines and to all points. The hotels are all located around the depot with but a few steps to walk, and the tired traveler gratefully gets immediate rest at the excellent caravanseries that the city keeps. It is money and convenience to the business and travelling public, and is one of those marked advantages that Atlanta has in such superabundance which have contributed to her remarkable growth, and which she fosters carefully and wisely, remedying all the disadvantages that might be supposed to environ such a condition, and converting such drawbacks into absolute instrumentalities of municipal expansion.

Monumental effigies have begun in Atlanta. The statue of the late Hon. Benjamin Hill, one of the most renowned

VENABLE BROS BUILDING.

of her senators, orators and lawyers, which once stood in the principal street, has been removed to the capitol. Mr. Hill rose gigantically from the farmer yeomanry, as did Joseph G. Brown and Alexander H. Stephens, and Atlanta was very proud of her adopted son. He was the great rival of Mr. Blaine in the forum of reason at Washington, and it was a pleasing incident in the life of the Maine statesman that he contributed liberally to help pay for his political foeman's statue in monumental stone. The late Henry W. Grady, who, also an adopted son, had devoted his life to the prosperity of the Gate City, and afterward to the pacification and glory of the whole Union, is also remembered in an excellent marble monument. He rose to sudden national fame by a single speech, under most trying circumstances, and, like the celebrated George Canning, but much sooner and at an earlier age, "lived in a blaze and in a blaze expired." His shining talents were displayed with pen and voice and

THE GAW BUILDING.

action. He was fecund of ideas for popular undertaking and knew how to inspire and energize his conceptions.

It was once bruited at Atlanta to rear a monument to the North and South in reconcilement. I believe that one suggestion contemplated sculptured wearers of the blue and gray uniforms embracing each other at the top of a lofty column. The idea never had material result, but now that Mrs. Grant and Mrs. Davis have had loving concourse at West Point it may be revived, and when the money pressure has vanished, take shape in reality. It was quite along the line of Atlanta conservatism and impartiality to greet General Tecumseh Sherman cordially, although he burnt out the city's heart and expelled women and children from their homes, and on another occasion to give Jefferson Davis a rousing and royal welcome. It may be recalled, collaterally, that Grady, who, in an exceptionally impassioned manner eulogized Mr. Davis to his face, later on proclaimed Mr. Lincoln "the typical American," and was willing to

CUSTOM HOUSE AND POSTOFFICE.

swear his son to fealty to the Union at Plymouth Rock, hard by the long waste of the Puritan sea. It is taken for granted that only a man like him and an Atlanta man could have bridged such a chasm with such daring oratory.

While alluding to the legislature, it would have been pertinent for me to have noted a most extraordinary occurrence. When Mr. Cleveland's first election was assured, the city of Atlanta literally went wild, and Mr. Grady and his colleague, Mr. Howell, invading the senate and house at the head of good-humored, excited and exulting citizens, displaced the presiding officers and announcing the news, adjourned the General Assembly. In ancient days and in other commonwealths this might have been a perilous proceeding, but everything was possible to Atlanta at that phenomenal epoch, and, though some of the old guard shook their heads and uttered deprecatory, if not imprecatory speeches, the majority of the people of the State laughed, for were they not all inebriated with joy, and was it not "just like Atlanta."

This audacious foray probably inspired the last words of General Toombs, who,

THE GRADY MONUMENT.

when informed of an exasperating protraction of the legislative session, grimly muttered : "Send for Cromwell."

I have sketchily referred to the press of Atlanta as a marvellous institution. In its formative period it was fearfully and wonderfully made, but always progressive, and is now exceptionally prosperous. The *Constitution* during the reconstruction period, under the guidance of Col. Avery, fixed its character for predominance in a marked degree, and later on, under the joint administration of Messrs. Evan P. Howell, Henry W. Grady and W. A. Hemphill, it grew like an intellectual banyan, projecting its branches not only over the State but over the union. Its latest editor, Mr. Clark Howell, quite a young man, has, if anything, magnified its robust character and power, as the recent presidential campaign proved, although the paper initially preferred Mr. Hill to Mr. Cleveland. The *Constitution* surpasses Hannibal in one function of good generalship. It knows not only how to utilize victory, but how to turn mistakes to triumph. One of the associate editors of the paper, Joel Chandler Harris, the world-renowned "Uncle Remus," is *sui-generis* in our literature, and one of the most modest and shrinking lords of the creation. It is a psychologic curiosity that Harris, with his presumed temperament for exclusive literature, should have blossomed into one of the masters of financial science and a pundit on the silver question. His articles upon this theme are fertile, learned, profound and aggressive. Your true man of genius is always a man of surprising resource and versatility. It may be with Harris, as with the late Professor J. D. B. De Bow. Up to his fortieth year, De Bow was addicted to romance. Suddenly he discovered an aptness for statistics and became the foremost writer of his day in this country upon such abstruse topics. Also on the *Constitution* are Mr. Wallace P. Reed, who has singular felicity in all departments of newspaper writing ; Mr. P. T. Moran, a prodigy of mental activity in various ways, and Mr. F. P. Stanton, who is one of the most prolific and most popular of recent lyric poets.

South of the Potomac, and in many pretentious places north of it, I doubt if evening newspaper enterprise has anything of the same experience as the *Journal* of Atlanta, which, though but a few years old, is rapidly becoming a rich and national publication. It is distinctively the rival of the *Constitution*, and owes its success chiefly to the powerful impression made by Hon. Hoke Smith, a young man, a lawyer by profession, a journalist by opportunity, and a politician by instinct. Within a brief period, Mr. Smith, by solid talent, untiring industry and boundless ambition, has become, on a most difficult theatre of endeavor in the State of Georgia, a leader in everything he determined to assert, reaching the position of Secretary of the Interior as the first public office he ever held, in consequence of adhering steadfastly to the nomination of Mr. Cleveland, and in entire accord with his financial views, which are not held by a majority of Southern politicians. The *Journal*, though for the present losing the immediate personal direction of Mr. Smith, retains his magnetism, and is ably conducted editorially by Mr. F. H. Richardson, who graduated on the *Constitution* and is one of the most versatile and brilliant of the younger generation of Georgians, assisted by a most energetic and accomplished staff. The *Evening Herald* is a recent aspirant for popular favor, and a very epigrammatic and vivacious sheet. It is under the management of Mr. Josiah Carter, who has an exceptional aptitude for journalism, assisted by Mr. B. M. Blackburn, a terse and forcible writer, who presents a well-founded claim of being "the original Cleveland man" of the last campaign, and whose zeal and sacrifice merited prompt recognition. All of these papers and several others less widely known, while in sharp conflict occasionally with one another, are thoroughly united for the common welfare of Atlanta.

Atlanta's faith in herself, and pronouncement of that faith exultingly rests upon solid and continuous achievement. In 1837 Atlanta was represented by one log shanty and a single family by the name of Ivy. It was then called

A PEACHTREE STREET RESIDENCE.

Terminus. In 1843 it was known as Marthaville and contained about a dozen families, with a railroad office, saw mill and two stores. In 1845 there were one hundred inhabitants; two years later it received the present name and had railway connection with Augusta and Savannah, while the Western & Atlantic road was progressing toward Chattanooga. In 1854 Atlanta contained 6000 souls and an annual trade of $1,500,000. In 1859 the census showed 11,500 people and a real estate valuation of $3,000,000. In the war period, despite the check to growth, this gallant little city did more than her duty in every respect, and was justly regarded as a citadel of the South. But for the displacement of General Johnston and substitution of General Hood in command of the army of defense, General Sherman's history would not be as at present fulminated, and the song of "Marching Through Georgia" might never have been written. As it is Atlanta has every reason to be content with her own intrepid conduct, and the page that the annalist has given her in that terrible martial epoch.

In all of that period and during the reconstruction era, worse perhaps than war, the people never lost their courage or their commercial instincts. They were confident of the future, and knew that upon the desolation of the conqueror there would rise a mighty and indomitable civilization. And yet, in 1866, the condition of Atlanta was such as to appal the stoutest will. With varying fortune, because of the aid and comfort of martial law established by unfriendly legislation at Washington, the foremost men of the State, Stephens, Gordon, Hill, Colquitt, Jenkins, Toombs, Cobb, and many others, backed up by the editors of the State, began the politcal agitation that finally eventuated in a complete recovery of home rule. The utterances of some of these speakers were likened by a once noted man as inopportune, "the wailing of children in the throat of a volcano," but the deliverance so yearned for and so fiercely demanded came at last.

In 1868, after the capital was established here, contemporaneously with the organization of the *Constitution* newspaper, Atlanta bounded toward the position of the second city in Georgia, and held that place in 1870. Her population at that time was 21,788, and, rising in every subsequent decade, is now the leading municipality with 104,421 people, having suburbs, legitimately her own, running the figures to 125,000. Between 1870 and 1890 the industrial and material expansion was so immense that it would require many pages of this magazine to enumerate intelligently. The tax returns for 1892 were $49,628,637, and over $2000 per front foot has been paid for city property. Large fortunes have been realized by holders of real property, and nowhere, perhaps, in the United States, without "booming," is such property, even at stiff and high rates, so promising. The tax rate is fixed at $1.50 per $100, and the actual worth of taxable property is estimated at nearly $70,000,000.

Since 1880 Atlanta's banking capital has increased from $850,000 to $7,500,000, with $8,000,000 deposits, $2,000,000 surplus and $10,000,000 loans. There are thirty-six banks, private bankers and private money lenders, of which nineteen are banks with $5,500,-

ooo capital. There are twenty-four loan and building associations, operating millions of dollars and erecting thousands of homes. From 1889 to 1893 the increase of bank capital in Atlanta was $1,484,500, of surplus $409,750, and of deposits $2,927,000. There could be no better test of development of every kind than these striking financial facts. The clearing-house transactions grew from $3,927,557 in January, 1892, to $4,666,817 in January, 1893. These are merely the transactions of the regular banks, and do not embrace the private banks or loan companies. This financial record is claimed to be without parallel in a city of the same size as Atlanta.

The taxable property of Fulton county grew from $52,345,972 in 1891 to $56,920,821 in 1892, or $4,574,849 in the one year. Atlanta has sixty-eight individuals and concerns working from $100,000 to $500,000. The number of tax returns increased 1050 in 1892 over those of 1891. The industries of Atlanta increased from 1880 to 1890 in number sixty-four per cent., in capital 215 per cent., in wages 235 per cent., and products 117 per cent. In 1892 there were 1061 new buildings erected at a cost of $2,500,000, the largest number of any one year. The 220 wholesale houses of Atlanta do an aggregate business of $91,000,000, while her retail trade has grown to $50,000,000.

As a live stock market Atlanta holds the second place in the country, employing 2160 cars for transporting stock valued at $5,462,500. In 1892 she had thirty lumber concerns with 2200 hands, shipping 100,-000,000 feet, and 129 wood manufactories working 2750 hands and making $10,000,-000 products. Her business runs to $150,000,000 annually, exclusive of the $33,-000,000 produced in her manufactories. Her wholesale houses sent out 1000 travelers. No less than 270,000 bales of cotton are entered here for shipment and compress. The manufacturing establishments numbered in 1891, were 633, with $16,190,000 of capital, employing 15,008 hands, chiefly skilled labor, and yielding an annual production of $33,000,000 in value.

The situation in cotton spinning may not be as favorable as that of Augusta, Macon and Columbus, because of the lack of water-power, but cheap coal has minimized this difficulty, and three cotton mills with 47,000 spindles and 1450 looms, working up yearly 20,000 bales of cotton, employing over 1000 hands, with a production of 27,000,000 yards of cloth a year, attest the city's capacity in this respect. So well satisfied are the cotton masters with the experiment that the mills are to be almost doubled in the near future to 70,000 spindles, and their proper compliment of 2300 looms, 2500 hands, turning 30,000 bales of cotton into 50,000,000 yards of cloth. The first mill, the Atlanta Cotton Mill, was built in 1879; the second, the Exposition Cotton Mills, in 1883; and the third, the Fulton Bag and Cotton Mills, soon after, and the shirtings and drillings of the first two are shipped North, to South America, Japan and China.

Atlanta has set her pegs for a half a million bales of cotton. Her local compresses can handle 600,000 bales a year;

A PEACHTREE STREET RESIDENCE.

there is storage capacity for 60,000 bales at a time; the cotton production near and tributary to her grows constantly; her railroad facilities are ample and increase steadily, and she has enterprising cotton merchants with plenty of capital, lead by the Inmans, the largest cotton house of the United States, who do a business of a quarter of a million of bales yearly and twenty millions of dollars. Close to coal, and with cheap rail carriage everywhere, Atlanta is making her cotton plants pay well enough to wish to duplicate them, while her rivals of half a century, with their handy water

A PEACHTREE STREET RESIDENCE

power, are satisfied to stand still. This result shows both her enterprise and advantages.

Four cottonseed-oil mills of large capacity, with $950,000 capital, work 550 hands to make the oil and as many more to buy the seed, at a cost of $900,-000 for the 60,000 tons used in the six month's season, and the product sells for $1,250,000.

This industry is daily becoming more important as new uses of the cottonseed are developing, which make it more valuable than as a fertilizer, giving it constantly growing price, and Atlanta, from its geographical position in the cotton region, is becoming the cotton-

seed-oil centre of the South, east of the Mississippi river. And this powerful fact is drawing to Atlanta the Southern headquarters of other large oil companies of every sort, and making Atlanta a great Southern distributing point for oil as for everything else.

Not satisfied to buy her vehicles abroad, Atlanta has eighteen flourishing carriage and wagon factories, besides agencies for the large concerns of the North, West and South, which use $300,000 capital, work 200 hands and turn out $2,800,000 products of the best kind, equal to any outside goods in finish and better in strength and durability. Considering that every element for this industry—the wood, the iron, the leather, etc., are within easy reach, of the best kind and inexhaustless quantity, it is no wonder that such progress has been made in this branch of manufacture, and that it has such a future here. The rich men drive superb carriages made here by home labor wholly out of home material. Nine furniture factories of Atlanta make all kinds of goods for the millionaire and freedman, and invades the Northern markets. In this business 750 men are employed, with a capital of $750,000 and manufacture $2,000,000 of magnificent goods that find ready sale everywhere and have solid repute for excellence.

There are 129 establishments—builders, planing mills, box factories, coffin, trunk, etc., makers, that work up wood in some form in the Gate City, using $2,275,000 capital, working 2750 hands, and making $10,525,000 products.

One of the most significant manufacturing successes in Atlanta, and full of import for the future, is the paying establishment of a factory for fine shoes by an enterprising young Atlantian, Mr. John M. Moore, who has solved this hard problem in the South, and practically demonstrated that we can compete with the North in the enormous shoe industry, which it has heretofore monopolized without rivalry. Mr. Moore has performed a signal feat in this success, the first of its kind in this section.

In iron working establishments and machine shops Atlanta is well supplied. There are manufacturers of cotton gins and presses, linters, car wheels and axles, bridges and other structural work, shafting, pulleys, boilers, engines, machinery for mining, for saw, grist, sugar and cottonseed-oil mills, agricultural implements and castings of every description. There are twenty-five such establishments, with $3,250,000 capital, working 3150 hands, with an output of $6,150,-000. Some of these are the largest and most vital industries of the country and the world, making the implements that plant, cultivate and prepare for market the imperial staple of the cotton fibre that so rules the world and is the monarch for a season of our commerce. It is significant of Atlanta's enterprise that she should have the great factories where the cotton gin, the cotton press and the cottonseed-oil mill are made in their perfection to supply the whole South, where the cotton alone is raised in this country and without a rival in the world.

The diversification of manufactures, especially in lines that require high-priced, skilled labor, accounts for much of the prosperity of the city.

As Atlanta is the unrivalled distributing centre of the State, because of superior railway connections and enterprising merchants and manufacturers, her trade is necessarily enormous, when compared with other cities in this section. Her commercial travellers, representing numerous lines of business, not only cover and control the territory presumably her's by right, but they invade the whole commonwealth and push into other States.

This leads us to the consideration of the leading quality of Atlanta's supremacy as the coming metropolis of the South. I have alluded to the fact that the great statesman Calhoun predicted the future of Atlanta when it was a spot of the virgin woods. His prophecy has been steadily verifying itself. It is literally true, as Calhoun foresaw and foretold, that Atlanta is the South's main railway centre. Calhoun wrought out the conclusion in his great mind from logical physical facts, from a luminous

conception of the topography of the continent. This was in 1845. As early as 1857 the intelligent minds of the country began to take in Calhoun's idea, and a convention of practical men in Charleston, after a thorough look into it, dubbed Atlanta the "Gate City of the South," which title it has since held undisputed by its central accessibility and the wheel of railways of which it is the hub.

From Atlanta by air line to an Atlantic port is 260 miles, to the Gulf 270 miles, to the Mississippi river 340 miles and to the northern line of the cotton belt 200 miles. Eleven lines of railroad diverge from Atlanta to these points. The Georgia Central, the East Tennessee, Virginia & Georgia, and the Atlanta & Macon run seaward with the Macon & Dublin. To the North run four rival lines, the Richmond & Danville, the Seaboard Air Line, the East Tennessee, Virginia & Georgia and the Georgia Railway. Four competing lines, the Central, East Tennessee, Atlanta & Florida and Georgia Pacific, reach to Florida and the Gulf. To the West extend the Western & Atlantic, (now the Nashville & Chattanooga) the East Tennessee and the Georgia Pacific, while the Marietta & North Georgia reaches out northwestwardly and the Georgia Railway extends to Carolina ports. As the focal point of all these railroad lines and the headquarters of the Southern Railway and Steamship and Southern Passenger Associations, it is no stretch of fact to call Atlanta the railway centre of the South.

This combination of railroad facilities has given to Atlanta a proportionate amount of trade. The city council recently spent $1000 in gathering information on this point and the facts are astonishing. In 1892 the five Northern cities, Boston, Providence, New York, Philadelphia and Baltimore, sent to the seven Southern cities, Augusta, Macon, Athens, Chattanooga, Montgomery, Birmingham and Anniston, 63,000 tons of freight, paying a revenue of $687,129. To Atlanta alone these five Northern cities sent 39,000 tons of freight, paying a revenue of $455,753. Thus Atlanta

TECHNOLOGICAL SCHOOL, ATLANTA.

received 38 per cent. of the tonnage and paid 40 per cent. of the freight as compared with 62 per cent. tonnage and 60 per cent. freight for the seven cities around her with three times as large a population as Atlanta. Ten Western cities, Cairo, Cincinnati, Columbus, East St. Louis, Evansville, Henderson, Louisville, Memphis, and Nashville, gave to the four Southern cities of Anniston, Athens, Augusta and Macon 167,500 tons of freight which paid $1,037,248 in charges, while Atlanta received from the same sources 169,500 tons, paying $943,873 freight charges. Thus Atlanta's share was 50.3 per cent. of tonnage and 47.7 per cent. of the charges. These are remarkable comparisons of commercial traffic, and they form a striking object lesson to prove Atlanta's commercial advantages.

Atlanta has had many recent evidences of her cosmopolitan destiny. The telephone company has found it necessary to adopt a costly system of underground wires. The new bridge on Forsyth street that spans the railroad from Marietta to Alabama street, extending two blocks, is a magnificent solid structure of iron and stone that has been two years building and is a model of permanence and science. The day of this writing the new water works are put into operation which give Atlanta as fine a water supply as any city in the South. And it is not an unimportant fact for business men to know that Atlanta has the lowest water rate of any cities of 20,000 people and over in the United States, save Rochester, N. Y., and Salem, Mass., which are about the same. Atlanta, on account of its railroad and hotel facilities, has become the home of conventions, which meet here in numbers to the profit of every interest. Atlanta has become the Southern headquarters for the great insurance, sewing machine, thread and other companies of the United States and the world, showing its value as a distributing centre. All the large insurance companies have general agencies here.

The country round about Atlanta is admirably fitted for contributing everything agriculturally needed for a great city's wants, but the farmers have caught the spirit of the age, and read with amazement no doubt the reported statement of the present Commissioner of Agriculture at Washington that they are lacking in any element of their calling. They would like the commissioner and some of his Nebraska friends to visit them at harvest time and report progress. Like all considerable cities Atlanta draws from a distance what she may lack at home. At all seasons of the year, but especially in the fall and winter, her streets are thronged with people from many miles round about who come to avail themselves of the city's trade as well as its diversions. An annual trade that reaches within a fraction of $200,000,000 at this time literally speaks for itself; and if one from an elevated place takes a bird's eye view of the railway movement, an idea of the importance of the traffic will be magnified.

The street railway systems of Atlanta are rapidly approaching 82 miles. Of these electricity is the chief motive power. The horse car will soon be extinct. The number of passengers carried last year was 6,650,000, and the earnings were about 6 per cent. on $1,833,000. These lines are largely developing the suburbs.

Educationally, Atlanta is on a very superior plane, with her seventeen public schools and numerous private academies and colleges. Ample appropriations are made, and the daily attendance is computed to be 7352 white and 5642 colored. There are two female colleges, the State Technological Institute, Neal's Georgia Military Institute, schools of languages, music and journalism, numbers of fine private elementary schools, two business colleges, three shorthand and type writing colleges, five medical colleges, a law institute, a dental college, a woman's medical college, and seven literary and theological colored universities, affording the highest instruction in every field of education, science, business and art. There are seventy churches, twelve of which are for colored persons. The investment of the white congregations is $1,900,000, with a seating capacity of 30,000. The colored investment is $250,000, with a seating capacity for

HIGH SCHOOL, ATLANTA.

20,000,—a total investment of $2,150,-000, and a membership estimated at 13,000.

With some suspicion of the old water supply and the pressure of numerous wells, subject to surface contamination, Atlanta had, despite these drawbacks, an extraordinary health record, the rate being nineteen per thousand of both races consolidated, and only twelve per thousand of the whites. This was in part due to her elevation of 1085 feet above the sea, good drainage, dry air and other atmospheric conditions. It was also due to the fact that many persons drank the pure water procured from the vicinity. With the present supply of water from the Chattahoochee, the death rate of Atlanta will very likely decrease phenomenally and constitute that city the healthiest spot on the globe. She has never shut her gates against any unfortunate fugitives from infected cities, has never had a sunstroke or epidemic; cholera and yellow fever brought here have never spread, and the portals will be wide open always to seekers after fame and fortune as well as health.

The governor of the State, Hon. William T. Northen, is a pronounced example of the Georgians who have made their State renowned since the war. He was a school-teacher in his earlier manhood and drifted into farming and politics. His writings on educational and agricultural subjects are expert and authoritative. He had the singular merit of being elected to his present position without a contest. He is in many respects after Mr. Cleveland's pattern, although there may be differences between them on issues of the day in regard to the currency.

The city government of Atlanta is being masterfully administered, and the present regime is a fine link in a succession of strong municipal bodies. It is safe to say that the astonishing progress of Atlanta has had its full measure of co-operation in her enterprising mayors and devoted city councilmen, and her present is one of the best she has ever had. The existing authorities, with that experienced and level-headed gentleman, Mayor John B. Goodwin, in the lead, are emulating the wisdom, enterprise, liberality and prudence of immediate predecessors, and they are loyally sustained by the people. They have most efficient and practical aid in the Chamber of Commerce and Commercial Club, under their able and public-spirited presidents, Mr. Stewart F. Woodson of the former, and Mr. J. G. Oglesby of the latter, both of them among Atlanta's best mercantile leaders.

This article would be extended beyond all reasonable limits, and insult the patience of the reader, if it entered into multitudinous details inviting the writer, and he is obliged to halt with a regret that many things and persons deserving of attention should be imperatively omitted. The advantages of Atlanta have been, in the main at least, elaborately presented for health at all seasons, for unrivalled situation for business, for freight and passenger distribution by unbroken lines to five South Atlantic and four Mexican Gulf ports, covering the entire cotton belt and "the most liberal, social and enterprising citizenship in the land." As I write, the morning telegrams state that one whole section of Kansas has been devastated by unfavorable seasons, and that thousands of ruined but adventurous people of that State are contemplating a flight to Dakota, and dread starvation if the government at Washington does not hasten to their relief. The best of these unfortunates would find that the country around Atlanta, or the State of Georgia generally is their true objective point.

The day is not far distant when the redundant population of the West will migrate Southward, and sometime in the twentieth century, the man who ascends the loftiest point of observation to behold the munificent domain circumferent to the basaltic crags of Stone mountain to the east and Kennesaw to the west, will exult at the tremendous extension of Atlanta, which, at such a period, must become not merely the first of the cities of Georgia, but the first of the South, and mayhap ranking among the first in America.

FORSYTH STREET BRIDGE.

PHOSPHATE BOULDER.

THE FLORIDA PHOSPHATE INDUSTRY.

By Edward H. Sanborn.

Since the early days of gold discoveries in California there have been few epidemics of mining fever equal in contagion and virulence to the outbreak of this disease that followed the announcement of phosphate finds in Florida a few years ago. And perhaps the most curious incident of this tremendous outburst of speculation is the almost universal ignorance concerning the character and use of phosphates. While it would be difficult to find an intelligent newspaper reader who does not have a pretty fair idea of the general characteristics of the great Florida phosphate boom, it would be almost as difficult to find a man, outside of those professionally or commercially interested, who has any intelligent conception of what is meant by "phosphates." To all except the thousandth man the term "phosphates" is meaningless, except in its connection with one of the most frantic spasms of mining speculation that this country has ever known. Not a few of the shrewd speculators who went to Florida, as well as some of the practically-minded business men who since have found profit in mining, were limited in their knowledge of phosphate to the consciousness that it was something to be dug from the ground. It was recently remarked to the writer, referring to the managers of one of the most prosperous phosphate mines in Florida: "They didn't even know how to spell phosphate when they came down here." It is in the frequency of questions about the nature, occurrence, mining and use of phosphate that the writer finds excuse for this article, the purpose of which is to answer these inquiries for the benefit of the every-day reader—not the miner or scientist.

Chemistry has been of inestimable value to the farmer by determining the composition of soils, by ascertaining what elements are withdrawn from the soil by vegetable growth, and by demonstrating how the fertility of the soil can be maintained by restoring artificially the elements removed by vegetation. So long as agriculture has been the chief occupation of man, the farmer has known, without reason, that the continued cultivation of certain crops impoverishes the soil, that the productiveness of various kinds of soil varies according to the crops that are planted, and that worn-out soil can be restored to fertility by the use of fertilizers, natural or artificial. All this has been part of the craft of farming for centuries, but . it has been simply a knowledge of results without any understanding of the cause. For centuries farmers strewed their lands with crushed bones and beheld more abundant crops, which they ascribed to the absortion by the soil of the gelatinous matter in the bones, but it was only fifty years ago that chemisty made known to the farmer that phosphoric acid was the only element of fertilizing value in bones. It was the establishment of this fact, after exhaustive experiments by the Duke of Richmond, that created a value for those minerals consisting of combinations of phosphoric acid with various bases. It was this discovery that caused the development of the present enormous fertilizer manufacturing industry and the allied industry of phosphate mining.

At first thought the amount of phosphoric acid taken from cultivated soil by growing crops does not seem to be an item of much magnitude. Chemistry, however, makes a revelation that startles us by mere arithmetic. Each 100 pounds of corn takes from the soil 1.55 pounds of mineral elements necessary for its growth, nearly one-half (45 per cent.) of this amount being phosphoric acid. In addition to this, each · 100 pounds of · corn stalk takes out of the ground 4.87 pounds of mineral elements, 12.66 per cent. of this being phosphoric acid. These figures, insignificant as they appear in the abstract, when applied to the great aggregate of our corn crop, show us that corn, in kernel and stalk, removes from the soil in a single year about 1,025,000 tons of phosphoric acid. In similar manner the other cereals deplete the soil of this element, the amount removed by each being about as follows : Wheat, 190,000 tons ; oats, 105,000 tons ; barley, 20,000 tons ; rye, 10,000 tons ; buckwheat, 6,000 tons ; the aggregate being in round numbers 1,356,000 tons. But this is only one-half of the story, for an average hay crop takes from the soil something like 235,000 tons of phosphoric acid. Thus

we find that the cereal and hay crops rob the soil each year of nearly 2,000,-000 tons of phosphoric acid. Even these stupendous figures represent the extent to which the soil is depleted by only two principal classes of agricultural crops—the grains and grasses. No account is taken of cotton, tobacco, rice, potatoes, and the infinite variety of other products of the soil. What wonder that the farmer has needed the knowledge of the chemist to show him the way to restore to his soil the elements his crops have withdrawn !

The depletion of the soil by the growth of vegetation being established the problem of restoring the necessary elements presents itself for solution. Bones, containing a large percentage of phosphoric acid in soluble form, have long served as one means of restoring exhausted soil, but the discovery of extensive deposits of mineral phosphates in various countries brought into use a new element and developed new industries of immense extent and importance. The element of value in these mineral phosphates is the combination of phosphoric acid and lime—phosphate of lime. In its natural condition this phosphate of lime is but slightly soluble by the acids of the soil, but by treatment with sulphuric acid in the fertilizer works the phosphate of lime is changed to "acid phosphate" or "superphosphate" which is quite soluble and therefore able to yield its valuable elements to the soil when used as a fertilizer. The manufacture of fertilizers, of which the natural phosphates form the base, is a diversified and somewhat complicated industry, too complex to enter into such an article as this, beyond mere mention of the principle involved, which is the rendering soluble of the insoluble combination of phosphoric acid and lime in the phosphate rock or pebble.

Although the deposits of phosphates in South Carolina have been worked continuously since 1868, it was only five years ago that the existence of phosphates in Florida was impressed upon the public mind with sufficient emphasis to attract capital and inaugurate the remarkable epidemic of speculation that

A DEPOSIT OF LAND PEBBLE PHOSPHATE, BARTOW, FLA.

swept the peninsular in 1890 and 1891. It was known to a few men for several years prior to 1888 that there were extensive and valuable phosphate deposits in Florida, but the knowledge of this fact did not arouse a frantic interest until five years ago. First, by the random discoveries of an engineer and the chance finds of a hunter, it was made known that phosphate pebble existed in quantity in the bed and along the shores of Peace creek—now risen to the dignity of a river—which starts near the centre of the State about the latitude of Tampa, and flows into Charlotte harbor on the Gulf coast. Then, the digging of a well near Dunellon, in Marion county, north of the centre of the State, revealed the existence of phosphate rock quite different in character from the smooth, water-worn pebbles of Peace river but of even greater value. In the five years that have elapsed since the first manifestations of the phosphate fever, all the western half of the State has been explored, pitted and prodded in the search for new deposits until the location of all the important beds has been determined. In the opinion of many whose experience qualifies them to speak, there are few valuable deposits now unknown, to which might be added that many deposits now deemed

of little value because of the inferior quality of the phosphate will eventually be utilized when some of the troublesome problems of phosphate mining and fertilizer manufacture shall have been solved.

There are two distinctive districts in which the phosphate deposits have chiefly been located. The "pebble" region includes the section traversed by Peace river in De Soto, Polk and Hillsborough counties and the "hard rock" or "high grade" region embraces the counties of Marion, Alachua, Levy, Citrus and Hernando. Ocala is the center of the hard rock region and Bartow is the central point in the pebble district. In addition to the two general divisions of rock and pebble each is again divided according as the material is taken from the ground or from the river beds. The phosphate of the pebble district is found in small smooth waterworn pebbles ranging from the size of a small bead to an English walnut, white or yellowish in color. The pebble in the land deposits is intermingled with sand and clay, the whole being covered with an "overburden" of ordinary soil several feet in thickness. In the river beds of pebble the deposits usually take the form of bars in the channel and the phosphate is comparatively free from foreign substances. The hard rock phosphate occurs in many and dissimilar forms. The two principal types, however, are the thin white or yellowish plates, resembling fragments of broken crockery, and the rough porous lumps like very porous limestone, irregular in shape and ranging from a few pounds to a ton in weight.

The methods of mining and handling the phosphates are about as diverse as the variety in the character of the deposits. When the first mining operations began the pick and shovel were about all the machinery that was used, and the attack upon the richest and most accessible deposits required little more for the time being. The growth of the industry, the working of deposits upon a larger scale, and chiefly the great drop in price of the product that has been occasioned by the discovery of the Florida phosphate beds, have necessitated more economical methods of mining, washing, drying and handling the phosphate, and a great deal of engineering skill and ingenuity have been displayed in devising methods and machinery for operating at the lowest

appliances. To one who looks for mining methods, in the ordinary significance of the term, the Florida phosphate region is a disappointment, for there is no mining, properly speaking. All the land workings are shallow pits, and the methods are chiefly such as would be used in handling gravel and loose rock in any economical excavation.

One of the simplest and cheapest methods of handling phosphate is that usually adopted in raising pebble from the river bed. A float is equipped with a boiler, engine and centrifugal pump and a revolving horizontal cylindrical screen. The flexible suction pipe of the pump is lowered from the end of the barge to the phosphate bed in the river, and the pebble is sucked up and discharged into the revolving screen. It is thoroughly washed by the accompanying water, the sand and mud pass through the meshes of the screen while the clean phosphate is delivered into a scow moored alongside the dredge boat, to be carried to the works on shore where it is dried and stored for shipment. The simplicity of this method

MINING PEBBLE PHOSPHATE IN PEACE RIVER.

cost. The entire industry is at present very largely in the state of transition from the crude methods and machinery first introduced to more economical methods and more elaborate mechanical

of mining and the very small cost of handling a large amount of material are its chief points, and this is really the only practical and economical method of mining river deposits.

MINING LAND PEBBLE BY HYDRAULIC SYSTEM.

In working the deposits of land pebble there is a greater variety in methods. The pebbles of phosphate are intermingled with clay and sand, sometimes in the proportion of four or five parts to one of phosphate, so that it is necessary to handle a large amount of material to yield even a moderate daily output of cleaned phosphate. The simplest and most extravagant way is by the use of shovels and wheelbarrows, still in use at some of the workings. In some cases the material is dug up by grapple dredges like those used in river and harbor excavations, running on a railroad track and loading the dirt and phosphate into cars which convey it to the washing and drying plant. Again the hydraulic system of the western gold mines is adapted to the requirements of the land pebble workings and the material is handled rapidly and cheaply. A mining plant of this character, in use by the Bone Valley Phosphate Company, near Bartow, Florida, is shown in a full page illustration accompanying this article. As this is probably the best method of working land pebble phosphate under given conditions, a description of the works will not be amiss.

A canal, formed by mining out a strip of the property, serves both to float the barge upon which the mining machinery is carried and to convey the phosphate from the workings back to the dry-house and storage bins. A dam closes the end of the canal at the point where the mining is in progress, and keeps back the water from a basin of an acre or more in extent from which the phosphate is being taken. The barge, moored against the dam in the end of the canal, carries a boiler, an engine, a centrifugal pump, a powerful pressure pump, and on the roof or upper deck there is a horizontal revolving cylindrical screen. The basin is free of water, save what is used in mining. Two streams of water from the pressure pump are carried down into the basin and by moveable nozzles are turned against the banks, breaking up the mixed pebble, clay and sand and washing everything to a well in the basin near the dam. The suction pipe of the centrifugal pump is placed in this well and the water, phosphate and dirt are lifted thence and discharged into the screen on the dredge boat, the sand, clay and water passing out into the canal or into the marsh land nearby, while the cleaned phosphate pebble is delivered into a lighter in the canal and carried to the drying house. This is a very simple and satisfactory method of mining, and the few men required to tend the machinery and streams of water can handle three or four hundred tons of material in a day at very small cost. This system is in operation at several points in the land pebble region with excellent results.

Probably the boldest · experiment in mining land pebble is that tried at Phosphoria, near Bartow, by the Florida Phosphate Company, limited, an English concern of large capital. The land, although high and removed from streams, is marshy, and the managers of the company determined to make use of a floating dipper dredge of the usual type used in land or water excavations. A shallow basin was dug and water was gathered by ditches from the· vicinity. The dredge, a ponderous machine of great capacity, was built and launched into this basin and then started to cut its way across the country. Water fills the excavations as fast as they are made, and in the course of a few years there will be a lake on the worked-out territory. Two floats are in use, one of them carrying the great dipper dredge and the other the machinery for crushing the lumps of earth and washing and screening the pebble. Each dipperful of material raised by the dredge is deposited in a hopper on the washer boat and passes between a pair of toothed rolls which break up the large lumps. Then the material passes through a long trough in which a shaft with blades thoroughly disintegrates the lumps of earth and phosphate. A copious flow of water washes out the sand and clay and the pebble travels to the end of the trough cleaned of most of the foreign matter. An elevator conveys the phosphate to a revolving cylindrical screen, which removes the remaining sand and the phosphate passes along to a scow which is towed to the dry house when loaded. Then a chain conveyor unloads the scow and delivers the pebble in a bin ready for drying. The works described are of much interest because of the novelty and boldness of their plan. There was something incongruous in the idea of building dredges in the pine woods where there was not water enough to float even a toy boat, but the expectations of the engineers have been fulfilled and the entire plant is operated successfully.

Leaving the pebble district with this brief view of the typical methods of mining, we may turn to the hard rock region and its mining features. The mining of hard rock phosphate is more difficult and more costly than the working of pebble deposits because of the harder character of the material and the irregularity of the deposits. Nearly all of the material is handled with the shovel in contrast with the wholly

DRY HOUSE AND STORAGE BINS ON PEACE RIVER.

DREDGING PEBBLE PHOSPHATE AT PHOSPHORIA.

mechanical handling of the output of the pebble mines. In some of the larger workings in the hard rock region the material is raised from the pits in buckets traveling on cables suspended between towers. At Dunellon this method has been followed on an extensive scale, and in one large pit the excavation has been carried to a depth of sixty feet. It is contemplated by this company to introduce a steam shovel by which material can be excavated much more rapidly and economically. Elsewhere in the hard rock region the material is handled in cars running on a narrow gage railway, which is moved from place to place as the work proceeds. In other mines, again, all the material is handled in carts or even in wheelbarrows. The varying character of the material, from coarse gravel to boulders weighing tons, and the lack of uniformity in the deposits which are sometimes thick beds of large area and again mere pockets of a few cubic yards, render uniform methods of mining and handling a matter of impossibility and in each mine the methods and machinery have to be adapted to the peculiarities of the deposit. Nowhere, however, is there such facility and economy in mining as in the pebble region. The nearest approach is the use of the grapple

or "clam shell" dredge in mining river rock.

All the land rock has to be washed and screened but the methods are somewhat different from those used in pebble mining. For washing, a "log" washer similar to those used for iron ore, is generally used. This, to the unitiated, may be described as a huge wooden trough in which are two parallel revolving logs to which are bolted strong iron blades. The blades on the two logs work together and between them the phosphate rock is thoroughly broken up and freed from foreign material which is carried out over the edge of the trough by a great volume of water. The cleaned phosphate is worked along to the end of the trough by the screw-like action of the blades and is then passed through a revolving screen for final cleaning and rinsing with clean water. These washers have been greatly improved in construction by the substitution of steel beams for the pine logs.

Before shipment all of the phosphate, whether rock or pebble, must be thoroughly dried. The drier chiefly used for pebble phosphate is a long iron cylinder, which revolves on small wheels. At one end of the cylinder is a furnace and the other connects with a stack. Inside the cylinder are ribs so arranged as to cause the pebble to travel along as the cylinder revolves. The phosphate is fed in at the end farthest from the furnace and is turned over and over as it passes towards the furnace, being constantly subjected to the flames and heat of the furnace which traverse the cylinder, until it leaves the drier thoroughly freed from its moisture. There are several styles of rotary driers, some of them enclosed in brickwork and heated both within and without, but the general principle is the same. In an ordinary unenclosed cylindrical drier as much as ten tons of wet pebble can be dried in an hour. Formerly all the hard rock was

phosphate is drawn from the bottom of the bins through spouts without any handling whatever.

The question that usually follows the first inquiry concerning the character of the Florida phosphate deposits asks about their origin. To this there have been several answers, some of them based upon the well proven teachings of geology, others mere conjecture. Dr. Francis Wyatt argues that the phosphate beds were formed by the action of phosphoric acid upon the limestone rocks of the early geologic era, the acid being derived from the abundant animal and vegetable life which per-

HARD ROCK PHOSPHATE MINING AT DUNELLON.

dried in the open air by making huge piles of alternate layers of rock and pine wood and burning the heap. From three days to a week was required to burn a kiln of rock in this manner, the piles often containing 1000 or 1500 tons. This method has largely been abandoned and the cylindrical rotary drier is being used instead, as more efficient and more economical. The pebble when dried is carried by chain and bucket conveyors to great storage bins, which are heavily timbered buildings often holding as much as 4000 or 5000 tons. When cars are to be loaded for shipment the

vaded that region. Mr. N. H. Darton, of the United States Geological Survey, advances the theory that guano was the original source of the phosphate of lime which replaced the carbonate of lime of the limestone. Professor N. A. Pratt is satisfied that the phosphate boulders are the fossil remains of a low order of animal life, which secreted a skeleton composed of phosphate of lime, just as the coral animal deposits a skeleton of carbonate of lime. Professor Cox expresses his opinion that the phosphate deposits of Florida are due to the mineralization of an ancient

DREDGING ROCK PHOSPHATE IN BLUE RIVER.

guano. Mr. Walter B. M. Davidson holds that the underlying limestone of Florida contained a small percentage of insoluble phosphate of lime which now remains after the carbonate of lime has been dissolved and washed away. From these various theories and opinions the reader may make his own selection. Abundant evidences of this swarming animal life are presented by the fossil remains in the phosphate deposits. Judging from the numerous quantities of these remains, it would seem as if this region once were fairly crowded with life, for the bones are unearthed by tons, huge mastodon bones, teeth and tusks, ribs of smaller animals and the teeth of sharks by millions. Occasionally bones in natural condition are found but most of them are of fossil character. Early investigators made the mistake of supposing that the deposits of phosphate of lime came from these bones, but it has been demonstrated that the reverse is the case, the bones having been fossilized by phosphate of lime derived from the surrounding deposits. There is much yet to be learned about the geology of the Florida phosphate regions, and future investigations doubtless will establish more clearly the origin of these remarkable deposits.

The discovery of phosphate in Florida inaugurated an era of speculation that is equalled only by the frantic struggle for gold and silver claims in the West whenever a big strike is made. It is unfortunate that the birth of such a great industry should be forever associated with the work of unscrupulous speculators and swindlers. So long as the fever raged it was amazing in its intensity. Pine lands that would have been thought dear a year earlier at $1.50 per acre, jumped to $200 and more per acre and even then were eagerly bought. Companies were organized in feverish haste and stock was issued by the ream. No enterprise was too big, no scheme too bold, no plan of development too costly to receive consideration and backing. The man who could not talk capital in millions and phosphate in thousands of tons, was of small importance. All this has passed, however, the bubble burst as rapidly as it inflated and, starting from the insecure foundation of the era of wild speculation, there has been built up an enormous industry that is doing business in a practical legitimate fashion and developing steadily and strongly. On paper there are probably 200 companies organized ostensibly to mine Florida phosphates. Hardly one-tenth of that number are actually in operation, producing and shipping stuff.

The first shipments of Florida phosphate were made in 1888, aggregating about 3000 tons for the entire year. In 1892 the shipments amounted to 287,821 tons and the output during the present year will largely exceed this amount. According to a recently issued report by the United States Department of Labor, the Florida phosphate miners control 193,348 acres of land, they have $4,705,582 invested in machinery and $14,366,067 in land.

Unfortunate as it may be that this industry should have been ushered in with so much of speculation and fraud, it is exceedingly fortunate that there exists a basis and foundation for an industry of enormous extent and importance. A few years of systematic development and honest, practical effort, like that now being put forth, will produce in Florida an industry that will far exceed in its magnitude and importance every other industrial interest in that State. The opportunities are gigantic, the progress is steady, the future is sure.

IN THE PATH OF PROSPECTORS.

A CREOLE GIRL'S FIRST BALL.

By Marie Louise Points.

She lived in the heart of Frenchtown, in the dim, dreamy Latin Quarter of New Orleans, which even in its decay retains an unmistakable aspect of ancient gentility that reminds one of the gloomy pride of a grand seignior, wrapping himself in the habiliments of faded glory, and stolidly standing out in gloomy isolation from the progressive spirit of improvement which characterizes the age. But it had been a great house in its time; one of those solemn foreign-looking edifices which somehow convey the impression that, while walking the streets of old New Orleans, one is not altogether upon American soil, but in the midst of a peculiar section and among people individually distinct from any hitherto met beneath the stars and stripes, yet seemingly an integral part of the whole.

The old mansion stood out upon the street, as all the characteristic Creole houses do. The lower façade, with its high arched framework and massive portal, gave it a decided ecclesiastical appearance, while above, in direct contradiction, a narrow quaintly stuccoed veranda ran midway along the front, and still higher, on either side, projecting beneath the several windows, were miniature reproductions of the gallery below. The house was old and gray and worn; a fresh coat of paint, or a missing shutter replaced, might have restored its appearance and removed the impression which gradually grew upon one that the place was altogether uncanny-looking from without, a fit abode for mice and bats and owls, or a favorite rendezvous for midnight ghouls and witches, rather than the home of the beautiful, dark-haired girl who stood upon the veranda that fair spring morning, culling the bright roses and geraniums that grew in boxes, cool, fresh and fragrant, overlooking the dim old street.

" Rat-tat-tat."

The postman lifted the curious brass knocker of the old-fashioned house, and its dull click reverberated along the corridors and galleries to the quaint attic room which Lalotte had just entered with her fresh bouquet. It was a large, airy apartment, with wide, open fireplace and deep dormer windows, through which the sunlight streamed and lit up the faded carpets and red jars of cactus and jessamines on the window-sills. The great four-posted bed, with its high mattress and brightly-figured counterpane; the curiously carved dressing table, surmounted by a low, wide mirror; the high-backed chairs, straight and prim; the faded prie-dieu, even the little altar, ornamented with a bronze statue of the Virgin and a few musty volumes labeled " Livres des Prieres," impressed one with strange, yet pleasing, incongruity, and told more plainly than words how each article had been placed there at different periods as relics of a dear vanished past. For every article in the antiquated room had its own peculiar history, some association which rendered it especially sacred to the inheritor, and prevented it from being relegated to a second-hand establishment and its place supplied by modern workmanship.

An old negress, evidently one of those privileged characters whose service and fidelity were recognized as part of this typical Creole home, entered the room just as the girl was placing her flowers before her little altar near the corner of the bed.

"Mam'zelle Lalotte," she cried in a breath, "one lettaire for you!" and she handed a dainty perfumed missive to the girl.

Now in the whole course of her life Lalotte had never received a letter, save the notes sent her by her mother during the four years she went as "pensionnaire" to the old Ursuline's Convent, whence she had been brought but a few weeks since to take her place in a world of which she knew as little as the white lilies that bloomed in the convent garden. She never dreamed of opening a letter addressed to herself, a privilege so dear to a woman's heart; in the convent the nuns always read the letters first, and true to her rearing she hastened to her mother, followed by the curious old negress, to learn its contents. A reception card bearing the conventional "R. S. V. P." was handed back to her.

She glanced at the card and her eyes lit up like twin-stars. "Un invitation au bal déguisé!" she cried; "et pour moi! ah! comme je suis contente! comme je suis heureuse!" and she executed several graceful figures about the room. "Mamma!" she continued, in pretty, half-broken English, a form of speech much in vogue in Creole homes since the gradual commingling of society in French and American New Orleans. "Mamma!" she repeated, in her pretty, coaxing way, "You go'ne let me go? eh? mamman! chère petite mamman! and she arrested with a kiss the protest that rose to her mother's lips.

"Mais, oui," cried old Zizi, stepping forward and taking the girl's part, "mais, oui! you make go for sure, Mam'zelle Lalotte! Ma foi! for what your ma bin tink for keep you lock up in dat convent so long time! Tiens! She was mudder for Jacques and Jules when she make not so old as you. Mam'zelle Lalotte, an' she love for go to ball, too, and for dance, and make fun! and de peep' day say: 'Mais elle est jolie!' but she is not one coquette, she one queen, one belle!" and Zizi rolled her eyes and clasped her hands enthusiastically in pleasure at the remembrance.

The old woman had guessed aright; the memory of her own youth touched a responsive chord in Madame's heart. She had not intended to bring Lalotte out until next winter, but she looked at the beautiful glowing face of the girl, the slender graceful figure, the soft, appealing expression of her eyes, and she decided that Lalotte should accept the invitation.

That decision marked a supreme moment in the girl's life. A first ball! truly an absorbing subject for the feminine mind in every locality, but all the more weighty in a community where a young girl's debut and accompanying costume are considered matters of the deepest social significance, and often from the amount of discussion involved, evidently as difficult a question to decide as the Bering Sea dispute or the Tariff Bill. With true Creole fidelity to and respect for customs and traditions, all of Lalotte's aunts and cousins were called into consultation upon the subject; modistes were interviewed, fashion plates from Paris critically scanned, and then, in sheer desperation the old French trunks in the garret were called upon to yield up their forgotten treasures—dresses that had belonged to the girl's great grandmother at sixteen, soft silk and filmy gauzes, powdered wigs and gilded tiaras were brought forth and held up to the light, while the aunts and cousins with continuous chatter and expressive gesticulations gave their unqualified opinions, and finally unanimously decided to lay these old treasures back in the dim garret with the pronounced verdict "trop vieux." What would suit a daughter of la belle France would scarce become a daughter of the beautiful exotic—this rare Louisiana product, with the complexion of France and the eyes of Spain.

At this perplexing stage of affairs one of the old aunts thought of grand-père— Mon Dieu, he had seen so much!—the grand balls at Versailles and the Tuileries, the gay festivities in the old French homes of New Orleans, when the old Latin Quarter was an acknowledged leader in society and dress, and her salons were as famous in the dim faubourg as those of the First Empire. So the old gentleman was brought in, and thus appealed to he carefully adjusted his spectacles and tremblingly took a pinch of snuff from his golden tabatière.

"Je me souviens," he said slowly—"d'un bal! un bal déguisé! Ah!" he continued, rolling his eyes and shaking his head, "that was something dat make peep' talk! dere nevaire bin one ball like dat in la Nouvelle Orleans! it bin took at de l'Opera Français, and all dem beautiful lady!. all dem fine costume! Mon Dieu!"

The aunts and cousins bent forward eagerly, and Lalotte's mother offered the old gentleman a glass of "eau sucré." He sipped it slowly, apparently heedless of the intense interest of his hearers, yet interiorly conscious of the momentous influence of his opinion as to what Lalotte should wear at her first ball.

"Je me souviens," he repeated slowly, as if thinking aloud, "d'un bal l—mais, dere was one I meet dere who look like one star, like one sun, she was so bright; she make represent one papillon, un beau papillon, with wings of gold! Et sa robe!—Mon Dieu! dat dress was magnifique, magnifique, magnifique! and mademoiselle she shine like a rainbow, et les rayons—ma foi! they went straight trou' my heart! Mais," he repeated, laying his hand softly on Lalotte's head, "she was belle, mon enfante, oui, oui! she was belle, dat beautiful papillon, dat beautiful girl—your gran'-muzzer!" and he leaned forward and kissed her, while the aunts and maiden cousins were visibly affected. Then the old gentleman drew himself up to his full height and held up his hand triumphantly; and gave his verdict with the air of a grand seignior:

"Our Lalotte shall be like her gran'-muzzer. She will go to de ball! She will be one papillon! un beau papillon!"

"C'est ça!" cried the relatives enthusiastically, shaking hands with one another and congratulating themselves upon the beauty and novelty of grandfather's suggestion. "C'est ça! voilà l'idée!—un papillon, un papillon!"

And a butterfly Lalotte represented, one of those brilliant winged creatures whose colors are so beautiful in Louisiana and vary with each changing

sunbeam as they flit from flower to flower sipping their sweets and telling their songs and stories. Her skirt was of rich creamy satin, her tablier of the fairest rose, and her bodice was the color of the sea foam when the moon is shining on it. She wore glittering wings of gauze that scintillated like a thousand dew-drops in the sunshine. A golden butterfly gleamed among the meshes of lace on her waxen shoulders and upon the toes of each of her tiny pink satin slippers. Here and there, fairy-like and transparent in brilliancy and coloring, appeared. the same fitful emblem, of every hue. and size, while triumphant and typical in the dark waving hair, darting forth its kaleidoscopic rays, shone a single golden-winged butterfly; that emphasized the entire make-up of the dazzling fairy-like costume, giving it life, tone, color.

She was beautiful! Her old nurse, Zizi, told her so as she tied the dainty ribbons above her pink-slippered feet, and her mother put the last golden pin in her hair and embraced her in a manner that spoke volumes. Down in the parlor where all her aunts and cousins were assembled, together with her godfather and godmother, who had come from their home near the bayou to congratulate her upon this occasion, grand-père, whose spirits rose with the evening, was talking volubly of his younger days and the balls then in vogue, the duels that would follow, and the chevaliers with whom he had measured swords, while off in a corner of the great window, the "vielle tante," who had never married because she was "trop difficile," detailed to a younger generation of "tantes" her coquetries and triumphs and the distinguished offers she had rejected.

Lalotte entered, smiling radiantly: "Comme elle est belle!" "Comme elle est jolie!" "Quelle figure!" and a dozen similar compliments greeted her simultaneously. Grand-père advanced and placed his hand upon her head, perhaps in silent benediction—who knows? Her cousin Jules smiled approvingly, and her brothers Jacques and Edouard kissed her on her cheek. From the kitchen at Madame's invitation came the old cook and butler, distinguished by life-long fidelity to the family, to see Mam'zelle Lalotte in her first ball dress.

That ball! Will she ever forget it? The long ride through the old French Quarter, the typical Creole home in the rue Royale, with its wide stuccoed veranda reaching far out on the banquet, the cool, paved court-yard with flowers blooming in parterres even in midwinter, and fountain playing in the moonbeams, and the grand salons thronged with the representative families of the old Creole regime. Garlands of evergreens festooned the walls and arches, smilax trailed over the broad, high chimneys, and above the low old-fashioned French mirrors, and dames and knights in powdered wigs looked down from their gilded frames and saw their prototypes in the bright smiling faces moving merrily around.

It was a veritable "bal déguisé." Here was a knot of gay Bohemians and troubadours, there a group of peasant girls in Normandy dress, gypsy fortune tellers, fair Marguerites, insistent Fausts and leering Mephistopheles, a laughing "diablesse." by the side of Marie Stuart, stately ladies of the First Empire holding gay converse with Richelieu and Marie Antoinette; and there were lords and ladies, soldiers and minstrels, genii and fairies,—but there was only one butterfly, as unique as she was beautiful.

And all were kind to her, for it was the first time she had spread her golden wings in the sunshine of the brilliant world, and it was a wonder, a revelation, a memory that would abide for aye. The hostess, though bound to Lalotte by only the slenderest tie of alliance, presented her affectionately to the guests as her "très chère cousine—la fille de Gabriêlle," and she met for the first time many "little cousins and aunts and uncles" of whose existence she was not hitherto cognizant, but whose claims to relationship were fully established by having espoused a cousin of a cousin-german or a brother-in-law of another. Her cousin Jules led her out for the first dance and her brother Edouard claimed her hand for the second.

Her mamma sat proudly near, anx-iously watching her every movement, while the host chatted grandiloquently of old days in New Orleans and, warming with his favorite theme, pointed out the chair in which Louis Phillipe sat when he visited New Orleans as the Duc d'Orleans and honored that house with his presence; he pointed to the room that he had occupied and the identical table at which was given the grand State dinner where the royal exile, looking around at the brilliant assembly of ladies in court costume, poured out a glass of sparkling champagne and proposed as a toast "Les Dames de la Nouvelle Orleans," and rising to his feet he quaffed off the goblet and bowing to his hostess said, "Ce n'est pas l'Amerique! Cést la France, c'est Paris!"

All this, too, he told to Lalotte as she sat next to him at supper, heedless of her "gombo aux huitres," as she listened with flashing eye and flushed cheek, and none of the butterfly's proverbial indifference.

"Beau Papillon! où allez vous?" said a deep voice at Lalotte's side as she rose from the table, "Rappelez ma valse!"

The music rose, soft, dreamy, persuasive strains that set the feet agoing almost involuntarily. They glided about the room lightly, gracefully, her wings glistening in the gas light, her eyes like tell-tale stars. Faint compunctions of conscience, doubts as to what the good Ursuline nuns might say, crossed her mind and troubled her in a vague, far-off way, but the music, the graceful swaying movement, the rhythmical, measured tread, seemed to her the essence of poetical grace, lulled her doubts and awoke forever in her Latin temperament that love of music and motion combined which has ever been a prominent characteristic of her race.

"Quelle valse!" her partner said dreamily as the music ceased, and proposed a promenade in the "conservatoire."

"Oh! non, monsieur," she exclaimed, drawing back in fear and surprise; and then, ashamed of her fears and thinking she had wounded his feelings, she naively explained that she could not go with him into the conservatory without her mamma or her brother Edouard. He bowed gallantly and escorted her back to her mother.

They drove briskly through the narrow streets back to Lalotte's old home that would seem so different now. She had entered that night into a new phase of existence. She would have henceforth other material with which to people her dreams, other food for thought than that afforded by the dim, gray convent, its gardens and chapel and study halls, and its quiet black-veiled inmates. The moon had risen high and lighted up the quaint old house, and the low, broad granite steps. Its beams fell athwart Lalotte as she alighted from the carriage and showed the gauze wings hanging limp and crushed, the butterflies detached and held by slender threads to her dress, and upon the banquet fell two or three specimens and lay there, a helpless, glittering mass.

"Voilà vos papillons, mademoiselle," cried her escort, gaily.

"Mes pauvres papillons," she repeated, looking down upon them half sadly, half laughingly, with a tear in her eye.

"Put them away, mademoiselle," he answered, picking up the butterflies and wrapping them carefully in her handkerchief. "Et demain," he laughingly added, smiling at the sympathetic face, "nous assisterons à l'enterrement des papillons."

"Yes," said Edouard, laughing heartily as he lifted the old brass knocker, "put them away, Lalotte, and tomorrow we will all assist at the burial of your butterflies."

But she only smiled still half-sadly, half laughingly, and caressingly repeated "Mes pauvres papillons!"

And then old Zizi could be heard coming slip-shod along the hall to open the door. Lalotte's mother and brother entered; for an instant she lingered, turning to wave a smiling adieu to the gentleman, and then the grim portal closed behind her; and that night, with a bunch of faded butterflies carefully hidden beneath her pillow, she buried her head in the snowy depths and dreamed such dreams as come but once to youth and beauty and trusting innocence.

NORTHERN SENTIMENT TOWARD THE SOUTH.

By Robert Adger Bowen.

For many years, now, the South and her people have been objects of interest to Northern minds, interest more or less generous and noble as the case might be, but an interest that is becoming every day more and more liberal and sympathetic. Old ideas are exploding daily under the searching light poured upon every vein and artery of the South from the great luminary truth. Slowly the tide begins to turn, and little by little, but surely and firmly, the South begins to receive a juster estimate of her past and present, to have the rags and tatters that slander so long has thrown about her torn away and to receive from minds generous and upright in themselves the only meed that generosity and uprightness, unclouded by the fumes of passion and false impressions, are ever willing to bestow—charity, sympathy, a brotherly toleration for mistakes and failures, and, moreover, a strong respect for the Southern people incompatible with the once existing belief in their degradation, brutality, effeminacy, and general inferiority.

Not until one from the South goes to the North and lives for several years intimately associated with the best intellect and intelligence there, can the fact of the widespread and generally accepted erroneous views concerning Southern life, conditions, habits and civilization be fully realized. Indeed, so great is the ignorance, so wide of the truth the impressions held concerning all things pertaining to the present of the South and to the past leading thereto, that at times it appears almost hopeless ever to expect to bring light out of such darkness. For more than forty years the pens of thousands at the North have been engaged in defaming the South, her people, her institutions, her customs. The shelves in her great libraries groan under the accumulated mass of "Rebellion literature," and it has only lately become a question to Northern readers whether both terms may not be sad misnomers. Against this heap of writing, in certain cases more or less respectable but in no single instance unbiased or free from the strongest sectional feeling, the South, with the exception of such monumental works as those of Jefferson Davis and Alexander H. Stephens, has contributed nothing of any decided importance towards her own vindication until very recent years. But that there now begins to be manifest at the North a general desire for information upon all points relative to the South, and that this desire is usually expressed interrogatively, goes to show that, underlying these early instilled impressions and beliefs, there yet exists a lurking doubt as to their probability, and an earnest wish to know what is really the truth about them.

There is a strange fascination, indeed, pertaining to Southern life, and especially Southern plantation life, which appeals peculiarly to Northern minds. True, these impressions are generally vague and intangible, like the imaginary flavor of Persian sherbets in the mouths of those who have never crossed the seas, but none the less—perhaps the more—on this account does a subtle spell linger over these picturings of the fancy, in which flower covered balconies, turbaned "mammys," palms, rattlesnakes, wild-turkeys and mosquitoes are woven into fanciful arabesques of more than Moorish wildness. Therefore, familiar as it all is to us of the South, our old homes, half-wrecked and decrepit as many of them have become, possess a charm and fascination that was not theirs even in happier days. There is nothing to be found elsewhere in America similar to these Southern homes, all of them more or less alike, peculiar to the people, yet each with an individuality, a personality almost, of its own. A stranger likes to hear of the low old plantation house, with its spreading piazzas, supported by long rows of white pillars, encircling the mansion as with an open hospitality, the high windows from ceiling to floor, the red chimneys, the queer old dormer windows on the roof, the rose vines on the piazza balustrade, the great oaks and elms sweeping the old roofs with their lower branches, its shade and coolness, its fragrance from shrub, tree and flower, its quiet and holy calm, the peace that broods above it, and the murmurous melody of bird and insect that wraps it round about in a drowsy, deep content.

The South is the romance land of the nation. It was always so; and the results of a terrible war, fraught to her with desolation and ruin, have circled her homes, as with a sacred halo, with the mystery of sorrow and suffering; have set apart her people, with their chivalry, their loyalty, love and devotion to their ideals, their noble endurance of unparalleled hardships, their courage, patience and unflinching perseverance against tremendous odds, as a race to be admired and respected even by their opponents in war and statesmanship. Hitherto the North has not thought about the South; she has but felt, and being sadly misguided by her leaders, she has felt for the most part bitterly and harshly, her feeling being untempered by definite knowledge. It is always an easy matter to work upon the emotions of the ignorant, and in the class of ignorance the North has undoubtedly heretofore stood in reference to Southern life, institutions, and habits of thought and feeling.

That the South herself may stand accountable for much of this ignorance on the part of the rest of the world of her inner life and customs, does not alter the case itself. She has paid dearly for her

conservatism, right though she may have been in her instinctive adherence to it. This conservatism in its essential characteristics is a part of the marrow of her bones, is a part of the contribution she is destined to make to the life and honor of the nation. Without it her people would not be. But an element of insulted pride, pardonable as it may be to her, entering into her dealings with the outer world at the most critical period of her existence, has cost her devoted people long years of calumny, misunderstanding, and an almost moral ostracism on the part of the world at large, but principally from her sister States of the North and West.

The absence of a literature in the South before the war may be looked on as a sad and strange fatality, readily explicable as it all may be. Conscious of her own rectitude, willing to raise her eyes to meet the full gaze of any, even the purest nation among men, yet bitterly wounded from far and near, her very virtues turned to steel against her own breast and her slightest error seized upon and, cruelly magnified, flaunted to her shame before the eyes of the world, she shut herself up in proud and sad determination to face it all and bear it all, but not to attempt to vindicate herself one whit. She was accused before the bar of nations and the world sat against her on trial, but proud in her consciousness of being the peer and not the vassal of any one of them, she spoke not. And to this day, and for many a sad day to come, shall the South suffer for this proud, though brave, misconduct. It was thus that books like "Uncle Tom's Cabin," and the host of nameless viperous stings that followed in its wake, could sweep the stern minds of men from their pedestals of right and reason, and by appealing to the overheated and misinformed side of their emotional natures, becomes a power in the land—not to free the negro but to condemn his master. It were needless to remind the South of what she has undergone since those days, of the long, terrible years of humiliation, suffering and agony through which she has passed as through a seven times heated fiery furnace, and from which she has emerged at last, her honor unsullied, her fame luminous before the gaze of the world, her hills and mountains, valleys, seas and skies dear to the hearts of her children as that for which they gave their best and costliest, as that is dear which is washed in the blood and agony of a great people dying for what they deemed true and right.

And now too she turns and begins to vindicate her past. And the world, asserting its independent manhood and right to use its own brains, where it has any, begins to listen, and listening thinks, and so begins also to doubt if there be not after all some good in Nazareth.

Thus while the South catches once again a glimpse of the dawn of brighter days, the North through travel and books and in various other ways comes to have a truer appreciation and sympathy for and with the South than perhaps ever before. To sensible Northern minds "Uncle Tom's Cabin" is no longer a prefix to their holy scriptures—not even an appendix. Southern students at the great Northern universities, far from finding their Southern birth a drawback to them, on the contrary are received with a warmer interest on that account, and have extended to them a generous hospitality with a delicate avoidance of all subjects that would by any means wound their preconceived ideas and beliefs, in a manner which would do all honor to that of which they are so justly proud, Southern courtesy and refinement. And it may be said in passing that these students attain the highest honors in the power of the faculty and the student body to confer—class presidencies, class oratorships, fellowships, editorships of university publications, etc.

Now, while there are one or two things about the South that a Northerner finds it exceedingly difficult to comprehend, such, for instance, as the true nature of the climate and scenery, her position towards the negro and the position of the negro towards her, there is undoubtedly this live interest developing about the Southern States, and an earnest desire to know the true status of things, not alone in the present but also in the past. Error and falsehood cannot per-

petuate themselves forever, and the Northern mind is far too keen and of too great an independent vitality, where it belongs to the thinking class, to feed itself any longer upon the dry chaff formerly administered as good grain by the party leaders. The most intelligent indeed may have a deeply rooted idea that all of the South is a vast bog of malaria, yellow fever, mosquitoes and ague. Tell them that in midsummer the heat there does not exceed, often does not equal, that to which they are accustomed in the North; tell them of rolling fields and meadowlands, of broad stretches of hill and valley, of miles of extended view over forest and plain to where the Blue Ridge lies like a great chain of uneven sapphires clear cut against the pulsing azure of the Southern sky, and the intelligence to them is new and strange. Stranger still to them the knowledge that portions of the South are visited in winter by ice and snow. This ignorance of the commonest details of Southern climate and scenery often evinces itself in delightfully refreshing *naivete*, though it conclusively shows how general and deep-seated the misrepresentation and misunderstanding concerning the South has become.

But, on the other hand, this desire for knowledge as to the truth of Southern questions means much. It means in in the first place a tacit confession of ignorance and a willingness to enlighten that ignorance. It means also a tacit withdrawal from the creed of their fathers or of their earlier days. The North acknowledges at last that she does not understand the negro, cannot understand him, never has understood him, knows nothing definite about him, acknowledges, moreover, that she does not like him. All this individually, of course, but does it mean nothing for the future historian? Their newspapers may continue to churn out froth about the "War of the Rebellion," and show a wonderful skill in the introduction into their columns of the words "rebels" and "traitors," but yet the universal respect, not the mere courtesy alone, shown to all Southerners by the true manhood and womanhood of the North, has a far truer ring and means far more. The North is proud of her prosperity and advantages; proud of her great cities and all the thousand echoes of material advance proceeding from them to all her towns and villages. She is ahead of the South in all this, immeasurably ahead, and knows it. But she is not ahead of the South, and never has been, in all that goes to make the man and gentleman, and she knows this, too, and, what is more, acknowledges it.

The South should not be less generous than the North. True, she has far, far more to forgive—to forgive and keep silent over. Forget she can never and should never. But she should strive to avoid the spirit of narrowness, loosen a little the outer girths of her conservatism and see good where good really exists. She should not feel that all Northern ideas are antagonistic to her and to her interests. She should not positively believe, or try to believe, that all Southern institutions, from the breakfast table to the halls of legislation, are superior to Northern ones. Pride is a shield that ofttimes wounds the wearer. Proud the South should be, must always be, but pride should not degenerate into self-satisfaction. She should remember that it is far harder for the North even tacitly to acknowledge error and fault in her conduct than it would be for the courtesy of the South openly and generously to forgive.

History works slowly, and truth does not rise in a day to the surface through the heated mass of all that has held it down for over a quarter of a century. But the bubbles that foretell its appearance should be encouraged charitably and generously, not stirred down again by too exultant a satisfaction. The South has borne her long agony of humiliation, sorrow and suffering so nobly and so heroically, her men and her women through long years of unparalleled ignominy, untrue accusations, and undeserved condemnations have ever been so perfectly men and women; from all the unwritten, unspeakable trials and persecutions of these lengthened years she has emerged so bravely and so well, that in the dawn of her day of triumphant vindication before the world —a vindication to be accomplished by the natural processes of truth and history—she should also stand in her uprightness, patient, generous and forgiving.

If it be asked where is to be seen the dawn of any such day, or even the faintest appearance of such a dawn, when day after day the press of the North and West reeks with bitter and unjust denunciations of all things Southern, the answer may be found in the fact that these defamations are beginning to be viewed with a proper sense of shame by the best natures of the North, and that they themselves would never be induced to use such language now. The greater spirit of the North, in its homes and by its firesides, no longer re-echoes such jackal attacks as those lately made by certain organs upon the memory of Jefferson Davis, and such eruptions of vindictiveness as that lately indulged in by Foraker over the tomb of General Grant not only failed to receive approval from his hearers but met with universal condemnation on all sides. Above all is the fact that the young men and the young women of the North, with independent minds unwarped by passion and personal animosity, are forming their own opinions of the most eventful period of the nation's history, are turning from the superlative accounts of rabid history-mongers with the instructive discovery of fraud which the youthful mind, and particularly the youthful American mind, is ever so quick to detect, and are feeding themselves from sources taking their rise in the South itself as well as in the more impartial mind of the North of today.

It would be too much to expect of the North an acknowledgment that she was in error in the great struggle that shook our country to its very foundations thirty years ago; it would be too much to expect that she should as yet even believe this to be so. And she does not so believe it. But when she is willing to admit that the South had provocation for what she did; when a history, dealing in large part with the war and its causes, is written by a professor in a great Northern institution of learning, and is received as a text book in many of the other large universities and colleges of the North, the title* of which excludes the talismanic word "Rebellion," and the contents of which are fairer and truer to the South than those of any book yet written on the subject— a book in which General Sherman and General Grant are mentioned not as gods, and in which the South is accorded the possession of a sense of right and justice and truth—surely this means much for the cause of the advancement of the South's fair name at the North.

And if it be further asked what reason there be to anticipate the oncoming of any such day of vindication for the South, can she not point to the halo of glory surrounding the memories of her great heroes, the white light of a reflected noble manhood that is shed abroad over the world from the lives and deaths of her great soldier-gentle-

*Division and Reunion, 1829-1889, Woodrow Wilson, Ph. D., L. L. D.

men, and to which all men reverently do homage? The respect, the honor, the glory which not the South alone, nor yet the North with the South, but which the entire world humbly and gladly pays to the great leaders of Southern thought and might and valor, is it only the meed which a magnanimous manhood accords to defeated traitors and rebels? Is it only the meed which a generous world accords to a misdirected sense of duty, to a distorted patriotism? Or is it not something at bottom far other than any of these things, an acknowledgment that the stainless purity and honor of a Lee, that the incorruptible, unflinching right-doing of the Titan Jackson, that the integrity and noble manliness of men like Davis and Stephens could never, by the very nature of truth and uprightness, lend themselves, nay, rather give themselves heart and soul, to a cause devoid of justice, patriotism and right?

"FLIM."

By Lull Martin.

"Oakdale!" screamed the train porter in tones rivalling the howling elements outside, at the same time ushering me into the driving sleet and rain of a dark ·November night. At half-past eleven o'clock I was deposited at this little wayside station in the northern part of Mississippi. Not a light being visible I could not discover a shelter of any description near me, nor a human being to whom I could appeal.

My home. was in Richmond, Va., where my mother, two little sisters and I had struggled bravely with poverty for two years after my father's death, each fighting daily against what we knew would sooner or later be inevitable, that I would have to leave home and apply my musical talent to a practical purpose. At last the day came when every dollar in our coffer had been spent, and there was no alternative left me but to procure employment. After several unsuccessful attempts, at last I obtained a position as music teacher with Prof. Hargrove, principal of Oakdale College, Miss., and left at once to begin work. I had a pleasant trip until I reached Memphis, Tenn., when I had to lay over a few hours. I tried to spend the time as pleasantly as possible by seeing something of the city; but imagine my consternation on returning to the station to find my train had left five minutes before. I was so distressed over this enforced. delay that the agent, who seemed a kind-hearted young fellow, told me another train would leave going south about eight o'clock that evening, ·but being a through train would not take passengers for the small places along the line. "Perhaps, though," said he, "I could get you a special per-

mit from the superintendent;" and requesting me to call again in half an hour. he said he would let me know the result. Of course I was on hand at the appointed time, and learned with heartfelt gratitude that the desired arrangements had been made in my behalf.

I had reached my destination at last, and at the same time was placed in the most terrible dilemma I ever experienced. I think I was born with a fear of darkness; it has always possessed inconceivable terrors for me. I could never be persuaded even to go into a dark room alone. Therefore it is easy to comprehend my feelings while standing there alone at midnight, and in a strange place. Everybody in the little village was sleeping as peacefully as if it were a veritable "city of the dead." I stood there perhaps fifteen or twenty minutes, peering through the darkness in every direction, so frightened my life seemed in danger from the rapid beating of my heart. At last I caught a faint sound of something approaching. Each moment I could hear it drawing nearer and nearer; I was not sure from which direction it was coming. My terror finally reached a state of frenzy, and without a moment's thought I grabbed my skirts and dashed through the darkness. I had not run more than twenty steps before I collided with an object of much more diminutive proportions than my own, which I clutched with an instinct of self-preservation, while together we rolled with alternating bumps down a steep embankment to—heaven knows where. At the same time there issued from the mouth of this small piece of humanity or imp of darkness, as the case might be, the most unearthly yells it has ever been my lot to hear.

"Oh, Lordy! dis is me. Oh, hab mussy on dis po' nigger! Dis is jes' Flim! Oh, Marse Lennox de debel is sho' got Flim dis time!" These and similar cries were kept up by the little negro (for such it proved to be) until we landed in the middle of a mud puddle at the foot of the embankment, when I caught him and shook him until he had no breath left with which to howl.

"Shut your mouth, you young rascal," I said, "stop your screaming and tell me where I am."

"Well you jes tell me who in de name o' the Lord you is, a knockin' a gen'leman down here at dis time of de night?"

"I am Miss Norton, the new music teacher at Oakdale College," I said in a more conciliatory tone.

"No, sah," he replied, "I b'lieve you is the debel's own se'f; for Marse Lennox say he knows Miss Norton is a bawn lady, jes' ca'se she is fum ole Virginny, but no bawn lady kin knock er feller as kerplunk' as you knocked me down dat 'bankment. I kin b'lieve you is de debel, but you sho' ain't Miss Norton."

In spite of Flim's complimentary opinion I determined to get out of my present predicament by his aid; therefore, summoning all my courage, I replied in a tone as commanding as I could assume under the circumstances:

"Now listen to me, Flim. I am really Miss Norton, and I am very cold and wet and tired, so wherever you are going I must go with you. If I stay here much longer I shall perish with cold, so move on at once." At the same time I grasped his shoulder firmly, rendering his escape from me impossible.

"I'se gwine to de doctor's," he said, twisting and squirming his small body under my hand like an eel. "'Cause Marse Lennox has been tuk mighty bad wid de cramps, an' I'se gwine ter git de doctor."

"Very well," I replied, "I will go with you."

"No, sah," he said, planting himself firmly on both legs. I ain't gwine to no doctor's house wid you dis night."

"Why?" I asked in some surprise.

"Ca'se we has ter pass right by de grabeyard ter git dar, an' dis nigger ain' gwine pass by no grabeyard les'n he kin see mighty well wha' kin' er comp'ny he's in. I'll jes' go toder way an' tik you to Mars Lennox's house fuss."

Fearing his master might really be ill, I was afraid to prevent him from going for the doctor, so asked him if he could not direct me to his home, thinking that perhaps I could find my way there alone.

"W'y to be sho' I kin," he replied, with as much eagerness and relief as if I had with one sweep of the hand cleared every vestige of cloud and darkness from the dripping sky.

"You jes' keep right straight down dis here railroad track 'till you comes to a great big pawn full o' water, an' you be mighty keerful, too, 'bout dat pawn, fer sho's yer drap in dar yer gwine ter drown. Den you tiks a paf dat runs right 'long de aidge o' de pawn, an' you follows it up de hill, an' you mus' be mighty pertic'lar 'bout dat hill, too, fer its done been washed putty nigh all 'way inter gullies, an' some pow'ful big uns run right frou dat paf. You'd sho' git yer nake broke if yer fell inter one in de dark. Den when yer reaches de top o' de hill you follows de paf dat runs inter de little skart o' woods, an' den dar yer is, right at de house."

As I did not feel quite ready to encounter the dangers he indicated, and having experienced enough horrors for one night, I told Flim he would have to take me to his home first and then come again for the doctor if his master were still suffering. Seing there was no alternative but to get me safely housed, he agreed more willingly than I supposed he would. We groped around in the dark and found the small grip I carried, and at last seemed fairly started home. Not a word was spoken by either of us until Flim came to a dead stop.

"I tell yer what, Missis," he said, "I'll tote dis here perlise an' tik you safe home, ef you'll promise ter bake me a mons'trous big cake fer my weddin'." This startling request, coming from such a small person at this uncanny hour, did not have a very soothing effect on my quivering nerves, and I became as much afraid of my guide as he had previously been of me. I don't think either of us would have been at all surprised if the other had mounted a broomstick and vanished through the clouds.

"You seem a very little boy to be thinking of your wedding day," I said, "how old are you?"

"Oh, I'se jes' nine year ole gwine on ten," he replied, "but I 'spects to git married when I gits grown, an' I sho' wants lots o' cake den. I'se heerd Marse Lennox tell 'bout de stacks an' stacks o' cake at his'n an' Miss Mary's weddin' in ole Virginny 'till gosh! it makes my mouf water here in de dark to tink 'bout it."

"I suppose your master and mistress are from Virginia then," I said, gaining courage from the mere sound of our voices.

"You bet dey is," was the prompt reply. "Some o' de rale ole ar'stocercy. Marse Lennox was bawn an' raised dar, an' so wuz Miss Mary, an' I 'spects Miss Sadie would ha' been too, only she wus bawn in Mississippi; but mussy knows she's sweet an' lubly 'nough ter been bawn in heben. You'se gwine ter bode to our house, fer I heerd 'Fessor Hargrove tell Miss Mary ef she'd tik you ter bode he'd let it pay fer Miss Sadie's schoolin' an' music, an' Miss Mary 'lowed she'd be mighty glad to do it, fer dey sho' is po', Marse Lennox and Miss Mary is. An' my gran'mammy gwine do yo' washin' too. She say she know you nice lady jes' ca'se you fum Virginny, an' she gwine charge you big price, ca'se she knows you too nice to jaw back at 'er an' jew 'er down, like dis po' white trash roun' here. My gran'mammy is sho' one good ole 'oman; she raised me, fer my mammy died when I wus bawn, an' my gran'mammy say she raised me by han'; she sho' did too, fer 'tween me an' you, an' de gate pos', it wus de tur'iblest spankin' han' I ever 'specs ter feel in dis worl'. Some fo'ks say my gran'mammy's mighty deef, but she ain't deef, she jes' hard o' hearin,' dats all. It makes my gran'mammy fu'ous ter say she's deef."

Listening to Flim's garrulous communications I found myself entering the "skart o' woods" much sooner than I expected. Suddenly the air was ringing with the voices of yelping hounds. "Mercy!" I exclaimed, "where are all those dogs?"

"Dey's jes' Marse Lennox's pack o' hounds."

"He must have a great many, judging from the noise they make," I said.

"No'm, he ain't got many now," said Flim, a quiver coming into his voice, "he's jes' got Uno an' Row, Tussle Up an' Tow, Juno an' her seben pups, an' ole Billydinktum, all de oders starbed to deaf las' winter while Marse Lennox wus sick wid de tarrified (typhoid) mala'ous fever."

Just then we arrived at the house, where I was warmly welcomed by Mrs. Buford, Flim's "Miss Mary." I was glad to find that Major Buford or "Marse Lennox" had so far recovered from his "cramps" that it was unnecessary for Flim to make another midnight expedition for the doctor.

The next morning I opened my room door in response to a gentle rap, and confronted the most ludicrous little figure I have ever seen, holding a bunch of violets in his hand. I could scarcely keep from laughing outright. Every vestige of clothing he had on seemed to have been made for some one either larger or smaller than himself. There was scarcely anything of him but skin and bones. He wore a swallow tail coat, the tails reaching to his heels. It must at one time have concealed the body of a man at least six feet tall, with a proportionate girth. His legs were encased in a pair of trousers I could easily have believed were made of sticking plaster, so closely did they cling to his bony little legs. I afterwards learned they had been a baby boy's first pair of pants, and was also told that Flim's grandmother did the washing for quite a number of families in the village, and frequently from her poorer patrons received old clothes in payment. This accounted for his incongruous attire. His shirt, shoes and stockings were in perfect keeping with the the remainder of his outfit. As he held the flowers up to me his little black eyes were fairly sparkling, and his mouth was stretched from ear to ear.

"Miss Norton," he began, "Marse Lennox 'quested me to persent you dese flowers with his best disgards, an' he hopes you feels bery much reproved arter yo' night's res'. An' Miss Mary say will yer walk in ter breakfas', I'se gwine ter show you de way to de dinin'-room."

On reaching the dining-room I found the family in which I was to make my home composed of only three members, Major and Mrs. Buford, and their daughter Sadie, a lovely, fragile girl of sixteen years, in whose face the evidences of consumption were plainly visible. One could see at a glance that not many lessons either in school or in this life would be learned by her.

After breakfast Sadie and I started to school. Flim was to accompany us each morning to carry Sadie's books and music. We had not gone very far before Major Buford passed us on his horse, with all the hounds following except the seven pups, but in a few minutes these young prodigies dashed by, yelping and whining and running as fast as their tottering young legs could carry them to catch their mother. As quick as a flash every book and piece of music Flim carried was dashed to the ground, and like an arrow he shot by us after the puppies, his long coat-tails held straight out behind him by the wind.

"Hi! yi! you young debels you! come back here," he screamed at the top of his voice, "you'll ebery one git kilt." By this time he had caught up with them, and grabbing one by the tail, another by its long ears, two by their hind legs, and knocking two more down and sitting on them, he secured six with only a slight skirmish; but the seventh was far out of reach, and with every step it took, seemed to kick back defiance at its young protector.

"Yes, you young lim' o' satan you, run on, I knows you kin run, you kin run mighty fas' too, but yer ain' gwine outdo dis nigger den. Marse Lennox! hi, Marse Lennox! you dribe ole Juno an' dat rapscallion ob a pup back home," screamed Flim, tightly holding the six puppies while angrily watching the seventh catch up with its mother. Ac-

cordingly Juno was started back in charge of her numerous progeny, and we proceeded on our way without further interruption.

Returning from school one afternoon I was startled by cries of "help! help!" from a deep gully near me. I ran to the edge, and looking down, saw Flim astride of another little negro, pounding his with all his strength.

"Flim! Flim!" I called, "stop fighting this instant! Arn't you ashamed of yourself."

"No I ain't, Miss Norton, fer dis nigger knocked all Miss Sadie's nice books out'n my han' in ter de mud." His indignation seemed to gather force with his words, and he struck his foe a parting blow on the nose that sent the blood flying all over his face. I thought this a good opportunity to lecture him on his fighting propensities which I noticed were aroused by the smallest provocation.

"Flim," I said, "why are you always so eager for a fight. If you were seriously hurt some time in a quarrel what do you think would become of you?"

"I do' no'm," he answered, looking down, and digging one toe into the ground. "I'se jes a natu'al bawn fowter, I can't help it; in runs in de fambly, jes lack you said de oder day, de music did in your'n. You can't he'p playin' de pianer, fer de music's right dar in yo' fingers, an' I can't he'p fowten, fer de fowten is right there in mine, an' I do' b'lieve it no mo' harm fer me ter fowt, den fer you ter play de pianer."

"Why of course it is," I answered, "for I always give pleasure when I play, while you only wound."

"Well, I ain't so sho' 'bout dat," he said, "fer de oder day when you kep' er playin' an' er playin' so long on de pianer, I heerd one man tell a 'noder, he did wish dat 'oman would stop dat blame noise, fer it was 'bout ter bus' his brain open."

Feeling that Flim had the better of the argument, I said no more, trusting that a few sound thrashings would put a more effectual stop to his hereditary trait than anything I could say.

Before June roses came, Sadie was

laid to rest in the quiet little church-yard. Her last words were to Flim, begging him always to remain with her father and mother, and care for them in their old age.

Thirteen long years have passed away, bringing many changes into my life. For five or six years I corresponded regularly with my two old friends at Oakdale, but as time passed the intervals between our letters grew longer, until they finally ceased altogether.

. Last summer while my husband and I were traveling gypsy style through the country, we came to a lovely little farmhouse, standing back from the road in a cool, shady grove. It looked so inviting we could not resist begging permission to rest from the noon-day sun. As soon as I entered the house, a sense of familiarity with my surroundings came over me, though I could not think when or where I had seen the little pieces of bric-a-brac, scattered so tastefully around the room. Even the pictures on the wall seemed to answer me with a glad smile of recognition. While I was trying to account for this home-like feeling I heard an equally familiar footstep in the hall, and looking around recognized in a moment my old friend Mrs. Buford. Time had dealt very kindly with her, had only scattered a few more silver strands through her hair; but in exchange had chased away the care-worn expression from her face, I so well remembered. I was soon in possession of the few changes that had taken place in her life. A relative of Major Buford's had left him as a legacy the small farm on which they had been living for five years. A heavy mortgage rested on the place when it came into his posession; but by perseverance and hard work Flim had paid it off, and to him more than to its owner was due the present fine condition of the place. He had been constantly with them since Sadie's death; never leaving them even for a few days. As a singular coincidence I will mention that the following eve he was to take unto himself a dusky-hued bride, and I was easily persuaded to remain for the happy occasion, and fulfill the promise made so many long years before.

TO A SOUTHERN POET.

By Anna McC. Sholl.

Poet, thou bringest from a Southern land
  The breath of roses and the glow of morn,
  The tender blushes of the day new-born,
The splash of white waves on the golden sand;
And with the magic of a poet's hand
  Thou turnest thorns to roses without thorn,
  And paintest sunsets on cold skies forlorn,
And green-robed hills by fairy rainbows spanned.

Oh poet young! when love has touched thy heart,
  Will the great world still gladder to thee grow,
  More red the rose, more tender blue the skies,
More bright the air through which the sunbeams dart?
  Or wilt thou turn from nature's pomp and show
  To see the universe in her sweet eyes.

'NEATH SOUTHERN SKIES.

By J. S. Rogers.

'Neath Southern skies, what clime so fair!
  Nor Arcadie, nor Palatine,
  Nor grape-empurpled shores of Rhine,
Nor Tempe kissed by balmy air;
Nay, nor Hymethian groves compare
  With all the enchantments that combine
    'Neath Southern skies!

But most of all—shall I declare?
  For me a paradise divine,
  'Mid corn and cotton, eglantine,
Is made by one who dwelleth there,
    'Neath Southern skies!

STOCK-RAISING AND DAIRYING IN THE SOUTH.

By H. B. Wetzell.

Those who travel from the rich prairie lands of the upper Mississippi valley region or the well cultivated districts of the Ohio valley, on their way to New Orleans, or to the winter resorts of Florida, will probably see but little along the route to impress them that the South, of which they have heard so much, is now, or is likely to become in the future, an important factor in stock-raising in the United States. The same may be said of the many thousands of tourists, business men and others—and many of them men of keen observation—who annually visit the far Southern winter resorts, following the Atlantic coast line railways to and from their points of destination. But let the latter class who come from Boston, New York, Philadelphia, Baltimore, Washington, and the territory tributary to those cities pass over the Shenandoah Valley, Norfolk & Western and the East Tennessee, Virginia & Georgia railway systems and they will get an entirely different impression from that gained . by going over the coast line routes, although the best impression which they get can be but an imperfect view of the present condition of stock-raising, and much less of the possibilities in that direction in the South. I mention this fact as a preliminary observation, for the reason that many Northern people—and indeed some Southern people too—who are unfamiliar with the true state of affairs, have wrong impressions as to Southern conditions.

An old friend whom I visited last summer in one of the Middle States, a rich farmer, stock-grower and dairyman, who was one of the tourist class I have mentioned, and who had received impressions of the South as a stock-raising and dairying region from a trip to Florida and New Orleans, and return by the coast line railways, said to me: "Why I didn't see enough grass to keep a cow, and at the hotels condensed milk and Northern butter were used." While the statement was largely a humiliating fact, yet I assured him that he should not form such an opinion of the South as a whole, and that if he would come with me I could show him not only good stock in the South, but lands admirably adapted for grazing and dairying purposes—and no small area either—and I could also find native butter and milk sweet and pure as that from his own dairy. I believe that the fellow thought I had a big job on my hands when I made him that promise, but not long ago I had an opportunity to fulfill my pledge.

The man had made considerable money in lumbering operations and timber land investments in one of the northwestern States and desired to make further investments in hardwood timber lands in the middle South, if I could find such a tract as he described, within a certain district. Several years ago I had examined a well-timbered tract with view of buying, but the boom period coming on about that time raised the owner's hopes and ideas beyond the reach of prudent buyers. Several months ago, learning that the owner had again become rational and "clothed in his right mind" for a trade, I examined the land carefully as to its timber and negotiated a sale for my friend, subject to his examination and approval. The land lay twenty miles distant from the nearest railway, but a new railway line, now under construction, will be completed within a few miles of the land in the near future.

We rode on horseback after we left the railway station, at times leaving the wagon roads and trails and striking through the dense woods on our way to make final examination of the tract of land. Every mile of the distance revealed new surprises to my friend. We passed places where proper attention had been given to the cultivation of the crops and promised a bountiful yield. The red clover was just ready for the scythe, and in places it was waist high; in others a thick matted and tangled mass, which had grown so rank and high that it had fallen down and covered the ground thickly, unfit for hay, but as good as a coat of manure for a fertilizer. The timothy and red-top and blue grass were thick, tall and rank. Exclamations of surprise came repeatedly from my companion, such as "just look at that grass; why that land is black and rich and loamy as the best prairie lands or Missouri river bottoms. I never saw the like of it before in a mountain country, and especially on high mountains like these. And the land is almost free from rocks. Why, on the mountains in my State, or at least the part of it that I am acquainted with, the land is so rocky and poor that you can't raise a disturbance on it, and if it is rich enough to raise huckleberries the owner thinks he is well off." My companion was not only well pleased with what he saw, but bought the tract of land, and is now negotiating for a large tract of land adjoining his purchase.

This land lies in one of the western counties of North Carolina, amongst the high mountains, and having for its surface rocks feldspar, hornblende and associate formation, containing the elements of potash, soda, lime and others rich in fertilizing material, and when decomposed and mixed with the constantly decaying vegetable matter which overlies it, becomes soil highly favorable for grasses, grain, vegetable, fruit and forest growth.

I cite this instance as somewhat characteristic of a large portion of the higher mountain districts and of the older geological formation in the States of West Virginia, Virginia, Tennessee, North and South Carolina and Georgia. When I first began exploring these regions for timber several years ago I was astonished, like my friend whom I have mentioned, at the wonderful fertility of the soil in many places, especially in the coves having northern exposure, the soil being a loose, rich, black or very dark loam. But when I ascended the higher mountains, and even to the summits of the highest peaks, found fewer surface rocks and the soil apparently blacker and richer, I was utterly amazed.

One will find this to be true, with few exceptions, of the higher mountain regions of the Blue Ridge and Smoky Mountain systems from West Virginia to Georgia. I remember a ride one early June day several years ago in company with Big Tom Wilson, a noted local character, who found the body of the lamented Professor Mitchell, who lost his life near the summit of the mountain which now bears his name, and the highest point of land on our Continent east of the Rocky Mountains. Mt. Mitchell is one of more than twenty peaks over 6000 feet high in the Black Mountains, a short cross chain about twenty miles in length, which shoots off almost at right angles from the main Blue Ridge range. It is situated in Yancey county, North Carolina. We rode up the mountain on the Cane river side, on horseback, over an old but now little used trail. Poplar trees of immense size, as well as other kinds of deciduous growth, covered the ground densely until about half way up the mountain, when the conifers set in, spruce and balsam, and thence to the very summit it was one dark, sombre forest.

As large timber is indicative of good soil, I wish to mention that on my way up the mountain I measured one poplar tree with tape line which had a girth of twenty-seven feet nine inches, one of the largest I ever measured, and it contained, according to calculations that I made at the time, upwards of 20,000 feet of lumber, board measure. On the summit of Mt. Mitchell, and not more than 100 yards from the then rude grave of Professor Mitchell, was a small patch of ground where the balsam timber had been removed a few years before. This ground was covered with a thick mat of most nutritious grass, and so early in the season was knee high. We tethered our horses in this grass plot, and I never saw any animals that apparently enjoyed grass more than this. Big Tom Wilson is the overseer of a large estate in the Black Mountains belonging to some New York gentlemen, and a large herd of cattle grazes upon these lands. Other parts of these mountains and adjacent ranges are almost equally as rich, and thousands of head of cattle grow fat· upon the native pasturage during the season when they are grazing, which is usually from about the 10th of April to the 20th or 30th of October. In my timber explorations during the grazing season, when often alone and in those vast silent forests, I was frequently reminded of some of the evidences of civilization which had preceded me, when I listened to the sweet music of the tinkling cow-bells in the distance, even though my bed at night was under the protecting branches of a friendly tree, and a fire my mute but cheerful companion.

The herders who look after the stock, salting them at regular times about once a week or sometimes less frequently and seeing that the animals do not stray too far away, take care of one hundred and fifty, to two hundred and fifty head for each man. The salting places are usually on, or near the summit of some mountain or ridge, or in some gap or depression of the same, and like deer and other wild animals of that class, the cattle frequently visit these salting places. Sometimes the timber is cut off from half an acre or more of land at these places, and soon thereafter blue grass starts up and covers the ground with a dense mat of nutritious grass, for it seems to be indigenous. On many of the higher mountains are bare places, or "balds," having no timber, nor have they had within the memory of the white race or legendary history of the red men, and these "balds" are covered with nutritious grass which affords good grazing.

There is one feature in this connection which must not be overlooked, for it is of much importance in grazing. There is an abundance of clear, pure water everywhere, and there is an almost entire absence of insect pests. If there is a better watered region anywhere I should like to know where it is. The whole region abounds in perennial springs, many of them of mineral or chalybeate character. When one reaches altitudes of 4000 feet and upwards above sea level, flies are seldom seen, and certainly are not troublesome to man or beast.

I traveled through these mountains for several years, and in all that time I do not remember to have seen, felt or heard a dozen mosquitoes on the higher altitudes, and not enough to annoy one on the lower ones.

There is a native plant growing in the rich, damp and dark coves, known as the "wild pea vine," which is wonderfully nutritious, and cattle, horses and mules grow fat upon it in an almost incredibly short space of time. My attention was first called to it and its nutritious properties soon after I began my explorations for timber. One day, about the first of June, I had been examining a tract of timber in a large rich cove, known as "Buckeye Cove." The poplar timber was magnificent, and toward the head of the cove there was some excellent cherry timber, but the predominant growth was buckeye, and hence the name of the cove. Let me here state that, as an evidence of rich soil in these mountains, I only want to know that there is an abundant growth of large buckeye timber. I have seen buckeye trees three to four feet in diameter, with smooth trunk without branches for more than sixty feet, and in striking contrast to the same species, the horse chestnut, which one sees as a shade tree in many towns and cities North and South, but these seldom attaining a diameter greater than twelve inches. I had heard the tinkling of cow bells all day in Buckeye Cove, and saw frequently some of the stock, mostly two and three-year-old steers, but amongst the number yearlings and cows from which the calves had been weaned but a short time. Many of them were short-haired, sleek, round and fat, and that was what astonished me, to see them in such good condition so early in the season. In the evening I came to the herders' cabin, and with that generous hospitality, so characteristic of the mountaineers in all conditions of life, they urged me to stay all night and remain as long as I desired.

They informed me that they were herding about five hundred head of cattle, and then explained that the stock had fattened so rapidly upon the wild pea vine which grew abundantly in Buckeye Cove.

Most of the stock which grazes upon these higher mountains is owned by men having farms in well settled districts, where they provide hay, fodder, straw and grain for the stock during the late fall and winter season. A number of farmers may join together in sending their stock to the mountains in charge of a herder and provide salt during the grazing season, and for his services in caring for the stock pay from $1.00 to $1.50 per head. The grazing privilege from the owner of the mountain land, together with the salt and herder's services costs the owner of the stock from $1.50 to $2.00 per head during the grazing season, which averages about six and a half months in the year. As soon as the stock is brought in from the range, buyers are usually on hand, and even sometimes while the stock is on the range, and they buy the two, three and four year old steers and many of the cows, most of which are in prime condition, and many fat enough for the butcher. The buyers then ship them to distant markets.

The grazing privileges on these mountain lands when held by non-resident owners is merely nominal. I am interested in the ownership of a large tract of timber land in one of the western counties of North Carolina, which is also a fine grazing tract, for the wild pea vine grows in abundance, and for several years we have leased the land for grazing privileges upon the payment of the taxes upon the land, which is relatively a small sum. Adjoining our land is a tract which is known as the "winter range," where the grass grows thickly under the dense balsam timber, and here is natural food and shelter for stock throughout the winter, at an altitude of more than a mile above sea level.

One reason for the grass growing spontaneously in the higher altitudes, and thriving so well, where the soil and exposure conditions are favorable, can no doubt be found in the humid condition of the atmosphere. The air is nearly always moist, and during the summer season the mountains, and especially towards their crests, are visited by frequent showers.

One may witness from the valleys below almost any day in summer upon the summits of the higher mountains a storm cloud or mist passing over or resting upon them. The reasons for this appear obvious. During the higher temperature of the valleys or on the lower elevation, the heated air rising strikes the cooler stratum of air above, which induces motion or movement often tending toward the direction of the mountains, and hence either condensation and precipitation or fog ensues, and the mountains get a full share. Of course at present we may look upon this vast grazing area to a great extent as being in a primeval condition, and I have treated the subject as such. But I think that I have indicated sufficiently that there is a basis for a great future grazing industry for those who shall subdue the wilder aspects of nature and bring this wonderfully interesting field into subjection and into the hands of the scientific and progressive stock-grower.

What I have said about stock has had reference to cattle. A volume might be written about the Southern Alleghany Mountain region as being adapted for sheep-raising. Few sections of our country surpass it in that respect. Possibly the ridge lands and the lower mountain ranges may be as well adapted for sheep-raising as the higher mountains on account of less humidity of the atmosphere, but I have seen as fine sheep on altitudes of 4000 feet or more above sea level as I have seen in the valleys. Probably nowhere do sheep reach a higher order of development, and people eat as good mutton as in England, where the climate is excessively moist. Here the fault of not raising more sheep is not lack of natural conditions, but the unwise laws that allow dogs, the enemies of sheep, greater privileges than the citizen.

I have given some of the essential features of the adaptability of the South as a stock-raising country. I do not mean the South as a whole, but that portion of the more elevated region embraced within the Southern Alleghany mountain system and some adjacent territory.

It is a lamentable fact that the South buys too much of that which she consumes from markets outside of her own territory, much of which—if not the greater portion—could be produced at home were the proper efforts put forth in that direction. And so long as this condition continues the South will be that much poorer in consequence. It is a very important question from an economic standpoint to every community, State or nation, when they send away their money to purchase commodities from foreign ports or countries that ought to remain at home. Within the last few months the question of the "balance of trade" being against us in our commercial relations with foreign countries has shown itself in an emphasized manner to the American people during these trying financial times. And the nation is simply the representative of aggregated communities.

In talking with the steward of a large hotel in one of our Southern cities a short time since, I asked him where he bought the butter used in the hotel. He replied: "Oh, I buy Elgin creamery butter. I can't depend upon the quality that I get in our home markets. Sometimes I get very good butter, while at other times it is not fit to eat. There is no uniformity about it, and to be sure of what I am going to get I buy the Northern Elgin creamery butter, and then know that what I get will give satisfaction."

Now this is but an illustration of a condition which is a humiliating fact, that applies not only to the city referred to, but the larger portion of the South, in respect to poor home-made butter. It is all the more inexcusable when we consider the natural advantages, many of them excellent, for making good butter, which a considerable portion of the South possesses. These advantages are good pasturage, an abundance of pure cold water, the lengthened season during which the cows may feed upon open pasturage, and other points of minor importance.

Butter-making is a science, and it is only the few in a community where butter is made for family use or for the market who appear to understand the science involved in it, unless taught by those who are familiar with good butter-making.

Even then, unless working under favorable conditions, the results may not always be satisfactory. Poor butter may be said to be the rule rather than the exception throughout almost the entire butter-making districts of the South. The chief trouble seems to be that it is not worked enough; too much buttermilk remaining, the butter soon becomes strong or rancid. Some of it is soft and mushy as warm lard, and is better suited for axle grease than for the table. As some one has expressed it, "they fail to put enough elbow grease into their butter." Some of the butter that comes to market shows attempts towards results artistic rather than scientific, in the manner displayed in impressions made upon the light-weight pound rolls or lumps from the working ladle. But an artistically indented or adorned roll of butter adds nothing to the quality, which is the prime essential.

It is not my purpose to enter into a discussion of the science of butter-making, but to say something of the opportunities afforded in the region referred to in the beginning of this paper, to those who may want to engage in a profitable industry in this neglected field. Probably nine-tenths of the farms in the section mentioned where grass grows, or can be made to grow abundantly and profitably with proper efforts in the right direction, have either cold spring water or clear running streams, admirably suited for dairying purposes.

Indeed, few countries surpass, if they equal, this region in that respect, so that the average farmer may be able to make good butter if he will give it the attention which it demands. This not only applies to the valleys, but even to the more elevated regions of our highest mountains.

With better roads and easier communication, so that milk can be concentrated at convenient points in the well-settled d stricts, in time no doubt creameries will be established in a great many places throughout the region. But at present, and until then, there are ample opportunities for many farmers to make good butter, which will at all times command steady and good paying prices throughout the year.

An erroneous impression prevails to a great extent throughout the farming sections that butter-making for the market is "a small business." It is in a certain sense, and because they make it so. It can be made of vastly more importance than they seem to realize. It is one of the most honorable branches of agricultural industry, and equally as profitable where the natural conditions are favorable and proper attention given to it. I see no reason why it is not equally as honorable employment, and as conducive to intellectual stimulus and enjoyment, as that of raising hogs, mules, corn and cotton. Where will one find in an agricultural community a more thrifty, intelligent, well-dressed, orderly people than where dairying is the chief industry? Where will one find better schools, more church buildings, better citizens, and where do the people live better and enjoy themselves more in any rural community than the dairy people? The weight of the argument is in favor of this industry instead of against it.

I could point out a number of instances to show that this dairying industry will pay well in the region referred to, but one will suffice to illustrate what I want to say upon that point. About ten years ago two unmarried brothers owned a farm with some wood land—limestone land—which they had brought under a fair state of cultivation by clover fertilization. It was good grass land, and a large spring of cold

water near the house was a prominent feature of the place. Here the original forest trees were allowed to remain about the spring, and in time a commodious stone structure, or "spring-house," was built. The brothers found that the milk and butter always kept cool in this spring-house, and they soon found that their butter was in demand. They increased the capacity of their dairy, but the demand kept ahead of the supply. They were intelligent men and studied the science of butter-making, and before long found a market for all they could make, and at fancy prices, too, with one firm in a city 300 miles away, to whom they shipped their product every day, though living six miles from the railroad.

Now the interesting part is to learn the result. Today these men are engaged in the dairying business more extensively than ever. Their butter is in greater demand, if possible. They have others to do the most of the work, while they are among the most highly respected citizens of their county. They entertain royally, have added greatly to their former holdings in land, are out of debt and have money in bank and income-bearing securities, and are in independent circumstances. Some of their neighbors who raised corn and wheat and hogs as selling products used to sneer at these two brothers who were engaged in "a mighty small business," but the tables are turned, for the dairymen own embellishments on several of their neighbors' farms in the shape of good-sized mortgages. I have often thought, as I enjoyed the hospitality of these men, what a lesson they should teach others in their own community, for the natural conditions for dairying in their case were no better than others in their section, and there are thousands of places equally as well adapted for dairying purposes by reason of natural advantages as that owned by these more enterprising men. But the majority of agriculturalists prefer to follow in the old beaten paths and ruts of their forefathers rather than to follow the advanced methods such as may be seen in all other industries.

There is a wide and profitable field for the dairyman in the South. The market for good butter and cheese is far beyond the available supply. The health resorts and summer resorts, such as Asheville, N. C., and many others, are increasing in number and in patronage every year, and these demand the very best article of butter that can be obtained, and for a prime article will pay a good price.

The population of the cities and towns throughout the South will increase, and they will consume large quantities of butter and cheese if they can get a good article. The nearest point from which the South Atlantic and Gulf coast, as well as much of the interior region, can draw its dairy supplies is, or should be, the region to which I referred in the beginning of this paper. With the development of the vast mineral and timber wealth of the South in the near future there will come new population, new activities and new industries, which will demand increased dairy supplies, and it is none too early to begin now to meet the future demands, even if there were no present demand.

THE SOUTHERN OUTLOOK.

An Unparalleled Opportunity for the South.

Disasters that are entirely without compensating features are rare. Every calamity that befalls mankind carries with it some element of advantage. Thus the present business depression and distress in the West present to the South an o'portunity for self advancement such as has never been presented before. We read daily of the thousands of unemployed, the losses of business men, the distress and dissatisfaction of the farmers, the idleness of the mechanics, in the West. Our first thought is one of sympathy and pity ; our second should be of the relief that these thousands could find in the South. In this situation lies the great opportunity for the South to help the unfortunate and at the same time benefit beyond measure every interest in the South. There has been an infinite amount of talk, argument and theory about getting desirable immigrants for the South. There is now an opportunity to accomplish this result in a simple and certain manner.

We are not advancing a theory, but stating facts that can be substantiated when we say that a little expenditure of money and well directed effort at this time will start a movement Southward from the afflicted portions of the West which will give to the South thousands of settlers of the classes most desired. There are thousands of farmers in Iowa, Illinois, Kansas, Nebraska and other Western States who are dissatisfied with their lot, with the climate, with crops and prospects. They are ready to go anywhere, if prospects of better conditions be offered. They own their farms or have sufficient money interest in them to give them a small amount of capital upon the disposition of their property in the West, and they can go to the South with money, energy and skill. They are ready and willing to take any steps that promise to better their conditions, and any section of the coun-

try that can secure these people will have a most valuable addition to its population and industry.

Here, then, is the tremendous opportunity of the South, a chance for practical work that will be more productive of results than a perpetual convention of Southern governors in Richmond. If the people of the South are in earnest in their desire to increase the population of their section by immigration of the most desirable character, here is a chance to fulfill their wishes. The stimulation of foreign immigration Southward is a big undertaking, requiring time, money, work, and the co-operation of several important forces, but the West offers an opportunity for securing immediate results by the expenditure of a minimun of energy and cash.

As regards the practical features of the situation, we have only this suggestion to make : Tell the people of the West what the South offers them—cheap lands that will raise a wide range of crops, a delightful climate that is unsurpassed by any section on this continent, and a ready market for all that is produced. Tell the Western people these facts in specific terms, not mere generalities, but definite information about what is now being done in the South by the Northern and Western people who have migrated thither. There have been books and books about the resources of the South and statistics beyond measure, but what the people of the West now want to know is what fruit lands are for sale in Georgia, at what price, and what they will yield in dollars and cents under average cond tions. They want to know what opportunity there is for planting rice in Louisiana and everything about it that is needful for a beginner to know. They want to know what an orange grove in Florida will cost, and what its crop is worth to the grower. They want to know where in the South cattle can be raised to best advantage, what the pasturage costs and what the cattle will bring. In short the people of the

West, who now are dissatisfied with their lot, want accurate, specific detailed information about Southern opportunities, down to the exact price and location of lands now for sale.

Put these facts into the hands of the Western farmers and mechanics by advertisement in Western papers, by carefully prepared phamphlets, by personal missionary work in the West if possible, by correspondence with every one in the West whose name and address can be ascertained. Fill the papers and magazines of the South with such facts as we have suggested and scatter them by millions in the West. Get the co-operation of the railroads in this work, and secure reduced rates for prospective settlers. Pay the expenses of a trainload of Western people for an excursion through the South, and the cost will be repaid a hundredfold. Do all of this and as much more as the united ingenuity of the best Southern minds can suggest, for this is an opportunity not to be neglected or wasted. It is the opportunity of a century, and if used wisely and fully it will benefit the South to a degree beyond imagination. But it is necessary to act now, not next month or in the winter.

The solution of the immigration problem is in the hands of the people of the South. If they realize the situation and act at once they can accomplish stupendous results.

Notes on Southern Progress.

The farmers of Georgia—and we may say of the whole South—are in a better condition today than they have been since the war. That is the testimony of all who have investigated the matter. We have it from the representative farmers themselves. They made good crops last year ; they have corn in their cribs and meat in their smoke-houses, and they have the promise of good crops ahead of them. They have been economizing in all directions ; they have been learning to live at home, and the financial stringency that is seriously affecting the people of other sections has no effect on them. "Hard times at the North?" said an old farmer the other day. "Well, them that give will have to learn how to take, I reckon. I've been havin' hard times at my house ever sence the war, inabout." An illustration is always better than a dry argument. The same farmer told with a chuckle of a little trade he had just made. He had an old sow which, after producing several profitable litters of pigs, fell int the habit of eating chickens. So she was fattened and killed and put through the process that sweetens home-made meat. The old farmer brought one of her sides to town—"middlin'," he called it—sold it for a barrel of flour and had forty cents to boot. He said he could turn that old sow into enough flour to enable him to have biscuit every day in the year. Naturally, there are no hard times at this farmer's house, for he lives within his means and has a little money over, and "the old woman," as he calls her, has nearly three hundred young chickens running loose in the barley stubble. Now, it stands to reason that a financial stringency which breaks banks in the West and closes mills in the East can have little effect on this man. He has as much ready money now as he had during the past twenty years, and not so much use for it. He is raising his own supplies, and if cotton goes down below the profit point he can afford

to hold it. Now, the condition of this farmer represents that of the great majority of farmers in the South, and, with such modifications as will suggest themselves to the intelligent reader, it represents the business situation here, where there are no bubbles to collapse and no speculative ventures to go to pieces. The business of the South is all on legitimate basis, and is in fine shape to face the contingency which has been forced upon it by the contraction necessary to place our financial system on a gold basis. Patriotism, patience and courage have made the South solid politically, and wisdom, prudence and economy have made it solid financially.—*Atlanta Constitution.*

It is estimated that the Georgia melon crop this year amounts to nearly $250,000 for the farmers and $100 000 for the railroads. About 8000 carloads have been shipped, bringing from $40.00 to $120 per car, the latter price holding at the beginning of the season.

The movement to secure the attendance of colored people at the Columbian Exposition promises to be successful. It is stated that the Pennsylvania Company has made arrangements, in conjunction with the Louisville & Nashville, to carry many colored people from Tennessee and Kentucky. The World's Fair committee of colored men which has been working up the scheme for some time, has completed the arrangements, and the first excursion from Nashville will be given August 21. About 10,000 persons have already been secured. Very low rates are to be given, and the crowds are to be gathered in Nashville, Lexington, Louisville, Bowling Green and other places.

A big coal contract was closed at Birmingham, Ala., July 28, by General Manager J. R. Ryan, of the Virginia & Alabama Coal Co. Mr. Ryan contracted for his company to furnish the Louisville, New Orleans & Texas Railroad with all the coal that line will consume for a year south from Elizabeth, Miss., amounting to nearly 100,000 tons, except a small amount which the Tennessee Coal, Iron & Railroad Co. sells that road for their Vicksburg bin. The coal will be delivered from the Coal Valley mines over the Georgia Pacific Railroad. The Virginia & Alabama Coal Co. have recently opened three new mines at Coal Valley, near Day's Gap, and it is from there that the Louisville, New Orleans & Texas Railroad will draw its supply of coal. Every mine of the Virginia & Alabama Coal Co. is running on full time, with a total output of 1500 tons daily.

THE city attorney of New Orleans has given an opinion that the ordinance to construct a sewerage system in the city, adopted during Mayor Shakspeare's term of office, is legal and should be carried out by the present city council.

HERE is a good view of the business situation in he South as seen by Capt. N. Weeks, president of the American National Bank, Galveston, Texas : "Failures in the South are comparatively light. This is owing much to the fact that the 'boom' fever did not prevail he e to the extent and in such a malignant type as in some other localities. Texas is especially well off. Owing to good crops and economy of her people collections have never been better from the country. What she owes will soon be paid off. Her cattle are already moving northward and her cotton will soon be coming to market. By early fall she will be free from debt, feel nothing of this stringency and be richer by far than ever before."

AN appeal has been sent to the Chicago roads from the Texas Immigration Association for weekly excursions to Texas from Chicago during the World's Fair period, for which a one-fare rate for the round trip should be made. A similar appeal was made last spring, but the Chicago roads then declined, because they said the brokers would use the low rate tickets to demoralize the market. They advised the Texas people to pass the anti-scalper law. They have passed the law, and again ask for the rate.

A TRIAL was made on July 25 of the machinery of the water works at Atlanta, Ga. Everything worked satisfactorily, and so soon as some of the smaller details of the plant are

completed it will be handed over to the city. This is one of the largest as well as most complete water works in the South. The pumping engines have a capacity of 10,000,000 gallons per day.

THE Atlantic & North Carolina Railroad is an example of what skillful and economical management will do for a railway. It has been in operation thirty-five years, but did not begin dividend payments until 1892, when $36,000 was disbursed to st ckholders. This year $36,000 more, or 2 per cent. of its capital, will be paid and about $20,000 left in the treasury as a surplus. The road is ninety-five miles long and is practically owned by the State of North Carolina, which holds a majority of the stock. Besides earning dividends and surplus, the road has earned enough to pay for extensive improvements to stations and additions to its rolling stock.

AN immense amount of moss is being shipped from Gainesville, Fla., to Eastern and Western points. The Spanish moss industry, already large, steadily increases. It is used for mattress filling.

A NUMBER of carloads of Florida pineapples have been shipped to Chicago this season, where they met with a ready sale at good prices.

WORK was commenced in New Orleans last week on the new elevator which the Illinois Central Railway is to construct in the Poydras-street yards. The elevator is constructed solely for the purpose of domestic trade. It will have a capacity of 250,000 bushels of grain, and will be constructed with all modern facilities for handling this product. Sufficient tracks will be built to the elevator as will render the greatest facility for handling grain. It is thought that the building of this elevator will create a better grain traffic, and prove a mutual benefit to local dealers and to the railroad.

THERE is more building going on in Milledgeville, Ga., at present than at any time since the war, and the demand for houses is unprecedented. Three blocks near the Central depot have been leveled off and over twenty houses erected thereon. Eight very handsome residences are now building on one block and four on the block adjoining.

THE improvements in the harbor of Charleston, S. C., are beginning to show a marked increase in the depth of wa'er in the channel. Important progress has been made in the work on the jetties, and in the Swash channel on July 7 the depth of water at low tide at the entrance was 15.9 feet, and at the inner shallow spot 15.7 feet. Add to this five feet of water caused by the rise of tide, and it figures up 20.9 at one point and 20.7 at the other. With a strong east wind, which is often blowing on the bar, the tide rises at least a foot higher, making the water 21.9 feet and 21.7 feet, respectively. The dredges are working at the mouth of the channel, and are excavating 2000 cubic yards of sand daily.

THE Northwestern Louisiana Land & Immigration Co. has been organized at Benton, La., with W. J. Hughes as president, and J. W. Martin as secretary. The stock is placed at $100,000, business to begin when $10,000 is subscribed. The company will at once engage in active work to develop Bossier parish, and has options on and control of an extensive body of land, to which it is proposed to induce immigration. An active agent will at once be sent to the Northwest for this purpose.

GOVERNOR LEWELLYN, of Kansas, has announced that he will appoint a commission to go to Chicago for the purpose of opening negotiations through the representatives at the World's Fair with the governments of Europe concerning the exchange of commodities with Kansas by way of the Gulf of Mexico. The governor says it has been proved that the railroads can carry freight from Kansas to Galveston, Texas, at a rate which would enable steamships from gulf ports to compete with lines from the Atlantic seaboard. The governor believes that by interesting foreign shippers in the project, the railroads which have gulf connections will abandon their pool relations with Eastern roads and put down rates so as to establish a permanent European carrying trade.

IMPROVEMENTS of a most important character in the harbor of Savannah, Ga., are about to be commenced. Work on the Marsh Island jetty has been begun by the United States engineer department under contract with the Atlantic Contracting Co. This jetty will extend from the lower end of Marsh Island to Kimzery's Point about opposite the beginning of Jefferson street, a distance approximating 9000 feet. From now on the work of construc-

tion will be pushed vigorously, and the jetty will be completed about September 1, when the work of dredging will begin, and the channel then obtained will hold and be a permanent one, affording relief and proving a great benefit to the Ocean Steamship Co., the Commercial Guano Co., the Vale Royal Manufacturing Co., the Southern Cotton Oil Co., the Southeastern Plaster Co., A. S. Bacon & Sons, Stillwell, Millen & Co. and many other corporations, firms and individuals.

THE Southern League of Building and Loan Associations, representing over $11,000,-000 of paid-in stock, held its annual session in Knoxville, Tenn., on July 19 and 20. Lookout Inn, on Lookout Mountain, was selected as the next place of meeting. The following officers for the ensuing year were elected : President, John Hanson Kennard, New Orleans ; first vice-president, Hon. J. T. Ellyson, Richmond ; second vice-president, Col. W. P. Washburn, Knoxville ; third vice-president, H. L. Atwater, Atlanta ; secretary and treasurer, B. M. Robinson, Bristol ; executive committee, John Hanson Kennard, New Orleans ; B. M. Robinson, Bristol ; W. H. Raymond, Nashville ; James B. Walker, Augusta ; C. E. Beach, Columbus ; Henry J. Lynn, Memphis ; J. P. Heap, Knoxville ; Malcolm Johnson, Atlanta ; Lawrence Cooper, Huntsville ; William G. Pascall, Atlanta ; Tracy Underhill, Louisville, and John Ott, Roanoke.

LYNCHBURG, VA., is enjoying a building "boom" of unusual size. Some of the structures now under way are four large stores with apartments for offices above, a hotel, a large brick warehouse, and a college building, which will be one of the finest in the South.

THE vineyards in the vicinity of Southern Pines, N. C., are reported to be in excellent condition and promise a large yield of grapes. Some of the vineyards near Raleigh N. C., have been badly effected by rot and mildew. The vines sprayed with paris green are in excellent condition.

A WORLD'S FAIR excursion party of one hundred or more will leave Augusta, Ga., Tuesday, August 15, to secure exhibits at Chicago for the Augusta Exposition and Georgia State Fair, which opens at Augusta October 17 and closes November 16.

CANAL STREET, NEW ORLEANS.

THE

SOUTHERN STATES.

SEPTEMBER, 1893.

COTTON INTERESTS OF NEW ORLEANS AND LOUISIANA.

By Henry G. Hester,

Secretary New Orleans Cotton Exchange.

The interests of New Orleans and Louisiana are so closely interwoven that to speak of one is practically to include both. While this is more or less the case with all large cities in their relations toward the commonwealths in which they are situated, the merging of interests between city and State is perhaps here more strongly emphasized than is usual. Of the total assessed values for the State, between fifty-five and sixty per cent. are within the city limits. The city not only controls the bulk of Louisiana's marketable products, but by reason of geographical position, and the energy of her merchants, handles and ships a considerable percentage of the cotton produced in a much larger section of the cotton belt. Hence, while Louisiana contributes an important share of the annual cotton crop of the South, we are accustomed to regard it generally in the light of a part only of the production of the New Orleans section, all of which pays more or less tribute to both city and State. This will be made more apparent by a glance at the following:

Year.	Cotton Crop. State of Louisiana. Bales.	Cotton Receipts. City of New Orleans. Bales.
1891-92..............	740,000	2,713,000
1890-91..............	625,000	2,270,000
1889-90, (census)....	659,000	2,148,000

Considering the State apart from connection with New Orlean's interests, while cotton is its most important crop, its influence is not altogether paramount; in other words, Louisiana is by no means an exclusive cotton grower, other staple products dividing with cotton the attention of her agriculturalists.

This has been most fortunate during the past two years of extreme depression in cotton, although there is no State in the South which affords better returns to the cotton grower. It is true, the past season's experience does not altogether justify this last assertion, but it must be remembered that 1892-93 will be regarded in the annals of cotton crops as synonymous with disaster to the fleecy staple, just as 1891-92 (the season preceding) will be considered the standard of perfection. What with floods in the great river and tributaries, covering vast tracts of the most fertile lands in the world, and weather conditions to the last degree unfavorable, Louisiana has suffered severely during the season now closing, in common with the entire lower Mississippi Valley. In fact, of the total decrease in this year's cotton crop, which will not amount to less than two and a half millions of bales, about fifty per cent. will fall on Mississippi, Louisiana, Arkansas, Texas and Alabama—all heavy shippers to and via

New Orleans. Louisiana alone will lose not less than 250,000 bales.

Taking, then, the year 1891-92, with its high conditions everywhere as a fairer criterion, Louisiana produced a crop of 740,000 bales out of a total of 9,035,000 for the United States. If we are to accept the United States Agricultural Department's figures revised to accord with the last census, this amount of cotton was grown on 1,158,000 acres, or say an average for the entire State of about sixty-four one-hundredths of a bale to the acre. Careful investigators consider that the government is at least 125,000 acres under the actual facts for 1891-92, but, even if this be the case, the average product would be fifty-seven one-hundredths of a bale, equal to 268 pounds of lint per acre. This would place Louisiana for the "bumper" year about the same as Texas and Indian Territory, twenty-two pounds per acre ahead of Arkansas and fifty-six ahead of Mississippi.

Compared with above, an average of 151 pounds per acre for Georgia, 160 to 164 for the Carolinas, and 172 for Alabama, the exceeding richness of the soil of the Pelican State as a cotton grower is strikingly illustrated. From a bale to a bale and a-half per acre is not uncommon; in parts of some parishes even two bales per acre have been reached, and results are obtained in other products as well as cotton, which justify the claim that Louisiana embraces the garden spot of the world, the fertility of her soil rivalling the far-famed valley of the Nile, a climate of sunshine and bloom with a temperature averaging 50° in the winter and 80° in the summer; long seasons and late frosts, affording the highest results with the least expenditure of capital or labor. No section of the United States holds out stronger inducements to the home-seeker. That the State does not rank higher as a cotton producer (that is, in total number of bales grown) is, as already stated, due mainly to division of agricultural industries, cotton, sugar and molasses and rice standing towards each other as follows:

APPROXIMATE VALUE OF LOUISIANA CROPS—1891-'92.

Cotton	$26,000,000
Sugar and molasses	15,000,000
Rice	3,000,000
Total	**$44,000,000**
Percentage, cotton	59
" others	41

It is true that much of the lands devoted to sugar and rice are better adapted to them than to cotton, but the State contains a vast area above and beyond overflow that may be converted into the finest cotton fields in the world, a result only retarded by lack of labor.

An important fact regarding Louisiana cotton production is the general superiority of staple, which gives it a value in proportion to length of fibre above cotton grown on uplands; and it has been found that careful selection of seeds from special plants has enabled planters to greatly improve even on the excellent bend staple, which has for many years held so favorable a name among cotton consumers.

It is proper to remark, however, that the premium for extra staple in American cotton has not been so remunerative within the last two years, the introduction of foreign long staples, principally Egyptian, having proven a serious drawback. Producers of these descriptions in a number of States complain bitterly of the difference, and it is likely if the situation is not speedily improved they will apply to Congress for relief.

As a rule the cotton grower inclines strongly to free trade, his interests being to sell in the dearest markets of the world and buy in the cheapest, both of which have been more or less interfered with by tariff legislation. But whatever his views, he has not complained vigorously hertofore against a tariff that forced him to buy his manufactured cotton goods from American mills at high prices. Now, however, growers of long staples are asking why the same measure of protection given home mills against foreign manufactures should not be accorded to them against foreign cotton growers. An address recently circulated freely among producers, claims that "the importation of Egyptian and Peruvian cotton not only affects the Sea Island of the Atlantic seaboard, which aggregates sixty to seventy thousand bales per annum, but has disastrously influenced values of all of four hundred thousand bales of good to extra staple cotton produced in the Mississippi valley. Mills that purchased thousands of bales of our benders and better staple cotton a few years since only buy a few hundred, and that at a small difference from the common run of staple. As the tariff has enhanced the price of every yard of goods we consume considerably over one-half, so has the free admission of foreign long staple cotton cut us down for those descriptions to prices that are ruinous. We do not wish to argue from the standpoint of free trade or protection. All we ask is to be placed on a level, as cotton growers, with the people who buy our cotton. If we are forced to trade with them, let them be forced to trade with us. If, on the other hand, the restrictions are removed and our markets are thrown open to the world, we are willing to take our chances, but have a right to insist that, until this is done, we should be placed on an equal footing, as an agricultural people, with the manufacturers of the East."

Much can be said of the superiority of Egyptian cotton for certain purposes by reason of its "smoothness, brilliancy of color, lustre and the silky nature of its staple;" but it is claimed that it is used in competition with American where the latter could be made to serve were it not a matter of price. Whatever may be the true state of the case, it is certain that apart from influences that have affected the cotton market as a whole, long staples have suffered, sharing in every depression, but experiencing little or no improvement in premiums over ordinary staples in periods of reaction.

The alleged superiority in ginning, baling and handling Egyptian it is said cannot be entirely accepted as the cause of its successful competition with American, although there is so much room for improvement on our part, the real fact being that we cannot compete with foreign pauper labor. This, of course, refers to extra staples and does not involve an acknowledgment of the South's inability to compete with the world in the production of cotton of a fair staple, body and color, necessary to supply the general demand.

There is undoubtedly much room for improvement in the cultivation, preparation and transportation of the fleecy staple which necessity will force in the future, all tending towards lessening cost of producing and marketing, and eventually confirming to American growers practical monopoly. Not the least of these will be the opening up of large belts of rich lands such as are embraced in Louisiana and adjacent States, where under proper care profits may be made not obtainable in less productive sections of the cotton belt.

While the trade of New Orleans has suffered greatly during the past year by reason of disaster to the cotton crop, the extent of the decrease has been officially overstated. This has been occasioned by erroneous over-valuation of cotton exports by the Bureau of Statistics of the Treasury Department for 1891-92, to the extent of about eighteen millions of dollars. How far similar errors were made in other customs districts, serving to create a false impression of the comparative trade balances of this and last season, it is not the purpose here to demonstrate, but it is a fact that cotton valuations furnished by collectors of other ports to the Treasury Department were in many cases absurdly high.

The Bureau's published figures for New Orleans made the average value of cotton exported for the year 1891-92 forty-six dollars per bale, or more than nine and one-quarter cents per pound, and that in a season witnessing the greatest depression known to the trade for forty years. The fault lies in the incorrectness of collectors returns, but if the treasury officials were cognizant of this the question is whether it would not have been best to have revised their published data for 1891-92 instead of perpetuating the errors. The treasury's methods of collecting this information, so far as relates to cotton, have been improved during the fiscal year just ended, (June 30th, 1893,) and this season's figures accord closely with facts. In a period like the present, however, when the reports for both years together are scanned closely to afford an index to the causes of the financial situation, the deductions are misleading. If, as is true, the methods in official valuation of export cotton up to June, 1892, were so loose, how far may the same system have been applied to other articles?

The cotton merchants of New Orleans have perhaps the most complete and perfect system for protection of cotton of any port in the world. Under the auspices of the Cotton Exchange, a thoroughly organized force of competent officials is engaged to watch and protect bales from the time of arrival, until they are placed in the hold of the outgoing ocean vessel. At each depot and press, or warehouse, men are stationed, whose duty it is to prevent waste or over-sampling; to see that all loose unavoidably made is gathered and stored, to be turned over to the receiver, and to report, when necessary, on condition and any other facts that may aid in preventing loss from careless handling or otherwise. Similar officials are stationed on the steamboat and ship landings to guard against petty pilfering, and daily reports are made and filed in the Cotton Exchange of the receipts on board every vessel during loading, with condition thereof, statement of weather and any matters that may affect the cargoes. These officials, under a competent chief and an assistant chief, are in the employ of the exchange. In addition to these, a force of picked men, answerable to the exchange, is engaged in the duties of night watching aboard vessels and on wharves. The result is that the fullest returns are made to growers shipping to New Orleans and complaints are seldom made of cotton shipped abroad from that port, unless it be of transit cotton beyond the control of the exchange officials.

The large spot business of New Orleans gives to that city special facilities for the purchase and sale of cotton for future delivery. As a natural cotton market, there is generally a sufficient stock on hand throughout the year to protect all contracts, obviating heavy outlays of capital for carrying cotton for speculative purposes. This modern method of hedging and insuring valuations, facilitating rapid economical handling of merchandise, is so interwoven with the world's trade, that no large centre can conduct business without it; and while the bulk of the contract purchases and sales are made in the great markets of New Orleans, New York and Liverpool, they include business for all other cotton centers with which they are directly connected by telegraph.

In spots, and cotton to arrive, New Orleans is the leading market on this continent, while the business in "future deliveries" which is steadily growing, has assumed an importance that divides the palm with Liverpool and New York. The cotton crop of the State is susceptible of great increase, which doubtless will result in time, through immigration, and the latter is likely to follow upon proper dissemination of knowledge of the State's remarkable fertility.

HARVEST SCENE IN A LOUISIANA RICE FIELD.

RICE GROWING IN LOUISIANA.

By Reginald Dykers.

On the broad prairies of Southwest Louisiana a great industry is being built up—an industry of ancient lineage and considerable renown. The strides it has made since its inception in that locality have been broad and rapid. It has brought together a population that is at once energetic, intelligent and progressive, such a population as Louisiana needs in her every section to develop her resources and bring her to that high place among her sister States that is hers by right.

Rice—pure, spotless, palatable, nourishing—should need but little beyond its own merits to make it the most popular form of grain in the United States today. As an article of food it is equal if not superior to wheat, and while it would perhaps be impracticable to substitute it entirely therefor, yet as an adjunct to our daily wheaten loaf what could be more desirable than one of those rare snowy pyramids of rice that our Creole kitchens know how to turn out in such a state of marvellous purity and toothsomeness.

The Burmese say that at the beginning of the world God made elephants and birds and fire and water and rice. This simple tradition shows what an important article it was to them. A Hindoo boy is fed on rice for six months after his birth as a process of purification, and then he is generally fed on it all the rest of his life because it is the handiest thing to eat. Even after he has trudged his way through the world and gone over the river to rest under the shade of the trees, his family prepares a "pinda" or ball of rice and offers it with many prayers and quaint fantastic rites to his departed spirit.

That the rice plant is of Indian origin there can be no doubt, and in the Shoo-King, or Chinese classics, the cultivation of it is mentioned as having taken place as early as 2356 B. C. It seems to have been introduced into Europe by the Moors in the Eleventh Century, and in

Georgia and Carolina its cultivation began about the year 1700. Its introduction into Louisiana is of very recent date, no rice having been produced there for purposes of sale until after the war, and there could be no stronger evidence of the success that has attended its culture on the prairies of Calcasieu than the fact that Louisiana today produces more rice than Georgia and Carolina, the crop for this year amounting to 7,500,000 bushels. On these broad, fertile lands, innocent of windy booms, untrammelled by the visionary lines of mythical corner lots, undisfigured by those blatant real estate sign boards that have sprung up all over the West, the hand of industry has wrought wonders. Where in 1880 there was only a sparse settlement, a lumber camp, perhaps, or a lone settler's cabin, there are today busy towns, a host of whirring saw-mills and—fairly miles of rice.

The population is composed largely of immigrants from Iowa, Illinois and other Western States, men who have come into Louisiana because they saw the advantages and the wealth that awaited them. With the latest and most improved machinery they have started in to make the southwestern part of the State a garden in which golden flowers shall grow. Steam plows, traction engines, pumps, windmills, all the busy panoply that one may see amid the wheat fields of Illinois, are puffing and whirring away beneath the soft blue sky of Dixie. During the last year more agricultural implements were shipped to Crowley, a little town in the centre of the rice-producing district, than to any other place in the State except New Orleans. Between seven and eight million dollars' worth of rice are shipped from Crowley every year and the amount is steadily on the increase.

One great advantage possessed by the Southwestern Louisiana soil is its capability of sustaining the weight of the various machines for tilling the soil and harvesting the crop, which the ground of Georgia and Carolina is too soft to bear. Clay predominates, with a subsoil of great hardness and consistency. The general character of the land is somewhat similar to the great

areas devoted to the cultivation of various kinds of grain in the Northwest. The surface undulations, however, are less marked, and the general aspect is one of more complete flatness. In their primitive state every depression formed a pond of slight depth, wherein vegetation of all kinds accumulated and decayed, making a deposit of great richness and fertility. Such a surface arrangement as this, where the water was held in natural reservoirs, would seem to be an ideal formation for purposes of rice culture, as the gully could be closed at some convenient point and the water allowed to run from one depression to another as suited the wishes of the rice planter.

One great drawback to such an arrangement, however, was found to be the superabundance of water which would at times accumulate in the basin, sufficient in its volume to break any ordinary levee erected to hold it in check. This danger is obviated, however, by an improved system of ditches and embankments consisting of a large ditch dug through the centre of the basin, with a strong gate at both ends, so that should any excess of water be present it can be safely and rapidly passed off, and prevented from overflowing the adjacent fields. Levees are also constructed on the outer edges of the field and the water conducted past them and stored for use when required. The great central drain has gates opening from it into each field, and there are also openings in the outer levee so that water can be let in at any time when it is desired and yet kept away from other fields where it is not wanted. The separation of different sections of the plantation by cross levees, thus cutting it up into plots of convenient size, is very necessary, especially at harvest time.

In order that some idea may be obtained of the enormous amount of ditching and leveeing required on a rice plantation it may be stated that Col. Screven, of Savannah, Ga., one of the best informed rice men in the United States, in his testimony before the Ways and Means Committee at Washington in 1890, calculated that a well equipped place containing 640 acres would have drains and embankments footing up to 115 miles. To make all these levees and ditches would be too great a task for the spade, and a ditching machine, consisting of a huge plow-like arrangement drawn with a capstan, is used. These machines cut a ditch two feet deep and three feet wide, and throw the dirt out to form the levee, which is completed and put into proper shape by a man who follows with a spade. Three men can thus make levees containing six or eight hundred cubic feet of earth in a day, and at an expense of about two cents for each yard of work. Everything is done systematically, and with an eye to reducing expenditure in every possible way.

To attain the best results rice should be planted towards the end of March, or in the early part of April, as earlier planting sometimes rots in the ground or is stunted by cold weather, and later planting as a rule does not yield so well. Climatic conditions, however, maintain a certain margin around every rule of this kind. The preparation of the soil before the seed is put in is a matter of great importance. Mr. R. S. Stoddard of Welsh, La., one of the most intelligent and progressive rice planters in the State, says in a recent

letter to the writer that to this imperfect preparation of the soil is due a vast amount of loss manifested by undergrowth, uneven ripening, and failure to come up through the ground. The soil should be thoroughly pulverized after ploughing, and the additional work will be amply repaid by the increased output.

The sowing in Southwest Louisiana is mostly accomplished by machinery of various makes, drills and broadcast seeders being both in extensive use. The White Honduras rice is the variety most commonly used, although the Carolina rice is very popular in some sections of the State. On rich soil between one and two bushels are generally planted to the acre, some planters differing from others in their opinions about the amount necessary to obtain the best results. The prevailing tendency now, however, is toward heavy sowing, and to endeavor to procure a good stand by planting more seed, instead of planting sparingly and expecting the rice to stool sufficiently to make a good stand. Conditions of weather and soil are not always favorable to this stooling process.

The time that elapses after the rice has been planted until it makes its appearance above ground depends

FLUME FOR CARRYING WATER FROM THE RIVER TO A RICE FIELD.

largely on the condition of the weather, but if all conditions of weather and soil are favorable it should show itself in about a week. Early planting is often slow to appear, while rice that is planted in the latter part of May or in June will sometimes be above ground in three days. Water is generally turned on the rice soon after it is planted for the purpose of making it sprout, and for that reason this first flooding is called the "sprout water." It usually is allowed to remain on the field some twenty-four hours, and has not only the effect of sprouting the rice, giving it an early start, but it settles the soil, filling up all the cavities and making the young plants come up evenly. Another flooding known as the "stool" or "stretch water" is turned on when the plants are about six inches high, and should only be about three inches deep to start on, being increased in quantity as the rice grows. When the growth has reached some two feet in height, if the weather is warm, deep water should be kept on it until the crop begins to get ripe.

In Louisiana, owing to the firmness of the soil, self-binding harvesting machines are used with great success and it is only a few of the small farmers who now use the sickle and cradle. An average yield per acre is about twelve barrels. A great deal of trouble is experi-

REAPING AND BINDING RICE.

enced from the attacks of "rice birds," which devour the grain with the greatest avidity, and produce the greatest amount of havoc. The damage that is sometimes wrought by these little pests is truly enormous and all sorts of means are resorted to to scare them away. Scarecrows answer the purpose after a fashion, and animated ones, armed with some sort of a firearm, generally succeed in dealing death and destruction among the pestiferous little creatures.

Very few, if any, planters clean their own rice. After it has been threshed it is shipped to a rice mill, either in New Orleans or some other point, and there cleaned. The process of cleaning is one requiring great nicety, and the value of the cleaned product is considerably dependent on how the milling is done. The rice is first screened to remove all trash and so forth, and is then conveyed to two stones, about five or six feet in diameter, and some eight or twelve inches thick, one of which revolves, while the other, called the "bed stone," is stationary. · The distance between these two stones is about two-thirds the length of a rice grain, and the theory is that the revolving upper stone produces a sort of air suction which raises the rice up on end at an angle of about forty-five degrees. The husk is broken open and the grain drops out, the chaff being blown away by means of a fan, and the rice is then taken by spiral conveyors to the pounders, egg-shaped vessels in which elongated cone-shaped upright pestles are continually working, and they remove by their continual agitation of the grain, the yellowish coating which it still retains, and impart to it a creamy tinge. The stuff that is removed is known commercially as "rice bran," and

commands a price of about ten or twelve dollars a ton. After being thoroughly pounded the rice is put through a system of screening and fanning processes which effectually separate the bran from the grain proper. The rice is afterwards carried to the brush or polishing machine, in which as its name implies, there is a rapidly revolving brush which rubs off the inner cuticle and imparts a polish to the grain itself, the residue being a fine powder or flour called "rice polish." A combination of graduated screens then divides the rice into the several grades by which it is known commercially on 'Change, and it is then ready to

RICE MILL STONES.

be barrelled and put on the market.

The prices that have prevailed for rough rice lately have not been what they should be by any means. The cause of this lies directly in the want of proper facilities for the storage of the crop, present conditions bringing about an enormous dumping upon the market at one time. What is needed are warehouses and elevators in which the rough rice can be stored and graded as is done with other grains in the North and West. This method would have the effect of straightening out things at once, and there is hardly any doubt but what it will be in vogue before very long, though the present tendency among the planters seems to be towards securing more mills and creating a greater competition for the rough product. This is a step in the right direction, but a sort of sidelong one, for were the warehouses and elevators to be erected, and the planter thus enabled to keep from rushing his crop immediately on the market, the mills now existing would be found amply sufficient for all purposes.

The necessity for reducing the cotton acreage gives rise to the question of whether rice can be successfully grown on a large portion of the area now devoted to cotton. What little experience has been had with its production not every part of South Carolina. We have seen it growing finely on the side of a mountain in this State. The experiment is well worth trying."

Certain fields that have borne cotton and have been sown in rice as experiments in parts of the Carolinas have yielded fairly well, and, in some instances, exceedingly well, and though no attempt has yet been made on a sufficiently large scale to set forth accurately the advantages of substituting it for cotton, yet it is safe to say that rice can be grown at a fair profit on lands now in cotton to a sufficient extent to reduce the present acreage of the fleecy staple at least twenty per cent.

Besides cotton lands there are in the

RICE POUNDERS.

on lands of this character would seem to indicate that it could be done. In response to a suggestion of Messrs. Dan. Talmage's Sons, one of the largest rice milling and dealing concerns in America, that some attempt should be made to substitute rice for cotton, the Charleston *News and Courier* of January 27, 1893, says: "The suggestion is a good one, we think; it is well sustained by the arguments of the gentlemen who offer it. There is probably no reason why the crop should not be grown on the uplands in a large part if South enormous tracts of land of a description fit for hardly anything but rice culture, and at present yielding no revenue, or, at any rate, but very little to its owners; in fact it is estimated that in eight of the Southern States there are between 70,000,000 and 90,000,000 acres of land on which rice can be grown. The State of Louisiana contains more of this character of land, of a marshy, and, for other purposes, valueless formation, than any other State. The enormous possibilities open to the rice industry in the United States are thus made plainly manifest, for were all these lands, the greater portion of which are now lying idle and going to waste, to be put in rice, the annual production of the country would amount to 80,000,-000,000 pounds. In this connection the following figures, compiled by Messrs. Dan. Talmage's Sons, of New York, showing the production for the whole United States from 1860 up to the present time, may be of interest;

CROP OF	CAROLINA.	LOUISIANA.	TOTAL U. S.
	Pounds.	Pounds.	Pounds.
1860........	103,600,200	1,679,000	105,279,200
1865........	7,500,000	2,746,490	10,246,490
1870.	40,800,000	14,088,880	54,888,880
1875........	42,460,800	41,400,000	83,860,800
1880........	59,927,400	51,941,590	111,8 8,990
1885........	50,450,000	100,050,000	150,500,000
1890........	49,000,000	87,750,000	136,750,000
1891........	45,887,400	109,778,200	155,665,600
1892........	*50,000,000	*205,000,000	*255,000,000

*Estimated.
"Carolina" includes that grown in North Carolina, South Carolina and Georgia.

Rice planted on uplands is grown without flooding, and is arranged with sufficient distance between the rows for a horse cultivator to be worked. Aside from the matter of flooding, its cultivation and harvesting are very much similar to the methods employed in the treatment of lowland rice, and the general character of the rice raised on uplands is very fine, the grains being hard and flinty, and able to take on a very high polish.

A few words about the food value of rice will hardly be amiss. Some data prepared by Dr. Frankland will serve to illustrate in a very forcible way the comparative value of different foods. He takes a number of common articles of nutriment and figures out what weight of each it will take to give sufficient strength to raise 140 pounds

10,000 feet high, as for instance, if a man weighing that number of pounds were to climb up a mountain side 10,000 feet, how much of each kind of food would he have to consume to enable him to do it. The following table is what he has arrived at:

Beef. ....3½ pounds.
Potatoes................. .5   "
Bread... ....2½   "
Wheat Flour................1½   "
Oatmeal....................1¼   "
Rice..... ....   1⅔   "

Oatmeal is the only one of these that is ahead of rice, and it is a tie between rice and wheat flour. Then, too, this test from a strictly muscular standpoint is hardly a fair one, as it is principally as a flesh producer and general nutriment that it excels. Very low grades of rice have been fed to stock with the most gratifying results. As a food for poultry it can hardly be excelled, though there is a foolish superstition that chickens fed on it lose their sight; but as no one can produce a fowl so afflicted, or even rendered so nearsighted that it will not perceive a grain of rice quite a distance off and run after it, the tradition seems to be entirely without foundation. Only sweepings and broken rice, however, are ever used for barnyard purposes. Looked at from any standpoint whatsoever, the cultivation of rice in Louisiana is an industry that has not only a great past but a glorious future, and the casual observer, the practical farmer, or the keen-eyed capitalist who traverses those fair and fertile rice fields near the Texas line, that stretch away until they get shadowy in the distance and the rice and sky blend together, cannot but foresee the grand harvest that is to be, the harvest that will overshadow in its greatness the products of China, India, Japan.

FRUIT STAND IN THE FRENCH MARKET, NEW ORLEANS.

LOUISIANA ORANGES.

By Henry H. Baker.

It may be a surprise to many to know that Louisiana is an orange growing State. Until very recently the pomologist of the Agricultural Department at Washington seemed to be ignorant of this fact, and there was no other means by which the public could procure statistical information regarding the Louisiana orange production. There are evidences, however, to show that citrus fruits were grown in the lower parishes bordering on the Gulf of Mexico by the earliest settlers, and the variety then must have been of a very superior quality, for the natives have studiously avoided the introduction of the so-called fancy varieties. The old "Louisiana sweet" could not be improved upon, they said. Orange planters in this State, of late years, however, have been awakened, as it were, and are experiencing the progressive spirit which is abroad in the Southland, and are introducing new methods not only in the cultivation and handling of the crop, but in forcing earlier production by propagating budded trees. The sweet seedling groves are no longer considered profitable as compared with those of the budded trees, and at the present time nine-tenths of the trees planted are budded on the sour and bitter-sweet stock. It is estimated that 20,000 or 30,000 young trees in this State were placed in orchards the past season, and as many more will be transferred from the nursery to groves the coming fall.

The section of Louisiana below the city of New Orleans, on the Mississippi river, is especially adapted to the propagation of citrus fruits. It is the most beautiful truck country in the South, being fertile beyond description and possesses the great advantage of being near a good market. This rich alluvial district would, no doubt, seem a veritable paradise to the struggling farmers of the far West, who year after year have had their homes made desolate by the frightful visitations of blizzards and cyclones. A Floridian who had heard of the fertility of the soil on the lower Mississippi, determined to visit that section of the State and ascertain the facts for himself. He was asked afterwards what he thought of the "Lower Coast" country, as it is called in New Orleans. He said:

"It would be almost impossible for the imagination to conceive of a more beautiful and fertile stretch of country than that which I visited below New Orleans on the Big Mississippi. This tremendous engine of mischief and peril to the residents of the upper parishes seems to lose its vitality and strength when it reaches the lower portion of the parish of Plaquemines, the orange district. There it lazily spreads itself out from bank to bank as if resting from its mad and cruel rush, and from its stillness appears more like a beautiful lake than like the mighty current which annually carries destruction and ruin to the upper country. The parish of Plaquemines is especially favored for the cultivation and propagation of citrus fruits. Its proximity to the Gulf of Mexico and river insures it almost from severe freezes and renders profitable orange growing almost a certainty." "If I owned any of this soil," said he, "I would ship it home and sell it as a fertilizer."

The Lower Coast produces annually great quantities of fruit and vegetables for the early market, and a large number of families are supported and educated upon the vegetable crop, which invariably is produced in the orange orchard. In other words, many poor laborers earning a dollar a day a few years since are now independent, having supported their families on trucking the ground while their orchards were growing.

In setting out an orchard as high a piece of land as possible should be procured and ditches dug a distance of 100 feet apart, then plow the land and sow down the place in cow peas. When the peas are in flower, turn them under to rot; then harrow, and you are ready to plant your trees. Young orange trees are very tenacious of life, and if one has the slightest idea of tree planting ninety-five per cent. of the trees will grow. If budded trees are planted you will be repaid by seeing them fruit the second year, and the third year quite a handsome crop will be the result of good cultivation and attention.

Louisiana produces annually about 450,000 boxes of oranges. This fruit comes into the market considerably earlier than either the crop of Florida or California, and therefore should command a good figure. The orange crop of the world is marketed in the following manner: Jamaica in August, Louisiana in September, Mexico in October, Sicily and Valencia in November, Florida in November and December, California coming in last in December and January. These delicious, juicy and delicately flavored Louisiana oranges are not known except to a favored few, who eagerly avail themselves of an opportunity to procure them, knowing the superiority of the orange to any other. With all the superiority that is claimed for the Louisiana oranges, it might appear strange to the uninformed that they are not more generally known. The reason is very obvious, however, to those who have the advantage of being posted in the matter and knowing the crude methods employed in gathering and shipping the crop. The Louisiana orange crop is generally disposed of in the months of May and June, after the fruit has begun to appear and when a fair estimate of the probable output of the grove can be made. The crop is sold upon the tree, and the purchaser has to pick it at his own expense, and pay in cash one-half of the price agreed upon at the signing of the contract and the other half in good bankable notes made payable before the crop is taken from the trees. It will be readily seen that the orange grower takes no chances; all the risks are assumed by the purchaser, such as are occasioned by storms and droughts, the visitation of which sometimes materially lessens the value of the crop.

When the harvest season commences in September a fleet of luggers is made ready to transport the crop to market as fast as picked, and Italians and negroes are employed to "break the crop," receiving as compensation from $1.50 to $2.00 per day. An expert hand will pick ten barrels per day. These hands are usually furnished with ladders with which to ascend the trees and with pouches or bags to receive the fruit. It is surprising to witness experienced hands "break" the oranges. It is done by a quick motion of the wrist after grasping the orange tightly in the hand. When the pouch is full it is taken down and emptied in a pile conveniently located for removal to the lugger which is moored to the levee in front of the grove.

This mound of oranges is sometimes left for days covered with a tarpaulin to keep out the dew or rain, as dampness is very damaging to the orange, particularly when confined in the hold of a boat. When ready to ship, the fruit is thrown into hamper baskets, which are carried to the lugger upon the heads or shoulders of the men, who dump their loads into the hold of the boat like so many potatoes. The lugger having received her load either proceeds to New Orleans under sail, or if the wind is unfavorable she is towed up by steam and landed at the space allotted by the city for a lugger landing at the French Market, where the oranges are again thrown into baskets, then into carts, which deliver them to their destination at some assorting warehouse. They are again basketed and dumped on the floor, where they are assorted, barreled and boxed and invariably marked "Choice Florida Oranges." The writer questioned a dealer regarding this deception and was told that Louisiana oranges were not known in the Northern market, and besides they did not have the keeping quality of the Florida orange, and therefore it was not desirable to have the fruit trade know that the orange was Louisiana grown. "I dare say," said he, "if the Florida fruit was handled like that of Louisiana it would be in as little demand."

The constant rough handling of this naturally delicate orange from the time of its picking until it reaches the market has done much to militate against its sale and depreciate the value of the fruit even here in Louisiana. This crude method of handling the orange in the lower Mississippi district of Louisiana was no doubt necessitated by the lack of adequate transportation, and also by the absence of intelligent buyers. There will be no excuse for this in the future. This rich alluvial orange section, which extends from New Orleans on both sides of the Mississippi river nearly to its mouth, a distance of over 100 miles, is now pierced by railroads, furnishing to the residents every facility of quick and cheap transportation.

There are several large orange groves on the lower Mississippi river below New Orleans, but the greater number are small properties, consisting of from 500 to as many thousand trees. The largest grove is about sixty miles below the city, and is owned by the Bradish Johnson estate. Through the courtesy of Mr. Chapman, the manager of the properties of this large estate, I was able to secure the following data regarding the output of their orange farm from 1880 to 1892, a period of thirteen years. I will give it here that the reader may judge of the value of an established grove. This grove occupies about 120 acres, and contains 12,582 trees, of which 9535 are bearing, the crop of

which has been sold from year to year in the following order:

1880	$ 12,000
1881	400
1882	9,000
1883	5,540
1884	9,000
1885	12,000
1886	700
1887	18,000
1888	20,000
1889	20,000
1890	23,000
1891	40,000
1892	25,000
Total	$195,000

In the year 1881 there was a freeze, which naturally affected the fruit, but otherwise did not injure the grove. The management of the Bradish Johnson Orange Farm has just perfected arrangements for the packing and shipping of the coming crop, which will yield, it is calculated, 35,000 or 40,000 boxes, and has been sold, it is said, for $30,000. The crop of 1890 yielded 18,781 barrels, and the crop of 1892, 17,713 barrels. This latter crop was allowed to remain on the trees, however, until many of the oranges fell to the ground and were lost, reducing the output considerably.

The modern system to be introduced on the Johnston place is as follows: The owners of the plantation will establish a packing house there adjoining the railroad track. A switch will be built sufficiently long to accommodate fifteen cars at a time. The fruit will be stem-cut by a patent clipper with a scoop attached into which the orange drops when the stem is cut, the picker's hand only touching the fruit once when he puts it into the canvas sack at his side. When the sack is full the man descends the ladder and puts the oranges in grove boxes which are set around the tree. A wagon comes and takes the boxes to the packing house where the fruit is poured into sizing machines. These machines are to grade the oranges to the number required to fill a box, varying according to the size of the fruit. So when one sees a box of oranges branded 176 it does not mean that some one has laboriously counted out 176 oranges and deposited them in the box—the machine has done the task. From the sizing machine the fruit goes to the packer in the house who stands behind the table or in the pit. This man takes an orange in one hand, the wrapper of paper in the other, wraps the orange and packs it in a box. When the box is full it is sent to the nailers and is nailed up. The box is then branded, the size marked on it, and it is then put into the car.

Orange Farm will produce from 100 to 115 carloads of oranges, making altogether from 30,000 to 35,000 boxes, or about 5,300,000 oranges. The crop will be taken off in about six weeks, commencing on the 15th of September. Messrs. Caron & Oteri, the purchasers of the crop on this place, have made arrangements with all the railroads running out of New Orleans to transport their crop without delay in refrigerator cars. They have registered a brand for the fruit they are to pack in the grove, and hereafter it will be sold as stem-cut Louisiana fruit packed in the grove. Messrs. Caron & Co. have interested with them a large dealer in Florida fruit who also owns plantations in Florida, and he, as well as his associates in business, ridicule the idea that the Louisiana orange will not ship as well as the Florida fruit. It is the opinion of those interested in oranges in this section that the introduction of Florida and California methods in picking the fruit will greatly enhance the value of the orange estates in Louisiana.

Budded trees give much quicker returns than sweet seedlings, such as constitute the grove of Bradish Johnson, that grove having taken at least ten or fifteen years to come into profitable bearing. Mr. James Wilkinson has a small grove of budded trees mostly Mandarins and Satsumas. They were two-year old sour stock with a one-year old sweet bud. He planted 500 trees in 1889, and in 1891 got from these trees 30,000 oranges which he sold for little over $300. He planted and cultivated vegetables among these trees to improve the land and keep the trees well worked, and the vegetables are sold for enough to pay for all the cultivation and attention given the orchard. Mr. Wilkinson estimates that his trees, planting, etc., cost him about $1 each. At the present time he has about 1000 trees and expects to get $1000 for the coming crop.

Messrs. Moore & Dameron, two young merchants in New Orleans, concluded to establish an orange grove on the Lower Coast. In March, 1890, they purchased about forty acres on the river and planted 3000 trees in the grove. Their trees were three years old when set out, that is, two year's sour stock with a one year old sweet bud. These amateur farmers had their work to attend to in the city, therefore of necessity had to have hired help, and they seldom visited the place more than once or twice a week. This little plantation is one of the prides of the Lower Coast and their success just goes to show what can be accomplished by intelligence and enterprise. This place is now coming into bearing and could be sold at any time at one hundred per cent. advance on their outlay. Last season they shipped to market not less than $1000 worth of truck. The present season they probably will not ship as many vegetables, but they will have over 5000 nursery orange trees to dispose of at $500 per thousand. The writer thought a statement from them might be interesting, and it is given here:

"In answer to your questions as to the usual method of starting an orange grove on the Lower Coast and the way to make the place self-sustaining until the grove comes into bearing, I will say that what information and experience I have is cheerfully given, believing that the more the advantages of the Lower Coast are known the greater will be the development. In commencing the grove, the ground is first plowed and put in good order, and, as good drainage is essential, ditches are dug to carry all water back to the lowlands. In December, January or February the young trees are planted in rows 16x16 or 20x 20 feet, according to the variety.

"Only budded trees on sour stock are recommended, as the sweet seedlings are subject to *mal de goma* or 'sore shin,' a root disease which has destroyed thousands of them in Florida, California and Louisiana. Budded trees come into bearing much earlier than sweet seedlings, and yield profitable crops in four years. Choice varieties of one year buds on sour stocks of two years old are bought at fifty dollars per hundred. These trees are in every way superior to those of the same age which we get from Florida. The orchard is not planted flat, the rows being slightly ridged to give surface drainage. Very little pruning is practised and a low growth is encouraged. Trees thus cultivated are hardier and less liable to be injured by severe cold. Clean cultivation in the orchard is practiced, and there is no better way to do this than by planting truck between the trees. After the truck crop has been removed, the ground is plowed and generally put in cow peas. Besides the large amount of nitrogen and potash they contain, they are of great benefit, acting as a mulch and keeping the ground cool during the hottest and driest weather.

"Cultivation is discontinued the last of August, in order that the trees shall not be kept growing too late in the fall. The scale insects, which have ruined so many orchards in California, are not nearly as destructive with us. The worst varieties we have never had. There are several very efficient emulsions that the scaly trees are sprayed with. When planting an orchard, care should be taken to buy trees free from scale, and little trouble will result. As to making a place self-sustaining, onions pay well, and there is no surer truck crop. They keep a long time and can be held for a good market. Sixty to eighty barrels per acre is a good yield, 100 barrels sometimes being made. They can nearly always be sold for $2.50 per barrel. Sweet and Irish potatoes pay very well, early cucumbers always do, and watermelons bring good prices and are safe to plant. All these crops, except potatoes, are very beneficial to young trees cultivated around them, and this should be taken into consideration in profits.

"One of the best methods of making a place self-sustaining is raising nursery trees, for which there is always a ready sale. The operation of budding is not difficult, though there is much to learn before one becomes expert. It costs from $30 to $50 to have 1000 trees budded. By following the policy of raising truck and nursery trees, any energetic and industrious man can make his place self-sustaining. Naturally the Lower Coast is superior in many ways to Florida or California, and only needs men of intelligence and energy. That she will have them before long is certain, and will soon be the garden spot of the South." ROBERT S. MOORE.

There has been question for some time among American horticulturists as to the extreme age at which orange trees will bear well and produce good fruit. Some maintain that an orange tree, no matter how much care is put upon it, will slowly wither and die after it has reached a half-century of growth. Others have argued that about seventy-five years is the limit of usefulness of a well-cared-for tree. Several American horticulturists, who have been traveling along the Mediterranean sea, have recently found trees over 120 years old that are still producing fruit of excellent quality. On the Island of Elba, where Napoleon was banished, there is an orange grove of over 700 St. Michael orange trees that were planted by an Italian in 1781, and it produced last year over 1800 boxes of fruit, but it produced four times that quantity twenty-five years ago. There are several small orange orchards in Southern Italy that are over eighty years old and are still productive of large quantities of fruit. On the Island of Malta, James Pellman, the famous American horticulturist, found one orange tree that there can be no doubt is 142 years old, and that yielded several boxes of fruit last year. It is even alleged that in the Azores there are orange and lemon trees over 200 years old that still bear fruit, but there is no good authority for the statement. Louisiana has quite a number of old groves, but it is almost impossible to ascertain exactly when the trees were planted. It was scarcely more than a century ago, however, that Florentine Buras planted the first regular orange grove in Plaquemines parish, at a place known as Tropical Bend, on the west bank of the river about sixty-five miles below New Orleans.

COLISEUM SQUARE, NEW ORLEANS.

NEW ORLEANS: THE SOUTHERN METROPOLIS.

By Frederic J. Cooke.

To the visitor who for the first time sees New Orleans, there are presented a thousand and one sights that are novel, curious, quaint, beautiful, picturesque, unlike anything that can be seen elsewhere upon this continent of ours. In certain elements of life, business, industry and politics our great cities closely resemble each other, differing rather in degree than in kind, but New Orleans presents at first sight and on close study, a never ending succession of scenes that are both novel and interesting. One's impressions embrace such a range of emotions and sensations that a record of first thoughts passes out beyond the limits of practical possibility. One is surprised by the striking contrasts in architecture, amused by the quaint shops and shop keepers in the French quarter, attracted by the enormous markets scattered throughout the city, astonished by the filth of the surface sewers in contrast with the extravagance of the

rose gardens, bewildered by the blare of seemingly continuous parades, allured by the curious old absinthe shops, captivated by the beauty and grace of the women, entertained by the shopping promenades, delighted by the dainty Creole cuisine of the New Orleans homes—in short, the stranger passes rapidly from one emotion to another until he travels the entire range of human sensations.

And the people of New Orleans, too, present nearly as many differing phases of character as their city shows. They are typical of the city in temperament and character. Reared to resent a personal affront and to protect their own and their family honor, they as quickly forgive and forget when the occasion demands. In public matters they are equally as impulsive, fierce in open denunciation of any miscarriage of justice, outspoken in mass meeting, saying nothing they will not carry out, and forgetting the whole occasion within twenty-four hours.

The sense of justice is perhaps more strongly imbedded in the hearts of the people of New Orleans than in any people in the country. The great labor strike of 1892, when 30,000 workmen went out and paralyzed the commerce of the city for nearly a week, besides putting every man, woman and child to personal discomfort, proves this assertion. For the first three days of this strike everybody in New Orleans took the whole affair as a huge joke, walked from three to eight miles to business or shopping, baked their own bread, used oil lamps or candles instead of the usual gas or electric lights, relied upon their neighbors for the news of the day—the daily newspapers having practically suspended publication—drove their own drays and carriages, and enjoyed the situation as much as the strikers. Yet, on the fifth day, smarting under a sense of oppression and the utter injustice and hostility of the leaders of this great strike, such ominous mutterings about righting the situation by the people were rife that the strike collapsed as suddenly and as peacefully as it started. It was because the people of New Orleans were aroused, and the leaders of the strike remembered the Italian episode of March, 1891. The next day everybody was in good humor again, and looking backward at the affair as a subJect for

ON RAMPART STREET.

bantering reminiscence. Such swift changing of human emotions is an indication of the temper of the people in New Orleans.

Social life in New Orleans offers an interesting field for study. It grades from the ultra-Bohemian set, at whose midnight orgies the wine flows fast and free, up to the ultra-fashionable class, whose entertainments equal in their lavishness and brilliancy the best that is found in metropolitan life anywhere in the country. The cosmopolitanism of the former set is equalled by the exclusiveness of the latter. Besides these two sets, which embody the gayety and refinement of the city, there are the literary, dramatic, musical and artistic circles as well as scores of clubs devoted to various specific purposes. Athletic and gymnastic clubs abound. Among the best of the social clubs are the Pickwick, Boston, Chess and Checkers and the Commercial, and the women also have their clubs. Socially New Orleans offers an infinite variety of entertainment, and the pleasure seeker need have no fear that time will hang heavy on his hands in this a pleasure-loving city.

During the winter there is a never-ending round of social events, ranging downward from French operas, cotillions and dinners to the mad frolics of the Bohemian sets. The curious commingling of work and pleasure is nowhere so manifested as in New Orleans. Mark Twain once said: "Half the city is always on a parade and the other half always looking at it." So it is, socially.

One of the chief charms of New Orleans is its streets, with the ancient little mule car, and the fervor with which the people cling to their traditions and customs, as well as to their promenades on the shopping avenues. Nowhere in an American city can a boulevard be found more brilliant by night or more interesting by day than the famous Canal street. There, of an afternoon, the whole city seems to resolve itself into an endless procession along the promenade. Here passes the dark-eyed Creole, the flower girl ·cries her boutonnieres and roses, the club men lounge idly in their chairs on the club galleries, the gamblers lean lazily against the iron posts on the banquette (sidewalk,) here struts by a tenor from the French opera, there a Creole dressed in black, with waxed mustachios and a red rose upon the lapel of his coat; now it is a party seeking the cafes where absinthe-anisette fascinates, the policeman lazily swings his club between whiffs of his cigarette, the music from the theatre orchestra floats out across the air—and thus the throng moves on. And in the neutral ground in the middle of the street, tinkle the bells of the picturesque mule cars passing in an eternal procession only equalled by the stream of humanity upon the sidewalk. Romance, beauty, gallantry, fondness of display, and all the pyrotechnic abandon of New Orleans are grotesquely pictured in this afternoon promenade on Canal street. After the promenade the little mule cars go staggering homeward freighted with the promenaders, and then New Orleans dines!

There is a world of meaning in that word. In the average American city, dining means no more than lunching, and a hurried lunch, too. But in New Orleans dining is a fine art, an exact science. New York may possibly possess the art as does New Orleans, but other American cities—never. With river shrimp, crawfish bisque, red fish court de bouillion, fish oulié, gumbo, chicken à la Creole, potatoes julienne, a salad, an omelette soufflée, cafe noir, some brandy, yes,—ah, my friend, you have never dined, you have not eaten the French Creole dinner? Then you have not yet lived, no. Such would be the Creole's thoughts with these dishes to select from. And the Americans, educated in their cuisine by the universal Creole cook, have grown to dine in the same way and with the same French customs, including the bottle of table claret or white wine. It is astonishing how universal is the use

of table wine at the New Orleans dinner table. Everybody, from the richest merchant in the city to the poorest laborer, enjoys his bottle of table wine with his dinner, and the consumption of claret is enormous. It is in New Orleans that the poor, in going to market in the morning, never forget to send the decanter or the empty bottle in the market basket for a refilling of wine for dinner. However frugal the dinner, the wine is omnipresent, as sure of everyday consumption as are the absinthe and the cigarette of the Creole.

Of public squares and monuments New Orleans possesses its full share, ranging from the famous equestrian statue of Jackson, facing the French market and backed by St. Louis Cathedral, to the monument erected to Margaret, a philanthropical woman of local fame, and the first woman in America to be honored with a monument. Then there is the well-known Henry Clay statue on Canal street, where great public meetings have been held for decades past, and which is now about to be removed to a more secluded spot through the machinations of the electric street railway companies, despite the protests of an indignant public. The Lee statue up St. Charles street cuts a magnificent silhouette against the blue sky, towering high above the streets upon a beautiful, chaste shaft. Facing the levee at the head of Canal street is a slender marble shaft raised in commemoration of the reconstruction period, when an engagement took place on this spot and

ON ESPLANADE STREET.

a number of lives were lost. In Lafayette Square, nearly in the centre of the city, rises a statue erected to the American philospher, Benjamin Franklin, while statues and monuments of minor importance are scattered throughout the city. The famous squares of Congo, Jackson, Coliseum and Lafayette are only excelled in historical reminiscences by the natural floral beauties of such public parks as Audubon and Lower City Park, the former squares being celebrated by great mass meetings touching public questions of importance, and Audubon Park as the scene of the World's Exposition, now transformed into a magnificent public resort, while Lower City Park possesses wonderful natural beauties as well as romantic traditions as the once famous local dwelling ground of the Creole population. As volumes might be written on these parks and squares from either an historical or sentimental standpoint, the mere enumeration of them is sufficient to recall tales and legends, and details must be left for the Louisiana historians.

THE MARGARET MONUMENT.

A feature of New Orleans life and one which every writer who visits the city singles out for description, is the quaint yet wonderfully convenient market system. Like most semi-tropical cities, New Orleans possesses markets which, for great size and the diversity of articles for sale, are veritable bazaars. Scattered over the city these markets meet you almost at every turn, tempting you to loosen your purse strings, whether it be for a cup of black coffee with the universal dab of fried dough, or a paper of pins, a bolt of calico, a basket of fruit, game, meat, fish or oysters for your dinner— anything, everything needed by humanity with a boutonniere thrown in for "lagniappe." For who would leave a New Orleans market without lagniappe? It is a delightful custom, this getting something "thrown in," and one which every true Lousianian expects as much as he does his cigarette after dinner. When the marketer completes his purchases for the day there is always something given him —a rose, a bit of confection, perhaps a bunch of lettuce for a salad or some petit peppers for the table, but always lagniappe. To abolish this custom in New Orleans would mean almost a popular uprising. And so it is when one visits any of the great markets from Dryades, Poydras, Magazine, Treme, or the far-famed French market, occupying a stretch of nearly three squares on the levee front, the purchases for the day are made, and lagniappe makes the heart happy.

To particularize these markets and picture all their every-day features and give them the flavor of romance they deserve is a difficult task. For years the French market has been a famous Sunday morning promenade for the French population of the city after early morning mass, and certainly no more distinctive phrase of New Orleans life can be found then by taking a stroll through this market between nine and ten o'clock on Sunday morning. Whether you amuse yourself at the café stand, the meat stalls, the oyster counters, or among the fruits and flowers, the dry goods bazaars or the vegetable booths, you will see the Creole beauties of New Orleans on the premenade laughing, gay, happy, at ease with the world and themselves. And the well-filled market basket goes home with dainties for the Sunday dinner which only a Frenchman or a Louisianian knows how to purchase. The other markets, less celebrated yet as extensive and complete, do their full share of traffic, and by noon time all are deserted save a few booths which have specialties for sale. For the city has made its purchases and is now looking for amusement.

Perhaps it is not amiss to speak here of New Orleans amusements, and particularly Sunday recreation. The city is a powerful church community, both Protestant and Catholic, the latter being the predominant influence. Yet the community is essentially gay, and Sunday entertainments are exceedingly popular with the masses. Among the churches, the St. Louis Cathedral, on Jackson Square, is one of the earliest, having been built in 1794. Its quaint Spanish architecture and its beautiful frescoes excite the admiration and curiosity of the stranger. Its founder was Spanish Don Almonaster, and to this day his memory is perpetuated by the weekly tolling of the great bell, whose mellow tones float across the square, over against the fruit and oyster luggers beyond the market on the levee, where swarthy Italians and devout Frenchmen cross themselves at the sound. And its great awkward towers and steeples stand out against the skies in grim array, while within, the soft lights of the tapers, the low music, the magnificence of the altar, the quiet of its galleries, the little confessional boxes, the absolute foreignness of its general appearance, are never-failing attractions to one who visits this historic building for the first time. Among the Protestant churches, there are the beautiful Christ Church on St. Charles avenue, Trinity Church on Jackson street, from which so many Southern bishops have emanated, and St. Paul's and St. John's, each distinctive in architecture.

THE HOWARD LIBRARY.

BUTCHERS IN THE FRENCH MARKET.

Yet, in spite of the strength of its churches, the city's populace seek amusement on Sunday to an extraordinary degree, more so, in fact, than any community in America. The picnic, a strictly New Orleans Sunday institution, attracts perhaps more than anything else. These are usually made more alluring in being given under the name of charity. Then the base ball, the theatre, the French Opera Sunday matinee at noon, the river and railroad excursions, Spanish Fort and the West End at Lake Pontchartrain, dances and soirees at similar resorts, the beer gardens, bars, cafes and restaurants catering to those who remain in the city, make New Orleans stand out as a peculiar type of an American city, intensely, almost madly, bent on Sunday pleasures. But with the philosophy of the Latin church, and the broad-mindedness of both Protestant and Catholic, these Sunday recreations evoke no special rebukes from the clergy of either church, and have come to be a settled fact in the life of New Orleans people.

Difficult as it is to describe briefly the varying characteristics of a city whose peculiarities are as strongly marked as those of New Orleans, there is nevertheless a never ending range of subjects and among them none more interesting than a study of the levees and life along them. Here may be found a sort of panorama that is always changing, never repeating and never tiresome. The great steamships bringing coffee from Mexico and South America; the tiny little Italian river luggers with their red sails and loaded to the guards with garden truck, the yellow orange or the Bayou Cook oyster; the down-east Yankee schooner, coming to this port for lumber; the great European "tramp" steamers entering this port for cotton and tobacco; the shriek of the tugs propelling other foreign vessels to the grain elevators; the enormous activity along the banana wharves, where Central American fruit is unloaded for Chicago and the Western cities; the consignments of the wealth of countries more tropical to the local dealers and buyers; the swish of the coal barges towed hither and thither; the fussy puff of the numerous ferry boats; the immense traffic in sugar and rice on the levee front; the activity of the hundreds of river steamboats, once the palaces of American inland traffic and still the pride of every New Orleans heart; the unique independence of the levee roustabout; the "hustling" abilities of the Mississippi river steamboat mate, whose profanity is proverbial and whose power, alas, is now somewhat curtailed—these and a thousand other strange sights are daily pictured along the twenty odd miles of levee front before New Orleans, while the Mississippi river flows past the city, calmly, peacefully, grandly, bringing the products of 20,000 miles of river and river tributaries as well as opening the markets of the world to her. And behind all this, backed by a system of levees which no high water can invade, the City of New Orleans in all its

thetic, industrious and economical. While they are far behind the American in progressive ideas, they are, nevertheless, good citizens. In New Orleans the Creole is usually employed in some clerical capacity. It is rare to see them occupying positions of responsibility; but this is due more to their lack of inclination than to scant ability. For this reason they are, perhaps, unjustly criticized. They love a life of comparative ease, and an assured income, and as a rule, do not possess the restless American spirit of speculation and development. So it is that New Orleans, having a Creole population of about one-half, advances materially on the one side and stands still on the other. In the banks, insurance offices, corporations and large business firms, Creoles will be found

CONGO SQUARE.

picturesqueness throbs with the commerce which pays tribute to her as the Southern metropolis.

When the writer stops to think of the people who founded New Orleans and who for years were the blood and sinew of Louisiana, it is proper to say something about the French Creole population. This element represents a very large proportion of the citizens of Louisiana and of New Orleans. The Creoles, like all French people, are patriotic, sympa-

keeping the books, doing the correspondence, taking care of the details of the business, while the American population is developing and stretching out for fresh conquests. But the Creole is a hard worker, steadfast to his employer, proud of his traditions and on the whole a good element in the population. In progress he must give way to the American, because he will not assume the speculations and responsibility, and the fault is his own if he be criticized.

Socially, the Creoles are lavish enter-tainers. They love high living, and their home life is marked by the highest refinement and most charming manners. To this element is due largely the repu-tation which New Orleans possesses as

you a palm leaf fan, an omelette soufflée and a rose.'

"New Orleans is unlike any other American city; her very name is a souvenir of gayeties, her breath is as sweet as a willow copse in June, and

OLD HOUSES IN URSULINE STREET.

a city of hospitality, and on account of their peculiar and delightful methods, the city will always retain a flavor of Paris and the European capitals.

In a recent sketch of New Orleans, Catherine Cole of the New Orleans *Picayune*, gave the following charming description of the charms of the city, a brilliant word-picture which only a New Orleans writer knowing the charms of the city could present:

"It makes not the slightest difference what is one's first impression of this quaint and sunny old city lying half asleep, blinking as it were under her luminous skies, luxuriously lounging on the elbow of the great yellow river; in the end one is sure to conclude that when she speaks, when first her tender message is breathed into the ear, it is an invitation something like this: 'I offer

something about her always makes one think of the opera and the bal masque, the carnival, the palm leaf fan, the omelette soufflée and the rose. She is not to be known in a day, and she will unfold herself slowly, petal by petal, growing in charm each day as Venice does—surely not to be comprehended in an eye flash.

"The æsthetic attractions of New Orleans are inexhaustible. At the end of the week you like the place; at the end of ten days you pace her streets wearing her rose colors on the lapel of your coat, singing the music of her opera house—the music of Verdi and Gounod and Meyerbeer, and at the end of a month you will swear by her Spanish daggers, by the beautiful eyes of her women, by the rose upon your balcony.

"There are famous old restaurants with chefs who are shrined as saints in the memories of gourmets; there are the attractions of the markets, the picturesque stalls piled with pineapples and pompanoes, cauliflowers and calico, garlic and bandannas; there are luggers laden with golden oranges and bananas; there are ways electric lighted and paths where only the firefly winks in flame. In the public parks you may have a rose, in a market stall a cup of French coffee brewed on a charcoal brazier, in the opera house the music of "Rigoletto" or "Les Huguenots," in the church the chanted mass and perfume of incense, in the ball-room beautiful eyes and a pink domino, and everywhere the breath of the sweet olive, the soft breathing of the sweet, salt sea winds from the Mexican Gulf, and overhead the luminous, radiantly blue and tender sky.

"The electric light shows the way to the opera, the French market, the cathedral, but out of the thoroughfare is a tiny cafe where the coffee might be bottled and sold for perfume. At the fringe of the town are convents that once were grand plantations, soon to be under the snows of sweet orange blossoms. The long, narrow, black tunnels of entrances to houses in Frenchtown give on open courts and pictures of most foreign-looking life. The song birds of the opera live here, the violet vendor has there her beds of purple bloom, and yonder the praline vendor concocts her rose leaf conserves or peels pecans for your after-dinner cup of café noir. A poet dwells in this big house, and across the way a ghost lives. A king once slept and snored in yonder haunted chamber.

"I look one way and see the salt-crusted funnel of an Indian steamer, or the red sail on the catboat of a Barataria oysterman; I look the other way and, pressed up by the dingy houses and the graveyard walls by the old basin, I see the charcoal schooners from the Mississippi bayous, their sails trailing like the broken wings of a gull. The air is warm and moist, it kisses the skin with a caress as tender as the touch of love,

A BIT OF OLD DAUPHINE STREET.

it is a whisper of the southland, and its breath is that of roses. A silver rod, old, faded golden rod, grown gray with age, self planted on the pent roof of Madame John's tumbling cottage, trembles in the wind, and at an early hour a plump market-woman goes clacking in her wooden sabots. A street-car bell tankles and then the car comes to a halt and waits politely while a would-be passenger rushes back into her house for something she has forgotten.

"Up in the Garden district, where the big, Southern mansions are, their verandahs and columns and gateways trellised with jessamine vine, all is sunshine and flowers. One may wander down the quiet streets, the shade trees arching overhead as if this were some country lane in an English shire, and never weary of the view nor lose the impression that this is New Orleans, the king, the queen, and all the royal family, of winter resorts.

"And so, with all her products and her commerce, her busy marts and her fine buildings, her opera and theatres, and her balls and routs, who desires that she shall offer you anything better than an omelette soufflée, a palm-leaf fan and a rose?

Beautiful, graceful as is this word-picture it cannot convey to the reader one-half of the delightful impressions that would rush in upon him during his first hour in New Orleans. Words fail under such a task and the utmost that can be told is but a suggestion of what can be seen. The sights that a stranger sees in New Orleans are never obliterated; its memories are sweet and fragrant, and the scenes that return to one's mental vision are full of beauty, grace and a charm that never lessens.

LOUISIANA'S ATTRACTIONS FOR IMMIGRANTS.

By M. B. Hillyard.

Louisiana presents almost peerless attractions to the immigrant. Her soil, climate and actual and possible products offer opportunities and inducements not yet fully explored, and almost incapable of enumeration. The Gulf of Mexico that laves her southern border teems with finny, crustacean and testaceous treasures, some of which have only lately been discovered and not yet exploited. There the oyster, shrimp (prawn) and diamond-back terrapin are found. To enumerate only a few choice fish—the Spanish mackerel, blue fish, red snapper, the pompano, there abound. In her rivers, streams and lakes, which are numerous, most of the fresh-water fish are found.

The forests and swamps of the State are full of timber, which in some respects has as yet received no attention from the manufacturer. Those woods which have awakened public attention have been an occasion of surprise by their beauty, durability, abundance, and the tardiness of their appreciation.

The merits of the coast climate are just beginning to commend themselves as a specific for neurotic complaints, and as curative or lenitive of rheumatism, asthma, catarrh, and bronchial or pulmonary troubles; while the climate of most of the State, though less pronounced in its salutary effects, is decidedly beneficial in these affections or diseases.

In agriculture and horticulture, and associated or cognate pursuits, active and almost exhaustive experimentation is constantly illustrating capabilities of soil and climate, to which it would be temerity to fix a limit. Thus, for illustration, it is only a very recent demonstration that the sugar-cane can be pro-

fitably raised in an area from which all former conception had eliminated it; that the tobacco, which has given such value and éclat to Western North Carolina, can be raised in equal quality, and with less expense, in the hills of North Louisiana; that the area of orange-raising is enlarged until its limit, for some of the hardier and more profitable varieties, has but a vague or hypothetical confine; that some of the choicest French grapes can be raised profitably and readily in the southern portions of the State, notably the Chasselas Doré, the Malaga, and the white muscat of Alexandria.

The reflecting and well-informed agriculturist and horticulturist will certainly agree that those demonstrations are startling triumphs of progress in their vocations. But it must not be omitted from mention that hops and buckwheat can be raised without difficulty, and the trucker will thank us for stating that celery, asparagus, horseradish and rhubarb or pie-plant may be added to a list of products that defies enumeration. The stock raiser and dairyman must not suppose that their opportunities are slender in Louisiana. Years before even Kentucky had attained anything like its present celebrity as the centre of the breeding of the thoroughbred race horse, Louisiana was noted in this regard. Her history in this respect has never been written. Her past and present record attest, besides, that the shorthorn, Jersey, Ayrshire, Holstein and Devon cattle can be successfully raised.

Of hogs almost every breed has been successfully raised, except the Chester White and Irish Grazier.

It is hardly necessary to say that the mule is easily and cheaply raised. Louisiana is an ideal State for sheep; in much of her area their fecundity, general healthfulness, quality, evenness and fineness of wool are demonstrable.

Stock-raising in Louisiana owes its capabilities to her climate and soil. Her rainfall, or precipitation, both in summer and winter, and the mildness of her winters afford the easy possibility of perpetual verdure for pastures. Added to this are abundant dews. Then, her numberless brooks, never-failing, and pellucid in her hills, and the larger streams there and her numerous creeks and rivers elsewhere add features to stock-raising rarely found in conjunction with her climatological and physical features.

The grasses and forage plants of Louisiana, natural and acquired, are incredible and beyond enumeration. It is even doubtful if botany includes a complete list of her grasses. In her natural, or naturalized grasses, the State presents a variety in abundance for eight months' pasturage in the year, and rich in all resources of sustenance for stock. To enumerate them here is impossible, but there are the sedges (at least two species), Japan clover, Bermuda, carpet grass (two or more species). These grasses, not to mention others, are widely diffused, and anywhere afford eight months' pasture, and in parts of the State nearly or quite year-long pasture. White clover, too, is becoming quite common. For winter pasture switch-cane is abundant in most creek and river bottoms, and is the usual reliance of most stock-raisers.

But it is amply demonstrated that the grasses so popular in the country at large are most admirably adapted to the State generally. Among these are the various clovers—red, white, alfalfa, California or burr clover, Kentucky blue grass ("June" grass of the West), orchard grass, red top or herd grass, and very many others.

This latter list of grasses may be called the winter grasses by way of contradistinction to the summer and natural grasses, such as Bermuda, Japan clover, carpet grass, etc. Thus, by combining these two classes of grasses, the stock-raiser and dairyman can have perpetual pasture in winter and summer. Thus the hay he has made can be turned into money and need not to be fed away to stock. Thus can be had butter, grass-flavored, the year round, worth at least twice what it is at the West and North. Thus his stock can be kept in superior health, because they do not incur the many complaints incident to shifting from green food to dry in winter and from dry to green in spring. Thus the wool of his sheep is of even fibre. Thus his fine beeves can be fat and ready for market for the West before they have become fit for shipment on pastures there. The poultry-raiser can here find a far more profitable field for his business than in the West or North. Fowls generally are far more prolific layers, healthier and of greater beauty of plumage here than there. New Orleans is a fine market for fowls, and many carloads are brought there from the West. The latter locality opens an opportunity here for raising spring chickens for the early Western market, as it does for early lambs, early fat beeves, early vegetables and fruits.

In what might be called specialism, Louisiana offers one of the most distinct fields for pursuits related to the soil of any State in this Union. A very large and most important class of her citizens are sugar planters. A much larger number are classed among cotton planters. Within a very short time, indeed, rice raising has become such a considerable industry, and so predominantly engrossing that its participants may be cast into the category of a class, and be termed rice planters. For several years a very considerable number of men have been engaged in trucking and gardening, raising early vegetables and melons for the New Orleans markets and those of the West. A few are largely engaged in orange-raising, but, as they are not distinctively so, and although the sum of their operation and that of numerous small producers is considerable, yet as few, if any, are orange raisers exclusively, or subordinate everything to it as an industry, they can hardly be thus classified. But it is probable that the day is not far distant when orange-raising will be a distinct vocation. Fruit-raising of late may be said to be one of the distinct industries of the State, a result of the development of the last three or four year. Dairying is a distinct business and confined almost wholly to the locality of New Orleans, where men, with a few head of cattle each, furnish milk to that city. The business of supplying eggs to New Orleans is a material help to the small farmers of southwest Louisiana, its importance there, relative to the State at large, dignifying it sufficiently to be classed as above. Poultry-raising ought to overshadow it there, if economic considerations were given due weight, but does not.

The raising of Perique tobacco is principally confined to one parish—St. James. It is claimed to be the peculiar product of that soil. Whether this be conceded or not, it is thought that its production is necessarily confined to a very limited area; and that a peculiarity of soil, of very limited territory, holds the monopoly of its production.

We expect to find, in the course of the next few years, the cultivation of the bright yellow or golden tobacco to have become so absorbing and alluring in various northern parts of the State as to constitute there a distinct industry or vocation.

While there is to be found here and there a raiser of one and another species of live stock, yet stock-raising may be said to be a disregarded industry. The field is broad, open, virtually unoccupied. It is too expansive a theme for the occasion, and must be suffered to pass with the glances heretofore bestowed upon it in this article.

From what has been said, it is to be deducted that the immigrant may enter the field of specialism in raising sugar, rice, oranges, fruits, vegetables or stock, dairying, making cotton, making hay, raising tobacco, or he can pursue the round he was accustomed to at home. More and more will this State adapt itself to utilizing the products of his former style of agriculture in his Western home. Will he raise hogs? Then new Orleans will buy them, as she gets most of her live hogs from the West. Will he kill and cure them at home? Either New Orleans or the country-merchant will take his bacon, because most of this meat comes from the West. Will he make hay? Either New Orleans will buy or some nearby purchaser will be found. Will he raise corn? He ought certainly to get a better price for it here than he got at home. Will he raise wheat? New Orleans will buy it; it is a new thing, but will develop. Will he raise oats? Either New Orleans or the local market will want them. Will he raise sheep? The Western market will take his early lambs, and at a fancy price. New Orleans or the local market will take his sheep. The country-merchant will eagerly buy his wool. Does his wife or daughter make good butter? He can certainly sell it for more here than at home.

He may be dazed at the discovery that the country merchant seems all for cotton, and if he gets disheartened he may raise it; and if he raises his own corn and pork, his vegetables and poultry, and makes his own butter he will do well at it. But the country merchant is shifty and adaptive. He has learned the true secret of his vocation—trade. He has learned that he must live by handling the products of the soil. He has grown up to adapting himself to his surroundings. In a country once all cotton-producing, the change has come to all fruit. The country merchant has come to buying fruit and shipping it. In a vegetable area the merchant sells his goods for potatoes and onions and barrels these and ships them. In a country that has become all rice-producing, the country merchant buys the farmer's rice.

We turn now to delineate, hurriedly, the areas that are given up, or we may rather say confined, to certain industries. There are three belts which admit approximately close delineation or demarkation. There is a territory beyond which demonstration of profitable production has not progressed. It would be rash to say that production is not possible beyond this limit. But qualifying circumstances must have play, and especially economic considerations. And with this definition or hint Louisiana is susceptible of divisions into her orange, sugar and rice belts.

We should hardly be willing to place New Orleans within the orange belt from the economic standpoint. That is to say, the tree is liable to great injury or death any winter, and it may pass several or many seasons unhurt, yet the growth of many years may perish. But the tree may soon be restored, hardly ever being killed outright. On the other hand, oranges are raised far west of New Orleans, and there are very handsome groves in Cameron and Calcasieu parishes. Perhaps it would be about right to say that the theoretical orange belt of Louisiana is on the latitude of thirty degrees from the east line to the west line of the State. In sheltered localities it might be moved nearly half a degree north of the latitude thirty degrees. Thus Lake Charles has many beautiful groves now. Many trees were killed there by the severe winter of 1885-86, which also killed many about New Orleans and far south. In Florida, on the south shores of Lake Arthur, in Vermillion parish, is another choice spot for oranges, and in some of the coves of the Queue de Tortue, in the same lovely parish, are spots where oranges are raised. On the Mermenteau river, at the railroad station of that name, in a sheltered cove in Acadia parish, is another location where oranges promised well, but were killed in the winter of 1885-86. One may take his chances within the lines we have mentioned, and many years may elapse before the oranges will be killed or even badly injured by cold, but there is always the risk.

It is probable that the hardier oranges in the future may be demonstrated safe anywhere in the belt above given—that is, in latitude thirty degrees sixty minutes from the east to the west line of the State. The matter needs further elucidating by the statement that in numberless localities in the above area orange trees are found more or less thrifty, according to soil, treatment, etc., and of course liable to those cold snaps that may "kill back" the tree or kill it outright, and yet from which quite a series of winters may be exempt.

The sugar belt of Louisiana, in general terms, may be defined to be from the mouth of Red river, south to the marsh bordering the Gulf of Mexico, and from the Mississippi river and its "country" west to the Vermillion. But the writer has seen superb cane in the pine hills in the eastern part of the State, and sugar cane is susceptible of profitable cultivation to the line of Arkansas, and some day most likely will be one of the most prominent crops in the northern part of the State.

The rice belt of the State is an entirely arbitrary area, based on the mere fact of culture, and dictated by no climatic consideration, and having for its most considerable, not to say determinate, cause or motive contiguity to water for irrigation. This for quite a time confined rice culture to the streams, and the area along the Mississippi and La Fourche rivers conspicuously were until very lately the chief seats of the industry. But within the last two or three years the very large body of immigrants, mainly farmers from the Western States, who have gone into the parishes of Calcasieu, Acadia and St. Landry, and very lately Vermillion, have devoted themselves mainly, almost wholly, to rice culture. Thus, a country which once raised only a little rice, and relied on rainfall exclusively, has in a short time been transformed into the great rice centre of the United States, and is the theatre of a more extensive system of irrigation than anything this side of the far Western States. There are many hundreds of miles of irrigation ditches; with constant additions, some notable canals, and many engines pumping water from the lakes and streams with which that area is blest. As Louisiana is full of streams for irrigation, and as there is no climatic bar, rice can be raised anywhere in Louisiana whenever need be. It should be stated, however, that a certain character of subsoil is necessary to rice-raising, so that the water put upon the rice may not percolate away. Of course, upland rice is a different species, and is raised or cultivated differently.

Because I have made this division of part of Louisiana's area into orange, sugar and rice belts, it is not to be supposed that that country is limited to these products. It is rather done to avoid misconceptions as also to discriminate her agriculture from the country at large and by particularizing products, dignify an area thus signalized. But not to be misunderstood, it may be said that in all this territory allotted to these three productions, orange, sugar and rice, there is one of the most beautiful of climates, with much soil of almost unrivalled fertility, and that everything common to the State at large can be produced there, except, perhaps, winter apples in the orange belt.

The writer has often wondered why Sea Island cotton is not raised along the coast parishes. There is no adequate explanation. It has been successfully produced a little further east along the coast between Mobile and New Orleans.

Professor S. H. Lockett, in his topographical map of the State of Louisiana has made a division of the State which is a great help towards a comprehension of its soils. The first division is the "coast marsh," a strip of territory stretching along the whole south border of the State, nearly or quite 400 miles on the Gulf of Mexico. It is of greatly variant width and out of all present consideration for purposes of immigration, except in a very limited sense.

The next grand division is the "wooded swamp," which, except for its great resources of timber, may pass without consideration here. The next grand division is "alluvial lands," constituted mainly by the valleys of the Mississippi and Red rivers, an area perhaps the most fertile on the continent taken as a whole. On the Mississippi river this area is leveed, and the overflows are being progressively subdued, and the same may be said, in a large measure, of the Red river. The area is preeminently the cotton region of the State. The "alluvial lands" of the State have immense treasures in their forests of oak, ash, hickory, gums, poplar, etc. These resources are as yet but faintly touched, a narrow rim only, as a general thing, having been cleared and brought into cultivation. This area is destined to be one of the most populous, as it is the most fertile, areas in the State. It is mainly situated on the great river of

our continent, which is becoming more and more a great thoroughfare for commerce and weds the West to the outer world.

The next grand division is the "prairies," an almost compact body of land in the southwest portion of the State. This area is the centre of the great immigration from the West, a movement that has greatly commended the State to settlement, and that has thickly peopled, in much of its area, a section of the State but thinly populated a few years ago. Their experience in many regards, especially of health, prosperity and hospitable welcome, has been of invaluable service in paving the way for expanded immigration to the State at large. Several million acres of this prairie have been taken by capitalists and immigrants, and the latter are numerous along the railroads in Calcasieu and Acadia parishes, and will soon be in force in St. Landres, LaFayette and Vermillion parishes, where fertile land, a hearty welcome and a lovely climate await them. And the same may be said of the other two prairie parishes of St. Martin and Iberia, as well as a portion of St. Mary parish.

The next division of Prof. Lockett is an unimportant one—"pine flats"— and may be passed without comment. The next is the "bluff lands." In this area lie the west half of Livingston and much of East Baton Rouge and the greater portion of West Feliciana parishes. The soil is "yellow, loamy, very fertile," and "washes badly." It is a great country for vines and has some fine timber. There are other unimportant areas of this character of soil scattered here and there over the State.

Another very considerable body of land is the "pine hills." There are two great divisions of these lands—the smaller one in the southwest corner of the State; the other in the west-central and centre of the State. Here is the enormous pine-timber repository of the State, a source of incalculable wealth, and as yet little invaded. The soil generally is "thin, sandy, poor." The water is good, surface rolling and hilly. There are many clear streams abounding in fish. The little creek bottoms are generally fertile. The soil is fine for fruits. In this character of soil is conducted the great fruit interest on the southern branch of the Illinois Central Railroad in the parish of Tangipahoa, in the eastern portion of the State. Here have sprung up considerable fruit and vegetable interests within the last few years. Many Western men have come in and founded new towns and enlarged old ones. They raise early fruits and vegetables for Western cities, and a large business has grown up. It has been amply demonstrated what a superb soil and climate these pine lands possess for peaches, pears, summer apples, strawberries, raspberries and grapes. It may be said in passing that the pine-hills area is an ideal one for sheep-raising. The wool clipped in part of the country has a distinctive appellation—"lake wool"—and is eagerly sought.

The next division of Professor Lockett is that of "good uplands." This is an area of the State that has received no consideration from Western immigration. Some immigrants have come in from some of the Southern States. But it has heretofore been out of the track of general railroad travel. It needs better openings to the West and will receive them. Two railroads give access now; one from Alexandria, north to St. Louis; another from Shreveport, north, called the "Cotton Belt" route. This "good uplands" belt stretches well across the Northern part of the State, from East to West; and this part of it is traversed by the Vicksburg, Shreveport & Pacific Railroad. Another section of this belt is situated in the north half of the extreme east side of the State. From near Robeline, in the western edge of Natchitoches parish, to Shreveport, in Caddo parish, this eastern area of the belt is pretty well opened up by the Texas & Pacific Railroad, one of the great trans-continental routes of the South giving direct communication with New Orleans on the south, and with San Francisco on the west. A narrow gauge railroad, between Shreveport, Louisiana, and Houston, Texas, penetrates southwest Caddo and northwest De Soto parishes.

The surface of this "good uplands" belt is variable in its topography, and ranges from gently rolling to hilly. The area is characterized by Professor Lockett thus: "Soil—sandy gray, or yellow loamy, or red ferruginous; subsoil—red clay; small bottoms—fertile; forest—oaks, hickory, ash, beech, maple, dogwood, gums and short leaf pine; water—good; products—cotton, corn, potatoes, small grain." Since that was written this section has been demonstrated to be a good fruit country. Besides the small fruits, peaches, pears and apples may be relied on, and even the cherry promises success. It offers great inducements to stock-raising and dairying. There are plentiful brooks and streams as a supply for water for stock. Kentucky blue grass, orchard, red top and the various clovers may be unhesitatingly sown in much of the area. It is a superb sheep country. In some of the parishes millions of acres can be purchased at very low prices, a good deal even at $2.00 per acre. And although much of this is worn out land, it is easily susceptible of restoration by the cow-pea, a far superior resuscitator of reduced soils than red clover. Besides most of this land is virgin soil and fertile.

The area opens an ample and tempting field for immigration, and if capitalists would combine, purchase these lands and open them to Western farmers, it would rapidly enrich them and confer an immeasurable benefit on the State by introducing thousands of good men who would be sure of health, prosperity and happiness. It ought to be said for this good uplands belt that there are many superb forests of hard woods within its limits, and, although it is classified so as to give little or no intimation to that effect, there is much superb pine timber in this picturesque area so rich and abundant in opportunities for cheap and healthful homes. The immigrant will find Louisiana well supplied in the main with railroad facilities, and with those already constructed and those projected and promising early completion, few localities will be found remote from this great benefit. It must be remembered, too, that the numerous navigable streams of the State have operated in the past as a deterrent to railroad construction. In much of the area of the State, steamboats ply past the very doors of the planters, and these make travel and transportation often very cheap.

In educational advantages, Louisiana ranks well. Male and female institutions for higher education are numerous and well distributed. Cheapness of building material is a matter of great importance to the immigrant. Hardly any State equals Louisiana in this respect and none surpasses her. The structural strength and durability, the ornamental beauty of her pine, as well as the lost merit in her cypress and other woods, are well known.

How does Louisiana rank in that most vital of all considerations—health? To answer this, I will quote from an address of Doctor C. P. Wilkinson, president of the New Orleans Board of Health, who draws from the census the following conclusions:

"Now as to the position which Louisiana occupies in the white list. I am very sure Vermont, Tennessee, Indiana and Texas have each of them enviable reputations for healthfulness, and a favorable comparison of Louisiana with any of the four would undoubtedly excite derision. What are the facts? Vermont has a white mortality of 15.12 per 1000; Tennessee, 15.21; Louisiana, 15.45; Indiana, 15.88; and Texas, 15.86; or, in this group of known healthy States, Louisiana stands superior to two and presents only a very small fractional inferiority to the others.

"Returning to official figures, and now excluding the large cities, we arrive at tables which meet our purpose—the relative salubrity of the rural portion of each State. The highest on record of percentage of deaths from malarial fever stands Florida, with 9.53 per cent. of its total mortality from this disease; the lowest Rhode Island, with only .08 per cent. In between these two extremes come the other States, those adjacent to our great streams showing a higher rate than the others. Arkansas has 7.65 per cent., Alabama 7.35, Mississippi 7.06, Louisiana 6.06, and Texas 6.04. Our own State showing more favorably than

any of our neighbors, save one, in a mortality springing from a disease largely preventable by ordinary attention, by the mass of the people, to the plainest and simplest laws of hygiene.

"The least infant mortality is exhibited in New Hampshire, which has 20.88 per cent. of infant to the total mortality; Maine 23.57, Vermont 24.10, California 25.31, New York 25.39, Connecticut 26.75, Massachusetts 29.21, Ohio 33.36, Rhode Island 33.69, Oregon 34.99, New Jersey 35.52, Wisconsin 35.61 Pennsylvania 36.15, and then Louisiana with 38.05, the list ending with Kansas and Nebraska, the highest rates in the Union—Kansas with 47.56 and Nebraska with 49.12 per cent. In this list Louisiana is not preceded by any Southern State. And should the calculation be based on the white population only, or an equal per cent. of colored to whites which exists in each of the Northern States ahead of her, her rank would not be fifteenth, but third or fourth. The infant mortality among negroes is enormously large, as from their habits it must be. Substitute a comparison between whites in the rural sections of the Union, North and South, and many of our Southern States would show that our people cared well for their young.

"The percentage of deaths of people over ninety-five years to the total mortality, or, in other words, the proportion of old people in a State, demonstrating beyond cavil the possibilities and probabilities of life in those localities, is exhibited by the census as follows: Vermont stands first with a percentage of .70 of old people to total mortality and Louisiana second with .62, Florida sixth with .53, Rhode Island tenth with .45, Tennessee twentieth with .27 and Nebraska the very last with only .03 per cent.

"From the foregoing facts we may conclude with certainty: 1. That Louisiana enjoys relatively to her neighbors a favorable position in regard to mortality from malarial fevers, being superior to Arkansas, Alabama, Mississippi and Florida, and only a small fraction inferior to Texas.

2. "That her percentage of deaths of children places her above any of

the Southern States, and, if like population be compared with like, her position will be third or fourth among all the United States.

3. "That her position in reference to lowest rate of deaths from consumption, a disease very dependent upon climatic conditions, is fifth.

4. "That her percentage of deaths of old people places her second among all the States for possibilities of long life."

The climate of Louisiana must pass with the remark of the best authority, Capt. R. E. Kerkham, the signal corps director of New Orleans: "There are few, if any, States in the Union that possesses a milder or more genial climate than Louisiana."

It ought to be said that Louisiana offers exemption from taxation for ten years to capital invested in manufactories, and that her taxes in general are a mere bagatelle.

It seems worth while to attempt to summarize a little here as to the prodigious variety of products possible to this State: In cereals, wheat, oats, rye, barley, buckwheat, Indian corn (and numberless maizes), rice, sugarcane (a great many varieties) and many varieties of sorghum.

In fibres we can produce cotton, flax, ramie, jute, silk, and, it is believed, hemp.

In grasses the list is simply legion.

In vegetables we may say almost every variety.

In fruits the list is almost endless— oranges, bananas, peaches, apricots, almonds, nectarines, olives, apples, pears, quinces, grapes, blackberries, dewberries, raspberries, strawberries, pomegranates, figs, Japan persimmons, plums, mayhaw, sloe. To which we rather believe the cherry, gooseberry and currant will some day be added.

Nuts include in the list pecans, chestnuts, walnuts, (English and black), many varieties of the hickory, the hazel and chinquapin. And we had like to have forgotten tobacco, ginger, indigo and tea, and a numberless variety of the field-pea, hops and the navy bean.

To the sportsman, Louisiana offers more varied attractions than any State in the Union. Everywhere, almost, quail, jack-snipe, wild duck, wild geese, brant, woodcock, are found in their season, and, except the first named, the coast-line teems with them. In the more thinly-settled areas, wild turkey and deer are plentiful. Everywhere the rabbit and squirrel are found, and the ubiquitous opossum and coon. And if the hunter wants danger he can find bear, wolves, wild cats and panthers.

The numberless bays, lakes, rivers and creeks offer pleasures in sailing and fishing which place the State above all rivalry.

The æsthetic side of Louisiana demands an abler pen. Her orange groves, her glorious skies, her never-failing flowers, the frolic blandness of her breezes, that "winnow fragrance and salubrity o'er her smiling landscape," are beyond the power of our hand to describe.

A PLANTATION SCENE IN THE LOUISIANA SUGAR BELT.

A VIEW OF THE WATER FRONT, NEW ORLEANS.
SUGAR EXCHANGE IN THE FOREGROUND; SUGAR REFINERY IN THE REAR.

JETTIES, LOOKING UP THE RIVER.

COMMERCE AND INDUSTRIES OF NEW ORLEANS.

By Major J. Henry Behan.

The advantages with which nature has endowed New Orleans have, in a measure, tended to retard, rather than promote her commercial prosperity. This chivalrous, intelligent and pleasure-loving people, inhabiting a land rich in climate and fruitful in resources, gathering in with gentle hands the riches which come to their doorway, might be compared to some great monarch awaiting the tributes of treasure and products demanded of the provinces conquered in warfare, unlike the civilian ruler who sends out his emmissaries inviting the people of the territories to aid in developing the commercial and industrial opportunities offered.

Think of a city lying near the mouth of the greatest river in the world, the *entrepot* of this fertile valley, reaching from the Gulf of Mexico to the great lakes, extending its mighty arms from the Alleghanies to the Rocky Mountains, gathering in with Ravanna-like avidity all the treasure of that vast territory, consisting of cotton, sugar, rice, grain, meat, coal, iron, precious metals, fruit and all the industrial handiwork of thousands of artisans, which, if loaded on barges, would float down this natural current of their own volition to the doors of the storehouses, and thence be distributed to the world. Without the power of steam or the new motor electricity, this favored city, with the benefits of water transportation enumerated, could keep her warehouses supplied and furnish cargoes to the numerous vessels always in the harbor.

The commerce of this city extends to every country on the globe. During the busy season, vessels from all ports, both coastwise and foreign, are lying at the wharves unloading their cargoes of merchandise to be immediately reloaded. The immense ocean steamers fill the lower portions of their hulls with from 30,000 to 40,000 bushels of grain, which is a regular export but is utilized as ballast, the between-decks being stowed with cotton for England, the Continent and even Russia. The other principal articles of export are cottonseed oil and cake, staves and tobacco. At one time this city controlled the market for the latter article, but some years ago disastrous failures diverted the trade and she now only handles it in transit for reshipping, and even under these circumstances the improvement in tobacco is so great from passing through the Southern climate, that the Germans, who are its principal importers, much prefer that quality which has acquired superiority in being transferred over the Southern route.

A city situated near the outlet of a great river, with a harbor of safety large enough to float the navies of the world, will in time, with enterprise, proper management and care, control all the commerce of the countries, including the coffee output, of South America.

The trade in fruit products from the islands and Central American States, consisting principally of bananas, pineapples and cocoanuts, which a few years ago required only two or three small schooners, has assumed proportions which now employ a fleet of about thirty first-class steamers. The Illinois Central, Louisville & Nashville and North Eastern Railroads have erected immense sheds and wharf accommodations for the exclusive use of this increasing and lucrative trade, from which, working day and night, are dispatched numerous fast trains of refrigerator cars, distributing these luscious fruits throughout the North, East and West, the latter territory being the principal recipient of the importations. Preparations are being made to establish a line of steamers with the Latin-American States which will control most of the commerce with those countries.

Not only is the Crescent City in the lead with tropical fruit, but it shares a large part of the Mediterranean trade, vieing in this latter with New York. New Orleans claims to be a better winter market for receiving and distributing the consignments on account of the warm climate and the ample and complete arrangements the railroads have

for unloading, rehandling and sending the cargoes North and West. The receipts here this year show an increase over last year and equal 1891, which encourages the merchants in the belief that their business will be still further augmented in this direction, with the hope of ascendency in the trade before much time shall elapse.

New Orleans is the natural outlet for the products of the Mississippi Valley, which furnishes Latin-America with the actual necessities of life, in exchange for agricultural, mineral and medicinal articles—namely, diamonds, silver, gold, coffee, mahogany, quinine, indigo, India-rubber and immense quantities of Demerara sugar and molasses for refining purposes, at this, their legitimate distributing point, a reciprocal trade which has unlimited scope and will be mutually beneficial.

A trade of much importance which is being largely developed is the extension of old saw mills with improved machinery and the erection of new and larger ones at advantageous points where felled timber can be floated to them during the seasons of high water, allowing the accumulation of a sufficient supply to keep them employed the entire year for the local as well as export trade to South America and England. These points develop into great magnitude the lumber and timber trade of the vast forests contiguous to this city from which it derives the principal benefit.

The Mechanics', Dealers' and Lumbermen's Exchange, an association formed for the better interchange of ideas in regard to building materials, has become a commercial necessity of consequence, affording ample protection to all parties using or furnishing articles for building purposes. To substantiate the general benefit derived, we quote the official record for the year ending June 31st, 1893, which "shows a total of 1192 buildings erected in New Orleans against 570 during the same period of 1891-92; 763 rebuilt, added to or repaired as against 873, with building permits calling for the expenditure of $2,940,473 as against $1,831,867. Making the usual allowance of one-third extra for the actual expenditure over the permit esti-

UNLOADING BANANAS ON THE LEVEE, NEW ORLEANS.

mates, the total amount spent on buildings during the year was $3,920,631 as compared with $2,422,489 in 1891-92, an increase of sixty-one per cent. There is an improvement in every line, 1161 residences having been built as compared with 551, while the number of stores erected increased nearly threefold.

This record is the best New Orleans has ever made. With due allowance for the loss by fire, decay, etc., it means an addition to the taxable wealth of the city in new buildings alone of $3,400,000 and an increase of 6200 in population. In a year of some general depression this is a good showing, as good relatively as any city in the country can make. And as real estate, when not artificially boomed, is the best test of prosperity, we may consider these statistics of New Orleans as bearing evidence to a solid, substantial and promising condition of affairs.

Much of this is due to the well organized and solid local building and homestead associations which have been instrumental in furnishing homes to a large number of the population unable to build or purchase property unless upon the instalment plan, the rule of these associations. This interest has become of such importance as to warrant the formation of a State Homestead League, which, now in its third year, has served to promote the financial status of the associations, whereby the confidence of the community has been obtained to the fullest extent.

Besides the commercial traffic extending all over the world as heretofore enumerated, there is considerable trade on the lakes and Mississippi Sound in charcoal, wood, sand, shells, tar, rosin, pitch, cresote, turpentine and other products of the pine forests, including large numbers of bricks for building and paving in this and the adjoining cities, and also for shipment to the interior. Realizing the inadequate quantity of this latter material, an enterprising firm has erected a mammoth brick factory within two hours' travel of the city by rail and water. The clay used in that vicinity is unsurpassed; work is pushing forward and the supply will hereafter be fully equal to the demand.

Near this deposit of clay for brick making is also another quality peculiarly adapted to manufacturing plain and decorative pottery and porcelain. The capital was furnished and a factory established near here, but for the want of patronage they have temporarily suspended work with a large amount of material on hand, and hopes are entertained that at an early date work will be resumed.

A casual observation has been made in regard to cotton and grain as cargoes for the immense ocean steamers that enter our harbor during the year It is necessary to impress upon the shippers of the West the growing importance of New Orleans as a grain exporting point. The Trans-Mississippi Congress, sessions of which were held in Denver, Kansas City, Omaha and New Orleans, has been of more vital consequence to this city than one would imagine at the first glance. The delegations from the West, particularly from Kansas City, upon their visits to New Orleans, saw and realized with their usual shrewd business acumen, the advantages of this port as an outlet for their grain and meat products. The large increase in the export of grain shows what energy and push will accomplish by making use of the favorable situation of this city. Grain transported by railroads is delivered at the ships' side and is transferred by the elevators at very small expense. That transported by the river in barges is landed alongside the ships and transferred by floating elevators at a nominal cost, making this the cheapest port for the export of grain, as it does not require rehandling. So well satisfied are the exporters of grain as to the cheapness and safety of the route via New Orleans from partial cargoes, they have in the last few years been making solid shipments by the largest of ocean steamers, which arrive at their destination and deliver the cargoes in Europe in as good condition as they were at the point of shipment.

In the year ending August 31st, 1891, the exports of grain from this port were: Corn, 2,108,919 bushels, and wheat, 3,244,459, a total of 5,353,378 bushels. For the year ending August 31st, 1892, they were: Corn, 6,192,006 bushels, and wheat, 13,055,682 bushels, a total of 19,247,688 bushels, showing an increase of 13,894,310 bushels. The exportation of grain for the ten months ending June 30th, 1893, equals the entire amount of last year, with a large stock on hand awaiting freight room.

We take pleasure in quoting the following pertinent remarks of Mr. A. J. Vanlandingham, commissioner of the Transportation Bureau in Kansas City:

"New Orleans possesses unrivalled natural advantages for trade; the Mississippi river and its tributaries afford not less than 15,000 miles of navigable waters communicating with a vast extent of country illimitable in its resources, exhaustless in fertility, and embracing nearly every variety of climate. Vessels drawing twenty-five to twenty-six feet of water can readily pass through the jetties, and have done so with the tide one foot below the average flood. New Orleans so far is the only Southern port that has proven its ability to handle grain at a profit to the shippers and the carriers, and it is to be hoped that the elevator capacity at New Orleans will be largely increased at an early date."

These words are an evidence of the superior advantages perceived by a shrewd and practical business man without prejudice or bias in favor of this port over any other. His wide experience as a railroad man makes this opinion of unquestionable value.

The increasing receipts of grain caused a demand for more elevator facilities, which was promptly met by the Mississippi Valley road, now part of the Illinois Central system, and the Texas Pacific Railway, the former increasing the capacity of the one at Southport, the latter erecting one at Westwego, which now makes five stationary elevators of 1,000,000 bushels capacity, besides the floating ones in the river. Numerous enterprises are on foot to increase the elevator and warehouse capacity in order to meet the growing demand for increased facilities to accommodate the anticipated larger shipments from the West and Texas. With plenty of water all the year from Kansas City; with the railway facilities for moving large quantities after the cotton crop is marketed; with the extension of the Missouri, Kansas & Texas Railway from Jefferson, Texas, to this city, and the Missouri Pacific from Alexandria, La., creating competition and giving two direct routes through the grain producing country; in a few years New Orleans will rank first in the grain exporting trade of this continent.

There is no danger of a blockade on the railroad, or an embargo on the river between here and Kansas City. The former can be relieved by the river, and if the water is low the cargoes of the barges can be reduced, the railways readily handling sufficient to supply the fleet of steamers awaiting shipments. It is surprising to note with what expedition vessels are unloaded and reloaded at this port; those arriving in ballast are ready to depart with a full cargo of grain and cotton or entirely distinct loads of either in a few days. We again repeat that nothing short of an earthquake can prevent New Orleans from becoming within the next five years the largest exporting city of the country.

With these unequalled facilities for receiving and handling the wheat of different grades, direct from the producing points at all seasons, it is a matter of extreme moment as well as surprise, to note the absence of flour mills. Here is a magnificent opportunity open to some enterprising man or company with sufficient capital to erect a mill or mills of large capacity on or near the river. Such a venture would undoubtedly be crowned with success from its advent.

The wholesale grocers carry large stocks, varying from one to two thousand barrels of flour, which during the wet season is subject to damage from climatic effects. The grain itself in elevators, with their improved bins which prevent it from heating, is a wealth of material conveniently at hand, and flour could be furnished fresh daily for local consumption as well as for shipment to Central and South America. Certain grades only are suited to these countries, owing to the effect produced by a long voyage and the change of temperature. The flour thus manufactured would necessarily be fresher and of a quality better adapted to the trade, being selected for those special orders. The raw material being transported in bulk at a lesser rate than the manufactured material in barrels, the difference in freight alone is enough to make it remunerative without further consideration.

The attention of millers and capitalists is called to this opportunity with the hope that it may lead to the early inauguration of this industry which assures success and profit. The question admits of close investigation without fear of the result.

It may not be within the purview of this writing to allude to the possibilities of a city so favored, but as the enterprise in question is an attribute of one of the principal and leading articles of its commerce, the utilizing of raw material at hand to manufacture a commodity necessary to all mankind, it is but the natural sequence of the situation attracting the attention of the casual observer, who says: "Here is the wheat, where are your flour mills?"

The industries of New Orleans are varied and numerous, a genial and salubrious climate allowing the manufactories to run in all seasons, so that the entire year is occupied by the busy hum of spindles, sewing machines, circular saws and other macinery in motion shaping material for use in the factories and for building. There are ten large saw and planing mills, several of them making sash, blinds, doors, molding and all necessary woodwork for completing and decorating the modern style dwellings. There are fourteen lumber companies in the city who are receivers, dealers and shippers of lumber; some of them controlling large mills in the immediate neighborhood, are able to execute orders for local trade and export with immediate and prompt attention. One firm, to accommodate the immense growing demands, constructed a railroad over fifty miles in length to facilitate the transportation of large timber to market or to tidewater for shipment. They are also owners of a mill on Pearl river, which has a capacity of 100,000 feet of sawed timber per day.

In addition to the pines which flourish in such exuberance on the uplands, down in the valley of the stream, or what is called "bottom land," we find an equally luxuriant growth of different woods susceptible of the highest polish, viz: the beech, gum, dogwood, ash,

SUGAR REFINERY, NEW ORLEANS.

wild cherry, white oak, red oak, pin oak, the majestic live oak, magnolia, white pine, hickory, cypress and others. Many of them are used in manufactories for furniture, office fitting and railway cars. An ample supply of well-seasoned lumber has placed the trunk and box making industry in the front rank with other cities and has secured immediate recognition. Packing cases and shooks of a smaller class (boxes for soaps and patent medicines) occupy much of the time of these factories, where also a number of women and girls are employed in making varieties of paper covered boxes. The goods made in the trunk factories are largely distributed throughout various States, and give entire satisfaction because of reasonable prices. The possibilities of development in store for all interests connected with timber is beyond prophecy.

There are located in New Orleans thirteen rice mills of large capacity receiving the rough material direct from the fields and preparing it for market. This is an article of our commerce which a few years ago belonged entirely to the Atlantic States, principally the Carolinas. At present this city receives and mills over a million sacks per year. New Orleans enjoys supremacy in the rice trade from the fact that the entire Louisiana crop is handled here. The yield is twice that of all the other States together, so this city may with justice be denominated the great market for domestic rice. The large amounts handled in New York are entirely of foreign growth. The development of this industry continues to increase yearly.

The swamps contiguous to New Orleans furnish moss in superabundance which keeps eight factories and numerous hands occupied in preparing it for mattress making, also for upholstering furniture. The many people engaged in gathering it from the trees, together with those employed in the factories, make quite an addition to the army of toilers whose labor tends towards the prosperity of a community. In connection with this subject should be mentioned four large mattress factories employing many expert hands in making these goods for local trade and for shipment. No inconsiderable quantity of this moss is shipped in its rough state, but most of it is rehandled by the city moss gins. This trade is also tending upward.

There are twelve foundries and

machine shops where the principal work for the sugar plantation and refineries, steamboats and steamships is done. They employ a great number of experienced mechanics, as well as many apprentices. The work done by the three leading concerns compares favorably with the best shops of the North, especially in sugar-house appliances, which require fine finish and precision. Separate from the foundries are a number of boiler-makers, and the constant din of the hammers heard far and wide gives the indolent sightseer an excellent idea of pandemonium.

New Orleans has always been the market for the two great crops of the South, sugar and cotton, but not until the past few years has any interest been displayed in either beyond the regular routine business of the commission merchant of receiving and selling, leaving the buyer to arrange his shipments without giving a thought to the fact that in a few weeks he would be purchasing possibly the raw materials in a manufactured state. This city has several immense sugar refineries, employing hundreds of hands, and two large cotton mills, with the whir of spindles and clatter of looms, new to the people but demonstrating more forcibly than a thousand pages of description the manufacturing possibilities there are in store for this place. The following statistics will give an idea of the output of one of the largest of our cotton mills: about 36,000 spindles and 1100 looms are in use; employment is given to about 900 operatives, who work up about forty bales of cotton daily, which is converted into various kinds of cotton cloth and hosiery yarns. Their production for the six months ending July 1, 1893, was about 1,968,424 pounds of yarn and cloth, the amount of cloth produced being about 7,873,000 yards. The amount of wages paid to work-people during this period was about $85,000.

Beside the promotion of manufacturing industries there is a humane consideration of much moment involved in the employment of women and girls, enabling them to earn an honest and comfortable living. In the manufacture of cigars and tobacco New Orleans now stands paramount. Fifty factories with a multitude of defthanded workmen and women turn out a fine grade of work, which is gaining an extensive reputation. Ten years ago not a woman or girl could obtain employment as a cigar-maker, but at the present time they are favored over the other sex. One firm alone has 700 women and girl employees, and they are considered peculiarly fitted for this vocation. With skilled labor and a perfect climate there is no reason why this city should not become one of the leading cigar centres in the world.

As we proceed, each new subject seems to grow in importance and claims to be a principal factor in promoting industrial wealth and prosperity. We find the clothing manufactories second to none in the value of their output. Orders are increasing year by year, as a large proportion of the clothing manufactured here can be made 25 per cent. cheaper than in New York. The chief branch of this industry continues to be the manufacture of jeans, which, on account of their reasonable price and durability, are satisfactory to the working people. No country store is considered complete without its large consignment of New Orleans made clothing in stock, and Mexico, too, is proving a profitable field for this industry, taxing to the utmost the factories, large as they are, for a sufficient supply.

Three knitting mills manufacture excellent hosiery, and although only recently established, have been very successful and are fast growing into favor. Orders for their goods are far in advance of the supply for local trade and shipment to Texas and Mexico. There is a bright future ahead for this young industry, as it possesses every element of success—capital, abundance of material, and cheap labor especially adapted to this class of work. The boot and shoe factories are improving their lines, both in material and style; business has advanced this year to the full satisfaction of those engaged in this line. The New Orleans trade is equally distributed in most of the Southern States with a steady increase towards those of Central America.

A small industry of local importance

has unexpectedly made a rapid stride into favor, and four factories are now engaged in putting up for table use what is known as "Creole Mustard," a piquant seasoning for salads and meats. It is sent out in jars ready for use without further preparation.

A few years ago we had to depend on Pennsylvania for our coal supply. It was transported in flatboats down the Mississippi and Ohio rivers from the mines near Pittsburg, often at a great risk from storms and other perils of the water. Since the opening of the new lines of railway in Alabama, coal from the mines of that State has become part of our commerce, and in such magnitude as scarcely to be believed unless one were standing at the North Eastern railroad depot counting the trains of ten and twelve cars each, "belted" to the Southern Pacific railway en route to Texas and Mexico. At first this trade was carried on via the river and Gulf to Galveston, but since the North Eastern changed its track to the standard gauge the shipments have been transferred direct without breaking bulk, which has increased the amount this year to nearly double the trade of last year.

Not many years have elapsed since the entire ice supply of this city came from the East in Maine-built ships, which were loaded at Boston and the cargo stored away on its arrival in buildings erected especially for this purpose. Later, the Western ice was added, some received in barge loads via the river and some by rail, all of which trade has lapsed into decadence, succumbing to manufactories now producing enough for home use and also supplying the summer resorts on the lakes and Mississippi sound, as well as many points in the interior. There are eight factories, two of them using water from driven wells, others the river water, boiled and filtered. There was some prejudice at first against using the manufactured ice, but that has passed away, and no questions are asked except by dealers, who naturally prefer to patronize the company in which they are interested as stockholders.

The dry docks, ship and steamboat repair shops, located in the fifth district, (what was formerly known as Algiers), do a thriving business the entire year and turn out work which compares favorably with the larger establishments in the East.

Within the past twelve years another enterprise, without attracting much attention, has grown to such importance that the brewers of the North and West, and even Europe, have observed the inroads made upon their once profitable trade by the New Orleans breweries. Formerly this city ordered its beer from the West and imported ale from England. While some yet is received from these sources, the amount is small in comparison with the past. The home consumption has not only increased but large shipments are being made to Mexico, Central and South America, showing how wide a reputation this incomparably fine malt liquor is gaining.

Cooperage is another industry which has extended its business considerably, until during this year a fire occurred which entirely destroyed the largest establishment and valuable property in the vicinity. This caused much discussion in insurance circles and attracted the attention of the city government, thereby delaying the permit to rebuild. This cooperage being a very estensive one the output has been much reduced in comparison with last year. While there have always been many small concerns owned by individuals who supply sugar planters with barrels and hogsheads by contract, not until recently were there any organized corporations, entering upon this industry on a large scale with all the modern appliances now necessary. There are, however, evidences of a renewal of the trade which is encouraging.

There are many smaller industries, common to all large cities which help to swell its trade and give employment to a number of workmen, from the skilled artisan to the ordinary day laborer. Passing over these we enter upon one of the principal factors which can promote or destroy a city's prosperity—the transportation companies. Six railroads have their terminals here; the Southern Pacific (Morgan line), Illinois Central, Louisville, New Orleans & Texas (now a part of the Illinois Central system), Louisville & Nashville, Texas & Pacific, New Orleans & North Eastern, which is the Southern division of the Queen & Crescent Route. The city has been at all times very liberal in granting privileges and facilities to these corporations, expecting an ample return by the increased trade relations with the territory through which their lines pass, but we are sorry to say in many instances this anticipation has not been realized nor the promises fulfilled. This question has been so often and thoroughly ventilated by the Board of Trade and Cotton Exchange, we will leave it in their hands or more properly in the hands of the Bureau of Freight and Transportation recently organized and incorporated by a regular delegation from all the exchanges. This association of business men was formed for the purposes enumerated in their published address, and surely an interchange of trade interests and mutual indulgences will result in a harmonious and equitable adjustment of the discrimination in rates against this city.

Another matter for serious consideration is the insufficient banking interest of New Orleans. During the season prior to the movement of cotton, sugar, etc., there is a great dearth of money for circulation which has a general depressing effect while it lasts. Though the stated amouut of capital seems tremendous, it is only a part of the money that can be used to advantage here. The institution of larger banking interests opens another broad path for enterprising and energetic capitalists, and will lead further on to the golden future which looms ahead for old New Orleans.

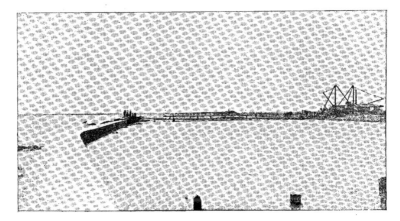

SEA WALL AT THE JETTIES

THE LUMBER INTERESTS OF LOUISIANA.

By Watson Jones.

The recent meeting of the "Forestry Congress" at the World's Fair in Chicago has brought into startling clearness the facts concerning the rapid denudation of our lands to satisfy the commercial demands for timber and lumber. A few years since the lumberman's call was "from Maine to Georgia" now it is from "Minnesota to Louisiana."

The remarkable adaptation of the alluvial bottom lands of the Mississippi and Red rivers running through the Pelican State to the production of the cane has for more than a half a century centered the business minds upon "sugar" as the dominant industry of the State. Thus until recent years its vast forest resources were slightly trenched upon. But of late the quick commercial instinct has discovered that Louisiana has within its bounds more than 50,000,000,000 feet of the best timber known. The capitalists, manufacturers and home seekers are finding out this fact, and eager inquiries are coming from all parts of the country as to the best location for investment or settlement.

Fortunately the ownership of these lands is in many hands, so that the monopolistic feature of large holdings is avoided. The conservative spirit of the old regime is dissipating with the advance of new era and "New South" ideas, and now quick response is given to earnest questions, and hearty welcome awaits any who bring money or self to aid in the development of the State.

An important fact affecting the lumber interests of Louisiana is that the character of her woods is of just the nature to satisfy the demands of taste and culture for decorative effect as well as strength. The cypress, the gums, the magnolia and the holly command prices that would have seemed preposterous a few years ago. True, many cargoes and thousands of carloads of yellow pine and oak have been taken, and thousands more will follow at increasing prices, but the quantities and values of the special varieties of the woods of Louisiana are realized by none and thought of by few.

It has been discovered that Louisiana is the cypress State, that while the wood is distributed through a wide extent of the Southern belt, the Gulf or red cypress of Louisiana is unequalled by that of any other section, so that already more than $1,500,000 is invested in the cypress branch of the lumbering industry alone. Large manufacturing establishments in New Orleans and other business centres of the State are this year consuming 9,000,000 feet of cypress to meet the demand for sash, doors, blinds and interior finish of this wood, so remarkable for its beauty and durability.

While it was not the intention of this article to be specific or statistical, a few words as to the location of certain of the principal woods of the State may be appreciated.

The long-leaf pine is found more or less over the hill country of the State, yet it may be said to have two important centres, the eastern and western. The former embraces the parishes of North St. Tammany, Washington, North Tangipahoa, most of St. Helena and East Feliciana. There is a considerable area of pine flats in North St. Tammany, South and West Tangipahoa and East Livingston parishes, and a narrow

430

rim in Southeast St. Helena parish and in Calcasieu. The western centre of the pine is situated in Northwest Catahoula, West Caldwell, Southeast Jackson, all of Winn, nearly all of Grant, except the narrow rim in the Red river valley in the southwest portion of the parish, Northwest and all West Rapides, a small area in Northeast St. Landry, all North Calcasieu, South and West Natchitoches and Southwest Sabine. Alexandria is near the geographical centre of

BLEEDING PINE TREES FOR TURPENTINE.

the State, and within a radius of seventy-five miles of this important railroad centre is situated the bulk of the great pine area of the State.

Until recently this great Western pine belt has been untouched. The Southern Pacific Railroad opened up Calcasieu parish mainly at Lake Charles and country contributing. The daily cut there now is about 300,000 feet. Later, the Texas & Pacific Railroad developed the lumber business along its line, but the mills, though of fine character and large cut, have barely made an impress upon the territory.

The Kansas City, Watkins & Gulf railroad now complete from Lake Charles to Alexandria will afford an outlet for the pine of North West St. Landry and South Rapides parishes, and if continued to its avowed terminus at Kansas City, is destined to develop great pine lumber interests in the parishes of Grant and Winn, which it will necessarily traverse.

The Houston, Central Arkansas & Northern Railroad, now running from Alexandria to Monroe, La., gives a very direct outlet to the West for the pine of Grant parish from north to south of its eastern area, of Southeast Winn, East Catahoula, Southeast Cladwell and Northeast Rapides parishes. This railroad opens up an extensive area of pine and is a most important factor in the development of the lumber interest of the State. In some parts of the pine belt the "cut" is very large, sometimes as high as 30,000 feet per acre, and not uncommonly 10,000. Sometimes many acres can be found where this last figure is exceeded. Few, if any, of these pine lands are now in first hands. Prices range according to cut and accessibility. They are about as follows: Lands cutting 3000 to 4000 feet per acre, distant from railroad, $1.00 to $1.50 per acre; for lands distant from railroad, cutting from 6000 to 10,000 feet, $3.00 to $5.00 per acre; lands near to railroad, $1.00 to $1.50 per acre for stumpage; lands away from railroad cutting 15,000 feet are

A LOUISIANA TURPENTINE STILL.

estimated to be worth $10.00 per acre.

The bulk of red cypress is situated south of the Red river and west of the Mississippi to the Sabine. The white cypress is a more generally diffused wood and is even found as far north as Delaware. In Louisiana it is to be found in all localities adapted to its growth. The sweet gum has no partic- ular locality. It is a considerable feature in most forests; is rather plentiful in the Mississippi bottom and the river parishes.

The tupelo gum is abundant in many wet bottoms of the State. The holly is everywhere as a scattering tree; the magnolia, though not rare as to a few specimens, is rare as to its quantity in any given locality. Both these woods have a great future value. The ash, hickory and various oak are common to the State. The live oak is found on the Southern or Gulf coast, on the Chenieres and Buck ridges and bayous and along the banks of the streams in many, if not all, the alluvial regions of the State.

No mention has been made of the ash which is scattered throughout many of the upper parishes of the State, also the maple, and in a few localities the black walnut. The pecan is quite common in small bodies throughout the State, and is commonly preserved for the greatly increasing value of the "thin-shelled Louisiana pecan nut." Great numbers are being planted, and the young trees grafted with the most per-fect samples form a profitable industry. Poplar and cotton wood are also quite generally distributed in the upper parishes near the river, the hackberry, dog-wood and sycamore likewise. In some localities the sassafras grows so abundantly as to deserve mention.

As to facilities for transportating and marketing the lumber, the primitive methods of river rafting and transportation are being rapidly supplanted by the railroads and every modern appliance. The Pearl river on the east and the Sabine on the west still serve as outlets for the principal exportation for foreign or coastwise business. The Jackson, or Illinois Central Railroad, is the oldest and still most faithful servant of the mills. The Great Eastern, or Queen & Crescent route, does some business for East Louisiana, but finds its great work in Mississippi. The Louisville & Nashville Railroad has very few mills, but is useful for its connections, while it has a small local trade. The Southern Pacific furnishes ready distribution of the cypress of the South and the yellow pine of the Southwest.

Two branches of the Southern Pacific from Schriever to Thibodeaux and Schriever to Houma are built. One is projected from Raceland to Lafourche and several others in the western part of the State, which will open up valuable timber sections.

The Texas & Pacific Railroad is most important for the Red river sections of the State. The "Vidalia Route" takes in the northern and uplands from the eastern border to Shreveport, which is a centre for all hard wood operations. The same may be said of the road from Delta, opposite Vicksburg to Shreveport. There is a narrow guage road from Shreveport running through De Soto and Caddo parishes, crossing the Sabine river at Logansport, which will eventually be made wide gauge and extended into Texas. It opens a vast pine district.

Thus, in extent, in variety, in favor, as to locations and facilities of transportation, the lumber interests of Louisiana merit the attention of the wealthy capitalist, the competent, energetic manufacturer, and above all, the man of family who seeks to make a home where opportunity to "grow up with the country" makes a small investment in the present sure capital for the future.

THE LOUISIANA OYSTER BEDS.

By F. C. Zacharie.

The great resources of Louisiana in its large production of sugar-cane, cotton, rice, lumber and fruits have hitherto kept in comparative obscurity what are generally deemed the minor—and wrongly considered the less remunerative—fields for the employment of capital and intelligent labor. Many of these are so regarded simply for the reason that the best locations for their development are remote from the centres of trade and great waterways, and in many instances difficult of access by quick transportation. This possibly accounts for the general ignorance of the great opportunities which these industries offer for highly remunerative investment. Prominent, if not the principal, among these neglected industries are the vast fishery interests of the State, which, under energetic labor and scientific cultivation, would in a few years equal, if they did not surpass in the way of pecuniary profit, the aggregate value of the entire agricultural product of the State. The extent of the oyster territory is so vast, the supply so abundant and cheap, and so little labor and capital are required for its development, that its wonderful advantages and enormous profits once known, capital and labor will inevitably seek employment in what must eventually become a leading industry, far surpassing that of any other State in the Union.

On the eastern boundary, starting from the Rigolets, the small gut or strait connecting lakes Borgne and Pontchartrain, and following the shore line southward and westward around the mouths of the Mississippi River to the Texas line, there is a coast of about six hundred miles in length, if measured on straight lines from point to point. Making an allowance for the curvatures of the coast, the shores of salt water bays, bayoux, inlets, lakes and islands, which fret this part of the State like net work, the littoral line will not fall short of fifteen hundred or two thousand miles. Taking into consideration the shelving, shallow beach adjacent to it, experts well acquainted with its geographical features estimate that the area suitable to planting and growing oysters is double the amount of acreage available in all the other States of the Union combined. By far the larger portion of this extended coast is dotted by expanded natural oyster beds, originally, that is in a state of nature, only distant from each other a few miles. Those most accessible to speedy transportation to market have been in some cases almost entirely denuded, and others seriously impoverished by the constant fishing in and out of season. In other instances the fresh water from chronic river crevasses has occasionally but only temporarily injured the productive capacity of these beds. These injuries, however, are but occasional and temporary, as we have just said. The fecund, recuperative power of nature, in no way more strikingly illustrated than in the immense reproductive capacity of the oyster, soon replenishes the stock, whenever the depredations of the fishermen or the overflow of the fresh water cease and the beds are allowed to rest for a time.

Besides these natural beds, the coast abounds in suitable places to which the mollusk can be transplanted from the seed bed, and under proper care developed into an oyster which for the delicacy of its flavor cannot be excelled

434

the world over. East of the Mississippi river these natural beds are still numerous and transplanting is carried on to but a limited extent. Not only do these beds supply the wants of the people of the Lower Coast, but small quantities are shipped to the New Orleans market, and hundreds of poachers or "pirates"—so called—from Mississippi carry away annually hundreds of schooner loads of the shell fish.

The flavor of these bivalves here taken, although of excellent quality, compared with those of the Atlantic States, yet is by no means equal to those taken from the choice planting grounds across the Mississippi, going west from the great river. Bayou Cook, Grand Bayou, Bayou Lachuto, Grand Lake, Bayou Lafourche, Timbalier bay, Last Island, Barrataria bay, Vine island lake, Vermillion bay, and the Calcasieu grounds furnish the best, those of Bayou Cook having par excellence the highest reputation in the markets of Louisiana and the neighboring States, and bringing a correspondingly higher price.

The manner of cultivation, if it can be dignified with that name, and the methods of fishing and forwarding to market are of the most primitive character, and by them capabilities of production have been as yet hardly broached. The fishermen are mostly uneducated Austrians, from the Slavonic provinces, commonly known as "Tackoes." Small colonies of them "squat" on any available shore, generally along some stream, bay or lake emptying into the Gulf, regardless of the ownership of the land, erect their huts, and with a capital of a couple of pair of oyster tongs, a skiff or two, and a small stock of rough provisions, usually advanced by the dealers in the city, embark in the trade of fishing oysters. Few of them own luggers, or engage in the business of forwarding their oysters to market. From time to time they recruit their helpers from the freshly arrived of their countrymen, who, knowing neither the language or the country, go to "learn the trade" at nominal wages in a sort of apprenticeship, receiving as part compensation for their labor board and lodging, such as it is.

The master fisherman or "captain" as he is termed, thus equipped and assisted, starts out in the planting season and transports from the natural bed skiff-loads of the shellfish, which he deposits in the brackish bayou or lake which he has selected near his cabin, marks his beds of "plants" with stakes to designate his ownership and keeps "watch and ward" over his possessions until his crop is ready to ship to market. Others do not plant at all, but only fish the natural oysters from the bed and sell to "luggermen." The planted oysters transferred from the natural beds where the sea water is very salt, soon feel the beneficial effect of their changed condition. The fresh water streams, draining the rich alluvial highlands, bring down in profusion infusiora and other low forms of vegetable and animal life on which the young oysters thrive. They commence immediately to fatten and alter the shape of their shells gradually from the lank and slim form somewhat similar to an irregular isosceles triangle, broad at the hinge and diminishing in breadth until they narrow down to what is commonly but erroneously called the mouth, forming somewhat of a wedgelike contour, to a more rotund or parabolic shape as they grow larger.

When sufficiently matured, say to an average length between four and six inches, the time of fattening and growth depending to a great extent on the size when transplanted and the richness and abundance of the food in the locality, the crop is ready for marketing. During the fattening process, however, the plants are subject to a variety of diseases, although not so numerous or so fatal as in the colder waters of the North Atlantic. Nor are they exempt from other destructive agencies. Schools of drum fish and sheepshead prey upon the beds, crushing the shells easily and devouring at times in a single night hundreds of barrels of oysters. Crabs also devour the young oyster, while a number of crustaceous borers find their way through the shells and kill the young brood. To guard against these depredations, although ineffectually in most cases, pens formed of stakes driven in the bottom of the stream are erected around the plants.

The planting we have alluded to consists in strewing the natural young oysters in thin layers over a hard bottom, which has been previously selected and located, or at times artificially created by deposits of old shells. In gathering or "tonging" the oysters from the natural bed twenty barrels per day is considered a good day's work per hand. This, however, is rarely reached, owing to the unreliability and inferiority of the labor. The "Tackoes" are by disposition not an industrious people, and like all the people dwelling near the shores of the Mediterranean and the Adriatic they are inclined to the "dolce far niente," and are peculiarly sensitive from their former habitats to the effects of the cold northers of the Gulf. Moreover, they are timid sailors and dread the sudden storms of our Southern waters. They are careless and heedless of waste, and it is a common practice, although contrary to law to "cull" the natural oysters and for that matter the plants as well, on shore or while under sail from the beds. The fatal effects in ruining the yield of oysters by this practice will be readily perceived when we state that it consists in scraping and knocking off the myriads of embryo young oysters which adhere to the older ones, and which should be dropped back into the water on the beds, to be thus preserved and matured, but instead are dropped on land or in the water away from the beds and there left to die. This is but one example of the thriftlessness of the ordinary run of "Tackoe" oyster fishermen. The report of the United States Fishery Commission of 1880 says: "The shipment of oysters from New Orleans has hitherto been of very small account and principally of fresh oysters. * * * Work is irregular because of the difficulty of getting oysters in sufficient quantity and when needed (owing mainly to the indisposition of the oystermen to work in bad weather.)"

There are no statistics at hand by which the total amount of the gathered crops can even be approximately esti-

mated. Prices vary very much, according to the weather and the season. Small natural unplanted oysters, commonly called "coons," suitable for planting, can ordinarily be purchased at from twenty-five cents to sixty cents per barrel, delivered free on board at the beds. Fully matured plants vary in price at the plant beds from one to two dollars per barrel, according ro the reputation of the locality from which they come. These "barrels," however, are what are technically called "bank measure," that is, two "bank measure" barrels make about three barrels when sold in market. When the planter finds that this crop is sufficiently matured and fat, ready for market, say six or eight months after being transplanted, he bargains and sells to the "lugger man" on the ground. A few planters own or have their luggers and ship for their own account. The "luggermen" transport their purchases to market, generally to New Orleans. The trip to the city usually takes from two to three days, a part of the journey consisting in threading narrow, shallow and tortuous bayoux. Adverse head winds sometimes delay the passage so long that the cargoes are unmarketable on reaching their destination. Sometimes where practicable "cordelling," or hauling the luggers by horse or man power, is resorted to, and at times steam towage is employed, all of which, of course, is an element of further expense.

Arrived at New Orleans, the "luggerman" disposes of his load to the dealers, who buy and supply the local trade and ship to neighboring cities. Prices range according to the supply. Favorable winds may serve to bring in on the same day a large fleet of oyster-laden craft to "lugger bay," as their landing opposite the French market is called. The market consequently becomes overstocked and glutted. If to this is added simultaneously a sudden change of the weather, from cold to warm, a not unusual thing in this climate, the "luggerman" is forced to sell at a very heavy loss on purchase price, or unload his cargo into the river. Besides these adverse contingencies, there are the ordinary accidents of navigation, such as grounding, and remaining so for days in the low tides in the shallow bayoux and lakes, and storms of several days duration, when the timid lugger-man, who shortens sail ordinarily on the slightest rise of the wind, now anchors or "ties up" and awaits its cessation. Then, too, the cargo is subject to considerable risk of being killed while in transit. A violent collision with the bank or another vessel, a violent hammering on the deck, and even heavy peals of thunder, have been known to deaden the whole cargo, and if the weather be warm and the market not close at hand there ensues a complete loss.

With all these disadvantages, however, which could easily be obviated by prudent and proper precautions for their prevention, and in spite of the heedless, thriftless and primitive manner in which the trade is carried on, these Austrians in nearly every instance amass considerable profits, make what to them are handsome and respectable fortunes, and usually retire to their native land, there to live, with their few wants and the Continental cheapness of living, the balance of their lives in comparative affluence for people of their class. These fortunes are ordinarily realized in a few years, seldom more than ten or twelve. On retiring, the fisherman's hut and outfit, oyster beds, tools, boats, etc., are disposed of, with the good will of an established business, to some relative or friend whom he has imported to the country for the purpose, or perhaps to some of his helpers who have saved a little money. In some instances good round sums are realized by these sales. In others, the retiring vendor retains a share in the future business and draws a portion of the profits, occasionally paying flying visits to this country to look after his interests.

Most of these men can neither read nor write English or any other language, nor do they speak or understand any tongue save Slavonic, and when dealing with others than those of their own nationality, require the services of an interpreter. These small fortunes which they amass in so short a time generally consist of sums varying from $5000 to $15,000 or more. Considering the small-

ness of their operations, the lightness of the labor, the exceedingly limited character of their business in every respect, the utter want of scientific or practical knowledge of oyster culture possessed by them, the acquisition of such sums in so short a time is marvellous. And yet when we consider their manner of life and their immense profits hereafter shown, it is easily comprehended. They "squat" on any lands, public or private, for which they pay no rent. Hitherto they have paid no rent or taxes of any kind. They pay nothing for their oysters if they tong them themselves. They subsist largely on fish which are plentiful and easily caught at all seasons, supplemented by poultry, which they raise, and game of all kinds, which abounds in proper seasons. In some cases they reclaim a small portion of the marsh land in the neighborhood of their cabins by filling it in, and cultivate vegetables thereon. During the "close" season, when only small quantities of oysters are illegally or surreptitiously marketed they engage in other profitable pursuits. Their expenses are almost nil, outside of a small amount for store provisions and rough clothing, and their proceeds are almost all clear profit.

In addition to the sale and shipment of fresh oysters, large profits have been realized by canneries, which have been established from time to time, but as the oyster supply in their neighborhoods has been diminished by indiscriminate and unseasonable fishing, and prices have increased, these establishments have removed to more favorable and lower priced localities, where their material could be purchased almost at their own prices. The canned oysters thus shipped from Louisiana have always been of the poorest and cheapest quality, subjected to the "bloating" process by continued "floating" in fresh water, and then canned by some imperfect process which imparts to them a "woody" and unpleasant taste. All these practices have combined to give Louisiana oysters an unfavorable reputation in markets other than those of the State. Properly prepared and of the better quality, connoisseurs have pronounced them equal if not superior to the best of Chesapeake bay or those of any of the other Eastern fisheries.

If we turn from this primitive, loose and careless method in which the oyster industry of Louisiana is at present carried on, and compare with it the skill, industry and science with which the cultivation is conducted in the Eastern States and in Europe, and then consider the vast area that the Louisiana oyster grounds present, the warm waters of the Gulf, the richness of the food, and the numerous other superior advantages which their situs affords, there dawns before us a field for investment, with such rich returns therefrom, as is scarcely presented anywhere else in the wide world in this or any other employment of men and money.

Let us for a moment illustrate the enormous profit accruing to these primitive planters and luggermen. A "bank" barrel of "coon" oysters will, when transplanted for six or eight months, increase to a barrel and a half by reason of the augmentation in size by growth. The "coon" oysters can be obtained free from the natural beds at no cost except the price of labor. If purchased they cost thirty cents per barrel. This barrel and a half is sold to the "lugger man" at from one to two dollars per barrel at the plant beds. When the "lugger man" sells at the city market he obtains from three to four dollars per "market" barrel, two "bank" barrels making three "market" barrels. Thus the bank "barrel" of fish which the lugger man has bought at $2.00, brings him a barrel and a half (market), or from $4.50 to $6.00 per bank barrel. If the planter ships himself, he would obtain $6.60 for what he has paid thirty cents, or obtained for nothing if he fished them. The same would be relatively true, only with a smaller amount of profit, where natural oysters are transplanted and so kept a few weeks simply to improve their condition by fattening before shipping.

As the trade is at present carried on, the planter gets the benefit of the first difference in the growth, and the lugger man the advantage of the difference between the "bank" and the market measure. Thus a person who both

plants and markets his oysters as we have said, would pay thirty cents a barrel "bank measure" and from that barrel he would gather a "bank" barrel and a half of mature, marketable oysters, which selling at say $3.00 he would get $6.60 for what he originally paid thirty cents. In other words a "bank" barrel of coon oysters worth thirty cents, expands into a "bank" barrel and a half of plants in six or eight months, which is two and a quarter "market" barrels, worth from $3.00 to $4.00 each. At $3.00 per barrel the thirty-cent purchase becomes worth $6.00; at $4.00 per barrel, $9.00. Of course these prices are predicated on the lowest average buying and selling rates and on the basis of large purchases and sales in an ordinarily favorable market. These profits would be immensely increased if the spawn were scientifically protected and the immature oyster were preserved from disease and other numerous enemies by proper precautions, now universally in vogue in the older countries and fully described in "The Oyster" by Prof. Brooks; Oelmer's "Life, History and Protection of the American Oyster"; the "Report of the United States Fishery Commission"; the reports of the Oyster Commissioners of many States and other American and European literature on the same subject.

That the field for investment is an inviting one, and is gradually becoming apparent as such to investors both within and without the State, (and must become still more so as the subject is investigated and studied), is shown by the formation of several incorporated companies who are now engaged in the development of the industry. Outside of many small individual efforts in that direction, several associations have been formed, prominent among which are the "Gulf and Bayou Cook Oyster Company, limited," which owns the major portion of the lands on Bayou Cook and the valuable planting grounds thereunto appertaining, and also the "Louisiana Fish and Oyster Co.," the latter of which is now in active operation, and the former will soon be, having just successfully terminated a long litigation with some of the Tackoe "squatter" fishermen. The legislature of the State has recently passed prudent acts for the protection of the fisheries, reserving the natural beds, not heretofore granted, for public use during the "open" season, providing for a proper police, as well as the leasing and sale of State lands suitable to planting at extremely moderate rates, and exacting a minimum tax to execute the law. The right of fishing oysters is reserved to citizens of the State alone. This law, although imperfect in not closing for a longer period in each year the natural oyster beds which have become well nigh exhausted, so as to allow them to recuperate and to be restored to their pristine fruitfulness, will probably be amended and perfected by future assemblies, as the legislative mind becomes more educated on the subject, as it has been in the older States that have undergone the same experience in this respect. Of course, such improvement will be strenuously resisted by the uneducated fisherman and the avaricious luggerman and dealer, who look no further than to the present profits of the day, and care not for the future, although if they did but know it, they are more vitally and immediately interested than all others in the prevention of the ruin of the fisheries.

Perhaps such obstructions to improvements are always to be expected from the ignorant. In New Jersey, where such an extended closure of seed-beds was similarly opposed, (as it was in France and other countries,) the commissioners tell us "all the opposition offered at the outset to this system of protection has now disappeared, and those who were loudest in their protestations have acknowledged their unfounded prejudice and error. * * * All the seedling grounds of Delaware

bay enjoy a rest of nine months and a half each year. As a result, the beds have increased in area, and new beds are continually forming, and the supply is increasing to a wonderful extent." If the legislature of Louisiana will follow the wise example of these older communities, also prevent the use of the natural beds except for seeding purposes, and thus compel and induce a proper cultivation of the oyster, a mine of untold wealth will be opened both for her own exchequer and her people.

The difficulties, dangers and delays of transportation are being rapidly overcome by railways and canals, some already built and others projected, penetrating the best oyster regions; and if capital be properly encouraged and protected in its investment, as it assuredly will be, the day is not far distant when the production will be immeasurably increased, the price for home consumption greatly reduced, and an export trade established which will supply the whole of the Western territory of the United States, from the Mississippi to the Pacific coast, at reduced prices. Not only to the capitalist is the field open, but to the skilled oyster culturists of Chesapeake and Delaware bays, Long Island Sound, and the shores of Connecticut, the State offers cheap oyster lands for sale or to rent, and a free supply of seed. To all such, with a minimum of capital and skilled industry and energy, she opens her arms to welcome them to a home on the verge of her "summer sea," beneath skies which hardly know what winter is, and to cheer them on to fortune and her own industrial development. This is no fair-seeming false promise, but one tendered in all sincerity, and based on facts which the writer has been careful to understate rather than to overestimate.

THE MOON ROCK AND JESSE WOOD'S BETHEL.

By Mrs. William B. Crenshaw.

Several years ago I made my first business venture in a small town in North Alabama as bookkeeper for a large lumber firm. I had been there but a short time when my employer came into the office one morning and requested me to go at once to Ashville on important business connected with the mills. "Court is now in session and you will most likely find all the interested parties there," he said. "My wife is very ill, and I cannot leave home just now; but I feel confident that you can attend to this business as well as myself."

Pleased with his confidence in my ability I willingly agreed to make the journey, glad of an opportunity to see more of the country.

Ashville was about thirty miles distant. The road leading to it lay across a spur of Sand Mountain, known as "The Backbone," and was too rough to be traveled in any manner except on horseback. This made me the more eager to go, as I was fond of riding and was provided with a good horse. Hurrying through my preparations, I set out to Ashville just as the hands of the great mill clock were creeping up to high noon.

Leaving the little town on the banks of the Coosa river, I rode slowly through the woods, enjoying their cool fragrance and listening dreamily to that weird, whispering music, never heard except in a pine forest. I reached the base of "The Backbone" and looked up its rugged sides, while tender recollections of my home in the Tennessee Mountains came trooping into my memory. A cool breeze, laden with the faint odor of sweet fern, rushed down to greet me, but a sudden burst of song from a bird near at hand startled my horse and dispelled my dreams.

I looked up. Before me was one of the most remarkable objects upon which my eyes ever rested. From the flat surface of the top of "The Backbone" rose a huge bluff. of sandstone, gleaming white as marble, its summit crowned with a rank growth of moss and ferns and masses of tangled vines which trailed far down its sidss. Of the two sides presented to my view, one was an irregular mass of broken stone, the other a broad, perpendicular, unbroken wall, whose whiteness was intensified by a large, dark-red stain upon its face in the form of a crescent moon. At the foot of this wall grew a large mountain oak, and under its thick branches was a mound of stones about six feet in height, so carefully arranged as to attract one's immediate attention and to suggest the work of human hands in its construction.

The sun was setting, and in the red glow of its level rays the bluff looked like a vast white palace against the soft blue summer sky. I was so lost in wondering conjecture that I did not hear the tramp of an approaching horse's feet, and was not conscious of any presence on the mountain save my own, until a hearty voice asked: "Well, you've struck a riddle, have you?" I turned quickly to face my questioner, who proved to be the village doctor from Riverside, and I answered: "Yes, doctor, one equal to the Sphinx. Perhaps you can read it for me."

The doctor twisted his mustache meditatively. He was my first acquaintance and friend in Riverside, a man in middle life, who had seen something of the world, and possessed a marvelous store of general information. I looked to him now for some explanation of the mystery which loomed up before us, for I was sure he could give me the information I desired. During a life-long residence in this country he had learned it thoroughly—its history and that of its people, its geology and its many incidents of war and adventure and tales of romance. He seemed weary now, and slowly dismounting he said: "We've only six miles further to go, and we can make that after moonrise. Let's rest here, and I will tell you all I know of 'The Moon Rock' and Jesse Wood's Bethel."

"You know," he said, after we were seated upon the moss near the mound of stones, "this entire country was once inhabited by the Creek Indians. Even when I was a boy, quite a number of them had their homes in the valley. One of the chiefs told me this legend of the 'Moon Rock':

"Long ago that beautiful valley was the home of a gentle, peace-loving people, known as 'the Beloved Children of the Great Spirit.' He often visited them in their homes and bestowed many benefits upon them. They lived in undisturbed prosperity until a neighboring chief, growing envious of their happiness, resolved to make war upon them. They, ignorant of any and every mode of warfare, were soon slain to the last man. This mountain top was the battlefield and hither the Great Spirit, hearing the death-cries of his children, hastened from the Happy Hunting Grounds, filled with mighty anger and grief. With the exception of the envious chief, he transformed all the painted, hostile warriors into the rattle-snakes which infest these mountains to this day. Then he laid the bodies of his murdered children tenderly away in the cavern under this rock, and shut them in forever, and no man has ever found an entrance to their sepulchre. From the chief's panting bosom he tore the heart, and with its warm, fast flowing blood he painted that crimson moon over their last resting place. When he had finished his work, he dropped the still bleeding, quivering heart upon that rock near you—see the stain it made—

where it was transformed into a vulture and fed upon the body it had once inhabited. And the Great Spirit's vengeance was completed."

A few moments of silence followed this recital, while the doctor filled and lighted his pipe. "Indian legends," he resumed, "have generally the two great characteristics of the people, blood-thirstiness and cruelty, and this one is no exception. No doubt it afforded to the savage mind a very satisfactory solution of that mystery of a crescent which is evidently beyond the reach of human hand. But a modern scientist will tell you that nature gave expression to one of her queerest freaks in the formation of that stone, and some day, when this vast area of mineral land is opened and all those little towns are populous cities, the Moon Rock will be to Alabama what the Natural Bridge is to Virginia." The doctor looked out over the valley, where the white moonbeams turned the river to silver and touched the village spires with their cool fingers, as if in his mind's eye he saw the cities of which he had spoken. But I did not leave him long to his musings.

"Is that mound of stones 'Jesse Wood's Bethel?' You spoke of it just now."

"Yes," he answered, "it is known over half the State as 'Jesse Wood's Bethel,' and was built by one of the most remarkable characters in its history.

"Jesse Wood's father was the first white settler in this part of the State, and Jesse, deprived during his infancy of a mother's love and care, grew up among the negroes and Indians, with scarcely more training than they. The father was a gambler and he taught Jesse all the tricks then known to the profession so thoroughly that when he reached his twenty-first year he was 'hard to beat' (to use his own expression), even by his teacher. During this time the country had received a great many more settlers, among whom the rough, gaming element predominated, and Jesse was soon the acknowledged leader of a band of young men, who by their lawless deeds terrorized the entire settlement for years.

"About the time my story begins, as they say in novels, a young evangelist, whose reputation for forcible eloquence had preceded him, began a revival in Ashville. With a fiery zeal characteristic of the preachers of those days, he waked the sinners to a realization of their danger, and reaped richly from the fields which he found 'white to the harvest'. The meetings had been in progress for perhaps ten days, when Jesse concluded that it was time he and his friends were 'having some fun' as he expressed it. With him, to think was to act, and that night he and 'the boys' filed quietly into the church, while the congregation eyed them askance and wondered what mischief was brewing. They had previously agreed to remain quiet until a call was made for 'mourners,' by which time their course of action would probably be suggested to them by some incident of the meeting.

"They had not intended to listen to the sermon, and probably none of them did, save Jesse. His attention was chained, and conviction entered his heart. When the minister finished his sermon, and coming to the front of the altar asked in thunder tones, 'Who's on the Lord's side?' Jesse's magnificent form rose to its full height and his rich, penetrating voice said, so distinctly that all might hear, '*I* am, from this day to the end of my life.'

"There was silence for a moment, the silence of astonishment; then his companions, construing this act into a signal for the fun to begin, laughed uproariously, and one of them, Jim Collins, said boisterously, 'Better git somebody ter shoot ye while ye air thar', Jess; mebbe ye'll stand some showin' fur heaven now.' 'I mean what I say,' said Jesse, in a firm voice, 'With God's help, I am going to be *a man*, 'en I wish ye all would choose, with me, the better way; but if ye air goin' ter stick ter the old life, we'll say goodbye now.' He waited a moment as if for some answer from them, then walked rapidly to the altar, while his companions silently, and with sullen faces, left the church.

"Jesse began to make preparation for entering upon the ministry, and, with that determination which was ever his distinguishing trait, he overcame every obstacle, and in two years from that

night he was an ordained minister. He became the beloved pastor of the church in Ashville, and once each month, in spite of wind and weather, he traveled this road to Riverside, where he preached to the plantation owners assembled in the little log church. He fulfilled every duty faithfully and conscientiously, and found peace and happiness as the years rolled by.

"His former comrades, in the meantime, had gone from bad to worse. Jim Collins had been tacitly given the leadership of the band, and his daring and deviltry stopped at nothing by which he could accomplish his ends. So it happened that when a band of robbers began to work these mountains, there were well-grounded suspicions that the two gangs were identical, and they were more feared than ever. Jesse, even in his wildest days, possessed a certain sense of right and honor, by which, with his great force of character, he had restrained them from doing what he would have termed 'dirty, mean tricks.' He had thought it perfectly right in the old days to win at cards and keep the winnings, provided the game was played fair, but highway robbery was quite another thing. His old friends steered clear of him, ''Cause we don't want none uv his durned preachin', Jim Collins declared. Jesse never sought them out nor attempted to preach to them, knowing that they had not forgiven him for what they considered his base desertion of them, and he hoped that time would soften their enmity.

"Jim Collins had once declared his intention of 'gettin' even with Jess,' and the opportunity was not long thereafter in coming. Jesse had filled his usual appointment at Riverside one Sunday in midsummer, and set out early Monday morning on his homeward journey. He was passing the village store when one of the planters hailed him, and going close to the horse's side said, 'Parson, I've a little package here which I would like for you to deliver to Lawyer Turner in Ashville. It contains three hundred dollars, and with you it will be safe from the robbers, for they'll never 'hold up' a poor preacher,' he added laughingly. Jesse took the package and after a short conversation he rode away, while his friend returned to the store, both unconscious of the fact that every word had been heard by one of 'Collins' Gang' on the opposite side of the street. Jesse was further detained by his horse going lame and having to be shod and it was late ere he left the village.

"The soft summer night had fallen and the golden light of a full moon was bathing the mountains in splendor when Jesse rode up the path singing:

'Rock of ages cleft for me,
Let me hide myself in thee.'

"He did not see a dark form lurking in the shadow of the Moon Rock, and he came fearlessly on sending the rich tones of his voice before him:

'In my hand no price I bring,
Simply to Thy cross I cling.'

"'Wall, ef ye haven't got it in yer hand hit's in yer pocket, pardner, en that'll do jest as well. S'pose yer hand hit over ter me, en ye kin jest keep on clingin' ez long ez ye like.' And Jim Collins stood out in the full moonlight face to face with his old friend. Jesse gave no sign of either alarm or astonishment as he drew up his horse and said quietly: 'I don't exactly ketch yer meanin,' Jim; couldn't ye make it a little plainer?' 'I kin make hit plain er'nough ef yer don't understand, though yer didn't use 'ter be so dull. Hit's jest this: I'm in despre't need uv that money ye're got, 'en whut's more I'm goin' ter have hit. 'Not from me, Jim,' said Jesse. 'You know what I mean I say, 'en you can't have that money unless you take my life with it.' The firm lips closed over the words and his determined eyes looked straight into those of his foe.

"There was a flash of steel in the moonlight and the unflinching form of the preacher was covered by Jim's revolver.

"'Wall, I kin mighty quick take that, too, 'en I don't know but whut I ought ter do hit, any way, fur yer goin' back on yer friends like ye did. Now hit's one uv two things—ye kin give hit ter me 'en make hit all right with the Squire, he believes so in you, 'en I'll

leave the State—er ye kin keep hit, 'en, well, dead men tell no tales. I'll give yer ten minutes.' 'If ye give me ten years, I'd answer ye jest the same,' said Jesse. 'Then, I s'pose ye air ready ter die, pardner, but I'll give yer time ter say yer prayers,' said Jim, mockingly. 'That's all I ask,' said Jesse, and, dismounting, he knelt down near that oak, then a tiny sapling. 'Time's up Jess,' said the robber at length, and the preacher rose and stood with folded arms before him, the light of a firm resolve shining in his eyes. Jim raised his pistol and aimed it straight at his old friend's heart. 'I'll give ye one more chance, Jess, while I count three. One!' The preacher's form was statue-like in the moonlight. 'Two!' There was a rustle in the vines overhanging the Moon Rock above the robber's head, but it was unheard by the two men. Jesse closed his eyes, as he thought, upon life. 'Three' was never spoken by the robber.

"Two huge rattlesnakes, engaged in fierce combat above him, rolled over the cliff, and loosened a sharp, angular boulder, which crushed robber and snakes to the ground in its fall. The report of the pistol woke startled echoes, which mingled with the dying groans of the would-be murderer and the terrible hisses and angry rattling of the snakes; but the bullet meant tor Jesse Woods had sped wide of its mark.

"He opened his eyes and beheld a scene which haunted him until his dying day. Before him lay the wounded robber, with the life blood oozing from a deep cut in his temple, while the maddened snakes writhed and twisted around him, burying their poisonous fangs in his face and neck. One glance at the stunned, bleeding form, half concealed by the bruised and quivering serpents, told Jesse that Jim Collins was beyond human aid. He hastened from the scene with heart and brain sick with horror, and rode swift as the wind to Ashville.

"Ere the dawn of a new day reddened the East he led a wondering crowd back to the Moon Rock, where lay the robber, still in the coils of the serpents, and rigid in death. The men made a grave under that oak, and buried the robber, placing at the head the stone which caused his death. It also marked the spot upon which Jesse Woods had knelt to commit his soul to God, and he made it the foundation of his 'Bethel.' Whenever he passed this place he paused to place a stone upon the grave, and to thank God for his merciful deliverance from death. During the Civil War, some soldier, supposing there was a hidden treasure under the stones, threw them to the ground, but Jesse persistently rebuilt the heap. He died at a good old age. No marble shaft marks his grave in the little church-yard, but here he has builded his own monument, and many generations will come and go ere Jesse's adventure is forgotton or his Bethel destroyed."

·Notes on Southern Progress.

THE new courthouse at Llano, Texas, is one of the finest in the Southwest. It cost $50,000 and has just been completed, It is three stories high and the materials used in construction were pink granite and white marble, giving it a very handsome exterior. It is richly furnished and artistically decorated within.

A CHARTER of incorporation has been granted to the First National Fire Insurance Co., of Fredericksburg, Va., with a capital stock of $300,000. The incorporators are John W. Bond, of Washington, D. C.; W. J. Mosley, of Philadelphia, Pa.; George D. Young, of Georgetown, D. C.; T. F. Meany, of Washington, D. C,, and W. E. Towles, of Culpeper, Va. The company has been organized by the election of the following officers : W. J. Mosley, of Philadelphia, president, and E. W. Wallace, secretary. The principal office of the company for the transaction of business will be at Fredericksburg, Va.

THE Jacksonville Clearing Association, of Jacksonville, Fla., which represents four national and two State banks, has been in existence about a year and has proved a pronounced success. For the year ended July 31, 1893, the total exchanges were $20,587,476, total balances $3,758,879, average monthly exchanges $1,715,623, average weekly exchanges $359,913 ; total business transacted during the year $24,346,356.

THE Galveston Chamber of Commerce will add an office building to the number of fine structures already erected in that city. C. H. McMaster has been selec ed chairman of a committee to make arrangements for its construction. The building is to be eight stories high and is to have all the essentials of a modern office building, with elevators, heat and light plants, etc. The ground floor will probably be used for a bank, and is to be provided with the necessary storage vaults, etc. This building will be the first of its kind in Galveston.

THE Mechanics & Traders' Insurance Co., of New Orleans, is now making the necessary alterations and improvements in their building on the corner of Carondelet and Common streets to fit it up as a first-class office building. When the changes are completed the company will have forty offices to rent, fitted up with all the modern improvements. There will be a wide and handsome entrance with tiled floor, and in addition a most complete and rapid elevator.

REPORTS from the vicinity of St. Augustine, Fla., are that considerable real estate is changing hands, and that much outside capital is being invested in the locality. In North City there is much activity in real estate transactions in the neighborhood of the San Marco Hotel. A tract of twelve acres just north of the hotel has been divided up into lots which are being sold rapidly. Half a dozen cottages are being planned by purchasers of the land and will soon be in course of construction.

THE Yazoo & Mississippi Valley Railroad Co. has applied for a permit to erect a $54,000 elevator in New Orleans. The site selected is bounded by Howard, Perdido, Feret and Poydras streets. The contract for the work has been given to the firm of James Stewart & & Co., of St. Louis, who built the two elevators at Southport.

SOME five or six years ago an English inventor sold to an American rubber manufacturer for a considerable amount a secret process for manufacturing cottonseed-oil into rubber. Since then this secret has become the property of the rubber trust. This process has been used ever since, and it is a matter of fact that large quantities of cottonseed-oil are now being used by at least fifteen or sixteen rubber factories in the United States to produce a substitute for rubber. This is in the United States alone. I do not know to what extent this process is being used in England and on the Continent, but as it originated in England it is probably used to some extent there also. By this process the converted cottonseed-oil costs about seven cents per pound. The admixture of this substitute has been limited to about fifteen per cent., as it is not deemed advisable to exceed this amount without deteriorating the quality of the rubber product. With an annual production of 3,500,000 to 4,500,000 tons of cottonseed, the greater portion of which now finds no more economical use than as a fertilizer or else is wholly wasted, the possibilities of the development of this new industry seem limitless. The new use for the seed of the cotton plant is a striking illustration of the economy of nature in providing nothing that is without its use to mankind. For generations cottonseed was regarded only as a nuisance and millions of tons of it were thrown away. Now it is a source of great profit to the planter, having sold during the past season as high as $22 per ton. As there are two pounds of seed for every pound of lint cotton the value of the seed to the planters has been as high as $11 per bale of cotton—a snug profit out of waste.

THE indications are that Atlanta will soon add another to the list of massive buildings which now attract so much attention in the Gate City. A military organization which includes many of the wealthiest residents is the Gate City Guard. Its present armory is not suitable, and the board of trustees is now examining sites with the view of erecting a building which will include an armory and a large auditorium for concert, theatrical and lecture purposes. It is proposed to expend about $85,000 in its erection.

THE exports of wheat from New Orleans during July aggregated 1,097,865 bushels, against 235,141 for the same month in 1895 ; and the corn exports for July this year amounted to 356,739 bushels, as compared with 111,998 in July, 1892. This gives an increase of 1,107,465 bushels for the two cereals, or nearly 300 per cent.

AUDITOR BLOOMFIELD, of the New Orleans custom house, reports the receipts of bananas at that port for the past fiscal year as follows : British Honduras, 17,500 bunches ; Costa Rico, 65,632 bunches ; Guatemala, 53,300 bunches ; Honduras, 165,654 bunches ; Nicaragua, 101,000 bunches, and Colombia, 110,300 bunches—total, 513,386 bunches valued at $160,834.

THE proposed system of sewers to be built by the city of Macon, Ga., promises to place that community among those having the best sanitary improvements in the country. Mr. Samuel Gray, the well-known sanitary engineer, of Providence, R. I., has been engaged to prepare the plans for the work, which will be under the immediate supervision of the city engineer. About thirty miles of pipe will be laid on the principal business and residence streets at an average cost of $6500 per mile. The probability is that vitrified pipe, such as is made in Macon, will be used, thus much of the $200,000 to be spent on the system will go to home industries. The surveys are now being made.

THERE has just been sawed at O'Neill's mill in Jacksonville, Fla., a cargo of Florida mahogany belonging to the South Florida Lumber Company of Cocoanut Grove. The lumber produced is capable of a fine finish, and is used for furniture, newell posts, balusters, etc. It runs small in size, but in quality and appearance resembles San Domingo mahogany.

"A RELIC OF THE OLD REGIME."——(SEE PAGE 479.)

THE

SOUTHERN STATES.

OCTOBER, 1893.

SOUTHERN LEADERS IN CONGRESS.

By Edward W. Barrett.

I. THE SENATE.

In the field of real statesmanship the South has always outranked the North. This has been true from the foundation of the government. It is true to-day. There are statesmen of great ability in Congress from the Northern and Western States, but taken as a whole the South has more conspicuous figures, more men of great ability in proportion to the total number in the legislative halls of this country than any other section. It is not that the soil or climate of the South is more productive of great men, but it is due to a custom which has always prevailed in the Southern States. They make few changes in their Congressional delegation. They retain their representatives in Congress just so long as they expand.

In the Senate the South has a larger proportion of great men than all other sections combined. It is because the South has elected and reelected the same Senators often. Such has not been the case among the Northern and Western States except in a few instances. Senator Sherman for instance, perhaps the ablest man on the Republican side of the chamber, has been a member of that body for twelve years, and Senator Morrill, of Vermont, has been in the Senate continuously since March 4, 1867. Senator Allison, of Iowa, and Senator Jones, of Nevada, commenced their

terms in 1873. But with these exceptions there are few Senators from the Northern and Western States who have served long terms.

The Southern States as a rule select Senators from the ablest of their men, who have devoted their lives to the school of statesmanship. As a rule Southern Senators have served in their State legislatures and afterwards have been governor or else served several terms in the House of Representatives.

At the head of the list of Southern Democratic Senators, and perhaps the ablest of Senators, stands Arthur Pue Gorman, of Maryland. He has been in that body from childhood, having begun his connection with it in 1852, when, at the age of thirteen, he became a page. As a page he served several years and was then made postmaster. After a term in the Maryland legislature, of which he was elected the Speaker of the House of Delegates, he was elected to the United States Senate in 1880. He was reelected in 1886 and again in 1892. His term expires March 3, 1899, and in all human probability he will be again returned.

Senator Gorman is now the recognized leader of the Democratic majority in the Senate. He attained this position by sheer force of ability. It was in the great fight the Democratic party made against the force bill that he first assumed leadership. By unanimous consent of the Democrats he was selected as the Senator above all others to prevent the adoption of that iniquitous measure. He rose to the occasion; night and day he stood in the fore of the minority forces battling every inch of ground. He contested with a stubbornness never before exhibited in that body for the rights of the minority. He blocked attempts to arbitrarily force a vote by unjust rulings of the presiding officer, and finally side-tracked the measure with the silver bill. It is to him that the credit is due for the defeat of the force bill. He saved the South from a return to the negro domination of reconstruction days. The South showed its appreciation of his work by sending many delegates to the Chicago Democratic convention for him for president, though he was not a candidate. Had he allowed the use of his name many of his friends believe he might have won. Could the South name the next Democratic nominee it would be Gorman.

ARTHUR P. GORMAN, MARYLAND.

Senator Gorman does not speak often. He only speaks when the occasion requires it. Then he is brief, but forcible. He attempts neither eloquence nor wit. His is the speech of the real statesman—strong, argumentative, logical. He is a natural leader of men, and his colleagues have implicit confidence in his judgment. When a legislative tangle comes he is the man sought to unravel it. He is for his party above all things. Under his management of the campaign Mr. Cleveland was first elected president. To his efforts were largely due the success of the party in the last election. It is upon him that the party now relies to settle the great struggle over the repeal of the Sherman law. Under his guidance and advice the solution of the perplexing problem will soon be attained.

Next to Mr. Gorman among Southern Democratic Senators ranks John T. Morgan, of Alabama, who achieved military distinction in the late war as general of an Alabama brigade.

Senator Morgan ranks among the foremost of the great lawyers of the Senate. He has been a member of that body for sixteen years, and is now chairman of the Committee on Foreign Relations. As an exponent of international law he has no superior. As a speaker he is the wonder of the Senate. He has no equal. He speaks without the slightest effort, physical or mental, and can speak continuously from one to seven hours. There is no repetition in his utterances; words and sentences flow in a steady stream for hour after hour, and, remarkable as it may seem, every sentence is well rounded, so perfect that the closest student of the English language could not suggest a change. They are models of logic. He has been known to continue one speech for seven days, speaking four hours a day, and in his entire argument from day to day as printed there would not be a repetition.

Senator Morgan is likewise a man of courage and determination. During the Hayes administration he first demonstrated these qualities to the Senate. It was during the expiring days of the Forty-fourth Congress. An Alabama bill in which he was interested had passed both houses of Congress and

JOHN T. MORGAN, ALABAMA.

was before President Hayes for his signature. Congress would expire on the fourth day of March. On the third he heard that the President intended to pocket-veto his bill. One appropriation bill was pending. The Senate must pass it or else an extra session would be necessary. At two o'clock on the afternoon of the third of March Mr. Morgan secured the floor and began to address the Senate. After he had spoken two hours the leaders became nervous. He was asked how long he intended to speak. In reply he simply stated he had a few remarks to address to the Senate and continued. At six o'clock he still had the floor and was proceeding without apparent effort. A second time he was approached by one of the leaders and asked when he would conclude.

"When the President signs my bill," he replied.

"But you cannot speak until noon tomorrow?" was suggested.

"Perhaps not," the Alabamian observed, "but I have a few more remarks to address to the Senate," and again the words proceeded to flow as though from an automaton.

At eight o'clock in the evening he appeared as fresh as when he began. The Senate leaders were in a wild state of excitement. A special messenger was despatched to the President to explain the situation. He returned with Mr. Morgan's bill signed. As he received it he smiled, and addressing the presiding officer remarked:

"Mr. President, I believe I have no further remarks to submit."

Mr. Morgan's term in the Senate began March 5, 1877.

Senator Isham G. Harris, of Tennessee, is silver-haired and serious. No one knows exactly how old he is, because he religiously refrains from stating in the congressional directory the date of his birth. He is supposed, however, to have attained his full four score years, though in appearance he might pass for sixty. He is the fighter of the Senate. He takes his positions and stands uncompromisingly by them. Unsociable, keeping to himself, he is without any personal friends, but admired by all his compeers in Congress. Like Cassius, "seldom he smiles, and when he does it is of such a sort as if he mocked his spirit, which could be moved to smile at anything." His seriousness over trifles at times makes him ridiculous, but withal he is one of the strongest, ablest and most reliable and conservative men in the Senate.

ISHAM G. HARRIS, TENNESSEE.

He is an ex-Confederate soldier, and he was wont, it is said, to swear roundly at his soldiers. It is told of him that during his second year in the civil strife he had given some command which was not obeyed. In his blunt way he began using his characteristic vigorous language to his regiment. It was then that young Charles Tard Quintard, now Bishop of Tennessee, but then a chaplain in the regiment, stepped forward and said before the entire regiment:

"Colonel, you should be ashamed of yourself. How do you expect your men to obey your commands when you yourself cannot command your temper." Instead of having the young priest court-martialed he said:

"You are right, Quintard, by God, I will not swear again until the war is over."

And he kept his word. This same resoluteness has marked his career in Congress. As president pro tempore of the Senate he rules with firmness and yet with justice, irrespective of party.

CHARLES J. FAULKNER, WEST VIRGINIA.

His speeches, while not notable, are always to the point and command the close attention of the Senators. He has served his State as legislator, presidential elector in 1848, United States Congressman from 1849 to 1851, as presidential elector from the State-at large in 1856, as governor from 1857 to 1861, when he volunteered as an aid on the staff of the commanding general of the Confederate army of Tennessee for the last three years of the war; was elected to the Senate in 1877, reelected in 1883 and again in 1889. His term expires in 1895. There will be an attempt to defeat him, but his uncompromising integrity and pugnacious

qualities on the stump will, in all probability, be the stepping stones to the Senate again.

Senator Charles J. Faulkner, of West Virginia, is one of the youngest men in the Senate. He is but 47. Though just commencing his second term, his good judgment and his popularity and ability have caused him to be ranked high up among the leading Democrats of that body. In the great force bill contest of the Fifty-first Congress he was the principal lieutenant of Senator Gorman. It was he who managed the details of the contest, marshalling the minority forces at the proper time and aiding materially in the manœuvres necessary to a successful contest. His first important speech was against the force bill. Through that he bounded to the front. In the silver contest he has also been conspicuous in bringing about a compromise.

Senator Faulkner was the successor of his present colleague, Mr. Camden, who was returned to fill the vacancy caused by the death of Senator Kenna.

Mr. Faulkner received his primary education in the schools of Paris, when his father was Minister to France in 1859. At the age of fifteen, in 1862, he entered the Virginia Military Institute. He joined the Confederate army with a company from that institution. He was one of a few survivors of his company at the battle of New Market. Afterwards at the age of sixteen he served as an aid to Gen. John C. Breckinridge. After the war he resumed his studies at the University of Virginia and graduated from the law school of that institution in 1868. Mr. Faulkner held but one public office before his election to the Senate, that of circuit judge in his State.

Senator Butler, the Adonis of the Senate, as he is pointed out to strangers

MATTHEW C. BUTLER, SOUTH CAROLINA.

on account of his physical attractions, is a picturesque character. His mental and moral make-up, as well as his physical appearance, all tend to make him a man of interest, one whom visitors to the capitol like to see and whom politicians like to conciliate. He is a South Carolinian, with all the faults and virtues which that term carries with it. Impetuous in speech, quick in action, uncompromising in integrity, loyal to his State and section, he stands in the Congress of the United States a unique figure, a relic of the war and the champion still of the old State's rights doctrine.

He was born in Greenville, S. C., in 1836. He studied law and afterwards practiced it with great success. He began his political career as a member of the legislature of his State in 1860. He laid down the pen and the scroll to take up the sword as captain in the old Hampton Legion in 1861. With a great military record back of him he surrendered as a major-general. A gallant Confederate officer is always dear to the South, but doubly so if maimed in the

cause which was lost. Butler was wounded and lost his right leg at the battle of Brandy Station. He was returned to the State legislature in 1866, and, with the exception of Wade Hampton, did more to overthrow carpet bag and radical rule than any other man in his State.

He was sent to the Senate in 1877 and has since been retained. His term will expire March 3, 1895, and that date will prove the most important in his life. Under the leadership of Gov. Tillman the old regime of the State has been struck down. Hampton was defeated in the revolution, and now all the efforts of the reform element are aimed at Butler. Tillman, after sending John Irby to the Senate, now aspires to the honor himself. He has never met with defeat, and should Butler succeed in overthrowing him, he will have struck a death blow to the third party movement in the State.

Butler is a farmer, but looks like a prince. He is good in rough and tumble debate on the stump and yet his speeches in Congress are as polished

WILKINSON CALL, FLORIDA.

as those of White of Louisiana. When advertised to speak the galleries are crowded and he is one whom the capitol police cannot prevent the throng

EDWARD D. WHITE, LOUISIANA.

from applauding. He is a free coinage man, believing too that the executive has no part in the legislative, and in his latest speech he declared that with Cleveland's message the duty of the man of destiny was done.

Senator Wilkinson Call, of Florida, is a native Kentuckian, but lacks the characteristic eloquence of the blue grass statesmen. He is essentially a plain blunt man, who talks right on and generally "tells you that which you yourselves do know." But withal he is one of the strong conservative members of the upper chamber, and his speeches are read with more interest than they are heard. He was born in Russellville, Logan county, Kentucky, in 1834, and by profession is a lawyer. He was elected to the United States Senate soon after the war, but was not allowed to take his seat. He was reelected in 1879, and his present term does not expire until 1897. He will be returned, as no man can be found in the land of flowers with sufficient strength to defeat the political veteran. He is a voluminous talker and has something to say on every measure which comes before Congress. He is the Buck Kilgore of the Senate, believing in carrying out the economic platform strictly, and for

retrenchment is eternally vigilant.

Senator Edward Douglas White, of Louisiana, is a good speaker and good liver. For a junior Senator still serving in his first term, he occupies a position of prominence gained usually with great labor after years in Congress. He is only forty-eight years old, but was the Senator chosen to make the fight against the anti-option bill. This gave him his reputation. He bore the brunt of the entire contest and finally defeated the bill as it was sent from the House, and returned it with the amendments too late in the session to be taken up again.

He has a judicial appearance, with a smooth face, good-natured smile and a nondescript eye which succeeds admirably in concealing his thoughts. He is one of the most graceful speakers in the Senate. His style is ornate, yet logical, abounding in metaphors and similes. He is a lawyer by profession, and from 1878 to the date of his election to Congress was associate justice of the Supreme Court of Louisiana.

He is one of the strongest advocates of the unconditional repeal of the Sherman purchasing clause. He is uncompromising against compromise, refusing to yield an inch to the opposition. He was born in La Fourche parish, Louisi-

GEORGE G. VEST, MISSOURI.

ana, and was educated at the Jesuit college in New Orleans. He was elected in 1890 to succeed Hon. James B. Eustis, receiving 119 votes, against eleven votes for H. C. Warmoth, Republican.

Foremost among the versatile orators of the Senate stands George Graham Vest, of Missouri. Mr. Vest is a Senator who invariably attracts a crowd when he is announced for a speech. He is a strong as well as an entertaining talker. His quaint manner of expression and originality of thought have made him a reputation second to no man in the Senate.

Mr. Vest has been a member of the Senate since March 18, 1879. Born and educated in Kentucky, he removed in 1853 to Missouri and began the practice of law. In 1860-61 he was a member of the Missouri House of Representatives, was afterwards a member of the Confederate House of Representatives for two years and a member of the Confederate Senate for one year.

EDWARD C. WALTHALL, MISSISSIPPI.

In size Mr. Vest is the smallest man in the Senate. In ability no man stands higher.

Senator Vest is noted for his generosity to new and timid Senators. Being an old member himself and ranking among the leaders, he is thoroughly familiar with senatorial methods. This trait of character has proven valuable to the Missouri Senator. A few years ago he was a poor man among rich ones. In his generosity of spirit he aided the late Senator Hearst in passing his little California measures through the Senate. Senator Hearst was a very modest man. He could not attend to these things himself. He showed his appreciation of

Senator Vest's interest in him by "carrying" the Missouri Senator in several large Western investments which realized handsomely, and now Mr. Vest has accumulated wealth sufficient to hold his own financially as well as mentally among his colleagues.

There is one man in the Senate who has no need to look after his political fences for some years to come. This is Senator Edward C. Walthall, of Mississippi. He has the longest time to serve of any member of that body. His term will not expire until way along in 1901. Down in his State the legislature meets so infrequently that it is necessary to take advantage of each session. The legislature of a year ago reelected Mr. Walthall to serve out the term which will not commence until 1895.

Senator Walthall is one of the idols of his party in his State and is renowned in the Senate for being the man with the most regular habits. Each night at nine o'clock he retires and no social temptation can make him depart from this custom. Each morning he arises at five o'clock and finishes a great part of his work for the day before his colleagues have opened their eyes or thought of awaking. He is as regular in his work as he is in his habits. No constituent can ask of him a favor without his giving it his personal attention. He probably does more favors, and with less blare of trumpets about it, than any man in Congress, and when the time comes for his people to return the favor by unanimous election, they are only too glad to do it.

Walthall's seat is seldom unoccupied, and no matter how dry the debate or how prolonged the discussion the Mississippi Senator is on hand ready to absorb any information that may flow from the lips of his colleagues.

Senator Zebulon B. Vance stands out prominently in the Senate as the quaint humorist of that body. Though he hails from Buncombe county, North Carolina, he deals not in "buncombe." When he speaks the Senate is invariably crowded. He has the happy faculty of interspersing his strong arguments and forcible statements of fact with repeated illustrative anecdotes which are as entertaining as effective. Among his colleagues he is noted as being the strongest and most popular man in America with the people of his own State. The average North Carolinian hold Zeb. Zance as second only to the Deity.

He has been a member of the Senate since 1879. Since his first contest he has had practically no opposition, and perhaps never will have serious opposition. No man in North Carolina has the temerity to stand against Vance before the people.

Senator Vance is 63 years old. He was educated at the University of North Carolina and began life as a lawyer. He was a member of the State legislature, and afterwards a representative from the State of North Carolina in the Thirty-

JAMES H. BERRY, ARKANSAS.

fifth and Thirty-sixth Congresses. He served one year as captain of a North Carolina company in the Confederate army, but left the army when elected governor of North Carolina in August, 1862. As war governor Vance made himself a life-long idol of the people of that State. He was reelected governor, and in 1870 was elected to the United States Senate, but was refused admission and resigned in 1872. He was then reelected governor of the State, and in 1879 was elected to the Senate, where he will perhaps remain the rest of his life.

Among the Southwestern Senators no man stands higher than James H. Berry, of Arkansas. Mr. Berry is a crippled ex-Confederate soldier, having lost a leg at the battle of Corinth, October 4, 1862. Mr. Berry served several terms in the Arkansas legislature, and was speaker of the House of Representatives. He was afterwards judge of a circuit court of Arkansas, and was elected governor of that State in 1882. When Senator Garland was appointed attorney-general in Mr. Cleveland's first cabinet, Mr. Berry was elected to succeed him. His term in the Senate commenced March 25, 1885. It will probably end only when his life ends.

Senator Berry is a true type of the

ZEBULON B. VANCE, NORTH CAROLINA.

JOHNSON N. CAMDEN, WEST VIRGINIA.

Southerner. He is serious in all things. He is a man who, when he assumes a position, never retreats. Though not a conspicuous figure in the running debates of the Senate, he is heard from on all great questions and is one whose words carry weight.

Always earnest in his attendance to his legislative duties, Mr. Berry devotes his entire time to them. His only recreation is the game of whist, over which he is an enthusiast. Whist is the only form of recreation which will cause him to abandon his studies. He is as earnest in his love of this game as some other Senators are in their devotion to the great American game of poker. But Senator Berry will play no game for money. He has never played a game of cards for money, bet on a horse race nor entered a speculation of any kind. Morally, however, he is not opposed. It is because he is so enthusiastic in his love of whist that he fears, should he play any game for a consideration, it would prove too great a fascination to resist. But the Arkansas Senator is an inveterate smoker. He is never seen without a cigar in his mouth. He smokes from fifteen to twenty Havanas daily. In smoke and whist he recreates.

Senator Johnson N. Camden, of West

Virginia, is now serving his second term in the Senate, having been elected by the Senate to fill out the unexpired term of the late Senator Kenna. Mr. Camden's former term in the Senate began in 1881 and ended in 1887, when he was defeated for reelection by John E. Kenna, then a very young man who had made an exceptionally brilliant record for himself in the House. Senator Camden is not a talker and has consumed very little of the Senate's time during his congressional career, but he has the reputation of being a shrewd politician and is respected by men of all parties for his sound common sense.

As a business man he has been a wonderful success, having done as much as any one man to develop the great resources of his State in oil, coal and lumber and by building railroads. His big operations in all these directions have brought him a great fortune variously estimated at from $5,000,000 to $10,000,000. Having had a hard struggle in his earlier career, he has been noted since attaining wealth and influence for extending a helping hand to deserving young men, and all over the State of West Virginia there are now substantial business men who owe their first start in life to the assistance of the Senator. This circumstance has

ROGER Q. MILLS, TEXAS.

given him a following in the State which no ordinary movement of politics can take away from him. Although a man of such large wealth and unusual business

cares, he is very simple and democratic in his habits, readily approachable and of very congenial manners. His present term will expire in 1895, but it is understood that he will be a candidate for reelection for the six-year term which will then begin.

Senator Roger Q. Mills, of Texas, stands out as one of the conspicuous figures of the Senate. Though he has been a member of that body but one year, no statesman's name is more familiar to the American people than that of Roger Quarles Mills. He began his career in the Texas legislature, was elected to Congress when a young man and served twenty years in the House of Representatives until he was transferred last year to the Senate.

In the house, for many years, he was a recognized leader. As chairman of the Ways and Means Committee and the author of the Mills Tariff Bill, his name became a byword throughout the country. His great speech in the House in advocacy of his tariff bill was so effective as to solidify his party, which before had been badly divided. His

ringing words and strong argument converted more than a score of previously dissatisfied Democrats, and upon the final vote but four Democrats, under the leadership of Samuel J. Randall, voted no. Three of the four were defeated at the next election.

Mr. Mills was a candidate for Speaker of the Fifty-Second Congress and was defeated by less than a half dozen votes. In the Senate he has not yet taken the conspicuous position that his ability entitles. Senatorial courtesy requires otherwise. His recent speech in advocacy of the repeal of the Sherman law was, however, one of the greatest delivered upon that question, and in time Mr. Mills' position in the Senate will be as prominent as that he occupied during the last years of his term in the House.

In personal appearance Mr. Mills is the true type of the Texan, six feet, two inches in height, ruddy complexion, with iron-gray hair and mustache. He is a hard student and deep thinker. As an orator he is one of those men who enthuses in his subject and carries his audience with him.

John Warwick Daniel, the senior Senator from Virginia, is the only representative in the upper branch of Congress of the old school of oratory to which Clay, Calhoun and Webster

belonged. For this reason he is a notable figure in Washington. He looks far more like an Episcopal prelate than a politician. His face is what might be termed angular; his skin is white, and in strong contrast to his black eyes and long flowing hair which he brushes in the old style, back from the forehead. He is the silver-tongued member of the Senate, and by far the most graceful and flowery speaker in Congress. He will always shine in the constellation of great orators who have reflected such credit upon Virginia. He is a brilliant man, drawing inspiration from a brilliant heart. All of his faculties are peculiarly alive, and there is no gift which nature has conferred upon him that Daniel has not perfected to his own use.

He is above all the classic orator now in public life. His record for oratory was made at his graduation at the University of Virginia, but the effort which gave him a world-wide reputation was a three hour's oration delivered at the unveiling of the recumbent statue of Lee, at Lexington, Va., in 1882. Not less than this, and perhaps more, was the profound but pathetic memorial to the illustrious Davis, in the capitol of Virginia. His recent speech in favor of the free and unlimited coinage of silver was one of the finest yet delivered since the present debate began.

Senator Daniel was born in Lynchburg in 1842. He served in the Confederate army in Northern Virginia throughout the war and became the adjutant-general on General Early's staff before the close. After four years of fighting he began to study law at the University of Virginia, graduating in 1866. His power of eloquence not

more than his depth of thought and application of deep research at once placed him among the foremost attorneys of his day. He is the author of "Daniel on Adjustments" and "Daniel on Negotiable Instruments." He first entered politics in 1869, when he was elected to serve in the Virginia House of Delegates. He was sent to the State Senate in 1875, and was an elector at large on the Tilden and Hendricks ticket. He entered the race for governor of Virginia in 1881 and was defeated by W. E. Cameron, the readjuster. He was then sent to the Forty-ninth Congress. He defeated William E. Mahone for the Senate and took his seat in 1887. He was reelected unanimously in 1891 and his term will not expire until March, 1897.

As Cleveland has said of him, "take him for all in all, he is the greatest of American orators today."

John B. Gordon, of Georgia, the soldier statesman, is a figure always pointed out to visitors to the Senate gallery. For years he has been the hero of the people of Georgia. His gallant service in the Confederate army endeared him to the people of that State, and immediately after the war they nominated him for governor, but it was during reconstruction days and he was defeated. In 1872, however, they elected him to the Senate, and reelected him in 1879. In 1882 he resigned his seat to accept the position of general counsel of the Louisville & Nashville Railroad, but resigned that and was elected governor of Georgia in 1886. He was reelected in 1888 and was returned to the Senate in 1890 to succeed Joseph E. Brown.

THE SPECTRE OF THE NEGRO.

By C. J. Haden.

Too much sophistry and sentiment and too little common sense have marked the discussion of the negro question. From Mrs. Stowe to Mr. Cable the advocates of the colored man have portrayed him as a martyr. All these writers, even including Judge Tourgee, have given their subject the stage setting of a story with its artificial colors and dramatic pathos. Let us look at his present relationship not through the false lenses of fiction but in the clear white light of truth.

Employed in squads under skillful direction, the negro is the best of laborers. As steamboat workmen, stevedores,. railway construction hands and plantation gangs this race excels all others. Not only will they do as great an amount of work in a given space of time, but they do it with less complaint and more cheerfulness, and are more amenable to discipline. Those who have had an opportunity to compare the negroes with other day laborers engaged in these capacities will concede the truth of this statement. Left to himself, the negro succeeds poorly as an independent farmer. Omitting a reasonable number of exceptions, the colored race is disposed to be improvident, and this accounts for his poor success as a manager in nearly all pursuits. Some great thinker has truly said that the Mongolian race lives in the past, the Ethiopian in the present and the Caucasian in the future. The black man is by nature disposed to imitate the butterfly rather than the ant, and this characteristic alone would bring him to defeat in a struggle with the white race, even if there were not other obstacles to handicap him. But against these the Creator has placed in his heart

the boon of contentment. While the great mass of laboring classes employed in the mines and work-shops of the North go to their toil with muttered threatenings of a strike, the colored man of the South goes forth to his daily task with a song on his lips.

For years the negro has been used as a phantom to frighten immigrants and investors from the South. Indeed this argument has been so often used against us that many of our own people have fallen into the snare and given the idea currency. The injustice of this is only equalled by that lack of decent fairness with which those inviting immigration to the Northwest have treated us. They distributed through Europe maps of the United States on which the whole South is labelled "fever swamps." Turn the subject over and over and scrutinize it with the closest care and no sound objection can be found why the presence of the negro here should hinder the incoming of money or white people.

Can we of the South, who were nursed in the laps of " black mammies " and as children played in the sand with the little " pickaninnies," object to the colored man's living on the same farm or in the same township? Can white men who have worked side by side with colored men in the fields or on the bricklayer's scaffold in peace for thirty years protest against the colored man's having a home on the public highway? Indeed, do they protest? Put this question to the millions of white men throughout the South and there will come back an unanimous answer in the negative.

Can the Northern people, who spilt their blood to make him a citizen, object to his enjoying a citizenship among them? Can the foremost writers and statesmen of the North, who in many cases have exerted their splendid talents in the vain effort to transform a slave into a saint by Federal enactment, deny him a right to a homestead among them? It is pleasing to note that, except in a few isolated instances, they have welcomed him. Is it reasonable to reckon that a people whose sentiments were crystallized in the civil rights bill will be stopped from coming to a land so inviting as the South because the negro is here? For my own part I believe not. The negro is a spectre set up to alarm timid men and conservative money against coming Southward.

The one thing which more than all others endangers capital to-day is a spirit of strikes among wage earners. Remember the recent wrecking of the Chicago, Burlington & Quincy railway system and the blood shed at Homestead, Pa. Men yet comparatively young recall the times when an oath-bound league of foreign laborers engaged in the Schuylkill valley mines was organized under the name of the "Molly Maguires." Officials of the Philadelphia & Reading railroad were special targets of this terrible clan. One by one they fell by the bullet of the midnight assassin, until none of the owners of that great anthracite region dared visit their property. At last the supremacy of law was re-asserted. Europe, from the North Cape to the Mediterranean, rests upon a muttering volcano of a discontented proletariat. Three years ago a hundred thousand French canaille, drunk upon absinthe, marched up the streets of Paris to proclaim Boulanger emperor, and failed because of Boulanger's cowardice. In the same year an organized uprising of the London stevedores blocked the commerce of the world's metropolis and threatened six million people with starvation, and the fate of millions of capital rested in the hands of a laborers' leader named John Burns.

Contrast all this with the peaceable relations between labor and capital which have for two decades existed in the Southern States. The white man of Europe and of the North sees in his lineaments his kinship of race and right with the rich and ruling classes, and he clamors for a new deal. The colored man, recognizing in the tints of his cheek the emblem of his inferiority, patiently submits to his lowly lot. And the fact that as time goes on he continues to perform the menial pursuits of life uncomplainingly is a conclusive guarantee that no organized outbreak will ever come from him. The friction between the races has been growing steadily less since reconstruction times. Looking back over an experience of fifteen years in the South I cannot recall one instance of an organized strike of colored laborers.

The negro is a lover of peace. Living apart from the whites in all social and religious matters he has his own churches, schools and lodges. His crimes are generally of the petty kind. The white man robs the bank while the darkey invades the chicken roost. The wants of the negro are few; no vaulting ambition goads him into rash undertakings. An extremely small percentage of colored men in the Georgia penitentiary are under sentence for arson or for the murder of white men. In the majority of cases it will be found they have been convicted for theft or for assault with intent to kill one of their own race. Deep in their conscience exists an awe for the white man and the respect and deference which spring from it. These, together with a predisposition to avoid strife, render the negro the safest of employes and servants. While, by emancipation his labor was changed from servitude into service, his feeling of dependence and respect towards his old master has but slightly altered.

The negro wage worker on the farm or in the factory is usually a spendthrift, trusting that when the evil hour of sickness befalls him his employer will come to the rescue. And to the credit of the employer be it said he has been rarely known to fail to support the colored worker during his time of misfortune. On this point I write from personal experience. A feeling of trust on the one hand and of responsibility on the other is a notable feature of the Southern industrial system. It has been inbred in the black man from the time he first saw civilization to lean upon the patriarchal arm of the master, and while there are reasons why this ought to be otherwise, yet it does one great good, it binds together the master and the servant on a peace footing. Moreover it is a warranty against strikes and their attendant evils.

To those of the North who complain of the social barrier thrown up between the races in the South I would respectfully point to the social conditions of the cities of the Eastern States. Between the well-to-do classes of New York or Boston and the German or Irish servants there is a chasm as wide and as clearly marked as between the whites and the blacks of the South. As often as the curb-stone orator of the South curses the negro the curb-stone orator of the North curses the Irish. White men of the great race which produced Emmett, O'Connell and Burke, when engaged in menial service in the city of Boston, are ostracised in the same way as is the black man in Atlanta. Even in the bitter days of reconstruction the negro was not held in check as are the Chinese of California. Looking back over a period of ten or twelve years I cannot recall an instance of a negro being lynched in any of the larger towns of Georgia. And for every case of lynching which happens in the remote and less enlightened districts, a like case can be found in the back-woods districts of Wisconsin or Michigan or the mining districts of the far West where a white man has played the leading part.

The unique political position of the South, growing out of the fact that we were the last of the Anglo-Saxons to maintain slavery, has caused a fierce light of criticism to beat upon us. For the purposes of carrying elections and of influencing commerce and immigration, volumes of false literature have gone forth to poison the mind of the world. At last truth is beginning to triumph. Out of the shadow of the night the South is coming back into the full day. Her resources, little known before, are being brought to the attention of the world. Three years ago the Hon. Chauncey M. Depew told the graduating class of the Yale college that the South was the best field for the enterprise of young men. Campaign slander, false maps and the phantom of the negro are slowly losing their efficacy as instruments of fright. A land where streams, unvexed by ice, turn factory wheels all the year, a land which enjoys a practical monoply of the clothing material of the world, a land teeming with timber, coal and iron and a soil capable of raising every useful plant known to the temperate zone, such a land when given an equal chance in the industrial race will bear the palm away. A State possessed of such enormous vitality and power of recuperation that it can lose and regain more than $500 per capita in thirty years is without a parallel in history, and this is the story of Georgia. To the thousands of Northern people who have settled in Georgia I appeal this case. To them I am willing to leave the question whether the negro is or is not a good laborer, a peaceful settler and a loyal citizen.

These abundant resources and this contented colored labor, brought under the skillful management of farmer, miner or manufacturer, are a fountain of wealth. Our splendid development in the last decade is but an index of things yet to be, for our face is turned toward the morning and the sunlight of a brighter day illuminates the pathway of progress.

LETTERS FROM SOUTHERN FARMERS.

[Frequent inquiries about Southern agricultural conditions, coming from farmers in the West and Northwest, suggested the gathering of letters from practical Southern farmers, giving their experiences in agriculture in the South. A great number of letters of this character have been secured by the editor of the SOUTHERN STATES Magazine, chiefly from men who have migrated from the North and West to the South and have been engaged in various branches of agriculture. The majority of these letters were written by practical farmers, some of them by correspondents who gathered their information from the farmers and others are from men whose intimate association with Southern agricultural interests enables them to write with authority. The letters published in this issue constitute the first instalment in an extended series, and their publication in this place is intended as an answer to oft repeated and urgent inquiries about the possibilities of agriculture in the South.—EDITOR.]

An Iowan's Success in Alabama.

JOHN MASON, Valley Head, Ala.— I have lived in North Alabama for the past twenty-one years. Previous to that time I resided in Iowa a number of years. I left Iowa to get away from the rigors of the severe winters and the extreme heat of summer. When the time came that I could leave, I looked at a great many localities and finally located where I am now living, on Lookout Mountain, four miles east of Valley Head, DeKalb county, which is on the Alabama Great Southern Railroad.

I find that the climate here is all that could be desired. The winters are not severe, and while the thermometer sometimes reaches 90° in the summer, the nights are always cool, giving assurance of a good night's rest after a good day's work, and this is a blessing which cannot be enjoyed in Iowa. There I have frequently seen the thermometer at 90° when I got up in the morning. All of this section is well supplied with running streams, so with pure air and good water we are entirely free from all malarial diseases, which is not the case in the Western States.

I have all my life been a farmer, and since moving to this place have raised successfully all the grains, grasses, etc., that will grow in this latitude, such as corn, oats, rye, barley, clover, timothy, herd grass, etc., and nowhere I have ever been will potatoes do so well, and yield so bountifully as here, both sweet and Irish potatoes. While in Iowa I paid considerable attention to the raising of Irish potatoes. When I reached the South, I found that the natives were not doing anything in that line; the sweet potato mostly was raised, and very good crops of that variety were and are raised. In Iowa the crop of Irish potatoes was, owing to the season, sometimes good, sometimes partially good and sometimes a failure. Since being here, I have raised Irish potatoes every year without a single failure, and raised from 300 to 500 bushels per acre, and one time I gathered Irish potatoes at the rate of 700 bushels per acre. The natives would hardly believe this, even when twelve of them assisted in measuring the ground and digging and measuring the potatoes. The ground was laid off three feet and the potatoes were cut up and planted one foot apart in the rows.

Blackberries grow here naturally, and all that is necessary to have them in abundance is to let the ground alone and they will soon come and thrive, and they build up the land very fast.

All varieties of apples, peaches and pears also do well, and garden vegetables and small fruits thrive. Some of the nicest cherries I have ever seen anywhere grow here.

There are many reasons to advance which prove that this is the place for practical farmers to locate. One of the main reasons is that here a farmer can live cheaper and keep up his farm cheaper than in the Western States, because there everything needed to build houses, fences, chimneys, etc., and even fire-wood, has to be hauled long distances, while here rock, fuel and timber of all kinds for all purposes are abundant. There is a very important consideration that must be taken into account by all practical farmers, and that is the question of under-drainage. Any real agriculturist knows that under drains prevent drowning out when there is too much moisture and mitigate the severity of a drought. In most Western and Northwestern States, and in some European countries, immense sums of money are necessarily spent in this manner to insure a crop, while here the natural formation is such that the under-drainage is perfect—better than all the money expended in the Western States could make it. This is a great item in the economy of farming, and everyone who understands the necessity for under drains will appreciate it, for it secures good crops under proper management and cultivation.

I find that it does not cost near so much to raise stock here as it does in the Northwest. All kinds of stock live well eight or ten months in the year on the natural range grass that grows in the woods. This will keep stock ten months except in cases of, comparatively speaking, exceedingly early and severe winters, and, like the people, the stock of all kinds are healthy. This land responds to fertilizing very readily indeed, and an old field that has been exhausted by improper cultivation can soon be brought back to fertility by a little manure and the judicious use of clover, rye and peas.

If any practical farmer will come here I will take pleasure in showing him all the advantages I here enumerate, and will, I am sure, convince him that my views are correct.

It is wonderful how soon this country recovered from the ravages of the late war. It was stripped of fencing and outbuildings, and of live stock and of men to a considerable extent, but everything has long since been replaced and much more added. If the seat of war had been in the Northwest as it was here, there would be a different tale to tell.

Health and Prosperity in North Alabama.

JOHN H. KEITH, Snake Creek, De Kalb Co., Ala.—I was raised in this county, and lived here until after I was grown and had a family. I moved to Kansas fourteen years ago, and remained in that State two years, raising two crops there, but the climate was so disagreeable and the winters were so cold, and the wind so severe, and the health of myself and family was so bad, that I left the State and went to Arkansas. I lived in that State three years, during which time I traveled over the most of the thirteen counties when not working my crop, trying to find a suitable place to locate, but I could not be satisfied, and after making three crops, I left Arkansas, principally on account of sickness and severe drought. I came back to north Alabama, where I was raised, convinced that in all points going to make up easy and cheap living North Alabama far surpassed any place I had seen.

The climate here is much milder in the winter than is the climate of Kansas, and it is cooler here in the summer than in Arkansas, and the general health here is a great deal better than in either of those States. Here we have pure air, and running water in abundance, and consequently are entirely free from all malaria or epidemic of any kind. Some portions of Kansas and Arkansas are more fertile than some places in North Alabama, but it takes much more to do a farmer there than here, because he has to feed all kinds of stock a great deal longer every year. Here all kinds of grain do well, and clover grows and holds well. So do herd grass and timothy; and in fact all of the cultivated grasses.

There is a natural grass growing in the woods all over this part of this country which makes a splendid range for horses, cattle and sheep. It is usually up in March, and lasts all through the summer and fall, and the stock thrive and grow fat on it. The timber is also plentiful, pine, poplar, chestnut in great abundance, and all the oaks. These trees bear acorns that keep hogs well through the fall and winter. Cattle here are all free from epidemics, and are far healthier and do better than in either Arkansas or Kansas.

All kinds of vegetables and small fruits do well here; so do both sweet and Irish potatoes, also apples, peaches, pears, etc.

A farmer can live and run his farm much cheaper than in either of the other two States, for here everything he needs for building houses, chimneys, fences, etc., is all around him in large quantities, and he has to feed very little. The people are civil, quiet and, generally speaking, industrious. Churches and schools are plentiful and, taken altogether, North Alabama is decidedly the best place for a farmer, particularly one of small means, I have ever seen.

Alabama Ahead of New England.

C. N. MAXWELL, Mentone, Ala.—I came to this country nearly fourteen years ago from the State of Maine. We have a delightful and healthy climate, good water and plenty of timber, such as pine, chestnut, hickory and various kinds of oak. The soil produces all kinds of fruits and vegetables, also rye, oats, wheat, millet and sorghum cane fully as well as in New England. With the same treatment I have raised without any special preparation as good rye as I ever saw grow anywhere.

We have a good range for cattle, hogs and sheep, and they can be raised cheaply. Hay and fodder are easily raised. The heat is not severe, the mercury rarely rising above 90°. In the valley it is warmer in summer than on the uplands.

The soil produces wheat, corn and clover better, but the land is held at a high price. The Alabama Great Southern Railroad traverses the county and furnishes us a market easily attainable at Birmingham and Chattanooga and other parts of the country.

We have no outlawry here. The people are hospitable and welcome industrious orderly people from any quarter of the world. As to politics, every man enjoys a perfect freedom in voting as he desires without persecution. I think I am safe in saying that a man can do much better here farming than in New England, and can situate himself comfortably with one-half the means, if he buys cautiously, that it would require there.

North Alabama a Poor Man's Paradise.

C. F. PARKER, Mentone, Ala.—I came to this part of the country seven years ago from Western New York, and located on the top of grand old historic Lookout Mountain, which is a plateau from five to ten miles broad and eighty miles long, with a general elevation of two thousand feet above sea level. It is a beautifully undulating wooded country, abounding in natural grasses and forest plants, affording excellent pasturage for cattle, sheep and other stock nearly the entire year. The forest trees are largely oak, chestnut and hickory, affording most seasons such an abundance of nuts that hogs grow and fatten with but little expense to their owners. Stock of all kinds, including poultry, are remarkably free from disease. Our cheap lands, though not rich, are easily made productive by proper tilling and fertilization, producing nearly all the grain, grasses, vegetables and fruits of the Northern States in perfection alongside of the more Southern productions, such as cotton, peanuts, sweet potatoes, etc.

We have the purest and most invigorating mountain air, long pleasant summers and short mild winters; no swamp nor malaria; an abundance of pure water from the mountain springs. Our society is about equally divided between the Southern and Northern settlers, who have long since given up sectional differences, and all are working with a single aim for the improvement of our section.

We need more farmers, more mechanics, more new enterprises, such as mills for utilizing our timber, fruit canneries, creameries, etc., and better stock.

I have lived in several of the Northern States, and am free to say that while they have generally a richer soil and better transportation facilities, and often better markets, and generally better educational advantages than we have in the South, yet we have enough to offset these advantages in our climate and variety of productions and the length of our working season. Farmers can successfully plow here every month in the year.

While the fuel question in many places West and North is one of serious consideration, here we have millions of cords of the finest wood decaying on our hillsides for the want of people to utilize the waste timber, and with an abundance of coal underlying our mountains the cold storms of winter have little to terrify us. Truly this is a poor man's paradise.

A Thriving Alabama Colony.

THURSTON H. ALLEN, Florence, Ala.—The little village of St. Florain is situated in Lauderdale county, Ala., and is the centre of as thriving a colony as can be found anywhere.

In 1878 a tract of 2000 acres of land in this county was purchased by Dr. Huser, a German Catholic priest, with the intention of settling colonies of his own faith and nationality upon it, and making it the nucleus of a community.

This land when purchased was a worn out tract, known as the "Wilson plantation," upon which the sole crop for many years had been cotton, and which had finally been turned out to grow up in broom sedge and briars as worthless and unfit for cultivation.

It was bought by Dr. Huser at about $4.00 per acre, partly for cash and partly on time, and was regarded as the poorest land in the county and completely exhausted. Dr. Huser built a church and a schoolhouse, and in 1878 divided the plantation into tracts of from ten to fifty acres each, and placed thereon some forty-five families, all German Catholics, from Pennsylvania, Ohio, Illinois, New York and other States, to whom he sold these lands at from $8.00 to $15.00 per acre, according to location and improvements. These colonists had experienced the rigors of the Northern and Western climates with the certainty of cold and drought.

They were all poor; their industry elsewhere had not hitherto availed them to any great extent. It had taken all the fruits of their labor to sustain them up to this time, so that most if not all of them were forced to go in debt for their land. Some of those who are now the most prosperous and independent commenced with mortgages upon their lands, and with but one mule or steer with which to break and cultivate the soil. To add to their troubles, Dr. Huser, not content with having sold them the poorest lands in the county, defaulted in the deferred payments, so that they were compelled to pay twice for part of their holdings.

There is no question that for the first two or three years the colonists had a hard time. The exhausted lands had to be nursed back into life, buildings had to be erected, fences built and improvements of all kinds made, while the want of ready money was terribly against them, but patient industry accomplishes wonders. Wood for fuel, fencing and building purposes was plentiful and cheap; the mild winters not only enabled them to wear lighter and less clothing, but to effect a saving of fuel, also to work during all seasons of the year out of doors.

The soil, it was found, had wonderful power of recuperation, took kindly to that great enricher, clover, and to other grasses, was easily worked and responded readily to intelligent treatment. The long summer enabled the farmer to grow and harvest two crops instead of one in each season, and it was found that even in winter there were products hardy enough to withstand the slight amount of freezing to which they were subjected. Vineyards and orchards were planted, and it was not long before a general improvement began to be apparent not only in the lands, but in the condition of the colonists themselves. As they gradually became more independent they built better houses and larger barns, adopted improved machinery and raised better stock; until today I am informed that there is not a family among them that is in debt.

They raise almost everything they need upon their own land and always have something to sell. They pay cash for what they buy and ask credit of no man. Their houses are comfortable, their barns and barn-yards in good order, their fences substantial, their horses, mules and cattle fat and sleek; their lands bring them every year abundant crops of wheat at the rate of twenty bushels to the acre without the use of commercial fertilizers, corn, Irish potatoes, clover, millet, vegetables of all kinds, while their vineyard afford enormous yields of grapes, much of which is made into wine of a good quality, for which there is ready sale.

In 1878 the Wilson plantation was a desert in the centre of fertile lands. To-day, while its surroundings have lost none of their fertility, it is noted for the heaviest crops and most prosperous farmers in the section. These lands, once turned out as worthless and exhausted, are now fully worth $50 per acre, and are not on the market.

The owners are prosperous, thrifty and contented with both soil and climate. They raise two crops per annum instead of one, such as two crops of potatoes, oats followed by corn, clover cut twice for hay and afterwards for seed or pasture. They find the region perfectly healthful, and they can average many more days for outdoor work than in the North or West.

That much of their success is due to the splendid perseverance and industrious habits of their race there can be no doubt, but these had failed them elsewhere, and that failure was what induced them to come to the more genial climate of Alabama.

Comment is unnecessary. A single glance at the thriving community is the best argument of a combination of energy, industry and patient labor with the more favorable adjuncts of such soil and climate as present themselves.

A Fine Country for Fruit.

WM. P. TRUITT, Deer Park, Ala.— I came here last January, and after looking at the advantages to be had here, I at once settled and commenced to plant fruit trees and grape vines, being satisfied that I had found the country to suit me. I have been eagerly watching the development of the present fruit crop, and am thoroughly convinced that for this business and the growing of vegetables this part of the South is equal to California, and as yet no insect enemies so destructive to the fruit crop have made their appearance, and not even a curculio sting is to be seen on the most tender fruits. The trees come into bearing early; near where I live peach trees, two years set, have a peck of fruit to the tree, and pear trees that have a full crop are now full of fruit. I have a fine lot of vegetables now (May 15) ready for the Northern markets—string beans, cucumbers, and a little later on, cantaloupes and tomatoes, all of which grow to perfection in this balmy climate, and will, in the near future, be raised on a large scale. All that is needed is industrious intelligent citizens with small means to make this the garden spot and fruit country of the world, and this I say from what I have seen since settling here. I have no land to sell, but would be glad to have my Northern friends come here and locate, as I know they could soon, on small means, be well off.

I had been sick previous to coming here for six months, and during all that time had not done a day's work, and could scarcely walk when I landed at Deer Park, but now am strong and can do a good day's work. The climate is equal to California, with a most refreshing breeze all the time. I expect to go extensively into the fruit and vegetable business, and would be glad to see the day when the Mobile & Ohio Railroad will be taxed to its full capacity to carry the products from these cheap lands to the North to feed those people so often frozen in by spring blizzards, none of which ever reach this delightful balmy climate. I find the society as good as the North, and the Southern people very friendly and anxious to have Northern people come and settle and assist in developing this big country with all its varied resources.

A French Immigrant in Arkansas.

JOHN BOUTT, Helena, Ark.—I can neither read nor write, but a kind friend of mine tells me you invite foreigners who have selected the South as a home to give their experiences for the benefit of others who may wish to come South. He writes this letter for me. I am a native of France; I came to America as a laborer and engaged in stave-cutting. The business took me to the woods, where I discovered the wonderfully rich lands of Phillips county, Arkansas. About 1878 I was able to buy and pay for forty acres of land, which I did, and began farming.

I have farmed for a living, raising corn, oats, millet, turnips, beets, onions, cows, hogs, sheep and mules, with cotton as a surplus crop. I can say that my mode of farming has proved a success. I have raised a family of eleven children, have never lost but one child, whose death was the result of accident. I have increased my farm to nearly 300 acres, and have it fully stocked with hogs, cows, mules and poultry. I have a handsome cash surplus in bank and will gather thirty to fifty bales of cotton within the next two months, which will add from $1500 to $2500 to my cash balance.

I have never needed for the best of friends and as good society as I had time to enjoy. All the luxuries which France can produce are available here—the grape for wine, apples, peaches, pears, strawberries, and indeed all the fruits grow luxuriantly, and no country equals this for beets, potatoes and turnips. Our lands are rich and we need no artificial fertilizers.

Cotton for a Cash Crop.

PETER MENGOS, Helena, Ark.—I am a native of France. I landed in New York, came to Ohio, went from Ohio to Indiana and then to Iowa where I took government land. I failed to be satisfied with climate and other surroundings in Iowa and came South, and for a time engaged in the timber business in Arkansas. When I got a few dollars

ahead I got a small farm in Phillips County, Arkansas, a few miles west of the city of Helena. My mode of farming was to produce on my farm something of everything that I wanted for my own support—corn, hogs, poultry, mules, horses, cows and sheep, potatoes and other vegetables, with cotton as a surplus. Having something of all of the farm products to sell, I have never had to buy such articles, and for that reason I have never needed a great amount of cash or currency. My principal surplus product has been cotton.

I can truthfully say my farming has been very satisfactory. If the cotton market does not suit me I can hold it, if I desire, to next season. It is with me a surplus, the proceeds of which I invest in additional lands, bank stocks or city property.

I have increased my farm lands to 600 acres in cultivation, which is worked by tenants, hired laborers, and share croppers. I encourage tenant and neighbor to produce first what he needs at home, with a surplus in cotton. I do not know a farmer in my country who follows this plan that is not thrifty and having his bank account. No hard times with any of them.

There is no country in the world which produces more of the comforts and luxuries of life than this, and no product of the farm as a surplus is so convenient as cotton. It will keep from season to season and transports at small cost and is always cash.

I as an individual can say that the recent hard times have not affected me. It is true I have heard great complaint from many in my locality, but I do not know a farmer, who has produced at home what he needs at home, who has reason to complain of hard times.

As to the matter of health, the country compares favorably with all parts of the world.

As to society, I do not believe I could have found warmer and truer friends in any community than I have found here among all nationalities, and particularly the natives of Arkansas.

Quite a number of French people are in this country, are doing well and are satisfied. Our French farmers are men who came to this country as stave makers ; their business in the woods made them acquainted with the rich lands; they have laid down the axe to take up the plow and hoe, and have made successful farmers and highly respected citizens. My countrymen looking South may address me in French or English at Helena, Arkansas.

From Indiana to Arkansas.

DR. G. D. JAQUES, Helena, Ark.—I think your invitation extended to people from the North, West or other countries who have located in the South, to give their experience, is a good thing. I am one of them and thank you for an opportunity to say what I know of the Southern people and the Southern country.

I am from Indiana and sixty-nine years old, and came to the South in 1866. I was a surgeon in the Federal army and, having seen the South during the war, I could not resist the desire to make it my home after the war. Accordingly I came South and I embarked in cotton planting. I planted for cotton alone; neglected every other farm product; indeed, I did not attempt to plant anything else. My land would have produced more corn, more hogs, more cows, more hay than Indiana land, but at the same time it would produce cotton, so I went for cotton and nothing else. The result of it was I busted at cotton raising and corn buying. I had unlimited credit and planted extensively, making a very magnificent failure.

Some of my neighbors who were French and Dutch, had no money, no credit, and could not speak English, made farmers of themselves ; they raised corn, hogs, turkeys, chickens, cows, potatoes, mules, sheep and a few bales of cotton. I speak from personal observation that they have succeeded. No more independent men, or luxurious livers, exist on earth than these men. It is a treat to be invited out to their farm houses where such plenty and comfort exist. They all have cotton as a surplus, but they have corn and hog first.

It is proverbial in this country that a man who has corn to sell always has money to lend. I retired from planting to the practice of medicine, which, with the aid of a small drug store, has made my support.

I, of course, was a Republican and had all the ways of a Republican, but my friends are by no means confined to my party. I must say that I have now, and have had all the time I have been South, as many and as warm friends as I could have had in Indiana.

I expect to be buried on one of the high hills at Helena, Arkansas, and the sympathetic tear of my neighbors will not stop to ask if I was a Northerner or a Southerner, a Democrat or a Republican, but will come full and free from my neighbors who are all my friends.

A Swede and Union Soldier.

N. J. FRITZAN, Helena, Ark.—Being a Swede by birth and a soldier on the Union side in the late war, I can give an experience which quite contradicts an impression which has been made to prevail among foreigners and particularly Union soldiers and Republicans as to the treatment we have received from the good people of the South who opposed us in politics. I have heard much of social proscription in the South. I was advised not to locate in the South for the reason that if not shot or hung I would be socially ostracized. The circulation of such stories as this has no doubt prevented thousands of my people from coming South. Had I listened to such stuff I would have probably gone West as thousands of my people did, but directed by a love for a Southern climate, and without the fear of rope or ostracism before my eyes, I came to Helena, Arkansas, in 1863, after being mustered out of the Federal service in 1862.

I engaged in the grocery business at Helena, and afterwards in the queensware trade. I have had no reason to complain. My business has been successful; my home has been a happy home; my children and my roses have grown under the genial influence of a Southern sun and vied with each other in beauty. I have not wanted for friends, and could not have more friends, warmer friends or truer friends if I had settled amid a colony of my own people or a colony composed of my Federal regiment. I was elected mayor of the city of Helena in 1888 and have been my own successor ever since. My last election was without opposition and unanimous.

I must say, and I speak from experience and observation, that no part of the earth offers greater inducements to the German, Swede, French or Italian farmer than the latitude of Arkansas, Tennessee, North Carolina and Mississippi. The soil and climate produce every product known or needed by the farmer, with the special product of cotton, which when produced as a surplus insures wealth and luxury to the farmer. As to health I will not betray my looks by telling that I am "nigh on to sixty," and notwithstanding this fact, that I offer a standing reward to the boy who with a fair start can beat me to a fire. I have not had to pay out much in such rewards, and it is generally known that the bantering chip is on my shoulder for anyone to brush off who wants a tussel.

Profits in Trade.

FRANK FORD, Helena, Ark.—I came to Helena, Arkansas, about four years ago. As a means of transporting myself and effects to the South I built a boat 14 by 45 feet, put all I had on it, including a young wife, pushed out into the stream and floated to Helena, Arkansas. I had a few goods, such as a small retail dealer needs, in stock. When I reached Helena it was not possible to get a store. I therefore took part of my stock and made a tent, set it up on a vacant lot and began business.

I sold for cash, and replenished my stock with cash and what credit I could safely risk.

A short term at this showed me the necessity for a store. I bought a business lot on time, borrowed money on the building and loan plan to build a brick store 20x60 feet, two stories high. A little more than one year in this store doing a cash business showed that my store was too small for my trade. I sold it and reinvested in a block of ground two squares out from the business streets and built again, giving myself four times the room I had formerly for the mercantile business and room for a corn mill adjoining my store.

I had made it a rule to barter goods or pay cash for anything that a farmer would bring to me, everything from a cord of wood to a load of cow bones, or a burnt out cook stove, corn, oats or shucks. I have now a full stock of clothing, shoes, groceries and such other articles as my trade demands. My corn mill grinds all the meal I sell, and I sell all I grind. The capacity of my mill is above my present sales, but I expect to increase sales to its full capacity. My trade being for cash I have not seen hard times, in fact my trade increases with the hard times, because many who had bought on time from others came to me with cash trade when their credit trade was cut off at other stores by hard times.

I must say I never saw a country that affords such advantages to a farmer. I do not mean a planter but a *farmer* who lives at home, buys what he wants for cash and puts away his surplus,—a farmer who sells spring chickens for twenty-five cents, eggs at twenty-five cents a dozen, sweet potatoes seventy-five cents a bushel, Irish potatoes fifty cents, beets, tomatoes for fifty cents, corn fifty cents. Of course, having all these things to sell, including lambs, cows, mules, colts and a surplus in cotton, he has but little to buy; he simply gets rich.

What the South needs is more farmers and fewer planters. Her 6,000,000 bales of cotton surplus means $300,000,000 gold surplus every year, ten times all the gold products of our mines and three times the gold and silver products of the United States. People to farm the South for all it is worth will settle the ratio and free coinage question with her cotton surplus. If the Western farmer will come South and feed himself on his own products and put away his cotton surplus, he will simply make a gold mine out of his own little forty-acre farm. Socially we have as good people as any part of the world, churches and schools, a mild climate and as good health as any part of the world.

$600 From 150 Peach Trees.

G. W. FLEETWOOD, Floyd Springs, Ga.—I am so forcibly struck with what you say about this being the opportunity for the South to get immigrants from the West by telling the Western people what the South has to offer them, that I will give a few facts showing some of the inducements offered by North Georgia. I will speak of fruit growing, especially peaches. Our mountain hills are wonderfully adapted to this fruit, but we are just finding it out. The range of hills is from east to west, giving us the north and south sides and the top for our trees. We rarely ever fail to have fruit. There is just enough iron in our hills to give the peach a color and size that cannot be surpassed anywhere. I sent a sample from my orchard to the World's Fair and received a letter from the chairman of the Horticultural Department stating that my early Crawfords were attracting the attention of peach-growers from all sections.

I bought 1000 trees six years ago at ten cents per tree—$100. I planted them on ten acres of fresh hillside land, terracing the hill before setting out the trees and running the rows with the terraces. I have cultivated the land every year except this in corn or cotton. I have gathered only two crops of peaches; last year I realized $100, and this year 150 trees of early Crawfords brought me $600. My Alexanders (early June) rotted on account of heavy rains just as they were getting ready to ship.

If any of your readers want to go into the peach-growing business, North Georgia is the favored section. Lands can be had at from $5 to $10 per acre.

Found Health and a Home in Georgia.

L. SHUMWAY, Fort Valley, Ga.—I came here from South Haven, Mich., four years ago with an invalid wife and daughter and little money. The first year fruit was a failure, and I had only a net half interest in a truck and melon crop, which yielded me $3000. There is no comparison between living here and in Michigan when it comes to cost, health and genuine comfort. My wife and daughter are in as good health as anyone, and so am I, and so far as this essential and this world's goods go, we are happy. A man can own his land here and live better and with more genuine comfort summer and winter than in any Northern State with which I am familiar, and that, too, at fully one-third less in actual expenditures and with one-half the labor required in the North, where it is so cold that the farmer's land and stock are idle during the freezing weather. Here we can work and have some money crop growing every month in the year, while our children can go bare-footed and play in the sunshine fully seven-eighths of the year, thus saving us the purchase of shoes, clothing and fuel necessary to keep them comfortable in the North. There is no need for me to advise my Northern friends to come down here and make Georgia their home, for they are coming as soon as the financial stringency slackens and they can get money enough to come. Right here let me say that the people who have always lived in the South—I mean people who live moderately—do not know anything about hard times, and the poorest people in the South are much better off today than are those in any section of the North. Any man with perseverance and energy can come down here from the North and become independent in a very few years. I would not exchange my Southern home for my old one in Michigan with a good many thousand dollars difference.

One-Half Less Expense for Living.

J. W. ANTHOINE, Fort Valley, Ga.—I arrived here over twelve years ago from Orange, Mass. I am satisfied with everything in this section. I own a little home and know I can live here more cheaply than any man in Massachusetts. I raise garden truck in abundance for my family and some to sell. I also raise poultry, make butter for my own use and some for sale. I can live fully 50 per cent. cheaper here than at my old home, and I am more comfortable all the time. The climate is splendid, and I am sure that on an average the Southern farmer is in much better condition at all times than are the farmers of Massachusetts.

The Uplands of Maryland.

O. F. Morton, Rockville, Md.—I am a native of Northern New England. I lived from 1866 to 1881 in Iowa and Nebraska; since then I have lived chiefly in Virginia and Maryland, spending about half of twelve years in each State. I have traveled considerably in both States and am familiar with most parts of them.

Since coming to these States I have met numerous home-seekers who have hailed from many directions. I can freely say that I consider the country, traversed by the Baltimore & Ohio Railroad, from the Chesapeake to the Ohio, to offer good inducements to home-seekers. It has the advantage of lying in one of the great thoroughfares between the West and the East. At one side are the large and rapidly-growing cities of Baltimore and Washington. Going westward from there we find many small towns rapidly increasing their manufacturing and mining interests. The markets are therefore good and improving.

The upland parts of Maryland have the best climate I have ever found. The summer season is not at all too warm, and, as the air is tonic, no Northerner need fear any enervating influence.

As between Nebraska and Maryland, I decidedly prefer the summers of the latter State. Here mosquitoes are so very few that no one thinks of barring them out of his house.

As to soil, it is idle to assert that this region is the equal of the prairie States. But while prairie soil is deep, easily worked and very durable, the yields per acre of the common farm crops are not so great as would seem to be the case. In this State I have seen growing crops which would equal anything I ever saw in the West, and such cases are not phenomenal. The varieties of soil and exposure which we possess favor diversified farming.

Here, as elsewhere in the South, there has been a tendency to farms of several hundred acres. This implies general farming, which at present prices is seldom profitable on a large scale. But the home-seeker who can content himself with from ten to fifty acres may do especially well in the region of which I speak. There is a good market for dairy products and eggs. Fruit does well almost everywhere. The canning of vegetables is an important industry. Fuel, both wood and coal, is cheap. Building materials are also cheap and land values are low.

Home-seekers should examine this region before going elsewhere. They will find good air, good water, and improving markets, and in scarcely any part of the country can they make themselves homes at more moderate expense. It is not a new country, yet it has many of the elements of newness. It is destined to be densely populated and a hive of industries, lying as it does so close to the commercial centres of the country.

Health and Fertility of the Gulf Coast.

William Sigerson, Ocean Springs, Miss.—I live on the Gulf of Mexico, eighty-five miles east of New Orleans and fifty-five miles west of Mobile, on the Louisville & Nashville Railroad, which is the trunk line from Mobile to New Orleans, and takes the travel through from the Mobile & Ohio Railroad and around all the vast territory from Florida and New Orleans and the east to the south. We have the loveliest climate on the globe. We are entirely exempt from overflow, tornadoes or cyclones; they do not occur this near the gulf. All the overflow we have here for ten miles back is the tidewater. Our timber lands are fine in Alabama and Mississippi, and our land is very productive for the cereals and vegetables, and as a fruit country it has no equal. Our pears this year are a perfect crop. I know one orchard of 100 trees of LeConte pears which have been planted eleven years and will yield 1200 bushels. The pears, peaches, grapes and figs are a perfect success.

We have no trouble in raising on our soil three or four crops on the same land in a year; we can, in a word, plow and plant every month in the year. When a crop fails all we have to do is to plow and plant again. For a grass country, we have no equal in my knowledge. Our sheep live and do well here the year through, and we will have the best wool-growing country in America as soon as we can get Northern men here to manage the industry. While people in the North are raising wool on land worth from fifty to $100 per acre, here our pasturage is free, in a great measure at least, for the land can be purchased from one to five dollars for fruit growing and sheep ranches. The country is fine for raising mules, which will be a fine industry as soon as it is found out. I have lived here on this gulf coast for eight years, and here we have the only perfect summer and winter health resort in America that I have ever found. Take the country from Mobile to New Orleans, a distance of 145 miles, and for twenty miles back from the gulf, and I am prepared to say there is no health resort like it. I came here from the North eight years ago, not for my health, but my friends told me I would not live six months. Well, I am in my eighty-fourth year and have not missed one meal because of sickness since I came here.

Grape Growing in North Carolina.

GEORGE A. WOODARD, Wilmington, N. C.—After a residence of nine years in the State, during which time I have taken special notice of its capabilities as to fruit growing, I have become fully convinced that North Carolina has all the advantages necessary to make the industry a complete success with wise and careful attention.

The climate, the soil and its proximity to good markets are all favorable. The season for growth is so long that fruits will come to bearing quite two years earlier than in the North. There is no danger of winter killing, and scarcely any from spring frosts. The soil, while not of great fertility, seems to be specially adapted to the various kinds of fruits, responding readily to the application of fertilizers. A large portion of the State being within twenty-four hours of the principal Northern markets gives an advantage over States farther South, ensuring the safe transportation of the most delicate fruits. All fruits ripen here at a time when none of the same varieties are to be found farther North, and almost without exception the prices realized are in advance of those received for Northern grown fruits, and coming so much earlier do not come into competition with them.

There is scarcely a fruit grown in temperate regions that does not flourish here. Grapes grow to perfection, the failure of a crop being rarely known. I have met parties who have lived and traveled in California, and who have informed me that they regard this State as the equal of California for grape culture. An English gentleman who was acquainted with the vineyards of France and Germany thought this State superior to either. It is as natural for the blackberry to grow here as it is for the pine tree. Strawberries flourish; there are growers near this city who have netted from $100 to $200 per acre. Peaches, pears, plums, figs, etc., all do well, and in some parts of the State seem to reach their highest perfection.

There is one portion of the State that is now attracting particular attention because of what is being done in fruits there. I refer to Moore county, situated on the Seaboard Air Line Railroad, running between Atlanta and Portsmouth, Va. At Southern Pines, sixty-eight miles from Raleigh, has sprung up within five or ten years a Northern town, intended at first as a health resort, which it continues to be, having already four hotels, with another to be completed during 1894, which is designed to be one of the finest in the South, barring the palatial hotels of Florida. Around this place, owing to Yankee enterprise, vineyards and orchards have sprung up, demonstrating fully that fruit growing pays well at this place at least.

I give here a few instances of what has been done this year. Dr. Weaver has netted $150 per acre from his Delaware grapes planted two years ago last spring. In passing I would say that I doubt if there is a place on the continent where this grape flourishes better than here. One other vineyardist, who paid $900 for five acres set with Niagaras and Delawares, after paying every expense, including his own labor, had left 20 per cent. on his investment. This was the first year of bearing, and of course the crop was light as compared with what it is likely to be in three or four years longer. Others did equally well on the choice varieties, which are the kinds to grow principally. Clusters of Niagara grapes grew here weighing twenty ounces. I saw fifteen pounds taken from a young Niagara vine as its first production. These grapes sell at twelve and one-half cents per pound. Not every vine does this, but it shows what is possible.

A company of Northern gentlemen is now engaged in putting out a vineyard and orchard to comprise nearly 300 acres. They began last spring by setting twenty-seven acres to Niagara grapes and now they have 100 acres ready for planting. Mr. E. Van Lindley and others less than two years ago cleared 350 acres of old pine forest land, setting in the spring 300 acres to peaches and fifty acres to pears. Many of the trees bore this summer. A good crop may be expected next year, and soon 200 or 300 hands will be required to harvest the fruit.

In June, Mr. H. P. Bilyeu sent to market his crop of blackberries. It consisted of 462 bushel crates of the Wilson variety, taken from eleven acres. His commission men returned him more than $1100.

Now, as to the cost of land, cost of planting, etc. Unimproved land, which in most cases is preferable, can be obtained at prices ranging all the way from nothing to $10 per acre. Mr. C. D. Tarbell offers to give every alternate ten acres of quite a large tract to any one who will settle on and improve it. Land in close proximity to the town will cost about $10 per acre. To clear this land free from stumps and roots, to plow twice and harrow, will cost from $15 to $20. To set with choice grape vines, such as Niagaras and Delawares, will cost from $12 to $20 more. Trellising, cultivating and fertilizing for three years will bring the total cost up to $125 or $150 per acre, the work being all done by hired labor. A vineyard prepared in this way will easily net $100

per acre yearly, and it would be difficult to purchase such an one after it began fruiting for less than $250 or $300 per acre; and it is quite probable that the value would soon increase to $500 per acre, judging from values of New York State vineyards.

If the land be set to best varieties of peaches it will cost not to exceed $50 per acre at three years of age; in blackberries, about $75 per acre.

With a variety of fruits it is possible to have the money coming in during nearly six months of the year, and I truly believe that with ten acres rightly managed as much can be made here as off the average 100-acre farm in the North and with far greater ease. The climate is healthy, the cost of living less than in the North, and labor can be performed in the field all the year around with scarcely the loss of a day.

The question is often asked: "Is there not danger that the business will be overdone?" I reply, this is a great country, with a very wide market, continually widening. More people are eating more fruits every year, hence I think there is but little danger of glutting the market with the more desirable varieties.

I will add further that the resources of this State are so varied and extensive that when developed it is likely to take high rank, making it one of the most desirable in which to make a home.

Twenty-three Years in South Carolina.

J. W. WOFFORD, Spartanburg, S. C.—The soil of this county is characterized by two distinct names. 1. The gray sandy soil. 2. The red clay soil. The sub-soil is red or yellow clay. The soil is of easy culture and responds readily to the use of commercial and other manures. The leading crops in this county are cotton, corn, wheat, oats, rye and peas. Cotton is the great money crop and brings the cash any day in the year at either of the seven cotton markets in the county. I have not known a failure in making a remunerative cotton crop (and I have been farming here for twenty-three years) where the land was properly cultivated. The boll worm is almost unknown in this county and the caterpillar seldom appears, and when it does it is always too late to affect the crop. The planting is simple and easy. No crop grown anywhere is more certain than the cotton crop in this county. The average yield per acre is about 300 pounds lint.

Corn for home consumption is grown here and does well on both upland and bottom land. The average yield for corn is about 15 bushels per acre. Wheat, oats, barley and rye grow finely and yield an abundant harvest. The average in agricultural reports seems rather low, but this is readily accounted for by the tenantry system which prevails here to a large extent. The average to the progressive farmer is very much larger in all the crops. Sorghum is a good paying crop and does well anywhere in the county, producing an enormous yield of syrup, sometimes as high as 150 to 175 gallons of first-class syrup to the acre. The ribbon sugar cane can be matured here to the height of four or five feet. Tobacco also is a money-making crop in this county. Peas, Irish and sweet potatoes, turnips and beets grow to perfection here.

Much of the soil is well adapted to the grasses, especially red, white, Lespedeza or wild, and the burr clover. The latter in connection with the Bermuda grass will meet each other, hence there is good grazing the year round on the same land. Vetch thrives here. The Means, orchard, Bermuda, timothy, herds, Kentucky and Texas blue, broom and crab grass do finely in this county, so do all the millets. Lucerne and the prickly comfrey do as well here, perhaps, as anywhere on the continent. The Spanish ground pea always yields an abundant crop on any character of our soil. So do the chufa and the artichoke.

Crop Yields Per Acre.

E. B. RHODES, Spartanburg, S..C.— I have been in Spartanburg three years. I came here from Boston, Mass., and a friend of mine was asking me about the lands and how much I could raise per acre. I told him I had made seventy-five bushels of oats to the acre, thirty bushels of corn and a bale of cotton to the acre, and, on some of my land I shall make two bales to the acre, and my land is not as good as some lands. Last year after I cut off my oats I cut off eight tons of fine crab grass hay and this year I shall double that. The land is a fine red soil, with a clay bottom and will hold all the fertilizer you want to use; and, as for climate, it is the finest in the world, and has the finest summer resorts in the South. All these statements are true, and if you will come to Spartanburg I think you will always stay here. The people are very kind and they will do all that lies in their power to make you happy.

Cattle Breeding and Bee Culture.

T. J. MOORE, Moore, S. C.—Spartanburg county affords unusual attractions to the cattle breeder and apiarist; to the cattle breeder because of the good price of beef, and especially because of the demand for good butter. In this connection I would say that there are in this county several fine herds of Jerseys and a very large number of grades. This is one of the finest sections for dairy farming that I know of. Clover and some of the ordinary grasses succeed, but for general purposes no grass is superior to Bermuda and Johnson or Means grass, the former for grazing, the latter for hay. This section produces both in perfection. Bermuda grass cannot be surpassed in yield and nutritive qualities. It pays me better than anything I have tried. Governor Haygood told me not many days ago, that on his Saluda Old Town place he made double the number of pounds of hay from Bermuda per acre than the census shows was made by any Northern State. It succeeds just as well here. Col. W. G. Childs, of Columbia, makes from three to four tons of hay per acre from the Johnson grass on his bottom lands. I propose to beat him. With butter from twenty-five to thirty cents per pound, which mine always brings, and Bermuda and Johnson grass, we are certainly to be envied, when you take into consideration with these our unrivalled climate, pure water, good health, school advantages, railroad facilities, and civil and religious privileges.

This county also furnishes great advantages to the bee keeper; honey producing plants are in the greatest abundance. The tulip or poplar, apple, peach, plum, blackberry, sour wood, persimmon, and so on to the end of the chapter, furnish an unlimited supply of honey. No winter protection is needed. Colonies will go safely through the winter in hives in which you can stick your fingers through the cracks. The finest quality of honey and the greatest quantity comes from the northern section of the county at the foot of the mountain.

Two Crops Per Year.

N. I. MAYES, Chattanooga, Tenn.— The writer has been engaged more or less in agricultural pursuits in the Southern States for forty years, and also in other pursuits. During this time, by study and comparison, much has been learned that may be of benefit to others. Fortunately it has been my privilege to travel through the North, East, West and Northwest, examining and comparing carefully the advantages for homes and business offered to settlers by various sections. It must be admitted that each section of our great country has attractions to offer, but I know that when our incomparable climate, health, productive soil, rainfall, temperature and social features are all calmly considered, the South offers the most attractive field for profitable, happy homes in all our broad land.

Northern farmers tell us that our farmers are shiftless, keep poor stock, have no barns, have poor houses, cultivate their lands badly, etc. Much of this is true. But there are many who make a great success at farming and stock-raising in the South because they do it right. One of the greatest drawbacks to the Southern farmer is that he owns too much land and tries to cultivate too much, resulting in poor cultivation and short crops. Where smaller areas are used and properly cultivated, good results are invariably obtained. Indeed, as much can be grown on one acre of land here as on the rich lands of the Northwest. Again, we can get much more money for our short crop than the farmers of the Northwest can get for theirs.

No doubt this will be denied. Let me explain: We can get two crops on the same land in one season. Here in Tennessee Irish potatoes are grown quite largely. The first crop comes off about the end of May. In June the second crop is planted, coming off about the end of October. Sometimes other crops follow the first crop of potatoes.

I have a neighbor who grew ten acres of Early Rose potatoes this season (1893). The yield averaged 100 bushels per acre, and they were gathered and sold for $1.50 per bushel, making $1500 for the first crop. At this writing (August) the second crop is very promising and indicates a yield equal to the first.

Another neighbor gathered and sold $15,000 worth of strawberries from thirty acres. Another sold a ten-acre crop of tomatoes at $1000 per acre, and after this was taken off the land was planted to corn and turnips, giving a full crop. These are examples of small areas properly cultivated and go to show what may be done in this country. I could give hundreds of reports of this kind if it were necessary.

But I stated we could get more clear money from crops in the South than from those rich prairie districts in the Northwest. How is it? Our climate being mild, it requires only half as much to build suitable residences and barns as in the cold North, half as much clothing for ourselves, half or one-third as much feed to carry our stock through the winter. Therefore we need to grow only half as much to be even with our Northern friends. But small areas properly cultivated will give as fine a yield in this section as in any part of the country.

Another beauty of this section is that any crop known in the temperate zone can be successfully grown here. Some sections are best adapted by nature to certain crops, but no matter what crops are desired we can suit the case with the necessary conditions. We have valley, ridge, plane, mountain and slope, any desired altitude, and an abundant supply of crystal-clear spring water.

Wheat, clover, timothy, orchard grass, oats, corn, potatoes—everything grows in profusion. Some sections are by nature adapted to the growth of tobacco, fruits, hops and vegetables, while other localities are best suited for grain and the grasses for hay. Three tons per acre is not an unusual crop of hay. No country in the world is better adapted for dairying.

It seems useless to discuss why our people do not engage more in these profitable branches of agriculture. It is known that they have not been educated to it, and it requires time to change the customs of a people. Besides, as a rule, they are land poor. What is needed is that others shall come and purchase at a low price part of their holdings, thus subdividing the land into smaller farms and improving the land and the crops. No fairer land can be found. The writer knows of some large tracts of excellent land that could be bought by a colony of farmers at low prices and on such easy terms that the rent would practically pay for the land.

The health of the South is proverbially good. In high altitudes pulmonary complaints are generally cured. Winters are mild and bracing, summers cooler than at the North. Among the happiest and most prosperous of our people are the Northern people who have settled among us. They are enthusiastic in their praise of the country, its health, climate and people.

Virginia's Commissioner of Agriculture.

HON. THOMAS WHITEHEAD, Commissioner of Agiculture, Richmond, Va.—I receive many letters from different places in all the Northern and Western States and foreign countries, making inquiries in regard to Virginia. Many have stated that a number living in the same county or township make inquiries with a view of buying and settling together. To most of these I have sent maps and publications setting forth the character of the soil, minerals, timber, market towns, &c. I shall state here as concisely as possible, the agricultural and mineral character, social condition and transportation facilities of the State, its climate and productions.

Virginia is an old State; much of its lands has been impoverished by continual cultivation; little improvement attempted. There is no-worn out land in it that cannot by proper management, with reasonable means, be made rich. It includes every grade of agricultural land, and its productions reach from the cotton and yellow tobacco crops, the grapes, melons, potatoes, peas and strawberries of the semi-tropical South, to the buckwheat, rye, barley, cabbages, potatoes, turnips, winter apples and vegetables of the frozen North, and between these on the warm slopes of the mountains and the velvet green valley of Virginia is a land of corn and wine, of meadow and orchard, of milk and honey.

Every class of agriculture succeeds in Virginia if properly conducted. Immigrants from other States, and many of our own people, have become well off by "trucking" in the tidewater country, or fruit-raising and canning in Piedmont, or by fine tobacco in the Southside, or cattle-raising and dairying in the Valley and Southwest. Virginia has every timber, and in my office in Richmond can be seen samples of all from their growth to their manufacture—from the cypress for shingles and sweetgum for lasts and handles in the swamps, from the maple for furniture and persimmon for shuttles, spools and machinery to the five-foot log of black walnut, poplar, white and heart pine, and white oak for lumber. Mines are now worked for coal, iron of all grades, gold, lead, zinc, copper, tin, manganese and pyrites, while there are quarries of the finest granite, slate, marble, brownstone, sandstone, soapstone, mica, asbestos and barytes, besides limestone, hydraulic cement, gypsum (land plaster), salt, earth paints, kaolin, and fire-brick clay, only awaiting capital. The climate has never been excelled for comfort and healthfulness, and for years its mountains have been famous for every variety of the most valuable mineral waters. The winters are mild, the summers pleasant. Large streams are rarely frozen over, and freezes are all of short duration.

Storms of any kind are of the rarest occurrence. Neither cyclones nor blizzards reach this "healthful shore and safe land." A good Providence has made Virginia the safest State in the Union. A hundred miles breadth of forest-covered mountain ranges secures us against the storms of winter, and the blizzards from the Northwest, and the cyclone and hurricane from the Southwest. Either would break harmlessly, and wear out against the magnificent range of grand mountains, rich in minerals, that shuts out our whole State from the fierce blasts that sweep the prairies. By the statistical map of the United States, Piedmont Virginia is the most healthful section of the Union, and most exempt from malarial diseases.

Virginia has naturally more recuperative agricultural power than any State in the Union. Her worn-out · fields—washed, gullied, deserted, left to broom-sedge and pine—reclaim themselves in time, and become as fertile as at first. Thousand of these reclaimed acres are for sale, and these lands quickly furnish abundant fuel and logs for building. Fuel is abundant everywhere. Common labor is abundant and cheap. Provisions are abundant and cheap. Mechanical skill is in fair demand.

Land is cheaper than anything else. We have greatly too much land for our population. Homes in the country and villages are cheaper than ever before. The land is dotted with churches and school-houses, mills and stores—every convenience of living for those that have the means, and are of any value to a country. There is a wonderful opening for large capitalists in the minerals, lumber, water-power, and facilities for manufacturing. Two grand trunk railways cross the State nearly from east to west, and two from north to south, while others of less length cut in other directions. Virginia has the finest harbor in the Union, and many others, besides a great bay and four large navigable rivers, and lines of steamers and sailing-vessels ply in all her waters. Our great need is good, honest, reputable, steady people, with families, to settle in good homes and become Virginians. To all such we offer this guarantee : Call meetings of those who desire to come South ; let them select and empower one or more of their number, who can correctly represent their character and means ; send the delegates to the Commissioner of Agriculture at Richmond, and I guarantee to have them shown these lands at fair prices, put them in the hands of Virginia gentlemen, who will not permit them to be deceived or defrauded, and where, if you have means to buy a home and live one year, you can do well financially and socially.

From a Former Iowa Farmer.

HIRAM CALKINS.—Becoming tired of the rigors of the Northwestern winters, and not possessing the best of health, I, in company with my father, concluded to emigrate to the Sunny South. So, in 1877, we left Hardin county, Iowa, and came to Virginia and purchased a farm of 350 acres, one and a half miles from Hampden-Sidney College, Prince Edward county. It cost us about what the buildings were worth. The highlands were badly worn out, having been rented out since the close of the war, and nearly everything carried off the place and not much returned to the soil. The soil having a good clay sub-soil, we thought it could be made to produce remunerative crops if the land was properly cared for. Our hopes have been fully verified. The past season we have raised very good crops of wheat, rye, oats, sweet and Irish potatoes, sorghum and tobacco. To improve land we have kept all the stock the farm could carry, depending principally on the manure for improving the land. The stock are kept under shelter during the winter and kept well bedded with forest leaves, straw, etc., to make all the manure possible. As soon as a field is improved sufficiently it is seeded down to clover and grass, in rotation. The past season we have cut two heavy crops of clover, and the third has made good grazing.

The soil of this section is of several varieties—dark and light gray sandy soil, red clay, mulatto color, &c. The bottom lands are alluvial and produce good crops of corn, and are kept fertile by the winter overflows of the streams.

We have met with a warmer welcome by the white people than we expected we would have, and I think all good Northern people will be welcome here.

When we came here we concluded that the people were about fifty years behind the North in nearly all branches of business, but since then considerable advancement has been made ; especially is this the case with the public school system. The State Normal school at Farmville affords a splendid opportunity for educating female teachers, and the ladies are availing themselves of the opportunity. Steam threshing machines are taking the place of the old ground-hog, the reaper and mower are displacing the cradle and scythe , so the good work goes bravely on.

Large Returns From a Small Farm.

A. JEFFERS, Norfolk, Va.—I recently spent a night and a portion of two days with a gentleman, formerly from Pittsburg, Pa., but a resident of this section of country for a period of twenty-three years. He is farming on fourteen acres of land, but we believe it is the liveliest fourteen acres of land in the entire United States. There may be, and no doubt are, trucking farms from which the owners get larger returns, but this little "pocket edition" of a farm is a regular dairy farm and truck farm combined.

I make mention of this little place simply to show what can be done on a little farm well tilled. The owner keeps from twelve to fifteen head of milk stock, two horses and a few pigs. He has this amount of stock on hand now, and never has less than at the present time. He makes every foot of his land grow two crops per annum, and has green feed for his milk cows growing in the open air all the year. Beginning in April, he plants corn, "Adams' Early," "Stowell's Evergreen," and other varieties, and from that time on during the summer he plants a new plat of corn about every two weeks and has green corn to feed until November frosts cut it for him.

He planted one acre of his land in corn the 6th of July last year, and on the 18th day of September following sowed clover among the corn, crimson clover, cultivating it in between the rows, afterwards taking off the corn. The clover made a fine crop, turning off fully three tons to the acre. The land was then plowed (in June) and planted to corn, which is now (September) cut and standing in the shock, and is good for sixty bushels of shelled corn to the acre. This land has had no fertilizer or manure for two years.

Thirteen years ago he bought his first family cow, a fine Jersey then fifteen months old. He has the same old cow in his herd, and his books show that of her calves he has sold $250 worth, and he has in the barn fully $240 worth of her descendants. In fourteen years she has had fourteen calves and has never been dry during this period. He cuts all his fodder with a one horse-power tread machine and a fodder cutter, and he also has a baby threshing machine to use in threshing out an occasional rye crop. He intends to add a mill for grinding his corn and other feed. We have seen all these appliances on many a farm, but never on so small a farm or scale as this. We asked our friend why he did not cover more ground, get more land, and he assured us that he would not attempt to farm another acre if it was given him.

The middle of August he sowed a patch to buckwheat,. and at the same time sowed clover and timothy. The buckwheat is now in bloom, as pretty a sight as one can imagine, and underneath its grateful shade is a perfect stand of clover and timothy, which he believes will turn him off at the rate of three tons of cured hay next summer at the first cutting, and nearly three tons more at the two later cuttings. The hum of the bees gathering honey from this field on the 23d of September was simply grand. We had heard of the "hum of industry," but this was the sweetest hum we ever heard, and one could hear it ten or fifteen rods away from the field.

We also saw here the "wonderful pea," so called from the great growth it makes. The peas sowed or planted on the poorest strip of his land here, and without fertilizer or manure of any kind whatever, had grown fully fifteen feet on either side of the rows and were still growing. The pea had just begun to bloom and form pods. It is surely the manure for this country, as it forms a great mass of vegetable matter to turn under to hold, renew and replenish the strength of the land made weak by long years of cultivation, or rather by long years of robbery. He had one acre in potatoes this year, from which he sold 131 barrels of prime stock and fed fourteen barrels of culls to his cows. The average price received was $2.75 per barrel. He sells his butter at thirty-five cents per pound. He grows all his forage crops on the farm, buying some ship stuff and cottonseed meal for a grain ration for his cows. He has no idle land, but as soon as one crop is off another one goes in the ground at once, both in summer and in winter. It is one ceaseless round of planting, cultivating and harvesting. It is astonishing to see what an amount of produce a man can grow here on a small area of land when he really tries his best. From a little field of the common red clover he cut this year at three cuttings fully five and one-half tons to the acre. These and many other facts in connection with his work show the advantage of cultivating small areas and doing it well, and also show the virtue in a liberal application of stable manure. The owner's name can be had on application, but he declined to let me use it in connection with this letter, as he has no time to answer the many idle inquiries he would get. We shall be glad to give his name and address to anyone who would like to know more particularly as to any matter in connection with his work. He is just as busy as the busiest bee in the buckwheat, and while the bees are making honey he is making money. Wish we had 10,000 like him.

A RELIC OF THE OLD REGIME.

By Val. Starnes.

See him gazing round about him,
　As though wandering in a dream,
While the mocking gamins flout him—
　He is of the Old Regime.

Failing energies he mustered
　Yesterday, to come and view,
Once again, the glories clustered
　In the city that he knew.

But he finds it, oh, how altered
　From the slow, old-fashioned town,
Down whose streets he strolled and paltered
　When the crinkly locks were brown!

Then, with whoop and merry chatter
　And the trace-chains' clanking din,
Sixteen mule hoofs all a-patter,
　From the West they rattled in

To the wagon yard's extensive
　Width of hospitable gate—
Ah, the memories throng, intensive,
　Through his poor bewildered pate!

Memories of the firelight flitting
　O'er the white tilts parked about,
While the jovial groups there sitting,
　With the banjo, song and shout,

Woke the echoes o'er the river
　On the Carolina side,
Made the dusky willows quiver,
　As they drooped above the tide.

Now, the cotton and provisions,
　E'en the mules, are shipped by steam—
Dim are ante bellum visions:
　Distant, dim, the Old Regime.

For the whole wide world has drifted
   Into newer life and law ;
All his unities have shifted
   Since the days "befo' de wah."

Before that war was waged,
   "Dey wuz really white folk's cities"—
So he says—but now he's aged,
   It is time for *nunc demitis.*

Since the mule has lost his power
   And the cotton comes by steam—
Round him evening shadows lower,
   Have enwrapt the Old Regime.

SECURITY FOR INVESTORS IN SOUTHERN BONDS.

By R. B. Sperry.

Much has been said on the subject of Southern investments, but one phase has been but scantily discussed, namely, the security afforded by constitutional and legislative restrictions as to State and municipal debts. Up to 1870 the creation of this class of indebtedness was not only an easy matter, but the privilege was sadly abused, and it was this more than all else that proved the bane of the South when she sought outside capital.

We all know how repudiation ran riot in the five years succeeding the war, and how the very mention of a Southern bond produced almost the same effect as shaking a red rag at a mad bull. It must be confessed that this feeling was in a great measure justified, as many of these bonds were issued at least with a semblance of law which could not have been done had the present wholesome restrictions prevailed. States, municipalities and counties were authorized to issue bonds in aid of railroads, canals and other enterprises under the guise of internal improvements practically without limit, and designing speculators were not slow to take advantage of it; and having received the bonds and foisted them on a credulous public, the enterprise for which they were issued was allowed to take care of itself.

Happily these conditions either no longer exist or are so modified as to reduce their danger to a minimum; and in States where they are not entirely forbidden the sober sense and past experience of the people may safely be trusted to prevent their abuse.

The following summary of constitutional and legislative restrictions of the eleven Southern States (taken only from a business man's standpoint, for I am not a lawyer) will be interesting:

VIRGINIA.

By the constitution of 1870 the State debt is limited to provision for existing debt. The State cannot lend or give its credit to, nor hold or own stock in corporations or associations. The legislature regulates the creation of debt and lending of credit of counties and municipalities, but such liability must be voted by the people.

WEST VIRGINIA.

By the constitution of 1872 the State is prohibited from creating debt except for public defense, casual deficit in the revenue or to redeem a previous liability. Neither can it lend or give its credit to, or become stockholder in corporations or associations. No municipality, county or other division can create debt in excess of 5 per cent. of its assessed valuation. Such debt must be approved by three-fifths of the voters, and must be provided for by an annual tax sufficient to pay interest as it accrues and the principal within thirty-four years.

NORTH CAROLINA.

By the constitution of 1876 the State cannot create additional debt until the bonds sell at par, except for public defense or a casual deficit in the revenue. Both the State and its sub-divisions may vote aid to, subscribe to and hold stock in railroad corporations when approved by a majority of qualified voters. The legislature regulates the creation of debt by counties and municipalities.

SOUTH CAROLINA.

The constitution of 1868, amended in 1873, forbids further creation of debt unless for ordinary and current business; nor can the debt of the State or its endorsement be given except with the approval of two-thirds of the qualified voters at a general election. The general assembly regulates the creation of debt by the sub-divisions of the State.

GEORGIA.

By the constitution of 1877 the State cannot create debt except for public defense, the payment of existing debts and to provide for a casual deficit in the revenue, and such deficit shall not exceed $200,000. The State cannot give or lend its credit or grant donations to any individual, corporation or association, nor can any city, town or county do so except for purely charitable purposes. County and municipal debts are restricted to 7 per cent. of their assessed valuation, except that where this limit existed when the constitution was adopted 3 per cent. additional is allowed. Debt can only be created with the assent of two-thirds of the qualified voters, and at the time it is made must be provided for by an annual tax which will pay the interest as it matures and the principal within thirty years.

FLORIDA.

By the constitution of 1868 the State can only create debt for erection of State buildings, support of State institutions and to provide for existing debt. Neither the State nor any sub-division can make donations nor lend or give their credit to nor be stockholders in any corporation or association. The legislature regulates the other questions of debt and taxation.

TENNESSEE.

By the constitution of 1870 the State cannot lend or give its credit to any association or corporation; otherwise there is no restriction. Counties, cities and towns may become stockholders in and lend their credit to corporations, provided three-fourths of the qualified voters assent thereto. The legislature regulates the amount of such and other debts and questions of taxation.

ALABAMA.

By the constitution of 1875 the State cannot increase its present debt except for public defense and a temporary debt not exceeding $100,000. Neither the State nor any sub-division can own or hold stock in, nor grant or lend money or credit to corporations or associations. Municipal and county debts are otherwise regulated by legislature.

MISSISSIPPI.

By the constitution of 1890 neither the State nor any sub-division can give or lend its credit to, or appropriate money for or hold or subscribe to stock in corporations or associations. The legislature regulates by general law other questions of debt.

LOUISIANA.

By the constitution of 1879 no additional debt shall be contracted by the State except for public defense, nor can State or any of its sub-divisions appropriate money, lend or give their credit to, or become stockholders in any corporation or association. The legislature regulates the creation of . debts by municipalities and parishes.

TEXAS.

By the constitution of 1876 the State cannot create debt except for public defense or a casual deficit in the revenue not exceeding $200,000. The legislature may grant aid in case of public calamity. Neither the State nor any of its sub-divisions can give or lend their credit to, appropriate money for, or become stockholder in any corporation or association. With certain constitutional restrictions as to taxation, the legislature regulates the creation of debt by counties and municipalities.

ARKANSAS.

By the constitution of 1874 the general assembly is authorized to provide for all just and legal debts of the State, but is prohibited from issuing any interest bearing treasury warrants or script. Neither the State nor any of its sub-divisions can give or lend their credit to, appropriate money for or own or hold stock in any corporation or association. No county or municipality can issue interest bearing evidence of indebtedness except to provide for debt existing at time of adoption of the constitution.

It will be observed that all these States, except North and South Carolina, absolutely prohibit State aid to corporations, and all except Virginia, West Virginia, North Carolina, South Carolina and Tennessee prohibit their counties and municipalities likewise; but in each of these States which do allow such aid charter limits of debt have been created by the several legislatures, which as I have already said reduce the evil to a minimum. Too much stress cannot be laid upon this feature, for instances are rare where Southern counties or municipalities have litigated any other class than their railway aid debts; and while it is true that the United States courts have come to the rescue of the bondholders, it is a matter of congratulation that this disturbing element has been removed.

That this is appreciated by investors is evidenced by the ready market Southern State and municipal bonds have found in the past five years, and by the high price they have commanded. Two prominent Northern institutions alone, whose financial committees are composed of some of the shrewdest and most successful business men in the land, hold nine millions of dollars of this class of bonds. As late as July of this year the State of South Carolina, through Baltimore bankers, refunded five millions of dollars of her maturing debt at 4½ per cent.; and this in the midst of the severest monetary panic this country has experienced in twenty-five years. Georgia 4½ per cent. bonds have sold as high as 116; Alabama and North Carolina 4 per cent. bonds at par. Cities like Richmond, Va., and Atlanta, Ga., have sold 4 per cent. bonds at par; while the bonds of cities of lesser importance have found ready market on a 4½ per cent. to 5½ per cent. interest basis, and why should they not in ordinary times?

Take for instance the bonds of Georgia municipalities. They are limited in amount to 7 per cent. of the assessed valuation; they must be approved by two-thirds of the qualified voters after thirty days public notice; they must be protected by a continuing tax sufficient to pay interest and retire the principal at maturity and they cannot be voted for any but municipal purposes. Can the investor ask more than this for his protection? The fact is he can get as good security and better interest on the same character of investment in the South than any other section of this great country.

"I'SE GOT MIGHTY P'TIC'LAR BIZNESS TER CONTRACK WID YOH SAH, MIGHTY P'TIC'LAR BIZNESS."

MURIEL'S RICH RELATION.

By Astley Palmer Cooper.

With Illustrations by the Author.

"Ez good ez er white man!"

"G'long wi' yoh pow'ful conceited notions! If er niggah are free an' low'd der sem priv'leges ez er white cit'zen, he are not so good, chile, ontil de brack jackass throw offen der lion's skin uv ign'rance."

Unc' Jasper sighed heavily as he finished this speech, and gazed contemptuously at a colored youth who had been daring enough to express an opinion and cross swords in debate with Unc' Jasper.

"'Spects yuse right, Unc' Jasper, 'spects yuse right," answered the abashed youth in conciliatory tones.

"'Spects I's right!" responded Unc' Jasper with offended dignity, "Course I'se right, yo ignoramus chile; I'se hed 'sperience 'nuff—'sperience in commershul life, 'n 'sperience in religion. Larn readin' books an' human nature, 'n don't stan' yere wastin' no time argy-fyin' wid marchents, ez hev hed 'sperience." With this final homily Unc' Jasper proceeded on his way, leaving the young colored boy to gaze after him in an abstracted frame of mind.

Unc' Jasper was a celebrated character in that North Carolina town. The residents could not well remember his advent, but they had a dim idea that the old man had peddled lemonade and cakes ever since the beginning of the town. Unc' Jasper was a curious being. While about the streets selling his wares he was always scrupulously clean and neat. He had no regular abiding place, but rested himself and took a meal when so disposed at the nearest residence of one of his race, and Aunt Hannah, or Bre'r Henry, or Sister Liza always welcomed him and gave him the best cheer their scanty lot could afford. Moreover, they felt amply repaid when Unc' Jasper gave some cookies to the children, accompanied by portentous words of advice.

Unc' Jasper, by reason of his age and "'sperience," was recognized as a sort of traveling Nestor by the colored population, and the words of his almost incomprehensible sermons were listened to in rapt attention akin to veneration. He never confided his secrets to anyone excepting Major Carr, a leading lawyer of the city.

"Er pow'ful larned gen'l'man, is de majah," Unc' Jasper would say, "wid er pow'ful heap uv books."

What Major Carr knew about the old negro's affairs or why they met in confidential talks so often nobody could surmise. The only biography of Unc' Jasper that was common property was that he was a freedman long before the emancipation days. Those who knew him intimately said that he was once the slave of a rice planter, Wilson by name, in South Carolina, who gave him his freedom for saving the life of his daughter Florence, at that time but a small child. It was also said that Mr. Wilson had started him in the business he since had followed. Gossip went further and told how Florence had grown into beautiful girlhood, the only child of her father, her mother having died during her infancy. One day she eloped with a dissolute and dissipated young man, a son of her father's most bitter enemy.

Mr. Wilson, who had strenuously forbidden an engagement, renounced his daughter, and her fortune-hunting husband soon dragged her down to degradation and misery.

After a few years of poverty, Florence's husband died as a result of dissipation, and soon afterwards she gave up the life struggle and succumbed to disease, caused by want and privation. A daughter was all that remained to recall the unhappy union, and she, poor child, would have been thrown on the cold and cheerless lap of public charity had not an anonymous rich relative

"THE COLORED BOY GAZED AFTER HIM IN AN ABSTRACTED FRAME OF MIND."

assumed her charge. This relative, by proxy, saw the remains of poor Florence buried, and also made arrangements for the care of the orphan child— Muriel. The identity of this relative became the subject of fruitless speculation, but all agreed that he must be both rich and generous.

Muriel's maternal grandfather had died before her birth, leaving his entire fortune to a nephew in New York City. This nephew had been at one time a suitor for his cousin Florence's hand, but his attention had been forbidden by her father, who did not sanction a union between cousins. Major Carr had interceded in the young man's behalf, and being now the agent through whom Muriel received her money, inferences naturally were drawn.

However, on the particular day on which this narrative opens, Muriel was at a private school in Virginia, and Unc' Jasper was pursuing the monotonous tenor of his merciful career. The old negro was turning into the most prominent business street when he met Major Carr.

"Bress yoh, majah, I'se glad ter see yoh, pow'ful glad; I ain't seed yoh fer 'r long wile. I'se got mighty p'tic'lar bizness ter contrack wid yoh sah, mighty p'tic'lar bizness."

"Well, Jasper," replied the major, "be at my office at five this evening and you can talk to your heart's desire."

"Thanky, sah," and Unc' Jasper replaced his old hat which he had removed out of respect to Major Carr's pow'ful larnedness.

The large hand of the clock, as though wearied and depressed by the excessive heat of the day, was crawling slowly up towards the hour of twelve, where it was scheduled to arrive precisely at the time its still more indolent companion, the small hand, reached the notch mark under the figure V, when Major Carr entered his law office. As he seated himself in the capacious easy chair before his desk, he noticed on the top of his afternoon mail a letter addressed in the angular hand of a college girl. He sighed as he opened it, a sigh in which pity and benevolence were mingled.

"Oho!" he ejaculated, after reading a few lines, adding emphasis to the remark by raising his eyebrows and again raising them as he read on. "Oho!" Major Carr seemed upset by the contents of the letter, and, laying it down, he snatched a cigar from the desk, and placing it, with its pointed end intact, between his teeth, he strode up and down the room in a perspiring agony of thought. And this is what the letter contained:

JUNE 2, ——.

My Dear Kind Friend—I have the greatest news to tell you. I am engaged to be married to the richest, handsomest man in town. His name is Clifford Read, and he says you knew his father before he died. Clifford is four years older than I. The girls here are all very good about it and are giving me the nicest kinds of congratulations. I am sure I can rely on you for your consent to a step which will insure your ward's happiness. How I wish poor dear mamma was alive to share my joy. We are going to be married from the home of Clifford's mother. She is a perfectly lovely old lady and has been so kind and considerate throughout. You must come over and give me away, as you are my near·st and dearest friend after "Cliff.". We are going to London and Paris and lots of places for our honeymoon after a short stay at Old Point Comfort.

Do you think my unknown benefactor will cons·nt? I hope so, as I need a t ousseau besides my graduating gown. Excuse haste as I have lots to think of and do.

With love, yours affectionately,
MURIEL.

P. S.—Of course you will be at the commencement with a handsome floral tribute for your happy and excellent ward.

M. W., soon to be M. R.

Major Carr's pacing of the room was interrupted by a knock at the door.

"Come in !" the major almost shouted. The door opened and ·the ebony face of Unc' Jasper showed itself, followed by the rest of Unc' Jasper with his lemonade pail and cooky basket.

"Here I is, sah, 'bout on time to de minit."

The major pointed to a seat opposite his own at the desk, and with a mournful sigh gazed out into the busy street. The old colored man sat down at the desk, and fumbled long beneath the bosom of his apron, tugging at something which proved to be a small-sized canvas bag, tied at the opening with a yard of wool cord. After a great deal of picking at knots, the cord was removed, and Unc' Jasper, with a triumphant smile on his face, poured out on the desk a torrent of coin, mostly of small denomination. The sound of the money aroused Major Carr from his reverie at the window and, turning hastily, he came over and sat at the desk. He glanced at the money and curtly asked:

"How much is there ?"

"Er hunderd 'n twenty-seben, zackly, majah," replied Unc' Jasper, fairly beaming with satisfaction, "er hunderd 'n twenty-seben, zackly."

Major Carr rested his head on his hand, and with a groan lapsed into another fit of abstraction.

"Is yoh taken sick, boss ?" queried the colored client, after gazing at the major for a few seconds.

"THE MAJOR GAZED OUT INTO THE BUSY STREET."

The major groaned again, and taking up Muriel's letter said : "No, not sick, Jasper, but worse. "I've just received a letter from Muriel, and she's going to be married."

"Gwine ter be married, sah ?"

"Yes, she's going to be married to a rich young man in three weeks from today."

Unc' Jasper only opened his eyes wide and stared at the major.

"And she is going to graduate and needs a graduating gown, and there are a quarter's college fees to be paid, and how it is all to be done with one hundred and twenty-seven dollars is more than I can tell. There is one thing certain, however, and that is she'll not be likely to need money after she is married."

"Is grandulating gowns berry 'spensive, majah?" asked Unc' Jasper, only realizing part of the speech.

The major took a pencil and commenced figuring. "If twenty dollars will pay for a graduating gown," he explained after a great deal of elaborate arithmetical exercise, "I think we can

MURIEL.

manage everything except the wedding, there's the rub."

"Does weddins cum costly?" asked Unc' Jasper anxiously.

"I am afraid they do, afraid they do," mused the lawyer aloud.

Both remained silent for some time and both gazed intently at the money, as if figuring by what means they could increase the size of the pile. Finally the lawyer spoke:

"Suppose, uncle, I stand the expenses of the wedding. I could——"

Unc' Jasper broke in with a deprecating gesture, "No sah, no, Majah Carr, dis ar er fambly affair, en wot de

'spense am ez ter be borne by me." Unc' Jasper paused for a moment and then continued:

"But yoh might 'vance de weddin' money ef yoh ar not skeer'd to trus' en ole cull'ed merchan' like Unc' Jasper."

"Very well," replied Major Carr, "I will advance it, and as soon as I can find out the cost of a wedding outfit"—"a hard matter for an old bachelor," he muttered, "I will send it to our ward as coming from her rich relative."

"Thanky kindly, majah. I do feel gretful to yoh fer de favor, en you'll never be regretful dat yoh done loaned de sum ter Unc' Jaspah."

In a pretty little Episcopal church in the suburbs of a Virginia town, towards the end of June, the month of brides and roses, a quiet wedding was in progress. The church was filled to its capacity, ladies largely predominating. Many comments, mostly of approval, were bestowed on the recently united couple as they passed down the aisle followed by the bridesmaids and attendants. The young wife was of the true type of Southern beauty, and her loveliness was enhanced by the simplicity of her bridal robe.

A familiar figure in the joyous procession that followed the bridesmaids was Major Carr, dressed with all the fastidiousness of a proud Southern gentleman of the old school. The major had done wonders with his usual appearance in honor of Muriel's wedding, and in order to do justice to the prominent role, that of giving away the bride, which he had just performed greatly to his credit.

In a corner of the church near the door was old Unc' Jasper, and he simultaneously smiled and wiped a tear from his dusky cheek, as he murmered: "Lord bress yoh, Missy," audibly enough for the bride to hear. She looked in the direction of the voice and nodded a look of pleased recognition at the old man, who, as she well knew, had saved her mother's life.

The congratulations in the church were soon over and the party drove to the residence of the groom's mother, where the wedding breakfast was waiting. Toasts of health, happiness and prosperity were drunk. Major Carr congratulated the young couple, giving them at the same time a bachelor's advice as to their future conduct.

The bride soon left the table in order to don her traveling costume, when a maid in the hall told her that an old negro from Carolina was very anxious to see her and persisted in his request. Muriel guessed correctly the negro's identity, and consented to see Unc' Jasper without delay.

The old colored merchant gazed at Muriel, his eyes beaming with pride as he surveyed her in all the grace and beauty of her bridal adornment, before he spoke, then reaching in his pocket he presented to Muriel a well-handled and much-worn roll of paper.

"I'se a pore ole cull'ed merchant, Missy, en I'se not able to gib yoh no val'able gif', but here am de mos' preshious doc'ment dat wuz ever given to any man, brack o' white—freed'm. Dis doc'ment made me er free cull'ed genl'man long 'fore 'mancipation; t'was gib me by yo' gran'father, chile, many years ago."

"Yes, Unc' Jasper," said Muriel gently, "for saving the life of poor mamma."

"Dat's er fac' Missy, dat's er fac;' yo' po' mammy wuz er l'il chile den." Unc' Jasper paused and seemed to lose himself in thought.

"But Uncle Jasper don't you wish to keep it yourself; you might need it some time to show."

"Not er bit, Missy," replied the old man, mistaking her meaning, "no need uv showin et now days, all cull'ed fokes is free; 'sides I ask yoh ter tek et ez er favor from er po' ole citzen who'se too po' ter gib yoh anyting mo' lab'rate."

"Very well, Uncle Jasper, I will keep it, but should you ever need the paper you can always get it."

"Thanky, Missy, my mind am easier now; keep it keerful en tell yo' chillun's chillun, wen yoh gits gray, de story uv how ole Unc' Jaspah 'came er free niggah, thanky, en God bress yoh, Missy."

Unc' Jasper bowed low and wiped his eyes again as he walked out into the glare of the noonday sun.

Six months had passed and Muriel and her husband were seated at breakfast in Venice. Muriel was reading a letter, and as she finished she drew her husband's attention from the gliding gondolas which he was watching.

"I've just received a letter from Major Carr with two pieces of news, one is that the money from my rich relative has now ceased forever."

"So much the better," replied her

"THE RICHEST, HANDSOMEST MAN IN TOWN."

husband, "as it makes you seem more to me and more mine own. And what is the other news."

"Do you remember Uncle Jasper who gave me his freedom papers for a wedding gift? Well, Major Carr writes that he is dead."

Muriel ate her breakfast that morning in silence, and as her husband gazed and wondered why her usual gaiety seemed subdued, he noticed a tear, which caught all the bright tints of the bright Venetian coloring outside as it rolled down her cheek a veritable pearl.

"Being cut off suddenly by an unknown rich relative would surely not account for that in a girl as unselfish as Muriel," he mused.

But Muriel's thoughts wandered back to a grave beside the swamps, a grave of a mother whose love had long since been withdrawn, and to the poor old colored man who had risked his life for hers, and she sighed inwardly, "poor Uncle Jasper."

A CAROLINA GARDEN.

By Robert Adger Bowen.

If you'd love a shady spot
　Where the garish light comes not,
And where thrushes sing in cedars all the day ;
　Where the mocker builds his nest,
　And the red bird's crimson crest
Makes within the orange foliage color gay :

　If in roses you delight,
　Red, and pink, and creamy white,
Or those damask ones whose blood red turns to black ;
　If your fancies so incline
　To the yellow jessamine,
Or to jonquils lying prone upon their back :

　If you'd like to sit with book
　In a dim and tangled nook,
With a mass of periwinkle at your feet,
　And while reading slow along
　Catch the rapture of the song.
Of the mocking-bird's wild music, fine and sweet :

　Then you'd love this garden old
　With its blaze of red and gold,
And its wide walks leading under cedar trees ;
　With its bamboo arbor seat
　Where the humming-birds all meet
And the honeysuckle bends with bumble-bees :

　Where you catch a distant view
　Of the mountains lying blue,
Seen o'er meadow lands agolden in the sun :
　Hear the nesting ring-dove's moan
　Making mellow undertone
Where the pine trees climb the hillsides one by one.

　There with finger marking place
　Where you'd stopped a moment's space
In the reading of some potent poesy,
　That the wondrous words might fall
　With their charm poetical
On thy heart with sweet repeated ecstacy ;

You might sit and dream away
All a golden summer day,
Till the whippoorwills called loud at eventide :
As the meadow lands grow shaded,
And the purple lights are faded
Where they lie in glory on the mountain side.

Do you think that you could love,
With its gold-blue skies above,
This old garden where sweet moods had come to you ;
Moods which all your after years,
And your trials and your cares,
Never could their lingering memories undo?

MISETTE.

"Can you tell me where Mr. Madère lives?" asked a young man as he drew up his horse at the gate of a little yard in Southern Louisiana.

The question was addressed to a young girl, whose absorbing occupation was pounding brick for scrubbing purposes, so dear to the heart of the Southern Creole. Kneeling before a large flat stone on which were heaped pounded brick, and bats, as she paused on hearing the voice, with hatchet upraised in slender, sunburnt hand, the sleeves rolled back from the rounded arm, a big sunbonnet pushed back from a pretty brown face, she might have posed as a novel study in art. Despite the fact that her rather scant and faded calico dress revealed a pair of shapely feet and ankles, she advanced with an ease and grace strangely at variance with her simple attire. Her utter want of self consciousness was the charm, neither was there the least forwardness, but a quiet dignity, peculiar to the Creoles, be they rich or poor. Her occupation, her costume, the yard and premises, denoted that Misette was of the latter class. While undoing the gate, she said:

. "My fader live here, hé Monsieur Madère. Entrez Monsieur."

Her voice, soft and gentle, rendered her broken English musical, and she raised her timid long-lashed eyes as she spoke. The stranger tied his horse and responding to her invitation followed her up the little path, to the barelooking gallery, newly scrubbed and liberally besprinkled with brickdust, which crunched unpleasantly beneath his boot as he walked. Misette offered a chair, and hoped that Monsieur would excuse her, while she went to call her papa, who had just returned from "Derrière," where he was making "Une recolte."

While waiting, the stranger glanced around and he could not but notice the utter want of adornment or taste about the little premises, not a trailing vine or flower of the most hardy kind. The French doors, opening on the gallery, enabled him to see that all the rooms bore the same aspect of bareness and brickdust. A Turkey red curtain flapped spasmodically in the open door and a clucking hen scratched most energetically for her brood of peeping chicks. The house was built according to the primitive style of architecture of the river coast. High gabled roof, built from the time-honored custom of keeping the house cool, and with an equally laudable idea of avoiding dampness the building was raised several feet from the ground on little brick pillars. Next his attention was attracted to a pile of dry driftwood, protruding from beneath the house, blanched in its course down the angry Mississippi. Perhaps for hundreds of miles it had turned over and over, buffeting with the current till many of the sharp angles had become rounded, and its body polished in the contest, finally to be arrested in its course to the Gulf, for this drift is considered by the poorer population as a special provision sent them by "le bon Dieu."

Mr. Madère appeared, presenting quite a contrast to his daughter. He was long and lank, wore his hair uncut, a pair of blue cottonade trousers, and a hat characteristic of its owner and his race; such a spiritless expression did it possess that it seemed to have grown on his head, part and parcel of himself. His chin stuck out in front, adorned with a scanty beard. He advanced to shake hands, saying interrogatively:

"You want see me, Monsieur——"

"Dickson," supplied the gentleman, "the United States engineer. And my good friend, the levee is in a very bad condition all along here."

Mr. Madère rubbed his chin and said: "Dat écrevisse, hey?"

"If you can spare a moment, I will show you the bad points I speak of. I want your advice as to what had better be done. I tell you, there's a big flood expected this year. You'll all be swamped by a crevasse the first thing you know."

Mr. Madère rubbed his chin the harder, and reflectively remarked: "My grandpa he live here, my pa he live here, and dere never been no crevasse. I tell you, dig him out," referring to the obnoxious crawfish.

"Well, my friend, you can take that job, I have seen that tried already." Which remark produced an appreciative laugh from the Creoles. They were interrupted by Madame Madère, a comfortable looking woman, whose motherly embonpoint was more to be admired than the plain calico gown, which was of a make of an anterior generation. The cut of the sleeve, the general squareness of its proportions, clearly demonstrated that her thoughts were not influenced by fashion's fickle sway. Her dark abundant hair was twisted at her neck, with little attempt at adornment. Extending a soft, plump hand to Lieutenant Dickson, she offered to shake hands, a "politesse" demanded by the Creole laws of hospitality.

"Bon jour, Monsieur," she said. "You want take my husband off wid you; he not yet had he dinner. You come sit down too, Monsieur."

As Lieutenant Dickson hesitated to accept this informal invitation, the grandmother of the family introduced herself with much sauvity of manner, wearing a "blouse volante" of Guinea blue calico, adorned with a foulard handkerchief, knotted at her throat in lieu of a collar.

"You speak French, Monsieur?" she asked, smiling, and on his shaking his head, continued:

"Mais quel dommage. The dinner is ready, Monsieur."

Without further circumlocution he found himself partaking of a genuine Creole dinner. Misette smiled a welcome and several thin little urchins slid in, with bare feet and faded shirts. He underwent the ordeal of shaking their limp little hands, as they were reminded by their mother to "dis bon jour donc." A steaming plate of "gumbo s'herbes" was handed him, a compound which at first he viewed askance, but took on trust on grandmère's remarking "c'est bon, oui." The green mass, a conglomeration of many herbs as its name implies, poured over a snowy mound of rice, he mentally compared to a minature mountain down whose sides ran a stream of green lava. But he found the combination most agreeable. Another savory dish also claimed his attention, which was pressed upon him by the name of "Jambalaya." When he left, it was with an agreeable impression of the culinary powers of the Creole dames. Also with the volubility of their adieux, Misette timidly adding, "Ah! When Monsieur come again."

The work of the family was recommenced. The old lady began to parch or "griller le café" which was a work of art, according to her prescribed rule. A large iron pot, a paddle, blackened by constant contact with the berry, and a fire built between bricks in the yard, were indispensable parts of the paraphernalia. The Creole women, in this portion of Louisiana at least, were thrifty, indefatigable workers, toiling at the accomplishment of household duties that could have been performed with one-half the trouble by the aid of modern labor-saving inventions and progressive methods, but all such were regarded by them as innovations and treason to the memory of their ancestors, for "Ma grandmère n'a jamais fait ça."

Misette, leaning over the unpainted banisters, slowly scraping the crumbs from a plate to the little chicks, suddenly called to her mother in that broken English the Creoles often drift into:

"Hey, Mama! Can't I go to school?"

"Qu'as tu, Misette? We too po', chile. You ain't got no nice dress," interrupted her mother.

"Mais, Mom, I can make some money. I can catch shrimps an' sell 'em; Madame B., what live en-bas, she want some."

"Va donc, Misette. De chevrettes no run yet."

"But oui," expostulated Misette, "I see Clemence yesterday, an' she say she get some."

"Fais comme tu veux, mon enfant," satisfied Misette. Her dreams that night were happy ones. Her newly awakened ambition called up visions of school triumphs, mingled with the shadowy form of a handsome prince bearing resemblance to Mr. Dickson, who smiled approval and crowned her with flowers, till slumber stealing each sense, the vision gradually faded away.

The first glimmer of dawn found Misette clambering up the sides of the levee, her shrimp bags hanging on her arm. These were simple arrangements made of common bagging, with hoops to hold them open. Her heavy dark braids hung half loose in the damp air, and on her cheeks was the flush of health. Her little brothers followed with basket and bucket, from which they took bait—corn meal or hominy. Misette quickly threw this into the bags as an allurement to the shrimp. While thus engaged the boys' little hands were busily collecting "shrimp weed," considered a necessary adjunct to a shrimp bag, but possessing no real merit save as an entanglement to the shrimp, preventing their egress from their prison. When these necessary arrangements were completed, Misette, holding one end of the rope that was attached to each bag, adroitly threw them into the river, one after the other, with a grace of movement and without apparent muscular effort, showing a familiarity with this occupation. She attached the ropes to stakes driven a short distance in the water, which necessitated the wetting of her bare feet. The boys seated themselves on the fascine work that protected the levee, dangling their feet expectantly. Misette seated herself on a bit of driftwood, and gazed

reflectively on the river, over which hung a dense fog. A steamboat at a little distance whistled plaintively at intervals as she groped her way. The fog lifted and she puffed into view. Misette woke from her reverie, and called to the boys:

"Ah! Va la Mable Comeaux. How I wish I was on dat boat." Then the shrimp bags claiming her attention, she drew them out of the water with loud exclamations of joy at her success. After repeated hauling in and throwing out, finding she had a sufficiency, Misette slipped her arm through the basket and trudged off to sell the result of her morning's work. Full of eager anticipation, she walked slowly along the dusty road with eyes cast down, watching the disappearing ground beneath her feet.

"Ah, cherie!" cried a sweet voice in her ear, and Misette's neck was encircled by a pair of arms, and a kiss was given by the merry Clemence, who was accompanied by a little mulatress whose greeting was: "Common vo, Moman?" Then, with smiles and pretty gesticulations the three girls walked on, talking rapidly, Clemence glibly relating the pleasure of her last fête.

"Oui, même," joined in their colored companion, in the curious patois of their race, unintelligible save to a Louisiana Creole. It is impossible to convey on paper a fair idea of the peculiar accent and rapid enunciation of this curious language. "Oui, même. Nous autre té couri en haut la levee. Nous tes aller loin dans champ di cannes, et nous autres té trapé di écrevisses dans fossé. Quel gala nous autre té fait, crase di mures avec di sire. Ah, cétait bon mo capable dit. Mo té gagner bon temps, oui."

Tearing herself from this recital of the delights of eating blackberries and sugar, catching crawfish, etc., Misette turned at the gate of a large yard and advanced timidly to the broad gallery where Madame B. and several of the family were enjoying the morning air. To the little shrimp-girl's surprise, her friend of the day before was there also. He greeted her cordially and showed much interest in her occupation, and watched her curiously as she modestly lifted the grey moss that covered her treasures and bashfully offered them to the lady of the house. They were easily disposed of and the gentleman's admiration was excited by the dainty way in which she lifted the little creatures by their long beards and measured them out in an old tomato can.

"And glad enough I am to get them," said Madame B., turning to her guest, who was contemplating Misette's graceful figure as she ran lightly up the side of the levee. He remained in a brown study so long that his hostess rallied him on his susceptible heart, when he said:

"I dined with her family the other day, but she seems superior to them. A disciple of Darwin would say that the strain of some far away ancestor was reappearing in her."

"True enough," replied the lady, with a little laugh. "Perhaps she inherits it from some mythical chevalier of the Court of the 'Grande Monarque,' for I notice that most of the old Creole families boast their descent from some distinguished origin, but their chief legacy seems to be family pride and great poverty. It's a pity she could not be given an education, she would then turn the heads of half mankind—as she has turned yours," said the lady maliciously.

Day after day Misette caught and sold her shrimps. Day after day the river rose, like some tremendous and mighty foe determinedly bent on destruction, not unlike a mighty Sampson feeling his power, striving and chafing in bondage, seeking to reclaim the territory snatched from its dominions by the hand of civilization. Anxious faces were met everywhere up and down the levee. Men carrying lumber, and the fastening of dangerous places were familiar sights. With the Madère family custom lent a security to their placid minds. Repeating with a shrug: "Il n'a pas danger. It is often time like dat, dans le temps de mon grandpère," they pursued their usual avocations, till one dark night the dreadful cry of "Crevasse! Crevasse!" broke the solemn stillness. Our friends did not need the

shouts and cries of their neighbors to rouse them from their fancied security, for the sullen roar of the crevasse and the gurgling of the muddy flood into the crevices of the house warned them to seek safety in flight with such household goods as could be snatched up in haste.

The morning beams fell slantingly on many a desolate group of people who had sought a temporary refuge on the levee in front of their submerged homes. Not the least sad among these were the Madères, sitting amidst a heterogeneous collection of household goods, dazed by the calamity which cast them ruthlessly from their home, over which now rolled a turbid stretch of water. The two women busied themselves with little arrangements for their present comfort, casting ever and anon pained glances at their forsaken home, a home no longer. Meagre as was their humble abode, it contained all they held dear; what more was left for regret? As fresh recollections of their losses presented themselves to their minds, they pathetically exclaimed:

"Et mes pommes de terre. Quel dommage! Et le mais. Comme elle belle," in a drawn-out plaintiveness of accent. Grandmère, who never in her time had experienced such a catastrophe, had nevertheless managed to save her "grec" or coffee dripper, and her "café grillé" had been her special charge in the scrimmage of collecting "ses butin." So that the hearts of old and young were solaced by a steaming cup of black coffee.

The top of the levee above the reach of the water was crowded with refugees from the flood. A sorry sight, indeed, they viewed. Here and there household treasures washed by the current, forgotten or neglected by the owners, floated or lay stranded on the piles of driftwood and debris. What a curious scene the levee presented. Kitchen safes lying on their backs served as substitutes for chicken coops, the inmates looking very crestfallen at their ignominious imprisonment. Here a washtub was turned over a squealing pig, there an inverted pine table did duty as a cradle, with several little tots tied securely in it out of harm's way. Poor creatures! How fortunate that their wants were few and simple, and their philosophy of a practical kind. Accustomed to none of the luxuries of the table, they accepted their portion of salt meat or hominy cooked on improvised furnaces, thankfully. They sat on the bare ground apathetically gazing at the eddying water, or aimlessly walking up and down the levee, the only promenade left them. True, the little dwelling they called home was destroyed and their meagre crops lay beneath the muddy flood. Perhaps they missed their weed-grown yards and tumble-down henhouse, but they knew that when the water subsided they could start again, catch plenty of drift wood for a new hen roost, scratch out some more ground for a crop, and be happy as they were before. Meantime they consoled themselves with the certainty of reveling in plenty of fish and shrimp, and of using their pirogues to advantage in slaying "grosbec" and other aquatic fowls. Ah, yes, a crevasse has many advantages to this class of sweptaways.

The news of the crevasse had spread far and wide, and as the day advanced, the broken ends of the levee became thronged with sightseers and anxious planters debating on the possibilities of stopping the break. In the crowd were many friends of the Madères who expressed their sympathy. Nor were their colored acquaintances less backward. "Common sa va commere, mo pas capable dit li common mo facher pour li" was the expression of many of that race. Among the planters visiting the crevasse was Mr. B. with his family. Their extensive crops were also doomed to destruction, but they had a kind word for their humble neighbors. They were joined by Lieutenant Dickson, who had been energetically directing the attempt to close the crevasse. He joined in expressing his regrets in seeing them among the sufferers, and smiled a kindly greeting to his young friend Misette, who was seated in her father's pirogue.

"Dat pirogue," said Madère, indicating the boat with his chin, and with a deprecatory smile, "You can ride in him ef you wan' to."

"No, my friend, we couldn't manage that craft," laughed Mr. B.

"Me, yas," continued the Creole. "I use him to mek one leetle hornt. I kill plen' grosbec me. I go back yonder in de bayou en catch plen' fish, yas."

During this conversation, Misette sat with downcast eyes, conscious, perhaps for the first time, of her bare feet and brown arms. Suddenly a sharp, agonized cry broke upon her ear. She turned and saw the form of a little child rapidly whirled away in the swift current. The next instant her pirogue was sweeping forward, avoiding with marvellous dexterity the obstacles in her way. The child was carried straight on to a pile of drift, upon which she lodged, one tiny hand closed convulsively over a projecting branch, and for a moment she was safe. Only for a moment, but in that moment Misette reached her side and had clasped the little garment that floated into reach.

How she got the child into the easily overturned craft she never knew. Then she turned her attention to extricating herself from the dangerous position in which they still were. The current twisted and rocked the little boat most alarmingly. Well was it for them both that Misette was such an adept in the management of a pirogue, or else two young and innocent spirits that hour would have left this sober world as yet so bright to them. As it was, her skill and strength were nearly exhausted when the boat grounded on the base of the levee. Eager hands seized it, voices sounded in her ear, with a vision of the white, agonized face of the mother as she clasped her baby frantically. Then, weak and trembling from excitement, but happy, Misette sought refuge in her own mother's arms to give vent to tears. Little notice was taken of the brave girl then, for no sooner was the little one discovered to be living, than with a few inarticulate words of thanks and gratitude, all hurried home with the restored treasure and our heroine was left to be scolded and petted by her family. The next day, however, Mr. B. returned with Lieutenant Dickson, and there was then no lack of substantial proof of their gratitude, but the Madères were modest and unpresuming, and the only recompense they could be prevailed upon to accept was a temporary shelter and that very day found them established on the B.'s plantation, to await the subsiding of the floods so that they might commence life anew.

In a luxurious parlor in New Orleans, surrounded by evidences of wealth and refinement, stood two ladies dressed for a reception. The crystal chandelier shed a radiance on the younger, whose grace of movement and downcast eyes reminded one of the little shrimp girl of the years before. Her arm was no longer bare and sunburnt, but encased in white kid glove, and about her wrist she turned a golden bracelet. Yes, Mrs. B. had proved a good fairy godmother to Misette. First attracted by her brave deed, and then by the sweetness of her disposition, she had interested herself in the girl, that eventful summer, taken her into her household as a companion and playmate for her child, and then had given her a few years of schooling and some training in the refinements of society. Tonight she was to make her debut into the world of society as the adopted daughter of her kind benefactors.

"You cannot hide it, ma fille," said Mrs. B., "your eyes show that you know who is coming tonight."

"Well, who is it, ma tante?"

"Why, Lieutenant Dickson."

Misette blushed and laughed. "He will not even know me. But, —." She stopped in confusion.

"But I will know him, you were going to say," laughed Mrs. B. "And here is our hero now," as the servant announced the lieutenant. He advanced, and she introduced them without mentioning the young girl's name. Misette flushed beautifully, glanced quickly, half shyly at him, then looked down embarrassed. In the fine gray eyes she did not discover the coveted recognition. His greeting was simply conventional and with a little laugh she threw off her feeling of disappointment and was soon conversing on indifferent subjects. At last Mrs. B. designedly drew his attention to a portfolio of drawings. He turned them over rather leisurely, till one of the drawings arrested his attention. It was a simple scene of a rustic girl pounding brick, and a rider at the gate. A flash of recognition broke upon him, and turning quickly, he exclaimed:

"Misette!"

"Oui, Monsieur," she replied a little demurely. Then they sat talking of the past, of her mother and of her dear grandmère's death. Nor was this the only meeting that happy summer, when something else was talked of besides mamma and grandmamma. When the gallant lieutenant returned to his Northern home he carried with him a lovely Creole bride.

AMONG THE GEORGIA POETS.

By Maria Louise Eve.

Georgia is justly proud of the rich contributions to literature by her adopted son, Paul Hamilton Hayne. Ever conscientious in his work and the exercise of his gift, he stands today one of the best known and most widely admired of American poets.

Paul Hayne not inaptly may be styled an apostle of nature, revealing her to men, so deep is his sympathy with all her manifestations, so magical his art as an interpreter of her many voices. As he walks through her leafy aisles he hears the flute of Pan and catches glimpses of Faun and Dryad among the interlacing branches of the trees. At every interview he gives some new knowledge of nature's secrets.

His descriptive powers are exceptionally fine, whether employed in sketching from inanimate nature or drawing scenes from the deeper drama of human life. Here and there a vivid piece of word-painting shows the strength of his imaginative faculty when called into bolder play, as in the following passage from the legend of "Cambyses and the Macrobian Bow," when the king, after lifting the bow:

"———— bent back its oaken massiveness,
Till the vast muscles, tough as grapevines, bulged
From naked arm and shoulder, and the horns
Of the fierce weapon, groaning, almost met.
* * * * * * *
Then came the sharp twang and the deadly whirr
Of the loosed arrow, followed by the dull,
Drear echo of a bolt that smites its mark."

In striking contrast with the above-quoted lines, and showing the lighter touch of the poet's pencil in delineating nature and embroidering her garments with his dainty fancies, are passages like this from one of the sonnets:

"I watch, unwearied, the miraculous dyes
Of dawn or sunset, the soft boughs which lace
Round some coy Dryad in a lonely place,
Thrilled with low whisperings and strange sylvan sighs."

The title: "Poet Laureate of the South," lovingly bestowed upon him by his admiring contemporaries, will always link his name with the land that is proud to claim him as her representative poet. A striking characteristic of Hayne's poetic gift was the magnetism that drew to him the hearts of his brother bards in bonds of friendship. There was a subtle quality that attracted alike those who had met him face to face and those who knew him only through his writings. He seemed to possess a genius for creating friendship. How highly he himself esteemed this gift is best attested in his own words:

"He who has found a new star in the sky
Is not so fortunate as one who finds
A new, deep-hearted friend. The stars must die,
They are but creatures of the sun and winds;
But Friendship throws her firm sheet-anchor deep
Beside the shores of eternity."

A marked feature of Paul Hayne's poetry is purity—purity of thought, purity of expression, purity of style. Writing only at the promptings of his genius, his verse never lacks poetic insight or the dignity that belongs to intuition. Whether setting rhythmic words and meaning to the mournful "music of the pines" or caressing the "bonny brown hand" of her who was his inspiration, the "bard of Copse-Hill" is always himself. It is interesting to know that his last words for the public were a full and simple confession of his faith as a Christian. In accordance with his desire, this declaration, to which he attached great importance, was published, shortly after his death in the *Sunday School Times*. It was Paul Hayne's parting benediction to the world.

It happens now and then that a poet is born into the world with a single message for it. He gives his message and goes his way, but the message stays. Richard Henry Wilde was one of those rare poets, like the authors of "The Old Oaken Bucket" and of "Home, Sweet Home," whose fame rests upon a single poem. He has written other poems, but they will perish. They possess some value, as coming from the same hand, with "My Life Is Like the Summer Rose;" otherwise they would remain unread.

This little, world-renowned poem, imperishable in its beauty, and which appeared at first without the author's name, possesses a history of unusual interest. The following particulars are from an authentic account given by Mr. Anthony Barclay, in a little volume published under the auspices of the Georgia Historical Society in 1871, of the "origin, mystery and explanation" of the alleged plagiarism. The charge was the unexpected outcome of a pleasantry practiced by him to mystify a few friends in Savannah, where he resided as British consul for many years. He translated the poem into Greek verse, naming it "The Lament of the Captive." The translation was so cleverly done that for a time it was accepted as genuine, and Wilde's "Summer Rose" was supposed to have borrowed its beauty from the Greek poet Alcæus.

In the meanwhile, the verses had become so popular in Europe that they were set to music, and claim had been laid to them by more than one aspirant for literary honors. Besides this, in one version, as if to confirm the story of its Greek origin, "the name of Tampa, a desolate sea-beach, on the coast of Florida, was changed to Tempe, the loveliest of the wooded vales of Greece," an error which has crept into many of the later copies.

These circumstances were, of course, a source of great annoyance to the author. At length, in 1835, more than sixteen years after the poem was written, he avowed the authorship and wrote to Mr. Barclay, with whom he had some acquaintance, a very courteous and elegant letter, asking from him a published statement of the facts, to remove the unintentional injustice under which he suffered. To this request Mr. Barclay responded very handsomely and gracefully, only resigned to his part in the affair "if the translator succeed in dragging the author from his concealment, and the event contribute to strip all masks and bestow honor where honor is due."

Notwithstanding that the poem is so familiar, it will not be amiss to quote here the closing stanza:

"My life is like the print which feet
  Have left on Tampa's desert strand;
Soon as the rising tide shall beat
  This track will vanish from the sand.
Yet still, as grieving to efface
All vestige of the human race,
On that lone shore loud moans the sea;
But none shall e'er lament for me."

It is safe to say that these footprints "left on Tampa's desert strand" will never be effaced so long as there are lovers of genius and of true art in poetry.

Of a widely different school is the poetry of Sidney Lanier. More complex in structure and in thought, Lanier's poetry is not of the kind that makes popular poems. Appealing to the intellect rather than to the affections and voicing no universal feeling of humanity, his audience is naturally limited. Yet it is not the language of one who feels no need of human sympathy, but rather of a soul with a unique individuality, and with needs differing from those of the world at large. The thoughtful and cultured and the lover of poetry for its own sake will always find much to admire in his exquisite imagery and finished verse. This musician-poet, in whose mind thought and sound are so intimately blended, would have all poetry conform to certain musical principles. Without feeling compelled to master the science on which his theory is based, the reading public may still enjoy the result in his rhythmic verse.

Fault has been found with some of the poems as being obscure and hard to understand. If at times the clear utterance of the thought is somewhat subordinated to its musical expression, let us forgive the obscurity for the fidelity to his intuitions. He never makes a mere jingle of words. The indwelling thought is never absent. But the meaning, where it seems least potent, is revealed through the captivating poetic imagery, like a living form half veiled in draperies.

In his best known poem, "Corn," he walks through the woods, "where the stately corn-ranks rise," feeding his mind with rich suggestions from the open book of nature. In "The Marshes of Glynn" he looks out upon the "beautiful glooms," gazing with a passionate, unsatisfied soul into the face of nature, asking her for that peace which she cannot give and pressing her with questions that she cannot answer. He walks by the low-lying marshes and muses:

"As the marsh-hen secretly builds on the
    watery sod,
Behold, I will build me a nest on the
    greatness of God."

The tide comes pouring in on the marshes and he cries:

"And now from the Vast of the Lord will the
    waters of sleep
Roll in on the souls of men,
But who will reveal to our waking ken
The forms that swim and the shapes that
    creep
        Under the waters of sleep?"

In a brighter vein is a descriptive passage of great beauty from the poem "Sunrise":

"And lo, in the East! Will the East unveil?
The East is unveiled, the East hath confessed
A flush; 'tis dead; 'tis alive; 'tis dead ere
    the West
Was aware of it; nay, tis abiding, 'tis un-
    withdrawn:
Have a care, sweet Heaven! 'Tis Dawn."

Thoroughly original in thought and in methods, Sidney Lanier had gained distinct recognition and a high place among American poets before death claimed him in his early prime.

Georgia surely has some vested rights in the poetry of another gifted son, James R. Randall, son of her adoption and her love, who has cast in his lot with her for so many of the best years of his life. For many of his soulful and stirring lyrics were written on Georgia soil, although his masterpiece, on which his fame chiefly rests, was inspired by his beloved Maryland in her hour of trial. It is to be regretted that Mr. Randall has not found time, in the busy life of a journalist, to collect his poems into a volume so that they would be more accessible to the reviewer as well as to the general reader. With the ardent temperament and the spiritual insight of the true poet, his poems are inspirations of genius rather than works of art. Ringing lyrics of action or tender and thoughtful strains, as suggested by the occasion or prompted by the mood of the writer, they bear the stamp, alike, of a high order of genius and a facile pen.

"Maryland, My Maryland". is so familiar to readers on both sides of the Potomac that quotation is hardly necessary. But what an exquisite line is this, as addressed to Maryland:

"And gird thy beauteous limbs with steel."

Note again this impassioned burst of song:

"Come, for thy dalliance does thee wrong.
She is not dead, nor deaf, nor dumb;
She breathes, she burns, she'll come, she'll
    come."

We are impressed with the versatility of Mr. Randall's poetic faculty when, after these martial strains, we read, in the legend of "Why the Robin's Breast Is Red," following the poetical version of the robin plucking away the thorn from the Savior's brow, this tender, devotional strain:

"Ah, Jesu, Jesu, Son of Man,
    My dolor and my sighs
Reveal the lesson taught by this
    Winged Ishmael of the skies,
I, in my palace of delight
    Or cavern of despair,
Have plucked no thorn from Thy dear brow,
    But planted thousands there."

Other poems of great beauty and imbued with that deep spirituality which is the source of so much of Mr. Randall's inspiration are "Eidolon" and "Resurgat." The author himself gives his patriotic poem "Arlington" the preference over his far-famed "Maryland."

·An interesttng sketch in the *Magazine of Poetry* furnishes a true history of Mr. Randall's famous lyric and how it came to be written. He was, at the time, (April, 1861,) the youthful professor of English literature and the classics in Poydras College at Pointe Coupée in Louisiana. Here he read the news of the attack on the Massachusetts troops as they passed through Baltimore. "I had long been absent from my native city," says Mr. Randall, "and the startling events there inflamed my mind. That night I could not sleep, for my nerves were all unstrung and I could not dismiss what I had read in the paper from my mind. I rose, lit a candle and went to my desk. Some powerful spirit seemed to possess me, and almost involuntarily I proceeded to write the song 'My Maryland.'" To a lady of Baltimore belongs the honor of adapting the words of "My Maryland" to the spirited air it needed to be the favorite war song of the Southern armies.

Mr. Randall certainly scored one of the victories of the war when his impetuous Southern lyric, which had added ten thousand soldiers to the Confederate armies, was declared by Oliver Wendell Holmes "the best poem produced on either side during the civil war." (See Eugene Didier in *Blue and Gray*.)

Charles W. Hubner, the editor-poet of Atlanta, has written nothing that is not elevated and elevating in its character. His genius seems to have been inspired by the same noble ambition with that of the poet Campbell, who desired to write "no line that, dying, he would wish to blot." If each poet has his own part assigned him in the great orchestra, Mr. Hubner's special gift would seem to be as a revealer of the spiritual in nature. The key-note to his poetic insight is best found, perhaps, in his thoughtful, unrhymed poem, "The Poetry of Nature," from which these lines :

"The gross in nature is but gross to sense,
For in the apprehension of the soul,
That which to our dull sense seems gross
    becomes
A subtile spiritual agency,
Wherewith God works the wonders of His will.

Becomes, indeed, a fair and holy thing,
Intangible to sensuous touch, but felt
By those fine filaments whereby the soul
Reaches 'through nature up to nature's God,'
Him apprehending in her poetry."

There are tender and reverential lyrics, patriotic and devotional, that would be quoted here if space permitted. To illustrate the author's happy handling of some of the lighter metric forms it will suffice to cite the sonnet commemorative of the death of Paul Hayne (between whom and himself a long and intimate friendship had existed), published on the seventh anniversary recently passed, and to quote the concluding lines of his admirable sonnet on the Death of Tennyson :

"Rest, Poet ! in thy royal sepulcher,
Thou, more than peer of England's buried
    kings,
With two wor'ds weeping round thy laureled
    tomb.
Thy spirit now, in some diviner sphere,
Straightway, its lyre celestial shall assume,
And ravish Heaven with its resounding
    strings."

But, to the mind of the writer, the most poetical is a fragment called "Vernal Prophecies." For downright beauty, these two lines on the first herald of the spring can hardly be excelled :

"Did not a crocus in the snow
    Foretell her coming, long ago ?"

Dr. Y. O. Ticknor, of Columbus, best known as the author of "Little Giffen of Tennessee," has contributed to the literature of Georgia a small volume of poems, from which the aforesaid, which is one of the favorite war poems of the South, and "The Knights of the Valley," may be selected for special mention.

An interesting note in the *Southern Criterion* says : "The story of 'Little Giffen' is said to be literally true. His name was Isaac Giffen, and he was born of humble parents in one of the hamlets of East Tennessee. His father was a blacksmith. 'Little Giffen' was terribly shot in one of the battles of Tennessee and carried far South with other wounded to be cared for. Sadly mutilated and so like a child in appearance as to seem to have been 'borne by the tide of war from the cradle to the jaws of death,' he was taken from the hospital in Columbus, Ga., to the home of Dr. Ticknor, five

miles south of that place. He remained
with the family a year, but was always
anxious to return to the war, which he
did in time to be killed near Atlanta, it
is supposed, and to be buried in one of
the many graves in Oakland Cemetery
bearing the melancholy legend 'unknown'.

A most tender and pathetic poem is
"Little Giffen of Tennessee." Told in
words so few and yet so fully told, it is
as if the writer knew that his tale needed
no garnishment. A few deft strokes of
the pen and the story of Little Giffen is
written in ink that never fades:

"Out of the foremost and focal fire,
Out of the hospital walls as dire,
Smitten of grape-shot and gangrene,
(Eighteen battles and he sixteen.)
Spectre! such as you seldom see!
Little Giffen of Tennessee.

" 'Take him and welcome,' the surgeon said.
'Little the doctor can help the dead.' "

This is followed by

"Months of torture! how many such!
Weary weeks of the stick and crutch,
And still the glint of the steel-blue eye
Told of a spirit that wouldn't die."

Then came news from the front that
soldiers were wanted, and—

"Little Giffen was up and away."

Then, how quietly and quaintly the end
is told. Taking leave, Giffen says:

" 'I'll write if spared.' There was news of
the fight,
But none of Giffen. He did not write."

It has been questioned whether
genius, and especially the poetic genius,
is ever hereditary. We need not go
far for an answer to this question,
while Mr. Hayne wears so gracefully
the mantle that has descended from
father to son, descended, yet in a different shape, for it is curious to note the
difference in the characteristics of the
poetry of father and son and the
distinct individuality of each. For the
flowing, mellifluous verse of the elder
Hayne, we have the terse, forcible,
multum in parvo style of the younger.

Mr. Hayne is one of the few Georgians who have, from the beginning,
made a distinct vocation of poetry. He
holds, with the great Roman lyrist, that
poetry should be regarded as an art, not

less than a gift. The artistic quality of
his endowment becomes more and
more apparent in his treatment of the
sonnet and other lyric forms of verse.
Widely known and much admired is his
apostrophe to "A Band of Bluebirds."
In the second and third stanzas are
found these lines:

* * * * *
" 'I dream that Heaven invites you
To bid the earth 'good-bye,'
For in your wings you seem to hold
A portion of the sky!
* * * * *
You leave melodious memories
Whose sweetness thrills me through—
Ah, if my songs were such as yours,
They'd almost touch the Blue!' "

A very charming lyric is "The Coming
of the King." Here is the first of the
two stanzas that compose the poem:

"Thrice happy am I, because
I have welcomed a king, today,
Who has kept aloof from my humble roof,
In a king's imperious way:
I have seen him oft, in dreams,
Yet he never has passed before,
With his robe of State, through my vine-clad
gate,
And entered my open door."

The second stanza reveals the personality of the king "whose name is Love."
The lines entitled "Cain (bronze figure
in the Pitti Palace)" are a fine example
of the quatrain, a form of verse in which
Mr. Hayne excels:

"A sombre brow, whose dark-veined furrows
bear
Remorseful fruit from God's curse planted
there.
Uplifted hands o'er eyes that look through
time,
Big with the burden of unshriven crime."

Mr. Hayne's poems are found in all
of the leading magazines.

Among the latest acquisitions to the
ranks of Georgia poets, and a very
attractive one, is Frank L. Stanton.
His poetry is not of the kind that
"smells of the lamp" or bears the mark
of the "file." It is just that rich, juicy
vein that seems to need only to be
tapped to bubble forth in spontaneous
rills of humor or pathos. "Wearyin'
for You" has that touch of tenderness
which belongs to all true humor and
brings a mist to the eyes even while
there is a smile on the lips:

"Jest a-wearyin' for you,
All the time a-feelin' blue;——"

In a different vein is "Weary the Waiting," from which these lines:

"Some time in the future, when God thinks best
He'll lay us tenderly down to rest,
And roses 'll grow from the thorns in the breast.
(But it's weary the waitin', weary.)

A rare bit of color in landscape painting is the pastoral depicting "Summer Time in Georgia," and beginning

"O, summer time in Georgy, I love to sing your praise
When the green is on the melon an' the sun is on the blaze.
When the birds are chantin', pantin' an' jes' rantin' round the rills,
With the juice of ripe blackberries jes' a-drippin' from their bills."

Frank L. Stanton was born in Charleston, S. C., but Georgia has been his home from early childhood. From her golden wheat fields and lowing cattle, from her clinging grasses and purple morning-glories he has drawn his inspiration. He has recently published his first volume of poems. His genius is manifestly in partnership with a spirit that is sweet and wholesome. Tender and reverential or playful and humorous by turns, his mood is never cold or bitter. Mr. Stanton's home is in Atlanta, where he is on the editorial staff of the *Constitution*, to which he contributes stories, dialect sketches, criticisms, witty paragraphs and poems.

An altogether unique contribution to the poetry of Georgia is a fragment from the pen of her able jurist, Judge Logan E. Bleckley, whose legal decisions read like poetry—the kind of poetry that goes to the core of the matter with its unswerving logic and reveals the true equity in which the law is rooted. In resigning his seat upon the supreme bench of Georgia, Judge Bleckley attached to his parting decision, fourteen lines, quaintly entitled in due legal form, "In the Matter of Rest, Bleckley, J."

This poem, which achieved the honor of being spread upon the minutes among the weighty matters of the law, comprises two stanzas, of which this is the second:

"Peace and rest! Are they the best
For mortals here below?
Is soft repose from work and woes
A bliss for men to know?
Bliss of time is bliss of toil,
No bliss but this from sin and soil
Does God permit to grow."

Judge Bleckley continues to vary his sterner labors with an occasional sortie in the field of poetry. By so doing, he not only secures entertainment to his readers, but doubtless also that "rest" which comes from exercise on congenial lines.

It is noticeable that there is in the work of the Georgia poets none of that crudeness of thought or expression which we might look for in the unfledged literature of a new people. There is, the rather, in the poetry itself, an indefinable air of having a long ancestry of old-world culture, with roots reaching away back into the iambics and trochaics of classic verse.

The fact that so many of these poems are the work of men with whom poetry has been an avocation rather than a vocation, that they represent the play rather than the work of their lives, goes far to show how different would have been the result had they not been bound down to the so-called practical pursuits of life.

To name all of the genuine poets whose thoughtful verse has, from time to time, graced the columns of the Georgia press would fill a volume. It is only within the scope of this paper to cite a few of those whose writings are most familiar, as examples of what Georgia has done and is doing in the flowery paths of literature. Another chapter should be devoted to the female poets of Georgia. Still another should include the younger aspirants for the bays, who are "fleshing their maiden swords" and making their mark in the magazines and periodicals of the day.

The Southern Outlook.

Northern Settlers in the South.

In this issue of the SOUTHERN STATES magazine is presented the first instalment of a series of "Letters from Southern Farmers," the publication of which is undertaken in response to numerous inquiries from people in the North and West who are looking Southward and are anxious to secure definite and detailed information about the South, particularly its agricultural conditions and possibilities. There are thousands of Northern people who have been dwellers in the South for many years, identifying themselves with all the interests of that section and making themselves one with the people of the South. With these incoming settlers from the North have come new ideas in agriculture and industry, and as a rule these Northern people have prospered in their new homes. In gathering material for the series of "Letters from Southern Farmers," effort was made to secure communications from Northern people who had made their homes in the South, in order to present to seekers after information views of Southern conditions from the standpoint most familiar to those for whom these letters are intended.

There are other reasons, also, why it is desirable to view the South through Northern eyes. The Southern-born farmer might reasonably be expected to present a view of the South in which there are no imperfections. Naturally his view would be regarded as partial, and on that account subject to large discount. A Northern man, however, is apt to speak pretty plainly and pretty 'ruthfully about the strange land which he enters and wherein he makes his home. Our own view of ourselves is always before us ; it is seeing ourselves as others see us that gives us the picture free from the bias of partiality. It is the view of a Northern man that is best calculated to interest a Northern inquirer, hence the selection of these letters.

The farmer is not presumed to be a literary man, therefore these letters are not presented as specimens of scholarly writing. They are the plain, straightforward statement of energetic men who toil with their hands and their brains as well. They are the testimony of practical men who have chosen the South as their home because of its manifold advantages, and are now telling the world what they think of the land of their adoption. A great number of letters of this character have been secured, and their publication in monthly instalments will constitute one of the most interesting features of the SOUTHERN STATES magazine during the next year.

Commerce of the Mississippi River.

Prior to the construction of railroads in the Mississippi valley the Mississippi river was the great highway of commerce between the North and South. Being the only interior means of communication, the river controlled all the internal commerce of the country between the North and South. The advent of the railroad, however, and the demand for more rapid transportation introduced a competing factor that has very largely lessened the prestige of the Mississippi river as a carrier of freight and passengers. The railroads have robbed the river of its passenger traffic, and great inroads have been made upon the freight business The magnificent river steamboats of a quarter of a century ago have given place to more common-place carriers of freight. The commerce of the great river has lost much of its volume, its profit and its attractive features, but it still remains as a great industry.

Steamboating on the river was at its prime during the fifteen years following the close of the war and during that period. The largest number of vessels built on the Mississippi and its tributaries was 460 in 1878, their aggregate tonnage being 62,928 tons, but in 1881 a total of 182 new vessels reached an aggregate tonnage of 81,189 tons. Since the latter year there has been a steady decline, both in number of vessels and their aggregate tonnage, with a small improvement during the last three or four years, as the following figures will show. These figures are from the records of the bureau of navigation, and represent the number and tonnage of new vessels built on the Mississippi and its tributaries during years ended June 30:

Year.	No.	Tons.
1878	460	68,928
1879	380	62,213
1880	135	32,791
1881	182	81,189
1882	152	35,817
1883	125	26,443
1884	93	16,664
1885	81	11,220
1886	76	10,595
1887	79	10,901
1888	84	11,859
1889	83	12,202
1890	104	16,500
1891	114	19,984
1892	99	14,800

The commerce of the Mississippi river, however, has not been killed by railroad competition, nor will it be destroyed. Its development has been temporarily arrested, but we expect to see a revival and further growth. The value of our internal waterways from a commercial standpoint is beyond calculation, and even the reduction in rates that has been forced by railroad competition cannot destroy their utility. Railroad rates have about reached minimum of cost, and it now remains for river commerce to adjust itself to the basis thus established. This done, we shall see an enormous expansion of the traffic of the Mississippi river and our other great internal waterways.

The Lesson of the Cherokee Strip.

The opening of the Cherokee strip for settlement presented a spectacle that can hardly be comprehended by those who consider the matter from a distance and in an entirely disinterested manner. Fortunately, this disgraceful scene will not be repeated as the last of the great areas of reserved land has now been thrown open for settlement.

Here is a vast area of virgin soil, subject to dry seasons that reduce everything to powder, torrid weather in which the temperature rises to that of a Turkish bath, and devoid of any special attraction, save fertility and the fact that the land could be had at $1.50, $2.00 or $2.50 per acre. Under these circumstances thousands of settlers flocked to the borders of the strip, awaiting the hour on which the land was opened for settlement, and then came the race for choice locations. Thousands and thousands of people scrambled into the strip in a chaos equal to that of a charge of cavalry in battle, and in the wild stampede scores of people were maimed or killed, either in accident or at the hands of companion boomers.

This event presents a curious phase of human nature. The most potent factor of attraction to this land was the mere removal of the restriction that forbade the settlement of this land. Had this same land been absolutely free for half a century it probably would have failed to attract the settlers who drove their stakes there a few weeks ago. It is hard to grasp the spirit of the occasion without a nearer view of the event. Thousands of people rushed to the strip, moved their belongings in wagons, camped on the border and then risked their lives for the sake of a few acres of land, which they will find hardly habitable before they reach the end of the first year. To say nothing of the price they paid for the land, the mere expenses of their journey, their long waiting and their final entry was more than enough to buy them fertile and productive farms in a desirable section of the South, where the soil would yield a range of crops impossible in the Cherokee strip, where the climate would permit of continuous cultivation from one end of the year to the other, and where the settlers could enjoy social and educational privileges that will not be theirs for years in the locality they have chosen.

Thousands of people swarmed into the strip upon its opening, and thousands dragged their weary way out of it again and sought their distant homes, disappointed and disgusted, but with a valuable lesson taught by experience.

The South has millions of acres of fertile soil that can be bought at less cost than that incurred by any one of the successful Cherokee boomers. As an object lesson in human nature the opening of the Cherokee strip was a prodigious success; as a struggle of home-seekers to secure choice quarter-sections under the impression that a slice of paradise would be theirs, it was a pitiful spectacle.

NOTES ON SOUTHERN PROGRESS.

KANSAS farmers are in a tight place because the Eastern money-lenders will not extend their mortgages on Kansas farms. The Provident Trust Co., one of the largest Eastern companies in this business, recently sent this notice to its agent in Great Bend, Kansas:

We are closing all our Kansas business as fast as loans mature, and an extension is out of the question. Most all companies doing business in Kansas are pulling out as fast as they can—not for want of business, but for reason that the legislation, sentiment and general antagonistic feeling toward a loan company is vicious and vindictive. Kansas loans will not sell in the East because confidence in them is all gone.

Without doubt a great amount of money will be withdrawn from the West both on account of the reasons given by the company quoted above, and because of the disturbance of confidence by the recent panic in the West. All of this money must find investment elsewhere, and the South ought to receive a large share of it more than ever before.

PRESIDENT WRIGHT, of the Macon, Dublin & Savannah, which extends from Macon to Dublin, Ga., is greatly interested in developing that section of the country with reference to fruit culture, and expects to secure much freight business from fruit farms he wishes to establish between Dublin and Savannah. Over 200,000 peach trees have already been set out near Macon, and as many more to be set out this fall. He is endeavoring to interest Northern fruit-growers in this section, and expects to settle a number of them along the line soon. As a fruit-growing country, President Wright says Georgia is better than California and has an advantage of forty per cent. in cheaper freights to markets. The country between Dublin and Savannah is even better adapted to fruit culture than that between Dublin and Macon, President Wright thinks, and when his road is completed in this direction he expects to make fruit-growing a special inducement to settlers from the North and West.

THE city of Knoxville's public improvements which are now being completed and which have been completed aggregate $550,000. One large item was $147,223.15, expended for iron bridges connecting various parts of the city. To this public expenditure can be added the money spent for a new sewerage system, which is in round figures $250,000. Then comes the paving system now under way and costing $125,000. Besides these, Knoxville has spent $250,500 in general improvements to streets, such as grading, paving and repairing. Most of this work has been done within a year.

THE experiment of cultivating the pineapple in De Soto county, Fla., appears to be a success. Only about three years have elapsed since the first slips were planted in this county, and now there are pines growing ranging from the little bloom in the plant to the ripe fruit. The severe winter having only injured the tip of the spines, the first planted have already produced crops eighteen months after the suckers were planted. The profit appears to be quite flattering. The soil is fine sand. Besides the pines, limes, lemons, oranges, guavas, citron and cassava all grow and yield in great profusion. The water is fine, consisting of large springs or lakes, which abound in bass and other fish. The timber is yellow pine and the land open bottom, so that comparatively little labor is required to prepare it for planting.—J. Flomerfelt, in *American Agriculturalist*.

THERE is considerable activity at present in the development of natural gas and the petroleum oil fields of the Petit Jean valley in Arkansas. At Magazine, in Logan county, natural gas has been struck at the depth of 270 feet, with a strong flow and good indications of oil. The work of drilling is being prosecuted with vigor. Besides those products a vein of coal was discove·ed at the depth of 200 feet in the same well. The vein is said to be seven or eight feet in thickness and equal in quality ·o any in America.

WE learn from the Macon *Telegraph* that it is proposed to bring several large excursions from the North and West to Georgia for the purpose of interesting them in that State and securing desirable settlers. This is a practical step in the right direction and such a course cannot fail to bring good results. There is nothing like object-lessons to convince the unbelieving.

THE contraction of silver-mining in the West is diverting a large share of attention to gold-mining, and in the increased activity in mining the yellow metal there may be some compensation for the blow that has fallen upon the silver industry. California papers state that the gold-mining industry on the Pacific coast is forging ahead. From Idaho, Washington, Oregon and all parts of California comes information of more prospectors in the field and of new mines being discovered and developed, while many abandoned mines are to be relocated and worked.

LAND in the vicinity of Rockport, Texas, is being sold for grape-growing purposes. It is stated that a number of tracts ranging from ten to 120 acres have been sold to parties intending to plant this fall. The cheapest of this land, unimproved, has sold for $15 per acre; one thirty-acre tract, improved with a few acres in grapes one year old, sold at $50 per acre. The purchasers are from different sections—some from Sandusky, the great grape region of Ohio. While there will be hundreds of thousands of cuttings and rooted vines for sale at Rockport in the fall, the supply will be far short of the demand. Such is the interest now felt in the grape business.

CROWLEY, the distributing point for the great rice fields of southwest Lousiana, has gr wn phenomenally with the development of the rice industry. In 1888 the property assessment was $45,395; in 1889, $73,290; in 1890, $77,515; in 1891, $93,080; in 1892, $219,530; in 1893, $330,035. The wealth of Crowley has increased a little more than sevenfold in these six years.

THE total assessment for Terrebonne Parish,

La., this year amounts to $1,752,290, an increase of $92,285 over last year's figures. It is gratifying to note this increase, as it speaks well for the growth of the parish during the past year. There are a number of new enterprises on foot which will not come under this year's assessment, but will be matured in time to swell the assessment rolls of 1894 considerably and probably bring the total assessment up to $2,000,000 or more.

THE past season has been the bes· in the history of the extensive truck farming interests in the neighborhood of Mobile, Ala. The cabbage crop was the largest ever raised in that district, the shipments being 136,799 crates, valued at $187,943, as compared with 110,387 crates valued at $137,983 in the season of 1892. The potato crop was good, with a large yield and fair prices, the shipments amounting to 73,325 barrels valued at $112,187, against 58,433 barrels worth $87,449 in 1892. This is the largest crop and value of any season on record with the exception of 1890, when 78,924 barrels worth $138,117 were shipped. The shipments of other truck crops during this season were as follows: 42,178 boxes of beans, 3923 boxes of peas, 2523 boxes tomatoes and 1447 packages of miscellaneous truck. These figures show an increase of 18,281 packages of last season and 37,510 above the season of 1891.

DURING the commercial year ending August 31, 1893, permits for the erection of 110 new buildings, valued at $131,329, were issued in Charleston, S. C. During the same time 120 permits for repairs, amounting to $52,640, were issued. The 1892 assessment shows a total property valuation of $21,987,122, as compared with $21,433,031 in 1891, a gain of $554,091.

THE year ended August 31 was a period of great building activity in New Orleans, the aggrega e value of structures erected during that time being more than a million dollars in excess of the value for the year preceeding. The figures given by the city surveyor show that during the past year 2168 frame and ninety-one brick buildings were erected, costing $3,172,707, which is an increase of $1,152,-675 over the year previous. Among the more expensive buildings erected this year are these: A $14,000 three-story frame building on Magazine street for the Pythian Hall Association, a $20,000 church on Louisiana avenue for Our Lady of Good Counci, a $48,492 brick hotel on Bourbon street owned by C. B. Solari, a

$65,000 brick wa ehouse on Front street for the Illinois Central Railroad, a $28,000 open shed on Magazine street for the New Orleans Traction Co., a $21,390 brick addition to the Lane Cotton Mills, a $100,000 six-story brick building on Baronne street owned by Louis Grunewald, a $36,200 five-story brick building on Baronne street owned by C. E. Fenner, a $32,350 convent building on Dumaine street for the Sisters of the Sacred Heart, a $22,000 brick store on Royal street owned by George Denegre, a $40,000 five-story brick building on Charties street owned by Leon Godchaux, a $50,635 five-story brick warehouse on Front street owned by Charles W, Zeigler, stock-yard buildings costing $80,000 owned by the People's Slaughter-house.

AUGUSTA, Ga., has a new factor of progress in the Young Men's Business League, which was recently organized in that city. Some 2 o of the active, progressive business men of the city came together and set this new organization on its feet with a great amount of enthusiasm and determination. The officers of the league are as follows: J. R. Lamar, president; D. B. Dyer, first vice-president; Charles S. Heard, second vice-president; Lamar Fleming, third vice-president; John D. Sheehan, fourth vice-president; John F. Harty, fifth vice-president; directors, Charles F. Degen, Augustus Beall, Hugh C. Middleton, Victor J. Door, J. U. Jackson, J. L. Wilson, T. R. Gibson, E. J. Costello, Paul Mustin, P. H. Rice; treasurer, E. S. Johnson.

THE list of enterprises which have been projected in Georgia in the last year is a long one, but it is continually receiving additions. The latest is an organization called the Henrico Land-Co., which has been put on foot by Messrs. H. F. Starke, W. E. Johnson, L. H. Moone and Hamilton Douglas, with a paid-up capital of $50,000, to be increased to $500,000. The object of the company is to build a manufacturing and residence suburb. The township site consists of about 500 acres of land on both sides of the East Tennessee road six miles from the city of Atlanta. A handsome depot, side tracks and other improvements will be put at the station, and negotiations are in progress for the establishment of factories, etc. A large canning factory plant will probably be erected at an early date, and it is also probable that a bicycle factory will locate there.

SAN ANTONIO, TEXAS, reports a fairly good real estate market and indications of a general revival and a smart business during the coming winter. The present demand is for modest cottages or low-priced lots on which to build small houses. Real estate dealers report a large number of inquiries from distant cities. There is a good deal of inquiry from Northern people who want to know about farming property in the vicinity of San Antonio. A good many farms are being sold to new settlers. Money is easier and can be obtained without trouble on good security.

REPRESENTATIVE S. B. ALEXANDER, of North Carolina, has been invited by the German capitalists who own the beet-sugar factories in California, Oregon, Nebraska and Utah to visit those localities and make full examinations of the manner of cultivating beets and abstracting the sugar from same. Mr. Alexander is a practical farmer, and the syndicate desires to obtain his views on the subject of the cultivation of the sugar beet in North Carolina, as they have thought that that State would make a very profitable field. The syndicate is desirous of extending its field of operations, and, in case Mr. Alexander thinks the beet can be profitably grown in the above State, will furnish several tons of seed for distribution among the farmers on condition that the farmer furnishes a report of the number of pounds of beets grown per acre and supplies a dozen beets for analysis. The invitation to Mr. Alexander has been accepted and he will make the desired inspection. If the experiment in growing the beets should be successful the syndicate intends to erect a number of beet-sugar factories in North Carolina.

THE DEER CREEK FARMERS' CLUB, of Harford County, Md., is considering the best means of attracting farmers to that section of Maryland. It is one of the great vegetable-growing parts of the South, and affords excellent opportunities to thrifty farmers. It is reported that farm labor is scarce and the large cultivators will offer liberal inducements to secure help. Hon. Herman Stump has offered to send twenty families to the country and the club will probably accept his offer.

MR. JAMES B. COUNCILMAN intends beginning work at once on the improvements he contemplates making at Mount Wilson, Md. He owns a track of 340 acres of land which lies very high and is in a healthy locality. Water is supplied from an artesian well, and a standpipe is being erected capable of holding 2 ,000 gallons. Mr. Councilman has let the contract for building five dwellings, which will be erected in a manner suitable for winter or summer use, and is having plans prepared for a summer hotel. The place is reached by the Western Maryland Railway, and it is understood that this company will co-operate to develop the new resort by making special rates, etc,, from Baltimore. Mr. Councilman intends building houses as fast as he secures tenants or owners for them.

THE Middle River Improvement Co. has begun the work of preparing its property in Baltimore county, Md., for erecting a hotel and several houses. The company expects to develop it into a suburban town. The route of the proposed electric road from Sparrow's Point to Baltimore is near the property, as is the Philadelphia, Wilmington & Baltimore road.

SIXTEEN carloads, amounting to 4000 barrels, of fall apples were shipped from Crozet Station, Va., between the middle and last of September. Winter apples are yet to be sold, and fully $75,000 will be realized from the apple crop in that neighborhood. The buyers, who are principally from Ohio, say they have hitherto bought their apples from Maine, and did not know before that such fine apples could be obtained in Virginia.

BEXAR COUNTY, TEXAS, of which San Antonio is the county seat, shows a gain of nearly $2,000,000 in taxable values for this year as compared with last. The assessment rolls for 1892 figured up $28,275,455, while the total of taxables for 1893 foots up $30,031,552. The principal increase has taken place in the roll

of non-resident property owners, which increased from $808.385 in 1892 to $1,253,550 this year, which may be considered as significant in showing increased investments in the State by outsiders.

AN Alabama man who is farming near Velasco, Texas, gives the Houston *Post* this striking account of what he is getting out of Texas soil: "This is my first crop in Texas, and before I came here I would not have believed any country could produce such cotton as I have raised with the hands I brought from Alabama. I have seventy-five acres in cultivation, and if this good weather continues, I am sure of at least 120 bales. I have already got out sixty-five bales, and am having six bales per day ginned at the Velasco Oil Mill's gin. Those bales all go over 500 weight each, and the quality of the lint and the 'turnout' from the seed is something astonishing to us Alabamians as is the yield per acre. Yet I hear people saying every day that the season has not been by any means a really good one on cotton."

THE first shipment of Florida oranges of the new crop to a foreign port was made on September 22 from Jacksonville by the Florida Fruit Exchange and consigned to its agents in Liverpool. The fruit was sent by rail via New York, and will be reshipped on the White Star Line of steamships. The exchange also made another shipment on the 27th ult., and one on the 4th inst.

AN interesting feature in connection with the North Carolina State Fair is the road congress which Governor Carr has convened at Raleigh for Octo er 18, when the State Fair will be held. He has requested the commissioners of the various counties to appoint two delegates and two alternates to represent their county at the congress.

SOUTHERN LEADERS IN CONGRESS.

By Edward W. Barrett.

II. THE HOUSE OF REPRESENTATIVES.

There are real statesmen representing Northern and Western States in the House of Representatives. Tom Reed, Bourke Cockran and Julius Cæsar Burrows are great men. But the South furnishes more men of political importance than all other sections. For this there are several reasons. In the first place, where boys and young men of other sections discuss local business affairs the discussions of young Southerners invariably turn to statesmanship. and to national affairs. Each Southern youth has his ideal statesman whom he copies either on the forum or in private life. The South is naturally romantic and its people are inherently hero worshippers. Each college and university has its youthful imitators of Calhoun, Clay, Ben Hill and other distinguished Southern statesmen. They have studied their lives, spoken their speeches, worshipped them as heroes. The young man of the South studies history and statesmanship. His Northern brother is for business. Such in both cases is natural. A young man to make anything of himself in the North must accumulate wealth. The people are wealthy. In the South it is different. The people are poor; money is not a requisite of social distinction or fame. Worshippers of the golden calf are the

exception. In consequence, instead of turning their attention to fortune they face about and strive for fame. From youth their minds are trained to statesmanship; oratory is natural to them.

Southerners are big-hearted as well as big-brained; and true statesmanship is a mixture of heart and brain. A real statesman is a man who can not only reason for his people, but one who has the great heart to feel for their condition and necessity.

When the people of the South choose a representative to Congress combining these qualities he becomes their idol. Once he gains their confidence it cannot be shaken. They retain him in public life; elevate him when possible.

Many of the Southern members of the present House have been in that body for from twelve to twenty years. In that time they have been schooled in statesmanship and versed in the science of legislation.

The House, that chaotic branch of Congress, is always seeking leaders. The South has furnished them. There is Crisp, the firm, courageous but conservative leader of men, one whose judgment is faultless, whose determination is powerful and whose coolness under fire phenomenal; Wilson, the scholarly and cultured chairman of the

Ways and Means Committee, the student in politics; Culberson, the wise legal light who presides over the Judiciary Committee; Sayers, the firm and economical, though fair and just chairman of the Appropriations Committee; O'Ferrall, the brave, generous and gallant chairman of the Committee on Elections; Henderson, of North Carolina, the silent, industrious, well-balanced chairman of the Committee on Postoffices; Blanchard, the polished and erudite chairman of the River and Harbor Committee; McMillin, the ready debater and man-of-all-things on the floor; Montgomery, the retiring but earnest, well-balanced, conservative and wise member of the Ways and Means Committee; Breckinridge, of Arkansas, the learned and experienced worker and ready debater; Oates, the one-armed veteran who has · carried off laurels in scores of partisan debates; Allen, of Mississippi, a combination of wit and wisdom; Compton, one of the mental athletes of the floor; Catchings, the parliamentary leader; Rayner, the eloquent orator, and a score of others distinquished for qualities of leadership in various capacities.

CHARLES F. CRISP, GEORGIA.

The House of Representatives of the present Congress is indeed the strongest body of men that has sat in that hall for many years. In it the South furnishes a large majority of the leaders.

Speaker Charles F. Crisp, of Georgia, stands out pre-eminently the great man of the House. Mr. Crisp is serving his sixth term. In his second he came conspicuously to the front as a man of judgment, ability and firmness. During his third term Speaker Carlisle dis-

covered his qualities of leadership and parliamentary knowledge and frequently called him to the chair. The House then admired his firm and determined bearing as a presiding officer. In the Fifty-first Congress, when Mr. Reed was Speaker, there were many Democrats who aspired to the leadership of the the minority. They took turns in striving for the honor but it remained for the Georgian, who came forward among the last, to demonstrate to the House that he possessed the true qualities of leadership and was the only man on the Democratic side who was more than an equal for the autocratic Speaker from Maine. In that Congress he was the acknowledged leader of the Democratic minority, and in the next, when the Democrats again controlled the House, he was elected Speaker. At the beginning of this Congress he was unanimously re-elected. The Democrats of the House have that confidence in him which causes them to rally about him and stand solid on all party questions. The Republicans admire him for his courage, determination, firmness and fairness. Under his hand the House has become a deliberative, orderly and active body. Mr. Crisp can probably remain Speaker as long as the Democrats control the House, but it is probable that his own State may send him to the Senate when the first vacancy occurs.

Mr. Crisp is a young man. He is just forty-eight years of age. Both his father and mother were of the stage. In his day his father ranked as Booth ranked among actors in later days. Mr. Crisp was born in Sheffield, England, when his parents were there on a visit. They returned a few months after his birth. He made his home in Schley county, Georgia, and at the age of sixteen

WILLIAM L. WILSON, WEST VIRGINIA.

entered the Confederate army and served as a lieutenant until captured and imprisoned in Fort Delaware. After the war he studied law and practiced in Georgia. He was elected solicitor general of his judiciary circuit, and afterward judge of the circuit court. He never served in the State legislature, but was elected to Congress at the age of thirty-six.

For twenty years Mr. Crisp has lived in Americus, Georgia, where he has a beautiful home and an interesting family. When he comes to Washington his family comes with him and they live at the old Metropolitan hotel, the Southern headquarters in Washington.

The Speaker is peculiar in his habits. Unlike most statesmen he invariably declines invitations to dinners and banquets. He does not like them. He prefers to remain in his private apartment at his hotel surrounded by his wife and children. The door of his parlor, however, is always open to his friends. They know it. No cards are necessary there. It is a sort of liberty hall. He is fond of young people, and the com-

panions of his children are often his companions.

A characteristic for which the Speaker is noted is that he never loses his temper. He is cool, calm and deliberative on all occasions. His judgment, like his temper, is faultless. Mr. Crisp is indeed one of the great men of this country.

An interesting question to the Speaker's colleagues in the House is whether or not he is eligible to the Presidency. The constitution says that none but a native born American citizen is eligible. Mr. Crisp's friends claim that he is an American citizen under the spirit of the constitution if not under the letter. His parents were American citizens, and he simply happened to be born while they were on a visit to a foreign country. It is, however, an interesting question, and the day may come when it must be decided.

William L. Wilson, of West Virginia, chairman of the Ways and Means Committee of the House, is probably the most learned and scholarly member of that body. He is an earnest, indus-

DAVID B. CULBERSON, TEXAS.

trious worker and a man of thorough knowledge of the details of the tariff schedule. He has devoted his entire time during his nine years' service in

CHARLES T O'FERRALL, VIRGINIA.

the House to the study of this question, and if it can be said that any one man has mastered it, that man is Wilson.

Mr. Wilson is just fifty years of age. His life before he entered Congress was spent chiefly as a college professor and college president, though a few years were given to the practice of law. Mr. Wilson served in the Confederate army as a private. After the war he was professor in the Columbian College. He resigned that to enter upon the practice of law in Charlestown. Just before his nomination for Congress in 1882, he was elected president of the West Virginia University.

Mr. Wilson is the author of the Wilson bill, repealing the Sherman law, over which there has been so much discussion. He is the recognized representative of the administration on the floor of the House.

David B. Culberson, of Texas, chairman of the Committee on Judiciary of the House is the sphinx of that body. Mentally this Texan is perhaps the ablest man in it. He is recognized as the greatest lawyer in either House of Congress. His opinion on legal questions is sought on all hands, but Mr. Culberson is not an orator; he speaks but little. His delivery is not good and he is diffident about taking

the floor unless he believes his entree into the arena of debate is absolutely necessary. However, when he talks every man listens, and the great mass of Democrats follow him like sheep behind a bell wether. Though Mr. Culberson speaks but little himself, he speaks often through others. Many of the younger members of the House consult with him about their speeches. He has a little habit of taking one of these young men on one of the seats in the lobby of the House and posting him for a speech. Then the distinguished old Texan sits by him and applauds as the young member utters his sentiments. Mr. Culberson is beginning his tenth term as a member of the House of Representatives. This is his nineteenth year of service in that body. He has been a lawyer and nothing but a lawyer all his life, except during his four years' service in the Confederate army, first as a private and then as colonel of the Eighteenth Texas Infantry. He served one term in the Texas Legislature before his election to the Forty-fourth Congress.

As well as a great lawyer and a statesman, Judge Culberson is quite a story teller and wit in his dry way. Here is one I heard him tell a few evenings ago:

"When Buck Kilgore first came to

ISIDOR RAYNER, MARYLAND.

Congress a few years ago, he asked me to help him select a boarding house. I carried him to one kept by an old lady who seemed to have very decided opinions of her own. She offered him nice rooms at a reasonable rate. He was delighted and agreed to accept them. Then the old lady asked: 'You are a member of Congress, I believe, sir. Where are you from?'

" 'I am from Texas,' replied Kilgore.

" 'Then you must have a recommendation or you cannot live in my house,' quickly retorted the old woman. 'I have had experience with these Texans before.'

"At this stage of the game I knew, of course, Buck would not have the rooms if she would give them to him, and for a little fun I encouraged the old lady.

" 'That's right,' said I, 'make him bring a recommendation. I won't give him one, but he may get one from somebody.'

"By this time Buck was ready to enter into the spirit of the thing with me and said :

" 'Why, madam, I understood you kept a free and easy sort of a place. That's the reason I came here.'

"At this remark the old woman flew into a rage and made a rush for a broom. We decided it was time to escape. That was Buck's last experience with a boarding house. He decided then to live at a hotel and he has lived at one since."

Charles T. O'Ferrall, of Virginia, is one of the orators of the House. Fearless in all things, firm in his convictions, able, wise and oratorical, he commands the respect of everyone, and, as he leads, many follow. Mr. O'Ferrall has made reputation for himself as a fair, just and firm man in his management of the contested election cases in the last two Congresses. He has been chairman of the Committee on Elections for three years. He is now serving his sixth year in Congress but will soon resign, as he has been nominated, and will be elected, governor of Virginia.

Mr. O'Ferrall was a colonel in the Confederate army and carries to this day several bullets in his body. He was wounded fourteen different times.

He studied law after the war and has practiced since that time.

As an eloquent orator no man stands ahead of Isidor Rayner, of Maryland. When Mr. Rayner came to the House he was practically unknown to the great majority of its members, but he had not been here very long before he became known to all of them. Without being disagreeably pushing he made his way to the front by dint of his fitness and energy. In committee as well as on the floor his unusual ability was quickly recognized. His oratorical powers alone would have given him a prominent place in the House, but many men make a hit as speech-makers who make very little impression as legislators. Sensible members of the House value the reputation they have among their colleagues for ability in · constructing legislation, a reputation which is gained in committee rather than on the floor, more than the transient applause which is the chief reward of mere oratory in the House. Mr. Rayner, being a sensible man, doubtless shares this opinion. The sincerity and honesty of the man have impressed those who have observed Mr. Rayner's career in the House even more than his abilities. His intense earnestness is one reason why he has succeeded both in constructive work in committee and in his oratorical attempts on the floor. Whether they agree with him or not his colleagues believe him to be entirely sincere, and this fact strengthens all that he says and does. As an orator Mr. Rayner is without a superior among the younger members of the House. Indeed it would be difficult to name a superior among the older members of the House. He never speaks without occasion or careful preparation. When he speaks his whole being seems absorbed in his effort and finds expression in a succession of brilliant sentences which seem coined on the inspiration of the moment. His voice is pleasing and his gestures graceful, and he gives pleasure as well as instruction to the House when he speaks.

Mr. Rayner is one of the young leaders of the House, being only forty-three, although he is now serving his third term in Congress. . He had the advantage of a thorough education given at the University of Virginia, where he also read law with such

NEWTON C. BLANCHARD, LOUISIANA.

success that he was admitted to the bar in Baltimore when he reached his majority, in fact a little before his twenty-first birthday. He has been practicing law with success since. In 1878 he went to the Maryland Legislature for two years, and in 1886 was elected to the State Senate for four years. With the beginning of the Fiftieth Congress he entered the House; has been twice reelected and it is supposed will continue indefinitely to represent his section of the city of Baltimore.

Newton C. Blanchard, of Louisiana, chairman of the Committee on Rivers and Harbors, has achieved much distinction in his management of the river and harbor legislation of Congress. It was under his advice and suggestion that the old system of making small annual appropriations for the improvement of rivers and harbors, which were soon expended and the results partially destroyed before another appropriation was made, was changed to the new system of awarding contracts for the completion of necessary improvements.

Under this new system, adopted by Mr. Blanchard, the government really saves money and achieves practical results. Instead of appropriating a few thousand dollars every year for the improvement of a river or harbor, the committee under his management contracts for the completion of desired improvements to be paid for as the work is done.

Mr. Blanchard is eminently a practical man in all things. He has demonstrated it in the management of his committee and upon the floor of the House. He is careful, studious and businesslike, all of which gives him the respect of his colleagues. When he reports a river and harbor bill the House knows there is no job, in it, and it is rarely amended.

Though but forty years of age, Mr. Blanchard is now serving his thirteenth year in the House of Representatives. He was born and raised in the Louisiana district which he now represents. He graduated in law at the University of Louisiana and was admitted to practice at the age of nineteen. He has been a practicing lawyer ever since. In 1876

WILLIAM C. OATES, ALABAMA.

he took an active part in the politics of his State and was largely instrumental in the restoration of the government of the State from carpet-bag rule. Several times he has been prominently mentioned for the Senate, and his friends believe it will not be many years before he is elevated to a seat in the Senate chamber.

Besides an industrious worker, Mr. Blanchard has the reputation of being the most skillful marksman in the House. He is a great sportsman and has the record of having brought down twenty-two quail in twenty-three shots. With a pistol he is even more expert than with the shot-gun. Occasionally he drops into one of the shooting galleries about Washington and, with a pistol, can hit the bull's eye of the target almost every time. He will toss a coin in the air and bore it with a bullet two out of three times. Once he was challenged to a duel by a political adversary in Louisiana. He accepted it with such celerity that the challenger was amazed. Within an hour he had heard of Mr. Blanchard's skill with the pistol and decided to withdraw his challenge. Fortunate for him that he did.

As an orator and a bold and fearless debater, few men stand higher in the House of Representatives than that one-armed veteran, William C. Oates, of Alabama. Col. Oates is serving his seventh term in the House of Representatives. He is the second man on the Judiciary Committee and is ranked among the great lawyers of the House. He is a close student, slow to formulate his opinions, but when once formulated he is as firm in the advocacy of his beliefs as man can be. In debate he is a power. Few men desire to cross swords with him in a running discussion. In sectional debates he is the South's most earnest defender. When he believes himself right he is firm unto stubbornness. His firmness was well illustrated during the Fiftieth Congress when the direct tax bill was under discussion. Col. Oates introduced an amendment to refund the cotton tax, holding that if it was correct to refund the direct land tax levied during the war the cotton tax, levied at the same time, should be refunded, especially as the Supreme Court had held the latter tax to be unconstitutional. Northern and Western members of the House of both sides opposed the refunding of the cotton tax. Col. Oates was firm, and with a few Southern followers he deadlocked the House for two weeks and defeated the passage of the direct tax bill. He was not opposed to refunding the direct tax, but he declared that it should not be done unless the cotton tax went with it. At the next session of Congress the direct tax bill passed, and it was through the influence of Col. Oates and the facts which he laid before the President in regard to the case, that Mr. Cleveland vetoed this bill as his last official act during his first term as President. The bill was, however, passed during the Fifty-First Congress and President Harrison signed it.

Col. Oates is fifty years of age. He was born in Pike county, Alabama. He is a self-educated man, having studied at home and then in a lawyer's office. He is one of the few Southern legal lights in Congress who accumulated wealth from the practice of his profession. He is one of the wealthiest as well as strongest Southerners in the House of Representatives.

Col. Oates served in the Confederate army as colonel of the Forty-eighth Alabama Regiment. He was wounded six times in battle, having lost his right arm in front of Richmond in 1864, in the twenty-seventh battle in which he was engaged. Before his election to Congress he served several terms in the Alabama legislature.

Col. Oates may close his career in the House of Representatives at the end of this Congress. He will probably be nominated for governor of his State, and the nomination means election. His friends expect that after serving two years as governor of his State, he will be sent to the Senate of the United States.

Col. Oates is not only a gallant soldier; he has had experience on the field of honor, and was as courageous and as successful there as he has been in parliamentary combats on the floor of the House. Twice he has accepted challenges for duels, and both times fought them. Though having only one arm he managed to wound his adversary each time, and escaped without a scratch. In one of the duels his adversary, slightly wounded at the first fire, demanded a second shot. It was accorded him, and this time Col. Oates wounded him more seriously. He, however, recovered.

"Private" John Allen, of Mississippi, as he is familiarly known, is the wittiest as well as one of the strongest men in the House. Allen is serving his fifth term in Congress. He made a reputation during his first term as a wit and has held it above all competitors. When he rises in his seat and says "Mr. Speaker" the House is all attention. They know a bright and witty speech filled with illustrative anecdotes is coming. Allen never disappoints his hearers. He has a new story for every day in the year, and he tells a story in his own inimitable style. He claims to be the only surviving private of the Confederate army, and from this claim he derives his title of "Private" John Allen. He says there were other privates during the war, but he has never been able to find one since. Mr. Allen is not always jocular; sometimes he surprises the House by his seriousness, and in his serious moments he occasionally delivers strong, argumentative and convincing speeches.

He was born in Mississippi, July 8, 1847, and received a common school education up to his enlistment as a private in the Confederate army at the age of fifteen. After the war he studied law and graduated at the University of Mississippi. Since that time he has practiced his profession at Tupelo. The only public office he ever held before coming to Congress was district attorney for the first judicial district of

JOHN ALLEN, MISSISSIPPI.

Mississippi. No man in Congress is more popular in his district than the "Private." The people will return him just as long as he cares to return.

There are, however, some people in Mr. Allen's district who do not realize the fame of the man. He was down home a short time ago, and visited one of the backwoods counties of his district where he had heard that opposition to him was being encouraged. While there on a court day he met old Uncle Billy Shanks, who had known him in his boyhood days. The "Private" had not seen Uncle Billy in ten years. When they met the old man embraced him and exclaimed:

"Why, John, where have you been all these years?"

"Don't you know, Uncle Billy?"

"No."

"Why, Uncle Billy, I. have been up to Washington in Congress!"

"The devil you have, John. I thought you might have been working over in Page county with your Uncle Ike."

At this latter remark Allen realized what a little man a Congressman might be in the estimation of some of his constituents. He told the story here a few days ago, and in conclusion asked: "After all, what is fame?"

Rufus E. Lester, of Georgia, is one of the silent, but industrious members of the House. Mr. Lester hails from the Savannah district of Georgia, and has proved a valuable representative for that district. Through his efforts an appropriation of nearly $4,000,000 has been made by Congress for improving the harbor of Savannah, the object being to improve that harbor to such an extent as to make it a great Southern port and thereby lead to the building up

RUFUS E. LESTER, GEORGIA.

of a foreign direct trade with the South.

Besides his work for his own district, Col. Lester is a conspicuous figure in the House. He is the author of a bill to repeal the ten per cent. tax on State bank circulation, for which he has made a strong fight before the Banking and Currency Committee, and which will probably be adopted by this Congress.

Col. Lester seldom enters the running debates on the floor. He is given more to strong, argumentative speeches. By profession he is a lawyer. Before his election to the Fifty-first Congress he had served several terms in the State legislature, having been president of the State senate for two terms. He was afterwards mayor of Savannah for six years. He is now serving his third term in the House.

There is one man in the House who rarely makes a speech. He is silent except when forced to the front, then he says what he has to say in as few words as possible. This man is John S. Henderson, of North Carolina, chairman of the Committee on Postoffices. In this position he has worked industriously for the improvement of mail transportation in the country, and in the South particularly he has almost worked wonders. By providing proper regulations and increasing the pay for transporting mails where it was necessary, the mail facilities of the country have been increased and quickened to a remarkable extent. A few years ago the time for transporting the mails between New York and New Orleans was forty-eight to fifty-two hours. It has been reduced under Mr. Henderson's guidance to thirty-six hours.

Mr. Henderson is purely a business man. The postoffice appropriation bill is drawn up by him upon business principles. He makes no set speech advocating it in the House; he simply explains its provisions in a business-like way and the House accepts it.

Mr. Henderson was born at his present home in Salisbury, January 6, 1846. He graduated at the University of North Carolina and served throughout the war as a private in the Confederate army. After the war he studied law and has since practiced. He served in the State House of Representatives and in the Senate. He is now serving his fifth term in Congress.

Alexander B. Montgomery, representative of the fourth district of Kentucky, is one of the silent leaders of the House, seldom speaking on the floor, never allowing an interview, modest, unostentatious, yet impressing his personality on every bit of legislation coming before Congress. He has many

JOHN S. HENDERSON, NORTH CAROLINA.

of the characteristics of Gorman, with the intrepidity of the Speaker, one of whose closest friends he is.

It was when Mr. Crisp was making

ALEXANDRE B. MONTGOMERY, KENTUCKY.]

his fight for the chair that Montgomery first became an important factor in the politics of the House. Standing out against the convictions of his State and his own constituency, he was one of the first men from his section of the country to declare for the Georgian. With great odds against him he soon had the majority of his own delegation in line and working in his silent way, became one of the most important factors in the race.

In recognition of his ability and services he was given a chairmanship and placed high on the Committee on Ways and Means. It is here that his best work has been done. He is peculiarly conservative, never allowing sectional or personal prejudices to mar has judgment or warp his vision.

His physical appearance is indicative of his inner self. Tall as the proverbial arrow, straight as the conventional ramrod, he passes through the halls of Congress a conspicuous figure. He looks the picture of the farmer and the judge, a mingling of the rustic and the judiciary. "What does Montgomery

think?" is a common question to be heard about the floor, and as often his advice is sought and as often taken. He has that peculiar faculty of differing with men without wounding their egotism. He never voluntarily offers advice, and when it is asked gives it straight without fear of consequences.

He is a Kentuckian with all the local pride which seems inherent in the natives of the Blue Grass State. He is a good churchman, a good horseman and understands the finest points of bourbon whiskey. He was born on a farm in Hardin county in 1837, where he has always resided. He was given a collegiate education at Georgetown College, Kentucky, graduating in 1859. In 1861 he graduated from the Louisville law school, but returned to his farm and lived the life of a planter. In 1870 he was called from the sickle to the bench and served as county judge until 1874. He served in the State Senate from 1877 to 1881, and by an overwhelming vote was sent to the Fiftieth Congress; since there he has been returned each time without serious opposition.

BENTON M'MILLIN, TENNESSEE.

Benton McMillin, of the fourth district of Tennessee, is a man the galleries love. He is always ready for a fight, and, in fact, is always seeking one. He never hits below the belt but watches his chance to clinch. He obeys none of the prize ring rules and scarcely the rules of the House. He is an all-round rough and tumble debater. He is sometimes called the Hercules of the House, on account of the enormous expansion of his chest, the stentorian tones and the muscle he displays in debate. He never seeks an under hold on his opponent. His voice not only fills the chamber, but echoes along the corridors, and some claim that it can be heard on the restaurant floor. He is no opponent for Reed's sarcasm or Burrow's parliamentary methods, but usually carries the day through sheer physical strength and honesty of purpose.

McMillin is one of those men who believe, when they hold an opinion, that others must hold it too. He does not understand that two men can think differently on any subject, given the same premises by which to arrive at a conclusion. It is this stubborness of character, this simplicity of faith that has kept him in national politics through seven Congresses and reelected him to the eighth.

He was born in Munroe county, Kentucky, in 1845; took a college course at Lexington, and studied law and began the practice of it in Celina, Tennessee, in 1871. He made his first appearance in politics as a member of the House of Representatives of Tennessee in 1874. He entered national politics as an elector on the Tilden and Hendricks ticket in 1876, shortly after which he was commissioned by the governor as special Judge of the Circuit Court. His personality was fully im-

pressed on all State issues, and when the election for the Forty-sixth Congress came around he was sent to be one of the body politic in Washington. He is a valuable member of the Ways and Means Committee, and during last Congress was a member of the Committee on Rules.

Clifton R. Breckinridge is the representative of the old Pine Bluff district in Arkansas. He is above all the bony and sinewy Breckinridge. He is a son of old John C. Breckinridge, Buchanan's Vice-President, and has the same slow way of arriving at conclusions and the same tenacity in sticking to them as the elder Breckinridge himself. He lacks the personal magnetism of many members of his family, but his opinions are usually sought by some of the more flashy members of Congress, and his advice has more than once been taken by the leaders of the House to extricate his party from some political jambaree. He is a member of the Ways and Means

CLIFTON R. BRECKINRIDGE, ARKANSAS.

Committee and is one of the scholars of this aristocratic club of Congress. Like Wilson, of West Virginia, but perhaps not to so great an extent, he is one of the polished scholars in politics. He shared the burdens of framing the Mills bill and was one of its strongest advocates on the floor. He does not speak often, but when he does is listened to with close attention by the members, though he seldom attracts an audience in the gallery. His speeches are prepared with great care and he possibly condenses more ideas in a short space than any other member on the floor. But he speaks so seldom that his average of ideas is considerably cut down within the session in com-

JOSEPH D. SAYERS, TEXAS.

parison with other leaders on the floor.

As his name implies he is a Kentuckian by birth, having been born at Lexington in 1846. He is one of the few
Kentuckians who served in the Confederate army as a private soldier and came
out without being a colonel. At the
close of the strife he was a midshipman
on duty below Richmond, Virginia. He
is a graduate of the old Washington
College, now the Washington and Lee
University. He chose planting as his
occupation and carried on a commission
business in connection with it. He was
an alderman of Pine Bluff and from that
post leaped over the heads of other
local politicians and was elected to the
Forty-eighth Congress from the State-at-
large. He was elected to the Forty-
ninth and Fiftieth Congresses and was
reelected to the Fifty-First Congress as
a Democrat, but was unseated by the
action of the House and the seat declared vacant. He was elected to the
Fifty-second Congress, and is now
serving in the Fifty-third.

One of the intellectual giants of the
House is Joseph D. Sayers, of Texas.
Mr. Sayers is the successor of Mr.
Holman as chairman of the Committee
on Appropriations. He was selected by
Speaker Crisp over all other men in the
House as the one man fitted by virtue

of business ability, force and character
for chairman of this perhaps most
important committee of the House. Mr.
Sayers is serving his fifth term in
Congress. He has been a member of
the Appropriations Committee from
his first term, and has done service on
that committee which entitled him to its
chairmanship. He is a man who has
the thorough confidence of the House.
When he reports a bill the House knows
it to be correct and will pass it without
question.

Before his election to the House of
Representatives he served several terms
in the Texas House of Representatives
and then in the Senate, of which he
was the president. He was chairman of
the State democratic executive committee, and was lieutenant governor of
Texas in 1879 and 1880.

In appearance Mr. Sayers is a typical
Texan. He is nearly six feet tall, stout
and ruddy. He has the reputation of
being the most industrious and hardest
worker of the House of Representatives.
He understands the financial situation of
this government as no other man of the
House, and under his management the
appropriations will be held down to the
very lowest possible limit, though he is
a man who will not do anything to
cripple a single branch of the govern-

THOMAS C. CATCHINGS, MISSISSIPPI.

BARNES COMPTON, MARYLAND.

ment. He does not pose as an economist, but he believes in doing what is just, right and proper.

Thomas C. Catchings, of Mississippi, the senior member of the Committee on Rules, and practically the leader of the House in parliamentary debates, is a man who has attained his position by sheer force of ability. From his first appearance in the hall of the House of Representatives in the Forty-ninth Congress, Mr. Catchings has impressed his colleagues with his judgment and ability. He is a man who talks only when he believes it to be necessary; then he speaks to the point and with an emphasis and force which carry his colleagues with him. He is not a great orator; he is simply a straight-away practical talker. He presents matters in the simplest language and in the most favorable style. His speech on the silver question, during its recent discussion in the House, was considered the strongest argument in favor of the repeal of the Sherman law during that memorable debate.

Mr. Catchings was selected by Speaker Crisp as one of the two Democratic members to serve with the Speaker himself on the Committee on Rules at the first session of the last Congress. The Speaker selected one Northern man and one Southern man to act with him. From the South he selected Mr. Catchings as the best representative on the floor.

Mr. Catchings was born in Mississippi, January 11, 1847. He was educated at the University of Mississippi, but left school to enter the Confederate army in 1861. He served throughout the war and was promoted on account of bravery to brigadier-general. After the war he practiced law in Vicksburg and served in the State Senate for four years, was afterwards attorney general of his State for a term of four years, and in 1885 was elected to the House of Representatives where he has since served.

One of the strongest men in the House is John H. Bankhead, of Alabama. Though serving only his fourth term he has been chairman of the Committee on Public Buildings for two terms, one of the hardest working committees of the House. Mr. Bankhead is an ardent advocate of bimetallism and stands among the leaders of that cause in the House. Though he appears but little in the debates, he is recognized as one of the leaders. He is conservative in all things. It was he who was largely instrumental in settling the silver contest in the House. The South-

JOHN H. BANKHEAD, ALABAMA.

ern men have confidence in his ability and integrity and he has a large following on the floor. Mr. Bankhead is not a lawyer. He is a farmer and merchant, though the larger portion of his life has been spent in public office. He served many terms in the State House of Representatives and the Senate, and held various other prominent positions under the State government of Alabama. He was elected from the Birmingham district to the Fiftieth Congress and has since been a member of the House of Representatives. Mr. Bankhead will probably remain a member as long as he desires.

Popular, gallant Barnes Compton, of Maryland, is a leader and an orator of the flint and steel variety. When he talks he strikes fire with every sentence. Soldierly in bearing, with a full and commanding voice, eloquent and ringing in his utterances, he is a picture in debate which makes his hearers applaud at every climax. His speech in vacating his seat in the Fiftieth Congress, when the Republicans unjustly turned him out to make room for Sydney Mudd, was one which will live forever in the annals of Congress. He went down, but with colors flying gallantly to the breezes, and his last words as he retired from the hall were words of denunciation of the unjust Republican majority which had deprived him of a seat to which he was legally elected. The House fairly rung with applause, and even the Republicans admired the courage of the man.

Mr. Compton was born at Port Royal, Maryland, November 16, 1830. He was educated at Princeton College. By profession, if it could be so termed, he

ALEXANDER M. DOCKERY, MISSOURI.

is a farmer. The majority of his life has, however, been spent in the public service. He was a member of the State House of Delegates and of the State Senate, having served as president of the latter body for two sessions. For eleven years he was State Treasurer of Maryland, and could have remained in that office for life had he so desired. He resigned, however, to accept the Democratic nomination for Congress. He served in the Forty-ninth and Fiftieth Congress. In the Fifty-first he was unseated after serving but a few months. He then served through the Fifty-second and was re-elected to the present Congress by a good round majority. No man in the House is held in higher esteem than popular "Barney" Compton.

Alexander M. Dockery, of Missouri, is a practical demonstration that a country doctor can evolve into a large and prosperous statesman. Mr. Dockery is one of the strongest members of the House. He is the economist of the Democratic party. He is a man full of original ideas and he never hesitates to try them on the government machinery. Many of them have proved valuable.

For many years Mr. Dockery practiced medicine in one of the little country towns of Missouri, and gradually arose to the distinguished position of county physician. He was full of nerve and pluck, and finding but little money in "doctoring country folks," he organized a bank, of which he was cashier until elected to Congress in 1883.

Mr. Dockery has served on the Appropriations Committee for years. He has the finances of the government at his finger tips.

HENRY B PLANT.

HENRY B. PLANT.

It is interesting to note the effect which is exerted upon the history of a country by its leading men. The people as a mass are the product of the ideas and customs which they have inherited and of the conditions of climate and soil where their lives are passed. But occasionally there are individuals who rise above their surroundings sufficiently to give a new impetus or direction to the national life. They may be generals or lawgivers, orators or prophets, poets or priests. It is such as these who in the past have thronged the historic stage or whose biographies load down the shelves of libraries. But through all time there have been at work, for the most part silently and unobserved, men whose minds and lives have been devoted to laying the foundations of their country's greatness or to ensuring its prosperity by the application of their ingenuity, their experience and their observation to the development of its resources. Their work is not done under the fierce light which beats upon a throne, or amid the thunder of cannon, the flourishing of swords and the flare of trumpets; they do not strut their fitful hour before a throng of spectators assembled to be amused, nor do they avail themselves of the modern facilities of newspapers and telegraph to impress themselves upon a world of readers. Silently and assiduously they go about their life's work, opening up new sources of beneficence for the plodding multitudes, combining the materials at hand into other and more valuable forms, widening the area of human productiveness, perhaps intent only on the work directly before them and themselves not fully comprehending the effect of their work upon those among whom they live or who are to come after them.

More particularly may this be said of those who have been termed the captains of industry, who have gathered into their hands the guiding reins of the chariots of commerce and have made the highways smooth and ready of access for all who would use them. Some of these men have acquired a more or less extended renown. In our own country we have had the Vanderbilts, Edgar Thomson and Thomas W. Scott, John W. Garrett and Jay Gould, men who have aggregated capital in vast sums for the accomplishment of their great enterprises, and in doing so have become the objects of popular attention. Such men are with us today, men like Geo. M. Pullman, C. P. Huntington, Chauncey M. Depew, Geo. B. Roberts, J. J. Hill and Pierpont Morgan. Their abilities, their energies have had an ample field for display and the results have been so stupendous as greatly to emphasize the measure of their success. In similar but less conspicuous fields of action, just such men have been and are at work in these broad lands of ours, among them one of whom a short biographical sketch would be of interest to the readers of the SOUTHERN STATES, since it has been with the varying fortunes of the Southern States that his own career has been identified from early manhood. That man is Henry B. Plant, the founder of the Southern Express Company and of the system of transportation by rail in South Carolina, Georgia, Alabama and Florida and by steamships on the Gulf of Mexico, of which he has for many years been president.

Born in Bradford, Conn., in 1819, of a Puritan ancestry, with blood as blue as their religion, as a youth he was employed on a steamboat between New

York and New Haven. Just as he had received promotion in that service he became incidentally connected with the express business which, in a small way, had been established by Harnden between New York and Boston, and this was the turning point in his fortunes. He shortly after entered the service of Adams Express Co., where his capacity and fitness for any position in which he was placed led to his rapid advancement. As an incident in this part of his career, it may be mentioned that, alternating daily with another expressman, he literally carried in two valises suspended from his shoulders by straps, a large sum in foreign gold, amounting in the total to millions of dollars ordered from the New York sub-treasury to the Philadelphia mint for re-coinage. Every other morning he took up his burden at the sub-treasury, was taken in a wagon to the steamboat for South Amboy, thence by rail to Camden, where, in another wagon, he crossed the ferry to deliver his precious charge after nightfall at the mint.

As the public value of the express service began to be recognized, its field of action became enlarged, and about 1853 the Adams Express Co. extended its lines into the South by way of steamship to Charleston, and Mr. Plant was sent there to look after their interests. There, associated with Henry Sanford, now the honored president of the Adams Express Co., he established the Southern division of that company. In this work he was engaged, with headquarters at Augusta, Ga., when the first shot was fired at Fort Sumpter. Casting his lot with the South, he became president of the Southern Express Co., a name familiar to every Confederate soldier indebted to it for the gratuitous delivery to him, even in the very trenches, of his box of clothes or food from the dear ones at home. The energy and thoroughness which characterized the management of this express company during the war was illustrated by the statement that when General Lee was operating north of the Potomac river, the Confederate government, desiring to make him a large remittance of money, proposed to ship it by express rather than to trust to its own means of communication, and the delivery was successfully made.

During the war, Mr. Plant made some considerable investments in Southern railroad bonds, a provision which afterward stood him in good account. After the surrender, when the South lay prostrate at her conquerors' feet, he did not lose heart; he had faith in her natural resources and in her people and he went patiently to work weaving again the network of express lines which ruthless war had rent asunder. As fast as the rails which Sherman's men had heated in bonfires made from the cross ties and twisted around the trees could be re-heated and straightened and put back in the track, a patched up locomotive and some weather-beaten old cars would jolt along over them, and there would be the Southern Express, carrying a few cotton samples to the factories and returning the greenbacks to start the cotton on its way to market.

In the reorganization of the railroad companies, bankrupted by the war, he rendered most valuable assistance, and his business forethought and capacity for organization had been generally recognized in Southern railroad circles, when in 1877 the failure of the Atlantic & Gulf Railroad Co. in southern Georgia found him with such an interest in its bonds that he was induced personally to undertake its rehabilitation. He reorganized it as the Savannah, Florida & Western Railway Co., relaid it with steel rail, provided it with new equipment and built a short line connection into Jacksonville, which gave Florida its first impulse into notoriety and prosperity. This led him to establish a line of steamboats upon the St. John's river.

From Sanford, which was the up-river terminus of this steamboat route, a narrow gauge road had stretched out a short way into the country. Taking this little road, the South Florida Railroad, as a beginning, he extended it across the peninsula through a wilderness, in which the cow-boy and the Seminole yet lingered, to the sleepy little village of Tampa, on the Gulf of Mexico. Situated at the entrance of a shallow river it offered but little in the way of business for a railroad, but Mr. Plant's mind had been set upon opening up the way to the West Indies and the Gulf of Mexico. He knew that there was deep water at the entrance of Tampa bay, and before he could prepare his plans to reach it by rail, he had established a mail route from Tampa bay to Havana, building for it the Mascotte, the first steamship with triple expansion engines that ever carried the Stars and Stripes into a foreign port. Following closely upon the establishment of this marine enterprise he carried the South Florida Railroad to deep water on Tampa bay, establishing docks for the purpose nearly a mile from the shore, where its warehouses, hotels and shops, built upon piling, seem to float, a miniature Venice, upon the glassy waters of the bay. The opening of this route to Cuba led to the establishment of cigar factories by Cuban enterprise with Cuban capital, and with Cuban artisans, at Tampa; a business which now employs thousands of men and has made Tampa one of the principal cities of Florida.

All this time, both on land and water, he was extending his transportation enterprises in South Carolina, Georgia, Florida and Alabama, until today there are some 1400 miles of railroad operated in what is known as the Plant System, as also steamship lines from Port Tampa to Mobile, to Jamaica and to ports on the west coast of Florida. Indeed, throughout this region, the well known orange and brown, the colors of the Plant System and its symbol, the Maltese cross, on cars and ships, on railroad stations and section houses, seem ubiquitous.

Previous to the extension of these transportation facilities in Southern Georgia and Florida the industrial pursuits of this sparsely populated region were mainly confined to the cutting of pine timber along the navigable streams and to the growth of a few thousand bales of cotton. The whole State of Florida, the largest State east of the Mississippi river, had not a town of 10,000 inhabitants within its borders. The commerce of its magnificent system of inland navigation, the St. John's river, consisted in 1868 of a few alligator skins, deer hides, sugarcane and an occasional bale of Sea Island cotton, bartered for necessary family supplies in Jacksonville. The facilities afforded for speedy transportation to distant markets have created orange groves, shipping fruit by millions of boxes, and farms producing early vegetables in equal abundance, pineapples and other semi-tropical fruit, and within the past two years the discovery of phosphate rock in south Florida, made available by this transportation, has opened up a new field for human industry in this once deserted region, comparable alone to the coal and iron industries of Alabama.

Associated with Mr. Plant in these enterprises were other men well known as masters of finance, Mr. Sanford, of the Adams Express Co., already mentioned, Messrs. Walters and Newcomer, of Baltimore, Mr. Haskell, of Boston, and Messrs. Jesup and Flagler, of New York. The same conjunction of ample resources with a creative mind, which induced Mr. Flagler to reproduce the architecture of Grenada and Seville in a marvelous group of hotels at St. Augustine, led to the construction by Mr. Plant at Tampa of a hotel of unique design and of a yet more pronounced Mooresque type, whose silvered minarets glisten in the rays of Florida's winter sun, above the verdure in which they are embosomed.

Here during the fashionable season, it is his pleasure and his relaxation to witness the enjoyment and gratification evinced by those who, hurried from the regions of a Northern winter, find themselves after a brief flight surrounded with all that can delight the senses; fruit and flowers and sunshine without, and within the comfort, the luxury and the artistic surroundings which characterize a modern private residence. With a most observant mind, always alert, Mr. Plant supervises his enterprises even to minute details, and this quality combined with his untiring industry, his business forethought, and his cordial relations with those around him, go far to account for his remarkable success in a region which, unnoticed before it had been developed by his enterprises, has since attracted the attention of other capitalists to undertakings that, but for his work as a pioneer, would have been either impracticable or unprofitable. The result of his labors, therefore, has been to people a large territory, before almost untenanted ; to open up a highway through Florida to the Gulf of Mexico, the West Indies and to Spanish America, the importance of which to the Southern States will only be appreciated as the products of the soil are manufactured in their boundaries and seek a near and favorable market ; to remove the sectional feeling, engendered by fraternal strife, by facilitating intercourse between the best elements of society amid the softening influences of a sunny winter clime, the reminiscences connected with the most romantic period of the early history of our country and all that makes our Southland so dear to its children and so delightful to its visitors.

Surely a man who has so largely contributed to these ends may well be considered as having given a new impetus and direction to the national life, to have opened up new sources of beneficence to our people, to have widened the area of their productiveness, and such has been the life work of Henry B. Plant.

LETTERS FROM SOUTHERN FARMERS—II.

[The letters published in this issue form the second instalment in the series commenced in the last number of this magazine. These communications are published in response to numerous inquiries from Northern people who desire to know more about agricultural conditions in the South, and what is being accomplished by settlers from other sections of the country. These letters were written by practical farmers and fruit-growers, chiefly Northern and Western people who have made their homes in the South. The actual experiences of these settlers, as set forth in these letters, are both interesting and instructive to those whose minds are turned Southward.—EDITOR.]

Good Soil and No Malaria.

E. H. SMITH, Citronelle, Ala.—My wife and I came here to find a home with a mild climate free from malaria with which we had both been troubled. We have both gained in strength since the first day we landed here. We have bought a forty acre tract two miles from Citronelle and are engaged in opening it up for a fruit and vegetable farm.

With over twenty years' experience in fruit and vegetable growing for profit in Illinois, Minnesota and Dakota, I have never found a soil better suited to the business, and the amount of fertilizer required is no more than is required there when fine crops are grown. These rolling lands I consider offer the best chances to growers of fruit and vegetables—cheap lands, perfect drainage and near shipping points. Our relations with the people have been very pleasant. They seem ready to give the hand of friendship to all.

Small Northern Colonies Could do Well.

G. H. JORDAN, Citronelle, Ala.—During the past three years I have spent the greater portion of my time in Southern Alabama. Coming from the State of Michigan, where winter prevails a good portion of the year, I think I more fully appreciate the gentle zephyrs of the South, and could enlarge at great length to my Northern friends upon the mild and healthful climate, cheap lands, good crops, good markets, etc., that can be found in this section of the country.

All kinds of fruit and vegetables thrive wonderfully here, and can be put in the Northern markets at a time of year when they bring the best prices. More money can be made here on a ten-acre lot than on an eighty-acre farm at the North.

We are located on the Mobile & Ohio Railroad, and all along the line of this road in Southern Alabama and the State of Mississippi there are thousands of acres of the best farming lands in the world that can be bought at prices within the reach of any industrious man. There is no place in the United States where one can secure a comfortable home at less price than here.

There is plenty of good timber and building lumber can be bought for $6 to $10 per thousand. The water is pure and good. Extremely hot weather is not common and the freezing point is reached only a few times during the winter season; twenty degrees above is the coldest I have ever known here and ninety-five degrees is the hottest.

There are some drawbacks here to be sure, but no more than one will find in any newly-settled country. Social advantages are not what one finds at the North. Schools and churches are not always up to the standard, but there is

531

an improvement going on in this direction all the while. As the natural resources of the country are developed the social and religious condition of the people will be elevated.

Hospitality and a cordial welcome are extended to all new comers. Political rights are respected and one can vote as he sees fit. Those who have been accustomed to the rigors of a Northern winter would be more than pleased with this delightful and agreeable climate. It is a health giving resort, as many can testify. Those who come here with weak lungs or in the first stages of consumption, after a few month's stay feel as if they had been "born again."

If several families would buy a tract of land and settle near each other, they could form a little colony and have many of the advantages which they have at the North, with this pure air, delightful climate and productive soil.

There are many industries neglected here now which could be opened up and made profitable. There is no better place for raising sheep; they do not require housing or feeding during the winter season. Those who engage in this business here have made large profits.

The canning industry would pay well, as there are no canning factories here, and at certain seasons of the year there is a large surplus of fruit and vegetables that go to waste. Any one looking around for a location to establish such an enterprise could find no better State than this, as figs, pears, peaches, tomatoes, cabbages, potatoes, cucumbers and every other fruit and vegetable are raised in abundance. I saw a cutting from a Le Conte pear tree recently nine feet long, the growth of a single year.

Lumber manufacture is not overdone and timber can be bought cheap. Northern enterprise, Northern pluck and Northern capital would revolutionize things about here in a few years.

An Illinois Farmer's Satisfaction.

T. J. GRAYBILL, Deer Park, Ala.—My experiments have proved satisfactory beyond my expectations. I moved with my family from Shelbyville, Ill., in January, 1889, my object being to find cheaper lands and a more genial climate than that of Illinois. I had looked over Kansas, Colorado, New Mexico, Arkansas and Texas; and spent considerable time investigating the West and South generally, before I went over the Mobile & Ohio Railroad through Mississippi and Southwestern Alabama. I find less objections to Southern Alabama than anywhere I have investigated. If that had not been true, I would not have invested and moved South.

I was raised on a farm in Southern Illinois, have been a farmer most of my life and think I am better qualified to judge of the agricultural resources of a country than to judge of it in any other particular, and I can honestly and candidly say, that I think the possibilities of Southern Alabama are greater than in any other part of the country I have ever seen. My conclusions are arrived at after four years of experimenting and observation.

While our soil in its natural conditions is not as productive as the soil of Illinois, yet with judicious handling it will produce good corn, Irish and sweet potatoes, cabbage, melons, and in fact all of the cereals that can be grown in the soil of Illinois. And these crops can all be matured at a time of the year that enables the producer to obtain big prices and stimulates him to plant more the next season.

In my judgment this is a natural sheep country. Thousands of head of sheep range through the woods of Southern Alabama and Mississippi throughout the year without attention or feed, except what nature has provided for them. There are no burs to damage the wool, no vermin to disturb the flocks, and there are no parasites even that affect the sheep.

I know of two men in our locality who own 10,000 head of sheep. All they cost them is a cheap hand to ride through the range and keep track of where they are. Raising cattle could also be made profitable by improving the stock on what it is now. My experience and observation have also taught me that as a fruit country Southern Alabama cannot be excelled by any section in the United States. I have tried various kinds of grapes, pears, peaches, apricots, quinces, and apples, and all seem to do well.

I do not think apples will pay to grow for the market, but I am satisfied that $300 per acre can be realized each year on pears, especially the Keiffer and Le Conte varieties. Small fruit do equally well; plums and blackberries grow spontaneously; strawberries are a great success.

We have an abundance of pure free-stone water as soft as rain-water, and we are especially delighted with the mild healthful climate. In four years and over I have not spent a dollar for medicine for my family, which consists of a wife and six children. I believe the climate of Southern Alabama will cure catarrh and rheumatism, and will greatly benefit all pulmonary affections. Nothing would induce my family to return to live in Illinois.

When I think of the large number of people in moderate circumstances in Illinois and the Northwestern States, who work all summer to accumulate enough to live on and shelter them in the winter, I wonder that they do not go and make homes in this country. I suppose some of them have the erroneous idea that they would be ostracised by society, and that their political liberty would be endangered; but if the Southern railroads will continue to offer inducements in the way of cheap rates, to get these people to go and investigate for themselves, it is only a question of time when this region will be sought after as one of the most desirable sections of the United States.

Why people will leave this land in Alabama and Mississippi, that can be bought from $2.50 to $10.00 per acre in a climate like this, on a trunk line of railroad that connects the centre of commerce in the interior of the United States with the great seaport of Mobile, land that they can make more money on than the $50 to $100 per acre lands of the Northwest, and stay and wade in mud and shiver half their lives, is more than I can understand, unless it is because they do not know of the opportunities there are here. Some people say the South is behind the times.

Admit that to be true, yet we cannot charge it to the country; it can be accounted for in other ways.

When I came here I was not looking for a country that was ahead of the times. I was looking for a place where I could get in on the ground floor, which I think is the best policy for people in moderate circumstances. We have here quite a large settlement of Illinois, Michigan and New York people who are prosperous, contented and happy, with their Southern neighbors. People of the South are glad to have Northern and Western people come to this country. We are all one people.

Thirty=four Per Cent. Profit in One Year.

D. C. GREEN, Lauderdale county, Ala.—In December, 1890, I purchased the farm of 400 acres which we now occupy and have cultivated since 1891, this being our third crop. The purchase price of the farm was $7000. We found it as most of the farms in this section, in a very poor state of cultivation, in consequence of having been tilled by tenants, in fact it was so poor that we hardly expected to pay running expenses for the first three years, but to our surprise, although the second year was a poor one for crops, it paid us net, after reserving fodder enough to carry the working stock through another year, about 34 per cent. of the original cost of the land. We find that we can raise corn at a cost of about $3 per acre or about fourteen cents per bushel in the crib. The first twenty-six acres we sowed in clover have given us in three years about $90 worth of hay per acre at the price of clover hay at the market at Florence, which has been no less than $15.00 per ton.

We have sold no corn for less than fifty cents a bushel and quite a quantity at sixty cents per bushel at the crib. So far as fruits are concerned, about six kinds of apples of good variety bear almost every year abundantly. About four varieties of the best pears do well here. The grafted peach is not a success, but seedlings give us a good crop in almost all years and some of the seedlings are very fine. The water is the purest I ever drank, being furnished by springs, usually at a temperature of about 56° in winter and summer.

The climate is very healthful and it was to get the benefit of that which brought us here. In 1890 Mrs. Green and myself traveled over portions of Kentucky, Tennessee and Mississippi in search of a place where the climate was sufficiently healthy to enable me to regain my health. Here we thought we had found it and the results prove that we were not mistaken.

Mr. Southworth, my partner in agriculture and stock raising, had been engaged in editorial work and had been a great sufferer from asthma for twenty years. He has not had an asthmatic breath since he arrived in Lauderdale county, in January, 1891. We both came from Woodstock, Ill. I had been engaged in the practice of medicine for thirty-two years, in which avocation I had lost my health.

I am satisfied that an industrious farmer of limited means, by judicious management, can realize upon his investment more than double the per cent. in a year that he can in any portion of the North with which I am acquainted, and I lived in one of the most prosperous sections. Besides, here we have a much more agreeable climate and can have upon our table fresh vegetables and fruits from our garden for at least nine to ten months in the year. This makes living so much more pleasant and it greatly diminishes the expense.

Those who wish to please the eye, as well as make money, will find the flora of this country very attractive. From early spring until mid-summer the forests are full with fragrance and beauty. We have the red bud, the dogwood, fringe tree, hawthorn, tulip tree, the mountain laurel, the fragrant spinkster and other blooming trees and shrubs, and the cultivated flowers of nearly all varities do exceedingly well, the rose especially. They live out-doors all the winter and are green nine months in the year, remaining in bloom from early spring until oftentimes the latter part of December or the first of January.

As to the condition of society, I would state that we have never found a more hospitable people in the world and so far as education is concerned the facilities in our town are equal to those of the towns of the same size in the North. We must regret that in the country provisions have not been made for the education of the children that we wish, but an effort is being made to increase the educational facilities in the rural districts throughout the State with promise of a fair degree of success.

All That the Heart Could Wish.

LEVI SHOEMAKER, Pea Ridge, De Kalb county, Ala.—I was born in Ohio. I have lived in Indiana and also in Missouri. I have seen a great deal of the country, from the Alleghany Mountains, Pennsylvania, to the Ozark Mountains of Missouri, and I have found no place where I like to live so well as I do on Sand Mountain, Alabama.

The climate is all that heart could wish for, and the water is the purest I ever drank, free from lime and other minerals. I can raise any crop here that can be raised in Ohio, and many more, such as cotton, etc. The best fruit I ever ate, such as apples, pears, peaches, plums, berries, etc., grow in abundance. There are no insects here to annoy man or beast. We are all a band of brothers here; churches and schools are good. We have the best range for cattle I ever saw.

North Alabama Compared With New York.

TIMOTHY P. DENISON, Springville, St. Clair county, Ala.—I was born among the White Mountains of the State of New Hampshire, not far from Mount Washington, but lived in Western New York from the time I was seven years old until I was about fifty years of age. My old home in Western New York was in a region with a climate very damp and very cold, the cold of winter feeling doubly keen because of this dampness, and giving the doctors much employment with cases of lung diseases, throat troubles, catarrh, disorders of the respiratory organs, rheumatism, etc.

I have had fairly good health for many years, but with weak lungs. For the benefits in general of an out-door life I went to Southern California, and afterwards to South Florida, living in each a few years. And then I concluded to try Northern Alabama. A famous traveler, while in the high altitudes and fine climate of Central America, wrote back that the average man could enjoy the most comfort and best health, either where he was then, or in Northern Alabama. I agree with him. I consider it fortunate that I came to the pleasant and healthful town of Springville, in Saint Clair county, where I met with the agent of the Alabama State Land Company and concluded a purchase with him of an excellent little farm of 120 acres—all in virgin forest growth at the time of purchase save a few acres, and these few acres I have added to and improved. And on this I have made my residence and home, most agreeably and contentedly, and in fine bodily health. For bodily comfort and prospects no consideration could induce me to exchange my pleasant Southern home for my dear and less comfortable home of old times.

Here in winter, the mercury never comes lower than 8 to 10 degrees above zero, and in summer but little if any above 90. The snowfall varies from the ordinary one to two inches to the very unusual extreme of eight to ten inches; generally lying on the ground from one day to five or six days—never sufficient in depth or quantity to produce floods or injury to property of any kind. There is just enough of change in the air and in the weather to remind the observer that we have our seasons of summer and winter here as elsewhere, but here more equable and therefore more healthful.

I suppose my lands, especially in this section, may be regarded as what are known as table lands, being at an elevation of some 250 to 300 feet above the neighboring valley lands. Soil is a vegetable loam, free and generous in return for the labor it receives, easily improved in fertility and productive capacity, and adapted to the usual crops of the country, wheat, corn, cotton, root crops, fruits, the grasses, etc.

In my purchase I intended devoting my labors to having a dairy farm and fruit farms, adding a flock of sheep afterwards, if I found I could make it pay after counting out the losses of sheep killed by dogs and lambs killed by hogs. Our chief drawback is the lack of markets for the sale of our produce and I write now the more readily with the hope that other Westerners and Northerners like myself may come here in sufficient numbers to aid in building up markets for our mutual good, one to the other.

Living is comparatively cheap here. Land, unimproved land or wood-land, is cheap here when we consider its nearness to the great cities North and East and West as compared with the far away cheap lands of the Northwest. We have good churches, good schools and good society. We can plant something every month in the year in this mild climate, either in the field or the garden.

We can sum up a few advantages of this region like this: We are nearer market than the cheap lands of the Northwest. All things considered, the climate of North Alabama is as good for a farmer as Southern California. The Lord sends rain here, and in Southern California millionaire land grabbers control the water that a man of moderate means irrigates his land with. Land is dear there, and you pay too high for climate and you are a week's journey from Washington or Baltimore. For all around climate ours is as good as South Florida where the sandy land is too poor and thin, too wet and too marshy, and too high in price, and farther than we from market.

Minnesota enjoys the reputation of an excellent climate because cold and dry. I know what cold weather is from Mount Washington, New Hampshire, to Western New York. Minnesota cold and dry is too much of a good thing. You cannot be out in the open air there in winter long enough at a time for the benefit of your health without being uncomfortably cold. Ours is a more excellent climate in that you can be out in the open air here comfortably all the year round.

Now if any intending emigrant wishes to know more of Alabama and its advantages and capacities, he must come down here as I did and we will undertake to show him about.

Profits in Fruits and Berries.

D. D. AMES, Avoca, Benton county, Ark.—I formerly lived in Ohio, and came to Benton county in 1881. When I came to Arkansas I was entirely without means. I bought a small piece of rugged hill land on credit, and with my own hands cleared it, fenced it and set it in strawberries and raspberries. I now have ninety acres in fruits. This land has cost me from $2.50 to $10.00 an acre. My berries pay me so well that I would not take $100 an acre for the land. I have several seasons realized this amount and more per acre from a single crop of berries; and some of my best fruits are on hillsides, which look very uninviting to those unacquainted with the productiveness of this land. I have realized $2700 net profit from twenty acres of strawberries. From four acres of Snyder blackberries I sold this season 217 crates at a net profit of $1.35 a crate. My advice to men who have but little means to begin with is to come to this country and engage in fruit-growing.

New York Apple Growers in Arkansas.

D. WING, of the firm of D. Wing & Bro., Rogers, Benton county, Ark.—In the summer of 1882 I incidentally learned through a friend of mine who was connected with the building of the railroad through Northwest Arkansas of the fine apples grown in that section. The crop that season in Western New York was almost a total failure. With my brother I was at that time engaged in the fruit evaporating business and we decided to investigate the Arkansas country with a view to locating our evaporators there. On the 4th of July my brother Stephen left Rochester and reached Rogers, Benton county, Ark., on the morning of the 6th. On the afternoon of the same day he telegraphed me that the prospect was good for a heavy yield of fruit. As rapidly as possible I shipped our machinery, and we erected in different parts of the country nine evaporators. We bought and evaporated that season over 100,-000 bushels of apples.

We were much pleased with our move, and our business was a great benefit to the country, consuming a great deal of fruit that would otherwise have been lost. We decided to remain in the country and bought land, partially improved, at $25.00 per acre, which we began at once to set in fruit trees. From that time to the present we have continued here in the evaporating business and from time to time have increased our orchard. In addition we now have eighty acres devoted to the nursery business, and our business in this line has been most satisfactory. We have filled large orders from dealers in the East, who regard our stock as something extra.

Our orchard is paying us well, many of our trees this season yielding us four barrels per tree of good shipping apples. These apples we sell readily in the St. Louis market at $3.00 per barrel. They are mostly of the Mammoth Pippin variety, which is unquestionably one of the finest apples grown. They are uniformly large, in color a light yellow, and of unsurpassed flavor. It is one of the apples which have made this country famous. We will add 1200 trees of this variety to our orchard this fall. Our Ben Davis, Wine Sap and other good winter-keeping apples we will gather soon, and expect to place several hundred barrels in cold storage to hold over till next spring.

We have found the cost of keeping up and caring for an orchard to be light compared with the cost in other sections. We have cultivated the land between our young trees in raspberries, blackberries and strawberries. These fruits grow here to great perfection, and we get them into the Northern and Western cities at good prices. We have had good results from our peaches, of which we have about forty acres. We believe that no part of the Union produces better peaches than this. We would not hesitate to advise all who want to engage in the fruit business to come to Northwest Arkansas.

All-Round Farming in Arkansas.

D. ·C. GITHENS, Rogers, Benton county, Ark.—I moved here from Des Moines, Iowa, in the fall of 1887. It was chiefly on account of health that I made the change. ·My wife and I found the winters too severe in Iowa, and both rapidly regained our health here and decided to make this our permanent home. I bought a farm near the town of Rogers at $25.00 per acre. The land has doubled in value. ·I am cultivating it in corn, wheat, oats and grass. I have never seen a country where clover does so well, and I get splendid crops of hay from ground that I have never seeded, the natural growth being luxuriant. This crop, like my clover, yields two cuttings in a season, but when I do not cut it the second time it gives me a good pasture throughout most of the winter for my cattle. My land in wheat yields twenty bushels to the acre, and I will gather fifty bushels of corn per acre this fall. I have a few acres of bearing orchard. In 1890 I sold from three acres $365 worth at fifty cents a bushel. I like this country very much. The winters are mild and the summers delightful. I could not be induced to return to Iowa.

From Canada to Georgia.

A. K. FISHER, Abbeville, Ga.—I came from Canada near Hamilton City. I make no claim to being a farmer, only as I have learned since coming South, mill and lumber business having been my occupation until the past few years when fortunately for me I changed. Before doing so I prospected over this State, the greater portion of Alabama. and ·Florida, and chose the pine and wire-grass section of Georgia. This section had no railroads until five years ago, but lying on Ocmulgee river it had water transportation for the cotton that was grown. But it was principally a stock country and thinly settled. They never fed either cattle or sheep'; these would become poor in winter, but by May all were in good order for beef or mutton.

Lands can be gotten for from five to ten dollars per acre. There are good openings here for farmers ; every thing in the eating line for man or beast commands good prices. Oats do well; we grow a rust-proof variety worth sixty cents per bushel. After the oats are cut in May we plow, harrow and roll the ground, and by using some fertilizers can cut from one to two tons of good hay per acre. All hay is worth $20 per ton, and the hay grown here is preferred to the Northern hay. It is called crow-foot grass or hay, and comes spontaneously after lands have been cultivated a few years. German millet does well; sown in March it is ready to cut in ninety days and is worth $20 per ton. In September this year I cut from the same land one ton good hay per acre from the native grasses without disturbing the ground after millet was taken off. No doubt alfalfa would do well here. I will give it a trial this fall.

The cattle and sheep are small, never fed in winter and never have been crossed with the improved breeds. The rule is and always has been with stock men to leave every tenth male for breeding purposes. This is a good section for fruit and stock farms. By crossing Shropshire or any good mutton buck with native ewes and feeding some during winter the lambs could be put in Baltimore market one month earlier than from Northern States.

By crossing some of the improved breeds of cattle with the native stock, good milkers can be obtained, which are worth here $40 per head. The steers by being fed in winter will bring in our home market ·fancy prices. Plenty of beef and mutton here in summer and very cheap. In winter our beef comes from the North (cold storage.)

Milk retails for five cents per quart, butter from twenty-five to forty cents per pound, and · eggs from fifteen to twenty cents per dozen.

There is no better section for peaches, pears and grapes, and some varieties of apples do well here.

This is about 31° north latitude. Lung diseases are very rare. I have lived in this county for the past ten years, and have not had a case of fever in my family or among my hands; neither have I given a single dose of quinine.

There are a few Northern families in this county. Any one coming from the North will be gladly received by the citizens.

A Well-known Ohioan in Georgia.

D. F. DeWolf, Madison, Morgan Co., Ga.—I have thought much of your inquiries and of the inquiries of those representing intelligent Germans, Danes, &c., who are now out of employment and want something more permanent than work by the day in factories. A number of such intelligent, industrious people would make this part of Georgia blossom and teem—its long seasons—I have sometimes plowed every week in the year—its great capacity for varied products—fruits, grains, cattle food, such as sorghums, of which this is the home; cow peas, whose grain and hay are the best of food for horses, hogs, and especially for milch cows. It is also the best of manures. Of the mammoth variety, which I mostly plant, I have measured 100 feet of vine from a single seed.

The land is so cheap here—$6 to $20 —more at $6 to $12 than at a higher price, all because it is owned in unprofitably large farms for the present system of labor. This renting method of tillage would bring the land of Ohio to $10 an acre in thirty years. The land responds to intelligent culture and manure the quickest of any land and retains the effects, since it is clay and sand in fitting proportions. There are millions of acres in Georgia which have never felt the healthful thrill of a plow proper, nor the quickening touch of manure, except as an occasional streak of diluted powders administered through an inch tube—a guano horn—may be called such. Plow deep. After wheat, oats, barley, &c., sow in early June, the peas. Plow these under for corn or cotton next spring. At the second hoeing of corn plant the peas to plow under in the winter. Or in September, after corn, sow red clover, which grows all winter, to plow under in April for cotton. Even if the peas and clover are fed or mowed, the long roots of both furnish a large amount of ma-

nure to plow under. The Bermuda grass makes capital pasture and winter hay. Yard and house cattle nights, and night and day in winter, for their manure, instead of buying guano exclusively. Raise corn for meal and for pork, and to feed mules at work. Raise fruits and garden stuffs to can and to sell fresh. Raise the wheat you want and for your help. All this is easily practicable to thrifty people who own farms not too large. The only difficulty is that the farms are so large and the custom of renting for cotton alone so inveterate that little of all this is done.

Hoping that we may be able to turn the attention of thrifty people with some—more or less—means this way to change all this, I have talked with our people of the necessity of selling small farms on payments. I think this will be done. All of the intelligence here sees the importance of this and would like to see the country so filled up. I find, when I go North, and through letters, the impression that the South does not desire this immigration. This is not true. And yet I can see how color is given to such a sentiment. As in any country, so here, there is occasionally a croaker who wants to buy all that joins him. He prefers that the country should look shabby that he may buy land cheap, forgetting how much more his life and the life of his family would be worth each year if the country were well filled up with prosperous, intelligent people. I think that a man with limited means, even, should have land enough to raise his corn for pork, for meal and mule feed; his grass, peas, sorghum, or fodder for cow food; his wheat for his family and his help. Poultry pays us well, though we sell neither chickens nor eggs. Our women manage to keep two to four score. They see that no kernel of grain is wasted. They lift the grubs and grasshoppers into our dinner pots. They sell well in the cities, as do butter, potatoes, turnips, etc. In short, I believe that an intelligent, industrious man can get a good living here easier than in any other country I know. People complain of hard times here as elsewhere. Why? Because they raise more cotton than the world wants, and they have to sell it too low. They also buy most of their food at an exorbitant price on credit, to be paid for out of this low price. All their meat, grain and canned goods, their potatoes, and turnips, even, for the most part, come from the North. Absolutely none of this need be. They can all be raised here easily and as certainly as elsewhere. I have raised 100 hogs in a year and bought no pound of grain to do it. I have fifty hogs now and 100 bushels of old corn at this date. It is simply a case of an easy custom on the part of large land holders to let their land to croppers who only know how to raise cotton, and who are induced to confine themselves to this for reasons given above.

Come and I will show you four adjoining farms on my street where hog and cattle food in variety and abundance is grown, as well as wheat, fruit, &c. The grain and meat raised here can be disposed of at better prices than at the West, and for cash, as they can always be used to pay labor to raise cotton, and the cotton always brings cash. But the more cows and hogs you keep to furnish manure, the more cotton you can raise per acre. Double the yield thus without guano, and the profit is almost double.

Michigan to Maryland.

W. H. BROWN, Annapolis Junction, Md.—It affords me much pleasure to give you some idea of the impression that this section of the country has made on me and my family since moving here from the State of Michigan last April.

Last October, being compelled to change our home on the account of sickness, I made an extensive tour of investigation, visiting the States of Ohio, West Virginia, New York, Pennsylvania, New Jersey and this State. And looking the country well over, I came to the conclusion, all things considered, especially the climate, that Maryland, and especially that portion of the State tributary to the Baltimore and Ohio Railroad, possessed more advantages than any part of the country that I had seen. I was so much pleased with the future prospect of this country that I decided to make it my home. I returned to Michigan, came back in March and purchased property at this place; and after being here not thirty days, could have sold out at a profit of nearly 33⅓ per cent.

The climate is all that could be wished for, neither too cold nor too hot, and vegetation and fruits of all kinds can be raised in abundance and which command good pay.

The opportunities for buying lands in this State are splendid. Improved farms can be bought at very low prices, on which the best paying crops can be raised, which find ready sale in the markets of Baltimore and Washington, D. C. Either city can be reached by good routes for hauling, distance 18 and 22 miles respectively, or by the Baltimore and Ohio Railroad, in time for the early daily markets; and as all kind of vegetables, fruits, melons, etc., are in demand, they command ready sales for cash. Trucking is one of the most profitable things that the farmer can do, and if he prefers can find a ready market at the canneries, which are located all through this country.

I also find that this State offers a great many inducements to small manufacturers in the way of sites, railroad facilities and labor; and to those seeking homes, new locations for manufacturing plants, would say that Maryland lands will bear investigation.

An Illinois Farmer in Mississippi.

T. B. GREGORY, Abbott, Miss.—I have lived here in Mississippi a little over ten years and have enjoyed good health all that time, and have known others who came here with poor health but became healthy and strong. I consider this part of Mississippi very healthy. As a farming country and for stock-raising and for truck-raising it is hard to beat. We have the finest of native grasses here for pasture on which stock thrive and get very fat.

Our climate is so mild that stock can be raised much cheaper than in the cold climate of the North, where they have to feed so long. I have grown red clover for five or six years and have proved it to be a success in this country beyond a doubt. The mint crop pays fully as well here as in Michigan.

We have good schools and churches all over the country in every neighborhood and here the society is good. Political liberties are just the same here as in Illinois and elsewhere. I am a third party man, or have been.

I was raised in Galesburg, Knox county, Illinois, and have spent a little time in Missouri and Kansas. I have farmed in all of these States and I believe this is the best country for a man of moderate means and plenty of grit.

Cheap Land, Cheap Stock, Great Possibilities.

C. S. Smith, Oak Lawn Stock Farm, Corinth, Miss.—During the last thirty-five years I have lived in Henderson county, Illinois; Washington county, Iowa, and Livingstone county, Missouri —all good counties. I have traveled over seventeen different States, and I believe this is the best country I ever saw for a poor man to live in. Any man who will work will get a home of his own here. It is a healthy and mild climate.

I have lived here five years. I did not sell my Missouri farm until last fall. It was a good farm, located within eight miles of Chillicothe, so you will see at a glance what I think of this country.

I will give you some prices: Milk cows from $5.00 to $15.00; young cattle from $2.00 to $8.00; from calves up to three-year olds; oxen from $10.00 to $30.00 per yoke or pair; it is a hard matter to give prices on hogs, for remember, they have the old-time kind. The rule for selling sows and pigs is $1.00 each for the pigs and the sows thrown in. Fat hogs, dressed, five cents, has been the price ever since I have been here, although but few are ever sold. Corn is worth fifty cents per bushel, hay from twenty-five to sixty-five cents per hundredweight, according to quality. Improved land here is worth all the way from $3.00 to $10.00 per acre, and you can raise nearly everything on it.

We do not make very big crops here and we do not make any failures. I raised eighty-one bushels and fifty-four pounds of corn on one acre last year. This is the best country for vegetables I

ever saw; sweet and Irish potatoes grow in abundance, and in fact all kinds of vegetables do well. Early and late it is a mild, pleasant climate to live in, and the people are very clever and sociable, and seem to be glad to see Northern people come here. I will say to my Northern friends there is plenty of room here and plenty of land to sell and rent. Any man who will work can buy himself a home here. You can buy cheap and on long time. I have all of my corn ground plowed. I have never seen a country where fall plowing pays as well as it does here.

I have a few words especially for my old army comrades. There are many army signs on my farm, and I frequently find relics of the war on my land. In Corinth we have a National Cemetery, which is very beautiful, nice and clean. None but Union soldiers are buried here or supposed to be. There are twenty-five acres of boys in blue buried here, with nice white marble slabs to mark the graves. There has been but one Decoration Day since I came South but what I visited the National Cemetery, and that day I was sick. The "Johnnies" always help us decorate. In order to show you there is no ill feeling between the North and the South, our crippled superintendent of the National Cemetery belongs to the Masons, Independent Order Odd Fellows, Knights of Pythias and Knights of Honor, and I believe he joined all of these orders in Corinth and holds an office in each. Comrades, you can plainly see whether a Northern man is held at arm's length or any ill feeling entertained towards Northern soldiers or any man who crosses Mason and Dixon's line.

After Eighteen Years in Minnesota.

H. F. Messer, Aberdeen, Monroe County, Miss.—I have lived nearly all my life in the North. More than twenty years ago I moved from New Hampshire to Minnesota, where I farmed until about two years ago. Then I came to this part of Mississippi on a prospecting tour, and being favorably impressed with the outlook, I returned to Minnesota and brought my family to this place last fall to spend the winter and spring and satisfy myself further as to investing here and making this my future home.

The farming seasons extend from February to the middle of October or November, and March, April, May, June, October and November are as delightful as any country. December here is similar to October in the Northwest.

Coal, wood and water are plentiful and cheap. The water is everywhere good; in many sections fine springs abound; everywhere good wells can be obtained at reasonable depths and cost, and artesian wells flowing cold streams can be had at moderate cost. On the prairie, owing to its healthful limestone understrata, the water is frequently "limed," but cisterns can be had at reasonable cost, which are filled by the winter rains, and the water is pure and cold and free from lime all through the summer, should anyone object to the lime.

In natural grasses and pasturage this portion of the country can compete with any, and is adapted to the cultivation and growth of everything that goes to make up the farmer's living. Though cotton has been the main growth, the farmers for the past two or three years have been turning their attention more to diversified crops, raising clover and stock.

The prairie soil here is peculiarly adapted to red clover and millilotus, and considerable portions of it are being sown with it. I have seen this spring as fine red clover growing here as anywhere in the North or Northwest, which means that it will be but a few years before this prairie land will be restored to its original fertility by being changed in clover and proper cultivation. It is also adapted to the growth of corn, wheat, oats and nearly all farm products, vegetables and fruits raised in the South, with railroad facilities as convenient as could be desired.

Horses, mules, cattle, hogs and sheep can also be raised as well as in any country. The healthfulness of this country will compare favorably with most any, as the appearance of the men, women and children will indicate. It is free from epidemics.

I find the people social, hospitable and neighborly, and doing all in their power to invite immigration to share in the advantages and develop the blessings of this climate and soil. These prairie lands, I find, were assessed for taxes before the war at from $30.00 to $50.00 per acre. They can be purchased now for from $8.00 to $15.00 per acre, and a few years in red clover and millilotus, with diversified crops and proper cultivation, will restore them to their original fertility.

As evidence of the Christian spirit and good morals of the people, you find here Methodist, Presbyterian, Baptist and Christian churches in nearly every neighborhood in the country, and the same in nearly all the towns, with the Episcopal and Catholic churches in addition. Free public schools, separate for whites and blacks, are established all over the State and much interest is manifested in them.

Mississippi for Farming and Stock-Raising.

E. V. HALL, Enterprise, Clarke County, Miss.—I am a Northern man; lived in Southern Minnesota thirty-three and a-half years. My occupation is farming. I raised small grain, stock, corn, hogs and hay in one county for over thirty years. Have been all over the North and West. Moved from Minnesota three and a-half years ago. Have been raising corn, cotton, stock, vegetables and hay since I have been here.

I consider it one of the best sections of country in the United States for farming and stock-raising. The soil is fair and can be made to produce enormous crops with a little commercial and home-made fertilizers. The timber and water are the best in the Union, and I believe it is the healthiest climate to be found. My wife and I have not been sick an hour since we have been here. Scarcely any sickness here at all.

I have succeeded very well since I have been here, and would not go North again to live under any circumstances. The whites as a class are very good people, kind, obliging and hospitable to all Northern people, and welcome them from whatever State they may come. I must say I am well pleased with the Southern white people.

Good land, with good timber and water, can be bought here cheaper than a settler could go West on the frontier and get it at government price. All things considered, it is a good fruit and vegetable country, and has many fine streams of pure sparkling water and plenty of fish and game.

There are many Northern people, who, if they only knew what advantages there are here, would soon be here to settle among us and enjoy the blessings of this healthy and genial climate.

Charms of East Mississippi.

W. F. LITTLE, West Point, Miss.— My experience in different parts of Mississippi and Louisiana is of six years' duration. I have spent ten years in the Mississippi Delta, and in my opinion East Mississippi and West Alabama is the most desirable portion of the South for Northern and Western emigrants to settle, for in this section they will find prairie lands equal to any of the prairies of Illinois or west of the Mississippi river. I consider them more valuable as they are equally as fertile, and in addition they are well supplied with all kinds of timber suitable for building and manufacturing purposes.

Fruits of all kinds grow luxuriantly and in abundance. Fruits fresh from the vines and trees are gathered eight months in the year. Vegetables can be had fresh from the garden twelve months in the year.

And at the present time, (September), while the pastures in Illinois and other Western States are parched and dried and farmers are compelled to haul water for their stock and feed them from the grain fields, our pastures are covered with fresh green natural grasses and all cattle are fat enough for beef. It is not only the case this year, but I have found it so every year since I came here. I have never seen it necessary to feed stock in the pastures, and nowhere is water more abundant than in this section, making it one of the finest stock countries in America.

We can raise any cereal or product that can be produced in any of the Northern or Western States and a great many other things that they cannot produce. I have peach trees three years old from the seed that have borne this year from one peck to a half a bushel per tree, and I have bearing grape vines three years old from the cuttings.

Another great advantage is that we have direct railroad communication to all Northern and Western markets, furnishing cheap transportation for vegetables, fruits and products of the truck farm. The Mobile & Ohio also connects with all lines to Eastern markets, and we are close with through transportation to the Southern and coast markets which are the best in the United States.

As a mild and delightful climate this is surpassed by none, not being as hot in summer as Northern Illinois, and seldom if ever does the mercury reach within ten degrees of zero in winter. People suffering with consumption, catarrh and bronchitis and other throat and lung troubles find almost instant relief and in many cases permanent cures, while scarlet fever and diphtheria are unknown here.

I would say to young men seeking homes who are unable to invest in the high-priced lands in the North and West, come South where you will find improved lands close to good markets for less than you can buy a homestead and improve the raw lands on the frontier, where you are compelled to haul high-priced lumber and fuel a long distance to improve the lands for which you have paid more than you can get farms all ready and fenced, with wells supplied with pure fresh water, comfortable houses, orchards and beautiful forests at the very door which afford fuel and good range and shelter for stock.

In the West they are exposed to the bleak winds and blizzards with frequently no other shelter than a barbed wire fence to split the wild winds and storms.

Here a man will find the comforts of life prepared for him as soon as he arrives, where he is free from such pests as flies, mosquitoes, buffalo gnats and green herd flies, such as he and his stock have to contend with in the North and West.

He will also find agreeable and desirable neighbors willing and ready to promote his interests in every way, and close to good schools and churches, instead of living on the vast prairies, with here and there an occasional house in the dim distance.

Well Pleased with Mississippi.

E. LeRugg, Tupelo, Miss.—I came here from South Dakota three years ago, and after looking around awhile located near Tupelo, Lee County, Miss. I found a very kind hearted and pospitable people intelligent and refined, good churches of all denominations, all working together in harmony which makes it very pleasant. Also the very best of schools; the graded schools are fully equal to any in the North. After living here three years among these people I must say I find very little difference between here and the North. A man or woman can have just such society as he or she seeks, and I wish right here to correct a prevailing feeling in the North, viz: that people from the North will be ostracized by society. Now this is a very great mistake and it is unjust to the good people in the South, and should these pages meet the eyes of any Northern friends, I wish. to say do not injure yourselves by harboring any such thoughts, for they are false in the main. I assure you that the Southern people will meet you more than half way.

As to politics I find no great difference here from the North. So far as I know all Northern people about here are Republicans and the Southern people are mostly Democrats and Populists. I am a straight-out Prohibitionist and no one has ever attempted to quarrel with me or any Republicans either. I have seen more jangling in the North than here.

Now a word about the climate. I have lived in Wisconsin, Iowa, Nevada and South Dakota, and my family and I have had better health in North Mississippi than in any of the above mentioned States. Good water, pure air and a more equal temperature are, I think, the main causes for our good health. I was always subject to rheumatism in the North but have nothing of it here.

About the resources of this country, if I should tell the truth, people would not believe it; therefore, I will simply say they are beyond computation. Such a variety of things can be successfully raised here, if rightfully managed, and marketed in the North before they can produce them and put them on the market. There are so many opportunities for raising two crops the same year, and there are but three months in the year that one cannot have fresh fruits on the table, of his own raising, if he will. Corn, oats, potatoes, and in some places wheat, do well here; also vegetables of all kinds. Floriculture is coming to the front in this part of Mississippi, and some of our women are making hundreds of dollars each year in this line.

Why will the Northern people still persist in remaining in that cold country when there are so many of heaven's blessings in store for them in the Southern country? I would not go back to the North to live even if I were offered the best farm as a gift. No, gentlemen, no more North in mine. I came South to make a home for myself and family, where the comforts of life can be enjoyed, and I can truly say to the South, "your people shall my people be, and your God shall be mine." Now if anyone will take the trouble to call upon me, three miles West of Tupelo, I shall be glad to see him, or if anyone writes to me I will cheerfully answer.

Good for Fruit and Stock.

Herbert A. Pennock, Goldsboro, N. C.—I have been living here over a year now, and formerly lived in Southeastern Pennsylvania. I am engaged in fruit-growing principally, but also am raising some shrubbery and nursery stock. The climate and soil seems to suit fruit and berries here finely. I think this is also a fine section of the country for stock-raising, especially for sheep and poultry. In this mild climate, with a proper selection of grasses, the stock-raiser could have pasturage nearly all the year round. I find the people here very hospitable and neighborly.

Around Chattanooga.

F. J. BENNETT, Chattanooga, Tenn.— The greatest opportunities for the average farmer lie in locations near cities, for here he always has a market for much of his produce, if not all, and as cities have ready traffic lines, the surplus can be handled at will to other markets. Then, of scarcely less importance is the great supply of cheap fertilizers.

No locality of all the Southern States offers so many substantial inducements to the small farmer as the Chattanooga section. The value of our varied soils has, until recently, been entirely overlooked and underestimated. Vegetable and fruit growing have been followed with marked success, and in every instance when the care and culture required have been given, paying results have followed, but recently tobacco, hops and peanuts are promising well. In fact, our people are just realizing the truth that our varied soils and range of elevation, mild climate, with its regular rainfall during growing season, are conditions which are seldom found and always desirable. Chattanooga has about 100 miles of macadamized and gravelled roads, which make hauling easy and rapid, and in place of 500 or 800 pounds making a full load one ordinary mule team handles from one to two tons at a load.

All of one-third more outdoor work can be accomplished here than in any Eastern or Northern State. All outdoor labor is infinitely more pleasant even in summer, for we never have sultry, oppressively close atmospheric conditions, such as prevail over most of the balance of the country. The temperature seldom reaches 95° in summer and averages above zero in winter. Lands are cheap, and any class can be had from first river bottoms, which will produce an average of seventy-five bushels of corn to the acre, to the thin, gravelly soils, which will not produce more than ten bushels. The lands range in price from $70 per acre to $5, but it must be remembered that for fruit and some of the vegetables the thin lands are much

more preferable. I have seen a net $100 per acre cleared from the $5 and $10 soils for successive years.

Profits in Virginia Hay Farms.

A. JEFFERS, Norfolk, Va.—Throughout almost the entire South the grass crop is either very sadly neglected or entirely ignored until it has become almost a general idea at the North, West and East that grass cannot be successfully or profitably grown at the South. Now I have spent a little more than fourteen years in the South, during which time I have been engaged in dairying, market gardening and general farming.

From my own experience, and from observation of the experiences of others, I am prepared to say that every acre of land within twenty or thirty miles of this city will grow clover as satisfactorily as any land in the United States. Much of it will grow good timothy, although, as a rule, the land is not quite stiff enough for timothy. Clover, orchard grass, millet, oats and rye can be grown to perfection. The vines of the peanut make most excellent hay for milch cows and mules. Ton for ton, it will make more milk than clover hay.

All, or nearly all, vacant lands in July send up a crop of grass called "crap" or "crop grass," because it comes in after crops maturing in midsummer have been taken off the land. Such grass yields from one to two tons per acre, and there is not a cent of expense attached to the crop except for cutting and storing it, and it is worth as much as clover hay, ton for ton, to feed on the farm. The white and red clover take the berry beds the third year after berries are set out, and sometimes the second year. Purely volunteer crops of clover have been sold standing at $20.00 per acre for the first cutting, and the second cutting was plowed under and the following February planted in potatoes, which brought to the owner a net profit of more than $100 per acre.

A few years since a practical Pennsylvania farmer came here to buy a farm. After looking the matter over thoroughly, he selected a farm at the price of $10,000, paying down one-fourth the purchase money and giving notes for the balance, payable $1000 annually. He is making his deferred payments in hay grown on the farm. Where else in the United States would a man be justified in attempting to do this? He raises about 100 tons of hay yearly. He sells it in this market at prices ranging from $15.00 to $18.00 for timothy, and $12.00 to $14.00 for clover, or clover and orchard grass mixed.

As this seaport city receives from the North and West about 2000 tons of hay per month, one can see that it would take a great many hay growers here to supply our home demand. It is estimated that we have within a 20-mile limit of this city between 50,000 and 60,000 acres of land used for market-gardening purposes, for which purpose no better lands nor better location can be found in the world. Within this same limit is another 50,000 or 60,000 acres of very fine grass land lying almost entirely idle. Our farmers are playing with might and main on a fiddle with only one string—truck. With thousands upon thousands of acres of good hay lands lying idle, we are allowing the other sections of the Union to send us from 20,000 to 25,000 tons of baled hay per annum. These fine hay lands range in price from $10.00 to $50.00 per acre, and if put into grass, by intelligent cultivation, they will pay for themselves with two annual crops of hay, and often with one crop. We can give any number of names of parties who are raising hay and raising it successfully and profitably.

Let the Michigan farmer come here and raise hay at $18.00 per ton instead of raising it for us in Michigan at $5.00 per ton. We have the soil, the climate and the market; all we need is the man. We want the men to intelligently press the agricultural button; nature will do the rest.

Virginia as a Fruit Country.

HENRY L. LYMAN, Charlottesville, Va.—It gives me pleasure to be able to say that the opportunities afforded Northern and Western people who settle here are as good as can be reasonably wished for by any active, enterprising class, if the active pursuits of life be followed, and as pleasant and beneficial as any I have ever read of or experienced, if the restoration of health or prolongation of life be the object. A locality which so happily combines the two features is hard to find.

The man who comes into this section and exercises the same elements of thrift and strict attention to business which necessarily characterize his actions in any other locality, finds more advantages and opportunities for making money than in any other known to me. We raise good horses and mules, live stock of all kinds, and especially sheep, garden truck, grains, hay, have good pastures with any sort of care, and our fruits are as good as the best from any part of this broad land. Then, too, the original outlay need not be large, as is the case in so many of the extensively advertised localities.

The special adaptability of our State for fruit culture is strikingly prominent this year, and we are favored with buyers from Cincinnati, Columbus, Chicago, St. Louis, Cleveland, Pittsburg, the far West, New York, Philadelphia, Boston and Europe. It may interest your readers to know that the shippers or buyers of apples here are claiming that the Chesapeake & Ohio Railway train service is better, their ventilated fruit cars are finer, and their rates lower than is the case from any of the Northern or Eastern points from which they have shipped heretofore; furthermore, these gentlemen say that they "have come to stay."

In this connection another important advantage presents itself to my mind, viz: In procuring empty casks, barrels, and other packages for shipment or stowage of crops and vintages, we find the supply over the Chesapeake & Ohio Railway comes to us at less cost, quicker time and at less freight than from the old points of supply. Anyone desirous of purchasing a home will do well to consider what better he can do than to take some one of the many good chances which are offering in our State. I will give the illustration of a farm offered last fall at a price which was entirely covered by the value of the crop of apples this year. I am happy to state that this is not the invariable rule, however.

No better element of American civilization exists than that which is found here, and any anxiety on the score of "ostracism" is as useless here as elsewhere.

A Pennsylvanian in the Shenandoah Valley.

J. K. SNAVELY, Harrisonburg, Va.— Having traveled through the State of Virginia for a number of years, I desire to give you my impression of the great Shenandoah Valley, the granary of the South, from a standpoint, for investment and stock-raising.

In Pennsylvania, where I resided, Lancaster county is called the "garden spot." Then in Virginia, Rockingham county certainly deserves the same consideration in which the city of Harrisonburg is located, being the county seat, in the vicinity of which quite a number of Pennsylvanians, with myself, have made investments, and believe there is no place where the outlook for profitable returns is more certain. The mineral and timber lands are much cheaper, in fact not 10 per cent. of the cost in Pennsylvania, and the opportunity for development with the prospects for coal in the mountains and in proximity to Harrisonburg is simply remarkable, and I see no reason why the products will not soon be brought into the market. As to farming, the farmers are a thrifty, well-to-do class, and probably no place in the United States feels so little the great financial depression now on the country. However, even with money in bank and practically out of debt, they are much worried about the present price of wheat, as this year they will lose by the low price.

Some attention has been given to stock-raising. In fact Harrisonburg is the great stock market of the State of Virginia, and I find men so engaged are making money. The proposed stock farm at Harrisonburg is regarded with a great deal of interest, as that would bring directly to their doors all classes of pure-bred stock, it being the intention to bring not only the best of sheep and hogs, but dairy and beef cattle, as well as all the varieties of light-legged horses. Owing to the proximity of the great cities, a large per cent. can be saved in shipment, and by having some of all kinds of live stock will be able to secure a steady business.

There is not a cheese factory in this part of the State, and as the merchants pay twelve and one-half to fifteen cents per pound at wholesale, there is a handsome market for anyone who will start in this enterprise.

As all kinds of fruits and berries are produced in this section in abundance, and the tomato and small vegetables grow luxuriantly, no better place could be found for a canning factory.

With an elevation of 1300 feet above sea level, Harrisonburg is filled with summer boarders and is practically a summer resort, being surrounded with the finest mineral springs in the world, the noted Massanetta Springs being within a few miles, and Bear Lithia, Rawley and Orkney Springs and many others of less note within easy reach. The climate is as noted for its health-giving qualities, as the people of this section are for their hospitality.

Although this is a white section, very little slavery having existed here previous to the war, especially in the county of Rockingham, the people are very evenly divided politically, the county giving Cleveland but one of a majority at his first election and Harrison several hundred, and again Cleveland carries it by about the same majority as Harrison.

Truly this is the heart of the Shenandoah Valley, surrounded by an agricultural section of from twenty to forty miles wide, and certainly nature has blessed it with fertility of soil and all that man could wish. The sheep men show 100 per cent. profit in their business. In fact, parties from the North are here now talking of buying a large tract of the cheap lands lying on the hillside to stock with sheep.

If these projected enterprises go ahead as they may be expected to, they will be the forerunners of many more, as the farmers are just waiting to go into the stock business.

Certainly no country on earth is better

fitted for the stock business than this section. The fine blue grass, the best friend the farmer has, and which he has been for years trying to kill by constantly raising corn and wheat, grows luxuriantly. The limestone soil makes it exceptionally rich in nitrogen, so valuable to make good growth of bone and muscle and fine mutton. Spring water on every farm ; markets at their door ; climate unexcelled. What more does one need to encourage them to buy a farm here and go into the stock business ?

HUMP-BACK, ·VA.

By Frank H. Sweet.

Massive and solemn, with its grand old head
    Uncovered to heaven and time's decay,
    Counting the ages as a passing day,
Guarding the valleys that its streams have fed,
And linking the peaks of the watershed :
    Now, clothed in its garments of winter gray,
    Then, shedding its gloom, and becoming gay
When its woods are dressed in their gold and red—
Forming bold eyries for the eagle's nest,
    And copse and covert for the beast and bird,
    And broad, green pastures for the farmer's herd ;
Calm and genial, and a place to rest
For the mountain folk, or the passing guest,
    Where the voices of mountain elves are heard.

"WILLER WAN'S."

By Rebekah M. Sayre.

It was noon in Alabama, before the war, and the old bell on the cane-brake plantation rang out, loud and clear: "ding-dong, ding-dong, ding-dong-dell."

The sound had a magical effect on the farm hands; all stopped work instantly, dropping their hoes in the half worked rows, and leaving the plough shares deep in the furrows. Even the mules understood, and remained motionless from the first sound until their dusky drivers were mounted, then ambled toward the quarters.

"Ding-dong, ding-dong," still rang out through the hot, sultry air.

"'Pears like dat bell got witch in it," said one of the hands, as he listened to a fresh peal.

"Yah," cried another, "doan tek no sich racket as dat ter lemme know when's dinner ready."

"Nor me, neither," grumbled others. But two pickaninnies who were trotting dangerously near the old gray mule's heels understood it all.

"Bet yer piece of sweet gum," panted the younger, "dats Marse Will, er little Missy, pullin' dat bell."

"Hi! whut yer tek me fer," cried the elder," did'nt dey tell me dis mawnin' dat dey wuz gwine fer ter do it?"

In the meantime the old horse-lot had been witnessing a busy scene. Marse Will was only a little barefoot boy eight years old that day, and very much excited at present, as he dangled to and fro in the air. The brown legs flew dangerously near little Missy's yellow curls in his efforts to keep his balance, but the short rope and heavy bell were almost too much for him.

"Get out the way, Win," he cried, as little Missy made a frantic grab at his coat so that she could help ring too. "I bet they heard that," he said triumphantly, as he let the rough rope slip from his little red hands. "Goodness! don't they sting," pausing to dip them into the old horse-trough bubbling over with cool water. "You need'nt tell Jim so," he added, "for he bet I could'nt ring it by myself, an' I did," and his big brown eyes sparkled with pride.

"But I helped, too," said Win, looking up wistfully from under a mass of curls, "for did'nt I bring the rocks for you to stand on?"

"Pooh! what good did that do?" cried Will, "I could have jumped high enough to reach the rope, 'cept I was 'fraid I might pop my new pants. Never mind," he said, as the blue eyes were beginning to moisten, "you know this is my birthday, and father promised that Jim and Tan could play with us after twelve, an' I promised to ring loud so they could hear real quick and—hooray! there they are now; bet I can reach 'em first," and off he ran.

The race was a short one, for five-year-old Winnie, who soon stumbled and fell, but being a philosophical little maiden she jumped up and seated herself on the edge of the trough to wait for the boys, and think of the "Sally Lunn" mammy had promised them for supper if they were good—when, "Hi, Win! look behind you," made her start, lose her balance and topple over into the cold water.

It was an old-fashioned trough, hollowed out of a huge poplar log, and Will heartily repented of his thoughtless prank before the little shivering sister was again on dry land.

"Better go ter de house an' lem

mammy dry yer," remarked Tan, as the crestfallen party looked blankly at each other.

"Oh, no," wailèd Win, "mammy's in the cellar makin' pickle, an' she said we couldn't have no cake for supper 'less

"I WOULD BE A REAL BOY IF IT WAS NOT FOR MY HAIR."

we were good until mamma an' papa came home, an' my dwesses are all locked up—boo-o."

Here a bright idea flashed over Will. "Say Win," he whispered, "would you mind wearing pants?"

"Haven't got any," sobbed she.

"But I have, an' if you'll hush crying an' steal in the back way, I'll show you how to put them on."

It had been the regret of Win's short life that she was not a boy, and the idea of playing one for awhile was not at all disagreeable to her, besides no one would know. Mammy was deep in tomato pickle and Sarah Jane, under whose care she had been placed, had charged her to be good while she stepped down the road to see if the wild goose plums were ripe, and Win knew by experience how long that would be.

"It is a good thing I noticed where mammy put 'em," said Will, when they had scampered into his room.

"Here they are," drawing out a small brown linen suit. "I've outgrown them, an' reckon mammy was going to fix them for someone else, but they will fit very well, if you roll up the legs a little. Now," he said, proudly, as she danced before the glass, "you would make a first rate boy, if it was not for those curls. Come on, but lemme go first, an' if the way is clear I'll whistle Dixie."

"All right," answered Win, absently, for her little mind had seized a great idea. She slipped in front of the tall mirror in mamma's room and took a long look. "Yes," she said, nodding approvingly at her other self, "I would be a real boy if it was not for my hair." Then she drew a long shining tress between her fingers, shut her eyes, and snip, snap from the sharp scissors and the pretty curl was gone.

Conscience here smote Win a little. "What would mamma think?" But then she had heard her say only yesterday that she wished girls' clothes were as easy to make as boys', and now she would have no more trouble.

Here the dying strains of Dixie were borne to her ear; no more time to wrangle with conscience. Clip, clip, clip, and the deed was done. "I don't look so pretty," she said, "but now I am a boy it don't matter. Won't papa be s'prised!" and jamming her big hat down on the shorn locks, she stole softly down the stair, leaving a muddy dress and a shining heap of curls on the floor.

"You were a mighty long time," whispered Will, "we're goin' down the branch, but won't the rocks hurt your feet?"

"Not much," said Win bravely, "an' p'raps Jim will carry me over the briers."

"Chillins, whut is yer doin'?" cried the well-known voice of mammy as they passed the cellar window.

"Sittin' on the grass, replied Will, promptly taking that position with great speed and causing unconscious Win to do the same.

"Dat's right, doan git inter no mischief, case I wants ter gib er good report to yer maw ter night."

"All right," answered Will, "can we go to the spring with Jim?"

"I reckon so, but tell Sary Jane not

ter let Missy git wet. I dun fixed yer lunch an' lef' it on de watermilion block; now be good chillins," and mammy was left with wrinkled brow wondering if it was one or two cups of mustard she had put in last.

"I'll tote de basket," volunteered Tan, when Will and Win had returned to the lot; "an' you can tote me Jim," cried Win. This was an unexpected pleasure to Jim.

"Whar, Sary?" he demanded, "I 'spec yer can't go widout her."

"Well the lunch can't go either," cried Win sharply, "for mammy said 'twas mine, too."

Tan closed the dispute by walking off with the basket, quickly followed by Will with a broken fishing rod, Jim and Missy forming the rear guard, the former "lowing he'd tote her part de way." On they marched through the shady lot and down the sunny lane and pasture, where Win stopped to count the little red and white calves knee deep in clover. Then on again beyond the great chestnut, where a halt was called to allow Marse Will time to extract the prickles from his feet, then on to the cool dark woods where the sun only broke through in fitful gleams.

"Now put me down, Jim," cried little Missy, "I want to walk some, the ground feels so nice," digging her little hot toes into the cold soft mud.

"Don't you think our spring is prettier an' Cap'n White's, Jim?" she added, as a sudden turn brought them to a spot where the sparkling water gushed from under the roots of a huge sweet gum.

"Course 'tis," answered Jim, "doan yer want some ter drink," and pulling a leaf he twisted it into cone shape and pinned it with a thorn. "Oh, it tastes so sweet and good," and the little cup was filled many times before thirsty Win cried enough.

"Now let's eat" met with a hearty response, and soon the great white flint rock, which Win called their table, was fairly loaded. To begin with there was a whole fried chicken browned just right, and ever so many sandwiches with the pinkest of ham peeping from the whitest of beds.

"An' I do b'leve there are lebenteen hard boiled eggs," declared Win, "besides a large loaf of ginger bread."

"An' now I finks I'll say grace" 'cause papa likes me to," she added, glancing around approvingly. Then taking off her hat she bowed her little head reverently and began:

"Dear Lord make us truly—" when

"WONDERING IF IT WAS ONE OR TWO CUPS OF MUSTARD SHE HAD PUT IN LAST."

"La Missy! whar yo' har" come in frightened tones from Tan. For a moment there was silence, then Will found his tongue.

"Winnie, what have you done," he cried.

Then Win began to whimper: "You need'nt holler at me that way, Will Gordon, I did it cause you told me to."

"I did'nt," cried Will, hotly.

"Well, you 'minded me of it, anyhow; you said that if I cut off my hair I'd be a real boy, an' I did it, there."

"You are a goosey," retorted Will, "and are no more a boy now than you were before, and—what will mamma say?"

Tan now luckily stepped in as peacemaker, for Will was very angry, and the tears were fast chasing each other down Win's rosy cheeks. "Doan cry so, Missy," said he, "yer har'll soon grow back, an' I'll run an' brung yer some plums, den we'll hab dinner." These words had a magical effect, and the good spirits of the company were entirely restored when Tan returned with Win's straw hat overflowing with big red and yellow plums.

How they did eat, for all had a sharp appetite, and there was a race to see who could eat the most.

"Listen ter dat bell ringin' mity peart," said Tan, as he nibbled a chicken leg discarded by Win.

"Hi!" laughed Jim, "dats fer de niggers dats got ter work, but we's big folks ter day. Come on, de plums is cold."

Soon they were all ranged round the mossy old spring, and four bright faces were reflected from its clear surface. Two were fair and two were dark; clear and distinct they were mirrowed for a moment, then the verging ripples blended them in one, and eight hands were plunged in in a flash. The ripe fruit was icy cold and met with a very warm reception.

"I wonder who first found this spring," said Will, meditatively, trying to decide between a red plum and a yellow one.

"I 'spose Unck' Jake did," answered Jim, "he foun' most all 'em round here."

"How did he find them?" asked Will, much interested.

"With willer wan's, of course, did you nebber hear tell ob dat?" with an air of pride at knowing something Marse Will did'nt know. "Yer tek er piece er willer jist three foot long an' peel it, an' den yer dip it in wateh ter let it know whut yer wants ter fin', an'—"

Here the story was interrupted by the arrival of Sarah Jane, who stolidly sat down and became a silent listener, while Win nestled behind Will so as not to attract untimely notice.

"Den," went on Jim in a solemn voice, "yer teks de wan' an' tu'n round three times wid yer eyes shet, an' den yer walk de way yer face is tu'n de las' time, an' when de wan' dip down, dere is de spring."

"Is that true?" cried Will.

"Course 'tis true, ain't I seen it myself?"

"Le's see if us kin fin' one in de cawn fiel'," suggested Tan, "I'll git de willers."

"Now whut mus' us do?" he asked, when he had returned with an armful.

"Peel 'em," answered Jim, producing a battered jack-knife which had been given him that morning by Will, who had found a bright pearl-handled one under his breakfast plate, while poor Tan, in lieu of something better, was forced to nibble the bark off his wand with his strong white teeth. Win tried that experiment, but found the bark so bitter that she decided to wait until Jim could do it for her. Then the length of the wand caused much discussion; how much was three feet. There were five pairs of feet present, but no two were the same size. Will thought Jim's too long and Win's too short, but Tan suggested they might find the spring quicker if the wands were longer, so they decided in Jim's favor and all four wands were dipped into the water.

"Which way mus' we go?" asked Win.

"I'm gwine in de cawn fiel'," said Tan.

"Yer dun no which way yer gwine," cried Jim, "yer tu'n roun' an' de way de wan' pint de las tu'n is de way; now tu'n."

All promptly began to turn.

"Sit down, Win," cried Will, "you can't go."

"I'LL GIT DE WILLERS."

"Why?"

"'Cause you are a girl and can't, sides mamma would'nt like it; you stay here."

"Can't Jim carry me?"

"Will wavered but Jim did'nt: "How could his wan' pint right if he had to tote Missy?" "Yer better stay here," he said solemnly, "somefin' mght hap'en; de wan' might pint in de crik or thro' pizen oak; no, t'wont do, Missy, but when I fin' de spring I'll come an' fotch yer. Now le's turn."

Little Win's eyes fairly swam through a mist of tears; the three boys became a dozen and the turns likewise multiplied. She threw herself on the ground and sobbed aloud. She could'nt go because she was a girl after all, and her pretty curls were gone too. "Sarah!" she cried presently, "Sarah Jane!" but a prolonged snore was the only answer.

"Well, if she has'nt gone to sleep a'ready," said Win, "an' right in the sun. I know what I'll do," and her eyes grew bright with mischief. "I'll go an' fin' a spring by myse'f, an' get back 'fore those boys."

Then standing erect as a general she paused, grasping the wand with both tiny hands, all unconscious of the sweet picture she made, the winsome face crowned with rough golden locks, a tear still lingered on her rosy cheek, the brown suit was almost black now, and only one trouser leg was rolled up. The pretty mouth smiled for a moment to think how she was getting ahead of the boys, but quickly grew serious again, her dark eyes closed and the mystic turn was thrice made. Then Win looked up, half expecting to see some strange country, but there were only the old spring and bit of woods, and through the open patches were the familiar fields of cotton and corn shimmering in the heat.

"Now, march!" she repeated sternly, remembering Will's words. Then she followed the wand through the woods into the fields beyond. The sun almost blistered her feet, and the wind made such a funny noise as it rustled through the grain, that Win was a wee bit frightened just at first. Then her hat was knocked off, and the end of the wand got broken, too, and it was hard to tell

which way it pointed. After wandering for a long time, Win noticed that the rows of corn seemed to be growing thinner, then abruptly stopped on the edge of a pine forest. Win climbed on the rail fence which surrounded the field and gazed around. To tell the truth, she did not like the looks of those dark woods one bit, but she was a plucky child, raised in the country, and as the end of the wand still pointed towards them, she followed with the blind faith of childhood.

"The walkin' is better, anyway," said Win to herself, for the cool brown needles that carpeted the ground were a pleasant contrast to the hot sand. But before long the glossy needles gave her several severe pricks, and she was finally forced to sit down and comfort her feet. As it was a pleasant resting place for her tired back, Win lay down and faced the dark trees and bits of blue sky. Presently a frisky squirrel whisked by like a flash of gray light, then a scarlet woodpecker startled her with his solemn tap, tap, and a musical tinkle was wafted to her ears, while a pair of eyes began to grow drowsy. "I'll shut them for a minute," thought Win, "then I'll find that spring, for I believe I hear it now," and she did.

But what of the boys all this time?

Hasty Will, in his excitement, had no time to note where his feet trod, provided that the precious wand was not interfered with, and he had several falls in consequence, and as luck had it, ran full tilt against mammy who was gathering sage in the garden.

"An' so yer done tore dem new breeches," she remarked severely as soon as she saw him.

"Geminetti! so I have," he cried in dismay as his eyes fell on a long snag. "How did I do it?"

"De Lawd on'y knows, I doan. Go straight ter dat house an' tek 'em off an' fotch 'em ter my room."

"What am I to wear?" interrupted Will, "all the rest is in the wash."

"No dey aint, dere's a pair I pit in yer room dis mawnin; its just scanderlus. Whut yer been doin'?"

"Huntin' for springs," was the mumbled reply.

"Huntin' fur springs! Dat Jim put yer up ter dat, I lay, an' I'll spring him wid er piece o' leather, and is Missy huntin' em too?"

"No'm, she's with Sarah."

"Well, go ter dat house an' stay till I come. Nebber seen sich er chile in my born life. Whut yer maw gwi' say 'bout dem new breeches?"

It was with a slow step and anxious heart that Will entered the house. He must leave his pants in mammy's room, so he proceeded to do so. He couldn't think of putting on his Sunday pair without permission, and Win had the others. What could he do? Win's dress was dry enough for her to wear now if she would only come back. The tears welled up in the little fellow's eyes; he knew that Jim and Tan had found lots of springs by now. Then his eyes fell on a gayly bound Robinson Crusoe, but it was not near so attractive now as it was that morning when his mother drew it from under his pillow. Will began to feel repentant; he was real sorry that Win fell in the trough, for after all that was the beginning of his troubles. "Well," he said, heaving a great sigh, "I can't get Win an' I can't get my pants, an' now I can't find any springs, so I b'lieve I'll slip up in the garret and read Robinson Crusoe till she comes back."

And what of Jim and Tan?

They had both followed their respective wands which were evidently possessed with restless spirits, and from the sudden turns they made were surely after the same spring, for though starting in entirely different directions both boys soon found themselves in the watermelon patch to their mutual astonishment.

"Hi! how cum you here," asked Jim.

. "De wan' pint dis way," answered Tan feebly.

"Dat's sure curyus," cried Jim, "yer start in de cawn fiel'; how kin de wan' pint two ways?"

"'Twuz jist de same way yourn did," cried Tan, "how yer tu'n roun' so peart?" But Jim declined to enter into explanations.

"Sho as I lib I b'lieve dat millon's cracked," pointing to a large green one basking at his feet. Whereupon Tan solemnly rapped it three or four times, and "'lowed if 'twar not cracked, 'twuz sure ober-ripe."

"I'll plug it an' see," suggested Jim, "case Marser tole Simon yistiddy not to

"BOTH BOYS SOON FOUND THEMSELVES IN THE WATERMELON PATCH."

bring air other rotten millon ter dat house."

"Hi! 'tis sure good," as the large plug was transferred to his mouth.

"No, niggah," in reply to Tan's expostulations of 'gimme er piece,' "dis un is mine, 'case I foun' it, but if dere is air other ober·ripe un yer kin fin' why yer kin hab it," and it is needless to say that Tan soon searched and found.

Sarah Jane napped long and sweet, until her slumbers were disturbed by a pig rooting under her feet in search of dinner. "Go long, horg," she said, giving it a sleepy kick, and settling herself for another doze. But piggy's sharp little nose had smelt chicken, and with a short grunt it returned to the charge, causing Sarah Jane to collect her scattered wits to some extent.

"Missy, ain't yer hongry?" she asked, after a prolonged yawn, but a grunt from the pig was her only reply. "Missy! Missee! whar is yer?" she cried; then, gazing blankly around, her eyes fell on the pig contentedly crunching a bone.

"Oh, Lawd!" she cried in terror, "I do b'lieve dat horg done eat Missy up; but no, dat aint nuttin but chicken laig in dat peeg's mouf. I 'spec' she gone ter de house ter mammy. I better go see; I'se hongry, too," and Sarah Jane sauntered up to the house. As she entered the yard she met mammy returning from the garden with a great basket of sage balanced on her head.

"Whar Missy?" she demanded at once.

"Aint her wid you?" cried Sarah.

"Course she aint wid me; did'nt I put her under your special charge dis mawnin, an' now yer dun loss her."

"No I aint, neither," retorted Sarah, "her wuz playin' down de spring wid Marse Will, an' I knows hers wid him."

"No she aint," cried mammy, "case I dun sont him up ter de house, and he lay dat Missy wuz wid you."

"Den her gone off wid dat no 'count Jim an' Tan, an I go fin' em."

"Well, yer better be quick, gal," cried mammy, "fer if she aint here 'fore marser comes home yer'll hab to hear whuts he got ter say ter folks dat purposely losses his chillin," and she hurried into the house to interview Marse Will.

"I nebber wuz so scairt sence de night jedgement start ter come, an' all de stars in de elements fall," mammy confided to Unc' Jake that night, "as whens I went up stairs an' fin' Missy's muddy frock an' har on de flo', and Marse Will nowhar foun'. I knowed dat ole rabbit did'nt jump out dem jimsin weeds an' cross my pa'f fer nuttin. An' dat idgit, Sarah, doan know nuttin 'bout em, an' we hunt, an' hunt, an' could'nt fin' em nowhar, an' den it grow late, so I walk out in de front yard so as ter be de fust

ter tell Miss', case I knowed de niggers ud scairt her. An' dere was dat triflin' Sary Jane skulking fust 'hind er rose bush den 'hind dem jasmines, makin' lik she still huntin', but I mistrusted her, an' fust ting I know she holler out, 'dere dey come,' an' say she run open de gate, an' I tel' Sary ter fotch some water, an' I'd go myse'f. But she dat aggervating she bresh pas' me, an' I hear her screech out: 'has yer foun' em', even 'fore de horses git ter de gate.

"An' Miss' tu'n so white I try ter pacify her tell'n how twuz jist dat no 'count Sary's fault gwine ter sleep an' lettin' dat Jim run off wid her. An' Miss' look so faint, marser tell her he fin' em directly, dey jist hide'n, an' den he holp her up stairs, an' call Sary ter bring some fresh water. An' yer b'lieve dat triflin' gal didn't stop to 'spute wid me bout totin in dem bundles, an' was tryin ter peek in dem ter see if Miss' dun forgot de dress she promised her.

"I was dat outdone I jist upped an' lam her sides the haid, an' dat ongrateful gal give sich er screech dat Marser cum runnin' down agin', thort some'in de matter wid his chillin. An' den Miss' fin' little Missy clothes an' har on de flo'; she holler loud as Sary. I aint nebber seen Marser so mad afore since Randy hit he ridin' horse. He eyes jist blaze, an' he look at me an' Sary like he could tar us to pieces; but he grit he teef an' did'n say nuttin to we, jist tu'n ter Miss' an' say some'n bout chillins' pranks, an' he fin' 'em d'rectly an' tell me not ter lef her, an' run down stairs."

"An' us war hidin' under de hen house," Tan told mammy afterward, "case little Tobe dun tell us bout de chillin', and so when Marser call us didn't ans'er, tell dat ole long Tom come stretch he-sef under de house an' grab us by de laig an' pull us out."

"An' Marser ax whar de chillin, an' us could'nt tell him, I thought he'd mos' go 'stracted. Den Sary say, 'Marse Will in de gyarden not so long go, an' he breeches whut he tore in mammy's room now.'"

"Den Marser tell big Tobe an' Sam ter hunt round de barn an' stables, an' tell Randy ter ax at de quarter, an' den tell me an' Jim ter go strait ter dat spring, an' show him 'zactly which er way us took, 'case her mought hev followed us. An' Jim did'n know which er way ter tu'n, 'case us wuz thinkin' bout dem millons, an' atter while he mek fer de cawn fiel', but he turn so menny times dat Marser gro 'spicious, an he grab Jim by he jacket an' say he doan want no more foolin', an' Jim gin ter cry, an' jist den I pick up er leetle handcher whut Missy dun chew up at de cornder, an' Marser snatch it, jist like t'war som'en gole.

"Den he pint at som' leetle prints in de groun', an' he say, 'dems my baby's tracks, but whut she doin barfoot,' an' I upped an' tole him bout Missy fallin' in de trof, an warin' Marse Will's clo'es an' cuttin' her har, an' he say nebber min' dat, jist so he fin' her. An' den I see one star cum out, an' de moon peeked ober dem pines jest as bright as day, but I knowed afore us wuz gwi' hab trouble, case I seen it fust time fro' dat swee' gum tree when I wuz drivin de cows from de pastur'. Den Jim went on, an' Marser right ahind, follerin' dose tracks, till dey run 'ginst dat fence by dat 'simmon tree, whar Randy ketch de bob-tail coon las' fall. An' I hear one o' dem scrich owls holler lik' somen' gwi' hap'en, an' I tole Marser her would'n gone ober in dem dark woods, but he dun jump dat fence wid Jim, an' I 'bleeged ter foller, 'case I skeered ter stay dere by myse'f.

Den Jim fin' er piece er willer he say cum off Missy's wan' but us did'nt fin' nuttin' else, do we hunt an' hunt, an' Marser call out all de names he could think on 'ter her, but her did'nt ans'er an' atter while he say us better tu'n roun' an' go back, an' I sure glad ter hear it, case dat owl 'gin ter holler ergin. Presen'ly I hearn some'n tinkle, an' I tell Marser soun' lik' runnin' watah, an' Jim la'f at me, but sure 'nouf dere wuz er branch, and Marser say dere mus' be wet wedder spring round dere, an' us foller it an' den I seen some'n white an' Jim 'low t'war er rock.

But when Marser seen it he aint say nuttin', he jist run up an' stoop ober it, an' sure 'nouf 'twar leetle Missy curled up in de pine straw fas' asleep wid her haid res'in on her arm, an' her look lik' sho 'nouf leetle boy in Marse Will's breeches an' short ha'r; an' in her odder han' she holt dat broken sweetch o' willer, an' 'fore gracious de end ob dat wan' pint rite ter dat spring.

"An' when her paw lean ober wid de lante'n, an' de light shine in her face, she open her eyes fer er minnit an' say: 'I knowed yer come an' fin' me,' an' when her nestle up in he arms she shet em ergin, an' nebber did tell howcum she fin' dat spring.

"Den her maw, wid Marse Will, cum runnin' down de road as soon as dey see de lante'n, an' Marse Will holler at her, an' ax her, 'whar she been,' an' her ans'er,' findin' springs,' jist as peart like. An' Marser whisper som'in in her year, an' she ax whar he been, an' Marse Will la'f sorter shamelike an' say: 'sleep in de garret.'"

A SOUTHERN SLUMBER SONG.

By Beulah R. Stevens.

> Wave, breeze,
> Thro' the trees!
> Sing a lullaby tonight.
> Bright star,
> From afar
> Send thy twinkling light.
> Moon, sail,
> Pure and pale;
> Watch our slumbers deep:
> Now, thro' all the night hours still,
> Loving vigil o'er us keep.

> Cloudlets float,
> Like fairy boat
> On a dark blue sea.
> Mock-birds sing
> Songs of spring,
> Carols blithe and free:
> Baby, rest
> On mother's breast,
> Close thy drowsy eyes:
> Star and moon and breeze and bird
> Sing thee loving lullabies!

> Primrose, wake
> By the lake,
> Lift thy golden head so bright.
> Moonflower fair,
> Kiss the air
> With thy lips so white.
> Wavelets toss
> Reed and moss,
> Lap thy banks so still,
> While thro' all the nightfall's hush
> Sounds the mournful whip-poor-will.

> Fairies, sing
> In your ring,
> Chant a merry round.
> Brownies all,
> Quaint and small,
> Elfin banjoes sound,
> Baby, rest
> On mother's breast,
> Close thy drowsy eyes:
> Flower and wave and elf and fay
> Sing thee loving lullabies!

"THE GHOST'S WALK."

By E. C. Lovell.

"'The Ghost's Walk!' Well, the title is gruesome enough; why is it so called?"

"Because the spirit of Lafitte walks there, guarding his buried treasure. Why, Nannie, you could not induce any one of the negroes to come here even in the daylight, they are so afraid of the old pirate's ghost."

"Not really, Louise?"

"Yes, indeed, it is true," answered the girl as they entered the shady arcade of the "Ghost's Walk."

Overhead the interlacing boughs of the live-oak trees shut out the daylight making the walk shadowy and gloomy. Involuntarily the two girls drew closer together, despite the familiarity of the scene to one and the eager interest of the other in a novel experience.

"Here is Lafitte's tree," said Louise Darell, placing her hand as she spoke upon a venerable live-oak midway the walk.

"Look, Nannie, do you see the Maltese cross?"

"Yes, large copper nails driven into the tree in the shape of a cross."

"Well, my dear, somewhere here the wonderful treasure will be found. Not a sou has come to light thus far, and, do you know, people have actually been so silly as to dig for it!" laughed Louise.

"Did you not say, Louise, that there was some legend, or prophesy, or whatever name you may choose to give it, about a ring and the finding of this hidden treasure?"

"Yes. The old family tradition has come down to us through several generations. Here are the verses:

"Be leal and loyal, man and mayde,
Who walk beneath the live-oak's shade;
If false the vow, from mayde or man,
Ye shall *feel* the pirate's hand.
When ladye fayre *shall wear the ring*
It will good luck to a Darell bring."

"But no one has worn 'the ring' and so our good luck is still in abeyance until it is found," laughed Louise.

"'Good luck to a Darell bring,'" quoted Nannie Morton. "Perhaps I may find it, Louise, for you know in our family we have the gift of the 'Bodach Glas,' and besides," she added laughingly, "I was born on Christmas Day."

"Oh, to be sure! It was Morton of Milnwood, your ancestor, who, in the reign of Charles II, bargained away his hopes of heaven for this gift of the 'Bodach Glas.'"

"Yes, and *one* in each generation has the power of the gift, and, Louise, I have it in mine."

"How delightful to read the future!"

"How terrible to know what will happen!" answered Nannie Morton gravely. "It is not a gift to covet, my friend."

"Why, girls, where have you been?" cried Mrs. Darell, as her daughter opened the sitting-room door. "Doctor Le Greè has been here and looked the picture of woe when you could not be found. He would have been here yet, but a messenger came for him."

"We have been in the 'Ghost's Walk,'" explained Nannie.

"So my little girl has been telling all about the old pirate, has she?" laughed the master of "Live-oaks."

"But, by the way, Miss Nannie, our

last 'strike'* takes place tonight and would you not like to come to the sugar house ?"

"Indeed I should !" exclaimed Nannie, "I have never seen anything of the sort, and have read descriptions only of sugar rolling."

Nannie Morton had never been South before, and to her the life of a sugar planter seemed idylic. A week's residence at "Live-oaks" had convinced her of the false estimates she had put upon Southerners and how little she understood a subject much ranted about among her own people—I mean slavery. Of strong Scotch descent, for her father was a Scotchman born, she had sat under the dry discourses of the Rev. Dr. McNaught, whose bête noir was a Southern aristocrat, and that "awful, terrible monster—a slave holder !" Hell, of which place the reverend doctor loved to speak, was filled with these "sons and daughters of perdition," and it was only after much persuasion on the part of the Darells that Nannie had been permitted to go into "these dwellings of the mammon of unrighteousness." Had not her physician's decree ordered her out of Boston, to winter in a gentler climate, the Rev. McNaught might have prevailed, and my story would not have been written.

She had met the Darells one summer North, and she and Louise Darell had kept up a friendship begun in the idle mornings at a seaside resort. Already she had felt the benefit of the climate, for "Live-oaks" lies below New Orleans, and the lake in front of the house bore witness to the nearness of the great Atlantic. Taking its name from the magnificent grove of trees, this home of the Darell's was a typical mansion of the Southern planter, two stories in height, and surrounded by the comfortable, wide galleries running on all four sides of the house, the lawn well kept and sprinkled about with orange trees, and here and there a banana and the pecan, while the ornamental trees, such as the crêpe-myrtle, the mimose and the magnolia, made this sloping lawn at "Live-oaks" a very beautiful one. A small boathouse gave mooring for a

*The last kettle-boiling of the season.

graceful sailboat, and all along the shore were dugouts and skiffs, for the "Live-oaks" people were as fond of water as ducks.

Katie was doing the honors this this morning and Nannie enjoyed her immensely. Katie undoubtedly belonged to that peculiar species of genus homo known as "tomboys." Her father laughed at her, her mother groaned over her boyish ways, she was her brother's chum, and as for Louise, she had been through the same pranks, so found much sympathy in the wild escapades of her fourteen year old sister. As for her mammy, Katie was her darling.

"Ain't you glad Rob's coming ? He's a dandy ! Oh, but won't we have good times ! I hope he'll like you."

"Well, I hope——Gracious ! For heaven's sake, Katie, what made you do that ?" For Katie had run into the water up to her thin elbows in the coolest manner.

"Oh, for fun, and to get Fluff," answered this youngest twig on the Darell tree, hugging a water spaniel.

"Well, I do declar'! Ef she ain' bin an' run in de water agin ! Lor' love de chile, I ain' nuver see yo' beat in my life ! What yo' reckon Miss Nannie gwine think o' you ?"

Pride as well as reproof spoke in Mammy's voice, and she added to Miss Morton in a low tone:

"Yo' see, mam, de chile hatter 'muse herse'f, she ain' got no chillen ter play wid," but to Katie she pretended to be very angry. "I gwine tell yo' ma, dat I is, dun spile yo' shoes, an' 'have diser-way 'fore Miss Nannie, who dun cum frum de Norf ; I 'shamed o' yo' dat I is ; cum long an' lemme git yo' some dry clo'es."

Mammy's look, as she fixed her bright black eyes on Katie, belied her words, and on this, as on many other occasions, Mrs. Darell knew nothing of the wetting.

It was certainly the reading of a new and most interesting book to Nannie Morton. She began for the first time to understand the strength and closeness of the bond between master and slave. The stories she had read, the tales of cruelty and starvation that she had heard certainly found no footing on this well ordered plantation. With plenty to eat, and light work to do, they were bright and happy-hearted, with a strong devotion to "de fambly," totally unknown to hirelings. "Ourn place," "we all's crap ;" so they spoke of "Live-oaks." Furthermore, the president himself was not nearly so important a person as "Marse Rob," and they took great pride in the beauty, the accomplishments of their young mistress, for whom they seemed to think no "gent'mans in de whole State wuz good 'nuff." Nannie had come South with a feeling of great sympathy for these "downtrodden creatures," as the Rev. McNaught always called them, and yet, inconsistent as it may seem, she felt great repugnance in their company.

"They are so ugly," she said to Louise.

"Ugly ! Why how can you say so ? Look at Uncle Phil, our carriage driver, why I call him distinguè looking. Where will you see a gentler face than Aunt Phebe's, what if her skin is black ? And Uncle Charles, why, Nannie, many a gentleman might take Uncle Charles for a model, and as for Mammy !—my dear old Mammy ugly ? To me she is beautiful !" cried the girl.

"But your Mammy is part Indian. I will retract my comment about her."

"Oh, Nannie, my dear, when you have been with us longer you will retract it all. When you see you will appreciate their faithfulness, their helplessness, and not feel that the love they give us and the affectionate care we show them are misplaced."

"I wonder what Doctor McNaught would say to all this ?" thought Nannie.

Robert Darell had come home, and his mother could sit by the hour and look at him, feasting her eyes upon her only son, and fondly believing, when the young doctor declared his pharmacopœia to be her only rival, that her boy was hers for a few years, anyhow. She never once thought of Nannie Morton as at all dangerous. In the first place the difference in religion was a drawback, for the Darells were Romanists ;

more than this, Nannie, though a charming girl, was not a Southerner, and besides, Robert's mother had already selected his wife. Had she not, in her mind's eye, actually built an addition to "Joyeuse," the home of sweet Mary Pelham across the lake ? Both the mothers had talked of this union more than once (though the young people had not) and from a possibility, their marriage, in the minds of their parents, had become a probability.

"Tomorrow is Halloween, and we will have our usual party," exclaimed Louise. "You, Nannie, with your Bodach Glas powers can tell our fortunes, will you not ?"

"Perhaps I can," answered the girl thoughtfully, "but, Louise, please do not joke about it, this gift is a very strange one."

"Why, my dear, you are actually superstitious," cried Louise, "Mammy has lots of signs and things ; you are as bad as she is. Just listen while I tell you some few of them : 'A rattlesnake's skin makes your hair grow.' 'Owls are old-time people.' 'If you step over a pin with the point to you never pick it up, walk around it, then get it, and,' " laughed Louise, " 'never, under any consideration, raise an umbrella in the house, else trouble will rain upon you.' 'The blue jay, poor wretch, makes a peculiar pilgrimage every month in order to carry sand to his Satanic Majesty,' and a 'dog with a jno-claw (extra toe) will never go mad.' "

"There," cried the young Louisianian, "I have simply hurled them at you, and I have as many more to fire at you on another occasion."

"Mine are not quite so childish, and I earnestly hope, Louise, that for you and yours, I may never read the signs of the Bodach Glas."

Brightly burned the fire of hickory logs the next evening, and merry and saucy was the talk that ran along the fire-lit circle. Nuts had been burned, fortunes told, and futurity peered into by many a pair of bright eyes, eager to find reflected in the mirror arranged for that purpose the bonnie face of one the heart held dear. With trepidation the girls had lifted their eyes when told to do so in sepulchral tones, and had, most of them, quickly dropped their glances and—was it the glow of the hickory logs that made them look so rosy?

It was Nannie's turn to meet her fate in the magic mirror. Robert had played his part in the game, and Mary Pelham's heart had beat with tremulous joy when his dark head was reflected beside her own. She pressed the tiny medal which she always wore in honor to Our Lady, and her childish faith whispered, "Oh, Blessed Mother, I thank thee!"

But now it was Nannie's turn. George de l'Orme was her chosen fate. She had been placed in the witching chair and was fully prepared to meet the roguish, dark-brown eyes of the young Creole, when, raising her lashes to look into the mirror, she met the deep, earnest gaze of a pair of gray eyes, which held, and in that fleeting moment told, a secret.

"How did it happen to be Robert?" asked Marie Paschoe.

"Someone called George away suddenly." At that moment Katie and George entered the room together.

"Now then, I am ready!" he cried. "Let me see my future lady! Why, Katie, you imp, you the future Mrs. de l'Orme! Upon my word!"

Robert and Katie exchanged looks; hers said "it's all right," and his quite as plainly, "Katie, you are a trump."

"Marry you, George? Well, not unless things go by contraries."

"Katharine!" said Mrs. Darell.

"He glad ter ax yo' bimeby, honey," consoled Mammy, "dey sut'n'y gwine pester yo' ma bouten yo', her Mammy's chile, dat she is. Hi, dat Marse George l'Ormy needn't be talkin' 'bout no imps; nuver min' what he say, honey," and from that time on Mammy had no use for this young man.

No words had been spoken between Nannie and Robert, indeed no opportunity had offered. Nowhere in the house could they find a quiet corner, she to listen he to tell the ever new, the ever sweet old story. Only when he bid her good night he had whispered "tomorrow," with a world of meaning in the one word that sent the blood into

her fair face, making her conscious of her blushes in the dim hallway. "To-morrow," she had whispered too, and was gone. Nannie Morton had surrendered, and, as is the case with all strong natures, the capitulation was complete. That one brief moment when the two had looked into each other's eyes—that full, precious moment—she guarded carefully and put it away, as we do a flower, a dear, sweet memory. She felt that Robert loved her, and she knew that he meant to tell her so. She could wait, for her faith in this man was entire, her confidence in him perfect.

The fire had sobbed itself out, and still she sat there, her revery unbroken. The distant slam of a door aroused her. She was rising from her chair when her eyes fell upon the charred and blackened logs, and she distinctly saw traced on them in gray-white of the ashes these words: "Robert Darell, July, 1863, Gettysburg."

"It is the Bodach Glas," she cried faintly, "but I do not understand it, only this—some dreadful thing will come to Robert in July, at Gettysburg. Why should the warning come two years and more beforehand? I will not tell him, no, not yet." Earnestly she prayed that whatever the doom he might be spared; she was coupling his troubles already with her own, and the thought that she was doing so called the warm red blood into her face again. She tried to cheat herself into believing that she had seen nothing—might she not have dreamed the words? Experience is a hard teacher, and do what she would, facts refreshed her memory of the many times that she had read the pale lettering of the Bodach Glas and its certain results. Only one thing she could do, and that was not to disturb the others with what no doubt they would call her foolish and even wicked superstition. This she resolved to do, for Nannie Morton's fine nature possessed that beautiful trait which we call unselfishness, and this new-born love made her already tender and sympathetic nature yet more so. She was not one of those who in fair weather look for rain, and yet—ah, if the gift of the

Bodach Glas had not been hers how happy she would have been!

Christmas day had come at last. For two weeks the whole plantation had been preparing for this grand frolic. The floor of the sugar-house was spotlessly clean, and the kettles all brightened up for the occasion. As one entered the long low room these kettles looked like immense flower pots, for the negroes had filled them with "Spanish daggers" and other evergreen plants, covering the furnaces with the soft trailing gray moss that waves from hickory, oak, and the dainty crêpe-myrtles. At one end was a raised platform whereon were placed chairs for the family "frum de house," and a large-sized table on one side of the hall sufficiently elevated the four musicians. There were two fiddlers, a banjo and a jewsharp, for this was the ball of the season and had to be fully up to the mark.

In great state "Wash" (Washington) received his master and mistress at the door, escorting them and their party to the seats of honor. On this occasion the namesake of the great general was in high feather. He was dressed in an old United States uniform, which he proudly informed you had been "wore by ole marster in de Mexican wah, sah!" A naval cutlass, which he had picked up from some of the vessels putting in at the lake, rattled at his heels, and a pair of huge spurs added greatly to his pride as well as his discomfort. He was a bandy-legged little fellow, very full of his own importance as master of ceremonies for this Christmas ball.

Two rival belles were there: "Cinthy," the "Live-oaks" favorite, and "Loo-Ella" from a neighboring place. "Loo-Ella's" star was in the ascendancy tonight. Mammy, too, was in great glee. How she sang, how she danced!

"O, lor' ladies ain't yo' sorry,
Krissmus cum an' yo' ain't marry.
De hoo—de ha—dat big-foot nigger
Wid er foot so big 'ee couldn't cut er figger."

Her song was but the key-note for many more.

"Hi-ho, my sweet gal, shake yo' leetle feet,
Dis one, an' dat one, is mighty hard ter beat;
Jes' like er yaller hammer tappin' on de flo',
Dis one, an' dat one, round an' round dey go.

O, mister buzzard, ef yo' len' me yo' wing
I kin dance or double shuffle ez well ez Sallie King.
O lif' yo' foots an' fling 'em high, an' turn round on yo' heel—
Fur dat de way dee dances in the ole Ferginy reel."

At 12 o'clock came the event of the evening—the supper.

"Are we going to their supper-room?" asked Miss Morton as, instead of going toward the house, she saw Mr. and Mrs. Darell turn toward the cane sheds.

"Certainly we are," answered Robert. "Why, it would hurt their feelings dreadfully if we were not there when they drink our healths."

"Ah," she whispered to herself, "how have these people of the South been maligned, and how misunderstood!"

In a long enclosed shed were spread the tables, and the delighted looks of the people as they caught sight of the good cheer emphatically announced good appetites, and delightful anticipation.

"Halt!" cried Wash, when all of the company were inside. This military order being promptly obeyed, "present arms!" followed.

There being no arms to present, except Washington's own cutlass, he held it for a moment dangerously near his nose, then waved it around his head, counting as he did so, "One! two! three!" Then such a cheer went up as made the rafters ring, and three times three the words rang out: "God bless our marster an' our mistis an' all de fambly." Then glasses were filled with foaming egg-nogg, and master and slaves wished each other a "Merry Christmas."

"And now, boys, good night," spoke Mr. Darell from the doorway. "Holiday for all tomorrow and God bless you."

"Twenty minutes after twelve," said Robert, looking at his watch in the brilliant moonlight. "It is the witching hour but nevertheless, Miss Nannie, I I am going to ask you to come with me to the 'Ghost's Walk.' I have so strong a desire to go there that I will not resist it, so will you come?"

"Do you know why I have brought you here?" asked Robert Darell, taking the hand that lay upon his arm into the warm clasp of his own. "Have you not· guessed my secret? Ah, yes! You must have done so. Must I tell you how many, many times the words have been on my lips, for my enforced absence, after that night when I took George de l'Orme's place, has not given me opportunity before. Can you, do you love me, Nannie, and will you be my wife? No other woman ever has filled, ever could fill my heart as you have done. Tell me, darling, have I found my treasure?"

"I think *I* have," she answered very softly, "and Robert I am very happy."

"What is that shining so brightly yonder? Reach it for me, Robert, there, just under that straggling root."

"Some bright pebble, I suppose ; certainly I will get it for you."

"What is it?" she questioned, as Darell uttered an exclamation. He did not answer, but rose quickly to his feet and taking her hand he slipped upon her finger a ring.

"The ring!" she cried, "the ring of the prophesy! How strange."

"When ladye fayre shall wear the ring
    It will good luck to a Darell bring,"
quoted Robert. "Ah, darling, I never had faith in the old verses until now when I've found my treasure by the pirate's oak."

In all her joy in Robert's love, she remembered the sign of the Bodach Glas. She was unselfish, even in this moment, and she did not tell him of the sign on the logs. Nannie sat looking at the pirate's ring. It was a love-knot of gold, the centre of the knot being a large and very pure diamond. It was the fire in the gem that had caught her eyes, as it lay hidden under the roots of the ancient live-oak.

How had it come there? Evidently it was, must be, the ring referred to in the old tradition. Good luck, good luck, and her's the hand to bring it. She took the ring off and read the faintly lettered words engraved inside— "until death us do part." She put it on her finger again, her marriage finger, where he had placed it, her sweet face rosy red in the light of the tall Carsell lamp.

The winter was swiftly passing, for the new-born year was a month old. Rumors, which had been as distant murmurings, grew into threatening facts. Alas, the cloud not bigger than a man's hand when Nannie Morton had come South now spread over the land and the crisis was at hand, for the cloud was soon to burst in that terrible storm— Civil War. All the young· men, and for that matter the old men, too, were holding meetings, organizing companies, and the "luxurious Southerner" was girding on his sword to defend his rights. The North made war upon the South, and renegades, indeed, would her sons have been had they not drawn their weapons in defence of their mother. Robert Darell had been no laggard. ·His was the first company registered from county, and he its captain.

Meanwhile, Nannie Morton had been summoned home. Her parents had not opposed her engagement until war was declared, and then it was that they wrote at the instance of the Rev. Mc-Naught, begging her to return as soon as possible. The letter was from her father, only a few lines and hastily written. The one following this commanding her to break her "engagement with a rebel" was never received. In four days Robert would leave. His father, too, was going to· join Beauregard.

"Nannie," he said to her suddenly, "I am going to ask you to marry me at once. My wife could come to me perhaps, if—if need be. Can you, dearest? Am I asking too much? Ah, Nannie, to know you are mine in law as well as in love—what would it not be to me? Will you, Nannie, will you?"

Nannie looked at him as he stood before her, so tall, so strong, so handsome. She did not speak, only laid her head on the new gray coat and answered her lover's question.

The priest came at eight o'clock the next evening and Robert once more put upon her finger the pirate's ring. Two days, two short days, and they were gone, and the three women clung to one another in the agony of mutual sorrow. They had given their all, their best, for our cause was holy and just, but oh! it tore the heartstrings, and the waiting of those left behind was a sore trial.

George d l'Orme, too, had gone in Robert's company, so even Katie, child as she was, was quiet and subdued, seeking Mammy for comfort.

"Nur min; honey, dee all gwine cum home, don' yo' fret, chile, dar is heapser fo'kes better 'n dat young Marse George. Dee kinnot pass my chile by; dere de cun'l's son, he er mighty fine." But Katie had rushed indignantly from the room.

"Hoity-toity!" mused Mammy, as she picked up the scattered clothing. "He dun 'sturb her er heap, dat boy is."

Washington had taken charge of the plantation; his master had left it under his care and management. To Charles came the greater responsibility in the protection of his mistress and her family. "I trust you entirely, Charles," his master said at parting. "I know you well, for we were boys together."

Charles made a promise which he kept, and the one regret which he had was not to be able to go with Col. Darell.

Months went by. News came of terrible battles, and the beloved ones were still unhurt; theirs seemed as charmed lives. At last, one day, came a message. Only a bit of soiled, brown paper, only a few words from George de l'Orme, but it said, "Robert is wounded, come." And after their long, long parting this was the way that Nannie Darell was to meet her husband.

By rail when she could, but oftener by wagon and horseback, the young wife traveled, Northward, Northward, toward Gettysburg, in the summer of 1863, for it was there on that awful Waterloo that Robert had been wounded. The Bodach Glas spoke true. George's few lines left her in terrible doubt, but oh! merciful heaven, spare him! The Angel of Death had hovered over this battlefield, and here the most precious blood of the South had poured out like water. While she was hastening to him, Robert lay on his bed, the great wound in his side slowly but surely sapping his life. "It is a question of days with him now," the doctor had

said, and left him for others with a stronger promise of living.

"Where is he—Captain Darell?"

"I fear you cannot see him, madam; he is badly wounded, and any excitement will but hasten matters—he is dying."

"I am his wife," she quietly answered. "Will you keep me from him now?"

The young officer much repented his explanation, as he met the questioning of a pair of dark blue eyes; he could not resist their appeal.

"Come this way," he said—"there, that door to the right; there is no one with him but the nurse."

She was by his side in an instant, her Robert, her own best beloved! Ah! she would have known him, for love's eyes are keen, but oh! how changed and how worn he looked. He stirred and murmured her name; bending over him she whispered, and he seemed to draw a long deep sigh. "I am his wife," she said, in explanation to the astonished nurse. "You may go. He is mine, mine!" she cried passionately. "Leave him to me!"

"She could not be here without permission," thought the nurse, as she gladly prepared to obey, for her vigil had been a long one.

"Will you ask the doctor to come to me at once, please, oh! hurry, will you not?" And the nurse, in pity, withdrew.

"Oh! my darling, my darling!" she moaned. "You shall not die, my love must hold you; ah! dearest, it shall, it shall!"

In a few minutes the doctor came. "Doctor," she said, "I want you please to open one of my veins—for him," she added softly.

"My dear young lady it will do no good; he is too far —"

"Will you?" she said, baring a round smooth arm and holding it toward him. "If it does no good it may not do any harm; will you? He is my husband; with him there is life, without him— ah! how worthless is mine!"

"It is dangerous," said the doctor.

"I know it," she answered, "but I would risk more for him."

"There, you can stand no more. Lie down and keep quiet, very quiet. I will send one of the nurses. You are a brave woman," he said admiringly.

"I love him," she answered simply.

The war clouds have rolled away, but the memory of those days will never die. Much has been told, much imagined, of the horrors of civil war, but with the Southern women it was experience. Who will forget the heroes of Manassas, of Cold Harbor, of Gettysburg? If they may not wear the conqueror's laurel, we will make our heroes wreaths of rosemary and pansies, a dearer tribute than the emblem of victory.

Again it is Christmas at "Live-oaks," and Robbie is to have a Christmas tree. They are all coming, Katie and George, the bride and groom of a week, for this is the first real Christmas since the war.

"Nannie," said her husband, "do you remember, darling, this night six years ago? Ah, how true the old tradition, for I did, indeed, find my treasure!" She only lifted her sweet face to his caress. Robert's eyes caught sight of a tiny scar on her wrist, and he added with deep feeling. "You did, indeed, bring me 'good luck,' for you gave me —life." He raised her hand to his lips, and the pirate's ring shone brilliant in the winter moonlight.

AT COCK CROW.

By Charles J. O'Malley.

Low crows the cock at twilight. Slender, white,
The young moon loiters at the port of night,
Filling her casks with dreams and crystal light—
　　A white ship moored at violet wharves of day.
　　　　O ship, out-flee!
Hasten from ports of dusk over the crystal sea!

Low crows the cock at midnight. Rimmed with gold
White flies the moon across the barn-roofs old;
The icicles within the beech gleam cold;
　　The broomsedge shivers on the hillside gray;
　　　　Winds flap the sea.
O gray-winged winds blow back great twilight's bark to me!

An hour ere dawn again the buff cock crows;
The moon has gone to harbors no man knows.
One white star burns, and home the brown owl goes;
　　The gray winds in the oakwood kneel and pray.
　　　　Pray, winds, for me;
The violet wharves return, yet sail nor ship I see.

"MOTHER OF STATES AND UNDIMINISHED MEN:" A GLIMPSE OF VIRGINIA.

By Louis Pendleton.

The tourist who enters Virginia from the North is at once struck by the contrast between what he sees and the industrial liveliness and bustle, the evidences of wealth and prosperity, the great and crowded cities, which he has left behind. If he be traveling overland, toward the famed and beautiful Shenandoah valley, and enter the State at the county of Frederick, he will remark that the turnpike is excellent, but that the country generally does not correspond. There are fine estates here and there belonging to those who were able to hold their own during the trying first years of the post-bellum period, or those of newly-acquired wealth, but the country for the most part strikes one as wearing a sad, poverty-ridden look.

This is not strange. Unhappy Virginia—battlefield of the war! Those who dwell upon the scarred bosom of this "mother of States" look backward from a lowly present to a lofty past. The last of the States to reluctantly turn her back upon the ancient confederation and cast her lot with the South, wherein she became the valiant leader and bore the brunt of the fight, she is also the last to find that her deeper scars are healing, the last to shake off the deadly lethargy and recover from the terrible prostration which followed an unsuccessful war.

Her sons and daughters, even those looking back from a third generation, love the memory and name of Virginia, looking beyond her poverty and sorrow to the bright picture of a glorious past, and they listen gratefully to the friends who wrote these noble words:

Virginia gave us this imperial man,
Cast in the massive mould
Of those high-statured ages old
Which into grander forms our mortal metal ran;
She gave us this unblemished gentleman.

What shall we give her back but love and
praise,
As in the dear old unestrangèd days
Before the inevitable wrong began?
Mother of States and undiminished men,
Thou gavest us a country, giving him.*

If Winchester—the first stopping place of the tourist who writes this article—will not stand industrial comparison with the Northern town, it has a quaintness and charm which the latter has not. And it has history. Is there another town since Agincourt and Crécy were fought, or since the Wars of the Roses of so chequered a fortune? Its inhabitants tell the visitor that from '61 to '65 it changed masters eighty-five times! From a hill-top in the suburbs the Blue Ridge with Ashby's Gap and Manassas may be seen, not to mention the valley of the Shenandoah, which incessantly resounded with the tramp of armies; battlefield of the war in very truth was this region.

In the adjoining county of Clark, a rich and rolling country, there are many old estates which saw their best days in the ante-war period, as "Mountain View," the old home of Bishop Meade; "Annefield," a stone mansion a century old,

*From "Under the Old Elm," a poem by James Russell Lowell, read in 1876 on the spot where Washington took command of the American army one hundred years before.

the carving and varnishing of which were brought from England; "Carter Hall," "Page Brook," "The Briars," "Grafton," "Long Branch," "Oakley," "The Glen," "Saratoga," etc., the last mentioned, as it was built and named during the Revolution, probably ante-dating the famous New York summer resort. The tourist observed that these names, among high and low throughout the countryside were as well known as so many towns or villages would have been.

In Clark county one does not say "at Mr. Lee's," for instance, but "at Grafton." In the present changed condition, the life lived by the dwellers on these ancestral estates is perhaps but a faint reminder of what it was when the family coach-and-four was seen on every country road, but the old flavor is not quite lost even in this age of the fast fading of distinctions. These gentle-mannered people who show lineage in their faces stand back from the popular tide, let the world flow on in its own way, and, even where poverty may·be knocking rudely at the door, resolutely maintain their old-time right of keeping the vulgar at arm's length. Here in rural Virginia may still be found a reminder of that charming Southern country life, medieval in some of its features, if you please, which was formerly so much depicted in the Southern novel, and which is now passed over by the realist as belonging to the domain of legend, or even—from the view of some critics—of what is purely imaginary.

The intention had been to visit the family at "The Briars,"* but it was learned in Winchester that since the father's death the household had been broken up. The oldest son was at the Virginia Military Institute, the daughter and younger son with their uncle at "The Glen." Not there, however, but at Millwood Church would they be found on Sunday morning, and thither the tourist went. This Episcopal church in the tiny village of Millwood, where the Clark county gentry† congregate on

*The home of the late John Esten Cooke, the novelist.
†It is not uncommon to hear the upper class so styled in rural Virginia.

Sunday morning, is an object of no small interest to the traveler who draws comparisons, inasmuch as it reflects an order of country life probably not to be found anywhere in America outside of Virginia. The stone edifice itself would not have been out of place in one of our large cities, while the well-dressed people had none of the air of country folk, and clearly were instructed men and women of the world.

During the time spent in this inter-esting region, the tourist was domiciled at "The Glen," the home of Mr. Wm. Page Carter, a brother-in-law to John Esten Cooke, cousin to Thomas Nelson Page, and himself a man of letters, known to magazine readers as a writer of touching verse in dialect. The road from Millwood Church to "The Glen" passes through the grounds of "Saratoga," now the home of another cousin of the Richmond novelist. As stated, this curious old stone dwelling, which seems good for still another hundred years, was so named by Gen. Morgan, of the Revolution, and was built by the Hessian prisoners in his charge. Tradition has it that the stone for this building was wheeled in hand barrows from a point three miles distant, and, too, that the work was not com-pleted until three months after peace had been declared and the laborers were rightly free. If this story be true, it serves up a bit of American history which we cannot smack our lips over, and which was well calculated to inflame the English. Indeed, it would seem that the Stamp Act, burdensome as it was, furnished us such good casus belli.

The tourist will not soon forget the first afternoon at "The Glen," and the quiet nook in the beautiful grounds, where John Esten Cooke's early and unpublished "Recollections" were read aloud, the soft voice of his only daughter imparting an added charm to the pecu-liar ease and flow of the style. The slight manuscript book, written somewhere about 1856, and devoted chiefly to the period of early childhood, was cleverly illustrated by the author's own pencil, and was distinguished by a simplicity and charm which one would hardly expect to find in a diary of a young man of twenty-one, particularly a literary young man whose leaning was decidedly toward romance.

"The Briars," some two miles distant, was visited the next day, Mr. Carter driving the tourist over. Many were the plantation gates to be opened, and rough was the road, for the course led away from the Winchester turnpike. His companion smiled as the vehicle jolted over the stones, and the tourist was told, with a half-sigh, that these were changed times; a light buggy was hardly the thing for these roads. No one had been aware, or if so had not cared, that the road was rough in the days of the coach and four. As the place came into view, it was recalled how "mammy" was wont, in the old days, to walk down this lane with the children, taking them to visit "Oakley" or "Page Brook" not far away.

One more gate and the visitor was at "The Briars." There was little about the old-time porticoed structure to impress the man of today; it belonged to the past—to Virginia's past—wherein the standard was different. And yet the visitor was impressed. Standing in view of this tree-embowered home where the historian and novelist of old Virginia saw his last, mayhap his happiest days, the visitor was conscious of a respect and reverence which no palace of a now-a-day plutocrat could arouse. Here lived the author of "The Virginia Comedians," the best Southern novel of the anti-bellum epoch; here was written "Surrey of Eagle's Nest" and those other war tales so full of thrilling action and romance; here, at a later date, came into life "My Lady Pocahontas," an idyl in prose, and here, after long labors, was produced that successful "History of Virginia," which was in very truth a work of love.

A tenant now occupied "The Briars," and Mr. Carter's recollections of many gay days and much fine company seen within those walls long ago were not without a suggestion of pathos. On the return, the conversation wandered to the novelist's poet-brother, Philip Pendleton Cooke, and the tourist listened to the story of his poem, "Florence Vane"

—the story of a proud and beauteous maid who would not be wooed, of the romanesque behavior of the poet in youth, of how he rode miles to place a bouquet of favorite flowers on the fair dame's windowsill at sunrise — and all for naught!

But even a poet may love more than once, and the widow of him who first sighed for the "fair, cold wonder" now resides at "The Vineyard," an old estate on the Shenandoah river within a few miles of "The Briars." The following is the poem:

I loved thee long and dearly,
    Florence Vane,
My life's bright dream, and early,
    Hath come again;
I renew in my fond vision
    My heart's dear pain,
My hope, and thy derision,
    Florence Vane.

The ruin lone and hoary,
    The ruin old,
Where thou did'st mark my story,
    At even told,—
That spot—the hues Elysian
    Of sky and plain—
I treasure in my vision,
    Florence Vane.

Thou wast lovelier than the roses
    In their prime;
Thy voice excelled the closes
    Of sweetest rhyme;
Thy heart was as a river
    Without a main,
Would I had loved thee never,
    Florence Vane.

But fairest, coldest wonder!
    Thy glorious clay
Lieth the green sod under—
    Alas the day!
And it boots not to remember
    Thy disdain—
To quicken love's pale ember,
    Florence Vane.

The lilies of the valley
    By young graves weep,
The pansies love to dal y
    Where maidens sleep;
May their bloom in beauty vying
    Never wane,
Where thine earthly part is lying,
    Florence Vane.

In the county of Albemarle, near Charlottesville, the far-famed "Monticello" was visited a few days later. The old home of Thomas Jefferson stands on the top of the mountain, Monticello (both mansion and mountain are so called), just two miles from the town as the crow flies. The drive leads out through a fine hill country, then up the green-clothed mountain side now brilliantly tinged with autumn coloring. Near the top the visitor halts before a great iron gate and the keeper's neat lodge of red brick. Pulling a knob attached to a wire, he sounds a large bell, not within the lodge but somewhere among the trees.

At last a small gate between the great one and the lodge is unlocked, and the keeper says that a fee of twenty-five cents must be paid before "Monticello" can be seen; these are Mr. Levy's orders. Who is Mr. Levy? He is the gentleman who owns "Monticello" and who lives in New York usually. While imparting this information, the keeper leads the way upward through heavily wooded grounds, for some half a mile, passing the old family burying place, in the midst of which stands a tall gray shaft in honor of Jefferson, erected by the neighboring university, which owes to him its origin. A little farther on the visitor passes through another iron gate into grounds more carefully kept than the outer park and follows a path strewn with white pebbles until the mansion is in view.

Monticello crowns the mountain top, a level plateau of perhaps less than two acres, commanding an extended view of the rolling country of Albemarle. The beautiful old mansion has been merely renewed, nothing altered, and probably looks just as it did in colonial days. It were idle to describe it. Everyone is familiar with the view of the west front, with the dome over the Greek-like portico; the very school geographies have published it. Nothing but the trees and the smooth lawn is visible from either front or side; not an outhouse anywhere. This is due to the fact that the servant's quarters on the left and the stables on the right are a little down the mountain and connect with the mansion by underground passages. The arrangement may have resulted in some inconvenience, but what a gain in beauty!

They cared for beauty more and for convenience less in those days—so thinks the visitor sitting on a garden bench and watching the old house. In such surroundings the imagination easily wanders back into the picturesque colonial period, peopling Monticello with the family of its master, with General and "Lady" Washington, and all the great folk of that day, their swords and cocked hats and knee-breeches, their short-waisted gowns and stately manners.

Walking round to the east front the visitor finds a surprise; for although it does not appear in the usual photograph it is handsomer, more striking than the other. The portico is wider, and there are more fluted Corinthian columns of gray stone with their lovely lotus-leaved capitals, and there is an old clock above the great hall doorway which has not been renewed and has truly an ancient look. The lawn here leads only a few rods away ere it looks steeply down the mountain, and is graced by a few fine old trees, beneath which two negro men are raking the dead leaves. A beautiful site for a home, but how lonely it must have been a hundred years ago; the place is isolated and profoundly quiet even now.

With a last look at Monticello and the wide rolling valley over which it has watched for a century, the visitor takes the downward path. Later in the day a lazy little horse-car carried the tourist from Charlottesville out to the university which was founded by the master of Monticello. A charming place, this University of Virginia. Having visited Harvard within six weeks, it was natural that comparisons should be drawn.

The grounds of the Massachusetts college are more extensive and highly improved and the buildings more numerous, larger, costlier and more modern, but there is a distinct charm about the Virginia college which the other has not—the charm of the classic. The Greek column rises before you everywhere, even in the students' dormitories, and the main building is modeled from the Pantheon. The external aspect would seem to be thoroughly in keeping with the careful attention given the classics in the lecture room; for, while the whole collegiate course is probably less wide in range than that of Harvard, it is said that a higher standard obtains in this particular.

The next place of sojourn was a town distinguished for its celebrities and beautiful for situation. Lexington boasts one of the greatest universities of the South—the Washington and Lee—and the only military institute of the whole country which West Point condescends to regard as worthy of recognition. Besides this, it is the home of Prof. James A. Harrison, author of the "Story of Greece"; of Mrs. Margaret J. Preston, the poetess, and of the family of General Robert E. Lee.

The Virginia Military Institute, familiarly called the "V. M. I.," is a place of great interest. The main building is an independent-looking old pile, all the more attractive for the flame marks of a reddish brown which plentifully stain its battered yellow walls. Not here alone, but in many places, does the valley of Virginia still show the scars left by the fire and sword of the Civil War. Walking among these flame-browned walls at sunset when the single shot is fired from the battery, it requires no great effort to imagine that the guns of that wild struggle are still thundering. The daily dress parade over the wide space of the lawn is almost a society event in Lexington. Ladies, young and old, with their escorts, promenade the walks bordering the ground, fondly looking on as the two hundred or more uniformed young men go through the drill in perfect order. And a stirring spectacle it is.

The Washington and Lee University, the grounds of which are within a stone's throw of the outer limits of the "V. M. I.," is less extensive in its buildings than the State College at Charlottesville, but its associations make it more interesting. First, the Washington College and later the Washington and Lee University; to its own merits it superadds distinction borrowed from these noble names.

Jackson's class-room and the battered old prayer-book which accompanied him through the war are among the objects which visitors wish to see; but it is not Jackson, nor Washington, but Lee that

one thinks of here. While squads of students are shouting and swaying about the campus in a game of football, the tourist goes into the chapel to look at the beautiful recumbent statue executed by Valentine. Now and then the swaying crowd on the grounds draws near and the muffled roar of young voices beats at the doors, but the stillness of the interior seems thereby rendered only the more intense, and the marvelous repose of the white figure becomes almost startling in its impressiveness. There is a nobility about this piece of stone as it lies there that is wonderful. One is reminded of the recumbent *Ariadne* of--is it Praxiteles?--which is said to seem to breathe. Dare one compare Valentine with Praxiteles? Who knows—it may be because it is Lee that this stone seems to breathe, because the observer would be moved in the presence of the rudest piece of chiselling if only it represented Lee? Let it be as it may, he goes away repeating, "It is wonderful, wonderful."

Close to the college grounds is the home which was the last on earth of the South's greatest soldier. A son and two daughters only live in it now; the former is president of the Washington and Lee, the latter are world-wide travelers, having seen, in the company of English friends, even so remote an object as the Great Wall of China.

Although robbed of their belongings at Arlington, they still have in this home many interesting relics of the Revolution and the colonial period, the family having inherited the Washington portraits and silver. There are portraits of the Washingtons, the Custises and of Martha Daudridge when young; of General Washington as a colonel in the king's army; of "Light-horse Harry"; of Lafayette as a young man (presented by himself to Washington), and many others, among them one of Col. Park, an ancestor of the Lees, who was Marlborough's aid-de-camp at Blenheim, and who rode with the wind, crossed the channel, and was the first to carry the news of the victory to Queen Anne. As a reward for this service he gallantly asked only for the queen's miniature, and this is to be seen upon him in the picture which was painted by her Majesty's command.

Two other portraits of great interest are recalled—the one of General Lee as a young man, than which nothing could be more noble-looking and handsome; the other of Pope Pius IX, the only monarch of any kind who officially recognized the ill-fated Confederacy. The latter was sent by his holiness as a present to the great Southern leader, for whom he cherished much admiration.

THE SOUTHERN OUTLOOK.

Western Interest in the South.

À gentleman in Nebraska, who received a copy of the October number of the SOUTHERN STATES Magazine in response to his inquiry for information about the South, wrote as follows :

The magazine is an agreeable surprise to me. It is just what is wanted, and deserves success and liberal patronage from both North and South. I do not even attempt flattery when I say that. Judging from the copy before me, the SOUTHERN STATES will be the means of materially increasing desirable immigration from the Northwest to the "New South." Pardon me if I suggest that those most interested have little or no idea of the demand for reliable information relative to Southern farming lands and the present condition of the South and the Southern people in this State as well as Iowa and South Dakota. It is surprising how little is known here of the resources of your country. If the land companies and those who have control of large tracts of Southern lands were to advertise them here one-third as much as these lands are advertised, I firmly believe they would be greatly and very agreeably surprised at the result.

This is but one from many similar communications that have been elicited by the series of "Letters from Southern Farmers," the first of which were published in the October number. Without exception these letters have been received with earnest commendation as a practical step in encouraging Southern immigration by awakening interest in that section among the people of the North and West. There never was a more active or more widespread interest in the South than prevails at the present time, and conditions never were more favorable to the success of any immigration movement designed to people the South with desirable settlers from the North and West.

Cost of Cotton Production in Texas.

Cotton is a far less profitable crop than is generally believed. It is a popular fallacy that the raising of cotton is a very profitable branch of agriculture. Under the most favor-

able conditions there is a fair margin of profit in the business, but the average profits are less than can be obtained in many less popular branches of agriculture. A plantation that raises a bale to the acre at a minimum of cost and realizes ten cents per pound can be considered a profitable institution, but they are very few and far apart.

This reflection is suggested by some figures relative to the cost of cotton production in Texas gathered and published by the Texas Agricultural Experiment Station. Figures of this character are so delusive as a rule that we involuntarily hesitate to accept them. Failure to comprehend the elements of cost and variety in methods of computing such data render most of such statistics practically valueless, and, as a rule, there is little to be learned from these figures. But these statistics issued by the Texas Experiment Station have the semblance of care and accuracy, and there is something to be learned from them. Efforts were made to ascertain the costs for each of the different soil sections of the State, but only a few careful, accurate statements were secured, and these, with results obtained at the experiment station, permit of some conclusions of value.

Summarizing the costs given by the seven actual producers we find the following :

	Cents per pound.
W. A. Clark, Temple, Bell county	4.09
Homer Clark, Temple, Bell county	4.62
J. M. McCrarv, Comanche, Comanche county	5.47
G. L. Stone, McGregor, McLennan county	5 24
J. F. Myers, Hutto, Williamson county	5 00
Jeff Wellborn, New Boston, Bowie county	2.12
W. G. Johnson, Reagan, Falls county	5.66

The cheapest cotton included in this list is that raised by Jeff Wellborn on Red river bottom land with no manure or fertilizer. The secret of the very low cost is the high productiveness of the land and the saving in labor by the use of cotton-picking machines. The details of Mr. Wellborn's statement follow :

COST	For one acre.
Rent of land..	$4 00
Breaking flat with two-horse plows in the fall...	1 00
Harrowing..	20
Planting..	15
Cottonseed..	10
Plowing-cultivating every ten days or after each rain, say eight times, at twenty-five cents each time..................................	2 00
Chopping..	40
Picking 1600 pounds of seed cotton by machine (Cunningham cotton harvester), including interest on investment or wear and tear on machine, ten cents per cwt...................	1 50
Marketing 500 pounds of lint...................	1 50
Ginning, bagging and ties.........................	3 00
Total cost, including rent of land.....	**$13 85**

PROCEEDS.	
500 pounds of lint at seven cents, actual price...	$35 00
1000 pounds of cottonseed at $6 50 per ton......	3 25
Total proceeds per acre...	**$38 25**
Less cost...........	13 85
Net profits per acre......................	**$24 40**

This is a striking statement and one that probably could not be many times duplicated. A profit of nearly $25.00 per acre on seven-cent cotton has the semblance of a phenomenon, but it is nevertheless a possibility, if Mr. Wellborn's accounts are s raight, and we have reason to believe they are. But some of the other planters show a larger profit per acre even at a much higher cost of production. A larger yield and higher price for the crop were the elements of advantage. Mr. W. A. Clark, of Temple, whose cotton cost 4.09 cents per pound, raised 650 pounds of lint per acre and sold it at nine cents, which gave him a net profit of $31.95 per acre on his cotton. But Mr. Clark's cotton followed a crop of English peas, which yielded sixty-five bushels. These brought $5.00, or nearly 50 per cent. more than the cotton, making the net profit $82.45 per acre. Mr. Homer Clark obtained 418 pounds of lint per acre which he sold at eight and a-half cents per pound, and his actual net profit was $16.18 per acre. Mr. McCrary's yield was only 250 pounds per acre, which sold at eight and a-half cents and brought a net profit of $13.68 per acre. Mr. Stone, whose cotton cost him 5.24 cents per pound, raised half a bale to the ac e, which he sold at seven cents, realizing only $4.39 per acre. Mr. Myers, whose cotton cost five cents per pound to raise, made 426 pounds to the acre on a 26-acre leasehold. He got seven and a-half cents per pound and cleared $10.64 per acre. Mr. Johnson made half a bale to the acre and got eight and a-half cents per pound, netting $7.10 per acre.

These figures show pretty clearly the range of possibilities in cotton production in Texas, and they demonstrate these two points—that

cotton is far less profitable as a rule than fruit or truck-farming, but that the e is nevertheless a good margin of profit in cotton at a low market price. The whole question hinges upon management.

The conclusions presented by the experiment station in the report from which we have taken these figures are as follows : "For a renter especially cotton planting presents an intricate problem. He cannot afford to fertilize the land on a short-time lease, and long leases for a term of years, so common in other countries, are here scarcely known. As a result of this the renter must depend upon thorough preparation, careful planting, persistent, proper cultivation and intelligent diversification of crops to insure a reasonable profit on the land he cultivates. For the independent homestead planter who depends upon brain and muscle to secure success, the problem takes a wider range and admits of easier demonstration. For all such the proper use of fertilizers and he combination of such other crops with cotton as will best economize labor, but admit of steady employment throughout the year, will furnish the key to the situation. As usual, in nearly all matters of importance, the average ability will find middle ground the safest. Contrary to a very prevalent belief, there is still money enough to be made in cotton growing, but it follows careful work and intelligent judgment, and will never come without an effort. The man who can and does diversify his farming interests without discarding cotton, as so many would advise, is the one who finds a profit in the staple one year with another."

Florida's Great Orange Crop.

The startling rate of increase in the Florida orange crop is creating several interesting questions about the future of this industry, and both growers and dealers are now beginning to ask what will be done with the crop a few years hence if the present rate of increase shall continue. The crop since 1884 has been as follows :

Year.	Boxes.
1885....................................	900,000
1886....................................	1,250,000
1887....................................	1,450,000
1888....................................	1,900,000
1889....................................	2,150,000
1890....................................	2,460,000
1891....................................	3,750,000
1892....................................	3,450,000
1893 (estimated)....................	4,500,000

In seven years the crop of Florida oranges has increased threefold, and if this rate shall cont nue we shall see Florida producing nearly

15,000,000 boxes in the year 1900. There is every reason to believe that the crop will increase as rapidly as it has in the past ; in fact, the increased acreage devoted to orange groves indicates that the production of oranges will increase even more rapidly than it has in the past few years. In the last three years the number of new trees set out has been greater than the number already growing, more than doubling the groves. Making allowance for the large number of trees that have not reached the bearing age, it does not appear unreasonable to expect that the crop will reach upwards of 20,000,000 boxes by 1900, unless some unforeseen disaster shall largely reduce the productive area.

In recent years we have several times seen the orange markets of this country glutted with Florida fruit. What, then, will be done with 20,000,000 or even 15,000,000 boxes a few years hence? This is a question that confronts the orange growers of Florida, and they already recognize that the future needs some consideration. The natural increase in American consumption of fruit consequent upon our growing population will absorb a considerable part of the increased crop of oranges, but it cannot be expected that the American taste for fruit will undergo sufficient expansion in the next six or seven years to make use of all

the great orange crop that appears in the near future.

The idea of making a foreign demand for Florida fruit, which has been much discussed in former years, is receiving more attention this year than ever before, and it is in this direction that the principal relief from prospect of a glutted home market seems to lie. Methods of handling the Florida orange crop have been greatly improved in recent years, and trade conditions have been materially improved by organization, so that the industry is now in good shape to undertake systematic solution of the question of disposing of the future great crops. A large quantity of Florida fruit will go to England this season under favorable conditions, and a very vigorous effort will be made to gain a sure footing in that market. An Amsterdam merchant, who called on us a few days ago, advised us that there should be a market in Holland for our oranges, as there is for our other fresh and prepared fruits. Florida oranges are not much known as yet in the English market, and the English taste has not yet been educated in this direction, but the infinite superiority of the Florida orange will soon demonstrate itself and win favor that will insure its future. With a sure foothold in the principal foreign markets there need be no fear of an overproduction of oranges, for there will be a demand for all our growers can supply.

NOTES ON SOUTHERN PROGRESS.

THE improvement of the Warrior river, in Alabama, is now progressing rapidly. Two of the series of locks and dams intended to afford deep water for navigation have been constructed, and the third is expected to render the river navigable into the coal country. The stream heretofore has only been deep enough for navigation between Mobile and Tuscaloosa.

THE Illinois Central has authorized J. F. Merry, assistant general passenger agent of the road, to prepare a book on New Orleans with the view of showing the advantages the city possesses for becoming the principal point of export for the Mississippi valley. Mr. Merry, who is located at Manchester, Iowa, has obtained an experience during his residence in the Northwest which will be of exceptional value in preparing the work, as he is well acquainted with the data which will be of the most interest to residents of Iowa, Minnesota, the Dakotas and neighboring States. The book will show the advantages New Orleans has over Eastern cities from a geographical standpoint, and the great future possibilities which the city has of increasing in population and in business ventures. It is to be entitled "The Commercial, Industrial and Financial Outlook for New Orleans."

AN important improvement at Memphis, Tenn., is an auditorium recently completed which will seat 6000 people. It was remodeled from another structure at a comparatively small cost, and is said to be the largest hall of its kind in the South. It will accommodate over 1000 more than the music hall being built at Baltimore.

·AT Bedford City, Va., a board of trade has been organized by the business men. G. C. Jeter is president, N. D. Hawkins and E. B. Stone, vice-presidents, and E. D. Gregory, secretary.

ARANSAS PASS, on the Texas coast, for which an improvement fund is now being raised by land companies and other concerns near Aransas bay, is an illustration of how the jetty system can be used to maintain a permanent depth of water in harbor entrances. The pass is 1000 yards wide and is situated between Mustang and St. Joseph's Islands. In front of this inlet lies Harbor Island, about five miles long and about a mile from St. Joseph's Island, to which it lies parallel. The body of water lying between these islands is what is usually called "the harbor." Within the memory of men now living the pass has moved southward nearly three miles by erosion of Mustang and accretion of St. Joseph's Island. The tides rushing in and out of Aransas and contiguous bays are confined to a narrow channel and the space between the islands is scoured to a depth of from twenty to forty feet. As the ebb tide rushes southward through this harbor it dashes against the head of Mustang, a sand Island, at a sharp angle, and is deflected at the same angle in obedience to the law of incidence and reflection. The sand cut from the island is carried seaward by the tide to where the ebb meets the littoral current and is there deposited, making the bar which obstructs entrance to the harbor. The erosion of Mustang served to lengthen St. Joseph's Island. The government has securely revetted the head of Mustang, stopping the erosion. The bar which has been formed still remains. It is a sharp sand ridge. The removal of this bar is the object of the present movement. At the commencement of the work last year there were eight feet of water on the crest of the bar, the depth having remained the same since the completion of the revettment spoken of. With the prosecution of the work last year the water deepened rapidly, there being full twenty feet at the end of the jetty, and the 18-foot contour extends 900 feet beyond the end, where eighteen months ago there were only nine feet of water.

It then shoals rapidly to the crest of the bar, which now shows a depth of ten feet, and then deepens rapidly to the gulf. The results are gratifying, and experienced engineers say there is no doubt that with the extension of the jetty to the crest of the bar a depth of twenty or more feet will be obtained. When the work is completed Aransas will be one of the best harbors in the United States for vessels of twenty feet draught and under.

THE Omaha & South Texas Land Co., of Houston, Texas, of which O. M. Carter is president and D. D. Cooley general manager, and which passed into the hands of a receiver in July last is again in the hands of its officers. The company, previous to its affairs going into the receiver's hands, had expended many thousands of dollars on Houston Heights. Among the manufactories located at the Heights were a car factory, a furniture factory, a brick and tile works, a spring-bed and mattress factory, electrical works, a saw mill, etc. The Consumers' Oil Co. has also located its plant there and is in full operation. Besides these, the company established drainage and put in water works, an electric light plant and an electric car line. The work at Houston Heights will be carried forward at once by the officers of the company according to the original programme. The projectors of the enterprise have great faith in the successful results of the undertaking and will prosecute their plans steadily towards perfection.

THE Freedman's Aid and Educational Association of Cincinnati proposes to establish a university at some city in Alabama for the education of colored students if sufficient inducements are extended in the way of a land grant for a site. The colored people of Mobile have organized a committee to try and obtain a site, and it is stated that several prominent citizens will donate sums of money if the university includes an industrial or mechanical department. The college is expected to cost $150,000.

THE increase of educational facilities in Georgia in the last twenty years is well shown by the annual report of the school officials of Bibb county, recently issued. There are 6164 pupils enrolled in the county, of which 2694 are colored. The yearly expenses for school purposes was $66,069.77. The value of school property in city and county is $150,000. In 1873, 1516 pupils were enrolled; the expenses

amounted to $21,715.02, divided among twenty-three schools with forty-one teachers. The present number of schools is forty-nine with 120 teachers. This is an increase of 400 per cent. in the number of pupils, 300 per cent. in the number of teachers and 300 per cent. in the amount of money needed for expenses.

THE pear crop of the coast country in Texas is the first on the market and usually brings good prices. The first picking of the strawberry crop in Texas reaches the market from two weeks to thirty days in advance of the California crop, and for that reason gets the very highest price the market affords. The strawberry season in the fruit section of the coast country lasts five months in the year, and is said to be the most profitable crop raised in the State of Texas. The most extended season in France covers only about seven weeks as a rule.

THE high prices for Virginia apples are arousing much interest among the farmers in the fruit growing counties, and the chances are that more attention will be devoted to fruit and less to other crops hereafter in many of the counties. New York buyers have taken all the apples offered by farmers in the vicinity of Bedford City. About $10,000 worth have been purchased thus far. A report from Page county states that every farmhouse has been visited by the buyers in quest of fruit. The prices range from twenty-five to forty cents per bushel, and the roads are lined every day with teams hauling apples to the railroad stations. The apple crop will be worth thousands of dollars to Page this year, and the good prices it is bringing will go far to supplement the low price of wheat.

THE Chinese & Mexican Commercial Co., an organization composed of wealthy Chinese in the country, has purchased a tract of 250,000 acres in the state of Sinaloa, Mexico, and on these lands it is proposed to settle 5000 of their countrymen. The land was purchased from Herrerra Bros. at a merely nominal figure. The tract lies back in the country about twenty miles from the Pacific coast line, and, it is said, is adapted to the growth of everything that has roots. In two or three months the company expects to have several thousand Chinese at work on the colony. To each one will be allotted sixty-four acres of land, and he will be expected to lay it out and plant it as soon as possible. It is not a co-operative colony, as every member will be expected to pay for his lands as soon as the profits begin to come in. The company will also, it is stated, establish several fac ories for the manufacture of boots and shoes, clothing, brushes, brooms and cigars, and as soon as possible will begin canning fruits.

THERE is quite an active development in real estate and building in Raceland, La. The mammoth sugar mill and refinery of Leon Godcheaux is nearly ready for operation. The sum of $130,000 has already been expended on new machinery and buildings. The work of grinding will commence on the 21st inst. A railroad bridge is to be constructed across Bayou Lafourche and a railroad connection established with the opposite side of the river in order that the sugar-cane may be brought directly to the Godcheaux mill. Mr. August Rantz is the manager of the Raceland mill and 150 men are now at work, 125 men being necessary to operate the mill the year around.

OUT of all the counties in Texas 180 report an aggregate increase in taxable values of $23,110,183 for the year 1892-93 as compared with the previous year.

THE vicinity of Luling, Texas, is considered one of the best for grape cultivation in the State. Next year the acreage in grapes in this section will be largely increased, and it is only a question of a short time until a wine press large enough to make up the grapes will be a necessity. The country extending along the Southern Pacific Railway from Flatonia to Kinsbury, and of which Luling is the principal market, seems to be peculiarly adapted to the growth of the grape. Thousands of acres of rocky and sandy hillsides that for years

have been considered worthless will soon be covered with vines, as this class of soil seems best adapted to them.

TEXAS people have long been alive to the advantages of securing a desirable class of immigrants, and in many of the counties they offer special inducements. Pasturemen of Refugio county favor immigration and will sell land from $6.00 to $10.00 per acre, according to quantity and quality, on reasonable terms to suit purchasers. Others are building comfortable dwellings and outhouses and enclosing fields to rent on shares. Owners furnish necessary implements, horses, etc., and expect from the rents one-half the crop when made. If renter furnishes everything only one-third of the corn and one-fourth of the cotton is demanded.

JACKSONVILLE, FLA., has shown a decided spirit of enterprise in issuing $1,000,000 of 5 per cent, bonds for city improvements. Eight per cent. city bonds amounting to $200,000 now due will be retired and the remainder will be applied to city buildings, improving the water-front, paving the streets, extending the sewage and water systems and otherwise adding to the attractiveness of the city.

SOMETHING new in the way of canning has been adopted by a South Carolina planter, who has determined to turn the greater part of his rice plantation into a truck farm. This gentleman has erected a cannery to handle the surplus truck grown and, in addition, to can rice. He proposes putting it up in cans varying from one to three pounds, cooked in real old Southern style, such as is only found in the rice-growing districts.

DOORWAY--MISSION SAN JOSE.

SOUTHERN STATES.

DECEMBER, 1893.

THE OLD SPANISH MISSIONS OF SAN ANTONIO.

By Elias Edmonds.

Actuated by a desire for territorial acquisition, so prevalent with European monarchs in the Sixteenth and Seventeenth centuries, Philip of Spain encouraged and fostered the pious zeal of the Franciscan Monks to establish their form of worship in the wilds of America, and extended to them for that purpose the aid and protection of the military arm of his government in the establishment of missions along the gulf and river courses of Texas. These missions, called "presidios"—meaning garrisons or forts—were founded in the latter part of the Seventeenth and early part of the Eighteenth Centuries, as far up the rivers of Texas as civilization dared to venture, and met with varied success, being subject to many vicissitudes of good and bad fortune, as the tribes of Indians among which they were located were friendly or hostile. The buildings were constructed with stone and mortar, and consisted usually of a small chapel for religious worship, cells for the monks, and houses or barrack-like wings for the soldiers and servants or domesticated Indians. They were surrounded, in most cases, by a stone wall for defense against incursions of hostile Indians, and within was a large open court or square. At first these missions were under the civil and religious control of the ecclesiastics, the troops being under command of their officers, in subordination, however,

to the orders of the superior monk in charge of the mission.

San Jose Batista, on the lower Rio Grande, was the first mission established in Texas. It was invocated in 1690, and the first mass celebrated in Texas was on May 25, 1690, by the monks accompanying Alonzo de Leon. In the same year the Mission San Francisco was projected at La Salle's old abandoned fort, St. Luis, on Lavaca Bay, but it was never built.

The next mission established in Texas, which in later years built the Church of the Alamo, was founded in the year 1703 by Franciscans of the Apostolic College of Queretero, and was first located in the valley of the Rio Grande, under the invocation of San Francisco Solano. Here it remained five years, but for reasons which do not appear and of which we have not even a tradition, it was moved to San Idelphonso, where it seems to have remained about two years, when it was moved back to the Rio Grande and reinvocated under the name of the Mission San Jose. It remained at this place under the spiritual guidance and temporal care of the good Father Jose de Soto until May, 1718, when, on account of the non-irrigability of the adjoining lands, it was moved 150 miles north to the San Pedro Springs, which is about one mile from the present centre of the City of San Antonio, where it was reinvocated under the name of San Antonio de Valero, after St. Anthony of Padua and the Duke of Valero, then Viceroy of Mexico. In 1722, "for the better protection against hostile Indians," we are told, it was again moved with the attendant garrison one mile, to the place now known as the Military Plaza, a place much better suited than the former for defense against hostile approaches, being protected on the one side by the San Antonio river and on the other side by the San Pedro creek, with vast open untimbered space around over which the approach of the enemy could easily be seen and the garrison put in readiness to repel assaults.

About the year 1730 there arrived at this point thirteen families and two single men, sent from the Canary Islands by order of the King of Spain. They

WINDOW—MISSION SAN JOSE.

were joined en route by others from the banks of Lake Teztuco, sturdy republicans whose ancestors the powerful Montezumas had never been able to conquer, and others also came from the new Spanish settlement of Monterey. These new colonists uniting laid off the main square, or Plaza of the Constitution, as it was called, immediately between the Military Plaza, then occupied by the garrison and Mission de Valero, and the

San Antonio river. Then they laid the foundation and built the old church San Fernando, which of late years has been modernized and greatly enlarged and is now the cathedral of this Roman Catholic diocese. It never was a mission nor designed for one, but only as a place of worship for the new settlers who did not choose to connect themselves with the missions. This new accession to the temporal strength of the missions, however, gave permanency and fixedness to the settlement and greater security from the Indians, so that from time to time colonists, both from Spain and from Mexico, arrived and settled around this locality and engaged in the cultivation of the rich irrigable lands about the place. Thus finding themselves crowded, and probably hampered and retarded in the prime object of their mission, the good monks of de Valero abandoned the location of the Military Plaza in May, 1744, and moved to the east side of the San Antonio river, where on the eighth day of that month was laid the foundation of the Alamo, the Spanish word meaning poplar or elm tree. Thus, after wandering from place to place a distance of over 150 miles in the wilds of this then unknown land for nearly half a century, seeking like "the weary dove" a resting place and finding none, these good fathers at last found for their mission a safe and sure lodgement and gave their church a name that formed the battle cry of the little army of heroes under Sam Houston and his noble compatriots at San Jacinto on that memorable day which ushered into being the Lone Star of Texas and gave to civilization an empire.

Situated as was this mission and church in the rich valley of the lovely San Antonio river, surrounded by gradually sloping hills, with vast tracts of irrigable lands extending for miles down the stream, it became noted at

to be wrested, however, from the original projectors by the Mexican when he accomplished his own independence, and in turn from the Mexican by his more powerful and enterprising neighbor, Brother Jonathan.

It is astonishing, permit me to say by way of digression, to note with what surprising rapidity communities grow, great historic events transpire, and nations are born and die. Two centuries ago this vast State—an empire now in territorial extent, population, wealth, and all things that go to make up a great civilization—was a wild and

MISSION SAN JOSE.

once for its great natural advantages and formed a nucleus for a great city, such as San Antonio is destined to be at no very distant day in the future. Possessing such advantages as I have faintly outlined—a veritable garden in the midst of a wild waste—immigrants from the old country and settlers along the coast and in less inviting localities soon swelled its numbers until the red man was driven from his haunts, and the secular and military arm accomplished what religious zeal had failed to do, although paving the way, a permanent, strong, and thriving settlement,

unexplored country, with a feeble settlement here and there next the borders of adjoining States. Five times hostile armies have traversed its borders, the flags of five distinct nationalities have floated from its bastions, and the blood of five distinct races of men have mingled upon its battlefields.

But to return to the Alamo, famous in history, the pride of Texas, the pride no less of all America—for the blood of its Travis, its Bowie and its Crockett, natives of other States, mingled with the sons of the soil in that ever-memorable fight, "the Fall of the Alamo," in

1836, before the invading forces of Santa Anna, 7000 strong, against 185 poorly-equipped defenders. Not one combatant was left to tell the tale of that heroic defence, the only surviving inmates of that doomed fort being the wife and infant child of Capt. Dickinson, one of its defenders, who died like his comrades in dealing death to the foe and giving his life for the liberty of his adopted State.

As the number of Indians under the charge of this mission increased, and, as they became civilized, they settled around the mission, thus forming a town on the east side of the river, where the company of San Carlos de Passos was stationed to protect the town and the mission from the incursions of hostile Indians, which were by no means infrequent. It had its own alcalde, or judge, for a long period of years, but in 1780, the converted Indians having been previously sent to the missions below the town from time to time as they were instituted, this mission, having no further missionary work to perform, was secularized and became an ordinary Spanish town, and its church a common parish church. The old mission walls and buildings have long since fallen to decay, except the church of the Alamo, which, strange to say, although used as a mission chapel from the time of its construction until 1783 and long afterwards as a parish church, was never entirely completed. We have no precise data regarding its actual construction: a rock in the front wall bears the date 1757, but whether this indicates the date of construction or was afterwards cut there to commemorate some other event, we are not informed. Certain it is, however, that the foundation was laid in May, 1744, as already mentioned.

The illustration gives a view of the church as it now stands, after being somewhat modernized by a sharp roof and gables instead of the flat roof which it is said to have had at the time of the bombardment in 1836. The walls of this mission, like all the rest, were constructed for defense against the Indians, and, although they were four feet thick, they afforded but slight resistance to artillery, and breaches were readily made by the light ordnance used by Santa

Anna in the memorial assault and butchery of the garrison. At what precise date it ceased to be used as a place of worship we are not informed, but in 1876 the entire property was leased from the Roman Catholic Church authorities by Mr. Honoré Grenet, an enterprising merchant, who converted the old church into a warehouse and built upon the grounds occupied by the old ruins of the convent a magnificent wooden structure for his mercantile business, which he pushed with great energy and success until his death in 1882. After this the leasehold passed into the hands of others who still conduct a large grocery business upon the very ground where the good old Franciscans taught wild Indians the church catechism and won them from their wild ways to civilization and Christianity. Thus, in the onward march of events the old and time-honored structures of the past gave place to the needs of commerce, and the shrines and altars reared to the Living God are desecrated and devoted to the God Mammon. The old church itself, the Alamo, dear to the heart of every Texan, was purchased by the State in 1883, and is now in charge of an officer who keeps it in presentable condition and shows to visiting strangers where Bowie fell and where Crockett fought his last fight for liberty and independence.

Soon after the arrival of the colonists who laid off the Plaza of the Constitution and erected the old San Fernando church, already alluded to, the great fertility of the land along the San Antonio river and its susceptibility to irrigation, together with the rumors of rich silver mines at no great distance in the interior, growing out of information derived from the Indians, began to attract attention and settlers poured into the country, so that it became necessary to establish other missions and presidios as a protection to these settlers in the cultivation of the land in vegetables and cereals for the support of the rapidly increasing population. Accordingly, preparations were made for the erection of the Mission San Jose de Aguayo, projected some years prior during the official term of a governor of Texas of that name, but not then built on account of

THE ALAMO.

the hostility of the Indians and the diffi-culty in procuring the necessary garri-son, because of the great need Spain then had for her military forces in other quarters. This was designed to be, and was in reality, the most elegant and beau-tiful of all the Texas missions. Cele-brated architects were sent over from Spain, and years were spent in carving the statuary and elaborate ornamental works upon the building. This orna-mentation is only imperfectly shown in the engraving, as the photograph was made after the building was in ruins and despoiled of much of its pristine elegance and beauty. This building was not com-pleted until 1771, and should be in a much better state of preservation, but neglect, aided by the corrosive touch of time and the hands of vandals, has de-spoiled it of its exterior beauties by de-facing the statue of the Virgin Mother and Child and other figures that adorned and graced its beautiful front. Yet in viewing it, those beautiful lines of the poet, although suggested by structures

reared for far different and less holy pur-poses, involuntarily creep into the mind.

"The roofless cot, decayed and rent,
Will scarce delay the passer by ;
The tower, by war or tempest bent,
While yet may frown one battlement,
Demands and daunts the stranger's eye ;
Each ruined arch and pillar lone
Pleads haughtily for glories gone."

This mission is situated on the right bank of the San Antonio river, about five miles below the town, upon a beautiful elevated plateau, and looks down in silent majesty upon a valley of irrigable lands, along which this beau-tiful river wends its murmuring way to the sea. Thus we float down the stream of time to the great ocean of eternal rest. Thus the minds that planned and the hands that built this grand old structure, with the pious monks who labored in its moral vineyard, have all gone, and soon not a stone will be left to tell after ages of the grand achieve-ments wrought out in the establishment and maintenance of these missions in the difficult and savage wilds of this far away land. After secularization the lands of this mission were contended for by Don Domingo Castillo, and after long suit they were vested in the Indians of the mission, as by purchase for $150, now worth more than as many thousands.

The missions Concepcion, San Juan and La Espada, were first located on the Guadaloupe, then known as St. Mark's or San Marcos river, but in consequence of the difficulty of procuring water for irrigating purposes, so indispensable for the raising of vegetables to supply the inmates and settlers around, Cosa Fuente, the viceroy of Mexico, commissioned the governor of Texas, the ex-guardian of the Apostolic College of Queretero and the president of the Texas missions, on October 29, 1729, to make a new settlement and location for them. After a general tour of inspection of the country, as far as practicable, considering the hostility of the Indians, they selected three sites, two in the vicinity of the missions already established on the San Antonio river and near the city which now bears that name, and a third about thirty leagues below, where at a later date a mission was

established and the town of Goliad was settled, which subsequently became notorious for the treacherous, cruel and bloody massacre of Fannin and his entire command by the Mexican forces of Santa Anna on Palm Sunday, March 27, 1836.

These commissioners then proceeded to the neighboring tribes of friendly Indians, to whom they explained the holy and benovolent purposes of these institutions and persuaded them to submit to the instruction and discipline of the padres or monks, and to aid in the construction of buildings for religious worship and instruction and for shelter and defense against the hostile tribes. Having thus completed the labors assigned to them, the commissioners reported to the viceroy and asked him to make the necessary decrees. The viceroy laid the report before the inspector of presidios for his opinion, and this functionary reported favorably on September 22, 1830, concerning the recommendations of the commissioners, with the exception of the location thirty leauges distant from San Antonio, which he considered so

MISSION DE LA CONCEPCION DE ACUNA.

far from the other settlements as to render the inmates liable to attack and massacre by hostile Indians. He recommended the removal and location of the three missions in the vicinity of the presidios of San Antonio de Bexar and the adjacent mission, San Jose. The viceroy, in conformity with this opinion, on October 2, 1730, decreed that the captain of the royal presidios of San Antonio should issue an order locating the three missions as recommended, using his judgment as to the location of the lower mission and ordering a guard of soldiers for each mission as long as their services might be needed for its protection. On the fifth day of December, 1730, the captain of the presidio of San Antonio de Bexar, in pursuance of this decree of the viceroy, remitted the same to Don Gabriel Castelles, captain of the presidio of La Bahia del Espiritu Santo (then temporarily located at what is now the town of Goliad, thirty leagues below San Antonio, as stated above) with orders to prepare to execute the same. Just here it is curious to note the quaint language and oriental style of this captain, Don Gabriel Castelles, in his return upon this order as illustrative of the great reverence and respect with which inferior officers in those times regarded their rulers. His return reads : "A dispatch was presented to me from the most excellent viceroy, through the captain of the royal presidio of San Antonio de Bexar, which I kissed and placed on my heart as a message from my king and natural lord, which with blind obedience I obey and am ready to execute whatever it commands."

Upon receipt of this return the captain of the presidio of San Antonio, on January 12, 1731, decreed, with all the ceremonies, formalities and circumlocutions which seemed to distinguish official proceedings of that day as well as the present, the removal and relocation of these missions. Thereupon, on March 5, 1731, nearly a year and a half from the issuance of the preliminary order of the viceroy, Captain Perez, of the royal presidio of San Antonio, accompanied by the officers of the presidio and Father Bergara, proceeded to

the mission grounds designated for La Purissima Concepcion de Acuña, and seizing by the hand the chief of the tribe of Indians, who had agreed to attach themselves to that particular mission, led him about over the locality and caused him to pull up weeds, remove and pile stones and do other acts of actual possession, in order that by virtue thereof he might not be despoiled without first being heard and defended by Father Bergara, president of the Texas mission, or his successors in office. After thus defining the bounds of the mission lands and investing the Indians with the possession thereof in the "due and ancient form" deemed necessary in that day, there were attached to the ownership of the land irrigating privileges, pasture lands, watering places on the river, and the further right of driving their stock out west for pasture so as not to interfere with the growing crops. It was the custom at that time to grant to each mission or individual settler one "labor" (177 acres) of land for farming and gardening purposes, and one "league" (4428 acres) for grazing purposes for such stock as it might be desired to raise.

On the same day and in the same manner other tribes of Indians were invested with the possession of the mission lands of San Francisco de la Espada and San Juan, located a few miles below San Jose and about seven miles below San Antonio river and San Juan on the east side, both having tracts of irrigable land which were long cultivated by the Indians. But after the secularization of these missions and the grant of the lands to individuals, the Indians being left without a directing head and being naturally lazy and improvident, many of them returned to the wild life from which they had been only partially reclaimed. The irrigating ditches soon filled up from nonuse and neglect, and these rich bottom lands are now covered with groves of pecan trees from which the present owners reap a goodly profit with no labor save that of gathering the pecans when ripe and taking them to market. Much of these old mission lands has been redeemed and is now in a high state of cultivation, without irrigation, however, affording an abundant supply of garden vegetables for market. But wherever a pecan grove has grown up it is protected with great care, because it is more productive and profitable to the owner than if the land were under cultivation.

As we have seen, on the 5th of March, 1731, the Mission La Purissima Concepcion de Acuña (so called from the Virgin Mother and Juan De Acuña, then viceroy of Spain in Mexico) was located and the foundations of its church and convent were laid. It is situated a mile and a-half below the city of San

modern structures in the city and repeat their orisons kneeling upon cushioned stools, rather than the hard stone floor of the mission chapel. The dome and turrets still stand, and access to them, as well as to the chapel, is through the principal door, which is surrounded by a triangular facade deserving of especial notice because of its rare workmanship. One tower contains a room in which the sacred vestments and articles not in daily use were kept, while the other was used as a baptistry, the walls of which were painted with various emblems, conspicuous among which are the cord

MISSION SAN JUAN.

Antonio on the east side of the river, but the prefix and annex of its name have long since been dropped, and it is now known simply as the Mission Concepcion. It has crumbled almost to ruins. A small and rudely-constructed chapel within the main building is still kept in tolerable repair and mass is said there by priests of the Roman Catholic church at stated intervals, but no priest has it as his especial charge. The worshippers in that vicinity prefer to attend mass at some one of the more

of the Franciscans, a serpent and the seven dolores (sorrows) which pierced the heart of the Virgin Mother. Those who are bold enough to ascend to the roof by means of a rickety old ladder can obtain a better view of the curious old structure, and at the same time behold a landscape of surpassing beauty. In full view are the broad acres of irrigable land where the Christianized Indians tilled their fields and drew water from the intersecting canals to irrigate their growing crops, while at a distance the blue hills lift their towering peaks to the sky and at your very feet gurgles the beautiful river, singing praises to the Almighty Giver' of all good. The walls and fortifications are all gone, only a trace remaining here and there to remind one of the shelter and refuge they long afforded to the weary traveler as well as to the Indians who had been converted to the Romish faith and taught to lift their simple hearts in worship and adoration to the one true God, instead of to the many manitous their wild and savage fancies had found in snakes and lizards and other disgusting reptiles.

The Mission San Juan Capistano is about seven miles below San Antonio on the east bank of the river, and is of a style of architecture quite different from any of the others, which indicates that it was built at a much later date. It was founded, it is true, in 1716, but was unfortunate in its first location and when removed to the present site in 1831 it was probably only fortified as a place of refuge, for we have no accurate account of its building. Like the rest of its compeers, if I may so speak, it has almost entirely fallen to ruin, but the chapel is still preserved with some modern improvements, and religious services are regularly held there, although at one time it was entirely abandoned. The lands around and about it are owned entirely by. Mexicans, the descendants of the original mission Indians who intermarried and amalgamated with settlers from Mexico and elsewhere. This mission seems never to have been successful and no historic events give it importance save that it speaks in common with the others of the zeal and energy and devotion of its founders.

The Mission San Francisco de la Espada (St. Francis of the Sword) is about three miles below San Jose and on the opposite side of the river from San Juan. From its title one would infer its mission was one of war rather than peace, but the old fathers, in selecting the names of their missions, often chose regardless of the significance of the name as applied to the purposes of the mission. At all events, if its purpose was warlike, it seems not to have

been noted for its great achievements, and we have but a meagre account of the spiritual benefits it brought to the wild savages. Nothing now remains to tell us of its original proportions and construction, except a portion of the front wall of the building, which we are told was sword-shaped, indicative of the name it bore, but even that has lost its original conformation. Time and neglect do not, in my mind, satisfactorily account for the rapid decay and ruin of these grand old structures. An inspection of the material and workmanship shows that these buildings were constructed of the most durable materials, put together in the most substantial and skillful manner, and when compared with buildings in San Antonio erected about the same time, that still withstand the ravages of time, the thoughtful mind is immediately led to the conclusion that the portions of the missions used for barracks for soldiers and for purposes of defense were more or less demolished by the advancing or retreating armies of Mexico in the war waged for the subjugation of Texas. It is true that neither history nor tradition supports this theory, but when we reflect that the population of this country in those early days was somewhat nomadic, and when we consider the overpowering sensation occasioned by such incidents as the storming of the Alamo and the wholesale butchery of Fannin at Goliad during the war of 1836, the minor bombardments or the abolition of the presidios at much earlier dates, or even at that period, may have appeared so very insignificant as to escape the notice of the historian, whose data were collected after the lapse of many years and were at best of a most unsatisfactory nature.

However this may be, the fact still remains that they are now mostly decayed and ruined, leaving but faint evidences of the great labor and skill employed in their construction and the untiring devotion of the Franciscans in planting the cross among the wild and savage Indians of this almost boundless waste of prarie, mountain and vale. The missions were all secularized in 1793, except the Alamo, which, as we have already seen, was secularized at an earlier day. The effect of this general decree of secularization was to take the missions out of the hands of the monks who had labored so in their establishment and construction and to place them under the control of the secular clergy. The lands at the same time were granted to the individual Indians constituting the mission flock, and soon for the most part they passed into the hands of others or descended to the children of such as had intermarried with the Mexican and Spanish settlers about the missions, some of whom still own large bodies of these lands. Soon after secularization most of the mission chapels ceased to be used as places of worship, but as the population of the country increased they were again opened for services, and such as are in safe condition still afford a place of worship for the Mexicans residing in their vicinity.

Strangers visiting this unique old town think they are amply repaid for a drive to these old missions by the curious architecture still discernable amid the ruins, and they often return from their inspection with heightened feelings of respect and reverence for the monastic orders and their sublime faith in Him who said to His disciples: "Go ye into all the world and preach My gospel to every people."

HON. PHILIP W. M'KINNEY, GOVERNOR OF VIRGINIA.

THE STATE OF VIRGINIA.*

By Hon. Philip W. McKinney,
Governor of Virginia.

Virginia is one of the Middle Atlantic States, lying midway between Maine on the north and Florida on the south. It is also one of the belt of Central States which runs across the continent from east to west. It is situated in latitude 36.31 to 39.27 degrees north, corresponding to that of Southern Europe, Central Asia, Southern Japan and California. Its longitude is from 75.13 to 83.37 degrees west from Greenwich. It extends 20.57 degrees north and south and 90.24 degrees east and west.

In soil, climate, productions, conveniences for transportation, educational and religious advantages, Virginia has no superior among all the States of the Union. Blessed by the finest climate, absolutely free from extremes of heat and cold, visited by neither cyclones nor blizzards, and famine and pestilence being unknown, Virginia offers a safe place for a home where expectations of comfort and prosperous continuance can be relied on. The average temperature of the State is 56.9, and the average rainfall 42.12, for ten years, and does not vary materially in any section.

The land of the State is cheap, from the splendid blue-grass region of the Valley of the Shenandoah and the Southwest, through the magnificent orchards and yellow tobacco fields of Piedmont to the cotton and peanut plains of the southern border, and the oyster beds and fishery shores of Tidewater. On the great rivers can be found good, cheap land—low-priced when compared with like lands in other States in the Union.

MINERALS.

The mines of valuable ores are richer and minerals are cheaper and the wood and timber can be bought for less than elsewhere, while in quality and intrinsic value they are fully equal to the best in other States.

For twenty years mineralogists have predicted that the time would come when Virginia would be ahead of all other States in quantity and quality of its minerals. These predictions have been verified and immense deposits of minerals, richer than any other State can show, and great coal fields for making coke higher in fixed carbon and more valuable for smelting purposes than any others, have been discovered, and this coke is being carried by rail to make cheap iron in other States. During the past few years there has been a great increase in the amount of capital invested, and a greatly increased activity in the mining of tin, gold, mica, clay, salt, pyrites, etc.

The number of prospectors and explorers for minerals is greater than ever before in the State, and more analyses and practical tests of minerals have been made, all with fine results. This discloses the fact that minerals in paying quantities and qualities are found in many localities not known as mineral bearing heretofore, and thus exceeding the highest expectations. These minerals are in many cases in close proximity, which lessens the expense of manufacturing when more than one kind of mineral is needed. For instance: Coking coal, iron, lime and manganese for

*A paper prepared for publication in a pamphlet to be issued by the governors of the Southern States.

cheap iron and steel; salt, coal, manganese and lime for soda ash and bleach; high carbonate marls and fine aluminous clay for cement; fire clay for furnaces, etc.; alkaline clay for vitrified brick; pyrite, coal and lime for sulphuric acid. Another consideration of value in this connection is that there is already railroad transportation through nearly all the mineral sections, with abundant water power where water power is needed.

The surface of the State rises by five steps from the ocean shore to an altitude of nearly six thousand feet. Under these steps are all the richest minerals. The first area includes the phosphate marls of Tidewater and the gold and more recent coal formation and sulphuret belt of Middle Virginia; then come the magnetic iron, lead, zinc and manganese deposits of Piedmont, the Blue Ridge and the Valley, and next the vast deposits of salt, coal, iron and gypsum in Appalachia.

The Commissioner of Agriculture, after four years' service, and careful investigation, reports as follows: "In Virginia there have been found, tested and developed immense deposits of minerals richer than in any other land. The coke from her immense coal fields is higher in fixed carbon and more valuable for smelting than any other, and has been carried hundreds of miles by rail to make cheap iron in other States. Her iron for steel, for cannon, for car wheels, for stoves, etc., has been given, upon test, the highest places. Her immense deposits of manganese stand before the world without a rival. Her zinc has long had a reputation based on a contract with the Italian government, and both the mines and the smelting are increasing. Her granite was accepted by the Federal government for building after an official test, and the finest pavements in many cities of our sister States are of Virginia Belgian block. Her large deposits of magnesian lime still furnish the celebrated James river cement. Her Buckingham slate stands without a rival in roofing. These all have had official and practical tests.

"Add to these minerals that have been developed and believed to have shown paying quality and quantity, the pyrite of Louisa, mica of Amelia, fire clay and ochre of Chesterfield, gold of the middle counties, baryta, soapstone, lead, copper, asbestos, plumbago, kaolin, gypsum, salt, lime, marble, lithographic stone and many others, and Virginia may well be proud of her mineral wealth."

In 1892 the Commissioner of Agriculture emphasized the above by quoting and repeating after another year's thorough investigation: "I would simply add that there is now an increasing development in gold, tin, mica, fire clay, soapstone and pyrites, while in iron, copper, zinc, lead, manganese and coal there is a steady continuance of the work. Petroleum has been discovered east of the Blue Ridge, beyond peradventure, in the coal section near Richmond. Many of the minor and scarcer and more valuable minerals have been discovered in developing and mining those well known.

"The stone of Virginia, granite, soapstone, marble and sandstone, are being more extensively developed and regularly worked than ever before, and the manufacture of brick in all qualities, tiles, drain pipes, etc., is becoming a large industry.

"Manufacturers of wood, iron and tobacco still hold the prominence, and are followed by many smaller manufactures attracting attention.

"Manufactures of wool are increasing, and fine woolen goods from Charlottesville, Bedford City and Buena Vista are well known in the markets of the Union, while smaller factories are springing up."

MANUFACTURES.

The number of furnaces for smelting the various ores is phenomenal, and as much as $50,000,000 has been invested, mainly brought in from outside of the State.

Railroads are being projected and built into sections where the richness and proximity of different ores and an abundance of fuel promise the cheapest product, and double the amount already invested can and will be invested in these mines.

Works for the manufacture of metals

are beginning to follow in the track of these furnaces, and towns like Roanoke, Buena Vista, Pulaski City, Radford and others demonstrate the advantage of such manufactures by their extraordinary life and growth.

The remarkable activity in the gold belt leads to the belief that Virginia will soon be famous for gold, as it is now for its mines of coal and iron.

Five years ago Pennsylvania and Maryland had a monopoly of the fire-brick trade of Virginia, and buff brick and vitrified brick came from the North-west. Now Chesterfield and Rockbridge counties supply much of the former, and Smyth and Powhatan are prepared to compete for the latter.

A valuable tin field was discovered in Rockbridge county some years ago, but for want of capital failed to be fully developed. Within the past two years the fact is assured that Virginia has a developed tin mine—large in quantity and exceedingly rich as to quality. Many tons have been mined, and some has been subjected to furnace tests and assayed. Capital alone is wanting to add tin to the natural products of Virginia, and tin-plating to her manufactures.

MINERAL WATERS.

Virginia has long been celebrated for its mineral springs, some of which rank with those found at the most noted resorts in the world. The number is yearly being added to, and each season brings large crowds from the State itself, who, with those who come from far and near, fill up every place in the search for pleasure or health.

These springs embrace chalybeate, sulphur, alum, limestone and lithia, and many combinations of these; also, hot and warm springs, while from mountains and hills gush the cold freestone water, clear as crystal.

TIMBER.

Virginia has extensive forests of pine, white or hemlock, spruce or yew, yellow pine and oldfield pine; thirteen varieties of oaks, besides cypress, cedar, locust, chestnut, hickory, juniper, poplar, cucumber, gum, maple, walnut, cherry, sycamore, beech, birch, persimmon, ash, cottonwood, mulberry. These all grow large enough for timber, and there are several distinct varieties of them, giving to the State more than thirty different valuable timbers. In some sections walnut, cherry, poplar, pine, ash, gum, oak and chestnut attain an immense diameter and height. Many smaller varieties are valuable for furniture and ornamental work.

The Dismal Swamp can supply the country with gum, cypress and pine for a hundred years to come; Middle Virginia and Piedmont, with pine, oak, chestnut, hickory and locust; while Appalachia, the Valley and Blue Ridge have the finest and largest poplar, walnut, cherry, beech, birch, cedar and ash in the whole country. The Valley has long been famous for its wagon timber, while immense quantities of poplar, walnut and cherry go by rail from Appalachia to Northern markets.

In the last few years large cargoes of timber have been shipped from our ports. The lumber trade of Norfolk alone amounts to $5,000,000 annually.

AGRICULTURE.

The agricultural products are varied and abundant. All plants that grow in any part of the temperate zone flourish here. Across the State there is an isothermal line; south of this line plants that come to perfection in the tropical regions yield fairly well—i. e., the fig, pomegranate and olive among the fruits, and cotton, peanuts and yams come to perfection. There is another isothermal line on the mountain side, several thousand feet above the level of the sea, beyond which the frost never comes. Above this line the productions belong to the extreme north temperate zone, and here rye, buckwheat, cabbage, turnips and potatoes attain their perfection. Between these two extremes may be found all the plants that belong to the temperate zone. Com. Maury says that "everything that can be cultivated in France, Germany and England may be grown here equally as well, with other things, such as Indian corn, cotton, tobacco, peanuts, broom corn, sweet potatoes, etc., which are not known as staples there." The *National Republican* says: "The soil of Virginia is as varied as the colors of a crazy quilt; parts of it produce wheat equal to Dakota, corn equal to Illinois, potatoes equal to New York, cotton equal to Georgia, while its tobacco is the best made."

This description is verified. The Commissioner of Agriculture of Virginia, in his reports from 1888 (made yearly) to 1892, makes the following comparisons:

Dakota reports for 1891, wheat average, sixteen bushels per acre.

Highest field yield, twenty-seven bushels per acre.

Average, 1892, twelve bushels per acre.

Highest yield, nineteen bushels per acre.

Virginia in 1889 reported three counties with highest field yield of fifty bushels per acre.

Eighteen counties, forty bushels per acre.

Twenty-nine counties, from twenty-five to thirty bushels per acre.

Eleven counties report many instances of a yield of over 100 bushels per acre.

Of corn, a majority of the counties report field yields exceeding fifty bushels per acre.

There are authentic yields of potatoes of over 400 bushels per acre, and individual crops of over 10,000 bushels.

Of cotton, Southampton county reported as the highest yield 2300 pounds per acre, and the census of 1880 gives the product of cotton in eight counties at 19,598 bales.

Every variety of tobacco can be grown in Virginia, of the finest quality, with the greatest yield per acre.

There are well authenticated reports of immense yields of oats, rye, buckwheat, peanuts, sweet potatoes and cabbages from the counties in different sections of the State suitable for their production.

There are many instances in which men of moderate means have, with the net proceeds of one year's crop, not only supported their households, but paid the entire price for the land. There are other well-established instances in which the entire price of the land has been paid from the net proceeds of a crop of tobacco made from the land.

Trucking in some sections, especially in Tidewater, has been exceedingly profitable, and there are thousands of acres of the peculiar land known as "trucking land" that can be bought at very low prices. There are authentic instances of from three to five paying crops being made from the same land in one year. From a thirty-acre farm the owner sold $15,000 worth of vegetables in one year; from three and four-seventh acres the owner sold over $1700 worth of vegetables in one year. Another year's crop consisted of kale, which brought $250 per acre, which was followed by the Irish Potato crop, which brought $225 per acre, and closing with a crop of corn planted the 20th of June, bringing twenty-five bushels per acre. From one and a quarter acres of this land the owner sold $6201 worth of produce in the five years beginning with 1883 and ending with 1887. Evidence of these facts, after deducting freight and commissions, can be found in the office of the State Commissioner of Agriculture of Virginia.

It is difficult to convince a stranger of these facts when he comes from a country where the annual rent of such land, with no better surroundings, is as great as the fee-simple price of Virginia lands. These lands are intrinsically cheaper than any public lands subject to entry anywhere, and with the advantages offered for trade, education and the comforts of a family, as a place for making a home, they are cheaper and better than any lands in the world.

There are manufactories, mills, shops and stores in every county, mainly in the cities, towns and villages, and they are fast embracing the utilization of every product of the State used, from canneries and dairies to furnaces and cotton mills, and the products of their works in cotton, wool, iron, zinc, lead, wood, tobacco, fruit and vegetables is not excelled in the Union.

The growth of the cities and towns of the State is marked, and her grand trunk lines of railroads and navigable rivers, leading to the largest, safest and most magnificent harbor in the world, surrounded by every appliance for trade and commerce, insure a rapid settlement around this wonderful 'haven for ships.'

The navigable waters of. Virginia afford ingress and egress to the commerce of the world. At Norfolk and at Newport News, Lambert's Point and Hampton Roads can float the combined navies of the world. In May, 1893, war vessels of great dimensions, representing many foreign countries, rendezvoused at Hampton Roads, and the leviathans of the sea can lay close up to the wharves at Newport News.

At Richmond, the beautiful capital of Virginia, on the historic James, can be daily seen large passenger and freight steamers from New York, Boston, Philadelphia and elsewhere in the United States, and sailing vessels from across the mighty deep, and West Point, on the York river, alike affords a safe and commodious harbor for the largest ships. Alexandria, Fredericksburg and Petersburg have lines of steamers and carry on a considerable trade by sailing crafts.

The whole State has fine facilities for transportation for freight and travel by rail and water, and there is every indication of an increase in railroads and steamboat lines as well as marked improvement in the turnpikes and county roads. Capital to any amount can ·find a safe investment in the mining of every metal, in the working up of every wood, great and small, known to the temperate zone, as well as in every manufacture of the products of the field and of the orchard.

FISH AND OYSTERS.

The rivers and creeks of Virginia are filled with excellent fish, varying in kind and quality from the mountains to the sea. In our tide-waters oysters and other shellfish are abundant, and are excelled in no part of the world. Our people are becoming interested in the propagation and cultivation of fish and oysters, and while it is now quite an industry, we have reason to believe that it is increasing and in a short time will become the greatest of Virginia's industries.

Oyster lands, suited for cultivation, are rented by the State to its citizens at $1 per acre. These lands are unsurpassed for this business, and it is believed that the cultivation of oysters will become a source of immense profit to those who take advantage of the present opportunity to secure these lands. The area of oyster lands controlled by the State is estimated to be from a million to a million and a-half acres.

GAME.

Many of the counties of Virginia are full of deer, and the pheasant and sora, wild ducks, geese and turkeys are in abundance in many sections. The "old hare" is abundant in every county and furnishes food second to none of its kind, and the partridge is everywhere to be found to animate the huntsman and add a dish to the table unsurpassed.

EDUCATION.

No State has better educational facilities than Virginia. All persons between five and twenty-one years of age who are residents of the State have a right to attend our schools, free of tuition.

The number of pupils enrolled in our public schools for the present year was 342,720, the number of teachers was 7795, the number of school houses in use was 6595 ; the value of school property is $2,763,637, the cost of the school system for the year was $1,636,982.

The school money is distributed among the counties and cities on the basis of the school population.

STATE INSTITUTIONS FOR HIGHER AND TECHNICAL EDUCATION.

University of Virginia, Charlottesville.

Virginia Military Institute, Lexington.

Virginia Agricultural and Mechanical College, Blacksburg, Montgomery county, Va.

State Female Normal School, Farmville, Prince Edward county, Va.

Virginia Normal and Collegiate Institute, Petersburg, Va. (For colored students of both sexes.)

College of William and Mary and State Normal School, Williamsburg, Va.

Institution for the Education of the Deaf, Dumb and Blind, Staunton, Va.

Medical College of Virginia, Richmond, Va.

Hampton Normal and Agricultural Institute, Hampton, Va. (For colored students of both sexes.)

The State appropriated for the fiscal year beginning September 30, 1892, the sum of $159,750 for the support of the above-named institutions.

There are various other schools and colleges of high repute in various portions of the State for the education of the youth of this country. Their names are not given here because we are speaking, in this paper, of those institutions which belong to the State. The others, above referred to, belong to different churches and charitable organizations of every creed, and all of them deserve high commendation, but the limited space given to this article will not allow us to refer to them except in a general way.

RELIGIOUS OBSERVANCE.

Virginia was first to declare for religious liberty. In no State in the great Union of Commonwealths is there a better regard of religious observances or a more general church-going people than in Virginia. The spires of churches of all denominations, and of both white and colored races, tower up in almost countless numbers in our cities and in the counties, at almost every crossroad and in every neighborhood can be seen churches, wherein every Sunday and on other days, the crowds that attend worship are evidences of the fact of religious liberty, for in these temples, dedicated to the God of all the people, can be found those who think as they choose about religion, and worship as they please, with none to make them afraid. The Virginia people are God-serving.

OUR PUBLIC DEBT.

This important question, which has been giving us trouble for many years, is now settled to the entire satisfaction of creditors and meets with the approval of our people. With the present low assessment on our property we can pay the interest and support the government and keep up our schools. The tax amounts to forty cents on $100 value of property, which is as low as that imposed in most of the States. With an increasing population and wealth, this will in all probability be reduced in a few years to a rate of taxation as low as that which can be found in any State of the Union.

NEEDS.

Virginia, like most of the old slave-holding States, languishes under a burden growing out of the ownership of large tracts of land by persons who have neither labor nor capital sufficient to cultivate them. All over the State these large plantations are growing up in pine and brush. With all the accompaniment of a cultivated and refined society, with conveniences for agriculture and trade, our people are kept down by paying taxes on over 15,000,000 acres of arable land, which, not being cultivated, brings in nothing, and is rapidly being taken up by pine and other wild growths. Every year adds to the cost of reclaiming and improving. To remedy this, at least 10,000,000 acres of land, not including homesteads, ought to be sold (18,000,000 would be better) to immigrants who are able to purchase, and who would also stock and cultivate the land after having bought it. Virginia wants men who want homes for themselves and families; it needs population; it requires good men—steady, industrious, law-abiding men—with their families. Thousands of acres of broad, fertile, unoccupied land await the coming of such a class of settlers.

IMMIGRATION.

A good class of immigrants would introduce small industries into the villages and thickly settled portions of the State. These industries should be suited to the families of men of small means, who find it necessary to have their children, if not their wives, earn something away from home. Virginia cannot afford to exchange her population for that of any other land or country. With capital there could not be found anywhere better farmers, planters, orchardists and truckers than the present agricultural population, nor better miners and manufacturers than she already has. But without complaint or mourning for the cause, her agriculturists and planters find themselves with large tracts of valuable land which they cannot utilize, and they do not wish to sell their homes, but such parts as they are unable to cultivate for want of means, and their taxation is a burden.

With this statement of facts concerning Virginia, showing the inducements she offers to immigrants, we invite all good and law-abiding people from the various States of the Union and from the various countries of the world to come and make their homes with us and to share with us our advantages of government, education, of soil and climate, and all the blessings which have been vouchsafed to our commonwealth, and bring with you your families, your friends and your household goods, and you will receive a cordial welcome from our people and from our government.

QUATRAINS OF THE SOUTH.

By Frank H. Sweet.

THE SOUTH.

A prolonged sleep, from which, at length,
  She wakes to find her dream unreal,
But shows the world the latent strength
  Which only mighty throes reveal.

HOSPITALITY.

Warm as the sun that seeks its land,
  Boundless as all its wealth may be,
Open as its extended hand,
  Is Southern hospitality.

THE EMIGRANT.

He rashly crosses plain and sand
  To some strange, unknown shore,
And leaves a pleasant, fertile land
  Knocking upon his door.

THE NEW SOUTH.

Out from the cocoon of the past
  The chrysalis appears,
Well tempered by the fiery blast,
  And fed by dormant years.

LETTERS FROM SOUTHERN FARMERS—III.

[The letters published in this issue form the third instalment in the series commenced in the last number of this magazine. These communications are published in response to numerous inquiries from Northern people who desire to know more about agricultural conditions in the South, and what is being accomplished by settlers from other sections of the country. These letters were written by practical farmers and fruit-growers, chiefly Northern and Western people who have made their homes in the South. The actual experiences of these settlers, as set forth in these letters, are both interesting and instructive to those whose minds are turned Southward.—EDITOR.]

Fruit on Chandler Mountain.

JOHN W. INZER, Ashville, St. Clair county, Ala.—I desire very briefly to call the attention of those who wish to grow fruits in Alabama, to Chandler Mountain. This mountain is one of nature's beauties, and is located some six miles north of Ashville. In almost every respect it is the best place to grow fruits I ever saw in Alabama. This mountain rises on the west bank of Little Canoe creek, on the line of Etowah and St. Clair counties, and extends southwest a distance of eleven miles, and then suddenly drops down. The table lands on its top are about eight hundred feet above its base. It is bounded on the east by the beautiful valley of Canoe creek, and on the north and northwest by Greasy cove. The mountain is from seven to eight miles across, and on its top are to be found beautiful table lands, in width from two to four miles. These lands are quite productive, well timbered and well watered, and produce, well, almost any kind of fruits or vegetables grown in this latitude. They hardly ever fail to bring fruits, being above the frost altitude. The small fruits, as well as peaches, apples, pears, etc., can be grown with great success up there, and thrown into the early spring markets.

The Alabama Great Southern Railroad runs at the eastern base of the mountain. It is within forty miles of Birmingham, and in less than sixty miles of Chattanooga. Fruits can be gathered on this mountain and placed on the Cincinnati market in less than twenty-four hours. Early peaches can be grown there and sold in Cincinnati for seven or eight dollars per bushel. Health is almost perfect; scenery beautiful. A public road crosses this mountain, leading from Steeles, a station on the Alabama Great Southern Railroad, to Greasy cove.

Some of these mountain lands belong to the United States government, and can be homesteaded. Almost one-half of the lands belong to the Alabama State Land Company, Birmingham, Maj. F. Y. Anderson, general manager.

There are a dozen or more farmers living on this mountain, and there are the best of reasons why there should be more than a thousand families there within the next three or five years. All manner of vegetables grow well on this mountain land. I could say much more, but will say no more now. This mountain is in townships 12 and 13 and ranges 3 and 4 east.

Climate, Soil and People—All Good.

N. JAMES INGERSOLL, Chunchula, Ala.—My sojourn of eight years in this locality convinces me that this is most decidedly a healthy section of country. I am not fully advised as to all the conditions that go to make it so healthful, but a reasonable trial must convince almost anyone that it is all that is claimed for it in point of health. As to soil for productiveness, we have not a large amount of vegetable matter in our soil, but it responds readily to the application of any good fertilizer. There is much to be hoped for from improved methods, soiling with green crops, using a good Yankee plow and perhaps a good Yankee behind it, has promise of material reward.

As to natural advantages, soil included, I cannot see that we are a whit behind Middle or Northern Florida; rather this section appears in a better light in regard to some of the most vital points. As to the social status, I speak with some interest; a more kindly or genial people than that which inhabits this section it would be hard to find. In this respect they are of the seed royal.

Our churches and schools are quite plentiful and our public school system is increasing in effectiveness. We have the true gospel in our churches, but we would like more people among us to help us build our "watch fires." As to political liberality, there may be political disturbances abroad, but this section is one of the most free from political excitement that has been my fortune to tarry in, and this statement I make after having sojourned in nearly half of the States of our Union.

Home-Seekers Will Find Welcome.

JOHN S. WHITEHEAD, Escatawpa, Ala.—We have as fine pine lands, rolling, table and flat, as can be found anywhere North or South, well adapted to the growth of any kind of fruits or vegetables that can be grown in any semitropical locality. Pears, peaches and strawberries are being successfully cultivated; corn, potatoes, peas, rice, cotton are staples now cultivated; a little tobacco is raised for home use, and it does well. Stock of all kinds does well on the range eight months in the year. The Escatawpa (Dog) river flows through a natural lake; we can get some fish, and generally plenty at almost any season of the year.

We have plenty of pine timber for all local demands and some for export. We have two good churches, Baptist and Methodist; our schools are not what they will be when we get more good people, but they average fairly with our country public schools generally. Home seekers will find some thrifty good people scattered through here who will welcome them and who realize the need of more good people among us. I am ready at any time to answer questions or otherwise aid to secure a good settler.

Intelligent, Energetic Men Wanted.

W. S. FORMAN, Springville, Ala.— Coming under the head of a Northern, or rather a Western man myself, having now been living south of the Ohio river longer than eight years, I will most cheerfully give you my opinions and the result of my experience of farm life in Alabama, its present condition and future prospects, together with the comparative advantages in the way of acquiring and possessing the ordinary comforts of life as produced from the soil. I think I will be able to convince any reasonable man that Alabama is the goal on which he should fix his eyes, both for his health and comfort and his cheapness of living. A farmer and the son of a farmer myself, the cultivation of the soil being my principal and favorite vocation, I speak from observation and experience.

Farming in Alabama, as well as elsewhere, demands industry and economy from all engaged in the business in in order to make it a source of profit. A man may make a living, hold his own with his neighbors and his merchant without practicing strictly either of the above leading principles, but they must be observed to make his labors a means of profit; but these principles require as strict observance to produce profit in every other industry as in that of farming. To some extent the lack of a rigid enforcement of them has thrown the farming interest in Alabama so largely in the background. Rapid changes, however, are coming over the minds and habits of our people, growing out of former mishaps and failures, so that we may most reasonably hope the

Alabama farmer may be found and classed amongst our most worthy and independent citizens.

While we have in a large measure quite a uniform climate, running into neither extreme heat or cold, we have every variety of soil as we have in general topography—mountain lands, table lands, valley lands and bottom lands along our principal streams, and a variety of soil. All of these soils are naturally adapted to the successful cultivation of all the cereals—more than demanded for home consumption—grasses, stock raising, with no better climate or country for fruits of all sorts, grapes and berries. What can you ask of any country more than Alabama soils produce for you? For all these, with ordinary care, can be produced in abundance.

From the foregoing it will at once be seen that our State is the place and home for the farmers, who are the bone and fibre of any country's population. We have neither in the towns nor cities, or in the country anywhere any locality subject to disease or epidemics of any class. Generally speaking the country is high, with dry, healthy atmosphere and abundance of pure limpid water gushing from the mountain sides, of which we have many in almost every vicinity.

All we lack in Alabama to make it the foremost State in the Union, saying nothing about coal and iron, is men—high-minded men, intelligent men, men who are not afraid or ashamed to roll up their sleeves, to make and eat their own bread, to make their homes attractive and happy, to make their own lives and homes living examples of thrift and happiness for others. We want just 100,000 such men to come into Alabama and take up their abode with us. We will guarantee homes for all. Lands are cheap, living is cheap—none cheaper anywhere, and the way is open to every good citizen.

A Maine Man in Arkansas.

J. H. TRASK, Helena, Ark.—I am a native of Maine and my home is now in Phillips county, Arkansas, a few miles south of Helena. I note with pleasure the effort which is being made by the SOUTHERN STATES to make known the great agricultural and climatic advantages of the South. Comparing agricultural pursuits in my boyhood home in Maine with the same calling in this country, one is impressed with a feeling of wonder that so few leave the old country to find homes in the sunny South. The advantage of climate and seasons which the South possesses over the North it would seem is enough to impress Northerners with a desire to come South, to say nothing of the great advantages of fertility of land and the opportunity to get cheap and comfortable homes.

In Maine we had one month in the year devoted to hay-making; here we have from May to October, all good hay-making months, while from May to November are grazing months, during which no hay or feeding is needed for stock not at work. From November 1 to March 1 a few days occur at times when shelter is needed for stock, sometimes a rainy week, sometimes a snow, but such weather is exceptional. It is rarely the case that stock if left to its own choice will not prefer the open fields to the sheltered lots. Vegetables and fruits of all varieties grow to great profusion. The Irish and sweet potatoes, beets and turnips may be produced twice a year, that is to say the first crop of Irish potatoes may be taken off and a new crop planted and matured, or the same ground may be planted in sweet potatoes, cabbage, beats, beans or turnips. A crop of corn and a crop of peas may be made on the same land. But little attention is paid to fertilizing; in many parts it is not necessary. I remember the great cost of fertilizing in Maine when I was a boy; more was expended for fertilizing than is required here to make a crop.

For many years the advice has been "Go West, young man, and grow up with the country." Now the word is "Come South." We want young men who want to accumulate and make homes comfortable. To such we can say do not stand on the order of your coming. Come determined to work half as hard as you work in Maine, come determined to work for your own comforts and you need not fear. If you have no money to buy a home with, rent your land and a mule the first year, raise what you want at home and a little cotton for revenue, and the second year you will be master. Land can be had at from $2 to $10 per acre. From $40 to $200 is what you need to buy a 20 acre farm. This is all you need, but, of course, as you grow in strength you will grow in wants and will buy the land adjoining you. Do not fear that you will want for good, kind, agreeable neighbors. Our people are refined and intelligent and sociable as the people of any part of the world. We want people to come and live with us and enjoy the riches which providence has planted in this country. Do not believe that your politics or religion or your Yankee notions will be in the way. The South is ready with open arms and outer latch strings to receive you and as-simulate with you. Bring all the Yankee notions and Yankee ways you have with you; we need them here to increase, if possible, the size of our turnips and roses, our potatoes and pansies, our pumpkins and petunias. Come and help us to mix our Yankee industry with Southern generosity. "Come with us and we will do thee good."

On the South Slope of the Ozark Mountains.

REV. H.W. ZENTZ, Mammoth Spring, Ark.—I am a native of Ohio. Leaving that State in my fifteenth year I struck out to make my way in life. I landed first in Indiana, about twenty-five miles from the city of Fort Wayne, in April, 1852. The country there was new then, game plenty and the luxuries of life but few. I had my siege of ague and fever in the Wabash bottoms with the crowd, who had to have the malarial diseases there as surely as children have to go through measles. After a precarious life in that wild country the war came on and I marched away with the rest of the boys to the front. I tried to do what I thought to be my duty, and returned home in the spring of 1865 and two years afterwards migrated to Iowa.

During my army life I had spent much of my time in Southeastern Missouri, Western Tennessee, Eastern Arkansas, parts of Mississippi and Louisiana, and during the year 1864 near Pensacola, Fla. I observed the climate, productions, etc., of the South and fully resolved if the opportunity ever occurred to make the South my future home. Finally in 1888 I bade farewell to Iowa, with her ice and snow and blizzards and frequent droughts and everlasting winds, and came to this point. I took up a homestead in Randolph county, Ark., purchased other lands and started in to improve them as I was able. I soon found that I had located too far from market, and "proving up" I soon found an opportunity to sell out advantageously.

I am now located on a farm in Oregon county, Mo., about two miles from the flourishing young city of Mammoth Spring, Ark. I am satisfied that I have found the best all-around climate in the world, and the best fruit country in the United States. The county I live in took the blue ribbon at Chicago for best peaches, and Fulton county, Ark., for the largest and best apples. The tree producing these apples grew about five miles from my home. The largest orchard in the Union is the Olden fruit farm in Howell county, Mo., about thirty miles north of me. We are on the south slope of the Ozark mountains. We have no droughts, no blizzards, no extreme heat or cold. Our winter is mild and does not last over two months. We raise all the fruits of the temperate zone, save the orange, lemon and such semi-tropical fruits. All the grains raised in the Northern States, potatoes, both sweet and Irish, tomatoes and all garden vegetables, grasses of all kinds, cotton of the very best variety—in short we show up successfully in a greater variety of grains, fruits, vegetables and grasses than any other locality in the Union.

As to health we challenge the world to show an all-round healthier climate than this. Diphtheria and scarlet fever are unknown, and typhoid and "spotted fever" or cerebro spinal menengitis almost equally scarce. The winds and cyclones I so much dreaded in Iowa are not feared here. Such a thing as a "cyclone cave" is unknown in this vicinity.

Our society, although made up of people from the North, the South, the East and the West, works harmoniously without respect to "race, color or previous condition of servitude." Of course what colored people we have among us know their place and are useful and docile; we are having no trouble in that line. I was cautioned before I left the North that, having been a Union soldier, I would have to "look a leedle out;" but I have eaten and slept with men who were opposed to me in the same battles; I hire them to work for me; we are members of the same church; they are my elders in the congregation and I am their pastor. We know no difference. The war is entirely over here. In conclusion I would say that for climate, scenery, productions, and especially for fruits, vegetables and stock-raising, for range for hogs, sheep, etc., for good hospitable society, for push and energy, morality and everything that goes to make life enjoyable with the minimum of drawbacks that must be met everywhere, I believe that the southeast slope of the Ozarks, and especially Oregon county, Mo., and Fulton county, Ark., will more nearly come up to "high water mark" than any other locality in this broad land of ours.

Led to Arkansas from the World's Fair.

D. A. COATE, Stuttgart, Ark.—After spending thirty-five years of my life in Marshall county, Iowa, and six years in Cloud county, Kansas, I was induced to visit Arkansas by having placed in my hands, in the Arkansas building at the World's Fair, a little book setting forth some of the facts about the State. After spending the best part of my life in the Northern States, where the weather is so changeable, where the summers are so hot and dry and the winters so long and so cold, I was desirous of changing the seasons about where the summers would be long and the winters short, or in fact where there would be no winter, and I came to Stuttgart. To the northern man who knows what the climate and crops are in the North, I want to tell just what I find here. I find a grand prairie, about

eighty miles long and twenty-five miles wide, with good soil and just rolling enough to drain the water, covered with blue stem grass that will make from one to three tons of hay to the acre. This prairie is dotted with groves of timber with from a thousand to five thousand acres of oak, hickory, catalpa, gum, walnut and many other varieties. The grass is green and makes good feed ten months. The mast in the timber makes fine feed for the hogs, making stock raising very profitable, as the expense is light. As to crops, the soil produces good crops of corn, oats, millet, wheat, potatoes—both Irish and sweet, cane and broom corn, in fact all of the crops of the North do splendidly when properly cultivated. Fruits of all kinds are plentiful; apples, peaches, plums, pears, apricots, figs, strawberries, quinces, dewberries, blackberries and in fact all kinds of fruits and vegetables grow very large and very fine. Five crops of potatoes are grown each year or planted five months in the year, and two crops of lettuce, radishes, onions, cabbage, etc. A good crop of stock peas is grown on the same ground you raise your corn and oats on, which is very valuable. As for climate, the weather is not so changeable as in the North. We have warm, pleasant days and cool nights, with no high winds, just a little breeze, and the winter months, January and February, are not cold. It seldom snows, but we have plenty of rain. The people on the prairie are mostly Northern men. There is good society, good schools and good churches. I am greatly pleased with the country, climate and people and can recommend it to my friends.

Among the Orange Groves of Florida.

C. J. K. JONES, DeLand, Fla.— Originally from New York, (Long Island,) I have been interested in Florida for over twelve years, and unless a change comes over the "spirit of my dreams," or circumstances prevent, I expect to live in the State for the balance of my natural life. I own an orange grove of twenty acres in West DeLand, Volusia county. Wild land in this locality comes high, but is well worth its cost in preference to cheaper lands situated at a distance from transportation. The Jacksonville, Tampa & Key West Railway branch to DeLand divides my twenty acres in two equal parts, thus affording exceptional advantages of transportation. On my place I can raise, or am successfully raising, the various varieties of oranges, grape fruit, grapes, guavas, Japanese persimmons, pears and peaches, the latter as fine as a man need wish.

I have owned my place since 1881, having bought the woodland whereon my trees now stand in February of that year. I have experienced all vicissitudes of the Florida climate in the past twelve years, but never have I seen reason for wishing to exchange my investment in a home in this delectable climate. More, I have never seen an instance where, being rightly located, a man has failed to "make" a grove who has persisted in developing it as the circumstances demanded. Florida has its failures. As men in other parts of the United States experience successful and unsuccessful seasons so do Floridians have their years of only partial success. In the twelve years of my varied experience and acquaintance with Florida I have never seen either a total failure of corps or a season wherein a man could not make a living from the soil.

It is not a State for a lazy man, nor for a man whose main capital is stupidity and brute strength; at the same time a man "diligent in business and fervent in spirit" can succeed with less necessary labor and have more time for leisure and social intercourse than in any other portion of our country. I have lived in New York, Massachusetts, California, New Jersey and Kentucky, and have found here the conditions of climate and soil more favorable for "home making" than in any one of the above named States.

The soil of my place was "bottomless sand" when I bought it, but under the method of green crop manuring I have pursued, has gained a body and substance that makes it exceedingly productive, as the trees and very heavy crops of "crab grass" (or "cocksfoot"

grass) annually witness. As to the heat of summer, which people unacquainted with the facts naturally suppose is unsufferable in its intensity and unremitting in its continuance, never was there a greater misapprehension. The past summer in Florida was one of phenomenal heat for this State, yet, going straight from my study, I worked in the hot sun for the entire months of July and August without any serious discomfort or consequence of ill. Hot? Of course it was hot! So was it in Dakota! I can and do perform hard manual labor in Florida during the summer season that I would not attempt for any consideration north of the Florida line. Physicians may account for it as they will. In New York State I have had two sunstrokes, and never a sensation of one in Florida. As a rule our nights are cool for sleeping, and in the mornings we awake to the new day refreshed by the breezes that from Gulf or Atlantic have fanned us all night long.

The health of our locality is excellent. It has never suffered from an epidemic of any kind. My family, never in the most robust health, have had less sickness and fewer ailments than in any other place we have ever lived. With care and prudence in selecting a home no one need have any more apprehension in living in Florida than in the healthiest portions of the North. Many diseases to which children are subject in the North are comparatively unknown here.

Our observation and experience have led to the conviction that a man can support his family from the soil more easily here than in the more vigorous climates. With plenty of water the family table can be supplied with some varieties of fresh vegetables the year round. Some wit and labor will have to be expended to solve here and there a difficulty, but there is not an obstacle that cannot be readily overcome. On a larger scale than the garden the farmer can, with the same diligence that elsewhere wins success, surely fill his corn-crib and smokehouse. With cassava, sweet potatoes and cow-peas growing bountiful crops almost for the planting, the addition of large yields of "crab grass" brought the farmer the nutritious provender necessary for his stock.

As to the "oozing out of Northern energy" which is popularly supposed to be a Florida disease of certain "death in life," I can only say I have never been less inclined to work here than in the North. On the contrary, stimulated by the pure air, rested by the cool nights, and refreshed by the cool breezes, I have no sense of inertia nor wish to be idle. I welcome work. As to the social, intellectual and religious side of the home question, I can speak only of what I know in and around De Land. Outside the larger cities and homes there are but few places in any part of our broad land so liberally provided with the opportunities for the highest life as are found here. I believe, from a pretty widely extended observation, that such is the case over a great part of the State along the lines of transportation.

We have in De Land public and private schools, kindergarten, the J. B. Stetson University, some six or more churches with settled pastors, and all the organizations for social and moral well-being usually found in older communities.

Tobacco Culture in Florida.

Mr. C. C. Chapman, Lake City, Florida.—(A letter to W. L. Glessner, commissioner of immigration of the Georgia Southern & Florida Railroad.) "You have often asked me to give my experience and opinion in regard to the growing of cigar-leaf tobacco in Florida, and I have heretofore declined—not because I lacked confidence in my ability to produce an article fully equal to the best Sumatra and Havana leaf, but I wished to fully demonstrate my belief by actual results. In my first year, 1892, I had fair success, but I found the curing of the crop attended with many difficulties, hence I wanted to wait until I saw the crop of 1893 before giving my opinion, as I do not wish to mislead anyone. My 1892 crop has been worked up by a Northern manufacturer of note, who claims it to be equal to the finest Sumatra. It has stood the test against Sumatra that cost $4.50 per pound. The first trial was three pounds of my leaf to ten pounds

of Sumatra. The cigars so wrapped were sold at $95 per thousand to the fine trade in a large city. After a time the proportion was raised to five pounds to ten, and later on to an equal quantity of each, and the manufacturer received many compliments on the fine character of his goods. This manufacturer is ready to buy a large quantity of these wrappers this year, and says they are the finest wrappers ever grown in this country. A recognized authority in the Connecticut valley, when shown a sample of 1892 crop, stated over his own signature that for fine glossy texture and evenness of color he had never seen its equal grown in this country, Sumatra or Cuba.

"I am well acquainted with all the tobacco-growing sections of this country, and have come to the conclusion that there is no section so well adapted to the cultivation of fine wrappers as that portion of Florida starting at Lake City and extending northwest to Lake Park, Ga., along the line of the Georgia Southern & Florida Railroad. Here we find a dark, sandy loam that is free from clay, lime or phosphate. The country is thickly dotted with small lakes, and the soil will produce, with a small amount of fertilizer, from 600 to 800 pounds of fine light-colored leaf that is bound to become very popular as a cigar wrapper. A man with a small farm, who grows other crops to live on, can grow this leaf at less cost than in any other section of the country. Labor is cheap and there is plenty of it. We can grow tobacco here with or without rain. I have set plants when it had not rained for two months and it did not rain for several weeks after setting, but my plants grew right along. I have cut tobacco fifty-five days after setting out the plants. I have leaves that will run from 150 to 350 to the pound. I find it a very safe country in which to grow tobacco, as there is no trouble from wet or dry weather. Capillary attraction and heavy dews overcome dry weather, while cultivation can be resumed within an hour after a heavy shower. We are not subject to hail or wind, and insects are easily taken care of. Out of 600 pounds, barn weight, stripping every leaf off the stalk, I got 515 pounds of fine wrappers and only fifteen pounds of fillers and binders. Lands can be bought cheap and on favorable terms.

"Coming as I did from New England, I naturally felt uneasy about my health in this country, but after two years residence in Florida I can truthfully say that I never lived in a more healthy climate. In the growing season I am in the field from sunrise to sunset, and. I have never been compelled to seek the shade on account of heat."

Profits in Pineapples and Tomatoes.

S. F. GIBBS, Melbourne, Fla.—I am in the pineapple business; have been since 1883. I plant from ten to fourteen thousand plants to the acre. It costs about $350 per acre, including land, slips, planting, care and fertilizers, until they come into fruiting the second year. I generally get from seven to eight thousand apples per acre, marketable apples, which bring from six to eight cents net. The pine slips sell at from $5.00 to $7.00 per thousand, according to size. They average four slips per plant, and about one extra sucker to each plant, which sell at from $10 to $12 per thousand. The pineapple responds to care and fertilizers as quickly as any plant I know of. I am also growing tomatoes and beans on hammock land, clearing from $150.00 to $250.00 per acre. Beans are very profitable; early planting that comes into market about December brings from $3 to $7 per crate, of about three pecks.

Pineapple Growing in Florida.

WILLIAM E. PABOR, Pabor Lake, De Soto Co., Fla.—I came from Colorado to this lake region of South Florida in July, 1892, to recover my health and engage in fruit growing and other pursuits. I found a soil that looked to be valueless for culture, · but on which· heavy pines and oaks were growing, with underbrush indicating that plant food was hidden in what seemed to be pure sand. I selected fifty acres on which was a small lake of perhaps ten acres in area and began clearing for a home. By fall I had a cabin up and three acres cleared, on which I set out 3,000 pineapple slips,

500 bananas, some mango and other trees of a tropical character. During the right season I had more land cleared and in March set out trees as follows; 50 peach, 50 pear, 25 apple, 100 plum, 10 kaki or Japanese persimmon, 10 fig, 10 kumquat, 10 mulberries. This was very late in the season to set out deciduous trees, but they all grew well during the summer just past except the kumquat which all died; but these I shall plant again this winter. Some of the plum trees, especially the Kelsey and the Excelsior, made vigorous branches. The peach trees already show buds setting.

During this season I have set out 4000 more pineapple slips. Since we had no frost in this section of Florida last winter, I am of the opinion that this fruit, of which 10,000 can be grown upon an acre and brought to maturity in two years, is far more certain than orange growing, besides being so much more profitable. An expense of $700 will return the amount originally invested in the first crop and fifty per cent. additional as profit; while the plantation will then, for at least ten years thereafter, net its owner above all expenses fully $500 per acre. Of course, where the pineapple will grow there also will the orange, lemon, lime, pomelo, (or grape fruit,) mango, guava and other tropical fruits succeed.

I am on what is called the high sand hills of the lake region, one of the most healthful in the land where the purest of water is abundant, where there is no malaria as there is no marshy land or stagnant pools, where even in the summer the nights are far pleasanter and cooler than in the North and West.

In the near vicinity there is land where rice, corn, sugar cane, sorghum, potatoes and other farm products can be raised as well as the grasses suited to the South.

I have visited nearly all the States of the Union, but am convinced that nowhere do the conditions of success exist in greater ratio to the general disadvantages of a country than in Florida.

In a very few years I shall have a lovely home and a pineapple plantation which will be an annual source of income, and it· has not taken over a .thousand dollars to do it. With a less amount even than this, it is easy, on account of climate, cheap lands, healthy surroundings, to found a new home in Florida. I shall be pleased to give further information to any one desiring it.

More Comfortable in Florida than Colorado.

JAMES HAVENS, Pabor Lake, Fla.— (A letter written to W. A. Tyler, Denver, Col.) When I left the North I promised to tell you all about tropical Florida and her resources. I have waited some time that I might not lead you to think me hasty in forming an opinion, but the longer I wait the more I am pleased with my surroundings and the brighter the future looks. As the soil here is so well adapted to the culture of all the tropical and semi-tropical fruits, flowers, etc., I started by setting out 10,000 pineapple plants, 100 banana trees, 100 grape vines and quite a number of orange, lemon and grape-fruit trees. The most of these were set out in January and March, 1893. All are doing well, and a few of the pineapples have commenced to bear fruit. As pineapples are destined to be one of the chief products of this section, I am clearing more land for their culture.

Florida has long been noted for her oranges, the demand for which is greater than the supply. Now the pineapples are in a fair way to overshadow the oranges; and to convince you that the market cannot be overstocked with that wholesome fruit, you have but to see the large number of ships that arrive annually from foreign ports laden with them. Then for further proof go and purchase one and you will find that fifty cents will buy a very poor, small apple. I dwell upon that one product only because it is something new to you. The other fruits you are better acquainted with.

In this section of the State there are numbers of little lakes covering from five to fifty acres of ground. The water is the purest I have ever met with; it is equal to the mountain streams of the Rockies, yet as soft and free from alkali as rain water. There is no mud whatever in the lakes, as the bottom is all white sand, and the inhabitants of the lakes would fill with rapture any disciple of Isaac Walton. Our forests are mostly pine, oak and palmetto, and a Nimrod can keep his table well supplied the year round with venison, turkey, squirrel and quail.

Another great point in favor of the colonists here is that the land can be bought at such low figures that there is no need of those dreaded mortgages which have been the ruin of so many men who were striving to make themselves a home.

But now you ask what of the climate? Is not the heat unbearable, and is not a Northerner at once attacked with malaria when he comes down here? I have suffered more with the heat in Denver, Col., and Chicago, Ill., than I ever have in Florida, and in the year that I have been here I have not seen one case of fever, nor have I heard of any south of Jacksonville. As to our nights, nothing can be more sublime; we always have either a sea or gulf breeze and a blanket is very comfortable to sleep under. The dry, hot, and sultry night of the North is not known here. Another time I will tell you how I am beautifying my home with different kinds of palm trees, beautiful tropical flowers and shady grape arbors, and will close by saying Florida is without any exception the best place where an industrious and enterprising man or woman could settle.

In the Land of Fruits and Flowers.

GEO. EDMISTON, Avon Park, De Soto county, Fla.—Avon Park is the only place in Florida of which I am qualified to express an opinion. I came here with my family three years ago from near New York City and we have lived here ever since. I think this place cannot be excelled for healthfulness; and I find the climate very pleasant even throughout the summer. Only a few times during the past year has mercury been up to 96° in the shade, and not once above it. My house is quite high above the lake and has broad, low verandas, and here in the hottest days we find grateful shade and the cooling breezes rarely if ever fail, certainly never for any considerable time. Here, in the delightful summer evenings we can sit a while before retiring and enjoy the refreshing coolness, without the slightest molestation from insect life for we rarely see or hear a mosquito. Our soil is poor, but it responds quickly and bountifully to the moderate use of fertilizers and plenty of water. During much of the summer the frequent rains furnish all the water needed; but there are many times in the year when it is a great advantage to have a good supply of water at hand which can be applied without too much expense. Since I came to Florida and Avon Park I have acquired sixteen acres of land fronting upon Lake Verona, have cleared it of trees and stumps and have a thrifty young orange grove of 400 trees growing and a three-acre vineyard of Niagara grapes which bore a few hundred pounds of fruit the second summer after they were planted and 2000 pounds or more the past summer. I have also 5000 pineapple plants 1200 of which (the earliest planted) bore fruit the past season which I sold here at from 8 to 25 cents each, mostly from 20 to 25 cents. I have also limes, guavas, mangoes and peaches growing. I have a patch of cassava growing which I find excellent for feeding poultry of which I keep a number sufficient to supply my family with eggs and now and again a nice chicken. I have found many varieties of roses to do exceedingly well here. Marechal Neil, Solfaterre, Cloth of Gold, Gloria de Dijon do splendidly as pillar or veranda roses. Many other varieties succeed quite as well as these. With the ground properly prepared and with good culture they will do as well here as in greenhouses at the North. With a comfortable home in a very pleasant community with good church privileges, and a good school soon to be opened in a nice new school house—with several new houses going up within sight, all giving evidence of growth and progress, I must say I am very well contented in Florida, and at Avon Park.

$1000 Refused for One Acre.

CHAS. WILKINSON, Avon Park, De-Soto county, Fla.—I came to Avon Park, Fla., less than two years ago from Holyoke, Mass., and first bought a one acre tract in which I have planted 5000 pineapples of a choice kind. For this one acre I was offered $1000 week before last, but I would not sell because I think I shall clear that next summer in the sale of fruit and slips. I have made a living during this time in painting, clearing land and planting for others, and I can say that I never was so happy in my life and free from care.

First Impressions of Florida.

EDWARD E. THOMPSON, Avon Park, De Soto county, Fla.—After a residence of twenty-five winters in Hartford, Connecticut, I decided to spend this one where freezing is unknown. I sailed up the St. John's river to Jacksonville, November 10, and arrived at this place 250 miles further south the next day. To a new comer there are many surprising things about this country. First, the roads, instead of being deep sand as expected, are generally hard and good, and one does not need to keep in the road but can ride or walk in any direction through the pine woods which hardly seem like woods, for the pine trees are scattered straight, not large, and there is no undergrowth, so one has a wide view for miles in every direction, and millions of brilliant wild flowers are always in sight. The sandy soil looks as though it would be useless for anything but building purposes to a Northern man, therefore one can hardly believe his own eyes on seeing orange groves loaded with large luscious fruit, some trees not six feet high with three hundred large oranges bending the limbs to the ground, also banana groves with fruit hanging in great bunches; lime trees—three of them producing thirty thousand limes this season and only five years old; acres of pineapple plants, some fruit growing at this late date. Surely this is not fancy but facts; not frozen facts but tropical truths and the old saw about depositing money in a sand bank would not be such a bad idea after all, if the sand bank were the sandy acres of Avon Park. It would be better than many national banks this year of our Lord.

But the greatest surprise of all is the people, of whom there are about four hundred from all parts of the Union, all thrifty, intelligent and industrious, and they approach a new comer with no stiff formalities but in a cordial way that is genuine and makes one feel that one man is as good as another and all are brothers together of one great family. At the neat little church here there are hardly seats enough for the people who assemble for service both morning and evening. The singing is led by a man who two years ago was a music teacher in Massachusetts but is now the pineapple "sharp" of Avon Park. He has an acre of pines planted out with the regularity of a checkerboard, enclosed with a neat picket fence and has a pretty painted cottage. He has lost none of his musical qualities and appears to be a very happy man. There are no stagnant ponds here as expected but a great many lakes with sandy bottoms and water so clear that one can see the big black bass gliding about at a great depth. Right in front of the hotel is a lake of sixty acres and ninety feet deep. One lake covers 1200 acres. All of this lake water is as good to drink as any we have in Hartford, in fact I like it better. For one who dwells near to nature's heart the climate here makes existence simply delightful. There is no chill in the air, yet it is tonic and full of the balsam of pine trees. There is no lifeless air, no enervating effects, but rather increased energy. One can always leave windows wide open all night and not get cold in his head ; window screens are unnecessary for there are no insects. Those who live here all the year are the most enthusiastic about the climate.

Eighteen Years in Florida.

E. B. Olmstead, Pomona, Fla.—I have been in Florida eighteen years next February and have been out of the State but once, and then for only four months. My family all enjoy good health most of the time. I have lived on this one homestead ; it is what is called high pine land and we can raise all the vegetables we want the year round by making a spring and fall garden. I keep cows and we make most of our butter. I have an orange grove, some of my trees being twenty years

old and twenty-five to thirty feet high. I have a good crop almost every year ; have only lost the crop twice in the time of my being here by the frost. We have men here who came here without a cent and now own fine groves, but they had health and plenty of push. What has been done can be done again without the hardships we had to go through when I came here, as we now have railroads, stores, churches and school houses. There is no excuse for a man to stay in the cold North without work and freeze there. There is plenty of land here and it is cheap.

What Some Connecticut Yankees Have Done in South Georgia.

(Contributed by Major W. L. Glessner, Macon, Ga.) About twenty years ago Mr. H. H. Tift moved from Mystic, Connecticut, into South Georgia, at a point now known as Tifton, but which was then an almost unbroken forest of yellow pine which had been opened by the Brunswick & Western Railroad. As he expressed it to the writer, his capital consisted of "a pepper-box saw mill and ten thousand dollars of debt." Three years after he was joined by his brother, W. O. Tift, and they went to work literally to hew (or saw) their fortunes out of the woods, and by energy, prudence and hard work they succeeded, until to-day they have one of the largest saw mills in the South, to which are attached dry kilns and planing mills. They own some 70,000 acres of land and have built out into the pine woods seventeen miles of railroad, laid with good steel rails, equipped with engines and cars, and upon which there is not a cent of debt.

Until within a few years the land in this section was considered valuable only for the timber which grew upon it, and there was little attempt made at farming, and that only in a crude way. But four years ago the Georgia Southern & Florida Railroad, running from Macon, Ga., to Palatka, Fla., was built through this territory, crossing the Brunswick & Western Railroad at Tifton. The projectors of this new road had faith in the land, and in order to test the productiveness of the soil proposed to establish a farm on which should be grown all the crops common to Georgia. To aid in this project Messrs. Tift donated to the railroad company one thousand acres of land nine miles north of Tifton, on which are now grown corn, cotton, rice, sugar cane, tobacco, oats, rye, barley, Irish and sweet potatoes, melons, peaches, pears, grapes, apples, cherries, plums, figs, and all kinds of vegetables. Where four years ago was a forest there is now a farm that is the wonder and admiration of the State. The Tifts also determined to demonstrate the fertility of the land, and to this end took a hundred acres of land from which the timber had been cut, and clearing it of stumps proceeded to break it up thoroughly and plant it in various crops. Twenty-eight acres were planted in grapes. This was in 1890. This year they shipped and sold off these twenty-eight acres 60,000 pounds of grapes, besides making a large quantity of wine. In 1892 they planted fifty acres in tobacco, and on ten acres made an average of 1200 pounds to the acre, the whole crop averaging over 800 pounds to the acre.

Eight years ago Ed. Tift joined his brothers, and also getting the farming fever, three years ago carved out a farm from the woods and planted it in peaches and grapes. This year some of his peach trees bore as high as three pecks to the tree. The Tifts were joined by Mr. Snow, a practical fruit-grower, and now W. O. Tift has forty acres in grapes and 10,000 peach trees. H. H. and W. O. Tift have about 1000 pecans, 800 pears and a number of English walnuts. Ed. Tift has twenty-five acres in grapes and about twenty acres in peaches. Tift & Snow have 40,000 peach trees, and propose to keep on planting until they have 80,000. W. H. Mallory, who came down from Connecticut last year, has 9000 peach trees. Two gentlemen from Pennsylvania have purchased 500 acres, which they will plant out in peaches and grapes. A party of practical and experienced fruit-growers from Ohio visited these orchards and vineyards last July and declared them to be the finest they had ever seen.

But the Tifts have not confined themselves to saw milling and farming. When the Georgia Southern & Florida Railroad was built an important junction was formed at Tifton and the little old sawmill station took on new life and growth. Realizing the importance of starting their town right and protecting it from speculating boomers, they laid out the town with wide streets, and sold lots only to those who would build and specified the character of the buildings. The consequence is that Tifton has more handsome residences and business blocks than any town of its size in the State, and presents an attractive appearance. There is a large and handsome hotel, fine churches, a good school building, the largest canning factory in the State, and the place has had a healthy, steady growth, attracting enterprising and intelligent people.

What the Tifts have done in South Georgia, others can do by exercising the same energy and intelligence. The opportunities are there awaiting the men.

In the Georgia Fruit Country.

R. P. Johnson, Smithville, Ga.—I removed to this place in Southwestern Georgia about thirty years ago from East Tennessee. Though a native of Virginia I never have had any inclination to return. We have a fine country here, delightful climate, hospitable, intelligent people, law abiding and church going. Of course our population is not all white people; some counties have a greater number of negroes than whites, though as a general thing they are all loyal and well behaved. We have a fine fruit country. Our melon and fruit crop; if it could be as systematically marketed as cotton, would bring more clear money to our farmers than the cotton crop. We cannot grow apples as well in this portion of the State as in the middle and northern portions, but peaches grown here are as fine as are grown anywhere. It is the home of the Le Conte and Kieffer pears. We have within a radius of four miles of our town 15,000 pear trees, most of them of bearing age. Shipments this season netted $3.55 per barrel. We have plenty of room for all good citizens who mean business, and would be glad to have them come. As to prices of land, they can find a place among us that will suit as to price and quantity.

A Charming Spot in Kentucky.

H. W. HUNTER, Kingsville, Ky.— When we came here, in the middle of autumn three years ago, one of the first things we did was to build an "ice dam," thinking that because October and November were so warm the next summer heat would be very oppressive. We were doubly disappointed, however, for, although we had been told that ice generally formed here in winter, it has never been more than an inch in thickness on our dam, nor have we ever felt the need of any, because we have an abundance of pure, cold spring water and the summer days are no hotter than they are in Pennsylvania where we came from, while the nights are cooler in this elevated portion of "the dark and bloody ground."

We are but a short ride on the comfortable trains of the Queen & Crescent route, from the "fields of yellow corn, way down in Tennessee," and in sight of numerous hills and knobs, but just about us the land is rolling, just enough so to abound in springs and brooks of clear, cold sparkling water shaded by oak, walnut, ash, poplar and other trees.

Our soil, which is a sandy loam with a clay subsoil, is adapted to corn, oats and other grains, also potatoes, both sweet and Irish, and tobacco, while for strawberries and grapes we think it is not excelled anywhere. All the various kinds of garden vegetables flourish here luxuriantly, and peaches, apples, pears, plums, etc., do well. Perhaps it may be superfluous to say that the people of this vicinity are English speaking and are quiet, industrious and law-abiding, as are also the German and Swiss settlers a few miles from us.

The Place for Young Men to Start.

J. E. GIFT, Corinth, Miss.—I fell in love with the country during my term of service in the Federal army, and returned South a few years after the war, and have lived in this country for twenty-three years. I have always gotten on nicely with the people, have never had any trouble in voting the Republican ticket when I desired to do so. We have very good lands at any price, plenty of timber, good water, good health, plenty of schools and churches, in fact, Corinth has more churches than any other town of its size in the State. I have lived in Ohio, Indiana and Illinois and have never seen as good a place for a young man or man with small capital to start in as this. There are several Northern families in this county, and all are doing well. Anyone coming here will do well, and be well received if they will half way try to do right. The people will almost give you a farm if you will take it.

No Ostracism in Mississippi.

A. G. LEACH, Enterprise, Clarke county, Miss.—I have lived here a little over seven years. I am an old soldier and belong to the Grand Army, Old Abe Post, No. 39, Lake Benton, Minn., having moved from there to this place. I have been treated very kindly by the people in every way. Some of my best friends here are ex-rebels or Southern soldiers. I am a Republican and vote the Republican ticket in national affairs all the time. I talk on all political subjects, bet on Harrison with any of them, and I have never had a man to say an unkind or insulting word to me since I have been here.

I think any man coming here with his family to make a home will be treated with all the courtesy due him socially and politically. And we have good churches of all denominations, and the people generally are a thorough going church people. We have also a good school building and a splendid school. We have good soft water and lots of springs, nice running streams, no standing or stagnant water, and as healthy a climate as there is in the world.

Thousands of people go to Minnesota for health, and Enterprise, Clarke county, is just as healthy, and the soil just as productive, and more so, as you can run two crops on the same land in one season, and sometimes three. People are now (May 19) shipping green peas and Irish potatoes. People have mostly finished shipping green peas and have planted the same ground in corn and cotton. I saw cotton up and growing nicely yesterday where a fine and paying crop of peas had been taken up and shipped this year.

The soil is very productive when properly fertilized, and easy to handle, the most of the plowing being done with one horse or mule or one ox. Lots of times you will see a man running a farm and raising a crop whose team and all his tools do not cost $50, and I could safely say in some cases not $25.

Fruit of all kinds does well here, apples, peaches, pears, plums, figs, grapes and strawberries. Peaches, plums, strawberries and pears are being shipped each year and give nice returns.

We also have fine quinces and berries of all kinds, such as blackberries, dewberries and raspberries. All can be shipped with a profit. I am in the fruit and dairy business in a small way, always have plenty of milk and butter, and can always get twenty-five cents per pound for all the butter we have to sell. I have done reasonably well since I have come here. Have a nice home and am making it nicer every year by planting fruit trees and by other improvements.

I like the climate and the people and am well pleased with the country generally, and know anyone coming here can get a home cheaper than any place I ever saw, and he can make that home just as fine as he pleases and do it all with his own labor. Any man who will come here and buy a home and work as people work in the West, can get rich and make a home as good as he wants.

One of the Healthiest Sections.

C. W. ROBINSON, Meridian, Miss.—I moved to Meridian eleven years ago. Prior to my removal to Meridian I had resided in Kentucky, Tennessee, Indiana and Ohio, and during all my life had suffered more or less with miasmatic fevers. During my residence in Meridian I have been entirely free from that trouble and from all forms of sickness.

Have only been confined to my room two days by sickness during the eleven years. I regard this part of Mississippi as one of the healthiest sections of the United States. When I came here Meridian was a struggling village of about 4000 population. Today it is a prosperous city of 15,000 population. I do not know of any man in Meridian, who is willing to work and who is sober and careful, who is not making money.

The free school system of Meridian is equal to that of any city of like size in the Northern States. All religious denominations have churches in Meridian. There is no such thing in Meridian as the open saloon, and consequently our population is a sober, moral class of people. The five railroads centering here afford excellent shipping facilities. We have some fifteen or sixteen manufacturing establishments, all of which are paying handsome dividends. The people of this section of Mississippi welcome settlers, and so far as I have been able to observe, there is no distinction made between the Northern or Western man and the native Mississippian in social, religious or business privileges.

Success With Fruit in Missouri.

S. W. GILBERT, Thayer, Mo.—In the fall of 1884 I left Fulton county, Ohio, to pay my father here a visit. Upon arrival I found a country with a glorious climate and a soil fairly productive, the whole surface (or nearly so) quite undulating and a greater portion covered more or less with stone. This stone is not usually large but runs in size from a pin point to as large as a man can roll. What puzzled me was to know how it could be possible for so much of the surface to be stony, yet, after digging six inches to a foot deep we strike a red subsoil, in which it is possible in places to dig twenty-five to forty feet and never strike a pebble, although in places we strike solid rock much sooner. The longer I remained here the better I liked the country, and finally I traded for sixty acres of land that is now known as "The Flint Hill Fruit Farm."

Unfortunately, I did not have a dollar to improve my place, and not until I attended our Missouri State Horticultural Society at West Plains, Mo., in the summer of 1888 did I become interested in fruit. In the fall of that year I began improving my place, notwithstanding I was in debt $125.00 to stores here for merchandise, etc.

I obtained a position with the railroad and followed line repairing for five years, putting all I could make into improvements on "The Flint Hill," and the first of March found me with too much on my hands to attend to my farm and railroad work, so I quit the road.

Now for results. Since 1890 I have had a few berries to sell every year which helped pay expenses. This year I have made the following sales: Strawberries, $382.59; raspberries, $821.18; apples, about $100.00; peaches, $1373.-32; besides strawberry and raspberry plants, of which I have 100,000 yet for sale, and corn and hay enough to feed my six mules. The above sales are net f.o.b. here. They are also the fruit sales from about twelve and one-half acres of land that was in the woods in the fall of 1888. With exceptions of the apples and a few scattering peaches that I took from two-year-old peach trees, the Flint Hill farm now has fifty acres in fruit, about 1500 apple, 3500 peach, 250 plum, 200 pear, fifty cherry and fifty apricot trees. My trade has grown faster than I have had capital to increase my plant, and this fall I secured thirty acres more ground and am now busy clearing fifteen acres of it for strawberries to be set next spring if we cannot get the ground ready before then. Some winters here are so mild that we can plant in midwinter. I have five acres of strawberries and four acres of raspberries for a crop next year.

Owing to proper study of shipping strawberries, I have found a berry that I have shipped 1500 miles and it arrived in perfect condition, and of course there is no end to the amount of berries that I can sell in the North every spring. Our berries commence ripening about May 1st, and continue for three to four weeks. I would like to see enough fruit growers come here with capital enough to put in enough berries to enable us to ship a carload every day. We could get better prices for them. I have been looking for some one with $10,000 capital to go in with me and make one of the best berry farms in the United States, but so far have failed.

There are a number of bargains here for those who want to get away from the long winters in the North. I would be glad to assist all who want to come and to get a good place. Can buy three or four farms if taken soon for less money than a man can put the improvements on the land were he to take it in the woods. Several have come in from the North this fall and many more are expected this month. There are ten or more families coming from one town in Minnesota alone. I would be glad to correspond with any who wants to locate here. We have no room for the speculator, but want men who will help develop the country.

We have a town of about 2000 people, good society, good graded schools and four churches, and our town is growing steadily and never has had a boom, or a bank or a business failure. Our people are well pleased with my exhibit at the World's fair. In peaches I was not excelled by any State in the Union either in quantity, quality or flavor. The State of Missouri took sixteen medals, being more than any other State received, and I was honored with two out of the sixteen for peaches and apples. This is of itself evidence of what can be done here.

Paradise for Rich or Poor.

G. A. DeBaun, Avert, Stoddard county, Mo.—I came to Stoddard county thirteen years ago from Central Illinois. I am now fifty-three years old and in my prime. I am now farming as I was raised to it in my boyhood days. I have lived in St. Louis and Chicago several years, and will say that so far as health is concerned this country is equal to St. Louis, and a man can make as good a living here and work one-half as much as he does in Illinois or any Northern State. There are old people here, well on towards the century mark, who say that they never knew such a think as a failure of the crops so that the county had to import anything in the shape of food for man or beast. This is a splendid fruit country. I have not failed to see peaches in the last thirteen years. We are in the great Ozark fruit belt, and it is a lazy man's paradise. If a man has the energy to hustle he can gain a competence in a few years. Land can be bought at $5 to $35 per acre, according to the improvements. There is plenty of room for immigrants and a man can get plenty to keep him busy here. We have room for farmers, mechanics and saw mill men—plenty of timber lands. A man can buy a farm on time or borrow money if he has real estate security. In fact this is God's country for the poor man or the rich man. We welcome all good citizens but no sharpers need apply.

A Good Ten Per Cent. Investment.

M. A. BLACKBURN, Corsicana, Texas. —I came to Texas last winter from Edgar county, Ill., and bought land in Navarro county at $22.50 and $23.00 per acre equally as good as land I sold in Illinois for $85.00 per acre. I rent my land for one-third the grain and one-fourth the cotton, and will realize 10 per cent. on my investment this year. The black lands hold moisture a long time, making it possible to raise a good crop during a dry year. Corn will yield forty to sixty bushels per acre; oats, sixty to 100 bushels; wheat, fifteen to thirty bushels; cotton, a half to bale, and prairie hay one to two and one-half tons. There is no risk to person or property; investments are perfectly safe. Schools and churches are everywhere, markets at your door, the people are law-abiding and moral, the climate is perfect, all of which make this the best country in the world.

Rich Lands at $1 per Acre.

JOHN F. ASH, Athens, Henderson Co., Tex.—Having moved from Pike county, in the southern part of Indiana, I have been asked to give my reasons for the change, also to state if this country has advantages over the North and of what nature. Here I will state my reasons for coming to Texas and the decided improvements, especially to the farming class of people. The greatest thing to be considered is the cheapness of land here. I have near four thousand acres of land, costing the same number of dollars. This land is now rated for taxes at $2.00 per acre while the Indiana farm is rated at $40.00 per acre; in other words there is more money invested in 160 acres of Indiana land than there is in 4,000 acres here.

With the same amount of energy, enterprise and push that is taught among Northern farmers, this land will net equally as many dollars to the acre as that of the North. Stock of any kind can be raised here for one-half the cost it can in the North. Very little preparation is needed for wintering cattle, as the native grass is sufficient to keep them in good flesh. I would urge the young man seeking a home to come to this portion of Texas where fruit and vegetables of all kinds grow abundantly, and where a people whose hearts compare with the great State itself will welcome you into their midst.

"BEHIND THE PONTOON TRAIN CAME THE PRISONERS"

A War-Time Christmas.
BY Bennet Carroll Shipman

(The incidents of this story are facts, gleaned fm the journal of a lieutenant, then acting adjutant of the Fourteenth New York Cavalry. The escort under General D—— was sent out to protect the gunboats and transports in the Mississippi sound around the Pascagoula river)

It had been a hard march. Two hundred and ten miles in fifteen days. I will leave it to any old soldier to say if that is not a good two weeks' march with such roads as we had. It was in the latter part of the year 1864, almost the last day of November, when we left Baton Rouge. We were ordered out as a guard to General D——. For the first part of our march we had fine weather and good roads. We were in pine woods, which, while the weather was good, made fair marching, but when the rain began—O Lord! It seemed to me as if I could never look with calmness on pine woods again. The layers of pine needles acted like so much sponge. How well I remember the first day of this miserable weather! After our stay in Baton Rouge, where I had again become accustomed to some of the comforts of life, this damp, miserable, slushy morning seemed doubly hard to us. Camp was broken at 6 A. M. with our brigade, the Fourteenth New York Cavalry, and our brothers in this raid, the Sixth Missouri, as a rear guard. A miserable column it was, too, that finally filed away in the rear of the pontoon train from our camping ground.

It was dangerous riding over such ground on this kind of a day, as we very soon had forcibly impressed upon us. One poor fellow of the ranks too suddenly reined up his horse which had started unexpectedly forward. Its hoofs as it reared up, slipped in the yielding soil. Backward fell rider and horse. The thud that followed was sickening, but such an event is among the least a soldier must behold. The horse struggled to his feet, but the rider only uttered a groan and lay still. Two companions were off their horses in an instant and found that he was only badly hurt, so he was immediately carried to the ambulance. The train continued, and in five minutes I doubt if a single man remembered the accident, so callous become the feelings when brought daily into contact with horrors. The riders, however, profited by the lesson and rode more carefully.

During the day we arrived at a creek, the bridge over which had been broken down by the retreating Southerners. General D—— was making himself very conspicuous, according to his custom. General D—— I might add in parenthesis, was not a favorite with our boys, nor we with him. I merely mention the following incident to show his self-sufficiency. After taking the work out of the engineer's hand and imagining that he was accomplishing it, he finally vanished to his quarters. Then the work began, and after a few hours' delay we crossed the new-made bridge and then entered the pine woods.

"He's a fool," disrespectfully commented Captain Cobb, ignorant of the honor soon to be bestowed on him.

"But wisdom certainly don't come out of his mouth," further commented Major Nobb. However, we soon had more cause to grumble than his mere lack of sense.

"That I will put down in my journal as Fussy's Creek," I said as I rode over the bridge, "named in honor of our illustrious general."

Several times during the day did our men have to dismount to pull and tug at the wagons. The roads were in a miserable condition, and men and mules tired and weary. Often, too, trees and brush had to be cleared out to allow the wagons to pass. To make these discomforts greater none of · us knew whither the expedition was bound. Its destination was a profound secret.

Towards evening an orderly came galloping up from the advance and delivered two orders to Major Nobb. After reading them he handed them to me to publish, which I did when the men were brought into line at the first clearing, a mile or two further on. One was an order detaching Captain Cobb and his company to act as body guard to General D—— (the honor before mentioned) and the other an order dismounting the Fourteenth New York Cavalry, for, as it stated, unsoldierly conduct, plundering, etc. The men received the latter in silence as indeed they were obliged to, but I should not like to have been the recipient of so many blessings as were silently bestowed on our general.

"What do you think of it?" I asked the doctor as I fell in beside him.

"It's a shame—a damned shame?" he said explosively; "besides, from a humane point of view, if this worthy general wants to do any fighting he is getting his men in fine condition for it."

"That's not the worst," said I as he stopped, "it is unjust; our men never committed any depredation; it was the train men. They would skulk off among the pines and hide till the guards passed and then begin plundering. And now we have got to suffer for them."

After a weary day's march we arrived in camp at 8 P. M., so worn out that some of the men seemed ready to fall from their horses. The animals themselves were in but little better condition. Pine woods still surrounded us and the weather was still rainy. In consequence, our beds that night were about as comfortable as a wet sponge. O, the beauties of a pine forest! May he who praises them experience them some time. That is the best and worst I can wish him.

Such was the average day's march during this wet season, varied, however, by different little unpleasantnesses; for instance, getting the wrong road and counter-marching. Occasionally, too, we would do without some meals, while the horses, poor beasts, had often to go without theirs. Yet some of our friends at home considered that a soldier's life at this time of the war was next to nothing at all. A few times on our march we sent out forage parties, but they were almost useless, as it was precious little forage one could find in pine woods. One of these parties brought back a few prisoners on one of their expeditions. Nothing except these things varied the monotony of our rainy way.

Behind the pontoon train came the prisoners—a very few, some ten or twelve. Among them was a man remarkable in more than one way. Our youngest lieutenant was the proud captor, for it was only after a hard fight that it was done. It happened in this wise: On the morning of Thursday, December 22d, at about half-past two reveille sounded. The camp was awake in an instant, and in a few moments "boots and saddles" sounded, together with the "assembly." Instantly all were in line and ready. The bugle sounded the advance, and we started out over a most desolate road. After a march of about nine miles, all the while keeping in the arc of a circle so as to strike our camp again near the Mobile road, Captain Martin's company, having the advance, ran upon the Confederate pickets and drove them in. Continuing further, we again ran upon them and soon after struck the main body of reserves stationed at Davis' Creek. They formed and followed our rear guard, under command of a lieutenant of the Sixth Missouri cavalry, and drove it in. We formed a battle line, the Fourteenth New York on the right and the Sixth Missouri on the left and opened fire. There was a lively time. At one time they attempted to turn our right flank, but Lieutenant Cole was sent by Major Nobb to protect it. The attacking party was commanded by the prisoner before mentioned, and our lieutenant had all he could do to hold the enemy at bay. However, he did, and a chance ball grazing the Southerner's head ended the fight at this quarter. He was very slightly wounded, however, and soon recovered. Then he found himself a prisoner. The enemy forced us back a mile, and had they then taken advantage of their position, could have captured us all. But they did not, and our artillery soon came up. This turned the tide in our favor, and we drove them back till the recall sounded.

The prisoner who had fought so valiantly was a captain, and he seemed in every way fit for his position. He never spoke unless spoken to, and then only in monosyllables. His inaccessibility was felt by all, prisoners and guards. One would as lief talk to a cold stone for all the satisfaction, or anything else, one could get. Most of the time he would walk with his hands thrust in his pockets and his eyes cast on the ground. What seemed to affect him the most was his inactivity; he never cared for the hardships. I have seen his lip curl with a scornful smile—and his smile was scornful, it cut like a knife—when some of our boys seemed ready to drop from their saddles with weariness. There was something pitiable about his dejected, proud manner. He seemed galled by the fact that all action for him was over. His well-defined features and haughty manner stamped him as a Southerner of culture, though from his poor bedraggled gray, one would have thought him less than the least of our privates. But he wore a captain's honors, and for my part I thought he would have made a better general than the one we had, providing, of course, he was on our side.

We had been moving since we left Baton Rouge and now, on December 23d, settled down, we hoped, to what we considered a well earned rest. We had been sent to East Pascagoula with dispatches for General G——, who was encamped at Franklin's Creek.

We had left the pontoon train, thank Heaven! We used to say: "Blessed are the pontoonians for, when the train is gobbled, we shall have rest." Not only had we been marching, but at Pascagoula we had unloaded two transports, rather tiresome work. So now we prepared for Christmas with all the enthusiasm of soldiers. Major Nobb, Captain Martin, the doctor and myself sent to the mill for boards. We wanted a shelter to protect us from the cold, for it was getting cold now. We sent the doctor out to forage for us, to see if he could not buy some chickens or better still, a turkey. He arrived before the boards did, and in a most excited state. He came running towards our group gesticulating wildly.

"I wonder what's the matter with the doctor now?" I remarked.

"Found a new case, maybe," said the major, "a beautiful compound fracture."

"More likely a new case of whiskey, which he has partaken of too deeply," commented Captain Martin.

Any one of these guesses might have been correct, for the doctor had but one way of expressing joy, and that was in the manner above described. So I concluded to withhold my verdict. He soon came up, puffing, red in the face, almost exploding with his discovery.

"Say, you fellows," he began, "I've struck it—I tell you! We'll spend our Christmas—jolly—wait—a minute—and I'll—let you—know all about it." The doctor paused, as indeed he had to, for he needed all his breath for breathing purposes. We stood expectant till he regained it.

"We'll enjoy this Christmas, boys, anyhow," he said when he could talk connectedly. "I hadn't got far down that road, round the bend there, before I saw a plantation house. It's nigh hidden in the trees, which is the reason, I suppose, that none of the boys have been over there yet. 'Well,' says I to myself, 'I'll find something around here.' So I went up to the front door and knocked, for you might as well ask for a thing before stealing it. An old

surgeon-general. In spite of his trembling walk and careworn face he looked proud as a prince. Indeed I thought it might have been best to take the chickens and say nothing about them. But I spoke up and told our wants."

" 'Sir,' he said in a tremulous voice as he caught hold of the door for better support, 'I can see from your uniform that your mission in this cruel war is to

"I SAW, COMING DOWN THE HALL, A WHITE-HAIRED GENTLEMAN."

auntie opened the door, but she threw up her hands in horror when she saw me." Here the doctor gave an imitation. " 'Fo' de Lawd, ole marse!' she cried, 'ef heah ain't a Linkum ossifer!' I was going to laugh, but I saw coming down the hall a white-haired gentleman. He was the 'ole marse.' I felt sorry for him, but I could no more have told him so than ask Lincoln to appoint me

save, not destroy. But those others,' he went on fiercely, 'who infest this country, those vandals are plundering everywhere'—he pointed to some blackened ruins—'but as a Southerner and a fellow creature, I offer you, who say you need it, my hospitality. My son, too, is in the war, but against you, and I would bless the one who aided him. You are welcome, then, sir, in his name to whatever I can give, and that is little, for little is left.' I felt like crying right there. However, I didn't, but managed to thank him and reassure him on the point of plundering. I wanted to bring a few things over to camp but he would not hear of it. We must go there and stay as long as our division is in camp here."

We all shook the doctor by the hand and congratulated him on his excellent manner of carrying out his commission. We were quite overjoyed at the prospect of a comfortable night. To have a good shelter and warm beds after all the rain and mud and pine woods we had endured was a luxury that could not be too highly estimated. We adjourned without loss of time to our hospitable Southerner's and received, as the doctor had forwarned us, a most royal welcome. The doctor introduced us. Our host, profiting by a hint he had let fall on his previous visit, had what was for us a magnificent supper. Charles Lamb has sung the praises of roast pork, but who can sing those of roast turkey with all necessary adjuncts? Truly, no one, we thought. Aunt Helen (pronounced Heelen) sent in plate after plate of delicious corn bread—your true Southern corn bread, none of your base imitations—and plate after plate of flaky hot hiscuit. Biscuit? I know you all immediately think of those heavy, round disks an inch or two thick. Nothing of the kind. You have never tasted true biscuit. Accept a soldier's eulogy till you can ascertain for yourself.

"Lord, major," said the doctor, as that worthy was demolishing his eighth biscuit, "you will be downed by this campaign; your stomach 'll never be able to stand this hot bread."

"Can't help that, doctor," returned the major, "these are too good not to be eaten. Yet it seems that I will have companions in my misfortune," he added, glancing around the table. But none could withstand such food, and we all ate—well, with the appetite of soldiers. Can I say more?

"Doctor," said I to him, for he sat next to me, "you remember one of our prisoners, that one you can't touch with a ten-foot pole?"

"Yes, what's the matter with him?"

"Don't you think he looks mightily like our host?"

"Why, bless my soul!" exclaimed the doctor, putting up his glasses, "When I come to look at him, it's so. I never thought to notice it before."

"Sir," said I aloud to our host, "I believe you said to the doctor when he was here before that you had a son in the army."

"I have, sir," he answered, "and a noble boy he is. Ever since the first shot was fired at Charleston he had been impatient to go and enlist, but I would not let him. I was too jealous of him, too fearful of losing him. Too soon, I feared, I would have to let him go. But I love my country, too, and I did not hesitate. Now, when our lines are being crushed in and our remnants of armies driven back, every man counts, and so he went, and so would more go if I had them, even myself if I were able; for, though I am entertaining you as guests, don't think that I have the slightest feeling or sympathy with you." "But," he continued, his voice softening, "I have never heard from him since he left. The Unionists have upset the whole country, and no news of him could reach me. I can only hope that no harm has come to him and that I may receive him back again safe."

"We echo that hope," said Major Nobb, interpreting the feelings of all. I had no idea, when I asked my question, that I would open such a fount of emotion. The embarrassing silence that followed was soon broken, but I promised myself to keep my mouth shut for the rest of the evening. The supper went on, each forgetting for the time that they were enemies or that a war existed.

"Well," remarked Captain Martin, as the conversation had drifted around to such a subject, "talking of negroes, although we have come to free them, I've seen some that fight pretty shy of us. And freedom isn't enough reward for them sometimes; witness that night we brought up the rear of the pontoon train. You may remember the night, Robert?" he said, addressing me. "We came to where the road split into three," he continued, "General D—— had not left a vidette nor blazed a tree, and so we did not know which road to take. A few of this African race offered to guide us for some of Uncle Sam's greenbacks. And we might have done better ourselves, for both the first two roads we took were wrong, and we couldn't have done worse. Oh, no; niggers are good enough to discuss as a political issue, but when you come to have dealings with them, excuse me."

"I am sure you will change your opinion," objected Mr. Rae, our host, "when you hear my old negro, Bonaparte. He can give you some old plantation songs, which at least will amuse you. He is one of the few who refused to leave me; Helen is another."

With conversation and music, for the major played and there were three pianos in the house, we passed the time very pleasantly. We had thought to celebrate our Christmas eve in some old shanty, rude at best, with whiskey, after the soldier fashion, but here we were enjoying some of the best of wine. "Uncle Bony" was brought up and induced to sing, accompanying himself on a fiddle. He professed to play the air, or as he termed it, the "chune" of each piece, but for the life of me I could not tell the difference between one "chune" and another. He sang all his songs to the—the—whatever it was he played. I can only remember the opening stanza of one, and it went somewhat like the following:

" I'se got a little dawg
    Wot won't bite me,
  But he bites ebery one
    Dat he do see."

It is needless to remark either on the sentiment or the metre of this. Uncle Bony then took a comprehensive survey of what his "little dawg" would do and wouldn't do. We had Uncle Bony presented to us in another light before we got to bed. Aunt Helen showed us our room, and naturally wanted to have a few words with us foreign curiosities. So she began telling us of Uncle Bony.

"Yaas, indeedy, Uncle B-b-bony is a good-hah'ted nigga' an' you'd think he'd be a Christian a'ter goin' th'ough all the troubles he's been, b-b-but he ain't; he's chuck full of Blackrockism; he'll go to de d-d-debil sho'ly."

"Blackrockism? What is Blackrockism?" asked the major puzzled.

"Why, Lawd! honey, doan' you know w-w-what dat is Why, it's when a nigga' b-b-bleebs what is, is. Uncle B-b-bony's done took many ob de mos' influenshal m-m-members f'um Lebanon ova' to Blackrockism. De d-d-debil has done tole him he kin do w-w-what he want." And Helen retired proudly, being conscious that she had interested "de Linkum ossifers."

"Well, boys," began the major, sitting down on the edge of his bed. . We were all put in one room at our request. Uncle Bony and Blackrockism having been disposed of, I've a proposition to make. A question first: what do you think of our host?" All voted him the finest old gentleman in the South. "I agree with you," continued the major. "We can't pay him with coin, nor, since we are enemies, in any other way either. But we would not have it said that a Union man was ungrateful for any favor received from the South?" (faint applause from Captain Cobb and the doctor, who were plus a little too much wine). "But," continued the major, emphatically frowning down the applauders, "I think I see a way of repaying him. I have an idea that our haughty prisoner is the son of our host. To make sure of it we can take Mr. Rae to camp tomorrow. If it is so, then by getting his release we will square accounts. What do you think of the plan?" It is needless to add that we all agreed, and with that we all turned in and slept soundly.

After another meal, in which more of the doctor's destructive bread figured conspicuously, Major Nobb said:

"Mr. Rae, I do not wish to raise false hopes in your breast, but I think—only think," warningly, "that I have seen your son lately. For you greatly resemble the man I refer to; but to make more sure I will describe him. Has your son dark auburn hair and brown eyes, straight features, and—?"

"Yes, yes!" cried the old man, eagerly starting forward, his eye glistening and his voice trembling. "It is he! It is he! O, where have you seen him? Tell me! Not dead! O God! not dead! He was my only hope and consolation." He stood with hands outstretched, his haughty expression flown and his face the very picture of entreaty. We respectively withdrew to the window. "Tell me, tell me it's not so."

"Sir," answered the major in that sympathetic voice he could so well exert, "I can enter into your feelings from loved ones at home; but remember I am not sure that this is your son. If it is he, then your son is safe and I hope will soon be restored to you. "Pray don't," he added quickly as he saw Mr. Rae's intention of overwhelming him with thanks, "I did not wish to appear as a benefactor at all, I only hoped to cancel our debt."

"It is no debt on your side," returned the other, all his hauteur again appearing. "Do you not know that it is the duty of every Southern gentleman to treat a guest as I have treated you, whether friend or foe?" But, he continued, softening, "if I may regain my boy through you I will owe you a life-long debt of gratitude.

"I regard it in a more practical light," returned the major. "One good turn deserves another; you have put us under more obligations than you think. However, if you will now come with me to camp we can soon settle all doubt as to the identity of your son."

With trembling haste Mr. Rae prepared to go out into the chilly air. Christmas was the very opposite of its eve. The latter was bright and beautiful, while the former was gloomy and dark. The weather, too, was colder, and altogether Christmas was a very unsatisfactory sort of a day. As we came out into the damp atmosphere a great deal of our Christmas enthusiasm evaporated. Dismal forebodings of orders to march through the pine woods and over muddy roads presented themselves to our imagination.

"Thank heaven!" said Captain Martin, "we've spent one night in comfort, and I for one am willing to do anything for Mr. Rae consistent with my duty."

"And I," exclaimed the doctor and myself in the same breath.

We were the envy of our brother officers when we arrived in camp. "Evidently," I heard Cole remark to a companion, "they are already moving in the F. F. S." But it was not the society they were envious of, but our quarters.

Martial rank had been more or less forgotten in our stay at Mr. Rae's, but now back at camp we naturally fell into our respective positions. Major Nobb alone accompanied Mr. Rae to the prisoner's quarters, while we dropped behind. Of the interview between the three I know nothing personally, but was told of it by an eye-witness, so that this account will be but poor at the best.

Mr. Rae and his son recognized each other immediately.

"O, father," cried the son, springing forward and embracing him.

"My son! my son!" was all the answer, but this exchange of words, meagre as it was, was sufficient for two hearts so full of love. The major turned and looked in another direction. There was nothing in the words, all in the tone.

"But, sir," was the next the major heard, delivered with the accustomed haughtiness, "my son is a prisoner, if these signs denote anything," and he waved his hands towards the guards.

"Certainly," answered the major; "how else could I have known of him?"

"True, true," said the father, "I had never thought of that."

"But what of it?" continued the major, "I intend to obtain his release."

"Sir," returned Mr. Rae, with a proud dignity that almost startled Major Nobb, "have you come this far South and yet do not know us? Do you think that, even should I agree, my son would accept his liberty thus? No. He must wait for an exchange, or till the war ends, which it soon must do." "For," he added sorrowfully, "our strength is nearly gone."

"I respect your wish," said the major, bowing. "So be it. I can only offer you my sincerest thanks for your hospitality, and I shall always cherish your memory as that of a dear friend. Again I offer you all I can—thanks for myself and companions."

"And I," replied Mr. Rae, with a stately bow that sat well upon his aged person and gray hairs, "I accept them in the spirit you give them. My hospitality has always been open to whomever has needed it, and I hope will always be." My boy, he continued, turning tenderly to his son, "I know you have fought bravely and done your duty, because I know you. That gives son in impotent longing, "I might have done so much more if I could have remained free longer. Why was I, out of all my company, knocked on the head and taken? I could have done so much, so much! But to march a prisoner here day after day and waste my energies for nothing is maddening,

" 'O FATHER!' CRIED THE SON, SPRINGING FORWARD AND EMBRACING HIM."

me as much pleasure as though you had won a general's position. Perhaps you have fought your last, as the war may soon be over, but at least you have the satisfaction of having done your best."

"But, father! father!" burst out the father! In my anger sometimes I feel that I could snatch a gun from a guard and make a break for liberty, fighting and killing till I fall. But it is madness. I fear I will become mad if this lasts much longer. I hope an exchange will soon be declared, and then, father, I can fight for our dear South again."

The major looked at the prisoner in surprise. His face was transformed; now he was all animation, and hope and courage gleamed from his eyes. But he also heard the words and believed him capable of attempting such a thing.

Then came the farewell. The major pretended to be watching a groom at the other side of the camp.

"Farewell, my son, bear all with a stout heart, and you will show a courage as great as that in battle line."

"You can truthfully say he fought well," said the major, as he went back to the house with Mr. Rae. "Lieutenant Cole should tell you of it, as he saw it, and I only know from hearsay, but I will tell you the best I can." And he related the skirmish and how the young man was captured. "You may be sure," he added, "that he did all the damage

he could. And," continuing laughingly, "altogether I am glad you did not take my offer." "But," again becoming serious, "you may be sure that I will treat your son as leniently as I possibly can, and he shall have all the comfort that I can get for him."

"God bless you!" said the old gentleman brokenly, wringing the major's hand, "God bless you! as I know he will. Farewell!" The major watched him enter the house supported by Bonaparte. "How near the grave are both!" thought the major as he strode back to the camp.

What remains to be told? Little. In a few hours orders came to move. The younger Rae was not exchanged as he had so hoped to be, but remained a prisoner till the end of the war, and arrived home in time to close his father's eyes in death.

THE WIDOW LIGHTFOOT.

By Kathleen Gray Nelson.

If you followed the rough winding road that led from Ellis Town, a road that was always dusty in summer and muddy in winter, you would find, just beyond the three-mile post, the picket fence that enclosed the home of the Widow Lightfoot. The fence had never been painted and had once been garish in its newness, but that was when John Lightfoot had first brought his bride there to live. Time, in the years that had followed, had made up for man's omission by gradually tinting it with nature's color until now it was a mossy green. The tall hollyhocks peered over it and bloomed in old-fashioned serenity during the long summer season, until you quite forgot there was any fence there. If you entered the little gate— the hinges did not work well, but by lifting it up you could open it—and looked beyond the trees and thickly growing shrubbery, you would see that the house had never been painted either, and sun and wind and rain had shaded it until it looked like a softened pen and ink sketch.

In the once neatly laid-out yard, where each flower-bed had been a diamond or a square in brilliant contrast to the sober colored house, flaunting peonies, roses, dainty larkspur and chubby touch-me-nots climbed over each other in the struggle for existence. The prim little many-petalled yellow rose of long ago, great purply red velvet roses and sweet pink roses mingled their fragrance in the air and enticed the bees from the row of hives on the side of the hill. These flower neighbors had all come up there so many seasons now that each had outgrown its allotted space and invaded the territory of its neighbor. That was why you found the sweet pea clambering unsteadily upon the sleepy pretty-by-nights and a daisy hiding its fair face in the lily's cup as if drunk with its perfume, while crowded out of the race the violets wandered far out into the walk. The Widow Lightfoot never rebuked any of these trespassers. "They ain't doin' no harm," she would say, placidly, "and I let 'em grow just where they want to."

A zealous hired man had once persuaded her to let him saw off several lower branches of the great oak tree that guarded the door, and although the wounds had healed and were now covered by the kindly moss, those poor green knobs were a perpetual reproach to her. "My conscience has allus hurt me for tryin' to improve on natur," she often explained, as she sat on the little porch, peeping regretfully out from behind the honeysuckles at the evidence of the hired man's handiwork. "It's just one of them things in life you can't undo, an' it ought to make us mighty careful how we act, 'specially towards things that grow just like the Lord tells 'em to."

Mrs. Lightfoot had been a widow for many years now, so long in fact, that as she expressed it, "she had forgot to be lonesome." "Yes, in Mr. Lightfoot's time she had been real well off," she would tell you with a suppressed sigh; "an' when he died he left her the home an' a bit of land, enough to live on, an' a nigger or two to work it. Then the war come on an' she seen hard times like all her neighbors; but she had somethin' to be thankful for, her home an' her land was left an' that was more'n some of 'em could say."

In her younger days she had been wont to go through the neighborhood and quilt the gay patchworks that delighted the good country dames of long ago, and she achieved such a reputation in that line that she was in constant demand. But of late years farmers' wives had grown sadly unappreciative of such utilitarian fancy work and quilting as a profession was not lucrative. Occasionally some one sent her a quilt, but in this age of hurry the order was to do it as plainly as possible. She told sadly now of Mrs. Higgins' "Mountain Rose" quilt, made of such lovely bright green and red calico put together with white, and of the wonderful pattern she had quilted it—vines and leaves and grapes, and each grape stuffed separately until it stood up in rotund perfection. And there was the "Alabama Wreath" of Miss Maria Peterson, and then Mrs. Lightfoot would wax eloquent over these gay covers of our grandmothers.

"The present gineration 'll never see the like of them," she would say, shaking her head. "Oh yes, she'd seen some of them white counterpins they have these days, but there wasn't nothin' pretty about 'em, not even a bit of color to cheer one's eye," and Mrs. Lightfoot sniffed contemptuously. "The calikers now wasn't pretty like they use to be, nor the eatin' as good," she would continue. "Yes, times had changed, but 'cordin' to her way of thinkin' it was for the wusser. She heard them tell how the world was gittin' wiser, but it didn't look to her like folks knowed as much now as they did in them days."

The Widow Lightfoot was very proud, so much so that when a gaping hole came in the elbow of her best cotton frock she wore a dolman to church that was long and ample enough to cover all defects in the garment underneath, although the thermometer told a story of summer heat, and a little stream of perspiration trickled constantly down her backbone. It was also on account of this same pride that when some of her front teeth became conspicuously absent she invaded the territory of denistry and made herself some weak and very troublesome ones of beeswax. She had

inserted them by a process known only to herself, and she was forced to laugh with great circumspection when they were in place. They were for ornament only, and it was rather inconvenient that she could not eat with them and had caused her some embarrassment. There was the time when she went to spend the day with neighbor Hornblower, and although she swallowed everything with a mighty gulp and much danger of choking, still, when the unsatisfactory repast was finished, she found that two of her teeth were missing. Since then she had worn them only on Sundays and other very important occasions, and the remainder of the time they reposed in the little left hand drawer of her old fashioned bureau.

There had always been a certain rivalry between Silas Green's widow and the Widow Lightfoot, both being left alone about the same time, and when the widow Green saw Mrs. Lightfoot's acquisition of teeth, she was overcome with righteous contempt of her neighbor's vanity. "Em," she said solemnly to her daughter, "the widow Lightfoot's growed some new teeth, an' at her time of life, too. Why she must be fifty-one if she's a day, for she's older'n me, an I'm only forty-nine. It's my opinion she's a dyin' to marry, an' I do believe she's settin' her cap fur James Turner. He's such an old fool he don't know no better than to be took in by them very teeth, neither;" and Mrs. Green smiled scornfully.

In the meanwhile Sunday came and found the Widow Lightfoot in her accustomed pew, enveloped in the charitable folds of the dolman. All unconscious of her neighbor's criticisms, she sang "I Would Not Live Always" in a high tremulous treble, with much satisfaction to her soul, and her heart experienced a thrill of satisfaction when she saw James Turner glance at her twice during the service. She had caught him looking at her several times of late, and it had always brought a faint pink tinge to her withered cheek. Who shall dare to say when sentiment dies in any human heart, particularly a woman's? For despite her fifty odd years the Widow Lightfoot's heart beat as quickly as any young girl's in the presence of her first lover, when she saw James Turner watching her with a look of approbation in his light blue eyes, and under his kindly scrutiny her hand trembled so she could hardly turn the leaves of her hymn book.

In the seclusion of her own home that day she took off her well-worn black bonnet and. put it carefully away, and she chuckled to herself as she rolled up her teeth with the same precision. "It's mighty lonesome livin' alone," she remarked to the purring cat, who was sunning herself in the doorway, for she had no one else to talk to, and later in the day she acknowledged to that same inattentive listener; "It's nice to feel somebody is interested in you agin." From which confession it will be easy to see that the Widow Lightfoot's heart was still young.

Mr. James Turner has been out West for several years, where he had accumulated enough to live comfortably the remainder of his days. Then the longing had come to him, as it comes sometimes to all wanderers, to pay a visit to his old home. True, there had been many changes since he left, old friends had died, children he remembered were now bearded men or happy mothers, but there were a few of those left who remembered and loved him, and "there's no friends like old friends" he never tired of repeating, as he dropped back contentedly into the old life.

"I've found out folk's hearts change less'n anything else," he would say, "an' friends once made is too good a thing to lose or let forget you. That's why I've come back where I was born, an' its made me young agin, too. Why, I remember everything 'bout here just like it was yestiddy; every tree on the old place that I ever climbed as a boy;. every turn in the creek, an' right where the best fishing grounds was; an' I remember, too, where old man Haskin's watermelon patch was," he would add, winking at Squire Bassett, his friend and comrade in those boyhood days. Then they would both chuckle gleefully at the remembrance of their youthful pranks. "I tell you mem'ry's a wonderful thing,"

the Squire would add, "the next best thing to youth."

"Widow Lightfoot's a pow'ful spry woman," Mr. Turner remarked meditatively one day, as he sat in a split bottom chair in front of Dave Winder's store at Ellis Town. "She gits around mighty lively for one of her age, though when I come to think of it, she ain't as old as she might be, not by a long sight. I use' to think a power of her when I was a boy, clerkin' at Abe Jones' store—it stood right around the corner from here, till it burned down, nigh onto fifteen years ago—an' he kept as pretty a line of things as you can find anywhere today."

"It was a good store, the finest in these parts," Squire Bassett assented, tapping on the ground with his cane as if to emphasize his words.

"I remember just as plain as if it hadn't been a week ago, how she use to look when she come a drivin' up there in her pap's two-horse wagon," Mr. Turner continued, his thoughts still with the Widow Lightfoot, "her eyes a shinin' at a feller, an' her cheeks so pink they made you think of June apples. My! my! when she would come in an' call for five yards of indigo-blue caliker with a figger in it, my hand would trimble so I couldn't measure it off, an' I never could count with her a-lookin' at me. Then she'd sometimes want to buy a dime's worth of striped candy; she was partial to peppermint, an' I'd allus pick out the biggest sticks for her, 'an when she went to pay for it I'd say, blushin' till I was redder'n any beet,—'Just take that for laps, Miss Becky.' Then I'd stand behind the door watching her as she drove off, an' the store would look mighty dark and cheerless the rest of that day. Strange what a difference a woman's presence makes anywhere. I seen her married, too, an' a prettier bride I never laid eyes on, an' folks all said Ben Lightfoot was a lucky man."

"That he was," Squire Bassett said, looking from his whittling to nod approvingly, "for Becky was a likely lookin' girl, an' allus mighty handy to have 'round. We allus set a great store by Becky."

"It all comes back mighty fresh an'

clear," Mr. Turner went on, "makin' me 'most forgit I've growed to be an old man since then. I went West the next year atter she married, an' since then I've been so busy, 'tween plantin' crops an' gatherin' 'em in gittin ready for wintcr an' then fixin' for the summer, that I ain't had no time to think 'bout women folks. Now I come back here an' find we're both growin' old, with nobody to care for us; it's a sad thing I tell you to outlive your friends an' have to walk alone to the grave just the time when you most need a bit of lovin' sympathy to make you feel that happiness ain't gone with your youth."

"Our old friends are gittin' pow'ful scarce now, Jeems," the Squire remarked, and if he had been a man of a less prosaic turn of mind he might have thought that Mr. Turner was waxing sentimental over the Widow Lightfoot, but the Squire had by this time entirely forgotten her connection with the conversation.

As the weeks went by the Widow Lightfoot began to think she had been mistaken about James Turner's looking at her with any particular favor, "tho' he allus was a pow'ful bashful man," she told herself, "an' I reckon the only reason he never got married was because no woman ever axed him, for I'm sure she'd a had to do the axin'."

One Monday morning, however, as the widow sat on her shady front porch, peeling the apples for her solitary pie, there were the sound of wheels approaching, and they ceased abruptly at her gate. "Mercy me, who can it be comin' here this time of the day," she thought, as she went to the steps and peered eagerly down the walk. The tying of the horse must have been a very difficult process for it occupied some time, and just as she was growing very impatient, she saw James Turner tugging at the gate.

"Just lift it up a bit," she called cheerfully, although as she afterwards expressed it, "her heart was beatin' like a churndasher." Thus advised, Mr. Turner succeeded in gaining entrance. As he came up the narrow walk Mrs. Lightfoot noticed that he was clad in his immaculate Sunday suit of shining black

broadcloth, and her trepidation increased with this discovery.

"An' I ain't got my teeth in," she remembered, with sudden dismay, as he neared the steps.

"Come right in, Jeems," she said, cordially, with a heightened color, keeping her lips as tightly closed as was possible under the circumstances. "I'm just makin' ready the apples for my pie for dinner, tho' it don't seem worth while to do much cookin' when you've only yourself to feed."

"No, no," Mr. Turner replied vaguely, as he took the proffered chair, crossed his legs, and looked meditatively at his newly blacked shoes.

"You know how lonesome it is to be alone," the widow continued, "so you can feel for me."

"Yes, yes," he agreed, still occupied with the contemplation of his foot.

The widow did not venture any further remarks for several minutes, and Mr. Turner grew perceptibly uncomfortable. Once or twice he cleared his throat vigorously, but an awkward lump had found lodgment there that rendered speech impossible. The widow at last took pity on his plight, and remarked through her tightly closed lips:

"It seems like old times to be settin' talkin' to you, Jeems."

"An' there ain't no times like old times, Becky," he supplemented, nodding his head slowly.

"That's what I've allus said, Jeems," the widow agreed, and again there was silence. Mrs. Lightfoot remembered what she had said about a woman "havin' to do the axin'" in his case, but somehow it did'nt seem any easier for her than it was for him. "It ain't a woman's place I know," she told herself, as she tried to screw her courage up to the necessary notch, "but its better than to lose him," and again she commenced the conversation.

"It's mighty nice to see you back here agin, Jeems. We ain't never forgot you if you did stay away so long."

"That's kind of you, Becky, to say that," he mumbled, never daring to look at her.

"The West must have agreed with you," Mrs. Lightfoot went on, unwilling to lose the advantage she had gained, "for you came back lookin' most as natural as when you an' me led the dance down at Mr. Higgins' quiltin' bee, that night when it rained so as we was a comin' home an' you wrapped me up in your coat lest I get wet. You had an awful cold the next Sunday, too, Jeems, an' I felt mightily distressed."

"Ah, them was happy days," he said, warming up at these memories. "Well do I remember old John Higgins' quilting bee, and how Lem Davis an' myself most fit right there 'bout which one should have you for a partner in the Virginy Reel. Lord, how proud I felt when you took me! An' how pretty you looked that night in some sort of a white dress, with your eyes fairly dancin', an' I thought angels must look just like you, 'cause I knowed they couldn't look any prettier."

"La, Jeems," Mrs. Lightfoot said, with a pleased smile, as a pink flush spread over her face and lost itself under her prim white collar. "We've both growed old since then," she continued, "an' the years tell their own tale in the gray hairs in my head and the wrinkles that has marked up my face."

"You look pow'ful natural still, Becky," Mr. Turner replied.

Again there was a pause in the conversation, so long in fact that the widow grew afraid of the sound of her own voice and sat in nervous expectancy.

"Becky, I've come to ax you somethin'," he said at last, just as she had decided that he never would speak, "somethin' that I've been kinder interested in for some time."

The widow felt a cold chill start at the very base of her brain, run quickly down her backbone and end in the tips of her toes.

"Yes, Jeems," she managed to say finally, in a weak voice.

Mr. Turner's face was very red, and he was perspiring profusely. He mopped his face vigorously with his hankerchief, took off his glasses and polished them until they fairly shone, put them carefully on again, but still did not look at the trembling Becky.

"It's been on my mind a good deal lately," he commenced again, "an' I thought as how it was best to start out the week by axin' it."

"Yes, Jeems," the widow said meekly.

"Well, what I've come for, Becky, is —is to ax—that is to say—oh, consarn it all—to find out—have you any Shanghai chicken eggs, Becky?"

The widow straightened herself up abruptly and gave a little snort.

"Jeems Turner!" she said sharply, "have you been settin' here a mortal hour, puffin' like a porpoise, tryin' to ax me if I had any Shanghai chicken eggs? No, I ain't, an' I don't want none neither!"

Mr. Turner looked at her deprecatingly, and twisted his handkerchief round and round his finger in an absent-minded way.

"I've got some, Becky," he ventured at last.

"Well, you're welcome to 'em," she snapped.

Mr. Turner shook his foot nervously, and turned in a very unhappy frame of mind, judging from the expression of misery on his face.

Mrs. Lightfoot picked up the pan of apples at her feet, and resumed her work with renewed energy, as if oblivious of his presence.

"I reckon I'd better finish these apples," she condescended to remark, "seein' as how the flies is a pestering of 'em."

Mr. Turner watched her for some time in silence, and then he said meditatively:

"I seen the Widow Green this morin' an' a very nice lookin' woman she is, too, Becky."

Becky responded with a scornful "humph!" At last she put her lips together firmly and said in a very decided voice: "I don't suppose you come here to tell me that the Widow Green was a fine-looking woman, Jeems."

"No, Becky," he confessed. "Maybe I'd better go if I'm not pleasin' you," he added meekly.

"Nobody said you wasn't pleasin' me," the widow replied, looking more amiably at the now thoroughly crushed Jeems. "In fact, Jeems, I'd be glad to have you all the time."

The deed was done! She picked up an apple and began peeling it furiously, never even noticing that she was cutting a peeling of enormous thickness. Mr. Turner seemed at first dumfounded by the suddenness of it all, and then he said eagerly: "Well, you can have me, Becky, for the axin'."

"It seems as how I've done that," she replied, for it looked like you couldn't git to the point by yourself."

"I'm mighty glad it's all settled," he said, with a sigh of relief, "for its what I come to say, an' it looked like I couldn't git it out. You allus was a quick-witted woman, Becky, an' you saved me a peck of trouble, to say nothing of the uneasiness of my mind."

"Don't say nothin' 'bout it, Jeems," she replied modestly, "I was just a leetle more nimble tongued, that was all."

"It's a heap of consolation to me to have it over," he said, "more'n you can imagine, an' now, 'cordin' to my way of thinkin', the sooner we have it clinched the better."

"I reckon you're right, Jeems," the widow responded.

And that was how it came about that Mr. Turner was seen driving rapidly through Ellis Town just at dinner time in company with Squire Bassett, and the wonderful news discussed the next morning in front of Dave Winder's store was that there was no longer a Widow Lightfoot.

GABRIEL'S TRUMPET.

By Hester Dorsey Richardson.

The house was one of the hip-roofed farm houses peculiar to the early settlements of Maryland. The roof, with its dormer windows, slanted nearly half way down the walls in conformity with the primitive idea of architectural beauty. The clapboards were whitewashed, the shutters painted green, and the roof, by far the most conspicuous part of the house, had been stained by time a dull weather-beaten grey.

Back of the dwelling there was an old-fashioned garden in which lilacs, holly-hocks and big red peonies grew side by side with potatoes, cabbages and climbing beans. Box bushes, planted decades before, bordered the path to the creek which flowed by the garden. The tall lilac bushes grew close to the walk on each side, so that their bloom-laden branches met in an arch overhead.

The front yard was given up to poultry. Beyond the low paling fence a beautiful stretch of green was the promenade of the flock of geese whose incessant cackle alone disturbed the serenity of the place.

Across a narrow strip of meadow land west of the house a quaint brick chapel of ancient design stood near the river bank in a grove of fine old trees, whose sheltering arms protected the little sanctuary and cast cool, restful shadows about the yard in which the dead of many generations lay buried.

One warm day in mid-June many years ago, the geese were not the only occupants of the grassy lawn, about which they waddled with lazy steps in front of the Webster farm house. Under a great spreading walnut tree an old cart stood in the shade; between the shafts hung an iron chain forming a swing, in which a slender dark-haired girl sat reading, scraping her bare foot along the ground to keep herself in motion. Through the dense foliage of the ancestral walnut the sun had found a narrow passage and darted a ray upon the head of the girl and aslant the page she was reading.

It was high noon.

Suddenly the book dropped from the girl's lap as she sprang to her feet. A peculiar rasping sound had fallen upon her ear recalling her from fairy-land. It was Gabriel's trumpet summoning the farm hands to dinner. The old man stood in the low doorway leading to the dining room, with his battered trumpet at his lips, sending forth the doleful call familiar to those who had labored on the farm during the past half century or more. No one but Gabriel had ever blown that trumpet. Others had tried, but with no better result than waste of breath for their pains.

"WITH HIS BATTERED TRUMPET AT HIS LIPS."

He alone knew the secret of its latent tones. Its duty done for the day, the horn was carefully placed in the little corner cupboard and the master seated himself in a low flag-bottom chair by the door.

Gabriel had passed his ninetieth birth-day, but he was still active, with all his faculties well preserved, for he was not as blind as Brutus nor so deaf as Hector, his two faithful watch dogs, lying before him on the grass, catching flies in a lazy desultory way. Little Polly Gooster, the orphan daughter of Gabriel's only child, was the one sign of youth at the farm. Many a time she had tried Gabriel's soul with her madcap pranks, but never a cross word nor a touch of the scriptural rod had he given her since the day when that most pitiable of creatures, a motherless babe, she had laughed in his wrinkled face with the merry eyes of his dead darling and kissed his tears away in infant glee. The tiny year-old tot had thus crept into her grandfather's grief-stricken heart and solaced it. From that day he had lived for her pleasure, and now between the man of ninety and the girl of fifteen there existed a bond of mutual love and confidence such as is seldom established between the old and young.

At the sound of the horn Polly threw her book into the cart and ran lightly over the grass to the house to put the last touches to the dinner table. As she passed Gabriel sitting in the doorway she dropped a swift kiss on his seamy cheek. The caress brought a happy light to the dim old eyes and a smile to the noble face which lingered there when nodding recognition to the men as they came into the yard nearly half an hour later.

Polly sang as she worked. She loved to handle the blue china plates, on which gallant beaux helped stately ladies across turbulent brooks shaded by weeping willow trees. She had always felt a sort of comradeship with these indigo men and women who had figured so largely upon her childish horizon.

Gabriel was one of twins. The homes of the brothers, although a mile or more distant by land, were exactly opposite each other, and but for the intervening stream they would have been within easy walking distance. It was Gabriel's custom to call on Reuben every morning unless the weather prevented, for Reuben had not borne the flight of years as well as he. There was no more familiar figure in the country side than that of

Gabriel Webster riding along the highway on his dapple gray mare "Fly," who, though thirty years old, still carried her master at a brisk little trot.

The old gentleman was always clothed in well-brushed broadcloth and wore an antique silk stovepipe hat, in which he carried his papers, spectacles and big bandanna kerchief. He rode with a cane in lieu of a crop, and was altogether a most dignified and interesting character.

The brothers always greeted each other with much ceremony. Reuben, standing erect in his blue army coat,

saluted Gabriel, whom he begged to be seated before resuming his own chair by the open fire. Gabriel would carefully lift the venerable silk hat so as not to spill its contents, and deposit it upon the hearth, and after inquiring for Reuben's health would bring the red bandanna into use, and proceed to discuss the latest news from Washington.

Polly was happy enough in the quaint, simple home of her beloved grandfather. She did not miss the presence of young people, for her surroundings had been dear to her as far back as she could recall. Since she had learned to

"SHE LOVED TO HANDLE THE BLUE CHINA PLATES."

read, as her grandfather's companion she could always find entertainments in the old-fashioned library with its wainscoted walls, bare rafters and big open fireplace. Here two capacious cupboards filled up the deep recesses on each side of the great chimney jam, containing the leather bound volumes which had put Gabriel so far ahead of his non-reading neighbors. And so Polly laughed at life during the long bright days of her fifteenth summer, like the birds chattering in the trees above her; she knew only the sunny side of existence.

But the summer drifted into gorgeous autumn. The meadow and the old church yard were aflame with golden rod, that flickered on its long stems like yellow torchlights in the wind. The leaves of the grand old walnut tree were falling and, dropping into the water of the cove, sped away like tiny elf-boats on the receding tide. The tall, stiff dahlias were abloom in the old-fashioned garden. The leaves of the mulberry trees in front of the house rustled in the grass, and the naked upper branches beat against the sloping roof with every gust of wind. The swish of the river on the shore sounded bleak.

The joys of summer had departed, and with them Gabriel's vigor seemed to have gone. Polly was quick to notice the change. She saw that her grandfather was failing. The mare had not been saddled for several days, and Gabriel showed no disposition to leave the house. He had not complained, but when one day he kept his bed an unspeakable grief settled upon Polly's heart. The village doctor was called in. He came every day, measured out doses of medicine, shook his head ominously and road away in his rattling gig.

Gabriel lay on the high, old tester-bed in the room beyond the dining room. He had slept there since his birth, and fashion had never induced him to give up his ground-floor chamber for one under the eaves. He suffered little or no pain and slept most of the time. Polly would scarcely leave him, and whenever his eyes opened they seldom failed to meet the loving gaze of the faithful girl.

One morning in late November, when Polly went to take news of her grandfather's condition to Reuben, her eyes were wet as she reported Gabriel "not so well."

"Wait, child, I'll go back with you," called Reuben's wife as Polly was pushing off in her canoe. Taking her knitting and tying on her quilted bonnet, she told Reuben she would "go to see how Gabriel fared," and, although suspicious of the canoe, was soon on the other side of the creek.

When, later in the day, Polly had "set her across the creek," the old lady said, "be sure to send if Gabriel gets worse to-night."

The girl promised, with a sob in her voice, as she faced for home in her little craft.

The sun was sinking in a cloud of glory behind the old church. An eagle's nest in the topmost crotch of a spare sycamore tree stood out a dark speck against the sky. Long shadows stretched up the stream from the broken piles of a dilapidated pier and the trees on the river bank were reflected in the glassy surface. An oyster "pungy" riding at anchor duplicated itself in the limpid water, while a gang of white ducks left long ripples behind them as they swam hurriedly homeward in response to the call of "hickey!" "hickey!" "hickey!" from black Maria on the shore.

The beauty of the peaceful scene was for once unheeded by the sad-eyed girl, paddling so rapidly toward the garden bank. As the canoe grated upon the sand and Polly stepped upon the log wharf, the sun dropped below the horizon, and a leaden grayness overspread the landscape.

Late that night the master lay dying. In the kitchen three old black crones crouched in the great open fireplace that yawned like a cavern across nearly one-half the room. They had drawn their frocks between their knees to escape the fire. All had round tin boxes in their hands from which they were dipping snuff with the aid of small sticks, on the flattened end of which they lifted the brown powder to their teeth. The three-legged pot hung from the crane over the blazing logs. It was a weird scene, and they looked like veritable witches as they moaned and rocked to and fro.

No sound was heard in the master's bedroom, save the ticking of the eight-day clock and the smothered sobs of the girl who knelt beside the dying man. He had passed beyond conciousness, and now her only duty was to watch and wait. A few hard gasps from the quiet figure on the tester-bed, and Polly was a second time orphaned, with the grief of a first great sorrow. She had not felt the loss of her parents, and the full measure of her love had been lavished upon her grandfather. She was stunned, crushed by the blow.

In her anguish she had forgotten her promise to her aunt. It came to her suddenly with a pang. Leaving the room softly she ran bare-headed to the shore. The moon was full and showed that the tide had gone out. Perhaps the old man's soul had gone with it.

The canoe was high and dry. How could she let Reuben know?

Forgetting she had never been able to blow it, she hastened back to the house and retraced her steps to the river bank with the dinner horn in her hand. Was it that the spirit of the departed had fallen upon his darling grandchild? For out on the midnight air acrosss the water, there arose and floated the solemn wail of the horn, startling into silence the dismal cry of the whip-poor-will that was making night hideous from his place in the walnut tree.

Reuben, who was a light sleeper, heard the sound, and getting quickly out of bed he opened the door to listen. "What is it, Reuben?" called his wife, suddenly waking and seeing her husband standing like a wraith in the moon-lit doorway.

"Gabriel's trumpet!" he cried with uplifted hands.

And then they knew the old man was dead.

"ALBEMARLE AND PAMLICO."

By Edward H. Sanborn.

First impressions count for a good deal. If not always correct, they are at least interesting, and they generally have something of significance. When Captain Philip Amidas, who commanded one of the ships sent to this country by Sir Walter Raleigh in 1584, wrote down his first impressions of the North Carolina coast upon which he had landed, he expressed himself thus: "A goodlie land, the fragrance of which, as they drew near the land, was as if they had been in the midst of some delicate garden abounding in all manner of odoriferous flowers." The first impression of one who visits the same section today is not likely to vary much from what Captain Amidas carried back to England in his mind, and there are pictures of a "goodlie land" in the minds of thousands who have never been nearer the North Carolina coast than the fish stalls and early vegetable stands of the New York markets. The four hundred years that have passed since Sir Walter Raleigh's men attempted to build a city on Roanoke Island, almost out in the Gulf Stream, have not lessened the "goodlie" character of the country bordering the Albemarle and Pamlico sounds, and to the practically minded man who loves to reckon net profit per acre, this country is immeasurably more interesting than it was four centuries ago.

During a recent hasty trip from Norfolk, down through a portion of the Albemarle section, over the Norfolk & Southern railroad, I was impressed with several features of the country that ought to interest practical men. It is a country that is most familiar, perhaps, to Northern sportsmen, and probably this fact is responsible for the pre-eminence that is usually given to the sporting attractions of this region. But the man who takes his sport with the cultivator and hoe can find this section as interesting as the man who hunts for his enjoyment with gun and dogs. Before I set foot in that portion of North Carolina that is washed by the waters of Albemarle and Pamlico sounds, this query arose in my mind: Above is Norfolk, the centre of our greatest trucking district; below is New Berne, the centre of another early vegetable region of great importance. What of the region lying directly between these two points? I have answered this question to my own satisfaction and I give the result of my observation and investigation.

What may be designated as the Albemarle-Pamlico section of North Carolina embraces ten counties bordering on the two sounds, namely: Currituck, Camden, Pasquotank, Perquimans, Chowan, Washington, Beaufort, Tyrrell, Hyde and Dare. These ten counties have an aggregate area of about 7000 square miles, of which about 2500 square miles is water, which in this part of the country is well nigh as productive and profitable as the land. The entire population of these counties is about 90,000, chiefly scattered, as the ten chief towns number only about 12,000 in their aggregate population.

Considering the chief characteristics of these counties and taking them as they are traversed in going southward, we first enter Currituck county, which forms the northeastern corner of North Carolina. Currituck sound, which slices a long narrow strip of sand from

"TRUCKING"
IN
EASTERN
NORTH CAROLINA

the coast, is the favorite shooting ground of many wealthy Northern sportsmen, who control the privileges of large areas of land and water. Snowden, on the Norfolk & Southern railroad, is the station from which the most frequented shooting grounds are reached. But apart from this attractive feature of Currituck county, its most important characteristic is the trucking industry, which will steadily spread southward from Norfolk along the lines of rail and water communication. The soil is a clay loam, which is better suited to corn, rice and truck than to cotton, although some cotton is raised here.

Camden county, lying next to Currituck, is a long narrow strip of country, running from the Dismal Swamp, on the Virginia line, down to Albemarle sound. The Pasquotank and North rivers lie on either side of the lower portion of the county, making a peninsular of it. The upper portion of the county is chiefly semi-swamp land with a great amount of short-leaf pine, gum and cypress timber. Some cotton and corn are raised in this county, the fisheries are important and the truck industry is developing into a large business.

Pasquotank county occupies a position similar to that of Camden, running from the Dismal Swamp down to Albemarle sound, with the Pasquotank and Little rivers on either side of its lower portion. Along the rivers are strips of swamp with gum, cypress and juniper timber, and in the interior there are oak, hickory, short-leaf pine, ash, maple, black gum and holly, these timber resources forming the basis of a large lumbering industry. The soil of this country is of great fertility, and while considerable cotton still is produced, the trucking industry is assuming the most important place in agriculture. The raising of early potatoes for Northern markets is one of the most important and most profitable industries. Communication by steamers on Albemarle sound, by canal through the Dismal Swamp to Norfolk, and by rail over the Norfolk & Southern railroad give this section exceptional facilities for shipping products of every kind to the Northern markets cheaply, quickly and conveniently.

Elizabeth City is the county seat and most important town, situated at the head of navigation on the Pasquotank river, at the southern end of the Dismal Swamp canal and on the Norfolk & Southern railroad. Large shipments of lumber, fish and truck are made from this point.

Perquimans county, which comes next in the series, is almost identical with Pasquotank county in all its characteristics. Its northern end vanishes in the Dismal Swamp and a large portion of the county is what might be classed as "semi-swamp," that is, wet land that is readily drainable and available for agricultural purposes. The soil ranges from a fine gray loam to black muck. The Perquimans river, an arm of Albemarle sound, runs up into the lower end of the county, dividing it into two promontories and affording excellent facilities for transportation by water. The conditions are exceptionally favorable for trucking and the fishing interests are of considerable importance. Shad, herring, rock-bass and other fish abound in all the bays, creeks and rivers of the county.

Chowan county has a long coast line, formed by the Chowan river, Albemarle sound and Yeopim river, which extend along three sides of the county. With these three bodies of navigable water and a railroad crossing its centre, the county is well supplied with transportation facilities. There is a large area of valuable timber land in Chowan county, including short-leaf pine, oak, ash, dogwood, maple, cypress, gum and holly. At Edenton, the county seat, which is located on Edenton bay at the end of the first link of the Norfolk & Southern railroad, there are very extensive saw milling interests, and the lumber trade of this section is of great importance. The fisheries of this county are among the most important on the coast, and great quantities of shad, herring, rock, sturgeon, perch and other fish are shipped to Northern markets.

Crossing Albemarle sound, we come to Washington county on the southern shore. Only the northern half of this county has been brought under cultivation to any extent, the southern portion still remaining in its primeval condition

and consisting largely of swamp lands heavily timbered. The cultivatable portion of the county has a very rich soil, producing a large yield of cotton, corn, sweet potatoes and rice. Along the shore of Albermarle sound there are large fishing interests, shad and herring being the principal catch. Phelps lake and Pungo lake occupy the highest portions of the great swamp region of the lower part of the county, and they are connected with the sound by canals which enable vessels to enter the interior of county.

Tyrrell county, which adjoins Washington county on the east, is of precisely the same general character except that it has a larger proportion of swamp land. Its cultivatable portions are rich and produce good crops of corn, potatoes, peas and rice. There is an immense area of valuable timber, chiefly cypress, gum and juniper, and the lumber interests of the county are of great importance. Cattle raising is a prominent industry in Tyrrell county, thousands of cattle running wild in the swamps where they feed on the rich green vegetation.

Dare county, which has an historical interest as the birthplace of the first white child born upon this continent and also as the landing place of the first expedition sent to this country by Sir Walter Raleigh, is the easternmost county of North Carolina and consists chiefly of water area, the land being made up of a succession of long narrow islands and peninsulas. The mainland is chiefly swampy, lying but a few feet above tide level and heavily timbered. All this country is well adapted for stock-raising, which can easily be made successful and profitable. The most important industry of the county is the fishery interests, which are of great extent. Nag's Head, a delightful summer resort, which is very widely known among lovers of seacoast life, is situated on the eastern shore of Dare county, immediately opposite Roanoke island, where Raleigh's expedition landed and established a colony.

Beaufort county, the most populous and probably the most important county of this section, lies further inland and is divided by the Pamlico river, an arm of the sound of the same name. There is a large area of heavily timbered swamp land within this county, but there is also a larger proportion of rich farming land than in any of the other counties of this section. The swamp lands lying at the head of the numerous streams which rise in the interior and flow into the Pamlico and Pungo rivers are easily drainable and are considered equal in fertility to the bottom lands of the Nile or the Mississippi, without being subjected like them to overflow or inundation. These lands are covered with pine, cypress, white cedar, gum, oak, maple, beech and poplar, and can be cleared easily and at small cost, the first crop of corn usually paying all the costs of clearing, with the timber as a profit.

Hyde county, lying east of Beaufort county, is fringed and indented by sounds, bays and rivers, and its middle portion is occupied by a large lake, Mattamuskeet. Alligator swamp also embraces a large portion of its land area. Around the shores of the central lake is a fringe of rich land that has been cultivated for more than a century and is still producing large crops of corn without manure or rotation of crops. The soil of Hyde county seems to be inexhaustible in its fertility and capable of almost limitless cultivation. The soil contains an unusual amount of vegetable matter and the intermixed earthy matter is in a state of extreme fineness. Lumbering and fishing are important industries.

This is but a hasty survey of the counties embraced in what I have designated as the Albemarle-Pamlico section, and it is designed only to indicate the principal characteristics of this region. To the uninitiated, probably the most striking feature, and at the same time the greatest element of disadvantage, is the predominance of water in this region. To one who does not know this section it will probably occur at first thought that a country so largely swamp and low-lying sea coast cannot be very healthy nor yet of great agricultural possibilities. This is the natural error of the stranger, but more intimate acquaintance with this region establishes the fact that this very predominance of

Tobacco

In the
Cotton
Fields

water constitutes one of the most desirable features of the country and one of its greatest sources of wealth. It is a fact, not readily appreciated by those who have experienced the miasmatic and malarial influences of Northern swamps, that the swamp lands of the South are not unhealthy, but as a rule free from all disease-breeding elements. For evidence of this take the county of Norfolk, in Virginia, the most famous truck growing section in the country. This county is threaded in every direction by small water courses and was long considered an unhealthy and malarial region, but the settlement and cultivation of that section have demonstrated that the locality is entirely healthful and especially free from the diseases usually attributable to reclaimed or submerged lands. The South is full of examples of the falsity of the generally prevailing impression regarding the unhealthful character of the swampy regions. One of the most striking examples is furnished by the great reclaimed region in the interior of Florida, where about two million acres of land that was formerly entirely submerged has been drained and made available for agriculture. The experience of those who worked in the swamps during the drainage operations and those who have since lived upon the reclaimed lands proves the entire healthfulness of the region.

Regarding the sanitary condition of the Albemarle-Pamlico region in particular, let me quote briefly from reports of Professor Ebenezer Emmons, a former State geologist, who said many years ago: "It may be inferred that as the swamp lands are so low and wet that they must necessarily be extremely unhealthy, or become so when drained and the vegetable matter begins to decompose. Experience, however, does not support this view. The testimony of those who have cultivated them for forty years is that their families have enjoyed as much health as their neighbors who lived at a distance. Persons who are in the habit of plunging into the swamp lands knee-deep for draining, and when drained to live in the immediate vicinity of the extended surface of black vegetable mold for years, are rarely

sick with fevers." There is much more that might be said upon this subject, but there are other points that call for attention.

The fishery interests of this section are one of its most attractive features. A remark by an officer of the Norfolk & Southern railroad, which operates several steamboat lines through the waters of Eastern North Carolina in connection with its railroad line, set me a-thinking. He said: "The water in our territory is nearly as productive of traffic as the land." When I came to look into the figures of the fisheries of the North Carolina coast, I saw that this could be true enough. Here are a few facts and figures, gathered from the recent report on the fisheries of the South Atlantic coast by Dr. Hugh M. Smith, published as a bulletin of the United States Fish Commission. The fisheries of the North Carolina coast give employment to 10,274 persons; the capital invested amounts to $1,243,988; the catch in 1890 aggregated 51,799,142 pounds of fish and oysters, valued at $1,027,142. The larger items in the catch for 1890 are as follows: 16,481,000 pounds of alewives (herring); 1,345,194 pounds of bluefish; 12,410,400 pounds of menhaden; 3,585,-981 pounds of mullet; 5,768,413 pounds of shad; 1,885,677 pounds of squeteague; 5,650,820 pounds of oysters. Dare county shows the largest catch for 1890, amounting to 7,856,196, while Chowan county yielded nearly as much— 7,494,274, the catch in the latter county being chiefly alewives (herring.) A book might easily be written about the North Carolina fisheries, but this brief mention must suffice at this time and place.

Coming back again to the starting point, let us look at the trucking industry a little more in detail. The counties of Northeastern North Carolina, which have been designated as the Albemarle-Pamlico region, were included by the census office in the Norfolk district, so we have no figures for the industry apart from the statistics for the Norfolk region. But these will show something that is of interest. In 1889—and the industry has grown greatly since then—there were 45,375 acres of truck farms in the Norfolk district yielding a product in that year worth $4,692,859. Add 50 per cent to the value of the crop in that year and you will get a better idea of the present state of the industry. The truck farms in the Norfolk district were valued, according to the census figures, at $6,148,312, or about ninety-eight dollars per acre. Employment was given to about 23,000 persons.

Here is a thought that is suggested by the average value of the trucking lands in the Norfolk district, as shown by the census figures—$98 per acre. Much of the land in the immediate vicinity of Norfolk is valued at two to four times this figure by reason of the large amount of labor and money expended in bringing it to its present high state of cultivation. On the outskirts of this great trucking region, where the development has not reached so high a stage, lands of equally good character can be purchased for prices that appear nominal in comparison with the values around Norfolk. The query naturally arises, then; why not raise truck more extensively on these cheaper lands, at less interest cost? All down through these counties that I have named, lands of high productive capacity, admirably suited for trucking can be bought at from $8 to $25 per acre. Interest on the investment in lands at these figures as compared with lands at $200 to $400 per acre is quite a consideration.

There can be no doubt that the entire region of Northeastern North Carolina, stretching from Norfolk, Va., to New Berne, or even down to Wilmington, will be a continuous truck garden one of these days. There is every condition requisite to this end, and it is only a question of time and development. Fertility, climate, cost of land, nearness

to markets and facilities for transportation meet all the requirements for the business. I do not believe there is a place in the country where a man can make his living more easily than right in this section, and where a lazy man can make an easy living, an energetic man can make his fortune.

In market gardening nowadays, everything depends upon the speed with which the farmer can get his stuff to market. With the present admirable transportation facilities throughout the entire eastern section of North Carolina, truckers can get their produce into the Northern and Western markets to the best possible advantage. From the centre of the Albemarle-Pamlico region the time to Northern markets is about as follows: to Washington by the Norfolk & Washington Steamboat Co., twenty-four hours; to Philadelphia by Pennsylvania railroad, thirty-six hours; to New York by Pennsylvania railroad, thirty-six hours; to New York by Old Dominion Steamship Co., forty-eight hours; to Boston by rail, forty-eight hours; to Boston by steamer, seventy-two hours. Thus the trucker has a choice of routes and time, according to his necessities, and can ship to the various markets in good time and in good condition.

This is but a fragmentary description of the Albemarle-Pamlico region of North Carolina, a region that has great attractions for a practical man. The writer found it of sufficient interest during a hasty trip to induce him to study it further, and he believes any man who enjoys the study of the resources of an undeveloped country would find similar pleasure in a thorough examination of this section so rich in all the elements requisite for successful and profitable agriculture by modern methods.

MARSE TOM'S ASLEEP.

By James Tandy Ellis.

Jes' back befo' de cannon's roah
    Wuz heard thro'out de lan',
I means by dat, some time befo'
    De niggah wuz free man;
I hain' gwine spick o' slav'ry, kase
    It doan' bar' on de case,
But I wuz happy in dem days—
    Dat doan' come out o' place.

Along about de early spring,
    When plantin'.time had come;
When birds begin to chirp an' sing,
    An' honey bees tu hum,
Marse Tom would beckon wid his han'
    An' say, "Now, Lud, you keep
De chillun quiet, understan',
    I'm gwine tu go tu sleep."

De couch wuz near de winder whar'
    De breeze cud tech his face,
An' when Marse Tom wuz sleepin', dar
    Wuz quiet 'bout de place;
De little niggahs go 'way down
    De holler fur to play,
An' ef dey cum too close aroun'
    You heah some o' dem say,
        "Marse Tom's asleep."

When summer come, an' 'long in June,
    When all de fields wuz green,
De dinner done, an' arfternoon,
    Dey all know what dat mean,
Ole Miss she teck her work upstairs,
    Miss Janie wid her go,
Marse Tom would drap de farmin' cares,
    An' purty soon you'd know
        Marse Tom's asleep.

        *   *   *   *   *

I'se sottin' here dis summer day,
    De same place I wuz bawn,
But forty years have slid away,
    An' all de folks is gone.
Marse Paul wuz kilt at Shiloh, an'
    Miss Janie—I doan' know
Whar she is now—I understan'
    She's married long ago;
Dat graveyard in de medder wide
    Whar all de ivies creep,
It holds ole Miss, an' by her side—
    Marse Tom's asleep.

THE SOUTHERN OUTLOOK.

The South in the Magazines.

In glancing through the Christmas numbers of the leading monthly magazines this year one cannot fail to note the prominent position occupied by the South both in topics and writers. Such a conspicuous Southern influence in the magazines as appears at this holiday season has probably never before been manifest. In *Harper's* there are three distinctively Southern features. There is a charming paper on "The Old Dominion," by Thomas Nelson Page, an exceedingly interesting retrospective article on Virginia, which deals chiefly with the eastern portion of the State. The insight into the social and political conditions of the antebellum days and the present time is one that will be appreciated by those familiar with the subject and enjoyed by those to whom it is new. Southern fiction is represented in the December *Harper's* by "The Phantoms of the Footbridge," a story by Charles Egbert Craddock, and "Bud Zunts's Mail," a romance by Ruth McEnery Stuart. Then there is the usual introductory story in the "Editor's Drawer," by Thomas Nelson Page.

The December *Century* is even stronger in Southern elements. The first instalment of Mark Twain's much-advertised serial story, "Pudd'nhead Wilson," discloses scenes and characters that are essentially Southern. The story opens at Dawson's Landing, on the Missouri side of the Mississippi river below St. Louis; the characters are distinctively Southern and the period is prior to the war. "By the Waters of Chesapeake" is the title of a striking paper by Dr. John Williamson Palmer, in which the life of colonial days in Maryland is delightfully portrayed. This article, with its beautiful illustrations, is one of the most striking features of the magazine. Miss Murfree appears again in the *Century* with the second part of her story, "The Casting Vote." Joel Chandler Harris contributes "The Baby's Christmas," a graceful and touching Georgia

story which presents several strongly drawn characters. George W. Cable writes of "The Gentler Side of Two Great Southerners," giving two incidents in the lives of Jefferson Davis and Stonewall Jackson, trifling in themselves, but revealing the gentleness of character that was concealed by the sterner exterior of these two great Sou herners.

There is but one distinctively Southern feature in the Christmas *Scribner's Magazine*, but this is of exceeding interest. It is a Christmas story by Thomas Nelson Page— "How the Captain Made Christmas," a delightful tale of a Christmas day spent in a Pullman car, southward bound and belated by a wreck. The characters are so natural and the scenes so close to life that we are forced to the conclusion that we have made the trip with the same conductor and porter. If not, we would like to make the journey under such circumstances as Mr. Page relates. The December *Atlantic*, while taking no recognition of Christmas as an occasion of literary attractions, presents another of Bradford Torrey's interesting Florida articles, this time dealing with the "flat-woods." This, like Mr. Torrey's previous articles, presents those pictures of bird life that would appeal most strongly to the naturalist, but there are sufficiently frequent diversions from the subject to rob the articles of any scientific stiffness or dryness. Charles Egbert Craddock appears again in the *Atlantic* with further chapters of "His Vanished Star."

The prominence of men and things Southern shown in the Christmas magazines has been sustained throughout the year as a glance backward through the files will show. Among other features the *Century* has had several instalments of Grace King's charming "Balcony Stories," with their graceful pictures of New Orleans creole life ; "Mr. Gadsbury's Brother," by M. Francis Swan Williams, a story of the stern, stubborn but sturdily honest character of a North Carolina mountaineer;

"Caught on a Lee Shore," the diary of a cruise on the Florida coast by Lieutenant William Henn, the skipper of the Galatea; "The Prince and Princess Achilles Murat in Florida," by Matilda L. McConnell; "The Redemptioner," an Eighteenth Century Maryland story by Edward Eggleston; "The Escape of the Confederate Secretary of War," by John Taylor Wood; "Mr. Cummins' Relinquishment," by Richard Malcolm Johnston. *Harper's* has had during the year a striking Southern feature in Julian Ralph's articles, somewhat "scrappy," to be sure, but albeit very readable. "In the Old Way to Dixie" he told of his trip down the Mississippi river by steamboat from St. Louis; this was followed by "New Orleans, Our Southern Capital," Our Own Riviera, (Florida,) and lately by an entertaining article on the Louisiana sugar country—"Along the Bayou Teche." Constance Fennimore Woolston's novel, "Horace Chase," which has been coming along in instalments during the year, is distinctively Southern in its scenes if not in all its characters. Last February Ruth McEnery Stuart's short story "The Woman's Exchange of Simpkinsville" attracted attention to one of the recent accessions to the ranks of Southern writers, and in October Charles D. Lanier told the readers of *Harper's* something about "Our National Game Bird," with a suggestion of the pleasures of partridge shooting in Virginia and Maryland. The only representation of the South in *Scribner's Magazine* during the year up to Christmas was in George W. Cable's charming story of "The Taxidermist," a tale of New Orleans life, with some of its quaint features and a good side of the lottery to which people are not accustomed. In the *Cosmopolitan* there have been several Southern articles of a material nature, such as "In Our Cotton Belt," by H. S. Fleming, and "The Great Florida Phosphate Boom," by Alfred Allen, and in fiction the South has been represented by Opie Read, Martha McCulloch Williams and several others.

What is the significance of this? It means that the South is producing more writers, who are gaining recognition by their merits, and that the vast wealth of the South in all the elements of literature is being more liberally drawn upon as it becomes better known in the world of letters. All this is good ; all this is helpful to the South, as it gives to the world truer pictures of life and conditions in the great South country.

Monticello and Mr. Levy.

The following letter is from the author of the paper entitled "Mother of States and Undiminished Men," which appeared in the November issue of this magazine:

Editor Southern States Magazine :

"In my random notes on Virginia which appeared in your November number, in the course of a brief description of "Monticello" occur these words:

"At last a small gate between the great one and the lodge is unlocked and the keeper says that a fee of twenty-five cents must be paid before 'Monticello' can be seen; these are Mr. Levy's orders. Who is Mr. Levy? He is the gentleman who owns 'Monticello' and who lives in New York usually. While imparting this information the keeper leads the way upward through heavily wooded grounds. * * *

"Although the intention in the above was merely to note the colloquy at the gate, without implied criticism, the inference, perhaps, may be drawn that fees are collected for purely mercenary purposes. It should, therefore, have been stated that on the back of the gate ticket the visitor is informed that the gross amount derived from entrance fees is devoted to charities in Albemarle county. This fee system is in every way a proper one, and is said to have been put in force at the request of the citizens of the county after other methods of protecting the place had been resorted to. It is doubtless known to many of your readers that the family of Mr. Jefferson Levy, the present owner, have been since the time of the immortal statesman the guardians of fair 'Monticello'.   LOUIS PENDLETON."

PHILADELPHIA. December 7, 1893.

NOTES ON SOUTHERN PROGRESS.

AN effort is being made to arrange a permanent exhibit of Virginia's resources at Richmond. It is believed that such a combination will be of much advantage from an advertising standpoint alone. Col. A. S. Buford, president of the Virginia World's Fair board, and Mr. Henry W. Wood, president of the State Agricultural and Mechanical Society, are interested.

THE board of directors of the Maryland Investment Co. held a meeting in Baltimore recently and elected Mr. L. M. Tough, president ; M. V. Richards, vice-president, and continued Geo. W. Booth as treasurer. A tract of ninety-four acres of land adjoining Laurel, on the Baltimore & Ohio Railroad, has been purchased by the company, subdivided into building lots and a number of dwellings are about to be erected. The company's capital stock is $25,-000, paid in.

A NEW industry for the South is being established in the vicinity of Savannah, Ga., by Mr. C. B. Warrand and his associates. They will erect a plant for the manufacture of lampblack and printer's ink. The company expects to use about 1500 tons of rosin wasted in handling on wharves and in the rosin sheds ; this waste is mixed with sand and dirt, and can only be used to advantage for lampblack. Lampblack factories on the same principal have also been established at Fort White, Fla., by J. E. Lee and at Kershaw, S. C., by McDonald & Co.

THE ship City of Montreal, drawing twenty-one and a-half feet of water, crossed the Brunswick (Ga.) bar without difficulty on November 24. It is stated the channel is now deep enough to allow a vessel drawing twenty-two feet to pass over the bar.

OLOF BERGSTROM, of Omaha, Neb., has been in Fort Worth, Texas, and it is reported that he contemplates buying a tract of 12,000 acres

in Tarrant county and locating small farmers upon it. Mr. Bergstrom has been extensively interested in land ventures in Kansas and at one time was land agent for the Union Pacific Railroad.

IT has been ascertained that the daily capacity of all the cottonseed-oil mills of Texas last year, when running at their full capacity, could work 1,800 tons of seed per day, and the new mills built during the past summer in that State have an aggregate capacity of 2,200 tons of seed per day. The aggregate capacity this year is then about 4,000 tons per day. It is stated that Texas alone will produce this year about half as much oil as was made in the entire South last year.

EXTENSIVE developments in the coal fields of West Virginia are promised in a project which has just been made public at Cincinnati, Ohio. Messrs. W. M. Green and C. Morris, of the latter city, and Mr. James W. Ellsworth, of Chicago, have already purchased 25,000 acres of land on the Gauley river, in West Virginia, and have a contract to secure 15,000 more. The lands are located near the Chesapeake & Ohio Railroad, and a branch line is now being constructed to them, a distance of sixteen miles. Messrs. Morris, Green and Ellsworth propose organizing a company with a large capital stock to develop these lands, and are now engaged on the matter.

THE Young Men's Business League of Augusta, Ga., is taking steps to have the legislature create a State bureau of information which will answer all queries from outsiders who wish to locate in Georgia. The editors of the several papers will be urged to assist it by favoring the plan in their columns.

THE Cherokee Land and Improvement Co., of Knoxville, Tenn., which controls a large tract of land in the vicinity of the city, is making preparations to improve the prope ty. It is reached by a steel bridge which the company built at its own expense across the Tennessee river. This bridge alone cost $75,000. It is proposed to build an electric railway line from the city to the tract for the convenience of suburban residents. Many of the company are Ohio capitalists, among whom are Benjamin Wheeler and W. W. Harper, of Zanesville, and James Reynolds, of Mansfield.

THE Waldensian colony established in North Carolina some time ago is gradually being increased by new arrivals, 166 members of this sect having arrived at New York on November 20 on their way to the Old North State. These people are reported to be th ifty, hard-working settlers, who will prove of great advantage to North Carolina. The South heartily welcomes all such foreigners, and every well-located colony that is established in that section will in time become a centre of attraction to draw others. The start in all immigration work, as well as in nearly all business enterprises, is the hardest part of the battle. The beginning has been made in immigration, and now we see nearly every day some new evidence of the Southward trend of population. The movement is very small at present, and no one need look for any great rush, but year after year we shall now see a steadily-increasing flow of immigration this way.

THE tropi al-fruit trade is rap dly increasing at Mobile. The banana dealers especially recognize the advantages that port possesses, and claim that cargoes can be imported and distributed at Mobile at more of a profit than at New Orleans. The Mobile & Ohio Railway Co. is making special efforts to secure the fruit shipments to the North and West by maintaining a fast-freight service and offering other inducements to the dealers. According to a large importer, the following differences in money and time are in favor of Mobile when compared with New Orleans : Wharfage twenty cents per ton ; quarantine fees during season, $20.00 ; coal $1.00 per ton ; discharging, one cent per bunch ; harbor master's fees, $20.00 ; pilot fees,$3.50 per draught boat ; time to Chicago, twelve hours It is estimated that from $400 to $500 can be saved on an average-sized cargo by unloading at Mobile, saying nothing of the time saved.

THE citizens of Nashville realize the great advantages to the community which a business organization can obtain, and have organized a board of trade, which includes a large proportion of the representative merchants of the city. One line of its work is to "build up" the city by increasing its industrial enterprises and adding to its wealth and population by every legitimate means. In this respect it has an excellent example in the city of Memphis. The officers of the Nashville body are : A. J. Harris, president ; Joseph H. Thompson, first vice-president ; B. Herman, second vice-president, and W. D. Gale, treasurer. The following constitute the board of directors : G. P. Thruston, William F. Orr, J. B. Morgan, F. T. Cummins, John J. McCann, W.L.Granbery, A. J. Harris, Joseph H. Thompson, B. Herman, Edward Buford, W. M. Cassetty, James B. Richardson, W. A. Wray, D. S. Williams and W. K. Phillips.

HON. S. B. ALEXANDER has returned to Charlotte, N. C., from his trip to the sugar-beet sections of the West. The result of Mr. Alexander's observations is that a number of counties in North Carolina can not only equal, but even surpass Nebraska in raising beets, and he is confident that the German syndicate now looking for Southern locations for beet-growing and sugar mills will decide upon North Carolina. Mississippi, Georgia and South Carolina are also making efforts to secure favorable consideration as a location for these proposed factories.

THE sisal-hemp plant is attracting considerable attention in some parts of Florida, especially in the vicinity of Fort Meade. A shipment of the leaves has recently been made to Paterson, N. J., where the fibre will be extracted and a comparison made with that produced in Yucatan and the Bahamas. It is believed that the cultivation of this plant will increase considerably in Florida in the future.

A CHICAGO syndicate is locating a French colony of about 100 families on tracts of land of ten to twenty acres at Rockport, Aransas county, Texas. The settlers will engage in cultivating the grape for wine-making.

THE business men of Greenwood, Miss., stimulated by the success of the Young Men's Business League of Memphis, Tenn., have organized an association to develop the town and to secure manufacturing plants, if possible. A pamphlet will be issued giving a map and description of the place, and showing up the fine timber lands, with the splend d railroad and river facilities possessed by Greenwood, which will be generally distributed.

SOME time ago Alderman Macdonald, of Greenville, S. C., wrote a letter to the *People's Journal*, of Dundee, Scotland, which circulates among Scotchmen all over the world. The letter described the advantages and attractions of this section of South Carolina, especially for sheep-raising. It was printed and favorably commented on, and Mr. Macdonald has received a number of letters of inquiry, some of which may have important results. The scope of the circulation of the letter is indicated by the fact that among the places heard from by Mr. Macdonald are Nairn, Dundee and Longside, Scotland, and New York, Philadelphia, and Omaha, Neb.

IT is announced that the Iron Mountain Railway's land sales in Arkansas are 100 per cent. greater than last year. The company owns land in forty-two counties in this State, and most of the new settlements this year have been made by Arkansas people who are improving the land for farm work.

A MEETING of the directors of the South-over Land & Improvement Co. was held in Savannah recently to consider the proposition of the America Promoting Co. for the placing of the land company's stock. The proposition of the promoting company was accepted with provisions, and the Southover Company's stock will at once be placed upon the market in the East. As soon as enough stock has been placed to leave no doubt of the success of the undertaking, the erection of the proposed 30,000-spindle cotton factory will begin.

ANOTHER real-estate organization is about to be inaugurated in New Orleans. The company will engage in the buying, renting and improvement of incorporated real estate in the suburbs of the city and conduct a general real-estate business. The capital stock of the new organization will be $100,000, divided into 4,000 shares of $25.00 each. A large quantity of the stock has already been sub. scribed, and the undertaking will be pushed to a successful issue. At a recent meeting of the stockholders for the purpose of electing officers and going into a permanent organization, the following stockholders were selected as a board of directors: Messrs. H. J. Ledoux, W. K. DePass, A. K. Amacker, E. J. Barnett, P. Schumacher, J. Transchina, Warren Kearney, William Demoraelle, R. H. Whitmore, Arthur Weber, M. D., and H. J. Malochee. An election for executive officers of the company resulted as follows: H. J. Ledoux, president; H. J. Malochee, vice-president; W. K. DePass, secretary; A. K. Amacker, attorney, and E. J. Barnett, notary. The company expects to be operating in a short time.

THE famous Timmons case, involving real estate in the aristocratic portion of Birmingham, Ala., to the amount of $2,000,000, was finally disposed of last month in favor of the Elyton Land Co. by Judge Toulin in the United States Circuit Court. Some twenty-five years ago John Timmons owned a farm of 200 acres, covering the foot of the Red mountain. This tract is now in the city of Birmingham, and is called South Highlands. It covered some magnificent residences, and it is the homes of the wealthiest and most intelligent people of the city. These property-owners purchased their places from the Elyton Land Co., and for several years they have been uneasy about their title. The heirs of John Timmons, residing in North and South Carolina and Tennessee, claimed that Timmons in his will only bequeathed a life interest in his farm to his wife; hence they brought suit to recover this land, which had in twenty years risen in value from $2,000 to $2,000,000. The case has been twice tried in the United States Circuit Court, at Birmingham, and has gone up to the Supreme Court of the United States. The decisions have all been in favor of the Elyton Land Co., except one by Judge Boreman, when the jury awarded the heirs $250,000. This decision was reversed by the Court of Appeals at New Orleans, and Judge Toulin dismissed the case from court.

DURING 1893, 435 buildings have been erected in Roanoke, notwithstanding the dull times.

A REPRESENTATIVE SOUTHERN SCHOOL.

The Horner School, at Oxford, North Carolina, founded by the late James H. Horner, M. A., LL. D., has been training boys for college and for active life nearly half a century.

The s and that students prepared at the Horner School have taken at colleges has been influential in bringing this school prominently before the public. Among the alumni of the institution are some of the most successful men of the Sou h. The most successful cotton manufacturer of the State, the president of the wealt iest and most extensive railroad system of the South, the president of one of the largest universities of the South, the lawyer whose professional income is the largest in the State, the most extensive tobacco planter of the South, are alumni of the Horner School.

The success of students of late years can be judged only by their college courses. Of fifty or more students representing this school in the colleges of the State during the past few years, a few are given here as representative.

J. CRAWFORD BIGGS.

Mr. Biggs was awarded first distinction in scholarship at the Horner School in 1887. He entered the University of North Carolina in 1889, being rather young to go to college when he finished the course at the Horner School. His first two years at the University entitled him to be ranked as valedictorian of his class. He won the *Greek Prize* during his sophomore year, and the *Maugum Medal* at the close of his senior year. He graduated at the head of his class in 1893. He is now instructor in Mathematics and Sciences at St. Alban's School of Virginia. President Winston, of the University, says: "Mr. Biggs was one of the best prepared students that ever entered the University. During his entire University course he maintained the highest average of scholarship reached by any member of his class. He was, besides, an accomplished athlete, a leader in social pleasures and the president of his class. Few men have made a record so excellent in all respects and so marked by variety of talent."

FRANK P. HOBGOOD, JR.

Mr. Hobgood was awarded first distinction in scholarship in the Horner School in 1889. taking a post graduate course, which enabled him to complete his course at college in two years. He entered Wake Forest College in 1891 and graduated in 1893 valedictorian of his class. He is now director in Latin and Mathematics in the Oxford Female Seminary.

STONEWALL J DURHAM.

Mr. Durham was awarded first distinction
in scholarship at the Horner School in 1888,
and entered Trinity College in the fall of the
same year. He graduated in 1892, with the
highest commendation of his instructors.
President Crowell, of Trinity, says of him :
"From parentage he received much, from the
Horner School he brought a very superior
preparation for college ; in college he discovered his own individuality and learned how
urgent the work of a new life really is." He
is now instructor in Latin and Mathematics at
the Horner School.

enjoys the rare and honorable distinction of
having reached grade 'one' in every study
during his entire course. His fine natural
talent and the excellence of his preparatory
training give promise of a record rarely surpassed in the annals of the University."

BURTON CRAIGE.

Mr. Craige was awarded first distinction in
scholarship at the Horner School in 1893, and
entered the University of North Carolina in
Sep'ember. He has yet to make his record at
college, but his instructors at school predict
for him a brilliant college career.

FRED. L. CARR.

Mr. Carr was awarded first distinction in
scholarship at the Horner School in 1891, and
entered the University of North Carolina in
the fall of the same year. During his first
year at college he made the highest average in
scholarship ever made at the University.
President Winston says of him: "He

LYMAN A. COTTEN.

Cadets Lyman Cotten, Stuart Carr and John
Carr are selected as representative students of
the school during the present session. Their
record thus far entitles them to first distinction
in scholarship. It may be of interest to know
that Stuart Carr and John Carr are not related
to each other.

C. STUART CARR.

The preparation of boys for college is not a matter of chance. A study of college records shows too plainly that early preparation has very much to do with the subsequent career of young men. Parents are invited to examine into the advantages offered at the Horner School.

The Chicago *American Trade Journal* for August 29, 1893, has the the following reference to the Horner Military School in its leading editorial:

HIGHER EDUCATION.

"During the past month this institution has been the subject of closest investigation at our hands, and trained representatives of the *Journal* have pursued rigid enquiry among highest unbiased authorities concerning its scope, method and achievements. In fact, all available information concerning its features have been sought. Those directly concerned in its management or financially interested in its success were not consulted, it being deemed advisable to obtain expressions entirely free from bias or self-interest.

"As a result of such fair and painstaking search we do not hesitate to select this admirable institution and to freely and unreservedly endorse it to every reader who seeks the best and highest in education and who would secure the greatest return upon his investment, for this excellent establishment has undoubtedly solved the important question of maximum returns combined with minimum of expense. It affords the highest practical education at lowest possible cost. Moreover, it is ably managed, thorough in methods and equipment ; in fact, all that could be asked or desired ; hence we do not hesitate to commend it in unqualified terms. We have no greater interest in this institution than in any other of its kind, but having by unbiased investigation assured ourselves of its superiority and worth, consider it a duty to subscribers to make such supreme merit known.

"Now is the time to consider selection of an educational establishment and the choice should be made after closest examination. This we have done, and in all candor we say to every reader that the claims of this institution cannot be ignored. It amply meets the requirements of the most exacting."

JOHN R. CARR.

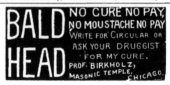

THE

SOUTHERN STATES.

JANUARY, 1894.

THE SOUTH AND IMMIGRATION.

The great question before the South today is immigration. Not the immigration of anarchists and socialists, nor even of the rougher elements of foreigners, who are neither anarchists nor socialists, but who are only fitted for the lowest order of work, but the immigration of comparatively well-to-do people —farmers and others in the North and West who are anxiously looking for a better land. Discouraged by the conditions surrounding them, by the poverty of the soil in some cases, by the ceaseless fight against the blizzards of the winter and the broiling suns of summer as in the Dakotas, by the distance from market, consuming in freights almost the entire value of the products, and by many other disadvantages, there are hundreds of thousands of people who would gladly move South if they fully understood the conditions of life and the opportunities for success in this section. The South has so long been misunderstood and misrepresented, its agricultural interests have been so closely identified in the public mind with the raising of cotton by negro labor. alone, that the great mass of American farmers outside of the South are almost wholly ignorant of the attractions and capabilities of this section for every branch of farming—for fruit raising, for dairying, for vegetable growing for Northern markets, for cereal production for all which some one or other part of the South is most admirably adapted.

About twelve years ago, when the Manufacturers' Record took up the work of making known to the world the industrial resources of the South, and in every issue predicted that the time was coming when the South would control many lines of manufactures, its statements and predictions were received with skepticism even by many in the South and ridiculed everywhere else. Convinced that it was right, it labored unceasingly week after week and year after year until it finally impressed upon the world that the South is to become the centre and controlling power in cotton manufacturing, in iron making, in woodworking industries and in other lines of industrial advancement. What the Manufacturers' Record has sought to do for the industrial and general interests of the South, the SOUTHERN STATES Magazine now proposes to do for the immigration and real estate interests of this section. Convinced that there is no other country in the world of equal advantages and resources, combined with equal attractions of healthfulness and climate, nearness to markets and all other things that unite to make possible success in life, it is proposed to push with unceasing vigor the work of making known throughout the North and Northwest as well as among the better classes in Europe, the attractions of the South for the farmer as well as for all others who are seeking a good location in the most promising and progressive section of America.

With a view to beginning the discussion of how to bring about the desired results, to secure the attention of farmers in other sections, and impress upon them the desirability of the South, the opinion of the leading railroad managers of this section was recently invited and we give in this issue letters from twenty prominent Southern railroad officers, discussing the question of immigration in all its phases. Out of this preliminary discussion we expect to see such interest aroused that this subject will become the predominant question throughout the entire South.

The attention of our readers is invited to the following letters, and from any one, either in the North or South who is interested. in the subject, we would be glad to have an expression of opinion upon the best means of attracting to this section the better class of settlers, not only farmers, but all others desiring a home where nature has . been most lavish in her gifts.

The Views of an Expert on How To Attract Immigration To The South.

Baltimore and Ohio Railroad Company, }
Baltimore, Md , January 2, 1894. }

The South is comparatively very little known among the masses throughout the North and West. We must therefore educate these people regarding the numerous opportunities awaiting them. They want to come, but where to locate is the vital question. Only those directly interested in the work realize what little knowledge exists about the South. This can only be accomplished by persistently advertising the merits of the country in general, and the advantages of particular localities. To do this rapidly and effectually there must be co-operation. Every railroad company should make special efforts to solicit persons to settle along its line; the citizens of each and every community should see that their particular section is well represented, and a good plan for them to work on is the organization of boards of trade, chambers of commerce, business men's clubs, and in fact any association of citizens who will work for the promotion of the best

interest of the community in which they reside.

We should encourage real · estate agencies. I do not believe that there is a field in the United States that offers better openings for reliable and practical real estate men than the South.

Compare counties, towns and cities in which there are reliable and hustling real estate agents, with those having no active agencies, and we find the work of the former manifested by the incoming of people seeking locations.

Lands should be placed in the hands of real estate men, and reasonable commissions paid for the sales thereof. It is a profession and the encouragement of it should be fully sustained.

I would lay great stress upon the necessity of real estate agencies in every county in the South. They have done much toward the settlement of the West, and I have seen the settlement of communities held back by reason of not having proper representations among the real estate fraternity. Land owners should place their properties on the market at reasonable figures, and the terms of sale should be easy to persons who will locate thereon and improve the property; the first payment should be small, and long time given on deferred payments.

If we could only move a small proportion of the real estate agents in the North and West to points in the South, a wonderful change would soon be visible.

Every Southern State should create an immigration bureau, placing it in the hands of some experienced and reliable immigration agent and continue the work for a period of years. This work can be carried on with a fund, the amount of which would be nominal considering the advantages which will accrue. It will take at least one year to organize the work, and immediate returns should not be expected. I think possibly one of the stumbling blocks in. the past, when soliciting immigration to the South, has been that our people expected too rapid returns, consequently the movement on the part of the States has been spasmodic. Great care should be exercised in placing at the head of

this work persons not interested either commercially, politically or otherwise in any particular section of the State which they represent, and it should be run on strictly business principles.

The work being done by the press and our immigration agents is convincing outside people that the South is the most desirable portion of the United States. This movement is merely in its infancy. In the next few years we can reasonably expect a great change in the condition of affairs. The increased capital and active population coming South will produce wonderful results.

The Baltimore & Ohio Railroad Company has been for several years circulating among the people of the North and West pamphlets, maps, etc., descriptive of the Southern States; the results have been very satisfactory. We have coming into our section of country daily people seeking homes, business locations, manufacturing sites, etc. Quite a number are delayed until they can dispose of their interests in the North.

M. V. RICHARDS,
Land and Immigration Agent.

More Advertising and More Push on the Part of Railroads Needed.

Frank Y. Anderson, Land Commissioner.
Vicksburg, Shreveport & Pacific Railroad Co.
Alabama & Vicksburg Railway Co.
Alabama Great Southern Railroad Co.
Birmingham, Ala., December 30, 1893.

Your favor of the 23d instant asking for an expression of opinion as to the best means to attract the better class of immigration—especially Western and Northwestern farmers—to the South, addressed to Mr. W. C. Rinearson, general passenger agent of the Queen & Crescent system, Cincinnati, Ohio, has been referred by that gentleman to me.

The Queen & Crescent system of roads controls over a million acres of lands in Alabama, Mississippi and Louisiana, and is naturally anxious to have these lands settled up by farmers, more especially from the Northwest.

Thousands and thousands of people who have grown tired of the narrow limits of the Eastern States and wished more latitude, moved to the West, where, after submitting to the suffering and extreme hardships of the blizzards

of winter, they sell out everything they have, and with the remains move South, and on account of our cheap lands are able to buy larger possessions with the balance of their money than they originally had. People who do this must necessarily be enterprising; hence those who come South from the Northwest are naturally of the better element. To reach this class more effectually, however, the railroad company should advertise more extensively; it should send its agents into the North and West, not only to distribute this literature, but they should be capable of explaining the many advantages the South has to offer.

The great good that the Manufacturers' Record and the SOUTHERN STATES Magazine that it publishes, devoted to the South, are now doing, should be more fully recognized and encouraged by the Southern people and those who have interests in the Southern States.

What we need is to enlighten the people of the North and West as to the true status of the South—its beautiful and general climate; its wholesome atmosphere; its cheap lands, capable of growing all the cereals raised in the North, with the addition of cotton and tobacco; its ready market for everything that can be raised almost at the door of the farmer, and the hospitable and hearty reception which every Southern man is ready to extend to the newcomer who may come to make his home with us.

In my opinion, the railroad companies of the South should combine and distribute literature which would explain these advantages to the people of the North and West.

F. Y. ANDERSON.

PRESIDENT R. C. HOFFMAN, of the Seaboard Air Line, has given the question of Southern immigration much time and consideration and is heartily in favor of all legitimate means to secure a desirable class of home seekers to locate in the South. Mr. Hoffman expresses himself as follows:

"The South offers exceptional inducements to settlers. Thousands of acres of land in North and South Carolina are today lying untouched from which abundant crops can be raised. Much of this land can be bought at from $1.00 to $5.00 per acre. In South Carolina, along the Georgia, Carolina & Northern railroad, there is a strip of country, from forty to fifty miles in length and extending fifteen miles on either side of the tracks, which is especially suitable for bright tobacco growing, as well as other crops. We have proved this by successfully cultivating the plants. But it has few or no settlers, and not a leaf of tobacco is now grown on it. South Carolina alone has miles of naturally fertile plantation land cultivated before the war by slave labor. The original owners have died, or have given up work on the land, and even the negroes have left it to follow the whites into the cities and villages. This soil will produce large crops, is easily tilled, and is located in one of the finest sections of the South as to climate and facilities for reaching market.

"These are but a portion of the localities where the small farmer can find land of a good quality and at a low price. The Seaboard Air Line will do everything possible to encourage the newcomers by giving them the best of transportation facilities and aiding them in other ways. The people will give them a hearty welcome. If a party of farmers think of going South let them send one man ahead to examine the country and see for himself. He won't find this an overdrawn picture I can assure you."

The Seaboard Air Line Expects to Begin an Active Campaign.

Seaboard Air Line, }
Portsmouth, Va., December 29, 1893. }

The Seaboard Air Line, in a quiet way, is making every effort to induce immigration along its line. So far we have not been successful, nor have we made a determined effort towards settling farmers; but it does seem to me that our line presents wonderful advantages to persons seeking farms. The land is very productive; the climate is unsurpassed, and the proximity to market, you know, is close. There is not a week during the year that plowing cannot be done. We find no difficulty in making excellent grass, fine wheat, oats,

rye, sweet and Irish potatoes, cotton, corn, tobacco, and in short, I believe everything that is grown on a farm anywhere in the United States. The people have been wonderfully successful in the growth of grapes and fruits. Last year, on a part of our line, parties had no difficulty in making $150 per acre in grapes.

We expect to take much more active steps towards immigration than we have hitherto done. I think the great trouble with the Northern and Western people heretofore has been that they have been unwilling to go South, on account of the predominance of the colored people—not being accustomed to them; but the Northern people who have settled here have found that the negroes in no way interfered with their successful farming, but on the contrary afforded them cheap and reliable labor.

I think the best means of attracting immigration would be for someone in whom the immigrant would have absolute confidence to come and see for himself, and make a statement of what he saw—the condition of affairs, the character of land and its price.

JNO. C. WINDER,
Vice-President and Manager.

A Wave of Immigration Moving Southward.

Richmond & Danville Railroad Company, }
Washington, D. C., January 5, 1894. }

The property I represent being purely a Southern institution, it affords me great pleasure to note the continuance of the interest heretofore manifested by the Manufacturers' Record and the SOUTHERN STATES MAGAZINE in the development of the South, and I assure you that this company is fully in accord with your work.

From the evidence which has come to my notice, I am quite sure there has not been for years, if at all, such a tidal wave of immigration towards the South —especially from the West and Northwest—as now exists. From the correspondence which is daily passing through my office, it is evident that the farmers in the cold and bleak Western States are fully aroused to the advantages which the South affords over the conditions in the Northwest for agricultural purposes. And not only this, but the climate of the Northwest is so severe that its inhabitants are seeking a more moderate temperature from a standpoint of health. Whereas in the Northwest they have only a few months of weather suitable for their pursuits, in the South they have almost the entire year, and can raise several crops on the same land.

To all inquiries in regard to Southern farm properties, we take the necessary steps to have the parties immediately supplied with printed matter, maps, etc., descriptive of the country, climate, soil, temperature, etc. We have been gratified to know that quite a number of parties who have come South as prospectors have purchased, and will locate.

I think the best means of attracting the attention of the Northwestern farmers is to have our country properly advertised throughout that section.

W. A. TURK,
General Passenger Agent.

A Difficulty That Can Be Overcome.

Norfolk and Western Railroad Co }
Philadelphia, December 27, 1893 }

I am very much pleased that you are calling attention to this important matter of immigration. Our road is much interested in the subject, but we are not at present taking any especially active steps.

There is one important difficulty met with in Virginia as well as in other Southern States in the fact that there are no lands belonging to the State or the railroads or the United States Government which can be taken up by immigrants. The result is that when a railroad, through advertisements or other means, calls attention to the agricultural resources tributary to its line, it can only be done in the most general way, and no practical way has as yet been suggested by which intending immigrants can be brought into communication with parties who have desirable lands for sale.

The reason the Western railroads and States have been so successful in disposing of their land to immigrants is that they have the land for sale and they are willing to dispose of it at prices to suit purchasers and parties desiring to locate can go directly to a well-established agency with a certainty of being able to select land at a reasonable price.

This is not the case in the Southern States. It may be that by calling attention to this difficulty some means may be found to overcome it.

F. J. KIMBALL, President.

Immigration the Greatest Need of the South.

Mobile and Birmingham Railway Company, }
Anniston, Ala , December 30, 1893. }

I have noticed with much interest your articles referring to the question of immigration from the West and Northwest to the South, and believe that you are agitating a question that is of vital importance to our section of the country.

I am satisfied that immigration of intelligent and energetic farming people is the greatest need of the South today, and I have been surprised that the railroad companies have not realized this to a sufficient extent to make an organized effort to secure such a class of people.

The effort of the railroad companies west of the Mississippi river to attract immigrants from the Southern States east of that river have been very marked and noticeable, and have resulted in drawing people by thousands from the States of Alabama, Georgia and Carolinas and locating them in the sections of country through which their lines run.

The railroad companies in the States named east of the Mississippi river have thoughtlessly facilitated the efforts of the roads west of the river, and have lost a large and valuable population which by all means ought to have been retained. There are a great many lands in Alabama and other South Atlantic States which are altogether suitable for diversified farming, and would prove attractive, on account of climate, to many people who are dissatisfied with their surroundings in the Northwest, and I believe that if the railroad companies would make an organized effort in securing options on lands at reasonable prices, and presenting their attractions to these people, there would be a great movement towards the South of a class of people that would be of incalculable benefit in developing her resources.

I learn of many inquiries made concerning lands in this immediate section, but I do not think that much is being done to draw the people this way.

I have had some correspondence with the managers of the systems of railroad being operated in the South, and I hope that yet something will be done to bring immigration of such people as may be able to introduce new methods of farming and thus greatly encourage our agricultural interests.

T. G. BUSH, Receiver.

Looks for Active Steps to Promote Immigration.

Atlanta & West Point Railroad, }
The Western Railway of Alabama, }
Atlanta, Ga , December 29, 1893. }

In reply to your favor and asking for my opinion as to the best means to attract immigration, I beg to say that this is a matter that in my opinion should receive more careful attention not only by railroad men, but by all who would be benefited, and I have no doubt that in the near future active steps will be taken to promote this movement.

JOHN A. GEE,
General Passenger Agent.

East Coast Line, }
Jacksonville, St. Augustine & Indian River Railway, }
St. Augustine, Fla , December 26, 1893. }

Your letter of December 23d has been referred to me, and I desire to State that our road, in connection with the Florida Coast Line Canal & Transportation Co., has tried for several months to draw the attention of settlers to our land along the East coast of Florida. I traveled through that part of the country from December last year to May this year, wrote an illustrated description of it in the English and Scandinavian languages, and sent about thirty articles about Florida to the papers in the Northwest. I had, also, an office in the Florida State Building at the World's Fair in Chicago, and distributed about 50,000 small circulars and 10,000 books to visitors who inquired about Florida. The result has been to awaken a widespread interest in Florida among Northwestern farmers, especially Scandinavians and Germans, and I could, at last, about fourteen days ago, start the first Scandinavian colony on the East Coast, near the St. Lucie

river. Since then it has grown to twenty-three families, and as each of them really is sent out as pioneer from a whole lot of friends and neighbors, who only await their report for coming, I expect to have a thousand here before next spring. The company has built an immigrant hotel and given the settlers very fair conditions for payment.

As I am hurrying back to the colony today, I shall prefer to send you a long article about the colonization of the South later on. I will, at the same time, send you through my office in Chicago copies of my book, as it is exhausted here. I send you, by this mail, a copy of an illustrated paper from the Old Country, (printed in Copenhagen, in 150,000 copies), which is found in nearly every family in Denmark, Norway and Sweden. You will find eight cuts from the East Coast, and an article in Scandinavian, written by me. Through this article I expect to draw the attention of farmers in the Old Country to the resources of the South and turn the stream of immigrants in this direction, and I have already received several dozen letters from people, who want to immigrate directly to Florida.

LOUIS PIO.

Deeply Interested in Immigration.

Louisville & Nashville Railroad Co. }
Louisville, Ky., January 3, 1894. }

I believe the SOUTHERN STATES can be used to great advantage by soliciting correspondence from farmers who have moved from the North and Northwest to the South, Southeast and Southwest, and allow these gentlemen, in their own language, to state the result of their experience in the South. We have recently inaugurated land-seekers' excursion rates, and tickets for these excursions will be sold January 8th, February 8th, March 8th and April 9th, at one fare for the round trip from our gateways, viz.: Cincinnati, Louisville, Evansville and St. Louis, to principal points in the South. These tickets will be limited to twenty days, giving the farmer ample time to investigate.

I think it would be well for you to note these low-rate excursions, and call the attention of interested parties to these low prospector's rates. We are deeply interested in immigration to the South, and are desirous of encouraging it in every reasonable way. There is a good deal of inquiry, especially from the Northwest, as to the South, and such parties as have settled on and adjacent to our line seem to me satisfied and prosperous.

C. P. ATMORE,
General Passenger Agent.

What the Plant System is Doing.

The Plant Investment Company,
New York, January 6, 1894.

Thinking that you desired full information on the subject of your communication I forwarded your letter to our General Land Agent, Mr. D. H. Elliott, who is in charge of the lands of the Plant Investment Company, and now enclose you his response which has come to me to-day.

H. B. PLANT,
President.

Associated Railway Land Department of Florida,
Sanford, Fla., Janua y 2, 1894.

Replying to inquiry as to what the Plant system has done and is doing to encourage immigration South, I would say :

The Associated Railway Department of Florida, which has charge of the lands of the railroad companies comprising the Plant system and the properties that are for sale, and of the lands, would reply that for several years we have been distributing advertising matter throughout the United States, which matter contains a description of this section of the country, its climate, resources and capabilities, a short treatise upon all the crops grown in Florida, either for market or for consumption, together with county pamphlets descriptive of the several counties in which we have lands for sale, containing a map and a description of the county by the county commissioners, township plats, being fac-similes of the United States Government surveys, and as full a description as it is possible to give of the character and quality of the land, its description and price.

In addition, we have made displays of the principal products of the State at the various expositions, more recently at the World's Columbian Exposition, and at the Southern Exposition at Augusta' Ga. A display of the products of Florida attracts considerable attention and enquiry for information in detail as to the resources and capabilities of this section of country, and in many persons causes a desire to visit and locate in Florida.

At present the correspondence of this department has greatly increased within the past sixty days, and we believe that we can say that it has materially increased each season.

Referring to opinions as to the best means to attract a better class of immigration, (especially the Western and Northwestern farmers), South : A means that would convince parties who desire to live in a warmer climate, a more congenial climate than that of the North and West, that they would exist in the extreme South the year round, and that they would never have to come in contact with and be socially equal with the negro, and their apparent fear and prejudice against living in the South with Southerners would be the most effective. We have distributed advertising matter both through the mails and newspapers, land map folders and county pamphlets, both in person and otherwise, that contain a plain statement of facts as to the resources and capabilities, climate and products, which should be convincing to any intelligent man, but still it appears not to be so, but a lingering doubt remains as to the reliability of the statements therein contained. The people in the North and West who read the newspapers are accustomed to look to them for information and they have confidence in the truth of their statements. We had conceived the idea that by having these editors visit this section of country, see it in person and exchange ideas with the inhabitants they would get, and would truthfully present to their readers, the conditions existing here, and by that means convince the people as to the true situation. With this in view, we have had several excursions visit the South and Florida, and I can see the result in the pertinent enquiries from people in the sections of country where these newspapers were published, as to the price of our lands, and the probability of their removing to Florida.

There is another element which enters into this question, and that is, as to how the people can get rid of their homes, or effect an exchange of their property in the North and West for property in the South. We have numerous enquiries to that effect: two today. It appears that there is no demand for their property, and they cannot sell except at a sacrifice; they are awaiting an opportunity, and when they can effect such a sale they will remove to Florida. Apparently they have become tired of the ext.eme cold and sudden changes of temperature. In personal interviews with farmers and others who have felt as if they would like to get into a warmer climate, they do not seem to understand how it is that, with so pleasant and equable an air in the winter months, a white person can exist or labor in the sun in the summer. It is not to be expected that all would understand climatology, and it is difficult to make them understand that we have such a temperate climate in the summer.

Having but few manufacturing interests in this State and but little demand for skilled labor, it is particularly from the intelligent farming class that we may expect immigration and the development of our wild lands. It is not the price of the lands that deters settlement, for we have offered to give forty acres if they will live upon it and pay the taxes thereon for five years, and we offer them either for cash or on time and will not dispute as to price. With the utilization of our phosphates in fertilizing, we will solve an important problem as to where they will get plant food for the apparently sandy lands which appear to the Western man as being unproductive. As to how the man of moderate means can make a living in Florida, it is a question that has been and can be readily solved, but how we can convince him that he can live comfortably in Florida, and that he will not be compelled to associate with nor live with the negro, is a problem that, to my mind, can only be solved by time. I can only say to these people come and see and try for yourselves. It would

appear that an intelligent person might be convinced of the fallacy of such ideas, but we do not seem to accomplish it and produce those results that our efforts would seem to warrant. Thousands of acres of good farming lands that are open and ready for cultivation are lying idle for want of labor. Large numbers of negroes, who, it seems, the present farmers think are the only people who can labor in the fields, have been tempted to the phosphate mines by higher wages, hence the farms are deserted by them with no one to take their places. Many farmers would say that they cannot make a living out of the farms, nor any profit in that business. Many orange growers will say that the present prices are unremunerative; that they have lost money on their groves this year, the care and fertilizers having cost more than the fruit sold realized. At the same time their groves are not for sale on a basis of less than 6 per cent. interest on a thousand dollars per acre.

An energetic and frugal person, with means sufficient to get himself established on a small farm in Florida, need have no fear but that he will make a good living, a happy home, and some money. As to the poorer class, if some arrangement could be made to give them some employment until they could get a home, it might induce an immigration and populate the section of country adjoining the phosphate mines, or wherever employment could be secured for foreign immigrants and the poorer class of white people, and let the negro go back to the farms.

I do not see that any white men could be induced to come to this section of country to accept employment on the farm, at the wages paid by the farm, or the wages which the farmer thinks he can afford to pay, namely, $8.00 to $12.00 per month and rations. The negro can accept these wages and his rations, and is no further trouble to his employer, except to see that he does his work, but a white man could not live on such rations, but must have food properly cooked, and a comfortable shelter and place to sleep.

There are many ideas that could be

advanced upon this subject, but whether or not they are practicable I am not at present prepared to say.

We have worked to a limited extent on all of them, but have not as yet produced very satisfactory results in either.

D. H. ELLIOTT,
General Land Agent.

Pushing by Means of Low Rates.

Missouri, Kansas & Texas Railway Co.
St. Louis, Mo., January 4, 1894.

Our line is making a vigorous effort to encourage immigration. We have placed very low round-trip rates in effect from all of our junctional points to the principal points in Texas on sale every day, and a half rate to points in Texas on the second Tuesdays in January, February, March, April and May.

An appreciation of this action is being substantially shown by the number of people that are taking advantage of these low rates.

JAMES BARKER,
G. P. & T. A.

The Letters In "Southern States" Doing More Good Than Any Other Advertising.

Savannah, Americus & Montgomery Railway,
Americus, Ga., December 30, 1893.

In my opinion all roads like the Savannah, Americus & Montgomery must do something towards the locating of people along their lines. We have, especially east of Americus, fresh and fertile lands that can be purchased at remarkably low prices. The climate, as you know, is mild, and the cost of building houses and fences, etc., very much lighter than in any other sections, on account of the proximity of saw mills and timber. With all this there are obstacles to be overcome, and in my opinion much hard work will be required in order that the end desired may be reached. There seems to be a prejudice in the minds of many Northern people against this section, and a short trip through our country sometimes strengthens the same instead of having an opposite effect. The accommodations offered such people, or in fact anyone, at many places are not the best and this may create an unfavorable impression at times when a party is prospecting. The letters from Northern people published

by the SOUTHERN STATES will perhaps do more good than any other class of advertising. Unfortunately for us, however, there are but few of these people on our line.

While I think this section, with its mild climate, cheap lands and building material, and convenience to markets, offers a good field to men who have a small capital, still their object can be accomplished only by hard work and economy. I have no doubt that the right class of people can be induced to come to this section in course of time if the proper effort is used. I think in order to do any good a list of valuable lands that are for sale, with full information in regard to price, etc., would have to be kept and advertising matter issued from time to time.

C. B. WILBURN,
General Freight and Pass. Agent.

General Tendency of Immigration South.

Jacksonville, St. Augustine & Indian River Ry,
Jacksonville, Fla, January 4, 1894

There seems to be a general tendency of immigration to this State. We are receiving almost daily inquiries from the West, New England and the Middle States, and some from abroad. We have been working through our agent at Chicago during the summer.

J. R. PARROTT,
Vice-President.

Wilmington, Newbern & Norfolk Railroad Co.
Wilmington, N. C, January 1, 1894

Our road has not yet taken any particular steps in the matter of encouraging immigration, though we expect to move in this matter before very long.

With respect to the best means to attract the better class of immigration of Western and Northwestern farmers to our section of country, on which you ask an expression of my opinion, I have not yet given as careful thought as the subject demands, nor have I heretofore had any experience in this matter. I should think, however, it would be necessary to circulate among the farmers whose immigration is desired a carefully prepared pamphlet, giving the conditions of our soil and climate, the prices of our land and the products best suited to them, their relation with respect to the different markets, means and terms of transportation and such other statistics as relate to this matter and would give such farmers information to be desired in the premises.

H. A. WHITING,
General Manager.

Good Results Following Persistent Effort.

The Missouri Pacific Railway Company,
St. Louis, Mo., December 29, 1893.

We have been working to secure immigration to the Southwest for the past ten years, and during that time have expended many thousands of dollars in advertising matter of various kinds, newspaper correspondence, through outside agents in the East and Northeast, by personal efforts and in every way possible.

The population of the States in which we are particularly interested has very materially increased during the years referred to, and there has of course been a steady increase in all valuations. The outlook at present for their future is decidedly encouraging, and we have no doubt whatever that all efforts made in the direction of their betterment will be amply repaid.

H. C. TOWNSEND.

Cotton Belt Route,
St. Louis Southwestern Railway Company,
St. Louis, December 26, 1893.

The great trouble with Texas has been that the people expect the railroads to do it all, and do not spend one cent to induce immigration. This line, as well as all other Texas lines, is doing everything in its power to induce people to emigrate to Texas. While there is a very large emigration at the present time going into Texas, it is principally from the old Southern States. I do not think there is much of a movement from the North. We have inaugurated a series of one fare excursions to all points in Texas, on the sec-

ond Tuesday in each month, until May; and we are in hopes that this will at least induce some prospectors, and there is no doubt but that we can succeed in locating some of them in Texas, with their friends.

We are also now making reduced round trip rates to many points named and this should attract some business to our section.

I would be glad to have any suggestions you may have to offer in regard to inducing people to immigrate to our country.

E. W. LaBEAUME,
G. P. & T. A.

Seeing is Believing.

Central Railroad & Banking Company, of Georgia,
Savannah, Ga., December 29, 1893.

We are endeavoring to place in the West such matter about the South as we can get hold of. We are not getting out any information ourselves but merely distributing matter gotten up by farmers and others located on our lines. In my opinion, the best way to induce immigration is to run a series of excursions into our country and let the Western people come down and see for themselves what we have to offer.

J. C. HAILE,
General Passenger Agent.

Seeking Information on Immigration.

The Atlantic Coast Line,
Wilmington, N. C, December 27, 1893.

Our line has spent a great deal of money in advertising the section through which we run in the interest of immigration. Our success has not been phenomenal; on the contrary it has not been so good as we had reason to expect. We are very much interested in any move that will actually develop immigration, but probably have not as yet been able to hit upon the correct method of doing so.

T. M. EMERSON,
Traffic Manager.

AN ECONOMIC CHANGE IN SOUTHERN FARMING.

In 1860 the South produced fully one-half of the total output of agriculture in the whole country. Having but one-third of the population of the United States and of whites only 6,800,000 out of 27,000,000, its farms yielded 358,000,000 bushels of corn or forty-four per cent. of the entire crop of the United States; all of the cotton, 5,196,000 bales; 351,000,000 pounds of tobacco, being over eighty-one per cent. of the country's full crop; all of the sugar and rice, 302,000,000 pounds of the former and 187,000,000 pounds of the latter, and all other crops in proportion. The cash value of its farms was $2,300,000,000 against $4,300,000,000 for the balance of the country.

In 1865 the South was bankrupt. Over $5,000,000,000 had been swept away from its people, and the burden of debts seemed beyond the power of human strength to bear. But piled on top of this was a disorganized labor system, and later there came the horrors of the reconstruction period. When the war ended Southern farmers found themselves in the deepest poverty, without stock, without farm implements, their fences destroyed and desolation everywhere. Money was offered to them as an advance on cotton before the seed was planted, or rather commission merchants or factors offered to furnish them with needed supplies for the home and farm taking a lien on the crop not yet planted. Necessity compelled the acceptance of these offers. By advancing money on cotton alone the factor virtually compelled the farmer to devote all of his attention to cotton and to buy his bacon and grain which the factor sold. Thus, the factor loaned money on credit at a high rate of interest, sold the far-mer all of his supplies at exorbitant prices, often averaging fifty per cent. or more above what the same store would sell the goods for to a cash purchaser. He required that he should have the selling of the cotton when ready for market and here he had a chance to charge drayage, storage, insurance, commission, etc. At the end of the season when settling day came, the farmer was in debt to the factor and must begin the new season under this condition.

From year to year his situation grew more desperate. He was in effect a slave. He was simply forced to raise more cotton, because cotton alone could be mortgaged in advance for supplies. A decrease in price meant still larger acreage in order that the aggregate results might make up for the shortage in value. To have encouraged diversified farming, the raising of corn, bacon and other products of this character would have been suicidal for the factor, because it would have meant the loss of the profit he made in selling Western corn and bacon to his customers. Very slowly, so slowly indeed that sometimes it looked as though no progress was being made, the Southern farmers gradually made a little advance towards a condition of freedom. Gradually they increased their production of foodstuffs, and in some measure at least reduced their indebtedness to their factors. But up to three years ago the advancement in the direction was very slow. When the crash of Baring Bros. failure came, followed by the great decline in values, cotton dropped to a lower point than it had touched for many years. In the following season prices continued low and bankers and factors found that they had advanced more money on cotton than it would sell for. This made them less disposed to make further advances and the great financial stringency added to their difficulties. Unwilling as well as unable to make much advance to the farmers, the bankers and factors by this course made it necessary for the farmers to practice the greatest economy, to produce their cotton at the lowest possible price and to raise their own foodstuffs. Thus, for two years the farmers of the South have been engaged in getting down on a rock-bottom basis of cost of production, buying little, living at home and paying off their debts. In brief, the whole farming interests of the South have been passing through a great economical revolution—changing from a credit basis with extravagance which ease in borrowing always begets to a cash system. The importance of this to the future of the South can scarcely be estimated. As the situation stands, Southern farmers are less in debt than for twenty-five years, while Western farmers are probably more in debt than ever before. As the bankers of any community are more intimately acquainted with its financial condition than anyone else, and this is especially true in small towns, we recently asked an expression of opinion from many Southern bankers as to the financial condition of the farmers. These letters are so uniform that one might serve for all, but as the testimony of many witnesses carries greater weight than that of one, we publish them all just as received. They deserve careful study especially by the thousands of Northern and Western farmers who will read this, and who are contemplating moving South.

A Transition Period from Credit to Cash.

ALABAMA NATIONAL BANK, Birmingham, Ala.—There is no unusual activity in any lines of business. We are in a transition state from the old long-time-credit methods of the past to the cash basis practically. It is most difficult to put aside habits and practices that have been welding for years and adopt new and unusual methods, but it is believed that the business methods of recent adoption are crystallized, and it must bring with it a new flow of health and

life when we have adjusted ourselves perfectly to it.

Farmers Nearly Out of Debt.

THE TREDEGAR NATIONAL BANK, Jacksonville, Ala.—While the business of this section of the country is dull, I think there is a general improvement. For the past three years our people have been living carefully, economizing and liquidating their indebtedness, and the result is that the bankers, merchants and business generally are on sound footings, as their strength during the recent panic shows, and the farmers are raising more food supplies, making crops cheaper, and are nearer out of debt than for years.

Farmers Out of Debt.

BENTON COUNTY BANK, Bentonville, Ark.—Slowly and surely we are recovering from the effect of the late war. We have large fields for investment and enterprise in this country, and if a people would come here who are used to factory enterprises and have not been intimidated by past hard times, i. e., a people who have not gone through a period without money and without credit, and who have not been compelled to lay away each dollar as an intended sweet token, we say if such people come there are any number of openings for capital and push. We grow no cotton in this part of Arkansas, hence have only food supplies and stock, both of which we have in excess of home consumption. We are justly called the apple-orchard section of America, no doubt the finest fruit belt in the South being in the Ozark mountains. We have a healthy climate; our farmers are nearly all out of debt and live well.

An Invitation to Thrifty Farmers.

FIRST NATIONAL BANK, Helena, Ark.—Owing to the usual small cotton crop this year business has not been as large as was expected, but as a rule it has been satisfactory.

The monetary crisis has not affected this section much as there has not been a single bank failure nor any mercantile failures either in this city or immediate vicinity.

The large timber interests here were slightly affected for a short time last summer, and the hardwood industry has not yet entirely recovered, but the demand for cottonwood lumber, which grows very rapidly here, is as great as ever, and all our saw mills are cutting to their full capacity. A cottonwood-box factory, which has for two years been idle, is now starting up again, and orders are coming in very rapidly. The farmers are now raising increased food supplies, and are in a better financial condition than for several years. A canning factory is about to be erected here, and if completed in time will enable our farmers to plant largely of tomatoes and vegetables, which are easily raised and can be produced in large quantities, from 250 to 500 bushels per acre. Our rich soil and temperate climate enable our farmers to raise two crops of potatoes and three crops of tomatoes a year, and if the demand justified it a million bushels of tomatoes could be raised here annually. Money is plentiful enough to supply all legitimate demands, as the paid-up banking capital of this city, which has a population of 6000, is $350,000 and the surplus $75,000.

For the thrifty farmer with a small capital, who is willing to work, no finer country can be found anywhere, and lands can be bought very cheaply. Cleared lands can be had at about $10 an acre within three miles of a railroad, and a good market for everything raised.

The all-cotton farmers have not been successful, and their number is steadily decreasing.

There is a fine opening here for a large canning factory, and for any factory using wood, as the supply of ash, oak, poplar, cypress and cottonwood is almost inexhaustible. The refuse of our saw mills would give a furniture manufactory enough cheap material to manufacture tables and chairs to supply a large scope of country. At present this goes to waste. The people are anxious to welcome all newcomers, and anyone who wants to erect a manufacturing plant here can obtain the ground free of charge. With three railroads

and the Mississippi river freight rates are low, and every market is accessible to us.

Farmers in Better Condition Than for Years.

HEMPSTEAD COUNTY BANK, Hope, Ark.—While there is less money in this country than usual, owing to the money panic and the short crops and low price of cotton the past two years, the farmers as a rule are in better condition and on a more self-sustaining basis than for years. More breadstuff, forage and pork than usual have been housed, and the farmer has made up his mind to less cotton and a more diversified crop. Trade at this particular point has been unusually good for the past three months. The weather is all that could be desired. Crops have been gathered early and in good condition. Fall plowing is fully under way, and I prophesy great prosperity the coming year. I fully believe that the low price of cotton and the panic, while a great hardship on the people of the South, will in the end prove a rich blessing, causing a complete reformation and a change in the mode of farming and living. Lands are rich and cheaper than for years. Good investments could be made here in timber and farming lands.

Outlook Very Bright—Raising their Own Food Supplies—Farmers are in Good Condition Financially.

BANK OF LITTLE ROCK, Little Rock, Ark.—The outlook for the future of this section of the South is, in my opinion, very bright. The financial condition of the farmers is much better than it was a few years ago. The very material reduction in the price of cotton has compelled farmers to produce their own food supplies to a large extent. As a result of this they are able to make a crop with very little assistance from their commission men or bankers. The result is that when a crop is marketed they have their money to use to pay their debts and to invest for their various needs. The towns and cities of the State feel this change, and all seem to be in a prosperous condition and doing a good, flourishing business. Little

Rock, the principal city in the State, has shown a handsome increase, notwithstanding the much-talked-about hard times and depression. The bank deposits of this city show an increase of nearly $250,000 over one year ago. Our wholesale trade is 50 per cent. larger this year than last. Our cotton receipts this year have been larger than ever before. The South certainly offers better attractions for the investment of capital than any other section in this country.

Enforced Economy Has Proved a Blessing.

NATIONAL BANK OF COLUMBUS, Columbus, Ga.—I very much regret that I cannot give that attention to the subject-matter of your letter which is warranted by its importance to the South. It is undoubtedly true that our people have studied economies during the last three years, which relieves them now from the enforced bankruptcy going on in other sections of the Union. I am told by our brokers that sales to farmers of salt meat are very greatly diminished; that much less corn and hay is engaged from the West. This would indicate that the farmers are depending more largely on home-raised supplies. Our section seems to support people who do not work. It will bring great rewards to those who settle here with the resolve to be industrious.

Farmers Exceptionally Prosperous.

THE FIRST NATIONAL BANK, Cordele, Ga.—In this section business is healthy, but very conservative. The farmers are in an exceptionally prosperous condition, being practically out of debt as the result of three years of rigid economy. They are paying great attention to the raising of everything needed for home consumption. In south Georgia the manufacture of lumber and naval stores is a great industry, and it has held its own quite as well as has any other line of business, and those engaged in it express themselves as confident of the future, and they find no difficulty in obtaining capital to prosecute their trade with during the dull winter season. While trade is not so active

yet, still all the signs are for better times, and business men are confident.

Farmers Have Paid Their Debts Better Than for Years, and are Prospering.

THE CITY NATIONAL BANK, Griffin, Ga.—Our local cotton crop for this year will be about equal to last year's crop, with the prices for the crop ruling a fraction less on the average than last year, which leaves us financially about where we were a year ago. But to better this condition growing out of the cotton crop alone, our agricultural interests are very much improved on account of the policy of our farmers, adopted within the last two years, of raising more meat and bread on the farm for home supplies instead of depending on the towns to furnish these supplies from storehouses filled from the garners of the West. Ten years ago the grunt of a hog would have been a frightful sound, but now we hear the lowing of cattle and the squealing of pigs around the barnyards of nearly every planter in our section, and it is a common thing to hear a farmer say, when he comes to town these cold days, that he has been killing hogs and had backbone and spare ribs for breakfast, with the usual accompaniment of pork sausage. Ask them about corn and they will tell you the crib is full and they will not have to buy this year. All this indicates a thriftiness on the farms that portends good for the future if this policy is adhered to. Our middle Georgia lands are capable of producing the most diversified crops of any lands in the Union. This may sound a little boastful, but we invite all who doubt to come and see. Market gardens do well; grape culture is a perfect success; peach-culture has proven successful; small fruits of every kind succeed well. At our Georgia agricultural experiment farm, a mile from town, we have seen as fine tobacco as we ever saw growing in Virginia. The milk dairy at the station turns out as fine butter and cheese as we ever saw. Cattle do well and can be kept at as little cost as anywhere, because they graze on the pasture until late in November and begin again in March. Corn, oats, rye, barley and peas are profitable crops. Wheat is raised here, but does not prove profitable like the other grain crops. After all this is said and the farmer can verily live at home by the products of his farm, then comes the old white-headed monarch, "King Cotton," and says to the farmer: "I command the gold in every market in the world. Pick me, handle me carefully, roll me up and bind me together so that I can travel, and I will return you the glittering gold from every nation on earth." So our farmers feel independent, and with peace and plenty at home and money in their pockets they have no fear of the sheriff or tax collector.

As to finances, we can say that for the unprecedented hard year of 1893 the farmers have met their bank paper better than for years past, and their credit is the very best. They are less in debt, more rigid in economy and more free from fret and care than we ever saw them, and our towns prosper as the farms prosper, and the credit of our section stood the test of the fiercest panic in forty years, unscorched and unimpaired.

Farmers Less in Debt than Ever Known.

THE EXCHANGE BANK, Macon, Ga.— In this immediate section our planting community seems to be in much better condition than for years. Their notes have been promptly met this winter; they have raised large grain crops, and in the majority of cases a good deal of meat. I think they have come nearer paying out of debt this year than I have ever known them. While the merchandise business here has been somewhat restricted this year, I think the merchants are in good condition, and the outlook for this immediate section is very good.

Farmers in Better Condition than Since the War.

CLEVELAND NATIONAL BANK, Cleveland, Tenn.—In my judgment, the Southern farmer is in better condition than he has been since the war. The Tennessee farmer can raise almost every article used on the home table, and while the farm products are selling at a

low price, the farmer can buy more for his products at present prices than he could have done at the time when his farm products sold at the highest figure, because every article that a farmer needs to buy for his farm or home sells at a low price. The agricultural districts of Tennessee are in good condition, and less money has been lost in the investments made in farming lands than in any other investments in our country. The Tennessee farmer gets a good home, a comfortable living, and can be the most independent fellow in the land. Our farming lands decreased in value somewhat from year to year up to five or six years ago, but the tendency is now upward. Our towns that have kept out of the booms and held to their normal growth are in fine condition, but the boom towns are suffering from overloading. Outside of the troubles immediately growing out of the boom, I think the State of Tennessee is in better condition than at any time for past ten years. In our own town of about 3,000 inhabitants we are prosperous. All merchants have very good trade, country people have plenty, banks are doing good business and all our manufactories are running on full time.

Farmers all Have Money.

THE PEOPLE'S NATIONAL BANK, Winston, N. C.—The farmers in our section all seem to have money and plenty of the necessaries of life. They are raising increased food supplies, and the outlook for them and for the townspeople as well is encouraging.

Business Gradually Increasing.

FIRST NATIONAL BANK, Johnson City, Tenn.—In this section business is still below normal condition, but gradually increasing. All our manufacturing plants in operation, but some with reduced forces. Our farmers are in this condition—abundance of wheat, oats, corn and live stock, but no surplus money.

Well Satisfied with the Outlook.

THE CITIZENS' BANK OF NORFOLK, VA., Norfolk, Va.—While it cannot be claimed that the business of this city and section is altogether as active as in recent years, Norfolk and the towns adjacent thereto have, in view of the late widespread depression in financial affairs, good reason to be well satisfied with their situation, financially and otherwise.

Our agricultural, commercial and industrial interests are in a healthy and fairly prosperous condition, and the outlook for the future is highly encouraging. Our farmers are comparatively free from debt. Crops were good and have yielded, besides ample stocks of food supplies for home consumption, sufficient quantities for marketing, even at the ruling low prices, to make them hopeful for the future.

Financial matters in this section are also in good condition, and the outlook for the coming year is encouraging. Our banks, supported and strengthened by their loyal, conservative customers, were enabled to pass through the recent severe financial panic without resorting to unusual methods to protect the credit of their friends, or restricting to any considerable extent the customary facilities to their patrons.

More Bountifully Supplied With Food Products Than Since The War.

FIRST NATIONAL BANK, Russellville, Ark.—This section has never, since the war, been so bountifully supplied with food products. The farmers are making their bread, meat, hay and corn at home; and, with but few exceptions, every house and home has an abundant supply and will be independent of the merchant for these supplies. The people generally have more and better stock than ever before. The home comforts are greater and there is more cheerfulness.

The prospects for business generally are good. Our people are getting out of debt, and a spirit of thrift seems to pervade the masses. In the towns trade has been exceptionally good this fall and a tone of activity and improvement is very manifest.

I am emphatically of the opinion that the back bone of the hard times is broken and that we are entering upon a period of prosperity and plenty. There

is here a fine field for the investment of idle capital in developing our fine coal interests, in factories, mills, &c.

Remarkably Good Showing for Bartow County, Ga.

FIRST NATIONAL BANK, Cartersville, Ga.—I beg to say that from the best information I can obtain, North Georgia is in better condition financially than it has been since the close of the war. Our farmers owe less money and are raising more corn, wheat, oats, hay, hogs and in fact more food supplies of every kind, and are raising them at less cost than they ever did before. They are also raising more mules than heretofore, and they are doing all this without reducing the usual amount of cotton, our chief money staple.

Our county (Bartow) is one of the best agricultural and mineral counties in the great State of Georgia, and we think the future prospects for successful business in many lines here are very inviting to the owners of the untold millions now locked up in the money centres of the world. Furthermore, we have an intelligent, refined, hospitable population that would gladly welcome and encourage good citizens to come and cast their lots in with us. We believe that we have right here in North Georgia the very best all-the-year-climate in the United States. The business of our merchants and the receipts of cotton at this point have been larger the past season than usual, and the business of the First National Bank has more than doubled since the panic.

Out of Debt, But Conservative Business Predicted.

PARKER & CO., Cullman, Ala.—The condition of the farmers throughout our county is better now than ever before at this season. During the past year they have lived at home and gone in debt less than ever before, and this, with fair crops, make them in good condition generally. The business outlook around here is good, merchants have paid debts promptly and the demand is good, and there is no doubt but that the farmer has more meat and corn at home than ever. We look, however, on account of the general depression in business upon a very close year; banks will hold their surplus, not making loans as usual, and the result will be that money will be almost impossible for the average man to get. This will be true in our judgment. Unless there is general brightening up all over the country business will be more conservative than ever.

More Diversified Farming and Fewer Mortgages.

THE NATIONAL BANK OF JACKSONVILLE, Jacksonville, Fla.—From the best information I have been able to procure, the farmers in this State are in as good a condition as they have been for years. While the price of cotton is low, only a small portion of the State is dependent on this staple for its money crop. In the cotton section for the past two or three years the farmers have been diversifying their crops, and this year the yield of general farm products has been excellent. The farmers are yearly becoming more and more independent, and this year there were fewer mortgages given on their crops than heretofore. In the orange section the crop is large. So far the prices have been low, but the market is stiffening and the net returns for the entire crop will probably not be much below the average.

The mining of phosphates, of which this State has an enormous supply, was commenced some two years ago and is steadily increasing. The mines are all working full time with ample demand at slightly better prices than last year.

In Jacksonville the wholesale merchants report sales fully equal to last year and collections good. Transportation lines all report increased business over same period of previous year. Bank clearings are about the same:

Week ending		Week ending	
Dec. 3, 1892	$395,427.00	Dec. 2, 1893	$330,297.00
" 10, 1892	414,532.00	" 9, 1893	414,771 00
" 17, 1892	415,019.00	" 16, 1893	407,781.00

In conclusion I can say the financial condition of the State is fully as good as it was a year ago and shows very little effect of the panic from which this State in unison with the whole country

was suffering during the past summer.

No People Out of Employment.

BROOKSVILLE STATE BANK, Brooksville, Fla.—It is my opinion from an acquaintance with nine-tenths of the citizens of Brooksville and Hernando county that as a rule the farmers have raised better crops of corn, oats, rice, sugar cane and vegetables than for ten years. Their stock—cattle, hogs, sheep and horses—which are all raised in the woods without grain, are in excellent condition.

The orange crop, which is our staple, is 30 per cent. greater in yield than last year, which was an average crop. This industry cannot be too highly encouraged. To the poor man or man of limited means there are no greater opportunities than in this industry in this county.

Our lands are rich, and choice lands are very cheap, while such favorable terms can be had on land and on trees to plant as to put the industry on a basis where a man of ordinary vim with limited means can, within a short time, be independent, own his own home and a property that will increase in value for years to come.

Trees ten years old often yield from five to ten boxes per tree annually, usually worth $1.00 per box on the tree, with from fifty to 100 per acre, or an average of $500 per acre yearly, and trees twenty years old will double this yield. It is my opinion that the thousands of people unemployed in the great North should "Come South." There are thousands of acres of land in Florida that can be had on terms within the reach of any man with common honesty.

Wages are good for all classes of work. Picking oranges is our harvesting time and no man need be out of employment. Many plant groves and work for wages to support themselves until groves will bear and sustain them.

Our farmers are in good financial condition. Our orange grove men were blessed with an abundant yield, and while returns are not satisfactory, the cause has been not with them, but in the condition of money matters in Northern markets. We have no people out of employment, and no people without means of support that are able-bodied.

The Only Even Partially Unfavorable Report.

HENRY JAMES, Farmers' and Merchants' National Bank, Abilene, Texas. The financial condition of farmers of this section is not very good this year, although a great many of them are in better fix than ever before. The farmers in this county are rapidly changing from wheat raisers to cotton farmers, and this country will in the end be a cotton country, though not exclusively so, as the crops here will always be diversified, and considerable stock interests in a small way will be general. Wheat raising has proven almost a failure in this section. The farmers and everyone have learned economy and conservatism from the panic, and I think will be prosperous from now on.

More Cash and More Supplies Than Since the War.

THOS. H. BATTLE, Vice-president Bank of Rocky Mount, N. C.—I would say that I think the prospect of this immediate section very good. Our people are in advance of some others in discarding the credit system and therefore feel less than they the depression that attends every radical change of system.

Some industries and towns will necessarily suffer—more or less permanently —but if the whole South will adopt the cash system its general prosperity will be assured. Our farmers have more food supplies and more cash in their pockets to start the new year with than any year since the war.

Brighter Outlook than Ever Before.

THE FIRST NATIONAL BANK, Lake Charles, La.—Louisiana generally is in better condition, I think, than any other State in the Union. It is true that our rice crop in this section was only about 60 per cent. of last year's crop, but the prices being considerable better, the rice planter was ahead in the deal. The sugar crop was simply immense; in fact a good many of the planters were unable to harvest all their cane before the frost came on. The timber trade in Southwest Louisiana has been very good for the past year, and promises to be better for the coming year. We found some difficulty in supplying the demand for money during the past three or four months, but at the present time money is plentiful. At no time in the history of this country have things looked so bright as they do now.

THE SOUTH'S COTTON MANUFACTURING POSSIBILITIES.

By Richard H. Edmonds.

There are about 15,000,000 cotton spindles in the United States. They represent an investment, including all classes of cotton manufactures, of over $400,000,000. Of this number the South has in round numbers one-sixth, or 2,500,000 spindles, and the capital invested is about $70,000,000 to $75,-000,000. The world has about 85,000,-000 spindles. If the capital invested were in the same proportion as in this country the aggregate would be over $2,300,000,000, but the capital of European mills is less in proportion to the number of spindles than in this country. The South produces nearly sixty per cent. of the entire cotton crop of the world, and if it manufactured this it would need over twenty times as many spindles as it has, or about 50,000,000, and the capital needed would exceed $1,300,000,000. The total annual value of the product of these mills would be equal to the present value of three full cotton crops. In the last eighteen years the cotton crops of the South have sold for an aggregate of nearly $6,000,000,-000. Before they reached the consumer their value had increased to $18,000,-000,000 or $20,000,000,000. This enormous business, creating wealth wherever established, is the prize for which the South has now commenced to contend. It is a prize worthy of the most vigorous efforts and energy of any country. The South holds the vantage ground; it produces the staple; it has an abundant supply of labor that readily takes to cotton manufacturing; it has water-powers sufficient to drive all the mills that would be needed to consume its full crop; it also has the cheapest and best

steam coal for mills that do not use water-power; it has a favorable climate; the cost of living being less than in other sections, it necessarily has a lower cost of wages; all these points combine to give the South exceptional advantages over both New England and Europe. Many years ago it was vigorously claimed by the cotton manufacturers of England that New England could never become a serious competitor with their country in cotton manufacturing; "our climate," they said, "is better suited for cotton manufacturing, especially for fine goods; our labor has had more experience and is more skilled; our capital is more abundant and is cheaper." To their minds these arguments were convincing, but while they argued New England went on building mills and making cotton goods. When the South first undertook to develop its cotton manufactures with any vigor the people of New England ridiculed its efforts and declared that the South could never develop a large cotton manufacturing business. "Its climate," they said, "is too enervating and hasn't the degree of moisture needed as ours has; it has no skilled labor; capital is scarcer than with us, and interest rates higher, and besides all these, our New England people are so energetic and so much better able to retain their business than Southern people are to win it away that the South will never become a serious competitor in cotton manufacturing." The people who said these things, and they included the leading manufacturers and business men generally, honestly believed their own arguments. After a few years they saw that something was wrong with their arguments. Matters were not working out in the way they had predicted. The South was rapidly capturing the coarse cotton trade and absolutely controlling it. Under these conditions it became necessary to find some new arguments, and then it was unanimously decided by all New England, following in the exact footsteps of Great Britain in its arguments of years ago as related to New England, that the South could possibly make coarse cottons successfully, but it was out of the question for it to spin fine yarns. "New England," they said, "will always retain its supremacy in fine cottons." Even today such claims are often heard, but they now sound like the graveyard whistle, intended to bolster up courage that is fast slipping away.

Starting without capital and without experience, the South has already practically monopolized the coarse cotton trade, and is pushing into finer goods with the determination to capture that too. It is needless for Great Britain or New England to argue against it. The logic of facts, of things already accomplished, disproves all of their arguments. No one pretends to say that the South will spin and weave every bale of cotton that it raises. New England, Great Britain and the Continent will continue as cotton manufacturing centres, but the future great growth of this industry will be in the South. Cotton production and consumption are not stationary. The world's needs are growing. Increasing wealth of the masses increases the requirements per capita of cotton goods. The extension of civilization into the dark places of the world opens new fields for cotton goods. Civilization's advancement is measured by the increase in cotton consumption. In the crop year 1878-79 the world consumed 7,485,230 bales of cotton of 400 pounds each ; in 1891-92 it consumed 13,194,000, 400 pound bales. This increase is progressive. It must go on constantly, and the 9,000,000-bale crop, which looks as big as a 6,500,000-bale crop did ten years ago, must be exceeded before many years by 10,000,000, and then 11,000,000 and 12,000,000, and gradually on, as the world's ever-increasing requirements shall demand.

With this growth, and even more rapidly than this, will the cotton manufacturing interests of the South develop. What has been done is but an indication of what will be done. What has been done is shown by the following census figures :

COTTON MANUFACTURING IN THE SOUTH.

	1880.	1890.
Capital...................	$21,976,713	$61,124,096
Number of mills...........	180	254
Number of spindles........	667,754	1,712,930
Looms......	14,323	39,231
Value of product..........	$21,038,712	$46,971,503

Making another form of comparison we have :

Years.	No. of spindles.	No. of looms.	Bales consumed crop year ending August 31.
1860................	217,291	5,615	10,502
1870................	416,883	8,203	94,085
1880................	667,754	14,323	233,886
1890................	1,712,930	39,231	573,844
1893................	2,550,000	54,000	743,848

While this increase in the number of spindles in Southern mills, from 667,000 in 1880 to 2,500,000 at present, was taking place, the increase in the rest of the country was from 9,986,000 to 12,777,000, the gain in the South being 270 per cent., and in the whole country, outside of the South, 28 per cent. In 1880 the South had one-fifteenth of the number of spindles in the country; now it has one-sixth of the number. As rapid as this growth has been, it must be still more rapid in the future. Fortunately, the building of cotton mills never became a town-booming feature, as was the case with iron furnaces; hence, there have been no financially-crippled mills to reflect on the South's advantages for cotton-spinning. Cotton mills are probably the most popular form of investment for local capital in the Carolinas and Georgia. Nothing else seems to appeal so directly and forcibly to all who have spare money to invest. The result is that the astonishing advance in mill-building in those States is due almost wholly to local capital. They are in nearly all cases earning good profits, thus steadily increasing the popularity of cotton mills as a safe place for money. Virginia, Alabama and Tennessee have given considerable attention to the development of their cotton manufactures, but their progress in the development of this industry has been very much slower than that of the Carolinas and Georgia. In the other Southern States some advance is being made, but it is to be regretted that so little has been accomplished in a field of such vast possibilities. About two-thirds of the number of spindles in the whole South are in the Carolinas and Georgia, pretty evenly distributed between them. Texas, with its 2,000,000 bales a year, has only 77,000 spindles, or less than one-sixth as many as Georgia or either of the Carolinas. Even Alabama, which led the South in energy and enterprise in industrial progress a few years ago, with a splendid climate, with good water-powers and the cheapest coal, has less than one-half as many spindles as either North or South Carolina or Georgia.

In iron-making the South has superior advantages over any other section, and must become the iron-making centre of the United States, but iron ore and coal are also found in other sections. With cotton the South's position is different. No other section of this country produces cotton, and the South's monopoly of the world's cotton trade was never stronger. Cotton manufacturing is therefore one business in which the South has every advantage. This is pre-eminently the South's rightful monopoly. No other large industry so justly belongs to any one section of our country as cotton-spinning and weaving does to the South. This is an industry that will create more wealth for the South than even iron-making. Every Southern State ought to press the development of cotton-mill building with tireless energy.

The relative growth of the consumption of cotton in Northern and Southern mills of late years has been as follows:

Crop Years.	Northern mills	Southern mills.
1892-93	1,687,286	743,348
1891-92	2,190,766	686,080
1890-91	2,027,362	604,661
1889-90	1,799,258	546,894
1888-89	1,785,979	479,781
1887-88	1,804,993	456,090
1886-87	1,710,080	401,452

The consumption of Northern mills last year, as shown by these figures, was the lowest for any one of these seven years—less even than in 1886-87, and 500,000 bales less than in 1891-92, though possibly, by carrying less stock than the year before, the actual consumption may have been a little larger than these figures indicate. How fared the South? Its consumption increased every year without a break, and almost doubled in the seven years. In the face of a decline of 500,000 bales in northern mills last year, southern mills gained 57,000 bales. Seven years ago Southern mills consumed less than one-fifth of the total for the country; last year they consumed nearly one-third. Then Southern consumption was only equal to twenty-three per cent. of Northern; now it is equal to forty-four per cent.

In view of the belief of many Northern people, who, having been converted to the side of the South's ability to control the making of coarse goods, are still determined to believe that that section can never compete in fine goods, prints, etc., it is interesting to note what one expert, who, having investigated for himself, says on the subject. Some months ago Mr. William C. Lovering, one of the leading cotton manufacturers of New England went South and studied the situation for himself. After doing so he addressed a letter to the labor committee of the Massachusetts legislature which must have caused the members to open their eyes. Mr. Lovering set forth very plainly the South's pre-eminent advantages, both natural and acquired, for cotton mills as compared with New England, and he added that if a new print-cloth mill were built in Georgia he "would guarantee to lay down in Massachusetts print-cloth at twenty per cent. less cost than at which it could by any possibility be produced by the best mill in Massachusetts." And yet New England people have been saying that the South could never compete in making prints. The statements of Mr. Lovering are fully confirmed by the results already accomplished. The South is moving forward with tireless energy in the development of its textile industries, and its progress in the past is only an indication of what it will accomplish in the future.

LETTERS FROM NORTHERN AND WESTERN FARMERS, GIVING THEIR EXPERIENCE IN THE SOUTH—IV.

[The letters published in this issue form the fourth instalment in the series commenced in the October number of this magazine. These communications are published in response to numerous inquiries from Northern people who desire to know more about agricultural conditions in the South, and what is being accomplished by settlers from other sections of the country. These letters were written by practical farmers and fruit-growers, chiefly Northern and Western people who have made their homes in the South. The actual experiences of these settlers, as set forth in these letters, are both interesting and instructive to those whose minds are turned Southward.—EDITOR.]

After Trying Many Western States Arkansas is Preferred.

D. S. HELVERN, Proprietor Rock Spring Fruit Farm, Mammoth Springs, Fulton county, Ark.—I was born in the fruit regions of Ohio where my father was a great fruit-grower. At the age of eighteen I started out in search of a fruit country, and went to Indiana, Illinois, Iowa, Kansas and Nebraska. Also looked over some parts of Western New York, Colorado and Utah; then took a trip South during the cotton centennial at New Orleans in the spring of 1885. In traveling around I generally stayed in each State long enough to become acquainted with some of the inhabitants and see the general outlook. I resided in Nebraska about twenty-one years, but was dissatisfied with that cold, windy and disagreeable country and came to Arkansas eight years ago and located in Jackson county, but not being entirely satisfied with the surroundings, I moved five years ago to Mammoth Springs, Fulton county, Ark., and have since been engaged in fruit-growing, making a specialty of the raising of berries and early vegetables for Northern markets, as we have a splendid outlet via Kansas City, Fort Scott & Memphis railroad to Kansas City and all northwestern cities. I have been very successful in my business, and think we have one of the finest fruit and berry sections in the United States. We are just below the Ozark range of mountains and our berries ripen the latter part of April and early vegetables are ready for market by the first of May, about four or five weeks before Kansas City home-grown come in.

I raise peas, beans, onions, radishes, beets, tomatoes, okra, cabbage, cucumbers, melons, cantaloupes, turnips, sweet and Irish potatoes, peanuts, egg plants, salsify, spinach, mustard, kohl-rabi, and, in fact, every kind of vegetable that can be raised in any other country. All kinds of berries, apples, pears, peaches, plums, apricots, figs, cherries, quinces, nectarines, grapes, scuppernongs, muskadines and all kinds of wild fruits grow in abundance. In all my travels I have never struck such a variety of fruits and vegetables as here, and I have never known this section to fail to produce a crop. Of course some years our fruit crop is lighter than in others, but we always have plenty and of the best flavor I ever sampled anywhere. California is nowhere in comparison. I sent some apples to the World's Fair at Chicago last September that weighed twenty-five ounces each and took the first premium there. They were raised within fifteen miles of our city. We also have the largest and best flavored pears that I have ever seen. In fact this is undoubtedly one of the finest fruit regions on earth. I raised tomatoes that weighed twenty ounces and at the rate of 400 bushels to the acre. I cleared on one and one-half acres of tomatoes in cash $87.75, and three and one-half acres of straw berries netted me $270. My grapes make about fifty cents to the vine at three years old, and I have several acres of these. Apples are always worth fifty cents per bushel and some years $1.00. This is the home of the peach, plum and berries. Blackberries grow wild here—one and one-quarter inches long, of fine flavor. The wild dewberry is also excellent and grows in great abundance.

Our crops of corn, wheat, rye, oats, field peas, etc., are very good, although not as good as we used to raise in the Scioto Valley in Ohio. This is a mountainous country with very rich valleys, and in these valleys and on these spring branches we raise fine truck; our hogs and cattle run out in the woods and take care of themselves most of the year. We begin to feed cattle about December 1st, and continue three months. Hogs mostly get their living on the wild mast, which is generally plentiful. Last year, at this time, I had only one old sow and two young ones, and to-day I have twelve hogs that will weigh nearly 200 pounds each, which are fat and worth four cents per pound, seven shoats worth $2.00 each and eleven pigs, two months old, worth $1.00 each, the product of these sows and the whole lot has never eaten ten bushels of corn. This is an increase of $121.00 in one year with little expense.

We have splendid society, schools, Sunday schools, churches in every neighborhood of every denomination, all clever and agreeable people; hardly ever hear an oath from any of our Southern neighbors, and they never say anything about your politics; vote as you please and nobody kicks. Last, but not least by any means, my family have been as healthy here as they were in

Nebraska, and my doctor's bill in eight years for a family of eight will not exceed $40.00. I held on to my Nebraska farm until last fall, fearing I might want to move back there to live, but now I have traded the 240-acre Nebraska farm for a 240-acre Arkansas farm. I am thoroughly located and would not exchange for anything. I am perfectly satisfied here to live and die. I came to this country for fruit and timber and to escape the cold sudden winter changes, and am fully satisfied. One word more; the coldest day has been three degrees below zero; hottest 102 in shade; these are the extreme limits, and these only occur about one day each winter and summer and only for a few hours each.

A Canadian's Experience.

J. J. CASSIDAY, Ailsa Craig, Ont.—Last spring I became so much interested in the South that I determined to visit that section. For one reason and another I postponed my trip until about the middle of June. For three weeks prior to this date I was in Central Michigan. During that time I thought over the matter a great deal before I could come to a final decision; and, when I reached Port Huron, June 15th, on my way, I found a letter awaiting me from my wife, advising me not "to go South —to death." I thought of my family at home, of the terrible heat, of the yellow fever and sickness I expected to find in the South. What if I should go down and be stricken! After a great deal of self reasoning, I at last concluded that it would be cowardly in me to turn back, so I decided to go. I was especially anxious to visit the country during the hot season, when the weather was most trying and the Mississippi river at the highest point it had ever been known, with one exception.

I confess that it was with considerable fear and misgiving that I started for Delhi, La. At Toledo I was very sick, and believe that my illness was the result of fear alone, as I had previously enjoyed the best of health. However, I started for Cincinnati, intending if I were worse when reaching there, to return. On my arrival at that place I felt somewhat better and continued Southward. I enjoyed the scenery and was pleased with nearly all of the country. On arriving at Chattanooga, Tenn., the end of my first day's ride, I was agreeably disappointed with the climate and temperature and felt in good health and spirits. I arrived at Meridian, Miss., next morning and found the atmosphere delightful. We reached Delhi on the twenty-first. I was now on the famous Macon Ridge, and took a stroll in the evening through the town and made arrangements for going out into the country in the morning. Next day, with my escort, I went twenty miles south through a beautiful country with abundance of fine timber. The land is gently rolling, and what drew my attention particularly, there were no cradle knolls that I could see in the forest. I have no doubt but the country was cultivated in some previous age. The soil seemed to be of the very best. The luxuriant growth of grass, shrubs, trees and the rich appearance of the foliage convinced me that the soil was very fertile. We came back on the twenty-third by another direction, visiting several old plantations that have been untouched for years, now covered with an abundance of grass and only awaiting some intelligent farmer to break the sod, sow the seed and reap an abundant harvest. What surprised me very much was that their potato crop was all harvested two weeks previously. I never saw finer bulbs. When I left Bay City eight days before, some were planting their potatoes and the corn was just coming through the ground in places, the most advanced being only about twelve inches high. Here in the South it was in many places over fifteen feet high and the grain commencing to glaze. The second crop of potatoes was planted on the same ground that the first crop was dug from.

We were nowhere within reach of a house to get our dinner and my friend, Mr. W. L. Cooper, was anxious on behalf of my stomach. I suggested making a dinner of blackberries, of which there had been an abundance, although they were now nearly out of season(23d of June). The Muscadine grapes were just beginning to change color and were hanging in the greatest abundance. The first crop of figs and peaches was gone. Pears were as large as good-sized tea-cups, and everything existed to prove that fruit of all kinds could be grown in abundance and got on the market long before there was anything in the North to compete with it. Tomatoes of the finest quality were ripe. The whole was an unexpected and pleasant surprise.

After making our meal of berries, we harnessed our pony, which had filled himself on Japanese clover and Bermuda grass, and commenced our journey toward Delhi. On our way we visited an elevation, the work of the mound builders, and climbed to the summit about thirty feet high, the surface of which comprised about one acre sown with peas. We reached Delhi about sundown.

Monday morning we started for the town of Floyd, twenty-five miles north of Delhi. We passed through a section of magnificent territory, heavily timbered. I saw a large number of oak and hickory trees girdled to make clearings. The timber on an acre of this land, if it were in the North, would purchase two acres of good farming land, but there it is considered almost worthless, as until the last two or three years there were no saw mills in that part of the country. Good pine lumber can now be had for $10.00 per thousand.

We called on several of the farmers on our way up and found them intelligent, sociable and hospitable. I kept my eyes open to discover if there was an effort to conceal any disadvantages the country had, but was satisfied that there was not. The health of the people is generally good, and I did not discover anything worse than mild fevers or dyspepsia, the latter caused by the diet, which in nearly every house was largely hot biscuit, corn bread, fat pork and black coffee. More fat pork is eaten there in each family in the hottest weather than in the North during the winter. More fruits and vegetables during the warm season would mean a freedom from dyspepsia. We drank from a good many wells during our trip of ninety miles and found the water good. I found that the people knew nothing of yellow fever amongst them, also that sunstroke was unknown so far as I could learn.

I found a pleasant peculiarity in the climate compared with ours. Get in the shade and you are always cool and the evenings are delightful. While in Port Huron during the two nights previous to my starting for the South the thermometer stood ninety-four. I slept in a house on the west bank of the river St. Clair not twenty feet from the water. My bed was between the door and window so as to catch the cool breeze; nevertheless I suffered from the heat. In the South I slept comfortably with a covering over me. Another feature surprised me. The first night I slept there the landlord showed me my bed and started away leaving the door open with no means of locking it. I asked him if it were going to be left open all night. Laughing at my fears, he said, "No person shuts their doors here." I took my purse from my pocket and placed it in the centre of the bed under the sheet and got on top of it. In the morning I found the money where I placed it, and during the remainder of my stay left it in my pockets and went to sleep without giving it a thought I had an idea that the colored people would transport everything movable. Mr. Cooper informed me that during his twenty-five years' residence there he had never suffered any loss from their depredations.

I found the land of the Macon Ridge rich and fertile and of uniform quality, capable of growing almost anything. A railroad line is surveyed along the entire length of the ridge, a telephone line was being erected, and every indication that in the very near future property must certainly be worth more than double its present price. At the present time plenty of land can be had for from $6 to $10 per acre, and less in some cases. At that price a man can go there with $1000 and be better off than he would be in the North with $5000. There would be no difficulty in making stock-raising a success with very little capital.

I left Delhi on the 26th for Pachuta, Miss., which is on the main line of the Queen and Crescent railway, between Meridian and New Orleans. I was met by a gentleman and taken to his planta-

tion of 5000 acres. After refreshments, he ordered two horses saddled and we rode all the afternoon, coming back next day after having seen a considerable portion of the country. I found the land more rolling than in Louisiana, but of an excellent quality of deep black clay, which seems to be as good six feet below the surface as at the top. The land is full of marine shells, indicating that either the Mississippi river or the sea once covered it. There is abundance of land for sale in this section. I saw and rode over the greater part of a plantation of 2500 acres, 1100 acres of which is cleared and without a stump, except some shade trees, and there is on it a fine large house and barn; 1400 acres of the land is well timbered with oak, hickory, gum and numerous other varieties of timber. The land is of an excellent quality, being a fine high rolling prairie. It is called prairie because of the formation of the soil, although it may be covered with a dense forest. This plantation could be purchased for $4.00 per acre or possibly less. There is a determination among the land holders there to sell the whole lot or nothing, but a party who would buy so much in a place is not the right kind of a man to develop the country. I presume a person could buy forty or eighty acre lots if he wished. Foreigners are scarce, the inhabitants being principally native born. This land must soon be known and will be purchased at a very sharp advance on present prices.

Good railway facilities, good markets, plenty of timber for fencing or sale, mild winters, the coolest weather known producing about one quarter of an inch of ice, temperate summers, no mosquitoes, plenty of water, very little malaria, few reptiles, a hospitable people, and a paradise for the stock man, make it a very desirable locality. The country must be seen by a Northerner before it is possible for him to realize that such opportunities exist in close proximity to him. During all my stay in the South, notwithstanding my fears previous to my departure, I suffered no inconvenience from the heat. I was out continually on horse back or in a buggy exposed to the heat of midsummer with the same clothes on that I wore in the North, a small rimmed hat and I never held an umbrella over my head. I came away alive and enjoying the best of health. My impressions were so favorable that I anticipate at an early date taking my family there to make a home.

A Northerner's Advice to Northerners.

F. DeWitt Smith, of Hohenwald, Tenn., writes of the highlands of Tennessee as follows: One of the most interesting spots in the South is the highlands of Central Tennessee, which is wonderfully endowed by nature with reference to healthfulness, climate, natural resources and picturesqueness of scenery. It is a country famed for its healthfulness, with pure water, invigorating air and mild climate, and has furnished homes for many from the less-favored section of the extreme North.

The highlands encircle the central basin of Tennessee and rise at an elevation of 1200 to 1400 feet above the level of the sea. A large part of it is level, but it is also diversified with hills and with valleys, through which magnificent streams of soft pure water, clear as crystal, flow over stony and pebbly bottoms, uniting finally in the great waterway of the Tennessee.

These streams are fed by innumerable springs which break from the hillsides. They furnish ample water power for manufacturing purposes as well as for domestic uses. While most of the springs are freestone, there are many mineral springs noted for their health-giving qualities.

To the lumberman, one of the most pleasing sights would be the thousands of acres of magnificent forests of timber which yet waits his coming. The timber is composed largely of white, red, black, post and tan bark oak, chestnut, poplar, hickory, pine, cherry, walnut and many other kinds. This timber can be utilized in many ways, and is well adapted for manufacturing high grade lumber, such as wagon material, hubs, spokes, bent work of all kinds, barrel headings, staves, crossties, etc. The refuse can be cut into cord wood and manufactured into charcoal and wood alcohol.

One of the great industries of this section which is being developed, and yet it is just in its infancy, is the mining of iron ore and the making of iron. The superior grade of brown hematite ore mined in this iron belt has made a reputation for superior quality of iron. In addition to this, thousands of tons of ore have been shipped to other furnaces in the South for mixing with the ores of their own section, thereby giving them the advantage of manufacturing a higher grade of iron. This is destined to be one of the greatest iron producing sections in the South. The fact that two large furnaces have been built in this locality during this year of financial distress and depression in the iron market is proof of the advantages which it holds out for producing cheap iron of a superior quality.

Lately natural gas has been struck in this ore belt and the indications are very favorable for oil.

Probably one of the greatest and most important discoveries that has ever been made in this State has been made in this section in Lewis county in the last few weeks in the discovery of a large deposit of phosphate, analysis of which shows it to be of superior quality.

To those who are tired of the long cold winters of the North and are looking southward for homes where the climate is more mild and genial, this section presents many attractions. It is especially adapted to those of limited means. It is not claimed that the soil of these highlands is as fertile as that of many other places, but it has its advantages in many other ways. Here we have cheap homes in a mild climate, where the cost of living is very small. All kinds of products that grow in the North grow here with the addition of tobacco, cotton, peanuts and sweet potatoes. Fruit, especially, does well and we can raise all kinds of fruit of a superior quality. All over the highlands is found a natural wild grass that furnishes for the greater part of the year pasture for cattle, horses and sheep and makes possible an industry which could be made very profitable.

We have two of the most important railroads of the South, the Nashville, Chattanooga & St. Louis, and the Louisville & Nashville Railroads, which furnish the means of developing the comparatively untouched resources of this section.

In closing, I wish to say as a Northerner to the people of the North who are looking South for either homes or investments that the erroneous impressions that are held by many Northern people of the Southern people in regard to their probably unjust treatment were they to come South, are without foundation. These, with other wrong impressions, have done much towards keeping people from seeking homes and investments in the South.

What Etowah County, Alabama, Offers To Farmers.

P. F. BRADFORD, Walnut Grove, Etowah county, Ala.—I am under obligations to you for your request of some statement from me for publication in the SOUTHERN STATES of my experience of farm life and its results as coming under my personal observation and supervision during my eight years' sojourn in Alabama. Part of my lands were purchased of Alabama State Land Co., of Birmingham, and known here as railroad lands, and the remainder commonly known as deeded lands—that is, lands procured direct from the government either by purchase or homestead entry by the original possessor. I am so well satisfied with the purchase I made that I am always willing to testify to the facts.

First, I may say I am highly pleased with my home in Alabama, after a residence of eight years or more; have never had better health myself and in my family in our lives and have had no use for doctors or medicines other than those peculiar to the ordinary household. My wife and children are all healthy and hearty and always ready for their meals when eating time comes, and as ready for rest and refreshing sleep when night comes.

Of the lands I cultivate, some are valley, some hillside and some plateau. The valley lands contain an admixture of soil, sand, vegetable matter and clay, about equal in parts, the latter sufficiently rich in lime to decompose the silicates and other constituent properties of the soil, to which add the annual surface accumulations with small additions of other plant food. We have an excellent enduring soil quite well adapted to the production of the various articles we cultivate in this neighborhood. I make my own wheat, intending corn to be my chief crop, having reference to my stock, horses, cattle, hogs, etc., cotton being my second or auxiliary crop only, this latter crop being the only article that brings us ready money. Our plateau and hillside soils are chiefly silicious vegetable loam, which, with some manipulation with properly prepared fertilizers of my own composting, are most liberal in their annual return with favorable seasons, and produce for us very much the same variety and proportion of crops as that in the valley, but ordinarily making larger yields of cotton per acre than the latter. But then we raise clover, millet and other grasses, and could set an example and make a boast of the several varieties of stock food we could profitably produce in this region had we more or larger markets for stock sales or for the food to subsist it. The first and foremost idea of the farmer should be, and which I try to do, is to make his farm self-sustaining in all the requisites for the supply of both family and farm; always something to sell or to barter for the need of the family and otherwise. He must have his meat and his corn crib at home and not in the hands of another. Herein is the secret of our success, if we have any, presuming we are all we should be in looking after and cultivating our lands and saving and storing our crops to see to it that we have produced all we need for home and home uses, as well as something to spare, living independently of the merchant, (the banker not coming at all in our line,) other than for clothing and other necessaries that we cannot produce and which are beyond our reach.

Now we can do all these things, for I am doing them. A fine driving horse which I own was sired on my farm and he is not the only good animal in my stable. I have excellent milch cattle. I am not so great a patron of the fine breeds as I am to groom, provide, to house, feed and improve the character of the several stocks I may chance to own. I am improving all my various stocks and breeds, and if I continue in these lines a few years longer I shall be able to place before the public some new grades and names of my own.

We have a fine healthy country, producing all sorts of fruits and vegetables. Individual success here, as elsewhere, depends very much on the energy and enterprise of the man. He must rely on his own personal efforts and management and not on those of his neighbor, except his neighbor should prove an instructive and profitable example to follow; feel that the burden of success rests wholly on himself; a determination to always look ahead, a point still further in advance being the object of his reach, squandering no valuable time, but estimating his energy and time his chief capital. These properly husbanded and employed in this section will bring to any man a competence in means and an independence of all ordinary surroundings.

But we have more than these; more than personal competence or personal independence. We have also all the facilities and requisites for the cultivation of the mind, the morals and the heart. We have most excellent schools— schools within the reach of all—from the primary to the higher grades. Nor are we behind other States or communities in our church advantages. We have prosperous churches of all our leading denominations—Baptists, Presbyterians and Methodists all around us— increasing in membership and influence from year to year. There are no more kindly people, no more honest and patriotic people in the United States than here in Etowah county, Ala.; besides, we have ample room and desirable lands for as many of those who are looking around the country for new and healthful homes, and all such should do as I did—decide and move to Alabama.

As for cost or cheapness of living no fairer or more correct inferences can be drawn than from the statements I have above made. There is no cheaper country to live in either for man or beast anywhere. I not only like this country very much but would not exchange my home in Alabama for either my old or any other in our broad sunny land.

A Western Farmer's Astonishment in Mississippi.

MR. C. F. S. NEAL, in Lebanon (Ind.) Pioneer, writing of Mississippi, says: "On the following day we were at Columbus, Miss., the location of the Girls' State University, some 600 in all departments. This city has 6000 people and looks much like a Northern one, but as at other towns, cotton was piled on every side. Fine farm lands lie all through this section, worth from $3.00 to $15.00 per acre. Good for corn, grains and grass. I never in all my travels before saw such great quantities of grasses, rich and beautiful. There are several kinds that I never had heard of before. One on which I heard the lavish praise of all, the lespedizia, is a grass of spontaneous growth and very much like our clover, and from actual tests richer than blue grass. Farmers here think nothing of two crops of potatoes or one of potatoes and one of cotton on the same land; three of hay, and many other crops yield two and three crops per year. The surprise to me is that they raise any crops at all. The lands are badly handled and when a Northern man comes in he makes farming win. Think of a corn crop for forty years on the same field. Well, that's just what they do, and do not break their lands either. They single furrow their plant and in two plowings the crop is made."

After Twenty Years' Experience South.

E. MASON, Mentone; De Kalb county, Ala., who has lived South for twenty years after twenty years spent in the West says: If a person knows of no country better than his own he is content. An exhaustive description of this table land would tend to cause many to form an erroneous idea of paradise and think that this must be paradise. The best way is to come and see with the eyes what nature has done. We have the most genial climate, just far enough South to insure three seasons of pleasantness and a short mild winter. The elevation above the sea is about 1800 feet. The soil is sandy naturally, thoroughly underdrained, and the air pure and water good, three requisites for the health of the people. Other natural advantages are timber, grass, coal, iron, clays and building stone, also water power, which has been used to a limited extent. The chief pursuits are farming, stock-raising, gathering tanbark, cutting crossties and barrel staves.

There are other things that North Alabama and North Georgia should receive credit for, and these are the almost total absence of mosquitoes, floods, droughts, grasshoppers, cyclones, "northers" or blizzards. We have no fear of any of these things, neither do political affairs ruffle or mar the peace and happiness of the rural districts. There is plenty of room here for a million people, and if any were to become dissatisfied they could never lay any blame on the country. The great wonder is that this section should have been passed by and almost unnoticed by the many, both Northern and Southern people, who are ever in search of health and summer and winter resorts.

Fine Openings for Dairying in Florida.

MR. D. R. PILSBURY, Sanford, Fla.— The peninsular form of Florida and the temperature of the waters that encompass it give to its different portions a varied climate and as varied productions. So while there are some crops fairly successful in all parts of the State, most productions are confined to greater or smaller sections of country.

Of important field crops, corn, sweet potatoes, rice, tobacco, sugar cane and cow peas are of the former class, and are profitable everywhere with proper culture. This can hardly be said, however, of any important fruit. Taking the north and west, including what is known as Middle Florida, the pear, peach, grape and fig are perfectly at home, and are grown (at least the first three) as a commercial crop in orchards of some size and are quite profitable.

In South Florida none of these fruits have as yet made a like success, though all are grown and in many cases with great satisfaction and profit. As it has been but a few years since they have been planted here, it is too soon to say just what their standing is to be as a market fruit. However, it must be said that the perfect adaptability of the orange and lemon to this region, and the well-known profit of its culture, have tended to prevent much attention being given to fruits less adapted and less surely remunerative.

The history of successful grape growing is of very recent date, and shows that while a few kinds do very well, are healthy and bear as well as anywhere, most of the northern sorts are unsuited.

Peach growing is a little older and the northern sorts are unsuited, the successful kinds being so far of peento, red ceylon, strains and Japan dwarf blood, all having different origin from the Persian, from which all northern sorts have come. The pears mainly grown in Florida belong to the same pear class as Le Conte and Keifer.

There remain two fruits to mention. The Japan persimmon does well everywhere, north and south, and on all soils. The fruit is exceedingly beautiful, bears shipment well, but what its place is to be in the market it is hard to say. It may be the apple of Japan, it surely is not of this country. The Loquat, long known as Japan plumb, is a most delicious fruit of apricot flavor, and is also a fine shipper. It is the earliest orchard fruit to ripen, coming in March and April. Peaches follow, last of April, May and June; grapes, June, July and August, with scuppernong sorts through September; the persimmon from August to January, and the pear, August and September. The only branch quite up to the times in South Florida is orange-growing that has absorbed all energy, thought and skill and money, too. Where location has been judicious, and culture wise, the returns are always satisfactory. With the acknowledged superiority of Florida fruit, the certain improvement in varieties selected for culture, the increase of knowledge in all matters of culture, so making a still finer fruit and extending its season, the outlook is such that growers are always extending their planting.

While orange ·culture is well up with the age, there are directions in which Florida is far behind any other section of the country. I refer especially to stock of all kinds and dairying. In North Florida something has been done to improve stock, and in some counties, notably Leon, there are very successful dairies with herds of well improved cows.

The native cow of Florida is inferior to the scrub stock of any other State, and right here lies the opportunity for hundreds, yes thousands of industrious and ambitious men with a little capital to build a competence or a fortune. What has been done in a small way in Leon county can be done and will be done all over the State. In this respect Florida is a new State, and it offers to the enterprising settler such chances in this direction as are not to be found in any State of the Union. It is not only the chances that belong to the pioneers in improving the farm stock of any region, but the special advantage of a region of perpetual grazing and crop growing.

The fact is the crying want of all this South country is more cows, horses, hogs, and poultry to utilize the unlimited pastures and natural food of the country, and then improved stock so good that it can't live on wire grass, but must have cultivated grasses and all feeding crops.

Can the finest butter, cheese, beef, pork be produced here? Certainly. Can forage and feed crops be raised in Florida to do this profitably? Surely. I raise for mule, cow, pigs and poultry, cow peas, and there is no better flesh, milk or egg producer in the land, quince corn, rice, corn, cassava, arrowroot, chufas and Spanish peanuts. Sow oats or rye in November for winter pasture. · A permanent pasture of Bermuda is better.

Chufas and peanuts may be harvested by the pigs and chickens in September or later. Arrowroot may be harvested by the pigs any time in winter, and all these crops thus utilized leave the ground in admirable condition for something else, and there is no time when some profitable crop may not be sown. If money crops are to be grown, the above crops may be followed by cabbage, onions, beets, &c., and later by Irish potatoes, corn, onions, melons, squashes and beans.

A Wide Variety of Farm Products.

JOEL RICE, Chattahoochee, Gadsden county, Fla.—I have been living here for nearly eighteen years, and can testify to the fact that this county is a most desirable place in which to live. We have no real wintry weather, though we do have a few killing frosts, enough to destroy disease germs, if any such should accidentally stumble upon us. We have great success in raising many kinds of fruit, though our main crops for marketing are the Le Conte and Keifer pears and watermelons; the marketing of peaches is yet in its infancy. Vegetables grow to perfection, while we raise an abundance of corn, sugar cane for syrup, real cane—not sorghum, and oats. Potatoes and all other root crops give immense returns, so that this is a paradise for truckers and farmers generally. Our part of the county (the western) has unequalled facilities for shipping, as we have three railroads centering at Chattahoochee River Junction, besides a fine line of steamboats from Columbus, Ga., to Apalachicola, Fla. Tobacco is also a great crop in this county, several hundred thousand pounds of the very finest wrappers and fillers being raised annually. Something in the soil and climatic conditions of this county causes the production of a finer quality of tobacco than in any other part of the State; our hammock lands are the finest known for this purpose. One outcome of the superior quality of our tobacco is the establishment in Quincy (our court house town) of a large cigar factory, where thousands of boxes of the most exquisite smokers in the United States are turned out every season.

A magnificent deposit of cement has lately been discovered near the Apalachicola river, in the western part of the county, said to be fully equal if not superior to Portland cement; a company is being formed to work it. Our county is finely watered and timbered, and we have a variety of soils—sandy lands, sandy surface with red or yellow clay foundation, and black river and creek bottom, and they can be bought for $2.50 to $8.00 or $10.00 per acre. We will welcome any number of new settlers who come with energy and determination to succeed.

An Ohio Dairyman in Mississippi.

F. R. HAMLIN, West Point, Miss.—I came from Bedford, Cuyahoga county, Ohio, to this place ten years ago. Have been engaged in the dairy business ever since. Am now milking fifty cows and think this country especially adapted to this business.

We have men at work in this town trying to establish a creamery here for the manufacture of butter by the centrifugal process.

I think the climate is all that could be wished. Schools A No. 1. Society in this vicinity is of the very best. Political liberty all that could be desired. I have always voted as I choose without fear or trembling and the Republican ticket at that. Market gardening a leading industry.

Views of a Former Illinois Man—A Fine Grass Country.

THEODORE EASTER, West Point, Miss.—I am from Banner, Campaign county, Ills. I have been here six years, own one-half section within one mile of West Point. Have engaged principally in the hay business and find several of the grasses grow to perfection in this section, among which I mention Bermuda, Lespedeza, timothy and herdsgrass; red clover is also a success on the black land, although I have not cultivated it.

Last year I raised fifty bushels of corn per acre. As a stock country this is the best I ever knew; stock can be raised here for one-half as much as it costs in many other sections. Vegetables of almost every kind do well, and during last season quite a handsome sum was realized by our people engaged in that line of business. I am convinced that the same care, cultivation and fertilization used in the Western States

as well as in other parts of the world, would make this one of the most famed farming sections on the globe.

The climate is very fine, and no healthier country can be found in the South. School and church facilities are unsurpassed, there being two first-class public schools in this town—one for white and one for colored chileren—with extensive faculties. There are five denominations that have excellent houses of worship.

As to politics, I will say that I have but little interest in that line. All elections since I have been here have been quiet, and all men can enjoy political privileges of all kinds without molestation.

I might say much more concerning the advantages to be found along the line of the Mobile & Ohio, but I suppose I have about covered the ground you desire.

Need of Energy and the Opening for Nurseries and Fruit Growing.

G. W. STAPLE, Meridian, Miss.— There is so much one might write that it is hard to properly know what to say of this country.

In a recent visit to the North, while inspecting many florists' establishments and talking with the proprietors, I found that the Southern people are noted for their love of flowers, and not only that, but what is more to the point, they buy them. One florist said that the Southern people were a regular gold mine to the Northern florists. If men of energy and capital would come into this country with the same economy and frugality practiced in the North, a greater part of all this business now flowing Northward would remain here.

But it is not so much in the florists' line as in the nursery line that golden opportunities are present. Northern nursery men are already feeling the advantages of a climate where long seasons of growth make vigorous and good-sized stock. A negro can plant nursery stock with his toes, and it will grow better than Northern stock planted and tended with the most thoughtful care. He can cut off a rose cane, jab it into the ground and come back the next year only to find a rose in bloom. It is absolutely essential for the growth of Southern fruit and orchard products to have Southern nurseries. Nurseries are springing up, but what is needed is Northern nursery training; a training beginning at childhood and growing with the plants. The ground is here; the climate is here; the atmospheric conditions are here; all that is needed is the trained mind, the frugal habits and the energy so characteristic of the Northern man.

What an opportunity for early fruit and vegetable-growing. · It would be too long a story to tell of each separate plant that is or might be raised for Northern markets, but suffice to say that I *know* the same care, bestowed on crops here that is bestowed on Northern gardens, would bring in double-golden returns. The more intelligent Southern people have not been so closely linked with the soil as men in the North, and there is needed this kind of blood to infuse new and progressive elements into the South. It is not common to see a finely-furnished house, with fine piano or other musical instrument in the house of the farmer here, yet it is just as much within the reach of the farmer here as in the North, where such is common. How can it well be otherwise when one considers the expensive buildings and surroundings of the Northern farmer in contrast to the simple and inexpensive methods necessary here? We in the South are abusing the generosity of nature instead of taking advantage of it. We are making bricks without straw while an abundance is at hand.

Stern necessity is a great invigorator of mankind, and it is because nature is so good to us that we abuse her confidence, take advantage of her kindness and scorn her so unjustly. Come down from the cold North, brother farmer, and show us what can be done.

The South is progressing with wonderful rapidity, and had it more of the sinews of war, sinews of vigor, sinews of frugality, there would be heard such a rushing sound of progress and advance as only the veriest dreamer can imagine. The amount of ignorance prevailing in the North with reference to the South is simply astounding. Not many years ago I met an old schoolmate just fresh from graduation at Harvard College. He asked me if it were safe for a man down here without carrying weapons. Such questions as that can only be answered by dignified silence, for any attempt to do justice to the subject by way of answer would simply strain the entire vocabulary of the English language.

Young men on graduation from Northern institutions of learning are scrambling for positions as school teachers at salaries not worth while mentioning, while here are openings— lucrative openings on every hand. It is an easy matter to open a private school most anywhere throughout this part of the country and realize a good income. Commercial schools are in demand ; all that is needed is a head to thoroughly organize and run them.

From New Hampshire to North Carolina.

C. D. TARBELL, Southern Pines, N. C.—Southern Pines, N. C., is a health resort and fruit-growing section combined. I came to this place four years ago from northern New Hampshire. I have watched the development of this section, and have seen the town steadily grow, and I have also seen the sick who come here for health grow strong and hearty. I wish, therefore, for the benefit of others, to make some statements, hoping they may be the means of bringing blessing to some. Many people who came here with consumption, and some whom physicians had given up to die, now enjoy quite good health, and have for years. Others came here with rheumatism and they, too, have become well, and whatever the sickness, none have failed to receive benefit unless the disease was too far advanced. If all the sick in the country could know of nature's power to heal in this piney sand hill, there would be as great a rush for this place as there was to secure homes in Oklahoma. This town is sixty-eight miles from Raleigh on the Seaboard Air Line, sixteen hours from New York and nine hours from Atlanta, and on the highest ground between Raleigh and the coast, 600 feet above sea level. It has a dry atmosphere, no mud and no malaria, and its water is filtered through forty to sixty feet of sand. The place contains four hotels, besides rooms and cottages to rent. Another large hotel is building to be ready for guests in the fall of 1894, and it is to be fitted up with all modern improvements.

It was early discovered by Northern settlers that this soil and climate were especially adapted to the raising of fruit, grapes, etc. Land is cheap. Labor only fifty to seventy-five cents per day including board, and it has been demonstrated that fruit and grapes and anything that requires a light soil grows and ripens here to perfection, and last year good quality Niagara and Delaware grapes brought thirteen and fourteen cents per pound, and peaches $3.00 to $4.00 per crate through the season.

Fruit in this section ripens in June and July, and comes in between that from the Gulf States and that of New Jersey and Maryland. So it will take many years to grow fruit enough in this section to glut the markets.

If you are seeking health or investments don't hesitate to come to Southern Pines, and if your experience is like the writer's the longer you stay the better you will like it, whether you are sick or well.

A Successful Immigrant Wants Others.

HENRY GUYER, Amherst, Va.—In 1868 I came from Europe to Lynchburg, Va., where I entered the service of a milk dealer. After staying there for one year and a-half, I bought ten milk cows to do the business of a milk dealer in company with Mr. Stump. Today Mr. Stump and myself are owners of a farm of 200 acres, with more than fifty milk cows and ten horses. We cleared off all the farm and planted a large number of fruit trees and grapevines, and both are good investments. We have fine crops of clover, wheat, oats, etc., and we are satisfied in every respect. There are a number of Germans and country people of mine living around us, all in good circumstances. We would like to have a number of Swiss and German settlers here, and especially as land is cheap, from $5.00

up, and is sure to bring good returns. Fruit trees and grapes do very well here. We have also good water and roads. In Lynchburg, a city of some 25,000 inhabitants, we have always a good market for our products. All industrious immigrants are welcome with us.

Prefers Virginia After Ten Years' Trial.

H. M. BRUBAKER, Roanoke, Roanoke county, Va.—In answer to your question how I like southwest Virginia, I will tell you. About ten years ago I left Dauphin county, Penna., for Florida, but stopped off at Roanoke, Va., which was then only a small place. I staid here only one week to look around. I liked the new town of Roanoke and the people of the town and county, and concluded to stay here, and will continue to stay here. I engaged in the trucking business, and still remain in it. The soil is good and the climate healthy. I would rather live here than in any other State I have been in. I lived two years in Iowa, and have been in Minnesota. And when a young man I traveled five years for a manufactory of cotton goods in Philadelphia, all through the States of Ohio, Pennsylvania and New Jersey.

It is useless for me to say any more, for I am satisfied to stay in Virginia, and would recommend it as a good State for a farmer or workingman to make his home in.

A Fruit and Grain Section.

ISAAC B. PARSONS, Adger, Ala.—I bought 80 acres of land in Jefferson county, Ala., from the Alabama State Land Company, of Birmingham. The land is excellent for all kinds of agricultural purposes. I can raise from 35 to 40 bushels of corn to the acre. Oats, wheat, rye and other grains grow to perfection. Grapes, apples, peaches and all kinds of fruit grow magnificently. All kinds of vegetables do exceedingly well. The timber consists of pine and oak principally, both of fine quality and abundant. Coal and iron ore abound and of first-class quality.

Dr. J. C. Jones, of this place, has a garden of about one acre and a quarter.

One quarter of an acre is well set in Guinea grass, which produces from four to five tons of hay annually. The other acre is planted in all kinds of vegetables, including corn, potatoes, beans, onions, &c., &c., which with a little fertilizer, annually, will realize, at market prices in last few years, at least $200 to $250, without any extra attention after cultivation. Four years ago this land was an old turned out field, the poorest land in the vicinity. From one peck of Irish potatoes he raised fifteen bushels. Other vegetables yielded in proportion.

ITEMS ABOUT FARMS AND FARMERS.

Sheep Raising in South Carolina.

A correspondent of *Home and Farm* writes from Fairfield county, S. C., as follows:

I have always been convinced that agriculture would never flourish in the South unless the raising of stock should be combined with the making of cotton and corn, and have therefore watched the raising of sheep with interest. I have never known an instance, where great profit did not result from sheep-raising when protected from depredations of dogs and in rare cases of thieves.

To a South Carolinian the success of Dr. Niz, of Mississippi, will certainly appear wonderful. The only drawbacks to sheep-raising in this State are depredations of dogs upon the flocks which can be remedied by the passage of a dog license law, and the trouble of fencing or herding sheep entail no cost except a little salt and a little cotton-seed in severe winter. Practically there is never any disease among sheep here. I will give an instance of what has been done in this county. In February, 1866, General J. Bratton bought a flock of forty-nine poor sheep. The shearing of that year he gave to his neighbors. In November, 1872, his flock amounted to 350 head, having bought no other sheep except a few Southdown bucks. In the meantime he sold $800 worth of wool and $900 worth of mutton, and had lived on mutton, not having had a chicken or pig on his place. With the sheep he had enriched thirty acres of land that would hardly sprout peas, so that it would make 1000 pounds of cotton to the acre. The only feed ever given was a little cotton-seed for a few weeks in the winter. Then he divided his flock, giving 175 head to a friend in another county to raise on shares. Since then his clover and timothy and lucern fields made by means of his sheep and herd of thoroughbred Ayrshire cattle have made his plantation resemble a Kentucky bluegrass farm.

Two Georgia Women Get Returns of $2000 From a Half Acre of Land.

The Guyton (Ga.) *Chronicle* tells a tale which it admits it would not believe had it not investigated the matter. The *Chronicle* says: "In Chatham county are two ladies, who personally and without assistance prepare, plant and generally work a truck enterprise which yields nuggets of money in results. The land consists of half an acre! It is under glass and is irrigated from an artesian well. They grow principally cucumbers and lettuce for the northern markets and attend to their careful shipping. The profit to these two ladies from this half acre the past year was $2,000! How does that strike our Effingham truckmen?"

Successful Orange Culture.

Here is the way D. C. Cutler, manager of the Meade orange grove near Ocala, Fla., makes a success of fruit and truck growing. He began ten years ago with a ten acre grove. This year's crop on thirty acres is estimated at 6000 to 10,000 boxes. He sent 200 boxes of fruit off in October and received $900 for the lot. His cucumber hothouse brings in about $600 in a season of three months. During six years he disposed of $22,000 worth of nursery stock. He grew swashes that paid him nearly $2200 a season. With it all he has now 140 acres in trees, and will fill out the remaining ten acres of his tract of 150 acres with "Parson Brown" and "Tangerine" trees. Last season he placed 600 orange trees, only one of which died. All the others are thrifty. He has 100 trees to the acre.

A Successful Farmer.

Col. M. McRae, of Maxton, N. C., makes farming pay, as the following statement from the *Robesonian* will show. Col. McRae has a one-horse farm, and the results secured from it in 1893 were as follows:

Exhibit of Money Value of a one-horse Farm by Col. M. McRae, for the year 1893.

467 bushels corn at 75c	$350 25
5000 lbs. fodder at 75c	37 50
25 bushels peas at 75c	17 85
125 bushels potatoes at 40c	50 00
7½ bushels rye at $1.25	9 37
40 bushels oats at 60c	24 00
12 gallons syrup at 40c	4 80
2,000 pounds hay at 50c	10 00
12 bales cotton (6000 lbs.) at 7½c	450 00
350 bushels cotton seed at 16⅔c	58 33
1000 pounds pork at 10c	100 00
60 gallons wine at $1.00	60 00
Dairy and poultry	50 00
Total	$1,212 10
Guano and labor	506 00
Profit	$706 10

Louisiana as a Fruit State.

Colonel A. W. Waite, a wealthy fruit grower of Fillimore, Cal., while in New Orleans recently, strongly advocated the advantages of Louisiana for fruit growing. Speaking to a Times-Democrat reporter, he said:

"Outside of California there is no State in the Union more favorable to general fruit raising than Louisiana. The soil and climate of this State would produce fruit of almost every variety, and of a flavor and quality that could not be equaled anywhere. Plums, cherries, pears, apricots, peaches, prunes and figs would grow here in profusion if properly cultivated and looked after. Experience has taught me that the average crop of fruit of all kinds will average about five tons to every twenty acres; and as the price obtained for it is from one and a half to two and a half

cents a pound delivered on the cars at your nearest station, the profit is very large.

"Oranges already grow here, and by a little grafting a superior fruit could be raised that would command a better market than any imported orange that is now sent into the country. This State is particularly adapted to the growing of prunes, and the soil is of such a character that the fruit produced would equal, if it did not excel, the California prune. Prunes always command a good market, and require only average care. The profit from them exceeds that of any other fruit which is consumed in like quantities, and from them alone a very large business could be built up with an exceedingly small outlay of money."

An Illustration of What Fruit Culture is Doing for the South.

The progress of the South in fruit culture and the possibilities of this industry are finding good illustrations in nearly every Southern State, but in none has there probably been a more rapid advance of any one branch of horticulture than that of peach growing in Southern Georgia. Peaches are attracting almost as much attention to that section as oranges did to Florida a few years ago. Many of the most successful growers are from other States, and among the companies organized within the last few years to operate along the line of the Georgia Southern & Florida Railroad are the Albaugh-Georgia Fruit Co., with 75,000 trees; the Ohio Fruit Land Co., with 100,000 trees; the Hale, Georgia, Co., with 100,000 trees, and the Tivoli Fruit and Land Co., now planting 80,000 acres in peaches at Tivoli. Georgia peaches reach Northern and Western markets ahead of nearly all other varieties, and as a result generally command profitable prices. A few years ago Capt. H. H. Tift, of Tifton, Ga., and his brothers, W. O. and Edward Tift, turned their attention to fruit growing. They planted a vineyard of forty acres of Delaware, Concord, Niagara, Moore's Early and other grapes three years ago, and in 1893 made a good profit from it, with every prospect of its being very profitable. Then they put out 750 pecan trees which are doing well.   Mr. W. O. Tift has a seventy-five acre flourishing peach orchard.   Messrs. Tift & Snow have a 200-acre orchard, and will plant fifty more in January. They also have a large acreage in plums and other fruits.   A number of Pennsylvanians have recently purchased 500 acres of land to put in fruit.   The growth of this fruit farming has, according to the Atlanta Journal from which we gather these facts, caused Tifton, which four years ago was simply the site of a small mill, to become a prosperous town of a thousand people with a canning factory and other industries.

Increasing Cultivation of Rice in Texas.

Mr. G. H. Mallam, secretary of the Texas Tram & Lumber Co., of Beaumont, Texas, in telling of the progress of rice culture in East Texas, says:

"While I am engaged in the lumber business my attention has been necessarily attracted in the direction of all the new industries that spring up in my immediate locality.   It is astonishing how popular and successful the culture of rice is becoming in Southeastern Texas, particularly in the counties of Jefferson, Chambers, Liberty and Orange.   I can, of course, speak more accurately of this industry in Jefferson, my home, than in adjoining counties.

"There is W. P. H. McFaddin, who has 800 acres in rice.   J. H. Broocks has about 1500; W. W. Green, 500, and will double his planting next year; W. A. Ward, 300, while fifty smaller farmers have begun the cultivation of rice.   In five years there will be 100,000 acres in rice in our immediate neighborhood.   Fifteen or twenty families have come over from the State of Louisiana and have embarked in raising rice."

An Attractive Part of the South.

One of the interesting features of the progress of the South is the trend of emigration from Illinois and other Western States to parts of Alabama and Mississippi.   The trucking and fruit-raising business in these States is attracting many people from other sections, and the outlook promises a continuation

of this immigration movement. Mr. W. W. Hose, of London Mills, Ill., writing of this movement, and of the attractions of a part of this favored section, says:

There is a great country bordering on the Gulf of Mexico, the natural advantages and resources of which are probably unsurpassed by any locality on the face of the globe.   The heart of this country lies in Southern Mississippi and Alabama and along the Mobile and Ohio Railway, and I shall select the vicinity of Citronelle, Ala., as an illustrative point.

Citronelle is situated 611 miles south of St. Louis, and is thirty-three north of Mobile.   It is a fine old town—more than half a century old at least—but has only just been touched with the universal spirit of improvement and development which is setting in all over the South.   Its population is now over 500, but a great deal of building is going on and it will only be a question of a few years probably when Citronelle will be one of the prominent cities of the South.

Already it is noted as a health resort, the Hygeia Hotel being crowded nearly all the year through; in winter time the guests are mostly Northern people who come here to escape the severe winters of the North, while in the summer people come from the large cities of the South to breathe the pure, free air of this elevated place and both winter and summer guests accord high praise to the health-giving waters of the wonderful springs here.   It is a common thing for people in poor health to come to this place and gain a pound of flesh per day from the time they arrive for a period of several weeks, and oftentimes confirmed invalids do this without any medical care after arriving here.   Citronelle is 350 feet above sea level, and located among fragrant long-leaved pines whose fragrant odors are a sure cure for colds, throat and lung trouble in their early stages, and all kinds of fevers.   This is not a description of Citronelle alone, but is applicable to all of this piney woods country.

Aside from its hotel advantages Citronelle has quite a number of cottages, belonging to Northern people, which are occupied every winter.   Mr. E. D.

Mann, of New York city, is completing a cottage here costing $30,000 before it is finished. He has 320 acres of ground and (while he is a wealthy man) is laying it out for profit as well as pleasure. He is putting out such fruit as pears, peaches, figs, pomegranates, pecans, grapes, etc., and is raising poultry very extensively. He is also raising small grain and hay. Many others will follow Mr. Mann's example and make Citronelle their permanent home, a good many wealthy people having already purchased grounds.

The resources of the country are so varied that it is adaptable to a large variety of industries and diversified employments. The first that presents itself is the lumber business, as the ground must be cleared before it can be put in cultivation. The timber is mostly pine, but has a good sprinkling of oak and hickory. Railroads are numerous and cheap labor can be had, so the lumber business ought to pay well, and apparently it does. It should be followed closely by woodworking shops, such as sash and door factories, carriage and wagon works, etc. Coal, wood and water can be had in abundance, the coal being shipped from further north in Alabama. Following this comes stock-raising. The climate and soil is especially adapted to this and the low price of land and great amount of it at present free range add to the inducements. This is particularly a grass country. But now to general farming. What can be raised? Well—corn, oats, sugar cane, all kinds of vegetables, hay and grass and fruits of every description. You can also get from two to four crops from one piece of ground during the year. I saw the fields which have this season produced twenty-five to forty bushels of corn to the acre and two tons of voluntary hay, which sprung up after the corn was gathered. And further, it must be remembered that corn is seventy-five cents per bushel and hay $15.00 per ton. This incident was on an Illinois man's farm, situated one or two miles from Citronelle. It is a sure thing to get two crops per season, and you can raise vegetables for the table all the year round. On Mr. Michael's farm are forty pear trees which will be bearing next year. There are 2000 trees five years old and $250 per acre would not buy the farm, and yet it has paid for itself every year since Mr. Michael owned it in the vegetables it has produced, besides the work being all hired labor. This is the same kind of land which can be bought in its raw state for three dollars to five dollars per acre and in some cases less.

But it is impossible in a brief article to give all the details of the advantages of this country, and much of it would scarcely be believed. All that is here stated, however, I am prepared to verify and much more also. Now, who should move South? An energetic man with $500 or more, who is looking for a home and willing to do some hard work in getting one. But the hard work is only the first year or two, and then he has a home that has increased ten-fold in value and a climate that cannot be surpassed.

A GENTLEMAN who is interested in the Aransas Pass section of Texas claims that all things considered that region is far ahead of California as a fruit country. It is now, he says, in about the same condition as Southern California twenty years ago, and is about to experience the extraordinary development in population, occupation and values that Southern California has passed through in the last decade. Its earlier seasons and comparative nearness to the great markets of the populous States gives the Gulf Coast of Texas advantages over California that have a money value. The fruit lands of the coast now being sold at $20 per acre have a greater intrinsic value, based on their productive capacity in money, than the same California lands sold at $50 to $300 per acre. It should be borne in mind that these lands are just as well suited for all the citrus and other sub-tropical fruits as for grapes, and most of the fruits of the temperate zone.

C. B. Sloat, assistant general ticket agent of the Rock Island Railroad, after visiting the Gulf Coast of Texas, is quoted as saying: "The people of that section are making special efforts to induce immigration, but I am inclined to the opinion that the prices at which the people hold their real estate are altogether too high to admit of the rapid development of the country. The owners of large tracts are cutting them up into smaller ones, but the price at which these small tracts are held is not sufficiently low to induce people to settle there."

THE cultivation of rice pays, according to Hon. Aladin Vincent, a native of Calcasieu parish, La., who planted 230 acres in rice ; most of the crop gathered was from 200 acres. He harvested 2000 barrels, of which he saved 175 barrels for seed and feed, and sold 1825 barrels for $3.00 a barrel, making a total sum of $5475. The total cost of producing the crop was $2000, the net profit being $3475.

MR. R. H. CARSON, of Monroe county, Tenn., writes very interestingly about the attractions of East Tennessee for small farming in preference to grain growing at present prices of wheat and corn. The big farms must, he says, give way to the small farms carefully cultivated, and then there is a good profit for the tiller of the soil. East Tennessee, says Mr. Carson, "is not only well adapted to dairying, but the character of the soil and climate make it almost an ideal section for apples, small fruits and vegetables. No other State in the union is better adapted to poultry-raising, and a few who have tried bees have met with most encouraging results.

"During the past few years a great many 'Yankees' have located in East Tennessee, and their truck gardens, vineyards and orchards should be lessons of value to our native farmers." May East Tennessee and the South in general soon have many thousands of these "Yankee" farmers. The more the better.

THE SOUTHERN STATES has received

many reports that the farmers of North Carolina are as a class better off than for some years. Col. Dave Settle, of Rockingham county, is quoted as saying that the farmers of his county didn't even know of the panic last summer except by reading of it. They had, he said, fine crops, plenty of money, plenty to eat and nothing to do until tobacco stripping time came around. Col. Settle mentioned a dozen or more men in Rockingham county who are worth over $100,000 each, and nearly every farmer in the county, he said, was out of debt and was doing well.

APPLE growing in Virginia has been attracting increased attention of late years because of the large profits made, especially in years when there has been a shortage in the Western crop. It is estimated that the apple growers of Albemarle and Nelson counties received about $500,000 for their apple crop in 1893, over $50,000 worth having been sent from Coverville alone. Mr. J. G. Martin of that place shipped 100 barrels to Liverpool and netted $5.21 per barrel on them.

ALL reports from the South show that the farmers are in better condition than for several years. The Cochran (Ga.) Telegram, referring to that section, says: "Nearly all the farmers in this county have harvested a fine crop of corn and other grain. The high price of meat has caused them all to raise their own meat, and the year 1894 will find nearly all our farmers with plenty of hog and hominy to run them through the year."

As a sample of what industrious colored people can do in the South, Louis Patton, a colored farmer of Bradley county, Ark., has been awarded three premiums at fairs in Memphis, Tenn., and Shreveport, La., within the last two years for specimen bales of short-staple cotton.

THE AGRICULTURAL AND HORTICULTURAL POSSIBILITIES OF TEXAS.

By John E. Hollingsworth,

Commissioner of Agriculture.

It has been one of my main efforts as commissioner of agriculture to collect in my department an exhibit of the various products of the State, together with such information as would be of use in exemplifying the agricultural and horticultural possibilities of Texas. While I readily admit the great value of our undeveloped resources and the importance of establishing factories, yet at the same time I am forced to the conclusion that the wealth of Texas consists in its incomparable agricultural and horticultural possibilities, pursuits to which our people are in all things adapted, and the soil, climate and season lend every aid. I do not claim to have completed my work so far as to give in full these possibilities, yet I think sufficient can be said to arouse an interest at home and to be exceedingly suggestive to all persons investigating such questions.

In beginning I will assert that in no place does experimenting with varieties and methods produce more startling results than in Texas. Often a man fails with one variety, where later on another man, by adopting a new method, using the same variety, makes a most signal success. When Mr. H. M. Stringfellow concluded to plant a pear orchard in Galveston county and make the Le Conte pear his principal one, his friends told him of those who had tried that pear and failed and to beware of danger and great loss. Having nothing to guide him in the way of other men's success and knowing what his friends told him was so, he concluded as a last resort to plant the pear orchard and rely on new methods for results. This year he has marketed 9127 bushels of pears off of thirteen acres, and has paid out nearly $100 per acre to his neighbors as wages for help and harvesting, and the crop netted him $5245. His new method was merely to fertilize his land heavily, using as much as a ton per acre and his results a fortune to himself and his descendants. I have in my collection one bushel of these pears, and they average 33 ounces each in weight, and will sell on account of excellence in any market.

In oats I can present some wonderful facts. They are winter oats and have been grown by Mr. John Harrison of Nash, Ellis county, for twenty-two years. As soon as he harvests his oats he turns over the stubble. His oats come up voluntarily, and he only sows when he desires to change his field for oats. The samples I have are the fifth crop from the sowing, on which one hundred mules were pastured all winter, and yet it made over seventy bushels per acre. His least crop in the twenty-two years was sixty bushels to the acre, and he has made as high as ninety bushels per acre. I also have the red oats, taken out of a four-hundred acre patch that averaged over 125 bushels per acre. Wheat, of which I have six varieties, shows a yield ranging from 25 to 48 bushels per acre. This comprises both spring and winter wheat, and the samples are excellent.

The grain lands of Texas are the black, waxy lands in the north and central portions of the State, and the black, sandy, chocolate and red lands of the west and north. As cotton is the prin-

685

cipal crop of the black, waxy lands, but little experiment on varieties and methods as to grain has been made. It is looked upon by all that a crop of grain is certain, and but little care is given to the preparation of the soil or the selection of the variety. In the west and northwest all credit for a crop of grain is given to the season and variety, and methods play but a small part, yet I have all kinds of grain perfectly grown and showing a large yield. In all the States where the people, on account of the density of the population and scarcity of land, have been forced to adopt methods and select varieties with a view to get all possible from the soil, the yield in grain has uniformly been doubled from what it formerly was. I think I can safely say that every indication points to similar results in this State. Here I have oats that have made 125 bushels per acre. The man who grew them put in a little extra time in preparing the soil. His neighbors made seventy-five bushels per acre, hence this little extra time paid him fifty bushels of oats per acre. Now let us add fertilizers and a little more time, and what then? In wheat I have forty-eight bushels per acre, against twenty-five for neighboring farms. A little extra work in preparing the soil paid twenty-three bushels of wheat per acre. Now, what can be added by varieties and fertilizers? In corn, barley, millet and rye the same results are shown. I am convinced that by experimenting on methods and a selection of the variety best suited the yield of grain in this State can be made phenomenal, and the grain crop of the west and northwest made as sure as the cotton crop on the black lands.

I have often advocated the diversifying of crops. I know there are portions of Texas that can make more out of crops that can be successfully grown there than of cotton. I have some fine samples of tobacco from many places in Texas, and it can be made a paying crop. A Mr. George Mayer in Dallas county is making $800 per acre on tobacco. The idea that tobacco grown here is not so strong and well flavored as that grown elsewhere is a mistake, because when properly handled and cured it has both strength and flavor. Texas tobacco is like all other kinds. It must go through sweats and other curing processes to bring out its qualities, but its qualities, when brought out, are perfect, and will sell anywhere. In east Texas and along the coast of Texas tobacco should be cultivated extensively, and with big profit. I also have flax. It decorticates perfectly with a fine fibre, and the yield of seed is large. Flax is extensively grown just for the seed, and the seed matures perfectly in Texas and yields a large amount of oil. Rice I also have, and there is quite a territory in Texas susceptible to rice culture. Texas rice is as fine as rice raised elsewhere and sells as well. Sugar is a paying crop in Texas, and is well known. Hops, though only raised on isolated vines, show that in Texas a vast hop industry can be started when the people feel so inclined.

As to agriculture, I will make the broad statement that my exhibit shows conclusively that no man has any possible excuse for not having fruits, flowers and vegetables around his house. I have fruits and vegetables of all kinds and many varieties from all portions of the State and grown on all kinds of soil. I have them from east Texas, beginning at Jefferson county and ending at Bowie. On the black lands they begin at Victoria county and end at Grayson and Cook, and from Amarillo to Rockport we have them from the west. Let no one think that I will stop at these general statements, for I shall not. It is my purpose here to give in detail what is, as a rule, referred to in glaring generalities. On horticultural products Texas has the markets of Denver, Chicago, Omaha and the West and Northwest until about August first without much or any opposition, and the railroads of the State give on carload lots rates exceedingly liberal and far below rates enjoyed by California to the same points. Along the coast from Orange to Corpus Christi in February vegetables of many kinds are ready for market, and from this on until the whole State has vegetables. Texas stands from thirty to sixty days ahead of the other States in the markets and this continues and extends to melons; while other States are laboring in expensive green houses to force a few early products, they are growing in our gardens to perfection. A late addition is celery, which grows in Texas whenever tried, and comes on the market just as the northern disappears. Celery has been successfully grown in Smith, Galveston, Waller and Tom Green counties, to come on the market about March, and in Potter county to come on the market in October. This can be made a profitable industry in our State.

Our strawberry season opens early and about thirty days in advance of all competition and the territory extends from Galveston to Denison. The sandy lands of East Texas are well adapted to this berry, and the annual net returns for some years have been $1000 to every three acres of berries. The blackberry grows over a much larger territory and by many have been found to be more profitable than the strawberry. Plums grow extensively in Texas and have paid in many places as high as $800 per acre. In June we enter the Chicago market with the Maimie Ross peach, selling them at $6 per bushel, and we hold the market on peaches in the West and Northwest until about August 1. Peaches this year have netted about $475 per car. Smith county alone reports a revenue in 1892 from peaches of $77,000.

The European grapes from around Rockport, which can be successfully grown from Port Lavaca to Brownsville, are ready for market by June 6 and sell at 25 cents per pound. They yield from thirty to over 100 pounds per vine and are grown on stubs without any expense for stakes and wires or training in any way. The American grapes grow all over the State, and when properly handled pay $100 per acre or over.

Pears are grown all over the State and successfully grown. The largest yield known is that of Mr. Stringfellow at Hitchcock, being 9127 bushels on thirteen acres.

I have apples from all portions of North Texas and that have grown on all soils large and well flavored. In a collection I have from Bowie, Montague county, are Ben Davis, Arkansas Black, Limber Twig, Wine Sap, Northern Spye, Nickey Jack, Winter Pearmain and Shockley. It was the opinion of ex-Governor E. O. Stanard, of Missouri, that these apples would sell in the St. Louis market at any time on account of their general excellence. Apples can be made an industry in Texas equal to that of any State and the profit much larger.

The melon crop is a very important and profitable one. Limestone county realized from 230 acres last year the handsome sum of $32,966. This county was equally successful with "garden truck," as it reports 399 acres valued at $130,660.

The fine cabbage sold in this State about February are grown on the coast. They are planted in September and make 400 heads to the acre. On onions from $100 to $200 per acre are made.

Of course I have many other kinds of fruits and vegetables, but I have mentioned only such as can be developed into an important industry.

One drawback to successful orcharding and truck-patching is the difficulty in getting sufficient persons interested to ship in carload lots, for low rates are always issued on large shipments. The expenditure of money advertising the great possibilities of Texas in other States will bring people, but will not bring the people we wish.

The men in other States who understand the value of intense farming as applied to varieties and methods are successful where they are, and we need just that kind. In France five acres is a large farm. In California ten acres is sufficient for any family. In Massachusetts twelve acres in cultivation is ample to base a good income, and Texas can surpass them all by the same methods. Men in west Texas are getting rich on ten acres of land. These facts are not known to the general public only as a matter of vague rumor, and in consequence many are saving and striving to get money enough to buy a 200-acre farm, when ten acres, properly cultivated would be worth more to them. The men to present these facts are already in Texas, but it takes a constant presentation, together with some educational features attending, to suggest the real facts. The markets we have and the rates given by the railroads, Texas should from February to August not send occasional carloads of vegetables and fruits, but sufficient people should engage in the business to send a fast special train over every leading railroad in the State every day in the whole time to the great West and Northwest. · Near the small towns along the roads men could buy ten acres of land for a few hundred dollars and get more out of it than they do now out of 200 acres. The women and children will be given ample work in packing and boxing fruit and other products and at increased wages. Bee culture, which goes hand in hand with fruit-growing, can be then made an important industry, and dairying in Texas will be carried on to a large and profitable business. Williamson county in 1892, from 2011 stands of bees, secured 100,264 pounds of honey, valued at $8641.

I have endeavored to set out a few of the possibilities of Texas from generalities, and as direct and certain as I could make them. Should my department ever be supplied with funds to collect a complete list of Texas possibilities, based on methods that have been successfully applied in the State, and varieties that do best and show the most profitable results, and then through the proper and most approved channel present these facts to the people of our own State, I have no hesitancy in saying that the State of Texas will awake to an importance in the markets little dreamed of to-day, and the annual product of fruits and vegetables will equal, if not exceed in value, our wonderful cotton crop at the present time.

"THE PARTING OF THE WAYS."

By A. Jeffers.

The late senatorial contest in Virginia has been an eye-opener in many ways. It has been an official notice served on the old "political wheel-horses" that the younger voters are to have something to say and something to do in the future political management of the affairs of the State.

This matter has not been brought about by any manipulations of any party or clique or faction. It is not the work of republicans, prohibitionists, populists or independents. It is confined strictly to the ranks of the dominant party of the State.

In this move some profess to see political trickery and more or less sharp practice, and charges and insinuations have been the order of the day, but from an unpartisan, unprejudiced and unselfish point of view we see in it nothing but the "parting of the ways" between the old and the new—between old Virginia and new Virginia.

Let us look at the matter for a few moments, divesting our minds of all prejudice, and look at the matter calmly, coolly and dispassionately, and what do we see? We see the shock of 1861 to 1865 rending the State as the lightning stroke rends the solid oak. We see the dead and decaying foliage and branches. We see the heroic efforts of the blighted tree to live. It has lost its vigor and its grand proportions, and much of its vitality. It is simply a touching reminder of what it once was. The people of the State in middle age at the time of the shock have never fully recovered therefrom, and can never recover, any more than can the noble oak of the forest recover fully from the lightning stroke. Since that time the tendency on the part of the people of the State has been to "look backwards" to that period of peace, prosperity and contentment that preceded the battle shock. It is but human nature to do this, and we are not speaking in the way of criticism or of fault-finding, but dealing with facts as they exist.

Since 1865 the people of the State have, strictly speaking, been looking backward, instead of forward. The burden of thought and expression has been "before the war," and instead of meeting the future squarely face to face, the tendency has been to "look backward," with regret and keen sorrow, rather than forward hopefully and earnestly.

It is fatal to success, in any and all undertakings, when one halts and looks backward. Those who live more in the past than in the present are not the best leaders, neither of men nor of thought.

The senatorial contest that resulted in the defeat of Fitzhugh Lee is nothing more nor less than the legitimate natural "parting of the ways." It means that the old leaf of history, blotted over with tears, regrets and with blood, has been forever turned, and a new page presented to the world. This new page requires new men, new methods, new ideas. The leaders of thought and action in Virginia in 1863-64 cannot, in reason, expect or hope to retain the leadership in 1893-94. More than a generation has passed away since then, and the world has moved rapidly on, while Virginia has lingered by the way, meditating regretfully and naturally of the past, without fully, firmly and fairly facing the future.

The times demand new men, younger men, schooled not so much in the arts of war or in the arts of the politician developed during and subsequent to the reconstruction period, as men schooled

689

in statecraft of more modern patterns and ideas. It is not because the State of Virginia thinks any less of the "old," but because she thinks more of the "new," more of what is in store. It may be truthfully said that the young South is in the saddle, but let us add, its face is turned forward instead of backward.

It is a very hopeful sign indeed. It may make some heart-burnings and not a few regrets, but it is the natural "parting of the ways," the division of the old and the new. It is just what takes place in the family, and among friends, relatives and acpuaintances the world over, and yet we see that, all things considered, it is for the best interests of all that such things should happen.

It is not because the people of the State think any the less of Lee or the past that he so ably represents, but because in "the eternal fitness of things" it is absolutely necessary, for the best interests of the State, that from this time forward the future should receive more consideration than the dead past. Our people have naturally awakened to this, and have acted accordingly. It is the most hopeful sign that has been seen in many a year. Let us interpret it aright, and "go forward" with our faces cheerfully and hopefully to the front, "with malice towards none, but good will to all.

THE GREAT SUCCESS OF A GEORGIA ROAD'S WORK.

Experience is always a good teacher and the experience of one Southern railroad in its effort to attract well-to-do immigrants shows how great a success can be made with the proper degree of energy and good management. From the Savannah News we take an account of what has been accomplished by the Georgia, Southern & Florida Railroad despite the many disadvantages under which it has labored. What this road has done can be done by any other road in the South. The country through which it runs has no unusual advantages, none not possessed by that along such lines as the Atlantic Coast Line, the Seaboard Air Line, the Richmond & Danville and many others. And in proportion as they exceed the Georgia, Southern & Florida in financial strength and magnitude ought they to exceed it in the scale on which they can profitably push the immigration business. The Savannah News in describing what this road has done says:

Railroads should be the natural developers of the territory they traverse, as upon that development must largely depend the continued success of the roads. It has, however, been too commonly the case that railroad managers have looked more to immediate results than future profits, and he has been regarded as the best manager whose net earnings were the largest, regardless as to how much he might be drawing upon future profits.

The management of the Georgia Southern & Florida road early recognized the importance of developing and building up the country along its line. Running through a new and richly timbered country, the lumber and naval stores naturally gave it a heavy freight traffic; but in time the lumber and turpentine must be exhausted and the road would have to look to other sources for its traffic. Recognizing this fact, Mr. W. B. Sparks, the president, inaugurated a policy which was calculated to convert the forests into farms and replace lumber and naval stores with agricultural and horticultural products that would put the traffic of the road upon a permanent basis. To this end a model farm of 1,000 acres was opened in the heart of the pine woods, for the purpose of showing the character of the soil and the variety of agricultural and horticultural products that could be profitably raised. Fruit trees and vines of all kinds were planted, the farm was stocked with horses, cattle and hogs of the best breeds, and the ground was cultivated with improved implements. The result has shown that the land of this section, which a few years ago was regarded as valueless except for the timber, is equal in productiveness to any in the State, and, as a consequence, new farms are being opened all along the line of the road. But the work of the model farm did not stop there. Its practical experiments showed the farmers that there was profit in products which had hitherto not been raised, it taught a better system of cultivation and instilled a spirit of enterprise and emulation into the people along the line. It is a great object lesson, and its work will be felt for years to come.

But the policy of the management of the road did not stop with the farm. Having demonstrated the productiveness of the land, it invited settlers to come in and cultivate them, and supplemented the invitation with offers of aid in the way of low freights upon building material and supplies. It established stations at convenient points, so that settlers could have all the conveniences of a railroad. As a consequence there are more new, growing and thrifty little towns along the Georgia Southern than on any other line of the same number of miles in Georgia.

About a year and a half ago a bureau of immigration was organized, and systematic effort has been made to induce Northern fruit growers and farmers to settle along the line. The result of this effort has been the organization of one orchard company, which purchased 800 acres and set out 50,000 trees and vines, another which purchased 1,500 acres and is setting out 90,000 trees and vines, and is preparing to erect a canning and crate factory, and another company is negotiating for 1,800 acres of land, on which it is proposed to plant 100,000 trees and vines. Besides these companies a number of individuals have been attracted to this section, have purchased lands and are improving them. Negotiations are pending for the establishment of two German colonies, who will each take up and improve from 2000 to 3000 acres. The owners of large tracts of land which have been milled and turpentined are clearing up farms and planting them in fruits, with the object of showing prospectors what their lands are capable of producing, and thus finding a sale for them. The adaptability of the lands along the line of the Georgia Southern has been extensively advertised, and hundreds of inquiries regarding them are being received and answered, while a number of excursion parties are being organized in the Northwest with a view of thoroughly inspecting the country. There are now about 500,000 peach trees and grape vines planted along the line of the road, which, within three years, will produce annually 1000 cars of freight.

Of course, this development has been somewhat at the expense of present net earnings, but it has been the policy of Mr. Sparks, both as president and receiver, to build up the road so that its resources would increase in the future and make it a profitable property for its owners, and in doing this he has fully demonstrated how greatly a railroad can develop and build up the country through which it passes. If all the railroads of Georgia would pursue the same policy, it would not be many years before Georgia would rank among the wealthiest and most prosperous States in the Union.

EDITORIAL AND NOTES OF PROGRESS.

Advice to People Contemplating Moving South.

There is a vague impression among many Northern people that the whole South is a sort of semi-tropical region where cold weather is unknown. They have an idea that once across Mason and Dixon's line they will immediately find a country of perpetual spring where the flowers bloom all the year round. The writer has met Western people in midwinter in the mountains of North Carolina who were amazed to find that it was not a region of ever-blooming flowers where cold weather was unknown. One day during a heavy snow storm some Cleveland people arrived at a mountain hotel and words failed to express their disgust. They had known so little of the country in advance and had so little appreciation of the increasing coldness as altitude increases that they expected to find Florida climate in North Carolina's mountains, and to find snow a foot deep called forth savage denunciations of the whole South. It should be fully understood that there are as wide variations in the climate of the South as could possibly be expected in a country of such vast area and where every elevation from the sea coast to nearly 7000 feet above sea level can be found. Moreover, it is not well to imagine that all of the South is equally desirable. As there is a wide variety of climate so there is a wide diversity of natural advantages. Some places are less desirable than others, and some less healthy than others. Don't imagine that the title "The South" covers a small region where every part is equally as attractive. In Virginia or North Carolina, for instance, you can find on the coast an ideal section for early fruits and vegetables, and even for figs and other almost semi-tropical products, and yet as you travel toward the Western part of these States and the elevation rises to 4000 feet and over, the agricultural productions are almost identical with those of Canada. In view of these facts it behooves every one contemplating moving South to make a thorough investigation on all these points in order that there may be no after disappointment. The SOUTHERN STATES is fully impressed with the fact that no other country in the world has such a combination of advantages as the South, nor does any other region hold out equal attractions to the man seeking a place for a home, but it wants every settler to be fully satisfied, knowing that this is essential to the permanency of the immigration movement now tending this way.

Busy Southern Factories.

Some interesting statistics, which show the number of unemployed wage-earners in 119 cities of the country, have been prepared by Bradstreet's. The total number is 800,000, according to these figures, of which New York city has 80,000, Boston, Mass., 30,000, Philadelphia 62,500, Pittsburg 75,000, Chicago 60,000 and St. Louis 30,000. Included in the estimate are twenty Southern cities, embracing Baltimore, Birmingham, Ala., Memphis, Tenn., Augusta, Ga., and other towns which are centres of manufacturing. The total number of unemployed in these twenty cities is 42,065, of which Baltimore, it is claimed, has 20,000, which we believe is too many. Comparing this section with cities in other parts of the country, we find that Philadelphia alone has 20,000 more idle workmen than the twenty cities, and 40,000 more than the nineteen outside of Baltimore; Pittsburg has 33,000 more than the twenty cities; New York has 38,000 more, and Chicago 23,000 more.

In the nineteen Southern cities outside of Baltimore we have a combined population of 1,575,000, which makes the percentage of unemployed 1.4; in Newark, N. J., it is 6.67; in Philadelphia, 5.9; in Buffalo, N. Y., 6.1; in Pittsburgh, Pa., 32, and Providence, R. I., 7.7. In fact, the percentage is lower in the South than in most of the larger cities of the country. At Augusta, Ga., Houston, Texas, and Mobile, Ala., the following report is made: "No wage-earners idle." These are the only places out of the 119 making such reports.

The statistics form another striking proof of the healthy condition of Southern industries compared with those in other parts of the country. It would be folly to say that lack of business has not caused many large furnaces and mills to shut down, but, as we have noted from time to time, a fair percentage have resumed operations, and more are resuming daily.

A Waste of Money by the Vicksburg, Shreveport & Pacific Railroad.

Mr. John M. Lee, land agent for the Vicksburg, Shreveport & Pacific Railroad, has submitted a proposition to the towns and parishes along that road, stating that the company has in view the organization of an immigration bureau. "The cost," he says, "of organizing and running such a bureau for sixth months will require about $200 to $300 per month," and the road will generously pay one-half of this if the counties and towns will pay the balance, and at once put competent agents in the field. Whether Mr. Lee or some other officer is the author of this scheme we do not know, but think for a moment of a railroad recklessly offering to spend $600 to $900 for organizing and running an immigration bureau for keeping competent agents at work for six months! Such extravagance, such wild waste of money, ought to call forth an indignant protest from the stockholders. Seriously it seems hard to believe that any railroad company would even consider the question of immigration and expect to spend the paltry sum of $600 or $900 on it. It is a waste of money, unless there was some one particular thing to be advertised. Such an expenditure is simply folly. The South can never attract immigration except by a very

much broader policy than that, and unless this money can be pooled with that of some other road, its use for the establishment of an immigration bureau would seem to be very unwise.

The Southward Trend of Population.

Never before was there such a general interest throughout the North and West to learn of the advantages of the South for farmers. Thousands of people in the bleak Northwest especially are preparing to move South, and the swelling tide of immigration promises to add vastly to the population and progress of this section all the way from Maryland to Texas. The railroads are all beginning to feel this, and each one is preparing to try to get a full share of this immigration movement. The Illinois Central and the Mississippi Valley Railroads have a land commissioner, Mr. E. P. Skene, located in Chicago, who has recently been in Memphis, and in an interview in the Commercial said:

The people over the North and West are beginning to turn their eyes Southward. They are tired of the rigorous winters and the severe drouths. The winters are too long. It is hard to work six months in the year to have enough to keep warm by the other six. In spite of the fact that our railroad company is holding its lands at advanced figures, it is finding plenty of purchasers. It is only a question of a few years when every portion of the Mississippi valley will be fairly teeming with life. Where virgin lands now stand the plow will trace its furrow. Forests will be replaced by towns.

Low Rates to Land Seekers.

The Southern Passenger Association has made a move which will be of the utmost benefit to the South by announcing a series of monthly low rate excursions from the North and West to Southern points. General Passenger Agent C. P. Atmore, of the Louisville & Washington, has been one of the most energetic workers to bring this about and the decision is in a measure due to his efforts. On February 8th, March 8th and April 9th tickets will be sold at one fare for the round trip by all roads having Southern connections. The time is limited to twenty days, but this is ample to give prospectors a chance to see for themselves what inducements the Southern States offer.

The greatest need of the railroads in the South is to secure settlers from the North and Northwest, as there are undoubtedly greater opportunities for successful agricultural pursuits in the South than there are in the North, and this interest pays better in the South than in any other portion of the country. The one-fare rate for the round trip is certain to draw a large number of landseekers to the South, and offers an excellent opportunity for colonization and immigration agents to arrange excursions at a small cost.

Atlanta and Its Proposed Exposition.

Of all the marvelous places for a union of energy and for public spirit, when it comes to any great undertaking calculated to add to the greatness of the city, which this country has produced, there is none greater than Atlanta. No one can study the history of Atlanta without being amazed at the power of combined effort to build up a city, for the growth of that place has been one of the wonders of the day, in that there has been no halting in the career of progress. In periods of depression following over-development, as in the great cities of the West, straight forward through bad times as well as good times the business men of Atlanta have carried forward the growth of that city.

A few weeks ago it was suggested that Atlanta ought to have a great exposition, not on such a scale as the Chicago World's Fair, of course, but something far ahead of what the South has ever had. The suggestion met a ready response. A public meeting was promptly called. Three hundred leading business men were on hand and promptly decided that such an exposition should be held. A committee of twenty-five was apppointed, with Mr. S. M. Inman, the head of probably the largest cotton house in the world, as chairman, to outline a plan. The next day the committee met, and men got up out of sick beds to attend it purely out of public spirit. No time was wasted. It was voted that Atlanta should have an international exposition in 1895, giving special attention to the South and to Central and South American exhibits; that a company should be incorporated with a minimum capital of $1,000,000, with the privilege of increasing to $5,000,000; that the charter be drawn up immediately; that a preliminary fund of $200,000 was needed, and this the committee practically pledged before it adjourned—such is the record of one week's work.

All honor to Atlanta, the typical city of the progressive South. It has undertaken a great scheme which it will carry to success, and which will prove of inestimable value to this section. The South has needed just such a grand exposition, where it can display as it has never displayed the amazing richness of its mineral and timber resources; where it can show its vast agricultural capabilities; where it can present to hundreds of thousands of visitors a concentration of all its advantages and resources for their investigation. Grand in conception, the SOUTHERN STATES predicts that it will be grander in execution, and that its value to the South will be beyond the possibility of estimating.

The committee appointed to carry out this great undertaking is as follows: Jos. Kingsberry, R. D. Spalding, Chas. A. Collier, R. B. Bullock, S. F. Woodson, Clark Howell, H. E. W. Palmer, J. G. Oglesby, E. B. Stahlman, W. A. Hemphill, H. H. Cabaniss, Anton Kontz, R. J. Lowry, J. W. English, E. P. Chamberlin, M. F. Amorous, Joseph Hirsch, W. D. Grant, J. R. Wylie, E. C. Peters, C. E. Harmon, John A. Fitten, Forrest Adair, Phil H. Harralson, Jacob Elsas, S. M. Inman.

"NATURAL advantages have ruined many a town," says a writer in the Houston Post. The truth of this admits of no question. The curse of many countries as well as of many towns has been found in the lavish gifts of nature. Countries and towns alike become imbued with the advantages of their "natural advantages" and, resting on this foundation, they go down to ruin, because "natural advantages" count for naught unless supplemented by the vigor and energy of a people who are determined to make these blessings only a means to an end. The South, more abundantly blessed by nature than any other section of our country, invites the people of less favored lands to come down and settle and take an active part in the creation of wealth by the utilization of its great natural resources. It is no longer content to boast of these advantages, but it proposes to make a vigorous effort to develop them to the fullest extent possible.

THE National Immigration and Colonization Association, of Washington, D. C., has been organized under Virginia laws for the purpose of developing the immigration business to the South from the North and West as well as from Europe. The capital stock is placed at $500,000, and Wm. T. Riggs, of Washington, D. C., is president; P. Donan, of Mississippi, vice-president, and J. W. Rarlett, of Washington, secretary. The plans of the company are on a very broad scale, and if carried out as projected, this company will soon be handling an immense business in locating settlers in the South.

MR. EDWARD ATKINSON, in a letter to the Manufacturers' Record asking for information about peanut cultivation in the South, says: "My impression is, that in the peanut, rightly treated, will be found a source of weath, now almost wholly unknown, exceeding the wealth that has been derived from the utilization of cottonseed."

TAMPA, Fla., tantalizes the dwellers in the North and West with the announcement of the "first strawberries of the season."

THE Rock Island Railroad is pushing its Texas immigration business and as one means to help on the work proposes to run excursions to Texas for homeseekers.

The general passenger department of the Missouri Pacific railway has gotten out an attractive book of ninety-six pages entitled "Texas." It is intended for free distribution, and gives a large amount of statistics and information concerning the State of Texas.

A Question for Northern and Western People.

Why should a farmer spend ten months of the year in the cold and frost cultivating wheat, when he may work in the sunshine of the South twelve months in the year, raising everything, from cotton to figs, from turnips to apples, from celery to tobacco? The idea that the Southern climate is enervating is the purest nonsense. An hour of work in the fields of the South brings greater compensation than five hours in the North. There is no economy in combating blizzards, when one may live in a country where the climate is ideal for the agriculturist. Zymotic diseases do not exist in the South, as they do in the North. The former is

far more healthy in every way. The statistics will show this. The financial depression under which the country has suffered for a year or more was much more serious in its effects in the North than in the South. The time is, therefore, ripe for the advertisement of the advantages of the South, and immigration and colonization societies snould be established in every Southern State and missionaries sent out. Such a movement would combine both business and philanthrophy.—Memphis Avalanche-Appeal.

How the Sugar Business is Growing in Louisiana.

The growth of Louisiana's sugar business has been very remarkable of late years, and referring to this the Attakapas Vindicator says of the progress in that vicinity:

"Alice C. refinery has exceed 4,000,000 pounds of sugar. That establishment expects to surpass 10,000,000 pounds this season. Ten years ago not a sugar-house in St. Mary produced 2,000,000 pounds; now the average is nearly 1000 per cent. above that of only a few years ago. Some of the sugar-houses in St. Mary are so full of sugar that moving room is scarce. Steamboats and railroads cannot take it away as fast as it is made. In many places large warehouses had to be erected so as not to prevent the establishment from shipping. A great many of our planters whose crops are larger than at first anticipated have been compelled to purchase additional quantities of fuel in the shape of large consignments of coal with which to further prosecute the process of making a large quantity of sugar from a medium amount of cane."

Fruit Culture vs. Wild Cat Stock Booming.

Tallapoosa, Georgia, which has been the subject of so much denunciation because of the fraudulent operations of the great land company that was booming the place a few years ago by wild and senseless exaggerations and deliberate misstatements, purposely made in order to let the insiders unload worthless stocks on a too confiding public—a land company, composed almost wholly of New England people, with the late Gen. Ben Butler, advertised as its president, and an ex-United States treasurer as its treasurer, is seeking to overcome the bad reputation which it has acquired. The place itself ought not to be charged with the misdoings of the land company. Tallapoosa will probably never become a great manufacturing town as the land company ceaselessly predicted, but it may become a good solid substantial town. It is in an elevated pine region, where the climate alone is almost enough to build up any place that is judiciously advertised. The adjacent country is well adapted for many kinds of fruit growing and recently this industry has received much attention. The Georgia Fruit Growing & Winery Association is pushing grape culture in that section, and, it is claimed, with much success. The company is doing a good deal of advertising and making very strong claims as to the advantages of that section for the industry, but the Tallapoosa Journal insists that all who investigate are more than satisfied. Probably there would have been no suspicion of the claims being too strong but for the memory of the old land company's unfortunate career. In this case, as in all others, a careful investigation is advisable on the part of every one contemplating an investment or a change of location. The Journal reports a number of sales of land for vineyards to outside people, including Mr. E. A. Latimer, of Springfield, Mass.; Mr. George Winderch, of Danbury, Conn.; R. E. Pines, formerly of Ceylon, India, who has settled in Tallapoosa, and Dr. J. W. Cooley, of Waynesboro, Ga.

San Antonio to the Gulf.

The San Antonio & Gulf Shore Railroad Co. proposes to build a road from San Antonio, Texas, to Velasco, through the counties of Bexar, Wilson, Gonzales, De Witt, Jackson, Wharton, Matagorda and Brazoria. The principal office will be at San Antonio. The capital stock is $2,000,000. The distance is 200 miles, and many sections through which the route is proposed have pledged subscriptions of land and money for the road. It is stated that the citizens of Matagorda county alone have $75,000 in cash to give as a bonus.

Low Rates to Southern States.

A general opportunity is afforded all who wish to see for themselves the advantages the South possesses by the action of the railroad lines in the Southern Passenger Association. A rate of one fare for the round trip will be made to purchasers of tickets on February 8th, March 8th and April 9th of this year. These tickets will be good for twenty days to all points in Kentucky, Tennessee, Alabama, Mississippi and points in Georgia as far east as Augusta, and in Florida west of River Junction. By means of this half rate prospectors for colonies and other parties of land seekers will be enabled to visit some of the most attractive sections of the South, and note by personal observation the quality of the land, the facilities for reaching market by rail and water, the climate and the general desirability for home location.

THE Hatteras whale fishery is one of the neglected industries of North Carolina, whose very lucrative profits are being reaped by New Englanders. Last July the steamer El Rio, Captain Quick, while on her regular trip from New Orleans to New York, passed through one of the whaling fleets off the Cape. The vessels were all schooners. Three had whales alongside and were cutting them up, or had whales in tow, while others were seen harpooning whales. Three lowered boats were in chase of those harpooned. The El Rio's crew saw a harpoon flash from a boat which had been pulling alongside a whale on the steamer's starboard bow, the prey went down with a great splash, only to reappear and race and race through the water, his hunters keeping pace at the end of a 500-foot line. Three hours later the vessel ran through another school of the monsters, three of which narrowly escaped collision with the vessel.

A few weeks later, on the 10th of August, Mr. Charles Hallock, the sporting author and journalist, happened to be in Provincetown when a portion of this same fleet arrived there with their fares. There were the schooner William A. Grazier, with 480 barrels of sperm oil; the George H. Phillips, with 380 barrels ditto; Baltic, 250 barrels; Rising Sun, 280 barrels; Alcyone, 300 barrels. They reported they schooner Carrie D. Knowles, with 500 barrels sperm and Sarah W. Hunt, with 350 barrels ditto, both of New Bedford—total 2540 barrels. These vessels had been out only four months in the most delectable season of the year, prosecuting without special risk an industry which has always been deemed extra hazardous, while their comrades in the Arctic were exposed to the hardship and danger of the ice during a period of two or three years. At the same time they were enriching themselves almost within sight of shore fishermen who were content with small returns, amounting to not more than $5000 in value, for porpoise fishing prosecuted in the colder months of the year.

A CONTRACT has been awarded to a Duluth firm to build a railroad sixty miles long from Pikesville, in eastern Kentucky, to Whitehall, on the Big Sandy river. The road will open up an extensive tract of valuable coal lands in Pike county which are owned by a syndicate of Duluth people.

THE Export Coal Co. of Pensacola finds its business of shipping coal from the Alabama mines steadily increasing. One contract on hand calls for 60,000 tons of coal, to be shipped from Pensacola at the rate of 5000 tons per month.

THE Caloric Reduction Co., of Blacksburg, S. C., is, according to the News, busy on its plant. The News says that the company broke ground last Monday. Brickmasons and carpenters are progressing rapidly. Materials of all character are arriving by teams and trains, and all indications point to the rapid completion of the company's first building of the extensive plant it is erecting. The completion of these works, which will comprise large fertilizing plant in connection with the crushing, concentrating and caloric reduction works, will be a valuable adjunct to the town of Blacksburg, and a forerunner of much larger and more extensive manufacturing industries, which have been attracted here by the favorable climate, railroad facilities and natural resources.

A MILL for the manufacture of woolen kerseys has been erected near Haight, Md., by the Oakland Manufacturing Co. The plant consists of a six-story building, 110 feet long by 61 feet wide, and another three stories high, 100 feet long by 40 feet wide, both for manufacturing purposes. A dyeing establishment, forty tenement houses and other necessary buildings have also been erected. Employment will be afforded to 200 hands.

J. D. HORNER, of Lumberport, W. Va., J. F. Allen, J. D. Kite, J. H. Davis, E. R. Davis and F. M. Jackson, of Clarksburg, W. Va., have incorporated the Ten-Mile Coal & Coke Co., with a capital stock of $1,000,000, for mining coal.

WORK has begun on the Chattanooga Western at the Chattanooga end of the line. The road is to be built by the Chattanooga Company, Limited, to the Walden Ridge coal fields. It will enter the city by an expensive steel bridge over the Tennessee river. English capital has been secured to aid the project,

the Chattanooga Company, Limited, being largely controlled by English people. The line will bring Chattanooga into close connections with coal fields and greatly reduce the cost of coal in that town. It is reported that the Signal Mountain Coal Co., in connection with this railroad, will develop large coal mines.

THE Gayton Coal Co. has been incorporated at Richmond Va., with a capital stock of $10,000, and privilege of increasing to $25,000, for the purpose of mining coal. John C. Haddock, of Glen Summit, Pa., is president; Ware B. Gay, of Boston, Mass., vice-president; W. J. Winegar, of Richmond, secretary, and W. S. Hurst, of Westfield, N. J., treasurer.

THE directors of the Augusta Cotton Factory, at Augusta, Ga., have declared a semi-annual dividend of 3 per cent., besides carrying a large amount to the company's surplus account.

A NEW milling combination has been formed at Nashville, Tenn., known as the Cumberland Mills Co., which controls the Union, Lanier, Nashville and American flour mills, with a combined capacity of 2,500 barrels of flour per day. The machinery in use is all of the latest patterns, and adapted to the production of the finest grades of flour. Mr. E. P. Bronson, of St. Louis, who was for seventeen years manager of the E. O. Stanard Milling Co., of that city, is the manager of this consolidated company.

In spite of the condition of business prevalent during the greater part of 1893 the dividends declared by Southern cotton mills show that this industry has been little affected by the "hard times" compared with the general industrial interests of other parts of the country. Taking a group of mills in Georgia and South Carolina, as reported by the Augusta Chronicle, the Augusta Factory, capital $600,000, paid six per cent. dividend; the Enterprise Manufacturing Co., capital $750,000, six per cent.; the Sibley Manufacturing Co., $1,000,000 capital, six per cent.; the King Manufacturing Co., $1,000,000 capital, six per cent.; the Graniteville Manufacturing Co., $600,000 capital, ten per cent. The Langley Manufacturing Co. has increased its capital during the year from $400,000 to $600,000, and will pay a semi-annual dividend of three per cent. on increased capital. The last two mills are in South Carolina.

IN reply to a letter, Mr. A. H. George, of Carrollton, Miss., writes us that he is representing a party of capitalists who intend erecting fifteen or twenty beet sugar factories in the South, if it is found, after careful tests, that the sugar beet can be grown successfully in Southern soil. The tests are to be made during the coming year and factories located afterward. Mr. George himself is of the opinion that this industry means a great deal to the country.

ONE of the most gratifying proofs of the re-established solidity and stability of business affairs in the South has been furnished, says the Philadelphia Record, by the steadiness of commercial and industrial growth during the late season of severe financial disturbance. No other part of the country has responded more promptly to improved conditions. Notwithstanding the continued low prices of such staples as cotton, iron and coal, Southern merchants, manufacturers and farmers are paying their debts as they fall due and preparing for the reaction that is sure to follow after prolonged depression.

THE Middlesborough Town Lands Co., of Middlesborough, Ky., has been reorganized as the Middlesborough Town & Lands Co., the change merely being a way in which to secure a legal assessment on the stock. This reorganization will give the company nearly $360,000 cash and put it in shape for carrying on its work of building up the town of Middlesborough. Misfortunes have followed each other in close succession at this town, but the place is by no means as dead as represented by some newspapers. It is a town with a future to it, and a very promising one, whenever the revival of the iron and steel trade justifies the starting up of its large steel plant and iron works.

THE Southern Female University is to be removed from Birmingham to Anniston, Ala., where it has secured the splendid Anniston Inn rent free for five years.

THE way in which Texas cities are growing is shown by statistics recently compiled in Fort Worth. The directory publishers estimate that its population is now about 32,000. According to the United States census of 1890 it was 22,078 in that year. This is a gain of 10,000 in three years. Bradstreet's reports 650 firms doing business in the city, compared with 585 in January, 1893.

THE Potts Valley Furnace & Mining Co., has been chartered at Charleston, W. Va., to mine iron and other ores, and to manufacture. The incorporators are O. S. Long, D. C. Gallagher, E. B. Dyer, J. M. Payne and Philip Frankenberger. The capital stock is $10,000, with privilege of increasing to $500,000.

THE new cotton mill of the Dilling Manufacturing Co., now building at King's Mountain, N. C., is to produce print cloths, and is the third mill of its kind in the South this year to be equipped by the Charlotte Machine Co., aggregating 25,000 spindles and 600 looms. The South is gradually diversifying the character of its cotton manufactures and producing finer goods.

THE development of the sugar interests of Louisiana under the bounty system has been wonderfully rapid, giving promise of the magnitude which this industry will reach unless crippled by unwise tariff laws. New Orleans has already received this season over 1,000,000 barrels, a gain of 243,000 barrels over the same time last year. The Times-Democrat estimates that the full crop will be at least 1,300,000 barrels, or 600,000,000 pounds, which will be the largest yield on record. Unfortunately this great industry is threatened with injury, if not destruction, by the Wilson bill, unless it is defeated or amended.

ROANOKE, VA., is one of the Southern cities which keeps pace with the times in the matter of public improvements. Of the total amount of over ten miles of sewers which have been laid in the city at a cost of about $60,000, by far a larger percentage of it was laid during the year 1893 than in any previous year. Contracts have been let for about five miles more of sewerage. Within the past eighteen months over eight miles of macademizing have been done upon the streets at a cost of about $78,500, or $9,800 per mile. The year 1893 has witnessed the completion of four public buildings and many improvements on other public buildings and property. The aggregate cost of these buildings amounts to $39,969.51. During 1893 electricity was substituted for lighting the streets in place of gas. The lights are now furnished by the Roanoke Electric Light & Power Co. at an annual cost to the city of $9,161.60.

WESTERN grain men have commenced to ship via Port Royal, one of the coming ports of the South, which has one of the finest harbors in the world. A week or two ago thirty-seven carloads or about 25,000 bushels of grain were shipped from Kansas City via the Kansas City, Fort Scott & Memphis Railway to Port Royal, S. C., for foreign export. This grain was sold by Messrs. Davidson & Smith to a firm in Liverpool. It was routed by the Kansas City, Fort Scott & Memphis to Memphis, Tenn.; Kansas City, Memphis & Birmingham to Birmingham, Ala.; Georgia Pacific to Atlanta, Ga,; Georgia Railway to Augusta, Ga.; Port Royal & Augusta Railway ᵗo Port Royal, S. C., and Johnston Line of steamers from Port Royal to Liverpool. This roᵘ te will shorten by many miles and many hours the distance between Kansas City and Liverpool.

THE phosphate industry of Florida is rapidly developing and becoming one of the great industries of the country. The following table shows the shipments from all ports in Florida and Georgia, giving also shipments by railroad and amount used in home consumption, with the comparative figures for 1892:

Point of Shipment.	1893. Long Tons	1892. Long Tons
Fernandina......................	126,694	125,012
Tampa......	104,407	70,214
Punta Gorda	88,467	63,123
Savannah, Ga	36,507	7,412
Brunswick, Ga	8,000	18,061
Railroads†......................	20,000	23,300
Consumed in Florida........	7,000	4,000
Total tons..................	391,075	311,122

†Estimated.

THE Bessemer Mining Company, of Bessemer City, N. C., is making extensive investigations on its property, having expended $15,000 since last April in opening up numerous veins of ore and in putting down shafts. The company lately voted $18,000 with which to continue its operations. Mr. Julian Carr of Durham, the head of the great Durham Bull tobacco house, is president of the mining company, while among the stockholders are some prominent Michigan capitalists interested in Lake Superior ores.

THE Florida Mining & Chemical Co., of Tampa, lately incorporated, expects to begin operations at that city about the 15th of January. It is stated that the capital stock is $1,000,000. A lease has been secured from the State for the right to mine phosphate from the east half of Lake Hancock, in Polk county. The company will use the old plant of the Tampa Phosphate Co. in Tampa for grinding and mixing the fertilizers. The capitalists interested in this company reside in New York and Charleston, S. C., fully one-third of the stock having been taken by large phosphate dealers in Charleston.

IT is reported that the Lake Drummond Canal & Water Co. of Norfolk, Va., formerly the Dismal Swamp Canal Co., will make extensive improvements to the canal by opening it to a length of twenty-two miles, sixty feet wide and ten feet deep, with locks 250 by forty feet at each terminus, at an estimated cost of $1,500,000.

· REAL ESTATE NEWS.

J. K. NORTON and L. C. Bailey lately purchased for $20,000 eighteen acres of land adjoining Alexandria, Va. The land will be sub-divided and improved.

J. M. KNOX, an extensive land owner along the line of the Rock Island railway, of Lincoln, Neb., and Fred Bush, of Bellville, Kan., a capitalist, have lately been in Texas with a view, it is reported, of investing in real estate.

A GENERAL improvement is reported in real estate interests in Fort Worth, Texas, and this is not confined to city property, but extends to farm lands in the adjacent counties. The Fort Worth Gazette has been interviewing a number of agents, all of whom report increased activity, and a number of them mention sales of farms to people who are moving in from other States.

Mr. W. R. Sanner thinks that the prospects are better than for the last three years and he has inquiries now from a number of Eastern people who contemplate investing in Texas property.

Mr. John A. Thornton reports that he has done more business in one week than previously for a month, and regards the prospects as more promising than for years. He has many letters of enquiry from outside people, and has just sold a large tract to one man.

SAN ANTONIO, Texas, is enjoying quite a revival in real estate matters since the money market has eased up. Improved and unimproved property is in better demand with quite an increase in the enquiry from Northern and Western people. For small farms there is said to be a big demand.

SPEAKING of real estate matters in New Orleans, Mr. Robinson, of Robinson & Underwood, said that the prospects for real estate this season are excellent. The solidity of the local banks and the general feeling of finan-

cial confidence that prevailed here during last summer's general distress has, he thinks, much to do with the present condition of the market. Numerous letters received by the firm recently show this to be the case, and the fact that this city is considered a good place to invest money is shown by the fact that the firm expects a delegation of gentlemen representing a syndicate of several millions of dollars to come here in a short time and make investments if they can secure satisfactory figures.

MESSRS. SWAYNE & ALLEN, referring to the real estate outlook at Fort Worth, say that the prospect for better times, while it does not indicate anything of a boom, is more encouraging than some time. Every indication is promising and a number of inquires are being made for property by outside investors. Good times are anticipated for Fort Worth and Texas during 1894.

MR. P. A. HUFFMAN, of Fort Worth, is quite enthusiastic over the outlook and reports that he has talked more business and effected more transfers the past two weeks than for the twelve preceding months. "I have," he says, "closed a number of important deals, both in the city and country, and now have several important transactions pending. Last week I sold a Tarrant county farm to a gentleman from Nebraska, and will soon close a sale with several other new-comers from Tennessee and Kentucky for farm property. There is any amount of demand for Texas property."

MR. SCHULTZ, cashier of the State National Bank, of Sedalia, Mo., has bought a business property in Fort Worth, Texas, for $10,000.

DURING 1893 there were 2450 new buildings erected in Baltimore. These figures give some indication of the great growth of this city, but they do not begin to tell the full story. Few cities in America are making more rapid progress in industrial development, in street railway construction, and in all else that combine to build up a great city ; but as yet this wonderful advance has had but comparatively little effect upon real estate values, and prices generally are not very much higher than before this new era of progress commenced a few years ago. The coming spring and summer will, it is believed, show a very decided increase in real estate matters.

MR. PARKER P. SMITH, of Jeannette, Pa., says that he would like to correspond with land owners in the South as he knows of a number of families who want to remove to that section.

L. M. DISNEY, agent of the Brazoria Land & Cattle Co. has sold over 10,000 acres of land near Alvin, Texas, to the Southern Homestead Co., which has been organized for the purpose of br nging in settlers to take up this land in small tracts.

THE Brownstone farm, two miles from Princess Anne, Md., was lately sold to Powell Brothers, of Shadeland, Pa., owners of what is said to be the largest stock farm in the United States. The price paid was $14,000.

THE bondholders of the East Carolina Land & Lumber Co. have purchased 173,000 acres of land, located in Dare county, N. C., belonging to the company.

MAJOR FRANK Y. ANDERSON, general land commissioner of the Queen & Crescent railroad system at Birmingham, has lately sold $100,000 worth of timber lands in Ouachita parish, La., to French capitalists.

MR. C. C. ROBERTSON, a real estate agent of Jacksonville, Fla., reports that J. H. Spring, of Philadelphia, has lately purchased between $30,000 and $40,000 of Florida property.

THE Robert Morris Land Co. has been chartered at Logan C. H., W. Va., for the purpose of developing coal mines and other mineral properties in Kentucky and West Virginia. The principal stockholders are S. D. Freshman, Audrian Vandevever, Alexander Boguy, George E. Walters and Teofilo Gimbernot, all of New York State.

OWING to the demand for dwellings at North Danville, Va., which, it is expected, will follow the completion next spring of the enlargement of the Riverside Mills, a company is to be organized to build houses there. It is reported that from 1000 to 1500 new hands will be employed.

THE Tennessee & Kentucky Land & Immigration Co., of Memphis and Paducah, has been incorporated by. Wm. L. Hull, of St. Louis, Mo.; Walter J. Hills, of Paducah, Ky.; George M. McFadden, of Kansas City, Mo.; Pitkin C. Wright, of* Somerville, Tenn.; Lee J. Lockwood, of Memphis, and Isaac O. Walker, of Paris, Tenn.

NEW ORLEANS BUILDING ACTIVITY.—The city of New Orleans is attracting more and more capital by the opportunities it presents for real-estate investment. One syndicate, in which Henry Maltby, a St. Paul (Minn.) architect, is interested, has secured ground, it is reported, for a hotel which is to cost $1,000,000. Of this sum it is expected that $800,000 will be furnished by people outside of the city. Still another company is reported to be planning a hotel to cost $1,000,000, to be erected by Chicago capital. The Liverpool & London & Globe Insurance Co. announces its intention of constructing an office building of the most modern type in the heart of the city, while the Morris Building and Land Improvement Association has had plans prepared for a 10-story building for offices, to be. fire-proof throughout and built after the most approved ideas in architecture. The Grunewald Hotel, nearly completed, will be another addition to the list of modern structures completed or to be built in the city. It will contain between 100 and 150 rooms and is to have all the appointments of a first-class resort.

NICHOLAS P. BOND, Hugh L. Bond, Jr., George Morris Bond, Thomas E. Bond, and Thomas M. Maynadier, all of Baltimore, have incorporated in that city the Mount Royal Construction Co. for the purpose of dealing in and improving land. The capital stock is $60,000.

MR. TULTO GORDON, of Laurel, Md., has sold 136 lots to Washington people.

ACTIVE work has been commenced upon the construction of the double track electric railway between Washington and Baltimore. This line will be about 30 miles in length or about ten miles shorter than the Baltimore & Ohio road between these two cities. The moneyed men who are building this line are

Mr. P. A. B. Widener and Wm. L. Elkins, of Philadelphia, and Mr. T. Edward Hambleton David Newbold, of Baltimore, and others. It is practically a part of the great system of roads owned both in Baltimore and Washington by the Traction syndicate. It is expected that the building of this line will open up and develop a wide stretch of country between these two cities, and that it will not be many years before there is practically almost a continuous settlement along the entire line. The remarkable growth of Baltimore in manufactures and the steady advancement of Washington justify the construction of such an electric line and assure a very active settlement of the country through which it passes. It is said that the road will cost about $3,000,000.

A DISPATCH from Augusta, Ga., announces that George Doleton, of Washington, D. C., has purchased a tract of land in the suburbs and will convert it into a cemetery to be called Rose Hill.

THE determination of Atlanta to have a great exposition in 1895, and the prompt subscription of $200,000 as a preliminary fund has awakened a lively interest in real estate matters, and agents report that deals which were hanging fire are being promptly closed up. The Constitution has been interviewing some of the real estate men, and from these reports the SOUTHERN STATES condenses the following points:

Mr. E. P. Black says that the immediate effect of this exposition surprises him. "The condition of affairs in the real estate market," he said, "which I take it is the best possible indication of the general business condition, has very greatly improved since this exposition movement has been st rted. There are very many more inquiries and holders of property are not nearly as anxious to sell as they were a few days ago."

Captain J. C. H ndrix said: "We are feeling it already. It seems impossible that that should be the case, but a very decidedly better tone prevails. We have had in the last five days more inquiries from would-be purchasers than we have in three times that long before."

W. A. Osborn said : "We see evidences of a decided improvement. Several deals that I know of which have been hanging fire for some days have been consummated since this movement has assumed definite shape. There is no business which gives quite so accurate

an idea of business in general of a community as this. The want of confidence which has been manifest for some time past seems to be passing away and things already are better and brighter."

E. M. Roberts: "We already feel the effects of it and there is a decided change for the better in our lines. The market has already brightened up very perceptibly and we are in receipt of many inquiries. This is, however, just the first strike of the good times that are coming in the near future. I believe the next two years will show a wonderful improvement and I believe the first steps towards Atlanta's reaching a greatness which it would seem foolhardy to claim now, but everybody in Atlanta has confidence in Atlanta and as long as that keeps up and we all pull together as we are going to pull on this exposition the result is bound to be beneficial."

Colonel George W. Adair: "There is no doubt that an exposition will do a vast amount of good to the city, in fact we won't have to wait until the exposition comes. There has unquestionably been a better tone in the real estate market since that meeting at the Chamber of Commerce and it has grown better each day with the increasing confidence that the exposition was a certainty. I myself could tell you a half dozen good trades that have been hanging fire, but which have been consummated since that time and the consummation of which, I am positive, was due very largely indeed to the exposition."

Colonel Samuel W. Goode : "We people in the real estate business know, perhaps, better than anybody else the benefits which accrue from bringing people in large numbers to the city. We in Atlanta have seen it in every exposition we have held and we have seen it in the history of every similar enterprise in the country. Why, every foot of ground in Chicago increased in value from the time there was a probability of the great World's Fair being held there. That increase is not fictitious, because the values will be retained. It was so with the cotton exposition here and you will find that it will be so to a much greater extent with the exposition we are to hold, as it is, international in scope and necessarily bringing here people from all over the world.

"I believe that right now the attention of capital is directed toward the South. We have, all of us, felt the business strain of the past few months, but we have felt it less than they have in any other section of the country, and in New York the splendid way in which the South weathered the storm has attracted the very general attention among the Northern capitalists."

"Atlanta," said Colonel A. J. West, "feels the effects of this exposition already. A better sentiment prevails, confidence has been restored and there has been unquestionably a livening up of matters in real estate business, especially since this exposition movement was inaugurated."

Mr. Frank Rice reported that "a better tone already prevailed. There are more purchasers and a great many more inquiries and everybody feels better. The good which these expositions do to Atlanta simply cannot be estimated. The people will come from all over the country and every one who comes will be a walking advertisement for Atlanta. A great many will unquestionably invest money in the South, and especially here. We are on the eve of better times and capital is going to be attracted towards the South."

W. M. Scott, in answer to the question as to the effect on real estate said : "Oh, I see the effect already. Why, I have just made a sale which two weeks ago I could not have made. I have in my hand papers of another one which has been hanging fire for several weeks, but the minute the exposition movement took practital shape the purchaser made up his mind he wanted the property and sent me word. I can tell you that in real estate circles there is a very much stronger tone and there is every indication of a lively market. People who have property are not near as anxious to sell, because they know everything is going to be better and livelier from now on, and the values are going to be very greatly enhanced."

SAN ANTONIO, Texas, issued 1102 building permits during 1893. The reported cost of the buildings, although far below nominal cost, was given at $662,335.

IN Cumberland, Md., 355 permits for new houses were issued in 1893, many of which were fine brick houses.

IMMIGRATION NEWS.

A Good Work in Texas.

The Southern Homestead Co. has been organized in Texas, with headquarters at Houston, by Messrs. L. Christensen and Wm. Wilcox, formerly of Chicago, and Mr. E. H. Porter, formerly of Galveston, and others. This company has purchased over 10,000 acres of land near Alvin, Texas, and will, according to the Alvin Sun, immediately put the land in shape for settlement. Contracts have been let for several miles of road grading and ditching. A fine graded road will be constructed around and through each section of 640 acres with a drainage ditch along one side of each road. Arrangements are now being completed for the establishing of a station on the land about four miles north of Alvin. The land will be sub-divided into tracts' of ten, twenty and forty acres each, with a forty foot graded road to each tract. It is the intention of the company to sell out the land in these tracts to settlers, and the arrangements made for good roads, drainage, etc., are worthy of careful study by others who own large bodies of land which they are anxious to settle up with thrifty farmers.

The South to Command Immigration.

Mr. H. L. Rogers, of Ohio, says: The South is attracting much attention in the North and West and the tide of immigration and capital will be to the South during the next few years. The West is conquered for the present at least, and everything has been overdone there, and the South certainly furnishes the best opening for the capitalist now. All that you people have to do to get both the capitalist and immigrant is to properly represent the advantages and splendid resources of the South.

The South has infinitely superior advantages over the West. It has almost inexhaustible mineral and timber resources. The West has little timber. The South has an established home market nearby, and all the markets of the foreign world are accessible through nearby ports, while the transportation on Western products to the consumer amounts to more than the cost of production.

An Excursion to Georgia.

The Macon (Ga.) Advertising and Information Bureau has taken an important step by arranging an excursion, which will start from Richmond, Ind., on February 13. Agents of the bureau are now working in Richmond and vicinity, and it is expected that between 600 and 1,000 would-be settlers will take advantage of the special rates and other inducements to come to Macon and see for themselves the advantages Georgia offers to home seekers. The Indiana papers are freely noticing the movement and giving it a liberal advertisement. The eagerness of the people to know about the South, and the readiness with which they agree to join the excursion party surprises even those at the head of the bureau.

THE rapid development of Port Royal now in progress will open up that district for trucking business and a letter from there says: "There is no better opening in all this country for truck farming than is to be found around Port Royal and Beaufort just now. The finest land for that purpose may now be bought at reasonable prices, right along the railroads, and on the banks of the rivers, where every convenience is offered for shipping all kinds of produce, and there is money in it."

Come to Georgia.

Disappointed farmers of the Northwest, who have suffered from the severe climate and have been unable to sell their products at living prices, are anxious to leave that section. An exchange says:

"Dakota farmers are turning longing eyes towards the East. A party of farmers from

705

Dakota are visiting Maryland with a view to settling there. All of them are land owners in South Dakota, but anxious to locate in the East, if they can be suited. They were originally from New England, and were induced to go West by the low prices of land and fair promises of success made. The severe climate of the far West has discouraged them, together with the low prices of farm products and the heavy transportation charges in reaching markets. The average price of wheat in South Dakota is 44 cents, corn 23 cents and hay $4 per ton."

These are the sort of people that Georgia needs, and that she could get if we had any organized colonization society. These farmers from the East and the Scandinavians, of whom Dr. Pope writes in his letter, which we published yesterday, have been greatly disappointed in the Northwest because of the scarcity and high price of fuel, and the long cold season, which requires heavy expenditures along the line. These same people, if brought to Georgia, would grow rich, and be delighted with the climate where they could work the whole year round in the open air.

The other day we published that Colorado had raised a fund of a quarter of a million of dollars to be expended in attracting immigration to that State, and everywhere the people are awaking to the fact that if citizens are wanted they must be gone after in a practical way. It does us no good to know that Georgia is a garden spot where industrious and intelligent application will repay the effort, unless the knowledge moves us to take some practical steps to bring this fact to the attention of those we would attract. We must not content ourselves with saying Georgia offers great inducements to settlers; we must convince the people of this fact whom we would secure as settlers. We must work as well as pray.—Augusta (Ga.) Chronicle.

THE Illinois Central Railroad is pursuing a very vigorous policy in its efforts to make known the attractions of the South to Western farmers, with the na'ural result that it is turning a great tide of immigration Southward just as any other Southern railroad can do when it pursues the same course with equal energy and discretion. On one day last month Mr. J. A. White, the traveling passenger agent of that road stationed at Cedar Rapids, Iowa, to work for immigration, took seventy-five home-seekers to points along the line from Jackson, Tenn., to Jennings, La. These are reported as well-to-do people who are looking for Southern homes.

G. W. McGANIS, land commissioner of the Mississippi Valley Railroad. with headquarters at Memphis, has sent throughout the country a number of maps and pamphlets descriptive of the Mississippi valley country, and offering settlers extra inducements to come South and buy homes.

MR. R. B. CHAFFIN, of Richmond, has sold an 800-acre farm in Amelia county, fronting on the Appomattox river, with 200 acres of river and creek flats, to Mr. John J. Cairns, of Washington county, Pa., for $18,500. Mr. Cairns proposes to bring about 200 Southdown sheep and make this a stock farm.

COL. OLOF BERGSTROM, of Omaha, Neb., who has had wide experience in immigration and real estate matters, having some years ago been land agent for the Union Pacific Railroad, has lately been making a careful investigation of Texas, with a view to turning immigration to that State. One of the enterprises on which he is figuring is the purchase of a 12,000-acre tract of land in Tarrant county, to be cut up into 100 and 200-acre farms and settled by Western people.

IMMIGRANTS are reported as arriving in Brazoria county, Texas, every few days, singly and in families, and it is said that immigrant trains are seen which must have depopulated entire communities. In nearly every instance these parties bring with them wagons, teams and farming implements. A great deal of new land is being enclosed and cleared, and several old farms in the neighborhood not worked since the war are being reclaimed and dedicated to corn and cotton.

JUDGE H. MASTERSON, of Brazoria, Texas, has bought a large plantation for $20,000, which he wishes to colonize by cutting up into small farms.

THE tide of immigration to Texas is said to be greater than it has been for years.

A PARTY of Illinois farmers under escort of P. R. Peterson, representing the Union Land Co., of Chicago, lately passed through Little Rock on their way to Prairie county. The party represented 250 families, mostly Russians, many of whom have been farming in this country for several years. They are in Arkansas to look at lands with the view of locating there. The Union Land Co. is said to be a large and wealthy concern, owning land in Arkansas and several other States. The company has already carried a number of families to that State from the Northwest, and Mr. Peterson, the agent, expects to place 300 families on Arkansas lands between now and spring.

MR. R. O. BEAN, traveling passenger agent of the Southern Pacific, with headquarters at Nashville, Tenn., lately passed through New Orleans with a party of sixty immigrants en route to Texas. He says that these immi- grants are going to Texas by the hundreds to settle. They do not go there to work for wages, but to buy or rent land and settle down. There is a great deal of State land in Texas lying idle, and these immigrants are taking advantage of this while they can get the land cheap, and are leaving other States where the land is higher and the work is harder to get. These immigrants are coming in by the Illinois Central, the Queen & Crescent, the Louisville & Nashville and go out on the Southern Pacific.

DR. O. A. HOUGHTON, of Syracuse, New York, says of the sentiment in his section : "Men who would not listen to talk about the coast country of Texas one year ago are now making their arrangements to come down. The cold-headed fellows, who talk cold- blooded business and never mix sentiment with financial transactions, are investigating Texas."

MANY Western farmers have lately been attracted to Plaquemines parish and several purchases of farms and homes have recently been recorded. A Colorado farmer who has just secured a farm there will cultivate vege- tables and flowers for the New Orleans market. He also proposes going into the culture of poppies, from which to extract opium for the public market.

THE Baltimore & Ohio Railroad Co., through M. V. Richards, land and immigrant agent, has lately sold a 300-acre tract of land in Hampshire county, Va., to a party of people from Western Pennsylvania. The purchasers are farmers who think the land especially adapted to their work and will settle upon it in a short time. They report that many other families are desirous of removing to the same locality in Virginia if land can be purchased at a reasonable price.

MR. J. A. P. MASON, of Deer Lodge, Tenn., proposes to visit Michigan, Wisconsin and Minnesota to try to draw settlers to the Cum- berland plateau of Tennessee.

HON. PATRICK WALSH, Col. D. B. Dyer and others of Augusta, Ga., expect to organize an immigration land company to purchase or secure control of large bodies of land for the purpose of settling it up with Northern and Western farmers.

MR. LOUIS PIO, immigration agent of the East coast line of Florida, has lately estab- lished a new colony on the St. Lucie river. He has already secured twenty-three families.

WHILE New Orleans has never been much of an immigration port as compared with Northern cities, there is considerable immi- gration there from abroad and more is looked for this season than in any former years. Commissioner S. A. Montgomery says that he finds the immigrants to be an intelligent class of laborers and artisans, and that they are, on the whole, desirable citizens. Cooks, garden- ers and mechanics are in the ascendancy from a standpoint of numbers. The steamship Havre, from Bordeaux and Marseilles, arrived lately with forty-six passengers who will set- tle in this country and a great many of them in New Orleans, if they can find employment in their respective lines. The steamship Break- water from Livingston, Belize, and Puerto Cortez brought forty-eight passengers. Twenty- seven of them were laborers and the others engineers and skilled mechanics.

WINTER immigration to Texas has com- menced. Forty-four immigrants arrived in Fort Worth one day and forty-seven were expected the following day. On their arrival they stopped over in the city a few hours and left in the evening in several different direc- tions. Mr. T. N. Bradburn, railway immigra- tion agent, says Texas is all the talk, and that thousands of immigrants would arrive there this winter.

MR. W. C. MOORE, of Liberty, Texas, writing to the Houston *Post* gives an inter- esting account of the rapid improvement of that town and the surrounding country. It is said that there is not a vacant house in the town, and the farming country surrounding the place is developing so rapidly as to insure a continuance of this prosperity. Immigrants are coming in almost every day and unloading their outfits at every railroad station, many of them from Iowa and other Western States. Rice culture is being pushed, and lands that were bought for five dollars an acre have yielded a profit this year of twenty-five dollars to thirty dollars an acre.

MR. J. P. GREIG, of Hockley, Texas, has sold his farm of 1300 acres to Messrs. Kerr, late of Illinois, for $10 per acre. Messrs. Kerr will put in a crop of canyagre root, a Mexican plant somewhat resembling the sweet potato and used in tanning the finer grades· of leather.

Mr. MATTHEWS, of Illinois, who recently purchased the Schleup place, near Hockley, Texas, is a practical farmer and stockman and carried with him some fine breeds of cattle, sheep, hogs, turkeys, geese and chickens.

MR. S. L. CAREY, general Western agent of the Southern Pacific, with headquarters at Manchester, Ia., lately took sixteen families from Iowa at one time to St. Charles and Lafayette La., and points between to buy homes and to settle along the line of the Southern Pacific Railroad.

MR. THOMAS WHITEHEAD, State Commissioner of Agriculture of Virginia, says: Our correspondence is simply immense. Already several parties have located upon Virginia soil and others have been here looking around for suitable property to purchase. Most of the immigrants are from the Northwest.

AN excursion of thirty-five arrived in New Orleans lately over the Queen & Crescent Railroad and left in the afternoon over the South· ern Pacific for points in Texas, where many of them will become permanent settlers.

REPORTS from Lexington, Va., say there is manifest in many sections of the Union an interest in the Valley of Virginia lands, and especially in this neighborhood. There are a large number of inquiries booked with real estate men from parties in the far Northwest, who want to come here for fruit, stock and grape-raising, while others want to locate near Lexington's fine schools.

TARRANT county, Texas, is rapidly settling up, and County Surveyor Goodfellow reports an unusual number of sales of real estate being made in the county at present. His force of surveyors are now behind in the work they are called upon to do. Mr. Goodfellow says as an illustration that Mr. S. C. Neill, of Mansfield, who recently owned 2000 or 3000 acres of land in the extreme southeastern part of this county, has in the last year sold all of this land in small farms at an average price of $20 an acre, and all these farms are now occupied by industrious farmers. On a recent trip Mr. Goodfellow counted from the top of a small mound eighteen new farmhouses that represented so many families now in possession who were not there a year or so ago.

OYSTER SLOOP RETURNING HOME.

MOBILE IN MIDSUMMER.

When I announced to my friends in the middle ·of last summer that I was going on a trip to the South and should visit the Gulf Coast, I was overwhelmed by a storm of protests. To go South in the month of August, and particularly to go to a place on the coast like Mobile, which I had stated would be my objective point, seemed to them to be little short of committing suicide. I was expected to perish in the scorching heat, and even if my case-hardened hide should withstand this test, I was sure to have every variety of fever and other diseases popularly supposed to be lying in wait for the foolish stranger who visits the Gulf in summer time. In spite of these warnings and the conduct of one of my companions, who solemnly measured me from head to foot "to get

a coffin of the proper size," he said, I packed my belongings, boarded the train and in due time, after a pleasant and comfortable trip was deposited in the early morning in the streets of Mobile.

Breakfast had not yet been announced when I reached the hotel, and while trying to make the best of the *mauvais quart d'heure*, which lay between me and the morning meal, I struck up a speaking acquaintance with a gentleman who, I discovered later, was the "traveling representative," or, as popularly known, drummer, for a New York firm. My new friend was very communicative, and I took advantage of this to draw out some information about the place.

"What do I know of Mobile?" said he, in answer to my question. "Well I guess I ought to know a good deal about it since my business has brought me here twice a year for the past ten years. Now I want to tell you something: People say Mobile is dead, no business and no get up about it, but they're way off. Why before the war Mobile was the largest shipping port in the South, and hundreds of vessels used to come up here and load cotton for the Northern markets and Europe. At that time, the largest private banking concerns in the country were located here, and the town did an amount of business that would astonish you. New Orleans simply wasn't in it. Every rich planter in this part of the country had to have a residence in Mobile or he wasn't in the swim, and, of course, society was represented by the best people in the country. Literature, art, music and all that sort of thing were cultivated, and to say that you were from Mobile was the same thing as now saying you're from Boston ; only nobody ever said Mobile people were made of ice. Of course the war busted things higher than Gilderoy's kite. Instead of the regular commerce, people took to blockade running, and what's more, they did it so well that the North couldn't stop it until the city was finally captured, though every effort was made to do so. You know the Confederate government regarded Mobile as such an important point that they literally filled the bay with torpedoes and every other conceivable obstruction, and right across the head, where the rivers run into the bay, they placed a double row of heavy piles, the top driven just under the water and sloping toward the south so as to sink anything that might come against them. On one side a passage

was left so that blockade runners could come in, but even this was risky business on account of the torpedoes. On the other side of the bay old Spanish Fort made things lively for Farragut when he came up to take the city, and after it had completely upset his plans and raised thunder until the materials played out, its garrison quietly departed, escaping the land forces which had come to help the navy. The funny part is that the Union forces were so afraid of the place that they didn't dare to tackle it for some time after it was empty. So far as its history is concerned, Mobile don't give odds to any town. Just chase around this section for a while and you can easily fill yourself up with history and not a few old relics, if you like that sort of thing, dating anywhere from the seventeenth century to now. Spanish, French and English have been here and each has left his tracks.

"About the city now ? Well, after the war things were terribly flat, and because of the obstructions still in the bay and damage done to business in general, recovery was awful slow. Why, even in 1870, there wasn't enough life in the streets to frighten a rat, so they tell me. But after that things commenced to mend a little, only New

A QUIET DAY ON THE GULF.

Orleans and other ports had drawn off the cotton trade, so there wasn't much they could do here. One thing they did get into was the lumber business, and this has been growing steadily until now it is about the largest of any port on the coast. The real improvement, though, has been in the last four or five

"Is it healthy? Now I know you haven't been here before! Why, Mobile has the record of being a remarkably healthy city. That's not just guess, but a matter of record, and in my opinion one reason for it can be found in the fine water supplied to the city. It's just about as pure as water is made.

TERRAPIN FEEDING.

years. Why, in that time business has almost doubled, and do you know what I lay it to? The little truck gardens that have been springing up all around. They tell me that some of those truck gardeners make as high as $200 net from one acre, and only have to work a few months in spring to do that. It's a regular soft snap, and there don't seem to be any end to it. The more that go into it, the easier it seems to be to dispose of their truck. All the railroads here run special trains to carry the truck North, and every day in the season they go out loaded. Then the sea trade is coming up again. A lot of coasting steamers stop here now, and two lines run to Nicaragua and one to Columbia, bringing in fruit for Chicago and St. Louis. Besides, there is a regular line of steamers running to Cuba and another to Mexico. All this has been bringing money in town, and general business has increased tremendously.

Now, I suppose, since you've never been here before, you expect to find the thermometer up around 200 all day. You're going to get left on that. I've seen the thermometer here at 97° in the shade sometimes, and that is the hottest it has been here for years, but the average for the past five years won't be much over 80° for August, and September is usually a little cooler. Even when it is hot here you don't feel it much. In the day there is always a nice breeze blowing, generally from the north in the morning and from the south in the afternoon and evening, and I have yet to find a warm night here. This place is way up top so far as that sort of thing is concerned. Now, if you want to see something of the town, just get on the electric cars and make a round trip and you'll surprise yourself."

By the time our meal was over, for part of the conversation was carried on at the table, I felt that I had learned something, and the sensation of being a possible martyr out on a pleasure trip had entirely left me.

The night before I had met on the train the sheriff of Mobile and a number of other county officials returning from the World's Fair, and we got to talking about fishing. I have been on a good many fishing excursions and am generally accounted a fairly good hand to keep my end up when the time comes to tell about them, but my stories were no where when heard alongside those which the sheriff and his companions recounted. For their benefit I fished pretty nearly everywhere in the country where I knew they had not been, and they, with one accord, lay the scene of their exploits in one place, even particularizing the locality which was around Cedar Point in Mobile bay and Mississippi sound. Down there they had caught red fish, sheepshead, pompano, bass, herring, mullet and a dozen other kinds of fish, many of which I didn't know even by name. The great game fish of the world (tarpon) was found there at all times, and drum fish, stingaries, porpoises, sharks and other monsters of the

A FAIR SAMPLE OF DIAMOND-BACK TERRAPIN.

deep could be found by merely whistling for them. The bay was literally alive with turtles of all kinds, from the savory diamond-back terrapin up to the mammoth turtle as big as a small island, and these walked over a solid pavement of oysters which covered the bottom of the entire bay. The enumeration of wonders

completely stunned me, and when I was finally invited to go down to this enchanted region and spend a week with the sheriff's father, I accepted with an alacrity which was more an earnest of my desire to go than of proper observance of social customs.

So that as soon as I had eaten breakfast I left my communicative drummer friend and started out to look up the sheriff. He was easily found, and arrangements for my visit to his father's house the next morning was quickly made. I was installed *pro tempore* one of the crew of the Governor Stone, an oyster schooner bound from Mobile to Cedar Point; distance thirty miles.

With a light breeze from the north we slipped slowly down the river past wharves where lay steamers and ships loading or discharging their cargoes, on by the great lumberyards and soon turned into the channel leading to the bay, silently stealing by the grim-looking snags which lined its sides, on to the lighthouse and then through the gap cut by the government in the double line of piles driven to keep intruders out of the city. Passing these we were out in the open bay, and as the wind had freshened we bowled along, the sails spread out like two great wings and the waters curling and hissing along the sides and under the stern.

Take a map of Alabama and look at the long broad stretch of open water leading to the Gulf. At the southwest corner of this bay, where it connects with Mississippi sound, there is a large island formed by Fowl river, and at the extreme south end of this land, which was named by the early settlers Mon Louis Island, a little promontory juts out between the bay and the sound, and right on the end of this there is a settlement called Cedar Point, the chief feature of which is a store, and this store was my destination. Our advent here about noon caused the usual commotion, and I received a cordial welcome from my kind host, which, supplemented by a hearty meal, made me feel as thoroughly at home as though I had always lived there. After dinner I adjourned to the gallery in front of the store both to enjoy the comforting pipe and to make the acquaintance of the "population," which was assembled in full force.

The following day was to be the first of the oyster season, and boats had been cleaned and their bottoms painted, and tongs and other tools polished up in readiness for the busy season. However, while all interest centered on oysters I found no difficulty in drawing out sufficient information about fishes and fishing to confirm me in the belief that while some of the largest fish in the country might live in these waters, the climate certainly bred the most startling fish stories.

But this day and the several following it were too full of pleasures and new experiences to attempt to detail them. There was so much to see that, enthusiastic fisherman as I am, this sport was left untried. One day I'd sail across the sound to Dauphine island, which for fourteen miles protects the inland waters from the fury of the Gulf storms, and walk through the forest of great pines to the Gulf side and climb the hills of sand blown up from the shore until they have covered the pine trees, leaving only the feathered tops standing above. From these hills one looks far out into the deep, blue waters of the Gulf, sometimes freckled white by the wind. What a gorgeous place it is for a plunge in the surf! The houses are all on the north shore of the island, and here is a beach fourteen miles long, of hard, fine dazzling white sand sloping gently down to the water line where the waves curl up and rush hissing

PINE TREES ON DAUPHINE ISLAND.

and curling in their spent force as the water flows back ready for another trial. I hope this beach may never be desecrated by a summer hotel and "board walk," but it is too enticing to escape. To sit in the cool shade of the pine trees enjoying their balsam fragrance, while the wind is whispering secrets through their tops, and look out over this beautiful beach with the never-ceasing surf beating upon it, and beyond the waters of the Gulf with here and there a sail visible! What an enticing picture and how the summer tourist would gloat over the circulars describing it! Imagine a lot of people dressed in the hideous regulation bathing suit; fat or lean, awkward and gawky, disporting themselves in this place ! It is worse than nightmare to think of it.

Another day I would visit the North Shore with its orange groves and pomegranates, pears and figs, grapes and berries of all kinds, bananas and a dozen other kinds of fruit. They don't grow wild, to be sure, but from the very small amount of cultivation they appear to have received one might say that they did. And then on the eastern end of the island, guarding the entrance to Mobile bay, stands Fort Gaines. a grim and forbidding-looking mass of brickwork, now deserted, except for a sergeant, who represents the. government and has a lonely time by himself. On its walls inside are the cannons, now dismounted and half covered with grass, which disputed Admiral Farragut's entrance to the bay, and all around lie cannonballs, rusting away. into their original state. To the curiosity seeker there is plenty about the fort that interests. Beneath the wall on one side is the oven that was used to heat cannon balls, and near it are some of these missiles which were being prepared for use. At another place is the magazine, heavily covered with brick and earth to resist a chance shell, and at still another is the "bomb-proof," a chamber as carefully protected as the magazine, where the inmates could stay in safety when compelled to leave the quarters. Standing on the top of the wall, Fort Morgan can be seen across the bay, and off to

the south the Gulf stretches into mysterious distances.

Nor is this all that there is to see. Starting from Cedar Point one can go over to Grant's Island, about a mile from shore, and chat with the quarantine inspector or the keeper of the channel lighthouse. The former can tell how to prepare all kinds of savory dishes from the oysters and fish at hand, among them the celebrated "jamboulaire," a dish which once eaten can never be forgotten, and the latter will tell about Grant's Island when it was Fort Fisher, and about the people buried under the little mound in the rear of the house. He will show where the magazine was and some of the loaded and primed shells which have washed down to the beach, or, if in the mood, he can tell stirring tales of war times, when he engaged on blockade runners and carried cotton to Cuba.

Then when you have your fill you can set out and sail on across the bay to Fort Morgan and watch the vessels loading lumber brought from Mobile on lighters; you can wander around the deserted fort and try to imagine the scene enacted thirty years ago, when Farragut's fleet steamed up the channel in defiance of torpedoes, and the storm of shot and shell rained from these now deserted walls. Then if you love sailing you can go from here down the wide channel toward the Gulf, passing Dixie Island, a crescent-shaped strip of land, and between it and the mainland, South Channel, where not many years ago in a great storm a large merchant vessel was lost, and with cargo and crew disappeared before assistance could be rendered. Then you steer off to the West and run under the lee of Sand Island, where you may be sure of a hearty welcome from the keeper and his assistant. It is not so much of an exertion to climb up to the top of the lighthouse, and once there all past difficulties are forgotten.

So far as fishing is concerned, well, all you need do

INTERIOR OF FORT GAINES.

is go down to the water anywhere and throw out a line. In the morning you can stand on the little wharf jutting out from the shore and watch the tarpon, or silver fish as they are called there, broach clean out of water in their efforts to catch the mullet, which swarm through the narrow channel as the tide runs out. If you don't feel in the humor for trying a line, borrow a casting net, one of the peculiarities of the Gulf Coast, and try one throw. You will not likely try another that morning as it will take until dinner time to untangle you from its meshes, but the experience is certainly novel and, to the looker-on, interesting. Finally, when you leave the place, whether you have been fishing or not, you will agree with me that one might travel long and far without finding a more perfect climate, purer air or a more delightful place in which to stay.

But something further should be said about Mobile's business. When you come to study the situation here, you are amazed at the combined commercial, industrial and agricultural advantages of the locality.

The harbor is one of the finest on the Atlantic or Gulf Coast. The city is but twenty-eight miles from the Gulf, with a channel twenty-one feet deep at mean low tide, and this depth is being increased by the work of the government year by year. The city has twelve miles of river frontage with thirty feet natural depth of water. A government engineer, commissioned to examine Mobile river and bay, reported that for a $3,000,000 appropriation he would guarantee a perfect thirty-foot channel to Mobile's wharves. There is regular steamship connection with points in Central America, Cuba, Jamaica, Mexico and other points. The coasting trade is very large and is expanding rapidly.

Mobile is the natural outlet for the coal of Alabama, and for such products of this and adjacent States as seek water to remote points. It should be noted as a factor of tremendous force in

Mobile's development that seven rivers, with an aggregate of more than 1000 miles of navigable waters, come together here and form the head of Mobile bay. These rivers, coming down from the coal and iron regions of the State, are

EXTERIOR WALL AND MOAT—FORT GAINES.

being constantly improved by the government and made navigable higher and higher up toward their source. A writer, not long ago, said: "There is not, elsewhere in the world, such combined industrial and commercial wealth upon water courses that feed a single port." In the shipment of coal and lumber and the importation of bananas and other foreign fruits, Mobile has built up an enormous business which is growing larger every day.

For manufacturing, Mobile is superior in its cheap fuel, and in its cheap raw material for cotton manufacturing, for lumber and wood-working factories of every sort, for ship-building, and for the canning of oysters, fish, fruit, vegetables, &c.

But probably the most noteworthy, as well as the most profitable and inviting industry of this region is truck farming, which, as my drummer friend remarked, seems to become more profitable as the number of truck farmers increases. The explanation of this, of course, is that as the business develops the railroads can afford to provide better facilities for getting the vegetables and fruits to the Northern markets quickly and cheaply; the Northern commission merchants can give more attention to handling the business, and, as the supply becomes larger and more regular, the market expands.

Mobile is becoming one of the great centres in the country for the production of early fruits and vegetables. Lands suitable for gardening can be had for much less than even the average farm prices that prevail in the North.

The railroads are rendering every possible assistance to settlers who buy lands for gardening. The business involves fewer risks with greater profits and greater certainty of profits than any other branch of farming. The Mobile & Ohio and other roads, during the season, run daily fast fruit and vegetable trains to the cities of the West and Northwest.

Altogether it may safely be said that Mobile is one of the great seaport cities of the future.

SAND ISLAND LIGHT.

LET THE EMIGRANT COME SOUTH.

By Gen. Thos. S. Rosser.

The word emigrant should be sacred to the heart and mind of every one of America's sons and daughters, for it was from him that we sprung and by him that the corner-stone of our great republic was laid.

He was the architect of the temple of free government which we are still engaged in building, and of which we proudly boast, and it was he who laid its foundation and in his own blood consecrated its holy mission.

The individual independence, the purity of character, the demand for fair-play, justice and toleration which mark the outlines of our manhood today, in all our dealings with the world and ourselves, was derived, by direct inheritance, from the old emigrant stock of brave, hardy, freedom-loving, God-fearing and king-hating adventurers, who first settled in the wilderness of America, and whom we delight to honor and revere as our forefathers, and as the wise political philosophers whose precepts are our best guides.

The right to speak for himself, to think for himself, to read for himself and to pray for himself was to him inherent, and filling his soul as an inspiration led him from home, from friends and from comforts in the Old Country to seek a new home in the new-found wilderness across the treacherous seas, and made the hardships and sufferings, dangers and cares, only sweet comforts under the skies of liberty.

Under the star of a new-found world was launched a new dispensation giving rise to a new Empire on a new plan which was surged into life and founded on a new faith and a new philosophy. It was the pioneer emigrant who fought for and won the right of self-government, from the combined wealth, power and assumed divinity of crystalized bigotry which had enslaved the children of men from the beginning of time and established the doctrine of political equality which placed the feet of every child born in the land on the highway of promotion, and awarded the palm only to the worthiest.

The genesis of the United States is the history of the emigrant, and as development after development has gone on, evolving territories and then States out of mere backwoods settlements, and a great nation has been built, yet there is still a task and a field for the same hardy, brave and enterprising emigrant, and although it is not in blazing the geographical lines and boundaries of States, it is equally important in advancing the frontier of development and extending the tide of the empire of wealth into richer and broader and more inviting fields.

To till the rich valleys and dig the gold of the sierras of the Rocky Mountains, the emigrant threw open the golden gate and bespangled our banner with the stately stars of the Pacific, and to reclaim the rich prairies from the hostile red man, and to send cheap bread and meat to the famishing millions of the old world, he crossed the Mississippi and planted the flag of his country on the great Western plains around which today are gathered the happy and prosperous millions of many proud States of the Union.

From the rock-ribbed hills of New England the father sent his sons to make a home and plant a new generation on the velvet fields of Illinois, but when the next generation came forward to divide the patrimony, thrift had so enhanced the value of realty that it was deemed best to sell the acres which had been acquired in Illinois by the first generation at one dollar and a quarter, for its increased price of one hundred and seventy-five, and with this the boys joined the Westward tide and begun life in the new fields of Minnesota, where a like experience following, the next generation planted itself in Dakota, then in Montana and on making its way Westward until the tide rolling out from the Pacific met the one moving West and finished the work of the emigrant pioneer.

The boy of the Eastern States now sits down and repiningly wails that there are no opportunities for him, and that times have changed from what they used to be when his father began life, and the work of the pioneer with all its rich fields and opportunities is now only an iridescent dream of the past, and while feeling that he would like to be a conqueror, concludes that there is nothing left of success to conquer.

But let me say to this young man, that there are yet fields replete with possibilities stretching out before him, as rich and as fruitful as any the past ever held, and whose scope will afford employment for all his energy, talent and ambition.

It is not far off. You will not have to sail the troubled seas to find it, nor to scale rugged or icy mountains, nor drive off the savage man or beast, but it is here in the midst of civilization and social refinement.

It is here in the sunny South, where the climate is equable and soil fertile—free from blizzards and cyclones—with the free navigation of rivers or sea from your door to the best Eastern markets. Here in the South you will find cheap lands, with a wealth of the best soil, or the wealth of forest and of mine far richer and more remunerative than the West can give, and without the merciless tax which that section is forced to pay for transportation to the Eastern markets and to the sea.

If you wish to be a "Cattle King" there are fields in the South where you may acquire the cheap lands capable of grazing in summer, and where you can cheaply feed in winter herds which will yield more profit than those which fatten on the mesquite or the gammee grasses of the Western plains in summer, and which, in winter, browse in gorges or cañons, and are only fit for market in the fall of the year, when, on account of the abundance, meat is so cheap as to scarcely pay the cost of transportation.

If you wish to raise sheep by the thousands, or tens of thousands, the South affords a better climate and cheaper and more wholesome food for them, and giving a greater and more profitable yield than the plains of Judith Basin of Montana can boast of. If your taste is for fine running or trotting horses, I can place you, for little money, by the side of studs in the South where even with much smaller investments larger results are reaped than anywhere else on the continent. If you wish to produce cotton, tobacco, grain or fruit, you may select you plantation or your farm already improved, and which will cost you less than the buildings standing on it would cost to build for cash, and these you can buy on long time, paying one-fourth cash, and the balance you may carry as long as you like by paying 6 per cent. for the use of the money.

I have been all over the West, I built the eastern end of the Northern Pacific and Canadian Pacific railroads, and resided for twenty years in Minnesota, and was a close student of agriculture and stock raising all the time, and I feel that I understand the problem as presented in both the West and the East. If you are in doubt go to the West and look around before you think of moving to a farm there, and if you are already out in the West and are not satisfied, I promise you that you will find health, wealth and contentment in the South, and her people cordially invite you to come and be one of them.

If you have not yet made your selection, I will tell you that life in a Western cattle ranch is isolated barbarism. None of the comforts of civilization, and no hope to make a fortune, that you may finally return with it East to enjoy friends and luxury. On a ranch the proprietor, the cowboys and the cows associate with each other and roam the plains, about as the wild Indians did in the days of the Buffalo. If you should conclude to settle on a prairie farm, let me suggest that you provide a deep cellar, so that when the cyclone signal is up you may retreat to it, while everything above the surface of the ground is called off on a long journey, from which they never return.

If you think of taking a bride with you to a Western prairie farm be sure and instruct her in the art of twisting bundles of hay and straw into tight withes, big enough and tight enough to serve as lightwood knots, for these are all the firewood she will have or you will be able to procure to cook with or to heat your room, or to cook for the Swede, whom you may be able to hire to help you clear away the snow which buries your trail from your door to your stable, or to dig your house itself out of a snow-drift so that daylight may shine on it after a blizzard has given it a call.

A man starting life in the West requires far more ready cash than one begining life in the South—even in the days of free homesteads; and now that grants to railroads and fraudulent preemptions have consumed all that is valuable of the public domain, an emigrant going West, looking for a home, will have to buy second-hand and pay from seven to fifty dollars an acre for lands, which are remote from market and all that can be produced on them are at the mercy of the nearest railroad or the elevator company—one robbing in freight tax, and the other in dishonest classification.

These taken along with the periodical grasshopper, alkaline water, black flies and prairie mosquitoes, and it will appear to him that the curses of an offended God are upon him and to abide forever.

Crops in the West cannot be diversi-

fied; wheat, oats, grass and vegetables limit the soil's yield—while in the South all of the plants, cereals, roots and fruits can be produced every year, and in abundance.

In Virginia, North and South Carolina, Georgia and Florida more wealth is being produced annually from "truck," consisting of vegetables, melons and fruits, than the entire wheat crop of the West is worth, and, while it takes an expensive plant to operate a wheat farm, "a mule and forty acres" along the Atlantic Coast will load a steamboat for Baltimore, Philadelphia or New York, and in the winter while the prairies are bleak and deserted the creeks and rivers teem with wild fowl, canvas-back ducks and wild geese, the marshes with woodcock, the fields with quail and the chaparal with deer and wild turkeys.

In this county of Albemarle in Virginia the product of the apple crop last year, (and this was saved mostly by immigrant Northerners) amounted to over $20,000, and besides the vast amount of peaches, pears, cherries, strawberries and grapes shipped North, annually, we supply the two wine cellars at Charlottesville with about three hundred thousand pounds of all varieties of wine grapes, producing the celebrated "Virginia Claret" and a rich Burgundy, known as "Norton," which has already found its way into the most fashionable restaurants, clubs and private cellars in the Union.

Many of the old colonial homes of large acreage now offered for sale in the South should attract the enterprising young farmer of the North, for nowhere else on earth are such inducements as they afford to be found.

Come as individuals or come as colonies, and come in the spirit of the immigrant who is determined to forge his way to the front and shape things around him to harmonize with his own high purposes, and we shall indeed have a new South.

THE INCREASE OF COTTON PRODUCTION.

By Richard H. Edmonds.

Cotton is the most remarkable of all agricultural products. No other crop could stand the bad treatment which cotton receives from the time that it is planted —for the majority of cotton-raisers never give it the attention which all farming operations demand—until, after being badly packed, it is rolled in the mud around country stations or left for weeks exposed to all kinds of weather. Neither heat nor cold, rain nor sunshine, nor even age, materially affects the quality of the staple in the belief of the producers, and hence they disregard all of the precautions given to the handling and marketing of all other crops. In reality this treatment is barbarous and wasteful, but cotton stands it as no other crop could. While it is one of the world's greatest agricultural staples, it becomes the foundation of what is claimed to be the most important industrial interest of the day. Its consumption measures the progress of civilization, and, as Henry W. Grady once said, the missionary of the gospel as he penetrates the wilds of Africa, opening it up to civilization, is but an advance agent for cotton goods. As civilization advances and wealth increases, the wearing of cotton clothes necessarily keeps even step in the march of progress.

Mr. Thomas Ellison, the great cotton authority of England, in writing on this subject, once said: "The cultivation of the cotton plant, the manufacture of its fibre and the distribution of its product afford employment to a much larger amount of capital and labor than any other branch of mechanical industry, and yet, so far as Europe and America are concerned, this vast agricultural and manufacturing system has been built up almost within the limits of the past century."

No other product of the soil can be depended upon with the same certainty of having such a uniform foreign demand and upon which we can safely rely to so large an extent in the settlement of balances due abroad by our country.

In studying cotton, however, we find that all of these facts are only a part of the sum total of its remarkable qualities. It was comparatively only a few years ago when the seed was considered a nuisance, to be hauled away to a dumping-ground. Now the seed is the basis of one of the most important industrial interests in the South—an interest that has many wide ramifications, reaching from the fattening of live-stock in competition with the West to the olive orchards of Italy, for whose protection the Italian government has waged war against cottonseed oil. Years ago Mr. Edward Atkinson, impressed with the value of cottonseed, then hardly more than a waste product, stated that if New England could produce cotton for the seed alone it would grow rich at it. Now the seed sells at from $10.00 to $20.00 a ton, and supports an industry in which probably over $40,000,000 are invested. As there are two pounds of seed to every pound of lint, $10.00 a ton for the former would practically mean adding nearly one cent a pound to the price of cotton, and with seed at $20.00 a ton two cents would be added.

So far as known, cotton is indigenous to the American continent. According to Mr. Thomas Ellison, it was found by Magellan in Brazil in 1519, by Cortes in Mexico in the same year and by De Vica in Texas and Louisiana in 1536. Bancroft reports that cotton was first cultivated in the South in 1621, but there is good historical authority for saying that it was grown in Virginia to a considerable extent some time before that. The cotton that was grown in the colonies furnished the raw material out of which the old spinning wheels and hand looms produced "homespun" goods, and it is reported of Jefferson that in his house was made over "2000 yards of cloth, which his family and servants required yearly. The first regular export of cotton was probably in 1784, when eight bales were shipped from Charleston, but two small shipments had been made in 1748-49 and 1757, though it is generally supposed that these were of West India cotton reshipped through Charleston to Great Britain. The first shipment of eight bales, which was seized by the authorities, who claimed that so large a quantity could not be of American growth, was afterwards sold to Messrs. Strutt & Co., of Derby, in whose mill Samuel Slater, the man who laid the foundation of cotton manufacturing in New England, was then working.

In 1739 it was testified in an English court that "cotton grows very well in Georgia, and that it can be raised by white persons without the aid of negroes." When the colonies undertook to encourage the manufacture of cotton goods the home government did everything in its power to hinder the progress of the industry, with a view to compelling them to confine their attention to the production of food and raw materials, and to purchase their manufactured goods from Great Britian. At the request of English merchants, who were disturbed by efforts of American manufacturers to export their goods, an act of Parliament was passed imposing a fine of £500 for every offense of exporting such goods, and, this not proving effectual, a law was enacted forbidding the exportation of textile machinery from Great Britain, in order to prevent American manufacturers getting cotton machinery. Despite all these disadvantages, however, more and more attention was given by Americans to the study of methods to develop the cotton industry. Massachusetts especially took active steps to encourage cotton manufacturing, and in 1786 the legislature gave £200 to two brothers to help them establish carding and spinning ma-

chinery. Later £500 was granted to assist another factory, and afterwards £2000 to another. Samuel Slater undertook about this time to establish a mill in Pawtucket, and his success has made for him the reputation of having been the father of the cotton manufacturing in this country. The South was not so prompt in taking up this industry, and the first mill erected in that section is supposed to have been one established in South Carolina in 1790. Up to this time the progress in cotton cultivation and manufacture had been very slow, and it was felt that some improved method of ginning cotton must be invented before the cotton business could attain much larger proportions. This was a subject of frequent discussion.

In 1795 Eli Whitney, who, though a native of Massachusetts, was then living in Georgia, succceded in making a gin that proved entirely satisfactory. With the introduction of the gin the cotton business in all branches advanced with leaps and bounds The South's crop jumped from 2,000,000 pounds in 1790 to 10,000,000 pounds in 1796, and to 40,000,000 pounds in 1800, or only four years later, while the yield of 1810 was 80,000,000 pounds, and that of 1820 160,-000,000. The rapid increase in the demand for cotton and the profitableness of its cultivation caused a concentration of the energy and capital of the South in planting, and industrial interests which had been flourishing declined under the craze for cotton-raising. In 1816 the tariff on cotton goods was largely increased, the measure being strongly supported by the South on the ground that it would promote the consumption of its cotton, while the Northern States opposed this advance in rates because of their large shipping interests—another illustration of how tariff sentiment changes as conditions change. From a crop of about 400,000 bales in 1820 production rapidly increased, the growth of this industry probably surpassing in extent and wide-reaching importance any other crop in Europe or America. The energy of the South was turned into cotton-raising, and production really increased in advance of the world's consumptive requirements. Other agricultural interests were not, however, neglected. Diversified farming was the rule, and the South was more nearly self-supporting in the way of foodstuffs—corn, bacon, etc.—than it has ever been since the war. In general prices were well maintained for forty years, though gradually tending downward after the beginning of this century. In 1801 the average New York price was forty-four cents a pound, and from this it slowly declined, often with an upward spurt for a year or two, to thirteen and one half cents in 1839.

With prices ranging from thirteen to forty-four cents, and averaging for forty years, from 1800 to 1839, a fraction over seventeen cents a pound, cotton cultivation was so profitable that we cannot wonder at the disposition of the people of the South to concentrate their efforts more and more on cotton cultivation to the exclusion of industrial interests. Beginning with 1840 there came a period of extremely low prices and the cotton States suffered very much from this decline. In that year the average New York prices dropped to nine cents, a decline of four cents from the preceding year, and this was followed by a continuous decline until 1846, when the average was 5.63 cents, the lowest average price ever known to the cotton trade. Even in 1891-92, when an enormous surplus of cotton following the depression that succeeded the Baring failure forced prices to what many claimed was the lowest point on record, the average at New York was 7.50 cents, or nearly two cents higher than in 1846. Moreover, in 1846 the seed was without value, while in 1891-92 the sale of seed added almost a cent a pound to the value of the crop and transportation was very much cheaper than in 1846. In 1847 the crop was short and prices advanced sharply, only to drop back to eight and then to seven and one-fourth cents, making the average for the decade, from 1840 to 1849, the lowest ever known in the cotton trade.

These excessively low prices brought about a revival of public interest in other pursuits than of cotton cultivation, and the natural tendency of the people to industrial matters, as evidenced by the history of the colonies prior to the Revolution, but which had long been dormant, was again aroused, and for some years there was a very active spirit manifested in the building of railroads and the development of manufactures. With 1850 a period of much higher prices was ushered in, and for the next ten years the average was about twelve cents. Then came the war with its accompanying scarcity of cotton and prices rapidly advancing until 1863-64, when the New York average was 101½ cents. When the war ended the world was bare of cotton. The demand was pressing and the prices continued very high. But the South was bankrupt. It had no capital on which to operate, its planters were burdened with debt, their houses and fences destroyed, their labor system disorganized, and in this condition they were in no position to buy foodstuffs, live-stock and agricultural implements.

Money-lenders were, however, ready to advance money on mortgages on unplanted cotton, but on no other crop. Most of them were factors or commission merchants who would agree to advance a certain sum of money, or rather a certain line of credit at their stores for merchandise of all kinds, on every acre planted in cotton. Under these circumstances diversified agriculture had to be abandoned, and the planter was forced to buy Western corn and bacon from his commission merchant. By the time he had paid more than double price over cash values for his supplies, paid interest on the money advanced, and commission, storage and drayage and insurance on his cotton when marketed, the planter usually ended the year in debt to his factor. The profits of the factor, though, were sufficiently large to justify him in continuing his credit, and by doing so the farmer was kept in debt from year to year. The negroes and the tenant class of whites could borrow money on cotton in the same way, and this developed into a tenantry system for raising cotton which prevented any attention being given to the improvement of the land. Year after year the farmer was forced into cotton-raising to the exclusion of everything else, until it became only too true that "the South kept its corn-crib and smokehouse in the West."

After 1880, although the Southern farmers were still heavily in debt, they commenced to give increased attention to the cultivation of grain and to the raising of early fruits and vegetables. The progress made since then has been very remarkable, but, despite this great increase, the production of corn in the central cotton States is not yet up to the yield of 1860. In the meantime the cotton crop increased rapidly, rising from 5,456,000 bales in 1881-82 to 9,035,000 bales in 1891-92. Summing up in tabular form the statistics of the cotton crop since 1840, we have :

Years.	Acres.	Total value of crop.	Net ℔s ℔ acre.	Bale ℔ acre.
1875 76	11,635,000	$399 445,168	177	0.39⅞
1876-77	11,500,000	252 602,340	171½	0.39
1877 78	11,825,000	255,768,165	181¾	0.40⅜
1878-79	12,240 000	236 586,031	185¼	0.41⅝
1879-80	12 680,000	313 696,452	206¼	0.45½
1880-81	16,123,000	356,524,911	188½	0.41
1881 82	16 851,000	304 298,744	145⅜	0.32⅝
1882-83	16,276,000	327,938 137	20.⅜	0.42⅝
1883 84	16,78 ?,000	288,803 902	157½	0.34
1884 85	17,426,000	287.253,972	150½	0.33
1885 86	18 379,444	313 723.080	165½	0.30
1886 87	18,581,01?	298.504.215	162½	0.35
1887 88	18,961,897	336,433,653	173½	0.37
1888-89	19,362 073	344,669,801	167⅞	0.35¾
1889 90	19 979 040	373,161,831	173¾	0.36½
1890-91	20,583,935	4?9 792.047	200⅞	0.42
1891-91	20,555,387	391.424 716	209⅝	0.44
1892-93	18,667,924	284.279 0?6	176	0.37

Years.	Crop.—Bales.	Consumption in U. S. Bales.	Exports. Bales.	Average price ℔ middling uplands in N. York.—Cents.
1840 41	1,634,954	267.850	1,313 500	9.50
1841-42	1 683,574	267,850	1,465,500	7.85
1842 43	2 378,875	325,12?	2,010,000	7.25
1843-44	4,030,409	346,750	1,629,500	7.73
1844 45	2,394,503	389.000	2,08?,700	5.63
1845 46	2,100.537	422,600	1,666,700	7.87
1846 47	1,778,651	428,000	1,241 200	11.21
1847-48	2,439.786	616,044	1 858,000	8.03
1848 49	2,866,938	642,485	2 228,000	7.55
1849 50	2,223,718	613,498	1,590,200	12.34
1850 51	2,454,442	485,614	1,988,710	12.14
1851-52	3,126,310	689,603	2 443 646	9.50
1852-53	3,416,214	803,725	2 528 400	11.02
1853-54	3 074,979	737,236	2,319 148	10.97
1854-55	2,982,634	706,417	2,244,209	10.39
1855 56	3,665,557	777,739	2,954,606	10.30
1856-57	3,093 737	819,936	2 252,657	13.51
1857 58	3,257,339	595,562	2,590,455	12.23
1858 59	4,018,914	927,651	3 021,403	12.08
1859-60	4 861,292	978 043	3,774,173	11.00
1860-61	3,849,469	843,740	3,127,568	13.01
1861 62 ⎫				31.29
1862-63 ⎪	............War Period....			67.21
1863 64 ⎪				101.50
1864 65 ⎭				83.38
1865-66	2 269,316	666,100	1,554,664	42.30
1866 67	2,097,254	770,030	1,557 054	31 59
1867 68	2,519 554	906,636	1,655,816	24.85
1868 69	2,366,467	926,374	1 46? 880	29.01
1869 70	3,122,551	865,160	2,2?6,480	23.98
187u-71	4,352,317	1,110,196	3,169,009	16.95
1871 72	2 974,351	1,237,330	1,957,314	20.48
1872 73	3 930 508	1,201,147	2,679.986	18.15
1873-74	4 170,388	1,305,943	2,840,9?1	17.00
1874 75	3 832,991	1,193,0?5	2 684,7?8	15.00
1875 76	4,6?2,313	1,351,870	3,234,244	13.00
1876 77	4.474.069	1,428,013	3,030,835	11.73
1877 78	4.773.865	1,489,022	3 360,254	11.28
1878-7?	5,074 155	1,558,329	3,181,004	10.83
1879 80	5,761,252	1,789,978	3,885,00?	12.02
1880 81	6,605,750	1.938 937	4,589,346	11.34
1881 82	5,456,048	1,964,535	3,582,622	12.16
1882 83	6 949 756	2,073,096	4,766,597	10.?3
1883-84	5,713 200	1 876,683	3,916,581	10.64
1884 85	5,706.165	1 753,125	3,947,972	10.54
1885 86	6,575,691	2 162,544	4 336,203	9.44
1886 87	6 505,087	2,111,532	4 445,302	10.25
1887 88	7,046,833	2,257.247	4,627,502	10.27
1888 89	6,938,290	2 314,091	4.742 347	10.71
1839 90	7,307,281	2,390,959	4,955,931	11.53
1890-91	8 652 597	2,632,023	5,847 191	9.01
1891-92	9,035,379	2 876,846	5 933 437	7.64
1892-93	6,700,365	2,481,015	4,402,890	8.24

Although a great deal of complaint is heard throughout the South about the decline in the price of cotton of late years, the average decrease has really been less than the average decrease in the price of wheat. The decline in average cotton prices since 1876 has not been as much as 30 per cent., although the average for 1891-92 by itself was more than this, but that was an exceptional year; whereas the drop in wheat since 1876 will average about 33 to 35 per cent. In both cases the heavy decrease in value was mainly due to the fact that production increased more rapidly than consumption. We kept on piling up a surplus of cotton and wheat, and a decline under such circumstances was inevitable, and it does not seem to have been proportionately greater than the increase in production beyond the consumptive requirements of the world. At present the consumption of both wheat and cotton is increasing more rapidly than the acreage or production, and under this, one of the laws of trade, which, given time enough, always brings about an equilibrium, we may reasonably look for a gradual improvement in the value of these staples during the next few years.

A study of the foregoing figures will show that seven years of successively increasing crops, as from 1885-86 to 1891-92, was unprecedented in the history of trade. It is doubtful if any leading crop raised can show such an unbroken increase for seven years. Jumping from 5,700,000 bales in 1884-85 to 6,500,000 bales in 1885 86, there was practically no halting, as the variations in two years were too small to be noticeable, to 9,035,000 bales in 1891·92, a gain of 3,300,000 bales, or nearly 60 per cent. advance in seven years. It ought not to have been expected that consumption could keep pace with such an increase. Fortunately there came a break, and we have now had two short crops. This will help to reduce the enormous stocks that have overweighted the market for several years. With surplus stocks worked off a fresh start can be made, and if next year's crop is moderately small the cotton trade of the world will then be on a sound basis for higher prices, because consumption will then have overtaken production.

In eighteen years cotton has brought into the South over $5,700,000,000, a sum so vast that the profits out of it ought to have been enough to greatly enrich that whole section. Unfortunately, however, the system which the poverty following the war developed, of raising cotton only and buying provisions and grain in the West, left at home but little surplus money out of the cotton crop. The West and North drained that section of several hundred million dollars every year, because it depended upon them for all of its manufactured goods, as well as for the bulk of its foodstuffs. Hence, of the enormous amount received for cotton, very little remained in the South. The increase in diversified farming, the raising of home supplies, the development of trucking and the building of factories are all uniting to keep at home the money which formerly went North and West. Whether the cotton-raiser himself be getting the full benefit of this or not, the South at large is necessarily doing so.

The figures given in the foregoing tables show that the lowest average yield per acre for the seventeen years under review was 145⅝ pounds in 1881, and the highest 209⅝ pounds in 1891. Had the yield per acre in 1891 been as low as in 1881, the crop would have been less than 6,700,000 bales, instead of 9,035,000 bales.

From 1840 to 1849 the average price in New York was eight cents per pound, a lower average for nine years than any single year since has shown except 1891-92.

The importance of cotton in our foreign trade relations can be appreciated from the simple statement that since 1875 our exports of this staple have been valued at $3,800,000,000 while the total exports of wheat and flour combined for the same period have been $2,500,000,000, showing a difference of $1,300,000,000, or over 50 per cent. in favor of cotton. Moreover, during the same period we have exported about $200,000,000 of manufactured cotton goods, making the full value really $4,000,000,000. Compared with the exports of wheat, flour and corn combined, the value of which since 1875 has been $3,100,000,000, there is a difference in favor of cotton of $900,000,000. Going back to 1820, it is found that the total value of flour and wheat exported for the last seventy-four years is $3,913,000,000, or $100,-000,000 less than the value of the cotton exported during the last eighteen years.

LETTERS FROM NORTHERN AND WESTERN FARMERS, GIVING THEIR EXPERIENCE IN THE SOUTH—V.

[The letters published in this issue form the fifth instalment in the series commenced in the October number of this magazine. These communications are published in response to numerous inquiries from Northern people who desire to know more about agricultural conditions in the South, and what is being accomplished by settlers from other sections of the country. These letters were written by practical farmers and fruit-growers, chiefly Northern and Western people who have made their homes in the South. The actual experiences of these settlers, as set forth in these letters, are both interesting and instructive to those whose minds are turned Southward.—EDITOR.]

The Many Advantages of Lakeland Vicinity.

MR. J. L. DERIEUX, Lakeland, Fla.— In this season when the blizzards sweep over the plains and the whole North is wrapped in snow and ice, let me speak a word to the shivering denizens of that section and tell them of a "better land" —where there are no cyclones, no blizzards, no flood, no mud, no slush, no zero temperature, no grippe, no pneumonia, no scarlet fever, no diphtheria, no labor strikes, no riots, but where the flowers bloom and the birds sing every day in the year, and the tenderest fruits and vegetables mature and ripen in midwinter—where life is not a burden but a pleasure.

But the first question that many will ask is, "What can I do in Florida to make a living?"

During the session of the Agricultural Congress at Chicago, Mr. Washburn of Florida said: "It is true we have swamps, and we have the everglades, but there is no malaria in the country; and we have less sickness there than in any other portion of the United States. A year ago last January I planted potatoes upon some of our poor land and I raised 220 bushels to the acre and sold them for $2.00 per bushel. In February I planted watermelons and took off a large crop. In May I planted the land with sweet

potatoes and I took off 500 bushels of as good potatoes as ever grew in the world, I think. So you see that we can raise two or three crops in a year, and that it pays us to fertilize the land."

In this light sandy soil a man can cultivate twice as much land as he can in the heavy soils North.

In this locality we raise corn, oats, rye, rice, sugar cane, sweet potatoes, cow peas, Irish potatoes, cabbage, cauliflower, tomatoes, string beans, okra, egg plant, garden peas, lettuce, cucumbers, strawberries, oranges, lemons, grape fruit, guavas, bananas, grapes, peaches, plums, figs, mulberries, Japan persimmons, and I believe on our highest hills we can raise fine apples without protection, for last winter, which was a severe one, I did not lose a hill of my tomato crop from frost, and my guava leaves were not touched, hence, I conclude that the highest hills in this locality surrounded by numerous lakes are as near frost proof as any in the State.

The following are the results of some of my neighbors' crops:

Richard R. Platt, on January 10, 1893, planted three barrels of early rose potatoes on one and a half acres of flat-woods land, and raised sixty barrels, which netted him four and a quarter dollars per barrel.

The Duvernette Bros. have been

raising cabbage for several years and their yield is from 100 to 200 barrels per acre, which they sold at from $1.00 to $1.50 per barrel f. o. b.

N. S. Gallaway, Walter Gallaway, Wm. Odurm and several others are engaged in strawberry culture. They say their berries, taking it one year with another, average them $300 per acre.

We produce about 600 gallons of syrup per acre, which is worth forty cents per gallon. Rice from twenty to seventy-five bushels per acre.

Mr. McDonald, from 250 orange trees this year, had 2121 boxes of fruit, which he sold for ninety cents per box on the trees. One of his grape fruit trees produced $70.00 worth of fruit this year, and $102.00 last year.

Mr. A. G. Munn this year sold from two grape fruit trees seventy-one boxes of fruit at $1.00 per box on the trees.

Of course we have here improvident men, as can be found everywhere, who do not succeed, but the above examples will show what can be accomplished in Florida by proper means and methods.

Our improved lands can be bought reasonably. Our unimproved lands can be had at from $2.50 to $30.00 per acre, according to quality and location.

Lakeland is a town of 1,000 inhabitants; is the highest point on the Southern Florida Railroad, and perhaps the highest on the peninsula.

The following altitudes are from the profile map of Southern Florida Railroad: Tampa, 10 feet; Seffner, 73; Plant City, 128; Lakeland, 217; Bartow, 114; Winter Haven, 170; Bartow Junction, 175; Kissimmee, 63; Orlando, 113; Sanford, 10; Richland, 97; Dade City, 85.

Lakeland is eighty-three miles from Sanford; sixty-three from Orlando; forty-three from Kissimmee; fourteen from Bartow; twenty-six from Dade City; ten from Plant City; thirty-two from Tampa. Here we have a high, dry and bracing atmosphere which is so favorable to the feeble and to invalids.

There never was a case of yellow fever here.

I don't think there has been a death in this community from fever of any kind for several years except two cases that were brought here from the cypress swamps.

The South Florida Railroad and the main line of the Savannah, Florida & Western Railroad cross here, and a third railroad is chartered to cross here.

The town is surrounded by rich phosphate mines, which are being opened very extensively and very profitably.

We have good hotels, churches, a graded school that employs three teachers, also a first-class weekly newspaper and a good solid bank, and the town is lighted with electricity.

There are nine beautiful clearwater lakes in a radius of one mile of the town. One of them is six miles long and three miles wide. These are filled with choice fish and are surrounded by beautiful groves and luxuriant gardens, and adorned with comfortable and happy homes.

In summer this beautiful, high and salubrious lake region is either fanned by good strong breezes from either the gulf or the ocean, and its happy denizens can lie down and sleep undisturbed by sultry nights or buzzing mosquitoes.

Our people are sober, moral, intelligent, energetic, progressive, and they welcome all good settlers, irrespective of their religious creeds or political affiliations. Come and see us.

A Farmers' Chance in Virginia.

A gentleman living in Norfolk writes as follows to the SOUTHERN STATES: Before me is a letter from a Michigan farmer asking what the chances would be for a man to buy land near Norfolk, Va., for the purpose of raising hay for the Norfolk market, stating that the Michigan price for baled hay was generally $6.00 to $8.00 per ton, and often the buyers were quite scarce at that price.

Now our port receives more than 2000 tons of hay each month from the North and the Northwest. 1 believe the producers of all this large amount of hay receive, as a rule, less than $8 per ton. It must be surely a losing business to grow hay at that figure, as it is calculated by the chemists that every ton of good hay shipped from the farm carries with it about $7 worth of chemicals. That is to say the soil is robbed or relieved of $7 worth of chemicals by each ton of hay grown thereon. If this hay is sold then the word "robbed" is rightly used, and the land of the farmer who sells his hay is being "robbed" at a rapid rate, and it is surely a losing business to engage in, viz: that of raising hay for market, especially where the price is only from $6 to $8 per ton.

Now our Michigan friends and farmers can come to Virginia and raise fully as much hay per acre as in Michigan, and often a great deal more, and get nearly three times as much per ton for it right here in the home market. The Michigan farmer gets $6 to $8 per ton for his hay and our farmers here get $16 to $18 per ton for theirs, and we can grow really more hay to the acre than can be grown in Michigan.

One can readily see the strong incentive or inducement for the Michigan farmer to come to Virginia to grow hay for the market. The same rule and the same line of argument apply to the grower of corn beyond the Mississippi. The Virginia truck farmer grows a fine crop of early potatoes, which, as a rule, brings fine prices, say from $25.00 to $50.00 per acre, clear of all expenses, and then puts the same land, the same season, into corn, which one year with another yields from thirty-five to fifty bushels per acre and commands fifty to sixty cents per bushel. In short, here we have the soil, the climate and the markets. What we want are the growers, the farmers from the North, the West and the Northwest to come here and utilize our idle lands and grow those products in demand here at the best prices in the United States, and for which products our soil is nicely adapted.

It is a generally known fact that the Western producer of wheat, oats, corn, hay, pork and beef, as well as of many other farm products, is very poorly paid for his work, and I know from long experience that the consumer here pays the highest market price in the United States for all such products. The great trouble lies in this fact. The Western "supply" is most too far from the "demand," hence the great margin between the price received and that paid.

When these and hundreds of other facts, plain business facts, are once generally known at the North and the West we shall see many of the producers from those sections knocking at our doors. We are indeed most highly gratified to see that the SOUTHERN STATES extends such pressing invitations to such to come.

Nature has decreed that this part of the Sunny South shall have a sixty day winter, and even that is not severe enough to stop plowing and planting, as the plows run most all the time, and there is not a month but some crop is planted. How different from that section where "old hoary headed winter" rules half the year, and often "lingers in the lap of spring" half of the next summer.

A Michigan correspondent, in describing the winter there, said it was "eight months winter and four months late in the fall." In such a climate as Michigan, Minnesota, Dakota, Iowa and portions of many other States, as well as in New York, Pennsylvania and all the Eastern States, the farmer is handicapped by a severe and prolonged winter. In the South these icy fetters fall off and a man has full use of hand and head all the year. The people are thinking of these matters—the "leaven" is working in the lump, and the lumps are coming Southward every day.

The Strong Points of the Norfolk Trucking Distict.

A. JEFFERS, Norfolk, Va.—I notice that your very commendable efforts to draw attention to the agricultural interests of the South are attracting wide attention in the North and West. We are truly glad to note this, as the more light that is let in upon the South the better it suits our people.

We are now in the midst of winter. The lowest dip of the thermometer, as shown by the government signal service station in this city, was 25° above zero, and that only on one day up to date. The last fifteen days, with one exception, have been as fine as we have ever seen, with the temperature during this beautiful stretch of weather from 30° to 60° above zero.

Truckers are now thinning out their kale and spinach crops, and instead of letting the "thinnings" go to waste, are shipping them to Northern markets. As soon as the frost gets his seal well set on the "greens" at the North and West, our people begin to find a market for our "greens," and the "thinnings" of the crops often pay the entire expense of the entire crop. A trucker friend of mine—a man who is only trucking in a very limited way—told me yesterday that he had shipped 150 barrels of "thinnings" from four acres of spinach, at $1.50 per barrel. This will pay for his entire crop, so that next spring, when he sends North 500 to 600 barrels of spinach, his returns will be nearly all profit.

It is to be regretted that more sheep are not kept in Southeastern Virginia. A farmer friend was talking yesterday about sheep. He only keeps a few, but they are good selected Southdowns. He has now about twenty head. He has his lambs ready to sell the first of April, and has no trouble to get ten cents per pound for them on this market, and his lambs at that time weigh from sixty to seventy-five pounds each. He says that there is a better profit for him on his sheep than on any other stock he can keep, tariff or no tariff.

Speaking of the tariff reminds me of an incident. Several men, for lack of anything else to do at the time, were discussing the very important question as to "where was the best place for a boil." One of the party argued ably for one portion of human anatomy, another for another portion, until finally it came to a member of the party who had said but little, but evidently had done some thinking. "Gentlemen," said he, "I have carefully considered the matter, and I have come to the conclusion that the best place for a boil is on some other fellow." And from the action of our iron men, our coal men, our lumbermen, our sugar men, our rice men and even our truckers, I am of the opinion that they all think that the best place for the "reduction of the tariff" is "on the other fellows." As long as the "tariff" was only a plank in the party platform it was simply a "theory," but when it gets into Congressional halls it is a "situation" that confronts us.

Of course all your readers know of the Smithfield ham. It is known all over the United States and also in many foreign countries. This brand of ham is prepared in Isle-of-Wight county, about twenty-five miles from Norfolk. Its originator left the manner of its preparation to his son, who still places it on the market at fancy figures. Recently I found this gentleman paying 16 cents per pound for green (uncured or unsalted) hams, as they came from the hands of the farmers of the surrounding country. Of course there were certain requirements as to size, age of hog, manner of keeping, &c., although the ham most in demand was from the hog who had "rooted" for himself and fattened largely on the mast in the woods. It occured to me that this was an object lesson. It is not in many places that a farmer can get sixteen cents per pound for uncured hams, and I know of no other portion of the country where pork can be made so cheaply as here.

I visited a gentleman's smokehouse in Isle-of-Wight county and saw 4000 pounds of nicely smoked bacon stored there. On being questioned the owner said that he had made that bacon at a cost of not more than two cents per pound all around for hams, shoulders, sides, etc.

It is true the results of truck farming often read like fairy tales, but some pig tales may be told too. In fact, the greatest need of this section of the South now is for a large number of "allround" farmers. If such will come here and engage in raising sheep, cows, hogs, poultry, grass and corn, they will find much greater profit than in raising these at any other point in the United States, because right here all such can be raised to perfection, and when raised they are at the very threshold of the best markets with the steadiest demand and the best prices in the entire country.

The gulf stream, with its immense volume of 70-degree water, flows steadily past our coast summer and winter without variation in temperature or volume or rate of speed and takes off the edge of both the heat of summer and the cold of winter, thus equalizing our temperature and giving us the best all-the-year-around climate of any point in the United States. There are many other great advantages, to which we invite the careful attention of the man who would better his agricultural condition. The splendid agricultural advantages offered by this portion of the South are not understood by people in general.

Our soil is nicely adapted to the growth of all the fruits, vegetables, grasses and grain found in middle latitudes; our climate ably seconds the efforts of our tillers of the soil, and our markets and facilities for reaching the same are really the best in the world.

We are nearer New York than half of York State, and nearer Philadelphia than half of Pennsylvania—nearer as regards freight rates and the time of getting there. When our advantages are but once even fairly understood, we shall be deluged with home-seekers, who, while desiring to escape the cold and frosty North, the unfertile and unproductive East and the "wild, windy and woolly West," do not care to go to the far South, can compromise on this point, as it not only gives the most desirable all-the-year-round climate, but at the same time leaves them within easy reach of the great legislative, educational, financial and commercial centres.

The Attractions of Eastern Virginia.

A. JEFFERS, Norfolk, Va.—It may not be generally known that the land on which Chicago, Cincinnati, Detroit, Milwaukee and many other Western cities stands, once belonged to Virginia. It may not be generally known that all the territory now embraced in the States of Ohio and Indiana was once within the State limits of Virginia. Such was the case, however, and in the year 1781 Virginia ceded all this vast territory to the general government, out of which territory the above-named States were afterwards formed.

Now Virginia not only gave the territory out of which to make these States, but she also loaned many thousands of her people to help settle up, populate and develop the same. So we see that Virginia, in addition to being the "Mother of Presidents" and the "Mother of Statesmen" can also lay just claim to being the "Mother of States" as well.

Now in the "fulness of time" conditions are changed, and Virginia is asking the West to repay that "old-time loan." The interest has been accumulating on the same for "lo, these more than 100 years," and it now has reached "a right smart sum," and as near as I can come at the facts in the case it will take about 5000 good families from each of these five States (25,000 families in all) to properly balance the account. We do not ask or expect this just and legitimate debt to be paid at once, but are content to receive it in instalments.

The writer has just returned from a tour in these States, and it is surprising to see how many have their faces turned toward the "Sunny South," and on every hand I heard the statement, "my grandfather or great-grandfather came from Virginia and we would like to return." The desire to study and to know about the South, and of Virginia in particular, is steadily increasing. The reaction has set in, and the Western movement has lost its force, and the tide is steadily setting in towards the South. People are reading, talking and thinking. A little well-directed effort and a small sum of money judiciously expended will enable the State of Virginia to secure immediate instalments on the debt above mentioned.

The climate of the West and the "long haul" to market are the principal reasons why so many would remove to the South. Then, too, the West is very hard on horses and on womankind. The farmer must board the men employed on the farm, and this makes slaves of the farmers' wives. In farming at the North all hands catch it hard, horses, men and women, all work hard. In the South the horses alone work hard, as they can work and are worked all the year. The farmer's brain is worth more to him in the South than elsewhere in the United States, consequently he need not work so hard, and woman is relieved from that worse than Egyptian bondage, boarding the hired help, as the laborers here board themselves. Therefore there are many sound, solid reasons why the Western agriculturist should come South. Here he can work all the year instead of being compelled to hurry the twelve months' work into four, five or six months' time.

Three great essentials underlie· successful and profitable tilling of the soil. These are soil, climate and markets. In two of these (the latter two) the entire South excels all other sections of the Union. And this particular portion of the South leads in all three essentials, as our soil in good hands and under fair treatment is the most productive in the entire United States.

When the people of the North, the West and the Northwest are once made to fully understand our many great advantages, our loan will be very soon repaid in full. A little wise and judicious legislative action on the part of our law makers, now assembled at the State capital, and a small appropriation, judiciously expended, and a little concerted effort "all along the line" will do much good. First, an official and hearty invitation should be extended to all. Second, full and reliable information should be disseminated, and it is in just this line that the work of the SOUTHERN STATES Magazine comes in, and I can assure you that it is highly appreciated by every one who has the real good of the South at heart.

Thirdly, there should be an official head in the State to direct the work, so that the greatest good may be secured to the greatest number. I have recently visited and talked with farmers 100 miles from Chicago, and still nearer Detroit and Toledo and other great commercial centres, who were really farther away from their markets than our people here are from New York, Philadelphia, Boston and other great seaport city markets. Our "water transportation" and the consequent "cheap haul" puts us squarely at the threshold of all the best markets of the North, while at the same time we are near enough or far enough South to get the full benefits of the best all-the-year-round climate in America. Our farmers are therefore working on inside lines. They have the inside track, the short haul, the cheap freight and the good soil. When the Western farmer once fully understands these matters he is coming here multitudinously.

We send a barrel of potatoes to New York for twenty-five cents and a barrel of cabbage for from fifteen to seventeen cents; everything else in proportion. Our people enjoy the cheapest freight rates and the best shipping facilities of any portion of the United States.

Florida's Sub-Peninsula.

WM. P. NEELD, of Pinellas, Fla.—On the west coast of Florida, about half way the State lies the little peninsula Pinellas. This section is famous for its tropical fruits, its fine fishing and its cool, breezy summers and its excellent society. Here are located many old groves of oranges, and orchards of tropical fruits. The low lands are adapted to the production of all kinds of vegetables and in a few years hundreds of carloads will be shipped from here. Pineapples are especially adapted to our scrub lands, and the time is not far off when thousands of acres will be planted to this crop. It is strange that no enterprising man has started a pinery here. There is a rich reward to the first man who puts in ten or twenty acres of pineapples. The sale from suckers and slips will be enormously profitable for many years. Florida is destined to furnish the United States with tropical fruits as well as oranges. Pineapple farms yield from $250 to $2000 or $3000 per acre according to varieties and management. No nicer or more profitable business can be engaged in than this. Once planted, they last for five or six years. A liberal fertilizing two or three times a year, and as many hoeings with scuffle hoe is all that is required besides harvesting the fruit and the suckers. Several small patches of this fruit have been set out here for five or six years and have proved wonderfully well adapted to soil and climate.

The mango is a most delicious tropical fruit, and grows here as well, perhaps, as in the East Indies or Mexico. Over

2000 boxes were shipped from here summer before last. Last season the crop was short and the home market took all that was offered. The Avocado pear does nearly as well as the mango, and is a most remunerative crop. Other tropical fruits are grown here besides these and the guava. Our oranges hang on the trees until March and April, when the market is at its best.

A Native of Connecticut Tells of East Tennessee's Attractions.

P. M. BARTLETT, Maryville, Tenn.— Coming from my native State, Connecticut, in the spring of 1869, in compliance with the call of the Synod of Tennessee (issued in 1868), to take the presidency of the Maryville College, founded in Maryville in 1819, and having in these many years visited much of the territory in this remarkable valley, it would seem that I have had ample opportunity to give reliable information about this part of the great American continent.

At the outset, let no one living in the little valleys of my native State measure our greatness by the cozy, narrow cradles among the New England hills. From northeast to southwest this valley is 250 miles long by 100 miles wide. It embraces thirty-four counties, and contains 13,404 square miles. It is larger than either New Hampshire or Vermont, thirteen times larger than Rhode Island, one and one-half times larger than Massachusetts, almost three times larger than Connecticut, and six times larger than Delaware. It abounds in rivers and creeks, affording water power enough to drive thousands of factories. There are single springs which flow water sufficient to run two or three mills. In my own county are mill sites which in New England would be worth $50,000. Of cultivated lands, the soil was originally good, and it has been poor tillage, which has not preserved the original fertility. Worn out lands can be easily recuperated. There are thousands of acres of rich bottoms along our streams. Timber of various kinds is abundant.

The mineral resources are unparalleled—coal and iron ore enough it would seem to supply the nation for centuries— variegated marbles of surpassing beauty in immense quantities are attracting the dealers all over the continent. Valuable beds of zinc, the refined products of which are sent to the Northern markets. Gold is found among the mountains, and beds of it are now yielding its yellow dust to the skillful miner. Extensive deposits of copper which have been reported to surpass any other as regards profitable investment in that mineral. Valuable beds of slate have been discovered in my own county, and expert miners from Wales declare no such immense deposits of the best roofing slate have been found elsewhere on our entire planet. Capitalists from Ohio are developing these deposits and can now measure the marvelous beds 200 to 300 feet in depth. How much more will be found no one knows. Parties are now leasing thousands of acres in the firm belief that natural gas and petroleum will be found in abundance.

The climate is between the extremes of heat and cold. Seldom does the thermometer reach zero, and then generally only for a day or two. When the thermometer is only 15° above zero it is called cold. Seldom do the frosts prevent farmers from plowing in the winter months. In December, January and February, usually plowing is done for spring crops. Oats are often sown in February and corn planted in March. But is it not very warm in summer? I never have known the mercury to rise as high here as in my native State. At our altitude (1000 feet) I have obser ᵉd in our hottest days how cool the bree ᵉs were that fanned us. A company ᵕf ladies reared in the North spent the entire last summer here, which to us was hotter than usual, and they remarked that the heat was not to them at all oppressive. Let no one keep away for fear of sickness, for my experience on this elevated plateau satisfies me that no more healthful climate can be found than ours in East Tennessee.

It is said that Thomas Jefferson declared it would pay anyone to make a voyage across the Atlantic in order to gaze on the grandeur of the Shenandoah river where it passes through the Blue Ridge Mountains. If the traveler wishes to gaze with rapture upon matchless scenery let him come to East Tennessee, and after he has. seen the Shenandoah let him come to Blount county and go with us for miles and miles along the Tennessee river as it rushes between the mountains far into North Carolina, and · I think he will exclaim, "There is nothing on this planet that can equal what I have seen among the mountains of Tennessee!"

When you come you will find a hospitable people whose horses and mules and homes are at your command, and you will not be asked to pay one-half what you would estimate the service to be worth. Such is the country and such the people we ask you to visit.

East Tennessee has the resources to make it one of the wealthiest sections of the globe.

Better Than His Former Home.

JOHN G. HAYDON, Clio, Ark.—I have been in Southeast Arkansas for ten years, and am pleased to say that the climate is delightful throughout the year ; the people are very hospitable. The soil is productive of corn, oats and cotton, sorghum and potatoes, and there is an enormous quantity of yellow pine timber lands ; in fact the yellow pine lumber trade is almost in its infancy. In a word, I would not exchange my home in Arkansas for my old home. We invite our friends from the North to come and mix with us, and we assure you we will make you feel at home.

Prefers Florida to Delaware.

FRANK THOMPSON, Avon Park, Fla. I have been in Florida between three and four years; at Avon Park nearly three years. I came from the city of Wilmington, Del.; am a ship joiner by trade. My work was such that in winter I suffered so much with the cold that I could not stand it, so I came to Florida and must say the climate is all that can be wished for, and Avon Park is a very healthy location and free from mosquitoes and other pests and well adapted to the growing of all kinds of tropical fruits with proper attention.

I have twelve different varieties of tropical fruits growing and one pineapple I have grown from the seed.

A German Settler in Virginia.

W. GROSMANN, Petersburg, Va.— I am glad to give my experience as a German settler in Virginia. I came to Virginia in the year 1879 and located in Lunenburg county, but afterwards moved to Chesterfield county, near the City of Petersburg.

On this farm, only one mile from the city, I directed my whole attention to the raising of vegetables, and I must say I succeeded beyond expectations. In connection with my farm I opened (seven years ago) a seed business in Petersburg, and two years later a real estate office was added, so that at present you find me busy as a farmer, seeds- · man and real estate agent. It is my honest belief and opinion that immigrants can do well here in Virginia, providing they do not buy too much land and do not go too far from a city or station ; and if. they would come in . colonies, buying large tracts of land for division, they would surely prosper. Our geographical location is A No. 1, and must, sooner or later, bring Virginia to the front.

I always have time to answer letters asking for information about Virginia, and the latch-string on our front door hangs out to everybody wanting to make Virginia their home.

Satisfied With the Country.

SAMUEL D. REES, Kuehla, Ala.—I have been planting cabbage, potatoes, &c., for the last ten years in Mobile county, and it affords me pleasure to write that I am entirely satisfied with my surroundings. Everything grows here if it has a fair chance.

I came from the vicinity of Cincinnati. I enjoy splendid health, and if there is anything the matter with this country I have been unable to discover it.

Southwest Virginia vs. Switzerland.

PAUL SCHERER, Coyner's Spring, Botetourt county, Va.—I have resided in Virginia for more than two years, and as I have traveled through the State a good deal I wish to give you an impression of Southwestern Virginia from the stand-point of a European.

In Switzerland, where I came from, farmers are proud to produce the finest meadows and to raise fine cattle and fruits. Truly there is no question that half the amount of energy used by the farmers in my home country will produce here more wealth through farming than anywhere else.

There is a general prejudice against the "worn out" land of this section, but I beg your readers to come and see what fine crops neighbors of mine raised by the use of lime.

We can get as fine clover as any-where and all grasses, including the famous blue grass, are growing abund-antly. Cattle are raised easily, and will compare favorably with any other beef cattle. The prospects of sheep raisers need no comment at all. Between Coy-ner's Spring and Cloverdale there are some of the finest and most flourishing apple orchards east of the Mississippi.

It is hard for me to understand why all the Europeans are going West and are not willing to settle in a country which offers cheap and fine land, nearer markets, good schools, and whose citi-zens welcome the honest newcomer.

The immigrant, coming from the mountains of Central Europe, can find here a country that when well develop-ed will stand very little behind that of his home country.

The advantages Virginia offers are in my mind far superior to those offered by any of the Western States, and I believe that the time is not far distant when the tide of immigration will be turned in this direction.

A Northern Man's Views of the Capa-bilities of Georgia Soil.

A. K. F., of Abbeville, Ga.—I learn that many persons in the North are anxious to hear from persons who have gone South and engaged in agricultural pursuits. I send you an experience. I am a Canadian. For many years I was en-gaged in the lumber business, but changed to farming a few years ago. After a pros-pecting tour I decided to cast my lot in the wire-grass pine lands of Georgia.

This is termed one of the new counties, as it had no railroads until five years ago, and but few settlers only within reach of the Ocmulgee river, which is navigable. Those were principally en-gaged in raising sheep and cattle. Land can be bought for from $5.00 to $10.00 per acre. There are good openings here for farmers. Most of the produce finds a home market at good prices. I raised last year 2,000 bushels of oats (rust proof), worth from fifty to sixty cents per bushel. I cut the oats in May, put on some fertilizers, plowed, harrowed and rolled the land, and cut from the same ground from one to two tons of first-class hay, worth here from $18.00 to $20.00 per ton. It is called crow-foot grass, and comes up spontaneously after land has been cultivated a few years. German millet also does well. Sown in March, it is fit to cut in ninety days, and finds ready sale at $18.00 to $20.00 per ton. In September, from the same land, I cut one ton of good hay per acre (na-tive grasses) without disturbing the ground after the millet was taken off. Alfalfa is not grown here as yet, but no doubt would do well; some parties are growing it successfully in some of the older counties. I shall try some this winter. The cattle and sheep are small, never having been crossed with improved breeds. The rule is and has always been with stockmen to leave every tenth male for breeding purposes. By cross-ing Shropshire bucks with native ewes, and feeding some in winter, the lambs can be put in northern markets one month earlier than from Ohio. By crossing some of the improved breeds of cattle with the native stock, in that way obtaining good milkers, which are worth $40.00 here, and keeping the steers fat until winter, they will bring in our home market fancy prices. There is plenty of good beef here in summer, and cheap.

In winter our beef comes from the North (cold storage). Milk retails for five cents per quart; butter from twenty-five to forty cents per pound. There is no better section for peaches, pears and grapes, and some varieties of apples do well here. This is about thirty-one degress north latitude. Lung diseases are very rare. I have lived in this county for the past ten years and have not had a case of fever in my family or among my hands; nor have I given a single dose of quinine. The citizens are very sociable and extremely anxious for farmers to settle, as they wish to change from raising cotton, but hardly know how to cultivate any other crop. Anyone coming from the North to this section will be welcomed by the citizens.

Mississippi Preferred to Illinois.

T. S. LITTLE, West Point, Miss.—I have lived in this State six years and find the climate all that is desired. The soil is good for all kinds of grain, wheat, oats, barley, potatoes, corn, tobacco, flax, grapes, peaches, apples, pears, plums and all small fruit. The people are kind and sociable. We have good schools and churches and a fine climate. Our political liberty is as good as elsewhere. I do not wish to return to the North any more, as I love this climate for health and comfort. We have fine timber on bottom land.

My former place of residence was Illinois. I am a carpenter by occupation. My political views are Republican. The people do not interfere with my opinions as is supposed in the North. The people are disposed to vote as they please. I hope that the people of the North will come South and see for themselves.

ITEMS ABOUT FARMS AND FARMERS.

Grape Growing on a Large Scale.

In the last issue of the SOUTHERN STATES some facts were given about Tallapoosa, Ga., a town that a few years ago gained an unsavory reputation throughout the whole country as the scene of a series of huge swindling operations in lots and stock. The natural failure of the effort to boom Tallapoosa as an iron-making town should not in any way discredit the farming attractions of the locality. These must be very great if we may judge from the work of the Georgia Fruit Growing and Winery Association mentioned in the last issue of the SOUTHERN STATES. The report of the treasurer of this company, made recently at the annual meeting of the association, showed that the aggregate business done by the association had been over $35,000, $17,000 of which had been received in cash. This amount of business represents aggregated sales of about 1,000 acres, of which 400 acres are now being planted to grapes and 100 acres to strawberries. In addition to the business done by the association nearly 3,000 acres of vineyard land has been sold by real estate agents and pri-

vate individuals, nearly 300 acres of which will be planted to grapes this season, and about fifty acres to strawberries; add to above the 500 acres of grapes and 200 acres of strawberries to be planted by the North Georgia Land & Manufacturing Co., and there is an aggregate of over 1,200 acres to be planted to grapes, and 350 acres to strawberries this season.

Mr. L. S. Bigelow from Brockport, N. Y., who is in charge of the planting for the Georgia Fruit Growing and Winery Association, is quoted by the Tallapoosa Journal as saying "that a vineyard in New York State that will not produce from 600 to 1200 nine-pound baskets an acre per year is considered a poor vineyard; this is equivalent to from ten to twenty pounds to the vine; yet the estimates made by the North Georgia Land & Manufacturing Company are only ten pounds to the vine and by the Georgia Fruit Growing and Winery Association fifteen pounds to the vine. Mr. Bigelow says further that he considers this section far superior to New York State for grape growing, both in nature of its soil and its climatic conditions, and above all the supreme advantage of coming into the market with the grapes when there is virtually no competition."

What Southwest Texas Offers.

N. A. Young, of San Antonio, Texas, claims that the country adjacent to that city offers unusual advantages for farmers. Mr. Young says:

"Our farmers most of them depend too much on cotton and corn, when they should diversify their crops and make it a point to have a little of everything to sell that grows, and also raise their own meat as well as bread, keep a few good hogs, keep a few good cows, and if cramped for pasture sell off the increase. Make your own milk and butter and have some over to sell. This is the method by which all the German families prosper, and there is no reason why any man here with a little farm of 100 or 160 acres should not in a few years become independent. Here where a man can work out doors eleven months or more in the year, and where the winters are so short that he only has to feed his loose stock but two or three months, I say there is no place in the United States to equal the country contiguous to this city in the varied advantages for the small farmer, provided, as in all vocations, he is not afraid to work.

I know an American who came to San Antonio in 1867 with no money, only a yoke of oxen, wagon and a few household effects and his wife. He first rented twelve miles east of the city and began farming, raising everything and always having something to bring to town to sell. I bought butter from him for six years. He built up from the start, raised a family of nine children, six of whom are now grown. He bought more land from year to year and as soon as one of his sons or daughters married he gave them each from 160 to 200 acres of land. He is now independent, rents out his large farms and is worth, after providing for all his children, who all live near him, $50,000. Can any country beat that? There is plenty of good farming land in Bexar county to be at had from $5 to $10 per acre, and on easy terms, and to all farmers who want a change let them

come to Bexar county, buy a small farm and grow rich and independent. What has been done once can be repeated and there are plenty more than the instance named to verify the statement that dry though it may be, yet still there is money and success to the man of pluck and courage in farming in old Bexar county yet."

Virginia vs. Western Farming.

Mr. A. G. Wilson, a farmer of Culpeper county, Va., writes to the Religious Herald about farming in that section: He says:

"You may offer a thousand dollars for a wike-awake, saving, energetic farmer who is not getting along well, and you will be in no danger of losing your money. All through Orange, Culpeper and other counties where I have been, I find that those who work at it succeed and find farming a very good business."

Contrast this with the debt-burdened conditions of many Western farmers who work as hard as they can possibly, but who are working against conditions that cannot be overcome. In one section everything favors the farmer—mild winters, nearness to markets, cheap land —while in the others "a winter eight months long," and distance from markets makes profitable farming almost impossible, except under unusual circumstances.

Alabama Farmers.

A letter from Eutaw, Ala., to the Birmingham News tells the same story of a better condition of farm interests that comes from every part of the South. It will be interesting to Northern farmers to be told in the language of this correspondent:

"Farmers are bestirring themselves. Much breaking up of black lands has already taken place, and all are busy getting up home-made fertilizers for the coming crop. Looking over the papers much is seen of farmers here and there who have made meat and corn enough to do them for another year. In Greene county—the white end of a black belt county—nearly all the farmers are in just that condition. I could name a great number of them who can live at home this year, except for a little flour, sugar and coffee, and many can leave out the sugar, as it is simply easier than anything else to make all the syrup and sugar needed by any family."

Contrast This With Western Farming.

Mr. C. P. Willingham, after a trip to Houston county, told the Macon (Ga.) Telegraph that it gave him a new lease on life to see the independence those Houston county farmers have, and their thriftiness. He says they are all feeling confident of a restoration of the "good old times," and are already giving themselves over to extensive preparations for next year's crop. "I look upon the middle Georgia farmer as the happiest of men," said Mr. Willingham, "and I believe he is in a more prosperous state today than in ten years."

Mr. Homer Eads, of the Missouri Pacific Railway Co., San Antonio, Texas, in a letter to the Manufacturers' Record, says: "We have had an exceptionally warm winter in Texas, especially in the southern portion of the State. At this writing the thermometer registers 75 degrees. New grass is coming up unusually early this year, especially in sections favored with sufficient rainfall, and in consequence, live stock, having access to new grass, is beginning to put on a little flesh. We have had no cold weather so far, and should it continue mild the balance of the winter season, there will be no stock losses in Southwest Texas to speak of, and the heavy runs of stock cattle that have heretofore gone to the Indian Territory for grass and water from this section during the months of January and February, will be held at home and shipped direct to markets. This is, of course, the brightest view to be taken, although present indications look very favorable."

Farmers in the frozen regions of the Northwest must read with a great deal of interest the following letter from Clermont, Fla., dated June 9: Early vegetables are commencing to come in, Mr. J. H. Compton being the first to make tomato shipments from this station. Returns on tomatoes are very satisfactory, none having sold so far less than

$5 per bushel crate. Messrs. Malloy & Wootsen have shipped between 300 and 400 bushels of string beans which have sold in the Western markets at from $3 to $5 per bushel crate.

According to the Greenville Banner Texas is not experiencing the hard times prevailing in other States; in fact Texas is prospering. The Banner says: This state of affairs is due largely to the preparation our people have made to "live at home and board at the same place." The crop of 1893 was varied more than that of any other year. Farmers have, as a rule, raised pork enough for meat during the next year, and some are selling to their neighbors and to the towns. There is a surplus of corn that will supply the demand. Oats are plentiful and the wheat crop will supply almost all the breadstuffs needed. While this condition exists here there is poverty and suffering in the North and East. In the North hard times have left their impress on the people, and starvation stalks abroad in the land. There is a remedy for this, and it can be found on the fertile prairies of the Southwest, and especially of Texas. There are millions of acres of untilled land in Texas awaiting the plow share.

Montgomery county, Texas, has been experimenting with tobacco cultivation, and the results are said to be remarkably satisfactory. The object sought was to produce a fine quality of Cuban cigar leaf. This has been accomplished in a number of counties. The crop of 1892 in Montgomery county sold for thirty-five cents per pound and averaged about 600 pounds to the acre. The first crop of 1893 sold for forty-one cents per pound and the second, or "sucker," crop is still in the hands of the producers, and for it they have been offered forty-six cents per pound, and this, too, on land without a particle of fertilizing.

Farmers in Shelby county, Tenn., are planting potatoes. That county is reported to have shipped away 50,000 barrels of potatoes last year. The crop comes on the market early in June and lasts for six weeks or more.

"TEXAS," said Colonel Walter Gresham, who represents the Galveston district of the Lone Star State, to a Washington Post reporter, "is in splendid condition. I do not believe there is today a more prosperous State in the Union. Our farming classes are particularly well off. The tillers of the soil are freer from debt than they have been in a long time, and many of them have snug bank accounts. Their crops have turned out better than was expected, and despite the low price of cotton they have been able to lay up money. Immigration has started up on a lively scale, and we are getting desirable people from every section. As a consequence the demand for farming lands has increased, and there has been a rise in values, particularly in the coast regions."

THE Madison Horticultural Society is being organized at Madison, Miss., by Dr. H. E. McKay, j. B. Yellowly, T. B. Briggs, F. L. Hay and other prominent fruit growers.

THE Charlotte (N. C.) News quotes a prominent farmer of Mecklenburg country as saying, that while 1893 was a bad year generally in financial circles, it was a comparatively good year for the farmers of that section. "I really believe," he said, "that our farmers are better off now than they have been in years past. They raised a surplus of everything, and instead of buying corn, you now see them selling it. Nearly every farmer of my acquantance has had corn to sell. They are less in debt now than they were a year ago, and are steadily swinging into a system of cash business."

THE Democrat, of Scotland Neck, N. C., lately made a canvass of the farmers in that section and found that the reports all indicated a better financial condition than for many years. Cash was reported as scarce, but nearly all farmers had a full supply of corn and meat on hand, and were prepared to make this year's crop at low cost.

ONE of the evidences of the good condition of Southern farmers is that they have returned to the custom of ante bellum days and are now raising their own foodstuffs. Southern railroads which have heretofore hauled thousands of car loads of Western grain and provisions to the South aunually are now feeling the almost total loss of this business, and Southern factors are finding that their business of furnishing farm supplies is this year nearly dead. Southern farmers, with full corn cribs and abundance of meat, with their cotton as a surplus cash crop, and with less indebtedness than for many years, can well afford to take a cheerful survey of life.

MR. G. B. D. PARKER, of Chinquapin, N. C., in 1893, had 100 acres in corn, from which he gathered 525 barrels, and on fifteen acres in cotton he made thirteen 500-pound bales of lint cotton.

WHILE Northern farmers are still freezing Southern truckers are putting in their spring crops, the truckers around Newberne, N. C., having already planted their peas to a large extent.

NORTH CAROLINA employs many of its convicts in farming, and last year the penitentiary farms produced an aggregate of 1191 bales of cotton, 50,000 bushels of corn, and 12,500 bushels of peanuts. But for a freshet which destroyed about 30,000 bushels, the corn crop would have been 80,000 bushels. There are now 1000 acres in wheat on these farms.

THE GROWTH OF A NEW INDUSTRY.

By D. A. Tompkins.

About ten years ago there lived near Alvarado, Texas, a young man named A. J. Vick. He had moved to Texas from West Tennessee. Returning to visit his old home he met Dr. Porter, of Memphis, who had known him as a boy, and they chatted with the usual interest of old friends long separated but recently met.

Dr. Porter was president of a bank in Memphis and also of a cottonseed-oil mill.

"You've got nothing special to do," said Dr. Porter to young Mr. Vick, "get in the buggy and go with me out to the Gayoso cottonseed-oil mill. I want to show you some of the headway we have made in manufactures since you left this civilized country and went West."

Mr. Vick got in the buggy and went to the Gayoso mill and after looking over the mill Mr. Vick said: "Do I understand properly, that fifty per cent. of the cottonseed is hull and that after paying ten dollars per ton for cottonseed you burn the hulls for fuel to make steam ?"

"That's exactly right," said Dr. Porter, "and it seems a pity that so good a looking product as cottonseed hulls can be put to no more profitable use than it can serve as a fuel."

"Would you consider a suggestion from a Texan worthy of consideration ?" asked Mr. Vick.

"Of course I would," answered Dr. Porter, "but I have some ideas on the subject myself and before you begin let me suggest. Would you undertake to try an experiment to learn whether these hulls have any value as a feed for cattle, either for producing beef or milk and butter. I have had an idea they might make a good substitute for hay, fodder and such like 'roughness.' It is not simply 'an idea;' I have had them analyzed and the chemistry of the thing is all right, but I don't want to try to push the experiment except through just such a young man as I take you to be. If I send you a couple of car loads of these hulls, pay the freight on them and guarantee to protect you in all expenses incurred, will you give them a fair trial as to what value they are as food for animals with split hoofs ?"

Without pursuing the conversation further, Mr. Vick agreed to receive the hulls and give them a fair trial. His experiments led to the conclusion that the hulls were a first-rate food for cattle and sheep and more especially so when mixed with cottonseed meal.

As a result of the experiment, about the year 1884, Mr. Vick sent from Western Texas to Memphis about 300 head of prairie steers which he put up and fed on hulls and meal to make cattle of them. The result was entirely satisfactory both as to the production of good beef and as to the financial outcome.

About the same time this experiment was being made Mr. Fred Oliver of Charlotte, N. C., and his friends were organizing the Southern Cotton Oil Company.

Mr. Vick made a contract with the new company to supply him hulls and meal to feed about 2000 head of cattle. These were successfully fattened and sold and in the following year Mr. Vick interested three other gentlemen with him and fed about 10,000 head of cattle. About this time the American Cotton Oil Company began to purchase and feed cattle in order to utilize the hulls from their mills. The dairymen in New Orleans had also learned the value of hulls as a feed for dairy cattle.

About 1890 the value of cottonseed hulls and cottonseed meal began to be generally understood as a feed for cattle and for milch cows, in Texas and Arkansas and to some extent in Louisiana. From this time on the cattlemen of Texas began to be very much more interested in the subject. The ranges were being narrowed down by increasing occupation of Texas land for farming purposes, and the question of carrying cattle over the winter grew to be a more and more important one. The cattlemen began to subscribe to the stock of oil mills in order to be able to get hulls and meal to carry their cattle over the winter. The cotton-oil business grew rapidly, especially in the southwest, until in 1893 cattlemen had come to consider an oil mill near enough to get food for their cattle as a necessity.

In the summer of 1893 there were probably not less than forty oil mills in Texas alone, and the chief motive in them all was the making hull and meal feed for cattle grazed on the plains in the summer, but requiring some food in winter in consequence of narrowing ranges.

The following table will show about the number of cattle fatted for beef in the South since 1883 on cottonseed hulls and cottonseed meal, and also the number of cattle fed for dairy purposes in the same time:

	DAIRY.	BEEF.
1884	....	300
1885	500	1,500
1886	800	10,000
1887	1,500	15,000
1888	5,000	20,000
1889	15,000	30,000
1890	25,000	50,000
1891	50,000	75 000
1892	75,000	125,000
1893	100,000	175,000

Mr. W. P. Richardson, ex State senator for New York State from Goshen, was amongst the first to appreciate the value of cottonseed hulls and meal as a feedstuff for dairy cattle. He finds that he can save three-quarters of his hay by the use of hulls and meal. Formerly he fed twenty to twenty-five pounds of hay per day, while now with the hulls and meal he uses only five pounds.

Mr. Richardson keeps seventy-five milch cows on his farm near Goshen, N. Y.

He finds that by the use of hulls and meal he can keep a larger number of cattle on a farm of a given size than he could without the feed. By its use he can produce more milk and more butter than he can with any other feed and at less cost. Its use is rapidly increasing amongst the farmers of his section.

The following data has been prepared by the American Cotton Oil Co., and published in a pamphlet about cottonseed hulls and meal as a cattle food.

"The advantages of cottonseed meal as a food and fertilizer have become so well understood, that we need not speak of its merits to those who have used it. To those who have not, we give below its fat and flesh producing qualities as compared with other articles, and as set forth by eminent agricultural and chemical authorities:

Food.	Flesh Producing.	Fat Producing.
Turnips...................	1	5
Carrots................... .	1	7
Straw....................	3	16
Potatoes.................. ...	3	17
Brewer's grain.............	6½	18
Rice meal.................	6½	77
Hay (early cut)............	8	50
Buckwheat................	9	60
Malt..................... ...	9	76
Rye...................... ...	11	72
Oats..................	12	63
Corn....	12	68
Wheat....................	12	97
Barley................	12	67
Bran & coarse millstuff mix..	31	54
Cottonseed meal...........	41	77

The following feeding value and manurial value is given as Mr. Lawes' estimate of the value of the manure from a number of foods, and with them the feeding values are estimated by Wolf:

	WOLF.	LAWES.
	Feeding values.	Manurial values.
Cottonseed meal.	$41 40 per ton.	$27 86 per ton.
Linseed cake....	34 40 "	19 72 "
Beans...........	15 20 "	15 73 "
Wheat bran......	20 80 "	24 59 "
Clover hay.......	14 00 "	9 64 "
Corn meal.......	22 20 "	6 64 "
Meadow hay	12 80 "	6 43 "
Oat Straw........	9 00 "	2 90 "
Potatoes.........	5 80 "	1 50 "
Turnips	2 20 "	86 "

The meal has great strength; therefore, we recommend that for several days after commencing its use give one quart at each feed, mixed with slop or bran. Gradually increase the quantity until two quarts or more are given at a feed. If thus fed, will give great satisfaction."

Every oil mill in the South is selling large quantities of hull and meal for cattle feed. The mills will work 1,500,000 tons of seed from which will come 750,000 tons of hulls. Each ton of hull with its pro rata of meal will make a fine fat beef of a lean steer.

The oil business is constantly increasing. It will not be long before there will be a million tons of hulls available, and of course this will not all go to make beef, much will go to dairy cattle for the production of milk and butter.

The consumption of this feed is not confined to the South, however. As stated above, Mr. Richardson, of Goshen, New York, has been using it with success for several years, and its consumption in that section is constantly increasing. The hull alone is now worth at the oil mills $3.00 to $5.00 per ton, and has sold at a price as high as $7.00 per ton. The meal sells at the mills at $20.00 to $22.00 per ton, and the mixed feed at a price aggregating the price of the hull and meal in the mixture plus the cost of mixing and sacking, and machinery has been developed and is built for putting it in sacks in good marketable shape and a large business has been developed in the sale of it, both in sacks and in carload lots in bulk.

NEW BERNE IN BLOOM.

By Charles Hallock.

The chance tourist who essays to follow the lead of the Chesapeake & Albemarle canal at the close of January, en route from Norfolk to New Berne, after a passage through the lone cypress swamp and a night voyage across the Mediterranean expanse of Pamlico sound, wakes up at his destination with a consiousness of strange contrasts in nature. In the crypt-like aisles of the Dismal Swamp all was stark, silent and lifeless. Not a pipe from a partridge nor a chirp from a sparrow disturbed the perfect hibernation; not a yellow jasmine or redbud opened its calyx to the raw atmosphere. At New Berne the mellow whistle of a blue bird greeted the new-comer, and blossoms of blue myrtle bespangled the glossy foliage which clustered by the stone walls. The sky was blue and devoid of a brumal cast. The air felt soft and warm, and truckers were found busily engaged in putting in their peas and potatoes for the initial crop. Some were shipping early cabbage and spinach to New York.

At this season of the year flurries of snow will come in Norfolk, and the prevailing atmosphere is gray; but at New Berne, mocking birds and thrushes warble in the hedges, yellow hummers and robins flit from tree to tree, crowds of old field larks rise from the standing stalks of corn, and the great pileated woodpecker makes the forest resound with the impacts of his bill. Such delectable conditions result from a simple difference of two degrees of latitude, which gives New Berne truckers an advantage of ten days over their Northern competitors, and by so much makes them the gainers.

Late in November 200 varieties of roses fold their petals for a six week's respite from perennial blooming, but persistent little buds, tweaked and deformed by morning frosts, hang on until Christmas. The clustering white blossoms of the Japan plum keep them quiet company, together with the creamy blooms and purple fruit of the Spanish bayonet, which so much resembles okra pods in shape and size, though not in color. After Christmas it is dead winter for three weeks. No presumptuous blossom ventures to disturb the restful hibernation of the flora except the purple winter violets which never cease to unfold their constant petals. Gay gallants and coy maidens pluck them for their buttonholes, cherishing them as souvenirs of brighter days. All winter long they bloom, these irrepressible flowers, without perceptible intermission nestling close to the ground amidst a thick frondage of green leaves. You can find them on any warm day. Cold merely chills, but does not paralyze them. Once, after a six days' freeze and superincumbent snow in the frigid January of 1893, with the surface of the Neuse river skimmed with ice, they bloomed out bravely as soon as the temperature rose, as fresh and fragrant as before.

In New Berne the winter climate is sufficiently warm without being enervating. Its average normal temperature is 44° for January, February and March. Snow falls are so rare as to be welcomed for their novelty. January, 1893, was an exceptional month. It was phenomenal. Snow laid on the ground for five successive days, and one morning there was sleighing! The oldest inhabitant had never seen the like. Thereupon, sleds and runners of the crudest construction were improvised. Cows were incontinently stripped of their bells to make a festive jingle on the road. Everybody was ecstatic. But the sport was only for a day; mud and slush supervened. In the previous winter of 1892 a single fall of less than an inch occurred. The current winter has been in keeping with previous records, and on January 10 the premonitory bluebird piped the advent of spring as usual. At that date hyacinths and fostoria are always seen in Southern exposures, followed on January 19 by flowering quince, orange, jasmine, a most fragrant shrub, spiren, jonquils and bridal wreath. Daffodils and narcissus appear the first week in February, and peach blossoms and dandelions by February 15. Weeping willows come to leaf by February 27. By March 1 the sweet bay and dwarf magnolia are in bloom, their pure white or purplish-pink blossoms showing in advance of the green foliage. Tulips and lilacs unfold a little later, and green pea vines stand four inches high. Potatoes and almost all vegetables are planted in February, and by the beginning of April, radishes, peas and asparagus are ready for shipment to the North.

In New Berne premises are many fruit trees, cherries, pears, apples, peaches, plums, apricots, figs and pomegranates, and by the first of April their branches are all aglow with pink and white blossoms. Wistaria then begins to hang out its white and purple clusters on the balconies and verandahs, climbing sometimes to the tops of the tallest elms, and the flowering almond illumines the terraces and parterres with its delicate floresence. From that time on development is rapid, and flowering plants, trees, vines and shrubs vie with each other in their resplendent garniture of color. Nearly all the shade trees which stud the lawns and overarch the streets are florescent with pink, blue, red, yellow, lilac, straw color and purple colors, the polonia, locust, crêpe myrtle and chinaberry being always prominent. Even the forests are aglow, not only with their own exuberance of bloom, but with the crimson, scarlet and yellow blooms of jasmine, woodbine, honeysuckle, trumpet flower, bamboo, sweet-brier, sarsaparilla and other vines, which clamber to their highest tops and weigh them down, sometimes spreading over a large area of frondage. Reputable botanists declare that no less than 1800 varieties of trees, plants, shrubs and vines bloom in North Carolina in the months of March, April and May!

The winter foliage of the forests and gardens is perhaps even more enchanting to the Northern visitor because more novel. Evergreens, not including conifers, of no less than thirty varieties, oaks and magnolias of several kinds, holly, yopon, haw, and euonymus, all brilliant with red berries, olive, laurel, cape jasmine, cherokee rose, bamboo vines, ivy, cranberry, gall berry in blue spangles, woodbine, fetter-foot, creeping whortleberry, honeysuckle, wintergreen, rhododendron, sand myrtle, mock orange, sarsaparilla, box and many others, with parasitic moss and mistletoe clinging to trunks and branches and polypodon climbing up the stems, all simulating summer in midwinter in the most captivating manner.

THE SOUTHERN RAILROADS AND IMMIGRATION.

The letters on immigration from officials of Southern railroads published in the January number have drawn forth widespread comment. The managers of the Southern roads were asked to give their views on the immigration to the South, the need of it and the best way to induce it, and to say what their respective roads were doing in aid of immigration. The promptness and fullness of the replies indicated much greater interest in the matter than had been looked for.

The two following letters came in too late for the January number, but they are too valuable to be lost and are given a place here:

What the Mobile & Ohio is Doing.

Mobile & Ohio Railroad Co.
Mobile, Ala., January 17, 1894.

Your favor of recent date regarding Southern immigration is received and the contents carefully noted.

In reply thereto I wish to say that the Mobile & Ohio Railroad has been doing more to attract the attention of Northern farmers to the South than all of the other Southern railroads combined.

We have had to do all of this immigration work without the co-operation of the other Southern railroads, and until the present month connecting lines in the North have persistently refused to join us in making through excursion rates.

During the past three years we have been making a land-seeker's rate of $10 for the round trip from St. Louis to Citronelle, Ala., giving the land-seeker over 1200 miles of travel on our road, with the privilege of stopping off at pleasure both ways, the tickets being good for thirty days. Since a few of the Northern roads have consented to join us in the land-seekers' excursions once a month, we have adopted a one-fare rate, and land-seekers' tickets will be on sale on a number of Northern lines to points on the Mobile & Ohio Railroad at one fare for the round trip.

If the Southern railroads will co-operate and use the same means for attracting immigration that have always been used by the Western railroads to settle up the West, there will be no difficulty whatever in inducing a great immigration to the South—enough to occupy the millions of acres of productive but unoccupied lands.

Some of the Southern railroads soon after the war spent large sums of money in endeavoring to attract immigration from the North. The conditions at that time were unfavorable, and prejudices existed both North and South. Today an entirely different condition exists. The Southern people want immigration and the Northern people are gradually finding out that their prejudices regarding the Southern people, climate and productions have been entirely erroneous:

Unaided and alone the Mobile & Ohio has been fighting this battle of immigration, until we have aroused an interest and started a movement so strong that nothing will ever be able to stop it. Today there are over 150 Northern farmers along the line of our road investigating opportunities for purchasing homes. In addition, there was an excursion party of over 100 land-seekers left St. Louis last night in charge of our general agent, Mr. F. W. Greene, for various points on our road through Eastern Mississippi and Southern Alabama. There is a very decided growth in the disposition of Northern people to come South, and a number of clerks in my office are kept busy answering letters and mailing literature to Northern farm-

ers who are making inquiries for information about this country and asking for
rates.

The immigration movement to the
South will, within three years, be greater
than to the West. There is going to
be another army of Northern people
come to capture this country, but this
one will be an industrial army. We
have found in our work that there is only
one way to fully overcome the prejudices
existing in the mind of the average
Northern farmer, and that is for him to
come down and see for himself. The
hundreds who have visited our country
during the past year have all been
pleased. I do not know of a single one
who has gone back dissatisfied with the
country.

It has been customary for many years
with the Southern railroads, in sending
out folders and other advertising matter,
to gorgeously decorate the outside with
a picture of a swamp, surrounded by
moss-festooned trees and ornamented
with a beautiful collection of alligators.
The result of this class of advertising
has been to create the impression that
the South is a country of swamps and
alligators. People visiting our road look
in vain for either, as we have not a single swamp on the entire water line of the road.
We run along a water shed, and the
country is rolling and as healthful as any
portion of America. In fact the greater
part of the country through which we
run is a sanitarium, where malaria is
unknown, and the climate will relieve
and cure many diseases incident to the
North.

The reasons for our being so successful in securing immigration from the
North, aside from our persistence in
attracting the attention of Northern
people to our country, are that we offer
greater shipping facilities in the way of
fast freight schedules and low rates from
interior points to the markets of the
North and West, especially on fruits and
vegetables, and take greater pains to
foster and develop the industries of the
new settlers than any other Southern
railroad; and we have a greater variety
of soils and more favorable conditions
than can be found elsewhere. Not to
mention the rich portion of Southern

Illinois, we cross the Western part of
Kentucky and Tennessee, a fertile section of country. We then run for over
200 miles through the rich prairie region
of Eastern Mississippi, the Egypt of the
South, where the conditions for general
farming are more perfect than can be
found anywhere else in America. This
is the portion of the country that is
especially attractive to the Northern
farmers. The improved farms in this
region are sold at from $10 to $15 per
acre, within a mile of the railroad stations. These lands in the hands of
Northern farmers produce enormous
crops of clovers and grasses, thus furnishing a basis for the most successful
prosecution of all branches of agriculture.

From Meridian, Miss., to Mobile, Ala.,
the country is rolling. The soil is a
sandy loam covered with long-leaf yellow pine. These lands can be bought
for $3 an acre, immediately on the road.
A more healthful location does not exist
anywhere, and the soil and climate are
especially adapted to the cultivation of
fruits and vegetables and the most of farm
crops. The farmer can get from two to
four crops every season from the same
land, and he can net more money from
each one of the crops than he will make
on the same crop in the North. Living
expenses are much less here than in the
North. The air is filled with the health-
giving odor of the pine trees. The
water, either from wells, springs or
brooks, is purer, clearer and softer than
any you will find elsewhere. The water
used in Mobile comes from a creek flowing down through the pine woods, and
is used by all the manufacturing chem-
ists here without filtering or distilling.
There is no day in the year when a
farmer cannot work in the fields with
entire comfort, unless it is raining too
hard to be out.

You can have a garden all winter and
go to it every day for green vegetables.
This is not only a great pleasure, but a
very decided help in keeping down the
family expenses.

A most difficult thing for the Northern
man to realize is that our summers are
cooler and more comfortable than they
are in the North, but this is true. The

nights are always cool, and the days are never so hot as they get in the North. A cool breeze is never absent, and sun-strokes are unknown.

The Northern people are beginning to find out these facts, and to know that they can farm more profitably and more comfortably in the South than they can in the North, and when these facts become generally known through the North there will be an immense immigration to this country.

There is little profit in farming in the North with their high-priced lands, while in this country a man of small means can get rich farming. I could give you numerous cases, but will only mention one that has come under my personal observation. A man started seven years ago with only $1000 capital. He bought twenty-seven acres of land and in the meantime has done nothing but cultivate this small tract. He has accummulated above his living expenses fully $40,000. Others have done equally well, and any one who is industrious can accomplish as much as this man.

There are only four things necessary to induce a great immigration from the North to any part of the South. First, you must have a desirable location for the immigrant. Second, you must let the Northern people know what you have to offer. Third, you must afford the people of the North and West every opportunity to visit the South and investigate at little cost by giving them as low excursion rates as the Western lines used when attracting attention to that section. Fourth, if the people of any section of the South are prejudiced against Northern immigration, the first work to be done by the railroads is to educate them to the advantages of Northern immigration and get their hearty co-operation, so that the people who come South shall be made to feel that they are welcome and are wanted as settlers and neighbors.

E. E. POSEY,
Acting Gen'l Pass. Agent.

Importance of Colonization.

Queen & Crescent Route. {
Cincinnati, Ohio, January 10, 1894. }

I have your interesting favor of the 30th ultimo in regard to the matter of future Southern development, and can unreservedly endorse your views as to such development depending largely for the next few years on the immigration movement from the North, and the growth and progress of farming communities and improvement of farming methods.

I am of the opinion that one of the necessary adjuncts to that process of immigration and settlement that shall be the entirely successful one in the South is colonization. As far as has been possible, the Queen & Crescent has given every encouragement to colonization enterprises in the past and is making increased efforts to do so in the future. A community of people, all with home ties and kinship to bind them together and to make their every-day life pleasant, will succeed, where an immigrant who enters a strange community alone will fail. This, I want to make plain, is not because of antagonism on the part of the South so much as from want of knowledge on the part of the Northern settler of Southern ways and habits.

The territory tributary to the line of the Queen & Crescent is rich in possibilities to the farmer. A ride of ten hours South from Cincinnati brings the man from Michigan or Northern New York into a locality where his stock can pasture for ten months a year, and where cattle and horses never suffer from cold weather or storms.

For fruit raising, a Northern man, when transferred to the hillsides around Chattanooga, can get a double price for his berries and other small fruits, because he gets them to market a month before he could possibly do so in the North.

The peach-raising industry is developing rapidly on the high lands of the Cumberland plateau.

Tobacco raising has proven signally successful on the land adjacent to this line between Meridian and New Orleans, and along the V. S. & P. division (in Louisiana) between Vicksburg and Shreveport.

This company has for sale over a million acres of land tributary to its lines in Alabama, Mississippi and Louisiana, which is selling at prices that cannot be touched in the North or West, and we stand ready to welcome new settlers and give them every assistance in our power.

Nor have our past and present efforts in this direction been in vain. For the last five years the counties through which the Queen & Crescent passes have shown unprecedented growth in population and wealth. A comparison between them and counties having a farming population in the Northern States, shows that while all the Southern counties grew in population and taxable values, many of the Northern counties did not increase at all, and the average is far below that of the South.

I certainly am at liberty, in the light of these facts, to say that the development of the South through the immigration of farmers from the North, and the growth of her farming interests is an established and present fact as well as a pleasant one, and will increase rapidly and surely in the future.

W. C. RINEARSON,
General Passenger Agent.

AN ANCIENT TEXAS PORT REVIVED.

Immediately following the Texas revolution of 1836 Linnville sprung into a flourishing seaport. It was the largest town in Calhoun county and did the biggest business on the Texas coast. It was located on a commanding bluff twenty feet high, overlooking Lavaca bay. A more healthful spot for a town could not be found anywhere. A big custom house was established by the young republic and vessels from the four quarters of the globe crowded her wharves. They came in numbers from New Orleans, the North Atlantic ports and Europe and the city had, it seemed, a most hopeful future. But the place did not last many years. It was completely wiped out of existence on a bright afternoon in 1840 by a band of bloodthirsty Comanche warriors, estimated at from one to two thousand. The people that did not escape to the vessels were massacred, and the destruction of the town forms one of the saddest chapters in American history; but no able pen has touched upon the event and who among even the intelligent people of the country has read about the town and its awful fate. Rival ports grew up and no effort was ever made to rebuild the town, and in all these long years cattle have peacefully grazed over the desolated site.

But strange as it may seem, modern capital and enterprise, will undertake the task of rebuilding the place. In the summer the Phillips Investment Co., of Kansas City, Mo., a wealthy syndicate bought all the country around Linnville. It has now been developed that the syndicate will locate a German colony on the property. The program will include the opening of a postoffice and stores, and the rebuilding of the town. The country around rivals the valleys of California in fertility of soil and climatic advantages. The colonists will be selected and fruit growing and the cultivation of vegetables for the Northern markets will be their occupation. The syndicate is subdividing the territory by avenues, roads and streets and will spare no expense to establish an ideal community of those thrifty people in this semi-tropical region. None but Germans will be allowed to buy homes.

AS TO IMMIGRATION FOR THE SOUTH.

By Andrew J. Howell, Jr.

The idea of immigration suggests a degree of thrift and prosperity, or at least encourgement of industry, which is interesting and pleasant to those who esteem material advancement as a worthy object of busy thought and constant endeavor. This to a large extent is due merely to our love of activity and novelty and the wish for rapid increase of wealth, and it is often carried to a degree at which sound jndgment and reasonable expectation will not sustain the zealous desire to secure immigration. There is, however, much that is reasonable and plausible in the plans and efforts for immigration; and results manifested in a multitude of instances in our country in the development of sections, great and small, have justified all the means that have been used for the accomplishment of ends reached.

Into the vast domains of the United States, unoccupied during the earlier years of its existence, immigration poured, filling the fertile fields and flocking to recently opened mines and centres of new industry, until there has resulted some of the most thrifty and substantial sections of the Union. Foreigners and those from other sections alike shared in the development of new districts.

Evil has resulted in some instances from such immigration in consequence of a lack of appreciation of their surroundings on the part of some immigrants, and the bad disposition of others, and from many other sources; but the good has far overbalanced the evil and furnishes an earnest of what might be done to advantage in other instances.

Now the United States may be generally populated. Frontiers have become developed communities, and all parts are united by quick means of communication and business relations. Their respective habits are formed, customs established, and each is marked by a fixedness of disposition, which is against the idea of frontier life.

Occasional disappointments as to expected success and many other reasons still prompt citizens to desire a change of residence, or removal from one section to another as immigrants. Foreigners, also, are still reaching our shores in the expectation of finding happy and profitable homes here. The Manufacturers' Record gives the information that numerous inquiries are received at its office from farmers and others from the West and Northwest as to desirability and encouragement for immigration into the South, and seeks advice as to how such immigration may be secured and judiciously controlled.

Many citizens, ardent with the idea of the South's progress, hasten to invite immigration to it, unqualifiedly and unconditionally, satisfied to feel that just so many men and women may be gotten to remove to their section. This, however, involves many serious errors. That immigration is desirable for the South is obvious; that advantages would accrue from it for the South's advancement and prosperity bears no question; provided, however, care is used in the selection of immigrants, in the encouragement offered them for removal here and in the assuming of an attitude toward them on the part of Southern citizens, with whom they would dwell.

The conditions obtaining in the South with respect to immigration are widely at variance with those of the Western and other sections. Here long years and peculiar mode of life have firmly established the characteristics of its citizens; and the conditions of soil and climate, the opportunities for industry and the advantages for commercial advancement differ widely from those of other parts.

What is needed, however, in an immigrant for the South? It noes not need labor other than what it has, except, perhaps, occasionally in its mining and foundry industries. Its interests are chiefly agricultural and commercial, and its native labor—the negro—is better suited than any other in these departments. Negroes are abundant, and there can really be no need for additional labor.

Does the South then need immigration of farmers? Yes, if they bring with them ideas of independent farmers' life and tend to develop its advantages for such by habits of industry and economical and judicious modes of life. Does it offer advantages for such? Unquestionably, it does. Not to speak of the long period of dependence very largely on its own resources prior to the war; for a few years subsequent thereto, when slavery was abolished and its conditions of life changed, and before commercial relations were established to a considerable extent with the North and West, and while it was repressed with a feeling of wounded pride at its defea, in the struggle which it had undergonet through a feeling of necessity, it supplied almost wholly its own wants and fared better and more comfortably than at least its agricultural interests do at the present time and for several years hitherto. The large food supply from the North and West, meat, flour, etc., were not then drawn upon and increased by the South's demands; its clothing and shoes were made by itself, though often times rudely, from its own stuffs; and the feeling of self-dependence furnished the means for supplying its almost every necessity. If it was then, in its crippled and impoverished state, capable of such self-support, what could it not do—how much more economically and better supply its own needs—now that conditions are so favorable to it? The secret

of a community's success is in its drawing upon its own resources as much as possible, and converting as little as possible into money wherewith to make purchases of others.

The South's climate and soil give it agricultural advantages and advantages for certain manufactures possessed by no other portion of the world. Details would be superfluous here.

Activity and prosperity are contagious, and upon the incoming of new citizens, with new determinations to do well, the entire community will eventually feel the effects of the leaven. Such, indeed, is begun to be manifested even with the small consideration given to immigration in the South. Increase of wealth and commercial prominence will inevitably follow such infusion of new spirit.

Now, as to the means of securing immigration of the proper kind.

None should be sought but intelligent, well-bred persons capable of sustaining themselves with such assistance as may be offered them. None should be had who feel themselves subordinates or merely laborers, but they should have a spirit of independence and honest industry. The peculiar temper of the Southern people, however, would not allow them to be patient and fraternal with overbearing and rough strangers. In other words, the only immigration that should be encouraged for the South is that which would easily commingle with its citizenship and aid in upbuilding its industrial interests.

Since immigration would be of undoubted and very considerable advantage to the South, and should therefore be sought, much and careful attention should be given to securing it, and in guarding the important fact that only suitable immigrants should be sought. The establishment of various immigration bureaus through the South would be advantageous; such bureaus to furnish information desired, to assist in securing homes for immigrants and to distribute wisely attractive advertising matter. The bureaus should be managed by competent men with proper conceptions of the ends to be reached. The importance of an occasional immigration commissioner is questionable; his service are too indirect and generally too wide in particular instances. For the proper management of such immigration matters, however, it would be well to have a central bureau to whom the district ones could report and by whom attention to particular localities could be directed for the gaining of local information. As to the appointment of these bureaus several methods may be suggested.

It will surely be a matter of a very short while before much attention will be given to immigration for the South, and it is most important to guard against the infusion of new elements which would be detrimental to its welfare and not conducive to its peaceful and substantial progress.

SOUTHERN DEVELOPMENT.

By D. B. Dyer.

It gives me great pleasure to write about the South, which is the wonderland of the United States. It abounds in all the natural elements of wealth and greatness; it evokes surprised admiration from all who investigate its resources, that have reposed for centuries, and it now claims those who came to only linger for a "spell" as its own loyal citizens. In its illimitable wealth of soil, (for its lands produce in rich abundance all kinds of fruits, vegetables and field crops,) in its iron, coal, lead, gold, timber, water power and other important items, there are great possibilities, great probabilities, which are solid and tangible.

Pioneers from the North, East and West have gone out and explored the country, and are now making their reports of the alluring resources of the region that is destined to be the greatest theatre of development during the next twenty-five years.

It is pre-eminently the most conspicuous field today for observation and study. When "the times are out of joint" the defects, the advantages, the resources of the country are subjects of sober consideration. A country that can stand in the front rank under such world-wide disaster as we have been witnessing makes a good impression abroad, and proves positively that it has stability and worth. The South has been the brightest section in the United States during this crisis. There have been fewer collapses, fewer reverses, less stagnation than in any other section.

During this prolonged epidemic of commercial and industrial depression through which the whole civilized world has just passed, the South has stood the storm in a manner which entitles it to the attention of investors. Such lessons teach people to be practical and admonish them to be prudent in seeking new locations for homes, or the starting of new industries. This section belongs by nature in the front rank, and offers superior openings to investors, as well as to those who have only small capital and are willing to work. Sectional feeling has gradually disappeared, and its citizens desire, and are determined to have, more people, more money, more brains and enterprise, and the good from every section are invited to come.

Slavery was a part of the social system, and incorporated into the government. The industrial institutions were shaped to its requirements; trade and commerce were regulated to harmonize with its influences, which ramified all branches. It is, therefore, easy to see that it was difficult, and required time to correct the effects of such an evil, diffused as it was so thoroughly by many years. Human power could not eliminate its influence at once, but time, experience and circumstances have changed the conditions and views of the Southern people, and they have sagaciously fallen into the procession, and invite home seekers and all kinds of manufacturers to come.

The era of great growth and development is just beginning; the golden opportunity is certainly at hand, not only for those who wish to buy cheap lands, but for the manufacturer, the banker, the merchant, the miner and the farmer. There is room for millions of people, more millions of money, and there is not on earth a safer or more certain opportunity for profitable reward. Think of one hundred millions of acres of productive land to settle up in such a climate at prices less than Western land, and you cannot but realize that the South is a gold mine, and as the country increases in population advances in prosperity and wealth, present values will be permanently enhanced.

Circumstances are rapidly paving the way to make the progress of the South for the next twenty-five years surpass that of any other section of our country for that length of time. The natural wealth of this section has been overlooked by investors, but just so soon as the industries of the country have sufficiently recovered from the present great depression to enable the people of the North and East to look about for investments, and to better their condition, it is my opinion that thoughtful, conservative men will turn toward the South, as nearly every industry known to civilization is still without full representation, although all thrive here if only the natural resources were developed, and then, too, if this were accomplished there would be no need to import anything for man or beast.

If the same eager energy and snap that are characteristic of the North was universally displayed in the South more real prosperity would exist and wealth could be accumulated faster here than there.

The absence of extensive factories for the manufacture of all kinds of goods and implements is not the fault of nature, neither is the demand for the product lacking right here at home, and everyone knows the value of a home market. This paucity may strike the reader as something quite remarkable; even a foreigner would find it hard to understand why the South does not manufacture a larger per cent. of the agricultural implements, furniture, clothing, boots, harness, stoves, machinery, crockery, etc., that it uses, instead of buying nearly everything from the North. This peculiar condition of affairs, so prominent, must necessarily attract the attention of investors. It seems to me that such wonderful openings for the profitable investment of

capital cannot much longer remain neglected.

It is, of course, necessary that the peculiar and exceptional advantages of the South be advertised, not spasmodically and at uncertain and irregular intervals and in isolated spots, but by every State of the whole South over the whole civilized world. As a result, instead of a few wandering pioneers—strangers seeking new homes—a regular army would take possession of the waste and unoccupied lands.

It is to the future that the South looks with confidence, for during the next quarter of a century it will be to Europe and the Northern States what the great West has been to Europe and the Eastern States for the past twenty-five years.

There are in the South at the present time better opportunities for the investment of capital than there has been for many years, perhaps, ever before. The South is only at the beginning of its greatness, and the population is sure to increase on an average of hundreds of thousands per year for many years to come. . This will advance all values greatly.

The South has a greater variety of crops, timber and minerals than any other section of our country. It has greater advantages than any other undeveloped country, and yet its lands are cheaper than lands of the West.

The basis of its prosperity is conspicuously permanent, in that its climate and soil permit the production in abundance of every known crop of grain and fruit of the North, as well as the fruits of the tropics. It has an inexhaustible store of coal and of nearly every useful mineral, and can truthfully boast of its great variety of virgin forests, grand water powers and magnificent rivers and harbors. .

With such peculiar, natural and unchangeable conditions governing the South its industries and activity of trade need not be at the mercy of caprice, nor hinge wholly upon any one kind of crop or mill or factory.

I have often remarked that people, not natural advantages develop a country, but circumstances govern the actions of individuals, and slavery was the reason why immigrants did not come and manufactures did not flourish before the war. It has been changing since 1865, slowly, owing to the impoverishment of Southern people, and the lack of the proper knowledge of the situation by Northern travellers.

Residents of the South import a large proportion of everything they use, and yet there is hardly a single article that they cannot produce or manufacture profitably.

Capital is required here as well as elsewhere to complete successfully any undertaking, and yet, where can you find in the United States another field where the products of large mills and factories can find a home market at their very doors?

Superior advantages are offered to all lines of manufacturing. In a region abounding in fruits and vegetables all canned goods come from abroad, and what is true in this case holds good in others.

The success of the cotton mills already established proves the practicability of location and should pave the way for others, as well as for numerous other industries, such as glass and chinaware works, paper mills, canning factories, furniture and wagon factories, and car works. The local consumption is large, and if that demand alone is supplied much money could be made.

Ship building will some day be one of the great industries of the South, as it would pay today much better here than in the North. The South possesses an unending succession of harbors, many of which are so land-locked that sea-faring men speak of them in glowing terms, as being equal to those of any nation. Its best seaports are open at all times and seasons for the largest ships, and this fact is fast putting the South in direct communication with the important trade centres of the world. The grain of the West is today being shipped over routes that have never been travelled before, and beef and pork must also find the shortest and quickest and cheapest route between the West and European markets. The South has looked long and earnestly for this desired accomplishment, as there was never any good reason why the exports and imports for the South should go through Northern ports, yet the few train loads of corn now coming from Kansas City to Port Royal are not much within themselves; they are only the pioneers; but the rattle of the trains that are to follow across the continent, the struggle of the great ships with the waves, form the frame and set the tune of the poem that will be sung through the centuries to come. But these are not all of the South's advantages; mines of all kinds are awaiting development; iron and coal are found in close proximity in exhaustless quantities, and can be utilized more cheaply than any where else, yet the field is only partially occupied. The South wants rolling mills, nail mills and stove foundries, and they will meet with immediate success.

The mining, smelting and refining of lead and zinc, (which are known to exist in large quantities,) as well as precious metals, can be carried on profitably.

I venture nothing in saying that there is no section of our country that possesses finer water power, which furnishes such a wonderful stimulus to manufacturing interests. The South is pre-eminently adapted to manufacturing, and it is certain in time will eclipse the East. It is in this direction coupled with the agricultural development that it offers the most attractive field that exists anywhere in the United States.

It is only necessary to state the situation and condition of the South with exactness and truthfulness to convince any one that in variety of resources and in abundance of natural wealth it is a wonderland; but these are not the only advantages it offers to the people of the North; its people are your brothers; they possess the same progressive characteristics of vigor and energy, and are today in line with the hope that animates our universal and uniform civilization.

EDITORIAL AND NOTES OF PROGRESS.

Organize Land Seekers' Tours.

The reduced rates of one fare for the round trip offered by railway companies in the Southern Passenger Association to persons wishing to visit the various States, afford an excellent opportunity to excursion managers to arrange trips through various sections. Thousands of people would take advantage of the low rate to visit the South but will not come because they fear the hotel and incidental expenses would be too great. The railroad fare forms but one item, and as would-be home seekers are not wealthy, motives of economy often prevent them from taking the trip much as they desire to.

Here is a suggestion we offer and which we believe will receive the hearty co-operation of the railroads. Form a sort of Southern colonists' aid company with live agents at various points in the West and Northwest where it is believed parties can be secured, arrange ten and twenty day tours through Southern sections where the best opportunities are offered settlers in the way of cheap lands, etc. Include the entire cost of the trip, such as railroad fare, hotel expenses, etc., in the charge and guarantee to take prospectors on these tours at a certain rate.

Such briefly is a scheme from which a good revenue can be made by those who start it, while the benefit to the South and the railroad lines cannot be over estimated. If a party of seventy-five or one hundred is secured, the cost of a tour would be less than one-third of the sum a single individual would have to pay. Southern hotels would make minimum rates, the railroad companies would help in every way and a company of responsible persons would have the co-operation of the commercial bodies and immigration bureaus throughout the South. These ex-cursions could be planned like to the Raymond & Whitcomb and Cook tours, only on a much cheaper basis. Every feature can be systematized so as to work to advantage.

As a sample of what agents can do in the West, an excursion is now being planned by which it is expected over 600 people will visit Macon, Ga., and vicinity, from around Richmond, Ind. If this result can be accomplished in that State, there is no reason why it cannot be more successfully accomplished in Iowa, Kansas, Nebraska, the Dakotas, Minnesota, Wisconsin, Illinois and Michigan, and all through New England.

If 600 can be brought on a single excursion from a single locality why not bring them from all over the North and West?

Cheapness of Southern Farm Lands.

At the January sales day of real estate in Spartanburg, S. C., nearly 2000 acres, made up of small tracts in different parts of the county, sold for an average of $4.70 an acre, one half cash and the remainder on time. And yet Spartanburg county, as the Editor of SOUTHERN STATES knows from personal experience, has a climate that is almost perfect and which the people of the Northwest would imagine almost equal to paradise itself; it is noted for its healthfulness; it is a very progressive county, having more cotton spindles than any other county in the South, numerous railroads, a regular rainfall without droughts or floods, beautiful streams of clear water fed by innumerable springs from mountains thirty or forty miles away. It is a county in which "every prospect pleases," where laws are well obeyed, where schools and churches abound. With all these advantages here is farm land selling at less than $5.00 an acre.

The very cheapness of it makes Northern farmers, accustomed to high prices, think that surely there must be something wrong. But on the contrary there is nothing wrong except 'an over-supply—more land than there are people to occupy it. As in Spartanburg county so all over the South. Millions of acres of land can be had at from $2.00 to $10.00 an acre, that in every respect will yield more profitable returns—more in money, a hundred times more in comfort and health than the high priced lands of other sections. Here is the great opportunity for farmers. The South is to them the most inviting country in the world. None other equals it in combined advantages and resources.

The Question of the Day.

The Montgomery (Ala.) Advertiser urges the forming of associations all over the South for the purpose of seeking to attract settlers now that there is such a general disposition in the North and West to move South. The Advertiser says:

"By proper efforts we could add many thousands of good citizens to our present number, through immigration from the Northern States, within the next few months. Do not put off the matter of forming associations to forward the interests of the locality in which you reside, but move in the matter immediately, and impress upon your friends, neighbors, etc., the necessity for their heartily joining in the matter, and giving good substantial aid for the printing and distribution of the cold facts as they exist, as to the fertility of the soil of your locality, and especially its healthfulness, churches, schools and people."

The whole South is waking up on this question, and the work which the SOUTHERN STATES is doing is not only seen in turning Northern and Western attention to this section, but it is equally noticeable in the interest that it has awakened in the South.

How to Secure Settlers in the South.

The Augusta (Ga.) Chronicle, which is seeking to arouse an interest in securing settlers for the agricultural lands in that section, gives the local people some advice which every real estate agent and every railroad officer in the South should ponder over carefully. Referring to how Dakota was crowded with settlers—not foreigners alone by any means—but with thousands and tens of thousands of progressive Americans, the Chronicle says:

"That Georgia has superior advantages over North Dakota needs no argument, and yet the latter State has been getting the immigrants and Georgia has not. Why? Because it worked for them.

"So it will be with other Southern States when the movement starts Southward. Those who work for the immigrants will get them, and Georgia, though the Empire State of the South, will not unless she organizes and works for them."

What is true of Georgia is true of every section of every Southern State. There must be active, vigorous work. The railroads must work, the land owners and real estate agents must work, and with united forces great results can be accomplished. As the SOUTHERN STATES is the only publication in the country devoted solely to attracting attention to the real estate interests and agricultural possibilities of the South it is necessarily the best medium through which to secure the attention of those who are looking to the South.

Rapid Growth of Cotton Manufacturing South.

In the last issue of the SOUTHERN STATES there was an article on "The South's Possibilities in Cotton Manufacturing," in which it was pointed out that although the South produces over 60 per cent. of the world's annual cotton crop, it has only 2,500,000 spindles out of a total of 85,000,000 in the world. The field for expansion is practically without limit, and the wealth which the development of this industry is destined to create in the South can be estimated in part only by the statement that it would require an investment of nearly $1,500,000,000 to manufacture in the South all the cotton produced there. This industry is rapidly extending, and every week sees some new mill company organized or the enlargement of some existing plant. Through the severe depression of the past year Southern mills ran steadily, turning out their full product and finding a market for it at a profit, as shown by the dividends now being declared. At present there is considerable activity in the enlargement of mills now in operation. Recent reports show that a Newberry, S. C., mill will increase its capital from $250,000 to $400,000 and put in 15,000 new spindles; a mill at Chester, in the same State, will add 5000 spindles, thus doubling its capacity; an Anniston, Ala., mill will spend $50,000 in enlarging its plant. At Augusta, Ga., leading cotton manufacturers have formed a new company with a minimum capital of $400,000 and a maximum of $1,000,000 to build a 15,000-spindle mill in South Carolina, and a $200,000 company has been organized to build another mill near Augusta.

Florida as a Possible Sugar Producer.

Several years ago the late Judge Kelley, of Pennsylvania, so long known as "Pig Iron" Kelley, because of his devotion to protection on iron, wrote a series of articles on the South for the Manufacturers' Record, one of which presented an exhibit of the capabilities of Florida as a sugar-producing country. Judge Kelley believed that almost as important as protection for the iron of his State was protection for the encouragement of sugar-growing in the South, in order that we might build up a sugar industry that, while adding vastly to the magnitude of our agricultural interests, would retain at home the many millions of dollars now paid out annually for foreign sugar. Judge Kelley's views as to the sugar-producing capabilities of Florida were in advance of the day, as he believed that that State could easily, with a continuance of a protective tariff, become the greatest sugar-making region of the world. The results since accomplished at the St. Cloud plantation, near Kissimmee, have demonstrated the correctness of his predictions. When Mr. Hamilton Disston undertook to reclaim several million acres of land in that section his own friends doubtless thought that it was a wild and visionary scheme, but it is now seen that it was one of the most broad-minded business undertakings of this day of great enterprises. After the work of reclamation had commenced, he started a sugar plantation to prove what could be done in cane-raising, then built a costly sugar mill, and now, fter several years of full trial, has proved what the possibilities of that section are. Mr. S. A. Jones, of Tampa, in a letter to the Tampa Times setting forth the results accomplished by Mr.

Disston, gives some facts that are worthy of national attention. There are in Florida, he says, by careful surveys, 4,000,000 acres of the "richest sugar land on the face of the earth, capable of producing 4000 to 6000 pounds of sugar per acre." This land can be reclaimed for $20,000,000, and with the maintenance of the bounty on sugar, or a tariff of two cents a pound guaranteed for fifteen years, private capital will undertake to reclaim this entire area. If sugar is put on the free list and the bounty system abolished, Mr. Jones thinks that as a national undertaking the government ought to appropriate $20,000,000 to reclaim this land in order to bring about the great wealth from sugar production which would follow. Mr. Jones, basing his figures on the equipment and the results of the St. Cloud plantation of 1000 acres, now turning out 60,000 pounds of sugar a day, and inviting the most careful investigation of the correctness of his statement, says:

A 5000-acre plantation would require one sugar mill complete ($200,000,) thirty miles of movable narrow-gauge railroad, five dummy engines, 200 cane cars, 175 carts, 600 weeding hoes, 600 cane knives, 350 mules, 600 common laborers and seventy-five expert laborers. Florida has 4,000,000 acres of the finest sugar land in the world that can be made ready for cultivation for $20,000,000. Counting 5000 acres to the plantation, we find that Florida will furnish 800 such plantations; which would employ 480,000 common laborers and 60,000 skilled or expert workmen, and would require 800 sugar mills at $200,000 each, making an aggregate of $160,000,000, and the machinery for them would be manufactured at home. The 800 plantations w uld require 280,000 head of mules and the produce to feed them, 140,000 carts for our home wagon-makers to manufacture, 200,000 plows and sets of plow harness, 480,000 weeding hoes, 480,000 cane knives, 24,000 miles of movable narrow-gauge railroad, 4000 dummy engines, 150,000 cane cars. The average cost today to the American consumer of sugar is six cents per pound The equipment for the production and manufacturing of 90 per cent. of the American consumption of sugar and the land on which it is grown is owned in foreign countries. Florida can produce the entire American consumption at three cents per pound and make a fine profit after her lands are reclaimed, and employ this vast army of working people and create the demand for this enormous amount of machinery and farm implements.

These figures give some idea of the vast sugar-producing possibilities of Florida.

A Satisfactory Reason.

The Wall Street Journal gives this reason for the decrease in earnings of several railroads:

Formerly the Southern farmer obtained his supplies almost entirely from the Northwest. Then the bad times in the South came along and the Southern farmer had no credit and had to start in to raise his own supplies. At the same time he began economizing and putting his affairs into shape. But now, when he has a little money on hand, he is not sending to the Northwest for his supplies, but continues raising them at home. The railroads have lost a good deal of traffic from this source that they will not get back again.

This, however, means a more prosperous country and a better financial condition of Southern farmers, which will eventually add far more to the business of the railroads than has been lost by the production at home of food supplies.

MR. L. E. EATON, of Willimantic, Conn., writes to the SOUTHERN STATES that "there are thousands of New Englanders who would go South if there was some one to start the ball rolling." Well, SOUTHERN STATES proposes to start the ball and never to let it cease rolling.

WHILE it is true immigration is turning to Texas as never before, Texas is not, as in former years, monopolizing the business. The whole South is now drawing home-seekers in great numbers.

THE enthusiasm of Texas newspapers in their devotion to the advancement of the State is illustrated in the determination of some of the State editors to get up an exhibit car of the State's resources and take it through the North this spring and summer.

A Record Hard to Beat.

An illustration of the profitableness of well-managed Southern cotton mills is found in the history of the Graniteville Manufacturing Co. of Augusta, Ga. Originally nearly all the Augusta cotton mills were constructed by the aid of Northern capital, but gradually the stocks of the various enterprises have drifted back to Augusta, until today there is not over one-tenth (average) of these stocks owned by Northern people. The institution among them all which all Augustans mention with especial pride on account of its being one of the oldest, and more especially on account of the wonderful success it has attained under the management of Mr. H. H. Hickman, who has been president since 1867, is the Graniteville Manufacturing Co. This company is capitalized at $600,000, and besides paying ten per cent. dividends for twenty-seven years—during

which time it failed to pay only two or three dividends—it has built from its earnings another mill, the Vaucluse, at a cost of $362,000, besides accumulating a cash surplus to March 1, 1893, of $322,520. The Vaucluse mill for many years has earned a sum sufficient to pay seven per cent. dividends on the entire stock of the company, leaving the bulk of the earnings of the larger mill, the Graniteville proper, to be applied to improvements and adding to the surplus. The company owns its own water-power and operatives' houses, besides 13,000 acres of land. The number of spindles is about 35,000; the number of looms, 959. It is difficult at all times to buy stock in this institution; sales, when made, vary from 145 to 155.

Another Texas Road.

Burkett & Murphy, railroad contractors of Palestine, Texas, announce that they will build a railroad line from Palestine to Dallas, about 100 miles in length, passing through Anderson and Henderson counties. They state that right of way has been donated for most of the distance from Palestine to the Dallas county line. At Dallas the new line would tap the Missouri, Kansas & Texas and Texas & Pacific, and at Palestine it would connect with the International & Great Northern, one of the Huntington lines.

Cottonseed Rubber.

Mr. C. B. Warrand, of Savannah, who wrote about the manufacture of rubber from cottonseed oil in the Manufacturers' Record, some months ago, writes now as follows on the same subject:

"The Elastic Product Co. has turned its whole establishment in only partly oxidizing the cottonseed oil and making varnish out of it. As I wrote in the article about cottonseed-oil rubber, the rubber trust bought the secret from an English inventor some six years ago, and its works steadily make its own cottonseed-oil rubber product at a cost of about seven cents per pound. The varnish made by the Elastic Company sells well and is as good as linseed-oil varnish. I know the secret how to make the rubber from cottonseed oil through my own researches, but it is of no value in the United States, as the rubber trust is the only purchaser of this kind of product, and the only patentable feature is an apparatus which has been patented in the United States. The whole process is very simple, and if I was assured of the sale of the product I could establish a plánt for the manufacture here and keep the process secret, or, if desired to manufacture it in Europe I would sell the secret."

Two More Hotels.

Two more hotels are projected in Southern cities, which, if built, will greatly improve the places where they are intended to be constructed. A company is being formed in Charleston, S. C., to carry out the plans of J. A. Wood, the New York architect who designed the famous Tampa Bay Hotel, to build a large hotel in Charleston. It is proposed to build a structure of brick and artificial stone, with steel girders, which will be fireproof. The hotel is to contain 300 rooms, with a large veranda around the outside and an ornamental rotunda in the c ntre. Two towers, each 160 feet high, are to be located on the front corners, and the interior is to be finis' ed in cypress and pine. The cost is estimated as between $400,000 and $500,000. Hon. D. H. Chamberlain, F. W. Wagner and W. M. Bird, all of Charleston, are among the capitalists interested.

To the Gulf Shore.

Captain William Davis, of San Antonio, who is at the head of the movement to build the San Antonio & Gulf Shore Railway, writes from San Antonio as follows:

"The San Antonio & Gulf Shore will run to Galveston and will be fifty miles shorter than any of the present lines, running through one of the best agricultural sections in the State and forming the only continuous line to both Velasco and Galveston."

THE News, of Irwinton, Ga., says that in 1889 eighty carloads of Western corn, oats and hay arrived at Sycamore, or equal, say, to about 60,000 bushels of Western grain for that one small town. In 1890 these shipments dropped off 35 per cent., in 1891 still lower; in 1892 only about fifteen cars were received ànd in 1893 not a single car of Western grain was received. The decline in the consumption of Western bacon has been equally satisfactory. This raising of foodstuffs at home means millions of dollars to the South; the decrease from 60,000 bushels of corn to nothing and the same decrease in bacon must mean the keeping in and around Sycamore alone of over $100,000 that formerly went West every year. All changes of this character at the first inflict hardship somewhere, and the local merchants who have sold this Western stuff and the rail-

roads that have handled it have temporarily lost business, but this will be much more than made up by the greater prosperity that this change is bringing about.

THE Tennessee Producers Marble Co., of which Hon. Redfield Proctor, of Vermont, is president, has commenced work on a large marble mill, which will cost complete, about $100,000.

THE Sal Mountain Asbestos Co. is mining asbestos near Demorest, Ga. A $15,000 plant is in course of erection, and shipments will commence about May 1.

THE Aiken Manufacturing Co. has been organized to build a 15,000 spindle cotton mill at Bath, S. C. Messrs. H. M. Dibble and F. B. Henderson, of Aiken, S. C.; John G. Evans and Thomas Barrett, Jr., and Charles Estes, of Augusta, Ga., are the incorporators. The capital stock is placed at $400,000.

WOLF & KING, of Duluth, Minn., have the contract for building sixty miles of railroad through the coal fields of Pike and adjoining counties in East Tennessee, to open up some large tracts of coal and timber lands bought about a year or so ago by Duluth capitalists.

THE Blacksburg Phosphate & Guano Co., with a capital stock of $100,000 has been organized in Blacksburg, S. C., by John F. Jones, T. B. Gautier and D. C. Ebaugh. The company will build phosphate works. Blacksburg has been fortunate in securing several very extensive enterprises.

THE production of coal in the South each year since 1884 has been as follows:

1884......	12,783,176
1885.	13,059,991
1886.....	12,696,614
1887.....	15,262,006
1888....	18,035,438
1889....	18,569,734
1890..........................	20,633,277
1891.....	24,772,665
1892........	25,484,036

THE old Peninsula Land, Transportation & Manufacturing Co. has been entirely reorganized, and will proceed to carry out its proposed land improvements and industrial projects, including an electric light plant, an ice factory, a hotel, etc. Alex. St. Clair Abrams. of Tavares, is president, and Jno. C. Soley, of Boston, Mass., treasurer. Jas. H. Mellen, of Worcester, Mass.; D. G. Ambler, of Jacksonville, Warren C. Spencer, of Boston, and others are interested. A trust deed for $500,-

000 has been executed by the company, with the American Loan & Trust Co. of Boston as trustee to secure bonds.

THE Central Coal & Coke Co. is erecting, at Texarkana, Texas, a saw mill of 150,000 feet daily capacity, a planing mill of 200,000 feet capacity, and two dry-kilns of 200,000 feet capacity. J. W. Ammerman will manage the plant. This company was organized last year with a capital stock of $3,000,000.

H. H. WHELESS, F. T. Whitehead, J. D. Pace, W. T. White and J. M. Augers have incorporated the Shreveport Manufacturing Co. for the purpose of manufacturing patent articles of wood and metal. The capital stock is $50,000, $30,000 of which has been subscribed.

MACON, GA., proposes to spend about $200,- 000 on a complete sewerage system.

THE Bridgeport Stove Works has been organized at Bridgeport, Ala., with a capital stock of $25,000.

PATRICK J. CONLEY, Edward E. Poole, Algernon S. Holderness, Jno. D. Dunn and William N. Alexander have organized at Fordyce, Ark., the Fordyce Nut Lock Co. The capital stock is $100,000.

THE Lett Copper Mine Co. has been incorporated for the purpose of developing a pyrites mine near Mineral City, Va. The incorporators are William F. Lett, Frederick R. Lett, Louis J. McKenney, William F. Lett, Jr., and M. M. Lett, all of New York. The capital stock is $200,000.

THE Georgia & Florida Investment Co., of Tallahassee, Fla., owner and operator of the Carrabelle, Tallahassee & Georgia Railroad, has decided upon the erection of a large lumber plant at the Ochlochnee bridge, on the line of the new railway. The plant will consist of saw mill, planing mill, dry-kiln. A number of dwelling-houses will also be built. The capacity of the mills will be 80,000 feet of lumber daily, and that of the dry-kiln will be 40,000 feet daily. The entire outfit of machinery has been purchased from the Georgia Iron Works, of Augusta, and the Standard Dry-Kiln Co,. of Louisville, Ky. The entire output of lumber will come from the company's lands, of which there are 160,- 000 acres. The Investment Company is also building a mill of 15,000 feet daily capacity at Hilliards, Fla.

THE new plant of the Lenoir Car Co., at Lenoir, Tenn., is rapidly nearing completion. The main building is 92x454 feet; blacksmith and ironworking shop, now complete, is 70x 260 feet, the power house is also complete, and is 62x66 feet; boilers are up and the engines are in place. The woodworking shop, 100x300 feet, has foundation finished, and the trusses and other parts are being prepared as rapidly as possible. The erecting shop is to be 120x300 feet, and the foundation is only partly in, but the work will be pushed. Eight or ten carloads of machinery, tools and other equipment have already arrived, and most of the balance is under contract.

THE Roane Iron Co., of Rockwood, Tenn., one of the oldest iron concerns, has just completed its new furnace, which has a daily capacity of 100 tons of pig iron. It is claimed that Rockwood has stood the industrial depression remarkably well, and the blowing in of the new furnace will add very materially to the volume of business of the town.

PLANS have been drawn by Paul J. Lietz, of Chicago, for the hotel it is proposed to build in Fort Worth, Texas, to cost $300,000. The plans are for a building of terra cotta, with steel beams, to contain 195 rooms. It is to be five stories high. McLean & Mudge, of Fort Worth, are interested.

THE Florida Fibre Co. has been organized at Dayton to build a fibre plant which will employ about fifty hands and consume from twenty to forty tons of raw palmetto daily. It is intended to add a brush mill and mattress-making when advisable.

A PARTY of fifty capitalists from New York were in Galveston and Laporte for the purpose of examining the Laporte and Houston Railway. It was rumored that they were going to buy the road and extend it into Galveston.

A DISPATCH from Mobile, Ala., announces that the Mobile & Ohio has determined at last to carry out the project of building a branch of its system into Birmingham from a point in Bibb county, Ala. The extension will be about fifty miles long and give Birmingham a new short route to St. Louis. The connection will be made with the Montgomery & Tuscaloosa branch of the Mobile & Ohio, now being built.

URIAH LOTT, of New York, has agreed to build a railroad from Little Rock, Ark., to Hot Springs.

REAL ESTATE NEWS.

How Norfolk is Developing.

The Norfolk Virginian has published some interesting statistics showing the commercial development of the city. In round numbers its trade for 1893 amounted to $82,000,000, compared with $48,000,000 in 1884, an increase of $34,000,000 in nine years. The exports for 1893 amounted to $10,696,556, a gain of $2,314,556 over the previous year. A total of 457,040 bales of cotton were received, against 345,709 in 1892, an increase of 32¼ per cent. The 1893 coal shipments were 1,774,040 tons, valued at $5,322,120. The clearing-house receipts were $49,000,00, $1,620,000 less than in 1892.

A Real Estate Object-Lesson.

The success of the Statesville (N. C.) Development Co. is a practical lesson of what can be done in Southern real estate. This company has paid to its stockholders 20 per cent. dividends in three years, and still has sold but a small portion of the real estate it holds in the vicinity of Statesville.

THE Omaha & South Texas Land & Improvement Co., of Houston, Texas, which is engaged in developing a large tract of land near that city, has lately had a very successful auction sale, the first day's sale having aggregated about $30,000.

KANSAS CITY parties are reported to have lately purchased some 4290 acres of land near Abilene, Texas.

THE gener l business outlook in Macon is reported to be very promising, brighter so local reports say than ever before in the history of the city.

THE Interstate Immigration Bureau has been organized in Chicago for the purpose of gathering information of interest to all who contemplate moving from one section to another.

E. A. CUMMINGS & Co., Clark and Washington streets, Chicago, lately advertised for a large tract of Texas land suitable for a colony.

IN Louisville, Ky., a decided improvement is reported in real estate matters, and an active spring trade is anticipated.

LAND owners around Roanoke, Va., are pursuing a very liberal policy; and people to whom land companies are indebted for farms purchased during the boom period and cut up into streets and town lots are reducing the amount of the last payments now falling due. B. F. Ammen, of Salem, voluntarily reduced his claim against the Victoria Co. just one-half; James Chalmers made a big reduction from the amount due him by the Creston Co., of Salem, and Capt. R. B. Moorman did the same thing for the Creston Co., of Roanoke.

MR. J. J THOMPSON, Yankton, S. D., writes to SOUTHERN STATES that he wants to move to Maryland or Virginia and wants to know if there are any real estate dealers who will send him catalogues of lands for sale.

MR. GEO. T. FRY, Jr., of Chattanooga, Tenn., has lately made a $60,000 purchase of improved property in that city.

REAL estate dealers of Fort Worth, Texas, report considerable demands for property. Quite a number of transfers, ranging in prices from $1000 to $5000, have lately been made, and also a number of sal s of country property.

YOAKUM, Texas, reports that several real estate deals have lately been made, including one, by Mr. L. H. Pulliam of his ranch, two miles from town, consisting of 509 acres of land, at $17.50 per acre, Mr. Charles Kerchell being the purchaser. The real estate market is said to be looking up.

A LETTER from Fort Smith, Ark., says: "At Fort Smith real estate is looking up and the same condition applies to all the towns in Northwest Arkansas. I found a perfect furore in the apple-growing country of North-west Arkansas. All around Rogers, Springdale and Fayetteville, people are locating from the Northern States. The World's Fair seems to have sent hundreds of people into the apple regions of Arkansas. The real estate men there are busy from morning until night show-ing buyers around. I find quite a number from the far Northwest, Nebraska, Dakota, and even California, but the majority are from Missouri, Illinois and Indiana. Quite a number of large fruit farm deals are on hand and parties are figuring on buying large tracts which will be operated by incorporated com-panies under one management. The people there are not crying hard times any more than they are in Little Rock. While there was a much smaller apple crop this year than usual, the crop brought big prices, some orchards realizing over $100 per acre. Apples sold for $1.00 per bushel on the tree. The wheat, oats and corn crops were very good."

THE rapid growth of the foreign trade of Port Royal, S. C., since the establishment of a direct line of steamers to Europe is attracting much attention, and is naturally resulting in an increased demand for real estate. The Port Royal Company reports sales of a number of lots with good prospects for increasing activity.

DAVID ANDERSON, of South Omaha, Neb., who was in Houston, Tex., a year ago has returned and is amazed at the steady growth of Houston. Ed. Early, of Columbus, Neb., is also with Mr. Anderson, He is ex-cashier of the First National Bank of Columbus, He spent two seasons in San Diego, Cal., but thinks the South Texas climate is as salubrious and healthful as Southern Califo nia, and that in every other respect the country is far supe-rior to California.

DAYTONA, FLA., is growing quite rapidly and the result is an active real estate market with much more liberal sales than had been known for some time.

THE San Antonio (Texas) Light says: Let-ters received in this city within a week past show an extensive inquiry for Southern Texas lands, for purposes of general agriculture, hog raising in connection with fruit farms, vegeta-

ble gardening, fine stock raising in connection with cereal culture, also lands for country residences adjacent to some good city where the advantages of home country life and that of city proximity might be enjoyed together. These inquiries are from people of abundant means in the Northern States, who have grown tired of the four months' deep snow and four months' more of cold weather. There is more inquiry for Southern homes this winter than ever before since the settlement of the country, and the great bulk of those enqui-ries are concerning Texas lands and advant-ages. This is an indication that before many years this whole region will be settled with good producers.

THE Oakley Planting Co., Limited, has been incorporated at New Orleans for the purpose of cultivating sugar-cane, etc., and the capital is $100,000. Andrew Hero, Jr., is president ; William S. Hero, secretary and treasurer, and Samuel M. Malhiot, manager.

THE Orleans Yarn and Hosiery Mills, Lim-ited, has been organized at New Orleans to manufacture woolen and cotton yarns and hosiery. Simon Mayer is president. The capital stock is $100,000.

THE Knoxville Sentinel says that there are more strangers in Knoxville looking for in-vestments of various kinds than have been there before for months past. Some of these strangers are Tennesseeans, living no great distance from Knoxville, who want to move in to take advantage of the city schools. But the most important of them are Eastern capitalists, who have been flooding the town ever since the beginning of the new year. Some of them are making inquiries for real estate investments, while others are asking questions about industries and enterprises of different kinds.

THE Lutherville Heights Co. has been in-corporated with a capital stock of $50,000, at Baltimore. The incorporators are Charles T. Bagby, H. Allen Tupper, Jr., Willoughby M. McCormick, R. A. McCormick and L. G. Turner. It is reported that the company will develop a suburban tract of land near the city.

THE property of the Americus Investment Co., Americus, Ga., is being sold off in order to wind up the affairs of the company. On account of the general scarcity of cash the prices realized are insignificant in compar-ison with the value of the properties. Unimproved pro erty in Americus, for which $20,000 was refused a few years ago, has just been sold to a Baltimore banker for $6000. Two plantations in Sumter county, Ga., comprising 1,300 acres brought only $3600. Twenty-two hundred acres of timber land in Tatnall county sold for $2100. Twelve hundred acres near Cordele brought $720. The famous DeSoto plantation in Sumter county, of 5180 acres, brought only $24,100.

At these prices the purchasers' ought to make enormous profits in the next year or two. There have probably never been known opportunities for investment with such promise of early and extraordinary profits as may be found in Southern real estate.

REAL estate seems to be pretty active at Houston, Texas. Among recent sales reported there are the following: Judge Henry Brashear bought recently for $45,000 three lots, fronting 100 feet on Main street and 150 feet on Capitol avenue. It is likely that an opera house and business block will be built on the property. It is reported that property on McKinney avenue has been bought for a new Presbyterian church, the price paid being $22,500. Messrs. George B. Lucas and Andrew Daw have just bought for $25,000 three lots on the corner of Capitol avenue and Travis street. Another transaction is a sale by A. P. Root and others to A. J. Vick, of an und vided three-fourth interest in seventy-five acres of land one and three-quarter miles northwest of the city for $27,000. The aggregate of the four transactions mentioned above is $119,500.

A REAL estate association has been formed in Richmond, Va., with the following officers: Edward S. Rose, president; H. Seldon Taylor, vice-president; R. R. Harrison, secretary and treasurer. Board of directors: Edward S. Rose, H. Seldon Taylor, E. A. Catlin, F. T. Sutton, J. Thompson Brown, N. W. Bowe, J. B. Elam, H. A. McCurdy, and F. D. Hill.

THE American Land and Title Register for January, in its review of the past year, shows that real estate has held its own during the depression better than any other class of property.

This might have been expected. Our cities and towns are growing all the time and must continue to grow. The demand for farming land is steadily increasing. Our population doubles in every generation, and as the supply of real estate is limited it must necessarily rise in value.

Periodical panics and depressions will come, causing business stagnation and retarding development, but the owners of real estate who are able to tide over the temporary monetary embarrassments will find when the storm blows over that they are in good shape.

Real estate in a city or town is something that cannot be duplicated. It is bound to increase in value, because in a new country like ours cities and towns must grow for centuries to come.—Atlanta Constitution.

THE State of Virginia exacts from real estate agents a license fee of $100, and, besides, the payment of a tax of one-fourth of one per cent. of the gross amount of all sales. This is in addition to such local license fees and taxes as towns and counties may impose. A bill has been introduced in the General Assembly to relieve real estate dealers to some extent from this burdensome taxation.

THE Buffam Loan & Trust Co., of Ocala, Fla., has bought a number of the islands along Sarasoto bay, on the Gulf coast, for the purpose of growing lemons.

A TRACT of land comprising 363 acres in Chesterfield county, Va., near Petersburg, belonging to the Chesterfield Heights Land Co., was sold recently to Messrs. W. M. Habliston, T. B. Underhill and Augustus Wright for $11,740.

J. P. ANDRE MOTTU, of Norfolk, writes to the SOUTHERN STATES: "Real estate is picking up a little and some sales have been made during the week."

IMMIGRATION NEWS.

A Prosperous Section.

Dr. R. S. Rust, a Cincinnati capitalist, while in Americus, Ga., lately, in an interview in the Recorder, expressed astonishment at the prosperity which he saw prevailing in the South and in Southwestern Georgia in particular. He says that the people there have nothing to complain of in the way of hard times in comparison with the North and West, where thousands of able-bodied men are almost starving and can get n · work.

In Georgia, the people have a year's store of provisions ahead, and the panic and suffering in the North have only an indirect effect upon this God-favored section of country.

Nothing has so forcibly illustrated the superior natural 'advantages of Southwest Georgia as the comparative freedom from the terrible depression that prevails in the North and West, and this fact is being recognized by every intelligent observer.

Resources of Texas.

The passenger department of the Fort Worth and Denver City Railway, of Fort Worth, Texas, has been kept busy sending advertising matter all over the United States. One of the pamphlets is entitled "Farmers' Guide to Prosperity; New Homes for a Million People in a Mild Climate; A Beautiful and Wonderfully Fertile Country Now Open for Settlement." The pamphlet is neatly gotten up and has a good map of the Panhandle country from Fort Worth up to Trinidad, Col., and a large amount of information about the Panhandle country. The other one is a book entitled "Texas," a complete and comprehensive description of the agricultural and stock-raising resources of the Texas Panhandle country, statistics in regard to its climate, etc. This book has 130 pages, and gives a detailed description of the Panhandle country, and is intended for the home-seeker, capitalist and tourist, giving facts about the climate, soil, farming, stock-raising, dairying, fruit-growing,

game and fish, &c. These books will be sent free upon application to the passenger department of the Fort Worth and Denver Railway Company, Fort Worth, Tex.

Moving from Wisconsin to Maryland.

Mr. M. V. Richards, Land and Immigration Agent of the Baltimore & Ohio Railroad Company, says that in spite of the hard times which prevail now, he is in receipt of inquiries from many people engaged in manufactures who were interested in the Baltimore & Ohio section several years ago and are looking about now with a view to locating when times brighten, and that as to settlers the tide is more than ever to West Virginia, Maryland and Virginia. Except the movement to California he knows of no such migratory movement in this country today, and it is part of his business to watch such things and know what is going on.

Recently he brought 180 persons, German farmers and their families, from Wisconsin to Maryland, where they bought small tracts of run-down lands, and by proper cultivation will bring them up again to high productiveness.

Immigration and the South.

The Age of Steel, of St. Louis, says: "It is plainly written on the face of present Southern conditions that immigration is one of its nearest and most urgent needs. Hitherto the drift of population, both home-born and alien, has been West and North. In response to this influx huge areas of territory have been reclaimed from primitive solitude and State after State added to the sisterhood of the republic. The footprint of man has been the track of Western empire, and in response to pick and plow wealth and prosperity have spread from Maine to California. So far the Moses of the modern exodus has had his face to the West. The next march is Southward. Here lies the area of an empire, the climate of a Canaan and the resources of nearly half a hemisphere."

The Southward Movement of Settlers.

J. C. Bonnell of Chicago, general immigration agent of the Chicago, Rock Island & Pacific Railroad, has been down in Texas the first time for thirty years, and while there, said in an interview: "This coast country is developing too fast for our road to stay out any longer. Our first venture into Texas has resulted most profitably, the people have given us a warm welcome and I am satisfied the managers will soon branch out and take in more territory. We are bound to get into Houston, and you mark my word, we are coming sooner than you people dream of. It is quite probable that the road will follow the course of the Trinity river and the greater part of the distance towards the South, and it may fork off into two divisions, one to Houston and the other to Galveston. I know some such plan is contemplated by the Rock Island, and it would have been started last year if the financial situation of the country had warranted the additional railroad building.

"I have just come down to look over Houston in particular and South Texas in general in my capacity as general immigration agent of the Rock Island. I have visited Galveston and La Porte, and yesterday morning took in that flourishing suburb, Houston Heights. This is my first visit this far South in about thirty years, and I am, of course, enthusiastic over the wonderful development that has already been made and that seems possible in the near future. The Rock Island is doing its share towards attracting immigration to South Texas, and we intend to continue in that line of business for some time yet.

Flocking to Texas.

Texas has caught her second wind and immigration is pouring into the State at a rate that has not been equalled in ten years. This is no wild statement, but a fact which is borne out by reports originating from outside the State as well as those resulting from observation within the State.—Dallas (Tex.) Herald.

A Colony of Swedes to locate in Mississippi.

It is said to be an assured fact that a colony of Swedes will be located at Centreville, Miss., in the near future, quite a number of purchases of land in small lots having been made there recently by three gentlemen (Swedes) from Rockford, Ill., representing 100 families, who wish to make their homes in the South. They sent these three representatives South to look out for homes for them, with a view to truck farming.

JAMES GAMAGE, agent of the Iron Mountain Railroad Land department, at Macomb, Ill., and his brother, a prominent lumber dealer of that city, while in Little Rock, Ark., told the reporter of the Press that he brought down another party of the best Illinois citizens, several of whom have already located, and all of whom will no doubt become citizens of Arkansas. There were thirty-two in the party. They were all from Macomb. These people brought all of their household goods with them and have purchased property on the prairie south of Carlisle a short distance east of Little Rock.

Bought a Farm.

Mr. S. S. Babcock, of Delevan, Wisconsin, has bought a farm of about 150 acres near St. Florian, close to Florence, Ala.

FARMERS in the neighborhood of Lonoke, Ark., are reported to have made their crops so much cheaper this year that despite the low price of cotton they all seem to have money left after settling up. Many well-to-do people from other sections have recently settled there. Many of these people came by railroad and brought their teams, etc. Many, too, have moved in by the wagon route, and from all appearances that county is likely, so a correspondent of the Little Rock Press says, to have a boom very soon. There is also considerable inquiry from other States as to the character and prices of land, which promises a good healthy immigration. Altogether the prospects are very flattering for another year.

G. B. RANDOLPH, T. G. Bush, J. W. Lapsley and other citizens of Anniston, Ala., are endeavoring to perfect an organization to secure settlers from the West to locate in and around Anniston. The county in that section is unusually attractive, and if the Anniston people will only secure the settling there of a few Western farmers, their success will be certain to attract others.

THE Louisville Courier-Journal, in an editorial on immigration, says: Our Kentucky farmer has been spoiled by the remarkable fertility of our soil and is not much inclined to nurse the less fertile places. He wants his crop to come as easily as possible. When he has worn out the best of his soil he is more inclined to pull up stakes and go West than to set to work to redeem neglected spots. In the bluegrass the wonderful recuperative qualities of the soil defy, abuse and encourage easy met ods. All over the State is a great abundance of fertile land that yields bountifully in return for even moderate care in cultivation. But in less fertile portions this disposition has been marked to pick out the more fertile spots, neglect the rest, take little care of the soil and finally become discouraged as the land wears out and go West in search of something easier.

There has been a great deal of this sort of emigration from Southern and Southwestern Kentucky, and there is a great deal of this half-neglected land all over the State, land that the easy-going Kentuckian disdains, but which the thrifty, painstaking, economical foreigner, accustomed to hard labor and contented with small beginnings, would make the foundation of a fortune. The soil is fertile enough to reward a fair amount of care, and it is cheap. If the immigrant wants a better class of land, he can find it in abundance and at reasonable price. We need such people. We need them to coax harvests from neglected lands and to plant vineyards and orchards on hillsides whose value we underrate. We need them to clear more land, to build homes, to raise stock. They would fare well with us and their coming would enrich our land. That they do not come is because they hear more of the lands of the Northwest and are trailed away to sections that really can not offer them so much, but which are more active in making themselves known.

J. C. BONNELL, general immigration agent, and C. J. Anderson, general passenger agent, at Topeka, of the Chicago, Little Rock Island & Pacific Railroad, were in Houston lately for the purpose of having a conference with General Passenger Agent Robbins of the Houston Texas Central in regard to immigration transportation. F. M. Boswell, traveling immigration agent of the Rock Island, who was in Houston at the same time with a large excursion party from the North, stated that the excursion next month promises to be double that of the past week.

THE Queen & Crescent route is selling land seekers' excursion tickets for February 8th, March 8th, and April 9th, from Cincinnati, O., and Lexington and Louisville, Ky., at one fare

for the round trip. The tickets have a time limit of twenty days, and are good to all points on the Queen & Crescent system of roads in Kentucky, Tennessee, Alabama and Mississippi, to all points in Georgia as far East as Augusta, and to New Orleans.

THE Citizens' Devolopment Club, of Shreveport, La., has received a letter from August Lehman & Co., of Kansas City, relative to the locating of a number of German immigrant farmers in that section, and expressing a wish to enter into negotiatons with the club to that end; also a letter from the European and Southern Emigration Company, asking for documents, statistics and other data, the purpose of the company being t establish colonies of white immigrants in desirable Southern localities. A committee of five, consisting of W. B. Jacobs, J. H. Shepherd, R. T. Cole, J. B. Slattery and Mayor R. T. Vinson, was appointed to furnish the needed information and devise ways and means to secure immigrants.

MR. W. H. WALKER, formerly of Lincoln, Neb., but now a resident of Houston, Texas, has recently visited Nebraska and to a representative of The Post said: "There is a great deal of interest in South Texas and especially the fruit-growing section of the coast country all over the State of Nebraska. The coming of the State officers and other prominent Nebraskans in o this section and their purchase in La Porte of what is called the Nebraska syndicate property was the beginning of the movement, and now the people up that way are well acquainted with the general resources and advantages of South Texas. I intend to make my home in Houston and just as soon as possible will bring my family here."

WHILE in San Antonio lately Mr. J. M. Rice, Freight Agent of the American Refrigerator Car Company, said that all over the Northern and Eastern States, homeseekers are moving to Southwest Texas, having heard of the wonderful possibilities it possesses as a fruit and early vegetable growing region.

THE Frankfort Land Company, of Morgan county, Tenn., has some 20,000 acres of land on which it is reported that it intends to colonize a lot of Swedes. There are already quite a number of Swedes located there.

J. M. EBERLE, Land and Immigration Agent of the Illinois Central Railroad, reports that there is every reason to believe that during the next few months a large number of people from the Northern and Eastern States will settle along the Illinois Central line in Mississippi. He has lately had a l rge number of applications for sites and locations. The winters of the North have largely tended to make the farmers of that section seek a warmer climate.

The San Antonio Light says there is no State of this Union that will see the advance within the lines of 1894 that Texas will. All the in ications are that an unusual stream of immigration will pour itself into the State within the next few months, and also that this immigration will not be a foreign one, but a domestic transit including some of the very best agricultural, manufacturing and commercial classes of the older States. Texas has a warm welcome for these new citizens and gives them a hearty home reception.

Amarillo Northwestern: The coming spring will bring many prospectors and settlers to the Plains. There has never been a greater demand than at present for advertising literature pertaining to the Panhandle.

Hon. Eric Johnson, of Omaha, chief clerk of the Nebraska House of Representatives, was in Houston, Texas, lately. Mr. Johnson is quite a noted immigration worker, and is on an inspecting tour of the South Texas coast country with a vi w to locating a number of settlers in that section. His parents were among the pioneer families to come to the United States from Sweden, since which time that country ha furnished thousands of people to America as settlers. Mr. Johnson states that on a recent tour of the farming section of Nebraska he found Swedes who had moved there four or five years ago among the most prosperous people to be met in that State. Many of them, when they arrived at Castle Garden, were actually in want, and under the present laws would have been refused admittance into this country.

A number of Norwegians have been in Fl rence, Ala., looking up farms. They announce themselves to be the forerunners of others.

A party of Norwegian prospectors have been in Lawrence county, Tenn., for some weeks prospecting. There were five hard-working prosperous farmers in the party. They were the typical Norwegians, the bu hy,

reddish beards characteristic of the race, almost completely covering their f ces, and they were attired in coarse but neat clothes, with warm caps for head coverings. All spoke the English language fairly well.

The spokesman of the party stated that on first reaching this country they settled in Missouri, but later went to Minnesota, where they bought farms and established themselves comfortably. They have prospered and saved money, but of late years have met with so many reverses from the severe winters that they determed to come South. Learning that land was cheap in Lawrence c unty, they went there to look around. The result was highly satisfactory to them all, and they found families of their own race already settled there and doing well. They selected a tract of land and will probably return with their families in the summer.

Mr. John Cramer, of Columbus, Neb., has been seeking information about land in Georgia, with a view to locating a German colony there.

La Porte, Texas, is attracting great attention among Northern and Western people. About the middle of January excursionists from Missouri, Iowa, Indiana, Nebraska, Ohio, Illinois New York and other States, taking advantage of the cheap railroad rates filled all the hotels and cots in private houses in La Porte. Over 100 excursionists were in town at one time.

The universal comment was said to be a full realization of their expectations, and that South Texas holds forth great inducements to the homeseeker. Many of the excursionists were surprised to see all manner of fresh vegetables growing in the gardens at this season.

A Home-seekers' excursion left Sioux City, Iowa, on the 15th of January for Kenner, La. These home-seekers stopped all along the line, as the tickets are good for thirty days. They were bought to Kenner, but they will make their way to New Orleans before they r turn, and if the country in that section pleases them they will possibly make it their home.

Mr. D. Hutchinson, of Rock Hill, S. C., wri es to the Southern States: "I am glad to learn of your efforts to induce reliable and desirable immigrants in the South. Every section of this country, almost, will offer inducements to this class of people and it will well nigh be impossible for them to make a mistake in locating. . We have here in our small place already three cotton mills, besides a number of other enterprises, and capable farmers can easily earn comfortable incomes right here with us. Keep up the good work.'

THE Tyler Texas Democrat-Reporter says : There is no doubt but that Smith county has lost the opportunity this fall of placing to its credit a great number of good families which it could have had just by a little organized effort.

For weeks past thousands of people have been pouring into Texas from the older States, and many of them are seeking homes in East Texas.

Some of these immigrants come expecting to rent farms ; others come prepared to buy. Several families have located in Smith county ; many others would have located could they have been provided with homes.

Organization could prepare places for these people; organization could present to other sections the advantages of a home here; organization could in a very brief time put a thousand new and good families in Smith county. Such an addition to our population would prove more beneficial than another trunk line of railway. Let us organize.

THE awakening of the South to the need of immigration is illustrated and emphasized in the following extracts from a recent editorial in the Augusta (Ga.) Chronicle :

"There are thousands of acres of arable lands in Georgia and South Carolina that are offered for sale for less than ten dollars an acre. Our people are land poor. That which should be most in demand, because of its intrinsic value—farming land—cannot find purchasers. This land will produce any crop profitably, except cotton at its present low price, with intelligent cultivation and proper care.   *   *   *

"We would favor an issue of bonds to the amount of $5,000,000 for the purchase of land to be divided into eighty-acre farms to be sold to settlers on ten years' time ; the bonds to run for twenty years and to bear a low rate of interest, and the purchasers to pay the State principal, interest and expenses. The details could be easily agreed on and the State amply protected.   *   *   *

"But when the legislature that has just adjourned refused to appropriate a dollar to publish the resources of the State, we almost despair of the future of Georgia. Such benighted indifference—to call it by no stronger term—is incomprehensible.

"The Young Men's Business League of Augusta has a grand mission before it. It should do in part what the State Legislature could do for the entire State. Let us agitate and arouse public sentiment. Lightning may strike the general assembly the next session. In the meantime let colonization societies and land and investment companies be organized with a view to inducing farmers from other S ates to settle in Georgia."

IMMIGRATION TO THE SOUTH.

The New Orleans Times-Democrat published recently the following editorial on Southern immigration and the work the SOUTHERN STATES is doing to promote immigration. The importance and value of the letters on this subject from the managers of Southern railroads, published in the January number of the SOUTHERN STATES, justifies the reproduction here of the Times-Democrat's summary of them, along with its comment :

The SOUTHERN STATES magazine discusses the question of "The South and Immigration" very thoroughly and interestingly.

This matter, and especially the best way of attracting immigrants to the South, was being very actively agitated here, a number of conventions having been held to consider it, when the financial crisis came upon the country and put a sudden and complete stop to all such discussions. As the crisis is not yet over it has been a difficult matter to again arouse the South to the importance of immigration, yet now is the very time to agitate it, as the South has proved during the crisis its solidity, and shown that it was better able to withstand the financial storm than the North, and has thereby established the fact that it is the best place for immigrants. Hence, any efforts made just now to assist immigration are more likely to be effective. This is the view taken long ago by The Times-Democrat, and we are glad to see the SOUTHERN STATES of the same way of thinking.

In its last number it publishes a number of interesting letters on the subject from leading railroad men, representing nearly 30,000 miles of Southern railroads. These gentlemen were asked to give their views on the question of what the South ought to do in order to attract immigrants and how to go about the work in a manner to secure the best results. This, indeed, is the great question of immigration. The advantages that the South offers settlers are generally recognized. The Southern people are enthusiastically in favor of immigration, and there is no need to canvass among them for it; but what are the practical steps that should be taken to induce Western farmers or immigrants from abroad to come South and settle here? This was the great question discussed at the Southern Gubernatorial Conference last summer, but we cannot say that anything very definite or conclusive was then decided on.

As the railroads are vitally interested in immigration, as much, indeed, as the people themselves, since many of them own large bodies of land which they are anxious to sell, and which can be sold to advantage only when immigration sets in, letters from their officials having charge of land matters must be timely, interesting and valuable.

Mr. M. V. Richards, land and immigration agent of the Baltimore & Ohio Railroad, thinks that the trouble is that "the South is very little known among the masses throughout the North and West. We must therefore educate these people regarding the numerous opportunities awaiting them. They want to come, but where to locate is the vital question. Only those directly interested in the work realize what little knowledge exists about the South. This can only be accomplished by persistently advertising the merits of the country in general, and the advantages of particular localities. To do this rapidly and effectually there must be co-operation. Every railroad company should make special efforts to solicit persons to settle along its line ; the citizens of each and every community should see that their particular section is well represented, and a good plan for them to work on is the organization of boards of trade, chambers of commerce, business men's clubs and in fact any association of citizens who will work for the promotion of the best interests of the community in which they reside. We should encourage real estate agencies." Mr. Richards lays great stress upon the necessities of real estate agencies in the South, and holds that the settlement of the West was largely brought about by them. He holds further, "that every Southern State should create an immigration bureau, placing it in the hands of some experienced and reliable immigration agent and continue the work for a period of years. This work can be carried on with a fund, the amount of which would be nominal, considering the advantages which will accrue. It will take at least one year to organiz the work, and immediate returns should not be expected. I think possibly one of the stumbling blocks in the past, when soliciting immigration to the South, has been that our people expected too rapid returns, consequently the movement on the part of the States has been spasmodic."

We quite agree with what Mr. Richards says about "spasmodic" efforts. The chief trouble ab ut this immigration movement in the S uth is that it has been spasmodic. We have gone at it heartily one year, to drop it the next, very much like s me of the government work on our rivers and harbors, whereas to accomplish any serious improvement the work ought to be pushed continuously for three or four years at least.

Frank Y. Anderson, land commissioner of the Vicksburg, Shreveport & Pacific, Alabama & Vicksburg & Alabama Great Southern Railroads, thinks that "the railroad companies should advertise more extensively; they should send their agents to the North and West, not only to distribute immigration literature, but should be capable of explaining the many advantages the South has to offer." Mr. Anderson believes that the main work should be done by the railroads, and he believes that if they would combine and devote themselves to energetically advertising the advantages of the South the best results would follow.

Mr. John C. Winder, vice-president and manager of the Seaboard Air Line, ann unces that his company has made some effort to induce immigration. It has not been very successful, he admits, but " we expect to take much more energetic steps toward immigration than we have hitherto done." He thinks that the large colored population in some portions of the South has had a deterrent effect on immigration, but that the Northern people no longer find the negroes in the way.

Mr. W. A. Turk, general passenger agent of the Richmond & Danville Railroad, thinks

that we may expect this spring "a wave of immigration. It has indeed already begun, and we believe that the present prosperous condition of the South as compared with other sections will have a favorable effect." More and better advertising is needed, he thinks, to encourage the movement of population southward.

Mr. T. G. Bush, receiver of the Mobile & Birmingham Railroad, notes that the Southern railroads east of the Mississippi have encouraged emigration rather than immigration. The Texas & Arkansas roads have made a bid for immigrants from the older Southern States, and the roads in the latter section have helped along this movement instead of end avoring to keep these people at home, not fully realizin how much they lose in them. Mr. Bush announces that he is in correspondence with the managers of a number of railroad systems in the South to see if some plan or policy of immigration cannot be agreed on among them, but he does not specify what his policy is.

Mr. Louis Pio, of the East Coast Line, the Jacksonville, San Augustine and Jordan River Railroad, says that his line made special efforts during the past year to secure immigrants, and has met with very satisfactory results. It distributed tens of thousands of books and circulars at the Chicago Exposition, and Mr. Pio himself traveled through the country, and particularly the Northwest, in the interest of immigration to Florida. He awakened a widespread interest in Florida among the Northwestern farmers, especially the Scandinavians and the Germans. He has already established a Scandinavian colony at St. Lucie, which he expects to see soon blossom into a large settlement.

Mr. C. P. Atmore, of the Louisville & Nashville, declares that his road is deeply interested in immigration, and has already taken important steps to encourage it. It has inaugurated a number of land-seekers' excursions, by which people from the North and West can come South at very little cost and examine the country with a view of settling here.

The Plant railway system of Florida worked actively at the Chicago Exposition circulating pamphlets about Florida, and has already secured promising results from its investment. Mr. D. H. Elliot, its general land agent, has decided views upon the line of policy that should be pursued by the South to secure immigration. He strongly advocates excursions, and especially those that will enable the Western and Northern editors to see the South in order to remove the prejudices they entertain against this section, and to convince them that it will suit their people. "With this in view we have had several excursions visit the South and Florida, and I can see the result in the pertinent inquiries from people in the sections of country where these newspapers were published as to the price of our lands and the probability of their removing to Florida."

Mr. Elliott further says: There is another element which enters into this question, and that is, as to how the people can get rid of their homes, or effect an exchange of their property in the North and West for property in the South. We have numerous inquiries to that effect; two today. It appears that there is no demand for their property, and they cannot sell except at a sacrifice; they are awaiting an opportunity, and when they can effect such a sale they will remove to Florida. Apparently they have become tired of the extreme cold and sudden changes of temperature. In personal interviews with farmers and others who have felt as if they would like to get into a warmer climate, they do not seem to understand how it is that, with so pleasant and equable an air in the winter months, a white person can exist or labor in the sun in the summer. It is not to be expected that all would understand climatology, and it is difficult to make them understand that we have such a temperate climate in the summer.

Mr. W. H. Whiting, general manager of the Wilmington, Western & Norfolk Railroad, thinks that "it would be necessary to circulate among the farmers whose immigration is desired a carefully prepared pamphlet, giving the conditions of our soil and climate, the prices of our land and the products best suited to them, their relation with respect to the different markets, means and terms of transportation, etc."

E. W. LeBeaume, of the Cotton Belt Railroad, differs from most of the other railroad men, complaining that too much is expected of the railroads, while the States themselves and the people do too little.

There are quite a number of other suggestions in these communications, too many, indeed, to review here. They show, however, a great interest in this matter and that the railroads are disposed to co-operate and assist materially in any scheme to assist immigration. Nearly all of them contain good ideas. The best result, however, is to be obtained, not by throwing all the work on the railroads, but by some policy of co-operation by which they, the States and people, can work together in this great cause. And, as we have already said, we do not know a better time for such work than just now, when the superior advantages of the South have been made so manifest.

Fruits in Central Georgia.

Mr. T. Skelton Jones, of Macon, Ga., writes to the SOUTHERN STATES as follows: I would like to call your attention to the wonderful progress made in Central Georgia in the development of the fruit-shipping industry. The shipment of melons commences about the 10th of June and extends to the 1st of August, and the average shipments for the season amount to about 10,000 cars, which go to all parts of the United States this side of the Rockies, as well as Canada. Having accomplished this much in melons, attention is now being turned to peaches, pears and grapes. It has been about six years since the first shipment of peaches was made from Georgia to the Northern markets, yet within that time the Georgia peach has attained a reputation that places it above all other fruits. There is not another crop grown that pays a better profit on the investment than Georgia peaches. One 200-acre peach orchard has returned to the owner fully $125,000 in five years, and in one of the years there was a failure of the crop. Nor is this profit confined to large growers; the small growers have done equally as well if not better. One grower with an orchard of eight acres sold his crop on the trees for $2500, or more than $300 per acre. Another small grower sold his crop on 100 trees for $500, and the buyer picked and packed them, while the buyer said he made $500 in the transaction. Georgia has many advantages over California in the marketing of fruits. It takes two or three days to transport a car of peaches to New York, and the freight is $160, while it takes nine days from California, and the freight is $320. Peach growing in Georgia offers to the man of moderate means greater inducements than any other industry in any other section. He can buy lands from $5.00 to $25 per acre. These lands are productive and easily cultivated; while the orchard is growing into bearing he can cultivate the land between the trees and raise enough produce to pay the cost of cultivation and support a family. With established fruit lines, cheap and rapid transportation, this section will within the next five years become one of the greatest fruit-producing belts of the country, which with the surety of crops, the nearness to the great markets and the earliness of ripening, gives to Central Georgia advantages that are fast making it a formidable competitor with California.

Transfer of 2,000,000 Acres.

The State of Florida has made a final transfer to the Atlantic & Gulf Coast Canal & Okeechobee Land Co., of about 2,000,000 acres of land, provided for in the contract entered into in 1881, by the State of Florida and Mr. Hamilton Disston of Philadelphia. Under this contract Mr. Disston was to drain and make available for cultivation an area comprising several thousand square miles of land in Southern Florida which was subject to overflow. The work of constructing canals and other drainage works has gone on uninterruptedly for the last twelve years, and all that Mr. Disston undertook to do has been accomplished. He has reclaimed for the State several million acres of available land, that, but for his enterprise, would have remained wholly worthless. Over eighty miles of drainage canals and open water works, from twenty-six to 106 feet wide and from seven to twelve feet deep, have been constructed. Rivers have been made navigable by the deepening of their channels and the removal of obstructions, and a vast amount of work done of incalculable value to the whole southern part of the State independently of the area reclaimed from overflow.

Much of the land that has been saved is shown by the testimony of experts to be the richest sugar land in the world. The climate, soil and general conditions of the country are pre-eminently favorable to the growing of sugar, rice, tobacco, vegetables and all subtropical fruits. The company owning this two million acres will colonize it with settlers from the North and from abroad. The reclaimed area is from twenty-five to seventy feet above the sea level.

Mr. Disston, while enormously enriching himself and his associates, has given a principality to the State.

A Book on Maryland.

The Baltimore Sun has issued a second edition of its little book, "Maryland; Its Resources, Industries and Agricultural Condition," which is of its kind the most complete and satisfactory publication the writer has ever seen. It is comprehensive, yet brief. It furnishes a clear outline view of the whole State, and a stranger to Maryland reading it will get more information and a better idea of the State than could be had from volumes of such matter as is ordinarily printed.

Lightning Source UK Ltd.
Milton Keynes UK
UKHW021327240119
336090UK00005B/585/P